The Professional Educator

A NEW Introduction to Teaching and Schools

Charles B. Myers

Peabody College
Vanderbilt University

Lynn K. Myers

Harpeth Valley Elementary School
Nashville, Tennessee

Wadsworth Publishing Company

IⓉP™ An International Thomson Publishing Company

Belmont · Albany · Bonn · Boston · Cincinnati · Detroit · London · Madrid ·
Melbourne · Mexico City · New York · Paris · San Francisco · Singapore · Tokyo ·
Toronto · Washington

Education Editor: Sabra Horne
Development Editor: John Bergez
Editorial Assistant: Janet Hansen
Production Services Coordinator: Debby Kramer
Production Editor: Cecile Joyner/The Cooper Company
Print Buyer: Karen Hunt
Permissions Editor: Jeanne Bosschart
Text and Cover Designer: Peter Martin/Design Office
Cover Photograph: Tommy Thompson
Copy Editor: Joan Pendleton
Photo Researcher: Laurel Anderson, Photosynthesis
Technical Illustrator: Richard Sheppard
Cartoon Illustrator: Renee Deprey
Compositor: G & S Typesetters, Inc.
Printer: Quebecor Printing Book Group/Hawkins County
Cover Printer: Phoenix Color Corporation
Credits continue on the last page of the book.

Printed in the United States of America
1 2 3 4 5 6 7 8 9 10—01 00 99 98 97 96 95

For more information, contact Wadsworth Publishing Company:

Wadsworth Publishing Company
10 Davis Drive
Belmont, California 94002, USA

International Thomson Publishing Europe
Berkshire House 168-173
High Holborn
London, WC1V 7AA, England

Thomas Nelson Australia
102 Dodds Street
South Melbourne 3205
Victoria, Australia

Nelson Canada
1120 Birchmount Road
Scarborough, Ontario
Canada M1K 5G4

International Thomson Editores
Campos Eliseos 385, Piso 7
Col. Polanco
11560 México D.F. México

International Thomson Publishing GmbH
Königswinterer Strasse 418
53227 Bonn, Germany

International Thomson Publishing Asia
221 Henderson Road
#05-10 Henderson Building
Singapore 0315

International Thomson Publishing Japan
Hirakawacho Kyowa Building, 3F
2-2-1 Hirakawacho
Chiyoda-ku, Tokyo 102, Japan

Library of Congress Cataloging-in-Publication Data

Myers, Charles B.
        The professional educator : a new introduction to teaching and
    schools / Charles B. Myers, Lynn K. Myers. —Rev. ed.
            p.   cm.
        Includes bibliographical references and index.
        ISBN 0-534-20574-7
        1. Teaching.   2. Education—United States.   3. Learning.
    I. Myers, Lynn K.   II. Title
    LB1025.3.M94   1995   94-23321
    371.1′02—dc20

To Cassie, Carina, and Cory

Brief Contents

Contents

UNIT 1

A First Look 2

CHAPTER 1

Teaching and Schools in America Today:
The Current Scene and Future Directions 4

U N I T 2

Students and Learning 148

UNIT 3

Historical, Political, and Philosophical Contexts 260

CHAPTER 8

UNIT 5

Teachers   552

CHAPTER 15

Professional Teachers: The Life and the Work   **554**

Preface

Anyone involved in teacher preparation in the United States must face the reality that teaching today, and in the years ahead, is and will be truly different from any other time in our history. Most classroom students and their families are noticeably unlike those of the idealized past. The responsibilities that society asks teachers and schools to assume are broader, more numerous, and more challenging than even in recent times. Expectations that teachers and schools educate *all* students to the maximum of their individual capabilities are persistently and forcefully voiced, even though today's students exhibit greater ranges of abilities and arrive at school with more serious needs than ever before. At the same time, the societies in which those students live and in which teachers teach are becoming increasingly complex, confused, and threatening—and at accelerating speeds.

Within the profession of teaching, knowledge about professional practice as well as about the content to be taught is expanding so fast that it is harder than ever for classroom teachers to keep up with new ideas, let alone translate them into practice. Even when new knowledge does "filter down" to the classroom, it often challenges teachers' assumptions and values, requiring them not only to learn new skills but to adjust their personalities. All of this is compounded further by a lack of consensus among educators about how best to prepare teachers, at the same time that citizens and societal leaders still believe that teaching is relatively easy to learn and to do.

These conditions require teacher education programs to prepare their students from the outset for a complex, ever-changing professional career that involves *lifelong learning* and *continuous personal development*. Those of us involved in preparing tomorrow's teachers must re-examine how our teacher education programs and courses can be structured to educate teachers who will be successful throughout their careers. How can we develop our students into professionals who care seriously about their students, are well informed about the field of education and subject matter, and are capable of applying continually emerging research data to real classroom practice? How can we teach skills and value perspectives that teachers can build upon as their students and the demands on their teaching change over time? How can we develop beginning teacher education students into professionals who truly *make a positive difference in the lives of the students* they will be educating over their twenty-five or more years in the classroom?

This text is our response to these questions—not a complete response, of course, but one that begins where teacher education begins—in the introductory course.

Guiding Assumptions and Goals of This Text

The ultimate purpose of any teacher education program is to produce graduates who succeed as educators in real-world classrooms. We believe that when teacher education programs are successful in helping their students develop intellectually, those students evolve into teachers who

■ *have a command of the knowledge bases of teaching;* that is, the relevant theory and research encompassing such areas as human development, learning theory, the nature of knowledge, effective teaching practices, educational philosophy, classroom organization and management, and evaluation;

■ *have the ability to form personal conceptual frameworks* that allow them to integrate information from many sources and absorb new ideas as their learning continues over a professional career;

■ *have the ability to apply theory and research creatively* to unique and ever-changing circumstances in actual schools;

■ *are lifelong learners, critical consumers of new information, and reflective practitioners* who can continually assess and improve their own performance.

These assumptions lead to the following goals for an introductory course in teacher education and for this text:

1. *Provide a* **substantial**, **integrated**, *and* **understandable** *introduction to the knowledge bases in the field of education that helps students connect theory and research to the practice of teaching and that establishes for them the relevance of doing so.*

   We see the first course in education as an *integrating introduction* that exposes students to the various areas of knowledge they will pursue in their subsequent study, and connects these areas to each other and to the practice of teaching. The course should start students thinking seriously about the ideas they will need to master to be successful in the classroom in the years ahead. This focus is consistent with recent, forward-looking proposals for the way teachers should be educated, including those of the National Council for the Accreditation of Teacher Education (NCATE), the American Association of Colleges for Teacher Education, the Association of Teacher Educators, the Holmes Group, the Renaissance Group, and the Association of American Colleges.

2. *From the outset, connect this study to real-life observation and experience.*

   Often education texts and courses describe teaching, classrooms, and schools as if they are static, far off, bland, and unavailable to students reading the texts and taking the courses. This is not really the case. Nearly all college classes have access to written case studies, as well as videotaped classroom and school episodes; and most college campuses have active pre-K–12 schools nearby. We decided to take advantage of these opportunities so that the use of this text could be more active for students. Frequent accounts of schools, students, classrooms, lessons, and teaching provide realistic examples of what students can look for in case studies, videos, and visits to schools. Chapter 2 and sections of several subsequent chapters teach students specific ways of observing and, more important, of analyzing classrooms from the perspective of a professional.

3. *Emphasize the process of lifelong learning and professional development, and begin to impart some of the skills future professionals need to be lifelong learners.*

   Learning to teach now requires that students become capable of understanding continuously developing research findings and also become skilled at applying those findings in their future classrooms. We believe that we can best start students along a path toward lifelong professional learning and continuous development by engaging them in the active intellectual processes of (a) relating the information they are studying to episodes drawn from actual classroom and school situations as well as their own recalled experience, and (b) reflecting persistently on the meaning of the ideas they are learning in terms of their future teaching. We have included several features designed to encourage students to become engaged intellectually from the start of their professional study in the interplay between theory and practice, and to begin developing the mind set of intelligent consumers of research. Consequently, we ask students to do more analysis and reflection than has been typical in introductory texts.

4. *Be an exemplar of good teaching practice.*

Finally, we assume that an education textbook (and course) should exemplify what we tell our students about effective teaching. Accordingly we have crafted this book to (a) meet students where they really are, with an understanding of the developmental sequence they go through; (b) provide a conceptual organization; (c) encourage active learning; and (d) continually relate what students are learning to the purpose being served—preparation for real-life teaching.

Organization and Coverage

In line with our assumptions and goals, this text is organized so each unit and chapter provides introductory information on a key area or topic typically studied by teacher education students. Its starting point is the level of understanding that we believe beginning students bring to their professional study; and its content and chapter-by-chapter organization follow what we believe is the development process that those students go through intellectually as they face the information, ideas, and issues about education, teaching, and schools that they need to know in order to be successful in the pre-K–12 classroom. The organization is our attempt to structure our teaching of beginning teacher education students just as we tell them they should organize their future teaching of pre-K–12 students—"Begin where the students are in terms of their present knowledge and interests, guide them toward the goals you have set for them, and structure the learning experiences in a way that assures that they succeed each step of the way."

We assume that as students start this text and introductory course they are intelligent and aware, but not knowledgeable in a professional sense about education, teaching, and schools; are not "blank slates" but rather come to the study of education with ideas and values based on personal experiences, gained from the perspective of a student, without a broader context or conceptual framework. In this sense, the text can be thought of as a *constructivist approach* to teacher education.

By providing an integrated survey of the field in a logical sequence, and by consistently relating the topics surveyed to the practice of teaching, we aim to give students a substantial foundation for their work in subsequent courses. Our own bias is that this approach is superior to trying to teach "foundations" first and "how to teach" later as if either one could truly be understood separately.

Of course, teacher education programs vary widely in structure and approach. We have tried to make the book a valuable text for instructors who share our assumptions and goals but either teach a first course with a "foundations" or "teaching" emphasis, or omit some of the topics in this book and include others. The unit structure enables instructors to assign groups of chapters in accordance with their syllabus, and chapters may be read independently or in a different sequence without loss of understanding. Further, we believe that this comprehensive survey will be a useful resource and review aid for students in education as they pursue

advanced courses, seek certification as teachers, and observe classroom interactions.

A brief description of the content of each chapter follows.

Unit 1: A First Look

This unit describes contemporary contexts that surround pre-K–12 teaching and
schools today, focuses student attention directly on classroom teaching and the
operation of schools, describes characteristics of teaching and schools that experts
believe are marks of good practice, and instructs students in several techniques for
analyzing teaching and schools from the perspective of a professional educator.
When students finish the unit, they should be well on their way toward changing
their perspective from that of students to lifelong-learning professionals.

■ **Chapter 1: Teaching and Schools in America Today: The Current Scene
and Future Directions** describes issues and trends in American education and
introduces students to the professional study of teaching and schools.

■ **Chapter 2: Inside Classrooms: Studying Teaching** focuses attention on
analyzing real classrooms and teaching (where the action is and where students'
primary beginning interest is); shifts student perspectives from that of previous
pre-K–12 student to that of a professional teacher; and provides them with the
beginnings of conceptual and observational tools for studying teaching.

■ **Chapter 3: Effective Teaching Practices** surveys what contemporary researchers and scholars say is good teaching practice so that students can integrate what
they learn in their coursework into this context.

■ **Chapter 4: Studying Schools as Cultures** focuses attention on how real
schools operate; provides students with an intellectual framework for understanding schools as unique cultural organizations with complex subcultures; and supplies
information on new ways of seeing schools as site-based, decision-making units
and learning communities.

Unit 2: Students and Learning

This unit focuses on pre-K–12 students, explains how they develop and learn, and
describes how teachers and schools function for the purpose of educating them.
This material anchors the topics to come in a basic knowledge of learners—who
are, after all, the focus of what teachers do.

■ **Chapter 5: Students Are Alike, but Not the Same** discusses how pre-K–12
students develop, how they are alike and different, how schools organize and categorize students, and the benefits and problems of sorting students into categories.

■ **Chapter 6: How Students Learn** introduces learning theory to provide a theoretical base for future study of both teaching and learning.

■ **Chapter 7: Learning for All Students: The Goals of Equity and Excellence**
pulls together ideas from all the previous chapters with a focus on the goals of
equity and excellence in the context of how the role of schools has evolved during
the last half of the twentieth century.

Unit 3: Historical, Political, and Philosophical Contexts

This unit explains that contemporary teaching and schools are the products of at
least three interacting influences: historical traditions, political pressures, and
philosophical assumptions and principles. We believe that this "foundation" mate-

rial is all the more meaningful because of the context provided in Units 1 and 2. When students finish the unit, they should be able to interpret the ideas they have learned about teaching and schools in historical, political, and philosophical terms and to understand the importance of these contexts.

■ **Chapter 8: The Historical Context: Traditions That Guide Teaching and Schooling** provides a historical context for understanding education, teaching, and schools in America in terms of four basic questions: Why have schools? Who is taught? Who are the teachers? What is the curriculum?

■ **Chapter 9: The Political Context: Pressures That Influence Teaching and Schools** describes the political environment in which teachers and schools operate, including local, state, and national legislation and regulation; court decisions; taxation and funding; legal rights and responsibilities of teachers and students; the impact of pressure groups; and schools as political organizations.

■ **Chapter 10: The Philosophical Context: Beliefs That Guide Teaching** surveys philosophical approaches to education, in a way that helps students begin to see the importance of their personal philosophy in the decisions they will make as teachers.

Unit 4: Content, Curriculum, and Instruction

This unit shifts students' attention to the principal elements of the practice of teaching. It explores the nature of knowledge and subject matter content, and explains how content is formulated into curricula, lessons, and teaching strategies. It describes how teachers plan, evaluate, and execute lessons. The unit ends with descriptions of five models of instruction that serve as examples of ways in which the various elements that make up teaching can be combined to educate students successfully. When students finish the unit, they should be able to integrate all the knowledge they have learned about teaching and schools from the text into their own view of what teachers do to educate their students.

■ **Chapter 11: Content: Knowledge, Skills, and Affective Learning** provides a conceptual framework for understanding the content taught in schools, including knowledge, skills, and affective learning.

■ **Chapter 12: The Curriculum and Lessons: Designs for Learning** explains curricula, in two ways: first, in terms of the ideas about content described in Chapter 11, and later as they lead toward lessons that teachers teach each day, as expanded upon in Chapter 13.

■ **Chapter 13: The Act of Teaching: Planning, Implementing, and Evaluating** pulls all previous study together with a focus on what teachers do to teach students, including planning, executing, and evaluating lessons. It emphasizes the critical role of the teacher as decision maker and the central element in the whole enterprise that makes learning happen.

■ **Chapter 14: Models of Instruction** describes five models of instruction that illustrate how some experts have combined all of the elements described in Chapters 1–13 into specific approaches to teaching and learning. It stresses that even these "packaged" approaches can be used by teachers only after much personal choosing and adjusting to fit personal priorities and local situations.

Unit 5: Teachers

The final unit describes a number of aspects of the lives and professional work of teachers now and in the years ahead. When students finish the unit, they should have a professional-level grasp of what teachers' lives are like both inside and outside the classroom. They should think of pre-K–12 teaching as a service to students and their community. They should also have a sense of where they fit personally in the teaching profession.

■ **Chapter 15: Professional Teachers: The Life and the Work** describes and analyzes teachers today in the context of all that has been studied in the first fourteen chapters of the text. Specific topics are images and concerns of beginning teachers; the roles teachers play in their classrooms, with students, in the general school environment, and with peers, administrators, and parents; the needs of students that teachers must address; job conditions; and professional group membership.

■ **Chapter 16: Teaching the Next Generation: Is It for You?** extends Chapter 15 into the future and sets a forward-looking context for students as they proceed with their study in subsequent courses. It asks students to reflect seriously on what pre-K–12 teaching will be like in the years ahead and on themselves as potential teachers. It includes information about getting a job, teacher supply and demand, and salary and compensation. It ends by asking students to answer for themselves, "Do I want to be a teacher?" "What would my life be like?"

Teaching Approach and Features

The teaching approach and features of this text are derived from the assumptions and goals as described earlier. Particularly important are our desires to provide an exemplar of good teaching practice—"to practice what we preach"—and to engage students in active, reflective study in their first professional course. The conceptual organization, focus on active learning, and other special features were all designed with these points in mind.

Conceptual Organization

In each chapter, we depict at least one realistic situation that exemplifies a rather broad aspect of education. That picture serves to ground the chapter's discussion in a way beginning students can reasonably grasp. We then move from concrete situations to step-by-step development of a more conceptual understanding. At the end of a chapter, students will not know all that there is to know on the subject, but they should have a solid foundation for future learning. Frequent links both within and across chapters helps to integrate the disparate areas of study they will encounter in their professional preparation.

Active Learning

This text is specifically designed to involve students actively in the learning process and to begin to cultivate the habits and skills of lifelong teachers. We ask questions, suggest that students read additional professional materials along with the text, direct them to analyze case-study situations, challenge them to form and reflect upon their own ideas, and urge them to continuously reformulate what they believe about teaching and schools. Several of the special features described below support this goal.

Special Features

Many textbooks include "boxes" and other elements that seem to serve little purpose beyond interrupting the narrative and, in some vague way, adding "interest" to the text. In contrast, the features of this book are carefully designed to work together with the text exposition to support both content mastery and active learning.

Unit Introductions.   The chapters of this book are grouped into logical units of study. Each unit begins with an introduction that describes the focus of the unit and lists the major concepts and cognitive skills to be mastered in each chapter.

Chapter Introductions.   Each chaper begins with a brief introduction that previews the focus, content, and organization of the chapter.

Snapshots.   A Snapshot—a realistic portrayal of a teaching or school situation that relates to the major ideas of the chapter—immediately follows each chapter introduction. The Snapshots help students visualize real-world settings that make theory and research relevant to practice. Each begins with general questions that stimulate and direct students' thinking. Frequently chapter sections refer back to the Snapshot to further reinforce the connections between the ideas students are learning and real situations.

Key Concepts.   Key concepts are highlighted throughout the text in several ways—as subheadings, as marginal notations, as italicized items in the text, and in lists of key terms at the end of the chapter.

Something to Think About.   Thought provoking data, situations, and dilemmas are presented throughout the text, always with guiding questions for students to consider. These activities reinforce ideas being studied in the respective chapters and ask students to apply what they are learning to real circumstances.

Reflecting on Practice.   Fifteen of the sixteen chapters contain Reflecting on Practice sections, in which students are asked to use ideas presented in the chapter to study a relevant episode or issue. These sections enable students to apply their learning to the analysis of specific case study situations and can serve as the basis for class discussions. Questions are provided to guide thinking.

Case Studies.   Case studies are scattered throughout the text. They appear in Snapshots, Something to Think About, and Reflecting on Practice sections, as well as within the narrative. All are based on actual situations, although several have been modified to illustrate particular points.

Educational Research.   Fourteen of the sixteen chapters contain Educational Research sections that describe specific aspects of educational research related to the chapter focus in some detail. The aim of these sections is to further cultivate students' ability to study and apply research findings to their teaching practice. They provide glimpses of the nature of research, strengths and weaknesses of specific research efforts, conclusions from some of those efforts, and ways in which the conclusions have affected teaching practice and schools.

Chapter Ending Items.   Chapters end with summaries, study questions, key terms, and lists for further reading. Notes for each chapter are gathered at the back of the book. These elements enable students to review, probe, and extend what they have learned from each chapter.

Profiles.   Full-color photo essays enhance the real-life quality of this text through candid profiles of two contemporary teachers, presented largely in the teachers' own words. Readers should be able to identify readily with third-grade teacher Sarah Smith, who is near the beginning of her career, while junior-high-school teacher Paul Ong represents a thoughtful professional with the calm wisdom of a lifelong teacher and learner. Their voices lend a special realism to several of the themes of the book.

Glossary.   The glossary at the back of the book reiterates definitions of new terminology introduced and defined in the text.

Appendix.   The Appendix of the text has two parts. Appendix A is a second analytical classroom observation system—The Teacher-Student Interaction Observation System—which is intended to extend student activities that are a part of Chapter 2. Appendix B is a list of the addresses and phone numbers of offices to contact in each state for information about teacher licensure and certification requirements.

Ancillaries

Instructor's Manual

The *Instructor's Manual* that accompanies this text contains chapter-by-chapter information, suggestions, and resources. Material for each chapter includes a chapter overview, outline, rationale, list of objectives—key concepts, generalizations, skills, affective learning, and other important information to be learned—suggested activities and procedures, and suggestions for extended learning. Graphics that can be photocopied to make handouts and transparencies are included for every chapter.

Test Bank

Test questions that accompany this text come in two forms: as a computerized testing system and in print. The computerized testing system is available in two formats: for Macintosh (LXR) and for IBM (Trilogy Systems). Questions are identified in the following ways: objective or idea being assessed; level of difficulty; thinking skill level (recall, comprehension, application, analysis, synthesis, evaluation); pages where the information being assessed is explained in the text; and whether or not the question is used as an example in the *Student Study Guide*.

Student Study Guide

The *Student Study Guide* that accompanies this text tells students in both general and step-by-step ways how to direct and manage their study of the text. It lists the objectives of each chapter in the form of concepts, generalizations, skills, affective learning, and information they are expected to learn. It explains how to decide which ideas are more important than others and how to reflect upon chapter content at higher-order thinking levels and apply it to real-world situations. The Guide carries on the *constructivist* characteristic of the text by asking students to connect intellectually the ideas they read in the text with their own personal background experiences and beliefs about teaching and schools. It includes practice test questions for each chapter.

And Finally, An Exchange of Professional Ideas

Because being a teacher, teacher educator, and a textbook author is a continuous process of learning and improving, we invite professors and students who use this text to join in an exchange of professional ideas. Our addresses are below. Write to us about your ideas, hunches, reactions, beliefs, opinions concerning this text, your teacher education experiences, and teaching in pre-K–12 schools in general. We will use your contributions as best we can, not only to improve this text, but, when it is appropriate, to compile and disseminate your contributions to others. We hope we can build a sizable network of teacher education students, teachers, and professors who use this text and want to share their ideas.

Charles B. Myers
Box 330, Peabody College
Vanderbilt University
Nashville, Tennessee 37203
Internet: MyersCB@CTRVAX.VANDERBILT.EDU

Lynn K. Myers
Harpeth Valley Elementary School
7840 Old Harding Road
Nashville, Tennessee 37221
Internet: MyersLK@CTRVAX.VANDERBILT.EDU

Acknowledgments

Teachers of many types have had a direct impact on our professional lives and on the writing of this text. They include our parents and children, our own elementary and secondary school teachers in Columbia and Wrightsville, Pennsylvania, particularly Elmer Kreiser, Dorothy Broome, Mary S. Groff, Dorcas Bortz, and John Filbey; our college instructors, especially Jack Allen, Kenneth Cooper, and Robert P. Thomson; our cooperating teachers when we student taught, Neil Everhart and Mary Miller; our teaching colleagues, especially Pauline Maderia, Sarah Rowan, Debbie Ladd, Marty McSwiney, Martha Copeland, Joyce Blair, and Joe Myers; our students from Grade 1 through graduate school. In various ways, all influenced this book and specific elements of its content.

We also acknowledge the unique, expert, and gracious participation of the contributing authors of both the initial and revised editions—Penny Brooks, Terry Deal, Carolyn Evertson, Marcy Singer Gabella, Brian Hansford, Alene Harris, Earline Kendall, Ann Neely, Jeanne Plas, Cathy Randolph, Debbie Rowe, Doug Simpson, Jane Stallings, and Nancy Vye. We asked each of these specialists and widely published scholars to explain major aspects of their respective areas of expertise at a level addressed to beginning teacher education students, within the limits of our specifications, and with the understanding that we would make changes in their work. They provided concise, focused ideas at a level appropriate for our readers and at the same time allowed us a latitude with their creative work that was truly admirable.

We want to express our appreciation to the professional colleagues who gave their talent and time in reviewing the manuscript in part or in whole: Morris Anderson, Wayne State College; David L. Bachelor, University of New Mexico; Joseph A. Baust, Murray State University; Carlton Beck, University of Wisconsin—Milwaukee; Sylven S. Beck, The George Washington University; Gloria Bonner, Middle Tennessee State University; Mary Jane Bradley, Arkansas State University; Richard Couch, Clarion University of Pennsylvania; Ron Elkind, Assumption College; John Georgeoff, Purdue University; Bruce Gutknecht, University of North Florida; Linda Houser, Ball State University; Karl Jost, University of Tennessee—Knoxville; Fred Kierstead, University of Houston—Clear Lake; Guy Larkins, University of Georgia; James C. Lawlor, Towson State University; Barbara M. Parramore, North Carolina State University; Kenneth Wulff, Kent State University; and Timothy Young, Central Washington University.

We thank Sarah Smith and Paul Ong for sharing with us their thoughts on teaching in the photo essays, and we thank their schools and their students for their cooperation.

We would also like to thank the people who helped us bring this revised edition to its final form: Janette Daugherty and Deloris Clark at Vanderbilt; Nancy Sweeney, Beverly Anderson, and Harry Griggs at Captiva Island, Florida; Suzanna Brabant; John Bergez, Sabra Horne, and Debby Kramer with Wadsworth Publishing; and Joan Pendleton, Robin Lockwood, and Cecile Joyner.

About the Authors

Charles B. Myers

Charles B. Myers is professor and former associate dean and department chair at Peabody College, Vanderbilt University. He teaches the introductory course for students preparing to teach in elementary and secondary schools as well as graduate level courses. He serves as advisor to the campus chapter of the Student Tennessee Education Association/NEA. In 1982, Professor Myers was recognized by the college as the faculty member who made the greatest contribution outside the classroom to student-faculty relations.

Dr. Myers has taught in junior and senior high schools in Harrisburg, Pennsylvania, and Nashville, Tennessee. At the college level, he has taught at Rider College in New Jersey and Armidale College of Advanced Education, New South Wales, Australia, and at Vanderbilt. He received his undergraduate education at The Pennsylvania State University in secondary education and social studies and his master's and Ph.D. degrees from Peabody College in American history and the teaching of history and the social sciences.

In addition to this text, Professor Myers has written and served as general editor for a number of elementary and secondary school texts including *The Taba Program in Social Science—People in Change;* a sixth-grade social studies text, *People, Time and Change;* and a high school issues-oriented text, *The Environmental Crisis.*

Professor Myers has held a number of national positions in teacher education and social studies education organizations. He serves as a member of the Unit Accreditation Board and Standards Committee of the National Council for the Accreditation of Teacher Education. He writes, speaks, and conducts workshops on teacher education, social studies, and the teaching of thinking and valuing skills.

Lynn K. Myers

Lynn K. Myers is a third-grade teacher at Harpeth Valley Elementary School in the Metropolitan Nashville Public Schools in Tennessee. She teaches basic subjects in a self-contained classroom. She also supervises classroom practica, student teaching, and internship experiences for college teacher education students. During the first fifteen years of her teaching career, she taught first and second grades at Fall-Hamilton Elementary School, an inner-city school that serves a high proportion of children from economically disadvantaged homes, and as a reading resource teacher. She has been designated a Career Ladder III teacher, the highest level in the Tennessee career ladder system.

Ms. Myers pursued her undergraduate education in elementary education at Rider College in New Jersey, Millerville State College in Pennsylvania, and Peabody College. She completed her master's degree in early childhood education and reading education at Peabody and has pursued further study at the Educational Specialist level in reading.

In addition to writing this text, Ms. Myers has served as a consultant and evaluator of elementary school language arts, social studies, and reading texts and supplemental materials. She has also been an evaluator of computer program software designed for elementary instruction.

Ms. Myers is active locally and nationally in reading education and teacher professional development efforts and has been building representative for her local unit of the National Education Association. She has developed a recognized system for student behavior management.

Contributing Authors

Although Charles and Lynn Myers are the primary authors of this text, a number of other experts in teacher education wrote chapters, parts of chapters, and initial drafts of chapters in their areas of expertise, for either the initial or this revised edition. Often their contributions were edited or rewritten so that the chapters would fit together smoothly, but each contributing author prepared a valuable part of the manuscript. Those authors and their contributions are as follows.

Penelope H. Brooks

Penelope H. Brooks, professor of psychology, Peabody College, Vanderbilt University, is a developmental psychologist with special interests in mental retardation and cognitive development. Her recent publications include *Bright Start: A Cognitive Curriculum for Young Children* (with H. Carl Haywood and Susan Burns) and several articles on children's development of beliefs about alcohol and children's safety. Professor Brooks wrote Chapter 5 and assisted with the revision of Chapter 6.

Terrence E. Deal

Terrence E. Deal, professor of education, Peabody College, Vanderbilt University, is an expert on school and organizational cultures. His publications include the national best-selling book, *Corporate Cultures* (with Allan Kennedy), and *Reframing Organizations: Artistry, Choice, and Leadership* (with Lee Bolman), which looks at organizations from four perspectives: human resource, structural, political, and symbolic. Professor Deal wrote the substantive parts of Chapter 6 for the initial edition, which remains relatively unchanged in this revised edition as Chapter 4.

Carolyn M. Evertson

Carolyn M. Evertson, professor of education and chair of the Department of Teaching and Learning, Peabody College, Vanderbilt University, is an expert and researcher on effective teaching and classroom organization and management. She is a fellow in the American Psychological Association. She has written widely on effective teaching and has co-authored *Classroom Management for Elementary Teachers, Classroom Management for Secondary Teachers* (both with Edmund Emmer and others); and *Learning from Teaching* and *Student Characteristics and Teaching* (both with Jere Brophy). Professor Evertson collaborated with Ann Neely in writing the planning and organization components of the initial edition of Chapter 13 and assisted with its revision.

Marcy Singer Gabella

Marcy Singer Gabella, assistant professor of education, Peabody College, Vanderbilt University, is a curriculum theorist interested in the cognitive consequences of employing diverse forms of representaton (e.g. visual arts, music, technology) in curriculum and instruction; and in the impact of the organization and culture of schools and classrooms upon students' subject matter understandings. Her recent publications include: "The art(s) of historical sense: An inquiry into form and understanding" (*Journal of Curriculum Studies*) and "Beyond the Looking Glass: Bringing students into the conversation of historical inquiry" (*Theory and Research in Social Education*). Professor Gabella collaborated with Catherine Randolph in revising Chapter 13 for this edition.

Brian C. Hansford

Brian C. Hansford, professor and head of the School of Curriculum and Professional Studies, Queensland University of Technology, Brisbane, Queensland, Australia, is an expert in classroom dynamics and communication. His publications include *Teacher and Classroom Communication*. Professor Hansford wrote the teaching section of the initial edition of Chapter 13 and the classroom climate section of the initial edition of Chapter 3.

Alene Harris

Alene Harris, research assistant professor of education, Peabody College, Vanderbilt University, is a specialist in classroom management and the analyzing of teaching. Her writing includes articles on classroom management and a study of effectiveness in teacher training programs. Professor Harris revised the Mastery Learning and Cooperative Learning sections of Chapter 14 for this edition, and collected data for and wrote a number of the case studies that appear throughout the text. She also reviewed much of the manuscript for the initial edition from the perspective of a secondary school classroom teacher of seventeen years.

Earline Kendall

Earline Kendall, professor of the practice of early childhood education and director of teacher education, Peabody College, Vanderbilt University, combines a longtime involvement in early education with teacher education interests. Her publications include "Family and School Coalitions: Surmounting Obstacles" and "Who's Vulnerable in Infant Day Care?" (with Virginia Moukaddem). Professor Kendall revised the High/Scope Cognitive Oriented Curriculum section of Chapter 14 for this edition.

Ann Neely

Ann Neely, associate professor of the practice of education, Peabody College, Vanderbilt University, and assistant provost, Vanderbilt University, is an expert in teacher planning. Her publications include two articles that relate directly to her contribution here: "Integrating Planning and Problem Solving in Teacher Education" and "Teacher Planning: Where Has It Been? Where Is It Now? Where Is It

Going?" Professor Neely collaborated with Carolyn Evertson in writing the planning and organization components of the initial edition of Chapter 13 and assisted with its revision.

Catherine H. Randolph

Catherine H. Randolph, research assistant professor of education, Peabody College, Vanderbilt University, is interested in understanding classrooms as social and cultural settings. Her writing includes explorations of the teacher's role in a writer's workshop, and, with Carolyn Evertson, work on redefining classroom management for learner-oriented classrooms. Professor Randolph collaborated with Marcy Singer Gabella in revising Chapter 13 for this edition.

Deborah Wells Rowe

Deborah Wells Rowe, associate professor of early childhood education, Peabody College, Vanderbilt University, specializes in the areas of early literacy development and whole-language instruction. Her recent publications include a research monograph, *Preschoolers as Authors: Literacy Learning in the Social World of the Classroom*. Professor Rowe wrote the Whole Language section of Chapter 14.

Jeanne M. Plas

Jeanne M. Plas, associate professor of psychology, Peabody College, Vanderbilt University, is primarily associated with doctoral training in school, community, and clinical psychology. She consults and writes extensively in corporate and organizational leadership. Her publications include *Working Up a Storm: Anger, Anxiety, Joy and Tears on the Job* (with K. V. Hoover-Dempsey) and *The Human Touch* (with W. W. Arnold). Professor Plas wrote Chapter 9 for the initial edition, which appears in slightly revised form as Chapter 6 in this revised edition.

Douglas J. Simpson

Douglas J. Simpson, professor of education and dean of the School of Education, Texas Christian University, is a philosopher of education. His publications include *The Pedagodfathers: The Lords of Education* and *The Teacher as Philosopher* (with Michael Jackson). Professor Simpson wrote Chapter 10.

Jane Stallings

Jane Stallings, professor of education and dean of the College of Education, Texas A&M University, is president of the American Educational Research Association and is known for her work in classroom research that links observed instructional strategies with student behavioral outcomes. Her current interests center on the delivery of and research on comprehensive school-linked services. Professor Stallings helped plan the initial edition of this text; wrote most of Chapter 10 for the initial edition, which is Chapter 14 in this revised edition; and provided much of the content for the initial edition of Chapter 3. Chapter 2 is also based substantially on her work.

Nancy Vye

Nancy Vye, senior research associate and assistant director of the Learning Technology Center, Peabody College, Vanderbilt University, and a member of the Cognition and Technology Group at Vanderbilt, is a cognitive psychologist and an expert in cognition and instruction. Professor Vye, as a member of the Cognition and Technology Group at Vanderbilt, was the primary author of the Technology-Based Anchored Instruction section of Chapter 14. Recent publications of the Cognition and Technology Group at Vanderbilt include *The Jasper Series as an Example of Anchored Instruction: Theory, Program Description and Assessment Data,* and *From Visual Word Problems to Learning Communities: Changing Conceptions of Cognitive Research.*

A Visual Guide to

The
Professional Educator

If you are contemplating a career in education, you face the reality that the challenge of educating today's learners is more complex and demanding than ever before. The responsibilities that society asks schools to assume are more numerous and diverse than they were even a few years ago. At the same time, the knowledge base that underlies the profession of teaching is constantly growing, leaving educators scrambling to keep pace with new research, new theories, and new debates.

Yet these challenges also help to make a career in this ever-changing field uniquely rewarding. Being an educator has always been an honorable and essential calling. Today, it is increasingly a *professional* calling that involves *lifelong learning* and *continuous personal growth*.

We have written this text to give you a clear, comprehensive, and realistic overview of contemporary education and the course of your future study if you decide to specialize in this field. Although mastering the content of the book is important, we believe that this material becomes meaningful only if it is related to real situations and the kinds of episodes you can expect to encounter as an educator. For this reason we have also included features designed to help you get started in actively *applying theory and research to real situations* and in acquiring the habits of a *continually learning, reflective practitioner*.

On the following five pages, we describe the elements of this text and how you can use them to succeed in this course—and, we hope, to become actively and enjoyably engaged in learning about one of the world's most important professions.

Charles B. Myers

Lynn K. Myers

To help you master essential content...

Chapter Outlines

list the main subjects to be covered in each chapter. Use the outlines to structure your study and to review the material after you have read the chapter.

Key Concepts

are highlighted as subheadings, as marginal notes (as seen here), as italicized words in the narrative, and in the Key Terms lists at the ends of chapters. These cues can be invaluable in helping you to check your comprehension of the material.

The Culture of Organizations

Like cultures in broader society, organizations—IBM, the Catholic Church, the United States Army, Harvard University, and P.S. 102 in Harlem—have their own ways of doing things, their own personality and identity. This organizational culture consists of a particular tone or feel that insiders usually take for granted but that outsiders sense strongly as they confront the organization for the first time (much as Laurie Renfro experienced her first day at Carson). Experts who study organizations label the tone or feel with such terms as *ethos, spirit, climate*, as well as *culture*. It is an elusive, hard-to-put-your-finger-on side of an organization, an aspect that many people simply do not see or comprehend.

Cultures develop in organizations, as they do in the outside world, because people require symbols and symbolic activity to give meaning to their life and work. People create cultures around themselves, which then guide, define, and shape what they do and believe. The transaction is two-way—human beings create culture, and they are shaped by it. The transaction evolves continuously as long as the community, corporation, hospital, school, or organization of any sort exists.

Learned thought and behavior

Symbols and symbolic activity

...and become actively involved

"Snapshots" introducing each chapter focus on real teaching situations to set the scene for the ideas to be covered in the chapter. Frequent references to the Snapshot within the chapter, together with many additional real-life examples and case studies, further reinforce the connection between theory and practice.

SNAPSHOT

The Snapshot for this first chapter provides pictures of two classes taught by the same teacher some years apart.[1] The first is from 1994; the second from 1978. During the intervening years, the teacher has changed teaching styles. As you read, consider:

- What seem to be the most important elements of each picture?
- How is the teaching of the two classes different?
- How is it similar?
- How would you account for the differences? For the similarities?
- What memories from your own elementary and secondary schooling does the Snapshot recall?

Fall-Hamilton School—1994

It is 10:30 A.M., October 14, 1994. Leonard Rucks is teaching English to his third-period class. Today is a review day. Mr. Rucks has planned for the students to teach language arts through the use of childre[n's] [lit]erature in what is called a "whole-language appr[oach]" but he also wants the students to master the indi[vidual] skills on the grade-level skills test. Today, he is a[...] "taskmaster." He expects all students to be in the[ir] seats before the bell rings, and he tolerates no n[on]sense. He follows a school-system-adopted matr[ix of] English skills that must be mastered, and he kee[ps] everyone on task. Usually he assigns homework [...] days a week, and he calls parents if it is not done[. He] assigns paragraph writing twice a week. He is a p[lay-] able teacher, friendly and fair, but he expects a l[ot of] his students.

Mr. Rucks teaches five classes of English. Each i[s] ability-grouped, based on grades and test scores [in] English from last year. Sometimes students get [moved] to other classes if they are ahead of or behind ev[eryone] else. This third-period class contains students in [the] middle of the ability groupings, but the range is [...] A few students are not doing well and will proba[bly be] moved to a lower group at the end of this gradin[g peri]od. But they are still trying. Two have failed gra[ding] periods so far. They already know they will prob[ably] repeat sixth grade in a "transitional" class; but th[...]

"Something to Think About" boxes offer you the opportunity to pause in your reading and respond to the information you've been presented with. You may find that these sections inspire lively discussions with your classmates.

Something to Think About

Russell is in the second grade for the second time, and he is failing again. He is a mainstreamed student in the class, has slight learning disabilities, and is mildly retarded. He is a little troublesome but not really disruptive at this point. He is just older, noticeably bigger than the other students, and more aggressive.

Because of recently instituted competency testing, Russell's teacher will not be allowed to recommend that he be passed on to a regular third grade, even as a mainstreamed special student. He simply does not have the minimum test scores required for promotion.

However, because Russell's assessments indicate that he is on the borderline for placement in a self-contained special education classroom, he could be classified as mildly retarded and be put into a special education class that is not graded. But if this is done, he will probably be labeled EMR for the remainder of his elementary school years and will not be able to return to a mainstream classroom.

Russell's teachers, the principal, the school psychologist, and his parents must meet to decide whether he should repeat second grade again in a regular class or be classified as EMR.

- What do you think should be done?
- What are the benefits and negative aspects of either action?

"Reflecting on Practice" sections

ask you to apply what you've learned to the practice of teaching. As you will learn, being an effective teacher means being a *reflective* teacher, one who is never satisfied with pat answers and continually adapts to the demands of unique situations.

REFLECTING ON PRACTICE

This chapter's Reflecting on Practice consists of brief glimpses into three different schools. Each is presented as a case study for you to consider as you think about schools as cultures and as effective institutions of learning. Consider each of the following questions as they relate to these schools:

- What characteristics of the culture of each of these schools is reflected in the descriptions? Why do you think each of these characteristics developed in that school?
- What characteristics of effectiveness are reflected?
- How would you assess the cultural atmosphere and degree of effectiveness of each school?

Although the schools are different—elementary and secondary; urban and suburban; public and private—they also typify schools in America today. The descriptions are necessarily brief and incomplete, so you will need to read between the lines and make assumptions beyond the observers' reports about the schools, students, and teachers.

"Educational Research" sections

provide a glimpse of the nature of research, specific research efforts, conclusions from some of those efforts, and ways in which these conclusions have affected teaching and schools. As a professional educator, you will need to be an intelligent consumer of research information from a variety of sources and to develop the ability to sort through it all and apply research conclusions to your everyday work.

EDUCATIONAL RESEARCH

An Ethnographic Approach

Much educational research, such as that emphasized in the first three chapters, is analytical in nature—at least to some extent, it involves experimentation. But anthropologists, those who study culture, often are more descriptive than analytical. That is, they study a culture by observing people and recording what they see. Then they interpret their descriptions by comparing those of one culture to those of another, offering explanations for similarities and differences. This type of study is called *ethnography*.

Therefore, to the extent that schools are cultures, they too can be studied ethnographically.[26] In fact, the Reflecting on Practice section of this chapter consists of brief segments of four school ethnographies; when you read those four descriptions and responded to the questions that preceded them, you were thinking ethnographically.

Following is a short example of an ethnographic account that was written not by an anthropologist but by a journalist. As you read it:

- How would you comp culture of Fletcher-Joh that of the four schoo already read about in ter?
- How would you comp the culture of the high you attended?

When you finish thinking Fletcher-Johnson in these consider the three questio follow the description.

The account is by Ma a Washington, D.C., journ

On Monday mornings Mr. Tolson greets his nint math students at Fletche Educational Center, they about their weekends. Th gun battles that interrupt sleep, arguments that ec the alleys, sirens and scre are the night sounds of th jects.

"They say things that shock your pants off," Ar Tolson said Tuesday. "Bu know, for these kids, it ju like a normal thing."

Fletcher-Johnson, a r brown concrete building o Benning Road in Southea rant of the city), doesn't f school in a ravaged, drug- neighborhood. It is a spra place of bright colors and computer equipment. It is free. Its halls are carpeted quiet. In its open classroo teachers need not shout

...and to learn in a variety of ways

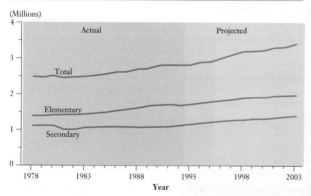

FIGURE 1-5 Numbers of elementary and secondary school teachers (public and private) since 1978 and projected through 2003.

Illustrations

in the form of tables, charts, and graphs give you another angle on the text content and visually organize a wealth of data. Actively work with these features by posing questions and asking what inferences can be drawn from the information they present.

Photographs

are more than attractive embellishments to the text. They have been carefully selected to present a vivid picture of the world of teaching. Use the images presented to develop your skill as an observer of education and to imagine what it would be like to be a professional educator.

And for added reinforcement...

At the *end of each chapter,* you will find:

A **Summary, Study Questions,** a **Key Terms** list, and **For Further Reading** section to reinforce the chapter's main ideas and provide you with sources for further study. Additionally, **Notes** at the end of the book acquaint you with the research base of teaching.

Study Questions

1. Think of one of the organizations in which you are or have been a member—fraternity, sorority, athletic team, church group, or the like. Then identify within that group the cultural characteristics of organizations that this chapter stressed—values and beliefs, heroes and heroines, rituals and ceremonies, stories and legends, and informal players. How and why do you think these specific characteristics developed as they did in this group?

2. Think again of an organization in which you are or have been a member, possibly the same one you used in Question 1. Then identify subcultures that exist or existed in the organization. Why do you think these subcultures developed in this group? In what ways was each subculture a positive and a negative influence in the organization?

3. Think of a school you know reasonably well. Then, using as your guide the six actions proposed for Carson High School in the section titled "The Carson High School Community's Task," propose six comparable things that people in that school could do to make the school better.

Also available:

A companion **Study Guide** that offers a resourceful collection of chapter summaries, self-tests, learning objectives, and review exercises to help you gauge your progress and prepare for exams.

(Ask your campus bookstore manager to order you a copy of this effective learning tool.)

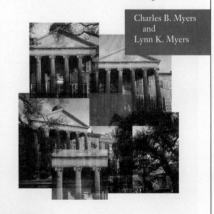

Study Guide for
The
Professional Educator

A NEW Introduction to Teaching and Schools

Charles B. Myers
and
Lynn K. Myers

1

A First Look

The Student Preface explains that the purpose of this text is to introduce you to the profession of teaching in pre-K–12 schools. Unit 1, Chapters 1 through 4, provides the beginning professional with points of view regarding three areas of study central to an understanding of education, teaching, and schools today and in the future: (1) the context in which pre-K–12 teachers and schools operate; (2) what happens in classrooms; and (3) how schools function. By studying this unit, you should gain new information in all three areas; begin to formulate your own ideas and views about education, teaching, and schools; and develop skills that you can use to interpret new information and ideas.

Chapter 1 explains why we have pre-K–12 schools and describes current events, issues, and trends that affect them. Chapter 2 looks at what happens in classrooms and shows you how to interpret those events. Chapter 3 describes what recent educational researchers say are good teaching situations and practices. Chapter 4 explains how schools function as cultural organizations and suggests ways you can study schools from that perspective.

When you finish each chapter, you should understand the following general concepts, and you should have begun to develop the skills noted.

CHAPTER 1
Teaching and Schools in America Today: The Current Scene and Future Directions

General Concepts

- Contemporary teaching and schools in America can be examined in terms of reasons for having schools, students served, subject matter taught, teachers, and the public's perceptions of schools.

- Teaching and schools in America are changing rapidly; in the 1980s, pressure for reform catalyzed the process.

- The changes involve different expectations, shifts in priorities, and new insights into the nature of teaching and learning.

- Predictions about teaching and schools of the future are based on new technologies, changes in teacher roles and education, and changes in the social and cultural environment.

Skills

- An ability to analyze key contemporary educational issues and trends that appear in the media

- An ability to relate contemporary educational conditions to the question, Will I like being a professional teacher in this context?

CHAPTER 2
Inside Classrooms: Studying Teaching

General Concepts

- Classrooms have characteristics that set them apart from all other group settings; although there are similarities among classrooms, each is also unique.

- Classroom teaching and learning can be studied and analyzed through systematic observation.

Skill

- An ability to analyze classroom teaching

from the perspective of a beginning professional

CHAPTER 3
Effective Teaching Practices

General Concepts

- Teachers often have a significant influence on the students they teach, but some teachers are much more influential than others.

- Recent research has identified teaching practices that are more effective than others.

Skill

- An ability to recognize effective teaching practices, such as appropriate use of time, classroom climates, use of active teaching strategies, and use of expectation and reward structures

CHAPTER 4
Studying Schools as Cultures

General Concepts

- Schools are organizational cultures that, when effective, are made up of people who follow certain patterns of behavior, possess common values and beliefs, and pursue particular goals.

- Key cultural characteristics of all schools are shared values and beliefs, heroes and heroines, rituals and ceremonies, stories and legends, and informal players.

- School cultures include subgroups, which must work together if the school is to be effective.

- If school reform efforts are going to succeed, they must attend to both the effectiveness and the organizational cultural characteristics of schools.

Skill

- An ability to view schools in terms of both effectiveness and cultural characteristics

Teaching and Schools in America Today

The Current Scene and Future Directions

*A*s you begin your study of education, teaching, and schools, you doubtless have many questions: What is teaching like today? What does it take to be a good teacher? Can I become one? If I do, will I be satisfied with the life and work? In a very direct way, this book is intended to help you answer these questions. We ask you to keep them and others like them in mind as you read the text and participate in the course in which it is used. Periodically, throughout the book, we prompt you to think about these questions.

In this first chapter, we begin by surveying the contemporary scene of teaching and schools in America and suggest ways in which you can begin your study of that scene. The overview includes sketches of current conditions, explanations of how these conditions developed, and predictions about trends for the future. All along, you are asked to think about what is being described and to formulate questions that will guide your study.

We ask you to do this for two reasons. First, teachers need to reflect upon and analyze ideas and then make professional decisions based on their thinking; we want you to begin that kind of thinking as soon as you begin to study teaching and schools. Second, we want your study of professional education to be interactive in an intellectual sense; that is, we want you to be able to develop *your own* ideas about the information presented, not just absorb what you read here.

After a Snapshot, the chapter begins with suggestions for approaching your study of teaching and schools. This is followed by a look at schools today, which includes the reasons for having schools, students, subjects taught, life in schools, teachers, and Americans' perceptions of schools.

After surveying the contemporary scene, we focus on recent efforts to analyze and address the perceived shortcomings of American pre-K–12 education, efforts that began in earnest in the 1980s and have been evolving and expanding since that time. In the process, we look at several national reports and proposals for revitalizing teaching and schools, and we describe several directions the reforms have been taking.

The chapter's last section shifts from today to the years ahead. Several predictions about schools and teaching in the future are made, and you are asked to think of how the predicted circumstances are likely to affect you.

The Snapshot presents two pictures, taken sixteen years apart, of a teacher and his classes of sixth-grade students. You are asked to compare the two pictures and to think about the differences between them.

The Reflecting on Practice box discusses concepts of teaching and schools that embody issues currently being debated. You are asked, first, to reflect upon these ideas and issues and to analyze your own personal thoughts about them; we anticipate that this process will allow you to monitor educational developments in the months and years ahead, including how your own views of them change. The Educational Research section provides an overview of contemporary research in education and sets the stage for more detailed investigations in later chapters.

The Snapshot for this first chapter provides pictures of two classes taught by the same teacher some years apart.[1] The first is from 1994; the second from 1978. During the intervening years, the teacher has changed teaching styles. As you read, consider:

■ What seem to be the most important elements of each picture?

■ How is the teaching of the two classes different?

■ How is it similar?

■ How would you account for the differences? For the similarities?

■ What memories from your own elementary and secondary schooling does the Snapshot recall?

Fall-Hamilton School—1994

It is 10:30 A.M., October 14, 1994. Leonard Rucks is teaching English to his third-period class. Today is a review day. Mr. Rucks has planned for the students to review the paragraphs they wrote yesterday, which he evaluated last night. When that is finished, he will drill the students on several spelling, punctuation, and grammar rules that a number of them do not seem to understand. He wants the class to be ready for the competency test that he will administer next week before the end of the report card period.

The test is part of a statewide achievement testing program that is administered to all sixth graders. One is administered each grading period. At the end of the year, Mr. Rucks will tabulate each student's test responses for all tests to determine which skills each has mastered. Students must master 75 percent of the skills for the year in order to continue on to seventh grade. The students take similar tests in mathematics. Up until a few years ago, virtually all sixth graders passed every year, but last year 15 percent failed at least one of the two tests and are repeating the grade.

Mr. Rucks has two specific goals for his English class, but they sometimes conflict with each other. He wants to teach language arts through the use of children's literature in what is called a "whole-language approach," but he also wants the students to master the individual skills on the grade-level skills test. Today, he is a "task-master." He expects all students to be in their seats before the bell rings, and he tolerates no nonsense. He

follows a school-system-adopted matrix of English skills that must be mastered, and he keeps everyone on task. Usually he assigns homework four days a week, and he calls parents if it is not done. He assigns paragraph writing twice a week. He is a personable teacher, friendly and fair, but he expects a lot from his students.

Mr. Rucks teaches five classes of English. Each is ability-grouped, based on grades and test scores in English from last year. Sometimes students get moved to other classes if they are ahead of or behind everyone else. This third-period class contains students in the middle of the ability groupings, but the range is broad. A few students are not doing well and will probably be moved to a lower group at the end of this grading period. But they are still trying. Two have failed the first grading period. They already know they will probably repeat sixth grade in a "transitional" class; but the more they master this year, the less they will have to repeat.

Mr. Rucks is a Career Ladder teacher. He attended special workshops in the summer of 1988 and was evaluated for a career ladder promotion during 1988–89. His ranking gives him a chance to make $7,000 more each year. Because he is a career ladder teacher, his lesson plans are reviewed and his classes are observed periodically by his principal and other evaluators. He is assessed according to state and school system guidelines and in terms of his own plans. How well his students behave in his classes and how well they perform on the tests are two of the criteria on which he is judged. The evaluation puts pressure on Mr. Rucks, and sometimes he distrusts the process. But he decided to participate because he wants the extra money and because he is tired of being paid the same base salary as some other teachers he considers ineffective. He knows he is good, and he intends to show it.

Wharton School—1978

It is 1:30 P.M., January 14, 1978. Leonard Rucks is teaching sixth-grade English to one of the classes that he shares with three other teachers in an interdisciplinary mini-school. The school is racially and economically integrated. All classes are organized heterogeneously. The other three teachers in the mini-school teach science, mathematics, and social studies. The same four teachers plan together and share the same students so that they can get to know each student better. This enables them to adjust their content and levels of expectation to fit the needs of each student. They are very happy with the fact that they have not failed a student for five years.

Mr. Rucks is singing a ballad to the class, a historical ballad from the period in England that the students are studying in social studies. He hopes to help the students feel what European life was like in 1688. The students are very attentive. They love Mr. Rucks. They know he cares about them. He is animated and always upbeat. When students do not do well on tests, he is always encouraging and tells them he knows they will do better next time. Happy faces abound in Mr. Rucks's class.

Although Mr. Rucks provides some full-class direct instruction, much of his instruction is provided to small groups and to individuals. The classroom is organized into learning centers and individual study corners. Students often work alone on programmed study sheets, which they take to Mr. Rucks for checking. Visitors tend to think

Mr. Rucks's classes are disorganized, but they are not. Students are simply working at their individual levels and at their own speed. He knows where each student is in terms of personal abilities.

Tests are infrequent in Mr. Rucks's classes except for the weekly spelling tests. Mr. Rucks assesses informally and continuously. He believes this type of evaluation is less threatening to students than formal evaluation, and he believes it is just as effective. His students' self-concepts are important to him. He wants them to believe they are successful.

Mr. Rucks and his mini-school partners run their classes as they see fit. Their principal has confidence in them and rarely "interferes." Although the principal is welcome in their classes, he rarely comes unless invited to a special class presentation. He rates their teaching performance from what he hears "as he walks the halls and talks to students and parents." He knows the mini-school provides a happy learning environment.

Studying Teaching and Schools

Anyone contemplating a career in teaching today is confronted with a field in ferment. Expectations of schools, teachers, and students are changing; and the challenges of the Goals 2000 legislation of 1994 reflects those changing expectations. The ferment, however, is not new. During the past decade and a half, teaching and schools in America have been scrutinized, criticized, eulogized, and "reformed." Nine major national reports on reforming schools appeared in 1983 alone, and many more have appeared since. Change has been the order of the day, and the impact of that change on students and teachers has been widespread, noticeable, and significant. Some of the specific changes that have occurred have been long in coming. Some have been rapid. Some have been consistent with each other. Some have been at cross-purposes. Some have been relatively easy to implement. Some have been traumatic. Some seem to have been successful. Some have failed.

Reform-generated changes have caused shifts in how teachers such as Leonard Rucks teach. In Mr. Rucks's case, he has modified his teaching methods; has shifted to whole-language instruction; and has become more demanding and precise in what he expects his students to learn, more structured in how he deals with his class, and more focused on academics. In the 1970s, positive student self-concepts were predominant classroom goals; in the 1980s, academic performance was a higher priority; now, he is trying to accomplish both at the same time.

So what do all these changes mean? What are schools and teachers in America like today? Why and how did they get this way? What ideas, principles, and assumptions guide them? What will they be like in the future? These are the questions addressed in this text.

However, be forewarned that the text raises more questions than it answers. It does so because there are no simple answers in the study of teaching and schools in the United States. There is no secret formula. To understand teaching and schools, you need to reflect upon what you already know, gather the information presented in this book, and seek complementary information elsewhere. Then you need to use that information to formulate your own tentative answers to these questions and many others like them. These answers will shape your own initial ideas about teaching and schools. Once you develop and refine them, you will be able to use them as benchmarks for further study and a more sophisticated understanding.

To begin, pause for a few minutes and consider the following questions. Jot down your thoughts.

Formulating questions

Tentative answers

- What were predominant characteristics of your own kindergarten through grade 12 learning?
- What types of things occurred in your pre-K–12 education that you now consider especially informative?
  challenging?
  enjoyable?
  sad?
  frightening?
  depressing?
- What good things did your teachers do?
- What bad or harmful things did they do?
- Of the students who went to school with you, which do you think benefited the most? Which benefited the least? What made the difference?
- If you do teach, in what ways do you hope to be like your own teachers?
- How do you expect to be different from them?

In addition, plan to read professional material that will keep you informed as you pursue your studies. For example, subscribe to the newspaper *Education Week*, which is published during most of the year, and read regularly one or two education journals, such as *Phi Delta Kappan*, which has been particularly up-to-date in its coverage during the last few years.[2]

Sources of information

The Contemporary Scene

This study of teaching and schools in America begins with a glimpse at the purposes of schools in historical context; then it shifts to a look at schools today. First, it is important to note that schools and what happens in them are not static. The two pictures of Leonard Rucks presented in the Snapshot at the beginning of this chapter highlight some of the changes that have occurred in recent years. As you read about schools today, think of how they were different in the past and how they will be different in the future. This look at schools addresses the following questions:

- Why do we have schools?
- Who goes to school?
- What is taught in schools?
- What else happens there?
- Who are the teachers?
- What are Americans' perceptions of teachers and schools?

Why We Have Schools

Schooling in the United States has always rested on the democratic and republican foundations of the nation. To state the point simply, the founders of the United States believed that its citizens should govern themselves, either directly or through elected representatives; that principle has guided the country throughout its history. As a result, all Americans need to be educated adequately so that they can understand the issues of the day, make informed judgments, and select appropriate leaders. They need to be educated well enough to get along with others and to be able to provide for their own economic well-being. This is the point made years ago by Thomas Jefferson when he said, "If a nation expects to be ignorant and free, in a state of civilization, it expects what never was and never will be."[3]

Schools are the primary agencies through which formal education occurs. They are the institutions that society uses to train its children politically, socially, and economically.

In comparison with other societies, the United States has been unique in trying to educate *all* its citizens. To be sure, that goal has not always meant what it does today, and it has not yet been attained. It is, however, closer to reality today than ever before. Over the years, women, slaves, poor people, those with limited abilities, those who could not get to a school, and those whose parents chose not to send them to school were neglected. But by the 1960s, all Americans of school age were expected to be in school, and nearly all of them were.

In recent years, Americans have realized that having most children *in schools* is not enough to accomplish what Jefferson had in mind. Children not only have to be in school, but they also have to be *learning*. In essence, this is the common theme of the reports on schools of the 1980s. These reports said that schools should be expected *to be successful in educating all the children* of the United States and that the people who operate the schools—elected officials, superintendents, principals, and teachers—are to be accountable for teaching all students well and teaching them the right things.

This expectation puts greater pressure on teachers such as Leonard Rucks. It requires him to teach academics more precisely and to show that his students are actually learning what is expected of sixth graders. As a result, in recent years, school systems have made modifications in how teachers teach and what students learn, and both continue to change. At the same time, perceptions of teaching, teachers, and schools have been noticeably transformed among teachers themselves, students, parents, and the general public. In short, teaching and schools are very different today from the way they were only a few years ago.

So, in general terms, what does it mean to say schools are expected to educate citizens politically, socially, and economically? Has the expectation changed over

Historical purposes of American schools

Schools for everyone

Learning for everyone

time? What does it mean today? How would you answer each of these questions at this early point in your study?

Because the United States is a democratic republic, all its citizens have the opportunity to participate in the decisions of the national, state, and local governments. In fact, for the system to work properly, a significant percentage of the citizens must participate actively in the government, must understand what they are doing, and must act responsibly. They must also get along with one another peacefully and positively. In other words, they must be *good citizens.*

But people are not born good citizens. Good citizenship is taught. It involves knowledge about government, people, relationships among people, and issues of the day. It involves positive values toward the goals of society, toward the system of government, toward other people, toward other nations, and toward active personal involvement in public affairs. It involves *skills* of effective participation.

Schools in the United States are expected to teach the knowledge, values, and skills of citizenship. Although they are not alone in this role, they have the broadest and most formal responsibility of any institution to fulfill it. In a sense, the schools' general civic mission is to transform self-centered young children into responsible, understanding, thoughtful decision makers.

Schools educate citizens through virtually every facet of their operation: when they teach reading, listening, thinking, geography, history, government, current events, vocational studies, and so forth; when they teach proper behavior, set dress codes, provide for peer social interaction; and when they train students for active participation in peer groups, club activities, sports, school government, and community projects. In fact, because the role of citizen is so broad and involves so many facets, it is impossible to separate the times when schools and teachers are educating for citizenship from those when they are educating for other purposes.

Most people think of the academic purpose of schools as their central reason for being. As they see it, students go to schools to develop their intellects, to become *educated;* that is, to learn information and ideas, to develop insights, and to put those ideas and insights to use as they explore new information.

The academic purpose of schools is reflected in how schools are organized. School days are divided by subjects—reading, arithmetic, social studies, science, language arts, music, art, English, world history, physics, algebra, computer science, and foreign languages.

In a sense, however, academic achievement is an *intermediate* purpose rather than an end in itself. It helps students to be better citizens, to be more successful economically, and to be more satisfied and successful social human beings.

Schools are also expected to train students for jobs. But how they should do this in today's world is a matter of debate. The debate usually centers on the degree to which the education is directed toward specific jobs rather than toward more general skills that are useful for a variety of occupations. For example, should high school students be trained to be sales clerks as part of their senior year, or would that class time be better spent on business math and accounting? Should a person who is weak in reading and mathematics be taught auto repair instead of additional reading and mathematics?

Most employers in recent years have favored more education in the "basic skills" and the "core academic subjects" rather than specific job training. They point out that if students are educated adequately in the basic subjects, they can be given specific training on the job—something that is difficult to do with trainees who are

Citizenship education

Academic achievement

Vocational preparation or training

academically unprepared. Employers also note that the rapidity of change in business and industry requires that employees be retrained often, frequently for jobs that did not exist when they were in school. As a result of those views, vocational education subjects have decreased in importance in recent years. At the same time, however, there is a strong push to tie high school vocational education to specific jobs for individual students, so that non-college-bound students graduate directly into a paying job for which they have been trained.

College preparation

For many students, the primary purpose of school, especially high school, is preparation for college. In this context, schools prepare students for more schooling, and that, in turn, prepares them for jobs. Along the way, students also learn to be good citizens, but their main objectives are getting into college, being prepared to perform well while there, and graduating into a profession. From one perspective, the college preparation purpose of schools is a combination of the academic achievement purpose and the vocational preparation purpose.

The college preparation purpose of schools is narrower than the other purposes mentioned here because not all students intend to go to college and because it is not easily identifiable as a purpose for elementary schools. However, because the typical highest-achieving students and the children of the most influential parents see high school learning as college preparation, that purpose for schools is the basis for many decisions made by school leaders. Probably the two most often mentioned measures of apparent success for schools are the numbers of graduates who enter prestigious colleges and how well they do in their studies there.

Personal and social development

In addition to these purposes, schools are expected to develop students into good individual and good social human beings—who feel good about themselves, who are capable of interacting with others in positive ways, and who are inclined to do so. Personal and social development as a purpose of schools parallels citizenship education but is less tied to civic responsibility and active political participation. This purpose stresses the fundamental worth and dignity of all people, even those not likely to become leaders. It teaches caring, sharing, and interpersonal understanding. It expects schools to instill in their students the American values of the importance of each individual, equality of treatment and opportunity, and potential for individual success within the American system.

In summary, our schools serve a variety of purposes. These purposes are derived from the beliefs and traditions of the United States. When viewed generally, they are consistent with one another rather than contradictory. Often they overlap.

But Americans expect much from their schools, maybe too much. Different people have different priorities and ask that schools emphasize different goals. Those priorities change constantly, and schools usually cannot adjust fast enough. As a result, although most Americans agree on the importance of schools and on their general reasons for being, they tend to be dissatisfied with the schools' effectiveness and are quick to suggest how schools can be better.

The multiple and conflicting goals for teaching and schools are phenomena that all teachers need to be able to live with. Because of persistent demands that schools do more than they can reasonably be expected to do and the increasing push for conflicting *outcomes*, teachers have to be capable of deciding what is best for their students and willing to act based on their professional judgment. To do this, they have to be knowledgeable, intelligent, reflective, and analytical decision makers and leaders. They must be able to sort through the confusion in order to serve the interests of their own students.

Who Goes to School

In the United States, almost everyone of school age is enrolled in school. For example, in 1995 about 50 million, or approximately 99 percent, of all school-age children were attending elementary or secondary schools. Of those, about 88.5 percent were in public schools; 9 percent were in religiously affiliated schools, primarily Catholic parochial schools; and about 2.5 percent were in other private schools.[4] Figure 1-1 shows school enrollment and enrollment projections between 1978 and 2003; Figure 1-2 shows a percentage breakdown of elementary and secondary school students according to race and ethnic background, based on data from the 1991 census.[5]

Percentage of school-age children in school

Table 1-1 shows the family income breakdown for students in public schools in terms of three characteristics used in 1991 census data: white, black, and Hispanic origin.

According to the 1991 census data, 21.8 percent of American children under age 18 lived below the poverty line—16.8 percent of whites, 40.4 percent of Hispanics, and 45.9 percent of blacks.[6]

Economic characteristics

As the decade of the 1990s started, about 16 percent of American households consisted of the ideal family—two parents who are married and two or more children.[7] In fact, only one-third of American households included any children under the age of 18.[8] Many households were made up of one or two older adults with no children, although children may have lived with them earlier.

Social characteristics

Also at the start of the 1990s, 24 percent of all children lived in a household without a father, and 60 percent of black children lived with a single parent.[9]

As these data indicate, students come to school from many different backgrounds. But in spite of those differences, teachers must help each child learn to the

FIGURE 1-1   Enrollment in elementary and secondary schools (public and private) 1978–2003.

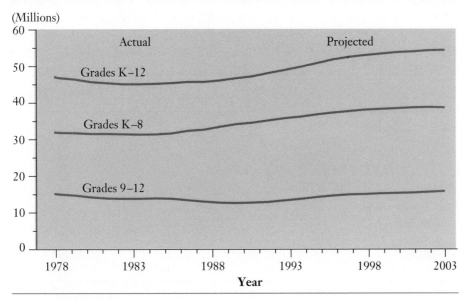

SOURCE: D. E. Gerald & W. J. Hussar. (1992). *Projection of educational statistics to 2003.* Washington, DC: National Center for Education Statistics, pp. 6–7.

FIGURE 1-2 Race and ethnic origin of population, ages 3–17 for the year 2000 (projected) based on 1991 census.

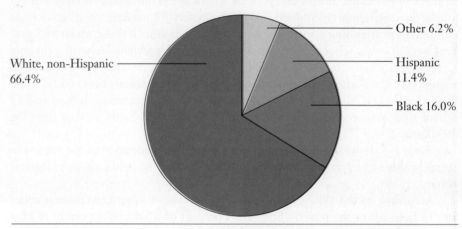

White, non-Hispanic 66.4%

Other 6.2%

Hispanic 11.4%

Black 16.0%

SOURCE: R. Kominski & A. Adams. (1993). School enrollment—social and economic characteristics of students: October 1991. *Current Population Reports*, Ser. P-20 (p. x). Washington, DC: U.S. Department of Commerce.

maximum of his or her ability. This task will be even more difficult in the years ahead. Greater percentages of students will come from cultural traditions different from those of their teachers and will have learning styles that the teachers do not understand. Teachers will have to learn more about their students' cultural distinctiveness so that those background characteristics become assets for learning, not hindrances. Concepts such as *diversity, multiculturalism, mainstreaming, inclusion,* and *learning styles* will be more important for beginning teachers than they were in the past. As you study later chapters and sections of this text, you will want to develop your own understanding of each of these ideas and begin to use them as you reflect upon and interpret educational developments in the real world of teaching and schools.

TABLE 1-1 Annual Family Income of Students in Public Schools According to 1991 Census

	Less than $20,000 (%)	$20,000 to $40,000 (%)	$40,000 and above (%)
Elementary School			
All students	34	36	29
White	29	36	34
Black	66	22	11
Hispanic	57	31	11
High School			
All students	29	33	37
White	23	35	42
Black	59	25	15
Hispanic	54	33	13

SOURCE: Extrapolated from R. Kominski and A. Adams. (1993). School enrollment—social and economic characteristics of students: October 1991. *Current Population Reports*, Ser. P-20 (p. x). Washington, DC: U.S. Department of Commerce.

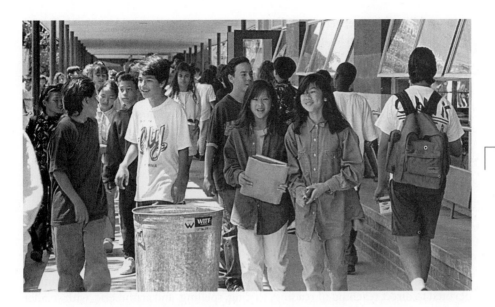

One of the challenges facing today's teachers is working successfully with students who are increasingly diverse—not only in ethnicity and culture, but in family background, attitudes toward school, and readiness for academic work.

What Is Taught in Schools

Over the past twenty-five years, American schools have followed two distinct patterns in what has been taught. During the 1970s, the emphases were on developing curricular flexibility, individualizing instruction, grouping students, teaching the "whole child," developing racial and ethnic identity, and enhancing the student's "self-concept." These emphases grew out of the philosophy of the 1960s that stressed the recognition of individual differences and the tailoring of learning to the different needs of the students. They were reactions to earlier times in which schools were more achievement-oriented and, according to some educators, "less humane."   The 1970s

The 1980s, particularly the years after 1983, saw a shift "back to the basics" and a more achievement-oriented set of educational assumptions. Students were expected to be more serious about learning. More "basic" academic subjects were required. There was less time for electives and vocational subjects. Those who did not achieve what was expected were more likely to fail. Students who failed subjects were prohibited from participating in school sports and in other extracurricular activities.   The 1980s

In recent years, schools have persisted in their achievement-oriented thrust, but some of that thrust has been tempered by the realization that funding is limited and that some students face dire out-of-school living conditions that make them especially difficult to teach. Educators as a group realize that improving the learning of students requires more than raising standards and flunking those who do not measure up. They know they need to assure that all students learn, but they also realize that resources and talents are limited and that they do not have all the answers necessary to succeed with all students.   The 1990s

In spite of these realizations, however, schools of the 1990s are expected to have identified learning *outcomes* that all students should achieve by the time they reach certain grade levels or they are ready to graduate. These outcomes are usually described in terms of the content that the students should learn; and, at least on paper, schools, teachers, and students are held accountable for this learning. That level of   Learning outcomes accountability for meeting clearly stated learning outcomes could possibly be the most powerful way in which pre-K–12 teaching in the next decades will be different from in the past.

Grade-Level Content

Typically, American students today study a relatively common pattern of subject matter as they proceed through the elementary school grades. In kindergarten, they are introduced to school and their school peers and are instructed at a readiness level in basic subjects—prereading skills, letter recognition, colors, numbers, rules of social behavior, and following directions.

Kindergarten

Often classes are relatively flexible, with play and naptime scheduled regularly. Lately, however, kindergartens have become more structured and more seriously academic in orientation. A higher percentage of students has enrolled in kindergarten, and more of them are attending for a full school day.

Primary grades

Most primary grades are still organized by grade level as self-contained classes with twenty to thirty students per teacher. Most primary-level instructional time is devoted to direct teaching of reading, writing, spelling, and arithmetic, with smaller amounts of time for social studies, science, art, music, and physical education. Basic skills have received increasingly more attention in recent years, and students, even in these early grades, are expected to demonstrate that they have learned minimum amounts of content in the basic fields before they move on to the next grade.

Upper elementary grades

The upper elementary or middle grades are either self-contained or departmentalized, based on local school preference. Typical class sizes are between twenty-four and thirty. Subjects taught are usually an extension of those at the primary levels. Basic subject content and skills are still stressed, but proportionally more time is provided for social studies, science, art, and music. Often, time is set aside for interdisciplinary studies and the study of topics generated by student interest. One approach to this latter type of study is "discovery time," or, as it is called in many schools, *exploratory* time.

Increasingly, elementary schools provide before-school and after-school day care for children to accommodate single-parent families and families in which both parents work outside the home. Especially where they serve poor communities, schools often begin the day by providing breakfast to the children. Nearly all schools serve hot lunches.

Middle schools

Middle schools usually include grades 6 or 7 through 8 or 9. Ideally, these schools are designed to fit the special student characteristics of preadolescents. Most are departmentally organized, but interdisciplinary classes are prevalent. Most provide a common curriculum with students grouped according to an ability ranking of some kind. At each successive grade level, the instruction usually focuses more on content and less on the student.

High schools

High schools usually include grades 9–12, although some do not begin until grade 10. Students usually follow discernible subject paths or tracks according to their assessed ability or their election of particular subjects. Typical high school courses of study are outlined in Figure 1-3.

What Else Happens in Schools

Schools are more than just places to learn. They are cultures in which children, youth, and a few adults live for a major part of five days a week, for approximately forty weeks a year. In that environment, students learn more than just the academic

The school culture

FIGURE 1-3   Three typical high school student courses of study.

College Prep Students

English/language arts—4 years
Mathematics—2 or 3 years (algebra,
    geometry, trigonometry, calculus)
Science—2 or 3 years
Social studies—2 or 3 years
Foreign language—2 years
Health/physical education—3 or 4 years
Computer science
Electives

General Studies Students

English/language arts—4 years
General mathematics—1 or 2 years
Science—1 or 2 years
Social studies—2 or 3 years
Foreign language—elective
Health/physical education—3 or 4 years
Computer science
Electives

Vocational Students

English/language arts—4 years
General mathematics—1 year
Science—1 or 2 years
Social studies—2 or 3 years
Health/physical education—3 or 4 years

Selections from
    Business education
    Commercial education
    Data processing
    Industrial education
    Trades
    Agriculture education
    Home education

content of the subjects taught, and they learn from more than just the teachers employed to teach them. They learn from the school environment itself, from their peers, and from the social and personal interactions that take place in the school society. In that environment, they grow, develop, and mature—physically, intellectually, emotionally, socially, and personally. They participate in classes, teacher conferences, lunchtime discussions, intramural and interscholastic sports, class parties and trips, debates, newspaper writing assignments, chorus and band, and hallway conversations. They learn about and sometimes become involved in fights, protection rackets, drug experimentation, and gang rivalries. They develop close friendships, lifetime attachments, love affairs, and bitter enemies.

Schools are age-grouped societies made up primarily of students but under the direction of a few institutionally imposed adult authorities. They have their own rules and folkways, their own social class distinctions, their own leaders, their own followers, and their own "underclass." In a sense, schools are at least two societies in one. They reflect the broad society from which their students come, but they also are societies of their own.

Students function in schools as individuals and as members of many subgroups. For example, at a given time, a hypothetical high school student, Mark David, could be all of the following: student, sophomore, class vice president, hall monitor, wrestler, track star, "big man on campus," "a macho hunk," son of Doctor Kenneth David, brother of Tim and Sherry David, class activist, and driver of the best-

Age-grouped societies

Subgroups

If you think back on the most important developments of your own school years, you will probably agree that schools are much more than just places to learn.

Personal and social development

equipped Pontiac Fiero. He also could be an average-achieving student, a member of Ms. Underwood's fifth-period physics class, a good writer, a smooth talker, a secure personality, a teacher's pet, the "steady" of Cassie Holloran, a friend of the principal, and a member of the "in group" of the school.

Through the course of the typical thirteen years of school, students learn from all events in their school lives. Some of those events are positive and stimulating; some are negative and inhibiting; some are bland and unimportant. Whatever those events are, they help transform the 4- or 5-year-old who enters preschool or kindergarten into a 17- or 18-year-old young adult. In that transition, students pass through a long sequence of personal modifications in which they actually become different people over and over again.

At age 17, the hypothetical Mark David is a different human being from anyone else. Much of what he is and what he will become was determined by what happened to him in school.

Good teachers, of course, take all of this into consideration. They care about their students as vulnerable human beings and see their professional roles as more than simply imparting knowledge and developing skills. They nurture their students, helping them succeed in more than just academics. They aid their growing up in all its dimensions. Probably the most devastating failures for teachers have little to do with flunked tests, but occur when they are not able to assist a student who is in trouble in a more personal way.

Who the Teachers Are

In January 1986, a United States spaceship exploded on takeoff at Cape Canaveral, Florida, killing all seven people aboard. One of those killed was Christa McAuliffe, a teacher from Concord High School, Concord, New Hampshire. She was one of the first "civilians" chosen for such a mission and was selected through a nationwide competition among teachers. President Ronald Reagan had established that selection process when he announced more than a year earlier that a teacher would be the first "civilian" in space.

Although political motives were involved, the fact that a teacher was designated illustrates to some extent the unique way in which teachers are perceived in American society, probably in all societies. More significant, however, was the reaction of the American public to the tragedy. News reports and most conversations about that explosion consistently referred to "the teacher and the other astronauts," and Christa McAuliffe became a name and a personal hero with whom many Americans seemed to identify. Christa McAuliffe's death was considered to be so traumatic for so many Americans that special media programs and special consultation services were established in communities nationwide to help people, especially students and young people, cope with it.

How teachers are perceived

The events that surrounded the death of the teacher in space illustrate very poignantly the degree of attachment that most people develop with some of their own schoolteachers and with teachers in general. Teachers individually, and as a group, are usually viewed as good, caring people who devote their time and energies to helping others. They are usually thought to be more honest, more "proper," more sensitive, and more "well meaning" than people in other professions. They are not usually considered to be the most intelligent professional group, but they are considered to be among the most dedicated.

Of course, nearly everyone remembers some teacher who does not fit the ideal. But, when people are asked which person had the greatest impact on their lives other than a member of their family, a teacher is mentioned 58 percent of the time, much more often than any other professional.[10]

In spite of this feeling, however, Americans express a curious ambivalence about teachers. They respect them and acknowledge their value but do not accord them the same status as they do physicians, attorneys, and other professionals.

So who are the pre-K–12 teachers of America? According to a National Education Association survey in the early 1990s, 72 percent are female, about 87 percent are white, almost 8 percent are black, 3 percent have Spanish surnames, less than 1 percent are Native American, and just over 1 percent have Asian or Pacific Islander family origins (Figure 1-4). Virtually all teachers are college graduates, and just over half also have a master's degree. Most became teachers through teacher-preparation programs at state colleges and universities, although some attended liberal arts colleges and became certified to teach later. The average teacher has been teaching fifteen years and is 42 years old.[11]

Teachers today

Patterns that reveal who becomes a teacher have fluctuated over time. Years ago, nearly all teachers in America were women; and, except in racially segregated minority schools, all teachers were white. Then, toward the middle of this century, more men and minority group members became teachers. Many were the first of their families to attend college, and they saw teaching as a step upward, socially and economically. Many of these teachers were returning World War II and Korean conflict veterans who attended college under the G.I. Bill of Rights of the 1940s and 1950s.

The population boom of the 1950s increased K–12 school enrollments so greatly that during the fifties and sixties teaching was a good field to enter. Nearly everyone with a college degree who wanted to teach was hired, and more than 20 percent of all those entering college said they wanted to teach.

Changing patterns

FIGURE 1-4   Racial and ethnic characteristics of pre-K–12 public school teachers. Compare these data with similar data about students in Figure 1-2. What do you infer from the comparison?

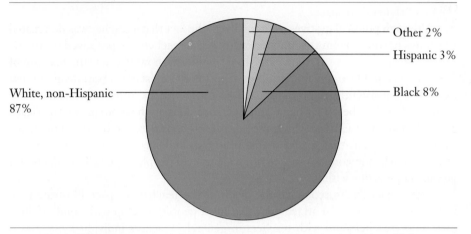

SOURCE: National Education Association. (1992). *Status of the American public school teacher: 1990–91*. Washington, DC: National Education Association, pp. 18, 78.

Then, by the early 1970s, the baby boom had run its course, and school enrollments dropped significantly. Few teachers were hired, and many were laid off. Fewer college students entered teacher education programs, and job opportunities in teaching faded.

At about the same time, employment opportunities expanded in other fields for women and blacks, two groups who traditionally gravitated toward teaching, in part because of discrimination against them in other professions. This situation had little impact on teaching while jobs in teaching were scarce, but it had tremendous impact by the mid-1980s.

During the last ten years, the children of the "baby boom children" of the 1950s have reached school age. These children are expanding school enrollments, especially in the southern and western regions of the country. At the same time, because fewer teachers were hired over the past two decades, more of those in the classroom are older, and greater percentages of them are retiring. (Figures 1-5, 1-6, and 1-7 show trends in numbers of teachers employed, student–teacher ratios, and school expenditures, respectively. Figure 1-1 showed student enrollment.) Because of this and because many of the people who traditionally would have entered teaching have been attracted to other accessible fields, a shortage of competent teachers developed about 1990 in some subject areas and in various locations across the country. As a result, in many regions people not prepared as teachers have been offered positions in classrooms by school systems that cannot attract qualified applicants.

Because of these trends, teachers in the United States as a whole are older than their counterparts of a decade or two ago. Lower percentages of college graduates enter teaching than before. Proportionally more academically strong women and minority group members are attracted away from teaching than previously. A greater percentage of teachers shifts to other professions after teaching only a few years. A higher percentage of untrained and noncertified teachers staffs classrooms. In short, the nature of teachers in pre-K–12 schools in America today is undergoing significant change.

Generalizations about teachers

FIGURE 1-5   Numbers of elementary and secondary school teachers (public and private) since 1978 and projected through 2003.

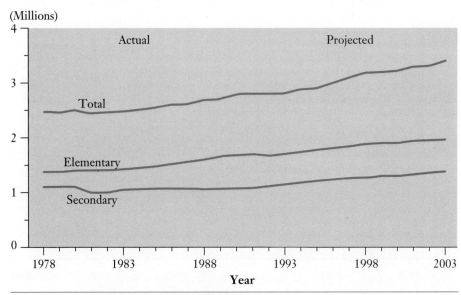

SOURCE: D. E. Gerald & W. J. Hussar. (1992). *Projections of educational statistics to 2003.* Washington, DC: National Center for Education Statistics, pp. 6–7.

FIGURE 1-6   Student–teacher ratios for elementary and secondary schools (public and private) since 1978 and projected through 2003.

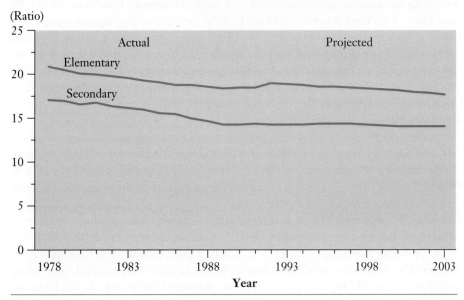

SOURCE: D. E. Gerald & W. J. Hussar, (1992). *Projections of educational statistics to 2003.* Washington, DC: National Center for Education Statistics, pp. 69, 71.

FIGURE 1-7   Expenditures of public schools in constant 1990–91 dollars since 1978 and projected through 2003.

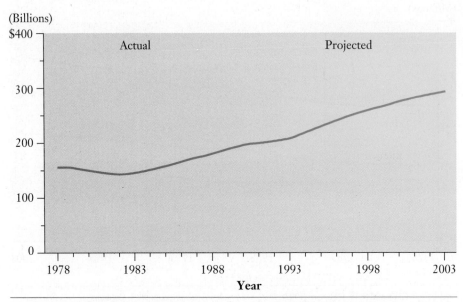

SOURCE: D. E. Gerald & W. J. Hussar, (1992). *Projections of educational statistics to 2003.* Washington, DC: National Center for Education Statistics, p. 76.

Perceptions of Schools

The rating of schools

For more than two decades, American attitudes about public schools have been reported each fall in an annual Phi Delta Kappa/Gallup Poll. This section is based on data reported in that poll in recent years.[12] When Americans were asked in 1993 to rate their local public schools on an A to F scale, 47 percent rated schools A or B, and only 15 percent rated them D or F. That rating was the highest since 1974, when 48 percent rated schools A or B. The 7 percent increase between 1992 and 1993 was the largest one-year improvement ever and represented a shift from the previous ten years, during which A and B percentages were rather stable in the low 40s. Between 1974 and 1984 the A and B ratings tended to rest in the low 30s. Tables 1-2 and 1-3 show the specific percentages for 1993 and comparison ratings between 1983 and 1993.

Interestingly, however, poll respondents rate American public schools nationally much lower than they rate their own local schools. As shown in Table 1-4, only 19 percent rate schools nationally as an A or B, and 21 percent gave them a D or F. The difference between the two ratings reflects a pattern in attitudes that has been consistent for many years of the survey.

On the other hand, when *parents* of public school students were asked to rate the school attended by their oldest child, 72 percent assigned either an A or B and only 7 percent responded with D or F. That 72 percent was 53 percentage points higher than their rating of schools nationally and 16 points higher than their rating of all local schools. Year-by-year ratings are shown in Table 1-5. As has been the case consistently over many years, the better people know the public schools, the higher they rate them.

TABLE 1-2   Americans' Rating of Local Public Schools—1993

	National Totals (%)	No Children in School (%)	Public School Parents (%)	Nonpublic School Parents (%)
A & B	47	44	56	37
A	10	10	12	5
B	37	34	44	32
C	31	32	28	41
D	11	10	12	9
Fail	4	4	4	11
Don't know	7	10	*	2

*Less than one-half of 1 percent.

SOURCE: S. M. Elam, L. C. Rose, & A. M. Gallup. (1993). The 25th annual Phi Delta Kappa/Gallup Poll of the public's attitudes toward the public schools. *Phi Delta Kappan*, 75(2), 138.

TABLE 1-3   Americans' Rating of Local Public Schools—1983–1993

	1993 (%)	1991 (%)	1989 (%)	1987 (%)	1985 (%)	1983 (%)
A & B	47	42	43	43	43	31
A	10	10	8	12	9	6
B	37	32	35	31	34	25
C	31	33	33	30	30	32
D	11	10	11	9	10	13
Fail	4	5	4	4	4	7
Don't know	7	10	9	14	13	17

SOURCE: S. M. Elam, L. C. Rose, & A. M. Gallup. (1993). The 25th annual Phi Delta Kappa/Gallup Poll of the public's attitudes toward the public schools. *Phi Delta Kappan*, 75(2), 138.

When Americans were asked in 1993 to list the biggest problem facing local public schools, for the first time since 1971 they ranked "lack of proper financial support" as the major problem. Twenty-one percent named it, 16 percent mentioned "drug abuse," and 15 percent picked "lack of discipline." More specific numbers are shown in Table 1-6.

Opinions about problems facing schools

TABLE 1-4   Americans' Rating of Schools Nationally—1993

	National Totals (%)	No Children in School (%)	Public School Parents (%)	Nonpublic School Parents (%)
A & B	19	20	19	15
A	2	1	3	6
B	17	19	16	9
C	48	47	49	48
D	17	16	17	15
Fail	4	4	4	12
Don't know	12	13	11	10

SOURCE: S. M. Elam, L. C. Rose, & A. M. Gallup. (1993). The 25th annual Phi Delta Kappa/Gallup Poll of the public's attitudes toward the public schools. *Phi Delta Kappan*, 75(2), 139.

TABLE 1-5 Parents' Rating of the School Their Oldest Child Attends—1993

	1993 (%)	1991 (%)	1989 (%)	1987 (%)
A & B	72	73	71	69
A	27	29	25	28
B	45	44	46	41
C	18	21	19	20
D	5	2	5	5
Fail	2	4	1	2
Don't know	3	*	4	4

*Less than one-half of 1 percent.

SOURCE: S. M. Elam, L. C. Rose, & A. M. Gallup. (1993). The 25th annual Phi Delta Kappa/Gallup Poll of the public's attitudes toward the public schools. *Phi Delta Kappan, 75*(2), 139.

TABLE 1-6 Americans' Opinion of the Biggest Problem Facing Their Local Public Schools—1993

	National Totals (%)	No Children in School (%)	Public School Parents (%)	Nonpublic School Parents (%)
Lack of proper financial support	21	19	24	13
Drug abuse	16	17	14	9
Lack of discipline	15	15	15	19
Fighting/violence/gangs	13	12	14	17
Standards/quality of education	9	9	8	18
Overcrowded schools	8	6	11	10
Difficulty in getting good teachers	5	4	7	3
Parents' lack of support/interest	4	5	4	3
Integration/segregation, racial discrimination	4	4	4	4
Pupils' lack of interest, poor attitudes, truancy	4	3	4	4
Low pay for teachers	3	4	3	2
Moral standards, dress code, sex/pregnancy	3	3	3	9
There are no problems	1	1	3	2
Miscellaneous**	3	3	2	*
Don't know	14	17	10	16

* Less than one-half of 1 percent.
** A total of 36 different kinds of problems were mentioned by 2 percent or fewer respondents.
Figures add to more than 100 percent because of multiple answers.

SOURCE: S. M. Elam, L. C. Rose, & A. M. Gallup. (1993). The 25th annual Phi Delta Kappa/Gallup Poll of the public's attitudes toward the public schools. *Phi Delta Kappan, 75*(2), 139.

This rating is interesting in the context of the twenty-five years of the survey. Those who interpret the poll describe the situation in these words:

> In the 25-year history of the Phi Delta Kappa/Gallup education poll, three school problems uppermost in the minds of respondents have been discipline, drugs, and finances. Between 1969 and 1985, discipline was the most frequently mentioned problem each year except 1971, when finances were identified as a major problem by 23% of the public. Drug abuse by students then became the most frequently mentioned problem for six years, 1986 through 1991. In 1992 drugs and lack of proper financial support were each mentioned by 22% of the respondents.
>
> In 1993 lack of proper financial support has clearly emerged as the number one public school problem. . . . Significantly, the respondents who most clearly recognized the inadequacy of school financing were college graduates, upper-income and professional and business groups, and public school parents. Concern about the problem of financial support was considerably greater in the West (30%) and the Midwest (29%) than in the South (13%) and East (15%).

Follow-up questions concerning finances for public schools elicited strong support for providing more funds for schools in poorer states and communities and a willingness to pay more taxes so this could happen. For example, 90 percent responded "yes" and only 8 percent said "no" to the question: Do you think more should be done to improve the quality of the public schools in the poorer states and in the poorer communities or not? And 68 percent said "yes" and 30 percent "no" to: Would you be willing to pay more taxes to improve the quality of the public schools in the poorer states and poorer communities? In addition, 88 percent replied "yes" and 10 percent "no" to: Do you think that the amount of money allocated to public education in your state, from all sources, should or should not be the same for all students, regardless of whether they live in wealthy or poor school districts?

Two survey questions asked about inner-city schools and willingness to improve them. In response, 81 percent said improving inner-city schools was "very important" and 15 percent said it was "fairly important." Sixty percent said they were willing to pay more federal taxes to improve inner-city schools; 38 percent were not willing to do so.

In other responses to the poll:

- 67 percent said they would like to see their children take up teaching as a career.
- 70 percent said they felt it is possible to establish a consensus to teach certain values in their local schools.
- 65 percent supported parental choice among public schools.
- 74 percent opposed allowing children to attend private schools at public expense.

Education Reform Since the 1980s

One way to understand teaching and schools in the 1990s is to think of education today as being, for the most part, in the third wave of a three-wave process of reform. That process began subtly in the late 1970s, was raised to national prominence by a report, called *A Nation at Risk*, in 1983, and has been played out ever since. This section describes the reform movement in two dimensions: first, in terms of the successive but overlapping three waves and then as the five paths that the change has taken. A few representative reports and proposals are described as illustrations of the waves and their thrusts.

As you read about the reform trends, think of ways teaching and schools changed during the time you were an elementary and secondary school student. How will the schools of students who just entered the first grade be different from your schools? How about the experience of students who just began high school? How will the teaching of new teachers be different from the teaching of your pre-K–12 teachers? What do you think of the changes you envision? What do you like in the trends? What do you dislike?

The first wave of reform was most visible for about three years beginning in 1983 and consisted of a succession of national reports that sounded nationwide alarms that the schools of America were in trouble. The second wave was made up of three parts: state-level reform efforts that were initiated to change the schools; a "second generation" of national reports that proposed specific, direct solutions to correct problems and suggested who should take those actions; and proposals for implementing specific changes. That second wave began shortly after the first and, in some cases, overlapped it. Much of its momentum has continued into the present decade. The third wave began as straightforward efforts at school system, school building, and classroom levels to implement what the reports and state-level regulations said should be done.

It needs to be pointed out, however, that the reform movement has not been an easy succession of actions beginning with the decisions about what to do and proceeding to agreed-upon solutions. Early in the process, problems were identified, and then many potential solutions were proposed. But those who tried to implement the apparent solutions to "the problems with the schools" quickly found out that the problems were usually different and more complex than had been thought and that the solutions would be more difficult to identify and implement. They found out, for example, that making schools better required attention to the out-of-school lives of children, the quality of the current teaching staffs, how teachers are prepared, how bureaucracies run, how politicians operate, and what citizens really want from their schools. Probably most important, they found out that making schools better costs a lot of money. As a result, the third wave has been proceeding unevenly and at many levels at once—in classrooms and schools where the real change needs to occur and at all of the levels from which resources, support, and direction for those changes must emanate.

The First Wave—A National Alarm

The first-wave reports, led by *A Nation at Risk*, were public calls to action. They were national in scope, general in nature, and in the form of printed documents whose releases were media events. Those reports attracted the attention of citizens and political leaders to "the weakened condition of our schools" and the "tide of mediocrity." They insisted on immediate emergency action and suggested, in a general way, what the action should be. First-wave reports included:[13]

A Nation at Risk
Academic Preparation for College
High School

A Place Called School
Horace's Compromise: The Dilemma of the American High School
First Lessons
Beyond the Commission Reports: The Coming Crisis in Teaching

A Nation at Risk (1983) was the most influential of the reports of the 1980s. It said that American schools suffered from mediocre performances and that this "rising tide of mediocrity" threatened the future of the nation and its people. It announced that because of these conditions, America was *at risk*. It cited, as *indicators of risk*, lower standardized test scores, lower SAT scores, higher illiteracy rates, lower graduation requirements, and the offering of more remedial courses in colleges.

Indicators of risk

The document was developed by the National Commission on Excellence in Education, which was appointed by Terrel Bell, U.S. Secretary of Education, who charged it with the responsibility to report to the people of the United States on the quality of education in America.

The *Nation at Risk* document represented a major event in the history of schooling in America. It reflected what many Americans felt about their schools, particularly high schools. It focused those sentiments into a condensed set of statements that made the condition of schools a national topic of concern.

A watershed

It said in part:

> Our nation is at risk. Our once unchallenged preeminence in commerce, industry, science, and technological innovation is being overtaken by competitors throughout the world. This report is concerned with only one of the many causes and dimensions of the problem, but it is the one that undergirds American prosperity, security, and civility. We report to the American people that while we can take justifiable pride in what our schools and colleges have historically accomplished and contributed to the United States and the well-being of its people, the educational foundations of our society are presently being eroded by a rising tide of mediocrity that threatens our very future as a Nation and a people. What was unimaginable a generation ago has begun to occur—others are matching and surpassing our educational attainments.

Rising tide of mediocrity

> If an unfriendly foreign power had attempted to impose on America the mediocre educational performance that exists today, we might well have viewed it as an act of war. As it stands, we have allowed this to happen to ourselves. . . . We have, in effect, been committing an act of unthinking, unilateral educational disarmament.

Educational disarmament

The report described the risk as follows:

> The world is indeed one global village. We live among determined, well-educated, and strongly motivated competitors. We compete with products but also with the ideas of our laboratories and neighborhood workshops. America's position in the world may once have been reasonably secure with only a few exceptionally well-trained men and women. It is no longer. . . .

Well-educated competitors

> We must dedicate ourselves to the reform of our educational system for the benefit of all—old and young alike, affluent and poor, majority and minority. Learning is the indispensable investment required for success in the "information age" we are entering.

Investment in learning

> Our concern, however, goes well beyond matters such as industry and commerce. It also includes the intellectual, moral, and spiritual strengths of

Something to Think About

In 1987, as American schools were beginning the process of reassessing their purpose and adjusting their programs and standards in response to early education reform agendas, a 15-year-old girl in Detroit wrote the following definition of the American dream:

To go to school and fenisch my Schooling without getting pregnant. (*Newsweek*, 1987, June 29, p. 19)

■ What are some of the implications of this statement for how schools should be improved?

A high level of shared education

our people which knit together the very fabric of our society. The people of the United States need to know that individuals in our society who do not possess the levels of skills, literacy, and training essential to this new era will be effectively disenfranchised, not simply from the material rewards that accompany competent performance, but also from the chance to participate fully in our national life. A high level of shared education is essential to a free, democratic society and to the fostering of a common culture, especially in a country that prides itself on pluralism and individual freedom.

Common understanding

For our country to function, citizens must be able to reach some common understandings on complex issues, often on short notice and on the basis of conflicting or incomplete evidence. Education helps form these common understandings, a point Thomas Jefferson made long ago in his justly famous dictum:

I know no safe depository of the ultimate powers of the society but the people themselves; and if we think them not enlightened enough to exercise their control with a wholesome discretion, the remedy is not to take it from them but to inform their discretion.

The progress of society

Part of what is at risk is the promise first made on this continent: All, regardless of race or class or economic status, are entitled to a fair chance and to the tools for developing their individual powers of mind and spirit to the utmost. This promise means that all children by virtue of their own efforts, competently guided, can hope to attain the mature and informed judgment needed to secure gainful employment and to manage their own lives, thereby serving not only their own interests, but also the progress of society itself. (*A Nation at Risk*)

To correct these problems, it recommended changes in five areas:

Recommendations

Content. That high school graduation requirements be strengthened and that all students be required to take the *Five New Basics* of (a) 4 years of English; (b) 3 years of mathematics; (c) 3 years of science; (d) 3 years of social studies; and (3) one-half year of computer science. That college-bound students also take 2 years of foreign language.

Standards and Expectations.   That schools, colleges, and universities adopt more rigorous and measurable standards and higher expectations for academic performance and student conduct. That four-year colleges and universities raise their requirements for admission.

Time.   That more time be devoted to learning the New Basics, including more effective use of the existing school day, a longer school day, and a lengthened school year.

Teaching.   That new teachers meet higher standards in teaching ability and in their academic discipline; teachers' salaries be increased; teachers be evaluated more effectively; teachers have eleven-month contracts; there be career ladders for teachers; people other than currently certified teachers be hired in areas of teacher shortage; incentives be used to attract outstanding college students to teaching; and master teachers design training programs for teachers and supervise new teachers.

Leadership and Fiscal Support.   That citizens hold educators and elected officials responsible for providing the leadership necessary to achieve these reforms, and that citizens provide the fiscal support and stability needed to bring them about. (*A Nation at Risk*)

The Second Wave—State Actions, More Reports, Proposals

The second wave of reform has consisted of three simultaneous types of activities: (1) state regulations and plans for action to correct "problems with the schools"; (2) additional "second generation" reports; and (3) second-wave proposals by well-known educational thinkers and leaders that outline specific plans for reforming schools and for implementing the changes already called for.

Second-Wave State Actions

The second-wave state-level reports were relatively specific sets of recommendations and plans for legislative or regulatory action to change conditions. Some actually had been issued before *A Nation at Risk*, but others surfaced later. Many have included annual updates of actions already taken. These plans produced the most significant activity of the reform movement during the 1980s. They told schools, teachers, and state agencies what should be done, and many have had the force of law to require compliance.

Because these reforms are so numerous and are still being enacted, it is difficult to describe them adequately here, but the following information should provide an illustration. In spring 1987, the following excerpt appeared in the newspaper *Education Week* as part of an article that described recent education reform action by the Indiana state legislature:

Student Testing.   The Indiana Statewide Test for Educational Progress will be expanded to cover grades 1, 2, 3, 6, 8, 9, and 11. Student achievement in language arts, mathematics, social studies and science will be tested each spring.

Students scoring in the bottom 16 percent on the test will be required to attend summer school, with the state picking up the full cost of remediation and transportation. Students will be retested at the end of the summer. If they fail to move out of the bottom 16 percent, they will be retained in their current grade.

*B*ecause this text is about the real world of pre-K–12 teaching and schools, the ideas, topics, and issues you study in it are not static. They are evolving and changing as you study them. Because of this change, you will want to keep ahead of contemporary educational developments in the area where you live and in places where you might want to teach. In a sense, you will want to direct your professional study along two paths: one based on the content of this text and the course in which it is being used and the other based on the issues of the day that you hear and read about in the media.

This Reflecting on Practice section is an effort to help you start along that second path—the one concerned with keeping abreast of the issues of the day. You are introduced to eight prominent ideas and issues in education that constantly come up in public discussions about pre-K–12 teaching and schools. It explores each briefly and suggests questions that might guide your thinking about each. By pursuing these ideas and issues, you will not only stay informed, but, more important, you will also develop an ability to integrate what you learn from this text and course with what is happening in the educational environment in which you are living. That ability will serve you well as you continue the lifelong process of learning as a professional educator. The ideas and issues discussed are:

- educational expectations
- accountability
- national educational goals
- school funding
- student testing
- opportunity-to-learn standards
- the privatization of schooling
- multiculturalism

As you read about each of these, consider two types of questions: the four general questions immediately following and the more specific questions after the discussion of each item.

- What understanding have you already developed of the idea at this early point in your study? How did you develop that understanding?
- In what ways is the idea as presented here different from your previous understanding of it?
- In what ways is the idea important to you as you study teaching and schools?
- How can an understanding of the idea help you interpret important educational matters in the weeks and months ahead?

Educational Expectations

These are the results (some people say *outcomes*) that students, teachers, parents, and those responsible for schools anticipate will occur because students are taught in school. Sometimes they are stated as graduation requirements, criteria for passing grade levels or courses, and lesson objectives. Educational expectations can be defined as what students should know and be able to do as a result of their learning.

Educational expectations are prominent in discussions about teaching and schools; many people feel that students are not learning as much as they should because teachers and school leaders do not have a clear enough idea about what they should accomplish. They say that clearer educational expectations need to be identified if schools and student learning are going to improve.

- What are some specific educational expectations that you have for all public school graduates in the United States?
- Should there be different levels of educational expectations if schools have very different types of student populations?

Student Testing

Issues concerning student testing involve types of tests and how student test scores should be used. Criticism of what graduates seem to know and be able to do has prompted many American citizens and leaders (particularly political leaders) to demand that students pass standardized tests in order to graduate or be promoted at certain grade levels. They also want the test scores to be compared from school to school and class to class in order to see which schools and teachers are successful and which are not. Many states have passed laws and formulated regulations to require the use of testing.

- Do you think all students should pass standardized tests in order to graduate or pass a grade?
- What content areas should be covered in the tests?
- What should happen if students flunk the tests in large numbers?

Accountability

Many Americans who want to improve schools say that those responsible for what students learn should be held accountable when students do not succeed. They frequently say that when students do not learn, they, their parents, their teachers, and their school leaders should be blamed and forced to improve or be "called to account."

- How would you assess blame if students do not learn what they should?
- What conditions would mitigate the blame?
- What consequences would you assess? Against whom would you assess them?

Opportunity-to-Learn Standards

Associated with efforts to raise expectations and assess accountability for student learning is the belief that public school students and teachers must be provided with the resources necessary for them to succeed. Those who believe in the idea of opportunity-to-learn standards say that public school leaders and government officials should be held responsible for providing qualified teachers and adequate facilities, equipment, and supplies for all students. They take the position that, if this is not done, the students who suffer have a basis for legal complaints, the students and teachers involved cannot be held accountable for lack of success, and the officials who fail to meet the opportunity standard should be "called to account."

- Do you think government leaders should be open to legal charges or removed from office if they do not provide the minimum resources for teachers and students to succeed?
- How would you decide what minimum resources are?
- How would you respond to the preceding questions if citizens voted down all bond issues and tax increases for schools, even when the bond issues are considered by everyone to be at the lowest level possible for adequate schools?

National Educational Goals

During the late 1980s and the early 1990s state governors and two presidential administrations adopted national goals to be achieved by all schools in the United States within the next few years. They were enacted into law by Congress in 1994.

Establishment of these goals was an attempt to form a nationwide commitment and focus energies to improve schools quickly.

- Do you know of any ways the national goals are affecting specific schools?
- What should be the federal government's role in establishing national goals? What should be its role in providing funds for schools to meet the goals?
- Who should be blamed if the goals are not met?

The Privatization of Schools

Partly because of dissatisfaction with public schools and because many students already attend private schools, there have been political pressures to use tax funds to pay private enterprises to run schools or provide contracted services for schools. The ideas that have been presented include disbanding local public schools entirely, contracting operation of specific schools in a school district to a private company, turning over control of individual schools to teams of educators who are paid one fee to run the schools, paying for the private schooling of individual students, and contracting with companies for specific functions such as food services and transportation. Various school systems and states are experimenting with forms of school privatization.

- What are your views on privatization of schooling and/or specific school services?
- What impact do you see the funding of private school services having on public schools?
- If you support some degree of privatization, how would you decide which privatization efforts are appropriate and which are not?

School Funding

Public school funding issues in recent years include questions about (1) the overall adequacy of funds needed for quality schools, (2) which level of government—local, state, national—should provide how much; (3) equal funding from school to school within a state; (4) the funding of private instruction for individual students when the public schools cannot provide appropriate instruction; and (5) the practice of governments requiring schools to provide specific services, such as some types of special education, without supplying funds to do so.

- Which school funding questions are prominent in your area at the present time?
- How well do you understand the various perspectives underlying the issues?
- What is your personal view and what is it based on?

Multiculturalism

Because American culture is made up of many racial, ethnic, religious, language, and social traditions and heritages and because of the diversity of the students who attend public schools, issues of how schools should teach, think about, and accommodate different heritages and cultural perspectives have been debated for a long time. The debates occur at all levels of government, have various levels of intensity, ebb and flow periodically, but never go away. The debates are critical for those who are interested in pre-K–12 teaching and schools for at least two reasons: First, they are an outgrowth and reflection of the very essence of America; and second, they help define why we have public schools and what we should expect them to accomplish.

- What school-related multicultural debates do you know about, and how well do you understand the issues?
- How are expectations of public schools influenced by the cultural diversity of America?

School districts that promote such students would lose a proportionate amount of state tuition support.

School Accreditation.   Beginning with the 1988–89 school year, schools will be accredited not only on the basis of "inputs," such as curriculum offerings and the length of the school day and year, but also on the basis of "outcomes," including student test scores, graduation rates, and the results of locally developed evaluations of teachers.

Schools that comply with existing "input" standards and perform at or above average for demographically similar schools on the new "outcome" standards will be accredited by the state board for a five-year period. Sub-par schools will be placed on probation. If the state board determines that improvements have not been made after three years of probationary status, it could ask the state legislature to approve the appointment of a state manager. In the case of low-achieving school districts, the board could ask lawmakers to force them to consolidate with other districts.

Merit Schools.   Schools that demonstrate year-to-year improvements in student academic achievement would become eligible for financial rewards.[14]

Second-Generation Reports

At the same time this state activity occurred, a number of second-generation national commission reports proposed actions to address the problems that the earlier commissions noted. Frequently, the second-generation reports spelled out steps to be taken and targeted the groups that should act. For example, the Carnegie Task Force on Teaching as a Profession, among a number of recommendations, proposed a national teacher-certification board and national standards for evaluating teacher knowledge and ability. It followed those ideas with efforts to establish a certification board and to develop a national teacher-evaluation plan. In somewhat parallel efforts, the Carnegie Task Force and the Holmes Group outlined new ways to prepare teachers and formed organizations to do so; and the National Council for the Accreditation of Teacher Education (NCATE), the national organization that accreditates college-level teacher-education programs, revised its standards and redesigned its accreditation process.

Second-wave reports include:[15]

A Nation Prepared: Teachers for the 21st Century (Carnegie)
Tomorrow's Teachers (Holmes)
A Call for Change in Teacher Education
Who Will Teach Our Children? (California)
Improving Teacher Education: An Agenda for Higher Education and the Schools
Time for Results: The Governors' 1991 Report on Education
The Nation's Report Card
The Redesign of NCATE
President Bush's and the National Governors' Association "Education Goals 2000"
President Clinton's "Goals 2000: Educate America" Act

A Nation Prepared   In 1986, the Task Force on Teaching as a Profession of the Carnegie Forum on Education and the Economy issued a report entitled

A Nation Prepared: Teachers for the 21st Century, which called for restructuring schools and overhauling teacher education. The report advocated

Overhauled teacher education

- establishing a national board of standards for those becoming teachers
- restructuring school responsibilities so that local teachers would control their schools
- restructuring the teaching force, with a new level of teachers who would be in charge of other teachers
- raising teachers' salaries and expanding career opportunities so that teaching would be competitive with other professions
- tying incentives for teachers to schoolwide student performance
- increasing the number of minority teachers

The report said that recent reforms in education had been intended to reverse the decline in the performance of schools and that future success in schools depended on creating a profession of well-educated teachers prepared to assume new powers and responsibilities to redesign schools for the future. To produce these teachers, it proposed

- requiring a bachelor's degree in the arts and sciences as a prerequisite to the professional study of teaching

National Board for Professional Teaching Standards

- a new master's degree professional program of study for all teachers that would include internships and residences in schools, probably requiring two years of study
- a National Board for Professional Teaching Standards to certify teachers

The group consisted of fourteen political, business, and educational leaders, including the presidents of the National Education Association and the American Federation of Teachers. Both organizations endorsed its recommendations and the Carnegie Foundation funded efforts to begin implementing the teacher certification board idea. That process has been a multiyear effort and is continuing with significant momentum. Its actual impact has yet to be realized but its work through the 1990s is worth watching by all interested in teaching.

Education Goals 2000   During the latter years of the 1980s, the National Governors' Association made the improvement of schools a major priority and established a mechanism to identify educational goals for all states so that, in their words, the United States would be "second to none." The governors worked with one another and with the Bush administration in developing a national agenda for improving schools. That agenda took the form of six national goals to be accomplished by the year 2000.

Formulating the goals and passing the relevant national legislation to pursue them involved unusual cooperation among many governors, the Republican Bush administration, and the succeeding Democratic Clinton administration. After preliminary activity among the governors, President Bush called an Education Summit in 1989, at which the governors and national political leaders agreed upon the six goals in tentative form. Then President Bush, in his State of the Union Address in January 1990, called for adoption of the goals. Several weeks later, the Governors' Association formally adopted the goals in slightly modified form and elaborated upon them by adding twenty-one more-detailed objectives that provided additional specificity for future action. Later, in the early months of 1993, after President Clinton replaced Bush, the Clinton administration reiterated its commitment to the goals, asked Congress to codify them into law, and recommended government

In a technological society, inspiring students to master science and mathematics is a critical goal for teachers and schools.

mechanisms to accomplish them. The key Clinton administration action was the "Goals 2000: Educate America" Act, which added two more goals to the list and passed the United States Congress in 1994.

The goals that were adopted are as follows:

- By the year 2000, all children in the United States will start school ready to learn.
- By 2000, the high school graduation rate will increase to at least 90 percent.
- By 2000, American students will leave grades 4, 8, and 12 having demonstrated competency in challenging subject matter that includes English, mathematics, science, history, and geography; and every school in the United States will ensure that all students learn to use their minds well so that they may be prepared for responsible citizenship, further learning, and productive employment in our modern economy.
- By 2000, the nation's teaching force will have access to programs for the continued improvement of their professional skills and the opportunity to acquire the knowledge and skills needed to instruct and prepare all American students for the next century.
- By 2000, students in the United States will be first in the world in mathematics and science achievement.
- By 2000, every adult in the United States will be literate and will possess the skills necessary to compete in a global economy and exercise the rights and responsibilities of citizenship.
- By 2000, every school in the United States will be free of drugs and violence and will offer a disciplined environment conducive to learning.
- By 2000, every school and home will engage in partnerships that will increase parental involvement and participation in promoting the social, emotional, and academic growth of children.[16]

"Goals 2000" has provoked two kinds of reaction. Nearly everyone realizes that all elements of the goals will not be attained by 2000, but most educators and political leaders believe that they serve an important purpose by providing national encouragement and direction for improved schools and better educated citizens. As you continue your professional study, you will want to monitor how well the goals are being pursued as 2000 approaches.

Second-Wave Proposals

Second-wave proposals for reforming schools have been developed by a number of prominent educational thinkers; and in many cases, they have followed research studies about school effectiveness by Ronald Edmonds[17] and ideas about changing schools recommended by Michael Fullan.[18] (More is reported on these studies in Chapter 4.) Specific second-wave proposals of this type include:[19]

The Coalition of Essential Schools (Sizer)
The Accelerated Schools Project (Levin)
School Power (Comer)
The "Success for All" Program (Slavin)

Each of these four plans is discussed here so that you can learn about potential schools of the future early in your study and then reflect upon these examples (and turn back to them periodically) as you learn more about teaching and schools today. These four proposals serve as "lighthouses in the distance" to help you come to grips with the question, Where are teaching and schooling of the 1990s headed if they are to get better? As you read about these four plans, note the key characteristics of each and form your own tentative judgments of their strengths and weaknesses.

Essential Schools Theodore Sizer of Brown University, a well-known educational thinker, critic, and reformer, formulated a plan to make schools, especially secondary schools, more effective; he also developed a network of schools and school systems to implement that plan. The plan is based on the adoption and pursuit of nine common principles that explain how schools should operate and what they should accomplish. The network is called the Coalition of Essential Schools.

Sizer's ideas achieved national recognition in 1984 when his book, *Horace's Compromise: The Dilemma of the American High School*, became a major influence in first-wave reform literature. Those ideas evolved after 1984 as the Coalition developed and expanded to include hundreds of schools and as Sizer and his colleagues refined their thinking. Sizer's 1992 book, *Horace's School: Redesigning the American School*, describes his ideas and efforts to bring about reformed, more effective, and, in Sizer's terms, "more powerful schools."

Coalition schools see themselves as well-integrated communities, with a clear understanding of what their graduates should have achieved, broad faculty decision-making authority, and integrated curriculum offerings. The nine common principles that guide Coalition schools follow.

- The school should focus on helping adolescents learn to use their minds well. Schools should not attempt to be "comprehensive" if such a claim is made at the expense of the school's central intellectual purpose.
- The school's goals should be simple: Each student should master a number of essential skills and be competent in certain areas of knowledge. Although

these skills and areas will, to varying degrees, reflect the traditional academic disciplines, the program's design should be shaped by the intellectual and imaginative powers and competencies that students need, rather than by conventional "subjects." The aphorism "less is more" should dominate: Curriculum decisions are to be directed toward the students' attempt to gain mastery rather than by the teachers' effort to cover content.

■ The school's goals should apply to all students, but the means to these goals will vary as these students themselves vary. School practices should be tailor-made to meet the needs of every group of adolescents.

■ Teaching and learning should be personalized to the maximum feasible extent. No teacher should have direct responsibility for more than eighty students; decisions about the course of study, the use of students' and teachers' time, and the choice of teaching materials and specific pedagogues must be placed in the hands of the principal and staff.

■ The governing metaphor of the school should be student as worker, rather than the more familiar metaphor of teacher as deliverer of instructional services. Accordingly, a prominent pedagogy will be coaching, to provoke students to learn how to learn and thus to teach themselves.

■ Students begin regular secondary school studies as they show appropriate competence in language and elementary mathematics. Students of traditional high school age who do not yet have appropriate levels of competence to start secondary school studies will be provided with intensive remedial work so that they can quickly meet those standards. The diploma should be awarded on a successful final demonstration of mastery for graduation—an Exhibition.

■ The tone of the school should explicitly and self-consciously stress the values of anxiety-free expectation ("I won't threaten you, but I expect much of you"), of trust (unless it is abused), and of decency (the values of fairness, generosity, and tolerance). Incentives appropriate to the school's students and teachers should be emphasized, and parents should be treated as essential collaborators.

■ The principal and teachers should perceive of themselves first as generalists (teachers and scholars in general education) and next as specialists (experts in a particular discipline). Staff should expect multiple obligations (teacher-counselor-manager) and a sense of commitment from the entire school.

■ Administrative and budget targets should include substantial time for collective planning by teachers, competitive salaries for staff, and an ultimate per-pupil cost not more than 10 percent higher than that at traditional schools.[20]

Accelerated Schools   Henry M. Levin of Stanford University, another educational theoretician as well as a professor of economics, has also formulated a plan for making schools more effective and developed a nationwide network of schools applying his ideas.[21] Levin's schools focus on improving the learning of at-risk and low-achieving elementary school students. They operate on the principle that these students should have enriched and accelerated instruction rather than remediation, and they concentrate their energy on prevention of learning difficulties so that remediation is not necessary. Their general goal is to raise poorly performing elementary school students to the typical performance of their age-group peers by the end of elementary school. To accomplish this, Accelerated Schools must help poor performers learn at faster rates.

Accelerated Schools work at improving themselves through an entire-school reform effort that stresses high academic expectations and achievement for *all* students. For the most part, their curricula are heavily language-based across all subjects and are designed to fit compatibly with students' out-of-school lives, backgrounds, and culture.

By the mid-1990s the number of Accelerated Schools that had personnel trained within the network reached several hundred; there were hundreds more on a waiting list, and many others that were pursuing Accelerated Schools ideas on their own. The key principles upon which Accelerated Schools function are

- *a unity of purpose* and common vision that is developed by all participants in the school community and that guides their decisions and actions
- *school-site empowerment* in which all school participants make decisions and accept responsibility for them, unhampered by intervention by higher-level school system officials
- *an approach to improvement* that builds upon school, student, parent, and community strengths rather than weaknesses[22]

School Power Even before the push in the 1980s for more effective schools, James P. Comer, a psychologist at the Yale University Child Study Center, had been developing a process for school improvement in a collaborative project with the New Haven, Connecticut, schools. The collaborative effort targets schools with high percentages of poor and hard-to-teach students and has had national success in a number of experimental school settings. Because of that success, schools nationwide have turned to Comer's ideas for help in their efforts to reach students who are not succeeding academically.

Comer's book *School Power* (1980) described his ideas, which, by the mid-1990s, were being tried in hundreds of schools nationally. His approach includes the following key ideas about students, schools, and school programs:

- In order to learn and behave well in school, students must be able to listen to instructions or receive information from their teachers and other responsible adults and children in a group. To be a learner, a student must be able to tolerate the frustration and disappointment of trial, error, losing, delayed rewards, and waiting without becoming unusually disruptive. Learners must be free and spontaneous enough to be able to use their existing knowledge in the initiation of activities or projects that can bring them new knowledge. They must be able to invest themselves in activities long enough to carry them through to completion and experience the intellectual and psychological benefits of having done so. To be able to work, learn, and play with others, a student must be able to appreciate and respond to the needs and feelings of others and must have the interpersonal skills necessary to negotiate respectful and helpful responses to his or her own needs and feelings.
- Most programs designed to improve schooling fail because they do not adequately address the developmental needs of children and the potential for conflict in the relationship between home and school, among school staff, and among staff and students. They do not consider the structural arrangements, specific skills, and conditions of the school that people need to address in the complexities of today's schools.
- Many school problems stem from the first difficult contact between home, student, and school, which initiates a process in which administrators, staff,

and students begin to struggle for power. Undesirable behavior and poor learning eventually occur.

■ Schools that recognize different or troubling student behavior as social underdevelopment or development appropriate for another setting and recognize low achievement as reflective of cognitive underdevelopment—and establish programs to develop children in a way that they can be successful in school—could eliminate the struggle for power and limit or reverse the downhill social and academic performance of many students who have had preschool experiences that did not adequately prepare them for school.

■ Because behavior problems generally initiate the downward spiral for student and staff performance alike, training that enables administrators, parents, and teachers to create a climate where behavior problems are reduced is critical.[23]

The Comer approach calls for the following:

■ organizing schools around concepts from child development, particularly social development
■ building a sense of community among all school stakeholders—teachers, administrators, students, parents, and so forth
■ drawing all who provide services to students—teachers, administrators, psychologists, social workers—into a team that addresses student needs and responds systematically, rather than in isolation from each other
■ close school–parent cooperation
■ an instructional emphasis on student social skills development through a program called "A Social Skills Curriculum for Inner-City Children"[24]

Success for All   "Success for All" is another program developed since the 1980s to help schools become more effective in reaching hard-to-teach low-achieving students. The program has been developed by Robert E. Slavin and his colleagues at Johns Hopkins University and their network of schools. Success for All evolved from Slavin's review of efforts to reach nonachieving students and his conclusion that many commonly used approaches—flunking students, pullout programs, special education programs, and even reducing class size—do not enable these students to regain lost academic ground. An article in *Educational Leadership*, "What Works for Students at Risk: A Research Synthesis" (1989), and a book, *Effective Programs for Students at Risk* (1989), outline the major points.

As a result of this review of research, Slavin identified potentially successful "preventive" approaches to teaching at-risk students before they fall behind. He found that two types of teaching methods seemed to be more successful than others: (1) continuous-progress programs in which students succeed at their own pace through a sequence of well-defined objectives and (2) cooperative learning projects in which students learn in teams to master material initially presented by the teacher. He also found some success among remedial tutoring projects and certain versions of computer-assisted instruction.

Key elements of the Success for All program include:

■ a school's belief that the entire institution is responsible for the success of every one of its students
■ a realization that success for all students is costly
■ an emphasis on preventing students from falling behind rather than on remediation

- a willingness to change instruction and adjust content in response to student needs
- the use of comprehensive and inclusive instructional programs that contain coordinated teacher manuals, testing materials, lesson plans, and appropriate resources
- the intensive involvement of students in their own learning, such as that associated with one-on-one tutoring and individually adapted computer-assisted instruction[25]

The Third Wave—Implementation Efforts

Third-wave efforts to implement the ideas of second-wave reports and proposals such as the four just described have been initiated in states, school systems, and individual schools throughout the country and have been implemented at various rates. Some states and schools started early and have maintained a fast pace, others have moved more slowly, and some have barely responded. Most third-wave efforts are still in progress. If successful, these efforts will produce the results that the reports anticipated. This section describes five paths reform movements have taken and examines the thrust of most of these efforts; later chapters include accounts of specific endeavors. However, the best way to understand current reform efforts is to monitor the developments occurring nationally and in your local schools and state. Recent issues of *Education Week* and *Phi Delta Kappan* should provide information of national scope. Your instructor can identify the best sources of information locally and at the state level.

A serious question of funding

Before we discuss directions of recent educational change, it is important to note that school funding has become both a major issue and a major question mark in the third wave of education reform. It is now obvious that accomplishing the goals of the various reform agendas will cost much more money than has ever been provided for public schools in America. With no more money than has been provided in the past, it is simply not possible to finance an excellent pre-K–12 education for *all* students so that every student reaches the educational outcomes set for him and her. In the past, even during very recent years, although some schools have done very well, other schools have had woefully inadequate resources, particularly in rural areas and urban centers; the underfunding of education has especially affected poor students, those with handicapping conditions, and those in systems with poor tax bases.

As the United States attempts to identify more clearly what it wants from the schools in terms of student learning outcomes, it regularly confronts the questions, What will it cost? Will we be able or willing to pay the price? During the last several years, courts in a number of states—most notably Texas, Kentucky, New Jersey, and Tennessee—have ordered state officials to provide quality education for *all* students of the state, ensuring that it is not just students in areas where tax sources are adequate who are well educated. In other states, legislatures are raising similar financing questions. Many state and local school systems are struggling to comply, but the process is complicated and success has not yet been demonstrated. (More will be explained on these points in Chapter 9.)

Paths of Change

The five paths of educational change generated by the reforms of the last decade and a half can be summarized as

1. back-to-basics, competency testing, accountability, and outcome assessment
2. greater professionalization of teaching
3. more effective schools and teaching
4. more equitable education for all students (not just equal amounts of schooling)
5. changing the content or subject matter taught

The ideas of teaching the basics and assessing students to determine what they have learned are not at all new, but reform agendas seem to have pushed especially hard in these directions. *A Nation at Risk*, the Bush–National Governors' Association "Education Goals 2000" program, and the Clinton "Goals 2000: Educate America" legislation all identified objectives for what schools should teach, the content students should learn, ways students should be assessed at regular intervals, and when the goals themselves should be reached. Similarly, many state actions of the late 1980s and 1990s prescribe what and how much students should know and by when. Most states specify subjects required for high school graduation, and basic academic subjects predominate—language arts, mathematics, science, and social studies. Tests have been mandated and are being developed in most of these areas for several grade levels. Students must know certain ideas, information, and skills to pass to the next grade and to graduate. Teachers must educate them effectively, or they will not pass.

Accountability and outcome assessment

According to those who support the thinking of many of the commission reports, teaching is being made more "professional" by the use of more evaluations

Professionalization of teaching

Something to Think About

The following is an excerpt from an article by Shawn Doherty.

Fighting Over a Principal:
A schoolboard tries to fire an innovative educator

When a bushy-bearded city slicker named Dennis Littky took over as principal of Thayer High School in Winchester, N.H., six years ago, the locals wagered on how long he'd last. The 250-year-old mill town had the region's highest welfare load, and the Thayer High kids were reputed hellions. That summer Littky hired a dropout to paint murals over graffiti on school walls, replaced study halls with new math and science requirements, and met individually with all 200 students to plan their schedules. By 1985 reading scores had jumped two and one-half grades. Today the dropout rate is half what it was in 1980, and more than half the kids go on to college—up from 10 percent when Littky took over. Last week, as parents watched their children dance at the spring prom, Thayer High seemed a happy place. So why is the school board trying to fire Dennis Littky?

Board members have a list of reasons. Littky permits class discussions of homosexuality and birth control. Board member Bobby Secord even heard Eddie Murphy's "Boogie in Your Butt" booming out of a classroom one day. "He runs things too loosely," says Secord, a local businessman who was Thayer's 1967 prom king but sends his two children to a nearby Christian school. The 42-year-old Littky, who received PhD.'s in education and psychology from the University of Michigan and ran a nationally acclaimed middle school on Long Island, also wears Khakis to school, lets kids call him "Doc" and chooses to live in a mountaintop log cabin without running water or electricity. ("I wanted to learn how to cut down trees and relax," he explains.) "He's the highest-paid individual in town and, instead of setting a dignified example, he acts like a tramp," complains former state legislator Elmer Johnson, a leader of the oust-Littky campaign.

. . . Mostly, however, the battle is a clash between old and new values. "Us old-timers resent liberal newcomers coming in and telling us how backwards we are," says Johnson, who lives in the same farmhouse he was born in 67 years ago.

However radical it seems to local eyes, Littky's transformation of Thayer does meet a call by a 1983 Reagan administration commission for a return to basics in public schools. Littky has imposed stiffer discipline and toughened academic standards at Thayer, and his efforts have been hailed by the National Education Association and the Carnegie Foundation. Theodore Sizer, a champion of new teaching methods and a Brown University education professor, named Thayer one of a dozen schools to participate in his national program of educational reform. The school board, however, yanked Thayer out of the program.

"Human Beings": For all his devotion to basics, Littky's style is reminiscent of the experimentalism of the '70's—and that is what has exercised many townspeople. Instead of lecturing from textbooks, Thayer teachers helped students excavate an 18th-century town and build a log cabin. Writing teachers assign journals. (One mother was so outraged to find vomit and child murder among the topics in her daughter's writing class that she organized a campaign to protest.) In a required course for seniors called Life After Thayer, kids discussed everything from sex to balancing checkbooks—though the board recently ordered teachers to get its approval before broaching sexual topics. Littky also won grants for an apprentice program that places students in beauty parlors, restaurants and garages; the board cut the program in half. "Thayer will never send the most kids to college or get the best test scores," Littky argues. "But our kids learn to think and become decent human beings."

In the clash of personalities and power, the kids are often forgotten. "Dennis has given these youngsters hope," says Brown's Sizer. Most of Thayer's students support Littky, who knows each of them by name and attended every basketball game this season. "Littky puts us before anything," says Terri Racine. "He's opened doors for us." Terri knows that better than most. She got pregnant during her Junior year and only Littky's support kept her in school after she had the baby. That semester Terri was elected class president, made the honor roll and undertook a special writing project about the town's attitudes toward teenage pregnancy. Littky's critics distributed her paper door to door to illustrate the immorality corrupting Thayer. But this fall Terri begins college—and that's why Dennis Littky thinks his job is worth fighting for.

Update—After two school board elections, Littky supporters won control of the school board and renewed his contract for another year. In 1993, he was selected New Hampshire Principal of the Year.

- What do you think are implications of situations such as this for changes in schools in the years ahead?
- Think of this situation as you read the recommendations of various commissions that are reported in this chapter. Which recommendations have caused or are most likely to cause conflict?

From *Newsweek*, May 25, 1987. © 1987, Newsweek, Inc. All rights reserved. Reprinted by permission.

and higher standards to assess who can become teachers as well as who can remain in the classroom. College preparation programs are becoming longer, more selective, and more demanding. Larger numbers of marginal applicants are being turned away. Practicing teachers are being evaluated more often and more thoroughly. Teachers are being paid better and respected more. The National Board of Professional Teaching Standards is establishing a new higher tier of teacher certification.

An increasing number of critics, however, challenges the notion that these movements produce greater teacher professionalization. They question how taking authority from teachers by subjecting them to more outside laws and commissions produces stronger professionals. This major aspect of education reform is at a crossroads formed by two questions about how to produce improvements: Should there be more laws and rules that tell teachers what they must do? Should teachers be given more freedom and support to do what they think is best?[26] More will be said about this in later chapters.

Schools and teaching will be scrutinized more closely than ever to determine which types of organization and means of operation, which approaches to teaching, and which teacher characteristics produce the best student learning. Characteristics of schools such as clear and common purposes, an ethos of achievement, a team spirit among staff, and quality leadership have been found to be good for student learning. Teacher characteristics such as good verbal ability, enthusiasm for subject matter, intelligence, and concern for students impress and influence students positively. Classroom techniques such as effective use of time, high time-on-task ratios, proper questioning, and appropriate use of pauses to stimulate thinking are said to produce high student achievement.

Effectiveness

The need to provide better education to poor, minority, non-native-English-speaking, and disabled students has been reiterated as a dramatically high priority for schools and teachers. However, among the reform ideas, this goal is still far from being achieved. Concerns are being expressed, plans tried, and resources identified, but significant results are still elusive. The United States has still not discovered how to educate children out of poverty and, as of the mid-1990s, is not sure if it is willing to pay the costs. Those who care most about the country's children, however, think it can be done and are still trying, as several of the plans described earlier indicate.

Equal education

In addition to the return to the basics, reform agendas include the teaching of certain content that most or all students are expected to master. Reading, writing, spelling, literature, most areas of common mathematics, natural science, biology, health, history, civics, and geography are usually among the subjects specified. And virtually everyone agrees that thinking skills must be developed. Also, most want more and better teaching of values, although there is much disagreement over which values warrant the most attention.

Content

Current Conditions and Predictions for the Years Ahead

In the 1990s, schools and teachers are still trying to respond to the pushes of the 1980s while acknowledging the American ideal of educating *all* students to their maximum. Nearly everyone agrees that schools need to be made better, especially as they try to reach students who have traditionally not been successful. Most also agree that the movements of the 1980s and early 1990s have built momentum and set direction.

The two dominant questions for the rest of the century and beyond are

■ In what ways should teaching and schools be changed?
■ How can the necessary resources be provided?

Some Predictions

Everyone knows that change is a fact of contemporary life. Changes in our lives are rapid and occur at an accelerating rate. People must prepare for and adjust to change. The future will be dramatically different from today.

If you begin teaching this year or in a few years and do not change professions, you will teach students as yet unborn. You will teach information as yet unknown. You will prepare students for jobs that have not yet been created and for a world environment that does not now exist. You will use teaching devices and techniques not yet invented.

Some views of schools and teaching and of the society in which schools will operate only a few years from now, early in the twenty-first century, follow. As you read these ideas, consider five questions:

■ Do you agree with these predictions?
■ What are their implications for teaching, for students, for you?
■ Will you be prepared?
■ Will you be able to adjust?
■ What are your predictions?

More questions to ask

Prediction One: Electronic Teaching

Much of what students now learn in school will be learned at home through computers, television, and other electronic devices. Students will learn primarily from computerized learning programs and will talk to their teachers electronically rather than sitting in classrooms.

Prediction Two: Early Individualized Learning

Small children will learn at home or in day-care centers almost from infancy. They will be exposed much earlier than they are now to sophisticated electronic recordings and videotapes, which will teach them sounds, shapes, and elements of their environment. They will be tested in evaluation centers so that individual learning programs can be written for them. These programs will help them learn material and develop skills that are particularly difficult for them and will enable them to forge ahead in their areas of strength. These children will arrive at kindergarten or first grade with a computer printout of their previous learning, which will be fed into a school's learning management system.

Prediction Three: Continuous Learning

Learning will be continuous, and it will occur everywhere. Students who attend school will learn not only in the classroom but also on the bus traveling to and from school, through the public address system while they have lunch, and through their headsets while they exercise. Adults will learn through audiocassettes that they play in their cars, through educational cable television channels, through rented or bor-

Something to Think About

Every Day in America

  2,740 teenagers get pregnant
  1,105 teenagers have abortions
    369 teenagers miscarry
  1,293 teenagers give birth
    700 babies are born with low birth weight
     69 babies die before one month of life
    107 babies die before their first birthday
     27 children die because of poverty
      9 children die from guns
      6 teenagers commit suicide
  1,375 teenagers drop out of high school
  1,849 children are abused
  3,288 children run away from home
  2,987 children see their parents divorced
135,000 kids arrive at school with a gun

  ■ What are the implications of these numbers for teachers in pre-K–12 classrooms?
  ■ In what ways do these numbers influence your thinking about teaching and teachers?

SOURCE: Children's Defense Fund. (1990). *Children 1990: A report card.* Washington, DC: Children's Defense Fund.

rowed videocassettes, and through telephone lectures piped into their home speaker systems. Electronic and print correspondence courses will be available on virtually every topic, for people of all ages.

Prediction Four: Eliminating Grade-Level Distinctions

Grade-level distinctions in schools will disappear as learning becomes more individualized and computer-managed. The amount of school time devoted to full class instruction will decline. Teachers will monitor and guide student progress more and instruct less. Students will learn more from peers in cooperative group arrangements.

Prediction Five: Differentiated Teacher Roles

The roles that teachers play will become more differentiated. Some will be "lead teachers" or "master teachers" who direct teams of assistants. Some will develop and refine curriculum packages, with only occasional contact with students. Some will record or present in-person lectures for classes. Some will specialize in student evaluation. Some will guide small group discussions. Some will counsel individual students. Some will train other teachers. All will be skilled in media and electronic instruction. Teacher salaries will vary greatly according to type of job performed, level of skill, and position of responsibility among the other teachers.

Prediction Six: Expanded Teacher Education

The education of teachers will be continuous, consisting of four or more years of "pre-education" study in the liberal arts and sciences, at least one subsequent year of professional study, an internship operated jointly by a college and a school system, and one or more years of apprentice teaching under a mentor teacher. Teachers will be employed for twelve months, will devote a substantial part of each school day to their own learning rather than interacting with students, and will continue on-the-job training throughout their entire professional lives. The nature of the specific functions that teachers perform will change substantially every ten to twenty years.

Prediction Seven: Larger "Underclass"

More students will be poor, urban, minority, and undereducated. More will have been born to teenage parents. More will come from families whose adults are unable to understand, support, or supplement the instruction of the school. More of these students will not find jobs or be fully employed most of their adult lives. More of them will be members of a social and economic underclass that year after year will become further separated from the educated, "successful" segment of society.

Prediction Eight: The Future Environment

The world outside the school will change radically, and those changes will have a significant impact on schools, students, and teachers. Everyone will be pressured by further urbanization, pollution, water and power shortages, population growth, prohibitive medical costs, international militarism, information overload, and similar conditions. Social priorities and values will be turned on end. But schools and teachers will still be expected to educate students for successful, productive lives in that future environment.

The New Teacher, Now and in the Years Ahead

Individual thinking about teaching

So, what does all this mean for a person considering becoming a professional teacher—a person like you? The question is not easy to answer, of course, and it probably needs to be answered individually and personally by each person thinking about pre-K–12 teaching as a career. The primary purpose of this text is to help you begin developing your own answer. Each chapter introduces you to information and key ideas from the *knowledge base* that education experts are providing through their research and scholarly thinking about education, teaching, and schools. As you read the chapters, you will be asked to engage in active learning by studying the information, using the key concepts to interpret what that information means for teaching and schools as well as for you as a potential teacher, relating what you read to your own knowledge about and experiences with real classrooms and schools, and formulating your own generalizations about education, teaching, and schools. This process will help you develop the reflective, decision-making skills needed for successful teaching. Various features of the text—Snapshots, Reflecting on Practice

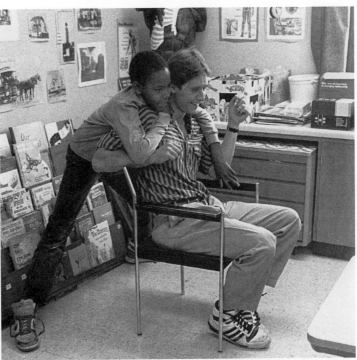

exercises, Something to Think About activities, and Educational Research sections—are intended to engage you actively and intellectually with the substance that makes up the knowledge base or accumulated knowledge about education, teaching, and schools. Do not skim over these features lightly. Use them to develop your own in-depth understanding and value perspectives about teaching and schools, now and in the years ahead, and to refine your intellectual and analytical skills as you become a lifelong learning professional.

Some terms often used to describe competent and successful professional teachers for pre-K–12 classrooms are:

intelligent	decisive	analytical	managerial
knowledgeable	reflective	skilled	
caring	artistic	role model	

As you think about the ideas presented in this text and pursue your subsequent professional study, you will develop deeper understandings, greater skills, and more positive value perspectives that relate to each of these dimensions of good teachers.

Words like "knowledgeable," "caring," and "role model" only begin to describe the many attributes of successful teachers. What words would you choose to express your image of the teacher you would like to be?

Conclusion

Teaching and schools in America today are a product of long-term policies and conditions and so reflect a continuity with schools of the past. Although conditions always change, the reasons why we have schools, the students, the subjects, life in schools, teachers, and some of the issues of the day are more like those of some years ago than they are different. Because of that continuity, schools have to be studied and understood in terms of their historical context.

EDUCATIONAL RESEARCH

Teaching and Schools

The Educational Research sections in this text introduce you briefly to aspects of educational research consistent with each chapter focus. This first section is general; others will be more specific.

Research is a careful and thorough search or investigation of something. It is intended (1) to discover new knowledge, (2) to correct interpretations of current knowledge, and (3) to revise previously accepted conclusions in light of new knowledge. Much of the research on teaching and schools that is useful to educators today is relatively new.

For centuries, teachers practiced their profession based on hunch, common sense, tradition, repetition from the examples of other teachers, and trial and error. And for a long time, the practice seemed to be working. Then, as research became more sophisticated in other fields, educators began to ask research questions about what they do. They asked: Why do we teach this way? Is it the most effective way? How could students learn this content most efficiently? Why do some learn it while others do not? What is the most practical way to organize this school?

Answers to these types of questions over the past thirty years or so have provided a pool of information, called a *knowledge base,* about schools and teaching, and that knowledge base has become the

intellectual "stuff" that educators need to know to improve teaching and schools. The knowledge base is growing, evolving, and becoming more sophisticated each year. All educators need to understand it and use it in their work if they are to be successful.

The 1970s marked a significant change in the nature of research on teaching and schools. Until then, much of the research was uncomplicated and tended to focus on the process of teaching, often on specific teacher behaviors. Typical types of questions included: What is the teacher doing? Why is the teacher doing that? Is he or she lecturing, asking open questions, monitoring seatwork?

In the last decade, however, research on schools and teaching has expanded to include a greater number of studies than ever before, and those studies are using more probing questions and substantially different investigative approaches. These increases in number, in complexity, and in variety of approaches have, of course, produced more useful information about teaching and schools. For example, one of the approaches, *process-product research,* compares what happens in the classroom with student outcomes. Instructional processes, such as the specific methods a teacher uses, what students do during the course of a school period, how time is divided among classroom activities, and the amount of homework assigned, are compared with such products as how much the students learn as measured on achievement tests.

This process-product research has led to documented conclusions that school characteristics, teacher

traits, and the specific nature of teaching make a difference in what students learn.

It has shown that some schools are better than others, that some specific school environments produce more learning than others, that some types of teachers influence students more significantly than others, and that some teaching techniques are more effective than others.

For example, in a study released in 1979, British researcher Michael Rutter and his colleagues reported, after intensively studying twelve London schools, that the nature of a school environment, or its *ethos,* is a factor in how well students learn. In *Fifteen Thousand Hours* (1979), he concluded that students in some schools performed better on tests and behaved better than expected in terms of their socioeconomic backgrounds.[27] In those schools, the principals established clear guidelines and monitored teacher work closely. The teachers expected high student performance and rewarded hard work. Rutter drew a connection between the students' test performance and behavior on one hand and the school conditions on the other.

Other process-product researchers have found that certain types of teaching methods contribute significantly to student learning. Some of those methods are (1) particular classroom management techniques, (2) direct and structured learning strategies, (3) a clear focus of instruction, (4) flexible instructional planning, (5) variation in teaching methods, and (6) a warm, enthusiastic, accepting teacher personality.[28]

But the idea that schools and

teaching make a difference in what students learn has not always been accepted. Two widely read and influential books of the 1960s and early 1970s, James Coleman's *Equality of Educational Opportunity* (1966) and Christopher Jencks's *Inequality: A Reassessment of the Effect of Family and Schooling in America* (1972), concluded in general terms that schools did not make much difference in what children learned.[29]

Coleman's conclusion stated, in essence, that the ability of the child to learn depends more on his or her socioeconomic background than on what happens in the classroom. Jencks said, "The character of a school's output depends largely on a single input, namely the characteristics of the entering children. Everything else . . . is either secondary or completely irrelevant" (p. 256).

These two studies led many educators to conclude that what happened in schools did not make much difference in terms of student learning, but that conclusion was erroneous. Schools and teachers might have to work against tremendous odds sometimes, but process-product research has shown (1) that they can make a difference and (2) that some ways of doing things are more effective than others. Some schools and teachers are more effective than others, and the differences between the effective and the ineffective ones can be identified. With that knowledge, the less effective can be made better.

Process-product research is only one of the approaches to studying schools and teaching that have proven useful in recent years. Among the others are ethnographic cognitive, sociolinguistic, and behavioral approaches. Each approach provides a perspective that illuminates different dimensions of teaching and schools. At this point, it is not important for you to understand all of the approaches mentioned, but it is important to realize that research on teaching and schools is continually producing information about what is and should be happening in schools. That information is important to all educators.

In the next two chapters, the Educational Research sections focus on research on classroom teaching. The section in Chapter 2 looks closely at the ways in which researchers study classrooms and teaching. The section in Chapter 3 reviews studies of teaching methods that have been found to be more effective than others.

On the other hand, circumstances surrounding teaching and schools have changed radically during recent years, primarily because of the education reform of the last two decades. Expectations of students, schools, and teachers have been modified, and what happens in classrooms has been adjusted to conform to these expectations. Teaching is changing and will continue to change, especially during the next decade or two, as reform agendas are implemented and modified. As a whole, the reform movement has, to an extent, redefined the purposes of schools.

Predictions for the future do not describe a return to more complacent times. Expectations and conditions in schools and in the environment that surrounds schools will demand constant change and redirection. Teachers will strive constantly to keep up and to do what is needed to teach well.

Constant change

Prospective teachers need to ask continually:

■ What is happening in schools and the profession of teaching?
■ In what directions are things moving?
■ What does this mean for me as a potential teacher?

Summary

Your study of education, teaching, and schools in the United States should involve formulating questions about the subject and using those questions as guides for investigation. Such questions will not have simple answers, but they can initiate a systematic approach to study that will make the topics more understandable and provide direction for further inquiry.

Schools in the United States are intended to provide citizenship education, academic achievement, vocational training, college preparation, and personal and social development. Virtually all school-age children and youth attend school. The curriculum is consistent across schools. The culture of schools affects students' and teachers' lives. Teachers are a varied lot of human beings, but many share similar general characteristics. Americans tend to be satisfied with schools, but they have been more critical in recent years.

The education reform movement that began in the 1980s has raised questions about schools, set directions for improvement, and started processes for change that are now being pursued. *A Nation at Risk* and other reports were most instrumental in initiating reform developments. Reform agendas include back-to-basics, accountability and competency testing, greater professionalization of teaching, more effective schools and teaching, more equitable education for all students, and changes in content. The most recent stage of this movement is reflected in Goals 2000 legislation. What actually happens as a result of the movement will be determined in the next decade or two.

Questions that dominate discussions about education, teaching, and schools are (1) In what ways should teaching and schools be changed? (2) How can the necessary resources be provided? Teaching and schools in the years ahead will be different from the teaching and schools of today. Predicted are more electronic teaching, more early learning, more continuous learning, fewer grade-level distinctions in schools, increased differentiation among teacher roles, different and more demanding patterns of teacher education, a greater need to educate poor children, and a radically different social environment.

Becoming a teaching professional for the pre-K–12 classrooms of the future requires in-depth understanding, skills, and value perspectives that must be developed through substantial study, active learning, reflection, personal decision making, and lifelong learning.

Study Questions

1. Review the "Goals 2000" objectives described in this chapter. Which of these do you think are most likely to be accomplished, even if not by the year 2000? Which are least likely to be accomplished? Why do you think so in each case?

2. In terms of your own priorities, which goals of education and which reform agendas will most need to be satisfied during the early twenty-first century? Why do you think so?

3. If your own children attend pre-K–12 schools or will do so during the next twenty years, what are the most important things you expect them to learn? Are these things also the most important for all children? If not, what are the differences and why do those differences exist?

4. Make a list of the ways in which teaching in pre-K–12 schools will be different in the year 2020 from teaching today. Explain and justify each item on your list. Decide whether each change is good or bad for students and teachers. Explain why you think so.

5. Make two lists of conditions concerning teaching and schools that will affect your decision about becoming a pre-K–12 classroom teacher: one that you think would prompt you to be a teacher and a second that would deter you from such a decision. Why do you list each item in the way you do?

Key Terms

Accountability
Apprentice teacher
Back-to-basics
Citizenship education
Cooperative learning
Culture
Decision-making skills
Diversity
Folkways
Inclusion
Knowledge base of
    education

Lead teachers
Learning outcomes
Learning styles
Mainstreaming
Master teacher
Multiculturalism
Opportunity-to-learn
    standards
Preventive approach
Process-product research
Professionalization of
    teaching

Reflective skills
Remediation
"Rising tide of mediocrity"
School effectiveness
School ethos
Self-concept
Time on task
Whole child
Whole-language approach

For Further Reading

Alsalam, N., Fischer, G. E., Ogle, L. T., Rogers, G. T., & Smith, T. M. (Eds.). (1993). *The condition of education 1993*. Washington, DC: Center for Education Statistics.

Children's Defense Fund. (1991). *State of America's children*. Washington, DC: Children's Defense Fund.

Education Week. Subscription Office, P.O. Box 2084, Marion, OH 43306-2084. (Newspaper on contemporary issues affecting teaching and schools, published 40 times a year—weekly during the school year)

Fullan, M. G., & Miles, M. B. (1992). Getting reform right: What works and what doesn't. *Phi Delta Kappan, 73*(10), 744–752.

Good, T. L., & Biddle, B. J. (1982). *Teachers make a difference*. Lanham, MD: University Press of America.

Haselkorn, D., & Calkins, A. (1993). *Careers in teaching handbook*. Belmont, MA: Recruiting New Teachers.

National Education Association. (1992). *Status of the American public school teacher: 1992*. Washington, DC: National Education Association.

Perrone, V. (1991). *A letter to teachers: Reflections on schooling and the art of teaching*. San Francisco: Jossey-Bass.

Phi Delta Kappan. (The Journal of Phi Delta Kappa that usually contains brief, informative articles on contemporary issues regarding teaching and schools. Each year the September or October issue contains results of the Phi Delta Kappa/Gallup Poll of the American public's attitudes toward public schools.)

Sarason, S. B. (1993). *You are thinking of teaching? Opportunities, problems, realities*. San Francisco: Jossey-Bass.

Zehm, S. J., & Kottler, J. A. (1993). *On being a teacher: The human dimension*. Thousand Oaks, CA: Corwin Press.

Inside Classrooms
Studying Teaching

*I*n Chapter 1 we looked at conditions that affect teaching and schools in general. Now we zero in on what actually goes on in classrooms. We present techniques that you can use to analyze teaching episodes that you read about, see on videotapes, and observe in local classrooms. Introduction to these techniques at this early point in your study of teaching puts you where the important action is— where teachers teach and students learn—and involves you actively in your studying. It helps you formulate your own ideas about teaching even while you read about those of others. It also provides you with skills for learning about teaching on your own.

Learning techniques for observing in classrooms this early in your professional study will also help you shift your perspective about teaching to that of a beginning expert from that of a passive spectator. It will help you see teaching differently from the way you saw it as a pre-K–12 student. You will not only see what happens but will also be able to interpret classroom events intelligently. Although you will probably not begin observing formally in classrooms for some time, knowing how classroom observation systems work will enable you to reflect upon the teaching that you experienced in more analytical ways. The observational and analytical skills you will develop will continue to be a key asset for you throughout your professional career.

The chapter opens with a brief overview of what happens in different classrooms and how classroom teaching is often perceived by those outside the profession. Then it instructs you in two approaches to thinking about teaching. The first approach suggests thinking about teaching in terms of four commonsense questions. It is a useful but not an expert approach to studying teaching. The second approach uses a technical observation system developed by educational researchers. For those interested in developing more expertise, a third technical system of analyzing teaching appears in Appendix A.

The Snapshot describes what happens in two Nashville classrooms. Trained observers provided both classroom portraits. The two descriptions are intended to start you thinking about specific classroom activity. The two Reflecting on Practice boxes serve as exercises for practicing your observation skills. The Educational Research section details how some researchers analyze teaching and classrooms.

SNAPSHOT

*T*he Snapshot for this chapter describes classroom activity of a few minutes' duration in two classrooms on a typical school day. One class is second grade; the other is eleventh-grade mathematics. As you read, consider:

■ What are the teachers and students doing?

■ Why are they doing these things?

■ What learning is taking place?

■ What do these episodes tell you about these teachers? About these students? About these classrooms?

■ What knowledge did you use to answer the preceding questions, and how did you gain that knowledge?

A Second Grade

It is 9:13 A.M., and school has been in session for more than an hour. Ms. Myers has completed her directed reading lesson to two of her four reading groups.[1] The Green Group has just assembled before her at the reading table in the front of the room. The class consists of twenty-three students today. Four are absent.

The seven students of the Red Group, who had their reading lesson first, are in the process of completing their worksheets. Two have already placed their work in the basket on Ms. Myers's desk and are beginning to read their books as Ms. Myers instructed and as the assignment written on

the board reminds them to do. Two others are talking and laughing while they stand at Ms. Myers's desk. John is getting a drink on the way back to his seat. Karrie is not quite finished but is working diligently. Tana is not nearly finished and is staring across the room at the bulletin board.

The five students of the Blue Group, who just finished the reading lesson, have returned to their regular seats and are writing their names on worksheets that will assess their ability to apply the reading skills that were just taught in directed reading. Vicki has already begun the first exercise. Shasta cannot find her pencil.

The six students of the Yellow Reading Group are at the listening center listening to a tape of *Sleeping Beauty*. After they finish the tape, they will complete a worksheet on which they will list the story's events in sequence. They will then write a short report about the story's characters and plot.

The five students seated before Ms. Myers open their books as the teacher directs. While they do so, she scans the room quickly, looking over their heads to check on the other students. She wants to know whether everyone is "on task" or at least appears to be. She tells the two at her desk to return to their seats and start the assignment quickly. She warns them that she will remove their names from the Good Helper list on the bulletin board if they do not respond promptly. She calls Tana by name and tells her to finish quickly. She notices that Karrie has not finished yet and that John is at the water fountain. She does not say anything to either of them but makes a mental note to check on them specifically on her next "visual sweep of the room."

Ms. Myers returns her attention to the reading group before her. She says, "Mary, please read the new words

for today." Mary reads the five new words from the chart, sounding out each. Ms. Myers compliments her. She then asks Mark to read the first page. When Mark finishes, she asks Candice to say in her own words what the story is about. She praises Candice for her insight. Then she asks Jason to read the next page.

When the last reading group is finished, Ms. Myers moves among the students to see how much of the morning work each has completed. She tells the children who have completed all assignments to put a star by their names on the "completed work chart" on the wall and lists the names of those not finished on the chalkboard. She suggests to them that they try to find time during the day to complete their work and says they may put a star by their name when they do. At the end of the week children who complete all the week's work will receive a reward.

Eleventh-Grade Algebra II

At the five-of bell, Ms. Bassler enters the classroom.[2] Bob and Tim are already seated; others trickle in. Cathy enters and explains that she cannot come for a make-up test today as planned; she asks if she may take it tomorrow and the teacher agrees. John enters and asks Ms. Bassler if she would like him to erase the board, but she says no because the problems at the top are part of today's work.

As the bell rings, the last of the seventeen students hurry to their seats; seven are absent today, taking AP tests. Fred and Cari go to the board and begin to put up problems from last night's homework. Other students get out their papers and books. Ms. Bassler checks the board work and pronounces it correct.

Ms. Bassler then reads the correct answers for last night's homework, and the students check their own papers. Fred frantically searches through his book but cannot find his work. When Peter asks the teacher to explain how one problem should be done, she does so and then continues on with the checking. As she reads, two students fill in answers to some problems they had not completed.

Ms. Bassler finishes reading the answers for the thirty problems and asks whether any students have questions. Several hands go up, and she answers the questions, using the board to illustrate each. At one point, she asks whether anyone worked a certain problem differently and got a correct answer. Marcia explains her different approach and receives praise for good thinking.

After dealing with questions about homework, Ms. Bassler reviews yesterday's lesson about inverse functions and works two examples. She asks Elizabeth whether she understands. She says she does. The teacher then tells Elizabeth that she had a conversation with her father last night, and she goes back to working an example.

After explaining the examples, Ms. Bassler gives the whole class a problem to work. All students copy the problem. Brad looks puzzled; Peter raises his hand. The teacher goes to Peter and gives help. Tom also raises his hand, and she goes to him.

When no more hands are raised, Ms. Bassler again goes to the board and reviews the process. She writes a new problem on the board. She makes an error in her example but catches her error and corrects herself.

Ms. Bassler now introduces today's lesson on finding first identities. After a brief explanation, she asks for a volunteer to build on what she has just demonstrated and find the second identity. Janie responds and is correct in her work. Ms. Bassler praises her. She then gives the class some tips on how to remember identities for exponents and for logarithms.

Ms. Bassler now refers to the problems she had written on the board before class and asks the class to give the answers for the first five. Students answer in chorus and the teacher leads a brief checking procedure for each response. Tom corrects the teacher on an error she makes, and she praises him for being observant.

Ms. Bassler next leads the students in working the second five problems dealing with the other identity. Students correctly answer all ten problems.

A student messenger comes to the door and hands the teacher a note. This student was once in the class but dropped it. Ms. Bassler teasingly asks if he wants to rejoin. He looks at all the problems on the board, declines, and leaves. Ms. Bassler and the class remind each other about what class was like at the beginning of the year. Ms. Bassler admits she was hard on the students and congratulates them for sticking with the course.

Ms. Bassler goes to the board and works a problem from page 378 in the text. She assigns the remaining problems on the page as classwork and leaves the room to make a phone call in response to the note brought by the student messenger. The students all work on their assignment. At first some ask others for help, and they give further explanations to each other. Then all settle at their own desks and work quietly and individually.

Ms. Bassler returns and asks if anyone needs help. Several students raise their hands, and she goes individually to each and guides the work.

Ms. Bassler assigns homework problems for tomorrow and calls for all of today's homework to be turned in. Fred now says that he lost his. Ms. Bassler says she believes him; he may turn in a piece of paper with an explanatory note on it and submit the paper if he finds it. As she says this, the public-address system interrupts with an announcement about awards.

The bell rings, and students begin to leave the room. Ms. Bassler stands at her desk and continues to help students who come up to her for last-minute help.

What Happens in Classrooms

Classrooms are places where students, teachers, learning materials, and ideas interact. In good classrooms, the interaction is purposeful, planned, and controlled by the teacher. If it is successful, students learn.

Classrooms are unique places

People read, talk, listen, question, respond, smile, frown, laugh, cry, gesture, daydream, and sleep in classrooms. As they do, personalities and ideas intertwine, often meshing, sometimes clashing.

Classrooms are places where children, adolescents, and teenagers live a major part of their lives, where they have to be even if they want to be somewhere else. In them, students study, grow, develop, mature, think, and learn. Classrooms are where *students* struggle, achieve, give up, fail, and try again.

Classrooms are also places where teachers practice their profession and apply their skills, where they inform, question, motivate, cajole, joke, understand, sympathize, and scold. Classrooms are places where *teachers* struggle, achieve, give up, fail, and try again.

Common Characteristics

Classrooms have common characteristics. In fact, throughout the United States they are surprisingly alike.

The hallmark of most elementary school classrooms is perpetual activity. The students interact constantly in a friendly, flexible, yet energized atmosphere under the patient and subtle direction of the teacher. Students participate as a total class, in small groups, and individually. They listen to teacher explanations, work problems at their seats, engage in "hands-on" experience at study centers, read assignments, write answers to questions, and complete worksheet exercises.

Elementary teachers such as Ms. Myers constantly manage a multitude of classroom events. They lead students through carefully paced sequences of experiences, with frequent changes in activities in order to maintain interest. They respond to correct student ideas with praise and other forms of encouragement. They monitor student progress and guide learning by asking questions and giving directions.

Because there is so much activity in elementary classrooms, successful teachers have well-developed plans of operation, consisting of rules and procedures, rewards and punishments, and patterns of communication with students that all understand. They use these devices to maintain classroom control, order student work, sustain learner interest, and stimulate learning.

Most secondary school classrooms are usually more "ordered," more focused on the content to be learned, and more noticeably purposeful than elementary classrooms. Some of these types of differences are reflected when Ms. Bassler's lesson described in the Snapshot is compared with that of Ms. Myers. In the academic subjects, teachers frequently stand at the front of the class or sit next to a podium from which they read lecture notes, follow along in the textbook, or study their teaching plans. Students typically sit at their desks, which are usually in rows facing the teacher, listening to the teacher, taking notes, socializing with each other, or daydreaming.

In secondary schools learning is overwhelmingly cognitive, and teaching is most often focused on the class as a group rather than on individual students. Teachers present facts and ideas, and successful students learn them, either by rote memory or through some higher level of thinking. In the process, students come to know and understand new information. When they have learned the information, students demonstrate what they have learned by answering questions, doing problems, completing exercises, writing papers, and passing tests.

Even when the subject matter involves more skill development than cognitive and verbal learning, common patterns are still present. Usually classroom instruction is still teacher-dominated; teacher-student questioning cycles still follow a pattern; and a common routine of teacher instruction, student practice, and student demonstration of skill and knowledge learned is obvious.

For the grade levels between elementary and secondary schools, classroom activity is a mixture of that found at earlier and later grades. Typically, there is less student-centered teaching and less student activity than at elementary levels and more than at higher levels. At the same time, there is more content coverage and

Elementary classrooms

Secondary classrooms

Middle school classrooms

You can practice your observational skills even with photographs of teaching situations. For example, how many specific differences can you find between these two classrooms? What factors do you suppose might account for them? What advantages and disadvantages do you see in these two learning environments? (Keep in mind the part of the classroom you don't see in the picture.)

more expectation that students learn on their own than there is for younger children. Students at middle school levels are in a transitional stage between childhood and young adulthood—entering adolescence or well into that developmental stage. At successful middle schools, the teaching is adjusted to fit the students' level of maturity. Because students mature at different rates, teaching varies greatly from grade to grade, class to class, and even within single classrooms.

Differences

But classrooms are also very different, and to some degree each classroom is unique. The differences result from variations in student age, abilities, and personalities; in teacher characteristics, styles of teaching, and personal philosophies; in the ways classes are organized, students grouped, and lessons conducted; in the family, school, and community cultures that envelop the classroom; and in the political, psychological, social, ethnic, racial, and economic ideologies and norms on which the classroom operates.

Besides the obvious differences in physical appearance of classrooms and the differences in the individual human beings who constitute a class, classrooms are also different in ways such as the following:

- the extent to which students are actively involved in their learning
- the amount and types of interpersonal interaction
- the level of abstraction and understanding at which learning takes place
- the ways in which students are grouped for instruction
- the type of social stratification within the classroom culture
- the amount of creativity
- the level of teacher tolerance of conflict, noise, and confusion
- the ways in which subject matter is organized and integrated
- the ways in which space and instructional materials are used
- the styles in which information and materials are presented

- the ways in which student behavior is managed
- the ways in which students are questioned and feedback is provided
- the degree of emotional support and physical contact
- the extent to which parents are involved
- the level at which special needs of students are recognized and met

Perceptions of Classroom Teaching

What is most important about classrooms is, of course, what happens to the students in them. If the right things happen, students learn what they should learn. What are the right things? What "should" happen in classrooms? What "should" students and teachers do? How "should" students learn?

These questions might seem simple. A typical member of the community, for example, might respond:

Teachers should tell students what they need to know; assign them work-sheets, exercises, and reading; make them do homework; ask them questions; correct them when they are wrong; compliment them when they are right; make them behave; give them tests; and assign them grades.

That might be the start of an appropriate answer, but, of course, there is much more to it. What people see in classrooms depends to a great extent on what they already know about classrooms, teaching, and students and on what biases and purposes they have as they observe. More knowledgeable and experienced observers tend to see more and understand more of what they see. But even experts observe from their own particular perspectives.

What observers see in classrooms

Even if you are very much a beginner in your study of teaching and classrooms, you are already an expert of sorts. You have some knowledge, and you have formed some perspectives about teaching. That knowledge and those perspectives will influence what you see when you visit classrooms that you observe. If you are like most people in the early stages of teacher preparation programs, your view of teaching and what happens in classrooms comes very much from a student's point of view.

Let's check on your perspectives. Think about one of your high school classes and teachers—not just a single class on one single day, but a yearlong class such as history, English, math, or science. Then consider the following:

- What are some of the things that happened in that class?
- What did the teacher do regularly?
- What did you and the other students do?
- Why do you think things occurred as they did?

Compare your thinking with that of other students in this education class.

Now, raise the same questions about a class or teacher from your elementary school. After that, apply the same questions to one of your college classes. Then consider:

- In what ways are your perceptions of the three classes similar to those of other students in this class?
- In what ways do your perspectives reflect the fact that much of your contact with teaching has been as a student?
- How might the views of more experienced and trained classroom observers be different from yours?
- How might your perspectives change as you continue your study of teaching?

Following are quotations from well-known educational researchers who study classrooms. The statements are reflections drawn from the researchers' classroom observations. Each comment reflects the particular researcher's perspective. As you read the comments, note the differences and identify the perspectives. Compare their comments to the way you responded to the questions above.

I stood in the open doorway of a classroom in one of the junior high classes located side by side down a long hallway. The day was a warm one and the doors of three of the classrooms were open. Inside each, the teacher sat at a desk, watching the class or reading. The students sat at table-type desks arranged in rows. Most were writing, a few were stretching, and the remainder were looking contemplatively or blankly into space. In one of two other rooms with closed doors, the students were watching a film. It appeared to be on the cause and prevention of soil erosion. In the other, the teacher was putting an algebraic equation on the chalkboard and explaining its components to the class. In visits to several other academic classes that day, I witnessed no marked variations on these pedagogical procedures and student activities.[3]

. . . each class and its inhabitants are in constant interaction with the social contexts in which they are embedded. The influences of family life, social class, ethnic and racial history, political and social ideologies reach the school directly each day through students and parents, teachers and administrators. The streets children negotiate to get to school, the people who live and work along the way, the houses or apartments where families live, the nature and quality of the social networks within the community are all important influences on the social, psychological, and educational forces at work in the classroom. Classroom life, therefore, is very much shaped and constrained by the norms, values, and traditions of the school; and likewise, the school is an integral part of the community which surrounds it. Each of these social systems—classroom, school, community—has its own structural arrangements, cultural idioms, and functional purposes, but each is also greatly influenced and sustained by the others.[4]

In general, these six classrooms exhibited certain basic similarities in language use, many of which would tend to indicate that they were fairly typical of classrooms observed in prior studies. Questions were primarily known information questions, although "real" questions were asked fairly often. Pupils answered most questions by providing non-personal information. Pacing of lessons, and extended development of question cycles through repeated or probing questions, increased as the school year progressed. Language use reflected more businesslike procedures in September and January and more informal procedures in December.[5]

Studying Teaching

Until recently, most educators had not analyzed what happens in classrooms closely, precisely, or scientifically. Instead, they tended to hold one of two oversimplified conceptualizations of teaching: the teacher as "born artist" or the teacher as "craftsperson." Either of these conceptualizations made systematic and thorough study of classrooms relatively unimportant.

The first of these conceptualizations rested on a combination of two assumptions about teaching: that teachers were "born, not made" and that teaching was an "art, not a science." This view of teaching included the belief that some people possessed an intrinsic talent for teaching. Somehow they knew instinctively how to teach; they were innately skilled. They did not need to be taught to be teachers. They were born artists. They needed only to learn the content they would teach to their students.

The second conceptualization rested on the assumption that teaching was a craft, much like those of the Middle Ages, such as carpentry and shoemaking. This view of teaching included the belief that people became teachers by watching other "master teachers" teach and by practicing the same techniques as an apprentice under the guidance of the "master." When the apprentices became good enough at the trade, they left the tutelage of the master for their own classrooms.

The nature of classroom teaching

With these mind-sets, teacher educators of the past tended to think of the task of preparing new teachers as a general three-step process:

1. Recruit intelligent, dedicated, compassionate young people.
2. Teach them some "subject matter" and a sufficient supply of "tricks of the trade" of teaching.
3. Send them to perform their art or practice their craft in student teaching and then on the job.

If these new teachers succeeded in the classroom, they were judged to have become "classroom artists," "skilled craftspersons," or some combination of both. They were expected to get better over the years, but that improvement would come from practice rather than from any systematic study of their effectiveness.

Although there is some validity to both of these ideas of the nature of teaching, educational researchers now know that they can study classrooms systematically. They can look for specific events and interactions, analyze what they see, determine which teaching is most effective, and develop ways to help teachers improve their performance.

Systematic Study

The study of almost any phenomenon is usually most productive if the people doing the study approach their task with some background knowledge and then do the study in an organized way. They begin with some general ideas about what they are looking at so that they can decide what it is that they see. Then they systematically observe, analyze, and interpret the phenomena under study.

One way of observing systematically is through a three-step process of (1) formulating questions to be answered, (2) brainstorming about the kind of data expected, and (3) constructing a system for gathering and categorizing the expected data. Such efforts at the start of an investigation provide guides for the analysis. They tell the investigator what to look for, what to record, how to record it, what to emphasize, and so forth. They help to assure that the correct and appropriate data are collected.

Observing

Once data are collected, they must be analyzed and interpreted. They must be made understandable and useful. Investigators must formulate them into meaningful conclusions and explain them in ways that others can understand. These tasks require skill as well as knowledge of both the data collected and the general phenomenon being studied.

Analyzing and interpreting

The importance of skilled, systematic observation, analysis, and interpretation of data can be illustrated by a look at the way many coaches and players on athletic teams analyze what they do. They first record their games on videotape and then analyze those tapes over and over again. Because they are knowledgeable, they know what to look for; but nevertheless, they look at the plays repeatedly, from different angles, and in slow motion. Several people look at each tape and interpret them from their individual perspectives. They compare notes and draw conclusions. Then they prepare for the next game in the hope of playing better and being successful. For purposes of comparison, think of how much more meaningful and valuable this type of analysis of a football game would be compared with off-the-cuff observations of a spectator attending a football game for the first time.

The same principles apply to the study of teaching. Knowledgeable, prepared observers see more in classrooms than do the uninformed and unprepared. They know what to look for, where to focus attention. They are able to understand more of what they see and can record their data more meaningfully than can the unprepared observer. Unprepared or unskilled classroom observers tend to miss or to misinterpret much of what happens in classrooms and to become confused because they see so much that they do not understand. They may also fail to see all that is going on.

Knowledgeable observers

In other words, just as with other types of analyses, raw data collected on teaching do not mean much in themselves. They have to be interpreted for meaning, and they have to be made useful. To do this, classroom observers of teaching must understand both teaching and the observation process. They need to be knowledgeable in a general sense, so that they know where to begin and what to look for; and as they proceed they must develop that knowledge and increase their sophistication so that they can attach appropriate meaning to the data they collect. In the end, they need to understand the data well enough to provide useful information to the teachers they observe.

The value of classroom observation

Jane Stallings, a national expert on the observation and analysis of classrooms, emphasizes the value of systematic classroom observation. The next few paragraphs of this chapter are based primarily on her ideas, as expressed in *Learning to Look* (especially pages 4–5).[6]

For teachers

When engaged in by a teacher on his or her own or through the help of another observer, systematic observation can help *classroom teachers* teach in ways that are consistent with the social, emotional, and cognitive development of children. For example, if a child is observed to be shy and introverted, the teacher might organize groups so that this child can work among friendly, nonaggressive children. If a child is observed to enjoy tinkering with machines and examining objects to see how they work, the teacher might direct that child to a good selection of exploratory materials in the classroom.

Systematic observation can also increase teachers' awareness of their own behavior and, when appropriate, can lead to changes. For example, observation can tell teachers how much they talk, how well they listen to student ideas, and what nonverbal messages they transmit.

For students of teaching

For students in the process of becoming teachers, classroom observation enables them to compare and contrast teaching styles. These students can learn a great deal from observing a master teacher handle difficult problems such as fights between children. Recording the observation in a precise way provides a concrete reference instead of just a general impression of how the teacher handled the fight. Additionally, students can compare different teacher behaviors with those recommended in a textbook, enabling them to decide which technique they prefer. But whatever the students decide, their knowledge and repertoire of teaching techniques will increase as a result of observing others teach in the classroom.

School administrators, who must evaluate teachers' performances each year, can use systematic observations in making judgments about teachers' proficiencies. For example, they can use their observations to identify and study relationships between teaching practices and children's achievement test scores. The administrator can also use the observation as a teacher training device by discussing it with the teacher. Such discussions of the observations are likely to be more helpful in providing feedback about classroom teaching techniques than are general, unsupported statements about the teacher's behavior.

For supervisors

Systematic observation also provides more accurate and precise pictures of classroom activity than do general and casual looks at teachers and students. This is particularly important because teachers have little time to reflect on or analyze their own behavior; and often their perceptions of their behavior and its effect on children differ widely from those of objective outside observers. John Goodlad and M. Frances Klein pointed this out in a study of elementary teachers when they said

> there seemed to be a considerable discrepancy between teachers' perceptions of their own innovative behavior and the perceptions of observers. The teachers [in the study] sincerely thought they were individualizing instruction, encouraging inductive learning, involving children in group processes [although the observers reported they were not doing so].[7]

Most of the remainder of this chapter is intended to help you develop your skills for analyzing teaching. The next section describes a general, beginning-level way of studying teaching, which we call a *Four-Basic-Question Approach*. Then we provide instruction in the use of a more technical and focused observation system that highlights specific aspects of teaching, the *Student On-Task/Off-Task Observation System*. A second technical observation system, the *Teacher-Student Interaction Observation System*, is presented in Appendix A.[8]

Skilled study of teaching

The Four-Basic-Question Approach to Observation

Let's assume you are going to study a videotape episode of the teaching of a lesson and report about what you see. You want to conduct the study systematically, and you want to be able to draw some meaningful conclusions about what you see; but you want to keep the effort simple.

Questions you might use for the study are

- What is the teacher doing?
- Why is he or she doing it?
- What are the students doing?
- Why are they doing it?

Before you proceed, however, let's look at these questions more closely. The four questions differ in at least two ways. One difference is the focus of the questions. Questions 1 and 2 focus on the teacher; Questions 3 and 4, on the students.

Formulating questions

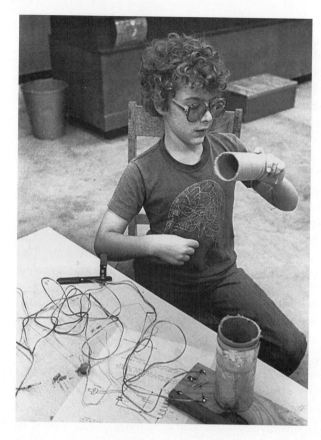

What is the student doing, and why? Becoming a skilled observer includes developing an awareness of the individual and environmental factors that may explain specific behaviors.

The other difference is less obvious. Questions 1 and 3 ask about *actions* of the teacher and students, respectively. Answers to them will be *descriptions* of what the people in the classroom do.

On the other hand, Questions 2 and 4 ask observers to make *inferences* about the actions they see. They ask them to *infer* the *reasons behind* the actions, to determine what motivated the teacher and students to do what they did. These *reasons* cannot be seen. Observers have to provide them. To answer Questions 2 and 4, those doing such a study must draw on their backgrounds and understanding of the situation to a much greater extent than for Questions 1 and 3.

What kind of data could you expect these questions to generate? A number of possible actions are listed in Figure 2-1 (Questions 1 and 3), together with a sampling of possible reasons for some of these actions (Questions 2 and 4).

Now, let's consider ways of gathering and organizing the data that you expect to find. One such way is a chronological log, shown in Figure 2-2.

At this point, you should have some idea about planning for and conducting a systematic study of teaching. Let's see if you have.

Look at the two descriptions of teaching presented in the Snapshot at the start of the chapter. If you were to observe these two episodes of teaching, using the four questions we've been working with:

1. What data would you record?
2. How would you gather and categorize these data?

Collecting data

Organizing data

FIGURE 2-1   Possible data from use of the Four-Basic-Question Approach.

	Teacher	**Students**
Actions	1. What is the teacher doing? standing talking pointing laughing saying "yes" giving instructions writing on the chalkboard telling Joe to sit down giving directions collecting homework frowning shouting	3. What are the students doing? sitting/listening reading sleeping walking to the trash can writing laughing whispering answering copying from chalkboard copying from another student
Possible Reasons	2. Why is the teacher doing this? She wants attention. She wants to be seen by all students. She is standing because she always stands when she lectures. She probably has not made a conscious decision to stand. She is presenting information to the students. She wants to tell them about the child in the play rather than take the time to have them read it. She wants everyone to get the same ideas about the play. She wants to emphasize certain ideas so that the students can see what is most important. She wants to hold student attention. She wants to reinforce some points that she mentions so that the students are more likely to remember them.	4. Why are they doing this? Most want to hear what the teacher is saying. They are interested in the lesson. They want to learn about the characters in the play. Two are not very interested in this play. They are more interested in their other subjects. (We do not know why.) The teacher has not stopped them. One is tired or bored. One is not concentrating and is restless. One is not paying attention. One wanted to interrupt the boredom. This child seems to be immature. Two are not interested in the lesson. One wanted to ask the other a question. The teacher often does not notice whispering.

Now, go ahead and practice using the four questions on each of the two Snapshot episodes.

1. Record responses to all four questions for each class.
2. Organize the data chronologically for each class.

A word of caution is in order here. In this illustration, you have been asked only to *begin* a process of studying teaching. You have been asked to *describe* actions and *infer* reasons behind these actions but not to assess the broader or deeper meaning of what you see. You were not asked to *interpret* data gathered in your study or to *draw conclusions* from them. This hypothetical illustration and the descriptions of

Interpreting data and concluding

FIGURE 2-2   Chronological log of teacher and student activity.

| Time | Teacher | | Students | |
	Action	Reason	Action	Reason
9:03	Standing	Wants attention	Most listening	Interested, want to learn
	Tells whole class what Bob did in the play	Wants everyone to know what Bob did	Most listening	Interested in play
			Two reading other material	Not interested in play
	Explains why Bob did it	Wants everyone to know why Bob did it	Most listening	Interested
			One sleeping	Bored, tired
			One taking paper to trash can	Bored, restless, immature
			Two whispering, not on subject	Not interested, distracted, bad
9:08	Watching students read	Wants them to practice reading	Most reading	Following teacher's directions
	Ignoring sleeping student	Willing to let him sleep	One sleeping	Tired
			Two day-dreaming	Bored, short attention span
9:13	Asking questions about reading	Checking for understanding	One answering	Was called on
			Most listening to the answer	Interested
			One sleeping	Tired
9:18	Giving directions for next activity	Transition to spelling	Most taking out paper	Following teacher's directions
			One sleeping	Tired

classrooms in the Snapshot are too superficial to permit interpretations or conclusions. Moreover, interpretations depend on knowledge that you will be acquiring later in the course. For this reason, practice in the skills of interpreting and concluding needs to be deferred.

The Student On-Task/Off-Task Observation System

Now that we have introduced informal observation techniques, we build on these to present a more technical system for studying teaching. Learning such a system should help you

1. gain a clearer picture of the idea of *systematic* studying of teaching
2. shift your perspective about classroom activity from that of an outside spectator to that of a beginning-level expert

REFLECTING ON PRACTICE

*I*f you have access to videotapes of teaching actual pre-K–12 classrooms or are able to visit such classrooms, this would be a good time to practice your observation skills. To begin, simply make a list of the four guiding questions:

- What is the teacher doing?
- Why is he or she doing it?
- What are the students doing?
- Why are they doing it?

Then arrange to view a videotaped teaching episode or an actual class. While doing so, record your observations in the form of answers to each of the questions, and see what happens.

Once you have done this and feel that you know what you are doing, you can add a second level of sophistication to your observing skills by interjecting the element of time. Continue to record responses to the same four questions, but do so every five minutes. Follow these steps:

1. Select a videotape (or choose a seat in a classroom) that will enable you to see the teacher and as many students as possible.
2. When you are ready to record your observations, note the time and immediately scan the class, making mental notes of what the teacher and students are doing at that specific moment.
3. Answer all four questions based on what you just saw.
4. Repeat the same scan-and-record process every five minutes for a full period, a complete lesson, or as long as you wish.
5. Review your notes, noticing not only what occurred each time you scanned the class but also how events changed over the time you observed.

3. more skillfully observe teaching in actual classrooms when you have a chance to do so

The Student On-Task/Off-Task Observation System is one of many used by classroom observers to focus on specific activities, analyze them, and interpret what happens. The systems are used primarily by teacher supervisors and peers to gather information about teaching and to supply that information to teachers, who can then better determine if they are actually doing what they intend to do. As noted earlier, teachers are often surprised when they compare observer reports with their own impressions of a class.

Different observation systems have different specific focuses, and all of them leave out much classroom activity that is not a part of that system's particular focus. Some systems, for example, concentrate on classroom patterns of talk, types of classroom language, teacher-student interaction, pace of instruction, student behavior, levels of student thought, and so forth.

We've chosen to introduce the Student On-Task/Off-Task Observation System because (1) it is a general system and easy to use, (2) you can use it with a video or in an actual classroom without knowing anything beforehand about the class, (3) it will help you shift your perspective about teaching from that of a spectator to that of a developing expert, and (4) it will begin to teach you how to use other observation systems. It is important to remember that your practice with an observation task this early in your professional education study is not intended to qualify you as a skilled classroom observer. It is, instead, intended only to help you look at teaching in a way new to you.

This observation system focuses on student on-task and off-task behavior. In slightly modified form, it is used by educational observers to analyze teaching in classrooms throughout the world. It was developed primarily by Jane Stallings.[9]

Although the On-Task/Off-Task Observation System is not difficult to use, it can produce significant, useful information for experienced teachers, teacher supervisors, and educational researchers. Once you learn the system, you should be able to make frequent and continued use of it with increasing sophistication throughout your teaching career. The system is explained and illustrated next; and then a Reflecting on Practice section provides an exercise so that you can practice using it.

The Student On-Task/Off-Task Observation System provides data on what individual students in a class are doing. Each student who is doing what the teacher wants is considered to be *on task*, and each student who is doing something other than what the teacher wants is *off task*. The form on which the observer records the observation data is the Student Off-Task Seating Chart, which is actually a seating chart prepared by the observer to conform to the seating arrangement of the class being observed. If the class is organized with desks in traditional rows, and the teacher is instructing the whole group, the chart might look like the one shown in Figure 2-3. (Note that the codes to be used by the observer are listed on the sheet for easy reference.)

Explanation

The purpose of the Student Off-Task Seating Chart is to record a sample of all students' off-task behavior and nonproductive use of time during a scheduled observation. Three types of data are recorded on the Seating Chart:

1. the off-task behavior
2. the type of activity in which the students should have been involved
3. the time the off-task behavior occurred

Nothing is recorded for students who are on task.

Off-Task Behaviors

The following behavior codes are used for activities other than what the teacher desires:

C   Chatting—Low-volume talking or whispering that is not part of the lesson, passing notes between students

D   Disruptive—Bothering other students, through loud talking, throwing things, pushing, fighting, and so forth

P   Personal needs—Sharpening pencils, going to the restroom, getting a drink, getting papers or books at times other than when the teacher expects

FIGURE 2-3   Example of a Student Off-Task Seating Chart.

STUDENT OFF-TASK SEATING CHART

Teacher: _____ School: _____

Date: _____ Time: _____ to _____ Number of Sweeps: _____
                (beginning)   (end)

(front of classroom)

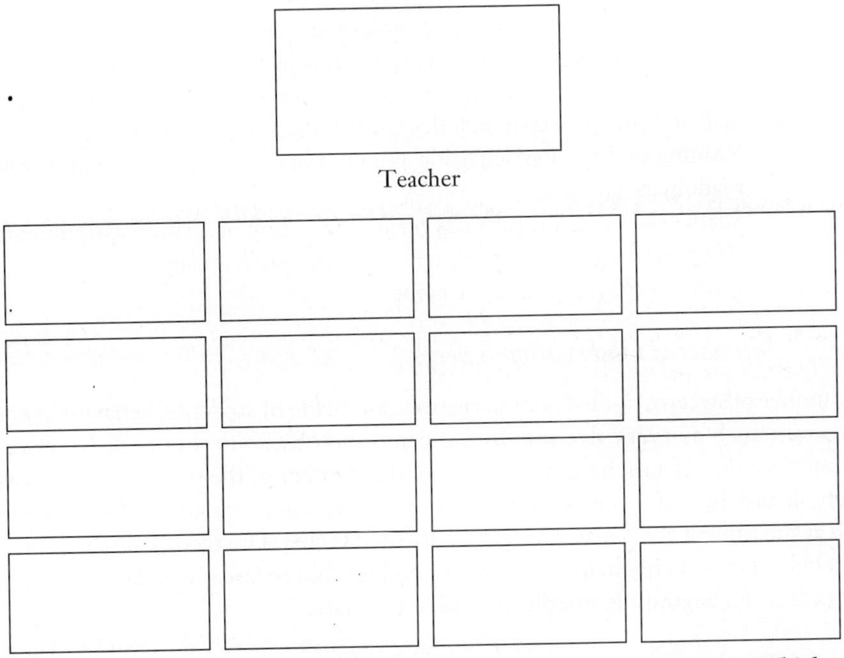

Teacher

Student Off-Task Codes	Activity	Sweep in Which Activity Occurred
C = Chatting	I = Instruction	
D = Disruptive	O = Organization	
P = Personal needs	Q = Question/Answer	
U = Uninvolved	R = Oral reading	
W = Waiting	S = Seatwork	
Z = Sleeping	C = Cooperative group	
	G = Game	

SOURCE: Jane Stallings.

U   Uninvolved—Doing something other than assigned tasks but not bothering anyone else

W   Waiting—Pauses that delay learning, such as sitting with hand up for the teacher's attention before being able to proceed, waiting for materials to be passed or for the teacher to review one's work, just being "stuck" until receiving the teacher's attention. (Note: This does *not* include raising a hand in response to the teacher's questioning and waiting to be called on. Such behavior is *on* task.)

Z   Sleeping

Activities

The following activity codes are used to record how students *should* be involved:

I   Instruction—Listening to the teacher explain subject matter or give directions about content

O   Organizing—Listening to the teacher assign work or explain organizing procedures; getting paper and books out

Q   Question/Answer—Listening to the teacher question students, answering a question, listening to another student answer a question, as in drill and practice; also includes students writing on the board

R   Reading orally—Participation as a member of a reading group that is reading aloud

S   Seatwork—Working at seats on silent reading or written assignments

C   Cooperative group—Working on a cooperative group task

G   Games—Playing academic games

Numbered Observation Sweeps

A number of sweeps, or observation records, are made of students' behavior at equal intervals, such as every five minutes, during one observation period. In order to know *when* the off-task behavior occurred, the number of the sweep is entered with each off-task behavior recorded. For example, if a student is *chatting* during *instruction* at the time of the *fourth sweep*, it is recorded C/I④. The record of when the off-task behavior occurred helps the observer and teacher to know whether students are off task at the beginning, middle, or end of the class.

What would a completed seating chart of this scene look like? How would it help an observer analyze what was happening in the classroom at this moment?

Directions

1. Prepare for the observation by developing a box-type seating chart for the class to be observed. (Refer to Figure 2-3.) The boxes need to be large enough so that several entries can be made in each. (Little or no space is needed between boxes because all recording is placed inside the boxes.)
2. Enter information on the form that identifies the class—the teacher's name, date, school, and the number of sweeps—so you will remember the context of the observation later when you return to your data.
3. As the lesson starts, record the time and immediately begin making the first scan, or visual sweep, of the room. Use the codes given in Figure 2-3 and record off-task activities for each student whose activity is not what the teacher desires. Record nothing for the students who are on task.
4. Make a slash mark beside each symbol just recorded (for example, C/).
5. Write in the space following each slash mark the symbol that shows what the student was supposed to be doing. (A notation of "C/I," for example, means that a student was chatting instead of listening to instruction.)
6. Place the numeral ① beside each entry to indicate that the off-task behavior occurred during the first sweep. Make the marks small enough so that several entries can be made in each box.
7. Use a watch or clock to check time and make visual sweeps of the classroom (repeating Steps 3 to 6) every five minutes for the length of time you had planned to observe. At each repeat of Step 6, make the circled number match the sweep number.
8. Record the time when you stop.

A sample seating chart that has been completed by an observer appears in Figure 2-4. (Normally it is not necessary to list student names in the seating chart. They are listed here so it will be easier for you to discuss the chart with your classmates and instructor.)

Summarizing the Off-Task Seating Chart Data

Notice in Figure 2-4 that each notation for a time when a student was observed to be off task has three elements:

1. the symbol for the off-task behavior (one of six possible)
2. the symbol for the activity in which the student should have been involved (one of seven possible)
3. the number of the sweep (for this observation, from 1 to 10, although no one was recorded as being off task during sweeps 8, 9, and 10)

With these data the observer can analyze

1. how often students are off task
2. which students are off task the most
3. which type of off-task behavior is the most frequent
4. during which activities in the lessons the greatest number of students are off task
5. which time during the class the greatest number of students are off task

Armed with these data, the teacher can make changes that may lead to an increase in the amount of time that students spend on task.

FIGURE 2-4 Example of a partially completed Student Off-Task Seating Chart.

STUDENT OFF-TASK SEATING CHART

Teacher: ____Ms. Jones_____ School: ____Kennedy_____

Date: __2/14__ Time: __9:36__ to __10:38__ Number of Sweeps: _____10_____
           (beginning)   (end)

(front of classroom)

Teacher

Flora	Mark	Betty	Joe

Jeff U/I ① U/O ⑤ U/S ③ U/Q ⑥	Susan	Robert	Dona

Ursula C/O ⑤ C/S ⑦	Daniel	Ellen	Bill U/I ① U/S ③ U/S ② U/S ④

Sharon C/O ⑤ C/S ⑦	Jack C/S ③ C/S ⑦	Lee U/I ① C/S ③ C/S ④ C/S ⑦	Mary

Student Off-Task Codes	**Activity**	**Sweep in Which Activity Occurred**
C = Chatting	I = Instruction	1
D = Disruptive	O = Organization	5, 10
P = Personal needs	Q = Question/Answer	6
U = Uninvolved	R = Oral reading	
W = Waiting	S = Seatwork	2, 3, 4, 7
Z = Sleeping	C = Cooperative group	8, 9
	G = Game	

SOURCE: Jane Stallings.

The data about a class as a whole can be summarized so that the material is easy to understand. A Summary Chart of off-task behaviors (Figure 2-5) can be developed; and the data from the Seating Chart can be transferred to it. To do this, the observer in the example would record in the appropriate box on the Summary Chart the number of times each behavior occurred and the number of times each activity occurred.

FIGURE 2-5   Example of a Summary Chart of off-task behaviors.

SUMMARY CHART
OFF-TASK BEHAVIORS

Teacher: _____Ms. Jones_____   School: _____Kennedy_____

Date: __2/14__   Time: _____9:36–10:38_____

BEHAVIORS	Chatting	Disruptive	Personal needs	Uninvolved	Waiting	Sleeping
Number of Sweeps = 10	9	0	0	9	0	0

ACTIVITIES	Instruc-tion	Organ-izing	Question/ Answer	Oral reading	Seat-work	Coop-erative groups	Games
	3	3	1	0	11	0	0

SOURCE: Jane Stallings.

For practice, use the information recorded on the Seating Chart in Figure 2-4 and on the Summary Chart in Figure 2-5 to respond to the following:

- How many times was it possible for an individual student to be off task during this observation? (Multiply the number of students by the number of sweeps.)
- How many off-task behaviors were recorded?
- Which students were off task most often?
- Which type of off-task behavior was most frequent?
- During which type of activity were students off task most often?
- When during the class period were students off task most often?

Calculating Off-Task Rates

The number of times students are off task compared to the total number of times they could have been off task is called the Off-Task Rate for the class. This rate can be found by dividing the total number of off-task behaviors of all students by the total opportunities that all students had to be off task. The total number of *opportunities* to be off task is determined by multiplying the number of students in the class by the number of sweeps. If the formula is stated in the form of a fraction, it looks like this:

$$\text{Total number of instances of off-task behavior of all students} \div \text{Number of opportunities for all students to be off task} = \text{Off-Task Rate}$$

Something to Think About

During her first week as a student teacher in a junior high school, a college senior was observing in several teachers' classes to get a "feel" for the school as a whole before she started her own teaching. As she watched in one eighth-grade history class, she compiled an informal Student Off-Task Seating Chart. At the end of the class, her data showed the following:

Of the thirty-one students,

- sixteen participated as expected for at least eight of the ten sweeps
- three slept for at least seven sweeps
- four chatted for five of the ten sweeps (in two different conversations)
- five were uninvolved for four or more of the sweeps
- three were disruptive for at least three of the sweeps

As the class left the room, the teacher approached the student teacher and said, "Well, that was a rather typical class. I noticed you were taking notes. What does that mean?"

If you were the observing student teacher, how would you respond? Why would you respond in this way?

REFLECTING ON PRACTICE

To help you practice using a technical observation approach, we provide an outline of the seating arrangement of a middle school English class (Figure 2-6) and a description of what each person in the classroom is doing at five specific times during a lesson. The teacher is teaching the whole class. The sweeps are at five-minute intervals.

FIGURE 2-6   Ms. Lloyd's English class.

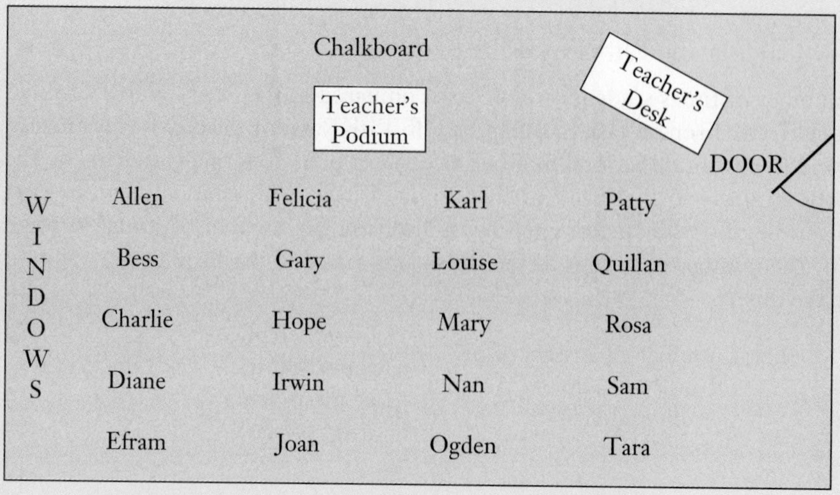

	Chalkboard			
	Teacher's Podium		Teacher's Desk	
				DOOR
W I N D O W S	Allen	Felicia	Karl	Patty
	Bess	Gary	Louise	Quillan
	Charlie	Hope	Mary	Rosa
	Diane	Irwin	Nan	Sam
	Efram	Joan	Ogden	Tara

Now that you have learned about the Student On-Task/Off-Task Observation System, record the student behavior that is described.

1. Make a Student Off-Task Seating Chart for the class, as in Figure 2-3.
2. Fill in the seating chart based on the class descriptions during the five sweeps.
3. Make and complete a Summary Chart as in Figure 2-5 and record the data from your seating chart.
4. Respond to the questions listed in the section "Summarizing the Off-Task Seating Chart Data."

Sweep #1

As the 9:05 bell rings, Ms. Lloyd closes the door of her seventh-grade English class and directs her students to copy the homework assignment from the side chalkboard onto their six-week calendar, to take out their red grading pens, and to exchange last night's grammar papers for in-class checking.

Allen opens his English folder to his calendar and begins to copy. Bess searches through her purse for a red pen as Charlie quietly studies the chalkboard in dismay. Diane tries to hand her paper to Efram, who leans back and stares out the window. Joan walks up the row and hands her paper to Felicia, while Gary and Hope discuss whether the assignment means up to or through page 67. Irwin sharpens his pencil. Karl, Louise, and Mary all copy from the board. Nan offers an extra red pen to Ogden, who ignores her as he and Tara comment on pictures of his new Great Dane puppy, Attila. Patty combs her hair. Quillan copies from the board. Rosa cannot see the board clearly and copies from Quillan's calendar. Sam searches for his calendar, cannot find it, and asks the teacher for another.

Sweep #2

At 9:10 students check last night's homework. Ms. Lloyd asks various students to identify prepositional phrases in sentences and to tell which words they modify.

Allen checks Diane's paper while Bess still searches for a red pen. Charlie raises his hand to volunteer for the next sentence, and Diane checks Charlie's paper. Efram did not have the assignment and therefore has no paper to grade; he sits and pokes at a rip in his book cover. Felicia explains number 6. Gary places a red check beside number 6, while Hope marks a red X on Gary's paper. Irwin's pencil breaks, and he gets up to sharpen it. Joan stares at Efram. Karl, Louise, and Mary raise their hands to volunteer for number 7. Nan watches Sam and Rosa's conversation. Ogden looks at the paper before him. Patty and Quillan both raise hands to ask questions. Rosa asks Sam whether number 4 had three prepositional phrases, and Sam says it did. Tara tries to get Sam's attention to show him the photos of Attila.

Sweep #3

At 9:15 Ms. Lloyd has finished collecting the graded homework papers and begins to introduce the adverbial use of a prepositional phrase.

In the first row, Allen and Bess take notes as the teacher lectures, Charlie and Efram stare intently at the teacher, and Diane takes a mirror from her purse and examines a cut on her lip. In the second row, Felicia and Gary study an example the teacher has written on the board; and Hope, Irwin, and Joan take notes. In the third row, Karl, Louise, Mary, and Nan all take notes, while Ogden tries to see who now has his puppy pictures. In the fourth row, Patty stares at the teacher; Quillan looks at pictures of Attila; Rosa squints hard at the board, then copies notes from Quillan's paper; and Sam and Tara take notes.

Sweep #4

At 9:20 Ms. Lloyd has finished her explanation of adverbial phrases, and students are working individually at their seats on the first five sentences of a twenty-sentence assignment. Ms. Lloyd walks around the room and looks over each student's shoulder.

In the first row, the teacher works with Efram to help him get started; all other students in the first two rows work independently on the assignment. In the third row, Karl, Louise, Nan, and Ogden pick out prepositional phrases, while Mary and Rosa discuss Attila's photos. In the fourth row, Patty and Sam both are stuck and have had their hands raised for help for some time; Quillan and Tara are finishing the fifth sentence.

Sweep #5

At 9:25 Ms. Lloyd has distributed a teacher-made crossword puzzle to students for review practice of *ie* and *ei* spelling words. Students may work on either grammar or spelling until the period ends. Ms. Lloyd has finally confiscated the puppy pictures, and she continues to walk around the room and look over shoulders.

In the first row, Allen, Bess, and Charlie work silently on the spelling puzzle; Diane works on spelling and asks Irwin how to spell several words; Efram stares out of the window. In the second row, Felicia and Hope continue on the grammar, and Gary and Irwin work on spelling; Joan stops to sharpen her pencil. Everyone in row three tries to fill in the spelling puzzle, and the teacher looks over Louise's shoulder. In the fourth row, Patty checks back in her folder notes on prepositions, Quillan and Rosa compare spelling puzzle answers thus far, and Sam and Tara work independently on their puzzles.

Conclusion

You should now have the beginnings of an analytical perspective about classroom activity and should be ready to study teaching from the standpoint of a developing expert. Of course, becoming a skilled observer takes practice as well as familiarity with new terms. Nevertheless, the two systems you have learned should enable you to recognize and understand a number of classroom events that might escape the notice of untrained observers. When you have an opportunity to do so, try either of these observation techniques on videotapes of teaching or during a visit to an actual classroom. If you observe a local classroom, make sure the teacher understands and agrees to what you will be doing. As you use these techniques, you will refine your observation skills, gradually see more subtleties in classroom activity, and develop deeper understandings about what is involved in teaching.

Remember, however, that we have not yet examined what constitutes good and bad teaching characteristics. Do not be quick to judge what you see. Observations can tell you what is happening, but only background knowledge about teaching and learning will enable you to judge appropriately what are good teaching practices and what are not. Chapter 3 begins to provide that background.

A second technical observation system, one on teacher-student interaction, is explained and illustrated in Appendix A. Now that you have learned one such system, you might want to learn to use that second one as well.

What We Know about Studying Classrooms

Educational researchers use classroom observations in their work, and the data generated are used to formulate conclusions about classroom effectiveness. Small-scale, teacher-conducted studies in their own classrooms, as well as more complex endeavors, are described in the following paragraphs.

As mentioned in Chapter 1, a study in the 1960s by James Coleman and others, *Equality of Educational Opportunity,* included comparisons of different factors that help determine how much students in a particular school learn.[10] The study asserted that *teachers are not as significant* in determining how well students learn *as other factors,* such as family background and the economic conditions in which the students live. This assertion led some readers of the study to jump to the conclusion that teachers and what they do in the classroom are not very effective in educating students.

But Coleman's findings did not justify such a conclusion. His investigation was a classic *input-output* study. Students were assessed when they entered school and again when they completed their studies. The data that were collected showed that student backgrounds and the abilities they brought with

them to school were more significant in determining what they learned than were the characteristics of the teachers who taught them and the ways those teachers taught. The data did not say teachers were ineffective, and they did not compare different types of teaching.

However, the Coleman data prompted other researchers to look at schools and classrooms more closely and to look at them in different ways. Some of these researchers have used *process-product* instead of input-output research designs. For example, they looked at different teachers, different teaching styles and techniques, different classroom environments, and different school organizations (all these are the processes of teaching); and they compared what they saw with how much the students in the various settings learned (the product of the teaching). They found that some of the things that teachers and schools do produce more student learning than others, and they found that these things can be identified and classified. Figure 2-7 charts some processes and their products.

These process-product findings mean that teachers and schools can make a difference in what their students learn. They mean that schools, classrooms, and teachers can be observed and analyzed in ways that lead to conclusions about the effectiveness of schools and teaching. They mean that the knowledge and skills used by the more effective schools and teachers can be taught to those that are less effective. Results from many of these studies are now being used

to change classroom practices, to change policies that govern schools, and to change the ways in which teachers are educated.

Often the direction of these changes appears in the form of policy statements about what teachers and schools *should do.* For example, "Teachers should plan thoroughly." "Teachers should monitor student work closely." "Teachers should have high expectations of students and communicate them clearly and consistently." "Schools should have a clearly established set of purposes that are agreed to by all of the staff." "Principals should be instructional leaders."

There is a potential danger, however, if this use of should-do ideas is pursued uncritically; and, unfortunately, many schools and teachers have suffered because of it. Those who have suffered have tended to adopt should-do principles as rigid *formulas* to be followed rather than as flexible guides to be applied sensitively to local circumstances. For example, during the 1980s, a number of schools and teachers incorrectly concluded from Stallings's research (some of which was referred to earlier) that there is a specific formula on the "best" percentage of classroom time to be used for interactive instruction. They then assumed that that percentage is the *correct* percentage for all classes, all teachers, and all contexts. Similar errors have been made in the misuse of findings from 1970s and 1980s research on classroom organization and management from Carolyn M. Evertson, Jere E. Brophy, and others.[11]

One reason research findings are turned into rigid formulas is the

FIGURE 2-7 A schematic representation of process-product research designs. Students enter the school and are affected *by some process, which produces a change in them. The change is the product.*

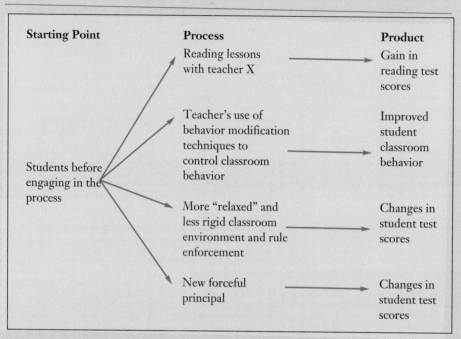

Starting Point	**Process**	**Product**
	Reading lessons with teacher X	Gain in reading test scores
Students before engaging in the process	Teacher's use of behavior modification techniques to control classroom behavior	Improved student classroom behavior
	More "relaxed" and less rigid classroom environment and rule enforcement	Changes in student test scores
	New forceful principal	Changes in student test scores

desire of educators for quick and simple solutions to problems. They want to improve their instruction, and they fall for easy fixes.

Another reason for the frequent misuse of research data lies in the nature of research itself. All research leaves more questions unanswered than it answers. Just as Coleman's input-output design left some dimensions of classroom instruction unexplored, so do process-product designs, as well as all other designs. The simple truth is all research designs have weaknesses as well as strengths. No research can "prove" how all teachers should teach.

Nevertheless, should-do statements, if considered to be guides rather than formulas, can be used effectively in schools and classrooms. This happens when school leaders and teachers apply research findings to a school or classroom, not as proven fact, but in the form of a new, small-scale, local research

study. In other words, when teachers try to follow a should-do idea in their classrooms to determine *whether* it works or not, those teachers are using research findings appropriately. They are doing a small-scale experiment of their own. They are testing the idea to see if it works for them in their setting.

For example, a teacher who decides to follow the research conclusion that *frequent positive feedback to students produces greater and quicker learning* can follow the practice and see how it works. If it does, that teacher has produced one more bit of evidence that the conclusion is valid, at least in one classroom. In addition, the teacher can now use the technique with some confidence.

Researchers who study classrooms follow the same basic pattern. They arrange for certain kinds of teaching, or they find classrooms where that kind of teaching is already occurring. Next, if they are us-

ing a process-product design, they observe those classrooms, using techniques such as those presented earlier in this chapter. Then they assess student achievement. Finally, they compare the observation data with the achievement data. When they find classroom activities and teacher behaviors (processes) that lead to increased levels of student achievement (product), they designate these activities and behaviors as *effective.*

Some specific things classroom researchers of the last ten years have been looking at include:

- the *academic content* covered—in the text, in a teacher's lecture, on the test, during a typical period, or during a whole school day
- teacher expectations of students
- the ways teachers communicate expectations
- student *academic engaged rate* (time spent actively on academic learning)

- the teacher's organizational and managerial plans and style
- the pace and sequencing of lessons
- time spent on *active teaching,* rather than on procedural or managerial tasks
- student *time on task*
- the relative value and appropriateness of whole class, small group, and individualized instruction
- the effects of grouping for instruction
- social status among students in classrooms

- the cognitive level of questions
- teacher reactions to student responses
- the ways in which teachers *monitor* seatwork and follow up homework assignments
- differences in the ways teachers interact with students based on their gender
- student socioeconomic status

The Educational Research section of the next chapter describes some of these studies and reports on their findings.

A good place for teachers to start looking at research that will be of value and interest to them are works by David C. Berliner and Ursula Casanova, titled *Putting Research to Work in Your Classroom,* 1993; David Hopkins, titled *A Teacher's Guide to Classroom Research,* 1993; and Nathaniel Gage and David C. Berliner, titled "Nurturing the Critical, Practical, and Artistic Thinking of Teachers," 1989.[12]

Summary

In many ways, teaching is similar from one classroom to the next, yet each teaching episode is also unique. To a great extent, perceptions of teaching and what happens in classrooms vary according to the point of view of the observer.

Teaching has been studied more closely in recent years than in the past. That study has led to the accumulation of data that can be used to change classroom practice and improve what teachers do.

Those who study teaching can better understand what they see if they approach their task with a set of guidelines about what to look for, a list of questions to ask, and background knowledge about both teaching and the process of observing. The guidelines and questions can be simple; for example, they may focus on what is happening and why it is happening. They can also be complex and may focus on specific classroom phenomena, such as student on-task/off-task behavior and teacher-student verbal interaction. Student on-task/off-task behavior can be calculated and reported by use of a classroom seating chart and the Stallings Student On-Task/Off-Task Observation System. Similarly, the Stallings Teacher-Student Interaction Observation System described in Appendix A can supply data on classroom verbal interaction.

Those studying teaching can learn best by observing videotapes of lessons or actual classrooms, using specific skills that make observation an analytical tool that is much more effective than simply reading books about teaching or being an unprepared spectator in a classroom.

Study Questions

1. Make a list of things that can be observed in classrooms or on videotape recordings of classrooms that would likely indicate that learning is not progressing. Make a similar list of things that would likely indicate that the class is functioning well. Defend your reasons for including each item on each list.

2. What are the advantages and disadvantages of guided classroom observations for

   ■ a teacher-education student who is doing the observing?
   ■ a teacher-education student being observed?
   ■ an experienced practicing teacher?
   ■ a school supervisor or principal?

3. How could classroom observation data be misused? What safeguards should be established to avoid such problems?

4. Lawyers, medical doctors, engineers, and other professionals seem to be more willing to analyze and critique their own and their peers' professional performance than teachers are. Even professional athletes videotape performances and criticize what they see in order to improve. Why do you think teachers seem to be more reluctant than other professionals to do this?

Key Terms

Academic engaged rate
Active teaching
Cognitive
Four-basic-question approach to classroom observation
Hands-on experiences
Inference
Input-output research
Knowledgeable classroom observation

Observation system
Observation sweep
Off-task behavior
Off-task rate
On-task behavior
Ordered classrooms
Researcher perceptions of classrooms

Spectator perceptions of classrooms
Student on-task/off-task observation system
Systematic study
Teacher as born artist
Teacher as craftsperson

For Further Reading

Barr, R. (1987). Classroom interaction and curricular content. In D. Bloome (Ed.), *Literacy and schooling.* Norwood, NJ: Ablex.

Barr, R., & Dreeban, R. (1988). *How schools work.* Chicago: University of Chicago Press.

Carew, J., & Lightfoot, S. L. (1979). *Beyond bias: Perspectives on classrooms.* Cambridge: Harvard University Press.

Denham, C., & Lieberman, A. (Eds.). (1980). *Time to learn.* Washington, DC: National Institute of Education.

Duckett, W. (Ed.). (1983). *Observation and the evaluation of teaching.* Bloomington, IN: Phi Delta Kappa.

Evertson, C. E., & Green, J. L. (1986). Observation as inquiry and method. In M. C. Wittrock (Ed.), *Handbook of research on teaching: Third edition.* (pp. 162–213). New York: Macmillan.

Flanders, N. (1970). *Analyzing teacher behavior.* Reading, MA: Addison-Wesley.

Goodlad, J. I., & Klein, M. F. (1974). *Looking behind the classroom door* (2nd ed.). Worthington, OH: Charles A. Jones.

Green, J. L., & Harker, J. O. (Eds.). (1988). *Multiple perspectives analysis in classroom discourse.* Norwood, NJ: Ablex.

Lortie, D. C. (1975). *School teacher: A sociological study.* Chicago: University of Chicago Press.

Morine-Dershimer, G. (1985). *Talking, listening, and learning in elementary classrooms.* New York: Longman.

Stallings, J. A. (1977). *Learning to look.* Belmont, CA: Wadsworth.

Stubbs, M., & Delamont, S. (Eds.). (1976). *Explorations in classroom observation.* London: John Wiley.

Weade, G., & Evertson, C. M. (1991). On what can be learned by observing teaching. *Theory into Practice, 30*(1), 37–45.

Effective Teaching Practices

For the first edition of this book, Jane Stallings developed a detailed outline for this chapter and prepared much of the first draft. She also wrote the Snapshot and the beginning of the chapter. Much of the chapter is based on her ideas, insights, and suggestions. Brian Hansford wrote the section titled "Classroom Climate."

Now that you have been introduced to the study of teaching, we present information about good teaching practices. The chapter has two thrusts: it surveys characteristics of teachers that make them influential with students and explains classroom practices that educational researchers have found to be effective in producing learning. The teacher characteristics discussed are primarily personality traits and ways of interacting with students. The classroom practices discussed represent four different aspects of teaching: learning time, classroom organization and management, active learning, and expectations and rewards for student performance. Study of this chapter will provide you with knowledge about teachers and classrooms that you can use to analyze the teaching you remember and observe, to think about as you consider what is good teaching and what is not, and to decide how you will teach if and when you become a teacher.

Before you start the chapter, however, a caution is in order. Teaching effectiveness as described here is not the solution to successful classroom performance. Many factors determine how much and how well students learn. Other factors are discussed later in this text, in Chapter 4, for example; and still others remain to be studied in future courses.

The Snapshot and the first few pages of chapter narrative provide illustrations and an overview of effective classroom practices. The Reflecting on Practice box describes an episode from a lesson and asks you to find the characteristics of good teaching that are included in what the teacher does. The Educational Research section cautions that much is still unknown about classroom effectiveness. Before you proceed, however, answer the following questions so that you can place what you are about to read into a personal frame of reference.

1. Think about your classroom teachers from the past. Who was the best teacher you have had? (The person might have been an elementary or high school teacher, a college professor, or a Sunday School teacher.)
2. Now list the characteristics that made this teacher so special that you remember him or her more than others. If appropriate, include personal characteristics and teaching practices on your list.
3. Choose five characteristics of your best teacher and write them down.
4. Compare your list with the lists of others in the class.
5. Keep your list and, as you read, compare it with the ideas described in this chapter. You will be asked to look at the list again at three points in the chapter—at the end of the first main section of the chapter, in the Conclusion, and in the Study Question section.

The Snapshot for this chapter describes short segments of observations of two classes: sixth-grade reading and ninth-grade social studies.[1] As you read, consider two things:

- In what ways is the teaching in the two classes different from classroom instruction you have experienced?
- Which elements of the teaching seem to you to represent characteristics of "effective teaching"? Why do you think so?

Sixth-Grade Reading

MS. SWEENY: Think, what does Langston Hughes mean by the line in the poem, "Life ain't been no crystal stair"? (Allows students a few seconds to think) Terry.

TERRY: That life has not always been perfect. There are problems sometimes.

MS. SWEENY: That's a good way to say it, Terry. What did the author say to make you think that?

TERRY: The mother in the poem said the stair of life had tacks in it and flat places.

MS. SWEENY: Good analysis, Terry. But what in the world is a tack in life? (Allows students a few seconds to think) Can you tell us, Joe?

JOE: Something that kind of tears you up.

MS. SWEENY: That's right, Joe. Have you ever had a tack in your life?

JOE: (Looks thoughtful and utters softly) When I didn't make the football team last fall.

MS. SWEENY: That was a very big tack, Joe, but you didn't give up. Did anyone encourage you to hang in there like this mother did with her son?

JOE: Yeah, my big brother.

This interaction is taking place in a sixth-grade remedial reading classroom in an inner-city middle school. The class has just read Langston Hughes's poem "Mother to Son," and the teacher is preparing them to read Hughes's short story "Thank You, Ma'm." The

teacher and students have read some passages aloud. With each reading the teacher asks questions that relate the students' background experiences and feelings to the characters in the story.

The teacher also explains some of the new words in the story to be read, each time checking for the students' understanding by asking them to use the words in the context of the story and in their own lives. For example:

MS. SWEENY: The author says one of the characters is a "purse snatcher." What is a purse snatcher, Billy?

BILLY: A person who takes someone's purse very quickly.

MS. SWEENY: Right, a purse snatcher steals purses quickly. This story has two characters: an old woman and a purse snatcher—one who took something quickly. Now I want you to feel what it would be like to be an old lady going home from work late at night and have someone run past and grab your purse. Visualize it and write a few words.

(All of the children look pensive and then write.)

MS. SWEENY: Everyone tell me, how did you feel?

SEVERAL STUDENTS: Scared, angry, tired, lonely.

MS. SWEENY: Read the next three pages to yourselves now, and see how the old lady surprises the purse snatcher. How would you feel if you were the purse snatcher? What would you do?

The teacher uses focusing questions to guide the students' silent reading. Student interpretations of passages are solicited and respected. Toward the end of the period she asks the students to write two paragraphs comparing how "Thank You, Ma'm" by Hughes is similar to and different from a Hemingway short story they read during the previous week.

Ninth-Grade Social Studies

In a rural midwestern school, a social studies teacher of current events is preparing to show a videotaped discussion of a tax-reform proposal involving state and federal politicians. He tells the students to think about how the tax reforms that will be discussed would affect them and their families. He gives students a structured overview chart showing major issues of the tax reform being proposed. The chart also has names of the politicians who participated in the discussion. The students are asked to listen and record statements and points of view on each issue made by each person in the discussion.

At the end of the tape, students are given five minutes to analyze which issues were covered and what the contrasting points of view are. Next, students meet in predetermined small work groups to collaborate on a report of issues covered. Each group is asked to develop its own point of view and some defenses of it. The teacher provides the groups with other sources of information (for example, newspaper and journal articles). After twenty minutes of group work, the recorders for each group make summary statements.

An argument develops about who would gain and who would lose if the tax reform is enacted. The teacher makes certain that multiple points of view are heard.

All students have a chance, but they must back up opinions with facts.

The assignment for the following week requires every student from each group to interview one of five people: an adult family member, a banker, an educator, someone representing the medical profession, and someone from the armed forces. Each interview is to focus on how the person being interviewed thinks the tax reform will affect him or her and the work that person does. The goal of the assignment is to learn about different points of view on a critical issue and to estimate how well people seem to be informed on the issue.

The stated goal of this teacher is to create knowledgeable, thinking people who can thrive in a democracy. Above the classroom door he has a sign: "You can fool some of the people all of the time; and all of the people some of the time; but you can't fool all of the people all of the time. Don't be fooled! Knowledge is Freedom!"

Good Teaching

All of the students in the classrooms described in the Snapshot were deeply involved in their lessons. That involvement resulted from the excellent preparation and planning by the two teachers. In each case, the teacher's expectations and objectives for the class were clearly specified on the chalkboard or in folders passed out in advance.

In the sixth-grade reading class, the teacher listed on the chalkboard the pages that would be covered and the written assignment to be completed during the 55-minute class period. For extra points, there was a riddle to be solved by those who entered class early. All needed materials were in stacks on the first desk of each row. When the bell rang at the start of the class, the teacher called for answers to the riddle while a student monitor took the roll with a seating chart. Materials were passed down the rows, and the lesson began within three minutes.

In the ninth-grade social studies classroom, copies of the tax-reform proposals were on the work tables. A question on the chalkboard asked: "How will tax reform affect teenage paychecks? See pages 48 and 63." Students entering the room started quickly thumbing through the materials. The room had five tables to which the students had been assigned so that high, medium, and low achievers were represented at each table. Each table of students formed a collaborative work group to carry out group assignments. The facilitator at each table took the roll and checked missing members on the roll sheet.

Both teachers involved their students in thought-provoking discussions. They used strategies that required all of the students to think and to participate. Their comments on students' contributions were low key, specific, and supportive.

Although the students being taught in both classrooms described in the Snap-

Sarah Smith

"You have to do whatever

comes from you*"*

*J*ust three years into her professional career, Sarah Smith can vividly recall her transition from lifelong student to classroom teacher—especially what she learned from observing accomplished teachers as part of her credential program. "I guess it's like going to art school," Sarah says today. "You're exposed to all sorts of artists, and you like this technique or that technique—but even though you use some of the things you learned along the way, in the end you have to do whatever comes from *you*.

Discovering what "comes from you"—translating professional training into something personally authentic—is a favorite theme when Sarah talks about developing as a teacher. And anyone watching her at work in her third-grade classroom can see that she is well on her way to blending her knowledge of research and theory with her own personal style.

*W*hat should observers look for when they visit a classroom? To Sarah, "One thing is, where's the teacher's personality? If somebody comes into my classroom, they're going to see 'She's into music.' Teachers need to have some *passion*—whether it's for jazz or football or math or science or whatever it is—some passion for life, because that enthusiasm really rubs off. You never know who you might touch that never would have taken an interest in a particular subject. And as an elementary school teacher, you can't miss—because you teach just about everything!"

*F*or someone as emotionally involved in her work as Sarah, a teacher's life has more than its share of ups and downs. "Some days everything goes wrong, the kids are the worst, and you go home and you're so drained and tired that you can't imagine going back for another day...

"Then the next day the kids are great and activities like our Greek mythology unit work like a charm, and you love it again—or at least you like it! That's the amazing thing about teaching. It's really that Scarlett O'Hara mentality: you have to have faith that 'tomorrow's another day.' Plus, there's that special quality of children, that sense of planting seeds. It gives me hope. It's very mutual—I need their energy, too."

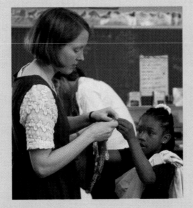

"You can't argue that being an elementary school teacher is not a worthwhile pursuit. It is."

"*W*hat makes it all worthwhile? Well, I guess it's the sense that you're doing something real, you're working where it matters. You're working with the future.

"School is a reflection of society. It's where everything is happening—I mean, *everything*. You name it, it's happening in your classroom. As a teacher, you're grappling on the most concrete level with society's problems, and you're part of whatever tiny successes happen at that level. It feels very real. It feels meaningful.

"You can't argue that being an elementary school teacher is not a worthwhile pursuit. It is."

shot were very different in age, cultural background, and subject matter, the two teachers were using similar instructional strategies. Many of their strategies have been identified through classroom research as being effective in keeping students involved in their studies and learning the required subject matter. Each teacher planned a variety of interesting activities for each class period so that the students would read, write, speak, listen, speculate, and visualize other times and places. When students are encouraged to engage in a variety of learning activities, they are more likely to stay involved in their lessons and are more likely to integrate their learning into useful intellectual patterns. When the teacher structures the content to be learned into patterns that the students can recognize, the students can more easily store the learning in long-term memory and retrieve the information in new situations.

Nevertheless, the extent to which the teachers described in the Snapshot were effective with students depended on more than the techniques they used in the classroom. The teachers also had to be perceived positively by their students and had to have an influence on them. If this were not the case, the students would have simply "turned them off." Therefore, before we turn to specific elements of classroom effectiveness, we examine teacher characteristics that researchers say have positive influences on students.

The Influence of Teachers on Students

A mid-1980s study by Mihaly Csikszentmihalyi and Jane McCormack of the influence of teachers on students reported a number of results about the extent to which teachers have an impact on students and the types of teacher characteristics that seem to generate the strongest impact.[2] Although the study occurred a decade ago and focused on teenage students and their teachers, its data and conclusions are still enlightening and apply to other school levels as well. The information in this section is drawn primarily from that study.

Teenage American students spend approximately three hours a day (weekends and vacations are factored in) with teachers. In contrast, they spend about two hours with other adults, including their parents, and about four hours with peers. Much of the time with other adults involves diverse activities (watching television and shopping, for instance), and comparatively little direct discussion or passing of information from the adult to the teenager occurs. Therefore, teachers have sufficient time and contact to have more of a significant influence on teenagers than do other adults, all else being equal.

Time students spend with teachers

As a result, teachers—at least some teachers—have significant impact on their students. In the study by Csikszentmihalyi and McCormack, "The Influence of Teachers," when teenagers were asked who or what influenced them to become the kinds of people they are, 58 percent mentioned one or more teachers, 88 percent said peers, and 90 percent listed parents. But further analysis of the responses shows that only a limited number of teachers actually produced the influence noted. The teenagers reported that only 9 percent of all their teachers had the impact that they mentioned. Ninety-one percent left no such mark.

The influential 9 percent

What distinguishes the teachers who have powerful influence over students from those who do not is, of course, important to improving teaching effectiveness.

Which of your teachers influenced you the most? Chances are they were like this social studies teacher in an important respect—they demonstrated enthusiasm for their subject.

Psychological and sociological theories suggest that influential teachers are those who are seen by students as having (1) control over resources that they desire, (2) power to reward or punish, (3) expertise in a particular area of knowledge, and (4) status and power in a general sense. But teenagers interviewed in the Csikszentmihalyi and McCormack study indicated that these teacher traits were not by themselves enough to influence them so significantly. Instead, these teenagers said the influential teachers also

1. *generated enthusiasm* for learning through their personal involvement with the subject matter and skill in teaching it
2. *communicated a sense of excitement* about learning the material
3. *made learning pleasant* instead of a chore
4. *explained things* in original or unusual ways
5. *were especially approachable*—easy to talk to and ready to listen
6. *instilled student self-confidence*
7. *showed that they really cared* about the students

Teacher's attitude is critical

In sum, the critical characteristics seemed to be the teachers' attitudes toward teaching, toward the subject matter, and toward student success in learning. The influential teachers exhibited enthusiasm, dedication, and energy that showed that they believed learning what they were teaching was worth the time and effort. Students in the study often described learning under these teachers as follows: "You learn a lot because it doesn't seem like work; it's something you really *want* to do." ("The Influence of Teachers," p. 419)

Making learning meaningful and worthwhile is important

This information about teacher influence seems to highlight a dimension of successful teaching that has not often been stressed in older studies or in much of the classroom effectiveness literature. Older studies have said that successful teachers are enthusiastic, accessible, caring, and friendly; and more recent classroom effectiveness literature (such as most of that reported later in this chapter) has added precision to those earlier ideas by identifying specific teaching strategies that produce more learning than others and by indicating how teachers can produce greater gains in student achievement. Since the 1980s, however, information such as that reported in this study adds to those ideas the belief that the most influential teachers are the ones who, in addition to being entertaining and caring and in addition to using the most effective techniques, also *make what they teach meaningful* and enable students to see *its inherent worth* to their own lives.

This means that especially influential teachers are those who teach so that students are *intrinsically* motivated to learn. Students come to math class because they want to learn math. They enjoy it and believe it is valuable to them personally. Teachers who have this effect on students do not just entertain and care about students *in addition to* their teaching, and they are not just effective or efficient in a technical way. They are teachers whose strengths are tied directly to what they teach. They might use extrinsic gimmicks to motivate students, and they probably use efficient teaching techniques; but most importantly, they make students want to learn what they teach. In a sense, they infect the students with their enthusiasm for learning.

More than entertainers and technicians

Before we turn to effective classroom approaches and techniques, pause and look at the list you compiled during the Introduction to this chapter of characteristics that describe your best teacher.

■ How closely do your characteristics match the points noted so far?

Characteristics of Effective Teaching

Despite widespread concurrence about the qualities of good teaching, precise research into what makes classroom instruction produce student learning is a recent phenomenon, and in many ways the 1970s and 1980s were watershed eras for this type of research. During those two decades, research into effective teaching focused primarily upon classroom organization, time management, classroom interaction, teacher planning, and teacher expectations. Researchers found that some of the characteristics generally considered to be part of good teaching, such as being well organized, can be evaluated relatively easily; but others, such as being caring and interesting, are harder to measure. As would be expected, the characteristics that are easier to measure have been researched more thoroughly than the others. In spite of that fact, however, data from the research have contributed significantly to the understanding of effective teaching, but much remains to be discovered.

This section of the chapter describes some of the teaching practices found to be effective in research studies. Those practices are divided into four categories:

■ use of time
■ classroom climate
■ active teaching strategies
■ teacher expectations and rewards for student performance

As you read about these four areas of effective teaching practices, it is important to remember that (1) classrooms and their occupants possess characteristics that set them apart from other types of group meetings, and (2) many of those characteristics are in place before the students and teachers arrive at the classroom door. Those characteristics or elements affect teaching and learning.

Classroom activities are different from other types of group meetings

One researcher, Walter Doyle, says, for example, that classroom environments contain the following elements:[3]

■ *Multidimensionality:* Large numbers of events and tasks occur because of the number of people present, the goals to be accomplished, the schedules to be met, the resources to be used, and so forth.
■ *Simultaneity:* Many things happen at the same time.
■ *Immediacy:* The pace of things is rapid.
■ *Unpredictability:* Many classroom events happen unexpectedly.
■ *Publicness:* Events occur in the open and are witnessed by all present.
■ *History:* Classes meet day after day, and classmates and teachers develop common experiences, routines, and norms, which guide future events.

All classrooms are not alike

It is also important to remember that all classrooms are not alike and that their differences have an impact on the effectiveness of specific teaching practices. Some strategies work better at lower grade levels, and some are better with older students; some are more successful with students of lower socioeconomic status, some with learners from more affluent backgrounds; some are appropriate with one type of teacher objectives and not others.[4]

In addition to these two reminders concerning the nature of classrooms, you need to keep in mind several other cautions regarding what will be said about effective teaching practices.

1. The effective practices reported here do not include all effective teaching strategies.
2. The extent to which each practice is effective varies from classroom to classroom, school to school, and teacher to teacher.
3. A preponderance of studies of teaching practice, including those that have led to the conclusions reported here, were conducted at elementary grade levels, in basic skill subjects, and with students of low socioeconomic status.
4. Many studies seem to overemphasize direct instruction and slight more interactive approaches.
5. In most cases, the primary criterion on which the effectiveness of the practice studied was judged is student academic achievement. Certainly there are other bases for deciding which classroom strategies and teaching methods are best; for example, the extent to which they enhance student self-concepts, peer group interactions, and the more affective outcomes from learning.
6. Research on effective teaching practice is relatively new and continuing. Data generated in the years ahead may require modification of present conclusions.
7. The general context in which learning takes place influences how much students learn just as significantly as does what happens in classrooms. For example, student socioeconomic status, intellectual abilities, physical conditions, and grade levels also make a difference.

Therefore, it is important not to overgeneralize from what is reported under the label "teaching effectiveness."

Use of Time

Our first focus on effective teaching practices is on how time is used. Several large-scale research studies conducted during the 1970s and funded primarily by the federal government started a movement toward the study of which teaching techniques, strategies, and situations produced the most noticeable learning. Those studies assessed the effectiveness of compensatory education programs such as Head Start, Follow Through, bilingual education, and special education. At that time, the government was funding many different models of education, and no one knew which approaches to instruction and specific teaching strategies were most effective in helping the targeted children learn to read, write, and compute. Because so little was known about effective instruction, most of these studies were correlational in nature. For example, in several studies, data collected from observing a large number of classrooms were compared to student test data, using a process-product design. These studies typically sought to determine what kind of instruction would be most effective for these special and economically deprived children.

In one cluster of correlational studies, when researchers found classrooms in which students were making unexpected gains in mathematics, they analyzed what the teachers of the high performers were doing that was instructionally different from the teachers of comparable students who were not achieving so well in mathematics. The findings of these different studies were quite consistent. The *use of time* in the students' instruction was a significant variable affecting how well the students performed. Although all the school districts studied had comparable amounts of time *allocated* for schooling, the districts, schools, and teachers *used* the time very differently.

The use of time was a significant variable

Because studies such as these looked at *time* as the variable to be studied, their results were easy to compare. Time is a universal. It is a factor in all instruction; it is constant (one minute equals one minute everywhere); and it is easily measured, quantified, and analyzed.[5]

Findings from studies such as these indicate that student academic achievement is *not* tied to the mere length of the school day or the length of a class period. Longer school days or longer class periods did not produce greater student achievement in either elementary or secondary schools. How the available time was *used* was the important factor.

Learning Time

Both common sense and research studies indicate that students of teachers who efficiently channel available classroom time to learning tasks usually learn more than students of teachers who do not. However, the actual amount of instruction time varies by teachers, as does the type of instruction provided within that time.

One of the first studies to investigate classroom time was a study designed to look at beginning teachers in California in 1978.[6] The study analyzed how teachers of second- and fifth-grade students used school time. Researchers first found that students were actually in the classroom only four and three-fourths of the six daily attendance hours. They considered this time—what is left after time is subtracted for lunch, for students passing in the halls from one class to another, and for recess—the *allocated time* for instruction. (See Figure 3-1.)

Allocated time

Having defined allocated time, they looked more closely at how teachers used that time and found that actual *instructional time* varied by teacher: Some teachers provided instruction for as much as four hours, others for as little as two. Not surprisingly, students who received more academic instruction in reading and mathematics achieved more in those subjects.

Instructional time

Next, researchers compared the time teachers were teaching and the time stu-

Student engaged time

FIGURE 3-1 A comparison of daily and yearly uses of classroom time.

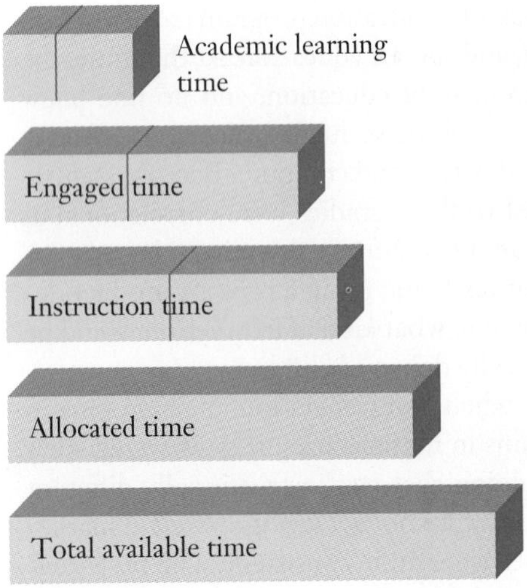

	Hours per Day	Hours per Year
Academic learning time	0.6–1.5	108–270
Engaged time	1.5–3.5	270–430
Instruction time	2.0–4.0	360–720
Allocated time	4.75	855
Total available time	6.0	1080

dents were learning and found they were not equal. Students were generally *engaged* in academic studies for one and one-half to three and one-half hours of the total school day—not the two to four hours teachers were providing instruction. As might be expected, students who were engaged in their studies longer made greater academic gains.

Maximizing engagement rates, however, is not simply a matter of making teachers aware of how they are using time. It also depends on the teacher's ability to organize and manage the classroom as an efficient learning environment in which academic activities are appropriate to the students' level of development, lessons are conducted smoothly, transitions are brief and orderly, and students take little time to be inattentive or to behave otherwise inappropriately.[7] Several techniques for accomplishing this set of optimal circumstances are described later in this chapter.

Once students' engaged time was studied, researchers found another time-related variable that is critical to student achievement. It has to do with the *rate of success* that students experience when they do their work. For example, if students practice problems for 30 minutes, it makes a difference if they get most of the problems right rather than do them all wrong. Therefore, the key idea that relates time to student achievement is *academic learning time* (ALT)—the class time students spend engaged in academic tasks they can perform at high success rates. It is derived from three other measures: *allocated time, engaged time*, and *student success*.[8] It is very important to note that in one study, students were found to be working at their ALT for only thirty-six minutes to one and one-half hours per day.

In sum, this line of research, in the 1970s and 1980s, has led to the generalization that students learn more if they are *engaged* in *quality* instruction at which they can *succeed*. This means that effective teachers need to engage students in academic learning, not just provide the time for the learning to take place. It means that the activities and subject matter must be set at the appropriate level of difficulty, the instruction must be paced appropriately, and the students must experience continuous progress.[9]

Part of the characteristic of success that is included in academic learning time is

Academic learning time

Optimal error rate

the concept of *optimal error rate*, the rate of correct and incorrect student responses that leads to the highest student achievement. Although the optimal error rate varies with the content being studied, some research indicates that when the purpose of instruction is to teach new knowledge or to review recently learned information, the most effective classrooms are those in which teacher questions yield a minimum of about 75 percent correct responses and in which seatwork yields about 90 percent correct answers for most students.[10]

The concept of *continuous progress* is also related to academic learning time. If students are to learn efficiently, they need to be engaged in lessons suited to their level of achievement, appropriate to the subject matter being taught, and paced at a rate that they can keep up with. Usually, the best lessons are those that permit the greatest number of students to progress continuously, in relatively small increments, with high rates of success, with a minimum of confusion, and without loss of momentum from step to step.[11]

Another major study concerning time investigated the variances of teachers' use of time and type of instruction.[12] In this study, reading teachers of grades 7 through 12 were divided into two groups: teachers whose students showed average academic gains and teachers whose students showed unusually high achievement. Observers studied how each group of teachers used time and found major differences, shown in Table 3-1.

Continuous progress

Time as a Teaching Technique

The preceding discussion indicates that teachers can use the teaching time available to them in a variety of ways, from least to most efficient; that is, they can maximize academic learning time. But time can also be used effectively in another sense. It can be used as a teaching technique in and of itself. One such use of time is *wait time*. Wait time occurs when teachers are questioning students, as in recitation or in discussion. It is the time between the end of a teacher's question and the time when a student *is called upon* to respond. It is the time when a teacher can logically expect all of the students to be thinking about the question because any of them might be chosen to supply the answer.

Typically, teachers wait nearly a second between asking a question and calling on a student. But when they wait about three full seconds instead (some researchers say three to five seconds), a number of positive things happen: The student who responds talks longer, more of the other students offer a greater number of unsolicited but appropriate responses, fewer students fail to respond, students demonstrate increased confidence in their answers, more of the students whom the teachers consider academically "slow" respond, and the student answers involve higher levels of thought.[13]

TABLE 3-1   Relationship between Use of Time and Achievement

Activity	Percent Class Time	
	Average Achievement	High Achievement
Active instruction	12	50
Organization/management	26	12
Student seatwork	50	35
Off task	12	3

Apparently there are no negative effects of using three-second wait time. It seems to be difficult for teachers to wait for three seconds when they first try to do so. In addition, teachers who try using a longer wait time report that the three-second pause seems as if it is much longer when they first start using it.

Classroom Climate

Now our focus shifts to classroom climate, its components, and the ways effective teachers create good climates. Although the physical setting and the types of instructional activities used in many classrooms seem surprisingly similar, classrooms differ widely, and a number of those differences can be attributed to classroom climate—that is, the psychological and social feeling of atmosphere that exists in each classroom. Some teachers create an atmosphere in their classrooms that is supportive, comfortable, friendly, and relaxed; others oversee challenging, competitive, and tense climates. It is difficult to describe precisely what creates a particular classroom climate, but research data suggest that a great number of interacting factors are involved.[14]

The paragraphs that follow show four clusters of variables through which classroom climate can be examined—ecology, milieu, social system, and culture.[15] All four clusters interact and have both positive and negative effects on classroom climate as a whole. (See Figure 3-2.)

Ecology

■ *Ecology*, as used here, refers to the physical aspects of a classroom—the things that make it up. It includes the classroom space as a whole, displays on the walls, chalkboards, the equipment present, and the learning resources.

Milieu

■ *Milieu* means the "feeling" or "interpersonal atmosphere." It includes the aspect of the setting that some observers call teacher and student "morale." The idea can be illustrated as follows: When both teachers and students have a high degree of satisfaction with what happens in their classrooms, a positive climate develops; and when they are unhappy, threatened, or "burned out," the climate has a noticeably different "feel" to it.

FIGURE 3-2 Variables involved in classroom climate.

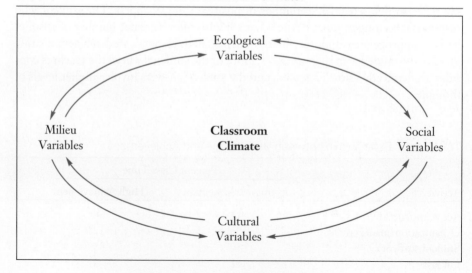

■ The *social system* relates to the informal and formal rules guiding inter-personal relationships in classrooms, as well as in schools generally. Included under the heading are student-teacher relationships, student-student relationships, principal-teacher interactions, teacher-parent associations, and so forth. An important variable in this aspect of classroom environment is the way in which communication between teachers and students is developed; for example, how well the teacher communicates information to students and helps them understand rules and policies and how extensively students are involved in or consulted on policy and rule formulation.

Social system

■ *Culture* refers to the values, belief systems, and norms existing in classrooms and the school as a whole. Variables included under this heading are expectations; teacher commitment; clarity of goals; and teacher use of praise, criticism, and rewards.

Culture

Because a good deal of power is vested in teachers, classroom climate is greatly influenced by the teachers' use of that power and their willingness to delegate some aspects of power to students. Although learning can and does take place in very oppressive classroom climates, in those classrooms where there is a positive socio-emotional climate, teachers and students are happier and less stressed, and there is greater student desire for participating in learning.

A positive classroom climate is not developed or maintained by chance. It develops from what teachers do and is affected positively by careful planning and thought—by classroom organization and management techniques. It is also influenced both positively and negatively by many of the day-to-day actions of teachers and students.

Classroom Organization and Management

In study after study over the last two decades, the areas of greatest concern for new and experienced teachers alike are classroom organization and management. These areas are often problem areas for teachers, and students simply do not learn effectively if classrooms are not organized and managed well.

But successful organization and management are not simple processes of setting down rigid rules and insisting on conformity to them. *Classroom organization* must arise from a well-developed, flexible plan of operation that has limits but that also tolerates exceptions and variations when goals and circumstances warrant them. In short, successful classroom organization and management are multifaceted processes that establish a classroom order that can be maintained while class goals, contexts, and events continuously shift.[16] The two classes and teachers described in the Snapshot for this chapter exemplify classroom organization and management in a number of ways. Think about those episodes and refer back to them as you proceed with this section. They should provide concrete examples for some of the ideas discussed. Effective management plans will differ from teacher to teacher, from grade to grade, and even from period to period. But although they may differ in specifics, all must address the following areas:[17]

■ arranging the room and materials to support instruction
■ planning and teaching both rules (behavioral expectations) and procedures (ways to get things done—for example, how to get a turn, head a paper, enter the classroom, etc.)
■ managing student work to increase student accountability

Effective teachers do more than "decorate" their classrooms; they design environments that support their instructional objectives.

- encouraging and maintaining good student behavior
- planning instruction
- maintaining student involvement throughout the lesson

At this beginning stage of your study, however, it is not appropriate to describe what recent findings say about all these areas. Instead, on the following pages we look at just two aspects of classroom organization and management: first at strategies that help minimize student behavior problems and then at effective approaches and techniques for handling student misbehavior when it does occur. We focus on these two because prospective teachers at all stages of their professional preparation tend to be especially anxious about student misbehavior and we want to show you that there are solidly researched, practical ways of dealing with these potentially worrisome situations.

Preplanned management plan

Minimizing Behavior Problems Research indicates that some organization and management practices are more effective than others in keeping students engaged in academic tasks. Successful classrooms generally have an organization and management plan developed ahead of time by the teacher, communicated to the students at the start of the school year, and maintained consistently throughout the year. They are classrooms in which efficient routines and procedures are clear and consistently followed, in which teacher and students clearly understand expectations about student behavior and consequences of inappropriate behavior, and in which the rules and procedures are enforced and reinforced.[18]

Effective classroom organization and management require that the teacher start off the school year right, and starting the school year right involves the establishment of successful *classroom structures* from the first day. That means announcing thoughtfully formulated rules and procedures, demonstrating them, enforcing them, and developing them into routines. To accomplish this, teachers must know what their management plan will be, teach it to the students, and watch over them closely (some researchers say "hover over them") until they have learned and accepted the system.[19]

One group of investigators looked intensively at how third-grade teachers who were known to be effective planners began their school year.[20] They found that these teachers not only planned thoroughly before school started, but they spent significant amounts of time during the first weeks of the year introducing rules and procedures and establishing schedules and routines. The researchers noted that the teachers actually *taught* these organizational elements as part of their classroom instruction; they did not just present them to the students as arbitrary rules of behavior. The effective teachers told the students what was expected of them, but they also explained their expectations clearly, modeled the procedures, responded to questions, and allowed time for practice.

In addition to developing management plans, establishing classroom structures, and following teaching routines, teachers considered to be successful classroom managers have also been found to be teachers who have *set the stage for teaching* in order to prevent behavior problems. In addition to the practices mentioned earlier, such efforts include arranging for well-paced lessons geared to student abilities and interests; setting up efficient routines for taking care of procedural tasks; and creating a classroom climate that is task-oriented, pleasant, and purposeful. Although these efforts do not focus directly on student behavior, they make classes successful because they minimize distraction from academic learning and keep students actively engaged in productive classroom work, thus minimizing the amount of trouble that they might cause.[21]

Many successful classroom managers have also been found to possess a characteristic that researchers have labeled *withitness*. They seem to know what is happening in the classroom all of the time and often can predict what is about to occur before it does. They can cut short small behavior problems before they escalate by constantly monitoring their classrooms from a position that allows them to see all of their students. Their students know these teachers are "with it"; that is, they know they can detect and deal with inappropriate behavior quickly and appropriately. The students know that if they act up, they will get caught.[22]

Often successful classroom managers are teachers who have the ability to *overlap* what they do; that is, they can do more than one thing at a time. For example, they can monitor the entire class with frequent eye contact while conferring with an individual student and can keep their instruction flowing without disruption while taking care of routine management chores or correcting a single student's behavior.[23] The episode of Ms. Myers's class in the Snapshot in Chapter 2 illustrates this.

Successful classroom managers usually maintain a *brisk pace*. As a result, students tend to stay on task and are unlikely to lose momentum and motivation. These teachers have all necessary materials in place before they need them, know what

Classroom structures

The teaching of routines

Setting the stage for teaching

Withitness

Overlapping

Brisk pace

they expect to do without consulting their notes, avoid giving confusing directions, and rarely have to repeat or backtrack in their instructions. Without disrupting the lesson, they watch for inattention and deal with it through eye contact, gestures, verbal cues, approaches to the inattentive students, and questioning.[24]

Student alerting and accountability techniques

Successful classroom managers also keep their students alert and accountable for their academic work through the use of certain techniques of presentation and questioning called *student alerting techniques*. For example, they mix the presentation of information with some questions. They state the question and look over the entire class *before* calling on a student to answer. This encourages all to listen and to think about the question because anyone might be designated to answer. They call on students in random order, but they get to everyone frequently. They intersperse individual responses with choral responses when those will work. They call on volunteers and on those whose hands are not up. They ask students to comment on other student responses. They ask follow-up questions.[25]

Lesson variety

In addition, successful classroom managers provide for variety in their lessons. They have whole group, small group, and individual activities; they present short lectures; they conduct recitation sessions; and they assign and monitor seatwork. They take time to explain ideas and directions and get feedback on academic content. They use different types of materials. They avoid monotony.[26]

Successful classroom managers are sensitive to student inattention; and they monitor student work for signs of confusion and lapses of concentration. They arrange desks to direct student attention. To avoid boredom, they vary activities, teach lessons of appropriate length, and provide for transitions that minimize wasted time.[27]

Arranging space

Finally, successful managers arrange physical classroom space to accommodate different types of learning activities, to make sure that all students are visible and can be reached for independent help, and to minimize traffic flow problems and congested areas.[28]

Teacher as ringmaster

This long list of things that successful classroom managers do to minimize classroom behavior problems has led some researchers to think of *teachers as ringmasters*. Like circus ringmasters, effective teachers constantly manage people, time, space, content, and materials. They make decisions and communicate directions virtually all the time. They do all of this within an overall system that includes

- attention to individual characteristics and differences
- organization of the classroom as an effective learning environment
- a flow of instruction that maximizes student engagement in learning
- implementation of workable housekeeping procedures and rules of conduct
- techniques of group management, motivation, and conflict resolution[29]

Handling Misbehavior   To this point, the discussion of effective classroom organization and management has dealt with approaches to teaching and techniques that tend to prevent misbehavior in the classroom. The focus now turns to approaches and techniques for handling misbehavior when it does occur.

Violent behavior

Although traumatic when they occur, severe types of disruptive behavior in schools, such as physical violence, theft, robbery, and vandalism, are rare in most schools. When they do occur, they usually happen in corridors, lunchrooms, and outside school buildings rather than in classrooms. If a teacher is present when they happen, the teacher must, of course, take appropriate action to (1) protect others, (2) stop the behavior, and (3) report the incident to school and/or legal officials.

The teacher's action should be cautious, sensitive, responsible, commonsensical, and forthright. In our judgment, the students involved should be turned over to other authorities.

The focus of the discussion here, however, is on the more typical instances of classroom misbehavior—tardiness, class cutting, inattention, talking, name calling, mild forms of verbal aggression, pushing, punching, neglecting academic work, and refusing to follow directions. These types of disruptive and uncooperative acts happen frequently in classrooms, and teachers are expected to deal with them as part of their responsibility.

Probably the key to understanding what should be done when classroom misbehavior occurs is to think of it in the context of what is expected in classrooms. Teachers are expected to teach; students are expected to learn. Therefore, teachers plan classroom activities in order to accomplish certain learning purposes, and they arrange what they and the students do based on those plans. When student behavior does not inhibit the accomplishment of the teacher's purposes, difficulties normally do not arise. Problems do occur when student behavior is at cross-purposes with teacher expectations. This then constitutes *misbehavior*.[30]

The classroom context

Sometimes the misbehavior is limited to a single student whose actions are inappropriate; other times, it is more widespread. Even a small degree of disruptive behavior is likely to be visible to other students, and this, in turn, means that it may spread to others in the class.

When misbehavior occurs, then, the teacher's tasks are to (1) prevent it from spreading, (2) extinguish it, and (3) get the class back on track. Teachers who are considered effective classroom managers of misbehavior intervene quickly and with the smallest possible amount of disruption to the normal flow of events.

Some effective *specific interventions* are nonverbal signals such as direct eye contact, frowns, gestures, and teacher movement toward the misbehaving student or students. Others are verbal *"soft imperative" suggestions or questions* such as "It's time to settle down." "Why don't you get your book out quietly?" Others include praise, manipulation of privileges, isolation, seat changes, and detention.[31]

Specific interventions

In addition to specific interventions, several general approaches to dealing with disruptive or uncooperative students have been found to be effective in some classrooms. One of these approaches is based on *cognitive behavior modification techniques*. This approach includes at least three key elements. It starts with the principle that appropriate behavior should be rewarded and inappropriate behavior discouraged and ignored. It applies the principle to classes as a whole, rather than to individual misbehaving students. It includes components that encourage students to think about their behavior and to control themselves, rather than respond only to external rewards and punishments assigned by the teacher.

Cognitive behavior modification systems

Effective cognitive behavior modification techniques tend to be more than simple rewards and punishments. They also stress teaching students to think about their behavior and accept responsibility for it. They teach students self-monitoring and self-control skills. Often they involve clear agreements and/or formal contracts with stipulated performance standards. Students are expected to do certain things to receive particular rewards; they are punished for unwanted behaviors. Since students know the consequences of their behavior ahead of time, they tend to see the system as a fair bargain.[32]

Another effective approach to dealing with disruptive and uncooperative behavior is based on ideas from counseling and psychotherapy. One such system is called

Counseling and therapy-based systems

FIGURE 3-3 Gordon's schematic representation of problem ownership and the acceptance line for student behavior.

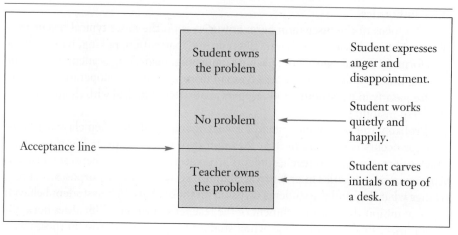

Teacher Effectiveness Training.[33] This system, developed in the 1970s by psychologist Tom Gordon, focuses on interpersonal conflict situations and provides a schema to analyze the conflict based on who *owns* the problem. (See Figure 3-3.) For instance, when a conflict occurs between a teacher and a student, it is analyzed to determine whether the problem is *owned* by the teacher (the teacher is experiencing the primary frustration), whether it is *owned* by the student (the student is experiencing the primary frustration), or whether the problem is actually *shared* by both. Determining what is and is not acceptable student behavior is important to this system. When student behavior is acceptable to the teacher (above the acceptance line), there is either no problem or the student owns the problem because of the limits imposed by the teacher. However, the teacher does not have a problem. The teacher begins to own the problem only when student behavior becomes unacceptable. At that point, the teacher must change the behavior (move it above the acceptance line).

Once the ownership of the problem is determined, Teacher Effectiveness Training provides interpersonal devices that the teacher can use to overcome the problem in such a way that neither the teacher nor the student "loses." The process involves a number of steps and includes two specific techniques—"active listening" and "sending *I*-messages."[34] More specific information about this system can be found in Gordon's book *Teacher Effectiveness Training.*

Another counseling-based system with a significant number of followers is William Glasser's *reality therapy*, which Glasser discusses in his books *Reality Therapy, Schools Without Failure,* and *The Quality School: Managing Students Without Coercion.*[35] This system provides guidelines for both general classroom management and solving problems with individual students.

In its revised form, Glasser's system for dealing with individual problem students involves ten steps to "good discipline," which he describes as nonpunitive, constructive, and no-nonsense. It holds students responsible for their behavior; sets fair and reasonable rules; requires consistent, fair, and firm enforcement; and assumes a positive, problem-solving stance by the teacher.[36]

A third counseling-based system, called *Assertive Discipline,* was developed by Lee and Marlene Canter around principles from assertiveness training. This approach includes the following key ideas:[37]

The Teacher Effectiveness Training approach

Reality therapy

Assertive discipline

1. Teachers should insist on appropriate, responsible student behavior.
2. They should not consider firm control of the classroom to be stifling or inhumane.
3. They should communicate behavior expectations to students clearly and follow up consistently.
4. Principals and parents should provide support.
5. Teachers should be assertive and not feel guilty about it.

According to the Canters, assertive teachers are positive, firm, consistent, and caring—caring about themselves to the point that they are not taken advantage of by students and caring about students to the point that they prevent them from behaving in ways that are harmful to their classmates or to themselves.[38]

Analysis in the late 1980s of thirty-six studies involving the programs of Teacher Effectiveness Training, reality therapy, and Assertive Discipline led those who conducted the review to conclude that these programs provide methods for dealing with threats to classroom order but are not adequate classroom management programs in and of themselves.[39] The reviewers felt that all these approaches fail to address day-to-day classroom management skills in ways that are needed to keep students productively engaged and to prevent minor problems from becoming major ones. In their view, teachers must also establish a comprehensive system of management and organization early in the school year for each of these approaches to be most effective.[40]

When you consider your own approaches to dealing with classroom behavior problems, it is important to remember that no approach or set of techniques works for all teachers or with all students. There are just too many variables involved. For example, the level of intellectual and social development of students has major implications for what is effective and what is not. In this regard, Jere Brophy and Carolyn Evertson identified four stages of student development, illustrating that different approaches fit students at different developmental stages.[41]

Too many variables

Stage 1 (kindergarten through grades 2–3). Most children of this age are compliant and oriented toward pleasing their teachers, but they need to be social-

In elementary school, students are generally compliant with established procedures like forming neat lines after recess—but not always perfectly.

ized into the student role. They require a great deal of formal instruction, not only in rules and expectations but also in classroom procedures and routines.

Stage 2 (grades 2–3 through grades 5–6). Students have learned most school rules and routines, and most remain oriented toward obeying and pleasing their teachers. Consequently, less time must be devoted to classroom management.

Stage 3 (grades 5–6 through grades 9–10). Students enter adolescence and become oriented toward peers. Many become resentful or at least questioning of authority, and disruptions resulting from attention seeking, humorous remarks, and adolescent horseplay become common. Classroom management once again becomes more time-consuming; but in contrast to Stage 1, the task facing teachers is not so much one of instructing willing but ignorant students about what to do as it is motivating or controlling students who know what to do but are not always willing to do it. Also, individual counseling becomes more prominent, as the relative quiet and stability that most students show at earlier ages give way to the adjustment problems of adolescence.

Stage 4 (grades 9–12). Most students become more personally settled and more oriented toward academic learning again. As in Stage 2, classroom management requires less teacher time and trouble, and classrooms take on a more businesslike, academic focus.

Although no single formula works all of the time, researchers have identified several common principles that can guide teachers as they deal with misbehavior. Those include:[42]

- respect for student individuality
- willingness to try to understand students' problems
- reliance on instruction and persuasion rather than force
- recognition that students have responsibilities as well as rights and that if they misbehave, they must suffer the consequences

Something to Think About

A group of high school students was having a discussion in a current events class. The topic was "life in school," and the conversation turned toward a particular teacher in the school and her relationships with students. The following dialogue took place:

TEACHER: In which classes in this school would you expect everyone to behave properly nearly all of the time?

CARIE: Ms. Daley's.

TEACHER: What do others think?
    (Virtually every other student in the class agrees with Carie.)

TEACHER: Why is this the case?

CARIE: It's hard to explain. (long thoughtful pause) Well, to act up in Ms. Daley's class is about like kicking a newborn puppy. It's some-

> thing you just wouldn't do. No one would. She would be so hurt, and you would be so sorry.
>
> JEFF: If someone would do something really wrong in Ms. Daley's class, the other kids would stop him. They would take her side.
>
> TEACHER: But why?
>
> DON: We respect her.
>
> ■ Can you visualize Ms. Daley? What would cause students to think of a teacher in this way?
> ■ Why are only a few teachers perceived in this way?

Grouping   We now turn to the classroom organization practice of grouping students. In some studies, various arrangements for grouping students have been found to be effective; but in general the results are mixed, primarily because there are too many other factors that influence what happens within and among the groups.

For example, teachers often group students by academic ability so that they can teach to different achievement levels at different times in the same class. There is some evidence that this leads to positive student achievement, particularly in directly taught skill subjects such as reading and mathematics.[43] But teaching different groups at the same time in the same classroom requires different types of classroom organization and management plans, as well as different teaching skills, than does whole-group instruction. It presumes self-directed study by the students. It also makes several assumptions about students' self-images, their motivation, and their perceptions of each other.[44]

Apparently many teachers teach differently to "lower" than to "higher" groups. For example, certain studies of language classes showed that teachers emphasized different instructions with different subgroups in a class. The lessons for "low" student groups placed greater emphasis on pronunciation, grammatical errors, and understanding single words; the lessons for "high" groups stressed "getting the meaning" and often ignored pronunciation and grammatical errors.[45]

Differential instruction

Another study reported that low-achieving students often receive more negative feedback, are given more directives, and are allowed fewer choices than are higher-achieving students. Higher achievers are the objects of greater expectations, are given more opportunities to demonstrate what they have learned, and are permitted more choices.[46]

Teachers who work effectively with multiple groups in the same classroom usually have successful classroom organization and management strategies that keep most of the students on task most of the time. They can handle several purposeful student activities at once because they have taught the students the appropriate routines. When student behaviors that require teacher attention occur, they can signal what is to be done, as well as what is acceptable and what is not. These teachers make it clear when students can ask questions and whom they can ask. They do not allow interruption of certain focused small-group instruction sessions. The students know the norms and understand.[47] The Snapshot episode of Ms. Myers' class in Chapter 2 illustrates this.

Grouping practices and classroom organization

One approach to grouping that has received much attention in recent years is *cooperative learning*, an instructional design that stimulates student peer interaction and student-to-student cooperation in the process of fostering successful learning

Cooperative learning

by all. Teams-Games-Tournaments, Student Teams Achievement Divisions, and Jigsaw are three versions of cooperative learning.[48] The general idea of cooperative learning is that students are organized into teams that include students of different abilities. Each team is expected to work together so that all students in each group learn the material being studied. Along with individual grades, students receive group rewards based on improvement. Cooperation *in* a team of individual members is stimulated by competition *among* teams. In effect, all students are rewarded if they help each other learn. (Cooperative learning is also described more thoroughly in Chapter 14.)

Other forms of grouping that encourage and reinforce student cooperation generally seem to have positive effects on student learning. For example, students engaged in peer tutoring (students provide resource help to each other) are involved in academic learning during more of the class time than are those in traditional classes. Also, classroom problem-solving lessons in which different students possess different pieces of information needed to solve the problem seem to motivate the students not only to cooperate but also to achieve.

Active Teaching Strategies

Another characteristic of effective teaching is the use of active teaching strategies. Students achieve more in classrooms in which their teachers actively teach and actively supervise them than in classrooms in which teachers leave them alone to work on their own for long periods of time. They learn more in classrooms in which the teachers follow a pattern of (1) presenting information and developing concepts through lectures and demonstrations, (2) elaborating and reinforcing ideas through feedback to students, and (3) preparing for seatwork through demonstrations and presentations of examples.[49] Look back at the chapter Snapshots for the first three chapters of the book to refresh your memory about how the teachers interacted actively with their students.

Teacher-provided content

Students learn more when the teacher personally provides the content to them instead of expecting them to pick it up on their own from their readings and assignments. The teacher talks a great deal when this occurs, but the talk deals with academic rather than procedural, managerial, or behavioral matters. This instruction is best when the teacher presentations are brief, not extended lectures, and when they involve questioning, recitation, and feedback on student ideas.[50]

Teacher presentations

The most effective teacher presentations are structured or organized in a way that the students can follow easily. Some elements of this type of presentation are initial overviews of content to be covered, advanced organizers, outlines, noticeable transitions, special emphases on the main points, summaries at the end of each subpart, and reviews of the main ideas at the end. Students also seem to learn more from well-paced presentations with a degree of *redundancy*—when the main points and key concepts are repeated several times.[51]

Seatwork

Several studies indicate that teachers who use active teaching and monitoring techniques while students are engaged in seatwork have better-managed classes and greater student achievement than do teachers who schedule long periods of independent, unsupervised seatwork. The effective teachers explain the seatwork with examples before the students start, demonstrate and model what is to be done, lead the students in guided practice, circulate among the students and monitor the work conscientiously, inspect individual papers frequently, provide timely and precise feedback, hover over the students, and usher the work along. For these teachers, seatwork is not a passive experience for the students or for themselves. It is not a relaxed, slow, inconsequential activity. It is serious, important classroom business, and students are kept on task.[52]

A number of specific things that many teachers do in their classrooms, called *teaching functions*, have been found by researchers to be noticeably effective strategies in helping students to learn and remember new information and to develop basic skills. Some functions that are especially useful when the learning is primarily memory level, when the students are young, and/or when the material is new to the students, are

Effective teaching functions

- structuring the learning experience carefully
- reviewing and checking student work daily and reteaching if necessary
- proceeding through lessons in small steps but at a rapid pace
- giving detailed and repeated instructions and explanations
- using a high frequency of questions and involving students in overt, active practice
- providing feedback, particularly in the initial stages of learning new material
- providing *prompts* (such as "Look at the 'e' at the end of the sentence. What does that tell you about the way the 'a' sounds?") during initial learning, enabling the students to respond to the prompt and in turn provide feedback
- setting levels of difficulty that provide for a success rate of 80 percent or higher on initial learning
- dividing seatwork assignments into small segments or devising ways to provide frequent monitoring
- providing for continued student practice (overlearning) so that they have a success rate of 90 to 100 percent
- conducting weekly and monthly reviews and reteaching if necessary
- offering praise if the answer is correct and providing correction if the response is incorrect.[53]

Teaching strategies that produce student understanding, rather than simple recall, are usually more effective than others; but, as cognitive psychologists point out, if students are to understand new ideas, they need to be able to link them to their previous knowledge and experience. Naturally, then, teachers who help students make these linkages are more effective at teaching for understanding than are those who do not. These teachers help students recognize new ideas, see how they relate to ideas they already possess, and assist them in storing the ideas mentally in a way that associates the ideas with previous knowledge and that enables them to be recalled easily for a long time.[54]

Mental linkages

Checking for understanding is an important specific teaching technique in this context.[55] If students do not understand, they are less likely to remember ideas or know how and when to use them again. To facilitate understanding, several research-based programs of instruction include steps that direct teachers to check for students' understanding regularly before proceeding to the next step in a lesson. If students do not understand, some programs direct the teacher to restructure the task and provide different examples and experiences to build the required background knowledge.

Checking for understanding

Questioning is also a significant aspect of active teaching, and when and how teachers use questioning significantly determines what students learn. For example, basic-skills instruction requires a large amount of drill and practice, and drill and practice is accomplished best with fast-paced questions that have right and wrong answers and can be answered quickly and correctly. On the other hand, instruction at higher cognitive levels requires thought-provoking questions that stimulate stu-

Questioning

How much more would you have learned in school if your teachers had always checked your understanding before moving on to the next step in the lesson?

dents to conceptualize, generalize, and evaluate ideas. They usually cannot be answered quickly and rarely have one correct response.

Research on questioning indicates that the more effective teacher questioners are not those who rely on one particular type of questioning. Instead, they use a variety of types of questions. They also fit questioning to their instructional purposes and adjust the level of their questions to both the conceptual level of the content they are teaching and the intellectual abilities of their students.[56]

Expectations and Rewards for Student Performance

Teacher expectations

How teachers set expectations and reward structures is another mark of effective teaching. Three decades ago Robert Rosenthal and Lenore Jacobson conducted a study of the relationship between teacher expectations and student performance and reported their findings in *Pygmalion in the Classroom.*[57] They found that students whose teachers expected them to perform well did so, and students who were expected to be low achievers, in fact, were.

Other researchers have looked at the same phenomenon and have found that some teachers behave toward low achievers in ways that communicate that they expect less of them. For example, Jere Brophy and Thomas Good report that teachers act differently toward students whom they perceive as high or as low achievers in the following ways: Slow students are frequently seated farther from the teacher than high achievers, are called on to answer questions less often, are provided less wait time to answer, are criticized more openly for incorrect responses, are praised less frequently for correct responses, are smiled at less often, receive less eye contact, are given less demanding work, are interrupted more frequently, and receive less instruction.[58]

Self-fulfilling prophecy

The point that teacher expectations of students are reflected in actual student performance is significant, but it takes on even greater importance when the relationship is explored more thoroughly. Researchers who have conducted more detailed research believe that the relationship is not just a correlation. There is evi-

Something to Think About

Some years ago Charles Myers, one of the authors of this text, approached one of his ninth-grade homeroom students, Gary, who had just received his midyear report-card grades. The grades showed that Gary had failed both science and mathematics every report-card period since the beginning of the year, and Myers expressed his concern.

Gary said he was not worried because he could pass on to tenth grade even if he failed both subjects. Although Myers knew Gary was correct about passing the grade even with two failures, he instead told Gary that if he failed the two subjects, he would have to repeat the grade and remain in junior high another year.

After some doubt, Gary accepted Myers's story as if it were correct. Then, the two developed a plan for Gary to try to pass science. (Gary felt math was hopeless.)

Near the end of the school year, Ms. Baxter, Gary's science teacher, told Myers that Gary was going to pass science because of a surprising turn-around in the quality of his work since midyear. She had asked Gary about this change, and Gary said he and Mr. Myers had a special plan that would help him pass. Ms. Baxter asked Myers to explain.

Myers described what happened, including the fact that he had lied to Gary in order to force him to take science seriously. He said that Gary still did not know he lied and asked Ms. Baxter not to reveal that he had.

Ms. Baxter was shocked. She stated, "But you deliberately lied to a student."

Myers replied, "Yes, I did, and it worked. Gary is studying science and learning as a result."

■ What does this episode have to say about expectations of students and their performance?

■ Should Myers have lied to Gary as he did?

dence that teacher expectations actually *cause* students to achieve or not achieve, at least to some degree. In some studies, students scored higher on tests after being changed from teachers who thought they were "slow" academically to teachers who thought they were stronger academically. The reverse happened when students were shifted from teachers who held high expectations for them to those who had lower expectations. In essence, the students' performances fulfilled the teachers' prophecies.[59]

Teacher expectations of students affect not only what teachers do to students and how those students perform but also peer perceptions of classmates. In at least one study, the way in which students were perceived by their classmates was influenced by the level of questions the teacher asked of them rather than by their actual achievement. In that study, a group of teachers was trained to ask higher-level questions of low-achieving students that elicited ideas, hunches, or opinions, rather than rote answers.[60] When students in the class were asked to select from the class roster the names of those who made good contributions to the class discussion, low-achieving students' names were checked. In classrooms where teachers

Peer perceptions

REFLECTING ON PRACTICE

This Reflecting on Practice box describes an eighth-grade science lesson in which the teacher, Ms. Copeland, uses a number of effective teaching techniques that have been explained in this chapter. Read the episode and respond to the following:

■ When in the lesson does Ms. Copeland's teaching reflect the following techniques?

positive milieu	visual prompts
preplanning	soft imperatives
overlapping	close monitoring
cooperative learning	checks for understanding
teaching routines	praise
student alerting	

■ Why do you think she uses each as she does?
■ Do you recognize in this lesson other effective teaching techniques in addition to those listed above? If so, which ones and when do they appear in the lesson?
■ When in the lesson could Ms. Copeland have used other effective teaching techniques? Which ones?

Before her eighth-grade science class arrives for fifth period, Ms. Copeland checks her lesson plan and her "list of last minute reminders." She uses a "list," as she calls it, as a final check before most lessons to make sure everything is ready. She started the practice years ago when she realized she needed a final check before lessons so that she didn't find herself without a necessary item in its proper place—a situation that complicates teaching and wastes time. Her student assignments to small-group teams and the classroom location where each team will meet are written on a transparency, the individual worksheets are on the "pick-up corner" of her desk, the times for different class activities are recorded in a corner of the chalkboard, all overhead transparencies are in order, the bulb in the projector still works, her teacher's manual lies open in the middle of her desk for quick reference, and all student desks are located as she wants.

The students enter the room chattering noisily, most pause to say "Hi," and proceed to their desks. She greets virtually everyone, calling them by name. When the bell rings, all are seated except Carina, Brittany, and Cory, who are talking near the door. She motions to them and they hurriedly sit down. Students open their science texts to the page written on the chalkboard as Ms. Copeland takes roll. She asks about two missing students.

Ms. Copeland begins instruction by reminding everyone about yesterday's lesson, mentioning several particular points to two students who were absent, and explaining that today's lesson is a continuation of their study of solid-waste disposal in the unit on the environment. She points to the general lesson topic on the chalkboard, "Waste generated by this school." Today the students will make individual lists of solid-waste items generated in the school, and those individual lists will be compared during a team activity later in the period. She explains the organization of the team activity by showing a transparency that reports the membership of five student teams and where in the room each team will meet. She tells the students she will describe what the teams will do when they get to that stage of the lesson.

Then Ms. Copeland gives directions for individual work, "Place your completed homework on the top right corner of your desk. Open your texts to page 217 and read the next section; be careful to follow the guiding questions. These pages in the text will provide information for a worksheet exercise that will come next and for the team activity later."

The students know from past practice that Ms. Copeland will pick up and check their homework as they read. They also know that she will ask about their reading and answer their questions about both the homework and the reading. Ms. Copeland continues, "If you get stuck or have questions, raise your hand. Are there any questions before you begin?" (Ms. Copeland pauses and looks around the room.) She notices that Cory has not yet opened his text and remarks, "Cory, page 217." Then, she says to everyone, "Okay, start your reading."

Ms. Copeland walks up and down the aisles as the students read, stopping at each desk to check homework, monitor the progress of each student's reading, question students about their understanding of the information, and answer their questions. She positions herself at each desk so she can talk quietly but also see nearly all students. She makes sure no student is out of her view for more than a minute or two. Between students, she scans the room for off-task behavior and raised hands. If she sees either, she attends to them before proceeding to the next student. At one point, she notices Jill staring into the distance and motions to her to return to her reading.

Except for short individual spells of inattention, all students read as directed. They realize that the individual exercises and team activities that Ms. Copeland mentioned will require knowledge from the reading. Besides, they like Ms. Copeland and think she makes science fun (although she is somewhat of an ecology freak). They also know that she does not tolerate "goofing around." Students who waste time or do not do as she expects lose "citizenship points" on their grades; and if they do not complete classwork, they have it assigned as extra homework. If this happens often, she has a "conversation with a parent" or, for parents who have e-mail at home, she "leaves a message." Even though Ms. Copeland is friendly and caring, and her "conversations" and "messages" are pleasant, students prefer to avoid them.

As Ms. Copeland completes checking with all students in four of the five rows, she notices that some students are nearly finished with the reading assignment. As she passes the overhead projector, she puts on a transparency with the message "When you finish reading, pick up a worksheet from the 'pick-up corner' of my desk and begin the individual exercise. Try to finish the worksheet by 1:25." Then she checks with individual students in the fifth row. As she does so, she points out errors, explains, asks students to explain their thinking, and compliments their good work. As she talks with Ken, she asks if he enjoyed the weekend with his father. (She forgot to ask yesterday. Ken lives with his mother, and he mentioned last Friday that he was looking forward to spending two days with his father.) As she passes Randy, she mentions that she has noticed how fast he has been growing lately and cautions him about stretching his long legs toward the center of the aisle where someone could fall over his feet.

As most students approach completion of their exercises, Ms. Copeland asks them to stop for a moment, while she explains the team activity. She refers again to the team assignment transparency and explains the task. She says, "When you finish your worksheet, take what you have written to the meeting place for your team and compare your responses with those of your other team members. As you do this, try to think of items that are not on anyone's list and add them to the list of one person on your team. When you have compared lists and made the additions you can think of, group your team's items (not just your items) based on the type of material they are made of. One person on each team should write down the items in a grouping and keep that list. Take turns until each person on the team has a list that is different from the others. Keep taking turns and compiling lists until 1:45 or until your group runs out of ideas. We hope that no team runs out of ideas. We will have individuals from each team report at 1:45. Everyone will report once. What questions do you have?"

After responding to several questions, Ms. Copeland says, "Return to your work and watch the time." She writes on the board, "Team Reports—1:45."

As students move to their team locations, Ms. Copeland spot-checks students worksheets to be sure all students have completed their individual assignments. Then, she monitors team conversations, provides guidance, and compliments those making good progress. She also makes sure everyone on a team participates and periodically asks students to explain their thinking in more detail. When she hears one team discussing a TV program, she calmly reprimands them for straying from the assignment.

By 1:45, all teams have at least five groupings of items and each student has a grouping to report. Ms. Copeland projects another transparency on the screen, which says

Reports and Groupings

When you report, tell us
    (1) The reason or reasons for your grouping
    (2) The items in your grouping.
Be prepared to answer questions.
As you listen, think of
    (1) The difference among the groupings reported
    (2) The ways in which similar groupings include different items.
Be prepared to ask and answer questions.

After the reports, Ms. Copeland assigns homework to follow from the class activity. She does so by pointing to the chalkboard on the side wall. It says

For homework, write answers to these two questions concerning your group:

(1) What do you think happens to the items in your group after we are finished with them at school?

(2) How could we change what we do at school so we would not discard so many of these things?

Ms. Copeland instructs the students to write both homework questions in their homework notebooks and to work on answering the questions until the bell rings. She tells them to raise their hands if they need help. She tells the students that their answers will be used for discussion tomorrow.

asked low-achieving students only simple questions, these students were not rated as making significant contributions.[61]

If teachers do not believe that students can take part in a higher-level discussion, those students are not given a chance. The behavior, then, carries over from teacher to classmates. In the case of high-achieving students, high achievement is reinforced; similarly, low-achieving students' low achievement is reinforced.

Rewards and academic achievement

Teachers reward appropriate student performance as a regular function of their classroom responsibilities. They do so to make students feel good about themselves, to motivate them to further and more complex study, and to direct or redirect their behavior. They do so to maintain desired classroom activities and an appropriate classroom atmosphere, as well as to provide feedback to students about their performance.[62]

Numerous rewards and incentives can be used effectively to reinforce academic learning. They include smiles, compliments, breaks from school work, a homework-free day, names of achievers on bulletin boards, parties, and so forth. Generally, when rewards are used appropriately, they increase learning across a wide spectrum that includes grade levels, types of school, student socioeconomic status, and types of community. For instance, studies have shown that when teachers use rewards to train students in the basic classroom learning skills of attending to what is occurring, staying on task, complying with directions, and talking with the teacher, those behaviors occur more consistently. More importantly, at least in the primary grades, the use of such rewards leads to increases in student achievement.[63] However, in using extrinsic rewards, specific guidelines must be followed to avoid adverse effects on student motivation.[64]

But to be effective, rewards must fit the context in which they are used—the classroom and school setting, the peer group culture, the instructional goals, and the type of student population. They need to be offered within a set of rules and arrangements that let the students know what to expect. The rewards cannot be arbitrary, whimsical, or unfair. Students must perceive them as valuable. For instance, praise from a highly respected, demanding teacher has more value than praise from a teacher who is not respected; and praise is received differently by an academically motivated high achiever than by a cynical, alienated student who is about to drop out.

Reward structures themselves are of different types, and the types vary in effectiveness depending on the context in which they are used and the purposes for which they are used. They can be classified as individual or group, and as competitive or cooperative. When *competitive reward structures*, such as grading on a curve, are used, the chances of rewards for some students are diminished when others receive awards. *Cooperative reward structures* function so that improved performance of one student can increase the likelihood of rewards for the other students. *Individual reward structures* are most effective when there are fixed criteria for reinforcement and when the probability of one receiving an award is unrelated to the probability of another's receiving a reward. Some studies indicate that low-achieving students respond to cooperative reward arrangements better than to competitive ones.[65]

Praise, as a specific reward, is often effective in directing behavior and encouraging academic performance, but it too must be used appropriately. It seems to be most effective when it is focused on specific student achievements, so that the relationship between the student behavior and the praise is explicit. It is more effective with younger children, with lower achievers, and with students from lower socioeconomic backgrounds.[66]

Some educators distinguish between praise and encouragement because praise expresses teacher approval of a finished product or successfully completed task ("I'm proud of you for making an A in math"), while encouragement focuses on student effort and improvement ("Your A in math reflects your hard work").[67] Encouragement is more effective in developing the intrinsic motivation that leads to increased self-esteem and lifelong learning.[68]

The four areas of effective teaching practices that you just finished reading about are examples of things good teachers do to produce the teaching and learning they want in their classrooms and for their individual students. You will probably not remember every one of these specific techniques when you are ready to have your own classroom. But they should serve you as concrete illustrations of the many teaching techniques good teachers use with every class, every day. They should also provide you with a ready resource to return to for review as you approach your own pre-K–12 teaching.

Reward structures

Praise

Conclusion

Early in this chapter, you were asked to list characteristics exhibited by the person you remember as your best teacher. The chapter described some of the characteristics of effectiveness that have been reported in relatively recent research studies. It is now time to get your list out again and make additional comparisons.

- In what ways is your list compatible with the research findings?
- Are there any incongruities?

More than likely, there is some parallel between your list and the research findings. But there probably also are significant mismatches. The extent to which there is lack of congruence illustrates the fact that good teaching is not merely the sum of a fixed list of proven effective classroom practices. Good teaching is more than that. (Hold on to your list a little longer. One of the study questions at the end of the chapter asks you to look at it one more time.)

Research is incomplete

Some of the incongruity between your ideas of good teaching and the research findings can also be explained by a point that was mentioned earlier: Researchers have studied some areas of classroom effectiveness but have neglected others. They simply have not had much to say, so far, about the effect on learning of the care that a teacher has for his or her students, of the teacher's love of subject matter, or of his or her sincere interest in students. These characteristics of good teaching are hard to study and difficult to document. But, despite the lack of documentation, all of us know intuitively that they are important.

Teaching is complex

Another reason for the incongruity has to do with the complexity of teaching. There are so many things for teachers to do, so many purposes to be pursued and goals to be achieved, so many student personality and character traits to be accommodated, so many classroom environmental influences to be managed, so many out-of-school influences to be overcome, and so many other intangibles that are not even recognized.

This complexity is illustrated in the writings of two scholars of the teaching process. A decade ago, David Berliner noted in one of his papers about teaching that

> researchers have found that teachers make about 10 significant decisions per hour. . . . These are not decisions about whether Johnny can go to the bathroom. Rather, they are decisions about whether Johnny should stop fractions and go on to decimals, or whether Jane should be moved into the fast mathematics group. These complex, professional decisions take place in environments where teachers have about 1,500 distinct interactions per day with different children on different issues, in classes where 30 students need to be supervised all the time, all day long.[69]

Nathaniel Gage has described teaching as part science and part art.[70] For him, the science part is the part that can be studied and analyzed for its underlying principles—the rules that, when discovered, will guide most teachers toward more effective practice. The part that is art is the part of teaching that extends beyond the underlying principles that can be studied.

According to Gage, a complete science of teaching is not attainable because good teaching will never be limited to an identifiable set of rigorous laws to be followed by all teachers. He says that teaching is more than science. It is also the artistry that involves the teacher's judgment and insight in day-to-day classroom

Much More to Learn

Until the type of research described in this chapter became available, educators who wanted to know the most effective ways of teaching and organizing classes needed to rely on either theories from educational psychology or personal experiences of other teachers. But many of the theoretical ideas of the researchers were developed outside real classrooms and were often found to be incorrect for many situations and impractical to apply in others. At the same time, many of the experience-based recommendations from practitioners proved to be unsystematic, incapable of being generalized, and contradictory.

However, recent research on teacher characteristics and classroom effectiveness as described in this chapter has changed that situation. We now have the beginnings of a body of knowledge about techniques, strategies, and approaches to teaching that work better in more circumstances than others do. Therefore, educational researchers are now at the point at which they know that teachers do make a difference in terms of what students learn, and they know that certain practices are more productive than others. Many of those practices have been identified in the main part of this chapter.

But at the same time, all educators—researchers, college instructors, teachers, and education students—must be careful not to inflate what is known about classroom effectiveness, and they need to guard against the temptation to latch onto a few practices as panaceas for a multitude of classroom teaching difficulties. These cautions are necessary because research also points out limits to what is known about teaching.

Consider the following five points.

First, the data from research are far from complete, and the principles being formulated do not apply all of the time. Students and teachers vary; classroom conditions and school environments vary; interactions among students and teachers vary. As a result, scientific rules and generalizations about classrooms are rarely precise and without exception.

Second, many assessments of the effectiveness of classroom practices and techniques in recent years have used student gains in achievement as their predominant criterion for success. But academic success, however important, is not the only goal of schools. For example, nearly all teachers and schools also want to socialize students and promote their affective and personal development. They want to keep poorly achieving students in their classes rather than have them drop out, even though having them in class lowers the achievement scores of the class and takes teaching time away from more immediately successful students.

Third, although teacher performance affects student performance, the link between the two is not a simple cause-effect chain. There are many variables and intervening complexities that both hinder and help the relationship—variables, for example, in the students themselves, such as their health, home environment, relationships with peers, ability to see or hear clearly, and general interest in the subject matter.

Fourth, events occur in classrooms with astonishing rapidity, and they occur among a group of twenty to thirty or more individuals simultaneously. In this context, teachers engage in hundreds of interchanges with students each day. Of necessity, many of these interchanges are spontaneous and intuitive, not theoretically based. They are not easily anticipated, predicted, or studied. Good teachers just seem to do these things well, often without thinking about them.

Fifth, teachers do not work in isolation, and sometimes the results of instruction do not show up immediately or evenly. A student may work at a particular mathematics operation for days or weeks before grasping it to the point of being able to do it correctly every time. In the meantime, explanations from another teacher, classmates, and parents may have stimulated the understanding. While studying the history of a particular period in grade 9, a student may develop insight into a novel from last year's English class. It is certainly possible that a student who has been to Europe and seen the Bastille will have a different level of understanding of the French Revolution than do classmates who have not had the same experience.

The point here is a simple one. Just as research is telling us more and more about schools and teaching, it is also telling us that we do not have all the answers. There is indeed much more to learn.

situations, the teacher's decisions on when to apply generalizations generated by research and when to ignore them, and the teacher's ability to make practical assessments of how the multitude of variables present at any moment in a classroom should be manipulated in order to produce significant learning. (More on this point is explained under the topic Reflective Practice in Chapter 13.)

In summary, more is known about positive teacher characteristics and effective teaching practices today than ever before, and researchers and practicing teachers are providing new knowledge every day. That new knowledge has helped and will continue to help teachers to teach better. Even though teaching will continue to get better, there is nonetheless no perfect formula for good teaching.

Summary

The degree of influence that teachers have over students and the classroom strategies and techniques that they use affect what students learn. Teachers spend more time with students than other adults do, and many students report that teachers have influenced them significantly. However, only certain teachers seem to have this influence.

Studies of classroom effectiveness show that teachers' methods, which vary greatly, affect learning. Many recent studies have investigated areas such as use of time, classroom climate, active teaching strategies, and teacher expectations and rewards for student performance. In each dimension, certain classroom practices have been found to be more successful in producing learning than others.

To a great extent, characteristics that make teachers influential with students and classroom strategies that appear to produce the most learning seem to be consistent across the country. But it is important not to generalize too sweepingly about "the best ways to teach" because no two teachers, students, or classrooms are exactly alike, and research data are still limited.

Study Questions

1. In what ways is teaching an art, and in what ways is it a science? Why do you think so?

2. Look again at your list of your best teacher's characteristics. Which of these do you think *all* students would think are positive qualities of teachers? Which characteristics would raise some disagreement? How do you account for the difference?

3. Of all the characteristics of effective teaching mentioned in this chapter, which five do you think are the most important? Justify your selection.

4. What standards besides student achievement should be used to assess classroom effectiveness? Which are, or might be, more important than student achievement? Explain your thinking.

5. Which changing conditions in teaching and schools and in society generally will cause changes in how effective teachers can be with students? In what ways will they influence teacher effectiveness? Why do you think so?

Key Terms

Academic learning time
Active learning
Allocated time
Behavioral expectations
Behavioral stages of
   development
Checking for
   understanding
Classroom climate
Classroom culture
Classroom routines
Classroom structures
Cognitive behavior
   modification systems

Correlational studies
Counseling and
   therapy-based
   behavior
   modification systems
Direct instruction
Instructional time
Interactive instructional
   practices
Learning time
Mental linkages
Optimal error rate
Overlapping
Praise

Prompts
Redundancy
Reward structure
Rewards
Self-fulfilling prophecy
Student accountability
Student engaged time
Teacher as ringmaster
Teaching effectiveness
Teaching functions
Use of time
Wait time
Withitness

For Further Reading

Berliner, D. C., & Casanova, U. (1989). Effective schools: Teachers make the difference. *Instructor, 99*(3), 14–15.

Brophy, J. E. (1986). Teacher influences on student achievement. *American Psychologist, 41*(10), 1069–1078.

Charles, C. (1991). *Building classroom discipline: From models to practice* (4th ed.). New York: Longman.

Csikszentmihalyi, M., & McCormack, J. (1986). The influence of teachers. *Phi Delta Kappan, 67*(6), 415–419.

Emmer, E. T., Evertson, C. M., Clements, B. S., & Worsham, M. E. (1994). *Classroom management for secondary teachers*. Boston: Allyn and Bacon.

Evertson, C. M., Emmer, E. T., Clements, B. S., & Worsham, M. E. (1994). *Classroom management for elementary teachers*. Boston: Allyn and Bacon.

Gage, N. (1978). *The scientific basis of the art of teaching*. New York: Teachers College Press, Columbia University.

Jackson, P. W. (1986). *The practice of teaching*. New York: Teachers College Press. (Reissued in 1991 by Teachers College Press.)

Kounin, J. S. (1970). *Discipline and group management in classrooms*. New York: Holt, Rinehart and Winston.

Lortie, D. C. (1975). *School teacher: A sociological study*. Chicago: University of Chicago Press.

Rosenthal, R., & Jacobson, L. (1968). *Pygmalion in the classroom: Teacher expectations and pupils' intellectual development*. New York: Holt, Rinehart and Winston.

Slavin, R. E. (1990). *Cooperative learning: Theory, research, and practice*. Englewood Cliffs, NJ: Prentice-Hall.

Slavin, R. E. (1992). Putting research to work: Cooperative learning. *Instructor, 102*(2), 46–47.

Studying Schools as Cultures

CONTRIBUTING AUTHOR
Terrence E. Deal

Terrence E. Deal wrote most of the substantive sections of the first edition of this chapter. Charles and Lynn Myers provided updates for this edition and the sections on school effectiveness, Something to Think About, and Educational Research. Alene H. Harris and Charles and Lynn Myers wrote the Reflecting on Practice section.

*I*n this chapter we shift our attention from classrooms to schools. As with Chapters 2 and 3, we examine guidelines on how to look at schools and information on what experts say characterizes good schools. The way we describe schools, however, is quite different from the way schools have typically been described in the past. For many years schools have been viewed as if they were families, factories, or blackboard jungles. This chapter describes schools as dynamic cultural organizations made up of many people and parts, all with a common purpose and common values and beliefs.

Until recently, educators often classified schools by dividing them into types based on characteristics such as level of instruction, size, type of curricular emphasis, and location. Sometimes the categories included affluence of the student body. Schools were labeled as primary, upper elementary, middle, junior high, high; large, small; academic, vocational, magnet, comprehensive; urban, suburban, rural; rich and poor. In at least two ways such descriptions seem to present distorted views of schools. They emphasize differences and obscure similarities across types, and they portray schools as being static.

Although this chapter addresses differences among schools, it stresses commonalities and the dynamics that most schools share. This emphasis enables you to develop a general mental image of schools everywhere, and it also provides you with a basis for understanding specific schools and for seeing how schools change over time.

The chapter is organized around a Snapshot of a fictional new teacher who enters a particular school culture for the first time, a report on what some experts say characterizes "effective schools," and descriptions of four different schools. The Educational Research section explains and illustrates ethnographic research.

SNAPSHOT

*T*his Snapshot describes the experiences of Laurie Renfro, a new teacher, as she assumes her first teaching position. As you read about her initial day at W. A. Carson High School, consider the following questions:

■ What things seem to surprise Ms. Renfro or strike her as being unusual? Why do you think this is the case?

■ What characteristics of the culture of Carson High School do you notice in the scenes described?

■ What conclusion can you draw about Mr. Grundig and Ms. Cohen from the brief glimpses of them presented here?

W. A. Carson High School

Laurie Renfro smiled as she stepped from her brand new car. "It's wonderful to think about life without the pressures and demands of exams, professors, and theories. Now *I* give the tests—whenever *I* want. From occupying the bottom rung to being the boss of my own classroom . . . I can hardly wait! And I'm even getting paid for it! Money for new clothes, a new car, an apartment, all mine . . . almost, anyway."

W. A. Carson High School looked like a friendly place, even from the outside: green lawns, well-trimmed shrubbery, and ample numbers of large lattice-paned windows. The fact that the school had been

built in the 1940s added to its charm. It gave the architectural lines character, something Laurie Renfro always liked in a building.

Entering the large-arched doorway, Laurie noted the familiar smell a school seems to emit in September before the students arrive. "Probably a blend of the newly waxed floors and the mustiness of being closed for the summer," she mused. In fact, the custodian was still standing in the corridor admiring the floor's sheen, knowing full well that the 1,200 pairs of new shoes scheduled to arrive within the week would quickly obscure his work of art with a mosaic of scuff marks.

"You must be the new social studies teacher," the custodian observed after sighting Laurie walking down the hallway in her obviously new suit, carrying a briefcase that could not have left the shelves more than twenty-four hours ago. "I think you'll like your classes," he continued. "But I hope you're not one of those new teachers with newfangled methods that deny the absolute fact that Carson students need discipline and the fundamentals. I'll be coming by to see how you're doing when school opens."

"Which way to the principal's office?" Laurie asked politely, thinking to herself that the custodian should stick to his floors.

"Down the hallway, two doors to the left," the custodian responded. "Oh by the way, my name is Mr. Grundig. And you must be Ms. Renfro. I heard that you went to the university. I sure hope they aren't stuffing your heads full of theories from a bunch of eggheads that have never seen the inside of classrooms like Carson. Now, if you ask me . . . "

"Thank you very much, Mr. Grundig, I'd love to chat longer, but I really don't want to be late to my first appointment with Mr. Bays."

"No problem, Ms. Renfro, I'm sure we'll have plenty of time to talk. I'll drop by your room often. It's delightful to have a new face on our Carson team."

"That's strange," Laurie thought to herself as she continued down the hall in the direction indicated by Mr. Grundig. "He talks almost as if he's in charge here. I'll bet he'll even read what I write on the chalkboard before he erases it. Well, I guess I don't need to worry about what the custodian thinks. . . . "

"Oh, Ms. Renfro! We're so delighted you're here." A cheery voice greeted Laurie as she walked past the opaque glass door labeled Principal's Office. "I'm Muriel Cohen, Mr. Bays's secretary." Mr. Bays is at a superintendent's cabinet meeting right now, and he always attends the Rotary Club every Tuesday at noon; so he'll be back around 2:00. In the meantime he's asked me to introduce you to Carson. He'll continue your orientation when he returns. Let me take your briefcase, and then we'll see the school. Would you like a cup of coffee before we start?"

As the tour progressed, Laurie was amazed at how much status Ms. Cohen seemed to have in the school. She knew everyone, and each teacher and staff person seemed to accord her unusual respect—cafeteria workers getting their equipment ready to produce the next year's sloppy joes and tuna boats, classroom teachers busy with bulletin boards and materials. Young teachers dressed in blue jeans, old ones dressed in tweeds, some very old ones seemingly contemplating how they could survive the last year before retirement—Ms. Cohen related easily to them all.

Laurie was also surprised at the variety of requests made of the secretary as she moved through the school. For questions about equipment, schedules, parents, children, and materials—Muriel Cohen had a ready answer. Many of her answers seemed to carry messages that let people know what they should be doing. Laurie also noted that Ms. Cohen asked her a lot of questions about her own background and ideas about teaching. "She seems as interested in educational methods as Mr. Grundig," Laurie thought to herself. "I wonder who really runs this school."

Finally, the two women walked up to a door with an opaque window marked 208. As Muriel Cohen opened the door, she turned to the new teacher. "This is your room for next year. What do you think?" As Laurie's eyes scanned the room from the bulletin boards to the metal desks arranged in neat rows on the newly waxed floors to the flag above the desk in the front of the room, her excitement rose. "Finally, my own classroom, my territory, *my* domain where I am the teller, not the told."

"It's wonderful, Ms. Cohen. I can hardly wait to get it ready for my students."

"I suspected that," Ms. Cohen said. "I'll leave you for a while to think about what you want to do. If you need anything, see me. Oh, by the way, I noticed among your references from the university recommendations from Professors Hall and Benstran. I just thought I'd let you know that they also wrote recommendations for Lance Snelling, your predecessor, who barely made it through last year. Very smart, he was. But he wasn't able to control his classes. That theory stuff seems to go over better at the university than it does here at Carson. I know you'll be different. There's a nice little place around the corner you may want to try for lunch. Just remember to be back at 2:00 for your appointment with Mr. Bays. And remember, anything that you need to know or have, come to me." With that, Ms. Cohen walked down the hall, turning her head only to acknowledge Laurie's thank you.

At lunch, Laurie mused over her introduction to Carson. The morning had been different from what she had imagined. She wondered why the custodian and secretary seemed so knowledgeable and powerful. She was surprised with the diversity of her colleagues in such things as age, dress, and personality. Each classroom seemed to have its own flavor, but even though the various subgroups seemed so different, something seemed to hold them together. Whatever it was, it made Laurie feel like an outsider, even though the people were all friendly enough.

She wondered how she would fit into the school and to whom she would be able to turn for advice and support. Learning the ropes might be more important and difficult than she had thought.

Not much happened at the meeting with Mr. Bays. Mr. Bays was a warm and charming man whose middle age was tempered with a dapperness and sense of humor that Laurie liked. But their conversation focused mainly on goals, objectives, district curriculum guides, school rules, discipline, evaluation procedures, and other matters that appeared to be only remotely connected to Laurie's main concerns or her morning observations. Mr. Bays was clearly in charge, but the things he was in charge of seemed unrelated to many of the questions that Laurie had formulated in the presence of Mr. Grundig, Ms. Cohen, and the other people at Carson. "Oh well," she thought. "It's only my first day."

As Laurie walked out the main entrance following her meeting with Mr. Bays, her thoughts moved back and forth between getting her classroom ready and understanding what made Carson tick. Thinking about the classroom brought exciting images of the year; the school itself just didn't seem to make much sense, at least not in terms of what she had originally expected.

Just as she opened the door of her car and carefully tossed her new briefcase into the passenger seat, Laurie heard her name being called. Turning, she saw a small group of other teachers in the parking lot. "Laurie Renfro?" an older male teacher inquired as he walked toward Laurie extending his hand. "I'm John Welch, and I teach mathematics. Welcome to Carson. Do you have time to have a drink with a few of your new colleagues?" "Of course," Laurie responded with a pleased look.

The conversation in the lounge cleared some things up but introduced new surprises. She liked the other teachers. They laughed affectionately when she told them about Mr. Grundig and Ms. Cohen. They asked her what Mr. Bays had covered in his meeting with her and then proceeded to brief her, as John Welch put it, on "the way we really do things around here."

Culture and Cultures

Values a people share

All schools, including Carson High, have their own *culture;* all organizations do. A culture is the pattern of behavior, assumptions, and beliefs that sets a group apart from others. The term *culture* encompasses the values a people share, the common patterns among the ways they think and behave, their sense of a common history, the body of traditions they accept, and the other characteristics that hold the group

A feeling of belonging

together. Those within a culture share a feeling of belonging that helps individuals identify with the group and lets them know how to act and how to fit in. It provides a sense of security for individuals that says they are not alone. Conversely, it is the element that is missing when a person leaves familiar surroundings, travels to a distant and different world, and senses that he or she does not know "how they do things here" or "what is normally expected." It is that part of Carson High that Laurie Renfro needs to absorb in order to become a part of it.

Culture is also a concept used in the social sciences to describe the character or feel of a society; to highlight the deep patterns of values, beliefs, and traditions formed through its history; and to explain why its people do things in a particular way. This concept is an intellectual tool that observers use to interpret and explain the ideas and behavior of groups and of people within groups. It has been used to study primitive tribes, urban gangs, the country club set, yuppies, Southern society, governmental bureaucracies, prisons, businesses, schools, and other formal and informal organizations.

A social science concept

The Culture of Organizations

Like cultures in broader society, organizations—IBM, the Catholic Church, the United States Army, Harvard University, and P.S. 102 in Harlem—have their own ways of doing things, their own personality and identity. This organizational culture consists of a particular tone or feel that insiders usually take for granted but that outsiders sense strongly as they confront the organization for the first time (much as Laurie Renfro experienced her first day at Carson). Experts who study organizations label the tone or feel with such terms as *ethos*, *spirit*, *climate*, as well as *culture*. It is an elusive, hard-to-put-your-finger-on side of an organization, an aspect that many people simply do not see or comprehend.

Learned thought and behavior

Cultures develop in organizations, as they do in the outside world, because people require symbols and symbolic activity to give meaning to their life and work. People create cultures around themselves, which then guide, define, and shape what they do and believe. The transaction is two-way—human beings create culture, and they are shaped by it. The transaction evolves continuously as long as the community, corporation, hospital, school, or organization of any sort exists.

Symbols and symbolic activity

Since the publication of two books in the early 1980s on this topic—Terrence Deal and Allan Kennedy's *Corporate Cultures* (1982) and Thomas J. Peters and Robert H. Waterman's *In Search of Excellence* (1982), the concept of culture has been a preoccupation with many businesses.[1] Firms across all sections of the economy—banks, insurance companies, hotel chains, and airlines—are struggling to identify, revitalize, and reshape their cultures. It is difficult to attend an executive retreat, annual conference, or business seminar without hearing the term used, misused, or abused. The concept of culture in corporate America has become a powerful management tool and probably has also become a management fad.

Culture in corporate America

Understanding Cultures

Because culture is an elusive entity, special concepts or a particular language is needed to help people understand it better, especially as it applies to modern organizations and schools. One way to begin that understanding is to think of organizations as tribes cloaked in a mystique developed over many years, a mystique that includes (1) shared values and beliefs, (2) heroes and heroines, (3) rituals and ceremonies, (4) stories and legends, and (5) informal players.

Shared values and beliefs

For instance, every tribe has something it stands for, a special character that sets it apart from other tribes. These are the *shared values* of the culture. They are often expressed in logos, symbols, or slogans. In American society, the Stars and Stripes, the Statue of Liberty, and the phrase "America, the land of the free" represent the value that we assign to the American way. The United States Marine Corps identifies itself with the motto "Semper Fidelis." The IBM Corporation anchors its business on service and dignity for the individual—values that it has adhered to since its inception. These core values are shared from the highest-ranking to the lowest-paid positions in the organization.

Heroes and heroines

Because values are intangible, tribes also identify and recognize *heroes and heroines* who embody the essential character of the organization. Just as primitive social groups had leaders who were often heroic, companies have chief executive officers, and school systems have superintendents, principals, and particularly well-respected teachers. Tribes also have additional prominent figures whose collective presence represents the full range of values that are necessary for survival and success. IBM has the late Thomas Watson Sr., the visionary hero who founded the company, and it also recognizes dark-suited, white-shirted marketers; unshaven, jeans-clad people who study and develop robotics; and the researcher who used to drive her motorcycle around the halls of one of its research and development units. In the aggregate, IBM's heroes and heroines provide role models that each person can look up to for guidance in determining how individual behavior can contribute to the company's success.

Rituals and ceremonies

In both primitive and modern organizations, *rituals and ceremonies* are important opportunities for individuals to experience shared values and to bond together in a common quest. The power breakfast or the afternoon gathering at a local watering hole enable people from different parts of a company to share an experience deeper than just eating eggs or drinking beer. Much as physicians and surgical teams for years scrubbed for seven minutes long after they knew that germs are destroyed in thirty seconds, people in modern corporations engage in many activities because of what those activities *express*, not for what they accomplish.

Typically, the clan members of an organization gather together once a year in ceremony to revitalize their commitment to its values, celebrate its heroes and heroines, enact its rituals, retell its stories, and fuse past and present together in a vision of hope for the future. For years the annual seminars held by Mary Kay Cosmetics included the awarding of Mary Kay–pink Cadillacs and diamond bumblebee pins to its successful beauty consultants, thus reinforcing the You-Can-Do-It spirit that represents one of its core values. Each year, members of the United States Air Force come together in their "rebluing" ceremony to renew their commitment to its traditions. Annually, communities conduct Fourth-of-July celebrations and families gather around Christmas trees, Hanukkah candles, and other symbols to celebrate spirit and traditions that are handed down in story and legend from one generation to the next.

Stories and legends

These *stories and legends*, in addition to being intertwined with rituals and ceremonies, have organizational significance of their own. They carry traditions, values, and miscellaneous reflections from generation to generation and lead to the time-honored history that develops loyalty among tribe members. They help current members identify with the corporate past and, in turn, anticipate a corporate future.

Informal players, or carriers

Every tribe has its network of *informal players*—the cast of "carriers" who preserve traditions, transmit organizational history, and reminisce. One of the roles of

Rituals and ceremonies are important in all cultures, including schools.

these players is to provide a powerful counterbalance to the power of the chief. They are typically older people who assure that occasions are enacted properly, that spiritual matters receive ample attention, and that history lessons are not forgotten. They are storytellers who weave the rich experience of a people into tales that transmit values in memorable ways. They are gossips who carry information from person to person, assuring that no one will be deprived of the important news of the day.

Informal players are found in all modern organizations. Although the title on their business cards or office doors may not formally recognize their unofficial roles, they transact their special business day in and day out behind the scenes or outside the formal boundaries of the organization. They plan the special parties, tell newcomers how things really are, and remind everyone of the reasons for starting and preserving specific rituals and traditions. They preserve the culture and help hold the traditional elements of the organization together.

All these cultural elements—shared values and beliefs, heroes and heroines, rituals and ceremonies, stories and legends, and the network of informal players—shape and give meaning to collective experience in families, sororities and fraternities, universities, armies, federal and state agencies, schools, and other organizations. They enable clan members, alumni, and workers to identify with a group that often spans time and distance. They provide a way for them to be part of the larger culture and to develop and maintain an attachment to it.

The School as a Culture

As one thinks of the elements of culture just mentioned—shared values, heroes, and so forth—it is obvious that schools embody culture as much as any organization. School visitors can sense it as they approach a school building and can almost smell and taste it as they walk through the doors. They can see it as they observe pictures hanging on the walls, students in the halls, exchanges between students and teachers in classrooms, and in student relationships on the playground.

Organizational saga

As early as the 1930s, Willard W. Waller discussed the importance of culture, beliefs, rituals, ceremonies, and values in schools; and he noted the roles portrayed by school folklore, myth, tradition, taboos, rites, ceremonials, collective representation, and participation mystiques in both the formal and informal parts of school life.[2] More recently, Burton Clark discussed the idea of the *organizational saga* in colleges, which he defined as a shared mythology rooted in tradition, reinforced by a charismatic leader, and possessing a cadre of faculty supporters, distinctive educational practices, a student subculture, and an external group of alumni and other believers.[3] According to Clark, as internal and external groups share their common beliefs, this saga creates links across internal divisions and organizational boundaries in schools. With deep emotional commitment, believers (teachers, students, alumni) define themselves by their affiliation with the school and in their bond to other believers. They share an intense sense of uniqueness. They display school colors, wear school rings, attend sporting events, and willingly announce, "I'm a Cougar." In an organization that possesses a strong saga, there is the group of those who "belong" and who are set apart from others outside the chosen flock. Such an emotional bond turns the membership into a community, even a cult.

School culture and change

Researchers note that school culture plays a major role in school change. Seymour B. Sarason documents the power of school culture—which he defines as behavior regularities and shared assumptions—in resisting and redefining educational innovations such as new math.[4] Terrence F. Deal and Ann Swidler demonstrate the importance of culture or shared symbols in the formation and operation of alternative schools.[5]

Deal notes that alternative schools have faced risky times because of their radical departure from conventional systems of education and because of their inability to create a new system of values and beliefs. His explanation suggests the following

"Go, Tigers!" There is much more to school culture than team nicknames and distinctive clothes, but participating in traditions like these is one of the ways in which students come to identify with a unique community.

scenario for new alternative schools: (1) Because of appearances of deviance from conventional ideas, alternative schools violate an implicit logic of confidence and thus come under careful scrutiny. (2) Confronted with hard questions, these schools try to respond with evidence to support their virtues, failing to realize that seeing does not always lead to believing. (3) Half believing in the prevailing myths themselves, alternative school participants begin to question the legitimacy of their endeavor. (4) Lacking strong sagas to support their conventional efforts, many alternative schools revert to conventional patterns of meaning and comfort. (5) Schools that are able to survive develop strong sagas—that is, their own identity.[6]

Swidler's study of alternative schools supports Deal's assertions. Swidler comments, "Watching teachers and students in free schools, I became convinced that culture, in the sense of symbols, ideologies, and a legitimate language for discussing individual and group obligations provides the crucial substrate on which new organizational forms can be erected."[7]

The same significance of school culture is supported by cases of exemplary schools. Effective schools are those that over time have developed a system of beliefs—a culture—that gives meaning to teaching, learning, and other school activities. Just as with businesses, these schools display shared values and beliefs, well-known and widely celebrated heroes and heroines, well-attended and memorable rituals and ceremonies, positive stories and legends, and a dedicated informal group whose members work diligently to maintain and strengthen the schools' mission.

School culture and exemplary practices

The Exemplary Center for Reading Instruction (ECRI) Program that Michael Fullan described in the mid-1980s is a superb example.[8] It focuses primarily on building a belief around teaching practices. In one elementary school, for example, the introduction of ECRI created a strong consensus and sense of community. Its heroes and heroines, such as the teacher who got polyps in her larynx from teaching so enthusiastically, were well known. A unique teaching ritual was observed across different classrooms even though individual teachers varied enormously in personal background and style. Positive stories of individual students' accomplishments (for example, a foreign student whose achievement gains were especially significant in a short time span) were told repeatedly by teachers, administrators, and parents.[9] These characteristics are strikingly different from patterns in less exemplary elementary schools.

In addition to anecdotes and examples, the case for a link between culture and performance in schools can be inferred from empirical research sources. Several of these consist of school climate studies that attempt to measure the effects of social atmosphere on educational outcomes. Edward L. McDill and Leo C. Rigsby document interesting linkages between school climate, student achievement, and student educational aspirations.[10] Similar findings are evident in school effectiveness studies, where both climate and ethos are consistently connected to measures of performance.[11] Although clear ties between student performance in school and school climate, ethos, and culture have not been specified in these studies, it is clear that something intangible about a school style, tone, and social atmosphere is related to student performance.

School culture and performance

Just as school culture affects school performance, it affects the lives of the people who live within it, and the extent of the influence is particularly noticeable to new arrivals. Each year thousands of new teachers like Laurie Renfro arrive at school with expectations of what their first assignment will be like. They are excited to have their own classrooms and are filled with ideas about how they can improve education and contribute to the profession of teaching. But many of these new

A complex human organization

teachers are simply not aware that they are entering a complex human organization with its own culture. They know that they will be around other people and will have to contend with goals, a hierarchy, rules, evaluations, and other well-known aspects of the formal structure of schools. But they underestimate the political intrigue and conflict that they will encounter in schools—or in their classrooms.

School culture and new teachers

It is easy to imagine the uneasiness, difficulties, and surprises one would feel when traveling for the first time in an unfamiliar land—the people, the languages, everything is different. The experience can be jarring and confusing. The same thing happens when a new teacher first enters school. In a sense, he or she is a foreigner who constitutes a possible threat—unless the culture can mold the stranger into its own likeness. For the most part, schools are successful at shaping new teachers. As Albert Shanker, head of the American Federation of Teachers (AFT) once remarked:

> Ten thousand new teachers each year enter the New York City schools as a result of retirement, death, job turnover, and attrition. These new teachers come from all over the country. They represent all religions, races, political persuasions, and educational institutions. But the amazing thing is that after three weeks in the classroom you can't tell them apart from the teachers they replaced.[12]

Organizational dynamics and forces

It is important for new teachers such as Laurie Renfro to understand the dynamics of their first days at school as well as the organizational forces that will continue to press upon them and their work. Otherwise, such a teacher will be confused and hurt; eventually young teachers may long for their old universities, where things seemed to make more sense. If such a teacher never understands that many of these feelings naturally accompany everyone entering an organization for the first time, the teacher may become one of the many promising young teachers who leave the profession.

Sources of School Culture

School cultures can be categorized in three ways: those that come entirely or in part from outside the school, those that are almost entirely indigenous to the school and pervasive throughout the school culture as a whole, and those that are primarily subcultures within the broader school culture.[13]

For example, a school in New York City would be more influenced by and more likely to react to different community values, expectations, and mandates than would a school in rural New Mexico. But at the same time, each individual school also develops a particular set of cultural values and activities that are likely to distinguish it from others in similar circumstances. As a result, schools in the same community or only a few blocks apart have different internal cultural characteristics. Some of those characteristics appear schoolwide—a seriousness about learning or the lack of it, for example, whereas others are found only among separate subgroups, which have formed around jobs performed at school, socioeconomic status, race, academic ability, personal interests, and the like.[14]

Subcultures within Schools

Just as each school is a culture, subdivisions or groups within schools are subcultures. As with cultures, these subcultures have their own patterns of behavior, assumptions, and beliefs. They are distinct enough that they are clearly evident to anyone who visits a school. For example, in any school, teachers, students, administrators, and service workers all have their own *circles of associates*, ways of doing things, shared values, group leaders, and so forth, even though they are part of the larger school culture at the same time. Evidence of subgroups can usually be seen when individuals in a school are free to choose where they spend their time. At lunchtime, for instance, teachers frequently cluster at a teachers' table, in a separate dining room, or in a designated lounge; students stake out their own territory in sets divided further by gender, age, race, type of personality, and friendship; and staff workers cluster with their own group in their own space.

Conversations in each of these clusters are quite different, as are the interpersonal interactions and presumptions about appropriateness of behavior. In fact, the behaviors are so distinct that nearly anyone could identify each subgroup blindfolded, simply by listening to the topics discussed and the language used.

In the general student subculture of a school, the actions and values of student leaders, or "heroes," are examples for others. These actions significantly affect the scholastic tone of a school and subsequently influence student behavior and performance.[15] Some students who are looked up to by peers reinforce studying, others denigrate it; some stress conformist behavior, others encourage deviance. In the process they establish subgroup norms, which influence scholastic performance and educational aspirations both positively and negatively.[16]

At the same time, however, the general student body of a school is not entirely cohesive. Each has its own groups within the group, and the influence of these groups within groups is also powerful. The smaller groups, or "gangs," have their own values, norms, language, patterns of dress, and informal rules for acceptable behavior. Differences among them are easily observed, especially in high schools where separate collections of "jocks," "druggies," "tree huggers," "head bangers," "groovers," and "brains" are clearly delineated. Here also the effect of student subculture membership on individual behavior is obvious. When subgroup norms are consistent with school goals, the behavior that is promoted supports school harmony. When the reverse is true, counterproductive individual behavior is fostered—cutting class, forming cliques, using drugs—and the school culture suffers.

The values, rituals, language, and beliefs of teacher subcultures are also well documented in the literature. For example, norms of autonomy and equality dictate how teachers relate to one another and may undermine efforts to introduce such innovations as peer observations, mentor teaching, open-space architecture, team teaching, or performance-based salary plans.

The teacher subculture can also directly influence teacher expectations and the amount of time teachers spend on instruction, thus influencing student performance and achievement. Some of this phenomenon was described in earlier chapters in discussions about teacher expectations and self-fulfilling prophecies. If teachers in a school expect a great deal from themselves and their students, most of them usually produce what they expect, and they tend to look down on those who do not. The reverse is typically true if expectations are low. Efforts of this sort have been seen clearly in the last decade as states have introduced career-ladder programs that attempt to distinguish between levels of performance quality.

The administrative subculture also has its own informal rules and procedures; and because of the position of authority of administrators, elements of that subculture permeate the school as a whole. For example, a principal's administrative style

Student subcultures

Groups within groups

Teacher subcultures

Administrative subcultures

A school's teachers develop their own subculture, with values and beliefs that are reflected in the way teachers relate to one another.

and general outlook affect the general operation of the school. If the principal is usually positive, supportive, and encouraging, teachers and students pick up the vibes and act accordingly; if the principal is too cautious, dull, and bureaucratic, they also respond to that message. At the same time, other subcultures in a school—for example, staff, teachers, and students—can support or conflict with that of the principal; and part of the principal's task is to make the cultures mesh.

As Harry F. Wolcott convincingly noted a number of years ago, some administrators become preoccupied with accountability, control, and change.[17] This in turn leads some to overmanage and second-guess teachers; they may also impose significant administrative burdens, especially in the form of paperwork. Such practices frequently put principals in direct conflict with teachers—a factor that can erode teacher motivation and effectiveness in the classroom. Principals also play key roles in encouraging or diminishing student performance. Some of their actions enhance productive activity and learning, and others hinder them. The principal's broad influence in a school culture may make teachers and students look forward to school or drive them away.

Parent and community values

Just as the values and traditions of parents and the local community outside the school affect the culture of the school as a whole, subgroup values from outside the school affect subgroups within. For example, although value orientations of both teachers and the community, as well as the extent to which parents are involved in secondary schools, are linked to student performance, so are the value orientations of street gangs. In essence, because community values differ and are championed by different interest groups or subcultures, the pressures they exert inside schools are not consistent and often are in conflict.

Generally, subcultures of all types inside a school can play a positive role in school performance, but they can also undermine schoolwide values, create subcultural battles, and neutralize each other. This is particularly true when subcultures, in the absence of schoolwide cultural strengths, vie constantly for supremacy and attention. For any school to perform effectively, shared values must keep various subgroups pulling in roughly the same direction. Otherwise, different subcultural influences will predominate, and both cohesion and performance will fall victim to a diversity of voices and special interests.

Now, let's apply these ideas to Laurie Renfro's experience. Had Laurie conceived of her first day at Carson High as if she were a new student entering college, a pledge entering a sorority, a long-term tourist traveling to a foreign country, or a germ entering a human body, her first day would have made more sense. She would have identified Mr. Grundig as a potential *gossip*. He shines floors but more importantly carries the word. In Ms. Cohen, she would have recognized the *priestess*, someone who would be of enormous help in her first year at Carson, enabling her to learn the ropes and avoid the traps. On the other hand, she would have also realized that both Mr. Grundig and Ms. Cohen could have made her life at Carson difficult. From both conversations, she would have noted that Carson High has customs and values that may or may not match those at the university. As the school secretary took her through the halls of Carson, Laurie had opportunities to note the various subcultures among the teachers and staff; for like any organization, Carson's culture hosts groups that may or may not buy into the core values of the place.

Laurie's cultural introduction

In her meeting with Mr. Bays, Laurie could have surmised that although principals are important, they are embedded in an intricate tapestry that was woven before they arrived and will remain after they leave. They may reweave a section or two, or tear a hole; and pieces of them may even become part of the mosaic. Though his meeting with Laurie may not have demonstrated it, Mr. Bays himself may realize by now that official policies often have little to do with actual behavior; that evaluation is as important a ritual as it is a straightforward task; and that his official title as principal, although bestowed by the board and superintendent, must be endorsed and augmented by his moral authority or symbolic presence. If Mr. Bays does not realize all this, the old guard that met Laurie in the parking lot will be running the school and shaping new teachers as they "learn on the job" and evolve their professional style.

The principal's role

Laurie Renfro needs to see all this for her own comfort and survival and for one more important reason. In a week, thirty-three high school students an hour will arrive at the door of her room. Each will look as strange as many of the teachers and staff she observed in her first tour of Carson with Ms. Cohen. Within the group will be small cliques, or subgroups, some planning to learn from Laurie but some already conspiring to find her weak spots and to use the class as an outlet for teenage attention getting. While all thirty-three students have had the summer to forget everything that their previous teachers tried to offer them, unconsciously they miss old familiar Ms. Ruby and resent this new young woman who is usurping her reign. For a classroom is a culture too.

Culture of the classroom

Laurie Renfro will be wise if she pays attention to faculty and staff concerns about the university and if she finds out what happened to Lance Snelling, her predecessor from the university who did poorly enough that he left or was terminated. The culture of Carson will make or break her first year and each year thereafter. Well-established cultural patterns have dictated the direction and performance of the school and they will continue to do so, with or without Laurie.

Past history

Something to Think About

Ben Stein, a journalist who observed in Birmingham High School, Van Nuys, California, for most of a year, wrote the following description of a lunchtime scene. As you read, consider:

- What subcultures are reflected in the lunchtime scene? On what basis do you think they were formed?
- In what ways does the culture of the school probably reflect the broader community in which the school is located?
- What does the description seem to show about the roles and relationships associated with the principal?

A word about lunchtime at Birmingham High School. Lunch is served at 12:30. It is served in a huge outdoor space with a roof but no walls. The students eat at large tables with benches, on the grass in a giant quadrangle, along rows of outdoor lockers. In contrast to my own memories of high school, there are no fights, no pushing matches and, most of all, no smoking in secret nooks and groves.

In an orderly way, the students divide themselves up into racial and ethnic groups. The blacks eat in the back of the eating room, near the soft-drink vending machine. The Mexicans eat on the grass and on benches near the grass. The prosperous white girls and boys eat nearer the center of the quadrangle or else sprawled on the cement near the student-activities room. There is also a row of blind, crippled and sad-looking students who eat by themselves along a wall of lockers near the faculty dining room, usually with a well-behaved Seeing Eye dog nearby.

The different groups rarely eat together. On the other hand, individual members of each group know each other and greet each other cheerfully as they pass by to get their trays or drop off their trays.

Jim Jameson, a fiftyish man who has been principal of Birmingham for about four years, walks through the cafeteria to make sure there is no butting in line and that occasional spats do not generate into anything worse. As Jameson walks by the students, they greet him and he greets each of them back, by name. Incredibly, he knows the name of almost every student among the 2,500 here. He also knows basic facts about each: "He's had a lot of trouble ever since his father died." "He's our best mathematician." "He's planning to go into the army." "She was out last week because she had a bad flu."

Jameson has been voted principal of the year by the board of education repeatedly. He walks around the campus not only as if he were in charge of it, but as if it were one large child of his own. Many events at Birmingham are occasionally touching, but the rapport between the principal and his students is always moving.

Seniors are allowed to leave campus for lunch. As far as I can tell, most of them do. They get into their cars—Rabbits and Toyotas and also a few Mercedes and Cadillacs—and head for the Round Table, Naugles, McDonald's and Bagel Nosh. A few go home if they live nearby and watch "The Young and the Restless."

Generally, there is a relaxed cheerful mood around lunchtime, as if the students lived in a world from which adult concerns had been permanently banned. . . .[18]

Differences among Schools

Because schools are often identified in writings by characteristics other than those associated with culture or effectiveness, it is useful to think of them at least briefly in some of these other types of contexts. To a great extent, school types differ because schools exist in a variety of cultural surroundings—locations; communities; regions of the country; degrees of urbanization; social, economic, and political climates; and so forth. Influences from these cultural surroundings naturally find their way into the school and its operation. The cultural environments of mid-Manhattan; Palo Alto, California; the Pennsylvania Dutch country; San Antonio, Texas; suburban Atlanta; Honolulu; and rural Puerto Rico are all American but all different. The schools in each of these locales reflect their special characteristics.

Types of schools

Schools also differ because of their size. More things happen in large, diverse schools of 2,000 to 3,000 students than in much smaller schools. The organizational structure, operating procedures, sense of identity, familiarity among students and teachers, and potential for getting lost in the crowd are just not the same. Neither are the breadth of course selection, the availability of advanced course offerings, the diversity of individuals, and the possibility of cross-cultural student interaction. Each type of school has its advantages and its drawbacks, and each has its distinctive elements.

Similarly, schools differ according to the age of their student body—elementary, middle, high; the focus of their instruction—academic, general, vocational, comprehensive; their type of funding and control—public, private, church-supported; the style and age of the building—old, modern, urban, brick, modular, spacious, crowded, state-of-the-art; and many other distinguishing factors. Among all these differences, however, are common elements as well—teachers, students, administrators, a sense of purpose, an institutional identity, and many other cultural components.

School Culture and Effectiveness

Even though all schools are dynamic organizations made up of many people who interact in ways described earlier, some schools are better than others, and experts who study schools have developed theories about what distinguishes good ones from bad ones. In recent years, many of these experts have measured the *goodness* of a school in terms of how well they produce academic learning or *academic achievement* in their students.

Academic achievement, however, is not the only standard by which schools can and should be measured, and some educators charge that it has been overemphasized by educational reformers since the publication of *A Nation at Risk*. Some of these critics point out that schools that instill positive self-concepts in their students, that teach citizenship and interpersonal skills well, and that prepare students for meaningful manual work after graduation should be judged just as successful as those that prepare students for college and SAT tests. In the years ahead, you will want to monitor the shifts that occur in the standards that educators and society at large use to determine which schools are good and which are not. (More will be said about this in Chapter 7.)

Two influential studies of school effectiveness in terms of student achievement conducted in the late 1970s and early 1980s,[19] plus parallel studies by other researchers, have led to a widely held belief that effective schools (1) accept the premise that *all* students can learn and therefore devote their energies to all students rather than just to those easiest to teach and (2) possess the following characteristics:[20]

1. a safe and orderly environment
2. a clear and focused school mission
3. noticeable instructional leadership
4. high expectations
5. opportunities for all students to learn and high rates of student time on task
6. frequent monitoring of student progress
7. appropriate home-school relations

Because these seven characteristics of school effectiveness have had such wide acceptance in recent years, school leaders throughout the country have tried to make them cornerstones of their school operations. The task has not been easy, however, and many of today's schools, if not most, would probably not be judged effective in terms of all seven characteristics. As Michael Fullan has pointed out, there is a big difference between knowing *about* school effectiveness and knowing *how* to make schools effective.[21] It is one thing to identify schools that have records of high student achievement and something else to create such conditions where they do not already exist.

One point that seems to be agreed upon by school-effectiveness experts is the belief that effective schools are more than places that contain a large percentage of skilled classroom teachers. Skilled classroom teachers are necessary, of course, but the school organization as a whole is also a primary factor in determining how well students learn.

Culture influences behavior

Although the concept of school culture adds a particular dimension to the literature on effective schools, that dimension was often overlooked by many educators concerned with improving schools during the 1980s. Those who recognize the importance of the culture of schools see that beneath the well-accepted organizational characteristics of effective schools lie cultural elements that influence the behavior of administrators, teachers, and students. By influencing behavior, these cultural elements affect how well teachers teach and how much students learn. By projecting an image of what the schools stand for, they also affect perceptions and parental and community confidence. Therefore, those who understand schools as cultures realize that cultural considerations are necessary if schools are to be made more effective.

Culture, Effectiveness, and Improving Schools

In the 1990s, efforts at school improvement and school reform have, for the most part, attempted to combine the ideas of school effectiveness and school cultures. You should be able to recognize some of this synthesis in the "second-wave proposals" described in Chapter 1. Look back at the descriptions of Essential Schools (Sizer), School Power (Comer), Accelerated Schools (Levin), and Success for All (Slavin).

It is important to recognize that both the effectiveness and the cultural aspects of school improvement efforts of the 1990s have come from the world of business and that both are an extension of activity in the 1980s. Some time ago, American business leaders were concerned about difficulties in their operations that did not seem to be present in competing businesses in Japan. So they looked at their Japanese counterparts for guidance. Two of the concepts they encountered were *total quality management* and organizational *learning communities.* Many industry leaders tried to integrate these two ideas into their own operations, and they are still doing so. In the process, they turned to the writings of William Edwards Deming and Peter Senge.[22]

It is not necessary for you to delve deeply into these ideas at this stage of your study, but it is appropriate for you to have a general sense of what the concepts of quality management and learning communities mean and how they are currently influencing school reform. Ideally, *total quality management* is a belief that what a business or school does is based on the primary goal of *serving its customers or clients.* All activity is assessed and evaluated in terms of how well it contributes to that goal. For schools, the *customers or clients are the students and their families;* so everything that a school does should be judged in terms of service to students. Because teachers are people in a school system who provide the main service—teaching and learning—they are "the first line of service providers."

Total quality management

This means their work—teaching—is the most important function of the school, and all other activities and personnel of the school exist in order to assist teachers teach. In short, principals, superintendents, custodians, and secretaries are all employed to help teachers and should be evaluated in those terms.

If a school operating under total quality management is to provide high-level-learning and to get better constantly, it needs to encompass at least four key characteristics, or elements, in its operation:

1. Everyone in the organization must accept responsibility for the overall successes and failure of the enterprise.
2. Management needs to be site-based, rather than centralized—that is, at the school, not at the central office.
3. Leadership must be located in a differentiated leadership team, not controlled in top-down fashion by principals or central office officials.
4. The whole enterprise has to be a *learning community;* that is, all participants must be constantly learning how to do their work better and be doing so in a way that enables everyone to learn from and teach one another. There is no top-heavy structure of officers who tell teachers how to teach as if they know secrets that teachers have not yet grasped.

Learning communities

As your study continues, you will want to monitor how these ideas play out in your local area and in schools where you hope to teach. The extent to which schools become quality-managed and learning communities will greatly affect what it means to be a teacher.

Maintaining a Positive Culture

Once schools are thought of as organizational cultures, those who are a part of the school culture can be seen as having certain roles to play or tasks to perform in order to maintain and enhance the school's work. To illustrate the idea of such roles and tasks, we return to Laurie Renfro and look at her as she becomes part of the Carson High School community. What are Laurie's tasks as she works at becoming a part of the school community? What are the school community's tasks for maintaining the Carson culture and for enhancing its strengths?

TABLE 4-1   Questions Laurie Renfro Should Ask about Carson High School

What does the school stand for?
What is its history?
What is its informing vision?
What do its architecture and spatial arrangements say?
What are its symbols?
How widely shared are its core values?
What are the images of the past?
What are the taboos?
Who are the heroes and heroines?
How are mavericks treated?
Are antiheroes and devils more highly regarded than positive characters?
What are the key rituals?
What values are expressed in daily behavior?
What happens in cultural ceremonies?
What stories are told and retold?
What are the stories about, and what do they mean?
What are the sacred myths?
Who are the gossips, the whisperers, the storytellers, and priests or priestesses?
What are the various subcultures, and how do their values deviate from core values?
How does behavior change when people enter the school?
Why do people stay or leave through the years?

Laurie Renfro's Task

Much of Laurie Renfro's success or failure in her first year will depend on how quickly she can become an accepted participant in the culture of Carson High School. So a major task that she faces is to learn about that culture and how to operate in it. To do this, she should systematically consider questions such as those in Table 4-1. As the school year passes, she should also consider similar questions regarding the culture of her classroom.

The Carson High School Community's Task

Making a school better

As Laurie becomes an accepted member of the Carson High community, she needs to join with Mr. Bays, Ms. Cohen, Mr. Grundig, and the rest of the staff to nourish, strengthen, and shape the culture of the school. Her initial observations suggest that Carson already has a strong, distinctive culture. But because cultures are made up of dynamic groups of many people and elements, their members must continually work at maintaining and increasing community strengths. Here are one observer's ideas about the tasks the Carson community could perform to make Carson a better school.

1. *Recreate the history of the school.* In New York City, several elementary schools convened groups of parents, teachers, administrators, students, alumni, and retirees in sessions to recall the stories of those particular schools. In these meetings people discovered their roots and realities. By placing past and present in juxtaposition, they created a shared sense of direction and a shared vision for the schools. In the aggregate, the schools showed dramatic im-

provements in test scores, attendance, vandalism rates, and other measures of school performance.

2. *Articulate shared values.* What a school stands for needs to be shared. In top-quality companies, slogans provide a shorthand means of making essential characteristics noticeable. Symbols, rituals, and artifacts represent intangible values. One school district, along with a local advertising group, made a commercial for its school. The intended audience was dual, as is often the case: Both consumers and workers were its targets. The response to the commercials was overwhelmingly positive. Efforts of teachers and students were recognized, shared, and reinforced.

3. *Anoint and celebrate heroes.* Every school has a pantheon of heroes—past, present, and future—and their anointment and celebration can provide human examples of shared values and beliefs. A recent phone call to Terry Deal, the contributing author for this chapter, from the new principal of his old high school offers a novel example:

   "We would like you to visit your alma mater," the principal said.

   "Why?" Deal responded.

   "Because you have done all right for yourself," she said. "And from all indicators you weren't supposed to. Your teachers remember you as a pain. Your classmates recall mischief and weren't big on your academic worth. The assistant principal notes that you spent more time in her office and the halls than you did in class. Your football coach was sure you'd end up in prison. In short, we want you on campus to show other troublemakers that there may be hope for them."

   Countless other similar opportunities to celebrate teachers, students, administrators, alumni, and parents who exemplify intangible values exist in any school.

4. *Reinvigorate rituals and ceremonies.* Rituals and ceremonies provide regular occasions for special learning and celebrating and for binding individuals to traditions and values. The parents of students at a public high school recently gave a banquet for its teachers. As the teachers arrived at the school's cafeteria, they were greeted with corsages and ribbons labeled with terms such as Guru, Mentor, and Exemplar. The cafeteria tables were draped with white linen tablecloths bedecked with silver candelabra and lighted candles. Some teachers and parents sang together at a piano while others mingled, drinking wine and eating cheese. The dinner was potluck; each parent brought a dish. The program following dinner called attention to the history, values, and vision of the school. The school choir sang. The event delighted the entire audience and transformed the school.

   In another such event, the principal of a large high school required his faculty to attend the annual graduation ceremony and to wear their academic robes. The district offered to pay the rental fee. Parents and students received the graduation ceremony with acclaim. The next year, attendance at graduation doubled. Student drinking and other behavior problems associated with commencement virtually disappeared. Parent confidence in the school has gone up dramatically.

5. *Tell good stories.* Faculty at a junior high school spent most of a faculty meeting telling stories about students and each other. As a result, several exem-

Rituals like rallies and celebrations of exemplary achievement help to ensure that a school's culture is continually renewed.

plary students were identified, one a student who had changed from trouble-maker to top student nearly overnight although he had had to overcome nearly insurmountable family and learning problems to do so. The faculty then convened an awards assembly to recognize exemplary students and to share their stories with the other students. The student whose achievements prompted the idea was awarded a large brass eagle. The eagle award now carries the student's name and is given annually to the student who has improved the most.

6. *Work with the network of informal players.* A collection of informal players, gossips, and storytellers is part of each school's culture; and their roles are

important to the successful operation of the school. When changes are proposed, these people must be involved significantly, or they may sabotage the effort.

Often these roles are occupied by nonacademics such as secretaries, service workers, and custodians. Those who fill these roles provide important linkages inside the school and are often direct conduits to the local community. These people need encouragement. They need recognition. One school did this by naming a new patio in honor of a custodian, a man who served an important role as a keeper of the history of the school, conveying to both teachers and students its rich legacy of past exploits and glories.

Carson High—Ten Years Later

As John Noble approached the entrance of Carson High School's brand new building, he smiled broadly. "What a school! Why did they pick me over all the other candidates? Just think, my own classroom, my own students."

As he walked through the sparkling clean entryway of the school, John noticed a distinctive banner hanging in the center of the foyer—Carson High School—Where Learning Is a Way of Life. His eyes moved toward a handsome plaque above the trophy case—Carson High School—An American School of Excellence. He beamed proudly. He also noted the pictures of a Mr. Bays and a Mr. Grundig hanging among others on the wall. "I wonder who those people are? Probably important people in the history of the school," he mused. As he walked across the freshly waxed hallway floors, he admired the student artwork and class portraits on the wall.

As he entered the door of the principal's office, an elderly woman greeted him in a cheery voice. "Welcome to Carson. You must be the new social studies teacher. I'm Muriel Cohen. Our principal will be back from the superintendent's office in a moment. While you're waiting for Ms. Renfro to return, let me show you around Carson."

Entering a school culture

Something to Think About

Ben Stein, the journalist whose description of lunchtime at Birmingham High School appears earlier in this chapter, wrote the following as part of the conclusion to his article about the school. As you read it, think of what his observations imply about the culture and subcultures of Birmingham High.

Here are some things I never saw:

There was a wide variety of students in classes I visited—rich ones, poor ones, kids from famous families, kids who did not know their fathers. I never, not once, saw one student tease another about being poor or being rich or not having a car or not having the right clothes. It might have happened, but I never saw it.

There were many times when teachers were clearly aggravated and tired. I never saw a teacher sharply criticize a student or try to belittle him or her because of a mistake. I never saw or heard a teacher even address the students in an angry voice. I never saw a student leave a classroom feeling ashamed or upset or humiliated.

The teachers were all busy with their life adjustment or their teaching or with something at all times. Yet I never saw a teacher turn away a student who wanted to talk or share a problem. I never saw a teacher who was unwilling to stay after class or after school to hear a child's tale of woe.

In a word, I never saw a teacher who was not working his or her heart out either to teach or to make the children feel better. The teachers were and are onstage all day long, struggling with extremely difficult audiences. You can wonder at what they taught or did not teach, but you could not seriously question the sincerity or intensity of their efforts.

. . . The students seem to be much happier, freer and more confident than they were in 1962, when I left Montgomery Blair High School in Silver Spring, Maryland. The students are incomparably kinder to each other, far more tolerant of diversity, far less ready to pass on their parents' or teachers' prejudices except in rare instances. The students seem to me to be more comfortable with themselves and with each other.

On the other hand, the students know precious little about how their society is organized, why a free society under law is unique and why the society is worth preserving. They also know little in the way of organized thought processes or even basic ways of solving intellectual problems. They often struck me as computers without programs or any clear way to be useful, even to themselves. This is probably what the '60's education critics intended, but it is a dangerous kind of human being to entrust with the future of society. A human being who has not been taught to think clearly is a danger in a free society.

Certainly, students who leave school knowing as little of thought or facts as the students I saw are going to have difficulty maintaining either the way of life they covet or a technologically advanced society. Still, there was a winning, ebullient cheerfulness about the students that consistently blew away negative thoughts. The boys and girls were so likable, so enthusiastic, so flush with the power of youth that it seems cruel even to guess that they will not get whatever they want.

In any event, my observations are those of an adult looking in for a few hours each day on the wholly separate and distinct country of youth. As my year in their world wore on, I became convinced that high school was not so much a system of teaching or learning as a state of mind—the magic state of mind of the last, fullest measure of youth. To try to understand more than bits and pieces of high school is like trying to understand youth. It cannot be done. All I could do, in my own way, was two things; first I could take snapshots and send them home to the land of adults, where we can look at them and marvel. And . . . I could and did learn to love the students at Birmingham High School as if they were my own children, to respect all the teachers I saw. . . . Whatever the shortcomings of the school and of the people in it, taken day by day and in person, they are as irresistible as youth itself.[23]

- Based on this chapter's two excerpts from Stein, how would you describe the culture of Birmingham High?
- From what Stein said here and from what he wrote about lunchtime in the earlier Something to Think About section of this chapter, how would you characterize the student subculture(s) of this school?
- What would you say are some of the basic values and beliefs that undergird the culture of Birmingham High?

*T*his chapter's Reflecting on Practice consists of brief glimpses into three different schools. Each is presented as a case study for you to consider as you think about schools as cultures and as effective institutions of learning. Consider each of the following questions as they relate to these schools:

■ What characteristics of the culture of each of these schools is reflected in the descriptions? Why do you think each of these characteristics developed in that school?
■ What characteristics of effectiveness are reflected?
■ How would you assess the cultural atmosphere and degree of effectiveness of each school?

Although the schools are different, they also typify schools in America today. The descriptions are necessarily brief and incomplete, so you will need to read between the lines and make assumptions beyond the observers' reports about the schools, students, and teachers.

Observation Number One: George Washington Carver Comprehensive High School

The following observations were made by Sara Lawrence Lightfoot in her 1983 book, *The Good High School: Portraits of Character and Culture.*[24]

George Washington Carver Comprehensive High School is in the southeastern section of Atlanta, the poorest area of the city. No matter what route you take from downtown Atlanta, you must cross the tracks in order to get to Carver. On the fifteen-minute journey from downtown, the scenery changes dramatically. Downtown Atlanta, with its bold new high rises and shiny edifices, symbolizes the hope and transformation of an emerging southern metropolis. In contrast, southeast Atlanta looks gray and shabby. Fast-food joints, gas stations, small grocery stores, and low-cost housing line the main streets. . . .

The Carver Homes crowd 5,400 people into 990 apartments. The two-story brick buildings lined up along nine streets were built twenty-five years ago as public housing. They do not appear as ominous and isolating as the high-rise public housing of Chicago or New York. There is something more humane about the scale of these buildings. There are stoops and porches to sit on and more possibility for neighborly contact. Yet the people here are just as poor and just as imprisoned by poverty and discrimination. What might have once been planted lawns and greenery has long since turned to gray, beaten-down dirt, and there are no sidewalks for people to walk on from house to house. Through the eyes of a northeasterner, the Carver Homes look semi-rural, even though they are part of a big-city problem. . . .

The student enrollment at Carver High School has fluctuated but seems to have stabilized at 890. As with all public high schools in Atlanta, Carver goes from eighth through twelfth grades. The five-year grade span is most vivid and visible with the boys. The young eighth-graders appear vulnerable and childlike in contrast to the tall, bearded senior boys, who seem to have suddenly shot into manhood. Except for one white boy, the students are all black. The teaching staff is predominantly black, with a small sprinkling of white faces. The white teachers are so thoroughly interspersed into the faculty that everyone I ask finds it hard to say exactly how many there are. None of the seventy-five teachers on Carver's full-time staff lives in the community. They travel several miles each morning from the more affluent middle-class sections of Atlanta and its suburbs. One teacher, who lives in a subdivision twelve miles away, is incredulous when . . . [an observer asks] him whether he lives close by. "I can't imagine living close by . . ." [he responds].

. . . The mood on campus is one of order and decorum. There is not the edge of fear or the potential for violence that one often experiences going into large urban high schools. Bathrooms are free of graffiti, hallways are swept and kept clean, and students express pride in the restored campus. Students gathered in groups do not appear ominous and threatening, but well behaved and friendly. . . .

. . . In many of the classrooms . . . very little of substance was happening educationally. Teachers were caught up in procedural directives and students appeared disinterested, turned off, or mildly disruptive. The institution has begun to emerge as stable and secure, but attention to the intellectual development and growth of students will require a different kind of focus, new pedagogical skills, and a profound change in faculty views of student capabilities. This most difficult challenge is connected . . . to the perceptions faculty hold of student futures and the place and station that students are expected to take as adults in the world beyond school.

Mr. Parrot, a slow-talking, slight man with a deep southern accent, teaches a social science course to juniors and seniors. The late-afternoon class is depleted by the absence of the seniors, who have gone off to rehearse for graduation. Five students, who have all straggled in well after the bell, are scattered throughout the large, well-equipped classroom. One has her head on the desk and is nodding off to sleep; another girl is chewing gum vigorously and leafing through a magazine; a third student stares straight ahead with glazed eyes. These three never respond to the teacher's questions and remain glumly silent during the class discussion. Two boys, Lowry and Richard, sit right under the teacher's nose and spend most of the class period being noisy and disruptive. Mr. Parrot hopes for other students to arrive, but finally decides to begin the class about twenty minutes after the bell. His opening remarks sound formal. He seems to be addressing his comments to more than the few people present. Standing behind a podium at the front of the room, he says, "Young people, let me have your attention quickly." Lowry and Richard quiet down momentarily, but the others appear to ignore his announcement. . . .

Although there are glimmers of more lively and skillful teaching going on at Carver and evidence of some sophisticated work done by a few students in biology, graphic arts, and literature, for example, the academic program seems to lag far behind the vocational training that is offered in the more than thirty shops at the school. . . .

. . . The academic side of life seems undeveloped and embryonic at the same time the vocational training feels rooted in history and clearly drawn. (pp. 32, 39, 52)

Observation Number Two: The Ensworth School

The following observation was recorded by Alene Harris at The Ensworth School, Nashville, Tennessee.

The Ensworth School is a privately financed, independent, coed day school with 460 students in grades "pre-first" through eight. It is open to all students regardless of race, religion, or creed. It began in 1958 in a former private home in one of the more prestigious sections of a large southern city. Since then, the original English Tudor residence has been expanded to include thirty-two classrooms, two art studios, two libraries, computer lab, gymnasium, exercise rooms, playing fields, tennis courts, playgrounds, and swimming pool on a well-manicured fifteen-acre campus.

Beginning at 7:30 each school morning, parents deposit carloads of bright and well-dressed children at the front porch of the school. Most students are white, but there are a few black and Asian faces. Academic entrance requirements assure that all students are of above-average ability, and virtually all are from above-average-income homes, although 6 percent receive financial aid to attend.

At 7:45, several teachers gather in the lounge, where they drink coffee and discuss pollen count, soap operas, and recent student illnesses. Two secretaries answer phones and collect notes from returning absentees.

As the day starts in Ms. Bain's first grade, work in the reading books is postponed as a student messenger delivers copies of this year's second issue of the student literary magazine. Each child receives a copy and immediately begins scanning the pages for his or her own writing and for writing of friends. Students read silently or softly to one another.

In Ms. Burgess's first grade, students sit in a circle on the carpeted floor for a show-and-tell session. Five students take their turns and share books, a poster, neon-bright shoelaces, a lost tooth, and a toy seal made of real fur. One boy questions whether a baby seal was killed to make the toy, and asks if it wouldn't be better to make toys out of old seals about to die.

Second-grade students in Ms. Kinnard's class write thank-you notes to two speakers who recently visited their classes. In Ms. McCall's class, students take their weekly spelling test.

Across the hall in Ms. Odom's third-grade room, the class listens as one class member recounts a recent experience of appearing on a local TV show to perform a winning song she wrote and entered in a citywide song-writing contest. The class then returns to its study of Egypt. Students are assigned to write a short paper from the point of view of a person either in the Egyptian court or on an archaeological expedition that discovered an Egyptian tomb.

Students in Ms. Sterling's fourth grade spend the first thirty minutes of their regular math period making colorful tissue-paper flowers as a part of a special service project for a school for the handicapped. They then take out their math workbooks and proceed to work at an individual pace on multiplication involving two- and three-digit numbers.

At 11:30, all children in grades 1 through 4 go to lunch. Teachers lead their students down the carpeted halls in quiet, single-file lines. Students eat family style at twenty-four tables, seated nine per table—two from each grade and one adult. Students take turns being servers and runners. The day's lunch is hamburgers and French fries. Students ask one another to pass the catsup; no one argues, pushes, or grabs.

At Table 21, there is one remaining gingerbread square and four would-be takers. Since the sharing of food is the server's responsibility, the second grader in charge for the week cuts the square in half and proceeds to raffle off the pieces through number guessing. All at the table accept her decision as fair. At noon, the elementary principal dismisses the children by class. Fifteen minutes later the fifth through eighth graders observe a similar lunch pattern, but with much more chatter and a bit less formality.

After lunch, two sixth-grade classes take individual oral French exams. Mr. El Amri sits at his desk with a semicircle of six students before him. The one student seated beside him shifts nervously in his chair as he labors to answer in French various questions posed by his teacher. The dozen students seated at their desks have survived their turn and either read French comic books, calculate their grade average, or engage in surreptitious English conversation.

The top fifteen eighth-grade math students who have been admitted to the Algebra I course take a break from their test review midway through their double-period class. As they do, one six-foot student asks the teacher if he may use the chalkboard to prove a theorem for his not-nearly-five-foot friend. Soon the board is filled with numbers and letters, and the teacher watches with amusement as the two boys use their break time to engage in academic challenge.

At 2:45 parents begin to line up their cars in the school drive, and at 3:00 students in grades 1 through 6 spill out the double doors in a jubilant yet somewhat orderly fashion. The seventh and eighth graders stay for an additional period of P.E. By 4:15, almost all students have left the school, and all have left with books and homework assignments.

Observation Number Three: Fall-Hamilton Elementary

The following observation was recorded by Alene Harris at Fall-Hamilton Elementary School, Nashville, Tennessee.

Fall-Hamilton is a modern public school in an urban location in Nashville, Tennessee. It houses 410 students from lower-middle- and low-income homes. About three-quarters of the children come from homes with poverty-level incomes and thus qualify for a hot breakfast and lunch at school. Only about one-third live in a home with both parents.

Although school will not begin for another hour, several teachers gather in the teachers' coffee room, where they discuss their weekend. At 7:15 the conversation is interrupted by a phone call, which a teacher answers. The parent on the line reports that her daughter will be late that morning. She wants the girl's teacher notified, but she does not know the teacher's name.

Ms. Tidwell, the school secretary, arrives at 7:30, turns on the easy-listening radio station, and tells the teachers that the principal will be absent today because his twins are sick. His wife stayed home from her teaching position in another school the last time they were sick, so it was his turn today.

At 7:45 eligible students who have been waiting outside the building enter the cafeteria for breakfast. They pick up their tickets and get in line. Several parents who have accompanied their children to breakfast wait for them to be served.

At the office, three substitute teachers have arrived to replace teachers who will be absent today; they sign in and are directed to the classrooms where they will teach. A mother brings a child who has had chickenpox to Ms. Tidwell to see if the child may return to school. The secretary declares the child well enough. A young student proudly shows Ms. Tidwell a wood carving he bought at the flea market over the weekend.

In the library, Ms. Ross checks the five centers she has arranged for students to use that day. Each teaches a different aspect of using the library. Her helpers assist her by returning books to the shelves. Several other students check out books and scan the shelves. One student is writing a book report at a table.

At 8:15, Mr. Stewart, the P.E. teacher, announces over the intercom system, "We will now have our pledge." Throughout the building, students and teachers stand and recite the Pledge of Allegiance and then observe a minute of silence. Mr. Stewart announces that P.E. classes will be inside today because of the rain.

As the day starts in the kindergarten classroom, fifty children are busily engaged at various learning centers. Some are reading quietly, some painting, some doing puzzles, and some working at the computer. The two teachers are teaching basic skills to two separate small groups.

In a portable classroom at the edge of the parking lot, Ms. Henkel is teaching reading to a group of her first graders. Another group is listening to a reading tape, and the remaining class members are doing phonics worksheets individually.

The teacher of another first grade is presenting spelling words, but few of the students are listening. Several are clustered in small groups, busily chatting with each other, as she methodically proceeds from word to word down the list on the chart.

A fifth-grade class passes by Ms. Williams's sixth grade as they go to P.E. Several wave to their friends. They hear the sixth graders giving reports on apartheid in South Africa. After the reports, Ms. Williams discusses the current problems in South Africa.

At 10:45 the first class arrives for lunch. The children pass through the food line, choosing between two entrees and moving on to their assigned tables. When the entire class is seated, the teacher proceeds to the teachers' dining room, leaving the cafeteria aide in charge. As other classes enter every ten minutes, the room becomes noisy. Children talk and laugh loudly, exchange food, and scurry back to the serving area for items they forgot. The aide shouts for quiet and pounds her hand on a table with a loud slap. The children pause for a moment but quickly resume their previous behavior.

Two students begin fighting and are sent to the office. Both names are recorded on cards. It is a first offense for one of the two; he is reprimanded and sent to his classroom. It is the second offense for the other; he is talked to more sternly and told to remain sitting in the office. A letter describing what happened will be sent home.

The students in Ms. Allen's fourth-grade classes are engaged in independent social studies projects. They are designing and painting dioramas. Ms. Miller's students are doing fractions. Some are solving problems in their workbooks, and others are doing so at the chalkboard under the teacher's guidance.

All eight children in the T-4 class listen as Ms. Ladd explains the rounding off of numbers. These students are in a "transitional class" because last year their third-grade teachers judged them unready for regular fourth grade. They are placed in a very small class in the hope that they will learn better with the close attention they receive from the teacher. Ms. Ladd writes eight examples on the chalkboard and asks each student to solve one of them. Then the class evaluates what each has done.

Ms. Tidwell announces, "No Boy's Club activity tomorrow; the bus has broken down. LaShonda Clay, walk to Jill's house after school today. Teachers, check your mailboxes for an announcement before leaving."

Children in each class line up for dismissal. When the buzzer sounds, their teachers dismiss them, and they scurry toward their assigned exits. The building quiets down quickly. Teachers pick up paper from their classroom floors and think about their plans for the next day. A few students wait in the entrance foyer for their ride.

Conclusion

This chapter has provided instruction on interpreting what happens in schools from a cultural perspective, as well as in terms of good practice as reported in school effectiveness literature.

Now that you have learned to think of schools as cultures as well as organizations striving to be effective, think again of the schools you know about from personal experience. This time, however, look for both characteristics of effectiveness and cultural concepts—the characteristics mentioned earlier in this chapter and

TABLE 4-2   Characteristics for Assessing Schools

Characteristics of Effective Schools	Characteristics of Cultures
Safe and orderly environment	Shared values and beliefs
Clear and focused school mission	Heroes and heroines
Instructional leadership	Rituals and ceremonies
High expectations	Stories and legends
Opportunity for students to learn and high rates of student time on task	Informal players
Frequent monitoring of student progress	
Appropriate home-school relations	

summarized in Table 4-2. Use both lists to make another assessment about what makes some schools better than others.

Having completed this exercise, you should now be prepared to analyze classrooms and schools from both an effective-schools perspective and an organizational-cultures perspective. The two perspectives should be useful guides as you continue your studies and when you eventually enter your own classroom. The cultural perspective will be particularly helpful when you are in Laurie Renfro's situation—starting your first teaching job. At that point, one of your primary tasks will be to become a contributing and effective member of the school's professional staff. You will not have to give up your individuality and your own personal values and beliefs, but you will want to make what you bring to the school mesh comfortably with the culture already present. To accomplish this task, you will want to ask questions such as those suggested for Laurie Renfro in Table 4-1.

EDUCATIONAL RESEARCH

An Ethnographic Approach

Much educational research, such as that emphasized in the first three chapters, is analytical in nature—at least to some extent, it involves experimentation. But anthropologists, those who study culture, often are more descriptive than analytical. That is, they study a culture by observing people and recording what they see. Then they interpret their descriptions by comparing those of one culture to those of another, offering explanations for similarities and differences. This type of study is called *ethnography*.

Therefore, to the extent that schools are cultures, they too can be studied ethnographically.[25] In fact, the Reflecting on Practice section of this chapter consists of brief segments of three school ethnographies; when you read those three descriptions and responded to the questions that preceded them, you were thinking ethnographically.

Following is a short example of an ethnographic account that was written not by an anthropologist but by a journalist. As you read it:

- Think of what terms you would use to describe the culture of Fletcher-Johnson Educational Center and its surrounding community.
- How would you compare the culture of Fletcher-Johnson to that of the four schools you already read about in this chapter?
- How would you compare it to the culture of the high school you attended?

When you finish thinking about Fletcher-Johnson in these terms, consider the three questions that follow the description.

The account is by Marc Fisher, a Washington, DC, journalist.

On Monday mornings, when Mr. Tolson greets his ninth-grade math students at Fletcher-Johnson Educational Center, they tell him about their weekends. They tell of gun battles that interrupt their sleep, arguments that echo through the alleys, sirens and screams that are the night sounds of the projects.

"They say things that would shock your pants off," Antonio Tolson said Tuesday. "But you know, for these kids, it just seems like a normal thing."

Fletcher-Johnson, a massive brown concrete building on a hill off Benning Road in Southeast [a quadrant of the city], doesn't feel like a school in a ravaged, drug-infested neighborhood. It is a sprawling place of bright colors and the latest computer equipment. It is graffiti-free. Its halls are carpeted and quiet. In its open classrooms, teachers need not shout to be heard over other classes a few feet away.

"We are out here in the forgotten land, surrounded by drugs," said George Rutherford II, principal since 1978. . . .

Last week, when Mayor Marion Barry visited Fletcher-Johnson to teach a science class, he asked students how many of them knew someone who had been killed. Fourteen of the 19 students raised their hands.

This week, Ronnell Monroe and Bobby Goloson, ninth graders and friends from the same block at 53rd and C streets SE, thought for only a few seconds about the last person they knew who was killed.

"Oh, yeah, this lady got kidnapped and he raped her and killed her," Monroe said. "She lived across the street. It got me a little down because my mother knew her. A boy, John, also got shot. Somebody messed with his girlfriend and he bought a .22 and shot at the fella. They ran through the alley. We heard it and my mother said to click off the lights and get down, get down, get down." Monroe said he spent about 10 minutes on the floor that night. "Then all the cops came and everybody went outside," Goloson said.

"You hear shots around our way mostly all the time," Monroe said.

"The lady's friends chased that man into the house and he didn't come out until the police came," Goloson said. "He only had a .22."

Children of all ages speak almost casually of pools of blood and screams that ricochet through the projects for hours.

The stories flow easily. And they are accurate: Deputy Police Chief Alfonso Gibson confirmed most of the incidents the children related; the others, he said, "are all realistic. These are not things the children dream up. . . ."

"A dude got shot," said Jermaine Griffin, 13. "He was high and he came and messed with other people and they pushed him and shot him. I knew his name and I felt sad. I was right around the corner. I was scared when I saw the blood."

"In my neighborhood, I always got to watch for people—crazy, drunk people running from the police. And mostly I'm scared of the police. I try to get away as quickly as I can. Especially now and in the summer. That's when people really get that stuff in them and get crazy. That's what it's really about—that drugs."

"I hear the shots and I jump and run around and peep out the window and go back to sleep."[26]

- In what ways would the out-of-school lives of the children at Fletcher-Johnson affect the in-school culture?
- How might the teachers and administrators of the school compensate for the troubled environment in which Fletcher-Johnson students live?
- Some people would say that teachers at Fletcher-Johnson simply would not be able to compensate for the out-of-school lives of their students, that the students are doomed to failure. What do you think?

© 1987 *The Washington Post.* Reprinted with permission.

Summary

In addition to looking at schools in terms of their effectiveness, another way of understanding schools is to think of them as organizational cultures—dynamic groups of people who follow certain patterns of behavior, possess common values and beliefs, and pursue particular goals. Although schools vary in many ways, looking at them as cultures provides an intellectual framework that explains them in terms more of their commonalities than of their differences. By using a cultural perspective, observers can look for key cultural characteristics in all schools—shared values and beliefs, heroes and heroines, rituals and ceremonies, stories and legends, and informal players.

When individuals, including new teachers in schools, enter organizational cultures for the first time, they face the task of learning how things are done in that culture. If they do not learn this, their stay in the organization is likely to be uncomfortable and unsuccessful. Frequently, they are not accepted as part of the group, and they find it difficult to mesh their personal values and goals with those of the organization.

Subcultures operate within schools, as they do in all organizations, and these affect the more general institutional culture both positively and negatively. Students, teachers, administrators, and service workers all have their cultures within the broader culture; and each of these subcultures has subdivisions within it. The extent to which all these groups work together greatly affects school effectiveness.

Efforts to improve schools today use both effectiveness and school-culture ideas. Many of these are experimenting with concepts such as total quality management, students and families as customers, site-based management, team leadership, and schools as learning communities.

Study Questions

1. Think of one of the organizations in which you are or have been a member—fraternity, sorority, athletic team, church group, or the like. Then identify within that group the cultural characteristics of organizations that this chapter stressed—values and beliefs, heroes and heroines, rituals and ceremonies, stories and legends, and informal players. How and why do you think these specific characteristics developed as they did in this group?

2. Think again of an organization in which you are or have been a member, possibly the same one you used in Question 1. Then identify subcultures that exist or existed in the organization. Why do you think these subcultures developed in this group? In what ways was each subculture a positive and a negative influence in the organization?

3. Think of a school you know reasonably well. Then, using as your guide the six actions proposed for Carson High School in the section titled "The Carson High School Community's Task," propose six comparable things that people in that school could do to make the school better.

4. What are some of the things that you think Laurie Renfro probably did during her ten years at Carson that would have led to her selection as principal? Why do you think so?

5. Think again of a school you know reasonably well. To what extent does that school exhibit the characteristics embodied in the concepts of total quality management, students and families as customers, site-based management, team leadership, and schools as learning communities? What changes would be involved if that school were to move toward each of these styles of operation?

Key Terms

Belief	Informal players	Stories and legends
Carriers	Learning communities	Subculture
Culture	Mystique	Symbols
Effective schools	Organizational culture	Total quality management
Ethnographic research	Organizational saga	Tradition
Ethnography	Rituals and ceremonies	Tribal mystique
Ethos	School culture	Value
Heroes and heroines	Shared values and beliefs	

For Further Reading

Bolman, L. G., & Deal, T. E. (1993). *Becoming a teacher leader: From isolation to collaboration.* Thousand Oaks, CA: Corwin Press.

Deal, T., & Kennedy, A. (1983). Culture and school performance. *Educational leadership, 40*(5), 14–15.

Erickson, F. (1987). Conceptions of school culture: An overview. *Educational Administration Quarterly, 23*(4), 11–24.

Fullan, M. G., & Stiegelbauer, S. (1991). *The new meaning of educational change* (2nd ed.). New York: Teachers College Press.

Kaufman, R., & Zahn, D. (1993). *Quality management plus: The continuous improvement of education.* Thousand Oaks, CA: Corwin Press.

Lieberman, A. (1988). *Building a professional culture in schools.* New York: Teachers College Press.

Lightfoot, S. (1983). *The good high school: Portraits of character and culture.* New York: Basic Books.

Murphy, J., & Hallinger, P. (1993). *Restructuring schooling: Learning from ongoing efforts.* Thousand Oaks, CA: Corwin Press.

Sallis, E. (1993). Total Quality Management in education. Philadelphia: Kogan Page.

Sarason, S. B. (1990). *The predictable failure of educational reform: Can we change course before it's too late?* San Francisco: Jossey-Bass.

Senge, P. M. (1990). *The fifth discipline: The art and practice of the learning organization.* New York: Doubleday.

2 Students and Learning

U nit 2, which consists of Chapters 5, 6, and 7, considers: (1) the nature of pre-K–12 students, (2) the learning process, and (3) the ways schools attempt to assure that all students learn. By studying the unit, you should be able to integrate the new knowledge about students and learning with the general purpose of American schools to serve *all* students.

Chapter 5 describes how students grow and develop, the advantages and disadvantages they bring with them to school, and how they appear to teachers on a day-to-day basis.

It notes that schools—out of necessity—artificially categorize students in efforts to serve all of them appropriately.

Chapter 6 explains theories of learning and how those theories guide classroom practice.

Chapter 7 puts ideas about the purposes of schools, the differences among students, and the learning process together. It analyzes the ways in which schools try to accomplish their purposes with the students they are expected to serve.

When you finish each chapter, you should have an understanding of the general concepts listed here and should have begun to develop the skills noted.

CHAPTER 5
Students Are Alike, but Not the Same

General Concepts

- Although students share some characteristics, each is unique.

- Because students are different in so many ways, teachers and schools need to know about their individual strengths and weaknesses in order to teach them appropriately.

- Because students are different, teachers categorize them according to certain characteristics; although the practice is often useful, it can harm children and must be done carefully.

- Categorizing students is an artificial procedure followed by schools and teachers; students are not born in categories.

- In addition to their personal qualifications, students possess varying levels of intellectual, educational, personal, economic, social, and cultural capital—all of which affect how they learn and how they should be taught.

Skills

- An ability to group students for instruction without overgeneralizing about student similarities and differences

- An ability to match appropriate teaching with individual student strengths and weaknesses

CHAPTER 6
How Students Learn

General Concepts

- Learning theories help explain how people learn and guide teachers in choosing the best way to teach.

- Teachers tend to select learning theories as their guides on the basis of their personal style of teaching and the characteristics of the students they teach.

Skill

- An ability to draw on learning theory to teach students appropriately

CHAPTER 7
Learning for All Students: The Goals of Equity and Excellence

General Concepts

- In recent decades the concepts of equity and excellence have guided schooling in the United States.

- American schools attempt to provide an equal and excellent education for all students in terms of their potential.

- American schools have still not succeeded in reaching the goals of equal and excellent education for all.

Skill

- An ability to combine the ideals of both equity and excellence in establishing goals for teaching and in planning instruction to accomplish those goals

Students Are Alike, but Not the Same

CONTRIBUTING AUTHOR
Penelope H. Brooks

Penelope H. Brooks is the primary author of this chapter. Charles and Lynn Myers provided the first part of the Snapshot and the Student Capital, Reflecting on Practice, and Educational Research sections.

T his chapter describes students in pre-K–12 classrooms from three perspectives. First, it chronicles how students grow and develop from birth through the high school years. Second, it points out that students come to school with different types and amounts of resources or "capital," which they can use to support their learning. Third, it notes that educators group students for teaching purposes and describes the categories that educators often use to characterize students whose special conditions influence how they should be taught—"gifted," "retarded," "disabled," and so forth.

As a brief overview, the chapter necessarily paints pictures of students with a broad brush, one that makes them appear to fit a common pattern when in fact they do not. Every human being is unique. The chapter title emphasizes this fact.

When teachers know how children develop and what causes the changes they experience, they can understand them better and anticipate certain events in their lives. As a result, teachers can better design the physical and social environments of classrooms. They can teach better. Therefore, this chapter summarizes both the cognitive and social-emotional nature of children at four different periods—infancy, early childhood, middle childhood, and adolescence.

The first part of the chapter is about normative development. Then, because no one is exactly "normal," the later parts of the chapter look at differences in students and how those differences affect teaching.

The intricacies of the weave between development and the role of environment are illustrated in the Snapshot and the Reflecting on Practice sections. In the case studies presented, parents, peers, and teachers had significant influence on the students involved—as did the traits and the ages of the students. From these case studies, you can see how students are alike in many ways, and also see how subtle, often chance, interactions affect their lives.

The Educational Research section describes a particular situation in which research data are used to influence policy decisions. The situation involves the issue of whether mildly retarded and other mildly disabled students should be taught in special classes or in regular classrooms.

SNAPSHOT

The Snapshot for this chapter consists of two short case studies.[1] As you read each, consider:

- What special needs do these two children seem to have?
- What could or should their teachers and schools do, or have done, to help them?
- What would you do if you taught the two?

Case Study: William, Sixth Grade

On the first day of school that year, William appeared to have wandered into the sixth grade by mistake. He was small, frail, thin, and pale. He slipped almost unnoticed into the classroom, sat at the back, and never spoke. When the teacher walked toward him, he seemed to cower; and when she asked if he would rather be called Bill, he whispered that he would rather be called William.

William was the second son of a wealthy physician. He had an older brother who was a high school football star, an honors student, and president of his class. William grew up in the care of a sitter. His parents entered him into nursery school when he was three years old, but he cried so much that his parents took him out and put him back with the babysitter. Discipline at home was strict. He spent a great deal of time in his room alone, playing with his dog and his pet turtle and talking to himself.

His family was quite proud of his older brother's accomplishments. They talked of his feats on the football field and took William to the brother's games. William did not appear interested in his brother's activities.

William's parents tried to help him develop other interests. He and his father joined the Boy Scouts, and his father became a scout leader. His father bought him a trumpet, but William did not care about learning to play. Other attempts failed—his father took him fishing and let him

experiment in his workshop. William was not interested in doing those things by himself, and his father did not have the patience to work with William and tolerate his mistakes. By sixth grade, William's parents quit investing time and energy in encouraging him because they thought it was wasted.

In class William was so quiet that it was easy to forget he was there. He was two grade levels behind in reading and writing. Before the fourth grade, teachers thought he was not trying. In the fourth grade, he was tested for learning disability and diagnosed as learning disabled. He was sent to a resource room daily for an hour of reading help. Although he worked diligently at the tasks the teachers gave him, his improvement was not sufficient to show up noticeably on achievement tests.

William's fifth-grade teacher decided that the previous teachers had been too lenient with him because of his family's prominence in the community. She insisted that he complete his work correctly; if not, he was kept in during recess or after school. His parents supported her efforts because they wanted him to eventually get into a good college.

William's performance still did not improve. By the beginning of sixth grade, he was still very shy. He sat quietly at his desk, rarely completed his work, and did not interact with the other children even at recess. His intelligence test (IQ) scores were high, but he showed absolutely no motivation to do anything.

Case Study: Sherry, Eleventh Grade

Sherry had been classified as "gifted" in the fifth grade. She performed well in all her classes and scored high on tests. Learning seemed to come easily to her. She was active socially at school but was also a serious student.

But by the time she had finished ninth grade, Sherry's academic performance was only adequate, mostly C's; and her school behavior was punctuated with mischievous acts and attempts to get out of class to engage in extracurricular activities that were only mildly interesting to her. The pattern continued in later grades. Sherry was extremely popular with her peers but an enigma to her teachers because she tried to get by with minimal effort in class. She seemed to know just how frequently and seriously she could avoid assignments and violate school rules and policies without major consequences. For example, she left the school premises when she thought she would not get caught. If caught, she would think of an excuse that seemed to satisfy the teacher. She and her boyfriend often kissed and hugged each other during classes they had together. On one occasion she sat in his lap when an important visitor came to observe the classroom. For her junior year she signed up for only one solid academic class—a required course in English. The others were classes in which she could get a C almost without trying—commercial art, recording studio, office aids. Sherry's parents were divorced and re-married. Her stepfather bought her a car so that she would not have to rely on her mother for transportation. Her mother, who also worked outside the home, had a great deal of difficulty setting and enforcing rules.

Sherry's life has been very socially oriented. She has been a cheerleader and a member of a high school sorority and other clubs. While in high school she has maintained a C average, but she failed algebra once and had to take it in summer school. She sees very little of her parents because she is constantly on the go.

When the time comes to take college entrance exams, Sherry will have very little mastery of the information and skills tested and will probably perform so poorly that she will not be accepted by any of the colleges to which she intends to apply. She is not concerned, however. She is not sure she wants to go to college anyway, and studying all the time does not appeal to her.

The Nature of Growth and Development

As William and Sherry's cases show, children do not grow and change in a conveniently predictable way. They are not like balloons, which gradually expand in a consistent, even, and symmetrical fashion. Rather, periodic examinations of children show growth and change at uneven rates and in spurts. Furthermore, it seems that a child may have qualitative differences during growth; the little person at age 3 or 7 may seem like someone else at 9 or 12. An obstinate, oppositional child at age 3 may be a thoughtful, cooperative student at 12; a small, frail child at 5 may be a handsome, well-proportioned adolescent at 16; an unmotivated, borderline-passing high school teenager may become a successful engineer or businessperson as an adult.

Gradual, continuous change

Experts in child development are just beginning to understand the dramatic ways in which children change. Sometimes they think of the changes as "stages," but many theorists are reluctant to use the term because it implies a static resting place in development where children stay for a while before they move on. In fact, there are probably no such pauses in development. Instead, the life span of a human being is analogous to the metamorphosis of a caterpillar to a butterfly. Change is continuous over time and consists of many small increments that are often difficult to notice. From one day to the next, it is difficult to tell that something has changed. When enough change has taken place for experts to notice, a new developmental stage is identified.[2]

The role of environment

Most changes in the developmental process are products of interactions with contexts provided by the environment; they do not happen automatically. Language is the best example of this interaction. Infants seemingly have a readiness to learn language. If language-speaking people are present in their environment, there is no way to keep most children from learning the spoken language. If infants are without access to language—either because they are deaf or because no one talks to them—they will not speak.

However, access to language alone is not enough. For instance, isolating children in a room so that they hear only tapes of Shakespearean plays would not teach them language. Language is "taught" by adults and older children interacting verbally and nonverbally with infants. According to language theorists, such "teachers" gradually program the level of difficulty so that they slowly increase the children's use of grammatic forms, vocabulary, and meaning.[3]

The environment plays an important part in shaping an individual's developmental progress, traits, attitudes, motivation, and values; and various elements of the environment can be examined for clues as to their influences on the ways in which people change. One approach to studying development, known as a *dialectical theory*, provides an understanding of the *interactions* (dialogues) between individuals and their environment by identifying four dimensions of these interactions—two personal and two environmental.[4]

Dialectical theory

Dimensions of Interaction between Individuals
and Environment (Dialectical Theory)

Inner Biological
Individual Psychological
Cultural-Sociological
Outer Physical

The *inner biological dimension* refers to physiological maturational changes or health changes within the developing child. These changes are responsible, in part, for many major life changes. For example, leaving home, marrying, and having children are made possible by the biological changes associated with adolescence.

The *individual psychological dimension* concerns what is ordinarily thought of as traits or tendencies. Sociability, shyness, values, sensitivity, and artistic talent are some of the characteristics that change as one gets older. These changes help determine relations between children and parents, husbands and wives, neighbors, classmates, teachers, and students.

Changes in the *cultural-sociological dimension* produce upheavals in people's lives if they change from a minority subculture to a dominant culture. This is especially so if the new dominant culture is quite different from the original cultural heritage. Immigrants entering a country often encounter such problems. Cultural-sociological influences include religion, laws, traditions, and communities.

Finally, the *outer physical dimension* includes such phenomena as climate, natural disasters, and terrain. These factors determine what people do with much of their time—following game animals, farming, and keeping warm or healthy. Changes in these factors—a famine, for example—cause major changes in the way people conduct their lives.

The coordination and *synchrony* in the dialogues among these four dimensions determine an individual's behavior at any given time. When the progressions of change within one or between two dimensions are not synchronized with those in other dimensions, a crisis takes place; examples would include pregnancy before physical or psychological maturity or a forced change from elementary to middle school before psychological or physical readiness.

Synchrony among dimensions

Crises are not necessarily negative events, but they usually do introduce upheaval as children or students struggle to reestablish some form of synchrony within the four dimensions. Thus, major events such as parental divorce, hurricanes, or serious illness can be crises in that they force children to renegotiate the dialogue they had with other aspects of their lives at the same time that they deal with the changes brought about more directly by the catastrophe.

The inner psychological dimension of development

Emphasis in the first part of this chapter is on the inner psychological dimension of change and development; and from that perspective, you will look at the ways in which experience and behavior change as a result of alterations in the other dimensions. In order to study child development closely, the inner psychological dimension is subdivided into two areas that will be discussed at some length: (1) the perceptual-cognitive-moral domains of growth and (2) the social-emotional or personality domains. The first refers to the ability of children to detect, transform, manipulate, and apply information from the environment. The second refers to two types of children's understandings—their understanding of their feelings and how they act on them and their understanding of their relationships with other children and with adults.

Two areas

Before you read the rest of this chapter, think for a moment about your own development.

- How have you changed since you started kindergarten—physically, cognitively, psychologically?
- What events or times in your life seem to be most significant in their effects on your development?
- Why were these significant?

Once you have done this, think of others who attended the same elementary and/or secondary school as you did, particularly those who were noticeably different from you. Ask the same three questions about them, and compare how you and those others developed and "turned out" so far in your lives. What are the similarities? What are the differences?

Perceptual-Cognitive-Moral Domains of Development

As children change and develop in response to interaction with their environment, they experience perceptive, cognitive, and moral growth. They develop refined abilities to detect, transform, manipulate, and apply information from the environment. This section explains how that growth takes place.

Perceptual Development

When we see things or events; hear sounds; feel surfaces, textures, or movement; smell odors; taste flavors; and detect the direction of gravity, we are involved in perception. We are noticing elements of our environment and gathering information from it. We acquire a great deal of information through perception.

When most adults interact with babies, they act as if the babies see the same things that they do. For example, parents usually believe that babies see faces, pets, and mobiles. Similarly, many beginning teachers believe that young school-age children see letters, words, and print and that they are aware of their own behavior, much as adults are. These beliefs are, in fact, wrong. The work of Eleanor and James Gibson shows us that children's perception is initially disorganized, inefficient, and undifferentiated.[5]

Think for a moment of the first time you looked at a night sky full of stars, examined a dental X-ray, ran your fingers over some Braille forms, watched someone communicate in American Sign Language, or listened to a symphony. At those times, you probably were in awe of someone who could distinguish constellations, read the dental X-ray, identify the Braille message, interpret the signing, or explain the symphony to you. Yet, the main difference between you and the "experts" was simply one of experience with the medium. They had already had learning experiences that you had not yet confronted. That type of learning has been called *perceptual learning*, and consists of learning to see, smell, feel, or hear. In a more technical phrase, it is "the education of attention."

For both babies and adults, the environment provides the same information. When a baby is shown the face of an unfamiliar person, that baby has available the same information available to an adult. However, the baby and the adult differ in the information they pick up. In other words, the baby and the adult differ in the ways they look at things, even though they look at the same things. Eleanor Gibson has delineated four ways in which young children differ from adults, ways in which naïveté differs from expertise.[6]

First, perceptual activity, such as looking and listening, becomes more searching and less captive as people develop. The differences can be illustrated if you think of someone flipping through magazines while waiting in an office reception room. That person's attention can be said to be *captive*—held by the objects being looked at, captured by the headlines, the graphics, and the highlighted displays. Compare flipping through a magazine with looking for a particular quotation or statistic in a magazine. In verbal shorthand, we contrast the two approaches by thinking of the first perception as looking *at* and the second as looking *for*. The distinction is one way to characterize the difference between the novice and the expert in many areas of experience—games, sports, art, music, and classroom activities. (Chapter 2 illustrated this difference in ways of looking in its description of the difference between inexperienced and expert observers' views of classroom activities.)

Second, perceptual learning consists of a change from unsystematic to systematic search. As children learn what to search for in the environment, they become more systematic in the search process. If they are given the task of looking for a word or a letter on a page, at first their eyes wander all over the page. With practice and perhaps instruction, their eyes begin to scan in a more orderly fashion, possibly from left to right and top to bottom, so that no area is covered twice while others are missed.

Third, perceptual learning consists of more and more specificity of information detection. For instance, when people first see identical twins, they look for differences between the twins so that they can tell them apart. With exposure to the twins, subtle aspects of their appearance or manner seem to become more noticeable, so that after a while, the twins no longer look as much alike as they did at first. This detection of details or differences with experience is one of the changes that are part of perceptual learning.

Fourth, perceptual learning includes an increasing ability to ignore irrelevant information. For example, when children learn to read different styles of type and handwriting, they have learned to ignore some differences and pick out what does

Becoming an expert at looking, hearing, and feeling

From looking at to looking for

Systematic searching

Detecting details

Ignoring irrelevant information

not vary across all examples. This is a formidable task for children who face it for the first time. They have to sort out many features of letters—straight lines versus curved lines, closed forms versus open forms, diagonals, horizontals, and verticals.[7]

Cognitive Development: Piagetian Stages

Educators know that most children learn to think as they develop, but they are not clear about what "learning to think" involves. They are not sure what thinking is or how people learn to do it, and they are further unsure where perceptual processes leave off and cognitive processes begin. One way to think of the difference between perception and cognition is to define *perception* as the detection of information and *cognition* as the transformation and manipulation of that information. This chapter uses that distinction.

Jean Piaget, 1876–1980

The study of cognition in children has been dominated by one approach for the last quarter of a century—the approach begun and elaborated by Jean Piaget, a Swiss psychologist. Because Piaget's ideas are so dominant in explaining students' development, his thinking is described in some detail here.

Adaptation in stages

Piaget viewed cognitive development as a form of biological adaptation. Species adapt to their environment by changing their behavior, not just their anatomy and physiology. Accordingly, as children grow, they become exposed to more of their environment; and as they perceive more of that world around them, they adapt to it by changing in certain ways. These changes occur over time as the children develop, and they occur in stages—stages that come about in response to interactions with the environment. The interchange between person and environment has two aspects—assimilation and accommodation. *Assimilation* occurs when children react to something new by finding in it something with which they are already familiar. *Accommodation* happens when children change their cognitive structure or knowledge to embrace the new facets of the encounter.

Assimilation and accommodation

According to Piagetian thinking, the way that assimilation and accommodation develop in children can be divided into four major stages of development: sensorimotor, preoperational, concrete operations, and formal operations.[8] See Table 5-1.

Sensorimotor Stage (Roughly Birth to 24 Months)

Change in motor and sensory acts

The sensorimotor period is a time of change in motor and sensory acts. Sensorimotor activities begin with single acts, such as looking, sucking, reaching, and grasping, and develop toward intentional, organized, flexible actions such as the entire sequence of reaching for an object, grasping it, and bringing it to the mouth. Cognitive psychologists now believe there are four or possibly five substages in the sensorimotor period. The four substages are typically identified as follows:[9]

1. the newborn period (until about 2 months), in which infants respond primarily to internal systems
2. the subjectivity period (until about 8 months), in which infants more readily respond to external stimuli but fail to separate objects in the environment from their own actions
3. the period involving the separation of means from ends (after about 8 months), in which infants learn that some actions have purposes
4. the period involving relationships between separate entities (after about 13 months), in which infants see objects as independent of actions that use them but also see that the two are related.

TABLE 5-1   Piagetian Stages of Development

Age	Stage	Characteristics of the Child
Birth to 2 years	Sensorimotor	Learns about the world through assimilation and accommodation Thinks "experimentally" as a "little scientist" Develops the concept of object permanence Begins to acquire language
2–7 years	Preoperational	Develops language Exhibits egocentrism Lacks the concept of conservation
7–11 years	Concrete operational	Develops a number of mental operations, including (1) reversing, (2) decentering, (3) conserving, (4) adding and subtracting, (5) ordering and sequencing, (6) classifying Controls own behavior
11–14 years	Formal operational	Begins more complex moral thinking Starts thinking abstractly and hypothetically Begins reasoning scientifically Exhibits adolescent egocentrism

The sensorimotor period culminates with the child's ability to represent actions internally. For example, infants no longer just *do;* they also have a primitive form of knowing.[10]

Preoperational Stage (2 to 7 Years)

Manipulating symbols

The next task for children is to learn to manipulate their newly acquired *symbols* (signals, language) or *representations* (images). At this point, the world a child has experienced is disorganized—disorganized in a way that you can probably understand easily if you can remember events that occurred when you were three, four, or five years old. The memories that you still have of these years probably consist of snippets—an image of a room, a person saying something, a feeling. There are no precursors and consequences of events, no sequence to the events. These gaps in memory are not necessarily faults of memory but might be simply reflections of your lack of cognitive skills at the time the experiences occurred. You were not able at that time to organize the original experience so that you can now remember all its context.

Concrete Operational Stage (7 to 11 Years)

The next few years witness several major related but *separable intellectual accomplishments:* (1) decentering, (2) the development of mental operations to apply to representations, and (3) the ability to control one's behavior.

Decentering

The first major intellectual accomplishment, that of *decentering,* "undoes" something that is characteristic of young children's thought. When solving problems, children tend to "center," or focus, on one aspect of a problem, usually a very

FIGURE 5-1 Piaget liquid conversion problem. Even though young children see liquid being poured from one of the shorter (and wider) glasses, they frequently say there is more liquid in the taller (and slimmer) glass. They do not "connect" the fact that the liquid just came from the other glass.

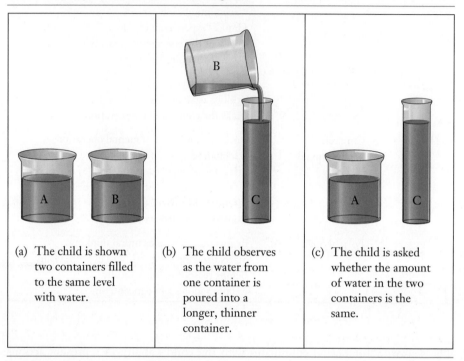

(a) The child is shown two containers filled to the same level with water.

(b) The child observes as the water from one container is poured into a longer, thinner container.

(c) The child is asked whether the amount of water in the two containers is the same.

SOURCE: From Goldstein, *Psychology* (Brooks/Cole, 1994).

visible aspect. Consider, for example, the famous Piagetian liquid conservation problem, shown in Figure 5-1.

1. Two identical glasses are filled to the same height with liquid.
2. When asked, a child will agree that the two glasses have the same amount of liquid.
3. The liquid in one glass is poured into a taller, thinner container in full view of the young child.
4. The child is then asked to say whether the two containers still have the same amount of liquid or whether one has more than the other.
5. The young child almost invariably says that the tall, thin container now has more liquid. When asked "Why?" or "How do you know?" the child almost always answers that the one picked is taller. The child almost never notes that the container is also thinner.

This is an example of *centering* because the child is focused on one dimension of the problem—in this case, the tallness of the second container—to the exclusion of other dimensions. Centering prevents children from considering several characteristics simultaneously because the child's attention is captured by the most salient aspect of the objects.

The ability to consider more than one aspect of a problem means that a child has begun decentering. This process is evidenced in many ways—not judging other people as all bad or all good, making judgments about whether two things—two letters of the alphabet, for example—are alike or different.

A second major intellectual accomplishment of the concrete operational stage, that of *developing mental operations*, allows representations (maps, symbols) to be organized and manipulated. Three mental operations of this type are (1) adding and subtracting, (2) ordering, and (3) classifying.

Developing mental operations

The mental operations of adding and subtracting allow children to solve the conservation problem that was illustrated in Figure 5-1. For children to know that the tall, slender glass contains the same amount of liquid as the original glass, they must *add* to account for the new height of liquid and *subtract* to account for the new diameter. Both calculations are necessary for the child to arrive at the "no change" answer because the two calculations cancel each other out.

The addition and subtraction operations have to be learned with respect to each dimension of objects—weight, area, amount, number. Substances that are continuous, like liquids, mud, wood, clay, or paint, are subject to one set of rules—known as *conservation of continuous quantity*—while those that are discrete (countable) are subject to a slightly different set of rules—known as *conservation of number*. Part of what children must learn is the degree to which substances can be changed and still keep the same identity or the same quantity.

A second mental operation that children learn to perform during the concrete operational stage is *ordering* objects along some dimension such as height, overall size, length, and darkness. This ability is demonstrated when children can order a series of sticks or strips of paper in increasing or decreasing length. To solve these problems of series, children have to understand that an object like a stick can play two roles at the same time; it can be longer than a shorter stick and shorter than a longer stick. Understanding both roles is necessary to see how a stick fits into its proper place in a *sequence*. This ability is necessary to understanding ordinal and interval scales based on increasing amounts—age, money, inches, pounds.

A third mental operation learned during the concrete operational stage is that of *classifying*. Classifying is the organization of objects and events into categories that help determine their meaning. Consider the following information made available to a young child:

> Fluff is the family dog. There are lots of dogs in the neighborhood. There are also deer, snakes, cows, birds, skunks, and horses in the neighborhood. Butch is the family cat. All of these are animals. Snakes are at the zoo. Giraffes, polar bears, and lions are also at the zoo.

How can the child organize all this information? It is highly disorganized as presented here; and no particular statement has a great deal of meaning. From these randomly available statements, however, children could produce the organized hierarchy shown in Figure 5-2.

As a result, when a particular animal is mentioned, the whole hierarchy is part of the meaning of the word. For example, Stripes, an aunt's cat, is probably a pet that lives at her house, is not a dog but is an animal. The classification scheme helps children identify what something is *not* as well as what something *is*.

A third major intellectual accomplishment of the concrete operational stage includes the ability to control one's own behavior—to tell oneself what to do and to obey that internal personal directive. This accomplishment is evidenced by children's increasing compliance to norms, by their ability to sit quietly, and by their

Controlling one's behavior

FIGURE 5-2   A representation of how a child might organize "animals" while using the classifying mental operation.

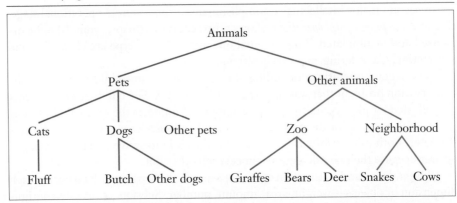

tendencies to reflect before acting. The process of *self-regulation* begins, according to Lev Vygotsky, in the form of commands or requests from other people—"Sit down." "Come here." "Bring Mommy her purse."[11] Children then learn to talk aloud to themselves; and finally, the language becomes internalized and behavior appears to be self-regulated, or controlled. Self-regulation is seen explicitly when children restrain themselves from doing something in order to get a reward later and when they talk aloud to themselves while solving problems.[12]

Formal Operational Stage (11 to 14 Years)

Hypothetical thinking

The thinking of adolescents differs from that of younger children in three ways: it can be hypothetical, it can consider several factors at once, and it can be considerably more systematic than at earlier stages. To think hypothetically means to think about possibilities—what might be. Because of the new ability to think about possibilities, adolescent thought appears idealistic and undeterred by practical considerations. Students at this stage can imagine themselves in many roles. They can create solutions to world problems. Often their images and solutions are unrealistic, however, because in the process of fantasizing them, young adolescents cannot consider the real obstacles to realizing them. For example, few know how much work it takes to become a ballet dancer, and almost none can understand the competing pressures involved in such political acts as peace treaties and negotiations for hostage release.

Reality gradually appears as part of adolescents' thinking, as they gain more experience in the activities they are thinking about and as they are able to take into account additional aspects of the activity. For example, they begin to realize that being an Olympic gold medalist involves not only glory but also hard work, long hours, not eating junk food, not taking trips to the beach, and not watching TV. It involves personal and financial sacrifice as well as personal commitment.

Adolescents also become capable of approaching problems through *systematic thought.* For example, in selecting answers on a test, they are able to consider one aspect of a problem at a time. If the problem requires varying two factors (for example, speed and distance), adolescents can learn to hold one constant while varying the other in order to find out how the two factors are related. The degree to which such a systematic approach carries over into other areas of adolescents' or adults' lives is not clear. At least, they have the capacity to solve problems systematically. Whether they use it in a desirable way may often be a matter of training and experience.

Development of Moral Reasoning

Just as children learn to reason about the physical environment of objects and their motion, they also learn to reason about human behavior. One of the most intriguing aspects of human behavior that children must learn about is moral behavior. Underlying moral behavior, however, are reasoning processes that may parallel general cognitive development.

If you have ever watched children learn to play games, you have probably noticed that very young children (preschool age) seldom understand the rules of games in the same way that adults do. For young children, rules are something that can be used at will, often only if they benefit the game player. They can be insisted upon, and they can easily be forgotten.

Then, some time around the age of 5, children almost suddenly begin to regard rules as sacred, written in stone, and made by some higher authority that "bestows" unchangeable rules upon a game. Indeed, to children at this age, a game and its rules are synonymous. Breaking the rules is bad, and following the rules is good. The essence of goodness, to them, is conformity and obeying rules.

At about age 8, many children begin to understand the role of rules in games and become more willing to change rules to adapt to situations. They start to see the purpose behind the rules and realize that it is important. For example, when they play scrub baseball games and pickup basketball, they adjust the rules to the situation. In other activities such as jacks, jump rope, hopscotch, and card games, they can see that rules have variations instead of being hard and fast for all occasions.

This developmental aspect of children's exceptions of rules was first noted by

Stage theories of moral reasoning suggest that the way children treat the rules of a game depends in part upon their developmental stage.

Jean Piaget, who recognized the pattern by watching children of different ages play marbles and through interviewing them.[13] Later, his ideas about how children view rules were expanded considerably by Lawrence Kohlberg.[14] Kohlberg saw that the rules of a game could be a model of the ways in which children understand other people's behavior. In his research, he and his students read a series of stories to children at different ages and examined their responses to those stories. The stories involved someone's having to make a moral choice. A well-known example is the story of Heinz, whose wife is dying of cancer. She can be saved only by a very expensive drug. He has no money and so cannot buy the drug. One night he breaks into the pharmacy and steals the drug for his wife. After hearing a story like this, children were asked whether it was all right for Heinz to steal the drug. If so, why? If not, why not? Based on children's answers to these questions about the moral dilemmas, Kohlberg distinguished six stages of moral reasoning. See Table 5-2.

TABLE 5-2 Kohlberg's Stages of Moral Development

Levels and Stages	Guides for Reasoning	Examples
Preconventional Level—Self-Interest		
Punishment-obedience	Obey rules to avoid punishment	"If I take the cookie, I'll be sent to my room." "If I rob the store, I'll go to jail."
Reciprocity-needs	Do what will be best for you in return	"If I tell him the answer for the test question, he'll give me answers when I need them." "I should take in his mail while he is away." (He does it for me.)
Conventional Level—Conventional Laws and Values		
Approval of others	Be a good person in the eyes of others	"Good boys don't fight." "They will expect us at church."
Rules—law and order	Do what the law says	"Speeding is against the law." "I shouldn't get on the plane until my row is announced for boarding."
Postconventional or Principled Level—Abstract Moral Principles		
Individual rights and standards	Follow rules and laws that make rational sense, but use own judgment when appropriate	"I'd rather lie than hurt his feelings." "I won't lie to cover for his alcoholism."
Ethical principles	Act according to own conscience based on what you believe is right	"I must convince her that abortion is morally wrong." "It's her body; she has a right to make her own decision."

In the first stage (usually children under age 5), children place a great deal of emphasis on punishment as a consequence of behavior. A child in this stage may say something like "No, Heinz shouldn't steal the medicine. He might get caught and be put in jail." Or, "Yes, he should steal the drug. His wife would get real mad at him and shoot him if he didn't." Note that both answers involve fear of punishment. It is also important to note that both "yes" and "no" answers are given by children. What is important in determining the stage at which the children are operating is the reasoning, the fact that children focused on punishment in their rationale.

Punishment-obedience

Children in the second stage begin to think of their own needs. They may give such answers as "No, he shouldn't steal the drug. If she dies, he can probably get another wife." Or, "Yes, he should steal the drug. He needs his wife to cook for him." Occasionally, children will show some evidence of awareness of reciprocal "backscratching" by answering something like "Yes, he should steal the drug. If he saves his wife, maybe she'll buy him a nice present."

Reciprocity-needs

In the third stage (usually between ages 6 and 10), children show concern for approval of others and for being "good." In answers to the question of whether Heinz should steal the medicine, children in this stage may say, "No, taking the medicine would make the pharmacist very angry." Or they may say, "Yes, he was only trying to make his wife happy."

Approval of others

Reasoning in the fourth stage demonstrates a respect for authority and duty. Children consider laws absolute; they are to be obeyed in all circumstances. Children in this stage might say, "No, he shouldn't steal the medicine because he would be breaking the law. Stealing is wrong." Alternatively, "Yes, he should steal the medicine. It's Heinz's duty to save his wife if he can."

Rules—Law and order

Most educated people probably reach the fifth stage in late adolescence or early adulthood. Reasoning at this stage involves the recognition of a contractual, democratic emphasis. Youth become concerned with individual rights and the general welfare of society. Responses to Heinz's dilemma might range from "No, he shouldn't steal the drug because, although he is desperate, the rights of the druggist must be respected" to "Yes, the druggist owned the drug, but his wife's need for medical care was more important."

Individual rights and standards

The few adults who reach the sixth stage show concern for living up to self-chosen principles such as "the greatest good for the greatest number" or the Golden Rule. For example, those who subscribe to the belief that the value of human life is the primary value would say that only one answer leads to an assignment to Stage 6: "Yes, he should steal the drug to save her life. Human life always takes precedence over property. If he had not taken the drug, he would not have been able to live with himself."

Ethical principles

The stages Kohlberg delineates appear to be good descriptions of the developmental sequence in thinking about moral issues. How people think does not necessarily determine their behavior, however. In the example outlined above, there are six reasons for both behaviors—stealing the drug or not stealing it.

Kohlberg's analysis of moral development has its critics, many of whom make important points. Several point out that Kohlberg's emphasis on the reasoning behind a behavior implies that the morality of an action depends more on the reasoning than on the action. Some have ethical problems with that idea. Another criticism is that by delineating stages, Kohlberg gives a false impression that clear boundaries exist between them. In fact, the stages flow from one into another; many children will answer some questions in the pattern of one stage but answer others as they would in another stage. A more telling recent criticism comes from Carol Gilligan's widely cited *In a Different Voice*.[15] She argues that Kohlberg's hierarchy may apply more to men, who are traditionally reared to be individualistic, assertive, and independent, than to women. (More is explained about this point later in this chapter.) Gilligan says that many women are more concerned than men with harmony in interpersonal relationships. For them, the maintenance of harmony and sensitivity to the needs of others are important determinants of decisions. While this focus on harmony looks like Kohlberg's Stage 3, Gilligan argues that it is in no way a lower stage of reasoning than Stage 4. Therefore, placing it at the lower level than justice implies a gender bias. She says it is a *different* kind of reasoning, but not a lower-level reasoning.

- What do you think of Kohlberg's stages of moral development? Is the reasoning behind moral behavior more important than the action itself?
- Do you agree with Gilligan that the developmental sequence may differ for men and women?

Social-Emotional Domains of Development

Children not only learn to think as they mature, but they also learn how to interact with other people, how to feel, and how to control their feelings in response to the actions of others. Consider the difference between a very young infant who alternates fussiness, sleep, and discovery and a diplomat who reads the behavior of others and very carefully controls his or her own behavior in public so as to convey the appropriate information. At home, the same diplomat may be naturally warm and outgoing, thus demonstrating flexibility in the ability to monitor and control emotions. What happens between infancy and maturity that allows and encourages such complex behavior to develop? Although only a few answers to this question are known, the following pages provide a survey of recent findings concerning this area of development.

Infancy and Early Childhood

When babies are born, they already possess many personality elements, but they learn others in their early years. Parents and other caretakers are dominant figures in this learning process and make many contributions through the preschool period.

As infants develop into the preschool period, venturing into the new world of peer relations, changes take place. These changes provide the opportunity for continued learning and development. Changes that occur during this period are determined in part by (1) what happened during infancy, (2) what the environment is like for the preschool child, and (3) the special developmental characteristics of the preschool child.

Infant temperament

The ability to adjust to the demands of a complex world has its origins in early infancy. Babies are born with at least three different dimensions of temperament—sociability, activity, and emotionality.[16] *Sociability* is the tendency of babies to prefer to interact with adults and to do so positively. Sociable babies smile, cuddle, laugh, and use charming ways to get adults' attention. Unsociable infants are miserly with their smiles and cuddliness; they avoid interactions. Only severely handicapped infants are totally lacking in sociability, but normal infants show a good deal of variation. *Activity*, as it is used here, means simply the extent to which a child is active. Infants vary in their activity level. Obviously, some are alert and in motion more than others. *Emotionality* refers to how easily an infant is upset or angered.

Common sense tells us that parents will want to spend, and will enjoy spending, more time with sociable, moderately active, easygoing infants and that parenting is more difficult with cold, inactive, or easily upset infants. Some infants, then, place greater demands on their parents and other caretakers than others. On the other hand, there is a relationship between mothers' temperament and their infant's temperament. This could be due to the way they interact with each other or to inherited characteristics.[17]

Caretakers, in turn, vary in their willingness and abilities to interact supportively with their infants. Those who can adapt their interactions to take into account the baby's individual eccentricities while still maintaining a consistent, nurturing, and interactive environment do their share toward launching appropriately adjusted infants. In fact, such caretakers foster in infants a basic trust in the events of the world.

Social contexts

The way caretakers engage infants in social interactions have been likened to a *conversational dance* or to *turn taking*, and they prompt in these infants the beginnings of social understanding. For example, when caretakers talk to babies and wait for the babies to respond by cooing, laughing, or wiggling, they are teaching the babies to maintain a conversation by taking turns and attending expectantly to the adult.

When infants need to know something—for example, the meaning of an unfamiliar event, such as a visit with Santa Claus—they have a person they can look to for information about what is happening and how they are supposed to react. This dependency is a product of many caretaking events over time, such as feeding, diapering, and conversational dialogues between the caretaker and the infant. The synchrony between infants and caretakers and success of these events depends on the ability and willingness of both parties to engage themselves in the conversation. Either a sick or disturbed infant or a chronically sick or disturbed caretaker can disrupt the dialogue to the extent that the infant's intellectual and social-emotional progress is seriously impaired.

Infants who possess a sense of trust in the adults with whom they interact are better able to take on the challenges of early-childhood and preschool experiences than are children whose infancies have lacked the supportive exchange that engenders trust. Early-childhood challenges include the broadening of the child's social sphere and the learning of the complicated rules associated with relations with peers, adults, and, perhaps, younger siblings.[18]

Physical contexts

At the same time that social contexts expand, physical contexts also expand into new realms—day care, birthday parties, car seats without restraining devices, grocery stores viewed from the floor rather than the seat in the grocery cart, other people's homes, nursery school, and kindergarten. Adjustment to this myriad of new experiences depends on a number of factors, but two are especially important: (1) having dedicated adults around as models and guides, and (2) the similarity of new contexts and experiences to familiar ones.

Adult reactions to any situation provide information about that situation to children. Adult reactions help children interpret situations, assigning them such values as threatening, matter-of-fact, or interesting. For example, adults demonstrate a variety of responses to threat—expression, reason, flight, or passivity. They demonstrate how to behave at numerous social occasions, such as football games, formal dinners, and dental checkups. They also tell children what to feel and how to behave—to be happy at others' good fortune, not to fight at a birthday party, and to act pleased when other children receive desirable birthday presents.

Self-control

Children internalize many of these instructions and admonitions over a period of time, thus forming the basis of self-regulatory control. Therefore, children appear at the school's doorstep with a wide variety of amounts and kinds of internalized rules and expectations. A child from a disorganized home or a home in which he or she has been overindulged may not understand the need for rules and may have a difficult time learning to follow them. "Why take turns?" "Why not shout?" "Why not run?" "Why not throw food?" "Why not hit?" "I do it at home." Also, the kinds of rules children conform to at home or in the neighborhood may not apply at school. Saying grace before meals may be common practice at home but difficult to manage at school. Water pistols may be allowed in the neighborhood but not at school. If the home and school environments are disparate, children cannot apply what they have learned at home to the new school context. As a result some children have trouble adjusting to school.

Middle Childhood

Middle childhood, roughly equivalent to grades 1 through 4, is often thought of as a period of inertia. Already during early childhood the speed and direction of a child's development were established, and now the child is coasting. One reason for this belief is that middle childhood encompasses no apparent sudden dramatic biological changes such as birth; instead it is characterized by rather smooth transitions. However, the smooth surface belies some very important social changes in social behavior, social cognition, and self-concept.

Social behavior

Children in middle childhood experience changes in their *social behavior* for a variety of reasons and in different dimensions. The sphere, or environment, in which they live expands. They assume more and different roles within the family. They develop strong and changing gender identifications. They establish new peer relationships, and group associations and popularity become much more important than they have been to date.

Social environment

It should come as no surprise that the social environment—parents, siblings, teachers, extended families—has tremendous influence on children. Directly and indirectly, these elements of the environment subtly control the course and rate of development. They do so by controlling the space in which the children act and what the children do in that space. Parents fence yards and provide toys, smile at some behaviors and scold others. Siblings expect some interactions and reject others, encourage some actions and tell their parents about others. Grandparents hug children sometimes and ignore them at others. Schools fence playgrounds and provide books and playground equipment, promote some activities, and prohibit or restrict others.

The conversational dance mentioned in the section on infants continues as children get older—but the roles given to children by parents, other caretakers, and teachers gets larger and larger. This expansion is intentional, the goal being to enable the children to think and behave independently in a mature and intelligent manner. Assignments, questions, and prompts are designed to lead children gradually toward this goal.

Vygotsky has identified an area of growth between a child's developmental
status at a particular time and what it could become with guidance as the *zone of
proximal development* (ZPD).[19] Ideally, all instruction should be aimed in this area;
but in reality, such precision is difficult for caretakers and teachers, especially if they
are instructing several children at different levels with varying ZPDs. William in
the Snapshot at the beginning of this chapter had parents who did not carry out
their interactions within William's zone of proximal development. Instead, they expected William to learn what his brother or father could master—sports, music,
electronics—and he was to do it on his own. When this did not happen, his father
got angry or changed the activity rather than interacting with his son in a more
appropriate activity or at a more appropriate level.

ZPD

Children assume different roles within their families, and as they develop and
interact with other family members, these roles evolve. For instance, the stereotypes
of firstborn or only children as more achievement-oriented and successful than
later-born children are not altogether wrong. In contrast, a second child might assume a more sociable, well-liked role; a third might be studious; another an isolate;
and another an irresponsible "black sheep." (Sherry, described in the Snapshot, was
a second child.) Later-borns are influenced by older siblings, and the nature of that
influence depends partly on the personality and gender of the older child as well as
the spacing between the siblings. For example, a young male may act more aggressive if he has older sisters, a strategy that might or might not be successful with big
brothers.[20]

Roles in families

The interactions of children with peers are gender-related, a point that is
discussed in some detail later in the chapter. However, it should be noted here that,
in grade school, children prefer same-sex friendships and groups. These peer affiliations serve several functions—companionship, a conduit of new information
(about sex, drugs, weapons, games), an audience for trying out new behavior (curs-
ing, rebellion), a source for expanding one's repertoire of jokes and riddles, a source
of items for collections, an environment in which to learn rules and the conse-

Gender-related interactions

*Did you favor same-sex
friendships in grade school?
How did these relationships
contribute to your learning
of "gender-appropriate"
behavior?*

MISS PEACH   © Mell Lazarus. By permission of Mell Lazarus and Creators Syndicate.

quences of breaking them ("Don't tell!" "Don't be a teacher's pet."). One of the most important functions of the peer group is to reinforce gender-appropriate behavior.[21]

Peer relationships

The status of the peer group and of a child within it depends on several characteristics of the individual child. For example, we know that physical attractiveness is one of the major determinants of status. Less-attractive children tend to have lower peer status and also more behavior problems than attractive ones. We also know that low peer status and behavior problems are often related, but we are not sure about the causes. Are both caused by the same social conditions, do the behavior problems cause the low status, or does the low status cause the behavior problems? This question is clearly analogous to the chicken-egg question. Being ugly may elicit ridicule, which produces low self-esteem, which produces problem behavior, which produces more negative reactions from peers, and so on. The cycle may continue as long as a child is in school.

However, attractiveness is not the only avenue to popularity in middle childhood. Popular children seem to have better social skills—for example, their ability to "read" a social situation before jumping into it. They are also likely to respond positively to other children who initiate contact. They are less likely than less popular children to reject others. They recognize implicitly that friendship is a long-term matter of trust and mutual understanding rather than a momentary agreement. Some of the other factors obviously involved in status are skill in sports, father's and/or mother's role in the community, status of siblings, and performance in school.

Social cognition

In addition to experiencing changes in their social environment, middle-childhood children develop *social cognition*. That is, they begin to learn rules about social relationships, a complex process that continues through adulthood. Because children are a part of the social environment of others, they affect what happens to others, and others affect what happens to them. Therefore, how children interact with these "others" is important to them. The behavior of children toward other children and adults is partially a product of their knowledge of social interactions in general and their knowledge of the motivations behind a particular other's behavior.

Self-concept

A third critical social change during middle childhood occurs in children's *self-concepts*, or beliefs about themselves. This change, as with the other changes, comes in response to the social environment. In short, children's concepts of themselves are also based in part on reactions of their immediate social environment to their behavior. That is, they view themselves as competent or incompetent individuals as a result of the extent to which they succeed or fail in their experiences. These experiences, in turn, help determine how willing they will be to risk failure in order to achieve success, how they will react to failure, and how persistent they will be in the face of difficulty.

MISS PEACH   © Mell Lazarus. By permission of Mell Lazarus and Creators Syndicate.

For example, in testing situations, children given easily solvable problems followed by more difficult problems will usually try to succeed with the more difficult problems. On the other hand, children given unsolvable problems to work first, followed by solvable but difficult problems, are more likely to fail at the later problems just as they did at the first. According to some investigators, this happens because children in the latter situation have learned to be helpless from their previous failures and are exhibiting a state called *learned helplessness*.

Learned helplessness

This notion of learned helplessness has been used as a partial explanation for some girls' seeing themselves as more helpless than boys in school. In a research project aimed at isolating sources of feelings of helplessness, Carol S. Dweck and her colleagues examined the feedback given to children in school.[22] She found that early in school, girls experience more success than boys and are criticized less. But she also found that the negative feedback that does occur is different for boys than for girls. The criticism directed at boys in those early years was mostly for conduct. In general, only about one-third of the criticism of boys was for intellectual misdemeanors.

On the other hand, 88 percent of teachers' criticisms directed at girls was for intellectual behavior. In other words, the criticism of girls focused on inadequate academic achievement and thus was more clearly a message about academic failure than was the more diffuse criticism boys receive. When girls were criticized, it was because of poor thinking, wrong answers, and so forth. Dweck also found that boys were more likely to be given positive feedback for the quality of their intellectual work in the classroom than were girls. These conclusions seem to indicate that many girls develop learned helplessness from negative feedback accumulated over time in the classroom and, therefore, experience declining interest in intellectual activities over the middle-childhood years.

Gender-related expectations

An element in the social environment of school-age children that has a powerful effect on self-concept is the fact that they get tested. This means they face structured and obvious chances to succeed and to fail. They must adapt to the situation and cope with the threat.

A factor that contributes to the way in which children cope with potential failure involves the circumstances to which they attribute the failure. Children can attribute *failure* to bad luck, to tasks that are too hard, or to their own inadequacies. Similarly, they can attribute *success* to luck, to their hard work, to their ability, or to some combination of factors. Children who believe that effort and ability are important to success and that luck and lack of effort contribute to failure are more likely to be achievers. But we may wonder where these attributions come from. Psychologists have not yet identified all the sources, but there is a consensus that they come from the hundreds of interactions with parents, caretakers, siblings, peers, and other significant people in children's lives—including teachers. (More

Coping with failure

explanation is provided on this point in the "Expectations and Attributions" section of this chapter.)

Adolescence

Along with infancy, adolescence is one of the two periods of the most dramatic change in social and emotional development. It is especially challenging because growth rates are uneven, and wide ranges of social behaviors are suddenly open to adolescents for the first time. Adolescents are no longer impaired by immature motor development or dependency on their parents. Society begins to expect maturity and, in turn, allows adolescents access to some of the freedoms (and related responsibilities) that adults have. But not all adolescents are equally prepared to encounter these freedoms and responsibilities.

Coping behaviors

As adolescents face their newly available freedoms, they display various types of *coping behaviors*—among them, egocentrism, the personal fable, and identity seeking. It is important to remember, however, that although the coping behaviors of adolescents follow common patterns, the individual experiences of each adolescent are different. Because growth is uneven during adolescence, some individuals have finished their pubescent growth spurt while others have not yet begun it. Although all adolescents experience changes in sexual characteristics and feelings and are affected greatly by them, these changes appear according to a schedule that has lain latent in each individual's genes for years. Although each adolescent's changes appear in approximately the same order, the timetable is different for everyone. Of course, the social-emotional changes are related to concomitant physical changes, and the interaction of the two further complicates the whole developmental process. As a result, adolescents often face major personality-social crises.[23]

Egocentrism

Adolescence is a period of increased self-consciousness, and people in this age range often engage in activities they never dreamed of in earlier years. The self-consciousness is often referred to as *egocentrism*, and the experimenting with different behavior is called *identity seeking*. The self-consciousness, or egocentrism, is characterized by the belief that other people are preoccupied with the adolescent's own appearance. This, then, often leads to a subsequent belief that others see the same things in individual adolescents as they see in themselves—the zits, the crooked nose, the soiled spot on the cuff of the blouse, the wrong brand name on the shoes. This imaginary audience that is believed to scrutinize the adolescent so carefully becomes all-knowing and ever present—always in judgment and always determining behavior.[24]

Personal fable

Consistent with this sensitivity to one's appearance is a second adolescent phenomenon that Elkind has labeled the "personal fable."[25] The *personal fable* is manifested in the adolescent's belief that he or she has unique emotional experiences and that these experiences are important to everyone else. Unfortunate events that happen to everyone else, then, cannot happen to the adolescent. It is other people who get pregnant, have car accidents, and get caught stealing. The personal fable begins with the knowledge that unfortunate things happen to others and that those "others" are like me; but the adolescent fails to finish the equation: *Therefore, those things can happen to me.*

Identity seeking

Identity seeking emerges from adolescents' growing sense of potency and independence. Many develop the idea that they can think better than adults—especially their parents and teachers. As adolescents they know what they are not, what they do not want, and that they do not want to be like the adults around them, but they often do not know what they *are* or what they *want to be*. This lack of definition results in a search for an identity or identities.

Affiliations with different groups are formed and then dissolved. They are frequently based on attention-attracting or status factors and may lead the newcomers into activities they would not ordinarily engage in (drinking beer, swallowing live salamanders, sexual experimentation) or into activities that are acceptable to their parents ("wholesome" social fellowship, respected athletic participation, health-oriented activities). These affiliations lend their identities to the novices, who can say, "I'm a Delta Phi"; "I'm a discus thrower"; "I'm liked by others"; "I'm accepted"; or "I belong." Initially, most of this sort of behavior begins as an attempt by the adolescent to be like and to be accepted by members of a group whose identity he or she is seeking. If such an identity involves drug or alcohol use, then drinking and drug use may take on such importance that they become the dominant force in the adolescent's life. The same is true if the identity involves team sports, running, dramatics, or church youth-group participation. At this point, think again about Sherry in the Snapshot. Might group affiliation needs explain some of her behavior?

Group affiliation

Social-Cultural Variations among Students

Even though students develop along consistent patterns, they arrive at school with a variety of strengths and weaknesses, and those variations affect how they learn. Schools try to accommodate those strengths and weaknesses among their students, and the extent to which they are able to do so has a direct bearing on individual student success. Three types of social-cultural differences that teachers need to keep in mind involve student capital, expectations and attributions, and gender.

Student Capital

Economists use the term *capital* to denote the money, equipment, facilities, and other materials that businesses use to produce the goods and services they sell. That idea can be applied to schools as well. When it is, the term *school capital* denotes the resources that communities need to supply to schools in order to provide for the education of the students who attend them: adequate buildings, heating, electricity, furniture, books, instructional supplies, a teaching staff, custodians, and money to pay for these and the other things needed to educate students appropriately. In essence, it is the "stuff" that schools need if good teachers are to be available and able to teach well. Different communities and schools have varying amounts of capital to be devoted to the learning they expect to take place.

The economists' concept of capital can also be applied to students; and, when it is, the term is used to describe resources that individual students need to possess personally or have access to in order to learn: resources in the form of previously learned knowledge and skills and other attributes on which they can build their continuing learning. For example, very young children need at least a minimum level of language ability to understand their teachers and to do their lessons; and content taught at nearly every grade level assumes that students have mastered prerequisite ideas and skills on which new instruction is based. For example, students need to know numbers in order to count; they need to comprehend abstract ideas in order to formulate hypotheses; they need some degree of self-confidence in order to lead study groups; they need money to buy books; and they need the support of family and friends to face personal challenges at school.

Student capital can be categorized as follows:

intellectual capital	personal capital	social capital
educational capital	economic capital	cultural capital

These six categories are presented here as a framework for assessing student strengths and weaknesses; they should also help you keep in mind the fact that teachers must always address a great number of differences among their students. The six categories can be thought of as two sets of three each. The first three are resources that are internal to the students who possess them, and the last three are resources that come from the students' external environment.

Intellectual capital

Intellectual capital refers to the "brain power," or intellectual abilities, that students possess. It consists of those abilities that are defined by the label "IQ." Obviously, some students are "brighter" or more intellectually capable than others, and those who are tend to learn more easily and more quickly.

Educational capital

Educational capital refers to the knowledge, skills, and values that students have already acquired. It is the content they have gained from experiences outside of school and in previous grades and lessons. It differs from intellectual capital because it consists of previous learning rather than an ability to learn. For example, a student who understands addition has more educational capital in terms of arithmetic than one who does not, and the student who does is better prepared to learn multiplication. Or, in terms of skills, a student who can dribble a basketball has more educational capital than one who does not possess that skill, and the more skilled dribbler is better able to play the game.

Personal capital

Personal capital encompasses what is often termed self-confidence, self-assurance, or self-concept. It is the reservoir of personal characteristics and personality traits that leads some students to believe that they can succeed in the face of challenge and, therefore, make them willing to try. All of us know people who are simply more confident or sure of themselves than others, and those individuals seem to accomplish more and to enjoy challenges more than their meeker, more hesitant counterparts. "Big men and women on campus" and "streetwise kids" seem to exhibit an abundance of personal capital in many of their actions and decisions. (The section titled "Expectancies and Attributions" helps explain this concept further.)

Whereas intellectual, educational, and personal capital are internal to students and pertain to resources that students seem to possess as individuals, economic, social, and cultural capital pertain to resources available to students from the external environment in which they live. *Economic capital* refers to the financial means

Economic capital

that help students learn. It is, in fact, not much different from *capital* as economists use the term; but in this case it is limited to financial means regarding education. Simply put, some students and their families have more money than others, and those who have more money to spend on things that affect learning tend to learn better. Some students can afford more nutritious food, better clothes, better health care, more books and magazines, videos, computers, a quiet place to study and sleep, and so forth. Typically, these "better conditions" are related to "higher status" among peers and teachers and tend to correlate with greater success at school.

Social capital

Social capital refers to resources available to students because of the social environment in which they live; that is, the family, circle of friends, neighborhood, and local community-based relationships on which they can rely for nurturing and social support. In a way, it has to do with whom the student knows and who knows the student. Some students have family members, friends, and other advocates who are in position to help them interact successfully with teachers and others in the school community, while other students are less "advantaged." For example, some students have older siblings who attended the same school and helped build ties between the family and the school; some parents are personal friends of teachers, are active in school functions, are well informed about educational issues, are at ease when talking with teachers, and are well known in prestigious ways in the school community. On the other hand, some parents never come to school and would embarrass their children if they did, are uninformed about teaching and schools and inarticulate around educators, and have virtually no social-economic status in the eyes of those who educate their children. Obviously, the students described first have more social capital than do the latter. (James Coleman and his researcher colleagues have been developing the idea of social capital in recent years.[26])

Cultural capital is similar to social capital, but it refers to the broader culture in which students live rather than to their family or local community. For example, many socioeconomic middle-class cultures tend to value schooling, learning, and academic success, whereas some teenage gang cultures have negative biases toward all these. If a particular culture prizes and reinforces learning, its children are more likely to achieve in school than are their counterparts from other cultural groups. This happens because the culture encourages students to approach their studies seriously, to behave appropriately in classes, to do homework as a matter of course, and to study for tests. Conversely, students with less reinforcing cultural backgrounds tend to be less learning-oriented and motivated. (Some aspects of this phenomenon are also explained in Chapter 4.)

Cultural capital

In recent years, significant attention has been devoted to the influence on learning of different American subcultures. Cultures receiving much attention in this regard are Asian American, African American, Native American, and subgroups associated with poverty. Illustrations of the positive impact of cultural capital include the high achievement of many Asian American students, particularly girls, and the impact of specially designed self-concept-reinforcing instructional programs that target young African-American students, particularly young men.

Remember that teachers should not blame students because they come to school with less student capital than some of their peers. It is rarely their fault. They and their families simply have fewer resources on which to build their learning. Therefore, they and their teachers have to work harder for them to succeed.

Don't blame the student

Expectations and Attributions

How individual students view themselves has already been touched on twice in this chapter: first as part of the discussions of "self-concept" and "learned helplessness" in the section on middle childhood and then in the description of "personal capital." Because of the impact that students' perceptions of themselves have on their learning, we return to it again. We do so this time (1) to stress how varied those perceptions can be among students, (2) to provide more detailed information about the phenomenon, and (3) to emphasize that teachers must recognize and make accommodations for these differences.

Explanations of performances

As part of their perceptions of themselves, students make personal assessments of what they are able to do, and these assessments form a basis for what they expect of themselves and the reasons they give for their successes and failures. For example, when students enter a class to take an examination, they usually expect to do either well or poorly; and when they try out for a sport, they expect to either succeed or not make the team. These expectations come from two related sources: (1) their past experience—how they did under similar conditions the last time they took an examination and (2) how they explained their last success or failure as well as all previous successes and failures in similar situations. These variations in *expectations* and *attributions* influence their learning and need to be considered by their teachers.

Causal attribution

Several prominent psychological theorists have proposed that all of us explain our behavior by attributing our success or failure to various causes. This is called *causal attribution*. For example, if you fail an examination, you can say that (1) you just are not very smart, (2) you were not feeling well, (3) the exam was exceptionally hard, or (4) you really did not study very hard. If you attribute your failure to your own lack of intelligence, you are more likely to expect to fail in the future because the lack of intelligence will probably still be there the next time you take an exam. If you attribute your failure to being ill, you will be less likely to expect to fail the next time because being ill is not a permanent condition and will probably not be a factor the next time you take an exam. If you attribute your failure to the exam's being extremely hard, you might expect to do poorly on the same instructor's exam next time, but probably would expect to do better on another instructor's exam. If you attribute your failure to not studying, you will probably expect to do fine on the next exam because you can control your grade by studying. In general, we make four kinds of causal attributions: (1) *stable internal*, such as intelligence; (2) *unstable internal*, such as illness, effort; (3) *stable external*, such as the teacher, the task; (4) *unstable external*, such as luck, family problems.

Attribution theory

One important conclusion to draw from *attribution theory* is that students' understanding of their academic performance is *extremely* important—perhaps more so than the performance itself. Its importance lies in how students account for their performance. Success is not likely to be a motivating experience if students think that it was due to luck, and attributing success to effort or ability is much more likely to assure success in the future. Conversely, if students believe that they cannot succeed no matter how hard they try or how much help they receive, their performance will probably not improve. They simply will not put forth the necessary effort to perform well.

Gender

Perhaps more than any other feature, gender is an individual's most significant characteristic, at least in terms of how the individual is treated by others. Why this is so is not clear, but it may have cultural roots so old that we cannot trace them. Although gender may be less important today than ever, it is a major factor in how people are responded to from the moment of birth. When a baby is born, relatives ask first, "Is it okay?" and then, "What is it?" Subsequently, gifts that celebrate the birth—flowers, cigars, and clothes—are designed specifically for the gender of the baby. Even signs for the parents' door or front lawn proclaim "It's a girl" or "It's a boy."

Infant behavior

Even though male and female babies' anatomies are different, there are no clearly defined sets of boys' *behaviors* and girls' *behaviors* during infancy that are caused by their physical differences. But parents and other adults treat them differently anyway. In the first place, parent perceptions differ depending on the baby's gender: Male babies are viewed by parents as being better coordinated, more alert; girls are seen as softer and more delicate. Parents cuddle girls more than boys and actively play more with boys.

As children grow, their behavior differentiates and begins to imitate gender-role stereotypes. In other words, they behave more and more like other members of their gender. Several theories attempt to explain this process. Cognitive theorists approach the development of gender identity with the concept of *schema*. A *gender schema* is a set of beliefs, concepts, and attributes that one acquires around one's gender. This develops from infancy through to the preschool years and comes from the different ways parents and others treat children of different genders, from different language (he/she, him/her, his/hers, mama/daddy), and from reinforcement and encouragement for behavior consistent with gender. As a child develops a schema for being either a boy or a girl, the child's behavior becomes more consistent with that gender-based self-image. A child then engages in more gender-stereotyped behavior and becomes more comfortable with it; in turn, the child receives more toys and more encouragement for being like a boy or a girl. Increasingly, the schema for one's gender becomes more elaborate.

Gender schema

This is not to say that children's gender-specific behavior has no biological basis, and some psychologists insist that it is hard to explain all gender differences as learned. In any event, there is evidence that many infant boys are more active and aggressive than girls and that they like toys that involve construction and manipulation more than girls do. Also, boys are more likely to create their own structure in

Some biological basis

Why are scenes like this more common among boys than among girls?

play and are less responsive to instructions from adults. Girls, on the other hand, play in a quieter, more cooperative manner and find the rough-and-tumble play of boys, as well as boys' resistance to social influence, frustrating.

Gender-based play

Gender differences in how children play may be the basis of the segregated gender groups that are found during the school years. Segregation by gender begins in the preschool years and becomes more pronounced as children get older. Subcultures develop within the same gender groups. Girls play almost exclusively with one or two friends while boys play in larger groups. The boys engage in rougher games and more competitive activities. They fight more and they engage in more dominance-related interactions. Girls, on the other hand, engage in more cooperative play, take turns with others, and talk about their personal lives more than boys. One theorist, John Archer, believes that girls get so frustrated with boys' play that they seek the play company of other girls, thereby isolating the boys.[27] Only later do boys seem to avoid girls. The explanation for this avoidance includes the loss of power associated with being or acting female. Some support for this idea comes from cross-cultural research findings: Young boys are most likely to try to dissociate themselves from women in societies where the power difference between men and women is the greatest.[28]

Sequential male roles

Deborah S. David and Robert Brannon have delineated the development of males' roles into three stages: (1) avoidance of femininity, (2) the physical role of boyhood, and (3) the adult male role based on achievement.[29] These three stages are viewed as being consecutive, and each is overlaid on the previous one. The avoidance of femininity occurs fairly early, around preschool and in the early school grades. The physical role of boyhood that involves dominance-seeking, rough play, and competitiveness comes next. At the mid-teen age, the third stage, achievement orientation, is superimposed on the other stages. This third stage has evolved only in recent times in Western cultures and apparently has come about because of industrialization, which means that many jobs no longer rely on physical prowess.

Sequential female roles

On the other hand, as girls' roles evolve, girls become increasingly interested in femininity, in dating, and in fashion, as they show a decreasing interest in mathematics, sports, and science. This change seems to be related to biological changes because early-maturing girls show this shift sooner than do later-maturing girls. According to the findings of a longitudinal study carried out in the 1960s and 1970s, there are no gender differences in mathematics achievement at the fifth grade, but after that boys pull ahead of girls.[30] This difference in achievement, then, parallels differences in interest in studying math.

In summary, gender-stereotyped behavior of infants and very young children leads to different play preferences of girls and boys. These play preferences lead boys and girls to segregate themselves into groups that further reinforce gender-typed behavior. This segregation, in turn, leads to elaborate gender-based schema that include preferences for school subjects, sports, leisure-time activities, and other activities.

Categories of Students

As this chapter has emphasized, children can differ in dozens of ways—partly because they are different to begin with, partly because they encounter different experiences as they grow, and partly because of the environmental conditions under which they function at any specific time. So, if they are so different from one another in so many ways, how can we think of such a thing as a normal or "typical" student? The answer, of course, is that there is really no normal or typical group of students. There is, however, a *range* of typical or normal behavior among students that teachers accept, allow for in their classes, and aim their teaching toward. Unfortunately, children who do not fit within the range of normalcy often suffer in classrooms with other children who are "more typical."

"Normal" range

You can get a feel for the difficulties involved in labeling students with the following exercise:

1. Reread the two case studies in the Snapshot at the beginning of this chapter.
2. Provide what you think would be the best possible label for each student.
3. Now think of the ways in which the labels you just thought of might convey impressions about William and Sherry that would *not* be appropriate.

In spite of the potential dangers, educators often group and label students in an effort to match them to the type of instruction considered to be the most appropriate for them. In the process such educators often put a name or label on the specialized needs of some students and then group students by these labels. Although this is usually done with good intentions, many professionals object to such labels or categories because they believe the labels do more harm than good. Those who object believe that labels cause people to behave toward the labeled person in predetermined, stereotyped ways. For example, the fact that some people are labeled "retarded" may influence how other people treat them; it may also affect the way "retarded" people feel about themselves.

Labeling students

Nevertheless, because instruction needs to be tailored to each student, the rest of this chapter examines several categories of students: children on both ends of the intelligence continuum—"gifted" and "retarded," children who have difficulties in learning, those who are emotionally disturbed, those who are physically disabled, and those who are called "average." Figure 5-3 shows a variety of ways in which students are grouped, emphasizing the range within each category.

Categories Based on Intelligence

People are often described in terms of how intelligent they are, and when this happens, adjectives such as "smart," "dumb," and "stupid" are used. Interestingly enough, no one knows what *intelligence* really is. Technically, it refers to scores on intelligence tests, but even the people who have constructed intelligence tests over the years do not know clearly what intelligence is. They have opinions about which abilities are necessary to succeed in school, and they have made up tests that supposedly test those abilities. But since intelligence tests were constructed in the early 1900s, there have been many different opinions and theories about the nature of intelligence. Even as those opinions shifted, however, the old intelligence tests have continued to be used because the scores (IQs) predict success in school fairly well: The lower the IQ, the less well a student tends to do in school.

Intelligence tests

Nevertheless, if everyone in the United States were tested on one of the most frequently used intelligence tests—the Stanford-Binet and the WISC-R—half of the population would score within a very narrow range, between 90 and 110. (The average score on both tests is 100; the maximum possible is 200.) Extremely high scores and extremely low scores are very rare. The theoretical distribution of intelligence scores is shown in Figure 5-4.

FIGURE 5-3 Different continua people use when labeling students. It is important to remember that students at the extremes of each continuum differ only by degree from other students on the same continuum.

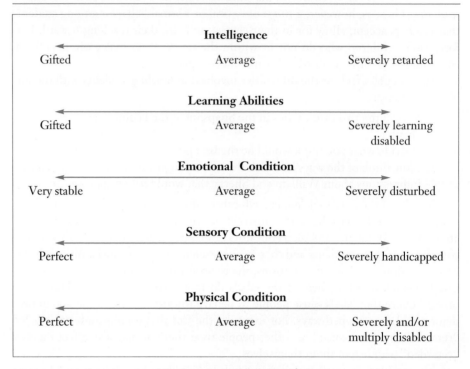

"Intellectually gifted" students

If children score about 145 on an intelligence test, they are considered by many to be *gifted* intellectually. Typically, these students, in addition to performing well on intelligence tests, are very creative and usually commit themselves wholeheartedly to a chosen task, whether it be music, athletics, or creative writing. A significant study on gifted children was begun in 1921 by Lewis Terman.[31] He selected 1,500 children whose IQs were 150 or greater and followed them for 50 years. (The study is still going on.) Most of the children became more attractive, healthier, and happier than average adults, and they tended to choose professional occupations.

A proposition that is often raised about the education of gifted children goes something like this: If these children can do so well in typical school situations, perhaps they could do even better if their instructional environments were designed specifically for them. Many educators, parents, and psychologists who raise this point feel that "gifted" children's abilities are underutilized in most regular classrooms and that these children need intellectual challenge to keep them interested in school and out of trouble. Such a belief calls for special programs: content acceleration, thoughtfully planned enrichment, guidance in selecting courses, the opportunity to work closely with other gifted children and youth, and the opportunity to work with mentors who have high-level expertise in the child's gifted area.[32]

The first task in providing special programs and resources for gifted students is the identification of the appropriate children for the program. This is not easy because not all children can be given intelligence tests, and IQ is not the only index of giftedness. While most schools use some combination of teacher nomination and

FIGURE 5-4   Modern IQ scores indicate where a person's measured intelligence falls in the normal distribution. On the WAIS and most other IQ tests, the mean is set at an IQ of 100.

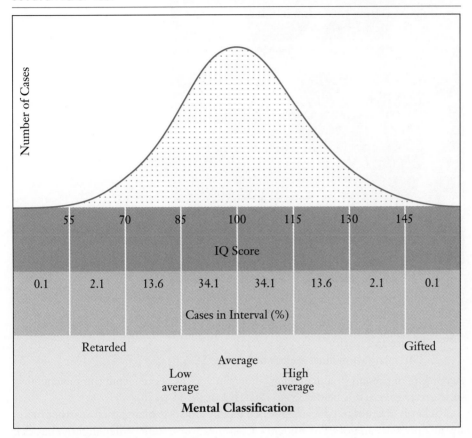

test scores, no identification system is perfect, and all of them will miss some gifted children. Isaac Newton, Leo Tolstoy, Frank Lloyd Wright, Albert Einstein, Pablo Picasso, Winston Churchill, and many other talented individuals either dropped out or flunked out of school.

Once gifted children are identified to participate in special programs, schools usually employ three strategies to provide the additional challenge thought to be appropriate for them: grouping the children who are selected so they can be taught separately from the others, accelerating the curriculum provided for them, and enriching their intellectual experiences in the regular classroom. The extent to which such strategies are effective in challenging these students and keeping them in school depends, in part, on the specific program, its goals, and the children themselves.[33]

Although official definitions for *mentally retarded* (MR) differ among states and schools within states, generally, if a person scores below 75 on an intelligence test, he or she may officially be considered mentally retarded. Usually, however, two other considerations have to be present for this designation:[34]

> "Mentally retarded" students

1. The person must also be deficient in at least two of the following technically defined areas: communications, self-care, home living, social skills,

Categories of retardation should not obscure the fact that retarded children are no less unique than children with normal intelligence.

community use, self-direction, health and safety, functional academics, and leisure and work.

2. The retardation must appear before age 18.

According to present practice, retardation can vary in degree from the subcategory of *severe/profound* (IQs below 35) to *mild* (IQs from 55 to 70).

Categorizing retardation

Schools attempt to educate retarded children by organizing their instruction to fit the different categories of students. Classification systems differ slightly, but the commonality across systems is substantial. Programs for mildly retarded children may be called *educable mentally retarded* (EMR) programs or *educationally handicapped* (EH) programs. Those for children with moderate (as distinct from "mild") mental retardation are considered *trainable mentally retarded* (TMR) programs. Those for children with greater retardation are simply called *severe* or *profound* programs. Through Public Law 94-142 (the Education for All Handicapped Children Act of 1975) as amended by P.L. 99-457 (1986), the federal government has mandated that all mentally retarded children must be served by schools.

Despite being classified as retarded on the basis of one, two, or three criteria, individuals who bear the "retarded" label quite often have no more in common than do people with no retardation. Like everyone, they vary physically and emotionally, and by personality, disposition, and beliefs. In fact, the reasons that they are mentally retarded are varied and numerous. Some causes of mental retardation are biological—caused by genetic disorders, such as Down's syndrome, or by injury such as brain damage. Some are environmental—caused by conditions such as extreme chronic poverty or physical abuse. Some involve both biology and environment.

Regardless of its type and its cause, no condition of retardation should be considered hopeless. Even the most severely retarded individuals (whose retardation usually has biological causes) seem to be able to benefit from an enriched environment. The children most likely to show IQ gains after extraordinary instructional efforts are those who score in the mildly retarded range.

Unfortunately, however, mentally retarded children often suffer from unfavorable stereotypes, probably because mentally retarded individuals are more likely than normal-range people to suffer from personality or behavioral problems; excessive aggression and depression are particular problems. This reaction by others simply adds a burden to the lives of retarded children; and that, in turn, often compounds the complex problems involved in educating them. It also causes some teachers to be apprehensive about having such children in their classes.[35]

Unfavorable stereotypes

Categories Based on Learning Difficulties

Sometimes children are in the normal or higher ranges of intelligence but still cannot seem to learn. They are not retarded, do not have a sensory handicap, and may be intellectually gifted; but they simply cannot learn a particular task. Usually, these children show no serious problems until they get to school, but then they have difficulty learning, especially to read or write. When this happens, it is often suspected that the child suffers from a *learning disability* (LD), which has been defined as

"Learning disabled" students

> a chronic condition of presumed neurological origin which selectively
> interferes with the development, integration, and/or demonstration of
> verbal and/or nonverbal abilities.[36]

Two commonly diagnosed specific learning disabilities are dyslexia and attention deficit disorder. *Dyslexia* is a disorder associated with reading. It is an inability to decode or interpret symbolic forms, such as printed words. *Attention deficit disorder*, which has only recently been identified, is like its name suggests, a problem with attention. It is a complex disorder, and a potentially high number of children suffer from it.

Do you remember someone in one of your classes in elementary school who just could not read aloud very well? The student would try to read but could not say the right sounds even after years of practice. Teachers and fellow students may have believed the student was not very bright. Today, that student would probably be diagnosed as dyslexic. Contrary to earlier beliefs, students with dyslexia have normal intelligence but have a special problem with human speech sounds.[37]

Dyslexia

People with dyslexia have problems in many different aspects of language—spoken language, reading, and writing. Investigators believe that all stages of processing sound-related information are involved, including the discrimination of one sound from another and the memory of sounds that have just occurred. Dyslexia appears to be inherited to a large extent and boys are much more likely to experience it than girls.[38]

Therapy for students who suffer from dyslexia involves remedial attention to all aspects of language—listening, comprehension, speaking, word identification in several modalities (multisensory). In addition, students can be taught effective learning strategies so they can circumvent particular problems.[39] For example, students who have problems with word identification may be taught to look at the context of the word, make a guess, and then see if it matches the printing on the page.

"Attention deficit disorder" is a label assigned to children who have serious and continuing problems in two or three areas: attention, impulse control, and (sometimes) hyperactivity. There are two subtypes of the disorder: Attention Deficit Hyperactivity Disorder (ADHD) and Undifferentiated Attention Deficit Disorder—ADD without hyperactivity. The disorder is a long-term problem that can begin in infancy and extend through adulthood. Some experts estimate that 3–5 percent of all school-age children are affected by it.

ADHD

To be diagnosed officially as having Attention Deficit Hyperactivity Disorder, a child must exhibit eight of the following eleven behaviors before 7 years of age: fidgets, has difficulty remaining seated, is easily distracted, has difficulty sustaining attention, shifts from one unfinished task to another, has difficulty playing quietly, talks excessively, interrupts others, does not seem to listen, loses things necessary for tasks, and engages in risky behavior. Most children with this disorder are diagnosed in middle childhood after parents cannot make them behave; teachers cannot get them to learn and follow routines in class; and peers are annoyed by their immature, attention-seeking behavior. The lack of friends and an inability to succeed may produce very low self-esteem. They may clown around to cover their difficulties in learning and coordination or appear not to care about their problems. They may try to control other children by bossing them, which may cause these other children to avoid them further. Many of the symptoms persist into adolescence, at which point students with this disorder may either become aggressive, have a high incidence of substance abuse, and defy authority; or they may become depressed and develop a sense of hopelessness.

ADD

Students who have ADD without hyperactivity have some, but not all, of the same symptoms. Inattention is primary, and they often have difficulty with organization. The disorder is also often associated with depression and irritability. Some experts believe that many children who suffer from this disorder are undiagnosed.

It is important to note, however, that not all children with symptoms that resemble ADD and ADHD have these disorders. Sometimes family problems, abuse, neglect, extremely unstructured home lives, and other circumstances produce the same behavior.

Teachers can take many actions to make life easier for children with ADD or ADHD, as well as for themselves. These actions include reducing distracting stimuli and disruptions in class routines, maintaining constant schedules, having clear observable classroom rules that are reviewed frequently, and providing a great deal of organizational structure.[40]

In addition to having difficulty learning at a normal pace, students with various learning disabilities often become frustrated, are easily distracted, are unable to stay on task, and seem to forget easily and frequently. The forgetting, however, may be more a matter of teacher perception than of reality. Instead of forgetting, the student may not have learned the material in the first place.

Students with learning disabilities also often have problems in the social domain. As you might guess from the descriptions of ADD, ADHD, and dyslexia, these students tend to have difficulties interacting with others and may be excessively shy, assertive, aggressive, and/or rude. These behavioral characteristics frequently lead teachers to stereotype learning-disabled students and to give up on the persistent and sensitive teaching tasks necessary to help them succeed. The characteristics try the teachers' patience and resolve at the very time when both are critically necessary if these students are to learn.

Something to Think About

Russell is in the second grade for the second time, and he is failing again. He is a mainstreamed student in the class, has slight learning disabilities, and is mildly retarded. He is a little troublesome but not really disruptive at this point. He is just older, noticeably bigger than the other students, and more aggressive.

Because of recently instituted competency testing, Russell's teacher will not be allowed to recommend that he be passed on to a regular third grade, even as a mainstreamed special student. He simply does not have the minimum test scores required for promotion.

However, because Russell's assessments indicate that he is on the borderline for placement in a self-contained special education classroom, he could be classified as mildly retarded and be put into a special education class that is not graded. But if this is done, he will probably be labeled EMR for the remainder of his elementary school years and will not be able to return to a mainstream classroom.

Russell's teachers, the principal, the school psychologist, and his parents must meet to decide whether he should repeat second grade again in a regular class or be classified as EMR.

- What do you think should be done?
- What are the benefits and negative aspects of either action?

Teaching practices used for children with learning disabilities have varied greatly over the years. Some educators advocate the establishment of highly individualized, incremental programs with close teacher supervision and guidance. Some procedures that target specific areas of functioning have been developed. Some of these are perceptual-motor training, multisensory training (an approach that uses all the senses to teach reading), language training that targets specific organic differences, and auditory-visual information processing. Except for the techniques mentioned for ADD, data on school progress for children instructed in many of these programs are not clear or positive enough to encourage widespread acceptance and use of specific procedures. Concurrently, some special education professionals advocate greater use of behavior modification techniques with learning-disabled students—including task analysis, reinforcement, modeling, and direct training.[41]

Various approaches to instruction

Categories Based on Behavior Disorders and Emotional Disturbance

If a student's behavior is bizarre, but the student is otherwise of normal intelligence, the student may be categorized as having a *behavior disorder* or as being *emotionally disturbed*. There are several kinds of behavior disorders and emotional disturbances—some extremely serious, some long-lasting, some transient. The behaviors range from conditions of fearfulness, hyperactivity, withdrawal, and mild aggression to more serious conditions such as being out of touch with reality (as evidenced, for example, by hearing voices or seeing things that are not there); showing repetitive exaggerated movements, inordinate aggression, and severe depression; and injuring oneself. Students who exhibit these behaviors in schools must be referred to specially trained professionals for diagnosis and intervention. Often special classrooms and schools are set up for children with serious behavior disorders or emotional disturbances. They are staffed by teachers and counselors specially trained in therapeutic approaches to instruction.

How do children become emotionally disturbed? Some scientists look to unhealthy home environments, while others look for biochemical problems. Still others believe that most forms of emotional disturbance have multiple causes. Currently, physical and sexual abuse are being examined as environmental causes of emotional problems in children, but much remains to be learned.

One puzzling aspect of the studies of emotional disturbances in children is that some children can experience the most abhorrent treatment early in life and emerge apparently unscathed as children and adults, while others suffer significantly from less extreme situations. Until much more is known about how children come to have emotional problems, teachers, as people essentially untrained in psychology and psychiatry, need to avoid guessing at the causes of emotional problems and blaming parents' behaviors, home environments, or recent traumatic events.[42]

Categories Based on Sensory Handicaps

Students with a *sensory handicap* are usually *hearing impaired* or *visually impaired*; that is, their hearing or sight is considered below the normal range. Although some students are completely deaf or blind, schools more often encounter milder forms of these and other sensory impairments. Nevertheless, they are especially vulnerable to being isolated socially by other students, a situation that often results in loneliness, lack of achievement, feelings of inadequacy, and other emotional consequences.

Students with mild or moderate hearing loss may adapt quite well in a classroom if they wear a hearing aid. Students with serious hearing impairment communicate with sign language, speech and lipreading, or a combination of both (known as *total communication*).

Visually impaired students also use a variety of communication modes, depending on their degree of handicap. Mildly impaired students may have their vision corrected with glasses and may need large print to read. Seriously impaired students most frequently use Braille as their primary method of reading, but they may also make use of sighted "readers," who read to them, or of "talking books."

The integration of sensory impaired students into regular classrooms poses special challenges for teachers. They must adjust their teaching so the impaired student can learn and must orient the classmates to the student's special needs. Teachers frequently need training in showing visually impaired students how to do things and in knowing when and how to offer help.

REFLECTING ON PRACTICE

*T*his Reflecting on Practice describes interaction between two junior high school students and football teammates.[43] One is deaf; the other is not. As you read, consider

- In what ways was James like other students?
- Why do you think the coaches kept James on the team?
- In what ways did contact with James help Chris?
- How do you think James's presence on the team affected the other players and the other students of the school?

Chris noticed James the first day of junior high school football tryouts. He did not pay much attention to him, however. He was too worried about himself. He wanted to make the team more than anything else in his life, and he was not thinking about the other guys.

Later that evening, as Chris reflected on the first day of practice, his thoughts turned to James. He could not see how James could make the team. Sure, he was big enough and skilled enough, but he was also deaf. How could a deaf person play football?

The next day, as Chris dressed for practice, James suited up nearby. They both finished at the same time and walked to the field side by side. Although they had attended the same schools for several years, the two boys did not know each other very well. They never communicated much. Chris always felt uncomfortable trying to talk with a deaf person.

When the two boys reached the field, a coach tossed a ball to James and told the two to warm up together. The practice involved many activities in which two boys worked together, and each time Chris and James were paired. This set a pattern, and they worked together every day.

James often did not understand what the coaches wanted him to do, but when this happened, Chris or one of the other boys would explain either by example or through gestures. As days went by, nearly everyone assisted James, but no one else did so as often as Chris. James was frustrated at times, but he appreciated the help.

Over the next three weeks, practice was hard and hot. Some boys quit, and others were cut. But through it all Chris and James persevered and succeeded. They also became close companions and good friends. They practiced together, showered together, and walked home together. In the process they developed their own system of hand signals to communicate with each other. Part of the system was actual sign language, which James had taught Chris, but much of it was a private code for Chris to tell James the plays and to explain coaches' instructions.

By the week before the final cut, Chris was sure he had made the team. He was practicing with the first team and doing well. James was also practicing with the first team most of the time, but Chris knew that the coaches were apprehensive about playing a deaf person. What would happen if he missed the play called in the huddle or when the quarterback checked off at the line?

The day before the final cut, the line coach called Chris aside and told him of his concerns about playing James. He also said he did not want to keep James on the team if he could not play him. He wanted Chris's assessment of how James would react to being cut. Chris said James would be devastated. He said that James felt that if he were going to be cut because of deafness, he would have been cut earlier. James knew he could play well enough.

Chris pleaded with the coach to keep James on the team and to play him. He explained the hand signals and assured the coach they would work under game conditions. It was an odd scene—a 13-year-old looking up to the coach with tears in his eyes pleading James's case. Chris said there was only one fair thing to do—keep James. The coach said, with unintended irony, "We'll see, but it's a shame he's deaf."

Chris did not sleep well that night. He worried: How would James feel if he was cut? How would Chris feel?

At two o'clock the next afternoon, Chris watched from a distance as the coach posted the final team roster. No one else was around. He had asked Ms. Miller if he could go to the lavatory and did so by way of the locker room. As soon as the coach left, he read the names. His name was there, but he knew it would be. Just under it was *James Haskins.* James had made the team.

Chris was waiting when James came out of his class. He flashed a thumbs-up sign and James knew instantly what it meant. He smiled broadly but then asked, "Are you sure?" Chris nodded. "Yes!"

The two boys gave each other high fives right there in the middle of the hall. When they realized everyone was staring at them, they got embarrassed and walked sheepishly toward the locker room. Chris did not know until several days later that James would not have been on the team if he had not begged the coach.

Chris and James played football together for the next five years and were good friends all the time. The hand signals worked almost every play.

The two boys drifted apart after high school graduation, when Chris accepted a football scholarship to Vanderbilt University. He could have gone to college closer to home, but Vanderbilt had a good program in special education, and Chris had decided to be a special education teacher and coach. There were many students like James, and Chris intended to help as many as he could.

Chris played college football for four years. He was a good player, and he performed even better off the field. When he graduated, he was prepared to teach special education and physical education. The other athletes elected him president of the Fellowship of Christian Athletes and in his senior year selected him for the award given to the college athlete who demonstrates the greatest concern for other people. The college faculty awarded him the Sullivan Award, given to the graduating senior who best exemplifies "a sincere interest in and concern for others."

Chris returned to his hometown as a high school teacher and football coach. He is successful and happy. His colleagues say he has a special talent for working with disabled and "problem" students. James is a successful construction worker and painter. The two men see each other periodically, usually when James attends Chris's football games.

The Physically Disabled Category

Cerebral palsy

Either because of birth-related problems, inherited abnormalities, abuse, disease, or injuries, a small proportion of students have *physical disabilities*. These disabilities, like hearing and visual impairments, vary in degree. Some students are so impaired that a caretaker must accompany them or a therapist must work with them. Others' disabilities may need something as technologically simple as a brace. Major kinds of serious physical disabilities are paralysis, frequently caused by injury; cerebral palsy (CP), usually caused by oxygen deprivation during birth; and spina bifida, an opening somewhere along the spine that allows neural tissue to bulge, thus causing serious motor problems. Less frequent disabling conditions include arthritis, muscular dystrophy, and injuries. As is the case with vision- and hearing-impaired students,

Spina bifida

teachers must not only adjust to serve the students with physical handicaps but must also orient their classmates.[44]

Teachers must constantly remember that physically disabled children are often quite skilled within or despite their limitations. They must be particularly mindful that students who have difficulty communicating may have average or above-average intellectual abilities. Even when severely impaired students cannot talk, sit, write, or type, their teachers must find ways to teach them and help them express their knowledge.

In recent years technological advances have become especially helpful with special students. Devices can be designed for individual students that are sensitive to such subtle responses as gaze direction, eye blinks, and head tilts. They allow severely disabled students a way to communicate with other people in and outside of the classroom.

Technological advances

The "Average" Category

Now that some of the educational categories used to group children outside the "normal" range have been described, it is important to comment again about students considered to be "normal," or "average." The point to be made is simple. *Normal students* tend to have fewer noticeably special or exceptional characteristics than do the children whose special characteristics have been described in this chapter, but each of them is a unique individual. Average students might be more alike than others, but they are still not at all the same.

EDUCATIONAL RESEARCH

Using Research Data for Educational Decisions

If the world of education were perfect, educators would make decisions about the best way to teach students on the basis of a sufficient supply of research information. They would read studies conducted by others, undertake some studies of their own, analyze the circumstances that affect the situation they face, and apply whatever ideas seem to be most appropriate to their task. Then they would design a plan of action, implement it, study the results, and make appropriate modifications.

Because the world is not perfect, the decision process is never that methodological or neat. Many things intrude: People do things in traditional ways and do not want to change, many have biases that they do not want challenged, information is usually incomplete, public pressure frequently requires action that is not supported by data, funds are always limited, and so forth. As a result, educational practices usually exist not because of conclusions from research but because of either (1) a desire to keep things as they are or (2) a strong enough dissatis-faction with the present situation to force a change. Sometimes the thrust of research information supports these practices; sometimes it does not.

This interplay between research and practice is illustrated in the following situation, which involves the question of how children who are different should be categorized and taught. The issue is whether certain students with special needs should be educated in separate special education classes and schools or whether they should attend regular classes.

During the 1960s students who were considered to have special learning problems were typically classified as having a particular type of handicap and were then placed in special, separate classes, where they were taught by special education teachers. The practice seemed to work well, even for those with mild handicaps, but over the years researchers turned up disturbing information. In 1968, after reviewing that research and analyzing current practices, one such researcher in special education, Lloyd Dunn, addressed a very pointed article to special educators, which he began with the following statement:

> In my view, much of our past and present practices are morally and educationally wrong. We have been living at the mercy of general educators who have referred their problem children to us. And we have been generally ill prepared and ineffective in educating these children. Let us stop being pressured into continuing and expanding a special education program that we know now to be undesirable for many of the children we are dedicated to serve.[45]

Dunn went on to say that separate, self-contained special education classes and schools for mildly retarded and other mildly disabled students had been established for the wrong reason—to get the "misfits" out of the regular classroom so that teachers could concentrate better on the other students. He said lip service was paid to the idea that this arrangement was best for the "disabled" student but that research reported that this was often not the case. Studies showed that special education classes were frequently composed of disproportionate numbers of minority students and students of lower socioeconomic status and that many students from disadvantaged homes were mislabeled as "retarded," "emotionally disturbed," "perceptu-

ally impaired," and "learning disabled."

Dunn said his reading of the data led him to believe that the process of evaluating and assessing children with learning difficulties was frequently conducted to find convenient labels for students in order to justify their removal from the regular classrooms. Often the goal was simply to get rid of them, not to formulate more appropriate educational programs for them. As a result, he stated bluntly:

> we must stop labeling these deprived children as mentally retarded. Furthermore we must stop segregating them by placing them into our allegedly special programs.[46]

Dunn stated what he believed to be the reasons that such mislabeling and segregating of these children take place:

> Regular teachers and administrators have sincerely felt they were doing these pupils a favor by removing them from the pressures of an unrealistic and inappropriate program of studies. Special educators have also fully believed that the children involved would make greater progress in special schools and classes. However, the overwhelming evidence is that our present and past practices have their major justification in removing pressures on regular teachers and pupils at the expense of the socioculturally deprived slow learning pupils themselves.[47]

To demonstrate that contemporary research did not support current practice, Dunn listed the following conclusions from a number of studies of his day:

1. Homogeneous grouping tends to work to the disad-

vantage of slow learners and underprivileged children.
2. Retarded children make as much or more progress in regular grades as they do in special classes, even though special classes tend to be smaller and to have more resources.
3. Diagnostic procedures frequently lead to mislabeling of students and their concentration in inappropriate homogeneous groups of children with supposed common problems.
4. Labeling children as "disabled" reduces teacher expectations that they will succeed.
5. Disability labels hurt children's self-images, contributing to their feelings of inferiority.
6. Special class placements create problems of acceptance of disability-labeled students by the other students in the school.

In response to these findings of weaknesses in current special education practice, Dunn outlined a possible alternative approach, which he proposed for development and testing. He advocated a moratorium on what was being done *until a better way could be identified:*

> it is suggested we do away with many existing disability labels and the present practice of grouping children homogeneously by these labels into special classes. Instead, we should try keeping slow learning children more in the mainstream of education, with special educators serving as diagnostic, clinical, remedial, resource room, itinerant and/or team teachers, consultants, and developers of instructional materials and prescriptions for effective teaching. The accomplishment of the

above *modus operandi* will require a revolution in much of special education. A moratorium needs to be placed on the proliferation (if not continuance) of self-contained special classes which enroll primarilythe ethnically and/or economically disadvantaged children we have been labeling educable mentally retarded. Such pupils should be left in (or returned to) the regular elementary grades until we are "tooled up" to do something better for them.[48]

In Dunn's view, an improved clinical approach to handling students with mild special education needs would include:

■ diagnostic and prescriptive teaching in which skilled educators would evaluate students more accurately and effectively, design programs for their individual needs, monitor the results of the programs, and make adjustments accordingly
■ resource rooms and itinerant teachers that would complement regular classroom instruction and replace segregated special education classes
■ a radically revised special education curriculum

Dunn's demand for discarding the present way of teaching mildly handicapped students rested on substantial research findings that showed the many weaknesses of the approach. Since he made his statements, his conclusions have been further supported by recent studies. However, Dunn's alternative approach was not grounded in significant research. It was a conceptual idea, not a tested and proven model. It sounded good, but solid evidence that it would work did not exist. Dunn acknowledged this fact throughout his proposals.

He felt he knew what did not work, but he did not claim that his new idea would. *He recommended only (and specifically) that it be studied and tested.*

Ironically, however, the Dunn concept quickly became the new way of doing things. School systems and states adopted some version of it without sufficient testing. In essence, they reacted to pressure to move away from the old, discredited approach, and a new concept was readily available. The new concept was called *mainstreaming.* But, even with mainstreaming, the labels and the labeling process continue.

As we describe in some detail in Chapter 7, mainstreaming is now the dominant approach to teaching children with special needs. But research results about its effectiveness are still incomplete and inconclusive.

Conclusion

The kind of information about students that was presented in this chapter is important to educators because it helps them make better decisions about how and what to teach. Knowing about developmental stages enables them to target their instruction at the appropriate levels for the age groups they face. Knowing about different types of learners helps them to adjust their teaching accordingly. Understanding commonalities across student developmental stages and within certain categorical groupings allows them to make common assumptions about what students can learn and do. As a result, teachers do not have to teach every student as if he or she is *absolutely* individual or unique.

Of course, teachers must be cautious as they make these assumptions about their students. They must avoid sweeping generalizations about them. Although no student is unique in every way, each is highly individual.

Once educators understand similarities and differences among students, they can organize their schools and classrooms and design their teaching to meet the educational conditions and needs of the children and youth who come to them. This involves a process of matching student capabilities with the established educational goals.

Summary

Children need to be understood if they are to be taught properly, and any attempt to understand them must include the realization that each child is similar to others and, at the same time, unique. Three of the ways children can be studied are by looking (1) at how they develop over the years, (2) at the variations in the resources or "capital" they bring with them to school, and (3) at how they are alike and different from others their age.

Dialectical theory describes development as a series of four types of interactions between individuals and their environment—inner biological, individual psychological, cultural-sociological, and outer physical. The individual psychological dimension consists of two parts—perceptual-cognitive and social-emotional development. Perceptual development involves a process of becoming less captive, more self-initiating, more systematic, more specific, and more able to ignore irrelevant information. Cognitive development, according to Piagetian theory, consists of four stages—sensorimotor, preoperational, concrete operational, and formal operational. Social-emotional development consists of four periods—infancy, early childhood, middle childhood, and adolescence. Each period has particular characteristics and events.

When students come to school, they bring with them wide ranges of variations in strengths and weaknesses. Some of these can be described as student "capital." Two other types of variations are those associated with "expectations" and gender.

Because children are different, educators often categorize them according to particular characteristics, and often the categories are formulated by fitting children in somewhere along a continuum of some sort. Some categories are based on intelligence—"intellectually gifted," "mentally retarded"; some on learning ability or disability—"hyperactive," "dyslexic"; some on degree of emotional disturbance, and some on the presence of a sensory or physical disability. All continua include a "normal" classification or range.

Although categorizing students is often useful to teachers, they must do it with caution and sensitivity. Any categorization involves overgeneralizing about the people involved and could be harmful.

Study Questions

1. Think about how your life would have changed if each of the following had taken place when you were in middle childhood or when you were an adolescent:

   a. Your family's income was cut off suddenly.

   b. You became seriously physically disabled.

   c. You had to move to another country—such as Chile or French-speaking Africa—without family or friends and without knowing local customs or the language.

   How might each change have affected your social-emotional development?

2. Contrast the ways in which a preschool child, an elementary school student, and an adolescent would approach this problem:

   Jim overslept one morning and found that he had only fifteen minutes to get to school. It normally takes him fifteen minutes to get ready and ten minutes to walk to school.

3. List some of the activities that students at your high school engaged in that you would consider "identity seeking."

4. What are some of the advantages and disadvantages of being in a special category of students?

Key Terms

Accommodation	Emotional development	Perceptual growth
Adaptation	Emotionally disturbed	Personal capital
Assimilation	Expectations	Personal fable
Attribution	Gender schema	Piagetian theory
Behavior disorder	Hypothetical thinking	Sensory handicap
Classifying	Intellectual capital	Social behavior
Cognitive growth	Kohlberg's stages of	Social capital
Coping behavior	moral development	Social cognition
Cultural capital	Learned helplessness	Social development
Decentering	Learning disability	Social environment
Dialectical theory	Mentally retarded	Student capital
Economic capital	Moral growth	Zone of proximal
Educational capital	Ordering	development
Egocentrism	Perception	

For Further Reading

Dunn, L. M. (1968). Special education for the mentally retarded: Is much of it justifiable? *Exceptional Children, 35*(1), 5–22.

Elkind, D. (1970, April 5). Erik Erikson's eight ages of man. *New York Times Magazine*, pp. 25–27+.

Flavell, J. H. (1985). *Cognitive Development* (2nd ed.). Englewood Cliffs, NJ: Prentice-Hall.

Flavell, J. H. (1992). Cognitive development: Past, present, and future. *Developmental Psychology, 28*(6), 998–1005.

Gilligan, C. (1993). *In a different voice.* Cambridge: Harvard University Press.

Kohlberg, L. (1970). The child as moral philosopher. In P. Cramer (Ed.), *Readings in developmental psychology today* (pp. 109–115). Del Mar, CA: CRM Books.

McCall, R. B. (1989). A.D.D. alert. *Learning, 17*(5), 66–69.

Sutherland, A. T. (1984). *Disabled we stand.* Bloomington, IN: Indiana University Press.

Wadsworth, B. J. (1989). *Piaget's theory of cognitive development* (4th ed.). White Plains, NY: Longman.

6

How
Students
Learn

CONTRIBUTING AUTHORS
Jeanne M. Plas
Penelope H. Brooks

Jeanne M. Plas was the primary author of the first edition of this chapter. Updates and revisions were provided for the revised edition by Penelope H. Brooks and Charles and Lynn Myers. Charles and Lynn Myers wrote the Education Research section.

This chapter examines such questions as how learning occurs and which conditions help to create good learning in schools. In part because much information about the human central nervous system and its relation to thinking and behavior is yet undiscovered, the chapter cannot explain everything we need to know about learning. It describes, however, several of the important learning theories that are available to teachers today. These theories are currently guiding classroom practice; new ideas are being developed and tested for possible future use.

The chapter explores two general theories of learning—behavior theory and cognitive theory, and several theories that fit within each, including Piagetian theory. Further, it describes the development of each theory and the ways in which teachers use each.

At several points during the chapter you are asked to think about applications of learning theory to classroom situations. The Snapshot provides a glimpse of an imaginary teacher from the past who had to cope without learning theories. Later in the chapter, you are asked to think again about this teacher and propose what she would have done if current theories had been available to her. At the end of the chapter, a similar case study of a future teacher provides another situation to consider. The Reflecting on Practice describes a conversation among three contemporary teachers that illustrates how learning theory can be used to address particular learning difficulties.

The Educational Research section describes the interaction among theory, research, and practice.

SNAPSHOT

The Snapshot for this chapter is about the first-year teaching experience of a teacher in 1859. As you read, ask yourself the following questions:

■ Why do some children learn more quickly than others?

■ Why might a child do well in one subject while doing poorly in others?

■ What is the relationship of motivation to learning?

■ What is the role of parents in the actual process of learning?

■ In what ways does this episode illustrate a teacher's need for learning theory?

Learning in the Wild West

Long ago, early on a crisp and sunny morning in a small western town at the foot of the mountains, Miss Priscilla Hope gave her long skirt a couple of brisk tugs and a yank. Having made sure that no part of either ankle was visible, she sailed through the schoolhouse door with an air of quiet confidence that was not exactly false, though it surely hid such things as her sweating palms and slightly irregular heartbeat.

Miss Hope was new in town and new to her job. In fact, her job itself was new—schoolteacher for the territory's children. And what a group of children it was! There were eleven in all. Caleb, the eldest, was 12 years old and the son of the territory's richest man, the owner of Peterson's General Store. Silas Peterson wanted his only son to learn "figures and readin' " so that he could be of help in the store. In fact, Mr. Peterson had been one of those who had insisted that the territory was ready for a school and a teacher.

Little Bertram Blevins was the youngest, the 7-year-old son of the area's most successful miner. Bertram did not talk much, and his father had reasoned that learning how to read would cause the boy to speak up more often. He further reasoned that spending more than three days a week at the school would be a waste of the boy's time, and he had been quick to let Miss Hope know his opinion when he had escorted her off the Overland Stage the week before.

Sarah Finn, age 9, was in school simply because her mother adored her and wanted her, as she said, "to be accomplished." The only other girl in the group, Amanda Suzette Todd, also 9 years old, was there because her mother was a younger sister of Sarah Finn's mother, who had insisted that Amanda accompany Sarah. ("It wouldn't 'do' to have only one girl around all those boys, you know.") Mrs. Finn had warned her sister not to be upset when Sarah learned faster and better than her cousin. She also had taken Miss Hope aside at the get-acquainted picnic to let her know that steps should be taken to protect hurt feelings when little Sarah outshone all the other children.

Most of the territory's children were not in school that first morning. They were helping their mothers and fathers—often taking care of young animals or young children. A couple of families thought that they might send their children over to the school in a month or two, when the weather got bad. Miss Hope planned to visit every family in the area to talk about the school and what their children could learn.

On that first morning, she began by calling on Ephraim Brook, whose parents wanted him to preach and had let

Miss Hope know that 9-year-old Ephraim was expected to learn to read the Book of Genesis before Christmas. When Ephraim was told to turn to the first page of the reader that Miss Hope had brought all the way from St. Louis, he just looked at her and began to cry. His crying scared Amanda so much that she began to cry even louder than Ephraim. Sarah became screamingly indignant at both of them, and Caleb took the opportunity to scoot out the door to hurl taunts at a passing dog. In the midst of all the confusion, not even Miss Hope was able to notice that quiet little Bertram was mouthing some of the words in the reader silently to himself as he began to hum and smile a little bit.

Eventually, Miss Hope learned much more about her students. She learned that under threat of physical punishment, Ephraim was not allowed to read anything but the Bible; Amanda was really good at spelling but could not seem to "add up" numbers at all; the adored Sarah seemed hopelessly slow in every subject; and Caleb always wanted to read the lines backward for some unknown reason. She also learned that Corey Laird, who could do nothing else with his head, was always able to get the right answer if he was measuring things or guessing at something like the amount of milk in a pail; that three of the oldest boys never wanted to come to school and so rarely did; and that little Bertram Blevins learned everything about an hour or a day before Miss Hope got around to teaching it. All in all, it could probably be said that the teacher learned more than her students.

By springtime, Priscilla Hope had decided that her three-month teaching course back in St. Louis had not really taught her a thing about what causes children to learn. And it certainly had not even addressed the issue of what makes them *want* to learn. When the spring planting began, she got back into an Overland Stage and headed out of the territory—which more or less got back to normal. Little Bertram Blevins was very quiet once more.

The Nature of Learning

Things have changed quite a bit in American education since Miss Hope got back into that stagecoach. Teachers today have a vast amount of knowledge compared to teachers of her time, and they can apply that knowledge to what they do. Part of that new knowledge comes from the study of how learning actually occurs, and the information is fundamental in most teacher education programs. Courses in learning and educational psychology often precede or are taught concurrently with teaching methods courses.

Theories, not facts

However, if the issues are much clearer for today's teachers than they were a century and a half ago, it is still true that a definitive understanding of the learning process remains elusive. Today we have theories of learning to guide teaching; that is, we have a number of reliable speculations on the nature of learning that help direct research programs and guide practical classroom approaches to helping children learn. Nevertheless, current research findings and the practical classroom approaches that have developed from them are still based only on theories. They do not rest on solid, quantifiable descriptions of what actually constitutes learning.

It may be some time in the next century before teachers will possess definitive information on human learning processes. For now, they must be content to master one or more of the currently accepted theories of learning and its various classroom applications.

In this chapter you will read descriptions of several of the most often relied-upon theories of learning available today—behavior theory, general cognitive theory, and sub-level theories that fit under each. The relationship of these theories to one another will also be addressed, as will their applicability to various teaching styles. Because this text is an introduction to teaching, a number of theories of learning, such as perceptual, Freudian, transpersonal, and humanistic, are not discussed, though you may study them in later courses.

Theory and teaching style

Just as most teachers bring to their classrooms a teaching philosophy, so each teacher brings a unique teaching personality, or style, to the classroom. Usually, that person's teaching style is more consistent with one of the theories of learning and its practical applications than with the others. Because there is no definitive approach to human learning, teachers are wise to take advantage of this situation and connect their unique strengths and habits of style to a learning theory that seems especially suited to those strengths and performances.

As you read this chapter, select the learning theory that seems to be most consistent with your own teaching personality and ideas about instruction. When you read Chapter 14, make a similar selection from any of the models of instruction that are described. After making both selections, compare your two choices and explore why you chose as you did.

Motivation

This chapter discusses the relationship between motivation and learning. The old saying that you can lead a horse to water, but you cannot make it drink has special meaning for schools and is applicable to all students. Even when we are sure of the best approach for teaching a specific subject to a specific child, that child's level of motivation can effectively retard or enhance the amount of learning that will take place. As you move through this chapter, divide your attention among three issues: the *how* of learning, the *why* of learning, and the *unique styles* of teachers and learners.

The Need for Learning Theory

Sometimes beginning teachers wonder whether it makes sense to study something if it is only a theory. Why learn something if we are not sure it is the truth? The answer is simple. We learn theories for two reasons: because they do help us, and because more solid information is not available.

That principle applies to learning theory as well as to theories in general. Although a clear understanding of the specific processes controlling learning are not available at the moment, teachers need guidance about how to produce or enhance student learning. In the absence of harder facts, the more important contemporary theories of learning serve as the best guides available. Therefore, it is necessary that teachers gain a working knowledge of aspects of various theories of learning that seem to have promise for the teaching situations in which they find themselves.

Kurt Lewin, an early pioneer of social psychology, once commented that "there is nothing so practical as a good theory."[1] Through this statement he made the point that theory directs our action. A good theory prompts action, shows us where to look for trouble spots, and suggests a course of remediation. Good theory is one of the best tools a teacher can have.

Theories as guides

General Theories of Learning

The theories discussed in this chapter offer suggestions concerning the hypotheses that might govern learning. They also offer suggestions for action when the hypotheses seem to be breaking down for a given child or for a given *kind* of child. Thus, these theories are tools that teachers need in order to become master professionals. At some point during the translation of theory into practice, master teachers transform the science of education into the art of teaching. Table 6-1 lists the learning theories presented in this chapter and their primary characteristics.

Behavior Theory

There are a variety of *behavior theories*. Each emphasizes a somewhat different set of circumstances surrounding human behavior, but all agree that behavior is learned. Thus, it is important to understand that, fundamentally, all behavior theories are learning theories. Behaviorists believe that even something as complex as personality, for example, is a learned phenomenon.

Although labels used over the years to identify types of behavior theory vary to some extent, this discussion relies on a conventional classification system that divides behavior theory into two types—*association theory* and *reinforcement theory*. The discussion emphasizes reinforcement theory because it has greatest applicability to schools and classrooms and because it is more often used within school settings. However, association theory is discussed first because it was developed first, and the later reinforcement theorists have often explained their beliefs about learning by comparing them with earlier associationist beliefs.

Association Theory

Ivan Petrovich Pavlov, a Russian scientist whose major contributions to science were in physiology, is probably best known today for a contribution that most

Pavlov, 1849–1936

TABLE 6-1   Primary Characteristics of Learning Theories

Learning Theories	Primary Characteristics
Behavior theory	Behavior is learned and is extrinsically influenced.
Association theory	An association of events stimulates memory and behavior; learning occurs because of associations among stimuli.
Reinforcement theory	Consequences of actions reinforce behavior; learning occurs because it is rewarded.
Cognitive theory	Thinking is an information-processing process; insight.
Information-processing theory	Identifies kinds of thinking processes and explains how they operate to help learning.
Cognitive-developmental theory	Describes how thinking processes change with development.
Piaget	Interaction with environment leads to adaptation, which includes assimilation and accommodation.
Vygotsky	Interaction with others in the environment leads to internalization of thought processes.

people consider psychological rather than physiological.[2] Shortly before the turn of the twentieth century, Pavlov and his laboratory workers were engaged in a study of the physiological processes that control digestion. Their subjects included dogs. In that effort, Pavlov happened to notice that after the dogs had become accustomed to the conditions and routines in the laboratory, they usually began to salivate at the sight of the food keeper, rather than at the time when the daily food allotment was actually presented to them. Pavlov, although initially uninterested in what he saw, reasoned that the process of digestion began to occur in the dogs' bodies earlier in the chain of events he was studying than had previously been suspected.

Conditioned reflex

Because of this phenomenon, Pavlov and his workers began to call saliva a "psychic secretion." He thought of the production of saliva in such an instance as a *conditioned reflex* and believed that dogs and other animals had no more control over salivation at the sight of a food keeper than they did when food was actually placed in their mouths.

As Pavlov pursued his study of the causes of salivation, he arranged for other things to happen at the time when the food keeper appeared or just before he appeared. For example, he rang a bell or showed the dogs a card with a circle drawn on it. After doing these things a few times, he found that the dogs salivated at the sound of the bell or at the sight of the circle. In fact, they salivated at the sound of the bell or at the sight of the circle even when food was not in sight or not likely to arrive within a specified period of time.

Pairing

Eventually, Pavlov reported laboratory results that demonstrated that dogs and other animals could, as it were, be taught to salivate at the sound of a bell or the sight of a circle on a card. All that was necessary was for the lab workers to *pair* the bell or circle with food for a period of time. Soon, the dog *associated* the bell or circle with food.

Pavlov's work is thought of as an associationist theory because the physiological responses that occurred when associations between stimuli were strengthened, such as the association between food keeper and food or a bell and food, were involuntary in nature. Pavlov showed that a great many physiological responses could be controlled by such associations. His studies provided the foundation for a revolution in psychological theory.

During the first part of the twentieth century, an American research psychologist named J. B. Watson further developed Pavlov's associationist ideas and adapted them for use with children.[3] Watson had an intense interest in animal psychology and believed that a thorough study of animals could teach us something about the psychology of human beings. This interest and the research work that it stimulated helped change the nature of psychology from a discipline considered to be similar to philosophy to one that was (1) heavily reliant on animal experimentation, (2) focused exclusively on behavior, and (3) oriented toward the eventual prediction and control of behavior.

J. B. Watson, 1878–1958

Animal experimentation

Watson and Rosalie Rayner conducted a classic and controversial series of studies on the *conditioning* of infant emotion. Albert B., an 11-month-old child, was the subject of the experiment. Albert was taught to fear a variety of items that had been paired with a white rat, an object that had initially elicited playfulness rather than fear in Albert. At the beginning of the experiment, Albert did not fear the white rat; he did, however, fear an unexplained clanging noise behind him. Then, Watson and Rayner repeatedly presented the rat to Albert at the same time as they made the loud clanging noise. That is, they *associated*—or paired—the rat and the noise. Albert quickly learned to fear the rat in a way that was similar to his original fear of the noise. After Albert had been conditioned to fear the rat, Watson and Rayner paired objects such as a seal coat, cotton wool, and a Santa Claus mask with the rat. The child eventually exhibited a fear response when viewing these objects by themselves, without the rat's presence.

Conditioning

Despite their belief that they could extinguish Albert's fear responses to the white rat and the other objects, Watson and Rayner did not do so; they did not help Albert to "unlearn" these fears. For this and other reasons, the Albert B. study has become a focal point in the literature concerned with the ethics of psychological research.

Watson and his followers believed that all emotions, pleasant and unpleasant, were learned. Indeed, they believed that all aspects of human functioning—exclusive of simple reflexes—were learned. In a well-known statement, Watson declared:

> Give me a dozen healthy infants, well-formed, and my own specified world to bring them up in, and I'll guarantee to take any one at random and train him to become any type of specialist I might select—doctor, lawyer, artist, merchant, chief and, yes, even beggarman and thief, regardless of his talents, penchants, tendencies, abilities, vocations, and race of his ancestors.[4]

One of the reasons for the popularity of behavioral approaches in American public schools probably lies in the attitudes reflected in Watson's famous paragraph. Americans have liked to think of their country as the land of opportunity, where people can become anything they choose regardless of such factors as specific hereditary limitations. The Watsonian prescription for learning seems to contain a sense of control over destiny. It may be that others exert the control, but it is a control that promises an important amount of power over the capriciousness of natural forces.

Edwin R. Guthrie, 1886–1959

Even though reinforcement theory has tended to be more popular in recent years than has been the earlier associationist theory developed by Pavlov and Watson, interesting and useful interpretations of associationist perspectives have continued to be developed over the years. For example, Edwin R. Guthrie is well known for his concept of *one-trial learning*.[5] Guthrie believed that people would associate and learn as a unit events that occurred together in time or space. In fact, he thought that a behavior could gain its full associative strength on the very first occasion that stimuli were paired. He argued that Pavlov's dogs learned the food-bell association the first time they were able to focus their attention on that association. The learning only *seemed* to require several pairings of those stimuli because there were competing stimuli in the environment.

Thus, Guthrie advised teachers to limit all distractions when encouraging pupils to learn. He also suggested that teachers should encourage the "inner speech" of their students in order to make sure that the important connections are actually being made. That is, students were to talk silently to themselves as they learned. In Guthrie's view, students needed "to be led to do" what they were to learn. Teachers needed to lead students toward the necessary mental connections. Recently, some cognitive approaches to learning have supported this view and specific classroom practices based on it have been developed (or rediscovered).

Association Theory: Some Classroom Practices

1. mnemonic devices
2. association of student hobbies and interests with course material
3. like materials presented together
4. associations of opposites
5. rhyming exercises

Acquiring associations

For behaviorists such as Pavlov, Watson, and Guthrie, the associations that animals and people make as they have experiences and act are of ultimate importance. For them, learning is fundamentally equivalent to acquiring associations. In the early associationist writings geared toward education, teachers were often advised to lead the child into repetitive exercises so that the appropriate associations would be sure to be made. Recitation of multiplication tables and spelling words are examples of some of the applications of this theory that seemed useful for the classroom.

In more contemporary educational programs, the strategy of *mnemonic devices* is influenced by association theory.[6] For example, music teachers often rely on the phrase, "Every good boy does fine," in order to teach that E, G, B, D, and F constitute one of the fundamental patterns of notes that must be learned in order to read music. When teachers associate a formula with something students are supposed to remember, it is valid to assume that an associationist learning theory is guiding the activity.

Reinforcement Theory

Consequences of behavior

While associationists concentrate on the association of events that *stimulate* behavior, the reinforcement theorists emphasize the consequences, rather than the antecedents, of behavior.[7] They are more concerned with the power of the events that *follow* a behavior. Their research has led them to conclude that the pleasant or unpleasant *consequences* of action help determine whether that action will be repeated. These theorists emphasize that Pavlov's dogs learned to salivate on hearing a bell mainly because the taste of the food that followed the bell was very good and, thus, very reinforcing.

E. L. Thorndike was the first prominent research psychologist during the initial third of the twentieth century to concentrate on behavioral consequences.[8] He wrote of a *law of effect* that governed important aspects of behavior:

> Of several responses made to the same situation, those which are accompanied or closely followed by satisfaction to the animal will, other things being equal, be more firmly connected with the situation, so that when it recurs, they will be more likely to recur; those which are accompanied or closely followed by discomfort to the animal will, other things being equal, have their connections with that situation weakened, so that when it recurs, they will be less likely to occur. The greater the satisfaction or discomfort, the greater the strengthening or weakening of the bond.[9]

Essentially, Thorndike told his readers that a behavior that is rewarded will tend to be repeated. At times, however, he shaded his interpretation of the part of the law of effect that deals with discomfort so that his readers took him to mean that punishment was ineffective in weakening a behavior—especially as compared to re-

E. L. Thorndike, 1847–1949

Law of effect

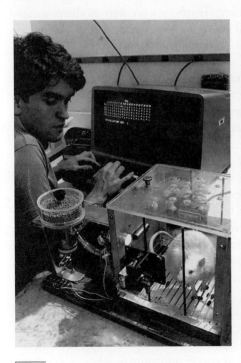 

What does a rat's bar-pressing behavior have to do with children's learning in school? According to B. F. Skinner (right), quite a lot. For Skinner, learning means behavioral change, and the same basic principles of learning apply across species, from rats and pigeons to humans. For this reason, carefully observing how animals respond to changes in their environment tells us more than we might think about how children learn in school—and in life.

ward. Currently, most reinforcement theorists hold that punishment can effectively reduce the probability that a behavior will be repeated; but they recognize that other unintended consequences can also be expected to occur, among them painful emotional responses such as fear.

Law of scatter of effect

Thorndike further claimed that a *law of scatter of effect* also guides behavior. Those behaviors that are similar to the one that is followed by reward will also tend to be learned. For example, a child who is effectively rewarded for producing neat spelling tests will tend to produce neat arithmetic and social studies assignments as well.

B. F. Skinner, 1904–1994

B. F. Skinner had the most important influence of any theorist on American learning theory.[10] In fact, in several polls during the 1970s and 1980s, Skinner was shown to be one of the most widely known American scientists, across all fields. He was most famous for the development of the concept of *operant behavior.*

Operant behavior

Skinner was originally concerned with the effects of reward on random animal behavior. For example, in his early experiments, chickens were placed in a box; when they happened to press a bar, food pellets automatically dropped into a nearby container. This increased the chickens' tendency to press the bar. Skinner began to think of this bar-pressing behavior as being *reinforced* by the consequence of the presentation of the food. The chickens pressed the bar again because they had learned that food appeared immediately after the behavior of bar pressing.

Skinner wrote that "teaching is the arrangement of contingencies of reinforcement which expedite learning."[11] In other words, learning occurs when appropriate rewards have been presented to the learner. Teachers who alert students to approaching tests to encourage studying and who later watch student reactions as the graded tests are returned understand Skinner's point.

Schedules of reward

In further studies, Skinner identified several *schedules of reward* that seemed to have different effects on behavior. For example, when chickens were placed on a *fixed interval schedule* (the reward arrived after a specified period of time, such as five minutes), they would learn to begin bar pressing only when the specified period of time was nearly over. On an *intermittent ratio schedule* (reward occurs randomly after various numbers of behaviors have been emitted, as in slot machine gambling), bar pressing would occur almost continually and intensely throughout the time the chicken was in the box.

Those who have reinterpreted Skinnerian work on reinforcement schedules for the classroom have used the idea to explain such phenomena as student study habits. They claim that when students are aware that an examination will occur every five weeks, studying will occur most prominently immediately before the test (fixed interval schedule). When students have learned that unannounced quizzes may occur at any time, studying tends to be more consistent throughout the semester (intermittent interval schedule).

Because he was interested in the ways that animals and humans operate on their environments, Skinner often used the term *operant behavior* to describe the kind of animal and human activities that his research investigated. Operant approaches emphasize the naturally active characteristics of people and animals while classical associationist approaches concentrate on the passive characteristics of research subjects. Thus, Pavlov thought of his dogs as *responding* to, and Skinner thought of his chickens as *operating* on, their environments. Associationist theory is interested in responses; reinforcement theory is interested in actions and their consequences.

Reinforcement and Learning

In applying reinforcement theory to the classroom, Skinner and his followers reasoned that many students were failing to learn because the typical student-teacher ratio was so great that large numbers of students were not receiving appropriate reinforcement for their efforts and achievements. As a result, they could not learn. In response, they developed programmed instruction methods, packages, and teaching machines to provide the opportunity for immediate reinforcement for the students.[12]

Programmed instruction methods and materials provide immediate reinforcement to the learner by arranging a series of questions so that the answers to the questions are close at hand. Each question builds upon previous information in an incremental way. Teaching machines apply programmed instruction methods through use of equipment capable of providing immediate visual and/or auditory feedback for a student's work.

Equipment such as this was especially popular in educational settings during the 1960s and early 1970s. Its emergence encouraged the hope that a major breakthrough in educational practice was at hand. Excitement prevailed because it seemed that science had provided definitive answers to fundamentally important questions about the basic processes of human learning. Unfortunately, the promise that some thought reinforcement theory held for education has not been fully realized. Gradually, it became apparent that programmed instruction methods were useful for teaching material associated with short, clear-cut answers, such as facts, definitions, and so forth, but not very useful for teaching abstract reasoning, synthesizing skills, and creativity. In addition, many students reported that they found

Programmed instruction

Despite efforts to create automated reinforcements, for many children a very potent reinforcer is still a teacher's smile.

programmed instruction materials boring. (In more recent years, computer technology has, of course, changed all this.)

Teacher-learner relationships

Limitations such as these prompted further educational research that began to identify the *teacher-learner* relationship as primary.[13] Those who conducted this line of study reasoned that the reinforcing, social responses from the teacher and their availability within human interaction were possibly the most reinforcing aspect of education for a large number of children. Although the machines could reinforce behavior, teachers could do it better. When one accepts that assumption, it is valid to conclude that materials and machines cannot successfully compete with the student-teacher relationship for most educational purposes. For many children, a smile from the teacher is worth far more than immediate feedback from a machine—even a machine that is lots of fun. In addition, teacher encouragement is likely to overcome the negative reinforcement of boredom.

While the limitations of reinforcement theory for classroom learning have reduced its impact on educational practices in recent years, some aspects of reinforcement theory are currently represented in most materials and models of instruction in widespread use in schools today. The power of the idea of reinforcement lies in its utility. Time after time, across a variety of settings and types of learners, positively reinforced learning tends to be acquired more easily and retained longer than nonreinforced learning. Thus, teachers and textbooks attempt to make their methods reinforcing; that is, rewarding. That such a technique has become almost second nature for many teachers is a sign of the utility of the idea.

Reinforcement Theory: Some Classroom Practices

1. using preferred student activities as reinforcers for less-desired exercises
2. letting students accumulate tokens, stars, or check marks that can be redeemed for free time, preferred activities, and so forth
3. ignoring undesirable attention-gaining acts
4. programmed instruction modules
5. computer-assisted instruction

Reinforcement and Classroom Conduct

Behavior modification

While reinforcement theory has been less pervasive in subject-matter instruction than some theorists anticipated, it has had a more profound impact on the way many teachers manage their classrooms. Indeed, some teachers see themselves as behavior managers; that is, people in charge of controlling the behavior of the children while they are in the classroom and school building. The strategies that these teachers tend to use are generally thought of as *behavior modification* approaches.[14] As mentioned in Chapter 3, teachers who use behavior modification techniques systematically reinforce behaviors that they consider as desirable for a given classroom setting.

In the most strict applications of behavior modification strategies to classrooms, a teacher assesses *baseline* behavior by counting the number of times that appropriate, or inappropriate, behavior occurs during a specified period of time. For example, a teacher might establish a baseline of target behavior for a specific disruptive child by counting over a period of time the number of times he or she raises a hand, rather than calls out, during a reading lesson. The teacher then reinforces hand raising by offering a social reward—smile, praise, or pat on the back—or a tangible reward—a gold star, colored paper for writing assignments, or extra time for recess. Sometimes, a token, such as a poker chip, may be given. In this case, the child adds the token to a collection of earned reinforcers and later exchanges a specified number of them for a major reward. The target behavior, hand raising, is assessed again after the intervention in order to see how much improvement has occurred. Such behavior modification strategies have proved to be very effective in managing the classroom behavior of problem children, and many teachers typically use these techniques to shape the behavior of an entire classroom group.

The most difficult aspect of behavior modification programs involves the choice of reinforcer. Each child possesses a unique set of responses to various rewards. Some children will find only tangible things rewarding, while others will change their behavior for a smile or a hug. A sizable group of children will respond to any kind of attention as if it were a reward—even negative attention that involves scolding or some other form of punishment. Thus, it is usually difficult to decide upon a reinforcer that is effective for all students in a group and at the same time nondisruptive.

Today, literature about the classroom application of behavior modification, or at least the use of it in the strictest sense, often raises ethical issues.[15] These ethical concerns exist for some people because the techniques seem to remove control over behavior from the individual student and effectively change that child's behavior to meet the needs of someone other than the child—usually the teacher. They feel that this creates a situation in which the development of appropriate behavior is habitually controlled extrinsically rather than intrinsically—that is, managed from outside the individual rather than from within.

Ethical considerations

Some time ago, a group of researchers reviewed behavior modification strategies in schools and concluded that they constituted an attempt on the part of educators to make children be still, be quiet, be docile.[16] Rejoinders to those studies have emphasized that all classroom strategies are designed to encourage children to adopt behavior that fits with a set of common values and those values include such things as consideration and cooperation.[17] Whatever position one adopts on these issues, it seems clear that a teacher's personal value system, the value system of the school, and that of parents are crucial in making a decision about using behavior modification techniques. It is important that teachers who consider using one of these techniques understand the ethical issues involved.

In summary, reinforcement theory is a type of behavior theory that concentrates on the *consequences* of behavior in an effort to ensure that learning takes place. These theories hold that learning occurs because it is rewarded. In contrast, the association theory emphasizes the importance in the learning process of forming associations among stimuli. Thus, association theories concentrate on the *antecedents* of behavior rather than its consequences. The impact of reinforcement theory applications has been so great that many psychologists and educators confuse behavior theory with learning theory in general. Although reinforcement theory enjoyed much popularity in American schools during the 1960s, its influence today, while pervasive, is found more often in classroom management techniques than in strategies designed to enhance the acquisition of knowledge and problem-solving skills.

Before you proceed to the next section of this chapter, pause for a moment to think again about Priscilla Hope, who was described in the Snapshot of this chapter. Assume she understood behavior theory and used it wholeheartedly in her teaching.

As a behaviorist, what would she have done to address some of the problems she faced in teaching her students? Write down your responses on a piece of paper, and keep it until later in this chapter. You will be asked to refer to it again.

Cognitive Theory

E. C. Tolman, 1886–1959

During the 1930s and 1940s, a research psychologist working within the dominant behavioral method began to make an impact on learning theory in a way that was unusual for those times. Instead of confining his attention exclusively to behavior, E. C. Tolman insisted that the *readiness* of the learner was important and that all behavior—even animal behavior—is *purposive:* Animals and humans do what they do in order to accomplish something.[18]

Purposive behavior

In a series of ingenious studies, Tolman demonstrated that a rat wandering about a maze evidently learns something about that maze, so that when food is placed at the end of one of the tunnels and other objects block off some of the routes toward that food, the rat seems to exhibit *insight* as it quickly and correctly chooses the only possible solution within the maze of paths. Many behavior theorists had trouble accepting Tolman's interpretation that animals engage in insight learning rather than trial-and-error learning; but despite the intense criticism, many found Tolman's work compelling, especially as the early promise of behavior theory seemed to fade. As a result, Tolman is credited with being one of the early pioneers of what has come to be called *cognitive psychology*, the scientific study of thought processes.

Information-Processing Theory

Cognitive theory began to develop at about the same time that computer science became important. The parallels between computer functioning and the operation of the brain were so fascinating to cognitive psychologists that another label for cognitive theory emerged—*information-processing theory.* Researchers interested in this area of study began to think of learning in terms of sensory input, encoding, and retrieval systems, using the same terms and models computer scientists used.

R. M. Gagné, 1916–

A classic human information-processing model was produced in 1974 by R. M. Gagné.[19] According to Gagné's model, which is illustrated in Figure 6-1, the environment provides stimulation for receptors located in the sensing systems (vision, hearing, and so forth). These receptors then pass on that stimulation to the sensory register. The sensory register feeds the data along to short-term and long-term memory. From there, responses are generated that guide the effectors (muscles, glands, and so forth), which act back upon the environment.

This early model has, of course, been modified and refined by other theorists, but it illustrates the basic theoretical idea accepted by information-processing specialists. It is important to remember, however, that the figure illustrates *processes*, not actual "things" that have specific locations somewhere in the body.

Many fascinating studies have resulted from the theoretical reasoning of information-processing psychologists. For example, the work of K. Anders Ericsson and Herbert A. Simon has shown that when people are asked to report verbally on the mental processes that they are using as they perform a complex task, the complexity of the total assignment seems to increase greatly.[20] However, when they are asked to comment on *what* they are doing, rather than *how* they are doing it, these same individuals find the overall demands to be far less difficult than in the first situation.

FIGURE 6-1   Gagné's information-processing model. According to this model, humans receive stimuli from the environment and pass it on to memory. Their responses are generated, which act on the environment.

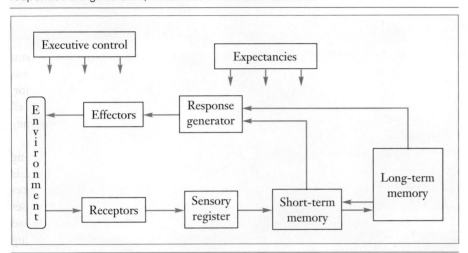

SOURCE: R. M. Gagné. (1974). *Essentials of learning for instruction.* Copyright © 1974 Allyn and Bacon. Used with permission.

Information-processing researchers have theorized that in the first situation, there is a greater burden on short-term memory. In the second situation, the subjects were asked simply to report whatever thought came into their minds as they performed the complex thinking task. This kind of thinking out loud apparently does not overburden short-term memory and, thus, does not interfere with the ability to perform the original task.

Theorists have focused much attention on the kinds of information-processing tasks that are involved in learning and necessary for success in school. While reinforcement theorists seem to have produced more models for teachers in the realm of classroom control, information-processing scientists have produced a good many data more directly related to learning—the acquisition of the subject matter that teachers expect their students to master. These school-based information-processing models, however, tend to be very detailed, cumbersome, and difficult to understand. The terms used are usually unfamiliar to the lay public and to teachers. As a result, reading about these ideas often leads the teacher to frustration rather than enlightenment.

This is unfortunate, because cognitive psychologists have important insights to offer classroom teachers. But it is understandable when one recalls that a sizable amount of work in cognitive theory has been available only since the 1950s. It is reasonable to assume that, as information-processing scientists continue to learn from their research, more easily understood explanations of their ideas, as well as more suggestions for classroom practice, will be forthcoming. In the meantime, a patient review of the available literature can often improve a teacher's understanding of the thinking processes that students may actually be using.

Ellen Gagné has produced an excellent summary of theory and research concerned with basic skill processes in reading, writing, mathematics, and science.[21] She reports, for example, that information-processing scientists believe that reading involves the processes of decoding, literal comprehension, inferential comprehension,

Ellen Gagné, 1947–

According to Ellen Gagné, one way to improve students' writing is to teach them to imagine an audience with whom they are communicating.

and comprehension monitoring. Each of these processes, in turn, has its own subdivisions. According to this conceptualization of reading, *decoding* involves the ability to match and to recode. When students *match*, they check the pattern of a word against word patterns that have been stored in their long-term memory. Matching skills result in production of a *sight vocabulary*, words that are recognized on sight, because they are matched with an already-known pattern. In contrast, *recoding* occurs when a word is sounded out. The resulting sound patterns activate the long-term memory, where the word's meaning may be stored.

Several approaches to teaching these reading skills have been produced. One common approach to teaching recoding skills places sound patterns typically occurring in words into a game that can be played on a microcomputer. Because sounding out words depends on a student's ability to group letters together within a meaningful sound unit such as "ism," "ing," or "con," cognitive theory suggests that practice at recognizing these sound units by playing the game increases the poorly skilled reader's ability to recode.

Although most of the information-processing models are highly technical, some of them offer assistance at a level that many teachers would consider practical. For example, when discussing the skills involved in composing and writing essays, letters, and the like, researchers have noted that goal setting is an important information-processing skill.[22] The ultimate goal of good writers is to communicate in a meaningful way; the goal of many poor writers is simply to dump onto paper all ideas possibly relevant to the topic. With this in mind, Ellen Gagné suggests that teachers should work with poorly skilled writers by teaching them to imagine an audience and to attempt to communicate to that audience.[23]

Cognitive Theory: Some Classroom Practices

1. emphasizing comparison and contrast
2. providing a context before introducing new material
3. using prompts, such as visual images
4. stimulating the use of more than one strategy for problem solving
5. emphasizing synthesis of parts
6. focusing on relationships between and among discrete bits of information

In summary, cognitive theory is concerned with mental processes. The development of computer science has complemented the development of cognitive theory; and, as a result, many cognitive theorists think of themselves as information-processing specialists. Within this field, researchers are concerned with those mental events that occur between the person's receptive sensory *input from* the environment and his or her active *response to* the environment. Cognitive theory is based on a view of human beings as active rather than passive. The majority of research in this area uses human rather than animal subjects, because it is presumed that people process information in a way that is functionally different from that of animals.

"Input from" versus "response to"

Information-processing theory is fairly new in psychological science, and its popularity is increasing dramatically. We can expect much more useful information for teachers from information-processing researchers in the near future.

Cognitive-Developmental Theory

Another branch of cognitive theory, called *cognitive-developmental theory*, is concerned with how children develop. Researchers in this area ask, When children's thinking develops, what changes? How can we describe the changes that take place in thinking processes?

An approach used to answer these questions, called *constructivism*, postulates that children *construct* reality through the give-and-take of their interaction with the environment. Infants interact with the nursery world of rattles, nipples, and fingers and construct an expectation for their own actions and those of the world around them. This theory suggests that early in infants' lives, they expect to hear a sound when an object is moved or to get milk when they suck on what they feel against their mouth. They then interact with the world according to that expectation. For example, they suck on almost anything put in their mouth. However, the world is never the same, and the environment does not respond the same way to each act: The thing the infant grasps does not rattle, but dings; the thing the infant's mouth feels does not give milk. Therefore, the infant's mind has to "go back to the drawing board" and change its interpretation of each encounter that does not produce the expected result. This process is not limited to infancy; it goes on throughout life and results in the beliefs and understandings that all of us have at any given point in our lives. In essence, what you need to remember about cognitive-developmental theory at this point in your studies is the idea that children *construct* a version of reality about themselves and the world around them based on their interaction with the external world.

Jean Piaget's close observations of individual children led to a far-reaching theory of cognitive development that remains highly influential even as it inspires criticism and additional research.

Piagetian Theory   The foremost cognitive-developmental theorist is Jean Piaget, whose work was discussed in Chapter 5. His ideas fit cognitive theory because they are concerned with the thinking events that are associated with learning. They also fit developmental theory because they carefully consider occurrences at each stage of growth and maturation as a student's capacity to learn changes.[24] Because of the developmental nature of Piagetian theory, a preliminary discussion of it was presented in the section on cognitive development in Chapter 5. Further consideration of some applications of Piaget's ideas are reported in Chapter 14, which describes instructional models.

Many of Piaget's ideas have been found to be useful for educators, physicians, psychologists, and other experts committed to enhancing the growth of children. In fact, virtually every approach to teaching recognizes the importance of Piaget's contributions. Kurt Lewin's comment that there is nothing so practical as a good theory is highly applicable to the theory of Jean Piaget—it has proved to be important because it has been so useful.

Adaptation

Piaget believed that developing children acquire the capacity for advanced thought as a result of their transactions with the environment.[25] Each stage of development depends on what has occurred in previous stages, as the child and environment mutually influence one another. As this happens, the child's mental functioning results in a useful *adaptation* of the child to the environment.

You will recall from Chapter 5 that, according to Piaget, *adaptation* contains two complementary processes—*assimilation* and *accommodation*. When assimilating, the child changes what he or she perceives in order *to fit it into an already-existing understanding* of the way things are. For example, consider the case of a child who has learned to classify as "bike" all two-wheeled machines with foot pedals. If the child should see a one-wheel apparatus with foot pedals and should call it a "bike," assimilation has occurred. That which is perceived has been assimilated into an already-existing cognitive structure. In contrast, accommodation involves *changing existing cognitive structures in order to adjust to a new perception*. If the one-wheel machine is perceived as something other than a "bike," possibly an acrobatic apparatus, and therefore becomes part of a new thought structure called "acrobatic props," then accommodation has occurred.

Assimilation

Accommodation

The processes of assimilation and accommodation can occur simultaneously. In all cases, they are complementary forms of adaptation to the environment. Piaget referred to the cognitive structures formed through these processes as *schema*. The cognitive schema of children change as they transact with their environments. It is through this continual interplay of person and environment that learning occurs. Because of the accommodations half of adaptation, Piaget's theory is considered a constructivist theory; that is, the child "constructs" a set of understandings about the world.

Schema

Piaget's theory of cognitive development has had a strong impact on many aspects of education.[26] His is a cognitive and a developmental theory that emphasizes the child's need to master age-related tasks prior to moving on to the next stage. The interplay between the child and the environment creates the opportunity for learning strategies to be developed. At first, the developing human being simply relies on his or her senses. Gradually, profiting from the manipulation of concrete objects, the child forms cognitive schema. Eventually, the adolescent child learns to abandon this reliance on the concrete, and abstract thinking then emerges. Piaget's influence on curriculum development has been pervasive and will continue for many years to come.

Cognitive and developmental theory

Criticisms of Piagetian Theory   Like all influential theories, Piaget's view of how children construct reality has had its share of criticism—much of which has been useful in stimulating new research and new ideas. The most controversial concept in his theory has been the idea of stage. According to Piaget, stages cover broad categories of cognitive behavior during a particular developmental period, when children can do certain cognitive operations and not others. For instance, he says that if a child is in the sensorimotor stage, that child cannot show number conservation, class inclusion, or mature object permanence. Recent evidence, however, has indicated that (1) children can master some tasks much earlier than Piaget had thought and (2) explanations for many Piagetian tasks seem to vary depending on the methods used to investigate the phenomena.

This point can be explained by looking at *object permanence*. Piaget said that if a person shows an object to an infant and then hides it from the infant's view while the child is watching, older infants will reach for the object in an effort to search for it, but younger infants will not. He explained the difference by saying the older infants believe the object still exists even though it can no longer be seen. He equated the children's reaching with their belief about the object—that it does or

Object permanence

does not exist. But there is now evidence that object permanence may be observed in young infants who are not yet able to reach; and, therefore, if the investigator uses a reaching task to measure the infants' belief that the object is still there, the test may be assessing the infants' ability to reach and search, rather than their assumptions about the object.

Breadth of intellectual abilities

A second criticism of Piagetian thinking involves the breadth of intellectual abilities associated with the different stages. In the American interpretation of Piaget's views, when a child is at a particular stage, he or she should be able to solve all problems that match the child's stage. Thus, if a child can solve the conservation problem in one context, he or she should be able to successfully apply those mental skills to all problems that require them. Although Piaget himself did not advocate this broad view, many have interpreted his theory in this way. One thing is clear, however: If a child has a particular concrete operational ability, it does not guarantee that he or she can solve all the problems to which that ability could be applied.

This discrepancy can be explained by looking at the balance scale problem popularized by Piaget. In the balance scale problem, weights are placed at various distances from the center. Children are asked to predict what will happen if one of the supporting blocks is removed and also to predict which side of the balance scale will go down when given weights are placed at given points.

Robert S. Siegler tested some children, aged 5 and 8, who initially solved the balance problem in the same way.[27] He gave these children experience with what he called "conflict problems." In these problems more weights were placed on one side of the scale, but the weights were at a short distance from the fulcrum (for example, four weights on peg 3); on the other side there were fewer weights, but they were placed at a greater distance from the fulcrum (for example, two weights on peg 4). In a problem like this, if children focus their thinking only on the weight, they reach one solution; but if they focus only on the distance from the fulcrum, they reach another solution.

From this study, Siegler found that this "conflict problem" experience benefited the 8-year-olds but not the 5-year-olds. He tried to find out why. One possibility was that the 5-year-olds did not know what to focus on in the problem. So he gave the 5-year-olds practice at representing the problem internally with instructions. "First you count the number of weights on this side—one, two, three, four. Then you count the number of pegs the weights are from the center—one, two, three. So you say to yourself, 'four weights on the third peg.'" After much practice using this technique and solving more conflict problems, the 5-year-olds were more like the 8-year-olds in their ability to solve the problem. It appears, therefore, that what was lacking in the 5-year-old children's initial performance was not achievement of a particular stage but their knowledge of what kinds of things to look for when they were trying to solve the problem. In this particular case, they were not likely to notice the distance (the pegs) until they had significant guided practice in doing so.

From this study we can see that, while Piaget's ideas about stage may be helpful in explaining how children learn to solve some problems, they are not adequate to account for all their learning. The children also need to know how to represent a problem; that is, they need to know what aspects of the problem are important for its solution.

Based on this research, Siegler formulated four rules that children follow in solving the problem:[28]

1. Predict that the side with more weights will go down and predict balance if there are the same number of weights.
2. Predict as in Rule 1 but also factor in the weights' distance from the fulcrum—that the greater the weights' distance from the fulcrum, the greater likelihood that side will go down.
3. Take into account both number of weights and distance from the fulcrum but do not have a consistent rule for integrating the two kinds of rules.
4. Take into account the number of weights and their distance from the fulcrum using a rule that integrates the two kinds of information.

Siegler found that younger children follow Rule 1; older children follow Rule 2; young adolescents follow Rule 3; and middle and late adolescents have an integrated rule that uses both number of weights and distance from the fulcrum. Siegler's explanation, in effect, breaks the problem into components that can be taught and learned by children one by one, whereas Piaget described the task in terms of a common pattern of generalized, systematic, hypothetical thinking characteristic of the "formal operations stage" (Chapter 5).

A third criticism of Piagetian theory deals with its emphasis. Piaget concentrates on how a person's own self-generated actions contribute to the construction of reality *inside that person's mind*. But, in fact, people do not develop in a vacuum. They are heavily dependent on their social environment for help in learning and developing. Piaget would not have argued with this notion; but he did not focus on the role of the social world in helping children develop their cognitive abilities—the roles of parents, peers, brothers, and sisters. Now, other theorists are elaborating on how the social world influences a child's cognitive development; and, in doing so, they are describing more of the interaction between the individual and the social environment. As they do this, they are, in effect, refining or building upon Piaget's ideas.

One group of theorists investigating this social interaction is made up of Russian psychologists who have been studying the interaction between children and their caregivers. The most influential of these theorists has been Lev S. Vygotsky. Vygotsky proposed the notion that parents engage in *regulating* their children through interaction.[29] For example, a mother guides her child in solving a puzzle that the child cannot do alone. The mother talks to the child about the puzzle and helps the child solve individual problems in the puzzle as they are encountered. This interaction between mother and child later becomes *intrapersonal regulation* as the child internalizes the words and strategies articulated by the mother and uses them without the mother's guidance. Once this happens, the child can use those internalized rules to guide future problem solving.

As you did a few pages ago, stop and think again about Priscilla Hope. This time, assume she knew developmental and Piagetian theories of learning as they have just been described and that she used those ideas wholeheartedly in her teaching. Also assume that she does not subscribe to behavior theory. As a developmentalist and Piagetian, what would she have done to address some of the problems she faced in teaching her students? After responding to these questions, compare your answers to the responses you wrote when you answered similar questions at the end of the section on behavior theory. How are your two sets of responses different? Why is this the case?

Impact of social interaction

Vygotsky, 1896–1934

Intrapersonel regulation

Something to Think About

Reread the descriptions of William and Sherry in the Snapshot for Chapter 5. Then assume that you are a colleague of two teachers who teach these students. Each comes to you and asks the same question: "I know William/ Sherry is in trouble but have no ideas about what to do." What would you suggest?

- How would you respond to each of the two teachers?
- Once you have decided what you would say, analyze the two responses in terms of what you just read about learning theory. Which elements of the various learning theories described in this chapter are you drawing upon in your replies?
- In what ways do your replies reflect your philosophy of education and your personal philosophy?

Learning Theories and Teaching Styles

Inevitably, teachers' learning theory preferences are influenced by four factors: the grade level they teach, the characteristics of their students, the curriculum they follow, and their personal teaching style. They need to consider all four factors as they select the learning theory or theories on which to base their teaching.

As teachers make these selections, they draw upon their knowledge of information presented in books such as this. For example, they consider what they know about student development, educational philosophy, various approaches to instruction, and curriculum patterns of organization. In a form of executive decision making, they put all these elements together and decide what and how to teach.

Grade level

Grade level is important because some of the theories emphasize the development of learning capacities prominent at a specific age while slighting those at other age levels. Those who teach at early childhood and early elementary levels often rely on Piagetian theory, because his most detailed writing is related to the thinking of young children. Adaptations of his work are particularly good for those who teach 7- to 11-year-old children—those at the concrete operational stage. In contrast, most of the reinforcement theory approaches have direct application to all age levels. Although the majority of the information-processing instructional models are geared toward beginning readers, a growing number of information-processing studies target high school and college learners. Thus, those who teach at the upper grade levels often find themselves relying on reinforcement and information-processing theories rather than Piagetian approaches. None of these choices is wrong or clearly better than the others.

Student characteristics

The unique characteristics of a classroom group sometimes require that a teacher search for approaches that differ from those that he or she has previously found useful. For example, it is not uncommon for a middle school teacher to be presented at the beginning of a school year with a group of children who seem unprepared to think in abstract terms—a capacity that is usually somewhat developed within children of middle school age. Adaptations derived from Piaget's work can often salvage the situation. Many remedial approaches rely on backtracking to stages of concrete manipulation before easing the child forward into abstract modes. In another case, a teacher may find a group of children of any age to be so unruly that little instruction of any type is possible. Reinforcement methods for classroom management can often help to create an environment where learning can begin to take place.

Curriculum decisions and choices among instructional materials are often made by supervisors or by groups of teachers who must consider such matters as the content covered, continuity across grade levels, cost, and sometimes political or religious and philosophical factors. Regardless of what influences the decision, however, the materials that are used by all teachers of necessity reflect an emphasis on a particular learning theory or a synthesis of several theories. Therefore, it is important that teachers have a clear understanding of which approach is reflected in the materials they use and that they evaluate the degree to which they themselves find that point of view to be useful.

Curriculum materials

Finally, successful teachers need to understand their own personal teaching style. For example, teachers who think of themselves as powerful classroom leaders who control students and who see the learner as a receiver of presented information often prefer reinforcement learning theory because that theory emphasizes the importance of the person who passes on the information and manages the behavior of his or her young "charges." These teachers often use applications of reinforcement theory in an efficient and productive way, both with subject matter learning and classroom management.

Teaching style

In contrast, teachers who study the nature of the learning process in some detail and are fascinated by the ways that children think things through tend to prefer Piagetian approaches. Often, this type of teacher expresses amazement at what children say and agrees that "kids say the darndest things." Piaget himself provides a good example of this kind of style. For hours at a time, he enjoyed quiet observation of the thought processes of his children.

Those whose teaching styles include a significant need for organization might respond well to information-processing approaches. These models tend to categorize and subdivide learning processes, and suggest step-by-step remediation strategies. For example, a typical information-processing approach to reading instruction will let the teacher know how many skills are involved in a particular reading task and will provide descriptions of the components of each skill.

Two important principles about learning theories to remember are (1) teachers need to rely on learning theories that complement their personal preferences and style and (2) their ability to adapt the theories they choose so they fit their particular teaching situation enhances the value of the theories. The adaptability of the theories increases teachers' understanding of them, as well as their utility as classroom guides. It is always true that a teacher's best teaching tool is the teacher's own self. Good teachers understand their own strengths, weaknesses, and preferences and are able to use these characteristics positively to enhance their students' learning.

REFLECTING ON PRACTICE

*T*his Reflecting on Practice consists of a hypothetical conversation among three teachers during their planning time. As you read, consider these questions:

■ How do you interpret this conversation and the situation with Jason?

■ What factors might have been influencing Jason's behavior?

■ What factors could the teacher have considered when trying to help Jason with his arithmetic study?

■ Was it a good idea for the teacher to give extra teaching time to Jason? Would you have chosen the recess period as the time to give extra help?

■ Based on this conversation, do you think a Piagetian approach might have been useful?

■ How would you have answered the primary-grade teacher's final question?

"Gee, Ann, you look awful today," commented Susan, a primary-grade teacher, to one of her colleagues, a fifth-grade teacher.

"I'm awful, all right, awful angry! Jason has driven me batty one more time. I've spent every recess period this week trying to teach him basic long division concepts, and we're still nowhere. Zero success. Then today I called him up to my desk when the recess bell rang, and he just informed me that he did not *want* to study arithmetic again during recess. He announced to me—to *me*—that he was not going to study during recess anymore. Then he just stormed out of the classroom. I just let him go. I knew I was so angry that if I started talking, I would just end up yelling and saying things I didn't really mean. Can you believe it? After I gave up all my afternoon breaks for four days, he has the nerve to *announce* to me that he doesn't want to learn arithmetic anyway, that he doesn't care about division, and—get this—he plans never to divide anything anyway as long as he lives!"

As Ann collapsed into a chair, her friend gave her an understanding look. Both teachers sighed.

"I can imagine that you're ready to string him up by those cute little suspenders of his, Ann. I know how much you care about him and how hard you've tried with him."

"You're darned right I've tried! And for what? So he can *announce* to me that he has no intention of studying arithmetic anymore."

Charlie, another fifth-grade teacher, joined the conversation. "What's going wrong, Ann?"

"Well," she replied, "he just doesn't get it. He's always trying to divide the bigger number into the smaller number or some other mistake like that. And when it comes to a remainder, forget it. He's just lost if a number won't divide perfectly into another one. 'Why do we always have to have something left over?' he says."

"You know, Ann," said Susan, "I used to have Jason in second grade, and I always thought his parents pushed him a lot. He's their only kid, you know. Maybe he's just rebelling or something like that."

"I've got three kids that are having a terrible time getting through this division chapter, too," said Charlie. "I'm doing the same thing with them that I did when I had trouble with the whole class last year when we came to this chapter. For one thing, Ann, you know that the textbook is particularly weak in this section—or at least, *I* think it is."

"I guess I agree with you," said Ann. "In fact, I don't think I like the whole book very much. There should be more pictures and more figures with problems.

Jason hates the book. I have to practically twist his arm to get him to read it. I guess that's true for some of the others in my class, too. But what is it that you're doing with those three kids, Charlie?"

"I'm using one of those Piaget approaches with them. I figured out last year that my group really needed to rely on concrete objects when trying to think through the arithmetic concepts. This year, I didn't waste any time when I saw that a few of them seemed lost in the woods on this division chapter. I got out my wood bars, plastic poker chips, and that other stuff you saw me making right before Thanksgiving last year. They seem to get it a lot quicker if they can actually see how the problems relate to concrete things."

"Well, that's certainly true of *my* second graders," said Susan. "But they're younger. Shouldn't fifth graders be able to work the problems through in their heads?"

Using Learning Theory: A Case Study from the Future

On a crisp, clear, late summer day early in the twenty-first century, Jennifer Hope Barnes found herself almost bouncing down the jetway of Flight 239 from St. Louis to Denver. Jennifer came from a family of teachers, and she had come to Denver to teach. It was to be her very first full-time teaching job—an especially important job in the life of all career teachers.

As she made her way to claim her baggage, she became strangely compelled by the memory of a great-great-great-grandmother, who was reportedly the first of the family's many teachers. This particular ancestor, Priscilla Hope, was said to have gone by stage to a one-room schoolhouse in a mining town somewhere. As she waited, Jennifer started wondering about Priscilla Hope. Had she been a good teacher? Had she felt just as Jennifer felt right that minute? What kind of woman would have traveled west in a stagecoach to live alone in a strange town? In response to her last question, Jennifer felt a moment of satisfaction, concluding that such a woman might be pretty similar to someone who would travel west in a jet for just the same reason.

Jennifer had been assigned to a primary-level classroom quadrant in a bright new public school building. Two of the teachers assigned to the other three quads were reportedly beginning teachers as well. Something about that seemed very comforting.

A few days later, just before entering the building on the first day of class, Jennifer gave her long granny skirt a couple of brisk tugs and a yank. She sailed into her quad with an air of quiet confidence that was not exactly false, though it surely hid such things as her sweating palms and slightly irregular heartbeat.

As the students settled themselves onto the floor or at a table, Jennifer looked out over them with a questioning glance. "Which ones," she wondered, "will need special help with their coding skills? Who are the ones who have memory register deficits? And who among these little persons can already reason abstractly when presented with one of the new Ray devices that have become so popular?"

As she began calling the children's names, she asked them to remember one thing that had already happened to them today. Attending closely to their answers, she began an almost automatic process of diagnostic listening. A part of her watched for early signals from those who would need special help with motivation. She was determined to become effective at teaching intrinsic motivation skills. She knew she would be good at using the older reinforcement strategies, but the newer approaches to intrinsic motivation seemed more challenging to her. She just did not quite understand what it was all about yet. However, she felt confident that after a year here under the guidance of her mentor teacher, she would know enough about it to be at least competent with these new strategies.

Jennifer silently blessed her university training program, especially the internship opportunity that she had experienced last year in Tennessee at one of the clinical education internship sites. She also silently wished that something truly definitive could be known about the complexities of the information-processing weaknesses in the dyslexia syndrome. "However," she thought, "I suppose it is quite enough for me that we have a pretty good idea now of how the average, well-motivated learner goes about the business of learning. I'm sure great-great-great-grandmother Priscilla had it a lot worse than we do today. She probably did not have any learning *theories* to guide her work. At least I have some facts—and good theories, too."

By the end of the year, of course, Jennifer knew which of her students were which, and she knew the learning strengths and weaknesses of each. She also knew a lot about the parents and a lot about what was going wrong for those who had a difficult time with such things as computer applications and abstract model building.

Throughout the swiftly passing year, Jennifer had marveled at how much these children knew compared to what she had known as a child. She also marveled at Priscilla Hope. Jennifer seemed to have an almost passionate curiosity about whether Priscilla had "made it." Had she been a good teacher?

By spring, Jennifer had stopped thinking so much about her ancient relative. What seemed much more important was that she herself had made it. She was awarded a beginning-teacher prize and offered a three-year contract that incorporated a salary increase. In addition to that, Karen Bradbury had actually learned how to compute in digital, analog, *and* synthesized—an accomplishment that no one thought would ever occur. And shy little Bert, who said and read little at the start of the year, had actually come up to her desk every day during the last week of class to read out loud for her what he had written.

Jennifer Hope Barnes was pretty sure that she was going to like teaching very much for a good many years to come. She looked forward to the challenges next year's students would present to her.

Conclusion

Teachers use learning theories to guide their teaching because research has not yet provided definitive answers to all questions about the best ways to teach. The theories presented in this chapter can prove useful in guiding teachers as they attempt to meet the goals they have set for their students; because they are useful, they are considered good theories. But the extent to which a theory is useful may change over time. Sometimes new ideas replace or enhance present thinking. The usefulness of a theory also varies from class to class and teacher to teacher.

Therefore, an important part of successful teaching involves choosing a learning theory or parts of theories as a guide for classroom practice. When teachers do this, they must know the theories that are available and must decide which are compatible with the students they teach and with their own personal teaching style. A good match of teacher and theory aids student success.

Teachers in the future will have more information at their disposal and possibly more theories to choose from as they confront teaching tasks. As a result, they will be better able to meet the needs of their students.

EDUCATIONAL RESEARCH

The Interaction among Theory, Research, and Practice

A main point of this chapter is that much of the knowledge that psychologists and educators have about how learning takes place is derived from one or more widely accepted learning theories. Stated rather simply, experts are not sure about how learning takes place, but they have some firm and broadly accepted hypotheses, and theories, about it. As researchers have tested these theories, conclusions from their studies support their thinking but do not confirm it absolutely. As a result, researchers continue to accept the theories as direction for their studies, the theories gradually evolve toward more refined principles, and forward-looking classroom teachers use the theories to guide how they design and teach lessons. Both researchers and teachers use these accepted theories about learning because, in the absence of more solid evidence, the theories are the best guides available.

This Educational Research section looks into the interaction among theory, research, and practice. In doing so, it extends points made in the Educational Research section of Chapter 5. This time our study focuses on *constructivism* as a theory about how learning takes place. Specific illustrations concern elementary school mathematics.

The section of this chapter on cognitive-developmental theory states that constructivists explain children's thinking as a process in which children personally *construct* meaning by interacting intellectually with their environment, including their classroom environment. For example, children see or hear something in their classroom environment (or experience it in some other way), interpret that new experience based on what they already know, and come to an understanding by connecting the new experience with their previous understanding. The result of the process is new knowledge, which is made up of three elements: (1) the new experience, (2) their prior understanding, and (3) their personal connection of the new and the old. This explanation of learning means that each person's understanding of something is personal because it is *personally* constructed in at least two ways: (1) the child's previous

understanding is unique to him or her, and (2) the intellectual connection he or she makes is also unique.[30]

This constructivist idea about thinking and learning can be illustrated as follows: Two young children witness a serious fire burning out of control and consuming a building. One of the two personally experienced a similar fire in the past and was seriously burned. The second had no such prior personal experience. Upon seeing the fire, the first child becomes emotionally upset and fearful; the second child is intrigued but neither upset nor fearful. The different responses can be explained by the idea that the two children *constructed* different meanings about the fire they were observing, each based on the understanding and experience they brought to the situation.

Constructivist thinking has tremendous implications for teaching because it undercuts assumptions upon which much current classroom teaching is based. In the words of two leading mathematics teacher educators, it challenges "a number of traditional beliefs about school learning; [including] beliefs about *how* students learn."[31]

A typical nonconstructivist, traditional view of mathematics instruction looks upon learning as a process in which teachers *transmit* information and ideas (from their own minds or from books they assign, for example) to students. The students absorb or take into their heads these ideas from other sources and, presumably, absorb them in the same form that they are understood by the person doing the transmitting (the teacher or the author of the book). Discounted are the facts that the students bring to their classroom lessons previous understanding different from that of the teacher, that they have different styles of thinking, and that they think on different levels. In this view, when a mathematics teacher teaches children the mental entity we call "four," the teacher's purpose is to have the children learn "four" as he or she (the teacher) understands it. The lesson is predicated on an assumption that there is an established way of understanding "four" and the children are supposed to learn what that is.[32]

In contrast, *constructivists* view the learning of "four," not as children *passively receiving* it from the teacher who puts it into their heads, but as children developing their own understanding of "four" through the three-part thinking process described above.

The constructivist view is different from the traditionalist view because it includes the following principles: (1) students learn by thinking in active problem-solving ways, rather than by passively absorbing information, (2) teacher communication does not *convey* meaning and understanding from the teacher to students but instead *evokes* the construction of meaning in students' heads so that students have to actively interpret what the teacher says and does, (3) learning must include understanding, (4) the understanding that students construct in their minds is not a replica-

tion of what the teacher has in his or her mind, (5) what and how students learn is affected by the social context in which it occurs, including the context of the classroom, and (6) the teacher's primary role is to coach or guide students, not tell them.[33]

For researchers in mathematics education, constructivist theory suggests that studies are needed to answer questions such as: If this is how students learn, how should mathematics curricula and lessons be organized? What should the class activities and learning materials look like? If teachers should not attempt to transmit their ideas to intellectually passive students, what should they do? Answers to these questions, of course, are not easy to find; but the questions give researchers beginning points for their studies.

These questions, however, are not the only ones. As is usually the case, when researchers have asked these and similar questions, they have tended to come up with additional questions rather than answers. One such additional question involves the issue of how much teacher guidance is enough and how much is too much. For example, if teachers should *guide* student learning rather than provide answers or describe the "correct ways of thinking about mathematics," then what kind of guidance and how much of it is appropriate? Responses can vary along a very broad continuum. At one extreme are those who suggest that teachers should "guide" students very directly and precisely; those who disagree say such guidance is merely a disguised way of telling students. At the other extreme are those who say teachers should allow students to "discover for themselves" with virtually no direction; those who

disagree with this stance say such an approach means students do not learn mathematics or do not learn it efficiently.[34]

A related additional question involves the classroom context in which mathematics learning takes place. For example, when students construct new knowledge based on prior understanding and experiences, much of the prior understanding and experience they draw upon occurred in mathematics classrooms (the current class the students attend and all previous classes). Those classes, of course, have differed from one another. Some were more traditional; others more oriented toward problem solving. Some stressed correct answers to mathematics computations; others emphasized higher-order thinking. Some accentuated individual seatwork and recitation; others encouraged student-to-student discussion and the interchange of ideas. If some types of classroom contexts produce student learning more effectively, how can those contexts be assured for all students?[35]

For mathematics teachers, constructivist theory requires a way of teaching that is very different from the traditional practice of passing on information from teacher to student and of students practicing the right way of doing mathematics. Constructivist theory calls for problem-solving classroom activities, student discussion and explanation of their thinking, intellectual challenges that develop higher-order thinking skills, and much more student understanding of mathematics.

To teach mathematics in these ways, teachers need to know more and have different skills than is typical for today's teachers. They need to understand how students learn mathematics, know their students' previous experiences with mathematics and levels of thinking skills, have a grasp of how classroom context affects learning, and be able to guide student learning without being too directive or too *laissez faire*. All of this has serious implications for teacher preparation and in-service education. It also has implications for how schools should be organized and what should be expected as students and teachers are evaluated.

Constructivist thinking has already greatly influenced the development of two sets of standards produced by the National Council of Teachers of Mathematics—*Curriculum and Evaluation Standards for School Mathematics* (1989) and *Professional Standards for Teaching Mathematics* (1991).[36] These two documents have been widely recognized as blueprints for how and what students should be taught, and both are being used for the assessment of mathematics achievement and competence tests for students and teachers. Both have been used by political and educational leaders as part of the Goals 2000 push to improve students' mathe-matics understanding and teacher accountability.

What happens next is a matter of conjecture and, for some, a matter of concern. Because constructivist ideas have influenced mathematics standards and Goals 2000 targets more quickly than they have influenced how mathematics is being taught in most classrooms, it is possible that students and teachers who will be expected to meet those standards will be held accountable for achievement that is, at least currently, unfair to expect of them.

Summary

Although much information about learning is yet to be discovered, learning theories based on what is currently known help explain how people learn and, therefore, serve as guides for classroom teachers. Currently, behavior theory, cognitive theory, and other theories that fit within each, including Piagetian theory, are relied upon most widely and have been found to be most useful. Behavior theories, including association and reinforcement approaches, emphasize the connections that are made between simple ideas and experiences and the consequences of active behavior. Cognitive theories more readily explain the dynamics of thought processes. Piagetian theory can be considered a cognitive approach, although it is more heavily developmental in focus than other cognitive approaches and is frequently thought of primarily as a developmental theory.

Teachers should choose from learning theories the ideas that fit best with their own personal styles of teaching and with the characteristics of the learners in their classrooms. By making an informed choice, teachers are able to meet the goals they identify for individual students and for a class as a whole.

Study Questions

1. Which of the learning theories described in this chapter is most appealing to you? Why?

2. Refer to Chapter 3 and make a list of ten to fifteen teacher classroom strategies or techniques that are described there. Then for each strategy on your list, select the learning theory in this chapter that the given strategy most noticeably reflects. Justify your connections.

3. Which of the learning theories described in this chapter would you draw upon most heavily if you faced the classroom situations described below? Explain your reasoning.

   a. A primary-level class has many students who are consistently off task—they talk among themselves a lot and frequently do not get their work done.

   b. Five of the boys in a fifth-grade class still cannot solve division problems in mathematics although the rest of the class is ready to move on to other lessons.

   c. Two ninth-grade students in a class of twenty-six rarely turn in their homework and almost never have it in on time.

   d. Three students in a seventh-grade mathematics class of twenty-seven are able to solve most word problems before the teacher explains how to do so. Most of the students learn how to solve them with explanation and some practice. Four never seem to understand.

4. How would you respond if a teaching colleague took the following position: "Behavioral approaches to teaching are wrong. They involve training and nothing more. Training is for animals, not humans. Students should be treated with more respect." As you respond, explain your reasoning.

Key Terms

Association theory
Behavior modification
Behavior theory
Cognitive-development theory
Cognitive theory
Conditioning
Constructivism
Fixed-interval schedule of reward

Information-processing theory
Insight
Intermittent ratio schedule of reward
Intrapersonal regulation
Law of effect
Law of scattered effect
Learning theory
Mnemonic

Motivation
Operant behavior
Pairing
Programmed instruction
Reinforcement theory
Schedule of rewards
Schema
Theory

For Further Reading

Biehler, F. R., & Snowman, J. (1989). *Psychology applied to teaching* (6th ed.). Boston: Houghton Mifflin.

Gage, N. L., & Berliner, D. C. (1991). *Educational psychology* (5th ed.). Boston: Houghton Mifflin.

Gagné, E. D. (1985). *The cognitive psychology of school learning.* Boston: Little, Brown.

Mayer, R. E. (1991). *Thinking, problem solving, cognition* (2nd ed.). New York: W. H. Freeman.

Mayer, R. E. (1992). Cognition and instruction: Their historic meeting within educational psychology. *Journal of Educational Psychology, 84*(4), 405–412.

O'Leary, K., & O'Leary, S. (Eds.). (1977). *Classroom management: The successful use of behavior modification.* New York: Pergamon Press.

Skinner, B. F. (1974). *About behaviorism.* New York: Knopf.

Strom, R. D., Bernard, H. W., & Strom, S. K. (1987). *Human development and learning.* New York: Human Sciences Press.

Learning for All Students

The Goals of Equity and Excellence

This chapter enlarges on ideas about the purposes of schools mentioned in Chapter 1 and relates them to differences among students (Chapter 5) and how they learn (Chapter 6). The focus of the chapter is on how American schools attempt to serve *all* students.

To review, the general purpose of American schools is defined by the nature of this country and the roles of its citizens. Because the United States is a democratic republic, its citizens need to be educated. They need to be able to understand ideas, events, and issues; to make judgments; to select leaders; to get along with others; to provide for their own economic well-being; and to be reasonably satisfied human beings. To provide the formal aspects of that education, we have schools.

But significant changes have occurred in recent years. Those changes shifted priorities for schools and raised new expectations about what schools should accomplish. Dissatisfaction with American schools surfaced especially during the 1980s; it became clear that they needed to be more successful in educating all children of the United States.

The information you gained about differences in students and how they learn from Chapters 5 and 6 needs to be placed in the context of purposes for schools. In this chapter we try to do so by explaining how the terms *equity* and *excellence* apply to the purposes set for American schools: having all students learn as much and as well as is possible.

To provide a perspective on the issues raised in this chapter, the Snapshot presents short case studies of three students from different backgrounds and with different abilities and needs. All three must be served by the schools they attend.

The Reflecting on Practice and Educational Research sections look at a special effort to serve students who are often missed by schools—an alternative high school for at-risk students. In those two sections you are asked to look at that effort both as a special service to students and as a research and demonstration project.

SNAPSHOT

The Snapshot for this chapter describes three students.[1] Each is different from the others, and all have different needs; but each must be served by the schools. As you read, consider the following:

- How should the schools serve each of these students so that each benefits as much as possible?
- In what ways should the instruction and instruction-related services provided for each of these students differ? In what ways should they be similar?
- How would you determine whether each of these students succeeds in school?

Mark

Mark is about to enter tenth grade in a comprehensive public high school. By most standards he is a successful student, although he is quiet and not a leader among his peers. He has solid A grades, ranks eighth in his class of more than 300, has taken most of the advanced courses available to him so far, plays second string on the soccer team, dates some of the popular girls at school, participates in several club activities, and is liked by his teachers.

Mark wants to be an engineer, knows he will go to college, and hopes to be accepted by an Ivy League university. He expects to be in the high school honors program for his junior and senior years. He will apply to be an intern in Washington, D.C., next summer.

Mark is one of three boys in a white, upper-middle-class family. Both his parents are professional educators—his mother is a college English professor, and his father teaches fifth grade. His home environment is supportive and educationally stimulating.

Mark's parents are reasonably satisfied with his schooling. He is achieving well; and they think most, though not all, of his teachers are good. They visit the school often and are active in the PTA. They frequently discuss Mark's progress with his teachers and counselors.

Sometimes Mark's parents wonder whether he would be achieving more if they had sent him to the private, academically challenging school they had considered. He would have had more stimulating classes, with more students who shared his interests and abilities. They decided to keep him in public school, however, so that he would interact with students from a variety of socioeconomic and racial groups.

Jamie

Jamie is halfway through second grade in an inner-city, public elementary school. His performance is below grade level, but so far he has not failed a grade. He tries to do what his teachers want most of the time, but not always. He hates homework and rarely does it. His teachers say he is noisy and aggressive much of the time. He has a slight perception problem that affects his reading, and he has asthma that flares up from time to time.

Jamie knows his primary teacher cares about him and wants him to succeed. He likes her. She devotes lots of time to helping him, calls his mother regularly, and sometimes gets very upset with him. At times, she even cries when he does poorly.

What Jamie likes most about school is the track club. He is a runner, and he wins most of his races, except when his asthma is bad. The physical education teachers at five inner-city elementary schools began track clubs last year, and this year Mr. Stewart, his P.E. teacher, personally asked Jamie to join. Whenever there is a Saturday competition with any of the other four schools, Mr. Stewart picks up Jamie and takes him to the meet.

Jamie lives in a small rental duplex apartment with his mother and an older brother and younger sister. His mother is head of the household, and the family is on welfare. His father is in prison for killing a man during a holdup. His older brother is often in trouble and usually skips school. Some people say his mother is a prostitute.

Jamie thinks he will probably flunk this year. He is far behind most students, and he cannot read well. He has to pass achievement tests to be promoted to third grade, and he already has failed most of them. He does not know what he will do when he grows up, but he is pretty sure he will not quit school, at least not until high school—and not while he can run in a track club.

Jamie's mother, who quit school when she was in the ninth grade, rarely comes to school, but she always tries to cooperate if a teacher calls her. She knows Jamie is difficult to handle and that he has problems at school. She does not want him to turn out like his brother. She thinks the teachers are good and appreciates the attention they give Jamie, but she does not really know much about teaching and schools.

Saundra

Saundra is in sixth grade this year and will go to middle school in the fall, if she passes. She works hard at school but is not very bright. She has some form of learning problem but no one seems to know what type. She has already failed two grades. She is 13—the oldest, tallest, and heaviest student in her class. The other students make fun of her and sometimes laugh at her clothes. The teachers like her and feel sorry for her.

Saundra knows she is not very bright, and she worries about flunking again. Lots of times she just does not understand things, no matter how hard she tries. Even when teachers give her special help, she never gets more than a C. She has a very frustrating school life.

Grades are not the only frustration, of course. The other students tease her because she is so fat. They also used to criticize her because she wore the same dress all the time—the only school dress she had. But the teasing about the dress is less frequent now, since one of the teachers gave her six new dresses—not really new ones, but new for Saundra. She told the teacher it was the nicest thing anyone ever did for her.

Saundra lives with her mother, two sisters, and a brother in public housing—"the projects." Although her mother works as a maid, they must also accept welfare. Saundra does not know where her father is and cannot remember him. Saundra's mother is a strong person. She has held the family together despite adversity. The children respect her, as do the teachers who know her.

Saundra's mother knows Saundra does not do well in school, but she expects her to keep trying. She also knows the teachers are doing all that they can. She worries about what will happen when Saundra goes to middle school. The new teachers will not know Saundra as well as her present teachers do, and she is afraid Saundra will quit school because it will be so difficult for her. She knows that Saundra needs as much attention as she can get.

Goals and Purposes

If schools were to meet the ideals set for them by Americans in general and educators in particular, they would provide an appropriate and excellent education for each of the students mentioned in the Snapshot; and they would do the same for all the other individuals who sit in classrooms across the nation. They would educate every single student to the maximum of his or her ability.

Ideal goals and the real world

Of course, education has never completely met these ideals. There is a great gap between these ideals and what schools can actually accomplish in the real world. American schools have simply not provided an excellent education for all children, and they do not do so today. Students such as Jamie and Saundra sometimes "slip between the cracks," and those such as Mark tend to make it without focused attention. Most knowledgeable observers believe, however, that through the years, schools have decreased the gap between what is expected of them and what they achieve.

In Chapter 8 you will read about schools and teaching in the United States' past—from colonial times to this century—and about the ideas, events, and people that shaped early American schools. For now, we can briefly summarize: As American schools evolved into and through the first half of the twentieth century, they increased in number, became available to more children, and expanded their instruction so that it became more useful to more students. Well before 1950, nearly every town had a school, and most rural children had access to a formal education, even if the distance to the schoolhouse was great. Nevertheless, many children did not have access to an education of appropriate quality. The children most often and most significantly slighted and neglected tended to be low-income, minority, and disabled.

Goals for Schools during the First Half of the Twentieth Century

Training the mind

At the beginning of the twentieth century, the dominant view held that American schools were meant to focus on *training the mind* and on teaching traditional academic subjects at the high school level. This view was articulated in 1893 by the Committee of Ten on Secondary Schools of the National Education Association.[2] The committee was composed mostly of college-level academicians who saw high school learning as a process of mental discipline that prepared students for college.

The committee recommended that the high school curriculum consist of nine subjects:

Latin	biological sciences (botany,
Greek	zoology, physiology)
English	mathematics
other modern languages	geology, geography
physical sciences (physics,	history, government, po-
chemistry, astronomy)	litical economy

In 1918, another group reported on what high schools should teach, and its focus reflected a significant change.[3] The Commission on the Reorganization of Secondary Education, also of the National Education Association, looked at student needs, interests, and abilities, as well as at the needs of society, and concluded that schools of the twentieth century should channel their instruction toward seven areas of life. Their report, titled *Cardinal Principles of Secondary Education*, called for high school instruction in the following areas: *Education for life, for all*

health	civic education
command of fundamental processes	worthy use of leisure time
worthy home membership	ethical character
vocations	

The *Cardinal Principles* stressed education of *all* students and for all aspects of their lives, not just education of college-bound students in demanding academic subjects. The report specifically mentioned that two-thirds of the students who began high school did not complete their studies and that they needed to be educated as well as those who were graduated.

This emphasis on educating the *whole child* continued into midcentury. In the *The whole child* 1930s, the Educational Policies Commission of the NEA issued a report, *The Purposes of Education in American Democracy*, which, influenced by the high unemployment of the Great Depression, reflected a concern for the out-of-school lives of all citizens.[4] It listed four broad issues of education, each of them focused on the individual:

self-realization	economic efficiency
human relationships	civic responsibility

Its general theme was similar to that of the *Cardinal Principles*.

In 1944, another Educational Policies Commission report, titled *Education for* *Life adjustment education* *All American Youth*, listed the *ten imperative needs of youth*.[5] It continued the schools' focus on the whole child and the child's *life adjustment* rather than on academic preparation and mental discipline. The ten imperative needs of youth were:

productive work experiences and	understanding of science and human
occupational success	nature
good health and physical fitness	appreciation of art, music, and literature
rights and duties of democratic	wise use of leisure time
citizens	ethical values
successful family life	ability to think rationally and commu-
wise consumer behavior	nicate clearly

The thrust of the report was reflected in the following statement:

When we write confidently and inclusively about education for all American youth, we mean that all youth, with their human similarities and their equally human differences, shall have educational services and opportunities suited to their personal needs and sufficient for the successful operation of a free and democratic society.[6]

Characteristics of the curriculum

In essence, ideas about *how* schools should meet the needs of twentieth-century American children and youth have varied from one extreme to the other—from a focus on teaching college-preparatory subjects to all students, with little attention to how those subjects apply to everyday life, to a focus on intentionally selecting and presenting content that meets individual needs, helps develop personal skills, and cultivates positive self-concepts.

Goals for Schools at Midcentury

Academic quality

By the late 1950s, American policymakers and educators began to have second thoughts about schools' emphasis on the whole child and the "less academic" ideas of the life-adjustment curriculum. Many began to feel that the schools' effort to educate everyone so broadly was resulting in an "average" education for most students at the expense of an education of true quality for anyone. They tended to assess quality, or the lack of it, in academic terms. Some noted particularly that schools seemed to be less challenging than they had been and that they apparently neglected the students who were most likely to become leaders of society. They demanded higher standards and more academically advanced instruction for the brighter students.

The cold war

This concern developed during the era that followed World War II and the Korean conflict, when Americans were competing ideologically with the former Soviet Union in the cold war and were intent on proving the United States to be superior in everything. Then in 1957, the Soviet Union launched the satellite *Sputnik*. Americans were appalled. They wondered at the Soviet ability to achieve a technological feat before American scientists could. They questioned the quality of the schools and saw a lack of commitment to compete and win. Americans were surprised; their national pride was hurt; and their security was threatened. They turned to the schools as a way to fight back.

Education and the national defense

Sputnik produced a national audience for academic critics who had been saying that schools lacked academic rigor, mental discipline, and challenging academic subjects. The critics wanted to replace "soft" life-adjustment subjects with more serious study. They wanted the schools to narrow their goals and to stop trying to be all things to all people. They said the national interest was at stake. Political leaders listened and responded.

Because of this post-*Sputnik* pressure, the national government funneled money to schools for teacher education, curriculum development, and equipment purchases through the National Defense Education Act. Better education became a matter of national defense. The areas of mathematics, science, foreign languages, and guidance received special attention, as did programs for academically talented students.

Balance

Nevertheless, the pendulum did not swing completely away from life-adjustment education. The shift was moderate, and the goals of educating the whole child and educating all the children were not lost. The change simply redirected educational priorities to a more balanced position between both goals.

James B. Conant helped initiate the shift and was partly responsible for its moderation. As president of Harvard University, chair of the Educational Policies Commission in the early 1950s, and author of several landmark studies of schools, he commanded much respect on school-related issues. He found in several of his studies, including *The American High School Today*, that although schools could be improved, they were not overwhelmingly bad and were already able to challenge talented students and simultaneously provide a comprehensive education for all students.[7] Conant's ideas set a tone for the times.

Ideas on how schools should be organized have also shifted back and forth through the century. Junior high schools were formed in the 1920s and 1930s to provide a transition for adolescent students between elementary school and high school. In the 1960s, middle schools began replacing junior highs in many communities, so that a similar close personal attention could be provided for students in transition, but this time for students in their preadolescent years.

School organization

The size of schools, particularly high schools, also has changed over the years. Small, somewhat constrained, multiple-purpose schools were replaced by consolidated county high schools with separate vocational wings and larger numbers of advanced and special courses than the small schools could provide. These, in turn, were succeeded by even larger comprehensive high schools with a myriad of courses and schools-within-schools. More recently, most decisions about school size have tended toward a middle ground. Schools are large enough to provide wide ranges of programs but are not so large that students get lost in the crowd.

School size

By the 1960s, the generally accepted mission of schools in America included a combination of purposes. Schools were expected to educate the whole child and every child to the maximum of each individual's ability. They were to help each student to strive for and reach *individual excellence*. John W. Gardner, educator and, after 1965, secretary of health, education and welfare under President Lyndon B. Johnson, stated the idea in 1961 when he wrote the following about striving for excellence:

Education for individual excellence

> There is a way of measuring excellence that involves comparison between people—some are musical geniuses and some are not; and there is another that involves comparison between myself at my best and myself at my worst. It is this latter comparison which enables me to assert that I am being true to the best that is in me—or forces me to confess that I am not. . . .
>
> Our society cannot achieve greatness unless individuals at many levels of ability accept the need for high standards of performance and strive to achieve those standards within the limits possible for them. . . . If the man in the street says, "Those fellows at the top have to be good, but I'm just a slob and can act like one"—then our days of greatness are behind us. We must foster a conception of excellence which may be applied to every degree of ability and to every socially acceptable activity. . . .
>
> And we are not going to get that kind of striving, that kind of alert and proud attention to performance, unless we can instruct the whole society in a conception of excellence that leaves room for everybody who is willing to strive—a conception of excellence which means that whoever I am or whatever I am doing . . . some kind of excellence is within my reach.[8]

Current Goals for Schools: Equity and Excellence

Since the 1960s, American schools have attempted to enable their students to reach the excellence identified by Gardner. They have sought to provide quality education for each individual child in terms of his or her capabilities. To accomplish this, they have delineated three concurrent goals for schools:

- that *all* children and youth be educated in the schools
- that they have an *equal* education in terms of their individual capabilities
- that each child's education be *excellent*

These goals mean that all three students described in the Snapshot of this chapter—Mark, Jamie, and Saundra—would have an equally excellent education, one that would be best for each of them individually.

Accomplishing these goals is not an easy task, however, and few schools would claim to have done so. Although the reasons for the difficult nature of the effort are many, we will examine only two at this time: the fact that resources for schools are limited and the fact that the meaning of *excellence* is not always clear in relation to schools and students.

Limited resources

All schools need appropriate amounts of *school capital*—the resources of all types (as described in Chapter 5) necessary to educate their students. But, in reality, nearly all schools face significant limitations on the resources that are critical to their success. Their funds are limited, and their leaders and teachers have limited amounts of energy, time, insight, commitment, and professional skill. They cannot pay for everything they want to do. They cannot assign the best teacher to every student. They simply cannot do everything. (How much schools can do is, of course, influenced by school finances, a topic discussed in Chapter 9.)

Trade-offs

This means schools must set priorities and make choices. They must decide which goals are most important and which are less so. In short, they must make *trade-offs*.

Equal and excellent, too

This need for trade-offs has led many school officials and many of those who support the schools to ask whether schools can possibly be equitable to all students and at the same time be excellent in all that they do. Some say they cannot. They say trying to be both equitable and excellent is too much. Some even see an incompatibility or contradiction between equity and excellence. Some go so far as to say that the two are mutually exclusive.

In fact, equity and excellence are not mutually exclusive, incompatible, or contradictory as goals for schools. They do, however, compete for attention and support, and this does result in a tension between them. But good school systems manage the tension, balance the priorities, and divide the resources evenly. They continue to seek both equity and excellence for their students.

Defining excellence

How well schools provide equity and excellence for their students also depends on the meaning of *excellence*. In a general sense, *excellence* means the best, and certainly everyone wants the best—the best schools, the best education for students, the best teachers, and so forth. But for the term to be useful to teachers and other school decision makers, it must be more precise. It must be made operational. Such questions as the following must be answered: Excellent in what way? Excellent by what standards?

Individual capabilities

The statement by John W. Gardner quoted earlier provides a first step in making the concept of excellence operational in the context of schools. It defines *excellence* in terms of the *individual capabilities of all students*. Students are excellent if they reach the upper limits of their own potential, and schools are excellent to the extent that they enable all of their students to do this.

A second step in making the concept of excellence operational involves the question, *Excellent at what?* Are students excellent because they pass the most sub-

By what standards should we measure whether a school has achieved "excellence" in educating its students?

jects possible, because they get the best grades, because they succeed in the most demanding courses, because they get into the best colleges, or because they turn out to be very likable people? Are their schools excellent because they offer the most courses, set the highest standards, have the best teachers, or graduate the most students who go to college?

In recent years, the *Excellent at what?* question has been answered most often in terms of what and how much students learn by the time they finish school. In that sense, schools are judged to be excellent on the basis of the quality or amount of learning they produce in their students. In educational jargon this is called the *quality of educational outcomes.*[9]

What students learn

When excellence is thought of in this double-sided way—in terms of individual student potential and amount of learning produced in all students—the ideas of equity and excellence are not competing goals for schools. They are a single standard. The challenge for all schools is to serve all students well.

Excellence—To serve all students well

An Emphasis on Equity

In the early 1960s, a genuine and widespread concern developed in the United States about the plight of the poor and other disadvantaged people of this nation. American society was successful and prosperous, yet some of its citizens obviously did not share in the benefits. Political and civil rights leaders asked why this situation existed, condemned it, and called for action to change it. The Kennedy administration began an attack on poverty and was perceived to hold racial equality as a cornerstone of its agenda. When President John F. Kennedy was assassinated in 1963, President Lyndon Johnson enlarged upon and continued the effort, steering through Congress a number of civil rights bills, declaring a War on Poverty, and calling for a Great Society, one in which all Americans shared in the wealth of the nation, both financially and culturally. Nearly everyone felt that schools should play a critical role in this advancement of prosperity and knowledge.

Because of this national effort to help those most in need, because of the critical role of schools in doing so, and because low-income, minority, and disabled children were so noticeably "disadvantaged" in both schools and society as a whole, the combined equity and excellence goals for schools were skewed during the 1960s and early 1970s. Matters involving *equity* were emphasized more than those that concentrated on excellence. As reported earlier, during the 1980s the emphasis shifted more toward excellence again, and since then the quality of schooling is again being judged more often in terms of student academic achievement. However, educators in general are still committed to both equity and excellence in schools and are still trying to accomplish both at the same time.

The Legal Mandate for Equity

Much of the push for equity in the schools was part of the civil rights movement of the 1950s, 1960s, and 1970s and came from outside the schools, especially through court challenges to inequitable school policies and practices and through national legislation. The watershed year was 1954, and the key event was the United States Supreme Court decision in the case *Brown v. Board of Education of Topeka.*

Brown v. Board of Education, 1954

The *Brown* case actually involved a combination of four cases then before the courts. The issues were many, complex, and overlapping. For the purposes of this discussion, however, we focus on the main points that relate to the issue of equity in the schools.

Plessy v. Ferguson, 1896

Since the *Plessy v. Ferguson* decision in 1896, most United States school systems had operated racially segregated schools because the *Plessy* ruling allowed them to do so. That opinion said that "separate but equal" facilities did not violate the Thirteenth and Fourteenth Amendments to the Constitution of the United States. Those amendments eliminated slavery and protected certain individual rights, including *due process* and *equal protection* of the laws.

The *Plessy* case did not arise from a question about schools. It came about when Homer Adolph Plessy sued a Louisiana criminal court judge who had convicted him for refusing to leave a "white-only" railroad car. A Louisiana law had required that white and "colored" passengers use separate public accommodations. Plessy, who was of one-eighth "African blood," had boarded a train in New Orleans, occupied a place in a "white-only" car, and refused to leave when he was ordered to do so. He was arrested, jailed, and convicted. (It is interesting to note that his action was essentially comparable to that of Rosa Parks, a black working woman whose refusal to move to the back of an Alabama bus in 1954 brought about a black boycott in Montgomery and ushered the future Nobel laureate, Dr. Martin Luther King Jr. to a position of national importance.)

The *Plessy* decision said that laws requiring separation between the races could be legally enforced. Courts could not interfere. Laws in many states segregated schools, as well as housing, transportation, and much of society as a whole.

In the unanimous *Brown* opinion, written by Chief Justice Earl Warren, the Court disagreed directly with the *Plessy* decision. Its two-part opinion said that:

1. segregation in public schools deprived the plaintiffs in the *Brown* case of "the equal protection of the law"
2. schools must correct the situation

Equal protection of the law

The Court based the first part of the decision on a series of assumptions and judgments:

1. Education was a critically important part of contemporary society of the 1950s.

2. Children probably could not succeed in life without it.
3. If states provided public education at state expense, they had to provide it equally for all children.
4. Even if most other aspects of education are equal for both races, segregation deprives minority children of an equal education because it denotes "inferiority" of the minority group.
5. A feeling of inferiority affects a child's motivation and mental development.
6. This deprivation results in depriving minority children of some of the benefits they would receive in a racially integrated school system.

Therefore, the first part of the *Brown* decision said that because separating children solely on the basis of race generates "a feeling of inferiority as to their status in the community that may affect their hearts and minds in a way unlikely ever to be undone," *separate educational facilities are inherently unequal.*

In the second part of the *Brown* decision, the Court said that schools that had been legally segregated had to begin a process of *correcting* the situation. It said they had to

Corrective action—
Desegregation

1. make a prompt and reasonable start toward desegregation
2. carry out the ruling of the Court in an effective manner
3. proceed consistently and comply in good faith at the earliest possible date
4. develop local desegregation plans

The *Brown* decision started a nationwide school desegregation process that directly affected nearly all American communities and most school students. At first, the schools that were most significantly affected were those that had been segregated by law or legal regulation—*de jure* (by right) *segregation.* Most such schools were in the South.

However, subsequent court decisions extended the *Brown* rulings to schools that were segregated not because of laws requiring segregation but because of other factors—housing patterns, the locations of schools, family choice, and local custom—*de facto* (of fact) *segregation.* De facto segregation rulings affected schools throughout the nation, especially outside the South.

When school systems and state and local governments delayed implementing the *Brown* directives—as many did—complainants turned to the courts for additional help. As a result, the courts insisted a few years later that desegregation proceed with "all deliberate speed." School systems and states were required to develop desegregation plans with timetables, to have the plans approved by the courts, and to abide by them. Often the courts found it necessary to monitor compliance closely. School officials who persisted in delaying were charged with contempt of court. The Civil Rights Act of 1964 authorized the United States attorney general to sue and to withhold funds from school systems that were not desegregating as expected or were otherwise discriminating by race, color, or national origin.

"All deliberate speed"

The most important Supreme Court case during the 1970s that involved school segregation was *Swain* v. *Charlotte-Mecklenburg Board of Education* (1971). The Charlotte-Mecklenburg County School District in North Carolina had technically desegregated its schools before 1971, but because of neighborhood living patterns, a number of district schools still had large concentrations of either black or white students. The Court said that, although under normal conditions school populations may reflect the racial composition of the neighborhood rather than the whole school district, in this situation schools should reflect the general racial composition of the population of the whole district. It declared that although neighborhood

Swain v. *Charlotte-Mecklenburg Board of Education*, 1971

Busing

Efforts to achieve educational equity through desegregation have involved disruption and conflict. In South Boston, a substantial police escort accompanied black students being bused to a previously all-white high school on the first day of court-ordered desegregation.

schools were a good idea under normal circumstances, the degree of racial imbalance in the Charlotte-Mecklenburg schools was such that the situation was not normal. Under these conditions, desegregation was more important than neighborhood schools. It said further that, although sending students to schools outside their neighborhood might prove inconvenient, transporting children by school bus would be an appropriate way to overcome segregation, because students already rode buses to school throughout the county. (It is important to note that it was the *Swain* decision that suggested possible use of busing, not *Brown*, and that *Swain* suggested busing and did not require it.)

After the *Swain* decision, the courts ruled in a number of other de facto school segregation cases, and their decisions were often inconsistent. These situations usually involved one central issue: Should serious imbalances in the racial composition of schools be permitted, or is racial segregation contrary to the constitutional guarantees of equality? The courts, Congress, and the executive branch of the federal government have often disagreed on how to answer the question.

Nevertheless, since the mid-1970s, the general movement of desegregation has been toward agreed-upon balances in the racial composition of schools, regardless of the cause of the imbalance. The means typically used to desegregate are those that restore balance with the least amount of disruption. However, nearly all such efforts involve a significant amount of disruption, consternation, and ideological conflict.

Desegregation, the norm

During the thirty years following the *Brown* decision, most schools in the United States were gradually desegregated, and as a result minority students in general have received more equitable educations than had been the case. The most obvious effects of the process have been the elimination of legally segregated public schools and/or public schools that are transparently unequal in quality. But broader, more subtle, and probably more pervasive changes have also taken place. Most white, black, and other minority students attend the same schools, interact fairly closely with each other, and experience the same teaching. Desegregated schools have become the norm, although many schools still have very high percentages of students of the same race and single-race percentages are increasing in many schools in the 1990s.

The Legal Mandate for Equity Applied to Students with Disabling Conditions

For several decades after the *Brown* decision, advocates for children and youth with handicapping conditions have demanded that the same principles of equity be applied to disabled children. Their insistence has resulted in court actions and legislation that have extended those same *rights of education* to such students. As with desegregation, however, the process has not been easy, quick, or smooth.

Although the *Brown* decision referred to the education of black children, it stated that when states choose to provide education for children, "it is a right that must be available to all on equal terms." This principle became the basis for litigation concerning the education of children with disabilities. In *Pennsylvania Association for Retarded Children (PARC)* v. *Commonwealth of Pennsylvania*, a landmark case opened in 1971 and ruled on in 1974, Pennsylvania agreed to a consent decree stipulating that it would educate mentally retarded children at public expense. The state agreed

> to provide a free public education for all its children between the ages of six and twenty-one years. . . .
>
> to place each mentally retarded child in a free, public program of education and training appropriate to the child's capacity.

Two related court decisions extended the *PARC* case principles beyond mentally retarded children to those with other disabilities. The ruling in *Mills* v. *Board of Education of Washington, D.C.* (1972) said the right of a free public education extended to children with all types of handicapping conditions. The *Wyatt* v. *Stickney* (1972) decision said children who are institutionalized also have a right to the same educational services as other children.

These and related court decisions, as well as several laws passed in the early 1970s, set the stage for Public Law 94-142 (1975), the most significant law in American history affecting the education of people with handicapping conditions. This law, passed in 1975, mandated that each state provide for the education of people with handicaps, that it follow a set schedule in implementing the law, and that it be in full compliance by the fall of 1980. The law stipulated that children with the following handicapping conditions had to be served by each state:

mental retardation	orthopedic impairment
hearing impairment	blindness
deafness	learning disability
speech impairment	multiple handicaps
visual impairment	"other health impairments"
serious emotional disturbance	

Public Law 94-142 specified that children and youth with handicapping conditions must be provided *a free appropriate public education* in the *least restrictive educational environment*. Under the law, the plan of education for each of these students

Education: A right for all

Public Law 94-142

Least restrictive educational environment

must be developed in the form of an *individual education program or plan* designed to meet his or her individual needs. The law also reaffirmed that the process of determining which educational services are to be provided for a specific child must be decided upon according to *due-process* procedures and with the direct participation of parents or guardians. It made states responsible for all educational programs for children with handicapping conditions and provided federal government funds to pay part of the costs. Subsequently, Public Laws 99-457 (1986) and 101-476 (1992) updated and reinforced the principles and stipulations of 94-142. (These and more recent parallel legislation concerning equitable education and educational financing are described in Chapter 9.)

Individual education program

Schools and Differences among Students

"The best for each"

As Chapter 5 showed, if schools are to serve all students equally and excellently, they cannot treat all of them in the same way. To do so would not only overlook the differences among students, but would also be naive. On the other hand, schools cannot treat each student as a wholly unique individual. They do not have the resources to do so. The challenge involved in providing both an equitable and excellent education to all students, then, is to provide the *best* education for *each* student.

Categorizing Students and Targeting Instruction

To approach the task of providing the best education to each student realistically, educators often group or categorize students, and teachers then target their instruction to those groups—high ability, low ability, college prep, vocational, and so forth. They do so because they believe that categorizing helps them teach better. In fact, they categorize subject matter, activities, and materials, as well as students.

Appropriately targeted instruction

When educators target instruction appropriately, the process usually helps everyone. Teachers teach better, and students learn better. For example, when the students who seem to have the best writing skills are grouped together for creative writing, the teacher can focus more intently on their particular skills than when such students are scattered among poorer writers. When those reading significantly below grade level are taught together, the teacher can target their common problems more exactly than when they are in heterogeneous groups. When students are permitted to elect some of their subjects on the basis of their personal interests and goals, their motivation to learn tends to increase.

When the categorizing and targeting are wrong, however, teaching and learning are inhibited. More importantly, students are hurt. For example, when all minority students are put into segregated classes, the placement is based on stereotypes, just as is the assumption that all girls are weak in mathematics. Similarly, when children with learning problems are assumed to be mentally retarded, they are incompetently diagnosed.

In essence, categorizing students to some extent is necessary, appropriate, and helpful. But categorizing must be done carefully, must be based on multiple criteria, and must be supported by complete and accurate data. The process must be seen as complex. The students must always be seen more as unique than alike.

An educator-imposed process

Chapter 5 explains that students do not naturally fall into homogeneous groups. Educators categorize them, and doing so involves an artificial process that imposes distinctions upon the students. Even when the categorizing is done well, with student understanding and approval, with the best of intentions, and with positive results, it necessarily overlooks some of the qualities of the individuals involved. Schools do this because they cannot meet all of the individual differences of all their students; and, when they cannot make the system fit the student, they find it necessary to make the student fit the system.

Remedial education is one of the ways schools try to enhance the learning of students who are not performing up to expectations for their age group. The practice, in essence, is one form of the processes of categorizing students and targeting instruction toward those students' particular needs. Students who are "performing below grade level" are placed in special classes or given extra instruction so they can *remediate*, or make up, whatever they did not learn earlier, when more typical students learned it.

Remedial education

When successful, remedial instruction does help students catch up, but often it turns out to be slower-paced instruction, and sometimes lower-level instruction, than that provided to other students. In less-than-ideal arrangements, remedial students frequently fall further behind as they proceed through their slower, less challenging classes while their age-level peers move on more quickly. Supporters of remedial education point out that even though students in remedial classes learn at slower rates and on more basic levels, they are likely to learn more and better than they would if they were placed in more typical classes where they would be both lost and frustrated.

Efforts to Serve All Students

This section of the chapter describes major efforts by schools to serve all students. Each effort focuses on a general category of students. Each is a way schools try to achieve the concurrent goals of equity and excellence.

Racial Desegregation

Although the *Brown* decision said that racially segregated schools could not be maintained and thereby started the process of desegregation, years passed before most segregated schools were desegregated and before large numbers of black and white students attended the same classes. In some schools and for many communities of parents, teachers, and children, the process is still not complete. As a result, schools, teachers, students, and our society suffer.

Though extremely regrettable, the length of the desegregation process is not hard to understand. The tradition of racial segregation had been ingrained in American society since white conquest and settlement began. Early on, a slave economy developed; and it created an erroneous view of differences among human beings—a view perpetuated by ignorance and fear and institutionalized by economic conditions, social norms, religious justification, public legislation, and common practice. Segregation was certainly not just a school problem. It occurred in schools because schools are a part of society and clearly reflect the values of the society.

An erroneous view of differences

Because state and local governments are responsible for providing public education and therefore decide how and to whom it is provided, it was they who estab-

Dual school systems

More than forty years after the Supreme Court's Brown *decision, equality in educational opportunity remains a distant dream for millions of schoolchildren in the United States.*

lished dual systems of schooling based on race. They decided when to build schools, where to build them, and how much to spend. They determined which students were assigned to which buildings, which classes, and which types of instruction. In doing this, they often made racially based judgments that were common in the society of their times. In short, segregated schools were not a result of educational policy; they came about because of the racially biased cultural expectations of the society.

Approaches to desegregation

In response to court orders and governmental legislation over the past four decades, school systems have tried a number of approaches to desegregation.[10] Some of those efforts were effective; some were not. Some have been "good-faith" responses; some have involved minimal compliance. Some have been obstructive. Among the efforts that have been effective, at least to some extent, are the following:

Freedom of choice, voluntary student transfer, and open enrollment	Busing across school district lines
Voluntary busing	Combining school districts
Compulsory busing	Establishing target ratios for schools
	Magnet schools

Obstructive tactics

Obstructive tactics have included:

refusal to comply	establishing white-only private schools
delays of legal actions	segregating students within schools
closing the public schools entirely	

White flight

White flight, a social phenomenon often associated with school desegregation, occurs when white people move away from neighborhoods that are in the process of absorbing additional minority group members. In the 1960s and 1970s this seemed to happen frequently as a direct result of school desegregation. When white children from one neighborhood were assigned to schools with high percentages of black students, their families moved to new neighborhoods.

More recently, however, researchers have found that white flight may be more complex than a simple negative reaction by whites toward blacks. Generally, people move to new neighborhoods for one of two reasons. When they move to "better" neighborhoods, they do so because they can afford it and because they want to improve their social and economic status in the community. When they move to less desirable neighborhoods, they do so because they are forced, usually because of economic circumstances.[11]

In this context, white flight is part of the mobility of families from "less desirable" to "more desirable" neighborhoods. Because white families generally tend to be economically "better off" than black families, whites more often move to so-called better neighborhoods. Frequently, blacks replace them. Of course, to the extent that people view schools with high concentrations of low-income, minority students as "less desirable," school desegregation is a motivation for whites to move away.[12]

Compensatory Education

Compensatory education is an effort by schools to provide special instruction for students whose out-of-school life is considered to be so different from that of most students that they are at a disadvantage in the regular school program. The types of deficiencies most often addressed involve economic and social deprivation associated with poverty, family instability, and other social conditions that hinder education.

Compensatory programs usually provide remedial instruction, special activities, and supplemental services intended to make instruction for disadvantaged students more effective and to produce greater achievement. Some of these are

For disadvantaged students

- *Early childhood education programs for high-risk students*, such as Head Start and Follow Through. Head Start programs are designed to provide early intervention and special academic help to preschool students who would not be expected to succeed in the primary grades under typical conditions. They provide special readiness instruction prior to first grade. Follow Through programs continue similar special instruction through the primary grades in an effort to sustain gains made at the preschool level.
- *Family intervention programs* that provide aid to children and parents of infants and preschoolers. Many of these attempt to prevent nutritional and educational impairments from developing at early ages.
- *Basic skill instruction*, especially in reading and early language development.
- *Bilingual education*, which provides instruction in a primary language other than or in addition to English.
- *Special counseling and guidance services* for students and parents.
- *Tutoring services* for students who demonstrate areas of academic weakness.
- *Dropout prevention programs*, including alternative schools, work-study arrangements, and on-the-job training.
- *Adult literacy instruction*, which by adding reading to the student's skills can enhance quality of life and ability to get or keep jobs.
- *Job training*, which prepares students to be able to get and stay on jobs.

Many current compensatory education programs were initially developed at the federal government level and enacted through laws passed during the 1960s as part of the response to the civil rights movement and the federal government's War on Poverty. Those early efforts typically provided federal government momentum,

Federal government initiative

guidelines, and funds but expected state and local governments to provide the programming.

As a result of federal legislation and comparable action at state levels, compensatory education is now provided for students from early childhood through adulthood. For the most part, the concept has remained strong from the 1960s into the 1990s; but, although Head Start remains very popular, during the last decade, funding in general has not kept pace with inflation as the federal government, particularly under the Reagan and Bush administrations, cut back on social programs. Several components of the Clinton administration's Goals 2000 legislation are efforts to channel more support to Head Start and similar activities.

Results are mixed

Although government officials and school leaders expect compensatory education programs to help meet the instructional needs of disadvantaged students, data from evaluation of many of those programs provide mixed results. In general, the findings do not show the gains in student achievement that have been anticipated. Unfortunately, it appears that despite tremendous efforts and much money, most compensatory education programs simply do not enable disadvantaged children to catch up with middle-class children in a significant or long-term way.

Something to Think About

The following is an excerpt from a news item by Frank Gibney, Jr.

The Gonzalez family lives in the lower Rio Grande valley in a cramped, dark and drafty three-room shack. Their home is in a *colonia* (neighborhood), an unincorporated rural subdivision. They have no heat or sewage system, and when it rains the colonia's rutted dirt roads and yards flood so badly that children must wade through a stew of water and raw sewage to get to the school buses. Even in the dry, 100-degree heat of spring kids have the wheezing cough of poverty.

That cough echoes up and down the U.S. border with Mexico, a poverty belt more desperate than even Appalachia. The heart of the squalor is in the lower Rio Grande valley, now the poorest region in the United States. In "the Valley," as it is known, Gonzalez and up to 250,000 other American citizens live in more than 400 rural slums. Unemployment in the colonias runs as high as 50 percent, water supplies are fouled and chronic diseases are rampant. Schools in the Valley's three main counties are hopelessly overcrowded. In short, the conditions in the colonias are the worst America has to offer. And the population is increasing so rapidly that studies predict it will double by the year 2000.

- How can schools provide an education for children of "the Valley" that will compensate for their living conditions?
- How would you describe or provide an "excellent" education for a child with this background?

This less-than-successful history of compensatory education programs is being investigated. Some researchers fault the breadth and "scattergun" thrust of some efforts; others say that specific programs are too small and short-term in scale; some raise questions about the instructional methods used and the qualifications of the teachers; and some say the task of educating the "children of poverty" in the United States is just too complex and too difficult to be accomplished through the kinds of programs already established.[13]

REFLECTING ON PRACTICE

*T*his Reflecting on Practice consists of excerpts from interviews of three people, a former student and two teachers, who participated in an alternative high school in a large city.[14] The alternative school was an attempt to reach students who are "at risk"—in danger of dropping out. As you read, consider:

- In what ways are the experiences described here success stories?
- What happens to students like Barbara when they do not have access to these types of programs?
- How do you think the current accountability pressures in education affect programs such as these?
- Programs such as these are usually very expensive. If you were asked for your recommendation by a school board that had to cut program budgets, would you suggest they keep this program and terminate others? Why or why not? Which types of school programs are less important to you than this? Which are more important?
- Would you want to teach in this type of alternative school? Why or why not?

Barbara

"You can be the scum of the earth," she says, ticking off each word as evenly as a metronome, "and these people would find something good about you. If you have anything good about you, that is."

Barbara is talking about an alternative program at a large comprehensive high school, a program that enabled her to graduate from high school a year ago.

"I never thought I would graduate from high school," she says, her hands busy flicking imaginary crumbs from the table. "Not until I got into this program." With a half laugh she adds, "My parents called it a miracle."

She describes her high school experience as a progressive journey toward apathy. "I went to school freshman year, got all my credits, and got good grades, although I didn't see the point."

Her attendance became extremely sporadic her sophomore year. "In the mornings I played Frisbee and in the afternoons I played pinball."

She explains with a question. "What was the point? My teachers could[n't] have cared less."

The outwardly obliging exterior she maintained her first year of high school began to disintegrate into [that of] a defiant, sullen girl who "partied" on school grounds within eyesight of teachers who left her and her friends alone.

After her sophomore year, Barbara interviewed for admission to a new program, an alternative program designed for students in danger of dropping out of school. She says her attitude changed.

"The teachers cared so much," she says, leaning forward and stubbing out her cigarette between two slender fingers. "They told you over and over that you could do it, they knew you could. And they said they knew that you knew too, deep inside." In her intensity, her voice breaks and she looks embarrassed for a minute, but then continues. "They kept us going. The classes were so small—about 8 kids—that we had to get along. And if we didn't understand something, they explained it. We did things over and over and over until they were right."

Pinching the rim of a paper cup, Barbara says, "It was hard." She wants me to understand that this was no easy ride; there were rules and regulations, more than in the regular school. A certain number of infractions and out you went. Period.

Without preface, she mentions her daughter. "Audrey is a year and a half now. I'm nineteen. I got pregnant when I was sixteen and I had her when I was seventeen."

. . . The first person Barbara told about her pregnancy was one of her teachers. She smiles as she remembers it. "She was great. She was wonderful. I was so scared. She told me all the options, all the things I could do. She told me it was all my decision. And she didn't tell anybody else. Not one single person." She adds, "She never told anything if you didn't want her to."

Opening her wallet, Barbara shows pictures of her daughter. Her face softens, showing them. "She was completely my responsibility. I took her to a baby-sitter on my way to school every day. I mean, can you imagine how tough this program was? If you were going to be late, you had to call them. Regular high school was never like that. They didn't care what you did."

To pay for the baby-sitter, Barbara worked during the afternoons in an office, which fulfilled one of the program's requirements that students hold a job. At night her boyfriend took care of the baby and she went to her second job as a waitress.

"I did it because I knew I had to. I knew this was my last chance. There wouldn't be any other. I had to graduate from high school. I didn't want to end up sitting in a room somewhere with a baby, watching TV and waiting for my welfare payments."

. . . Barbara describes her pregnancy as a miserable experience. "Some mornings I would wake up and cry. I didn't want to go to school pregnant. The jocks would all look at me and say, 'Wow! She's pregnant!'"

Her eyes pull back and cloud over. "One day this lady on the street gave me this awful look. I was nine months pregnant and out to here"—she motions about two feet in front of her—"and I knew how I looked. But I wanted to say to her, lady, don't you look at me that way. I have a job and I'm going to graduate from high school and *I'm not on welfare*." . . .

"Well, I did do it," she says. "I have a job, I graduated, I support my daughter . . ."

Her hands are finally still, clasped in front of her on the table as if she is going to pray. "Someday," she tells me, "someday I'm going to go to college." . . .

. . . as we both get up to leave, she smiles at me again. I thank her for telling me about how she got through school; I tell her she is a strong person. I want us to both leave with a feeling of optimism. Barbara is, after all, a success story.

"I'd do anything for those people," she says suddenly, as we emerge into the white sunlight of midday. She is referring to her teachers in the alternative program. "Anything. Because they did so much for me."

Mike and Susan

Barbara's teachers radiate the conviction that they are doing something worth-while. They work with at-risk students, a population characterized by a variety of problems. But Mike and Susan are unified in their enthusiasm.

"These kids are so much more rewarding to teach," Mike says. "We find working with them to be more interesting, more creative. And the program gives us so much more flexibility and freedom. We're not boxed into a mindset that says we absolutely have to cover a certain amount of ground by a certain time, no matter if it isn't understood."

Susan chimes in. "One thing you can feel, when you work with these kids, are the rewards. When you teach in a regular classroom, as we both have, sometimes you get the feeling that those kids will make it no matter who's standing in front of them."

Susan and Mike teach in an alternative program . . . constructed around a 5-point system which governs student behavior. Each negative behavior earns the student 1 point. At the accumulation of 5 points, the student is terminated from the program. However, there are chances for redemption built into the point system. A steady week of perfect behavior results in having a point erased from one's record.

Points are meted out for "clearly inappropriate behaviors," according to Susan. "If you don't call in before school starts to say you're sick or going to be late, or if you break a window, do wheelies in the parking lot, fight with other kids—each of these constitutes a point."

Attrition is not a severe problem. "We lose about 4–5 juniors a quarter," Mike says, "but not many seniors. They can see the end in sight and can operate under the system."

What works to make these kids turn their attitudes around? Susan says, "We personalize a lot. We remember their birthdays, things like that. And we do a lot of counseling. If a kid isn't in school, we call him or her up at home and find out why not. If a kid seems depressed, we take some class time to find out what's wrong." . . .

Susan, an English teacher, gives assignments rooted in reality. "Every February when the kids think they can't go to school another day, the school board starts talking about cutting our funding. We say to the kids: Maybe we won't be here next year. That's when the juniors write letters to the school board members."

"It's the best writing assignment I ever give, because they know how important it is to state their case carefully. They know why they have to write their letters over four times until they're perfect. We also invite people in to speak who are responsible for funding and the kids have to present their case orally. That's the very best communication instruction they could get."

Building a team spirit among the kids in the program isn't difficult, according to both teachers. "At the beginning of the year we do a lot of outdoor activities which focus on group cohesiveness," Mike says. "We take them out into the woods and present them with a situation where there's a log suspended over their heads by two ropes. We make it very immediate. Their task, for the good of the group, is to figure out how the entire group is going to get over that log. It has to be a group decision, and the kids have to come up with a plan."

"Right away you see who the leaders are. They all have to help each other; they have to touch each other and lift each other. This activity, like all the others we have them engage in, is designed so that no one can do it alone. This builds an incredible spirit among the group."

Susan responds to the notion that critics might consider their program a holding operation. "I tell the parents of my kids that they're learning more English here than in a regular classroom. I have these kids for two years and I always get excited their senior year when I see how much they've learned. I know exactly what they need to work on, what they're capable of and how far I can push them."

"Having a small class makes it possible to take difficult assignments and make sure every kid knows what to do because we are able to work one-on-one a lot. . . . You wouldn't think of our kids as being shy, but a lot of them have a shyness that is based upon their negative view of themselves. They feel they're not really very good at anything. They've never been good at school and they've been in trouble at home. Shyness is a way to avoid failure."

In this program they find they can go out and have a very positive experience and get a great recommendation from an employer. Once they've gone through a couple of these experiences they start having a more positive opinion of themselves."

The team spirit among the teachers in the program is just as compelling as that demonstrated among the students. "We're supposed to meet every day for one hour," Susan says. "It always ends up being three hours. We support each other, talk to each other. It also helps that we're all full-time in the program. We don't have to split duties elsewhere in the school, so we're able to stay focused."

Mike concludes, "In general, if you ask if teachers want to work in these programs, the answer is no. But we think if they knew how great the rewards are, how positively you as a teacher can feel about what you're doing, there would be more teachers opting for an alternative program."

Used by permission of Anne Turnbaugh Lockwood. Excerpted from interviews conducted by Anne Turnbaugh Lockwood and reported in *Newsletter: National Center on Effective Secondary Schools*, School of Education, University of Wisconsin—Madison, Fall 1986.

Bilingual Education

Bilingual education can be thought of as a form of compensatory education targeted toward non-native-English-speaking students who might fall behind others in class because of a linguistic barrier to communication. Early bilingual programs were intended to teach students whose primary language was not English in their native language until they developed skills in English. The concept was enacted into law in the 1960s as Title VII of the Elementary and Secondary Education Act of 1965 and in the Bilingual Education Act of 1968. It was reinforced through subsequent legislation.

Lau v. Nichols

Momentum for bilingual education was fueled by court cases in the 1970s. In 1974, the United States Supreme Court in *Lau* v. *Nichols* addressed questions about (1) the extent to which non-native-English-speaking students face a language barrier in schools and (2) what schools should do about it. The Court ruled that the San Francisco, California, schools were treating non-native-English-speaking students unequally when they required them to use the same materials and facilities as English-speaking students. As a result of this decision and subsequent mandates by the U.S. Office of Civil Rights, school systems must identify students whose primary language is not English and must provide language instruction for them in their primary language. They must help them learn by means of their primary language until their English is adequate.

When bilingual legislation was initially passed in the 1960s, the predominant non-native-English-speaking group of students in the schools used Spanish and were concentrated in California, the Southwest, and New York. Since then, many more Spanish-speaking students have entered the schools, and, more significantly, "new-immigrant," non-native-English-speaking families have arrived in the United States from southeast Asia and other regions of the world. Because of the increased numbers of non-native-English-speaking students and the broad array of primary languages, bilingual education took on a new significance in the late 1970s and 1980s.

"New-immigrant" students

In recent years, bilingual education programs have involved at least one of three emphases: (1) the teaching of English as a second language (ESL), (2) the temporary use of the primary language along with an intensive teaching of English so that students can quickly shift their primary language to English, and (3) the teaching of English with a parallel goal of helping the students retain their native language and culture. Programs that use the primary language only temporarily, until the students have learned adequate English, are called *transitional programs.* Those that strive to balance skills in both languages and cultures are called *maintenance programs* because students are expected to maintain skill in their initial language.

Three different phases

Generally, bilingual programs in the regular school curriculum, as distinct from those intended for adults, for example, contain elements of both transitional and maintenance approaches. They strive to teach English skills; to help the students adjust to an Anglo-dominated culture; to preserve and enhance the students' native

What goals do you think should be served by bilingual education?

language, cultural identities, and heritage; and to make them feel good about themselves and their cultural background.

Since the early 1980s, bilingual education has been engulfed in controversy emanating from at least two issues. First is the question of the overall effectiveness of bilingual education programs. Do they actually help students learn? Second, educators and politicians sometimes disagree about the purpose and role of bilingual education. How strongly should it "Americanize" students from families new to the United States, and how strongly should it work to preserve the students' cultural traditions?

Central to the latter debate is the question of how long a student's primary language should continue to be used as the means of instruction in the schools. Some people stress the importance of integrating students as quickly as possible into the use of English. Others place more value on retaining the primary language and its accompanying cultural traditions.[15]

Multicultural Education

Throughout much of American history a primary, stated purpose of schools was to provide a *melting pot* for the pluralistic population of the country. People came to this country from many countries and ethnic backgrounds, with distinct languages and with rich cultural traditions; but they were expected to change, to become "American." They were expected to give up their language and customs and to replace them with the English language and "American" values. They were expected to send their children to school for socialization and acculturation, to acquire the cultural characteristics that would enable them to succeed socially and economically in the new environment. In short, the children were expected to become Anglo in speech, dress, and social demeanor; and schools, in large part, were expected to effect the transition.

Of course, cultural diversity did not disappear during those years. For a long period, new immigrants kept arriving; and as they did, they perpetuated old-world characteristics and values. Some groups—Irish Catholics, Jews, Mexicans, and Native Americans—were large, geographically concentrated, and persistent enough to preserve their identities. Some resisted the melting pot idea so much that they avoided sending their children to public schools.

During the 1960s and 1970s, social observers and educators alike began to question the value of the melting pot idea in general and the melting pot purpose of schools in particular. They began to recognize more clearly the value of cultural diversity in society. They found *forced assimilation* of students, as well as the *artificial separation* of subgroups from one another, to be contrary to American ideas of equity. They noticed negative effects on children when schools placed common cultural expectations on non-native-English-speaking, nonwhite, ethnically varied students. They realized that such practices stifled enthusiasm, harmed self-images, created alienation, and encouraged social exclusion among peers.

In response, *multicultural education* has replaced the melting pot as a major goal of schools. *Cultural pluralism* has replaced assimilation as the ideal to be sought. With this shift in ideals has also come the notion that education should provide equal opportunities for diverse students; no longer are all students to be treated as if they were the same.

Because of this new perspective, at least ideally, today's teachers try to (1) accommodate student differences, (2) teach the inherent value and respectability of all cultures, (3) inculcate in their students a belief in the importance of cross-cultural understanding, and (4) cultivate an appreciation for personal uniqueness and individuality. To the extent that they accomplish the ideal, they educate students so they can make the most of their own backgrounds and abilities and can succeed in their own way.[16]

Multiculturalism is one of the major topics identified in the Reflecting on Practice box in Chapter 1. As you pursue your teacher education studies and as you monitor current education developments, you should reflect on this issue. As you do so, consider what you have just studied about the principles of equity and excellence.

- How do you think schools and teachers should provide appropriate education for students with diverse backgrounds, cultures, and traditions?
- How important is it to provide common content and skills for all students regardless of their backgrounds?
- How important is it for schools to teach students with particular cultural backgrounds and traditions about these elements of their heritages?
- How important is it for students to learn about the backgrounds, traditions, and heritages of students and people different from themselves?
- How do your responses fit with the overall goals of schools in America?

Gender-Related Aspects of Education

When American schools were expected to provide a melting pot to make children more like each other, they taught them to understand and conform to long-accepted social norms that had become ingrained in social behavior and had served as the guides by which society functioned. People who understood and conformed to the norms were more likely to be successful and happy.

One deeply ingrained set of norms had to do with *gender-role expectations.* Girls and women were expected to value and do certain things, and boys and men were supposed to value and do others. Therefore, when schools taught boys and girls how to conform to cultural expectations, those expectations were clearly different for each gender. In their extreme form they taught that boys were expected to be aggressive, tough, and mechanical; they were supposed to become medical doctors, attorneys, farmers, engineers, and industrial workers. Girls were expected to be sensitive, reserved, and caring; they were supposed to become nurses, teachers, secretaries, and homemakers.

> Gender-role expectations

In recent years, however, these and many other gender-related expectations in American culture have been questioned and challenged. Frequently, schools have been asked to help counteract, not reinforce, those felt to be harmful and restrictive. Generally, schools have taken up the challenge, but there has been much controversy.

Two aspects of gender-related issues that concern schools involve specific questions: Which gender-related concepts and values should be taught? In what ways should boys and girls be taught?

> Gender-related concepts

The gender-related concepts that are taught in a given school usually reflect the school's purposes, the teaching staff's perceptions, and the expectations of the broader society. In today's schools those influences tend to produce a mixture of concepts that perpetuate traditional gender-role biases and that challenge them. At times this creates confusion for students. For example, in most schools girls are not expected to participate in sports to the extent that boys do, but they are encouraged to participate more than they would have in the past. Fewer girls are expected to enroll in high-level mathematics classes even though they are encouraged to consider such professions as engineering. The same point holds for boys' participation in cheerleading and business education classes.

Most schools today probably teach that rigid gender-role identification and stereotypes are unfortunate and harmful. They teach students to question the validity of these ideas and to find their weaknesses. They show that gender-related roles have usually evolved from previous cultural practices, not from biological factors or other unchangeable conditions. They encourage students to analyze these practices and to think for themselves.

Nevertheless, schools continue, often unconsciously, to perpetuate many traditional gender-related values. The roles expected of males and females in many classes are the "typical" roles much more often than not. Textbook mothers and fathers, little boys and girls, aunts and uncles, waitresses and busboys tend to play traditional gender roles (as is described in Chapter 5).

Gender-related treatment of students

The ways in which boys and girls are treated while being taught usually follow the same pattern, sometimes reflecting old values and sometimes encouraging the new. For the most part, schools try not to reinforce the old heavily biased assumptions. They try to treat boys and girls alike instructionally. But old stereotypes and traditions continue to creep into practice. Boys have long been expected to be difficult to manage, girls to be emotional. The personal interests of students are often guided toward traditional gender classifications. Future job and career probabilities tend to carry gender-related assumptions. In short, schools today usually try to avoid gender-role stereotypes in dealing with students, but they are only somewhat successful.

Educating Students with Disabling Conditions

Stimulated by *Brown* v. *Board of Education, PARC* v. *Pennsylvania*, and Public Laws 94-142, 99-457, and 101-476, schools today try to educate children and youth with special needs or handicapping conditions more appropriately than ever before. Often the efforts are successful, and the targeted children benefit noticeably. But the degree of commitment, amount of activity, and attainment of results vary greatly from region to region, state to state, and school to school.

Free and appropriate public education in least restrictive environment

As mentioned earlier Public Laws 94-142, 99-457, and 101-476 require that all children with handicapping conditions be provided with a *free and appropriate public education in the least restrictive environment*. This means that disabled children from ages 3 or 4 to 21 must be educated at public expense in settings as close as possible to regular or "normal" classrooms. It means that many students with special needs and handicapping conditions can and should be mainstreamed into regular classrooms.

Mainstreaming

Mainstreaming is the practice of placing students with special needs in regular classrooms and schools when possible. It is done so that these children can experience a "near-to-normal" classroom environment and so that they can interact with non-disabled peers. Usually, mainstreamed students attend "regular" and "special" classes during the day or week and receive additional services beyond those of the mainstream classroom. The term *mainstreaming* is used for a great variety of situations—in fact, for nearly any arrangement in which students with special needs are taught for some part of the school day in the same classes as students not classified as having special needs.

Nearly all knowledgeable educators agree that placing special needs students in classes with "more typical" students whenever possible has positive educational and social benefits for all students. But, much controversy surrounds mainstreaming, and that controversy often flares up over two specific situations: (1) when decisions are being made about what is the most appropriate type and amount of mainstreamed instruction for a particular student and (2) when proposed mainstreaming arrangements are seen as so burdensome that they weaken the learning of the students involved.

In recent years, mainstreaming efforts have given rise to a desire on the part of a number of educators that schools follow a policy of *inclusion* in educating special needs and disabled students. By *inclusion* they mean a policy that allows all special needs students to be educated (1) in schools where non-special-needs peers attend, (2) in age-appropriate classes, and (3) under the supervision of regular classroom teachers with support from special education teachers and support personnel. Proponents of inclusion agree that any educational setting for special needs students that does not consist of these three characteristics is not equitable for the student with special needs. Their antagonists respond that full inclusion is often not possible or in the students' best interest.

Inclusion

Mainstreaming legislation also guarantees that children with handicapping conditions be provided with due process of the law to assure that they are treated equally with normal students when they are identified or classified, when they are placed in a particular instructional setting, and when educational services are made available to them. This guarantee helps to keep schools from misidentifying students, placing them in inappropriate educational settings, and neglecting them outright. The laws require that students and/or their parents or guardians participate in deciding what instructional plan is best.

Due process of the law

The laws also specify that the instruction provided for each child with handicapping conditions must be based on that student's abilities and needs. There must be an *individual education program or plan* (IEP).

Individual education plan

Changes that have followed the mainstreaming legislation represent the most significant developments in the long struggle to obtain equal education for children with handicapping conditions. In the nineteenth century, these children usually were either ignored by society or sent to separate institutions to receive special (and segregated) instruction, often some distance from home. The burden of the costs often rested with the student's family. Sometimes these arrangements meant that the students were educated well, but often they were simply "warehoused," and at times they were mistreated. Then, early in the twentieth century some communities began to allow mildly disabled children to remain at home and to be taught in special classes in the local schools. The practice was based on the idea that these children would be better able to function as adults in the community if they were not segregated from it for their schooling. But the instruction was still typically provided in separate classes and differed in kind from that provided other students.

The 1960s witnessed an increased interest in the education of people with disabilities. Under President John F. Kennedy federal government funds were used to train teachers in special education and to build and expand special education facilities. By the end of the decade, millions of students who were impaired by mental retardation, speech and hearing problems, emotional disorders, and other health-related disabilities were being served.

The federal government efforts of the 1960s, however encouraging, were voluntary for state and local school systems; and as a result, the quality of services varied greatly, and many needy students were not served. It was not until the legislation of the 1970s and 1980s described earlier that significant numbers of states expanded and equalized educational services to children with disabilities.

Even today's school systems face major problems as they attempt to serve children with handicapping conditions. These problems seem to be of four types: public indifference, high costs, inadequate numbers of skilled teachers, and the difficulty of correctly identifying and classifying students.

Results are not clear

At present, most schools commonly use a combination of mainstreamed instruction and supplemental special services to educate students with handicapping conditions when those conditions are not so severe that more restrictive learning environments are necessary. But data from comparative research on the outcome of mainstreaming and segregated special education are not conclusive. It is not clear which produces the greater learning or the better self-esteem in the disabled student. Mainstreaming, however, does appear to improve the social acceptance of the students with disabilities by their nondisabled peers. At this point, it may be that the benefits of any approach to educating students with handicapping conditions are best determined on an individual basis.

Educating Gifted and Talented Students

American educators, as well as the broader society, have been inconsistent in their approaches and attitudes toward educating children and youth who are academically stronger and more talented than most other students. At times they look at these students in contradictory ways—both as future societal leaders and national human resources who are being neglected by schools and as fortunate individuals who can succeed on their own without special help.

The special education movement seems to have convinced most educators that *something special* should be provided to serve these *special* students, but what should be done is not at all clear. Underlying this lack of clarity are at least four types of ambiguous conditions:

1. Ideas about how important it is for schools to provide special services for gifted and talented students have fluctuated over time, usually in response to shifts in the public's view of the most important purposes of schools and the availability of funds.
2. Identifying gifted and talented students seems to be as difficult as identifying those with disabilities.
3. Scholars and parents vacillate about separating gifted and talented students from their social and chronological peers.
4. The type of special instruction that is best for these students is not clear.

Priorities

When *Sputnik* went into space in 1957, Americans looked into what their schools were teaching as part of the effort to find out why the United States was apparently losing technological superiority to the Soviet Union. In the process, many determined that the schools were neglecting the best minds and the most talented students. They demanded that the situation be changed and more attention be paid to bright children.

As a result, the education of academically advanced and talented students became a higher priority of schools. New programs were developed and financed. Special sections of classes were organized for bright students. A greater number of advanced classes was offered in various subjects. Efforts were begun to help bright students who couldn't afford to go to college.

But the momentum did not last long. In the 1960s, at the same time that questions were being raised about education for the gifted and talented, concern also developed over the education of low-income and disadvantaged students. These concerns got more attention from the public, politicians, and educators than did the interests of gifted students. Low-income and disadvantaged students were at more risk, and their needs were considered to be more critical. By the late 1960s, the United States space program was on track, the cold war was thawing, and gifted and talented students were not so noticeably neglected as they had been.

Nearly two decades later, the educational reforms of the 1970s and 1980s swung the pendulum back a bit toward a greater interest in the education of the gifted and talented. But this time, these students were thought of more as a group that had to be educated better within the general school population, rather than as a special group of students that needed special, segregated instruction.

As with other students, it is difficult to determine which programs and classes are best for which gifted and talented students. Although these students might be classified as being alike by certain criteria, they differ in many other ways. For example, not all who have exceptionally high mathematics test scores might fit comfortably in the same advanced calculus course. Some might benefit more from individual instruction, some from additional free time to pursue nonmathematical interests, some from more time directed to other subjects, and some from the regular school program and environment.

Which programs and approaches are best?

In recent years, the instruction of gifted and talented students has been an important topic among educators, but their actions have varied greatly. Often what is done in a specific school or school system is determined by one or more of the following; the number of gifted and talented students needing attention, the influence of their parents and advocates, the priorities of the school leaders, the availability of skilled teachers, and the commitment of funds.

Educating "Average" Students

The *average* students in any school can be said to be those whose unique characteristics are not recognized as being significantly different from those of students in general. Of course, average students are just as unique as others, and often their uniqueness is recognized. Their uniqueness is just not significantly different enough to attract special attention from the system and its decision makers. Therefore, the normal or typical instructional programs and services serve them. In a sense, they fit into the normal routine of the school easily, so they are expected to succeed without special consideration.

A matter of recognition

Because there are more average students than there are students of any other classification, schools direct more of their efforts toward these students more of the time. Therefore, they tend to serve these students as well as, or better than, they serve any others. School decision makers have them in mind most often. Regular school operations accommodate them most easily. Teachers target their instruction and expectations toward them most consistently. Average students and the programming based on their needs are probably a major reason that so many schools look so much alike.

Likenesses and Differences among Students—A Reminder

This discussion of attempts to serve all students began by stating that schools first categorize and then focus somewhat different instruction and instruction-related services toward each group of students. It is important to remember, however, that students do not fit into the categories naturally. No matter how they are grouped

1. Students within any group are significantly *different from others in the same group*.
2. Students in any particular group are more *like those in other groups* than they are different from them.

The categories that schools use are school-developed, artificial, and arbitrary. Schools use them only because they cannot accommodate each individual student in a truly individualized way.

EDUCATIONAL RESEARCH

From Experimentation to Common Practice

Now that you have read Educational Research sections for six chapters, you should be developing insights into what educational research is and how it produces knowledge about teaching and learning. You should also realize that research findings do not explain everything and that they must be used with caution.

This Educational Research section traces in a very general fashion (1) the ways in which research ideas lead to experiments and (2) the ways that conclusions from experiments can affect what teachers and students do in classrooms. It also outlines how you, as a classroom teacher, can be involved directly in the process.

Educational research projects are tests of ideas about how to improve teaching and schooling. Generally, the process works as follows: Researchers form hypotheses (sometimes they begin as hunches) about what they think are or would be better ways of doing things in schools. They design ways to test these ideas under conditions that will show if their ideas are valid or not. Next, they conduct the experiment, collect data, and formulate conclusions. Then they share their work with colleagues by writing about it in professional journals and making presentations at professional meetings. Other researchers react to these reports, offer suggestions, and possibly try the experiment themselves. The exchange of information and further testing eventually leads either to the rejection of the idea or to the broader acceptance of it in some form.

If an idea begins to be accepted as a better way of doing things by a number of educators, those who believe in it often develop demonstration projects to show how and why they believe it is so good. These projects also become examples of how the idea can be put into practice and how it can be refined to assure the best results. As a result, the demonstration projects are often a bridge between experimenters—who test ideas—and regular classroom teachers—who must decide whether the ideas are worth using with their students. They provide firsthand evidence about the feasibility of an idea and encouragement for local teachers to give it a try.

Eventually, good research ideas are gradually accepted by a broad range of educators and are adopted by increasing numbers of schools and teachers. At some point, the ideas are recognized widely as being successful and become common practice.

The idea of alternative schools for high-risk students described in the Reflecting on Practice of this chapter as well as the different compensatory education programs also mentioned in the chapter are examples of ideas that have passed through the research–demonstration–common practice process. So are the effective teaching practices identified in Chapter 3.

Unfortunately, however, except for a turnaround in the last twenty years or so, research and demonstration efforts have not had the important roles in education that they should have. For a long time, many teachers taught year after year rather uncritically, much as they had been taught; conversely, they jumped at untried fads with no more than a superficial analysis. The Educational Research section of Chapter 5 alludes to the latter of these situations when it describes how quickly school decision makers adopted mainstreaming lock, stock, and barrel long before solid data were gathered.

Today, educators at almost every level can participate in research and demonstration projects if they choose to do so, and it is important for the improvement of teaching and schools that they do. When they do, they not only help students, but also generate and spread ideas that uplift the profession of teaching generally. Teachers can become involved in research and demonstration efforts in many ways, including the following:

■ Read research journals regularly.
■ Volunteer to participate in local experiments or demonstration projects.
■ Conduct in-classroom trials of personal hypotheses, even if they seem to be unsophisticated.
■ Share information about research and demonstration projects with colleagues.

As a teacher in the years ahead, you, as well as all educators, will have to include experimentation and demonstration as part of what you do to remain up-to-date in the profession. Change is occurring too fast to do otherwise.

Conclusion

Since the 1960s schools in the United States have attempted to provide equal and excellent education to all their students. Because those students differ and some have special needs, schools have to teach their highly varied students in a number of differing ways if all of them are to succeed. But because it is not realistic for schools to provide an entirely individualized program for each student, schools categorize students into groups and target different types of instruction and services to the groups.

The process, of course, is not perfect. Sometimes students are served well, but at other times they are misclassified, neglected, or otherwise dealt with inappropriately. However, today's educators and Americans in general recognize the need to provide equally excellent education for all students and seem to be committed to developing better ways of doing so.

Today's idea of excellence in education is not that of providing the same or equal services to all students. It is, instead, the idea of providing differentiated services to students, so that each of them can benefit equally well. The equality is not determined at the point of input (what the schools do for students) but at the point of determining results (what the students get out of it). The goal is that all student learning be excellent. If all of it is excellent, it will be equal. (Of course, all education is affected by school finances, a point that is discussed further in Chapter 9.)

Equal and excellent results of schooling

Summary

The goals for American schools have shifted during the twentieth century from a focus at the turn of the century on "solid academic" coursework that trained the mind to an emphasis in the 1930s and 1940s on life adjustments and, eventually, to a focus, since about 1960, on the relative balance between the two ideas. During the century access to schools has broadened to include virtually every child, and schools have attempted to provide an equally excellent education for all. In recent decades, educators have thought of equal and excellent education as that which enables each child to learn to the maximum of his or her potential.

Court rulings and legislative mandates have required schools to provide equal education to all children regardless of race, gender, and disabilities. The greatest push in these directions came in the 1950s and continued through the early 1970s.

To try to serve all students, schools often categorize them into groups, and then undertake special efforts to meet the needs of such groups. Those special efforts have been extended toward students in the form of racial desegregation, compensatory education, bilingual education, multicultural education, gender-related education, mainstreaming, programs for students with disabilities, and programs for gifted and talented students. Most such programs are intended to serve average students as well as those considered to be special in some way.

Study Questions

1. Form a mental picture of a hypothetical student for a particular grade in school. List five ways in which that student is like most students and five ways in which he or she is special or different from most students. Now describe ways in which that student should be treated in school that accommodate both the student's average and special conditions.

2. Suppose you are teaching a high school class of very successful students. The students include a number with very secure backgrounds, a lot of study help at home, and no noticeable disabilities. The class also includes:

   a. a student who is virtually blind but otherwise normal

   b. a student from a severely deprived family background who is otherwise normal

   c. a student with a terminal illness who is otherwise normal

   Suppose further that the final grade the students get in your class will help determine whether they get into the college of their choice and receive a scholarship. Would you give the three students described special credit for doing the same level of work as the other students? Why or why not?

3. What would you do as a school administrator if parents approached you with the following two requests? How would you justify each decision?

   a. Although my daughter might not qualify for the honors group in English next year, I would like her placed there. We immigrated five years ago from Thailand, and English is not her native language. She has done very well in school despite this disadvantage. Being with top academic peers will be beneficial to her.

   b. Although my daughter might not qualify for the honors group in English next year, I would like her placed there. We are a professional family of long standing in the community. She has done rather well in school, and being with peers from her own social class who also perform well academically will be beneficial to her.

4. How will the decision made concerning the students described in Question 3 affect other students in the class and school?

Key Terms

"A free appropriate public education"
Acculturation
"All deliberate speed"
Alternative school
"Average students"
Bilingual education
Compensatory education
Cultural pluralism
De facto segregation
De jure segregation
Desegregation
Due process of law
Educational outcome

Equal protection of the laws
Equity
Excellence in education
Follow Through Project
Gender-role expectations
Gifted students
Head Start
Inclusion
Individual education plan
"Individual excellence"
"Least restrictive environment"
Life adjustment education
Magnet schools

Mainstreaming
Melting pot
Multicultural education
Remedial education
"Separate but equal"
Socialization
Sputnik
Trade-off
"Training the mind"
War on poverty
White flight
Whole child

For Further Reading

Berne, R., & Stiefel, L. (1994). *Educational equity: The unfulfilled promise.* Boulder, CO: Westview Press.

Butts, R. F. (1978). *Public education in the United States: From revolution to reform.* New York: Holt, Rinehart and Winston.

Commission on the Reorganization of Secondary Education. (1918). *Cardinal principles of secondary education.* Washington, DC: Government Printing Office.

Conant, J. B. (1959). *The American high school today.* New York: McGraw-Hill.

Cremin, L. A. (1961). *The transformation of the school: Progressivism in American education 1876–1957.* New York: Knopf.

Cuban, L. (1982). Persistent instruction: The high school classroom. *Phi Delta Kappan, 64*(2), 113–118.

Educational Policies Commission. (1938). *The purposes of education in American democracy.* Washington, DC: National Education Association and American Association of School Administrators.

Educational Policies Commission. (1944). *Education of all American youth.* Washington, DC: National Education Association and American Association of School Administrators.

Entwisel, D. R. (1994). *Children, schools, and inequality.* Boulder, CO: Westview Press.

Fantini, M. D. (1986). *Regaining excellence in education.* Columbus, OH: Charles E. Merrill.

Gardner, J. W. (1961). *Excellence: Can we be equal and excellent too?* New York: Harper and Brothers.

Graham, P. A. (1993). What America has expected of its schools over the past century. *American Journal of Education, 101*(2), 83–98.

Kozol, J. (1991). *Savage Inequalities.* New York: Crown Publishers.

National Education Association. (1893). *Report of the committee on secondary school studies.* Washington, DC: Government Printing Office.

3 Historical, Political, and Philosophical Contexts

Unit 3, which consists of Chapters 8, 9, and 10, examines the historical, political, and philosophical contexts in which teaching takes place, students learn, and schools operate. This broad overview allows you to consider (1) the traditions from the past that have affected how schooling evolved in America, (2) the political pressures that influence teaching and schools of the present and past, and (3) the ways in which philosophical ideas guide the educational process. After studying this unit, you should be able to interpret what you have learned about teaching and schools in historical, political, and philosophical terms and should be ready to evolve your own philosophy of education, teaching, and schools.

When you finish each chapter, you should have an understanding of the general concepts listed here and should have begun to develop the skills noted.

CHAPTER 8
The Historical Context: Traditions That Guide Teaching and Schooling

General Concepts

- Schools in the United States developed from traditions of Western civilization that include religious and civic purposes for schooling.

- Americans think of schools as a community responsibility and as a service available to and appropriate for all children.

- Because of our democratic and republican form of government, common schools are needed to educate the citizens of the United States.

Skill

- An ability to interpret current activities concerning teaching and schools in their historical context

CHAPTER 9
The Political Context: Pressures That Influence Teaching and Schools

General Concepts

- Pre-K–12 public schools in the United States operate under the constitutional, regulatory, judicial, and financial authority and control of federal, state, and local governments.

- Political pressures on schools include efforts by government agencies and others who influence government policy to control the operation of schools and the content of instruction.

- The press for equal access to a quality education for all students has been a dominant political pressure on pre-K–12 schools during the second half of the twentieth century.

- A major component of the political context for schools involves individual, academic, and professional rights, responsibilities, and freedoms.

- The professional work of teachers is guided by legal issues, including those concerned with contracts, tenure, student rights, and liability.

- Schools and school systems are political as well as social and cultural systems.

Skills

- An ability to negotiate effectively through the multitude of political pressures that impinge upon teachers and their classroom teaching

- An ability to use the political context that envelops schools and teaching to enhance teaching performance and personal professional development

CHAPTER 10
The Philosophical Context: Beliefs That Guide Teaching

General Concepts

- Philosophical beliefs are answers that people provide for fundamental questions; philosophical beliefs relating to education inform the ways teachers teach.

- All teachers have philosophies of education that they have developed over time and have revised as they find it appropriate to do so.

- When teachers form their philosophies of education, they tend to be eclectic rather than follow one philosophy consistently.

Skill

- An ability to relate current approaches to teaching and schools to underlying philosophical principles, including your own beliefs and values

The Historical Context
Traditions That Guide
Teaching and Schooling

Chapter 8 focuses on the historical contexts within which schools and classrooms operate and in which students learn. The chapter reaches back into early recorded history to outline the historical setting in which schools of the United States developed. What teachers and students do in pre-K–12 classrooms today has its roots in historical events and movements. Emphasis is on schooling in Europe from ancient Greek times to the founding of the English colonies in America and on American schooling from colonial times to the twentieth century: These are the places where the roots of American schooling lie.

This focus does not mean that early schooling in other parts of the world was not important. Educational traditions evolved in China, Japan, and the kingdoms of Africa; in the Inca, Aztec, and Mayan civilizations of pre-Columbian America; and elsewhere. Those traditions, however, have not had as significant and direct an influence on contemporary American schools as have had traditions inherited from Europe and earlier periods of American history.

As you read each chapter section, ask yourself these four questions:

- What were the purposes of schooling during these times?
- Who was educated?
- Who did the teaching?
- What was studied?

Also look for the ideas and traditions that have molded American schools and teachers into what they are today.

The Snapshot describes the schooling of an imaginary student in ancient Greece, and the Reflecting on Practice describes a colonial American classroom. The two descriptors are intended to provide historical pictures of schooling that (1) illustrate the concepts explained in the text and (2) supply contrasts to what you see in schools today. The Educational Research section describes a historical study of secondary school teaching practices.

SNAPSHOT

This Snapshot describes the schooling of a boy in ancient Greece.[1] As you read, consider:

- How was Alex's schooling different from yours?
- Why do you think it differed in these ways?
- How was it similar? Why do you think this is the case?
- What were the primary purposes of his schooling?
- In what ways does schooling reflect the general culture of the times?

Schooling in Ancient Greece

Alex began his schooling at age 6 when his father arranged for a man who was a local teacher to take him into the school he conducted in his home for other Athenian boys. Alex's father had selected this particular

teacher because of the subjects he taught and because his reputation as a teacher was good. Alex's father agreed at the outset on the fee to be paid and the thrust of the instruction. Alex, unlike many other Athenian boys who studied different subjects under different teachers, was to be taught most of his subjects by the one teacher.

Alex studied reading, writing, literature, music, drawing, painting, and gymnastics. Before he could read, he listened to others read Homer and Hesiod; and when he learned enough of the alphabet, he began to read on his own. When he learned to write, he recorded passages read aloud by the teacher and copied some from the scrolls hanging on the walls.

Much of his learning consisted of memorizing. At first he did not understand much of what he wrote and memorized, but gradually he understood more. At times the teacher and students discussed the passages, and these discussions enabled him to grasp the elements of history and geography embedded in them.

For much of the school day, the teacher sat on a chair at the front of the room, and the boys sat on backless chairs facing him. Each boy had a wax tablet and stylus for writing and a lyre on which to practice his music. When Alex was 12, his father contracted other teachers to teach him at a more advanced level. One of the teachers had come to Athens only a few months earlier, but he had developed a good reputation quickly by lecturing at various public locations in the city. For a short time, the teacher's lectures were free because he was unknown to most of the citizens. As his reputation as a speaker, thinker, and teacher spread, more young men came to hear him and to discuss ideas with him. When he felt he was attracting an appropriate number

of potential students, he rented a room, began charging admission, and changed his approach from mostly lecturing to include more varied forms of teaching.

At this age, Alex studied oratory, composition, rhetoric, literature, music, history, law, arithmetic, geometry, the use of the abacus, and weights and measures. He also regularly participated in exercise and physical training, but these were provided at a different location and Alex was escorted to and from them by a "pedagog," in this case, an elderly slave. Lectures and discussions were the predominant means of instruction for certain subjects, but there was also much memorizing, writing, and calculating. Frequently, Alex and his schoolmates were expected to prepare and present speeches to their friends and families, as well as to the public.

At age 18, Alex left school to begin the two-year military training required of all boys by the city-state.

Schooling from Ancient to Modern Times

Because so many of the traditions that have formed pre-K–12 schools in the United States have roots in ideas about schooling and schooling practices that developed in Europe, this chapter looks first at some of those European ideas and practices. It begins with ancient Greece and then traces developments, in a very general way, through Roman times, the Middle Ages, the Renaissance, the time of the Protestant Reformation, and the Enlightenment. (Figure 8-1 is a time line showing that development.)

The Greeks—500–146 B.C.

Although schooling in Europe began some time earlier, the beginning point for this historical survey is in Greece about 500 B.C. At that time, wandering teachers, called *sophists*, traveled from place to place teaching young men of important families. Their students were the future citizens and leaders of the Greek city-states. They taught about civic issues and helped their students develop communication skills, especially in speaking and writing. Alex, who was described in the Snapshot, learned from teachers of this type.

Sophists

The purpose of this teaching was to provide the young men with the tools they needed to be effective leaders—tools that would be means to achieving political

FIGURE 8-1 Time line of key influences on teaching and schools in Western history. The influences, ideas, and individuals listed on the time line are considered important to teaching and schools today.

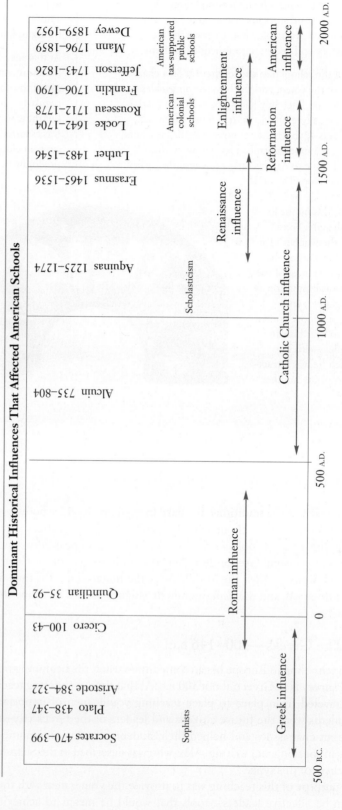

Dominant Historical Influences That Affected American Schools

power, social prestige, and wealth. Typical subjects were rhetoric, argumentation, logic, and the Greek language.

Unlike the teachers who succeeded them, the sophists reasoned cautiously. Most did not "search for truth" in their own study and did not inculcate the idea of doing so in their students. They simply taught information their students, such as Alex, needed to know and trained them in skills needed to gain positions of leadership.

During these ancient times, two of the Greek city-states, Athens and Sparta, developed organized approaches to schooling. In both places, boys and young men attended schools for physical, moral, and civic training. But Spartan and Athenian education had different emphases. Sparta stressed training for the military, emphasizing the physical and moral development of strong, loyal soldiers. Service to the state was paramount, and characteristics of obedience, patriotism, and courage were sought and praised. Athenian schools placed more emphasis on intellectual, cultural, and aesthetic goals than did those of Sparta. But there, too, military training played a sizable part in a young man's education for citizenship.

In the fourth and third centuries B.C., Athens produced three of the greatest teachers of the Western world. The first of these was Socrates. Socrates traveled around Athens teaching young men and boys the same subjects as the sophists taught. But he was significantly different from the sophists, both as a thinker and as a teacher. He was intellectual, and they were technical. As an originator of ideas, he raised questions they ignored or never thought of.

Socrates, 470–399 B.C.

Socrates sought to find universal principles, truth, beauty, and goodness in his study. He taught his students to do the same. He urged them to seek a life of moral excellence. He believed that, as a teacher, he needed to do more than train students to gain positions of authority. He prepared them to lead their citizenry toward a good and morally just life based on a set of ethical ideals. His method of teaching— a questioning of students in dialogue style—is known today as the *Socratic method.*

Socratic method

Guided by his principles and his search for truth, Socrates clashed with the civil authorities when his ideas conflicted with theirs. He believed that if ideas were to develop and if citizens and the state were to improve, it was necessary for all thinkers, including Socrates himself and his students, to be free to think and question.

Those in political power often disagreed and saw Socrates' social criticism as a threat to their power. Eventually, his questioning of civil authority led to his being put on trial for opposing the government; he was found guilty and given a choice by those in authority: Either he had to conform, or he had to die by his own hand. He held fast to his principles and committed suicide by drinking hemlock.

Plato, a student of Socrates, followed in his teacher's intellectual footsteps. He, too, sought truth, beauty, goodness, and justice. He believed the purpose of education was to develop the abilities of students so that those abilities could be used to serve society. He identified *ideals*, or universal concepts, that he said existed in the abstract, serving as goals toward which all people and states should strive. He thought of people, the state, and the other elements of the known world as imperfect representations of the ideal. Education was a means to make those elements more perfect. He wrote about his concept of the ideal state in the *Republic.*

Plato, 428–347 B.C.

Aristotle continued Plato's teaching, particularly his idea that the purpose of education was to improve people and society. In fact, he believed that the quality of life in a city and the quality of its government were direct results of the quality of

Aristotle, 384–322 B.C.

For Socrates (pictured here with his son), education had a profoundly moral purpose.

education. Education increased people's civil and humane capacities, led toward better governments, encouraged a cultivated society, and moved the city-state toward the ideal.

Aristotle was an abstract thinker like Socrates and Plato, but his teaching was more objective, practical, and scientific. He taught Alexander the Great and founded a philosophical school called the Lyceum. He wrote on many subjects, including astronomy, physics, botany, zoology, politics, ethics, logic, and metaphysics. His writings, like those of Plato, have had a powerful influence on thinkers and teachers through succeeding centuries.

The Romans—146 B.C.–A.D. 476

Rome conquered Greece in 146 B.C. Over the next century, Greek educational ideas became a part of Roman thinking, and schools became part of Roman society. As in the Greek city-states, the main purpose of education was civic in nature, with an emphasis on training new political leaders. But Roman schooling tended to be more utilitarian and practical and less philosophical and aesthetic than was that of Athens.

The Romans were very concerned with developing the leadership skills that were needed to administer their expanding empire. Therefore, their more advanced schools included training in rhetoric, grammar, mathematics, law, and administration. Those who completed schooling usually entered careers in public service, as lawyers, senators, teachers, and the like.

Cicero, 100–43 B.C.

Cicero and Quintilian were among the most distinguished of Roman teachers. Cicero was a Roman senator whose educational ideas combined the practical skills of debate, argumentation, and law with the more Greek elements of a liberal education, including ethics, philosophy, history, and astronomy. For him, the purpose

This heroic view of Plato and Aristotle was painted during the Renaissance, a time of deep respect for ancient Greek learning and culture.

of education was to serve the republic. The most important tools were oratory, a command of Latin and Greek grammar, and a knowledge of history.

Quintilian represented the Roman Empire rather than the republic, and he was primarily a teacher, not a political leader. He saw learning as a developmental process and outlined a sequence of education that recognized developmental stages. He stressed speaking but also believed in a broad liberal education and expected good orators to be ethical and moral people. Quintilian described his thinking on education and outlined his recommendations for Roman education in the twelve-book work *The Institutes of Oratory (Institutis Oratoria).*

Quintilian, A.D. 35–92

The Middle Ages—500–1300

By A.D. 500 the primary purposes of schooling in Europe were quite different from those of Greek and Roman times. By then, the Roman Empire had fallen, and church leaders had replaced political leaders as the main sources of authority. The primary political and social unit of society was the feudal manor or principality rather than the city-state or the empire.

Church influence

Schooling was intended to train for church and military leadership and to provide for the understanding of religion and church teachings. Much of this education occurred in monastic and cathedral schools established by the church with the support of feudal lords. In addition, two separate types of training were provided for knighthood and for craftspersons. The latter was usually conducted by guilds, which, in the form of apprenticeships, taught young men the tools of the trade through long, unpaid terms of training with merchants or master craftspersons.

During the early centuries of the Middle Ages, Charlemagne, ruler of what is

Alcuin, 735–804

now France, consolidated power in Europe by conquering many small fiefdoms and forming the Holy Roman Empire. Education in his kingdom was probably the most sophisticated in Europe at that time. Schooling was centered in his palace school and was directed by his chief advisor on education, Alcuin, a former teacher in England. Alcuin's palace school was intended to teach the children of the empire's royal class and, in doing so, to train the next generation of church and political leaders.

Alcuin's educational ideas and plans for schools served as models for centuries. He also is credited with developing, or at least popularizing, script writing as a substitute for earlier ways of forming letters. But his efforts tend to be overlooked by historians, who consider the Middle Ages a time of educational neglect. It was at this time, however, that education focusing on the seven liberal arts became a common curriculum. The liberal arts consisted of grammar, rhetoric, logic, arithmetic, geometry, music, and astronomy. They served as the basis of what is referred to as the *liberal arts* today.

Schooling in Europe during the Middle Ages was not limited to Charlemagne's court, however. It also occurred in the manors of many lower-level princes and in the monasteries scattered throughout the countryside. Generally, this type of schooling was practical training for court and church leaders, as well as for craftspersons and merchants. The subject matter included a heavy religious emphasis, along with training for the students' intended station in life.

By the eleventh century, a clearly identifiable type of education, called scholasticism, had developed. *Scholasticism* was an approach to study that combined faith and reason. That is, it combined a reliance on religious faith and the use of one's intellect to search for truth and meaning. It used a process of questioning, or inquiry, by which thinkers would come to understand their world and their God.

Scholasticism rested on the beliefs that God made the world knowable and that the mind is capable of discovering that meaning through deductive reasoning. Learners would gather ideas from the teachings of the church, from church authority, and from the revealed word of God. Then they would use their mind to discover meaning in what they studied.

Scholasticism evolved from the teaching of monks and priests, who were called *scholastics*. Saint Thomas Aquinas, a Dominican theologian, philosopher, and teacher who taught at the University of Paris, was its most noteworthy practitioner. Aquinas integrated church doctrine and Aristotelian philosophy into a way of studying the world in which he lived. He was the ideal teacher: a thoughtful scholar, an involved actor in the learning process of his students, someone who knew his subject matter and was sensitive to human nature. He considered schooling as something more than the informal learning that took place as children grew up and believed it should be provided by many agencies of society. Schooling was formal, planned learning that was based on definite principles and acknowledged subject matter. It led students to draw conclusions from their study.

Scholastics used *syllogisms* both to order knowledge for themselves and as a teaching device. Their curriculum included theology, church dogma, moral philosophy, metaphysics, logic, mathematics, and science. Students of the scholastics prepared to be monks, priests, scribes, court officials, and administrators.

As scholasticism developed, the schools in which scholastic teaching occurred grew into medieval universities. Gradually, they added law and medicine to their curriculum. Over the next few centuries important universities evolved at Paris, Orleans, and Toulouse in France; at Bologna, Padua, and Naples in Italy; and at Oxford

Margin notes:

Seven liberal arts

Scholasticism

Thomas Aquinas, 1225–1274

Universities

and Cambridge in England. Others were founded in Scotland, Spain, Germany, and other European countries.

The Renaissance—1300–1500

By the fourteenth century, a reaction had set in against the teaching of the Middle Ages. Scholars and their students grew tired of the heavy church dominance over schooling and scholarly thought. They shifted their attention from what would happen in the next life to an investigation of this world. Rather than relying on the revealed word of God and the church for intellectual authority, they turned more directly and more often to the writings and ideas of the ancient Greeks and Romans and to a spirit of free inquiry that they read about in the Greek classics. Gradually, their *classical humanism* replaced the thinking of the scholastics.

Renaissance thinking developed in synchrony with the rise of commerce in Europe. As expanding trade created centers of wealth in cities, especially those of northern Italy, the wealthy sought new learning in literature, the arts, and architecture. The wealthy commercial class began to sponsor teachers, artists, and writers; and they saw themselves as custodians of the new knowledge. As such, they became a cultural elite with a status that gave them a social position that was comparable to the positions of those with church authority and military might.

To preserve the intellectual and cultural elitism, they turned to court schools for their children and others of social and political position. These schools, which had actually existed for some time, were now relied on more than in the past to educate *courtiers*, people who were learned in the classics, polished in style and elegance, and of service to the court, particularly as diplomats. The curriculum consisted of literature, especially the classics, art, architecture, and Greek and Latin grammar.

Over time, however, schooling and formal education became a goal unto itself instead of a means to the greater end of true learning. Erudition replaced substance and understanding. To know the right thing or the correct style became more important than the pursuit of new knowledge or true investigation.

Classical humanism

Court schools

The concept of a "liberal arts" education dates back to the Renaissance and its love of humanistic learning. Only later, however, were the benefits of education extended to women and to members of less privileged classes.

Desiderius Erasmus of Rotterdam in the Netherlands was a noted Renaissance scholar and also its most telling critic. He was a teacher, philosopher, writer, and social critic. His most famous work, *In Praise of Folly*, satirically attacked the schooling and culture of both medieval and contemporary times. He said theologians and philosophers were more interested in showing off their intellectual gymnastics than in finding new meaning in life and the relationship between God and human beings. He said teachers stressed unimportant facts and precise intricacies of grammar rather than teaching their students meaningful knowledge.

Erasmus advocated the teaching of classical languages, history, etymology, archaeology, astronomy, and the Scriptures. He also acknowledged the importance of early learning and suggested that parents begin the education of their children by teaching the children themselves at an early age. He was aware of the importance of developmental growth in students, and he recommended that teachers use certain methods of instruction.

In response to the writings of Erasmus and others, later Renaissance thinkers and teachers developed ideas that still influence education and schooling today. Those ideas involved the nature of knowledge, purposes of education, the role of schooling, specific approaches to teaching, and the place of the liberal arts in the curriculum. Probably most noticeable of the specific legacies of the Renaissance is the place that Latin has held in the secondary schools of America into recent times.

Although schooling during the Renaissance broadened to include more diverse students than did the schooling of earlier times, it was still elitist and intended primarily for men. It was directed only to that class of people who might be expected to be able to appreciate it. The social critics it produced did not challenge the roles, stations in life, and importance of the powerful elite. Renaissance schooling did not stimulate concern for the life of the peasant. It did not challenge the assumptions of the rigid social class structure or the customs and privileges that accompanied it.

To the contrary, it criticized mediocrity, those who lacked social polish and status, and the uneducated. For the people of that time, education was tied to social class because of the elitist opinion that it would be wasted on the unsophisticated. Members of the other classes trained for jobs but were not schooled, in the finer sense of the term.

Renaissance schooling was not open to significant numbers of women. Daughters of aristocrats might study certain "ladies' subjects" in court schools or with private tutors, or they might be taught in convents or convent schools, but most had no schooling at all. Those who were schooled studied art, music, needlework, poetry, and dancing.

The Reformation and the Rise of the Middle Class—1500–1700

The rise of a commercial middle class, the development of modern nation-states, and the Protestant Reformation in Europe brought about a reorientation of schooling in the sixteenth and seventeenth centuries. The schools that evolved were less tied to the aristocratic classes, less bound to cities to the exclusion of the countryside, and no longer under the rules and tradition of a single church.

Schools needed to serve a variety of religious purposes. They were needed to teach as many people as possible to read the Bible, not in Latin, but in the local language—the vernacular. Whereas Catholic Church leaders had considered it unnecessary for each person to read and interpret the Bible, because that was the re-

Something to Think About

Some educational historians draw parallels between early European schools and select, private boys' schools of today.

- What similarities do you see between these two types of schools?
- In what ways are they different?
- Do you see parallels between these schools and the school depicted in films such as *The Dead Poets' Society?*

sponsibility of the clergy, Protestants insisted that their followers read the Bible themselves. Strict obedience to church authority was not at that time their practice.

Therefore, schools were needed to instruct religious followers and to help them spread their beliefs to others. Even the lower classes had to be reached so that they could learn their religion and live according to its precepts. Schools existed for a serious purpose, not for the stylish reasons of the Renaissance courtiers: Reading the Bible was believed necessary for salvation.

Economic conditions also necessitated the spread of schooling. If people were to trade and travel more, they needed to know more about other places and people. They needed to be able to write and to communicate in their own and in other languages. They needed to be able to compute and to handle their other business affairs.

Commerce

Protestant leaders such as Martin Luther and his early followers recommended basic schooling for children of all classes and both genders. They went so far as to urge government-supported schools. They proposed that instruction beyond the elementary level include both the local language and Latin, as well as history, music, science, mathematics, and physical education. Schools were seen as instruments of religion, but that was not their sole purpose. There was also a civic purpose—to develop useful citizens.

Martin Luther, 1483–1546

In the denominational schools of the times, teaching tended to conform to a rigid question-and-answer format and was often organized around the official catechism. The important religious denominational precepts were memorized and ingrained. As the schools spread, two levels of instruction became the norm—common "grammar" schools for all, including girls, and "classical" schools for the upper classes, those who were educated for church, civil, and commercial positions of leadership.

The greatest legacy of schooling during this period was the concept of universal education, or schools for everyone. The schools of the first European settlers in America were based on that principle.

Schools for everyone

The Enlightenment—1700–1800

In European history, the eighteenth century is known as the Enlightenment or the Age of Reason because the influential thinkers of the time emphasized the power of the human mind. These philosophers—among them, John Locke, Jean-Jacques

Age of Reason

Rousseau, David Hume, and Voltaire—believed the thinking mind could understand the universe and all in it. They thought that thinking people could develop the means to make the world and human life better. These ideas had a direct and powerful impact on all American institutions, including both the American form of government and its schools.

Scientific method

Enlightenment philosophers saw the universe as a gigantic machine that was guided and operated by a set of constantly operating *natural laws*. Humans could use their minds to learn about these laws and, once they did, could formulate principles that would bring all life into harmony with them. By using a pattern of thinking called the *scientific method*, they could come to understand the natural laws of the universe. The scientific method meant forming hypotheses about all phenomena and then testing the validity of those hypotheses. Those that proved accurate could be preserved and used as tools of understanding. Those not valid could be discarded or reformulated and retested.

The idea of progress

Thinkers of the Enlightenment believed that the world and life in it could be made perfect and that *progress* could gradually be made toward that goal. Through the use of reason, civic leaders could improve their institutions or find better ones, could improve society, and could perfect human life. People needed only to learn enough, and the human mind would discover how to make things better. Of course, if reason and the scientific method were going to reform society and make life better, schools were a critically important civic responsibility.

The impact of the Enlightenment was much greater, however, than its influence on schools. In fact, the greatest impact of the Enlightenment was the more general effect it had on the nature and form of government and on the relationship between governments and the people they governed. In this context, the ideas of equality, human rights, and governmental responsibility to citizens were most significant.

Jean-Jacques Rousseau, 1712–1778

Jean-Jacques Rousseau was a French philosopher of the Enlightenment whose ideas concerned both education and government. He believed that humans were in their best condition when they are in their "natural state." He stated, "Everything is good as it comes from the hand of the author of nature; but everything degenerates in the hands of man." Men were "noble savages." Free men were uncorrupted, but society and its institutions corrupted them. Therefore, he believed that education should return man to his *natural state*. It should allow him to follow natural inclinations.

Rousseau believed that education was a natural process if people would not disturb it. In his eyes, young children were naturally good and needed to be allowed to grow. He did not accept the prevailing traditional idea that all humans were sinful and that education had to counter that sinful nature. He expressed his educational ideas in many works, among them a novel, *Emile* (1762), about the education of a young man.

Rousseau's ideas about the nature of people and government became part of the philosophical justification for the eighteenth-century revolutions in America and France, and they molded the governments formed after them. His philosophical works *On the Origin of the Inequality of Mankind* and *The Social Contract* attacked social inequalities as artificial conditions based on property, wealth, and prestige, all of which were perpetuated by the institutions established and preserved by the powerful. He supported the revolt of the common man for a better economic, social, and political life. He saw education as a means to bring that about.

John Locke, philosopher and scientist, was the premier thinker and writer of the British Enlightenment on both education and government. In his writings about the human mind, he stated that at birth a human being's mind is a *tabula rasa*, or blank slate, without any ideas. As people grow, they learn from their environment through their senses. Gradually, simple ideas are replaced by more complex ones, as the person thinks, associates, compares, abstracts, and generalizes. Locke saw learning as an active, inductive process that uses a rational, scientific method involving investigation, the gathering of information, and the formulation of sophisticated ideas. He expressed these ideas in *An Essay Concerning Human Understanding*.

John Locke, 1632–1704

Locke presented his ideas about schooling explicitly in *Some Thoughts Concerning Education*. He wrote that education begins early in life, that it should proceed gradually, and that it involves physical as well as intellectual elements. The purposes of education are a sound mind and a strong body. The environment in which a child grows up is important. The subjects that he said should be studied at an early age were reading, writing, and arithmetic; later, English, French, mathematics, history, government, and physical education were to be added. His goal for schooling was an individual who could participate effectively and ethically in government and business.

Locke expressed his political philosophy in *Two Treatises of Government*. He said that governmental authority rests on a *contract* between the people and the government and that the sources of that authority come from the people. He challenged the idea of a divine right of kings. For him, kings and all governments derived their power not from God, but from the consent of the governed. Since that is the case, the people have a right to withdraw that consent if the government does not fulfill its part of the contract. He also asserted that all people have inalienable rights of life, liberty, and property. These Lockean ideas, along with those of Rousseau, formed the basis for the American Revolution and the form of government that followed it.

Consent of the governed

Schooling in America

Although schooling occurred on the North American continent before English colonies were established and much schooling also took place throughout the seventeenth and eighteenth centuries outside of those colonies, schools in the English colonies provided the primary historical basis for pre-K–12 schooling in the United States. This second section of Chapter 8 traces ideas about schooling and schooling practices from colonial times to the early days of the twentieth century. Because much of that historical tradition was narrowly focused on white, male students, the chapter includes additional information on the education of women and minority group members.

Colonial Schools

The types of schooling established in the English colonies in America during the seventeenth and eighteenth centuries provided the foundation for development of today's schools. Those schools reflected a combination of two types of traditions: (1) the political, social, and religious traditions of the people who settled the different colonies and (2) the ideas from the Enlightenment about the makeup of the universe, human nature, government, and education. Those ideas in combination determined the purposes of schools, who attended them, what was studied, and who did the teaching.

Influence of the Enlightenment

According to Enlightenment philosophy, schools were necessary because people needed to understand the workings of the gigantic machinelike universe in which they lived. If they understood the machine and its operations, they could adjust their lives to fit its patterns. If people were in harmony with the laws of nature, life would improve.

The thinking of the Enlightenment also required schools so that people would be educated citizens led by knowledgeable government leaders. If power derived from the consent of the governed and if civic leaders were responsible to the people who selected them, then the people had to know enough to select appropriate representativeness. The representatives in turn needed to be informed and skilled enough to govern effectively and honestly.

Enlightenment values also led to the expectation that schools would develop liberally educated human beings—that is, people who would be knowledgeable about and sensitive to the finer things of life. These people would be responsible for their own well-being and for the well-being of others, especially the less fortunate. They would work as partners with others in their local communities and in the broader world to make everyone's life better.

Religious influence

Religious beliefs and traditions of the Protestant Reformation that developed in England and northern Europe in the sixteenth and seventeenth centuries also made schools necessary in colonial America. According to these beliefs, people were individually responsible for their own religious faith. They had to be able to read and interpret the Bible. They had to select, follow, and understand their religious leaders. Some had to be the educated people who could serve as those religious leaders.

Because all people were considered sinful, and the devil was ever tempting, people needed to be brought up properly. They needed to be able to recognize sin and righteousness in themselves and in their neighbors. They needed to follow the correct path. Therefore, everyone needed to have at least some education, and community leaders were responsible for seeing that it was available.

New England colonies

In the New England colonies religious influences on schooling were more dominant than the ideas of the Enlightenment philosophers because of the religious backgrounds of the people who settled there. For example, the Puritans, who began the colony of Massachusetts Bay in 1630, quickly established community schools. They did so because they believed, according to the teachings of John Calvin, that all human beings were predestined at birth for either eternal salvation or eternal condemnation. Accordingly, those selected for salvation would exhibit their status by behaving correctly or properly. To act properly, they had to read and follow the dictates of the Bible. They had to avoid being deluded by the devil. They also needed the guidance of educated ministers.

The Puritans also believed that those selected by God would expect proper behavior from all their neighbors and, since their neighbors included those who were not selected for salvation, rules of behavior had to be formulated and enforced. Religious principles and civil laws were intertwined. Everyone was expected to conform. All who lived in a town were expected to abide by the laws enacted by the selectmen, to work hard enough to be productive economically, and to respect the dignity of their fellow citizens.

Colonial schoolteachers were most often young men, but a number of women conducted dames' schools in their homes for both girls and boys.

Common elementary schools were established in the towns of Massachusetts Bay to provide a basic education in reading, writing, arithmetic, and religion for all children, although girls and children from lower-class families attended less frequently than did middle-class boys. Children usually attended from about ages 5 or 6 to 13 or 14.

Common schools

The schools were usually one-room, wooden structures built on public land and owned by the town. The teacher typically sat at the front of the room on a tall stool behind a high desk or pulpit. A rod for discipline was always close at hand. The children sat on benches, usually studying in silence.

Younger children learned the alphabet and beginning reading from a hornbook, which was so named because it was covered by a thin transparent sheath of horn, and older children read the *New England Primer*. The students spent much of the school day copying letters and sentences, practicing numbers, and memorizing religious and commonly accepted maxims: "With Adam's fall, we sinned all"; "Idleness is the devil's workshop"; "The idle fool is whipt at school."

Hornbooks and the New England primer

While most studied silently at their seats, the teacher called children individually to the desk for recitation of the memorized lesson. Discipline was strict and corporal punishment commonplace. Laziness, idleness, and lack of learning were considered outward manifestations of the devil within, and teachers were expected to beat the devil out of students who exhibited these traits.

Usually, teachers were young men at the early stages of their working life. Most intended to move on to other careers. Many were in the process of studying for the ministry and had paused in their studies in order to make some money. Others used their salaries to repay money they had borrowed for passage to America. Often their dispositions and training were not suited for teaching. Frequently—and with communal approval—they used fear, embarrassment, and the rod to motivate their students.

Sometimes girls, especially those from middle-class families, attended dames' schools instead of the common schools. These schools were conducted by local women, usually in a room in their homes, and they included male students. The girls studied reading, writing, religion, and rudiments of arithmetic. The atmo-

Dames' schools

sphere was less stern than in the common schools, though it did not deviate from the contemporary moral norms.

Latin grammar school

After boys of higher social and economic levels received their basic instruction in the common schools or from private tutors, they frequently moved on to the town Latin grammar school. There they prepared for positions of religious and civic leadership. These schools were essentially secondary schools whose purpose was preparation for college—at that time and location, usually Harvard or Yale.

Typically, boys attended the Latin school between ages 8 and 16. They studied Latin grammar, composition, and the Latin and Greek classics—Cicero, Livy, Virgil, Caesar, Horace, Isocrates, Hesiod, and Homer. As time permitted, they also learned mathematics, science, history, and moral philosophy. Their teachers were more learned than those in the common schools, and their approach to teaching was less rigid and less reliant on corporal punishment.

Public schools

The town schools of colonial New England were called *public schools* because they were established by the townspeople as a public service, and at least the common schools were essentially open to the children of the town as a whole. They were not funded by public taxes, however.

Nevertheless, town schools were more than readily available institutions for those who wished to use them. Townspeople had moral and civic duties to provide them. Parents were expected to send their children. Children were expected to attend, behave, and learn. These expectations were written into law, and those who disobeyed were punished.

Two laws passed in the early days of the Massachusetts Bay colony illustrate the commitment to schooling in colonial New England and reflect the premises on which that schooling was based. Both served as models for other colonies. The first law was enacted in 1642, only twelve years after the first Puritans arrived on American shores:

> This Cort [Court], taking into consideration the great neglect of many parents & masters in training up their children in learning . . . do hereupon order and decree, that in euery towne ye chosen men . . . take account from time to time of all parents and masters, and of their children, concerning their . . . ability to read & understand the principles of religion & the capitall lawes [sic] of this country.[2]

"Old Deluder Satan"

The second was passed five years later, in 1647, and is known historically as the Old Deluder Satan act. It required all towns of significant size to provide schools.

> It being one chiefe project of ye ould deluder, Satin, to keepe men from the knowledge of ye Scriptures. . . . It is therefore ordred, yt evry towneship in this jurisdiction, aftr ye Lord hath increased yr number to 50 householdrs, shall then forthwth appoint one wthin their towne to teach all such children as shall resort to him to write & reade . . . & it is furthr ordered yt where any towne shall increase to ye number of 100 families or househouldrs, they shall set up a grammar schoole, ye mr [aim] thereof being able to instruct youth so farr as they shall be fited for ye university.[3]

Middle Colonies

Generally schooling in the Middle Colonies—Pennsylvania, New York, New Jersey, and Maryland—was similar to that in New England. Most children received basic instruction in the four R's (reading, writing, arithmetic, and religion) and many middle-class boys proceeded to higher instruction in preparation for college and careers as ministers and government leaders. These similarities resulted from the facts that the Middle Colonies were also English in origin and that the settlers

Something to Think About

Nearly all states and communities today have laws that require parents to be fined if they do not send their children to school. In many ways the laws are similar to those of the Massachusetts Bay colony. To assess your feelings about such laws, consider these two situations.

- John is in third grade, but his parents rarely see that he gets to school. He will fail unless he attends more regularly.
- Curt is in tenth grade but rarely attends. He is failing in every subject. He expects to quit school at the end of the year when he becomes 16.

If you taught each of the students, what would you do? Why would you do so?

were also primarily northern Europeans who sought a new life on an undeveloped continent.

But the schools in the Middle Colonies also possessed a number of different characteristics that have been incorporated into the schools of America. The differences were based on three factors: (1) the people of the Middle Colonies were more religiously, culturally, and economically diverse than those of New England; (2) they settled either in the harbor towns of the coast—Philadelphia, New York, and Baltimore—or were scattered throughout the farmland of the interior, rather than living in small, closely knit towns; and (3) they established their early schools about 50 to 100 years after the first schools of New England were established.

The European settlers of the Middle Colonies were English, Dutch, Swedes, German, Scotch-Irish, and French Huguenot. They were Quakers, Dutch Reformed, Lutherans, Presbyterians, Baptists, Roman Catholics, Jews, and members of small Protestant pietistic sects. They were farmers, traders, bankers, and craftspersons. They had many reasons for immigrating to America—not just religious ones.

Because of this diversity, settlers in the Middle Colonies tended to separate religion and government, and they were more tolerant than New Englanders of different religious beliefs. Communities rarely had a single government-operated town school, and they did not insist that everyone attend. Schools were more the responsibilities of different church denominations than of the government. The churches established denominational schools for the children of their members, as well as for children who were poor and unconverted. Middle-class parents who did not send their children to denominational schools hired private tutors.

Denominational schools

During the eighteenth century, the Society of Friends (Quakers) of Philadelphia sponsored a loose system of schools that were forerunners of American public schools. These Friends Public Schools were operated by their teachers (one per school) and were housed in rented rooms and teachers' homes at scattered locations throughout the city. Often a school would operate for only a short time, but a number of them were functioning at all times during the century. At various times, spe-

Friends Public Schools

REFLECTING ON PRACTICE

*T*his Reflecting on Practice consists of an excerpt from a description of a colonial American elementary school classroom written in 1750 by Christopher Dock, a teacher of German children in Pennsylvania.[4] It appeared in a document called *Schul-Ordnung*. As you read, consider:

- What historical European roots of American schooling seem to be reflected in this description?
- What cultural and societal norms of the times are reflected?
- In what ways is the teaching you observe in schools today different from that described here? What are some reasons for the differences?

The children arrive as they do because some have a great distance to school, others a short distance, so that the children cannot assemble as punctually as they can in a city. Therefore, when a few children are present, those who can read their Testament sit together on one bench; but the boys and girls occupy separate benches. They are given a chapter which they read at sight consecutively. Meanwhile I write copies for them. Those who have read their passage of Scripture without error take their places at the table and write. Those who fail have to sit at the end of the bench, and each new arrival the same; as each one is thus released in order he takes up his slate. This process continues until they have all assembled. The last one left on the bench is a "lazy pupil."

When all are together, and examined, whether they are washed and combed, they sing a psalm or a morning hymn, and I sing and pray with them. As much as they can understand of the Lord's Prayer and the ten commandments (according to the gift God has given them), I exhort and admonish them accordingly. . . .

After these devotional exercises those who can write resume their work. Those who cannot read the Testament have had time during the assemblage to study their lesson. These are heard recite immediately after prayer. Those who know their lesson receive an O on the hand, traced with crayon. This is a mark of excellence. Those who fail more than three times are sent back to study their lesson again. When all the little ones have recited, these are asked again, and any one having failed in more than three trials a second time, is called "Lazy" by the entire class and his name is written down. Whether such a child fear the rod or not, I know from experience that this denunciation of the children hurts more than if I were constantly to wield and flourish the rod. If then such a child has friends in school who are able to instruct him and desire to do so, he will visit more frequently than before. For this reason: if the pupil's name has not been erased before dismissal the pupils are at liberty to write down the names of those who have been lazy, and take them along home. But if the child learns his lesson well in the future, his name is again presented to the other pupils, and they are told that he knew his lesson well and failed in no respect. Then all the pupils call "Diligent" to him. When this has taken place his name is erased from the slate of lazy pupils, and the former transgression is forgiven.

The children who are in the spelling class are daily examined in pronunciation. In spelling, when a word has more than one syllable, they must repeat the whole word, but some, while they can say the letters, cannot pronounce the word, and so cannot be put to reading. For improvement a child must repeat a lesson, and in this way: The child gives me the book, I spell the word and he pronounces it. If he is slow, another pupil pronounces it for him, and in this way he hears how it should be done, and knows that he must follow the letters and not his own fancy.

Concerning A B C pupils, it would be best, having but one child, to let it learn one row of letters at a time, to say forward and backward. But with many, I let them learn the alphabet first, and then ask a child to point out a letter that I name. If a child is backward or ignorant, I ask another, or the whole class, and the first one that points to the right letter, I grasp his finger and hold it until I have put a mark opposite his name. I then ask for another letter, &c. Whichever child has during the day received the greatest number of marks, has pointed out the greatest number of letters. To him I owe something—a flower drawn on paper or a bird. But if several have the same number, we draw lots; this causes less annoyance. In this way not only are the very timid cured of their shyness (which is a great hindrance in learning), but a fondness for school is increased. . . .

As the children carry their dinner, an hour's liberty is given them after dinner. But as they are usually inclined to misapply their time if one is not constantly with them, one or two of them must read a story of the Old Testament (either from Moses and the Prophets, or from Solomon's or Sirach's Proverbs), while I write copies for them. This exercise continues during the noon hour.

It is also to be noted that children find it necessary to ask to leave the room, and one must permit them to do this, not wishing the uncleanness and odor in the school. But the clamor to go out would continue all day, and sometimes without need, so that occasionally two or three are out at the same time, playing. To prevent this I have driven a nail in the door-post, on which hangs a wooden tag. Any one needing to leave the room looks for the tag. If it is on the nail, this is his permit to go without asking. He takes the tag out with him. If another wishes to leave, he does not ask either, but stands by the door until the first returns, from whom he takes the tag and goes. If the tag is out too long, the one wishing to go inquires who was out last, and from him it can be ascertained to whom he gave the tag, so that none can remain out too long.

To teach the uninitiated numbers and figures, I write on the blackboard (which hangs where all can see) these figures.

1   2   3   4   5   6   7   8   9   0

far apart, that other figures can be put before and behind them. Then I put an 0 before the 1 and explain that this does not increase the number. Then I erase the 0 and put it after the 1, so that it makes 10. If two ciphers follow, it makes 100, if three follow, 1000, &c. This I show them through all the digits. This done I affix to the 1 another 1 making 11. But if an 0 is put between, it makes 101, but if it be placed after, it makes 110. In a similar manner I go through all the digits. When this is done I give them something to find in the Testament or hymnal. Those who are quickest have something to claim for their diligence, from me or at home.

As it is desirable for intelligent reading to take note of commas, but as the inexperienced find this difficult, I have this rule: If one of the Testament pupils does not read on, but stops before he reaches a comma or period, this counts one-fourth failure. Similarly if one reads over a comma, it is one-fourth failure. Repeating a word counts one-half. Then all failures are noted, and especially where each one has failed. When all have read, all those who have failed must step forward and according to the number of errors stand in a row. Those who have not failed move up, and the others take the lowest positions.

cific schools came under the sponsorship and loose control of church officials when the church subsidized their operation on the condition that they serve poor children free or at a nominal charge.

The Friends schools were intended primarily for Quaker children, both boys and girls, but other children, including blacks and Native Americans, were admitted as a matter of faith and practice. Their curriculum usually involved the four R's and sometimes the beginning elements of commerce and agriculture. It reflected the strong Quaker commitment to nonviolence and peace, characteristics that led to criticism during the American Revolution as colonists chose sides and took up arms.

Because Quakers believed that everyone possessed an "inner light" (roughly, the conscience and inspiration) that needed to be nourished and developed and because they rejected the Puritan concept of inevitable human depravity, they did not believe in corporal punishment in the schools. The classroom atmosphere was quite different from that of the town schools of Massachusetts Bay.[5]

The Middle Colonies also had higher-level schools for boys who pursued schooling beyond the four R's. Most of the students in these schools prepared for college and careers as ministers and civic leaders. But as Philadelphia and the other colonial cities developed into trade centers, more students looked toward business and commerce. In response, the schools added instruction in navigation, surveying, bookkeeping, Spanish, French, and geography.

Franklin's Academy

The Franklin Academy, a Philadelphia school begun in 1751 at the urging and under the guidance of Benjamin Franklin, stressed these broader purposes. It became the prototype for the American secondary schools of the next century. Its purposes and curriculum were to prepare students for employment rather than for college. Students studied English grammar and composition, rhetoric, public speaking, classics, mathematics, science, and history. Some were also trained for specific trades, such as carpentry, shipbuilding, and printing. Before the academies, boys had received manual training through apprenticeships with craftspersons rather than in schools, a pattern begun in the Middle Ages.[6]

Southern Colonies

Life in the Southern Colonies was significantly different from that in both New England and the Middle Colonies. Southern settlers usually came to North America for economic rather than religious reasons. Most came from England and were members of the Church of England rather than churches that had been persecuted. Many of those who arrived in the early days of the colonies came without families and expected to return to Europe after a few years. Others saw their settlements as outward extensions of the port cities of England. They intended to send their children back to England for schooling.

Through the seventeenth and eighteenth centuries, however, the economy and lifestyle of the Southern Colonies changed. Settlements that began as small commercial outposts for trading companies failed; and large tobacco, sugar, rice, and cotton plantations took their place. Many people scattered over the countryside rather than clustering into towns or cities. The plantations and such port cities as Charleston, which connected them to the rest of the world, became the centers of southern colonial life. That life evolved into a three-level society of planters and wealthy traders, poor farmers and craftspersons, and slaves.

Schooling was usually private and limited to the children of the wealthy. It was provided through plantation tutors (which included indentured servants), privately operated boarding schools, or schools established by Anglican missionary societies. Children of poor back-country farmers and slaves received no formal education. No continuing system of schools developed until well after independence.

Schools of the New American Nation

Civic purposes

The American Revolution replaced British rule with a representative democracy, and in the minds of the American founding fathers that change required a shift in the purposes of schools. Although religious purposes for schools continued, civic ones became more important. The schools of the new nation had to educate citizens. Only knowledgeable and understanding people could participate effectively in government, preserve liberty, and provide for the general welfare.

Thomas Jefferson, who was influenced by the political and educational ideas of John Locke, expressed this American philosophy of education: "If a nation expects to be ignorant and free, in a state of civilization, it expects what never was and never will be."[7]

Jefferson believed that schooling was a state responsibility, that it had to be available to all, and that at least part of it should be provided at public expense. To implement his idea, he developed a system of education for the commonwealth of Virginia from the primary grades through college. But his ideas were too advanced for the Virginia legislature, which failed to enact them into law.

Thomas Jefferson

In order to teach the three R's during the early years of the American republic, towns in every state either continued community primary schools that had been founded during colonial times or started new ones. Many towns also established secondary schools much like the earlier Latin grammar schools or academies. The primary schools were often free, at least for the poor. The secondary schools usually charged tuition.

Because of a particular sequence of events, schooling in America became primarily a state and local responsibility. Local community groups started early schools to serve local needs. Often they were in operation before the Revolution and, therefore, before states and the nation came into being. During the Revolution, state constitutions accepted responsibility for schools. Next, the federal Constitution, adopted in 1789, which could have claimed responsibility for schools for the national government, did not do so. Finally, the Tenth Amendment to the Constitution, the last in the Bill of Rights, reserved direct power over education to the states.

State and local control

But even in those early years, the national government demonstrated its support for schools. Shortly after the Revolution, Congress, under the Articles of Confederation, adopted a national plan to provide for schools in the territory of the West. Under the Ordinance of 1785, the land of the Northwest Territory was surveyed for development. That land, west of Pennsylvania and north of the Ohio River, was divided into townships of thirty-six square miles each. The townships were then subdivided into thirty-six sections, each one a square mile in size. When the federal government sold the land, the money paid for section number 16 in each township was set aside for the funding of schools.

National government-funded territory schools

As the American nation grew during the early years of the nineteenth century, a distinct sense of nationalism developed. And as a result, schools were expected not only to produce educated citizens but also to produce *Americans*—that is, citizens who were different from the people of Europe; who were individualists; who believed in the emerging American principles of government; who would succeed as merchants, artisans, laborers, or professionals; who could conquer the frontier; and who could demonstrate the viability, vitality, and basic rightness of the new country.

"American" schools

During the nineteenth century, emphasis on education for citizenship and for jobs gradually increased, while that on religious training continued to decline. Industrialization and the continuing flow of immigrants made the need for a *common* education for all as important as ever. People needed jobs. They needed to be able to get along with each other. In the minds of many, they needed to be made into true Americans.

Toward Free Public Schools

The most significant trend in education in the United States during the nineteenth and early twentieth centuries was the movement toward free public schools for everyone. Schools were different from state to state and community to community, and they developed at different speeds; but all seemed to be evolving in similar directions and seemed to be following about the same three-stage process. The trend affected elementary schools initially and secondary schools later. First, communities and states passed laws that *permitted* free, tax-supported, public elementary schools. Next, the laws *encouraged* the establishment of the schools, the school boards to operate them, and the taxes to finance them. Finally, the laws *required* that schools be provided and funded. By 1900, more than half of the children in the United States between 6 and 13 years of age attended elementary schools.

Nineteenth-century academies

Secondary schools of the early nineteenth century were much like the academies of earlier decades, but they included in their curricula college preparatory as well as practical studies. They were privately funded and operated. They usually admitted many types of students, had broad and sometimes ill-defined programs of study, and were of varying degrees of quality. Usually they were run by a board of trustees or overseers and a rather strong schoolmaster. Some were partly public in the sense that they received supplemental public funds, typically to cover the cost of educating poor children.

Public high schools

Although the first public high school was established in Boston in 1821, it was not until the latter third of the nineteenth century that secondary schools spread rapidly, much as elementary schools had done a few decades earlier. In that process, tax-supported public high schools replaced the academies as the most common secondary school. The academies that continued tended to evolve into private, select, college-preparatory institutions for children of families able and willing to pay their fees.

American high schools were unique institutions. They were tax-supported and free of cost to the student. They admitted girls as well as boys. They attempted to educate children for the world of work, for future college studies, and for their roles as citizens. Once the courts ruled in the 1870s that states could levy taxes for schools, most states quickly decided to do so. Not long after that, states passed laws requiring that high schools be established, rather than be left a matter of local choice.

Schools for immigrants

American high schools were influenced by the people and the times of late-nineteenth-century America. That period was a time of immigration, industrialization, and urbanization. The schools were expected to Americanize and help assimilate the immigrants into the melting pot of society. They were expected to prepare students for jobs in factories and in businesses. Many were expected to prepare American youths for lives off the farm and in the newly developing cities. In response, the high schools added vocational or career courses alongside college preparatory subjects. These new areas of study included clerical and commercial courses, manual and industrial arts, and home economics.

Schools for jobs

Social integration

Whereas secondary schools in other nations focused on college preparation for a select few or methodically separated the academic students from those who would soon leave school to take a job, American high schools tried to accept and serve all students between 14 and 18 years of age. They tried to help students advance economically and socially at the same time that they served as places where youths from different cultural backgrounds could interact socially. Despite these intentions, poor and lower-class children often did not attend in large numbers.

With two notable exceptions, high schools were remarkably successful in achieving their goals. The exceptions involved racial segregation and a lack of services for people with handicapping conditions. As Chapter 7 discussed, especially in the South, black and other nonwhite students were relegated to separate schools, usually not at all equal to those provided for white students. Physically and intellectually impaired students were ignored.

Segregation

What the Public Schools Taught

The content of instruction in public elementary schools in the United States did not change radically from the mid-1800s through the first half of the twentieth century. The three R's provided the focus for the primary grades, and the upper grades usually consisted of a combination of advanced basic skills and increasing amounts of science, history and geography, art, music, and physical education. Instructional changes that were made were more often than not in teaching methods and in the updating of the specific content.

The situation was different in the high schools, however. Because public schools had a number of purposes and attempted to serve so many types of students during the latter part of the nineteenth century, high school curricula tended to be confusing mixtures of offerings. To remedy this, the National Education Association established a Committee of Ten in 1892 to recommend what high schools should teach. Charles Eliot, president of Harvard University, chaired the committee and was its major force. The committee's recommendations in 1893 set the curriculum pattern that has dominated high school instruction for the 100 years since they appeared.

Committee of Ten (1893)

The Committee of Ten recommended eight years of elementary school and four years of high school. It proposed a high school curriculum much like the traditional college preparatory program of the past; and, although it outlined four alternative tracks, it suggested that the same general type of instruction be provided all students. Committee members believed that similar subjects were appropriate for both college-bound and terminal students because those subjects "trained the mind." That is, they improved the ability to remember, observe, reason, and express ideas. The committee believed these capacities contributed to the students' personal well-being and to their ability to serve society as citizens, workers, and parents.[8] (The specific subjects are listed in Chapter 7.)

In the early decades of the twentieth century, as more states passed compulsory attendance laws and more students entered and remained in high school, some educators began to question the value of the Committee of Ten's high school curriculum for non-college-bound students. These people felt that the curriculum was not sufficiently comprehensive. They were less concerned about mental discipline and more concerned about the direct utility of the subject matter.

Comprehensive education

In 1918, this view was incorporated into the *Cardinal Principles of Secondary Education,* a report of the National Education Association Commission on the Reorganization of Secondary Education. The report stated that a comprehensive reorganization of secondary education was imperative at that time and proposed what that organization should be. It called for a more differentiated curriculum in which business, commercial, industrial, agricultural, and domestic science thrusts would

Cardinal Principles of Secondary Education (1918)

not be overshadowed by preparation for college. The commission wanted a more truly comprehensive curriculum.[9] (The specific areas of the proposed curriculum are listed in Chapter 7.)

The *Cardinal Principles of Secondary Education*, along with the earlier ideas of the Committee of Ten, established the framework for the curricula of high schools in the United States through the twentieth century. Although there have been shifts in emphasis and innovations added over the years, these changes have occurred within that established framework. Typically, high schools have offered four curriculum thrusts or tracks:

- Academic or college prep—English language and literature, mathematics, foreign languages, sciences, and social studies (including history)
- General—Courses with the same titles as the academic program but modified for lower-achieving students on the assumption they will not attend college
- Commercial or business—Shorthand, typing, bookkeeping, secretarial training, marketing, distribution; in more recent years, computer applications
- Vocational—Industrial arts, home economics, agriculture, building trades, electronics, automotive repair, graphic arts

American Colleges and Universities

Colonial colleges

Colleges and universities in America were established in colonial times to educate ministers and upper-class gentlemen, many of whom became political and social leaders of their communities. The colleges were organized along the patterns of the major European universities, especially Oxford and Cambridge in England. Students studied English, Hebrew, Greek and Latin (language and literature), rhetoric, logic, mathematics, geometry, astronomy, natural and moral philosophy, metaphysics, ethics, and music. Harvard was established in 1636, William and Mary in 1693, and Yale in 1701. By the time of the American Revolution most colonies had their own colleges. It is important to note that these early colleges were chartered by the king and their charters were rendered secure in the new nation by virtue of the *Dartmouth College* decision by the Supreme Court in 1819.

After independence and through the early decades of the nineteenth century, new colleges were established regularly throughout the states and on the frontier as the size of the population and the desires of the people required. The colleges were usually denominational, but often publicly chartered, and with a liberal arts curriculum.

Normal schools

Beginning in the 1820s and 1830s, two-year normal schools were established in many states to educate teachers. They were patterned after such schools in France as the *Ecole normale supérieure*, from which they got their name; and since students entered directly out of elementary school, they gave the appearance of specialized academies. At first, students prepared only for elementary school teaching. Courses in the philosophy and history of education and in teaching methodology provided the core of their curricula.

Over the years, more subjects were added, the schools began to prepare teachers for secondary schools, and subject-matter departments were added. By the early twentieth century, most normal school programs had expanded to four years, and many had begun to call themselves state teachers' colleges. At the same time that normal schools were evolving into more comprehensive institutions, state colleges and universities added teacher preparation to their purposes and opened departments of education.

College education in general shifted significantly toward the middle of the nineteenth century when changes in society brought on pushes for education in the mechanical and agricultural sciences, for an extension of college instruction to a broader representation of society, and for greater direct government involvement in and support for higher education. As a result, the national government passed the Morrill Act of 1862, which established land grant colleges. The act, named for its sponsor, Representative Justin Morrill of Vermont, gave each state 30,000 acres of land for each of its senators and members of Congress. The income from these land grants was to be used to support one or more state colleges that would provide mechanical and agricultural education. The act immediately brought college education to most of American society and expanded the college curricula to engineering and the applied arts and sciences.

Land grant colleges

Between the 1860s and the 1940s, the pattern of higher education remained relatively constant. Colleges consisted of denominational liberal arts colleges, state colleges and normal schools, and land grant colleges. Slowly over the years, more institutions were established as the numbers of students increased.

Then, in the mid-twentieth century, the federal government passed the GI Bill of Rights to provide funds for returning World War II military personnel to attend college. Enrollments skyrocketed, and a college education became possible for a whole new group of Americans.

The GI Bill of Rights

The Schooling of Women and Minority Group Members

Throughout much of history, women, minority group members, and people with disabilities have not had the same access to education in the United States as have nondisabled, white, English-speaking males. These omissions have been reflections of social and cultural attitudes of the times. Gradually, however, the exclusion and neglect of all three groups has shifted toward inclusion in the American educational mainstream.

Of the three groups, women were able to enter the mainstream first, particularly if they stayed in traditional roles. Minority children were included much more slowly, much less predictably, and much more grudgingly. Disabled children have gained regular access to schools only in very recent times.

Leaders in the colonial and early national periods considered the education of girls less important than the education of boys. Some girls attended primary school, but many did not. Few continued schooling beyond the four R's and "ladies' subjects."

Women

However, in the 1820s and 1830s, attitudes changed significantly. Academies for "young ladies," normal schools, and special women's colleges were established, and many existing boys' institutions became coeducational. Emma Willard opened Troy Female Seminary near Albany, New York, in 1821, and Mary Lyon established Mount Holyoke Seminary in Massachusetts in 1837. Both schools and others that shortly followed were essentially academies for girls. These academies offered courses in modern and classical languages, music, art, science, mathematics, and domestic science.

The high schools that replaced academies usually admitted girls, and gradually more and more parents sent their daughters along with their sons. At first, the girls studied a separate curriculum in different rooms from the boys. Then classes were integrated, and the curriculum became more common.

Except for normal schools and finishing schools, the collegiate experience for women was similar to the earlier experience for women at the high school level. First, women attended separate women's colleges; they were later admitted to co-educational institutions. Their curriculum was initially different from that for men, but the differences were reduced with time.

Minorities

Schooling for the largest minority groups in America—black, Native American, and Hispanic—was usually neglected or, at best, grossly inadequate prior to the middle of the nineteenth century. Even since then improvements have been slow.

Native American students

Colonial missionaries provided schools for Native Americans as part of their efforts to convert them to Christianity. These efforts, although often well intended, were usually patronizing (students were taught as members of a lesser culture than that of the controlling group) and limited to the four R's. In the late 1800s, when the government took a serious interest in educating Native Americans, it did so in order to assimilate the tribal children into the dominant culture. But the schools available to Native American children were most often poorly constructed, inadequately staffed, and underfinanced. Frequently, the instruction was in English and based on dominant cultural assumptions. Teachers and those who hired them considered the Native American culture inferior and the students deprived.

Decades before the Supreme Court ruled "separate and unequal" schools unconstitutional, W. E. B. DuBois championed the right of blacks to rigorous, quality education.

Most early American children of Spanish descent who attended school received primary instruction and the rudiments of religious training in Catholic mission schools. As towns developed over the years, Catholic parishes were established in many of them, and most parishes had Catholic parochial schools. Often these schools were more attractive to Spanish-speaking families than were the public schools because of their religious focus and their Spanish and Mexican traditions. Frequently, Hispanic parents wanted their children educated in a context that preserved their religious and cultural heritage. Therefore, many avoided the Anglicizing experience of the public schools.

In more recent decades, children from Spanish-speaking families have attended integrated public schools in greater proportions. But the experience has rarely been without difficulty. Clashes between non-Hispanic and Spanish culture have persisted. Because Hispanic children often grew up in poor neighborhoods, the public schools available to them have often been weaker than those in predominantly white suburbs. Their buildings tended to be worn, their teachers less experienced, and their supplies more scarce.

Schooling for most black Americans was generally neglected or prohibited until Black students the end of slavery and the Civil War, although black children in northern states attended school prior to that time. At the end of the Civil War, the federal government attempted a major effort to educate freed slaves and their children through the Freedman's Bureau. Although that agency lasted for only a few years, one of its efforts was the establishment of schools for the children of former slaves, much like the town schools of early New England. But these schools were not really community schools. They had little local support. They were set apart from other schools. Their teachers were often volunteers from the North rather than people of the community.

From the period of Reconstruction through the middle of the twentieth century, the education of black students in America was primarily separate from the education of white students. Not only did black children attend segregated schools, but the philosophy of education in those schools also was often different from that elsewhere. In the last decades of the nineteenth century, that philosophy was embodied in an attempt to "uplift the poor, unfortunate former slave." Later, it evolved into an educational philosophy that called for "education for work" and "education for economic security."

Booker T. Washington was the predominant spokesperson for the "education-for-work" philosophy. He believed that vocational education—for farming, manual trades, and teaching—was the most useful education for black children. He felt it was premature for blacks to hope for careers in law, medicine, and political leadership. In essence, he espoused a compromise position with the white southern aristocracy that strove to keep black people in lower social and economic positions.

Although Washington's ideas fell on receptive ears, those of another black spokesperson, W. E. B. DuBois, did not. DuBois argued for an intellectually rigorous education for blacks and spoke emphatically about the need for well-educated teachers to staff black schools and colleges. He considered Washington's views to be accommodations to a repressive system of segregation.

The education-for-work philosophy, the cultural mores and laws of a Jim Crow society, and general racial prejudice determined the type and level of schooling usually available to black students. Instruction was basic and vocational. Expectations of student abilities were low. Schooling was segregated by custom and by law. In 1896, the United States Supreme Court upheld the constitutionality of the concept of "separate but equal" in the *Plessy* v. *Ferguson* court case. In so doing, it solidified a dual, segregated school system for America for the next half century.

Pressures to change the dual system of education persisted through the first fifty years of this century, however, and they came to a head at the end of World War II. As described in Chapter 7, nine years after the end of the war, in 1954, the Supreme Court in *Brown* v. *Board of Education of Topeka* agreed that separate education facilities are "inherently unequal" and that they engendered "a feeling of inferiority." Since then, federal and state laws have led toward the dismantling of segregated schools, and local norms have gradually shifted toward racially integrated public schooling in the United States.

Since the *Brown* case, the courts have also forced states and local communities to provide disabled people with access to regular schools. They have said that all Americans have a right to a "free appropriate education in the least restrictive environment." Therefore, schooling in the last three decades has been made available to children of school age who have physical, emotional, and educational conditions that in the past would have excluded them from receiving educational services. Today the mainstreaming of disabled students into schools and classrooms with nondisabled children has become common practice and generally accepted policy.

Separate is unequal

Students with handicapping conditions

Today's classrooms reflect a continuing effort to achieve the ideal of educational opportunity for all.

A Historical Approach

Like anthropologists, whose study of schools and classrooms was described in the Educational Research section of Chapter 4, historians also study teaching and schools. They investigate, describe, interpret, and explain events and practices of the past in an effort to provide ideas that will be useful for the present and future.

The following excerpt is from a historical study of teaching in high schools since 1900. The author describes how he conducted the study, what he found, and the general conclusions he drew.

I examined high school classrooms at the turn of the century, in the two decades between the two World Wars, and from the mid-1960s to the present. I chose these years to help me develop a series of impressions of what high school teaching was like before the Progressive movement, during the high point of the reform impulse within public schools in the 1920s and 1930s, and, finally, during and after a second effort to improve instruction that began in the mid-1960s. More specifically, for the years at the beginning of the century, I drew from both secondary and primary sources to construct a composite nationwide portrait of what teachers did in these classrooms. For the decades between the two World Wars, I focused on classrooms in Denver, New York City, Washington, D.C., and in many rural areas. For the 1960s and 1970s, I studied classrooms in New York City, Washington, D.C., North Dakota, and Arlington, Virginia. . . .

I concentrated on classrooms in the academic subjects: English, history and social studies, science, foreign language, and mathematics. I examined how classroom space and furniture were arranged, the manner of grouping for instruction used by the teacher (whole class, small group, etc.); classroom talk by teacher and students, instructional activities in the classroom (recitation, discussion, tests, lecture, film, student reports, etc.), and the amount of physical movement allowed students within the classroom. I chose these categories because they were visible signs of what happened in classrooms and could be recovered from a number of sources. Moreover, these visible signs of what occurred in classrooms coincided with varied patterns of teaching behavior that had been identified in the literature. . . . At no point did I equate these visible signs of instructional activity with the complexity of what teachers do daily with children, the classroom climate and culture, the richly textured social interaction between students and teacher, or the social system of the classroom. My intent was to map out in a crude way an important part—but far from the whole—of the classroom terrain.

To collect data on classrooms that no longer existed, I examined what teachers had written, student recollections, photographs from student yearbooks, newspaper articles, reports of principals to superintendents, formal studies of classrooms, self-reports from questionnaires given to teachers, and surveys of school systems. From these sources, I collected information on nearly 2,500 different high school classrooms in the three periods. . . .

My information on schools at the beginning of this century had to be reconstructed from a number of sources, since no historians have examined closely what teachers did in classrooms. In slightly more than 6,000 high schools enrolling just over 500,000 students, teachers (most of whom were male) often taught more than one subject in a curriculum plainly geared to preparing young people (the majority of whom were female) to attend college. Clues about what went on in classrooms appeared in the form of rows of bolted-down desks, rooms designated for "recitation," and master schedules allotting the bulk of the instructional day to this formal activity. Using accounts from school surveys, reports from principals, and stenographic transcriptions from more than 100 classrooms, I assembled an admittedly blurred but nonetheless distinguishable portrait of what teachers did in their classes.

Generally, teachers taught their classes as a single large group. Teacher talk dominated verbal expression during the period (64% of the time, according to Romiett Stevens). Student movement in the classroom occurred only with the teacher's permission. Classroom activities clustered around teacher lectures, questioning of students, and chalkboard exercises or in-class assignments from the textbook. Science classes that included laboratory work were an exception. Expectations for uniform behavior and respect for the teacher's authority were demonstrated in the rows of students facing the chalkboard and the teacher's desk.

I then jumped two decades to examine what happened between World Wars I and II in Denver, New York City, Washington, D.C., and rural schools across the U.S. I chose the first two cities because of their national reputations for leadership in embracing progressive practices, [and] the other sites were selected for comparative purposes. In addition to gathering accounts of what teachers did in the various high schools, I examined national surveys and state studies of teaching practices in the 1920s and 1930s. Despite the variety of research designs, methodologies, and sources of data I studied, there was a remarkable similarity in the results.

These interwar decades displayed an explosion of enthusiasm for the project method, joint teacher/student planning, small-group work, independent study, and curriculum revision. The Eight-Year Study, for example, targeted curriculum and instruction for reform in 30 high schools that volunteered for the study. Yet, with the exception of Denver and scattered urban and rural high schools elsewhere in the U.S. (where some versions of activity programs and projects, varied classroom groups, and substantial revisions in course content occurred), few progressive practices reached the typical classroom.

Most high school classrooms showed traces of progressive ideology that had been transformed by the realities of the 30 to 40 students per class, five to six classes daily, and teachers' additional extracurricular responsibilities. There was some change in course content often in English and social studies. The stiff formal repetition of the text at the teacher's command was replaced by the less formal discussions, students leading classes, and reports or debates by students. The student-centered philosophy could be seen in greater student participation in classroom talk, occasional trips to places in the community, subject matter that touched student concerns or life beyond the school house door. But the percentage of time allocated to subjects—except for those schools that experimented with core curriculum or general education for part of the school day—remained the same. Even with the advent of portable furniture, the most common classroom arrangement continued to be that of the teacher's desk dominating the front of the room facing rows of movable table-arm chairs or pedestal desks. . . .

By the beginning of World War II, little had changed in the typical American classroom. The instructional patterns that used the entire class as the primary teaching vehicle, a question/answer format and reliance on the textbook—all of which had characterized classrooms at the turn of the century—seemed basically the same. By 1965 another wave of reform pumped ideas, money, and new faces into U.S. public schools. Informal education, the open classroom and alternative high schools became required reforms, especially if a district wished to be viewed as *au courant*. The reforms of the Sixties were similar in many ways to the progressive impulse of a previous generation. I examined alternative and regular high schools in various settings, including New York City and Washington, D.C., again using sources similar to those employed for the earlier period.

Although the alternative school concept became quite popular and many districts were fairly quick to create their own, most students still attended regular high schools. . . .

Hundreds of teacher accounts, interviews, student publications, newspaper articles, and numerous other sources painted a composite portrait of high school teaching during the Sixties and early Seventies that was not unlike that of the previous generation. Teachers still spent most of the class period talking to the entire class, listening to students answer their questions, and assigning portions of the textbook to the class for homework. It was the same instructional diet of meat and potatoes—occasionally supplemented by a test, lab work in the sciences, some field trips, or a film—that had been served consistently in high schools since the beginning of the century.

Finally, I examined the period after 1975, when the reform impulse had been buried under a new set of slogans about "back to the basics." In one middle-sized school district I found little change from the late 1960s and early 1970s. Two other sources included two major pieces of research sponsored by the National Science Foundation (NSF): One, a series of 11 case studies of high

schools and their feeder schools; and the other, a survey of teachers and administrators on classroom practices. The case studies included many accounts of social studies, math, and science teachers. After mentioning the occasional artistry of a teacher who hooked the attention of a class and steered it gracefully for an hour, the writers noted the fundamental similarity in teaching that swept across subject matter, class size, teacher experience, or curricular group. . . .

What conclusions can be

drawn from this quick and narrow portrait of high school teaching since the beginning of the 20th century? The overall picture is striking in its uniformity: persistence of whole group instruction, teacher talk outdistancing student talk, question/answer format drawn largely from textbooks, and little student movement in academic classes. . . .

Used by permission of Larry Cuban. Excerpted from "Persistent Instruction: The High School Curriculum, 1900–1980," by L. Cuban, *Phi Delta Kappan, 64*(2), 1982, pp. 113–118.

Conclusion

By the middle of the twentieth century, the early goals set for schooling in America were, in fact, being practiced, and virtually all children of school age were being served. The system was still far from perfect, but nearly all children had access to schools, and the instruction provided was appropriate for most. As noted in Chapter 7, there was, and still is, a serious commitment to a quality education for all.

The education provided in today's American schools is the result of a long evolution—an evolution based in traditions that include (1) ideas from classical Greece to the present, (2) principles of Christian religious education and citizenship training, (3) Enlightenment concepts of the nature of the universe and the nature of human beings, and (4) Jeffersonian and Lockean beliefs about democracy and education. Contemporary schools, like the activities of teachers and students in them, did not develop by accident. They have a past that has made them what they are.

That past guides educators when they decide who should attend school, which subjects should be taught, how students should be disciplined, which students should be enrolled in which courses, how much latitude teachers should have in deciding what they do, which teaching methods should be used, and so forth. Because of that history, the decisions that are made are slightly different for present-day American schools than they would be in other times and places.

The influence of history

Summary

Many of the roots of American pre-K–12 education sprang from educational ideas developed in early Europe. Ideas from the classical Greeks and Romans and from the Middle Ages, the Renaissance, and the Enlightenment all played a part. Those ideas included religious and civic purposes for schooling and incorporated the ways in which thinkers of various times viewed the nature of the world, the needs of society, and the process of education.

Since American colonial times, schooling has been considered a community responsibility. Over the years, civic purposes for schools have gradually overshadowed religious ones; more students have attended schools; and the nature of schooling has become more diverse. In a sense, the main historical theme reflected in the development of schools in America is the realization of the idea of the common school. Schools have become almost entirely available to and largely appropriate for all children.

Study Questions

1. In what ways and to what extent has Thomas Jefferson's idea that a democracy needs educated citizens guided the development of pre-K–12 schools in America?

2. Why do you think American schools have tried to serve all students when that has not been the case in most other countries?

3. It is often said that the history of schools in America is a story of schools' adjustments to the changes in American society and the needs of the people. What have you learned from this chapter that supports this idea? What contradicts it?

4. Why do Americans think the ideas of (a) a common school, (b) comprehensive high schools, and (c) equal education for all are so important?

Key Terms

Age of reason
Apprentice
Apprenticeship
Aristotelian philosophy
Cardinal principles of education (1918)
Classical humanism
Committee of Ten of the National Education Association
Common schools
Comprehensive education
Comprehensive high schools
Consent of the governed
Contract (John Locke's idea)

Dames' schools
Denominational schools
Enlightenment
Franklin's academy
Friends public schools
Guild
Idea of progress
Ideals
Jim Crow
Land grant college
Latin grammar school
Learn by doing
Moral education
Natural laws
Natural state of humans

Normal schools
Object lesson
"Old Deluder Satan" act
Ordinance of 1785
Protestant Reformation
Public schools
Renaissance
Scholasticism
Scholastics
Scientific method
Seven liberal arts
Socratic method
Sophists
Syllogism
Tabula rasa
Vernacular

For Further Reading

Button, H. W., & Provenzo, E. (1989). *History of education and culture in America* (2nd ed.). Englewood Cliffs, NJ: Prentice-Hall.

Butts, R. F. (1978). *Public education in the United States: From revolution to reform.* New York: Holt, Rinehart and Winston.

Cremin, L. A. (1961). *The transformation of the school: Progressivism in American education, 1876–1957.* New York: Knopf.

Cremin, L. A. (1970). *American education: The colonial experience, 1607–1783.* New York: Harper and Row.

Cremin, L. A. (1988). *American education: The metropolitan experience, 1876–1980.* New York: Harper and Row.

Cuban, L. (1982). Persistent instruction: The high school curriculum, 1900–1980. *Phi Delta Kappan, 64*(2), 113–118.

Cuban, L. (1993). *How teachers taught: Constancy and change in American classrooms, 1880–1990* (2nd ed.). New York: Teachers College Press.

Dewey, J. (1916). *Democracy and education.* New York: Macmillan.

Dewey, J. (1938). *Experience and education.* New York: Macmillan.

Gutek, G. L. (1992). *Education and schooling in America* (3rd ed.). Boston: Allyn and Bacon.

Pulliam, J. D. (1990). *History of education in America* (5th ed.). Columbus, OH: Charles E. Merrill.

Ravitch, D. (1983). *The troubled crusade: American education 1945–1980.* New York: Basic Books.

Rippa, S. A. (1984). *Education in a free society: An American history.* New York: Longman.

Spring, J. (1986). *The American school 1642–1985.* New York: Longman.

Spring, J. (1991). *American education: An introduction to social and political aspects* (5th ed.). New York: Longman.

The Political Context
Pressures That Influence Teaching and Schools

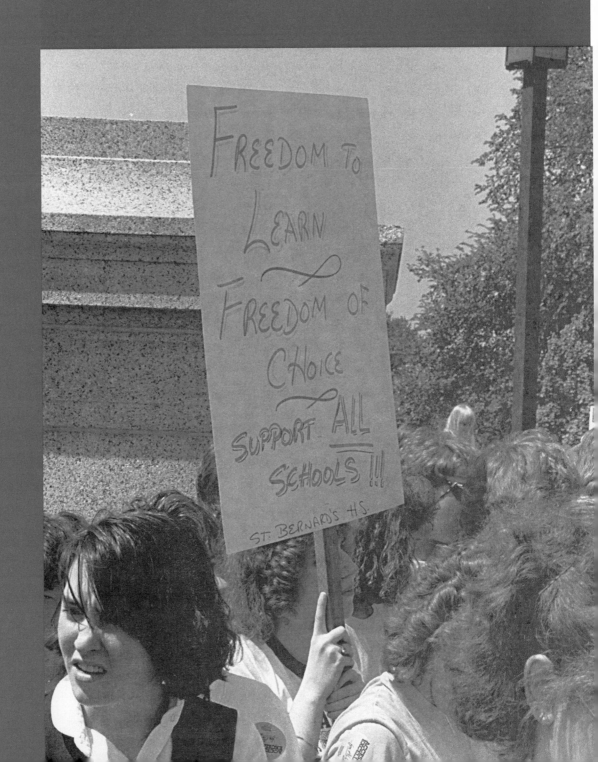

A realistic understanding of pre-K–12 education in the United States must include the recognition that teachers and schools function in a *political* context: an environment of politicians and elected officials as well as of less obvious forms of power and influence. This environment affects how schools are run and teachers teach. Because schools are established or approved by society, much of this power and influence emanates from outside the school.

Formally, external power is vested primarily in governments—at local, state, and federal levels—and is expressed through constitutional, legislative, regulatory, judicial, and financial means. But many nongovernmental power brokers also influence schools: high-status citizens; economically important business leaders; student, teacher, and citizen advocacy groups; issue-oriented pressure groups; and producers of curriculum materials. All these sources of power help define the authority, responsibility, and day-to-day activity of teachers and schools. Power and influence also develop inside school walls just as they do in any human organization. While external power authorizes, controls, and influences what teachers and schools do, teachers and schools use the power they possess to accomplish their mission of educating students.

Chapter 9 provides an overview of the political context of teaching. It first describes types of governmental authority over schools and the relationships between schools and each of the three main levels of government. Next, it traces some of the major impacts federal court decisions have had on schools and teachers. The third section of the chapter examines sources of school financing and their influence on how schools operate. The fourth section looks at laws that directly affect the work of teachers as employees and as professionals. The following section looks into pressures and influences from outside government that affect teaching and schools, and the final section describes schools themselves as political organizations.

The political context of teaching and schools affects all teacher decisions—decisions about being a teacher, where to teach, what subjects to teach, what content to cover, which perspectives to emphasize, how to interact with students, which academic and behavioral expectations to enforce, and so on. It also affects teachers' personal lifestyle choices. Understanding and dealing successfully with the political environment can make the difference between a satisfying and happy teaching career and one that is neither satisfying nor pleasant.

The chapter Snapshot presents three situations in which teachers face professional decisions with significant political overtones. The Reflecting on Practice box describes an interesting use of "data" about schools by those who influence public opinion. The Educational Research section explains the interaction between educational policy, research, and what is expected of teachers and schools.

The Snapshot for this chapter consists of three short case studies in which teachers, two very new in their careers, had to make politically sensitive and professionally risky decisions. As you read each, consider:

- How was each situation affected by the political context in which it took place?
- Did the teacher do the right thing? Why do you think so?
- What would you have done? Why do you think so?

Donna Dunlap: Student Teacher

It was early March, and Donna Dunlap was almost to the midpoint of her student teaching in a large urban New Jersey high school.[1] As she arrived at school that particular morning, two very different thoughts ran through her mind. Her student teaching was going well; everyone said she would be a good teacher, and she was beginning to believe that they were right. Tragically, however, a student in the school had died the day before from a drug overdose, and the news had hit the morning papers. Donna did not know the student, but she was sure many of the students in her social studies classes did. She would have to postpone her history lesson and let the students talk about the situation. She felt uncomfortable not knowing what to expect.

Surprisingly, the day went along well under the circumstances, although each class became quite emotional at times. Most students did not say much about the news, but her "current events" lessons were more draining than they had ever been prior to that day.

At the end of the day Donna headed toward the exit feeling somewhat relieved. At that moment, Greg, a student from her fifth period, approached. "Can I talk with you?" he asked. When she said "Sure," he was abrupt and to the point. "That dead dude? We did crack together. He died after I left. I'm hooked. I need help or I'm gonna die. Please help me but don't tell anyone. I'll go to jail." Stunned, Donna felt she would never forget his words or the tears in his eyes as he struggled not to cry.

Donna and Greg talked for a long time. She promised to help and agreed not to tell anyone, although she had no idea what to do and knew that New Jersey law required that she report Greg to authorities. She asked Greg to give her until the next morning to work something out. Then it occurred to her that she needed to tell some people in order to get help. Greg agreed that was okay as long as she did not talk to anyone who would turn him in.

Early the next day, Donna explained the situation to her cooperating teacher and her college supervisor of student teaching. The cooperating teacher reacted first. "Don't touch it," she urged. "It's not your problem. They don't pay teachers enough for this kind of thing. If you get involved, you could be prosecuted. The kid's hooked. You probably can't help anyway."

Donna said she felt she had to help. She could not live with herself if she turned the student down.

The teacher responded, "If you do, don't involve me. In fact, don't tell me." Then she left.

Donna felt she was about to cry. Kindly, the college supervisor said he felt the decision was Donna's and that he would support her either way. As they brainstormed possibilities, Donna explained that a friend had given her the phone number of a counselor who worked with troubled youth in a nearby city. Her friend thought the counselor would be willing to help Greg if Donna made the contact. Donna and the supervisor agreed that Donna would make the call, identifying herself only as one of Greg's teachers.

Within an hour, Donna and Greg met as the college supervisor looked on from a distance. What she told Greg was rather mysterious. "At 11:30 today, during lunch, be standing on the curb in front of Watson's store. A yellow pickup truck will drive up. The driver will ask you if you are Greg. Ask him his name. If he says "Larry," get in the truck. Do not mention my name or how you learned about him. He will see you get the help you want."

Greg was not in class during fifth period. Another student said he was in school for morning classes but seemed to disappear during lunch. A week later a note from the school office said Greg had dropped out of school. A teacher said she heard he was in drug rehab.

Tom Johnson: First-Year Teacher

Upon graduation from college, Tom Johnson accepted a position teaching secondary school English in a small

Ohio town.[2] He was fortunate to get the job. His new wife had grown up in the area and was about to finish her senior year in a nearby college. She would not have to transfer as they had assumed.

As the year progressed, Tom settled into a very satisfying situation. He liked the town, the school, and his students; and his teaching evaluations were very positive. Teacher colleagues and a number of parents let him know that they thought highly of his teaching and leadership work with his classes.

Although Tom had entertained thoughts of going to divinity school after his wife completed college, he was changing his mind. Maybe teaching really should be his permanent career. When the time came, he requested a renewal of his one-year contract; and he and his wife began talking about settling down in the town.

Then a disturbing thing happened. The editor of the school newspaper, a student in one of Tom's senior English classes, was publicly reprimanded and removed from her editor's position by the school principal after the paper printed an editorial criticizing the school administration and school policy. The principal had suspended a group of students who had conducted a protest march on school property. The suspensions and the action against the editor precipitated a schoolwide crisis that spilled over into the town.

Although Tom had no faculty role with the newspaper, students in his classes raised the issue as a topic for discussion and the now-removed editor consulted with Tom outside of class. Through all of the discussions in class, Tom tried hard to be impartial and not sway student opinion. He saw his role as helping students analyze the value positions involved, and he hoped they could formulate their own judgments through an orderly and rational process. In his meetings with the former editor, however, he indicated in response to her questions that he believed she had a basis for appealing her dismissal by the principal to the board of education.

The student decided to appeal to the board, sought legal counsel from a local attorney, and asked Tom to appear before the board on her behalf. Tom agreed to support the student's appeal and to speak on her behalf before the board. He worried about doing so, but he felt she deserved to be reinstated as editor and believed he would have been a poor role model for his students if he did not speak out. He and his classes had discussed the concept of due process extensively, and it seemed to fit in this case.

Tom's concerns were heightened when a fellow teacher took him aside and explained to him confidentially that several school administrators, at least some board members, and "important people in town" were upset with the likelihood that he would speak before the board on behalf of the student. His colleague said that the renewal of his contract was probably in jeopardy. Tom's father-in-law received a phone call from an influential citizen of the town that conveyed the same message.

After a great deal of soul searching, Tom spoke before the board and vigorously advocated the student's reinstatement as editor. The board, however, voted not to overrule the principal. The student was not reinstated. Tom's contract was not renewed.

That summer, Tom, his wife, and newborn son moved to California, where Tom entered divinity school. He is now a minister on the West Coast. He and his family regularly visit the Ohio town where he taught for that one year.

Adele Jones: Algebra Teacher

Adele Jones had been teaching high school mathematics for more than ten years and had tenure when she was fired in 1993 from her teaching position at Sussex Central High School in Georgetown, Delaware.[3] She was fired after her Algebra II students consistently received what her school administrators believed to be too many D's and F's. Ms. Jones believed the grades were true reflections of the test performances of the students. The school principal said they were "negative grades" that damaged student self-images. He felt Ms. Jones should have graded on a curve and assigned greater percentages of student grades to class work and projects. Ms. Jones responded that she did not *give* grades; students *earned* them.

Ms. Jones's students did get D's and F's in high proportions: In 1990–91, 42 percent failed, and 21 percent got D's; in 1991–92, 27 percent failed and 26 percent got D's. The principal felt these numbers showed that Ms. Jones was flunking students out of mathematics rather than helping them learn. He said she should start her Algebra II class at "Algebra I and a half" if that was where the students were. Ms. Jones disagreed. She saw the class as college preparation and questioned earlier grades for students who finished Algebra I not ready for Algebra II.

After a three-day hearing, a hearing officer agreed that Ms. Jones was incompetent and insubordinate. On June 21, 1993, the school board, on a 6–4 vote, fired her.

With legal representation provided by her union, the Delaware State Education Association, Ms. Jones appealed her firing. As a result, in the fall of 1993, a superior court judge ordered the school board to reconsider its action on procedural grounds, pointing out that it had not reviewed all the documents in the case. He also ordered one board member to abstain from voting because the member's child had received a poor grade from Ms. Jones.

In March 1994, the school board reinstated Ms. Jones on a 5–4 vote. Three of the five votes to reinstate were cast by new board members elected after the earlier dismissal vote. Ms. Jones received full back pay and prepared to resume teaching.

Governmental Authority and Schools

As has been mentioned often in this text, pre-K–12 schools in the United States are agencies of the government. Public schools are established and operated by the government, and private or independent schools must be authorized and approved by the government. This arrangement stems from the idea that schools are a *public good*. That is, schools provide something (education) that the people of the United States think is so important that the society at large should make sure that everyone can get it. As a matter of public policy, Americans force citizens to pay taxes for public schools and require children and youth to attend classes whether they want to or not.

Schools for the public good

This concept of schools as a public good has a long tradition. As we have seen in previous chapters, Americans have historically considered schooling to be good for individual students, for the communities in which they live, for the employers for whom they will work, and for the children to whom they will give birth. In addition, schooling has been considered essential because all citizens are potential voters and public decision makers. For all these reasons, the government controls and is responsible for public schools and the education they provide.[4]

Areas of Governmental Authority and Responsibility

The government acts to carry out its responsibility in our schools in a number of ways. Here we introduce four types of governmental authority over schools that we explain in more detail later in the chapter: (1) constitutional, (2) legislative and regulatory, (3) judicial, and (4) financial. These four types of political control and responsibility are not mutually exclusive; rather, they are highly related, as you will see.

Constitutional Authority

Although the Constitution of the United States does not list schools or education as a responsibility of the national government, several of its provisions have had significant impact on public policy regarding education. The Constitution does say that the government should (1) provide for the general welfare (Article I, Section 8), (2) guarantee freedom of religion and speech (First Amendment), (3) prohibit laws respecting an establishment of religion (First Amendment), (4) assure that no one be deprived of life, liberty, or property, without due process of law (Fifth Amendment), and (5) guarantee that no state deprive a person of the equal protection of the laws (Fourteenth Amendment). In the Tenth Amendment, it also says, "The powers not delegated to the United States by the Constitution, nor prohibited by it to the States, are reserved to the States respectively, or to the people."

As applied to schools, these constitutional clauses have the following implications:

- Unlike many other nations, the United States does not have a national school system operated by the federal government.
- Because all states in the United States have codified in law the powers associated with education that were reserved to them by the Tenth Amendment, the primary legal authority and responsibility for schools rests with the states.
- Nevertheless, because all levels of government must abide by and operate under the Constitution of the United States, the Constitution does affect the way state and local governments handle school and education matters.

Legislative and Regulatory Authority

From the highest reaches of the federal government to the lowest tier of the local school district, elected officials or officials selected under their authority pass and implement laws and regulations that govern the operation of both public and private schools. They determine what type of schools there should be, where they should be located, how they should be run, what should be taught, who should teach, and, to a limited degree, who should attend. By far, the major authority to do all this rests with the states. The procedures for making these decisions and seeing that they are implemented are different from state to state as well as within states and from time to time, but there is remarkable similarity across the country in both how schools are governed and the thrusts of the regulations and laws that guide what is done in schools and classrooms.

Judicial Authority

Because schooling and education are provided through governmental authority and are considered to be important both for the general welfare and as a matter of individual rights, courts and judicial decisions have a major influence on education. Two constitutional bases for the role of the courts in affecting teaching and schools are the concepts of *separation of powers* and *judicial review*.

The principle of *separation of powers* is established by the Constitution, which organizes the national government into three branches—legislative, executive, and judicial—and assigns separate responsibilities to each. The judicial branch is specifically charged with resolving issues of interpretation and conflict concerning the Constitution itself, laws of the United States, controversies in which the United States is a party, controversies between states, and controversies between states and citizens of other states. This constitutional concept means that the federal courts can be called upon to issue decisions on many points of disagreement that affect schools and the education of school-age citizens. At various times, courts have been asked to adjudicate questions about the rights and responsibilities of teachers, students, and parents. Should laws require all students to attend high school? Should schools teach about contraception even if parents object? Should students be al-

Separation of powers

lowed (or compelled) to pray in public schools? Should students be required to pledge allegiance to the American flag? How much expense should a school system shoulder in order to provide equal education to a special-needs student? On these and many other issues in the United States, courts have been asked to decide what is fair, appropriate, and constitutional.

The principle of *judicial review* is the basis upon which the U.S. Supreme Court and other federal courts rule on the constitutionality and appropriateness of lower court decisions. The principle was articulated by Chief Justice John Marshall in the 1803 court case, *Marbury* v. *Madison*. In essence, Marshall said the Constitution gives the Supreme Court the authority to interpret the Constitution—to judge when court decisions, laws, and other governmental actions are consistent with or contrary to the intent of the Constitution.

Judicial review

The federal courts have been asked to rule on a number of disputes involving education that have constitutional implications. Frequently, these disputes concern fundamental rights that Americans hold dear, such as freedom of speech, freedom of religion, freedom from arbitrary governmental action, equal protection of the laws, and due process. Court decisions in each of these areas will be explained later in this chapter.

Many school and education issues come before the courts at local and state levels as well. As with the federal courts, local and state courts must decide matters of fairness, justice, equity, individual and civil rights, due process, individual rights, and freedoms. They must also decide who is at fault when students, teachers, and school officials sue each other.

Financial Authority

Because schools cost money, the expectation that governments provide schools for children and youth includes both the responsibility to fund these schools and power over how that money is spent. State and local governments decide how much money to raise for public schools, do the raising, oversee how it is spent, and determine what strings are attached to the funds; and the federal government, for many years, has also supplemented that state and local funding. Schools depend on the funds and, therefore, are under the financial control of every level of government that controls the purse strings.

Because of this *power of the purse*, governments can influence areas of school-level decision making that go far beyond the authority allotted to them by statute. They can simply refuse to appropriate funds for buildings, materials, salaries, and activities they do not like. Or they can threaten to withhold funds, a tactic that often has the same impact as actually withholding funds. Conversely, they can withhold needed funds, or threaten to do so, in order to force school decision makers to do something that the school officials would not normally do if left free to decide for themselves.

Power of the purse

Those who use the power of the purse in these situations, as well as those who feel the pressure, tend to avoid discussing this form of influence or even admitting that it exists. Yet, examples of decisions that are affected in this way occur regularly. They include where schools are built, how pray-in-school policies are worded, who becomes principal of which school, whether condoms are distributed to students at school, which textbooks and library books are purchased, and what is included in the curriculum—sex education, bilingualism, multiculturalism, ethnic studies, and so forth.

TABLE 9-1 Representative Educational Roles and Responsibilities of the Three Levels of Government

Major Governmental Unit with Education Authority	Roles and Responsibilities
Federal Government	Help States and Local Governments Provide Equal and Appropriate Education for All School-Age Citizens
Congress	Formulate national educational policies and guidelines
President	Provide funds to states and local school districts for particular efforts
Department of Education	
Federal Courts	Encourage schools to improve
	Assure that states and local school districts comply with constitutional requirements
	Compile and distribute educational data
	Conduct research and evaluation projects
	Speak to public on education matters
State Government	Authorize, Support, and Maintain Schools of the State
Legislature	Establish state educational policies
Governor	Represent citizens of the state in making education decisions
Department of Education	
Chief State School Officer	Enact education laws, statutes, and regulations
State Board of Education	Formulate and apply rules and regulations for school operations
State Courts	Ensure school compliance with state laws, statutes, and regulations
	Interpret and explain state education laws, statutes, and regulations
	Monitor operations of school districts
	Grant state approval to schools
	Establish state standards for schools, students, and teachers
	Assess school performance and student and teacher competence
	Accredit teacher education programs
	Levy and raise state taxes
	Allocate funds to school districts
	Regulate and oversee school use of funds
	Determine curriculum
	Conduct research and evaluation projects
	Assure that schools comply with state and federal constitutional requirements
Local Government	Operate Local Schools
City Council,	Establish local educational policies in accordance with state directives
Town Committee,	
or County Commission	Identify local educational priorities
Mayor	Represent citizens in making education decisions
Local School Board	Enact local educational laws, statutes, and regulations
or School Committee	Establish local standards for schools, students, and
Superintendent	teachers

(continued)

TABLE 9-1   (*Continued*)

Major Governmental Unit with Education Authority	Roles and Responsibilities
Local Government (continued)	

Formulate and apply local rules and regulations
   for school operations within state guidelines
Levy and raise local taxes
Formulate and manage budget
Operate Schools
   Manage day-to-day school affairs
   Hire staffs
   Build and maintain buildings
   Allocate funds
   Oversee expenditure of funds
Determine curriculum within state stipulations
Evaluate schools, teachers, curriculum, and students
Ensure compliance with state and national directives
Assure that schools comply with state and federal
   constitutional requirements
Conduct professional negotiations about employment
   matters with teachers and other employees
Maintain working relationships between schools and
   other governmental units and community agencies
Maintain positive public relations between citizens
   and schools
Speak publicly on behalf of schools

Levels of Government and Authority for Schools

Even though states have the primary constitutional responsibility for education, all three levels of government influence schools significantly in ways that are more intertwined than discrete. One way to sort out these influences is to think of the predominant roles typically played by each level of government. Table 9-1 provides a general idea of these roles; but, remember, they vary from state to state and with each local government.

State Government and Schools

Although there are strong historical and sentimental traditions behind local political control of schools in America, states have always had more official authority over schools and that power is increasing. As the power increases, of course, so does the responsibility.

Reasons for the recent increases in state power involve a number of interrelated trends and events:

Increasing state power

1. As described earlier in this text, educational reforms of the 1980s targeted state governments for action.

2. States have increased their proportions of school funding while the local and national proportions have declined.
3. State politicians have become more active in and expert about educational matters.
4. Teacher unions and education-oriented pressure groups have gained strength and are more powerful at the state level.
5. Education policies of the Reagan and Bush administrations pushed substantial amounts of federal control and responsibility for funding onto the states.
6. In the late 1980s the National Governors Association (led by Governor Lamar Alexander of Tennessee, who later became Secretary of Education in the Bush Administration, and Governor Bill Clinton of Arkansas) made improved schools a top priority.
7. State business leaders clamored for higher standards for schools, teachers, and students as part of their push to maintain the United States' economic leadership in the world and attract new businesses to their states.

As a result of this increase in power, state governments have exerted more control over high school graduation requirements, student achievement testing, the content of curricula, teacher licensure and certification, and standards for approving teacher education programs in colleges.[5]

The trends toward greater state control and the lessening of local power, although accelerating in recent years, are not new. Both trends have existed for more than a century, even though their pace has varied from state to state and from time to time. During the nineteenth century, most states created school districts, established academic requirements, and legislated compulsory attendance. All these measures crossed local school system jurisdictions and imposed expectations from above. Early in the twentieth century, many states set statewide standards for teacher licensure. As described in Chapter 7, federal civil rights policies in the 1960s added to state law enforcement and funding responsibilities, a development that caused increases in state education bureaucracies. Then, during the 1980s and early 1990s, the efforts of the Reagan and Bush administrations to reduce the federal government's role in schooling, along with their more general push for less government regulation, forced additional responsibilities for schools from the federal to the state level. Along the way, state governors, legislators, and business leaders decided that better schools would help state economies. By the 1990s, school reform had become a major state responsibility.[6]

The ways in which states pursue their educational activities vary, but several educational policy experts have seen patterns in how states operate and believe there are connections between those patterns and the evolution toward greater state control. A number of years ago, one such expert, Lawrence Iannaccone, separated state policymaking processes regarding education into four types: (1) local disparate, (2) monolithic, (3) fragmented, and (4) syndical. Iannaccone maintained that state policymaking gradually evolves from the first type to the last type. In the *local disparate* process, local school leaders such as board members and superintendents form relationships with state politicians, and the two groups of officials cooperate to make political-educational decisions. In the *monolithic* process, political-educational decisions are made by a coalition of statewide educational groups, such as state teachers' organizations, superintendents' associations, and possibly business leaders. In the *fragmented* process, political-educational decisions tend to result

State patterns of operation

from clashes among various statewide interest groups and agencies, which often pursue different agendas and frequently disagree. Decisions in the *syndical* process are made through statewide cooperative efforts among government officials, interest groups, and other citizens.[7]

More recently another policy expert, Joseph McGivney, described a similar four-part evolution toward increasing state control. His early stages are similar to Iannaccone's but he characterizes the last stage as a statewide bureaucracy that includes education lobbies, legislators, and state department of education officials.[8]

Specific ways that state control has increased in many states in recent years include state minimum competency testing of students and teachers, more precise teacher certification regulations, increased course requirements for high school graduation, tighter state control over curriculum specifications and textbook selection, and increased specificity in state-imposed guidelines such as the length of the school year, how students with special needs are to be accommodated, and rules that tie student academic performance with eligibility to participate in sports. Probably the most significant trend that reflects increased state power over schools is the fact that states are gradually paying more of the costs of schooling in comparison with both the local and national governments. With this higher funding comes greater control. (More is said about this later.)

This shift in control is important to teachers—because it means that those who have direct impact on what teachers do are changing; and, at least in some cases, the people at the state level are becoming more intrusive. The shift, however, is not necessarily bad, as many educators seem to assume. State monitoring and regulation can be better than local authority, if it results in better education for students and better support and guidance for teachers.

Local Government and Schools

The term *local government*, as it pertains to schools, can be used to refer to any governmental entity more local than the state level. It includes governmental role players with general responsibilities, such as mayors, county executives, city councils, township supervisors, and the local judiciary. It also includes those bodies and individuals that are more directly responsible for schools, such as school boards and school superintendents.

Even though local governments have less legislated authority over schools than do their state counterparts, they still retain much control and powerful prerogatives, especially those that deal with day-to-day school activities and the lives of teachers and students. For example, school boards and committees at the city, county, town, or township levels hold the authority to select and employ superintendents and teachers, appoint principals, set tax rates, approve budgets, build and maintain school buildings, buy equipment, set school calendars, and negotiate salaries. Although their responsibilities are circumscribed by state and national rules and policies, their actions are the ones that typically affect teachers, students, and learning matters directly.[9]

Control of day-to-day matters

To a great extent, the ways that local governments deal with schools are results of local political patterns and power structures, the cultural makeup of the community, and the ways in which community activists choose to involve themselves in school matters. So, one way to develop an understanding of the relationships between local government and schools is to analyze the political character of the community.

Local power structures

Some time ago two experts who studied local community power structures, Donald McCarty and Charles Ramsey, divided these structures into four categories: (1) dominated, (2) fractionated, (3) pluralistic, and (4) inert. *Dominated* communities are controlled by a single strong community leader or a few powerful people. *Fractionated* communities are divided by two or a few competing power groups. *Pluralistic* ones have multiple competing power groups. *Inert* communities have no visible power structure. According to McCarty and Ramsey, each type of community tends to have a school board and local school system that have parallel power characteristics.[10] In other words, dominated communities have school boards and school policies that are heavily influenced by one or a few community leaders, and superintendents usually follow their wishes; fractionated communities and pluralistic communities have boards and policies that are caught among competing factions, and inert communities let the superintendent run the schools with little interference or guidance.

Whatever the community characteristics, the degree to which local government leaders involve themselves in school matters depends on such factors as the personalities of the individuals, what else is happening locally, and whether or not school-related controversial issues have surfaced recently. Some researchers believe that, when schools are running smoothly, local educational policy is actually conducted almost exclusively by the school superintendent.[11] Other investigators have noted the rise in power in recent years of some teachers' unions over policy decisions.[12]

"Hot" issues

On the other hand, local school events and situations often stir enough public interest to prompt citizens to get involved in school matters when under more normal circumstances they would not do so. Frequently, this type of involvement concerns issues such as the adequacy of tax support for schools, locations of new buildings, controversial curricular decisions, and questions about the appropriateness of specific teacher actions. Such instances might arise and dissipate without lasting impact on a community; but they might also become very volatile, cause lasting turmoil, and lead to the resignation or firing of school officials. Examples of these types of situations are reported in virtually every issue of *Education Week*—tax issues, Bible reading and prayer in schools, distribution of condoms, instances of violence, charges of unethical teacher practices, and teacher and student safety. When controversies arise about schools, the local governmental officials feel the heat.

Two current school reform trends are beginning to change the political landscape in some school systems: school system decentralization and site-based management. If their momentum continues, both movements are likely to have lasting impacts on who controls schools and how schools operate. Both movements have come about because of dissatisfaction with schools in general and school leaders in particular. Both have been pursued by those who hope to improve schools by putting control over them into the hands of citizens, professional educators, and parents who have more stake in the success of particular schools than do central office administrators and district school boards.

School district decentralization

School district decentralization involves dividing large school systems into subunits and assigning much decision-making authority to those units. In some cases, citizens in the subunits elect their own nearly autonomous school boards. Decentralization has occurred most often in large urban school districts, such as Chicago and New York. Those who support the concept hope that placing authority over schools closer to the schools themselves will make them better run, safer places and will improve student achievement. They think decentralization helps develop parent and student loyalty and identity with their schools, avoids at least some bureaucratic delays, and stimulates the formulation of clearer school purposes and priorities.

So far, results of school district decentralization have been mixed. Local citizens often do show a renewed interest in their schools, but improvements in the school environment and student achievement that can confidently be attributed to decentralization are rare. Some of the more frequent problems that have surfaced are clashes among the local stakeholders, cultural conflicts across ethnic lines, continuing bureaucratic delays, apathy, distrust, and inadequate funding.

Site-based management is a way of running schools that places as much decision-making authority as possible in the hands of the professionals and parents at individual school buildings. In its ideal form, each school building is allotted a lump sum of money and is authorized to spend it with very few limits as long as those making the decisions at the building level accept responsibility for their choices. The concept is drawn from experimental management efforts in business and is tied to research on effective schools.

Site-based decision making usually involves a team of decision makers—teachers, principals, other school staff, parents, and sometimes other community representatives and students. When run according to ideal form, team decisions are equitably and mutually arrived at, without dominance by any particular individual or group; for example, parents and students may have votes equal to those of the professionals. However, because site-based schools are new and in transitional phases from more traditional ways of operation, in most cases so far team decisions are not usually as equal or mutual as the ideal concept describes.

As with school district decentralization, the success of site-based management remains to be determined. Difficulties encountered include an inability by principals and other administrators to share power; reluctance by teachers, parents, and others not previously in positions of power to exercise their new authority and accept responsibility for doing so; lack of skill, perception, and time for the decision

Site-based management

Site-based management requires parents, teachers, and principals to forge new ways of working together and sharing power over school decisions.

makers to do what is expected of them; conflicts with central bureaucracies that continue to run things the old way; a tendency by the new decision makers to follow old patterns in spite of the changed circumstances; differences of opinions and priorities among team members; attempts by pressure groups to dominate and intimidate local teams; and inadequate funding.

If these problems dissipate with time, site-based management will spread and might become a normal way of running schools. You will want to watch these developments closely because, if they happen in most school systems, they will greatly affect the roles and responsibilities of teachers in the future. Teachers will be more in charge of what they do and how their schools function, and that increased authority will occur at the expense of principals, other administrators, school boards, local political leaders, and possibly taxpayers. A number of educators believe that if site-managed schools become a reality, professional educators, especially classroom teachers, will actually control teaching and schools for the first time in history. The implications of such a shift in power from local government to professional educators are monumental for teachers of the future.

Two representative illustrations of things that are happening with shifts toward site-managed schools occurred in Nashville, Tennessee, during the summer of 1992. With the employment of a new superintendent, the procedures for selecting new principals and teachers were changed radically. Under the old bureaucratic system, old-line administrators chose principals by advancing those in the system based on seniority, while teachers were selected through personnel office interviews and reviews of credential files. Teachers were not directly involved in either process, nor were parents. Neither process was open to the public, and those selected were announced when the processes were completed.

The new process for selecting principals is organized around a school selection team made up of six individuals, five of whom are tied directly to the school—two teachers, two parents, one non-parent citizen from the neighborhood served by the school, and one central office administrator. All have one vote. That team chooses three candidates from all applicants, who must publicly apply for the position, and recommends the three to the superintendent, who makes the final selection. As a result of the new process, a large majority of the twenty-two principals selected in 1992, as well as those chosen since, are individuals who would not have been selected under the old system. Conversely, many principal hopefuls who had played by the old rules in anticipation of eventual advancement were passed over.

The new process for selecting teachers in Nashville centers on a team of classroom teachers from the school that has the vacant teaching position. In an open procedure similar to that for principals, the team and the principal jointly select the new teacher colleague. Although it is not clear if this process leads to selecting candidates other than those who would have been selected previously, it is clear that it requires a new professional role for teachers, is time-consuming, and is much more rigorous—the search is more thorough, the review of credentials more complete, and the standards higher.

Two interesting developments concerning teacher selection during the first year of implementing the new process point out just how different the new arrangement is from the old. In one case, teacher selection team members unanimously agreed that they personally would not want to go through the same rigorous selection process they had just used to choose their new colleague and, as a result, would probably not seek a new teaching position in the school system during the rest of their teaching careers. They also felt that they, themselves, could not have met the

Teacher empowerment

criteria they imposed on the applicants. In a second situation, when the new colleague chosen proved during his first year at the school to be a poor choice, every member of the team who selected him refused to serve on a selection team the subsequent year. They said, in essence, we did not do well in making our choice last year, so we do not want the responsibility a second time.

These illustrations of newer ways of selecting principals and teachers reflect a trend toward stronger roles for teachers in the professional decisions that affect how they do their job. As school systems decentralize and as school building management becomes more site-based, teachers will be making more decisions, have more control, and shoulder more responsibility. New teachers will need to be prepared to accept these new tasks.

The Federal Government and Schools

The ways the federal government affects pre-K–12 education are indirect rather than direct, but they are very noticeable and powerful nonetheless. Federal actions primarily establish broad social policy goals and guidelines that have implications for what schools should and should not do, enact laws to pursue these policies, enforce these laws on lower levels of government and on individuals, and fund endeavors consistent with the policies, guidelines, and laws. These federal actions affect schools directly even though states have the primary responsibility for schools. One way to understand what the roles mean in practice is to review national education policy trends over the last several decades and note (1) the shifts that have occurred with changing times, (2) the ebb and flow of influence exerted by different pressure groups, and (3) representative government actions.

The direction and shifts in federal government education policy since the middle of the twentieth century, as well as the political pressures that caused them, can be categorized in general terms as shown in Table 9-2.[13]

Another way of characterizing the last several decades of federal education policy is to look at that policy in terms of successive presidential administrations. The Democratic Kennedy and Johnson administrations (1960–1968) whose constituencies included members of minority groups and low-income citizens, pursued active antipoverty and civil rights agendas and used federal education legislation and financial help for schools as ways of accomplishing them.

Shifting administration policy emphases

The Republican Nixon and Ford administrations (1968–1976) were less activist and often distracted from educational matters by the Vietnam War and the Watergate scandal, but they maintained relatively high support for education funding and legislation to educate students with handicapping conditions.

The Democratic Carter administration (1976–1980) returned to an activist federal stance on education matters and worked cooperatively with the professional education establishment, especially the National Education Association. During this time, the federal Department of Education was established as a separate Cabinet office.

The Republican Reagan and Bush administrations (1980–1992) changed direction radically toward a much more conservative federal role in education and were openly critical of schools and school leaders. Both administrations advocated higher standards for schools, teachers, and students, but they continued some support for the education of disabled students. They reduced funding, shifted some of the federal oversight of education from Washington to the states, courted private and fundamental Christian school supporters while publicly attacking public school advo-

TABLE 9-2 Federal Government Policy Thrusts, Pressures Behind the Policies and Governmental Actions by Presidential Administrations

Thrusts of Education Policy	Pressures Behind the Policies	Sample Governmental Actions
1950s		
Emphases on improving mathematics, science, and foreign language education	Military and industrial leaders	National Defense Education Act, 1958 (NDEA)
	Anti-communist politicians and pressure groups	
Focus on students who will be national, scientific leaders		
Improved teaching		
1960s		
Reduce poverty through better schooling	Civil rights groups	Elementary and Secondary Education Act, including Title I, 1965 (ESEA)
	Anti-poverty alliances	
End segregation in schools	National Education Association	Training of Teacher Trainers Act, 1964 (TTT)
Educate "disadvantaged" students		
		Teacher Corps, 1965
1970s		
Career and vocational education	Business community	Education for All Handicapped Children Act, 1975 (Public Law 94-142)
	Disabled persons advocacy groups	
Education of students with special needs		
1980s		
School effectiveness	Business community	*A Nation at Risk*, 1983
School choice	Conservative religious groups	School voucher plans
Education of students with special needs	Conservative political groups	Education of the Handicapped Act Amendments, 1986 (Public Law 99-457)
	"Education politicians"	
	Private and church school advocates	
	Disabled persons advocacy groups	

(*continued*)

TABLE 9-2   *(Continued)*

Thrusts of Education Policy	Pressures Behind the Policies	Sample Governmental Actions
	1990s	
Student academic achievement	School accountability enthusiasts	Goals 2000, Educate America Act, 1994
School accountability	"Education politicians"	School-to-Work Opportunities Act, 1994
Education of students with special needs	Disabled persons advocacy groups	Disabilities Education Act, 1990
Education and jobs	National Education Association	Individuals with Disabilities Act, 1992 (IDEA)
	American Federation of Teachers	

cates, and openly fought with the National Education Association. Some political experts and editors suggested that the two administrations used anti-school and anti-teacher union attacks as means to gain support from right-wing constituents.

In its early years, the Democratic Clinton administration has continued the push for more school accountability, but, unlike the Reagan and Bush administrations, has done so in ways that educators see as more positive and cooperative, such as by increasing federal support for school initiatives and making serious efforts to cooperate with teacher unions and the educational establishments at all levels. Indicative of its educational stances are its strong vocal support for the Head Start Program, School-to-Work Opportunities, and Goals 2000.

Ironically, it appears that the Reagan administration's efforts that created *A Nation at Risk* and the Bush administration activities that led to Goals 2000 may have provided the most significant federal boosts for public schools in the last quarter of the twentieth century. These efforts raised concern about schools and identified some of the objectives public schools need to meet in the years ahead. The Clinton administration seems to be continuing these emphases with a "friend of schools and teachers" style rather than with confrontation and without assuming significantly more direct federal authority over schools.

In a second apparent twist of irony, it also seems that the moves Reagan and Bush made to push much educational activity that had clustered in Washington back toward state governments has not only increased state educational power in comparison with Washington's but has also increased state educational power at the expense of local governments.

The Impact of Federal Judicial Decisions on Teaching and Schools

In an early section of this chapter, we described the bases for judicial authority over schools. Now, we analyze the impact court decisions, particularly those of federal courts, have on schools and teaching as courts have exercised that authority. We do this rather comprehensively for three reasons: (1) because judicial decisions about

TABLE 9-3   Clauses in the Constitution of the United States That Have Significance for Education

Article I, Section 8
The Congress shall have Power to lay and collect Taxes, Duties, Imposts and Excises, to pay the Debts and provide for the common Defense and general Welfare of the United States.
First Amendment
Congress shall make no law respecting an establishment of religion, or prohibiting the free exercise thereof; or abridging the freedom of speech, or of the press.
Fifth Amendment
No person shall . . . be deprived of life, liberty, or property, without the due process of law.
Eighth Amendment
. . . cruel and unusual punishments [shall not be] inflicted.
Fourteenth Amendment
No State shall make or enforce any law which shall abridge the privileges or immunities of citizens of the United States; nor shall any State deprive any person of life, liberty, or property, without due process of law; nor deny to any person within its jurisdiction the equal protection of the laws.

education have great significance for the political context in which teaching occurs and schools operate, (2) because judicial decisions have both quick and long-lasting impact, and (3) because they cut across the education authority of all levels of government.

The federal court decisions reviewed here are clustered around four primary issues: (1) access to schools and equity of instruction, (2) religious freedoms, (3) student and teacher rights, and (4) school finance equalization. The selection of cases we describe is by no means exhaustive: instead we focus on cases that are especially significant and representative of the kinds of issues the courts have addressed.

Nearly all Supreme Court decisions that deal with education and school matters are based on the key clauses in the Constitution of the United States shown in Table 9-3. Because of these constitutional principles, the Constitution requires that (1) when states provide schools and systems of education, they must do so equally for all; and (2) those schools may not infringe on student and teacher rights and freedoms, including the right of due process. As applied by the federal courts these principles affect all pre-K–12 schools to some extent, but they apply most directly to public schools.

Access and Equity

Equal protection of the law

Supreme Court decisions concerning access and equity typically derive from the *equal protection* clause of the Fourteenth Amendment. Such cases include, among others, those dealing with racial segregation, services to students with special needs, instruction for non-native-English-speaking students, and school finance equalization. The first three types of cases are described on the next few pages; school finance equalization is presented separately later.

Several of the court decisions mentioned here were first introduced in Chap-

TABLE 9-4   Representative Court Cases Concerning School Access and Equity

Case	Issue	Decision
Racial Desegregation		
Brown v. *Bd. of Education of Topeka* (1954)	May public schools be racially segregated?	Public schools may not be segregated, and segregation must be discontinued at the earliest possible date.
Green v. *Country School Bd.* (1964)	Are freedom of choice plans appropriate means for desegregating schools?	Various means for desegregating schools may be appropriate, but they must lead to actual desegregation.
Swain v. *Charlotte-Mecklenburg Bd. of Education* (1971)	What racial composition of a school constitutes desegregation?	The racial composition of every school does not have to match the racial composition of the whole school system; busing is an appropriate means for desegregating.
Keyes v. *School District No. 1, Denver* (1973)	To what extent does it matter if schools are segregated because of past *de jure* segregation or *de facto* segregation?	It no longer makes a significant difference because desegregation decisions should be based on principles of equality of education, not past practice.
Milliken v. *Bradley* (1974) "*Milliken I*"	May school districts be required by courts to desegregate across school district lines?	School districts do not have to cross school district lines to desegregate.
Milliken v. *Bradley* (1977) "*Milliken II*"	May school districts be ordered to provide remedial education to compensate for past *de jure* segregation?	School districts may be required to provide remedial education to compensate for past *de jure* segregation.
Equal Education for Students with Special Needs		
Pennsylvania Association for Retarded Children (PARC) v. *Pennsylvania* (1974)	Are mentally retarded children entitled to an education equal to that of nondisabled students?	A mentally retarded child is entitled to an appropriate, free, public program of education.*
Mills v. *Bd. of Education of Washington D.C.* (1972)	Are children labeled as having various disabilities entitled to an appropriate public education?	School districts may not exclude students with behavioral problems and other special students from schools.

*This determination was by consent decree rather than a court decision.

(*continued*)

TABLE 9-4   (*Continued*)

Case	Issue	Decision
Equal Education for Students with Special Needs (continued)		
Wyatt v. *Stickney* (1972)	Are institutionalized special children entitled to an appropriate public education?	Institutionalized children are entitled to an appropriate, free, public education.
Bd. of Education, Hudson Central School District v. *Rowley* (1982)	How much special services are school districts required to supply for its education of disabled students?	Schools are not required to provide a particular level of benefit above a "basic floor of opportunity."
Equal Education of Non-Native-English Speakers		
Lau v. *Nichols* (1974)	Must schools teach students who are not native English speakers in languages that are more comprehensible for them?	Schools must take steps to help non-native-English speakers who find their classroom experience incomprehensible because they do not speak English.
M. L. King Jr. Ele. School Children v. *Ann Arbor School District* (1979)	What are schools expected to do to teach students whose primary language is not standard English (such as "black English")?	Schools are required to take into account the home language of children when teaching them English.

ter 7 in connection with the major constitutional and legal reasons why pre-K–12 schools try to educate all children. We revisit them here to illustrate the political context and pressures under which schools and teachers function. Table 9-4 summarizes important decisions concerning access and equity.

Desegregation Issues

As explained in Chapter 7, the *Brown* v. *Board of Education of Topeka* (1954) decision established the principle that, when states provide education, they must do so equally for all students. Although the decision dealt primarily with racial segregation, the principle it established applies to all students. As a result, the decision has served as a precedent for cases involving a broad range of issues, including educating students with special needs and ensuring gender-related equity.[14]

A number of important successive Supreme Court decisions concerning racial desegregation of schools followed the *Brown* case. Those decisions have elaborated upon, extended, and sometimes confused matters; and, at the same time, they have provided the guidelines and directions by which specific school systems have developed and pursued plans to desegregate their schools. Many of the decisions have focused on two points: what schools should do to accomplish desegregation and how fast they need to act.

Following the *Brown* decision, the Supreme Court issued several decisions that forced reluctant school systems to actively desegregate. For example, in 1964 it instructed schools not to drag their feet, authorized the federal government to sue systems that were not desegregating at appropriate speeds, and said systems that continued racial discrimination could be denied federal funds.[15] Four years later, it said desegregation plans were not all that was required of schools; the plans had to be realistic and actually result in real desegregation.[16]

During the 1970s, the Court broadened its desegregation orders in two ways, both of which significantly extended the impact of desegregation orders outside the South: (1) It introduced the idea that busing could be used to create more racial balance in schools,[17] and (2) it applied desegregation rulings to situations of *de facto* segregation as well as those resulting from *de jure* segregation.[18] The latter point was particularly important because it based court desegregation decisions on the principle of equality of education, not on the fact that schools had become segregated because laws in the past required segregation.[19]

Decisions in terms of equality of education

As the Court extended the application of its desegregation rulings to more and more situations, it began to face two continually recurring questions: How much must systems do to correct situations of racial imbalance in schools? How long must desegregation rulings remain in effect before school systems can be declared in compliance and come out from under direct court supervision of their student assignment policies? Through the 1970s, 1980s, and into the 1990s, the Court has ruled on many individual cases that address these two questions; and the decisions have not been clear-cut. For example, it has supported plans for the cross-district busing of students in some areas and not in others.[20] In recent years, however, the Court has signaled a willingness to be less intrusive in local and state decisions and, in a number of situations, has declared that several school systems under court-ordered desegregation plans have met their goals.[21]

Issues Concerning Students with Special Needs

In *Pennsylvania Association of Retarded Children (PARC)* v. *Commonwealth of Pennsylvania* (1974), the courts, through a consent decree, extended the equal education principle of the *Brown* decision to mentally retarded students. As part of the court settlement, the State of Pennsylvania agreed "to place each mentally retarded child in a free, public program of education and training appropriate to the child's capacity." As was explained in Chapter 7, other court decisions, including *Mills* v. *Board of Education of Washington, D.C.* (1972) and *Wyatt* v. *Stickney* (1972), extended the equal education principle to students with other handicapping conditions.[22]

Probably the most powerful effect of these court cases was their stimulation of federal and state laws that required and provided for more attention to the education of students with handicapping conditions and disabilities. Most noticeable of these laws, of course, were the Education of All Handicapped Children Act, 1975 (Public Law 94-172); Education of the Handicapped Act Amendments, 1986 (Public Law 99-457); and the Individuals with Disabilities Act 1992 (Public Law 101-476).

As with desegregation issues, when access and equality principles have been applied to students with disabilities in different situations and under different circumstances, the courts have been asked to rule on (1) which educational practices are most appropriate in given situations and (2) how much effort and expense is required to assure equity. For example, in *Board of Education of Hudson Central School District* v. *Rowley* (1982), the Court attempted to indicate how much special service for students was enough when it said the law "does not require a particular level of

Degree of effort required to assure equity

benefit above a basic floor of opportunity."[23] The case involved a deaf student who was being provided special instructions but also demanded a sign-language interpreter for her academic classes. The decision, in effect, made three important points:

1. There are limits to how much special services schools should be required to supply, and they do not have to match the best program available.
2. What should be required should be judged in terms of its "educational payoff for the child."
3. It is appropriate to have the courts decide what is appropriate in individual situations.

During the 1980s and 1990s, court decisions across the country about how much is expected of schools and teachers to assure the equal education of disabled students have not been consistent in a way that provides clear directions for school decision makers. Many of the decisions seem to be based on circumstances specific to the cases being judged; but there is also evidence that all courts do not agree, and some judges seem to be unsure of themselves.[24] You will want to follow the deliberations as they unfold in the years ahead.

As that happens, schools will continue to try to serve students with disabilities, and the courts will continue to be asked questions such as, What is required? How do we do it? How much is too much to expect? In the process of responding, the courts are likely eventually to formulate more useful guidelines than those that now exist. It is not likely, however, that clear general answers to any of these three questions will emerge in the near future. In the meantime, teachers will need to do at least two things: (1) stay informed so they can do what is expected by the courts, and (2) strive to provide students with disabilities with the best possible education in a setting that is as close to that of nondisabled students as is appropriate.

Issues Concerning Non-Native-English Speakers

The Supreme Court extended the principle of equal education to non-native-English-speaking students in the *Lau* v. *Nichols* decision (1974). The Court said the San Francisco Schools were required to take steps toward teaching Chinese-speaking students in their native language if instruction in English would not be comprehensible to them.[25] In effect, it said that attending the same schools and having the same teachers, textbooks, and curricula as other children was not equal education if the students still did not have an equal opportunity to learn because of their language difference. As noted in Chapter 7, the decision gave a boost to bilingual education programs and promoted bilingual legislation.

The general concepts of the *Lau* case were applied to other educational equity situations that concern students' language and background. Specific issues include questions about English-based instruction and the use of English-based tests for non-native-English speakers, for speakers of "black English," and for those whose family environment is heavily influenced by dialects to the extent that their use of standard English is affected.[26] When taken together, these decisions seem to say that schools need to make sincere efforts to provide equitable educational experiences and assessments for students who may be having difficulty understanding standard English; but they do not have to provide special instruction to the extent ordered in some of the cases concerning special education.

So, how should we summarize all this information about the impact of federal judicial decisions on access to schools and teachings? One way is as follows: (1) As

Language and equity

Language and testing

interpreted by the courts, federal and state constitutions specify that all school-age children and youth must have access to an appropriate and equal education; (2) when politicians, educators, and society in general question these principles because of the effort needed to meet them, the courts have held those people accountable and expected compliance up to a point, but what that point is on each issue is still not consistent or clear; and (3) when it is not clear what compliance means in specific situations, the courts have decided.

Religious Freedoms

Whereas federal judicial decisions concerning issues of access and equity typically tell schools what they are required to do to educate students, decisions involving religious freedom issues generally try to strike a balance between two constitutional guarantees: access and equity on one side and religious rights on the other. For example, because students are assured equal access to public schools, all have a right to be in a public classroom; but they arrive at that classroom with different religious preferences and different ideas about how they should act out their religious beliefs in the public school setting. For instance, some want to engage in public prayer and see the teaching of prayer as part of their education; others object to being exposed to such practices. So, which religious freedom takes precedence, a right to pray in school or a right to avoid prayer in school? The key point to such an issue is the fact that the First Amendment constitutional provision of freedom of religion guarantees both the right to practice one's religion and the right to avoid the practice of religion.

It should also be noted that many of the disagreements about religion and the public schools arise from clashes of opinions about the role of schools in a society whose Constitution insists on a separation of church and state. As described in Chapter 8, many of America's first schools in colonial times had central religious purposes, but that was before the adoption of the U.S. Constitution in 1789; those schools were not tax-supported; and for the most part, students were not compelled by law to attend. At issue since 1789 has been the question: How does American society educate its children and youth according to society's ideals and purposes when many of those ideals and purposes are based in religious beliefs and traditions, *but* the society also insists on a separation of church and state?

It is this clash of basic American values that prompts most, if not all, court cases about religious freedoms and schools. Contrary to what some public commentators often imply, these cases usually do not come about because people have devious motives. They happen because sincere people place higher priority than their counterparts on one or the other of two Constitutional guarantees: (1) to practice your religion freely and (2) to be free of having a religion imposed upon you.

Because most school activities are conducted under the direction of school administrators and teachers, rather than by the free choice of students, many decisions that have been asked of the courts concerning religion-in-school matters involve an official school policy that some students challenge on religious freedom grounds. Also because a great number of the school policies that are challenged are policies that institute some official religious or religious-related activity rather than forbid the free practice of religion, the challenges tend to be requests not to engage in religious practices in schools rather than requests to do so.

All of this has direct implications for teacher and school administrator decisions and actions at least two ways: (1) Teachers and administrators must know and follow

Separation of church and state

the Constitution and the law in what they do, and (2) they must decide what to do when the application of court decisions to the specific situations they face is not clear. Every situation cannot be deferred to higher authority and should not be. So, what should teachers do when confronted with clashes of religious freedoms and perspectives in their schools? We suggest the following: (1) Know the applicable court ruling and the law; (2) make sure you understand the issues being disputed and the beliefs behind the positions being advocated by both sides; (3) respond to the specific situation carefully and rationally and in a way that avoids serious confrontations, angry words, and hurt feelings.

Each time teachers are confronted with value conflicts of all types, including those concerning religious freedom issues, they are called upon to make a professional judgment—a decision for which they are responsible, one on which they might be second-guessed and openly criticized. In the political context of schools, that criticism can be very public and emotional, and the teacher's decision may be wrong. Nevertheless, there is no way for teachers to completely avoid these dilemmas. They are part of the professional responsibilities that go with the job.

The issues explained below are grouped according to four types: (1) compulsory schooling and religious freedoms; (2) the use of public school facilities and public funds for religious purposes; (3) prayer, Bible reading, and religious displays in schools; and (4) curricular content that some people question on religious grounds. Table 9-5 summarizes important decisions concerning these issues.

Compulsory Schooling and Religious Freedoms

Nearly two-thirds of a century ago, in *Pierce* v. *Society of Sisters* (1925), the Supreme Court decided that, although states can require all students of certain ages to attend schools, they cannot require them to attend the *public* schools. The Court said that an Oregon law of 1922 requiring all children between the ages of 8 and 16 to attend public schools interfered unreasonably "with the liberty of parents and guardians to direct the up-bringing and education of children under their control."[27] The Court said states could restrict parents' choices to *state-approved* schools but not to only *public* schools.[28] In essence, the decision allowed for religious-based and church-operated schools. The following year, in *Farrington* v. *Tokyshige* (1926), the Court said non-public schools had the authority to make decisions on matters relating to teacher selection, textbooks, and curricula.[29]

These two decisions, in effect, set several guidelines concerning the authority of schools. In addition to allowing religious schools to exist, they (1) recognized state authority to approve and, therefore, to control non-public schools, (2) acknowledged that states could compel students to attend school, and (3) allowed states to certify teachers, regulate curricula, and inspect and examine schools, teachers, and students.[30]

An issue that the *Pierce* and *Farrington* decisions did not settle was, What happens if specific religious beliefs conflict with the standards states use to approve schools and regulate education? In *State of Wisconsin, Petitioner* v. *Jonas Yoder el* (1972), nearly fifty years after the *Pierce* decision, the Court took up that question when a group of Amish children argued that the state law that required school attendance to age 16 conflicted with their religious beliefs. The children's advocate opposed schooling beyond grade 8. The Court ruled that, although states could compel students to attend school, the authority to do so has limits. It said the state had to justify its rules in terms of how they assured that students were being pre-

Constitutionality of private but state-approved schools

TABLE 9-5   Representative Court Decisions Concerning Schooling and Religious Freedoms

Case	Issue	Decision
Compulsory Schooling		
Pierce v. *Society of Sisters* (1925)	May states require all students to attend *public* schools?	States may not require students to attend a *public* school, but may require all students to attend a state-approved school.
Farrington v. *Tokyshige* (1926)	How much authority free of state requirements do private state-approved schools have?	Non-public schools may decide matters relating to the selecting of teachers, textbooks, and curriculum.
Wisconsin v. *Yoder* (1972)	May a state require school attendance beyond grade 8 if the requirement contradicts Amish religious beliefs?	Amish students who challenged a state attendance law did not have to attend school beyond grade 8.
West Virginia v. *Barnette* (1943)	May states require public school students to pledge allegiance to the American flag if it contradicts their religious beliefs?	Children who are Jehovah's Witnesses and who object on religious grounds may not be required to pledge allegiance to the American flag as a public school ceremony.
Use of Public Facilities and Funds		
Illinois v. *McCollum* (1948)	May students participate in religious instruction on public school property if the teacher is not a public employee?	Students may not receive religious instruction on public school property even if the teacher is not a public employee.
Zorach v. *Clauson* (1952)	May students leave school during school hours to receive religious instruction at non-public locations from teachers who are not public employees?	Students may receive religious instruction during school hours if it is not on school property and is not at public expense.
Cochran v. *Louisiana* (1930)	May a state supply free textbooks to students in private, religious schools?	States may supply textbooks to students in private, religious schools if the effect of the action benefits the students without promoting the establishment of religion.

(*continued*)

TABLE 9-5 (*Continued*)

Case	Issue	Decision
Use of Public Facilities and Funds (continued)		
Lemon v. *Kurtzman* (1971)	Under what conditions may public funds be used for students in private, religious schools?	Public funds may be used for students in private, religious schools when the use has a secular purpose, does not advance or inhibit religion, and does not "excessively entangle" government and religion.
Everson v. *Bd. of Education* (1947)	May public funds be used to transport students to and from parochial schools?	Public funds may be used to transport students to and from parochial schools.
Wolman v. *Walter* (1977)	Which school services at religious schools may be paid for with public funds?	Educational services at religious schools may be paid for with public funds when they benefit individual students rather than support the operation of the school.
Mueller v. *Allen* (1983)	May states allow parents to deduct from their state income taxes money they pay for school expenses at private as well as public schools?	Parents of students at private schools may deduct from their state income taxes expenses for tuition, textbooks, and transporttion if the same deductions are allowed for public school parents.
Kiryas Joel Village School District v. *Grumet* (1994)	May a community establish a public school district for the purpose of using public funds for religious education?	The citizens of Kiryas Joel Village may not establish a school district for religious education purposes.
Prayer, Bible Reading, and Religious Symbols		
Engle v. *Vitale* (1962)	May a state authorize a public school practice of having students participate in the reading of a state-composed prayer?	The state may not authorize the public school practice of student participation in the reading of a state-composed prayer because it, in effect, imposes prayer on students.

(*continued*)

TABLE 9-5   (*Continued*)

Case	Issue	Decision
Prayer, Bible Reading, and Religious Symbols (continued)		
Abington School District v. *Schempp* (1963) and *Murray* v. *Curlett* (1963)	May public schools require the practice of Bible reading and reciting the Lord's Prayer?	Public schools may not require the practice of Bible reading or reciting the Lord's Prayer because both are religious practices.
Lee v. *Weisman* (1992)	May public schools conduct religious ceremonies such as invocations, blessings, and benedictions at school events?	Public schools may not conduct religious ceremonies such as invocations, blessings, and benedictions at school events.
Stone v. *Graham* (1981)	May schools post the Ten Commandments if public funds are not used?	Schools may not post the Ten Commandments.
Bd. of Education, Westside Community Schools v. *Mergens* (1990)	May schools prevent students from meeting on their own on school property to pray?	Schools may not prevent students from meeting on their own on school property to pray. Their activity should be treated as other extracurricular activities.
Religion and Curricular Content		
Epperson v. *Arkansas* (1968)	May a state prohibit the teaching of the Darwinian theory of evolution in public schools?	The state may not prohibit the teaching of the Darwinian theory of evolution.
Mozert v. *Hawkins Co. Bd. of Education* (1986) and *Smith* v. *Bd. of School Commissioners of Mobile County* (1986)	Must schools discontinue use of curriculum materials that some students find objectionable on religious grounds?	The school may continue the general use of curriculum materials that some students find objectionable on religious grounds, but must provide alternative materials for the students who object.
Edwards v. *Aquillard* (1987)	May a state require schools to teach creation science?	States may not require schools to teach creation science.

pared to become citizens in an open political system and self-reliant members of society. In the specific *Yoder* case situation, the Court ruled that an eighth-grade education was adequate to satisfy the state's responsibilities and that, beyond that point, the Amish children's religious beliefs took precedence over the state's interests.[31]

In addition to deciding when students are required to be in school, court rulings about compulsory attendance and religious freedoms have also dealt with issues concerning what schools and teachers can and cannot require students to do while in school. A landmark case of this type was the *West Virginia State Board of Education v. Barnette* decision (1943). The case involved a challenge to a state board of education regulation requiring children to say the "Pledge of Allegiance" to the flag of the United States. Children, and their parents, who were members of the Jehovah's Witnesses religious denomination objected to the regulation because they considered the pledge to be contrary to the biblical admonition against graven images. The Supreme Court declared the state regulation unconstitutional because it was an abridgment of First Amendment freedoms.[32]

In effect, on the matter of compulsory attendance and religious freedom, the courts have said that states can require that children and youth attend school, but they cannot be too prescriptive about which school they attend and about what students are compelled to do once in school. It has said further that one of the factors that, at times, has precedence over compulsory school attendance is religious belief. Other issues have been addressed in other cases, some of which are described in Table 9-3.

These decisions have a clear message for teachers and school administrators that can be summed up as follows: The state has the authority to force students to attend school, but those students do not relinquish their fundamental freedoms because they are in a school and classroom. Teachers and school leaders must respect and protect those student rights.

Something to Think About

At the start of the first day of his second year of teaching, Charles Myers, one of the authors of this text, was approached by Maria, an eighth-grade student in his homeroom. "During the summer," Maria said, "my mother joined the Jehovah's Witnesses religion and she doesn't want me to say the Pledge of Allegiance to the flag." Maria seemed uncomfortable about raising the issue until Myers said he understood, that the Constitution gave her that right as a freedom of religion and that the two of them could work something out.

Maria and Myers brainstormed three options: Maria could leave the room when the other students said the pledge at the start of the day; she could remain seated and say nothing when the other students stood up; or she could stand with the rest of the class but not say the pledge. Maria selected the third option.

Myers asked Maria to explain their discussion to her mother and, if she agreed, to ask her to write a note making the request that Maria not say the pledge, explaining why she was making the request and indicating that she wanted Maria to follow the course of action that Maria and Myers had agreed upon. He said he would keep the note in his desk drawer in case anyone asked about the arrangement. Maria brought the note the next day, and Myers kept it as he said he would.

Several weeks later, it occurred to Myers that he should inform one of the school administrators about the situation, so he told Mr. Grey, the assistant principal. Mr. Grey's response surprised him. Mr. Grey got red in the face as he shouted about unpatriotic people who ought to get out of the United States if they did not love it and who did not appreciate how much he and other war veterans had given for the country.

Myers countered by saying that he felt that the student and her mother had a right to do what they asked; that the Constitution assured them of that right; and that he, Maria, and her mother had worked out an appropriate plan. He said he felt the matter was settled unless Mr. Grey wanted to make an issue of it, knowing that Mr. Grey always avoided controversy when he could.

Mr. Grey said the Supreme Court was wrong and it should not be telling educators how to run their schools. He said he certainly would not have agreed to Myers's plan if he had been consulted.

When Myers asked Mr. Grey if he wanted to take up the matter with Maria's mother, Mr. Grey said it was probably too late to reverse what Myers had agreed to. Myers offered to make him a copy of the letter if he wanted one. Mr. Grey indicated that was not necessary. The conversation ended and the matter never came up again.

To this day, however, Myers wonders what would have happened if he had consulted with Mr. Grey or deferred the decision to Mr. Grey when Maria first raised the issue.

- Do you think Myers should have consulted school policy or school administrators before working out a plan with Maria and her mother?
- What would you have done? What risks would have been involved in your action?
- How should teachers decide when to make politically sensitive decisions on their own and when to consult superiors?

The Use of Public Facilities and Funds for Religious Purposes

The Constitution of the United States is quite clear in prohibiting religious education in public schools; but, as we have seen, the courts have also held that students cannot be required to attend public schools. Given these broad principles, the courts have been asked to determine under what conditions public support is allowed for children whose parents want them to have religious education outside the public schools. In a more general way, the courts have been asked which school practices fit safely somewhere between those that are unconstitutional because they *support* the establishment of religion and those that are unconstitutional because they *interfere with* students' free practice of their religion.

Over many years, judicial decisions on these matters have been based on three primary considerations: (1) Does the religious education take place on public school property? (2) Are public funds used? (3) If public funds are used, do they benefit the child irrespective of religion or do they support religious practices and institutions? Court actions that address these points are described below.

Because some parents believe that the education of their children should include the inculcation of certain religious information and values, they have tried to arrange for religious instruction of their children alongside their public school secular education. One way they have done this is through plans called *released time for religious education*. Under these plans, public school students whose parents want them to receive religious instruction during part of their school day are released for a certain amount of time each week from the regular school program of instruction, during which a person who is not paid with public funds teaches them religion.

Released time for religious education

The Supreme Court first ruled on one version of this practice in *People of the State of Illinois ex rel. McCollum* v. *Board of Education of School No. 71, Champaign, Illinois* (1948). It said the practice in that situation was unconstitutional because it violated the principle of *separation of church and state*.[33] But a few years later, in *Zorach* v. *Clauson* (1952), the Court permitted a New York state arrangement for released time instruction.[34] The significant differences between the two cases was that, in the *McCollum* case, religious instruction occurred in public schools, even though the teachers were not public employees; while, in the *Zorach* case, the students left the building for their religious instruction. As a result of the two cases, the courts have said released time arrangements for religious education are acceptable if the instruction is not on school property and not at public expense.

Child benefit theory and private schooling

Released time arrangements do not satisfy parents who send their children to church schools but want some degree of public funding for their children's education. One arrangement that has been permitted by the courts in certain circumstances rests on an idea called *child benefit theory*. The theory makes a distinction between public money paid *to students* and funds that go *to schools per se*. The concept has been used most noticeably in recent years in school voucher plans, whereby each child is given a voucher worth a certain amount of money (from taxes) that can be spent at a school of his or her choice.

The child benefit theory was first expressed in *Cochran* v. *Louisiana State Board of Education* (1930) when the Supreme Court allowed the State of Louisiana to supply textbooks to all school children, including those in religious, private schools. The court ruled the benefit was to the children, not the religious schools, and that it was similar to the benefit received by public schools students.[35] Subsequently, the court has used the child benefit theory as a basis for approving the expenditure of public funds for various kinds of costs for private religious education.

The Lemon test

Probably the decision that set the clearest guidelines regarding the use of public funds for private, religious education was *Lemon* v. *Kurtzman* (1971), which listed three questions that need to be addressed in such cases: (1) Does the function for which funds are being spent have a secular purpose? (2) Does the primary effect of the function either advance or inhibit religion? (3) Does funding the function excessively entangle government and religion?[36] The three questions have become known as the *Lemon test*.

Since the *Lemon* decision, courts have decided that tax funds may be used for bus transportation to parochial schools,[37] for the purchase of textbooks and tests, for special testing services, and for remedial instruction at *neutral* sites.[38] They have allowed disabled students at private religious colleges to receive tax-based financial aid[39] and for parents to deduct private school expenses for tuition, textbook, and transportation from their state income taxes.[40] They have disallowed use of tax money for the purchase of instructional equipment such as maps and projectors,

Our society guarantees education for all, but for many people education without religion is incomplete. How can these values be reconciled with the constitutional ideal of the separation of church and state?

for remedial instructional services at non-public schools, for field trips, for leasing parochial school buildings so public school teachers can provide remedial instruction in those buildings,[41] and for full-time Title I teachers in parochial schools.[42]

There is a pattern to these decisions that reflects the *Lemon* test. If the funds are viewed as going to the students so they receive education equal to that received by students in public schools, the arrangement is likely to be approved. If the funds are viewed as supporting religious schools, the arrangement is likely to be denied the use of tax money. In short, taxes can be used for equal education but not to support religious endeavors.

One of the most interesting cases on the issue of where to draw the line concerning public funds for religious purposes wended its way through the courts during the first several years of the 1990s. The case may prove to be a classic example of how hard it is for courts to draw a clear line. In 1994, the Supreme Court heard arguments in *Board of Education of the Kiryas Joel Village School District* v. *Grumet*. In the 1970s, a group of Orthodox Jews of the Satmar Hasidic sect established a small village in upstate New York as a refuge from the urban environment of New York City. In order to receive state funds to educate the disabled students of the town, the townspeople sought to organize their own, self-controlled public school system; and legislation to that effect was passed by the state legislature and signed by the governor in 1977. Almost immediately, the law was challenged as an unconstitutional state concession to a religious group. There was fear the legislation might lead to a proliferation of similar religious-operated, publicly funded school districts. The New York Supreme Court said the law unconstitutionally advanced religion as its primary purpose. In 1994, the U.S. Supreme Court agreed.[43]

Because the courts have taken on the task of drawing the line between the use of tax money to support religious education and the use of tax money to provide equal education in non-public school settings, many specific cases are likely to come before the courts in the years ahead. You will want to watch for them. A key guiding question you may want to ask is, Is each decision consistent with the *Lemon* test or does it signal a new direction for the court on this issue?

Prayer, Bible Reading, and Religious Symbols

Court decisions about public school prayer, Bible reading, and religious symbols are based on the same constitutional principles as those concerning the use of public funds for religious purposes, but they are less clear and harder to explain. At their core, they are yet another set of attempts by the courts to assure school neutrality on matters of religion. In a way, they are on the opposite side of the neutrality line from the *Barnette* case. In *Barnette*, the courts said schools could not *require* students to pledge allegiance to the American flag: in these cases, the court usually tells school officials what religious-oriented activities they *may not allow*.

Organized school prayer

In the 1960s, in *Engle* v. *Vitale* (1962), the Supreme Court disallowed the New York state-authorized practice where students read a state-composed prayer in school even if those who objected were permitted to leave the room. The decision said the official state practice imposed prayer on the students, even though the prayer was not denominational and was voluntary. It suggested that the state should not write or officially sanction prayers.[44] The next year, in two other cases the Court disallowed reading the Bible and reciting the Lord's Prayer as school practices.[45] In 1985, the Court overturned an Alabama law that authorized teachers to lead students in a prescribed prayer if the students willingly participated.[46] In 1990, it said schools may not prevent students from meeting on their own to read the Bible on the school campus, because the activity was considered to be similar to other extra-curricular activities.[47] In 1992, in *Lee* v. *Weisman* the Supreme Court ruled against religious invocations, blessings in which a clergyman invokes a deity, and benedictions at school events.[48] In all these cases, the courts seem to be basing their decisions on the extent to which the activities under scrutiny are either religious or secular and whether they are school practices or individual students' personal religious activities.

In the 1992 *Lee* v. *Weisman* decision, Justice Anthony Kennedy, who wrote the majority opinion, signaled that there is a limit to how much religious practice the Supreme Court would reject, but where the Court will draw the line is still not clear. Kennedy said the court did not intend to disallow all religious practice simply because someone complains and did not mean to exclude religion from every aspect of public life.[49] What this means for religious-related practices in schools, particularly for moments of silence, remains to be seen. You will want to keep up with current developments because what the courts decide will directly affect what classroom teachers are expected or required to do.

Religious scenes and symbols

Court rulings about religious scenes and symbols have dealt with public, governmental settings in general, rather than just schools. For example, in *Stone* v. *Graham* (1981), the Supreme Court struck down a Kentucky statute that required the posting of the Ten Commandments on school walls, although they were purchased with private funds.[50] In another case the Court barred a Nativity scene in front of the Allegheny County (Pennsylvania) Courthouse because the Court considered it religious rather than secular.[51] Shortly thereafter, a federal judge in New York state used this ruling to require the Schuylerville School District to remove a painting of the Crucifixion from one of its buildings.[52] The dividing line the courts have been using in these cases is the determination whether the scene or symbol is primarily religious or primarily secular. The items that are judged to promote religion in schools are unconstitutional; those that are judged to be secular are not.

Religion and Curricular Content

The issue of what is religious instruction and what is more secular than religious has also confronted courts considering the curricula of schools. The direct teaching of religious content for religious purposes is unconstitutional, as we have already explained; but, what about instruction that some people object to on religious grounds and others see as nonreligious? For example, in *Mozert et al.* v. *Hawkins County Board of Education* (1986), fundamentalist Christian parents charged that the reading textbook series assigned to their children contained material offensive to their religious beliefs.[53] They said that selections in the readings—*Wizard of Oz, Rumpelstiltskin,* and *Macbeth*—contained explicit materials that taught *secular humanism* values contrary to their religious beliefs; and they contested the schools' rule that required their children to read these selections. In a similar case, *Smith* v. *Board of School Commissioners of Mobile County* (1986), Alabama parents challenged forty-four textbooks as advancing the religion of secular humanism and excluding Christian contributions to the American way of life.[54] In both cases, the courts' decision rested on judicial decisions concerning what content is religious and what is not. For instance, is secular humanism a religion? If parents believe that exposing their children to certain literature contradicts their religion, is the practice unconstitutional? An indication of the difficulty involved in such decisions is the fact that the courts of appeal in both cases overruled the lower court decisions that found in favor of the parents. This is an issue on which courts still differ. To date, the courts have not yet drawn clear lines.

Secular humanism

On another curricular content issue, in *Edwards* v. *Aquillard* (1987), the Supreme Court ruled unconstitutional a Louisiana state statute that required the teaching of creation science—the biblical explanation of the origin of the human race—whenever evolution was taught. The court ruled the law advanced religion.[55]

Creation science

So, what are the courts telling teachers and school administrators about religion and curricular content in public schools? The response has two parts: (1) If the content is clearly religious in nature and teaching it has religious purposes, the practice is unconstitutional, (2) if the issues involved in a case revolve around deciding if the content is actually religious or not, clear guidelines have not yet been drawn and decisions seem to vary from case to case. This is another situation you will want to monitor carefully in the future.

We also think you will want to be careful as you teach ideas and use materials that might be found objectionable by some religious groups or their opponents. On one side, you do not want to be intimidated to an extent that it influences what and how you teach; but, on the other hand, you do not want to offend students and parents unjustifiably. Clear, rational professional judgment is required. This admonishment is especially important because issues associated with religion and content in recent times have become very volatile and very political. In many situations, advocates on both sides of these issues have resorted to political pressures to get their way; and, at times, politicians have used the emotional issues to garner votes. In the process, some teachers and other educators have been hurt.

We can summarize the impact of federal judicial decisions on the relationship between schools and religious freedoms by making two points: one about the nature of the judicial process and what it means for teaching and schools and a second about the general thrust of the decisions described above. First, because courts in the

United States get involved in issues only when there is an official complaint about a specific situation, it is often difficult to formulate general principles and guidelines for future action. By the same token, it is hard to apply general principles to specific situations because all situations are unique to some extent. Therefore, all court guidance for teachers and educators is open to interpretation and adjustment in the face of local conditions. Second, the guidelines that the court actions described above seem to be providing are as follows: (1) The courts insist that all students attend state-approved schools unless specific exceptions are granted, but they try to see that what they do in these schools neither establishes religion in our society nor interferes with individual student's religious freedoms; (2) they try to prevent public funding of religious practices without denying equal funding to students whose parents choose to combine their education and religious teaching; and (3) they attempt to prevent one child's religious beliefs from being forced on other students in the same school. In essence, the courts try to balance several very important basic American rights and freedoms that are guaranteed under the Constitution of the United States.

Student and Teacher Rights

As with religious freedom, students and teachers have a number of other rights as citizens that are guaranteed by the Constitution of the United States. Because schools have power over both students and teachers, there is always the potential for school authorities to require or forbid something that infringes upon one or more of these rights. When people think this happens, courts are called upon to decide if the action in question does, in fact, deny the student's or the teacher's rights. As with the judicial decisions already described, the task for the courts is to decide where to draw the line between school authority and individual freedoms. Although incidents such as these seem to affect public school students and teachers more than those in other schools, all teachers can be affected. Table 9-6 summarizes important decisions concerning student rights, and Table 9-7 summarizes those concerning teacher rights.

Student Rights

In addition to decisions about religion, the federal courts have rendered important decisions concerning student rights in a number of areas, including the following: a person's right to attend a public school, speech and student expression, search and seizure, drug testing, suspension from school, and corporal punishment. Each area is touched on briefly in this section.

Right to education
based on residence

For many reasons already noted in this text, school-age children and youth who reside in the United States are provided access to free public schools. They are allowed to attend schools that serve the geographic area in which they reside. They and their parents or guardians are not required to pay taxes; *residence* is the criterion. In *Plyler* v. *Doe* (1982), the Supreme Court ruled unconstitutional a Texas law that denied free public education to children of undocumented aliens. The court said that denying schooling to these children would unfairly impose a lifetime of hardship on them and would result in societal problems such as unemployment, high welfare costs, and crime.[56] It, in essence, said residence is the only criterion for attending a public school.

TABLE 9-6   Representative Court Decisions Concerning Student Rights

Case	Issue	Decision
Plyler v. *Doe* (1982)	Are undocumented alien children entitled to a free, public education?	Undocumented alien children are entitled to a free, public education because the right to education is based on residence, not status as a citizen.
Tinker v. *Des Moines Independent Community School District* (1969)	What free speech rights do school students have?	Students have the right of free speech unless there is a good reason for restraint, such as if it disrupts classes or invades others' rights.
Bethel School District No. 403 v. *Fraser* (1986)	May students be suspended from school for inappropriate public speech at school?	Schools may limit lewd, indecent, or offensive speech as part of their education function.
Hazelwood School District v. *Kuhlmeier* (1988)	May schools censor and regulate content in a school newspaper?	In this particular case, the student newspaper was judged to be a supervised learning experience, rather than a public forum and, therefore, could be censored.
Bd. of Island Union Free School District v. *Steven A. Pico* (1982)	May school boards remove library books from schools because they do not like the ideas expressed in them?	Boards have the right to select books for school libraries but may not do so with the intent of suppressing political ideas.
New Jersey v. *T.L.O.* (1985)	Under what circumstances may schools search students?	Schools may search students if the search is justified and if the scope of the search is consistent with the objective of the search.
Odenheim v. *Carlstadt-East Rutherford Regional School District* (1985) and *Anable* v. *Ford* (1987)	May schools require urinalysis of students?	Because urinalysis requires partial disrobing, it is a search and, therefore, may not be done unless there is a reasonable suspicion of illegal drug use.
Schaill v. *Tippecanoe School Corporation* (1988) and *Brooks* v. *East Chamber Consolidated Independent School District* (1989)	May schools require urinalysis of students participating in extracurricular activities?	Schools may require urinalysis of interscholastic athletes (Schaill) but not random urinalysis of students in other extracurricular activities (Brooks).

(continued)

TABLE 9-6 (*Continued*)

Case	Issue	Decision
Goss v. *Lopez* (1975)	May students be suspended from school without due process?	Students may not be suspended from school without due process.
Wood v. *Strickland* (1975)	May school officials be held liable for damages if they suspend students without due process?	School board members may be held liable for damages if they suspend students without due process.
Honig v. *Doe* (1988)	Do the regulations of the federal laws concerning the placement of disabled students apply in cases involving the suspension or expulsion from school of disabled students?	The regulations of federal disabilities laws apply to suspension and expulsion of disabled students.
Ingraham v. *Wright* (1977)	May schools administer corporal punishment to students?	The federal constitution does not prohibit corporal punishment of students if it is sanctioned by state and local laws and regulations.

Freedom of speech and student expression

The *Tinker* v. *Des Moines Independent Community School District* decision (1969) is probably the most significant student free speech decision and the one in which the Supreme Court established students' rights to free speech. Its key phrase to that effect was that students do not "shed their constitutional rights of free speech or expression at the schoolhouse gate."[57] The court said that the suspension from school of three students for wearing anti-Vietnam War armbands was not appropriate unless the school authorities showed that the students' actions interfered with the operation of the school and other students' right to learn.[58] On the other hand, in *Bethel School District No. 403* v. *Fraser* (1986), the court allowed to stand a school district's suspension of a student who used sexual innuendos in a nominating speech for a fellow student. The Court said schools had the authority to prohibit the use of vulgar and offensive language. It noted that the student's speech was not an expression of a political point of view, as in the *Tinker* case, and said that the school could determine that its prohibition of vulgar and lewd speech was part of its basic education mission.[59]

The *Tinker* decision is especially significant because, in it, the Court addressed student constitutional rights rather than using a "reasonableness" test to judge the school policy and actions that were being challenged. Until the *Tinker* case, the courts tended to assume schools had the authority to handle school matters without significant court interference or interpretation.[60]

In *Hazelwood School District* v. *Kuhlmeier* (1988), the Supreme Court ruled that schools may regulate the content of a school newspaper, saying that in the specific case the newspaper was a supervised learning experience rather than a public forum.

In its decision, the court also said the school had censoring authority in a number of circumstances—for example, to protect other students and to prevent publication of poor student writing.[61]

In *Board of Island Union Free School District* v. *Steven A. Pico* (1982), the Supreme Court ruled that school board members could not remove a number of books from the school library because they did not want students exposed to the ideas contained in them. The books removed were on a list circulated by a group of politically active conservative parents, and their authors included a number of prominent African American writers as well as Kurt Vonnegut Jr. The Court considered the action a partisan politically based move, a suppression of ideas, and a denial of students rights.[62]

Book censorship

The *Tinker, Bethel, Hazelwood,* and *Pico* cases all indicate some of the points on which court decisions have tried to balance school authority and students' freedom of expression—if the student activity is a political statement, if it is a supervised learning experience, if it hinders other students' rights to learn; if the school's action involves a suppression of ideas, or if it fits under the school's basic education mission. But there are many school situations that are very hard to classify according to these ideas and both teachers and administrators must exercise their judgment. One of the areas in which even the courts are not consistent is that of student dress and dress codes. Watch for more decisions in the years ahead.

Court decisions about search and seizure issues usually arise from clashes between the Fourth Amendment rights for students—against unreasonable search and seizure—and the responsibilities of educators to keep schools safe and accomplish their education mission. Because of violence in schools and the use of drugs, school authorities have increasingly instituted and expanded the use of metal detectors, X-ray machines, alcohol breath tests, and visual searches of lockers and book bags. And, in many specific cases, courts have been asked to decide which actions are justified and which go too far. The Supreme Court set two important guidelines on searches of school students in *New Jersey* v. *T.L.O.* (1985): (1) The search must be justified and (2) when conducted, the scope of the search must be consistent with the objectives of the search. The case involved a principal's search of a student's purse for suspected evidence of smoking, which resulted in finding evidence of marijuana use. The court supported the principal's actions.[63] Other court decisions have established two other key guidelines: (1) School lockers are considered school property rather than student property and, therefore, can be searched for reasonable cause; (2) strip-searches of students are unconstitutional.[64]

Search and seizure

For the most part, courts have used the two-part *T.L.O.* decision to determine if schools may require urinalyses of students. In *Odenheim* v. *Carlstadt–East Rutherford Regional School District* (1985) and *Anable* v. *Ford* (1987), the courts disallowed urinalyses because they involved partial disrobing.[65] In *Schaill* v. *Tippecanoe School Corporation* (1988), it allowed urinalyses of athletes; but, in *Brooks* v. *East Chambers Consolidated Independent School District* (1989), it disapproved of urinalyses of members of an extracurricular club that did not involve athletics.[66]

Drug testing

Issues over the suspension of students from school focus on *due process* and on the question, Do students have a constitutional right to an education at public expense? Before 1975, students could be suspended or expelled permanently from school at the discretion of school officials, but the courts took up the issue in *Goss* v. *Lopez* (1975), a case in which nine secondary school students were suspended from school for several days. The suspensions were according to Ohio state law but were

Due process and suspension from school

without an official notice and a hearing. The Supreme Court said the students had a legal right to a public education that could not be taken away from them without due process and that that process included public notice and a hearing. It ruled that, before students can be suspended for up to ten days, they must be given (1) an oral or written notice of the charges, (2) an explanation of the evidence (if the students deny the charges), and (3) a hearing in which the students can defend themselves. The Court implied that the procedures can be somewhat informal but that longer suspensions require more formal procedures. It also acknowledged that in cases where students might be threats to themselves, to others, or to property, they can be removed from school before the hearing is held.[67] In *Wood* v. *Strickland* (1975), the Supreme Court said school board members can be held liable for damages for the expulsion of students without due process.[68]

Because of provisions in legislation concerning students with disabilities, the Supreme Court ruled in *Honig* v. *Doe* (1988) that schools may not remove specially placed disabled students from their officially agreed-upon placement without implementing the due process provision of the legislation. In doing so, the court also ruled that suspension did not constitute an official change of placement for these students. The key point of this decision is that special education students must be dealt with according to special guidelines.[69]

Constitutionality of corporal punishment

The questions of the constitutionality of corporal punishment such as paddling in schools pertain to the prohibition of cruel and unusual punishment in the Eighth Amendment of the Constitution of the United States. In the *Ingraham* v. *Wright* decision (1977), the Supreme Court ruled that disciplinary corporal punishment in the public schools does not violate the Eighth Amendment and is permissible if sanctioned by state and local laws and regulations. The "if sanctioned" part of the ruling is important because a number of states and many school districts have outlawed corporal punishment. In the decision, the Court said the Eighth Amendment was intended to protect convicted criminals, not students; and that the openness of public schools offers safeguards against physical abuse of students. The Court also ruled that the due process clause of the Fourteenth Amendment does not require a notice and hearing before imposing corporal punishment because to do so would significantly intrude into the school's educational responsibility.[70]

In summary, the following statements can be made about court decisions concerning student rights. Students have individual rights that are protected from abuse by school authorities, but the courts have allowed school officials rather wide discretion as they deal with students. The courts have tried to balance school responsibilities to educate with students' individual freedoms. On the matter of corporal punishment, although many schools have prohibited it, it is not unconstitutional under the federal constitution.

Teacher Rights

There are numerous ways of categorizing the many federal court decisions that concern teachers' rights. The representative cases presented here are grouped into three areas: (1) relationships between teachers and their employers, (2) classroom and teaching issues, and (3) teachers' personal rights.[71] Other issues that, to an extent, parallel these groupings but at the same time cut across all three are employment contracts, dismissals from teaching, academic freedom, teachers' personal beliefs and lifestyle, and due process.[72]

TABLE 9-7   Representative Court Decisions Concerning Teacher Rights

Case	Issue	Decision
Teacher Employment and Dismissal		
Indiana ex rel Anderson v. *Brand* (1937)	May states enact laws to remove previous laws that establish teacher tenure?	States may not repeal tenure laws because tenure is a contract and once entered into cannot be ended unilaterally.
Board of Regents of State Colleges v. *Roth* (1972) and *Perry* v. *Sindermann* (1972)	Must school boards follow due process procedures in dismissing teachers?	School boards must follow due process procedures in dismissing tenured teachers but not when they do not rehire a nontenured teacher.
Goldberg v. *Kelly* (1970) and *Cleveland Bd. of Education* v. *Loudermill* (1985)	What constitutes due process procedures needed in situations involving teacher dismissals?	Due process procedures include a statement of charges, time to prepare a defense, a fair hearing, legal counsel, opportunity to prepare a defense and cross-examine witnesses, access to transcripts, and a right to appeal.
Teacher Free Speech and Academic Freedom		
Pickering v. *Bd. of Education of Township High School* (1967)	May a school board dismiss a tenured teacher for publicly criticizing the administration on matters of school policy?	School boards may not dismiss tenured teachers for public criticism about school policy.
Connick v. *Myers* (1983)	May a school board dismiss a teacher for publicly criticizing personnel decisions that affect his employment situation?	The First Amendment does not protect a teacher who publicly criticizes the administration concerning personal, personnel matters.
Bd. of Education v. *James* (1972)	How free are teachers to show their personal political views in their classes?	Teachers may voice or display personal public views at school as long as they do not interfere with normal school activities.
Keefe v. *Geanakoe* (1969) and *Parducci* v. *Rutland* (1970)	May a school board dismiss a teacher for using instructional materials with objectionable words?	Teachers have some latitude in deciding what materials to use, but school officials may impose some limits.

(*continued*)

TABLE 9-7   (*Continued*)

Case	Issue	Decision
	Teacher Free Speech and Academic Freedom	
Mailloux v. *Riley* (1971) and *Celestine* v. *Lafayette Parish School Bd.* (1973)	May a school board dismiss a teacher for using or having students use "taboo words" in class?	School boards may dismiss a teacher for using or having students use "taboo words" in class, but courts have decided both ways on this issue depending on circumstances particular to each case.
	Teachers' Personal Rights	
Adler v. *Board of Education* (1951)	May teachers be dismissed from their positions because they belong to certain groups?	Teachers do not have a constitutional right to their jobs and may be dismissed because of the groups they join.
Shelton v. *Tucker* (1960)	May states or schools require teachers to list the names of organizations they belong to?	States and schools may not require teachers to compile a list of organizations they belong to.
Keyishian v. *Bd. of Regents* (1967)	(Same issue as *Adler* v. *Board of Education*)	School boards may not dismiss teachers because they belong to certain groups (overrule of *Adler* decision).
Morrison v. *State Bd. of Education* (1969) (decision of the California Supreme Court)	May a state revoke a teacher's teaching certificate for private behavior that some consider "immoral"?	States may not revoke teaching certificates and teachers may not be dismissed for private, personal behavior not related to their professional work; private behavior that does not affect teaching is a teacher's own business.

Teacher-employer contracts and property rights

Normally, when public pre-K–12 school teachers are hired, they and their employing school districts sign a legally binding contract that specifies the terms of employment. This agreement, as with all contracts, is then protected by the Constitution of the United States, under Article I, Section 10, which says, "No state shall . . . pass any . . . Law imparing the Obligation of Contracts."

This protection means, in legal terms, that the teacher has a *property right* to the teaching job specified in the contract. The contracting school district can take the job away only under restricted circumstances: (1) when the school board proves a teacher is unfit, or the board can show that it no longer needs the teacher's services because of declining school enrollments and (2) after due process proceedings have been completed. In most states, the three accepted bases for determining that a teacher is unfit are incompetence, insubordination, and immorality.

New teachers typically sign a one-year contract and continue with successive one-year contracts until they have taught without interruption for the number of years specified by state law to reach *tenure*. In most cases, this pretenure time, or probationary period, is three years. Once the teacher is hired for a year beyond the tenure point (the fourth year usually, according to the laws of most states), the contract runs continuously until the teacher resigns, retires, or is dismissed for cause.[73]

Tenure

Contrary to popular belief and the outcries of some politicians, tenure laws do *not* mean teachers cannot be fired. They do mean that tenured teachers have continuing contracts with school boards and can be fired only for justifiable reasons and through appropriate legal procedures. (Tenure is explained in more detail later in the section, Professional Teachers and the Law.)

Understanding contractual arrangements is important to understanding teacher rights because the primary power that school boards have over teachers is the threat to take their jobs away. The Supreme Court, in *Indiana ex rel Anderson* v. *Brand* (1937), recognized this and stipulated that once states provide teachers with tenure, they cannot eliminate tenure by passing a new law because doing so negates the contracts already signed with tenured teachers. In other words, it takes away their property rights to a continuing job.[74]

Therefore, the most significant federal court cases concerning teacher contracts and dismissals have asked the courts to decide (1) what are adequate reasons for firing teachers and (2) what are appropriate due process procedures for doing so.

The courts have spoken a number of times in precedent-settings ways on the first of these points. In doing so, they have tended to allow teachers freedom to criticize their employers on public matters but have been less lenient on matters of employment. One set of these rulings deals with teachers' public criticism of their employers. In *Pickering* v. *Board of Education of Township High School* (1967), the Supreme Court said a teacher cannot be fired for publicly criticizing the school board and superintendent on matters of school policy.[75] In subsequent decisions, it said a teacher could not be fired for criticizing school policy on a call-in radio program, for criticizing a school district's desegregation plan, and for speaking out about collective bargaining issues.[76] However, in *Connick* v. *Myers* the Court said that, although teachers are protected when they speak out on matters of policy and public concern, they are not protected when they speak out as employees about their own employment situation.[77]

On other teacher employment issues, the courts have said that teachers can be fired if they do not complete advanced college coursework as stipulated in contracts and if they strike illegally.[78] They let stand a New York state regulation that denies teacher certificates to aliens.[79] They have also ruled on a number of employment discrimination matters, in which their general stance has been to oppose racial, gender, and age discrimination. For example, they said school boards may not force teachers to take unpaid maternity leave for a fixed length of time, and they may not force teachers to retire simply because of their age.[80]

On the issue of what is involved in due process, the Supreme Court, in a number of cases said that due process rights include (1) a statement of charges, (2) sufficient

Components of due process

time to prepare a defense, (3) a fair hearing before a tribunal (which, for teachers, is usually a school board), (4) legal counsel, (5) an opportunity to present evidence and cross-examine witnesses, (6) access to transcripts, and (7) a right to appeal.[81] In addition, the Court said due process must be followed in tenure-involved dismissal cases but that nontenured teachers can be treated differently. It said a school board decision not to offer a nontenured teacher a new contract does not violate a property right and, therefore, does not require a due process procedure.[82]

On matters of what teachers teach and how they teach it, the courts have tried to draw a line between public sensitivities and state or school board policies and guidelines on one side and teacher professional judgment on the other. Issues tend to be of two types: (1) questions about content specified to be taught in the school curriculum and (2) questions about materials and expressions used by individual teachers. Different courts have come down on both sides of both issues; patterns are hard to detect. Often they rely on the testimony of professional experts.

In *Epperson* v. *Arkansas* (1968), the Supreme Court declared unconstitutional an Arkansas statute that prohibited the teaching of the Darwinian theory of evolution in a state-supported school.[83] Although the case involved the potential firing of a teacher, the Court based its decision on the establishment of religion clause of the Constitution. In *Mozert et al.* v. *Hawkins County Board of Education* (1986), an appeals court sided with the school board when parents complained on religious grounds about the contents of an elementary school reading textbook series.[84] In terms of specific teacher actions, the Supreme Court supported a teacher of high school literature who refused to stop using a magazine article that contained language others considered vulgar, in *Keefe* v. *Geanakoe* (1969);[85] and in *Parducci* v. *Rutland* (1970), a federal district judge sided with an Alabama high school teacher, Marilyn Parducci, who had been fired because she continued to teach a Kurt Vonnegut Jr. satire after her superior ordered her to stop doing so when parents complained.[86]

Lower-level courts have supported school districts that have taken action against teachers for presenting objectionable content. For example, an Ohio court agreed with a school system's severe restrictions on an English teacher's assigning of several novels, and a West Virginia court supported the suspension of a teacher for inadvertently distributing a sexually explicit cartoon.[87] In *Board of Island Union Free School District* v. *Steven A. Pico* (1982), the Supreme Court overruled a school board decision to remove a number of library books from the school library.[88]

On the matter of teaching methods, courts have tended to avoid second-guessing teachers who do something that causes controversy if experts testify that the teacher's decision can be justified; but the line is fine and different courts disagree on specifics. For example, a circuit court sided with high school English teacher, Roger Mailloux, when he used the term *fuck* to illustrate "taboo words" in *Mailloux* v. *Kiley* (1971), but a court in Louisiana refused to reinstate Allen Celestine, who was fired for requiring fifth-grade students to write the same word 1,000 times as punishment for using it in class in *Celestine* v. *Lafayette Parish School Board* (1973).[89]

Because public school teachers are government employees and because of their leadership roles with students, they are often expected by the public at large and their school system superiors to conform to certain codes of personal behavior that are not usually imposed upon other adults. When these expectations become matters of dispute, the courts are asked to decide which requirements of teachers are

Due process and tenure

Instructional content

Teaching methods

Teacher personal behavior

justifiable and which are not. The issues are often divided into two categories: public behavior and private lifestyle and behavior. In general, court trends are similar on both. They are moving toward greater protection of teachers' individual rights.

In the 1950s, strong anti-Communist sentiment swept the country, and one of its impacts was a nationwide desire to keep people who belonged to subversive groups from public employment, including teaching. As part of that effort, a State of New York law prohibited people who belonged to certain groups from teaching. When the law was challenged, the Supreme Court, in *Adler* v. *Board of Education* (1951), upheld the law, saying teachers did not have a constitutional right to their jobs and were not denied due process in the case of this specific law.[90] Several years later, the Supreme Court upheld the firing of a teacher of twenty-two years who refused to answer questions regarding affiliations with Communist organizations. It said the questions could be asked to determine the teacher's fitness to be a teacher.[91] Then in 1960, in *Shelton* v. *Tucker* (1960), the Court struck down an Arkansas law that required teachers to compile annual lists of organizations they belonged to. The Court said the law was too broad and went beyond the state's interest to see if teachers are fit for the job.[92]

Loyalty oaths

In the late 1960s, however, the Supreme Court moved further toward protecting teachers' rights by reversing the *Adler* decision in *Keyishian* v. *Board of Regents* (1967). In this case involving faculty of the State University of New York, the Court said loyalty oath statutes that make membership in an organization sufficient for termination of employment are unconstitutional.[93] Four years later, in a case involving a loyalty oath in Florida, the Court became more precise by saying that the state could require public employees to affirm that they support the federal and state constitutions, but they could not require that they swear they do not believe in the overthrow of the federal or state governments.[94] The following year, the Court, in *Board of Education* v. *James* (1972), upheld a teacher's right to wear an anti-Vietnam War armband in class. In doing so, it used as its standard the question of whether the teacher's action interfered with normal school activities. When the lower court decided it did not, the Court supported the teacher's action as freedom of expression.[95] This basis of judgment was in line with that of the *Tinker* decision about students' freedoms of expression a few years earlier.

Teachers' freedom
of expression

Over the years, the court decisions described above shifted from the assumption that states and other governmental authorities can require certain conformity by teachers just because they are teachers to the belief that what teachers do should be judged in terms of its effect on the teacher's teaching performance. Although that evolution is shown here in terms of loyalty oaths and teachers' freedom of expression, the implications are much broader and affect other aspects of teachers' lives.

Except for the fact that teachers can be fired for committing a felony, court decisions involving the private behavior of teachers that does not affect their teaching and their students are less frequent than needed to show a clear trend. This is probably because teachers who were fired in the past due to private personal behavior tended not to turn to the courts. But one state court decision in the late 1960s indicates a shift in sentiment and may reflect an actual turning of the tables on the issue. It may have sent such a clear signal that the current absence of court cases may be a result of fewer firings or reprimands of teachers because of their private behavior. In short, maybe teachers are not being fired on these grounds, at least not openly.

In the key case on this matter, the California Board of Education revoked Marc Morrison's teaching certificate on the grounds of immoral and unprofessional conduct when it became known that he had had a brief homosexual relationship sometime earlier. The board said it revoked the certificate because teachers need to be models of good conduct and homosexuality was contrary to the standards of the people of California. The California Supreme Court ruled in favor of Morrison, in *Morrison* v. *State Board of Education* (1969), saying (1) the board's use of "immoral" and "unprofessional" were dangerously broad, (2) the teacher cannot be dismissed for personal, private behavior that is not clearly related to his professional work, and (3) when a teacher's private behavior does not affect his teaching, it is his own business.[96]

You will want to monitor court decisions about teacher public and private behavior as you consider professional teaching as a career. Although the courts have shown an increasing tolerance for not intruding on teachers' personal freedoms, there are many vocal and powerful groups in the country who do not like that trend and are using their influence to reverse it. At some point, courts will be drawing new lines that say what teachers can legally be told they may not do.

So, how should we summarize the impact of federal judicial decisions on student and teacher rights? In the case of students, the courts seem to be recognizing students' individual rights and freedoms more than they did in the past; but they are still trying to balance students' rights with the schools' responsibilities to educate. Students' rights must be respected, but their freedoms are limited if they interfere with the schools' mission.

The courts in recent years seem to be treating teachers more like other citizens. They assume teachers' employment rights are similar to those of all other citizens. They allow teachers reasonable discretion when they make professional decisions about what and how to teach. More than in the past, they are allowing teachers to separate their professional responsibilities from their private, personal behavior.

Despite these trends, it is important to remember that courts at all levels of government, as well as those who lodge complaints about teachers with the courts, have much power over teachers. Society insists on that power because teachers educate children and youth, and society wants its children protected. Although the courts currently appear to be less intrusive into students' and teachers' lives than in the past, they have not relinquished any of their power or authority.

The Courts and School Finance Equalization

Recent federal and state court decisions have said that the school systems of many states are not providing an equal education for all the states' children because their ways of funding schools are not fair. As a result, major statewide changes are being forced on many states. The repercussions over the next few years are likely to be as dramatic as those created by the *Brown* decision and the judgments about desegregation that followed it. The five most significant school finance equalization decisions are discussed below and Table 9-8 summarizes those decisions. The next section of the chapter further explains the general subject of financing schools.

In 1971, in *Serrano* v. *Priest*, the California Supreme Court ruled that the California system of financing schools, which, like that of most states, depended pri-

TABLE 9-8   Representative Court Decisions Concerning School Finance Equalization

Case	Issue	Decision
Serrano v. *Priest* (1971) (decision of the California Supreme Court)	Property tax financing of schools results in disparity in the quality of education, which hurts students in poor districts.	California's school funding scheme unconstitutionally discriminated against the poor.
San Antonio Independent School District v. *Rodriguez* (1973) (decision of the U.S. Supreme Court)	(Same issue as *Serrano* v. *Priest*)	Differences in local property taxes in a state are not unconstitutional under the federal constitution but might be unconstitutional under state constitutions.
Rose v. *Council for Better Education* (1989) (decision of the Kentucky Supreme Court)	(Same issue as *Serrano* v. *Priest*)	The entire Kentucky system of schools was unconstitutional, and the legislature had to create a new and more efficient one.
Edgewood Independent School District v. *Kirby* (1990) (decision of the Texas Supreme Court)	(Same issue as *Serrano* v. *Priest*)	Texas's method of funding schools was unconstitutional and the state had to equalize its funding of schools.
Abbott v. *Burke* (1990) (decision of the New Jersey Supreme Court)	(Same issue as *Serrano* v. *Priest*)	New Jersey's funding of schools was unconstitutional, and the state had to equalize its funding.

marily on local property taxes, resulted in unconstitutional differences in expenditures for schools between wealthy and poor school districts. The ruling said that the system discriminated against poor students who lived in poor neighborhoods.[97] As a result, California was forced to change how it financed schools in order to bring the expenditures in different districts into closer balance. Almost immediately, similar suits were filed in many other states.

> Unequal funding is unconstitutional

In one such suit in Texas, *San Antonio Independent School District* v. *Rodriguez* (1973), a federal court found the Texas financing arrangement similarly unconstitutional. This decision, however, was appealed to the U.S. Supreme Court, where, by a 5–4 vote, the Court found (1) that disparities in school expenditures across school districts in a state are not unconstitutional under the federal constitution because all students within a poorer district suffer equally, but (2) the situation might be unconstitutional under state constitutions. This, in effect, left cross-

> A state rather than a federal issue

What are the consequences for schoolchildren of inadequate funding for schools? To what extent would equalizing funding across schools and districts solve these problems?

district finance equalization matters for state courts, rather than federal courts, to decide.[98]

Three post-*Rodriguez*, state-level court decisions illustrate what has happened since. The Kentucky Supreme Court, in *Rose* v. *Council for Better Education* (1989), declared the entire Kentucky statewide school system unconstitutional under the state constitution. It also (1) ordered the legislature to devise a new and more appropriate state system, (2) rejected the property tax as the main basis for funding schools, and (3) directed a higher per-student spending amount for all school districts.[99] Within the next two years, the state legislature put an entirely new state education system in place with much higher funding. Shortly thereafter, the Texas Supreme Court, in *Edgewood Independent School District* v. *Kirby* (1989), threw out the Texas school financing system;[100] and the state court in New Jersey, in *Abbott* v. *Burke* (1990), declared its state system unconstitutional.[101]

As a result of these decisions, three significant issues about financing schools have been emphasized, and argued about, in recent years: (1) Is it appropriate to require all schools in a state to have comparable levels of funding or can taxpayers in one district choose to provide more funds than others? (2) What taxes should be used if finances are to be equalized—property taxes, sales taxes, income taxes—and in what proportion? (3) Does increasing funding lead to better education? (This last question is the focus of the Educational Research section of this chapter.) In addition, nearly all states are reexamining how they are financing their schools with an eye toward equalization.

The Financing of Public Schools

At the start of this chapter, we mentioned the financial authority that governments have over schools and labeled it the *power of the purse*. In the last section, we described briefly the impact of recent court decisions concerning the equalization of school financing within states. Now, we look at how public pre-K–12 schools are financed, the roles played by different levels of government, and some of the issues and conflicts associated with school funding.

The financing of pre-K–12 schools is a matter of public concern and debate, and the concerns and debates greatly affect the political context in which schools function. The key questions involved include: How much money do schools need? Who should pay? How should the revenues be collected? How should they be distributed? Is it important that all schools be funded equally? Should tax money go to private schools? What would happen if citizens in one area agree to tax themselves heavily for good schools and those nearby refuse to do so, and, therefore, have noticeably poorer schools? Should tax money from affluent school districts be shared with poor school districts? You will want to monitor school funding trends and issues locally, in your state, and nationally because what happens is likely to affect your decision about teaching and, if you do teach, the conditions under which you will work.

As you read about school financing, think about three concepts that you studied earlier, which are particularly significant to financing issues: *school capital, educational accountability*, and *opportunity-to-learn standards*. Remember we defined these ideas as follows: school capital—the resources that communities need to supply to schools for them to educate their students adequately; educational accountability—being responsible for the successes and failures of schools; opportunity-to-learn standards—the expectation that school leaders and governmental officials provide to schools the resources necessary for students to have an equal opportunity to learn. Use these ideas to guide your study of this section.

Sources and Distribution of School Funds

The money used to finance public education comes from taxes levied by governments on their citizens for the purpose of providing a *public good*—schooling. All three levels of government assess taxes for this purpose. Of the amount provided in most years, on average, state and local governments each supply 40 percent or more and the federal government supplies between 5 and 10 percent. Primarily, three types of taxes are levied—property taxes, sales and other user taxes, and income taxes. Local governments rely primarily on property and sales taxes for education funds; states rely mostly on sales and income taxes, and the federal government relies on income taxes. The main dilemma that governments face in providing funds for schools involves their need to provide enough funding for education without alienating taxpayers, some of whom always believe that the taxes they pay personally are too high. Figure 9-1 shows the average per pupil expenditures in each state for the 1993–1994 school year.

State Funding

Because states have primary responsibility for schools, most states supply a major portion of the funds provided for schools. For more than half the states, that amount is more than 50 percent of the total, but in some areas local funds significantly outdistance those from the state. Figure 9-2 shows the percentage of funds from each level of government for the nation as a whole at representative years during the twentieth century. Table 9-9 shows those percentages for each state for the 1993–1994 school year.

FIGURE 9-1   Estimated per pupil expenditures for each region of the United States and each state for 1993–1994.**

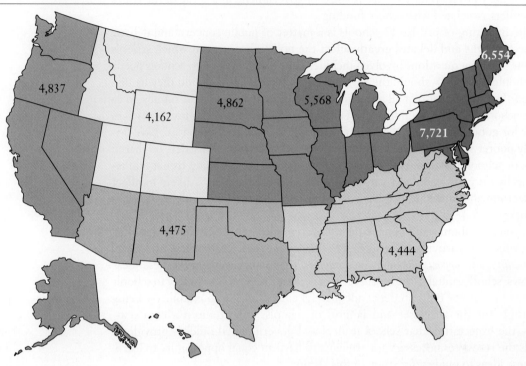

Region/State	Expenditure ($)
New England	
Connecticut	7,991
Maine	5,709
Massachusetts	6,151*
New Hampshire	5,498
Rhode Island	6,223
Vermont	6,922*
Atlantic	
Delaware	6,040
Dist. of Columbia	7,387
Maryland	6,028
New Jersey	9,429
New York	7,642
Pennsylvania	7,583
Great Lakes	
Illinois	4,940
Indiana	5,423*
Michigan	6,028*
Ohio	5,570
Wisconsin	6,260

Region/State	Expenditure ($)
Southeast	
Alabama	3,815
Arkansas	3,657
Florida	4,890
Georgia	4,174
Kentucky	4,677
Louisiana	4,371*
Mississippi	3,297*
North Carolina	4,653
South Carolina	4,242
Tennessee	3,903
Virginia	5,198
West Virginia	5,352
Plains	
Iowa	5,167
Kansas	5,189
Minnesota	5,350*
Missouri	4,187*
Nebraska	4,885*
North Dakota	4,263
South Dakota	4,430

Region/State	Expenditure ($)
Southwest	
Arizona	4,018*
New Mexico	4,469
Oklahoma	3,889
Texas	4,662
Rocky Mountains	
Colorado	4,584
Idaho	3,954*
Montana	4,727
Utah	3,203
Wyoming	5,570
Far West	
Alaska	8,501*
California	4,571
Hawaii	5,550
Nevada	4,541
Oregon	5,600
Washington	5,385

* Data estimated by National Education Association.   ** For each student enrolled.

SOURCE: National Education Association, Research Division. (1994). *1993–94 estimates of school statistics.* Washington, D.C.: National Education Association, p. 40.

FIGURE 9-2   Percentage of total school revenues provided by each level of government, 1919–1920 to 1989–1990.

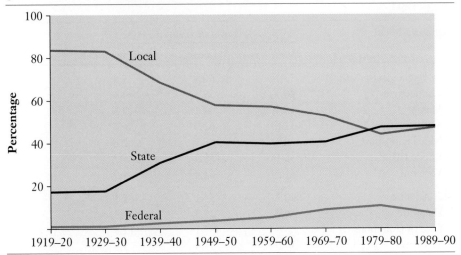

SOURCE: Snyder, T. D., & Hoffman, C. M. (1993). *Digest of educational statistics 1993.* Washington, D.C.: National Center for Education Statistics, p. 151.

The two greatest sources of state funds for schools are *sales tax* and personal and corporate *income tax.* Across all states, sales taxes produce about one-third of all revenues raised by states for all purposes, and income taxes produce almost as much.[102] In 1990, all but four states had statewide sales taxes and all but four had state income taxes.[103] In all states, a great proportion of state-generated revenues are spent on education, more than on most other specific state activities.

Sales taxes are a good source of education funds because they are broad-based and rather easy to collect; revenues increase automatically with inflation because they are calculated as a percentage of sales; the taxes are assessed on all who spend money in a state, including visitors and tourists, not just residents. The weaknesses of sales taxes are that revenues fluctuate with the economy and, therefore, these taxes produce less revenue in times of recession; and they affect poor people more than those who are affluent because poor people spend more of their income and save less. This last point is especially true if the sales tax is imposed on food and clothing.

Sales tax

State sales taxes range from 2 to 8 percent, and some states authorize local governments to add additional percentages on top of these amounts as a source of local revenues. In recent years, in order to increase the amount of revenues from sales taxes, the percentages have gradually increased from an average in 1970 of 3 percent to a level of over 5 percent in most states. During the same time some states have continuously added services to the list of things to be taxed.

State income taxes vary from state to state and, in recent years, the rate of personal income taxes has not increased as continuously as sales taxes. Patterns are more erratic and hard to generalize about because income tax levels are caught between the states' needs for more revenue and taxpayer revolts against high taxes. The situation is described in more detail later in the chapter.

State income tax

In addition to sales and income taxes, states gather revenues from other sources such as license fees—motor vehicle, corporate, housing, fishing; severance fees such as charges for mining and oil extraction; gift taxes; and lotteries. Except for lotteries,

TABLE 9-9 Estimated Percentages of Total School Revenues Provided by Each Level of Government for Each Region of the United States and Each State, 1993–1994

Region and State	Revenue from		
	State	Local	Federal
New England	33.7	60.9	5.4
Connecticut	40.1	55.3	4.6
Maine	48.3	44.1	7.6
Massachusetts	31.0*	62.9*	6.1*
New Hampshire	8.3	88.9	2.8
Rhode Island	36.5	58.3	5.2
Vermont	31.7*	63.4*	4.9*
Mid-Atlantic	40.7	54.1	5.1
Delaware	66.4	25.3	8.3
Dist. of Columbia	...	87.1	12.9
Maryland	39.0	55.4	5.6
New Jersey	42.9	53.6	3.4
New York	39.5	54.7	5.9
Pennsylvania	42.1	53.2	4.6
Southeast	52.7	38.1	9.1
Alabama	65.7	21.6	12.7
Arkansas	62.7	27.9	9.4
Florida	48.7	41.9	9.4
Georgia	47.9	44.3	7.3
Kentucky	68.3	21.7	9.9
Louisiana	55.4*	32.9*	11.7*
Mississippi	51.8*	30.5*	17.7*
North Carolina	64.3	28.2	7.5
South Carolina	47.4	43.3	9.3
Tennessee	48.6	41.8	9.6
Virginia	34.4	60.7	4.8
West Virginia	67.1	25.0	7.9
Great Lakes	37.4	56.4	6.2
Illinois	32.8	59.1	8.2
Indiana	51.2*	43.6*	5.2*
Michigan	32.1	62.2	5.7
Ohio	40.1	53.9	6.0
Wisconsin	37.1	58.3	4.6
Plains	45.7	48.4	5.9
Iowa	51.6	42.9	5.5
Kansas	49.8	44.8	5.5
Minnesota	50.6*	45.1*	4.3*
Missouri	37.4*	56.2*	6.4*
Nebraska	46.3*	47.6*	6.1*
North Dakota	42.6*	45.7*	11.8*
South Dakota	27.1*	60.9*	12.0*

(*continued*)

TABLE 9-9   (*Continued*)

Region and State		Revenue from		
	State		Local	Federal
Southwest	46.7		45.5	7.8
Arizona	42.3 *		48.9 *	8.9 *
New Mexico	75.3 *		11.9 *	12.8*
Oklahoma	63.3		29.4	7.4
Texas	43.2		49.5	7.3
Rocky Mountains	48.4		45.2	6.4
Colorado	42.8		52.3	5.0
Idaho	62.4 *		29.4 *	8.3 *
Montana	36.7		53.9	9.4 *
Utah	55.6		37.5	6.8
Wyoming	50.9		43.2	5.9
Far West	56.5		35.3	8.2
Alaska	63.6 *		23.8 *	12.6*
California	54.3		36.9	8.8
Hawaii	90.3		1.8	7.9
Nevada	36.0		59.3	4.6
Oregon	41.0		51.7	7.3
Washington	71.5		22.6	5.8

*Data estimated by National Education Association
SOURCE: National Education Association, Research Division (1994). *1993–94 estimates of school statistics*. Washington, D.C.: National Education Association. p. 38.

these other revenues are not usually earmarked for education; and state profits from lotteries typically account for no more than 2 percent of state education funds. This last point is significant because many statutes that authorize state lotteries were originally passed as efforts to fund education.

State education funds are usually provided to local school districts in the form of *state aid*, which is distributed in two ways: *general aid* and *categorical aid*. General aid is given to school districts as a single large amount, and the local district has wide latitude in determining how it is spent. Often it is provided through a *foundation program* formula, whereby the state funds are matched by a certain percentage of local taxes to provide a per-pupil amount of money that is considered to be the foundation level (minimum amount) needed to educate each child adequately. Local districts that can afford to do so usually provide additional revenues beyond the matching money from their own sources to increase funds above the foundation level. In theory, general aid funds are supposed to finance relatively equal levels of education for each student across all school districts in a state, but matters rarely, if ever, work out this way because of two circumstances: (1) The actual amount of state funds distributed to school districts each year is often well below the foundation level specified, and (2) the funding formulas usually provide the same amount of money for all students even though some students are much more expensive to educate—for example, disabled students and those in vocational education programs that require expensive equipment.

During the last few years, states have tried to modify their aid formulas to make the funds actually spent per student more equitable, but these efforts have not been

General aid

very successful because some school districts are very revenue-poor and those that have more money are reluctant to have the funds that they consider to be their share spent on children in other districts. This issue of funding equalization is what prompted the court decisions about funding already described. More explanation is also provided later.

Categorical state aid is distributed to school districts for specific purposes and programs and is earmarked as such. Examples of categories used by most states are school transportation, vocational education, special programs for disabled students, equipment, and buildings. Typically, categorical aid is provided to make up for the inadequacy and imbalance of general aid and to encourage specific endeavors that state-level influential groups advocate. Often categorical aid requires some amount of local matching money.

Categorical aid (margin note)

Local Funding

Even though local funding of schools is now superseded in most states by state funds, the local portion of school revenues is sizable. (See Table 9-9.)

Property tax (margin note)

On a nationwide basis, three-fourths of local taxes comes from *property tax;* and in some states, particularly those in New England, the percentage is over 95 percent.[104] Property taxes are annual assessments that property owners pay based on the estimated value of their property. The assessing process works as follows: (1) The *market value* (the price the property could sell for) is determined, (2) a certain percentage of that amount is calculated according to a local tax index to determine the *assessed value* of the property, and (3) a local *tax rate* is applied to the assessed value. For example, if a property that has a market value of $200,000 is in a school district with a tax index of 0.25, the assessed value of the property is $50,000 ($200,000 × 0.25 = $50,000). If the tax rate is *25 mills* (a mill is one one-thousandth of a dollar), the annual taxes owed are $1,250 ($50,000 × .025 = $1,250).

Property taxes have become one of the focuses of public controversy about school financing, and those controversies include the following circumstances: (1) Property tax increases usually require public votes and people do not like to vote themselves more taxes, (2) widespread continuing increases have led citizens to believe that they are taxed too much, (3) over recent years the proportion of property owners who have school-age children has dropped dramatically while those living on fixed incomes has risen, and (4) citizens in general have developed a widespread distrust for politicians, including those who raise taxes and fund schools. More is explained about this later in the section on funding issues of the 1990s.

Other local education funds come from a variety of sources. Some areas have local sales taxes, most have a variety of special license and permit fees, some have per capita taxes (a flat tax on each citizen), and some charge students for some services, such as those for textbooks, athletic participation, and laboratory equipment.

Federal Funding

Although the federal government has supplied small, intermittent amounts of aid to schools throughout its history, that funding was not substantial or consistently provided until the late 1950s. Even since then, the federal amount has never reached 10 percent of the total revenues spent for schools, and the amount provided usually is targeted for special purposes[105] (refer to Figure 9-2 and Table 9-9).

A primary increase in federal funding occurred since the 1950s, which can be explained in two ways: (1) The federal government actively pursued social programs, such as the Johnson administration War on Poverty, that relied on schools and required financial aid for schools in order to accomplish their goals, and (2) federal laws required school districts to undertake particular efforts such as desegregation, compensatory education, and bilingual instruction, and the government provided some of the funds to do this. The amounts of federal funds gradually increased between 1958 and 1980 and then tapered off between 1980 and the early 1990s.

It is important to remember, however, that federal funding for schools is not limited to the last forty years. As described in Chapter 8, under the Articles of Confederation, Congress provided funds for schools as early as 1785, several years before the Constitution of the United States was adopted. The federal government also supplied funds for state Land Grant colleges in the 1860s, for vocational education beginning in 1917, for a variety of education-related relief programs during the Depression years of the 1930s, and for the education of returning war veterans in the 1940s. The National Defense Education Act (1958) and the Elementary and Secondary Education Act (1965) both involved large infusions of federal money into schools in the 1950s and 1960s respectively.[106]

Until 1981, most federal money was distributed to state and local governments in the form of categorical grants—the money was designated for specific purposes. After 1981, with the Educational Consolidation and Improvement Act (1981), the Reagan administration shifted the distribution from categorical grants to *block grants*. These grants supplied states with funds with fewer earmarkings and strings attached. States had more discretion over how the money would be allocated.[107]

Block grants

Funding Issues of the 1990s

Stated simply, school funding issues revolve around two conflicting desires on the part of American citizens: (1) the desire to have good schools and (2) the desire not to pay high taxes. As a result, financing conflicts often involve disagreements about the sources of school revenues, how much money is needed, and what constitutes "good enough" schools. In the next few pages, we look at four types of current funding issues, each associated with a particular type of funding problem. Each concerns a question that political and educational policy leaders must face:

1. What should be done to finance schools in very poor school districts?
2. What should be done, if anything, about the imbalance of school funding from state to state?
3. How much taxpayer support for schools is fair to expect of citizens of a school district or a state?
4. Should tax revenues follow students to private schools?

Poor School Districts

In some areas, tax revenues are so meager and citizens' abilities (or desire) to fund schools are so low that there simply is not enough money for adequate schooling. These situations occur most frequently in large urban and very rural poverty areas, where property values are low, there is little business activity, and unemployment is high. As a result of these conditions, property taxes, sales taxes, and income taxes are all inadequate to produce enough revenue for the local schools. The court equalization cases already described are an outgrowth of these situations; and all of those cases, in essence, attempt to broaden poor school districts' tax bases to increase their funds.

Part of the problem of financing schools in poor areas can be illustrated briefly with the two situations described below. One involves an urban situation and focuses on differences in property values; the second is about a rural situation and differences in sales tax revenues.

In the Los Angeles, California, area, the same rate of property tax in Beverly Hills produces much more money per square mile than it does in the section of Los Angeles with the lowest property values; and the poorer areas invariably have more children for the public schools to educate.

In Tennessee, the state assesses a sales tax on most goods and provides for a "local option" whereby local communities can levy an additional amount of tax on sales. If the local government exercises this "local option," it keeps the additional money raised. This provides a good source of money for county school systems in which large volumes of goods are bought and sold. But it does not help rural counties with few stores and no shopping centers. In the 1980s, a new Wal-Mart store opened next to a county line in rural east Tennessee. People from both counties shopped at the store in substantial numbers. However, all the local option sales tax money collected at the store went to one county school system (in which the store was located); none went to the other. In one year's time, the taxes paid by that one store surpassed the total local taxes collected for the county schools across the line. In effect, each time citizens crossed the county line to shop, they helped finance the schools in the next county and denied that money to their own children's schools.

Because of situations like these, the amount of money provided for the education of each child varies greatly from county to county within every state.

Funding Imbalances from State to State

Just as there are imbalances in school funding from school district to school district, imbalances also occur from state to state. These imbalances, however, have not raised as much concern among the public as have those within states. But, it should be of concern to you as you consider teaching as a profession and think about where you will look for a job.

Imbalances in school funding occur from state to state because property values, the total statewide values of sales of goods, and personal incomes vary from state to state; and of course, different states tax their citizens at different rates. For example, in 1993–1994, the per pupil expenditure for education was near or above $8,000 in the highest states and below $3,500 in the lowest states (refer to Figure 9-1).

When you make comparisons, however, it is important to remember that the costs of living vary greatly from state to state as do personal incomes. It costs more to live in Alaska and Connecticut than in Utah, Mississippi, and the other states at the lower end of the list reported in Figure 9-1, and there is a comparable difference in the amount of income people earn. As you analyze these numbers, also remember that in all states, even those at the bottom of the expenditure lists, many taxpayers believe their taxes are too high, and few are ready to volunteer to pay more.

Taxpayers and School Taxes

Since the late 1970s, vocal anti-tax groups have forced governments to limit taxes and government spending in every state and many local school districts. The movement started noticeably in 1978 when California and Idaho voters passed referenda that required tax limits and continued through the 1980s as many other states enacted similar legislation. These actions resulted in decreasing property taxes nationally during the 1980s, but there have been subsequent increases in the early 1990s. They also have been a prime reason for increases in the proportion of education funds coming from state rather than local sources. You will want to monitor local tax and budget situations as you continue with your studies because what happens in various locations around the country will affect your decision if and where you seek a teaching position.

Tax Revenues and Private Schools

Related to the issues of taxes for public schools are the debates over *tuition tax credits*, educational *vouchers*, and *school choice*. Taxpayers and parents of school-age children become frustrated with both perceived high taxes and less-than-satisfactory public schools. They demand more for their money, and the parents begin to consider sending their children to nonpublic schools. Then, the parents begin to ask themselves, If I have to send my child to a private school to get the level of education that I expect, why can I not have some of my tax money follow my child to that school? Of course, responses to this type of question are multiple and contradictory. It is not possible or our intention as this point to try to supply answers, and each of the topics is touched on elsewhere in this text. However, it is important that you consider all these topics as you reflect upon school funding issues in the 1990s.

Tax credits, vouchers, and school choice

Professional Teachers and the Law

Much of the political context in which teachers work is shaped by the laws and regulations that prescribe teachers' rights and responsibilities. In addition to the statutes, court decisions, and constitutional principles already reviewed, there are a number of laws and regulations that affect teachers as professional workers. This section describes in a general way the legal context of teaching in the following areas: (1) qualifying for a teaching position, (2) contracts and tenure, (3) unions, negotiations, and strikes, (4) physical and verbal abuse, (5) academic freedom and freedom of expression, (6) negligence and liability, (7) reporting child abuse, and (8) copyright laws and computer ethics.

Qualifying for a Teaching Position

In order to be considered for a permanent teaching position in most public school systems and many private schools, teacher applicants must possess a state-issued initial teaching license or certificate. (Some states use the term *license* and others use *certificate*.) To qualify for a teaching license or certificate, a person must have completed either (1) an approved college or university teacher-education program or (2) an approved alternative route to certification. For most teachers, the path of choice is through an approved teacher-education program at a state and, possibly, a nationally, accredited college. Others, in states where they are approved, have pursued one of a number of alternative teacher-preparation paths.

Teaching license or certificate

State-approved college teacher-preparation programs are evaluated periodically by state departments and/or state boards of education according to state-developed standards. These processes usually lead to a listing of areas in which each college is approved by the state to recommend new teachers for licensure or certi-

State approval of teacher-education programs

fication. As you prepare for a possible career in teaching, it is critically important that you know which teacher licensure or certification areas your institution is authorized to offer. You will want to be sure that your studies at your institution lead to the teaching license or certificate you anticipate. Appendix C lists the addresses for the teacher certification offices in all states. (To avoid redundancy, in the paragraphs that follow, we will use the term *certificate* to mean both license and certificate.)

State reciprocity of teacher certification

To a great extent, a state-issued teaching certificate from one state can be used to obtain a certificate to teach in another state, but the process is not automatic. In some cases, teachers seeking jobs in different states from the one in which they got their initial certificate are required to take additional college courses or tests. Currently there are several national efforts at making the state-to-state transfer of teaching certificates more easily reciprocal.[108] You will want to monitor these developments in the years ahead.

National accreditation of teacher education

There is also a movement to broaden the national accrediting of college programs in teacher education through the National Council for the Accreditation of Teacher Education (NCATE).[109] As this movement progresses, more institutions that prepare teachers will become NCATE-approved, and more states will require that they do so. At some time in the near future, a significant number of states may require those seeking state teaching certificates to have completed programs of NCATE-approved colleges and universities. Many of the better-paying school systems already either require NCATE-approved training or give preference to applicants who have it. You will also want to monitor these developments in the geographic areas where you think you might want to teach.

Alternative certification

During the last two decades, alternative routes to teacher certification have been established in many states. They vary greatly and include virtually any path toward teacher certification that deviates significantly from the traditional ways in each state for qualifying for a teaching license. Some are slight modifications in coursework in teacher education institutions and others involve little or no professional study on a college campus. Some politicians and educators sing their praise as means for bypassing rigid certification procedures that they believe have hampered capable prospective teachers from entering the profession. The alternate paths tend to differ from state to state and changes are being made yearly, often in politically charged atmospheres. What will happen in the years ahead is a matter of conjecture, because politicians and state agencies are pushing in inconsistent ways. Two of the most general conflicting pushes are a demand that college teacher-education programs raise their requirements, at the same time that the standards for newer state-adopted alternative paths are nebulous and allow prospective teachers to avoid nearly all entrance criteria. Some educational observers believe that alternate routes will decline in popularity over the next decades as several projected trends continue: (1) the attraction to teaching of more bright, well-qualified prospective teachers, (2) the supply of qualified teachers catches up with the demand, (3) regular teacher-preparation programs and the state regulations under which they operate are modernized, and (4) requirements for entrance into teaching, at least in well-paying school systems, continue to rise.

Possibly the most interesting political development for you to watch in the years ahead concerning how prospective teachers qualify for teaching positions is the way in which the *opportunity to learn* idea in the Goals 2000: Educate America Act (1994) is implemented. If, as some educational leaders hope, that legislative provision means that school systems will be held more accountable for the competence of their teachers, it could cause school systems to be more cautious about whom they hire and to whom they grant tenure. The impact could be even greater if parents and guardians of students see the provision as a basis for suing school systems that do not provide students with noticeably competent teachers.

In addition to the requirement that prospective teachers be properly educated or trained, teacher-certification procedures in most states also include competency tests, which often cover basic skills, content knowledge, and professional knowledge, and character checks into applicants' backgrounds, usually for evidence of criminal behavior, child abuse, and drug use. In some cases, school systems do similar checks if they have not been done because of state regulations.

Competency tests and background checks

Some teacher applicants who have not passed these competency tests or character checks have challenged their use on constitutional grounds. Those challenges have led to two types of guidelines: (1) Competency tests and general character background checks have usually been approved for administration to all applicants, but states and school systems have been required to show that they do not discriminate unfairly; (2) specific tests such as physical tests for drug usage have been limited by some courts to situations where there is an "individualized suspicion" for using them.[110]

Contracts and Tenure

Earlier in this chapter, we looked at teacher contracts and tenure in the context of federal judicial decisions. Here we add a few general points.

The nature of teacher contracts in many school districts is determined through negotiations with the local union. In all cases, the contracts must comply with federal and state nondiscrimination laws. If contracts are broken, the aggrieved party may sue for reinstatement, restitution, and damages.

Tenure for teachers is secured by law in most states. Those laws stipulate that teachers who have taught a minimum number of years continuously (usually four) are presumed to have a continuing contract and may not be fired without appropriate cause and due process procedures. Tenure came about as an effort to replace political patronage as a basis for teachers' having jobs; to protect teachers' academic freedom; and as a result of rather persistent local practices in some school districts, whereby teachers were fired or threatened with a loss of their job for reasons unrelated to their teaching performance. Horror stories include requirements that teachers be members of a particular political party, participate in specific political campaigns, become affiliated with a specific church, shop at designated business establishments, and provide a variety of personal favors to school board members and their friends. Dismissals occurred over teaching specific content that some community members or groups did not like, personal lifestyles, and how a teacher treated or evaluated specific students.[111]

Reasons for having tenure laws

Unions, Negotiations, and Strikes

All teachers are permitted to belong to professional associations and unions, and most states have passed legislation guaranteeing unions the right to negotiate contract conditions with school boards for their members. These negotiation arrangements vary greatly from state to state, but they all contain authorizational guidelines for unions to bargain collectively or represent teachers less formally concerning contract items. Some states allow teacher strikes under rather prescribed conditions, but, because of the importance of the *public good* element of teaching, strikes by

Negotiated contracts

Since teachers' strikes are not only highly disruptive but often illegal as well, a decision to strike is a momentous one for the teachers involved.

teachers are often illegal and can always be challenged in the courts. The courts can force striking teachers back to work and assess financial damages against the individuals and the union.

Physical and Verbal Abuse

Laws concerning physical and verbal abuse affect teachers two ways: They protect teachers from abuse, and they prevent teachers from abusing others. Abuse in both directions between teachers and other adults is, for the most part, treated as any other abuse case in adult society; but abuse situations involving students are typically looked upon as special cases.

Abuse laws
are two sided

In the past, when students abused teachers, such as by physically hitting them, verbally attacking them, damaging their property, or threatening to do so, the incidents were often treated as in-school matters of school discipline. With the increase of violence in society and less close school-home contact, however, the arrest of students for abuse against teachers and other students is more commonplace. Laws nearly everywhere allow teachers to protect themselves from abuse from students, particularly physical harm, by taking defensive physical action and filing charges against abusers; but school cultures, school-based policies, and teacher preferences are as important as laws in determining whether or not students who abuse teachers are arrested. These decisions are often left to the discretion of the teacher affected, and that teacher's decision often takes into consideration the nature of the offense, the offending student's previous behavior, and the extent to which the student's future behavior can be corrected without severe punishment.

Abuse against teachers

Teacher abuse of students, whether physical, verbal, or through intimidation, is wrong, a misuse of the teacher's authority, and punishable by law. Most issues that surround teacher abuse of students focus on three questions: Did the teacher actually do what he or she is accused of doing? Is the action actually abuse? What is the appropriate level of punishment? What actually constitutes abuse is always a matter of debate and interpretation. Punishments range from slight reprimands, to firing, loss of teaching credentials, fines, jail sentences, and assessment of damages. Teach-

Teacher abuse of students

ers have been dismissed from their jobs for embarrassing and ridiculing students, speaking derogatorily about them and/or their ethnic or racial group, or for punishment that their teaching peers and superiors have declared inappropriate.

It is not possible to outline here all the guidelines that might prove valuable to you as you deal with students, but the following points might serve as a beginning: Do not physically punish a student without the prior approval of a superior and other appropriate individuals and without witnesses. Never hit or push a student out of anger. Never confront a student in a way that can be interpreted as having sexist or sexual overtones. Do take reasonable measures to prevent a student from hurting others. Do protect yourself but do not act beyond a point of self-defense. Reprimand students as you judge it appropriate to do so, but do not say anything to a student you would not repeat in front of your peers and the student's parents.

Suggested cautions

Academic Freedom and Freedom of Expression

Academic freedom and freedom of expression are particularly affected by court decisions, as explained earlier in this chapter. Here we will add only a few additional comments. Because of the nature of academic freedom and freedom of expression, laws that apply to these matters tend to be broad and generally worded. Many court decisions are decided in terms of the specific circumstances and the local situation, and most times the courts give great weight to teachers' professional judgments. Other factors typically used by courts to decide whether content is or is not appropriate are (1) the maturity and age of the students, (2) the overall relevance of the material to what is being taught, (3) the length or frequency of the passages or words being questioned, (4) whether the material is required or optional for students, and (5) the existence of school policy pertinent to the use of such materials.

Teachers' professional judgments are key

Negligence and Liability

Tort laws are the laws that govern civil suits brought by people who charge that they have been harmed by someone else. In those suits, the person bringing the charges sues for damages. Teachers may be the target of such suits. They may be charged when someone, usually a student, is harmed because of their negligence or intentional action. When such complaints are brought, the teacher, the school administrators who oversee that teacher, and the school board are usually all made a party to the suit.

Civil suits

In suits under tort law, several key ideas usually apply: reasonableness, standard of care, statutory responsibility, proximate cause, foreseeability, and tangible loss or damage. In most tort situations, the courts hearing the cases ask, Is it *reasonable* to find the teacher liable for the harm in this case? In trying to answer this question, the courts typically consider several subsidiary points—What is the legal *standard of care*, or standard of performance, that is expected of the teacher in this situation? Is the teacher *statutorily responsible;* that is, responsible according to the law? Is there a relationship, *proximate cause*, between what the teacher did or neglected to do and the harm that resulted? Should the teacher have *foreseen* the potential danger? What is the negative effect, *tangible loss or damage*, or extent of the harm?

Principle of "reasonableness"

For many years, teachers and schools were judged in most tort cases primarily in terms of the reasonableness of their actions. The main points considered were, Was the teacher reasonable and prudent? Lately, however, in an American society that seems to encourage civil suits at the drop of a hat, negligence suits accuse teachers of being liable for actions that are their fault in only a minor way, if at all.

Increase in negligence suits

For example, a child slips on a wet floor that the teacher does not know is wet, or students are injured in an automobile accident after sneaking out of school for lunch contrary to school policy and the teacher's specific orders.

What should teachers do in this climate? Our advice is straightforward and rather simple. Be very careful, prudent, and cautious; and take out liability insurance just as other professionals do. Nearly all school systems carry liability policies that cover themselves and their teachers, and both national teacher unions—N.E.A. and A.F.T.—have liability insurance as membership services.

Educational malpractice

Educational malpractice suits are a special type of educational civil suit that have begun to surface rather frequently in the news. They are cases in which whole school systems have been sued because individual students did not learn as expected. For example, a student sued a school system because he was never taught to read beyond a minimal level although he passed each grade and graduated from high school. So far, none has led to a judgment against a school system because no court has found all the questions raised above answered in a way that brought about a judgment of liability against the educators involved. But some malpractice verdicts that find schools and teachers liable are likely in the future. Their implications, especially for individual teachers, remain to be determined.[112]

Reporting Child Abuse

As cases of child abuse—physical, sexual, and psychological—have increased in number, teachers have become agents of detecting and reporting child abuse crimes. This is only natural. Teachers see children each day and can be taught to recognize the signs of abuse, even when those signs are subtle. But the situation is also troublesome for teachers because of the conflicting pressures it places upon them. Teachers must report suspected child abuse for the good of the child and because of state law; but erroneously reported instances cause grief and hardship for all. Our advice on this point is, Proceed cautiously, report your suspicion without making accusations, and remember it is less serious to err in an effort to protect a child than to err by not acting.[113]

Copyright Laws and Computer Ethics

The development of photocopying, audio and video recording, electronic transmission of printed and video materials, and the exploding uses of computers and computer software in many directions all have created new opportunities for teachers to bring into their classrooms materials that earlier generations of teachers only dreamed about. But all these opportunities have also raised questions about what is fair, legal, and ethical teacher use of the creative work of others. Today, the 1976 revision of United States copyright laws and the use of less formal *fair use* guidelines—for example, the use of an author's idea but not his or her exact expression of it and use for nonprofit educational purposes that do not affect the item's potential sales—serve as guides for teachers. Probably the best specific guide at the present time can be found in the four criteria that the 1976 copyright law lists for courts to consider in cases involving fair use:[114]

1. The purpose and character of the use, including whether such use is of a commercial nature or is for nonprofit educational purposes
2. The nature of the copyrighted work
3. The amount and substantiality of the portion used in relation to the copyrighted work as a whole

4. The effect of the use upon the potential market for or value of the copyrighted work

But these principles are rapidly becoming dated and are frequently disregarded.

Because this is an introductory text, it is not the place for us to try to be prescriptive about the do's and don'ts of legal and fair use at this stage in your teacher preparation. However, we do want to admonish you in three ways: (1) Be sure you use others' work legally and ethically, (2) always cite the original author, and (3) be prepared for continuing updates as to what legal experts designate as both legal and fair.

Political Pressures and Influences on Teaching and Schools

Because of the importance that citizens place on the work of teachers and schools, those citizens, as individuals and as interest groups, want to influence what teachers and schools do. This is to be expected in America's open political system, and, for the most part, education leaders listen to those with influence and try to be accommodating when they can. Problems arise, however, when those who exert pressure push in directions that others believe is not in the common interest, when different groups have conflicting agendas, and when a group's power is too strong.

In this section we survey briefly some of the sources and directions of political influence over schools in terms of (1) types of groups that actively exercise influence, (2) what they seek to accomplish, and (3) their apparent motives. In addition to the government leaders and school officials discussed earlier in this chapter, four other types of groups significantly influence what schools do: (1) professional educator groups, (2) business interest groups, (3) other specific interest groups, and (4) groups that use school politics for other political motives.

Professional Educator Influences

The most dominant professional educator groups that influence schools are the two national teacher unions—National Education Association and American Federation of Teachers—which together encompass a membership of about three million. They seek a combination of improved benefits for their own members—better salaries, working conditions, and teacher control of school decisions—and improved education for the students they serve. As is described elsewhere in this text, they are organized and use their power at all levels of government.

Unions

Both unions have been very visible at the national level, including in national elections and in the national education reform movements since the 1980s. At times they have been criticized by politicians as obstructing efforts to improve schools, but they have actually been more active in pushing for reform than slowing it.

Nearly all recent assessments of teacher union power describe an increasing influence over both national and state policy and over day-to-day operations of schools.[115] If school site-based management becomes commonplace, it is safe to predict that teachers, acting through their unions, will continue to have more power over schools and the education profession as a whole than ever before. In addition to influence over schools, a primary goal of teacher unions is to control professional teacher education in a way comparable to the way medical doctors control their profession.

Other professional groups

There are many other professional education groups that exert political influence besides the two national unions, some of which are listed in the last chapter of this book. Most are organized for other primary purposes, and attempts to influence decisions are secondary reasons for operating. A number of these groups are organized around the type of jobs their members perform—principals, curriculum supervisors, superintendents, school board members, and so on. Some coalesce around subject-matter specialties (science, mathematics, English, social studies), and some around specific causes (gender-related issues, environmental education, global perspectives, religious studies). Each of these groups seeks improved instruction in its area of interest.

During the last few years of school reform, several of these groups, particularly those with content focuses, have become very powerful in setting curriculum standards and in establishing criteria for admitting teachers into the profession. They have been fashioning curriculum content outlines and competencies for teachers that are being used as the bases for developing national assessments for students and teachers.[116] The standards of the National Council of Teachers of Mathematics are best known at the present time. As these groups continue their standard-setting efforts, their influence will expand well beyond any power position they have held in the past. Those influences will have direct impacts upon you in the form of tests that you and your students will be required to take.

Advocates for national certification

Possibly the most intriguing national development among professional educator interest groups is an effort by the National Council for the Accreditation of Teacher Education, the National Board of Professional Teaching Standards, the Council of Chief State School Officers, the two national unions, and a number of other organizations to devise a national plan for licensing and certifying teachers and for accrediting colleges and universities that prepare teachers.[117] If this effort succeeds, professional educators, through these organizations, will probably control who becomes a teacher, where teachers are prepared, and how they are prepared to an extent parallel to that of the medical profession.

Business Influences

Business leaders have always had disproportionately powerful influences over schools at all levels when they are compared with other non-educator professional groups. Their influences tend to be personified in the form of local school board members and vocal "movers and shakers" on local school issues, and in groups of individuals who have noticeable power over state and national education policy. Their power likely comes from two sources: (1) because they are usually visible to their customers and typically considered to be successful because of their position, they are looked to for advice in many areas, including education and (2) as business leaders, they have a direct interest in how schools spend tax money and how well they educate potential employees and consumers.

Economic interests and educational reform

Business power has become even more noticeable than ever before in education matters since the education reform movement of the 1980s. In fact, the primary "sounding of an alarm" of *A Nation at Risk* was couched in the economic terms of how well the United States can compete with other nations. Areas in which the influence of business interests continue to be felt in very observable ways are (1) the ways in which schools are administered, (2) the push for better teaching of basic skills and vocational education, (3) the adoption of school-to-work plans, (4) local tax questions, and (5) the teaching of private enterprise ideology.

Special Interest Influences

Special interest groups that influence schools come in all types and sizes. Some are large, well-financed political action arms of nationwide public and private activist groups, while others are much smaller; some have very general agenda (school reform, better care for children, lower taxes); others are more focused (advocates for more multicultural education, access for disabled students, less secular humanism in the curriculum). To illustrate the effects of such groups on teaching and schools we will describe a selection of groups that represent a range of political perspectives.

One category of especially important special interest groups consists of those that advocate particular cultural, racial, ethnic, and religious perspectives in society. For the most part, their goals are similar, but their specific focuses differ. They want a good education for the students who represent their group; they want their cultural perspective taught; and they want the rights and sensitivities of their children protected.

African American, Hispanic, and Native American organizations are among the most visible of this type of group, as are those of the religious right and advocates for disabled persons. Legislation at federal, state, and local levels for the last two decades is replete with examples of the results of their efforts. They have insisted on laws and regulations that assure fair educational treatment of their children and specify that certain curriculum content is covered—black history, for example. They have also opposed curriculum perspectives that counter their beliefs, such as the heavy emphasis on English traditions in American history.[118] Although most education communities try to accommodate varying culture-based pressures, when strong groups of this type are offended, they can marshall political offensives that can be fierce. Successful politicians rarely confront them directly.

Racial, ethnic, and religious groups

Another type of special interest group is the type that focuses primarily on the costs of schools. More of these tend to oppose taxes in general or the specific allocation of tax money than advocate for increasing funds for schools, but groups exist on both sides of arguments over spending. In many cases, tax referenda are passed or defeated directly because of their activity.[119] The education press, in fact, contains pages of stories about these activities each year. You will want to monitor those reports in your area.

Pro- and anti-tax groups

A third type of special interest group that influences schools consists of the groups that advocate better lives for children and society as a whole and see good schools as an important means to that end. Many such groups have been very active since the 1960s years of the War on Poverty. Examples today are the Children's Defense Fund and several promoters of Head Start and other early education programs. The results of their influence include the continued governmental funding of early education and Title I programs.

Advocates for children

Ideology-based special interest groups are a fourth type. Examples of these are the Heritage Foundation, Eagle Forum, and the Moral Majority—all of which push conservative causes—and the National Organization of Women, People for the American Way, and National Association for the Advancement of Colored People—which are liberal advocates. These groups have argued on both sides of issues such as prayer in school, tax support for private schools, and school choice legislation.[120]

Conservative and liberal causes

A fifth type of special interest group consists of the single-issue promoters who want schools to teach a certain perspective. Groups of this type coalesce around many issues, such as environmental education, private enterprise econ-

R E F L E C T I N G   O N   P R A C T I C E

This Reflecting on Practice section describes an interesting use of data by those with an influence on public opinion who wanted to push a particular point about problems in schools. It is based on a study by Barry O'Neill, which appeared in the *New York Times Magazine*, March 6, 1994. As you read consider

- How important is it that the two lists were more folklore than scientific data?
- Do you consider the people who used the data dishonest and misleading, or were they just misled themselves?
- What are the implications of this story for the idea that schools function in a political context?

In a story titled "History of a Hoax," Barry O'Neill described two lists that appeared on a bulletin board at Yale University. The lists compared top disciplinary problems in public schools in the 1940s with those of the 1980s. The two lists follow:

1940	1980
1. talking	1. drug use
2. chewing gum	2. alcohol abuse
3. making noise	3. pregnancy
4. running in the halls	4. suicide
5. getting out of turn in line	5. rape
6. wearing improper clothing	6. robbery
7. not putting paper in wastebaskets	7. assault

The lists were not unique to Yale University. As O'Neill's investigation found, they appeared, sometimes in slightly modified form, in speeches, interviews, and nationally syndicated columns by very prominent politicians and opinion leaders. Those who used them include conservative commentator Rush Limbaugh; former Secretary of Education William Bennett; columnists Anna Quindlen, Herb Caen, Carl Rowan, and George Will; former Harvard president Derek Bok; former New York City school chief Joseph Fernandez; conservative cause activist Phyllis Schlafly; former California governor George Deukmaijan; Senator John Glenn; CBS News; *Time* magazine; *The Wall Street Journal*; and many more. They presented the lists as fact, although most did say that they were quoting someone else.

O'Neill wondered why people as prominent as these individuals would use the lists without firmer evidence that they were accurate, especially when he realized that several of the points did not seem right. For example, the 1980s list did not match National Center for Education Statistics data or the Phi Delta Kappa/Gallup Poll data for the 1980s, and some points did even not sound right. Was rape really a major school *disciplinary* problem? Was suicide a school *disciplinary* problem by definition?

Through extensive investigation, O'Neill found that one of the originators of the lists was T. Cullen Davis of Forth Worth, Texas, who used them in fundamentalist Christian attacks on public schools and passed them on to his sympathizers. He said he developed the 1940s list from his recollection of his own schooling and the 1980s list from reading the newspapers. He clearly admitted that they had no scientific base.

Interestingly enough, O'Neill found striking similarity between the Davis (and Yale) 1980s list and responses to a questionnaire of school principals by the National Center for Education Statistics in the mid-1970s. As O'Neill points out, however, contrary to the way most users interpreted the information, that questionnaire was a survey of principals' *opinions* and did not provide actual data about school discipline problems. He also notes that the survey was conducted in the 1970s, not the 1980s; the principals were asked to report on *crimes* in their schools, not *disciplinary problems;* and the order in which the items were initially reported was by nature of crime, not the frequency with which each was mentioned.

In all, O'Neill found almost 250 versions of the lists. At various times they were labeled "disciplinary problems," "offenses," "top problems," and "worries." No one seemed to question calling suicide a school discipline problem. Somehow, through many translations, the recollections of T. Cullen Davis and survey responses of principals about crime in the schools in the 1970s became quotable facts about school discipline problems of the 1980s.

O'Neill raises a question you might want to consider as you reflect upon the political context of teaching and schools: Why have Americans found lists such as these so attractive? You might also ask, Why do opinion makers use lists such as these when more accurate data can be obtained? You might also want to consider how you would respond as a teacher if parents or other people in the community quoted "facts" about school problems in discussions with you.

omics, women's studies, global perspectives, and the teaching of individual foreign languages.

Special interest groups influence teachers and schools in many ways. Sometimes their message is sent via subtle persuasive mail campaigns to teachers and school officials, sometimes it is general and sent through the public media, and sometimes it is presented directly through political referenda and elections. Whatever form the pressure takes, it affects what teachers teach, how schools function, and what students learn.

The Use of School Politics for Political Gain

A fourth type of political influence on teaching and schools involves groups and individuals who use school causes and school elections for ulterior motives, usually to get elected or push a cause not directly tied to schools. Examples of causes used in this way recently are (1) anti-tax campaigns, (2) criticisms of specific school policies, such as condom distribution, school prayer, funds for religious schools, and charges of secular humanism in the curriculum, and (3) attacks on specific school leaders. These groups and individuals are different from those mentioned earlier, not in what they advocate, but in why they take such positions. They do so to gain political power rather than to advance the political causes that they say are their focus.

Use of school politics for political gain

The use of school issues in these ways typically occurs at the local level but it can affect state and even national politics as well. There are political and educational observers who charge that the Reagan and Bush administrations' advocacy of private schooling, school vouchers, school prayer, and morally conservative positions on a number of curricular issues were more political efforts to win votes than efforts based on the substance of each the issues. Other observers suggest that the Clinton administration's support for women's issues is similarly motivated. There is little reason to think that future office holders and aspirants to political office will refrain from using educational issues for their own purposes.

The Political Context in Schools

In addition to the political contexts that surround schools, teachers also feel political pressures and influences from within the school building and school system where they teach. Much of this is alluded to in Chapter 4 where the nature of schools as cultures is explained, but additional explanation that emphasizes the political aspects of that culture is provided here.

Differences in power levels

As with any organization, schools and school systems have people and groups of people who possess different amounts of power, levels of authority, and degrees of responsibility. Therefore, some individuals tell others what to do more often than they are told what to do; and, obviously, others are at the other end of the who-tells-whom continuum. For example, teachers have more power over students than students have over teachers. Building administrators have more authority over custodians than vice versa; superintendents and union leaders have more responsibility than do the people they were chosen to lead.

Official power

Some individuals have power and responsibility because authority over others is assigned to their position officially, legally, and organizationally. For instance, certain administrative individuals hire, supervise, advise, reprimand, and fire others. Teachers have formal authority to demand a whole host of things of students, and some teachers, such as department chairpersons and lead teachers, can require some compliance on the part of other teachers.

Ideology and personal style

Ideology and personal style are also strong determiners of both status and power. Some administrators and the teachers who work *under* them simply believe each has a role that dictates who should do what and how things should be done. Some of these delineate that the administrator is *in charge* and that the roles should not be mixed or confused. Others believe in less formal relationships and act accordingly. They are more interested in getting the job done than in who does it. They call each other by first names, are friends more than employers and employees, and see each other as team members. Possibly the clearest way to illustrate these two perspectives is to mention that some administrators and teachers "pal around" socially and others always act as employers and employees, even in social settings.

Informal power

Other person-to-person power is informal: the principal needs an extra teacher sponsor at an athletic event, a colleague needs her last period "covered" because a club trip is leaving early, a teacher needs a custodian's help with a minor repair. Many of these informal requests seem on the surface to be simple requests for "favors," but often there is more to the request than that. Frequently, the person asking for the "favor" has more power than the person who is asked and that power relationship relates directly to each individual's expected role. For example, a teacher would not normally ask the principal to cover a class when a teacher colleague is available or ask a colleague to deliver a note to the office if a student is available. Apart from formal status in the organization, a person's power over another may derive from such factors as seniority, age, status in the union, personality, and who "owes" whom.

Informal players

Informal power also explains why some people are more influential than their status or place on the organizational chart would indicate. Secretaries, custodians, activist parents, and even very personable students can be key players in the politics of the school environment.

Power among students

Students can play important power roles in at least two ways: (1) in their relationships with teachers and school officials and (2) among other students. Every class of students has its leaders, and teachers who are in tune know that power structure and use it. Two personal examples that we witnessed in our teaching careers serve to illustrate the point.

Some years ago, one of our student teachers was not able to get her high school history students to complete homework assignments necessary to present individual reports to the class as she had scheduled. When not a single student was prepared for the first day of reports, she became visibly upset and somewhat tearfully tried to dramatize the importance of the assignment. At that point, a star football player, actually nicknamed Bruiser, stood up in class and announced to everyone that they would be prepared for their reports beginning the next morning or they would answer to him. After that, every report was ready on time, except for that of one single-parent mother in the class who asked and received permission from Bruiser (who consulted with the teacher) for a one-day delay because her child was sick.

In another situation a high school principal suspended an exceptionally popular senior class honor student and cheerleader for a minor dress code violation that had rarely been enforced. The student's classmates became so enraged they walked out of school the next day, an event that became the top local news story of the day. Things did not settle down for weeks and, in the process, the principal lost much status with students and among members of the community.

The internal political pressures of a school that we have described often have direct ties to the power and influences of the broader community. Some parents of students and their friends are also political, business, and social leaders and influential activists in the community, as are teachers, their spouses, friends, and associates. As we said at the start of this chapter, political influences in the community at large permeate school walls.

What does all this mean to you as a potential teacher? It means that as a teacher you will be part of the political milieu of the school, and at least some of your success will depend on your understanding and influencing that political context. Although every setting is different, every school and school system and every community has its power configurations and power relationships. You will want to be able to size up the political milieu of the school where you teach. Developing a knowledge of what to look for is the place to start.

EDUCATIONAL RESEARCH

School Funding and School Outcomes

*T*his Educational Research section illustrates the interplay between research data and educational policy and, at the same time, points out that it is not always clear what research data actually mean. It relates a current debate concerning the question, Does increased funding for schools, particularly funding calculated in the form of per pupil expenditures, lead to improved school outcomes? In other words, when per capita expenditures increase, do students learn more?

For many years, conservative critics of public schools have argued against increasing funds for schools by saying that more spending will not mean students will learn more. Often they have pointed to research engaged in for more than a decade by University of Rochester professor Eric Hanushek, who conducted meta-analyses (analyses of other research studies) about the relationships between the input of school resources and student outcomes. After studying more than thirty research efforts that date back to the 1960s, Hanushek concluded that no systematic relationship exists between the amount of resources provided for schools and school outcomes.[121] However, Larry Hedges, Richard Laine, and Rob Greenwald, three researchers at the University of Chicago, reanalyzed the same data that Hanushek studied, using a different set of research assumptions. They reported in 1994 that they believe that Hanushek's data "support exactly the opposite conclusions and demonstrate that expenditures are positively related to school outcomes."[122]

Who is right? And what does the debate mean for arguments for and against increased resources for schools? In the following paragraphs, we describe the two studies and their conclusions. See what you think.

In articles written between 1981 and 1991, Hanushek reported on his analyses of many articles, books, and studies that investigated possible ties between certain types of school resources or inputs and school outcomes.[123] He identified seven types of resources that were frequently studied and clustered the studies into groups based on the seven types: (1) teacher-student ratios, (2) teacher education, (3) teacher experience, (4) teacher salary, (5) per pupil expenditures, (6) administrative inputs, and (7) facilities. His primary question was, When results of all these thirty-plus studies are synthesized, are there positive relationships between each of these seven types of resources and school outcomes? For example, do higher per pupil expenditures correlate positively with higher student achievement?

In his synthesis, Hanushek recorded each time a relationship was reported between one of these seven inputs and school outcomes in every one of the studies he analyzed. Then, he compared the number of times a statistically significant positive relationship was found with the times there was either no statistically significant result or the relationship was negative.

Hanushek found that, when all the elements of all the studies were clustered into his seven groups, there were never more positive relationships than the combined total of nonrelationships and negative relationships. For example, he found 65 incidents across the thirty-plus studies when per pupil expenditures were compared with school outcomes. Of these 65, only 13 reported positive correlations (more money spent correlated with better school outcomes). This meant that increased per pupil expenditures correlated positively with improved school outcomes in only 20 percent of the cases, and it did not correlate positively 80 percent of the time. (Notice that this 80 percent represents all *nonpositive* results, *not negative* results. There were many results that were not significant either way.)

Among the other six comparisons, the highest positive correlation that Hanushek found was 29 percent for teacher experience (40 of 140 studies), and the lowest was 7 percent for teacher education (8 of 113 studies). Because of these low percentages of positive correlations, Hanushek concluded that "there is no strong systematic relationship between school expenditures and student performance."[124]

Hedges, Laine, and Greenwald synthesized the same studies and used the same data as Hanushek, but conducted a different type of analysis. Instead of comparing the number of statistically significant positive results against all others, they compared them against the number of positive results that would have appeared simply by chance (that is, if there were no relationship between the two items being studied). The reason they made this kind of comparison rests on two basic assumptions about statistics. First, if two things that have absolutely no relationship with each other are compared a sufficient number of times, the lack of relationship will be reflected most of the time, but not every single time; sometimes a correlation will appear because of chance or coincidence. Second, in correlation studies in general, when chance is the only factor, about 95 percent of the time no correlation will show up, but through chance alone correlation will show up in the remaining 5 percent and that 5 percent will be divided evenly between positive and negative correlations 2.5 percent each way.

Applying these ideas to the data of Hanushek's study, Hedges, Laine, and Greenwald concluded that there is reason to believe that higher per pupil expenditures and more teacher experience do lead to better school outcomes in the form of student achievement. Some of the other types of input also seem to have positive effects. Acknowledging that money must be spent wisely, they argue that "money does matter after all."[125]

Our point here is not to settle the issue about money and learning, but simply to warn you against drawing conclusions from partial or disputed evidence. As you monitor the debate about more money and improved student learning, remember even researchers still disagree, not only about their conclusions, but also about how to study the issue and interpret the data.

Conclusion

As is the case with all professionals, teachers work in environments that are permeated with political pressures and influences. Some of those powers are set by the Constitution, by law and regulation, and because of funding authority; but other aspects of power relationships are more flexible and specific to certain situations. In all these environments, governmental authorities, individuals, and groups of individuals who have power use that power to accomplish their goals.

For the most part, those goals are honorable and tied to what the people exercising the power believe the school and school system should accomplish. But rarely do all interested parties agree upon what a school should accomplish or how it should accomplish it. When there are disagreements, the agency and people with the most power usually get their way. Often some get their way even when their motives are self-serving or what they want is clearly contrary to the best interests of students and teachers.

Successful teachers usually are very much in tune with the political contexts of the school and school system in which they teach. They know what the Constitution, laws, regulations, and judges say. They know who has power, what the power-holding people typically push for and against, how they use their influence, and how they can be dissuaded or successfully opposed when they are wrong. Successful teachers also coalesce their own political power, as individuals and as they form groups with other individuals, particularly in their professional associations and unions. Then they use this power to accomplish what they think is best for their students and themselves.

Understanding political power

As the idea of site-based management of schools develops further in the years ahead, school-based teacher groups and individual faculty members in individual schools will gain unprecedented power. People entering the profession will need to know how to use that power.

Summary

Teachers and schools are influenced by and feel pressures from the political context in which they operate. That context revolves around the concept of power. In essence, those with power over schools authorize, control, and influence what schools and teachers do; and teachers and schools use whatever power they can muster to educate students.

Power over teaching and schools is exerted in a number of ways. Governments at local, state, and national levels have constitutional, legislative, regulatory, judicial, and financial means that they use to require teachers and schools to do certain things and to avoid others. Courts exercise particularly strong power over schools and teachers because, under the Constitution of the United States, they determine many responsibilities that schools must shoulder and the student and societal freedoms and rights that they may not intrude upon.

States have the most legal authority over schools; but state, local, and federal governments have overlapping responsibility for schools, and all three levels of government provide tax-supported funding for pre-K–12 public schools. All three levels also have regulatory authority over private schools. That governmental authority over schools is derived from the belief by American citizens that pre-K–12 education is so important that it must be secured and guided by official government actions.

Influence over teaching and schools is also exercised by groups and individuals outside of government, although they often use governmental channels to make their influence felt. Those with noticeable power include high-status local citizens, business leaders and groups at all levels, professional education associations and unions, student advocacy groups, special interest pressure groups, and many more.

Teachers also work within a political context inside their school and school system, a context in which there are individuals and positions that possess differential amounts of power. Those with more power and authority are able to influence those with less power; in most cases, in fact, they are expected to do so as a function of their job.

Study Questions

1. Make a list of issues that require some type of decision about what teachers and schools should and should not do. For example, What should be covered in sixth grade mathematics? How long should the school year be? Should school open with a morning prayer? Then divide the list into three categories with the following headings: Should be decided by teachers and school officials, Should be decided by governmental officials outside the school system, Should be decided jointly. Explain your categorizing decisions.

2. If you were a federal judge, which type of restrictions would you agree could be placed on teacher behavior (in and outside of school) as long as a person has a teaching job? Which types of restrictions would you disallow? Justify your decisions.

3. Suppose you are a school principal and one of your teachers subtly is doing one of the following. What would you do? Why?
   — Advocates the support of one political party and unfairly slants negative information about the other party in his or her high school lessons
   — Openly says his personal religion is better than others and suggests that his or her high school students should convert
   — Frequently says that one racial group in America is better than others and is condescending toward students from other races
   — Is openly biased against one gender and seems to pick on students of that gender

4. What would you do if you taught a child of a school board member and that board member pressured you to give the student a higher grade than he or she deserved? Are there some conditions under which you would do so and others when you would not? If so, what makes the difference?

Key Terms

Academic freedom	Alternative certification	Categorical aid
Accreditation of teacher education	Authority	Child benefit theory
	Block grants	Compulsory schooling

Computer ethics
Constitutional authority
Copyright laws
Corporal punishment
Correlation
Creation science
Dominated
   communities
Educational malpractice
Establishment of
   religion
Fair use guidelines
Financial authority
Freedom of expression
Foundation program
   formula
Fractionated
   communities
Fragmented type of
   state policymaking

General aid
Inert communities
Judicial authority
Judicial review
Legislative authority
Lemon test
Local disparate type of
   state policymaking
Loyalty oath
Monolithic type of state
   policymaking
Non-native-English
   speakers
Pluralistic communities
Power of the purse
Property right
Reasonableness test
Regulatory authority
Released time for
   religious education

School capital
School district
   decentralization
School financing
   equalization
Separation of church
   and state
Separation of powers
Site-based management
Syndical type of state
   policymaking
Teachers' private
   behavior
Teaching certificate
Teaching license
Tenure
Tort laws

For Further Reading

Data Research. (1993). *U.S. Supreme Court education cases* (3rd ed.). Rosemount, MN: Data Research.

Data Research. (1994). *1994 deskbook encyclopedia of American school law.* Rosemount, MN: Data Research.

Fischer, L., Schimmel, D., & Kelly, C. (1991). *Teachers and the law* (3rd ed.). New York: Longman.

Mills, C. D. (1993). Important education-related U.S. supreme court decisions (1943 to 1993). In G. Cawelti (ed.), *Challenges and achievements of American education; 1993 yearbook of the Association for Supervision and Curriculum Development.* (pp. 187–192). Alexandria, VA: Association for Supervision and Curriculum Development.

Odden, A. R. (Ed.). (1992). *Rethinking school finance: An agenda for the 1990's.* San Francisco: Jossey-Bass.

Rossow, L. F., & Hininger, J. A. (1991). *Students and the law.* Bloomington, IN: Phi Delta Kappa.

Spring, J. (1991). *American education: An introduction to social and political aspects.* (5th ed.). New York: Longman.

Spring, J. (1993). *Conflicts of interests: The politics of American education* (2nd ed.). New York: Longman.

Swanson, A. D., & King, R. A. (1991). *School finance: Its economics and politics.* New York: Longman.

Zirkel, P. A., & Richardson, S. N. (1988). *A digest of Supreme Court decisions affecting education* (2nd ed.). Bloomington, IN: Phi Delta Kappa.

The Philosophical Context
Beliefs That Guide Teaching

CONTRIBUTING AUTHOR
Douglas J. Simpson

Douglas J. Simpson is the primary author of this chapter. Charles and Lynn Myers provided the Educational Research section.

P eople generally recognize that a person's philosophy of life directly and indirectly affects individual decisions, activities, and values and results in a particular lifestyle. Likewise, a teacher's philosophy of life and lifestyle influences his or her educational philosophy and style of teaching. For instance, if people value fairness, they will not only honestly evaluate political candidates but will also honestly judge the performance of students and fairly evaluate disputes between professionals. Consequently, what people believe to be true, real, and valuable will affect the way they teach, how they interpret issues, and what they emphasize in class.

This chapter, therefore, seeks to illustrate as well as explain how teachers with various philosophical beliefs may teach; at the same time it seeks to demonstrate that stereotypical thinking about the proponents of different philosophies should be avoided. The chapter covers two main topics. The first section—"Philosophical Beliefs and Teaching"—describes philosophy of education as a set of intellectual activities and shows how philosophy is relevant to teaching. The other major division of the chapter—"Systematic Views of Education"—describes particular philosophies of education as intellectual beliefs that affect the ways in which teachers teach.

The chapter Snapshot and the Reflecting on Practice sections are designed to illustrate practical aspects of educational philosophies. They demonstrate how the beliefs of teachers affect everyday life in the classroom, and they provide examples of the important questions that educational philosophies address. The Educational Research section describes one aspect of research in philosophy of education.

SNAPSHOT

T he Snapshot for this chapter describes the teaching styles of three teachers who differ in their personal and educational philosophies.[1] As you read it, consider the following:

■ How are the teaching styles similar? How are they different?
■ In what ways might the different styles reflect philosophical differences of the teachers? Are some of the differences possibly the result of personality, rather than philosophical differences?
■ What strengths and weaknesses do you see in each style?

■ How do the teaching styles compare with your own views of teaching?
■ Why do you want to teach? How will your reasons for wanting to teach affect your teaching?

A Science Teacher

Ms. Aycock teaches science in a private, coeducational boarding school in the Northeast. Unlike most of her colleagues, she is tolerated more than she is appreciated by the school administration and board. The reasons for the lack of appreciation are not immediately obvious. Her students do extremely well on standardized achievement tests, enjoy her classes immensely, and are awarded more university scholarships in scientific fields than are students at similar schools. In addition, her headmaster and colleagues describe her as a competent teacher, well-educated person, and likable individual, even if a gadfly in meetings.

Upon talking with students and faculty at the school, a visitor soon learns that Ms. Aycock's credentials, pedagogical methods, and coverage of content are not in question. Instead, it is her *questions* that are questioned. For example, she has on various occasions asked her colleagues such questions as the following: (1) Is the government's list of priorities for scientific research a form of mind control? (2) Why do we have so few female and minority students and children of teachers at this academy? (3) Shouldn't the faculty and students have more input into institutional policies, decisions, and practices? (4) When are we going to begin preparing our students to think and act morally? (5) Why don't we purge our library of sexist and racist literature?

In her classes, Ms. Aycock also asks many unsettling questions, such as: Is it moral for companies to build nuclear power plants and jeopardize the lives of present and future citizens? Does it make sense for the government to allow millions of people to live along the San Andreas fault when disaster is inevitable? Should billions of dollars be spent on space exploration when millions, perhaps billions, of people in the world are poorly nourished, clothed, and educated? Is government controlled by the rich and powerful or simply by leaders who are morally insensitive to the consequences of acid rain, fly ash, and industrial waste? Why does the government allow the ruling class to exploit the masses by monopolizing natural resources, land holdings, and economic growth?

A brief visit to one of Ms. Aycock's classes illustrates her professional orientation, practice, and concerns. She begins the class by saying, "Yesterday our field trip gave us a firsthand view of some consequences of acid rain that are mentioned in the textbook. Among other things, we saw the erosion of invaluable statues and historic buildings. The absence of vegetation and fish at the dead lake may still be fresh in your minds, too.

"Today I've invited Mr. Evergreen, an environmentalist, Ms. Cupidity, an industrialist, and Ms. Coddleston, a legislative aide, to discuss issues surrounding acid

rain. After all three have spoken, you'll have an opportunity to raise questions. Tomorrow we'll break into buzz groups to discuss ways of dealing with acid rain in the various kinds of environments it affects—the ecology, the economy, government, and so on. Keep in mind the distinctions and the connections between scientific, ethical, and political matters."

Ms. Aycock's friends and detractors sometimes describe her as an iconoclast, a social reconstructionist, a Socratic questioner, a neo-Marxist, a critical theorist, a socialist, and a communist. She usually responds, "It's obvious that you cannot recognize a Presbyterian with a social conscience when you see one."

A Social Studies Teacher

Mr. Reinhold's classes think he is an exciting and stimulating history teacher. They do not, however, always sit on the edges of their chairs, especially when he asks them to learn lists like this:

> 1001 Eriksson visits North America
> 1271 Polo travels to China
> 1487 Dias rounds the Cape of Good Hope
> 1492 Columbus travels to the Americas
> 1497 Cabot reaches North America
> 1513 Balboa sees the Pacific Ocean
> 1519 Magellan starts trip around the world

He says he uses such lists to give students an overview of a period, to provide a skeleton for a cognitive framework to be developed at a later time, and to introduce students to key explorers, dates, and places.

Mr. Reinhold's major goal is to develop the rational powers of his students. He is noted for being exceptionally flexible in the way he pursues his goals. That is, he uses museums, films, libraries, lecturers, projects, computers, programmed textbooks, discussion groups, and so forth. He knows students will forget much of the information they learn in his classes, but this does not trouble him. He is more interested in their learning to think rationally and critically about the economic, political, religious, philosophical, and ethical issues humanity has faced over the centuries. He also wants his students to evaluate past ways of dealing with problems and to learn how the past affects the present and the future.

Mr. Reinhold thinks it is not only his responsibility to pursue these objectives, but it is also his duty to direct students to see that there are enduring values worth passing on to each generation. If the students properly grasp these values—freedom, justice, respect, understanding, rationality, tolerance, compassion, and so on—they have guideposts that might help them change the present and direct the future.

A glimpse into Mr. Reinhold's classroom, where students are learning about early white settlers and Native Americans, suggests his emphasis on these values. At the conclusion of a film on the causes of conflict between the two groups, he says, "Now I want you to discuss four points with your partner. In the morning, I'll ask you for a written summary of your conclusions. The first question: Which ethical principles are relevant to an appraisal of Native-American–settler relationships during the period from 1500 to 1700? Second, identify particular cases of people either ignoring or adhering to these principles. Third, explain why, as far as you can determine, certain individuals followed or ignored these principles. Finally, decide which of these principles are and are not pertinent to human relationships today."

Reinhold does not feel he is alone in his goals for his students. All teachers of basic subjects—science, social studies, English, mathematics—should have overlapping concerns. Working together, teachers can help students decide to be rational, independent thinkers, morally responsible persons, and intelligent users of the basic branches of knowledge.

Hardly anyone would question whether Mr. Reinhold is a successful teacher. Most principals, teachers, and parents would be delighted to work with him or to have him teach their children. Yet he says he does not have a philosophy of education. His colleagues teasingly tell him he is either a confused essentialistic perennialist or a muddled perennialistic essentialist.

An English Teacher

Ms. Alvarez's students are seldom bored in her English classes. Her electrifying approach to life spills over into her teaching. If you can believe her students, she makes verbs vivacious, commas comical, adverbs agreeable, spelling splendid, and writing wonderful. She is a model for new teachers, the idol of her students, and an inspiration to the entire school staff. She does so many things well that it is easy to see why her friends believe she is a natural, a born teacher. Instinctively, she seems to know what to do, when and how it should be done, and which steps to take with each student.

Her first love as a teacher, however, is not punctuation, spelling, capitalization, writing, and grammar. She does an outstanding job teaching these topics, but she would spend all of her class time studying literature with her students if she had a choice. Although she knows basic communication skills are invaluable, she believes that the quality of life in society is enhanced by an immersion in great literature. In addition to the intrinsic value she sees in literature, she thinks the themes discussed by great writers raise important social and philosophical issues. She has been known to say more than one time, "You may excel on standardized tests, win a merit scholarship, build an outstanding practice or corporation, and achieve international recognition, but you are less than successful as a human being if you are ethically indifferent to the problems around you and if you lack the courage to act on your moral principles." "Don't be a Prufrock," she quickly adds.

When social, political, and ethical issues arise in her classes, students sometimes ask, "Aren't values personal, Ms. Alvarez?" Her most recent response is along the following lines: "*Personal* can mean at least a couple of things. First, it may mean that values are totally up to the individual and each person can do whatever he or she pleases. Second, it may also mean that values, after they have been debated and justified, must be personally decided upon and acted on if they are to have meaning. Those who subscribe to this second viewpoint think value judgments are at least partially rational, like other types of judgments."

Continuing the conversation, Ms. Alvarez adds: "Is it ethically acceptable for a person to discriminate against Hispanics, Baptists, Yankees, and aliens just because it pleases her? Is it possible we are violating transcultural moral principles if we murder or rape someone? Is it fair for me to award one of you a grade of F when you have earned a grade of B?" Her questions almost always spark further discussion in an atmosphere of open reflection and respect for the autonomy of each person.

When Ms. Alvarez was pursuing the M.Ed. in graduate school, one of her classmates said he thought she was an idealist. She thought for a moment and said, "If I am, please don't stereotype me and attribute all of that historical luggage to me. I'm a neoidealist with a mind of my own."

Philosophical Beliefs and Teaching

Have you ever wondered why teachers such as the three described in the Snap-shot teach differently? Is it because in their early lives they had different role models and culturally diverse backgrounds? Is it because teachers have distinct personalities and different subject specialties, types of students, and school principals? Do the various kinds of colleges and universities that teachers attend or the types of teacher-education programs they go through partly account for the differences among them?

Teaching styles

No doubt these and other variables do make a difference in the way any person teaches. But other factors also seem to be involved. If teachers have both the freedom and the courage to be themselves at school in the ways that Ms. Aycock, Mr. Reinhold, and Ms. Alvarez do, their philosophies of life and resulting educational philosophies should account for some differences in their professional activities. Many teachers, of course, in spite of differing educational philosophies, have essentially similar teaching styles. Their discussions of predicate nominatives, assignments in algebra classes, methods of teaching reading, and activities with students don't vary in any great degree. Samuel de Champlain, Francis Drake, and John Smith may appear in a social studies curriculum regardless of the teacher's philosophy. Geometry teachers have their students study segments, angles, triangles, polygons, prisms, and pyramids even when among themselves they have radically different educational perspectives. The Milky Way, the atom, and metamorphic rocks are standard fare in most earth science courses. Teachers who span the entire spectrum of philosophical thought use films, tapes, computer software, and chalk. So teachers sometimes teach similarly even when their worldviews differ. Conversely, teachers whose worldviews are essentially the same teach differently at times.

Similarities

Moreover, teachers as teachers do differ in many respects, and some of their differences are in part attributable to their philosophies of education. This is inevitable if one recalls Socrates, Martin Luther, Jean Jacques Rousseau, Johann Herbart, Thomas Jefferson, George Washington Carver, Maria Montessori, and some of the other major educators and thinkers they have studied. One must remember, too, that early educational institutions—Latin grammar schools, Franklin's Academy, women's seminaries—and many present ones arose for different philosophical reasons. The same idea may be said of textbooks, laws, and statements of educational goals by professional associations. It is important, therefore, for teachers to understand what educational philosophy is and how it contributes to their professional lives in covert and overt ways.

Philosophical differences

The Nature and Value of Educational Philosophy

One informative way of thinking about philosophy of education is to consider it to be a set of intellectual activities that lead educators who engage in them to build a particular product. In this context, we call the set of intellectual activities *philosophizing*. Philosophizing may result in *a personal philosophy of education.*[2] Philosophizing, then, involves at least four elements: (1) *clarifying* educational discussions by mapping out concepts that make abstract ideas about education more understandable and more useful as professional guides, (2) *justifying* educational decisions by providing compelling arguments and supporting evidence for them, (3) *interpreting* educational data in order to determine their significance for educational policy and

Philosophizing

TABLE 10-1 The Nature of Philosophy of Education

Intellectual Activity	Major Questions
Clarifying	What do you mean?
Justifying	How do you know?
Interpreting	How should these data be understood?
Systematizing	Do these findings form a coherent pattern?

practice, and (4) *systematizing* educational discussions, decisions, and data into a coherent understanding of what education is or should be. Each activity can be summarized by the questions listed in Table 10-1.

Each of these intellectual activities is an important part of the broader professional life of the teacher. Each helps the teacher come to grips with two questions: What am I as a teacher? Why am I doing what I am doing in the classroom?

Clarifying

"What do you mean?"

When teachers are encouraged to use a procedure or to pursue a goal, it is important to determine precisely what they are being encouraged to do.[3] For example, what is the speaker encouraging when teachers are told they should meet the needs of the whole child? Are financial needs included? Probably not. What about material needs? Our answer may be slower in coming. How are teachers to be involved, if at all, in meeting the social, religious, and emotional needs of students? What is included in the concept of educational needs? Can a teacher meet all of a student's educational needs? Do priorities need to be established? Is "the whole child" a clear concept?

Any advice can confuse teachers if it—and the ideas that make it up—is not analyzed carefully. Proponents of various educational ideas enjoin teachers to teach the basics, develop creative students, cultivate independent thinkers, pass on lasting values, pursue students' natural interests, nurture students' moral reasoning, and allow students to study whatever is meaningful to them. In some educational discussions the concepts of intelligence, indoctrination, education, learning, conditioning, self-actualization, tolerance, socialization, knowledge, censorship, and authoritarianism become muddled.

Imagine for a moment teachers who have been instructed by their principal to make certain their students learn "the basics" by March. Understanding their local situation, the teachers might surmise that the principal used the term *basics* to refer to the material on the achievement tests that will be administered in April. Suppose further that some have just started teaching their seventh-grade class a required unit on sex education. The material in the unit does not appear on the mathematics, science, language arts, and social studies tests, but they know the reason for the new unit: Twenty-one percent of the eighth-, ninth-, and tenth-grade girls in their school system became pregnant last year. They may be well advised to ask their principal, "Which is more basic, high scores on the achievement test or low scores on the pregnancy test? Do we discuss punctuation or impregnation? What do you mean by 'basics'?"

These situations illustrate the reason that asking "What do you mean?" is useful to teachers. First of all, raising the question helps teachers obtain a clear picture of what they are told they should or should not do. Being clear about what their instructions or challenges mean allows them to decide not only how, but also whether, they ought to pursue an objective. Second, an analysis of educational language can reveal how naïve some decision makers, policymakers, speakers, and writers are about the educational enterprise. Often they demand the impossible and the indefensible of teachers. When a teacher knows something unreasonable is expected or demanded, the teacher may be unhappy; however, the teacher will also be better able to argue against the decision or policy. Third, an analysis of statements on teaching procedures, structures, goals, outcomes, and content may on occasion reveal naïveté or hidden values and conflicting claims. Consequently, raising some form of the question "What do you mean?" eventually leads teachers into other kinds of philosophical questions.

Justifying

Because schooling is an intrinsically value-laden endeavor, teachers may frequently raise some variation of the question "How do you know?"[4] The teacher will want to ask, "What reasons and evidence support your views, policies, goals, and practices?" "Is the research that supports these ideas accurate and valid?" In essence, the teacher is asking for a justification of an educational idea, belief, or practice. Imagine, for instance, a school board meeting that is about to conclude. The chair praises the other members for their contributions to the new educational-excellence plan. As the board prepares to approve the plan, a member asks for a review of the list of criteria that will be used to judge excellent high schools. The following criteria constitute the list:

"How do you know?"

1. the percentage of students who pass the proficiency test on their first attempt
2. the percentage of students who score above the national average on standardized achievement tests
3. the percentage of students who score above the national average on the ACT and SAT
4. the percentage of students who attend a university on merit scholarships
5. the percentage of students who graduate from a university
6. the percentage of students who attend professional schools and become lawyers, psychologists, physicians, optometrists, dentists, engineers, and business leaders
7. the percentage of students who receive state or national recognition for outstanding accomplishments after graduation

After the criteria are read aloud for the entire board to hear, the member asks if the board will consider substituting an alternate list of criteria, which she proposes. Her list follows:

1. the percentage of students from low-income families who pass the proficiency test on their first attempt
2. the percentage of students from low-income families who are not arrested or incarcerated before graduating from high school
3. the percentage of students from low-income families who score above the national average on standardized achievement tests
4. the percentage of students from minority and low-income families who graduate from a university
5. the percentage of female students who enter male-dominated occupations

6. the percentage of university graduates who eventually become teachers, clergy, social workers, nurses, auto mechanics, cabinet makers, and farmers

7. the percentage of former students who contribute annually to charitable causes

Before discussion of this new list of criteria begins, the school board member distributes a list of questions she thinks the board members need to address: Why should the board believe filling cavities, removing plaque, and attaching braces are more valuable activities than teaching science, stimulating creative thought, and challenging students to use their knowledge for the betterment of humankind? Why should the board place more emphasis on ACT scores than it does on teaching students to live by the values of respect, freedom, compassion, and justice? How can the board justify the conclusion that people who grow food for thousands each year are less significant than those who defend a few hundred prospective criminals each year?

Much practice is unexamined

Questions of this sort take the school board—and the teacher—to the heart of the issue of the real nature and purpose of schooling. They force thinking teachers to recognize that much of what goes on in educational circles is largely unexamined. Related philosophical questions for the teacher to consider are: Why do we require four units of English and only two units of mathematics for high school graduation? Why are mathematics, science, social studies, and English-language studies considered core subjects and art, music, physical education, and foreign languages considered peripheral subjects? What are the major goals and objectives of schooling? Should schools be organized differently than they are? Why do some school systems and states not allow teachers to serve on school boards in systems where they teach? Does the same logic apply to doctors, lawyers, and psychologists serving on professional boards? When are teachers and principals going to be granted the freedom to redesign schools to better meet the learning needs of students and the professional needs of practitioners?

Educators who think independently

The utility of philosophizing in this realm is clear. As professionals, teachers want sound reasons for attempting to carry out their responsibilities. They want to know they are not blindly following tradition, being swept up in the most recent educational fad, or unethically pursuing even the best objectives. Educators who think independently can sometimes influence the actions of policymakers and decision makers by unearthing their underlying assumptions and, when appropriate, challenging them and their application to educational practice. Ultimately, the ideal is that teachers, by asking sensitive, probing questions about the underlying bases for educational decisions, policies, and practices, will make a difference in the processes, the content, and the outcome of schooling. In the long run, teachers are attempting to make a difference in the quality of life for students and society.[5]

Reprinted with special permission of King Features Syndicate.

Interpreting and Systematizing

Early in life, people in all cultures are gradually initiated into a set of values, beliefs, and perceptions common to their own culture. The process is called *socialization*. The impact of socialization varies, depending upon a number of factors. Some people are so conditioned by the process that they can seldom see things through the eyes of others or even have a thought of their own. Others, for a variety of reasons, rebel against their cultural orientations. They reject their origins and become critical of their social and intellectual heritage. Still others are challenged by their cultural environments and progressively sift through their values, retaining ideas they find defensible and discarding those they believe to be indefensible.[6] If the process is a rational, thinking process, the individual considers questions that rest on philosophical concerns in three domains: (1) concerns about the nature of reality (metaphysics), (2) concerns about the nature of knowledge (epistemology), and (3) concerns about the nature of values (axiology). Figure 10-1 lists questions that define these philosophical domains.

In each case, the socialized individual adopts and refines a set of beliefs that provides the means for interpreting and systematizing new experiences. These beliefs, in one sense, constitute an elementary philosophy of life; and that philosophy of life becomes a filter, an interpretive frame of reference, through which the individual perceives and organizes reality. The competition of influences between cultural socialization and education is illustrated in Figure 10-2.

As an individual's philosophy of life, or frame of reference, develops, it should help the person understand new experiences and ideas, thus broadening his or her perspective. It may, however, have a restricting effect if the individual does not learn "to see with more than one pair of glasses" or at least to understand that he or she is wearing glasses. If vision is significantly restricted, the individual does not become a philosophizing person who has learned to ask, "Am I looking at this too narrowly? Am I depending on just one viewpoint? Would some other approach help

Socialization

"How should these data be understood?"

Assimilating a cultural legacy and making it our own is part of the process of developing a uniquely individual outlook on life.

FIGURE 10-1   Philosophical domains, their primary foci, and key questions they consider.

Philosophical Domains		
Domains	**Descriptions**	**Major Questions**
Metaphysics	Nature of reality	What is real?
Epistemology	Nature of knowledge	How do we know?
Axiology	Nature of values or ethics and aesthetics	When is something good or bad, right or wrong, beautiful or lacking in beauty?

me understand this more fully? How do I learn to think and see from another perspective?"

As people begin to think philosophically about life, they raise questions about their developing philosophical views, questions such as:

1. What do I mean by discrimination, bias, open-mindedness?
2. What reasons and evidence do I have for my values, religious beliefs, political allegiances?
3. Is this policy consistent with what I believe?
4. Do I have a coherent set of beliefs about teaching?

The result or end product of thinking in an interpretative, systematic way is a useful philosophy of life, or, when applicable, of education.

When teachers philosophize about professional matters—when they ask themselves "How should this effective schooling data be explained? Why should these things matter? Is more than one interpretation possible or legitimate? If so, are they compatible? Do these new pieces of educational thought fit together with my existing ideas?"—they are essentially seeking answers to three questions: "Are these data worth considering? If so, how am I to fit these findings into my meaning system? Do these notions, theories, and data form a coherent view of education?"

FIGURE 10-2   A continuum of rationality. When individuals develop their philosophical positions, they base them on influences that are derived from cultural socialization and from a more reflective education. In a sense, the two types of influences compete for dominance as individuals decide upon their philosophical stances.

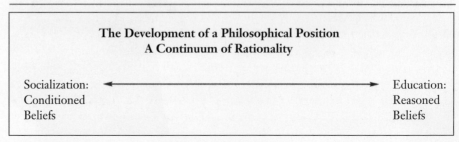

**The Development of a Philosophical Position
A Continuum of Rationality**

Socialization:
Conditioned
Beliefs

Education:
Reasoned
Beliefs

Three words—*understanding, coherence, relevance*—summarize the utility of interpreting and systematizing educational phenomena. To *interpret* educational findings and experiences is to come to understand education better and, ideally, to become a better educator. To *systematize* educational phenomena is to pull together what one understands about a variety of topics into a viewpoint that promotes intelligent, consistent, professional behavior. In so doing, teachers construct their philosophies of education or, as some prefer to say, their theories of education, which influence their entire lives as educators, including their instructional activities, curricular decisions, personnel choices, educational objectives, professional commitments, and ethical conduct.

"Do these findings form a coherent pattern?"

A Hypothetical Query

The four elements of philosophizing described can be illustrated in the following questions posed by a newspaper reporter to a governor who has just made a speech about education:

clarifying	Governor, now that you have finished your address, could you briefly tell us what you mean by "good teachers"?
justifying	Likewise, can you elaborate on why you believe many teachers are not doing a good job? And, in the light of your criticism of teachers, could you explain how it is that achievement test scores are above average across the state?
interpreting	
systematizing	Finally, please comment on how you reconcile your views that the state has too many inadequate teachers with your proposal to allow any university graduate into the teaching profession.

Systematic Views of Education

Teachers can study a number of philosophies of education if they wish to identify, clarify, and evaluate their own developing views on education. Thus far, no one has proved conclusively that a particular educational philosophy is true in a way that makes all competing views false. In fact, some might argue that this is nearly impossible, especially if they accept the premise that systems of thought limit as well as enhance the teacher's ability to understand educational issues.

Present-day options

This is not to say that all educational philosophies are equally true or reasonable. Nor is it to say that all positions offer the same degree of illumination. Some educational philosophies are based on such weak arguments and limited evidence that they merit little consideration. Others are strongly supported and deserve considerable attention.

Any philosophy of education probably offers some value; but an ideal philosophy of education is one that is stronger than others, more reasonable than others, and more useful than others. Prospective teachers who are developing their own positions should review the competing educational philosophies.

The philosophies that are surveyed in a cursory fashion in the rest of this chapter fall into three general categories: historical, modern, and contemporary. Each philosophy is explained from the viewpoint of a present-day educational philosopher even if a particular philosophy's intellectual heritage goes back to antiquity. The historical philosophies discussed are *idealism* and *realism*. The two modern philosophies treated are *pragmatism* and *existentialism*. The contemporary positions presented are *perennialism, essentialism, behaviorism, reconstructionism, futurism, evangelicalism, Marxism,* and *critical theory.*[7]

Problems to avoid

In reviewing philosophies of education, two overlapping problems often arise. The first problem is that of *stereotyping* the adherents of a specific philosophical position. This form of stereotyping usually is based on the belief that proponents of a particular philosophy agree on every detail of their views regarding metaphysics (the nature of reality), epistemology (the nature of knowledge), axiology (the nature of values), and education (the nature of schooling). When this happens, proponents of similar positions may be depicted as mindless conformists, all doing the same thing at the same time all over the world. Thus one may erroneously conclude the following: Mary Stone is an essentialist; therefore, she believes in a, b, c, and d, teaches with goals 1, 2, 3, and 4 in mind, and utilizes methods w, x, y, and z to reach her goals. The simple fact is that most teachers are somewhat *eclectic* in their philosophy and *creative* in their teaching; that is, they *synthesize* and create their own philosophic position from various philosophic views.

A second, and related, difficulty results from neglecting philosophical and pedagogical similarities across the schools of thought in order to emphasize their distinctiveness. As a result, a person can be left with the impression that only Variety A teachers lecture; only Variety B teachers think values are easily changed; only Variety C teachers have an interest in religion; only Variety D teachers are concerned with the autonomy of students.

Because of these two potential problems in understanding philosophies of education, it is worth repeating an idea stated earlier. Teachers with similar beliefs differ, as well as agree, on a variety of matters. In like manner, teachers with different beliefs agree, as well as disagree, on issues. These two potential problems in understanding philosophies of education—stereotyping or ignoring similarities across systems—can be overcome to some degree if educational philosophical positions are viewed in much the same manner as one would view religious denomination and political party affiliations. They are convenient labels that often hinder as well as help in understanding particular individuals. They refer to some common features of adherents, but they ignore differences that are sometimes as important as the similarities.

Historical Philosophies

In the Western world, probably the oldest philosophical positions that underlie educational theories are *idealism* and *realism*. The intellectual roots of both reach back to ancient Greece, Africa, and the Middle East. Present-day exponents, while connected with the past, express updated philosophical and pedagogical versions of the two positions. Table 10-2 summarizes the role of the teacher in each of these philosophies.

TABLE 10-2   Historical Philosophies of Education

Philosophy	Role of the Teacher	Illustrative Thought
Idealism	To foster the development of the spiritual person	"Teachers should model the qualities that they want students to develop."
Realism	To promote the development of the rational person	"Teachers should help develop the rational or religious essence of students."

Idealism

Idealism, as in the case with other philosophies, is not a single position but a general outlook that is represented by a number of individuals with somewhat similar views. Plato, who was also a realist, is often considered the founder of idealism, but later contributors are many—René Descartes, Benedict Spinoza, Immanuel Kant, and Georg Hegel. American idealists include Ralph Waldo Emerson, Mary W. Calkins, and Edgar S. Brightman. Educational philosophers noted for expounding the viewpoint include Herman E. Horne, J. Donald Butler, and Theodore M. Greene.[8]

Philosophically speaking, idealists are best known for their *metaphysical beliefs* (beliefs about the nature of reality), especially those beliefs that deal with the realm of nature that is beyond the physical. They argue that the physical world is not *ultimately* real. Although the material world is real to an extent because it exists and can be experienced, it is not ultimately real because it must be further analyzed and explained by reference to a more basic, fundamental reality or substance. The physical world, therefore, does not exist in and of itself but is contingent upon and is an expression of another substance, or *ultimate reality* (Figure 10-3).

REALITY

What is this ultimate reality that sustains the material world? A number of terms have been employed to refer to ultimate reality—ideas, mind, consciousness, form, thought, energy, and others. But the basic notion is that reality is ultimately *nonmaterial*, or *spiritual*. This reality is characterized by intelligence and energy.

Spiritual reality

FIGURE 10-3   This is an illustrator's representation of an idealist thinker. Is it consistent with your ideas about idealists in light of your studies?

Supreme being

Personal idealists, philosophers who may constitute the largest group of American idealists, think this ultimate reality is a person, an absolute mind, a supreme being, God. They see this supreme being as the source and sustainer of the remainder of the universe, including other persons. This rational being produced the material world and its inhabitants by willing an idea of them into existence. Ultimate reality, therefore, is a society of people who live in a universe that was produced and is maintained by the supreme being.

TRUTH AND VALUES

This theory of reality is the foundation for the idealist's view of both the nature of knowledge and the nature of values. Knowledge stems from interpreting both ideas and experiences in the light of the truth that an absolute mind exists. Idealists usually agree that reason is at least a key to arriving at truth, but they differ on whether the following ways of arriving at truth are either possible or desirable: recalling latent ideas, listening to an innate conscience, intuiting ethical principles, discovering information through scientific inquiry, and learning from sacred literature. In the end, however, regardless of how the idealists arrive at their own views of truth, they usually state that truth fits together in an inclusive, consistent meaningful system.

Universal values

Included in the idealist's point of view is a *theory of values.* The most important values for the idealist are the unchanging universal ones that are found in a rational, understandable universe and are grounded in the nature of society, human beings, and their concept of God. While such values as personal preferences and cultural mores are worthwhile, they are of secondary concern. Eternal, universal values receive more attention than temporal, relative ones. From an idealist's point of view, schooling should be based upon this understanding of truth, values, and reality. Schooling exists primarily to teach these eternal truths, these universal values—to teach this concept of reality.

PEDAGOGY

Although some literature suggests otherwise, the educational views of idealists are not rigidly dictated by their philosophical beliefs. Philosophical beliefs, however, do establish a context for schooling, teaching, and learning; they also provide latitude as well as limits for the professional educator. Although idealists who are educators have been historically associated more with certain teaching techniques, subjects, and goals than with others, present-day idealists can employ any method that is consistent with their value system. While modeling the intellectual and moral excellences of the absolute mind is important, contemporary idealists do not discount educational technology and other available pedagogical options.

Evolution of great thinkers

Today's idealists recognize that any curriculum that promotes the self-actualization of the student may be studied, and all subjects can contribute to an integrated view of reality. No bona fide subject is ignored, even though idealists have traditionally stressed the value of history, religion, literature, fine arts, and mathematics in enabling students to achieve self-understanding, self-realization, and the actualization of their intellectual, moral, social, and spiritual potential. An idealist, then, may value highly a liberal education and at the same time argue for the importance of specialized and vocational studies on very different grounds. It would be consistent with idealists' beliefs to promote, in any field of study, the emulation of great thinkers in an effort to assist students in realizing their potentialities.

As a teacher, the idealist:

- encourages students to imitate the thought of great people
- points out the moral and spiritual significance of ideas that are discussed
- attempts to model desirable qualities for students to emulate

- promotes independent thought in students by asking thoughtful questions
- stresses lasting over transitory values in decision making
- seeks to develop both the thinking skills and decision-making powers of students
- directs the intellectual and moral growth of students toward a condition of excellence

Because the student is viewed as a unique person who possesses many of the qualities of the absolute mind, the idealist-teacher believes each student should be treated as an immortal, rational creature, a person who is increasingly capable of making his or her own decisions. As the student matures, the emphasis of schooling should shift from the teacher's instructing to the student's self-directed learning. The growing responsibility of the student, when supported by early instruction and training, will enable him or her to utilize personal potentialities and become a creative, autonomous person. The primary goal of schooling, then, is to develop people who understand themselves and their world and who live in ways that are consistent with the ultimate reality of a spiritual universe.

Students who understand themselves and the world

Realism

Realism, like idealism, is a contemporary philosophical position with a rich heritage. Many think Plato and Aristotle first formalized the position. After them, a distinguished line of thinkers diversified and refined the viewpoint. Among these philosophers are John Locke, David Hume, St. Thomas Aquinas, Bertrand Russell, Alfred North Whitehead, and Ralph B. Perry. Educational philosophers who have promoted the position include such diverse thinkers as Jean-Jacques Rousseau, Maria Montessori, Jacques Maritain, and Harry Broudy.[9]

REALITY

Realists can be divided into two general groups: (1) materialists, those who emphasize that reality is completely material; and (2) traditional realists, those who believe in the reality of abstract ideas (Table 10-3). *Materialists* think the differences detected in reality or the material world are all a matter of degree, never of kind. Ultimate reality, in all of its variety, is impersonal, nonmental, and material. *Traditional realists*, can be subdivided into two groups—*classical realists* and *religious realists*—but, regardless of whether they are classical or religious realists, they believe abstract ideas are not just labels or names for things; they are instead descriptions of the essential features of a group or class of things. Rather than only naming, abstrac-

Material reality

TABLE 10-3   Realism and Reality: Three Perspectives

Type of Realist	Perspective
Materialistic realists	All reality is of the same kind and is material, impersonal, nonmental, or nonspiritual.
Traditional realists	
Classical realists	The essential nature of each entity is reflected in the abstract language used to label it and distinguishes one entity from another.
Religious realists	Each kind of reality, whether material or spiritual, is a reflection of the creative design of a supreme being.

FIGURE 10-4   Is this illustrator's representation of a realist thinker consistent with your thinking? If not, how would you change it?

tions describe the characteristics of things as they actually are—that is, the nature of specific things (Figure 10-4).

Human rationality

Although materialists differ with idealists over the nature of reality, some classical realists seem close to idealists, even though they still reject the proposition that ultimate reality is spiritual. For other traditional realists, namely religious realists, there are two kinds of reality—both material and spiritual reality. All realists agree that the ability of humans to reflect upon their own thoughts sets them apart from the remainder of known reality. And religious realists add that both rationality and spirituality distinguish human beings from the remainder of reality. These religious realists believe that the physical world exists in its own right, just as does the spiritual world. Each realm is equally real, even though substantially different.

These two strands of thought within realism—the materialist and the traditionalist—illustrate to some extent the diversity found in realistic thinking. Additional diversity will be described in the next few pages, as the philosophy is further clarified. For the moment, it is sufficient to note the differences between the two kinds of realism: One kind consists of those who see reality as completely material and a second kind includes those who see it as a combination of the material and the spiritual.

TRUTH AND VALUES

The position of realists on the nature of knowledge probably identifies them more frequently than any of their other positions. Realists largely agree that an objective, material reality exists and can be known. Particular things can be known and distinguished from ideas of those things. A particular item is not known, however, until its *nature*, or *essence*, is understood or perceived. In order to understand the essence of a particular thing, a person must first understand the class of things to which it belongs. A particular person, for example, is understood only after his or her essence, or nature, is understood. Therefore, a person cannot understand a particular human being unless that person has some understanding of human beings as a group.

The diversity among realists is as apparent in the realm of values as it is anywhere. Broadly speaking, values—or at least the moral ones—may be determined in several ways. *Materialistic realists* may argue one of two positions. One opinion is that moral values are determined by the social context and are to be judged in terms of consequences upon society. Society, therefore, is free to change its values if it can verify the need. A second, and quite different, opinion expressed by some materialistic realists is that just as natural order reveals natural laws, it also reveals moral laws. By studying human behavior and its consequences, we can discover natural moral laws. The good moral life consists of living intelligently by these laws, experiencing the benefits of the resulting life, and avoiding the natural consequences of violating them.

Among traditional realists, *classical realists* generally think that some moral values can be arrived at by rigorous rational thought. As they see it, an agreed-upon set of ethical principles can be determined, defended, and applied to human problems in any culture, although sometimes it is difficult to do so. The principles provide invaluable guides to maintaining a just and free society.

A third group of realists, *religious realists*, do not offer a uniform approach to ethics any more than do other realists. Some have a great deal in common with classical realists, emphasizing the role of reason in determining moral values. Others combine reason and revelation, believing that, since the absolute mind is a rational being, values are rational as well as revealed in sacred literature. Another set appears to think that natural law, reason, and scripture are all helpful in constructing sound ethical theory because God established natural law, exemplifies sound reason, and inspired scripture.

Regardless of the particular orientation of specific realists, they, along with many nonrealist philosophers, increasingly stress that there are several kinds of values and that those values need to be distinguished. They classify values, for example, as *preferential* (questions of taste), *prudential* (questions of wisdom), *aesthetic* (questions of beauty), and *ethical* (questions of morality). They say these types of values are substantively different and should not be reduced to one kind (Figure 10-5).

Because realistic educational thought cannot easily be described in an introductory text, our discussion of realistic educational philosophy at this point is confined to two perspectives, the educational views of present-day classical and

Materialistic realists

Classical realists

Religious realists

PEDAGOGY

FIGURE 10-5   Types of values, concerns addressed by each, and examples.

Types of Values		
Types	**Concerns**	**Examples**
Preferences	Likes and dislikes	Convertibles, baseball
Prudence	Wisdom and folly	Frugality, vacations
Ethics	Right and wrong	Justice, compassion
Aesthetics	Beauty and lack of it	Sculpture, music

religious realists. Other recent derivations of realism—Marxism, perennialism, behaviorism, critical theory—will be analyzed when we take up contemporary educational philosophies.

Cultivation of thinking

Classical realists believe that education is understood only when the nature of the human being is understood. The human being is believed to be uniquely a rational creature, a creature who, when fully developed, is capable not only of thinking but also of evaluating thought. Schooling, therefore, is fundamentally concerned with cultivation of thinking, regardless of the other responsibilities attributed to it by society—responsibilities such as social, physical, and emotional development.

Even though the major goal of schooling is to promote thinking (or reasoning), that goal need not be narrowly defined. *Reason* is not limited to thinking for its own sake. It is critical in understanding any subject—social relationships, emotional development, physical growth, and so on. Reason, furthermore, is necessary to thoughtful choices and independently selected ways of living, and that includes understanding values and selecting from among them.

Classical realists believe that teachers need to understand the process of thinking, need to be subject matter specialists, and need to be effective instructors. They argue that teachers cannot be effective unless they understand the rational processes involved in a particular discipline. Because classical realists are keenly interested in developing students' rational abilities and their understanding of themselves as rational creatures, the humanities, the arts, and mathematics are prime candidates for a core curriculum. A society's way of thinking are contained in these and other subjects.

As a teacher, the classical realist

- develops the essence of students as people by focusing on their rational growth
- is dedicated to getting students to live in the light of a reasoned answer to the question of what kind of life is appropriate for a rational creature
- assists students in realizing that a commitment to reason is the way to autonomous choosing and living
- guides students toward finding objective rational grounds for making value and truth judgments
- organizes learning activities so that students will come to see that particulars belong to classes of things
- promotes evaluative thinking as the appropriate means to social, physical, and emotional development
- helps students see the differences between preferential, prudential, aesthetic, and ethical value judgments

It would be a mistake, however, to suppose that contemporary realists are uninterested in the scientific pursuit of knowledge. Classical realists recognize that any intellectually rigorous study can develop students' rationality and, thereby, enable them to become more completely human and to search for solutions to human dilemmas. Toward this end, realists who teach employ a variety of methods to provoke thought, stimulate inquiry, and awaken the rational powers of their students. Just as with idealism, no one method is prescribed, and many can be used to good effect.

Religious realists, while common in most Western and some Eastern religions, are best known in educational circles as shapers of Catholic educational thought. Often known as Thomist philosophers, they largely base their thinking on the teachings of the scriptures, the doctrines of the church, and the writings of St.

Thomas Aquinas (from whom they got their name). Most Thomists are basically united in their belief that a personal God is the author of reality, reason, and revelation. This belief is fundamental to Catholic thought and to Catholic philosophy of education.

Neo-Thomists, as some contemporary Catholic thinkers are labeled, express diverse opinions about education but are largely in agreement that the general aim of education is to develop the person as a person. In order to accomplish this aim, the teacher needs to understand the holistic nature of education. *Holistic education*, in this context, refers to learning that (1) combines belief in God with giving reasons for one's faith, (2) stresses the significance of intellectual development and the value of manual labor, (3) balances the spiritual and the worldly life, (4) cultivates rationality and morality, and (5) integrates so-called secular forms of inquiry with Christian truths.

Because God is author of all truth, a neo-Thomist education is appropriate for all students even though students will vary in the degree they profit from it. Included in the conception of liberal education may be both religious and vocational education, not just the traditional study of the humanities and the sciences. The integration of these fields, Thomists believe, should assist students later in life as they seek to form a just and free society. The teacher is also to cultivate and model the virtues of faith, hope, and love and, thereby, nurture the love of God and humankind.

As teacher, the religious realist

- models the virtues of faith, hope, and love
- challenges students to recognize that they are principal partners in learning
- teaches students to understand that God and reason are the sources of permanent values
- teaches students that reason and revelation are complementary ways of discovering truth
- seeks to develop the student as a whole person by cultivating her or his rationality, spirituality, and morality
- uses mechanical drills as well as memorization when promoting greater goals in education
- relies upon divine and human resources to transform students into complete persons

Students must be led to recognize that they are the principal partners in learning. They are the ones who actively learn as they are informed by the teacher and illuminated by divine grace. They are endowed with reason and freedom and must choose to utilize both their human and divine resources if they are to be transformed into complete persons. The learning of facts and truths, while necessary, does not in and of itself bring about the goal of education. Mechanical drills by the teacher, if needed, must always be supplemented by a loving concern for the development of each child. The student, therefore, both is and must become autonomous through a liberating education.

Modern Philosophies

Pragmatism and existentialism are newer systematic philosophies than idealism and realism, although some of the ideas and attitudes in each have been present throughout human history. With the rise of pragmatism and existentialism in Western intellectual circles, a turning point occurred in philosophical and educational

Holistic education

Autonomous humans

TABLE 10-4 Modern Philosophies of Education

Philosophy	Role of the Teacher	Illustrative Thoughts
Pragmatism	To guide the development of the reflective person	"The teacher's goal is the continued growth of students."
Existentialism	To facilitate the development of the authentic person	"Students must create their own values and lives by choosing for themselves."

thought. The two ways of thinking not only changed philosophy in and of itself but also stimulated the formulation of additional and more varied philosophical and pedagogical positions. The role of the teacher in each is summarized in Table 10-4.

Pragmatism

Heraclitus, the ancient Greek philosopher, was perhaps a seminal pragmatist, but it was nineteenth- and twentieth-century philosophers such as Charles S. Pierce and William James who commanded the attention of contemporary philosophers and educators alike.[10] John Dewey, also identified as an instrumentalist or an experimentalist, contributed significantly to pragmatic educational thought and practice. Together, along with other like-minded thinkers, these philosophers expounded a new way of interpreting reality and education.

REALITY

Pragmatists have generally agreed that the universe is a natural, dynamic entity that can be partly known through human experiences and transactions. Human beings, as part of the natural universe, have evolved and become more complex than most of reality, but they are not substantively different from the rest of the universe. Humans, of course, have evolved to the point at which they can think and exercise choice; but their development, as far as can be determined, is purely natural and not supernatural. However, individual humans only partly experience reality because that which any single person knows and experiences is limited. Because a person cannot experience the whole, a general view of reality is beyond the realm of anyone's knowledge.

Reality is limited to the physical

TRUTH AND VALUES

For the pragmatist, truth is conceptually different in a number of ways from the views proposed by idealists and realists. To begin with, there is no absolute truth. Truth, both in itself and as we know it, is changeable, never final. This is so because the knower and the universe are in a process of change. Second, truth is discovered by using the scientific method to solve problems. Thus truth is discovered by its function—its use in solving the quandaries of society. Third, knowing the truth is a process that involves a direct transaction of the knower with sensory data. Knowing, therefore, is a *process* of inquiring, not a static state. Finally, truth is relative to the knower's experience with the available data (Figure 10-6).

Truth is changeable

Knowing is a process of inquiring

Because pragmatists base their concept of values on their concept of truth and knowing, they do not believe absolute values exist. Therefore, the Absolute does not prescribe right and wrong. Instead, pragmatists determine values by testing hypotheses about conduct; that is, they test behavioral patterns to determine their worth. If the evidence supports the conclusion that an action is valuable, then it should be cultivated. If not, it should either be discouraged or allowed to disappear.

Some interpreters of pragmatism understand these comments to mean that one individual's view of reality, truth, and value is just as good as anyone else's. That is to say, philosophical beliefs are purely a personal matter. But pragmatists themselves generally disagree with this; they introduce an element of objectivity into their

FIGURE 10-6   Does this illustrator's representation of a pragmatist thinker make sense to you? How might you portray pragmatists differently?

thought by determining values, not through personal preference but by means of scientifically demonstrating what is socially expedient, that which leads to the growth of society. Truth, rather than being determined by individual whim, is decided by public examination of the data.

The general educational goal of pragmatic teachers is the development of *reflective thinkers* who employ the *scientific method* to solve personal and societal problems. Reflective thinking involves identifying a real problem, collecting pertinent data, formulating a tentative hypothesis, deducing testable consequences, and verifying actual consequences. Ideally, a solution to one's problem is discovered. If resolution of the problem is not obtained, the individual proceeds through the reflective thinking process again.

Pragmatic teachers achieve their goal by guiding their students' learning experiences because learning is fundamentally a process that involves active problem solving. The teacher, at least at times, arranges learning situations for students around problems related to the subject matter or environment. On other occasions, students are given the freedom to select personal or social problems to study. The teacher has the freedom to allow or encourage any learning experience that has been judged to produce personal or societal growth. The teacher's focus, then, is on the *process of learning and thinking*, not the content to be learned. It is important not to misunderstand this emphasis, however; there is for pragmatists no dichotomy between process and content. The school curriculum, including the so-called traditional subjects, affords students the opportunity to investigate as reflective thinkers the scope of human understanding. Students work as thinkers who see hypotheses to be tested in every field of inquiry.

PEDAGOGY
Scientific method

Reflective thinkers

A study of traditional subjects, therefore, may or may not be of interest at any given moment to the pragmatic teacher. If the study of these disciplines can be incorporated into activities leading to the resolution of problems, they are welcome. In fact, the resolution of many problems demands an interdisciplinary frame of reference; students therefore need to acquire information from a variety of fields if they are to solve complex problems. The pragmatist values the information, however, for its *utility* and may employ any methodology to pursue it as long as the students are actively engaged in the learning process.

Utility of information

As a teacher, the pragmatist

- assists students in understanding that truth in itself and as it is known is changeable
- trains students to utilize the scientific method to search for truth and solve problems
- arranges problems for students that require an interdisciplinary approach for resolution
- guides students' learning so that the outcomes will involve personal and social growth
- promotes learning activities that require the student to be directly involved in the process of inquiry
- involves students in value questions in an effort to lead them to develop a concern for societal growth
- prompts students to look for the utility of what they learn

Progressive education

Although pragmatists contributed extensively to progressive educational thought and practice, pragmatism and progressivism are separate entities.[11] The progressive education movement, built partly upon the thinking of John Dewey and such pragmatists as William Heard Kilpatrick, coalesced largely around an opposition to a perceived rigidity in schooling—authoritarianism, conservatism, dogmatism, traditionalism, and absolutism. Leaders of the movement were noted for their support of pedagogical principles that were considered to be progressive: (1) a classroom centered on the child, (2) a curriculum based on interests, (3) a methodology oriented toward discovery, (4) a school focused on life, and (5) an environment shaped by cooperation. The movement eventually went far beyond, if not astray from, a rigorous pragmatism, and pragmatists were often mistakenly blamed for the excesses of sloppily practiced progressivism.

Romantic humanism

During the middle of the century, many progressive notions were incorporated into, and perhaps distorted by, the romantic humanism of such thinkers as A. S. Neill, Carl Rogers, and John Holt.[12] These individuals may also have been influenced by the existentialism of European thinkers of the nineteenth and twentieth centuries.

Existentialism

Existentialism, while treated here as a systematic philosophy, is actually a way of viewing the world (and schooling) that rejects the notion of a self-contained system of educational thought and practice. Its elements, or to state it another way, the existentialist *attitude*, can possibly be identified in the highly diverse writings of such thinkers as Søren Kierkegaard, Friedrich Nietzsche, Karl Jaspers, Jean-Paul Sartre, Paul Tillich, and Albert Camus. Existentialists who have written on pedagogy include Martin Buber, Maxine Greene, and Donald Vandenberg.[13]

REALITY

Existentialists generally argue that reality is too complex and paradoxical and that education is too unpredictable and personal to fit neatly into a rational and comprehensive system. Their thinking is characterized more by themes such as "humans are free to create themselves" and "life appears to be meaningless in terms of rational explanation" than by systematic and confined opinions. Actually, existential thinking varies tremendously. Two main streams of existentialist thought, religious existentialism and nonreligious existentialism, flow from the views of Kierkegaard and Sartre and others who can be roughly grouped with one or the other. The two groups represent two different understandings of reality. Kierkegaard, a nineteenth-century theologian, felt that the orthodox Christianity of his day was impersonal, meaningless, and irrational. Sartre, a Nobel laureate who lived from 1905 to 1980, had significant influence on twentieth-century thought. Far from the theism of Kierkegaard (who died fifty years before Sartre was born), Sartre declared existence to be insignificant, worthless, and absurd. (It is necessary to understand that he defined all these terms in his work and did not use them as they are commonly used.) It is also important to note that Sartre found ways to justify and dignify existence and that these were not always identical even with those of his close existential friends, such as Albert Camus. Most existentialists, however, share Kierkegaard's and Sartre's feelings of initial despair and their pursuit of hope.

Hope for some religious existentialists is found in a redefinition of the Christian: a person noted not for intellectually consenting to a set of beliefs but for a personal relationship with God. This redefinition created a new view of faith and reason. Reason may provide conflicting opinions about the existence of God and may lead to atheism, but each person can reject a purely rationalistic world to discover God by a *leap of faith*. The leap transcends reason, overcomes doubt, and secures meaning. *Religious existentialists*

Nonreligious, or secular, existentialists, facing what they consider to be a meaningless, absurd, objective reality, have assumed that meaning must be found without belief in a godlike entity. If the secular existentialist finds hope, it is in the individual's freedom to choose. Each person may find meaning in deciding to be a person—a thinking, feeling, willing, valuing being. The conscious, subjective person, who can create his or her essence by deciding what and who he or she wishes to be, is radically different from the objective, material world. *Nonreligious existentialist*

For some existentialists, truth is purely subjective. Others believe there is objective truth, as well as objective reality. The whole truth, however, is likely to be paradoxical, less declarative and more textured than that of many philosophical systems. Existentialists stress that all knowledge and perception has not been examined because it is not even available to the individual. Even if it were all open to analysis, existentialists maintain that, as traditionally understood, it would be worthless. Moreover, religious existentialists insist that truth, even the fact that God exists, is meaningless unless the individual personalizes it and is changed by doing so. Experiencing, accepting, and appropriating truth as part of one's personal beliefs is important. Passively accepting it as given is not important. *TRUTH AND VALUES* *Truth is paradoxical*

Values, like truth, are totally a subjective matter for some existentialists, whereas they are objective in part for others. In the former case, existentialists emphasize that each person creates his or her own values. In the latter, existentialists may refer to an objective set of ethical principles or criteria but once again add emphatically that intellectual understanding alone is insufficient. Values, like truth, must be personally accepted before they can be meaningful. *Personally accepted truth and values*

Among those existentialists who believe all values are entirely personal are philosophers who seek to avoid a whimsical view of morality. Values, they argue, are *worthwhile only if they are good for others as well as for oneself.* Freedom and choice do not lead to moral anarchy but to personal and social responsibility. Thus, good is found in compassionate choice and action for others. Evil is the choice to conform—to conform to societal, familial, or peer pressures and values.

In one sense, it makes no difference whether existentialistic teachers are nonreligious or religious, for the aim of schooling is to facilitate the development of what Sartre might call authentic people. *Authentic* people are individuals who recognize their freedom, utilize their options, and accept their responsibility. At the same time, authentic people reject an exclusively objective, impartial, rationalistic, deterministic, logical, and scientific philosophy of life. They passionately involve themselves in the selection, application, and appropriation of ideas, theories, and values. They courageously affirm the style of life that accompanies their philosophy of life (Figure 10-7).

Existentialists have not generally addressed educational theory and practice. They are nevertheless clear on a variety of educational issues. First, their educational aim is well defined—to cultivate the authentic person. Second, the curriculum in the school is conceptualized as a tool for the student's self-realization. Perhaps the most useful studies for this purpose include dialogues, discussions, and discoveries about such existential concepts as authenticity, love, freedom, responsibility, death, values, conformity, alienation, and meaninglessness. Art, literature, religion, philosophy, history, and cognate areas may be helpful realms to examine and personalize.

Obviously, teachers are not autonomous in the eyes of the existentialist. They

FIGURE 10-7   Are there critical ideas about existentialism that this illustrator's representation misses? If so, what are these ideas?

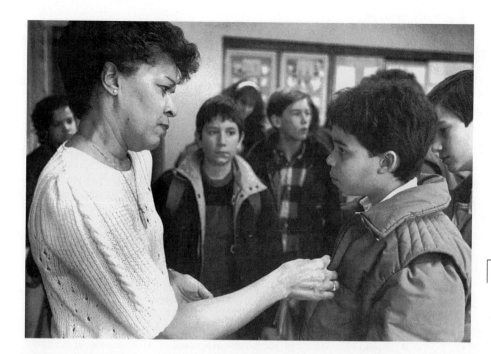

Existentially oriented teachers challenge students to assume responsibility for their own freedom and to make authentic choices.

enjoy freedom but are more concerned with their responsibility to facilitate the growth of students toward an autonomous life. In creating environments that enable students to become more authentic, they value person-to-person interaction. They also internalize what they learn and challenge each student to ask, "What do these facts, ideas, and so forth mean to me? How should they affect my feelings, attitudes, decisions?" Further, they strive to see that all interaction is based upon a mutual respect by all parties. They recognize that the pursuit of truth is valuable but are always aware that each student is dehumanized if the content to be learned is considered more important than the learner.

As teacher, the existentialist

- wants students to recognize that meaninglessness in life can be overcome by creation of a personal meaning or by a leap of faith
- expects the student to live with the paradoxical nature of truth
- asks students to keep this question before them: "What does this idea or material mean to me?"
- encourages discussions and dialogues about human tragedy, alienation, responsibility, and freedom
- nudges the student toward becoming an authentic human being
- challenges students to accept the responsibility and the results of their behavior
- strives to develop mutual respect among students engaged in the learning process

Contemporary Philosophies

In the discussion of historical and modern philosophies of education, contemporary idealists, realists, pragmatists, and existentialists were mentioned. In fact, each of these philosophies was explained from the stance of living, contemporary, educational thinkers. Therefore, the term *contemporary*, as used here, simply refers to phi-

Something to Think About

Brian Lynd teaches ninth-grade social studies and science to three double-period classes of inner-city students, nearly all of whom come from very poor economic home situations. He is committed to doing all he can for his students. He realizes that knowing the content that he teaches is important to their future success and that they face end-of-year tests they must pass in order to pass on to tenth grade. He also realizes that most of his students face tremendous out-of-school problems and face great likelihood of defeat or failure in much that they do, in school and out.

Brian almost constantly faces decisions about what is best for his students—decisions such as what and how much information to cover, how to grade, what to do with students who try but still get most answers wrong, how often to allow class discussions to ramble on subjects about the out-of-school lives of the students instead of the planned topic, how much to get involved in student personal matters, and so forth. In the last week Brian had to decide the following:

- Should he allow a full-period discussion about AIDS instead of his planned science topic on nuclear waste when a student raised the issue and most of the class seemed interested?
- Should he allow Bobby to sleep all period because he works five nights a week?
- Should he tell the students who asked that he and his fiancée live together?
- Should he give everyone in third period a passing grade on the last science test, since nearly everyone actually failed, with about equally poor scores?
- Should he skip the social studies lessons on due process and judicial review because they seem so abstract?
- Should he deal with the fact that Debbie is usually high on some substance in class?
- Should he ask Donald how his terminally ill father is and offer himself as someone for Donald to talk to if he would like?

In what ways do you think teachers who subscribe to each of the philosophies described so far in this chapter—idealism, realism, pragmatism, existentialism—would respond to these situations?

Which teachers who have different philosophies would respond in similar ways? Why? Are you sure?

Which would have significantly different responses? Why? Do you know of examples that run counter to your answer?

After you complete the next part of this chapter, on contemporary philosophies, return to these questions and consider them in terms of those philosophies.

losophies that have developed more recently. They may be seen as outgrowths of idealism, realism, pragmatism, and existentialism, but they have some special features of their own. One of those special features is a tendency to focus on pedagogical and/or societal questions. Another feature is that, with a few exceptions, beliefs about the nature of reality (metaphysics), the nature of knowledge (epistemology), and the nature of values (axiology) embedded in them are implicit rather than explicit. Table 10-5 presents the contemporary philosophies and the role of the teacher under each of them.

Reconstructionism

Reconstructionism, which evolved in part from pragmatism, has been espoused by George S. Counts, William O. Stanley, and Theodore Brameld.[14] Reconstructionists believe that the acute crises of the world require changes in both society and schooling. They say it is necessary to create a new world or a new order, one founded upon democratic principles and patterns of government. Failure to do so will lead to the self-destruction of humankind.

Create a new world

They therefore insist that teachers should become involved in creating this new world. To do this, teachers should show their students that it is imperative that they

TABLE 10-5   Contemporary Philosophies of Education:
The Role of the Teacher and Illustrative Thoughts

Philosophy	Role of the Teacher	Illustrative Thoughts
Reconstructionism	To develop builders of a better democratic world	"Teachers must address cultural crises and help build a new social order."
Futurism	To prepare students for the world of tomorrow	"Students must be taught strategies for adaptation and survival."
Behaviorism	To shape student behavior along prescribed lines	"Teachers should shape students into people who can contribute to society."
Perennialism	To produce rational beings who live according to traditional values	"The writings of great thinkers contain ideas and intellectual processes that all students need to understand."
Essentialism	To equip students with intellectual tools for productive lives in today's world	"Students need specific competencies and information if they are to live intelligently as citizens and workers."
Evangelicalism	To produce mature Christian thinkers	"All truth, including Christian beliefs, should be integrated into the thinking, choosing, and living of each student."
Marxism	To produce socialists who will build a classless world	"Teachers should help break the control of the ruling class over schooling."
Critical theory	To cultivate critical thinkers who will resist the antidemocratic forces in society	"Democratic schools should be created to liberate both teachers and students."

control their own destinies, not abandon them to the care of large corporations, which are driven largely by profits, and political officials, who may be motivated by personal ambition and guided by the principle of expediency.

For the reconstructionist, therefore, a fundamental goal of the school is to convince students that they should become eagerly involved in building a new society that includes the international community. This goal is critical, because such problems as nuclear weapons, hunger, nationalism, and racism can easily lead to the destruction of worthwhile life on the planet. Individual affluence is not a goal of schooling. Instead, international cooperation and compassion are major goals.

Solve world problems

Most reconstructionists strongly recommend studies that help students understand current world problems and their potential solutions. Social studies, the social sciences, and problems courses are central to the curriculum of reconstructionists. Additionally, they believe scientific and technological knowledge are necessary to help meet the needs of the world's people. If the objectives of reconstructionism are to be realized, schools need to prepare intellectually sophisticated and morally sensitive individuals.[15]

Futurism

Strictly speaking, *futurism* is a perspective that is both a predecessor of pragmatism and more inclusive than the ideas spawned by pragmatists. Conversely, both pragmatism and reconstructionism have contributed in important ways to futurism. Thus, even though educational thinkers throughout history have been interested in the influence of the school upon the future, only recently has a group of thinkers known as futurists made an impact upon educational policy and practice.

While understanding the past, controlling the present, and shaping the future are aims expressed by both pragmatists and reconstructionists, futurists move beyond these positions to argue for another proposition—namely, that the person of tomorrow must be intellectually and emotionally capable of living in a strange new world. Because Alvin Toffler, Harold Shane, and Robert Theobald argue or imply that the person of tomorrow should possess a prescribed set of characteristics, they are sometimes labeled *normative* futurists.[16]

Adaptation for the unknown

Normative futurists often stipulate that schools should constitute and promote participatory democracy both through what they teach and by their example as operating institutions. Rather than prepare students for a past that no longer exists or a present that is rapidly disappearing, teachers should, by their teaching and their example, prepare them to live in a democracy with many unknowns. Students, in order to live satisfactorily in this future, must acquire strategies for adaptation and survival. Adaptation, in particular, will require that students learn to think for themselves. Independent thought by the adult of tomorrow involves, among other abilities, thinking ethically and creatively.

According to futurists, the school that cultivates independent thinking should also stimulate autonomous decision making. More than ever before, the future will belong to people who think and choose for themselves. This aim—developing tomorrow's thinkers and choosers—is partly an outcome of schooling that attempts to produce both liberally educated people and highly trained specialists. It is aided by students who recognize both the autonomy and the responsibility implied by the concepts of studying and learning. Students who learn to think independently, live democratically, choose ethically, interact tolerantly, and act wisely offer hope and promise for the future.

Behaviorism

Behaviorism, with its base in materialistic or scientific realism, is a widely known system of psychology and was presented as such in Chapter 6. The theories of past behavioral psychologists such as Ivan Pavlov, John B. Watson, Edward Thorndike, and B. F. Skinner, however, have been expanded from a philosophy of science into a worldview and, by some, into a philosophy of instruction.[17]

This instructional philosophy is based upon the premise that all behavior is caused and therefore predictable. Because teachers are commissioned to change the behavior of students, they should use the most effective and efficient means possible. Teachers are behavioral engineers, responsible for controlling the educational environment of students and, thereby, what students learn. Teachers are therefore key participants in building a planned, scientific, and promising society.

In order to control students' learning, teachers must do several things. First, they must conscientiously identify their educational objectives and state them in behavioral terms. In doing so, they must specify the student performances that will demonstrate that particular objectives have been achieved. They also must break complex behaviors into small steps so that the total behavior can be learned. Second, teachers must reinforce those observable responses of students that indicate learning is occurring. They believe that rewarding correct student responses will result in those responses being practiced and that discouraging or punishing incorrect responses will cause students to abandon them. Third, teachers must carefully review the progress of each student to determine whether further goal analysis, new reinforcers, other curricular designs, and/or reinforcement schedules are needed. Because teachers cannot continuously observe each student as that student learns, they will want to consider using programmed textbooks, compartmentalized learning areas, teaching machines, computer programs, and behavioral contracts to help create desirable learning outcomes. These techniques, they believe, enable the teacher to apply the principles of a scientific pedagogy and to avoid one based upon tradition, opinion, or chance.

Teachers as behavioral engineers

Reinforcement

Perennialism

Perennialism, an offspring of realism and, to a lesser degree, idealism, focuses on a set of perennial truths and values and espouses the idea that education should liberate and fulfill students by developing their common essence, their ability to think and to choose. Many perennialists attempt to do this through studying the Great Books of the Western world and have been influenced greatly by the thinking of Robert Hutchins, Stringfellow Barr, and Mortimer Adler.[18]

This aim is achieved by providing each person with a liberal education that cultivates rational thought and responsible choice. One method of doing this is to provide students with the opportunity to study the works of outstanding writers in all fields—art, mathematics, music, philosophy, logic, history, language, ethics, religion, and science. Through this approach, students can be introduced to the wisdom of the past and to the truths and values they need to understand. This exposure helps them learn to think critically, prepares them for life and its accompanying duties, and enables them to contribute to society as citizens.

Rational thought and responsible choice

Teachers, therefore, are accountable to some extent for their students' rational development. They teach reading, writing, computing, and other subjects in the lower grades; as the students mature, they raise provocative points, design stimulating exercises, question unexamined assumptions, discuss conflicting theories, and initiate critical analyses. They also focus attention on permanent values, pass on perennial truths, demand reasons for opinions, insist on evidence for conclusions, and inculcate a love for precise thinking. For the perennialist, education is a cooperative enterprise that sharpens a person's rational powers and stimulates his or her potential for making good choices.

The responsibilities of teachers, however, cannot readily be realized unless students choose to develop and utilize their intellectual capacities. That is, students must assume partial responsibility for their own learning. Perennialists argue that the educated person is neither an accident of socialization nor a mechanical product of education. Instead, a person becomes educated by choosing to use the resources of school and society to cultivate his or her intellect.

Essentialism

Commonsense schooling

Essentialism, unlike most contemporary educational philosophies, cannot be easily and neatly tied to a historical philosophy. Some suggest that it is, in part, a by-product of idealism and realism. Others think it is simply a commonsense interpretation of schooling—a theory of education that stems from the thinking of the average intelligent person. The association of such people as William Bagley, William Brickman, Arthur Bestor, and Hyman Rickover with the philosophy may support the latter opinion.[19]

The emphases of essentialism are straightforward:

Teach the basics
and thinking

- The teacher should be an effective instructor and disciplinarian.
- The curriculum ought to be based upon "the basics" and other useful information.
- The student should become a self-disciplined learner and responsible student.

More specifically, these ideas imply that the elementary school teacher is concerned with teaching the skills of listening, reading, writing, and computing. The secondary school teacher reinforces previously learned skills and passes on information from the fields of history, mathematics, science, literature, and language.

What is the desired outcome of education from an essentialist viewpoint? Answers vary, and the fact that they do distinguishes many essentialists from perennialists. But, it is safe to say that many essentialists think schools should prepare students to live intelligently and successfully in today's society. A high school graduate should be prepared to act as an informed citizen, work as an efficient employee, and live as an informed and aware human being. In order to ensure that this outcome is accomplished, many essentialists focus their attention on the need for schools to pass on technical, scientific, and, occasionally, vocational skills and information. Still the essential teacher does not think this is all there is to schooling, for to live as an intelligent human being implies at least an introduction to the ideas, events, and people that shape the present and that offer insight into living itself.

Evangelicalism

Evangelicalism, as might be expected, is built largely upon the philosophical foundation laid by religious realism. It is a diverse movement based upon a common set of Judeo-Christian beliefs that include the following: God is a personal, rational, creative being; humankind is made in the likeness of God; nature and scripture reveal truths that are otherwise impossible to know; life has purpose and meaning in the love and service of God and others; ethical principles are based upon the rational and moral nature of God; human beings are alienated from God and need to be reconciled in Jesus Christ. Contemporary exponents of the viewpoint include C. S. Lewis, Frank E. Gaebelein, Ruth Haycock, and Paul Kniel.[20]

Mainstream evangelical philosophers appear to think that a primary educational goal is the development of mature Christian thinkers. Mature Christian thinkers, they believe, should have a liberal education that leads to an understanding of issues surrounding the reliability of sacred literature and the credibility of the Christian faith. Additionally, the mature Christian thinker should be able to apply Christian principles and knowledge from all branches of understanding to personal, social, political, and religious issues. Thus, mature Christian thinking should result in a lifestyle that appropriates all truth.

Mature Christian thinkers

From an evangelical perspective, the role of teachers is vital. Evangelicals believe that teachers should not only challenge students to discover honest answers for themselves but also be responsible for modeling the attitudes, dispositions, and skills of a liberally educated Christian. These may include a healthy self-image, concern for the poor, commitment to social justice, and conservation of natural resources. Ultimately, teachers provide students with a model and rationale for developing into mature Christian thinkers who act in the light of their worldviews.

More conservative evangelicals, who are known as *fundamentalists*, think the goal of the school is to produce separated, Bible-believing Christians. They believe the teacher is charged with passing on beliefs such as the following: The student ought to avoid involvement in non-Christian amusements, reject ideas founded upon the theories of evolution, abstain from certain kinds of clothing, shun liberal ecclesiastical and political ideas and affiliations, and oppose practices and beliefs that stem from anti-Christian worldviews. As a rule of thumb, many fundamentalist teachers inculcate these views by quoting scripture or lecturing on specific topics. When teaching any subject, the fundamentalist works to develop in students a respect for the scriptures by indicating how they apply to particular issues, solve problems, and answer questions.

Bible-believing students

Marxism

Marxism claims that reality is exclusively material, that society is involved in an ongoing class struggle, and that socialism is inevitable. Marxists theorists include in their thinking Karl Marx's views of the historical development of societies and the need of the oppressed to escape exploitation by the ruling classes. The writings of Samuel Bowles, Herbert Gintis, Kevin Harris, and Rachel Sharp clearly demonstrate these ideas.[21]

When contemporary Marxists apply their ideas to education itself, they focus a great deal of attention and criticism on schooling. At least in most of the Western world, Marxists see schools as a part of the culture that exploits the proletariat, the class ruled over by others. The bourgeoisie, or ruling class, controls the purposes and practices of schooling—and thereby its outcomes as well.

Schools are part of the problem

This happens because public schools in capitalist societies are institutions controlled by the government, which in turn is greatly influenced by the ruling class, by big business, and by the interests of industry and technology. Through the schools, the capitalist ruling class sees that certain kinds of knowledge are taught, thereby legitimating its own cultural values and guaranteeing its own future and its position of control. The result is that socially, economically, and politically powerful groups continue to control all material—physical, political, educational, economic, cultural—conditions, and employment opportunities.

The role of the Marxist teacher in a capitalist society may not be immediately obvious, but several generalizations are possible. First, the Marxist teacher should awaken students to the reality that encompasses them. That is to say, the teacher should help students recognize that they have been inducted into a capitalist mindset and are blind to the real world. They have had, and continue to have, their personalities, values, beliefs, and aspirations imposed upon them. They have been convinced they are free, but they actually live enslaved to the wishes of the ruling classes.

Second, the Marxist teacher should enable students to understand that they cannot realize their own potential in a world that deprives them of personal freedom, social justice, and material circumstances. Potentiality cannot become actuality without conditions that both allow and encourage development. Therefore, teachers should prepare students to counter the oppressive system.

Work for a classless society

Finally, the Marxist teacher can contribute greatly to the liberation of all peoples by encouraging students to work for a classless society, a people's democracy. That classless society would come about when each person is valued for his or her contribution to life in a communal environment. It would be a political entity that is governed by people who are concerned with everyone and with everyone's real needs. The teacher, then, is a necessary factor, for students must be awakened to the political ideology that engulfs them, to the material conditions essential to self-actualization, and to the type of government concerned with justice and respect for all people.

Critical Theory

Early in the twentieth century, a group of European intellectuals began arguing openly against the injustice, coercion, and oppression that was obvious in their countries. With roots in Marxism, their criticisms of society and its institutions evolved in ways that orthodox Marxists would never have envisioned. They probed into every area of life and society to uncover privileged groups, whether caused by birth, gender, age, race, class, occupation, inheritance, religion, or education and to expose authoritarianism and oppression regardless of whether it resulted from governmental, economic, political, professional, educational, or familial circumstances. Herbert Marcuse and Erich Fromm, among others, contributed much to this position. Others, such as Paulo Freire, Jurgen Habermas, Peter McClaren, Joe Kincheloe, and Henry Giroux, have continued this tradition in the field of education.[22]

Counter authoritarian oppression

Critical theorists are interested in nearly every topic that seems to explain how society and schools are organized, arranged, and configured; and they search for oppressive motives within each. For instance, they have examined school curricula, teaching methodologies, educational research, institutional management, district governance, physical arrangements, and fiscal policy in an effort to uncover ways in which women, teachers, students, parents, and minorities have been oppressed by the state and its agencies, which, in turn, are viewed as mechanisms that have been established by controlling interests in a country. Nearly every aspect of schooling has been described as either an informal or formal way of exploiting oppressed peoples, such as children, youth, women, minorities, the economically disadvantaged.

Although critical theorists have been criticized for reducing every pedagogical issue to a political problem and for lacking specific suggestions for the improvement of schools, these criticisms may be less valid today than they were in the past. Today, critical theorists may be found recommending democratization of the entire educational enterprise; ethnic, economic, and gender sensitivity in curricular development; increased productivity in action research; elimination of authoritarian relationships among students, teachers, administrators, and school boards; and recognition that all truth or knowledge is socially created and interpreted.

Critical theorists encourage teachers to scrutinize their everyday activities to identify and eliminate ideas and elements that contribute to the advantage of privileged groups and their values. In essence, they want teachers to help students bring about the transformation of schools and society by purging what they believe are the unfair and undemocratic practices, beliefs, policies, and laws that dominate educational, economic, political, and social institutions.

EDUCATIONAL RESEARCH

A Philosophical Perspective

This Educational Research section asks you to pause in your study of research on teaching and schools in order to think about how research is affected by philosophy and how philosophy is affected by research. It describes some of the ways philosophers look at research, and it uses ideas from other Educational Research sections as examples.

Philosophers, like other specialists who study teaching and schools, examine education from particular perspectives; and points of view influence the way they analyze and evaluate what they learn. The perspectives also enable them to offer advice to other educators. For instance, philosophers warn that teachers do not adopt a teaching style, learning theory, or curricular design simply because of a research report; and researchers do not engage in a specific kind of research simply because of an idealized theoretical idea. Philosophers remind us that all individuals who work with educational phenomena begin with a cluster of philosophical beliefs that, with or without their awareness, shape their professional choices, including their selection of techniques, materials, hypotheses, explanations, and recommendations.

Especially important influences on educators establishing research agendas and interpreting research data produced by others are their beliefs about human nature. For example, because theorists such as B. F. Skinner, Wolfgang Kohler, and Jean Piaget made separate assumptions about human nature, they approached their studies differently, and the elements of learning theory that they generated do not consist of a single set of coherent principles.

Because of this—the fact that beliefs influence research—philosophers make a number of observations and recommendations about evaluating research. Among these recommendations are the following:

- An educator's beliefs affect research and interpretations of research.
- The effect of a researcher's philosophical beliefs on his or her studies should be carefully assessed.
- Alternatives to a researcher's philosophical beliefs, hypotheses, and interpretations should be considered and evaluated.
- The relative merits of a researcher's work should be decided in view of philosophical beliefs.
- The knowledge gained from research should be used judiciously.

A second way in which philosophers' perspectives influence their view of research can be illustrated by reexamining Lloyd Dunn's criticisms of separate special education classes, as reported in the Educational Research section of Chapter 5. Dunn, although not a philosopher, concluded that it is morally wrong to classify students and then separate students with handicapping conditions into special education classes. His rationale for concluding that the practice is wrong is related to what he saw as both the intentions of educators and the outcomes of the separation. The intention of some educators was to get hard-to-teach students and minority group members out of "normal" classrooms. The outcomes that he considered reprehensible included lower achievement by disadvantaged students, reduction of teachers' expectations of these students, damages to children's self-images, and an increase in inferior feelings in students.

Although Dunn concluded that the practice of separating special needs students was not effective educationally for students, suppose for a moment that he were incorrect. Assume instead that the research data had indicated that the practice significantly enhanced the learning of handicapped students. Further, assume that all of the intentions of educators had been noble. If both of these assumptions had been correct, however, the separate-class approach to educating special needs students would still have had a negative impact upon the self-images and feelings of these students. In this hypothetical situation, research would have prompted a serious conflict of values—the practice would have worked in terms of educational

gains, and it would have been well intended, but would it have been ethical?

Several philosophical points surface from this example. First, educators need to be concerned with the morality of educational practice, as well as with teaching effectiveness; and the morality of the practice should have priority. (Just because a practice works does not make it right.) Second, although researchers as scientists describe what *is* or *was*, rather than what *ought to be*, their work frequently involves ethical issues. (Dunn argued that segregating special needs students was morally wrong. When he did, he spoke not as a scientist but as a moral philosopher.) Third, the soundness of researchers' ethical positions is as important as the soundness of their research design, and both need to be analyzed. Fourth, moral issues, while partly informed by ethical principles, human intentions, educational outcomes, and related matters, are also dependent upon facts. (Without the outcomes Dunn identified, it would have been much more difficult to conclude that separate classes for special needs students are wrong.)

Although philosophy guides research and the ways in which research findings are used, the reverse is also true. Research also influences philosophy. In fact, any

educator's philosophy of education can and should profit immeasurably from educational research; and educators who are so rigid philosophically that they ignore research data do so at their own peril and at the peril of their students. For example, research on classroom environments and interactions, which is discussed in Chapters 3 and 13, may cause teachers to alter part of their philosophy of teaching; to be more specific, they may reject the belief that students who do not talk in class are necessarily less capable than those who do so. When educators change their views like this, they use research to reassess their beliefs and to discard ill-founded ones.

In the best of circumstances, teachers want to determine whether their philosophical positions are consistent with the findings of educational researchers. If they are, their ideas are confirmed; but if a coherent body of research findings is incompatible with their philosophical beliefs, they are well advised to reevaluate both the research and their philosophies. Likewise, teachers are well advised to determine what difference their philosophy makes upon research efforts and the use of research data. In this way, educational research can challenge philosophical beliefs as well as be challenged by it.

Conclusion

Building a philosophy of education is a long, ongoing process. The original idealists, realists, pragmatists, and existentialists did not wake up one morning with their complete systems of thought ready for distribution. Nor did the developers of reconstructionism, futurism, behaviorism, perennialism, essentialism, evangelicalism, Marxism, and critical theory hastily arrive at their destinations. To the degree that they consciously philosophized, they sought answers to fundamental questions over a period of years, if not throughout their lives. They consistently asked questions of themselves and others:

- What precisely do I mean?
- What evidence and arguments support my views?
- What philosophical beliefs led to the discovery of these data?
- How should these data be understood?
- Do these findings form a coherent pattern?
- Is the pattern consistent with my worldview?

Prior to their philosophizing, they groped for answers, probed for clarity, wondered about evidence, and looked for reasons.

Fortunately, most teachers also construct their own philosophies of education over time, revising them as necessary. In doing so, they draw on all of their studies and experiences. Some such studies contribute directly and others indirectly. Studies in educational psychology, learning theory, instructional methodology, classroom management, and curriculum development are particularly informative. Also important is the contribution of teaching itself to an educational philosophy. Teaching contributes by providing fresh insights, testing suggested strategies, discrediting questionable assumptions, and confirming research findings.

Experienced teachers quickly realize that some philosophies of education address the realities and concerns of secondary teachers more than they do those of early childhood educators. Experience also shows that some educational philosophies better answer the questions raised about certain types of students than do others—for example, students at different grade levels, those with weak academic backgrounds, those from affluent homes, and those in religious schools.

As you develop professionally, you will want to engage in a concerted, focused study of educational philosophy. The descriptions of philosophies given here are intentionally phrased in terms as positive as possible, given our own biases. Of necessity, not all philosophies were included and only a limited number of viewpoints were seriously considered. The continuing search into philosophy of education will provide you with intellectual stimulation, an element in the lives of teachers that is often missing from less challenging professions.

REFLECTING ON PRACTICE

*T*his Reflecting on Practice section describes a teacher, Mr. Pavid, who is insecure and who constantly adapts his views, values, and practices to those around him. The example alludes to a variety of problems that future and beginning teachers may encounter, whether they are insecure or not. As Mr. Pavid changes his teaching positions and practices to agree with those of his colleagues, he combines incoherent and inconsistent ideas from a variety of philosophical and pedagogical positions. As you read the account, think about possible answers to the following questions:

- In what ways do the philosophical beliefs you studied and the perspectives you examined in this chapter throw light upon Mr. Pavid's personal needs, habits, and teaching potential?

- Does Mr. Pavid really have a personal philosophical viewpoint? Explain why you drew this conclusion.
- Which appears to be the greater problem for Mr. Pavid: his prior life experiences or his philosophical viewpoint? Can the two be separated? What makes you draw this conclusion?
- If you were Mr. Pavid's principal or supervisor, how would you guide him during the school year? What suggestions would you make? Would your advice constitute an attempt to get him to adopt a different philosophy of life and teaching? Should a person ever recommend a different philosophy to another person? What makes you think so?
- Because many teachers, like Mr. Pavid, are eclectic in their philosophies of education, what kind of cautions do you think teacher education students and novice teachers should be given by professors and experienced teachers? Would these cautions have been helpful in Mr. Pavid's case? Why?

A Third-Grade Teacher

Mr. Pavid, a beginning third-grade teacher, considers himself an eclectic existentialist with a deep appreciation for some insights he has gathered from other philosophical and pedagogical positions. His beliefs were radically altered during his junior and senior years at the university when he learned that other college students were ridiculing his so-called unfashionable and traditional ideas. Initially, he resented their remarks, but gradually he modified his views so that he would be more acceptable to his peers. Unfortunately, in his eyes, nothing he did seemed enough to make them accept him. He always seemed to feel he was different and unaccepted.

As Mr. Pavid began his first teaching assignment as a third-grade teacher, he listened carefully to other teachers to find out what they did in their classes. He frequently made statements or raised questions along the following lines, "How do you handle a student when she misbehaves? What do you think I should do with students who don't participate? When you have a student who cannot understand what he reads, what do you do? Do you think it is fair to punish the entire class when several act out? My supervisor told me she thinks that I haven't learned to integrate the various components of the curriculum into my teaching activities. Can I observe you sometime to see how you do it?" To the best of his ability, he attempted to follow the advice of all of his colleagues.

As the year progressed, it became increasingly clear that Mr. Pavid was questioning and observing other teachers so he could almost unreflectively emulate their styles of teaching. The insecurities that appeared while he was an undergraduate student and led him to assume the outward stance of an existentialist now lead him to select eclectically an assortment of habits and beliefs from his colleagues. In the process of selecting ideas and practices from his teaching peers, he now keeps mixing thoughts and activities that are logically inconsistent and pedagogically incompatible. His general dissatisfaction with teaching and lack of comfort in the classroom have become increasingly clear to students, parents, supervisors, and colleagues. Regardless of the situation he finds himself in, he always seems to be trying to please those around him, but never fully achieves his goal for obvious reasons. His future as an educator seems much in doubt.

Summary

This chapter surveyed some of the most fundamental ideas in philosophy of education. First, it noted that teachers teach differently from one another and that these differences are partially attributable to their philosophical beliefs. Philosophical differences are reflected, too, in various kinds of educational institutions, laws, and textbooks.

Second, the chapter illustrated educational philosophy as a set of intellectual activities in which teachers engage. These activities are clarification, justification, interpretation, and systematization. Taken together, these activities enable teachers to think clearly, logically, ethically, and comprehensively about educational concerns.

Third, the chapter analyzed some of the main Western philosophies and their connections to philosophy of education. Although some historical roots were noted, emphasis was placed upon understanding contemporary idealists, realists, pragmatists, existentialists, reconstructionists, futurists, behaviorists, perennialists, essentialists, evangelicalists, Marxists, and critical theorists. The views of each group of philosophers on metaphysics, epistemology, axiology, and pedagogy were noted. All of these ideas were presented with the goal of preparing you to formulate your own philosophy of education.

Study Questions

1. Which philosophy do you prefer at this point in your thinking? Why do you prefer it? In terms of education, what is the greatest *strength* of the position you like *least?* What is the greatest *weakness* of the position you like *most?*

2. What would you do if you were told that your educational philosophy is out of place in the school where you teach? Is it ever fair to restrict the implementation or application of a teacher's philosophy of education? If so, when?

3. If you were free to organize a school completely as you desired, would you welcome teachers with different philosophies from yours? Why or why not?

4. Are school accountability efforts, teacher evaluation, and student assessment programs covert ways of manipulating schooling and imposing a particular educational philosophy on teachers and students? If so, should teachers resist such attempts? If so, when?

5. Do you find yourself combining ideas from a number of educational philosophies? If yes, why do you take this combinationist approach? What are the advantages of this approach? And the disadvantages?

6. Should teachers have a social mission? If so, what is it? If not, why?

Key Terms

Aesthetic value judgments
Aesthetics
Authentic people
Axiology
Behaviorism
Clarifying
Classical realists
Coherence
Contemporary philosophies
Critical theory
Eclectic
Epistemology
Essentialism
Ethical value judgments
Ethics
Evangelicalism
Existentialism

Futurism
Idealism
Idealists
Interpreting
Justifying
Leap of faith
Marxism
Materialistic realists
Materialists
Metaphysics
Neo-Thomists
Perennialism
Philosophizing
Pragmatism
Preferential value
  judgments
Realism

Realists
Reality
Reason
Reconstructionism
Relevance
Religious
  existentialists
Religious realists
Socialization
Spiritual reality
Systematizing
Traditional realists
Ultimate reality
Universal values

For Further Reading

Apple, M. (1993). *Official knowledge: Democratic education in a conservative age.* New York: Routledge, Chapman and Hall.

Aronowitz, S., & Giroux, H. (1991). *Postmodern education: Politics, culture, and social criticism.* Minneapolis: University of Minnesota.

Barrow, R., & Woods, R. (1988). *An introduction to philosophy of education* (3rd ed.). London: Routledge.

Chambers, J. H. (1989). *The achievement of education: An examination of key concepts in educational practice.* Lanham, MD: University Press of America.

Duck, L. (1981). *Teaching with charisma.* Boston: Allyn and Bacon.

Fitzgibbons, R. E. (1981). *Making educational decisions: An introduction to philosophy of education.* New York: Harcourt Brace Jovanovich.

Giroux, H. (1991). *Border crossings: Cultural workers and the politics of education.* New York: Routledge.

Griese, A. A. (1981). *Your philosophy of education: What is it?* Santa Monica, CA: Goodyear.

Gutek, G. L. (1988). *Philosophical and ideological perspectives on education.* Englewood Cliffs, NJ: Prentice-Hall.

Hamm, C. (1989). *Philosophical issues in education: An introduction.* London: Falmer Press.

Hare, W. (1993). *What makes a good teacher?* London, ON: Althouse Press.

Kincheloe, J. (1993). *Toward critical politics of teacher thinking: Mapping the postmodern.* Westport, CT: Bergin and Garvey.

McLaren, P. (1989). *Life in schools: An introduction to critical pedagogy in foundations of educations.* New York: Longman.

O'Neill, W. F. (1990). *Educational ideologies: Contemporary expressions of educational philosophy.* Dubuque, IA: Kendall/Hunt.

Ozmon, H. A., & Craver, S. M. (1990). *Philosophical foundations of education* (4th ed.). Columbus, OH: Charles E. Merrill.

Peterson, M. L. (1986). *Philosophy of education: Issues and options.* Downers Grove, IL: InterVarsity Press.

Portelli, J., & Bailin, S. (Eds.). (1993). *Reason and values: New essays in philosophy of education.* Calgary, Alberta: Detselig Enterprises.

Pratte, R. (1992). *Philosophy of education: Two traditions.* Springfield, IL: Charles C Thomas.

Simpson, D. J. (1994). *The pedagodfathers: The lords of education.* Calgary, Alberta: Detselig Enterprises.

Simpson, D. J., & Jackson, M. J. B. (1984). *The teacher as philosopher: A primer in philosophy of education.* Toronto: Methuen.

Sockett, H. (1993). *The moral base of teacher professionalism.* New York: Teachers College Press.

Stanley, W. (1992). *Curriculum for utopia: Social reconstruction and critical pedagogy in postmodern era.* Albany: State University of New York Press.

UNIT

4

Content, Curriculum, and Instruction

Unit 4 consists of Chapters 11 through 14 and has two thrusts. It provides information about the content or subject matter teachers teach and explains how that content is organized into curricula. It also describes how teachers produce successful lessons by putting content together with the other elements of teaching that you have studied.

After studying the unit, you should understand the nature of content and how teachers fit content with purposes for schools, characteristics of students, learning theories, the culture of the schools and classes, and educational philosophy so that all these elements form a plan for conducting lessons. You should also understand how planning, teaching, and evaluating lessons are intertwined.

Chapter 11 describes the nature of content in terms of three dimensions: knowledge, skills, and affective aspects of learning. It explains each of these dimensions further as facts, concepts, generalizations, thinking, skills other than thinking, values, feelings, sensitivities, and decision making.

Chapter 12 explores ways that content is organized into curricula, units, and lessons and how it is combined with teaching strategies, classroom activities, and instructional materials to produce learning. The chapter describes different approaches to organizing curricula on a continuum from primarily subject-centered to primarily student-centered.

Chapter 13 asks you to draw upon all that you have read so far in this text. It describes what teachers do to create learning as a multifaceted process labeled *the act of teaching*. It explains how teaching and learning take place in classrooms and what teachers do to make the right things happen. It portrays the act of teaching as a three-step endeavor of planning, implementing those plans, and evaluating.

Because Chapter 13 focuses on classroom teaching, pause as you study this chapter to reflect upon how your ideas about classroom teaching have developed since you started this text. In Chapter 2 you began shifting your thinking from that of an "outside observer" of teaching to that of a "beginning expert." Notice how much you have learned and how much more sophisticated, reflective, and analytical your thinking has become; also think of how your ideas about teaching and teachers have changed since you sat in pre-K–12 classes as a student.

Chapter 14 contains descriptions and analyses of five models of instruction. Each model stresses different combinations of educational philosophy, learning theory, views of students, and instructional objectives. The five models illustrate ways various educational experts suggest lesson sequences be developed and taught. They represent ways some experts suggest teachers pursue *the act of teaching*.

When you finish each chapter, you should have an understanding of the general concepts listed below and have begun to develop the skills noted.

CHAPTER 11
Content: Knowledge, Skills, and Affective Learning

- The content taught in schools can be thought of as having three dimensions—knowledge, skills, and affective learning.

- All three dimensions need to be taught to all students, in all subjects, at all grade levels.

Skills

- An ability to connect intellectually different types of content—knowledge, skills, and affective learning—with approaches to teaching that are appropriate for each

- An ability to recognize classroom teaching that is compatible with different types of content

CHAPTER 12
The Curriculum and Lessons: Designs for Learning

- The school curriculum is a framework developed by educators to integrate all the dimensions of content into a teachable pattern.

- Students learn more in school than the content planned for them in the prepared curriculum; some of this is called the hidden curriculum.

Skills

- An ability to fit levels of content and teaching strategies into appropriate curricular patterns and sequences

- An ability to detect how school culture and the hidden curriculum affect student learning

CHAPTER 13
The Act of Teaching: Planning, Implementing, and Evaluating

- Teaching is a complex act in which teachers take all the ideas and elements affecting education that are available to them and formulate them in a personal way to produce learning in their students.

- Teaching is a multifaceted process that includes thorough planning, implementing those plans as classroom lessons, and lesson evaluation. Teaching can be thought of as a process of communication between the teacher and students.

Skills

- A beginning ability to plan lessons that pursue objectives and lead to appropriate student learning

- A beginning ability to evaluate the effectiveness of lessons

CHAPTER 14
Models of Instruction

- Models of instruction are designs for teaching based on particular purposes of schools, theories of learning, and philosophies of education; their purpose is to help teachers accomplish specific learning goals.

- Teachers tend to pursue models of instruction that are consistent with their own ideas about teaching and learning.

Skill

- An ability to analyze models of instruction in terms of learning theory, philosophy of education, and goals of instruction

Content
Knowledge, Skills, and Affective Learning

*T*his chapter is devoted to the content taught in schools. The first part describes content as a whole, and a second part explains content in terms of three dimensions—knowledge, skills, and affective aspects of learning, such as values, feelings, and sensitivities. The skills dimension is further subdivided into thinking and other types of skills. Later, Chapter 12 describes how content is fitted together in a school curriculum.

Educators today express a number of competing views about what actually constitutes the subject-matter content of schools and what that content should be. These differing views then affect their beliefs about how content should be related to the other ingredients in classroom teaching—classroom processes, theories of learning and instruction, philosophies of education, and so forth. Because of this state of flux and because this text is designed to present you with general conceptual frameworks that you can use to understand developing ideas and trends now and in the future, the chapter treatment of content is historical. For example, instead of focusing on currently competing ideas about content, the chapter devotes considerable attention to the subject-matter ideas of Jerome Bruner, Hilda Taba, and John Dewey, educators who were most prominent in the 1960s and earlier. The authors believe that those ideas will provide you with useful ways of understanding how content fits into classroom activities. You will likely study contemporary issues and trends in other courses.

Although the term *content* is often thought of narrowly, as only the *information* students are taught, here it is considered in a much broader sense. This chapter uses the term to mean everything students are taught—or as a high school student once explained, "Content is all the 'stuff' teachers teach to kids."

The chapter Snapshot is an excerpt from a classic satire on what is taught in schools and its relevance to the real lives of students and society in general. The Reflecting on Practice asks you to apply the ideas presented in the first two sections of the chapter by developing possible lessons. The Educational Research section looks at studies of a particular aspect of content—the teaching of history.

SNAPSHOT

*T*he *Saber-Tooth Curriculum* is a satire of education in a fictional primitive society where the content taught to students was not modified as life conditions changed over time. The now-classic work was written in 1939 by educator Harold Benjamin, who used the pseudonym J. Abner Peddiwell.[1] It is paraphrased in the Snapshot for this chapter. As you read consider:

■ To what extent is the situation described similar to situations that occur today when educators make decisions about content?

■ In what ways does the content in schools you know about reflect present social conditions, past traditions, and individual priorities of public policymakers?

■ What would be the most appropriate justification for each of the subjects that you studied in high school? In elementary school? In college?

■ What parallels do you see between this story and the case of Dennis Littky described in Chapter 1?

The Saber-Tooth Curriculum

According to J. Abner Peddiwell, there lived in Chellean times the world's first educational theorist and practitioner, one New-Fist-Hammer-Maker, who was known locally as New-Fist. New-Fist was a talented and educated maker of fine hunting clubs of stone. He was also a thinker and an idealist who wanted to help the people of his stone-age society improve their lives.

As a student of society and education, New-Fist often sat by the early morning fire studying how adults in his community went about meeting the basic needs of life—food, clothing, shelter, and security—and he tried to devise a way of making their work easier and their lives better.

Eventually, he thought that if the children were provided with a systematic education, they could help the tribe meet its needs in better ways. To accomplish this, he decided to teach his children three subjects:

1. fish-grabbing-with-the-bare-hands
2. woolly-horse-clubbing
3. saber-tooth-tiger-scaring-with-fire

These subjects would eventually provide more to eat, more skins for clothing, and more protection from the dangerous tiger.

As he taught these subjects to his own children, other parents followed his example. For a time, conservative tribe members objected because of religious principles, but gradually more and more parents were won over to New-Fist's ideas. Soon it became obvious that the students trained as New-Fist recommended were leading more successful lives, and eventually the whole tribe became prosperous and more secure.

If conditions in the society had not changed, New-Fist's curriculum would probably have served the tribe well forever. But conditions did change.

As a new ice age approached, a glacier crept close to the headwaters of the creek that ran through the tribe's valley. This caused dirt and gravel to be collected in the stream's water, clouding the clear creek with mud. No one could see fish in the muddy water. Even the best-educated fish-grabbing students could not catch the fish.

The additional water in the stream made the land near the village wetter than before, and this caused the woolly horses to migrate to drier land, away from

the tribe. Antelopes replaced the horses, but they were more shy and speedier than the horses. They also had a keener scent for detecting approaching hunters. As a result, horse-clubbing hunters returned day after day to the village without their prey. Even those who were taught the most efficient club-hunting techniques returned empty-handed.

The dampness from the glacial conditions gave the saber-tooth tigers pneumonia, and they died. When the tigers were gone, ferocious glacial bears entered the area. The bears were not frightened by fire and could not be driven away by even the most advanced methods of tiger scaring taught in the school.

The community was in a very difficult situation. The people had no fish or meat to eat, no skins for clothing, and no security from attacking bears.

Faced with these circumstances, several of New-Fist's more thoughtful descendants devised ways to overcome the difficulties. One devised a crude net to catch fish in the muddy water. Another invented a trap to snare the swift antelopes. A third dug camouflaged pits in the bear trails to catch the threatening animals.

Fortunately, the people of the tribe learned the new techniques. They caught fish in nets, snared antelopes in traps, and killed bears in pits. The community was once again well fed, clothed, and secure.

When some thoughtful people asked why net making, trap setting, and pit digging could not be taught in school, those in control told them that such subjects were not appropriate education. After all, these sorts of things were practical, life-preserving skills, which should be taught outside school. They were not *education;* they were *training.* They did not qualify to be taught in school.

Moreover, school leaders pointed out that the school curriculum was filled with the traditional cultural subjects— fish grabbing, horse clubbing, and tiger scaring. Students needed to study fish grabbing because it developed agility.

They needed to study horse clubbing because it developed physical strength. They needed to study tiger scaring because it instilled courage. Unlike more practical training, these subjects provided general education that carried over into all affairs of life.

Some radical villagers were not satisfied. They continued to object. They pointed out that times had changed and advocated that more up-to-date activities be tried

in school. They even suggested that these new subjects might have significant educational value.

The elders replied, "If you had any education yourself, you would know that the essence of education is timelessness. It is something that endures through changing conditions like a solid rock standing squarely and firmly in the middle of a raging torrent. You must know that there are some eternal verities, and the sabertooth curriculum is one of them!"

The Nature of Content

When most people think of the subject-matter content taught in schools, they usually think of information—the facts and ideas taught to students. But content is not limited to information. It also consists of thinking skills, a wide range of other skills, and components from the affective domain. For example, schools teach the thinking processes of comprehension, analysis, and synthesis; the skills of reading, writing, word processing, library research, speaking, and dancing; and such affective content as the values of justice and equity, the feelings of anxiety and frustration, and the sensitivities of sympathy and empathy. Therefore, when schools are successful, their students learn not only information but also content of several different types.

Information as Part of Content

Before devoting attention to the various dimensions of content, however, we must take a closer look at the nature of *information*. That look should clarify two persistent misconceptions about what information is and what its place in the processes of teaching and learning is. The first misconception is the confusion of information taught in schools with academic disciplines. The second is the failure to distinguish between information that is something to be *learned by* students and information that is a device teachers *use to produce learning in* students.

Different from academic disciplines

Often, information taught to students in schools is thought to be identical to what is studied by academic researchers. Tenth-grade biology is considered to be the same as research biology; high school algebra, the same as the content of the theoretical mathematician; and school French, the same French as that of the college French linguist. These things are simply not the same.

Selected information

Information taught in schools is drawn from the scholarly disciplines, but it is not taken indiscriminately. It is *selected* by educators who have *criteria* in mind when making their selections. It is chosen to fit the students being taught, to help them learn what the teacher has in mind. Therefore, the history taught by elementary and secondary school social studies teachers is more general, more selective, less detailed, and less precise than the history studied in college and investigated by research historians. Similarly, the physiology taught by high school science teachers is different from that of research physiologists; and the elements of drama taught by English and language arts teachers are different from those used by playwrights or drama critics.

Purpose and use of information

The difference between information taught in schools and academic disciplines derives from the *purpose* or *use* of each. Academicians and researchers use knowledge to investigate, to create new knowledge, and to organize that knowledge. Teachers use less complex versions of that knowledge, and they translate the information into terms that their students can understand. They use only part of the information, the part that they believe will help students learn and understand. Although their roles overlap, disciplinary scholars stress the probing and exploring aspects of their work, while teachers stress presentation and explanation.

Information taught in schools is also often thought of simply as the "stuff" that students are expected to know. That idea makes sense and is valid to a degree, but it is too limited. It creates the image that when teachers teach, all they do is pour information into the heads of students, whose only function is to absorb that information. Of course, teachers and students do more than this.

Earlier chapters have demonstrated that learning is a process of change in people. That change has many dimensions, only one of which is acquiring new ideas. Because this is the case, instead of thinking of information only as ideas to be poured into students' heads, it is more useful to think of it also as a *device* that teachers use to promote the opportunity for many kinds of learning in students. With this perspective, information becomes a means that teachers use to get students *to do things with ideas*—things such as analyzing their thoughts, refining their thinking abilities, assessing their values, becoming more aware of others' feelings, and so forth. Students who do things with ideas do learn new information, but they also learn much more.

Device to produce learning

Here are some ways teachers use information as a device to create several kinds of learning:

- History teachers can use information about the American Civil War not only to teach facts about that war but also to teach the concepts of war, conflict, patriotism, slavery, sectional loyalty, tradition, militarism, human values, freedom, equality, and so on. By doing this, teachers use information about the Civil War to produce broader, more meaningful, and more useful learning than would be provided if a lesson contained only specific information about a specific war.
- Teachers of literature can use a novel as a basis for discussing a variety of ideas, insights, and values about people in general, not just about those in that particular piece of literary work.
- Biology teachers can have students study the anatomy of a frog to teach anatomy and physiology of animals in general, including humans.

When teachers see information as a means to accomplish many educational goals, rather than only as an accumulation of ideas to be absorbed by students for their own sake, they can produce more significant and more varied learning. They can make content more dynamic and learning more active.

Deciding What to Teach

Because the primary purpose of education is to change students in certain expected ways, educators select content that they believe will help them change their students in the ways they desire. When they do this, they base their decisions on a number of factors:

Subject matter and educational objectives

1. the availability of content that can be taught
2. the values of the society that the school serves
3. their knowledge of the students they teach
4. their understanding of the nature of the teaching and learning processes.

For the most part, they select content that will

1. add to the knowledge, understandings, and insights that their students already possess
2. develop students' thinking abilities
3. enable students to attain skills that they could not otherwise use
4. help students develop certain values, feelings, and sensitivities in an on-going process of development.

As the process is explained in current educational terminology, teachers choose content for their classrooms that will enable their students to reach desired *outcomes* or *educational objectives*.[2]

The remainder of this chapter explores the three dimensions of content; then, Chapter 12 says more about the process of selecting content to be taught. As you study the rest of this chapter, remember that content is not the end product of learning; it is, instead, something used by teachers to produce learning in students—that is, to change students in many ways.

Also as you read this chapter, keep in mind the message of the chapter Snapshot on the saber-tooth curriculum—content must be appropriate for the students and the community in which they live and function. In these current times of rapid change, the content students study must be revised continually, or it will quickly become dated.

Knowledge as Content

At the beginning of this chapter, *content* was described as consisting of at least three dimensions—knowledge, skills, and affective aspects of learning. This section of the chapter looks at each of these dimensions. It focuses first on *knowledge*—the area that consists of the facts and ideas that students are expected to acquire.

The knowledge dimension of content is not simply a mass of facts to be pushed into students' brains. Although there are, of course, millions of facts to be taught and learned, some of them are more important than others, and some are more useful to student understanding. Also, facts are not isolated or separate from each other. They are interrelated in a multitude of ways, and they can be used to generate concepts, generalizations, models, theories, and laws and rules.

If knowledge were only a collection of similar but unrelated facts, it would be impossible to remember and understand all of them. There would be too much to know and no rational way to approach the task.

The Structure of Knowledge

Fortunately, knowledge has structure—structure that people use to learn and to understand, structure that teachers use to determine what to teach and how to teach it. The structure has been developed by academic scholars as they have studied their various fields, and it has evolved over many years. As a result, knowledge is organized into categories and hierarchies, and the parts are arranged so that they have meaning.

Two views of the structure of knowledge are described below. Scholars often use the two to analyze and explain their areas of expertise; teachers use them to

TABLE 11-1   Knowledge Organized by Discipline

Humanities	Mathematics	Social Sciences	Natural Sciences
Language	Computation	History	Botany
Composition	Algebra	Geography	Zoology
Speech	Geometry	Economics	Chemistry
Literature	Trigonometry	Anthropology	Physics
Art	Calculus	Sociology	Geology
Music		Psychology	Astronomy
		Political science	

educate students. The first perspective classifies knowledge into fields of study, or *disciplines*. The second separates knowledge into *levels of abstraction*, the layers of which are called facts, concepts, and generalizations. In a way of speaking, the first perspective places knowledge into vertical categories, and the second into horizontal layers. Table 11-1 represents the first configuration, and Figure 11-1 shows the second.

FIGURE 11-1   Knowledge organized by level of abstraction. Although experts often disagree over the question of which are more abstract, generalizations or concepts, this text arbitrarily shows generalizations as more abstract to provide this graphic illustration.

LEVELS OF ABSTRACTION

High Level

Generalizations

Reptiles often frighten people because of their appearance; quiet, slithery movement; and reputation for harm to humans.

Poems are writings intended to be read for pleasure; for delight in sound, rhythm, and meter; for emotional experience; and for understanding of the poet who created the work.

Concepts

Reptiles

Animals that are cold-blooded vertebrates, with lungs, have an outer covering of horny scales or plates, and produce young in eggs.

Poems

Literary compositions in which words are chosen for their sound and suggestive power, either in verse or having the intensity of imagination and language common to verse.

Facts or Items

Specific Reptiles

turtles
snakes
lizards
crocodiles
alligators

Specific Poems

Frost's "The Road Not Taken"
Hughes's "Mother to Son"
Fitzgerald's "Cobb Would Have
    Caught It"
Sandburg's "Chicago"
Wylie's "The Highwayman"

Low Level

Disciplines

Its own content

Each academic discipline is a category of knowledge that has two main characteristics that distinguish it from other disciplines. A *discipline* has its own content and its own specialized method of investigation. For example, the *content* of physics consists of such topics as matter, energy, force, and dynamics; that of economics includes scarcity, supply, demand, and price. The *methods* of the chemist center on empirical analyses of substances under laboratory conditions; those of the anthropologist concentrate on searching for artifacts and interpreting objects and documents.

Disciplinary categories, however, are artificial. They separate data that when found in nature, are not really separate; and they differ from each other *by degree* rather than *in kind.* For instance, although sociologists, economists, geographers, political scientists, biologists, chemists, and geologists might all study different aspects of a community, that community does not really consist of seven separate parts. The community exists as an integrated entity, and its components all overlap. The people who live there do not act sociologically in the morning, geographically in the afternoon, and biologically later in the week. They simply act.

The disciplinary scholars who study that integrated community, however, separate what they see into terms that fit their disciplines. They focus on different components of the community, stress different things, conduct different types of analyses, and form different conclusions. At the end of their studies, each individual disciplinary scholar understands one aspect of the community better than other aspects; but a reasonably complete understanding of the community develops only when those separate ideas, analyses, and conclusions are combined.

Academic disciplines serve elementary and secondary school students in ways similar to the ways they serve scholars, but obviously on another intellectual level. They help make a vast, complex, interrelated world more understandable (1) by separating it into parts that can be studied one at a time and (2) by providing a way of looking at each part that helps explain it. Because disciplines play these roles in

Although this village in Kenya is a single, living entity, a "disciplines" approach makes it the focus of separate investigations in anthropology, agriculture, ecology, history, and so on. What are the advantages and shortcomings of this way of organizing knowledge?

learning, school instruction is based to some degree on them, as can be seen in a review of school schedules, which typically divide instruction into subjects that rest on disciplines—English, science, mathematics, social studies, graphic arts, and so on.

Levels of Abstraction

Knowledge also consists of different layers (Figure 11-1). According to one way of looking at those layers, the lowest level is that of specific facts, things, actions, and events: for example, the parts of the human body, the capitals of states, the correct spelling of words, the dates of historical events, and the answers to simple mathematical computations. These are often referred to as the *basic facts* of a subject. They are the "fundamentals" that many traditional educators say should be "covered" for an elementary understanding of a topic.

Basic facts

Although individual items at this level of knowledge are less significant than those at higher levels, facts are important. They are the building blocks for the development of ideas. People cannot learn if they do not know at least some of the facts.

Concepts are a higher layer of knowledge than facts. They are mental categories or groupings into which facts can be placed. For example, the following are concepts: human beings, animals, government, conflict, and whole number. They are general *ideas* instead of specific items. For instance, the concept *war* is a general category that includes the specific item *American Revolution*, and the concept *insect* is a general category that includes a specific *fly* on the classroom wall.

Concepts

Although concepts as a group constitute one layer of knowledge, the range of difference among them is great. At one extreme are concepts that are narrow and precise; at the other end are general and abstract concepts. The range begins just one step above specific facts and continues to the most general and abstract ideas people can think of.

All of the terms in Figures 11-2 and 11-3 represent concepts. Those at the bottom of each diagram are more narrow and less inclusive than the increasingly

FIGURE 11-2   Levels of concepts based on degree of generality. This illustration shows two columns of ideas. All items in each column are labels for concepts, but the items at the bottom are less inclusive (or smaller) than those at the top. They become more inclusive (or larger) each step up the columns.

LEVELS OF CONCEPTS BASED ON DEGREE OF GENERALITY		
General	Part of the universe	Global confrontation
	Element of the world	War
	Inhabitant of the earth	Battle
	Living thing	Skirmish
	Animal	Argument
Narrow	Human	Disagreement

FIGURE 11-3   Levels of concepts based on degree of abstractness. This illustration shows instances of the concept "fear." Those at the bottom are rather specific; those nearer the top are categories of "fear"; at the top is a general definition for the term.

	Abstract Concept of "Fear"			
Very Abstract	Fear—a feeling of distress, apprehension, alarm, anxiety, or concern			

General Categories of "Fear"

Fear from being startled	Fear of harm to others	Fear of harm to self	Fear of pain	Fear of death
Fear of loneliness	Fear of sadness	Fear out of concern for others	Fear of the unknown	Fear of danger
	Fear of failure	Fear of disappointment		Fear of punishment

Particular Instances of "Fear"

Fear shown in a novel when a person is awakened at night by the noise of a thunderstorm	Fear shown in a film when a person sees an automobile accident	Fear shown in a video when a burglar pulls a gun on a shop clerk
Fear experienced by a mother when she says goodbye to her son who is leaving for war as a soldier	Fear experienced by a child going to summer camp for the first time	
Fear experienced by an adult about to undergo open-heart surgery	Fear experienced by relatives of a person about to undergo open-heart surgery	Fear of failing an examination
Fear of not being picked for the cheerleading squad	Fear of being grounded by parents for staying out too late	Fear of being sent to jail for selling cocaine

Relatively Specific

general and abstract ones higher up. As you study the two figures, remember that the nature of concepts means that any attempt to arrange hierarchies among them, such as in these illustrations, is necessarily arbitrary and artificial. Which ideas are more general and more abstract than others simply depends on what different people have in mind when they think of the ideas. However, the illustrations are presented here so that you can see an example of some ways in which concepts of different degrees of generalization and different levels of abstraction might fit together. The particular orders shown are the orders suggested by a group of educators polled by the authors.

Generalizations, or *general principles*, constitute a third layer of knowledge, and according to the scheme presented here, a higher level. They are valid statements that describe relationships among concepts. They are statements that people use to organize concepts and facts into an intellectual system that makes sense. They look and sound like sentences that explain things.

In the following examples, the key words (those in italics) are key concepts, and the statements explain ways in which those concepts are related. If a person understands these statements and accepts them as valid explanations, he or she probably knows something more about the ideas described than a person without a comparable understanding.

- All *people need food, clothing*, and *shelter*.
- Under *normal environmental conditions, roots of plants* usually *grow* toward *water* in the *soil*, and *stems* and *leaves* usually *grow* toward *light*.
- *Intelligent people* usually become better *teachers* than *stupid people*.
- *Teachers* rarely *make* more *money* than *medical doctors*.

Some scholars who study the nature of knowledge have identified other levels in addition to these three, some organize the levels differently, and many would probably say that this three-level description is much too simplistic, but it is adequate for this stage of your study. The main points to remember are (1) knowledge contains a number of levels, (2) people use those different levels in their thinking, and (3) teachers can teach students best if they select different levels of knowledge when they select the subject matter they teach.[3]

Teaching the Structure of Knowledge

The idea of the structure of knowledge had special significance for educators of the 1950s and 1960s who were confronted with the realization that the traditional guide for what to teach—"the important facts of each subject"—was not possible or appropriate for elementary and secondary schools. The "information explosion" showed that there were just too many facts to teach, that more facts were being generated every day, and that the new information was changing some of the "correct answers" of the past. In their search for a new way of doing things, educators turned to ideas expressed in 1960 by Harvard psychologist and educator Jerome Bruner in his book *The Process of Education*.

The Process of Education crystallized thinking about how knowledge should be taught and greatly influenced the content of school curricula in subsequent years. Its main thesis is that students should be taught *the fundamental structure of knowledge* instead of a collection of basic facts and incidental information. For Bruner, this meant they should be taught

1. key concepts
2. fundamental principles or generalizations
3. methods of inquiry of the disciplines

Although there are more recent and more complex ways of thinking about knowledge and how to teach it, Bruner's ideas are presented here because they seem to be more useful than most for beginning teacher-education students. Once you

Generalizations

Fundamental structure of knowledge

Jerome Bruner's view of education inspired many teachers to deemphasize conveying information in favor of helping students learn how to learn.

Learn how to learn

Spiral instruction

understand Bruner's views, you should be able to use them as a way to develop an understanding of other ideas that you will encounter in future study.

Bruner believed that the learning of the fundamentals of knowledge would produce greater student understanding, encourage students to inquire into issues and solve problems independently, enable them to transfer ideas learned in one situation to another, and help them *learn how to learn.* He said learning to learn was critical for students who faced life in the era of information explosion. He urged teachers to make students *problem solvers* by putting them into situations in which they could use fundamental ideas to find meaning in the data they studied. He stressed that students should engage in a *process of discovery.*

Bruner believed that students who are taught in this way could learn relatively complex concepts, first at a beginning level and later with more sophistication. As he saw it, students who possessed an initial understanding of concepts could return to them again and again in their studies, each time learning more at more advanced levels. As students proceeded through school, they could reencounter the fundamental ideas in a manner resembling a spiral.

Bruner's ideas were not entirely new, of course, and the 1950s and 1960s were not the first time educators worried about which important aspects of knowledge to teach. Scholars in classical Greece, in medieval and Renaissance times, in the Enlightenment, and twentieth-century scholars dating as far back as the 1920s explored similar ideas, especially in social studies and science. But Bruner's writings were especially significant because they caught the attention of leading educators at an opportune time for change.

Because of *Sputnik,* the 1960s was a time of radical change for school curricula. School systems, states, and the national Office of Education all engaged in substantial curriculum-rewriting projects, and many of those that gained broad followings based their approach to teaching content on the ideas of the structure of knowledge. Many adopted Bruner's framework in total. Frequently, the projects set new directions for which content was taught and how it was taught, directions that persist today in many classrooms. The greatest impact was at the secondary school level, particularly in science and mathematics.

Since the 1960s, the idea of teaching the fundamental structure of knowledge has provided curriculum committees and teachers with ways of selecting content that stress big ideas rather than simple facts. This has freed them from the compulsion to cover everything and has enabled them to choose content based on how intellectually useful it is for students. It has also provided a framework on which curriculum developers can put the ideas in sequence to be taught from kindergarten to grade 12 by supplying a range of concepts and generalizations in each subject.

Using structure to select subject matter

Using structure to sequence subject matter

The idea of structure means that teachers can organize knowledge to introduce facts, concepts, and generalizations in the same lesson and can build on those ideas in future lessons. It means they can arrange ideas to be learned according to their complexity and degree of abstraction. In fact, they can teach information and the skill of thinking at the same time.

Teaching information and thinking together

When taught the structure of knowledge, students are not restricted to studying subjects just to find out what is already known. They can learn a *process of investigation* as well. They can learn the *methods of inquiry* of the disciplines and ask questions much as scholars do. They can engage in beginning levels of research, becoming young historians, linguists, biologists, and so forth. In the process, they can *learn ways of thinking* that will help them understand new ideas and solve intellectual problems throughout their lives.[4]

Ways of thinking

Something to Think About

Which content to teach has been a persistent question for educators through the ages, and answers, of course, have varied from time to time. During the latter part of the 1980s, several vocal educators said that American schools were neglecting to teach students a particular *common core* of ideas and information that they need to know in order to communicate effectively as American citizens and to feel a part of American society. One of these critics, E. D. Hirsch, said schools need to teach more subject-matter knowledge and should return to a more traditional, fact-oriented curriculum.[5] He said literate Americans share a certain amount of discrete information and that that knowledge makes them *culturally literate*. Students who are not taught it are *culturally illiterate* and, therefore, disadvantaged.

Hirsch proposed that schools identify a basic core of subjects and information that all students should know and then set out forthrightly to teach it. He did not propose that this common core replace other basics such as reading, writing, thinking skills, and values. He said it should be in addition to those other efforts.

- Do you think schools should teach a common core of knowledge to all students?
- Do you think they are neglecting to do so at the present time?
- If school instruction should include a common basic core, what should be in that core? Why do you think so?

Before you continue on to the next section of this chapter, pause for a moment to think about the nature of knowledge as it has been described on the preceding pages. Compare that idea of knowledge to

1. how you would have described the content taught in schools before you started reading this chapter or before you began this course
2. the content of the saber-tooth curriculum of the chapter Snapshot.

Skills as Content

Skills margin note: Skills

Skills are abilities to do things. They are competencies that people possess that enable them to perform in certain ways. Skills are different from knowledge in that they require more than just knowing. They require *doing*, with some degree of proficiency.

Skills, however, are just as much school content as knowledge. They are part of what students need to learn and part of what teachers must teach. Skills differ from both knowledge and affective learning and are taught differently, but they are an important dimension of school instructional programs and are central to the reasons that schools exist.

Thinking

In at least two ways, *thinking*, which is a complex skill or combination of skills, is especially important as content to be taught in schools. First, all students must learn to think; second, the extent to which they do affects all their other learning.

When experts explain *thinking*, they usually use technical terms. Many say it involves at least three elements—intellectual processes, mental activities, and cognitive strategies. In combination, all three help people make sense out of the information and other stimuli that they encounter in their lives and relate new information to ideas they already have. Thinking involves skills that people use to do all of the following: to impose intellectual order on disorder, to gain insight, to predict consequences, to propose solutions to problems, and to decide what to do when faced with a decision.

margin note: A human trait

Some educators say thinking is a uniquely human trait, that it is the most significant characteristic that separates humans from other forms of life because human thinking is at a higher and more sophisticated level than that of other worldly creatures. These higher levels of thinking are described in many ways and often with highly specialized language. Some of the more common general labels are *critical thinking*, *systematic thinking*, *theoretical thinking*, and *abstract thinking*. More specific terms that define particular aspects of thinking are *conceptualizing*, *comprehending*, *computing*, *inferring*, *interpreting*, *analyzing*, *synthesizing*, *problem solving*, *generalizing*, *applying knowledge*, and *evaluating*.

What actually happens inside the human mind when people think is a matter of much uncertainty, research, and debate. But despite a lack of certainty, educators and society in general believe that people need to learn to think effectively, that thinking is a skill that can be taught, and that schools should teach it. They also believe that teaching skills of thinking accelerates mental development and makes students more autonomous, creative, and productive people.[6]

margin note: Schools and thinking

How can teachers improve students' thinking skills? One way is to attend to how *students think as much as to* what *they think.*

Teaching Thinking

When people think, they have to think *about something;* and when they acquire knowledge, they also develop their ability to think. In short, learning knowledge and thinking skills are interdependent and mutually reinforcing. Therefore, the effective teaching of knowledge includes the teaching of thinking and vice versa.

The two illustrations of specific types of thinking skills that follow—problem solving and conceptualizing—are intended to provide more precise ideas of what thinking skills are and to show how they can be taught in schools. The two are thinking strategies that people use all the time, and they can be taught across subjects and grade levels in elementary and secondary schools. The examples do not represent all kinds of thinking or all ways of teaching thinking. They are only brief introductory glimpses at the thinking-skill dimension of content.[7]

Problem solving and *scientific inquiry* are terms that describe a type of thinking in which people confront new information and situations as ideas to be explained or problems to be solved. The process begins with the assumption that humans are by nature inquiring beings who seek answers when explanations for puzzling situations are not readily apparent. This natural tendency motivates them to *discover meaning* in that which they do not understand.

Problem solving

As people pursue this process of discovering meaning, they seem to pursue intellectual paths that have a common pattern and a recognizable sequence. Although experts have described the process differently over the years, they agree in a general sense on what it involves. Sometimes it is called the *scientific method.* The best-known and most traditional form of the process is probably the one articulated by John Dewey in the 1930s.[8] The steps in the process outlined below parallel that idea.

When people solve problems, they typically do the following:

1. recognize the problem
2. analyze it
3. propose possible solutions
4. test consequences of those possible solutions
5. select a solution
6. evaluate the selected solution

In more pedestrian terms, they (1) face a problem, (2) gather information, (3) figure out what is wrong, (4) think of ways to fix it, (5) try some of them, (6) decide which solution is best, and (7) remember the solution so it can be used again.

People use problem solving all the time, sometimes in complex, sophisticated ways and sometimes almost automatically. For example, a TV repair person who turns on a television set and sees that nothing happens might typically do the following: turn the switch off and on a second time, wiggle the switch, push the plug tighter into the socket, check the electrical circuit, tighten possible loose contact points, replace possibly bad parts, and so forth. If the TV comes on in response to any of these actions, the problem is solved (unless more needs to be done to prevent the difficulty from occurring again). When a solution to the problem is found, the repair person uses that information to decide what to do while working on the next television set that does not work.

People act similarly in all sorts of situations—when the baby will not stop crying, when friends will not play with them, when the car will not start, when there is a detour on the road, when the roast did not taste the way it should have, and when the appliance coming off the assembly line does not work. Sophisticated experts such as nuclear physicists, engineers, medical doctors, and teachers act similarly in their work when confronted with difficulties that require interpretation and appropriate action. For them the processes might be more theoretical, complicated, and time-consuming, but the basic steps are about the same.

Because problem solving is a type of thinking that involves skill, it can be learned, and people can improve through practice. Therefore, it can be taught in schools. To do this, teachers present problems to students and focus their attention on *how* the students think about the problem rather than on *what* they think. They use the students' natural desire to discover as motivation. They help students interpret the problem in a way that makes sense to them, develop guesses or hypotheses about solutions, test them, and evaluate the results. They lead their students intellectually and encourage imaginative and resourceful thinking. They guide the students as they practice the skill.

A well-known approach to teaching problem-solving thought is the Inquiry Training Model developed a number of years ago by Richard Suchman.[9] In designing the model, Suchman analyzed how research scholars solved their problems, translated the steps they used into forms meaningful for school instruction, and developed teaching strategies for teachers to use to guide their students through the steps.

Table 11-2 outlines a teaching sequence based on the Suchman model. By teaching according to this sequence, teachers guide students through classroom activities that include (1) recognizing a problem, (2) searching for data appropriate to solving the problem, (3) processing the data, and (4) applying the data to the situation. Then the students engage in the most important part of the whole exercise.

Teaching problem
solving

TABLE 11-2   A Lesson Sequence for Teaching Problem Solving

Step 1: Presenting the problem	**Step 2: Collecting and verifying data**
Teacher presents students with a problem that does not have an obvious answer (through observing actual situations or viewing open-ended films, pictures, or stories).	Teacher helps students verify the nature of the problem by answering questions about information on specific objects, properties, conditions, or events of the problem; but does so only by responding "yes" or "no." (Students formulate "yes" or "no" questions.)
Step 3: Experimenting with data	**Step 4: Formulating a hypothesis**
Teacher encourages students to isolate specific variables and look for relationships in the problem. Students may also begin to develop their hypotheses.	Teacher guides students toward developing formal hypotheses or explanations for the problem.
Step 5: Evaluating the hypothesis	**Step 6: Analyzing the problem-solving process**
Teacher points out invalid parts of the students' hypotheses and prompts them to evaluate their thinking.	Teacher helps students analyze what they did to solve the problem in order to understand the problem-solving process better and to become more skilled at using it.

They analyze the inquiry process they just used in order to understand what they did. By doing this, they become increasingly skilled at the process.

Conceptualizing, or *developing concepts*, is a type of thinking that involves putting things into categories or groups; people do it almost constantly. It is a basic level of thinking on which other cognitive processes depend. For example, everyone categorizes *things* in the environment into groups such as trees, buildings, vehicles, furniture, animals, humans. They group *events* in their lives into work, play, useful, silly, patriotic, distasteful, harmful, tragic. People think of *ideas* in such conceptual terms as liberal, conservative, concrete, abstract, exciting, and foolish. They divide *people* into concepts such as female, male, short, pretty, macho, bright, white, Italian.

Conceptualizing

People do this so that they can understand something about the items that they group and then make predictions about those items. For instance, even if a person never saw a specific tree before, knowing that it is a tree tells him or her a good deal about it. The same would be true about a piece of furniture, an automobile, or a dog. In the same way, knowing that a person you are about to meet for the first time is a conservative thinker, a religious zealot, a terminally ill patient, or a grouch is also helpful. When you know which groups people are generally in, you may be able to interact with them more effectively. At the same time, however, it could lead you to prejudge and stereotype them.

Conceptualizing is such a common thinking process that it occurs spontaneously. You cannot stop yourself from doing it. When you walk across campus, you think to yourself—this is the shortest path to that building; that is an expensive car; he is an attractive man; she is a pleasant person; that is an ugly sweater. When you listen to a lecture you think—that is a vague idea; his terms are too abstract; this topic is dull; none of this relates to the real world of teaching; classes like this are boring. When you see students in a school, you think—he is short; she is shy; they are black; he is slow; she is sharp; they are poor; they are trouble-makers.

When people conceptualize, they engage in three mental operations:

1. They notice differences among the mass of information their senses provide for them, and they separate that information into discrete items or objects.
2. They look at the characteristics of the various items and use those characteristics to lump each of those items with others that have the same characteristics.
3. They put a label on that group of items.

For example, when individuals think about things, events, and people in their lives, they decide that some things are alive, some rough in texture, some dangerous, some unexplainable; some events are celebrations, parties, conferences, classes; and some are fun, sad, long, tedious, important, obligatory; some people are female, young, rich, socially polished, depressed, Spanish-speaking, English-speaking.

Although conceptualizing is spontaneous and people do it all of the time, some people conceptualize better than others. They conceptualize better because they have learned how to do so—they have been taught. Conceptualizing can be taught in schools at any grade level and in any subject, as long as students are engaged in thought above the recall level. Because conceptualizing is a skill, it is taught through practice. Teachers provide students with information and have them work thoughtfully and conscientiously through the steps in the process. That is, they ask them

Teaching conceptualizing

1. to notice aspects of the information before them
2. to group items together because of common characteristics
3. to propose labels for the groups

All through the process the teacher helps the students analyze what they are doing and why they are doing it so that they refine both their understanding of the process and their skill in using it.

An approach to teaching the skill of conceptualizing called Developing Concepts has been used in schools for some time. Developed by Hilda Taba and her associates at the Taba Curriculum Development Center in California in the 1960s, the approach involves a sequence of teacher questions that stimulate student thinking and discussion.[10] Those questions are outlined in Table 11-3.

Thinking about Thinking

Metacognition

For the last several years, educators have devoted significant attention to the process of thinking about thinking, which is called *metacognition*, and doing so has led to newer approaches to the teaching of thinking. These newer approaches focus on the process of thinking as a subject to be taught. In addition to learning and practicing thinking in a variety of subjects, students actually start a unit or take a course called Thinking. The idea is based on the assumption that learning about thinking improves thinking, and it is drawn from research indicating that a major difference between expert problem solvers and less capable ones is that the experts understand and can explain their own thinking, whereas the others cannot.[11]

Specific areas of metacognitive research concern the ability to monitor and regulate thought processes. For example, research in reading comprehension and

TABLE 11-3   A Lesson Sequence for Teaching the Skill of Conceptualizing

Teacher Questions	Student Responses	Student Thinking
Prior to the discussion, the teacher assigns or conducts an intake activity, one through which students learn information.		
1. What are some of the things you read about in the story?	Enumerate items	Recall information
or		Differentiate among items
saw in the film?		
or		
found on the playground?		
The teacher records student responses as they are given so that they can be seen by all. The teacher then cycles through the following two questions several times.		
2. Which of these items can be put together in a group because they are alike in some way?	Group items	Identify similar characteristics among items
3. What labels could be used for this group?	Label group	Synthesize and generalize about groups
Throughout the discussion, the teacher asks the students to explain their thinking by asking follow-up questions, such as "Why do you say that?"		

SOURCE: This illustration is based on discussion sequences described in H. Taba, M. C. Durkin, J. R. Fraenkel, & A. J. McNaughton (1971). *A teacher's handbook to elementary social studies* (2nd ed.). Menlo Park, CA: Addison-Wesley, pp. 65–70; and C. B. Myers (1973). *Introduction to people in change and the Taba program in social science.* Menlo Park, CA: Addison-Wesley.

study skills shows that good readers employ a wide variety of metacognitive strategies or skills. These strategies include the following:

1. adapting one's reading behavior in a particular situation to one's purpose
2. predicting and identifying main ideas of the text
3. monitoring ongoing reading to make certain that comprehension is occurring
4. changing one's strategy (approach to the reading task) when comprehension is not occurring. [12]

Poor readers often continue their reading when they are not comprehending, which can be a waste of time. They do not monitor the results of their efforts and change strategies to fit their purposes. Poor performers do not plan the strategies they employ and do not assess the effects those strategies have on their comprehension. Instruction in metacognitive skills can help these students improve their reading and studying techniques. [13]

Other Skills Taught in Schools

Skills, of course, are by no means limited to thinking. They exist in many forms— in so many forms, in fact, that it is virtually impossible to categorize them. Some are more complex than others, some are more physical than others, some are more closely tied to particular subject knowledge than others, and so on. Frequently, they overlap with each other and contain common subskills. A number of categories, each containing a list of skills, appears in Table 11-4. The categories are not dis-

TABLE 11-4   Skills Taught in Schools

Learning/Study Skills	Interpretative Skills
Reading	Reading maps and globes
Listening	Interpreting charts, graphs, and
Analyzing data	diagrams
Synthesizing data	Computing scales and distances
Evaluating data	Recognizing symbols
Taking notes	Interpreting timelines and calendars
Outlining	Organizing events chronologically
Skimming and scanning	
Writing	

Research Skills	Communication Skills
Using a dictionary	Speaking
Using a table of contents	Listening
Using an index	Writing
Identifying sources	Observing
Locating materials in library	Giving directions
Gathering data from other sources	Questioning
Organizing data	Signing (hand signals)

Social Skills	Motor Skills
Leading others	Developing eye-hand coordination
Interacting pleasantly with others	Drawing
Conforming to rules	Coloring
Controlling one's emotions	Handwriting
Cooperating with others	Typing
Following directions of others	Running
Making decisions	Jumping
Helping others	Throwing
Acting appropriately	Dancing
Assuming responsibility for actions	

Artistic Performance	Citizenship Participation Skills
Drawing	Staying informed
Painting	Analyzing values
Sculpting	Formulating opinions
Singing	Stating own views
Playing a musical instrument	Judging opinions and actions
Dancing	Making decisions
Acting	Persuading others
	Leading others
	Cooperating
	Following others
	Accepting responsibility
	Voting

T his Reflecting on Practice section asks you to think about teaching the knowledge and thinking-skill dimensions of content presented so far in the chapter. It directs you to select topics covered in subjects taught in pre-K– 12 classrooms and then to brainstorm how that content could be taught if you use the two approaches to teaching described earlier in the chapter. The first part of the exercise focuses on the problem-solving approach, the second on developing concepts. Both approaches combine the teaching of knowledge and thinking skills in the same lesson.

Problem Solving

1. Select a subject taught in elementary or secondary school and a specific pre-K–12 grade level; then identify a problem-related topic from within your chosen subject, making sure it is appropriate for the grade level you have in mind. For example, for a seventh-grade social studies unit on the environment, street litter; for a high school physics class, the need to move (with limited resources) a large and heavy object.
2. Review the steps in the problem-solving approach to teaching outlined in Table 11-2.
3. Formulate a specific problem that you would have the students investigate, again remembering the grade level of the students you have in mind. For example, how can street litter near the school be reduced? What strategies can be applied to move the heavy object?
4. Using Table 11-2 as your guide, sketch out the six-step problem-solving lesson.

Developing Concepts

1. Select a subject and grade level as you did in Step 1 above; then identify a grade-appropriate concept from your chosen subject. Refer to the earlier descriptions of concepts if you wish. For example, choose domestic animals from primary-level science and types of fear from a high school literature assignment.
2. Review the steps in the developing-concepts approach to teaching outlined in Table 11-3.
3. Devise an intake activity that will provide students with the needed background information. For example, have the primary children look for pictures of animals in magazines, or read them a story about animals; for the high school literary assignment, assign the piece of literature to be read, or show it in the form of a video presentation.
4. Again using Table 11-3 as your guide, make a rough sketch of what your three-step concept development lesson might look like.

When you have completed brainstorming about both of these potential lessons, do three more things:

■ Assess the ways in which the lessons you have sketched would teach knowledge and also ensure that the students would practice some type of thinking.
■ Write about how you felt as you engaged in the exercise, making particular note if you felt frustrated at times and why you think you felt that way.
■ Record how you decided on the focus of the two lesson sketches, how often you changed your mind, and why you did so.

Save what you write. You will be asked to refer to it again in Chapter 13.

crete, and the lists are far from complete, but they provide a glimpse at some of the components of this aspect of content.

Skills are developmental. Students learn them over time, through a combination of instruction and practice. They typically start with little or very low levels of proficiency and gradually get better. Observers can witness this phenomenon by comparing a student's proficiency at a skill over varying lengths of time. They would normally see little difference in ability from one day to the next but would see noticeable gains from month to month or year to year.

Observers sometimes miss this developmental aspect of learning skills when they watch experts performing a particular skill. The experts perform so smoothly and effectively that their efforts appear deceptively simple. They are not simple at all, a point an observer would recognize immediately if he or she could compare the expertly performed routine with the performer's first practice session.

Most skills are more than mechanically performed habits that are learned through drill and practice. They are, instead, complex, highly organized, integrated patterns of behavior that can be demonstrated with proficiency only when the skilled person combines significant knowledge of what is involved with practice over time. In short, most skills need to be understood to be performed well.

Some skills are so complex that experts still debate their exact nature. Reading and writing are good examples. These types of skills are really clusters of many subskills or components, and each of the components requires instruction, understanding, and practice.

A cursory look at how children often learn the skill of writing can serve as an illustration. In the primary grades, children learn to write letters, words, sentences, and eventually short narratives. In many programs, they begin by learning how to hold the paper and pencil correctly. Then they start actual writing by making straight and slanted lines and forward and backward circles. Next they learn and practice the correct formation for upper- and lowercase letters. After they make letters correctly, they copy short words and practice spacing those words on paper. Later they group individual words into short sentences. After much practice writing short sentences, they combine sentences into paragraphs. Eventually, they organize paragraphs into larger examples of writing, such as short essays or descriptions of events ("My Summer Vacation") or creative stories.

In the process of doing all this, students learn not only the skill of cursive writing but also a vast array of writing subskills that are integrated into a complicated act called *writing*. As they continue to write, they extend and refine their writing abilities, a process that continues throughout their lifetimes.

Teaching Skills

When students learn skills well, they usually do so through planned instruction. They learn them through a process that includes instruction about the skill as well as a sequence of directed practice, assessment, feedback, and further practice. They rarely attain high-level competence automatically, spontaneously, or incidentally, as by-products of being at school.

When teachers teach skills, they *supply basic knowledge* so that students know what they are doing, and they *provide experiences* so that students can practice. Teachers arrange information and experiences in sequences of increasing difficulty and present them one step at a time in a developmental pattern appropriate to the

Skills involve understanding

Clusters of subskills

Writing: An illustration

Planned sequence

students' level of understanding and ability. The teaching consists of explanation, demonstration, and guided practice so that students comprehend what is done, observe how it is done correctly, and work at doing it well themselves.

Because skills are learned through practice, much skills instruction concentrates on having the students use the skill under the guidance of and with explanations from the teacher. This practice makes it possible for the learner to become sophisticated at the task and to perform with greater competence, ease, and confidence. Although practice does not ensure improved performance, it provides opportunities for it. Under normal conditions teacher guidance, explanation, and encouragement help the student improve.[14]

Guided practice

Now that you have concluded the section on skills as content, pause for a moment to think about the skills that present-day high school graduates need. Think of how different these skills are compared to the skills that were necessary to function in society ten, twenty, or a hundred years ago. To highlight extremes, think of survival skills of the 1990s in contrast with those of a real saber-tooth-like primitive society.

Affective Learning as Content

The affective dimension of the content taught in schools consists of values, feelings, sensitivities, and choices. It includes such concepts as right, wrong, beauty, goodness, and priorities; and it includes the skill of making decisions. Although it has cognitive aspects and sometimes involves skills, it differs from other dimensions of learning because of its predominant emotional and evaluative overtones.

Affective learning is part of content because schools are usually expected to teach students to "do the right thing"—that is, to behave correctly according to community standards. To do this effectively, students must study the following:

1. the values espoused by their culture and others, as well as their own personal value system
2. the feelings of others, as well as their own
3. the sensitivities of others and what it means to be sensitive
4. how to make responsible decisions

Values are those aspects of life to which people attach worth or esteem. They are standards that people endorse, maintain, and try to live up to. They emerge from the very nature of societies and cultures and are passed on to younger generations through the process of *socialization*. They serve as general guides for behavior. Some of the commonly accepted values important to Americans include the following:

Values

human dignity	hard work	consent of the governed
honesty	achievement	getting along with others
equality	material success	due process of law
tolerance	interdependence	justice
freedom	freedom of expression	truth

Because values such as these are widely accepted throughout this culture, there is a fair amount of agreement about the role of schools in teaching them. However, other values are more controversial. They often seem in conflict at least with each other and/or with general cultural norms and traditions. When this happens, the role of schools in teaching them is frequently questioned. For example, schools in America are expected to teach all of the following ideals, even though those in the first column often clash with those in the second column:[15]

cooperation	competition
honesty	avoiding hurting others' feelings
loyalty to friends	reporting of wrongdoing of others
personal success	care for the feelings and welfare of others
conforming to social norms	creativity, individuality, and personal
ethnic identity	autonomy
sincerity of personal religious	acceptance of and respect for others
beliefs	tolerance and acceptance of others' beliefs
freedom of political expression	patriotism and national loyalty
nationalism	peaceful cooperation among nations
nonviolence	standing up for what one believes
appreciation of diversity	rejection of deviant behavior

Feelings

Feelings are internal emotional and moral sensations that people experience as they respond to others and to events and circumstances. People acquire feelings from their interaction with their social and cultural environments. They are usually expressions of the values that individuals hold and the sensitivities they possess. Because feelings are internal and individual, we "learn" them in different ways than we learn "knowledge." We discover, generate, cultivate, extend, and, sometimes, repress them in life's experiences.[16] Common feelings include the following:

joy	hurt	disgust	sadness
fear	belonging	alienation	anxiety
loneliness	acceptance	disappointment	admiration

Sensitivities

Sensitivity is the capacity to respond to others and to situations in a perceptive, humane, and empathetic way. It involves such abilities as seeing others as they see themselves, putting oneself in someone else's shoes, and communicating positively across personal and cultural barriers. It is a characteristic that runs counter to ethnocentrism, prejudice, and the rejection of values and behaviors just because they are different from one's own. Sensitive people understand the values, feelings, and aspirations of others and are able to empathize with them.[17]

Decision making

Decision making is the process of making choices; and good decision making is the ability to choose appropriately among alternatives in rational ways, resulting in solutions to dilemmas with a minimum of conflict. The process involves assessing values, ordering priorities, anticipating potential consequences of possible actions, and personal choice. Skilled decision makers seem to be able to select more beneficial courses of action, more often, more efficiently, and with less stress. They tend to decide for themselves more consistently, rather than defer to others, and they seem to accept more responsibility for their decisions.[18]

Teaching Values, Feelings, Sensitivities, and Decision Making

The affective domain is part of the content taught in schools because what students need to learn in this area is too important to be allowed to develop by happenstance. Students need to be helped to understand the emotional and evaluative aspects of their lives; to accept, extend, and modify their beliefs and feelings; and to be able to make good decisions. Schools teach in such areas by providing information and experiences that encourage values, sensitivities, and feelings to develop and appropriate choices to be made. By so doing, they help students analyze and develop their values, explore and come to terms with their feelings, cultivate and deepen their sensitivities, and practice making decisions.

Frequently individuals and groups express public concern about the teaching of values and other aspects of the affective domain; and sometimes, when they do so, they say that they believe schools should not teach values, that values should be taught at home or through a church. Invariably, however, their concerns are not whether schools should teach values but which values they should teach.

When most of society or a local community agrees on a value, schools are expected to teach about it and either advocate it or teach that it is wrong. For example, schools are expected to support justice, equality, and honesty and oppose murder, racial and sexual discrimination, and cheating. If a value is less broadly accepted or rejected in a community, schools may be expected to teach *about it*, without advocating or rejecting it. For instance, schools usually teach about but do not advocate specific religious beliefs, particular political party positions, and similarly debatable positions that have evolved from cultural traditions, such as how strict or lenient parents should be in child rearing.

When communities are split on particular values or otherwise unsure what their school-age students should be taught, schools usually avoid the issue. Sex education has often been avoided in the past. Now, however, the impact of the media and the spread of AIDS have caused community leaders and educators to have second thoughts about what to do, and in most communities schools are expected to provide some form of sex education.

Contrary to what people may think, schools have had substantial responsibility for affective learning across cultures and throughout history. Schools everywhere were established as *socializing institutions*, institutions founded by adult generations for the purpose of transmitting cultural values to younger generations and instilling in them a commitment to those values. In addition to teaching knowledge and skills, they were, and are, intended to teach *cultural expectations*—what the culture values and the behaviors that are expected of its members.[19]

Of course, schools are not the only socializing institutions that provide affective education. Families, churches, peer groups, older generations, traditions, rituals, and print and broadcast media do so as well. But in the complex and rapidly changing environment of recent times, many of these institutions have been changed, and their educational roles have become less clear than in the past. Similarly, some of these institutions, such as television, have much more strength than in the past. In response to such changes society has turned more directly to schools.

Marginal notes:

Which values?

Cultural expectations

Other socialization institutions

Something to Think About

The 1980s controversy over bilingual education reflects a number of perspectives as to which dimensions of subject-matter content—knowledge, skills, affective learning—are most important for students, and each of those perspectives is tied to similar assumptions about the purposes and goals for schools. For example, consider the four statements below:

MR. ALLEN: The idea of teaching children in their primary language when it is not English is critical. If young students do not understand their lessons in the early grades because of language barriers, they run the risk of never catching up.

MS. BATES: If students are going to learn as they should in public schools, they need to be able to understand English. Teaching them in primary languages other than English slows the process. Besides, schools that try to teach in several languages cannot provide as intense and sophisticated instruction in the other languages as they can in English. Teaching in non-English languages is a disservice to students who have to compete in an English-speaking society.

MS. CAIN: When students from homes where a language other than English is the primary language are taught only in English, they are being told that they are handicapped and not as good as their Anglo classmates. This hurts their self-image and stifles learning. Of course they achieve less.

MS. DODGE: I cannot understand why a child who learns fluent Spanish in school is considered a high achiever and one who learns fluent Spanish at home before entering school is considered deprived.

- How would you react to each statement?
- In which ways does each statement relate to each of the three dimensions of content described in this chapter?

Careful planning

Schools that provide the most effective instruction concerning values, feelings, sensitivities, and making responsible decisions plan carefully and follow intentional patterns. They realize that providing information is only part of the task. They also know that techniques of "preaching" and indoctrinating have limited or counterproductive value in school settings. Frequently, they teach through example, case studies, and the expectations they set for their students. By doing so, they put students into situations in which they experience or witness conditions that are value-laden and emotional in content and/or response. They arrange experiences for students that require them to

- think about values, feelings, sensitivities, and choices
- analyze and clarify their own positions, perspectives, and emotions
- compare their ideas and emotions with those of others
- put themselves in others' situations
- experience the feelings involved in situations, especially those likely to be emotionally laden
- develop their own skills at valuing and decision making.

Despite careful planning, however, school instruction in most subjects and at most grade levels is not usually organized initially around affective objectives. Instead, curriculum planners and teachers plan their lessons around knowledge—concepts and generalizations—and then plug into that content the affective learning

Instead of treating affective learning as an afterthought—or resorting to preaching—teachers can plan experiences that encourage students to empathize with others and to compare life situations, emotions, and values.

they believe should take place. For instance, history teachers typically decide to teach an event from the past primarily because of the knowledge it will transmit. They then determine how they can also teach values, feelings, and sensitivities in the same process. Similarly, many language arts teachers teach a particular literary work because they want their students to know the work or its writer. Only after they have selected the work to be taught do they consider the value lessons involved in the particular work. Unfortunately, the fact that the affective education decisions frequently come second in the planning process has led some educators to think they are of second-level importance. They are not.[20]

Second in the planning process

Teachers use many teaching strategies to teach affective dimensions of subject matter. Some are more appropriate for certain grade levels, subjects, and teaching styles than others. Illustrations of two of these appear below. The first helps students explore feelings, and the second helps them analyze values. When teachers use either of these strategies, they actually teach three kinds of learning: (1) knowledge about feelings and values, (2) analytical skills that students can use to study their own feelings and values and those of others, and (3) the emotional and evaluative overtones of feelings and values. The two strategies are based on the curriculum development work of Hilda Taba and her associates at the Taba Curriculum Development Center in the 1960s.[21] They are presented here as examples because they have been used long enough to have stood the test of time in actual classrooms, are used widely in classrooms throughout the United States, and can be plugged into many different lessons across subjects and grade levels. They fit into instruction any time a classroom topic touches on feelings or values, and they work with any students who can discuss ideas in a group-discussion setting.

Illustration: Exploring Feelings

The teacher presents to the class an intake episode that describes people in a situation involving significant feelings.[22] Such situations as those that follow could be read to the students or the students could read them or see them on video.

Lesson Topic	Situation
Second-grade social studies lesson on neighborhoods	A new child arrives in the neighborhood and knows no one.
Fourth-grade science lesson on pollution	An older woman in a crowd at a zoo slips on a banana peel just tossed on the ground by a teenager.
High school literature lesson on the antebellum South	A reasonably well-meaning woman from an aristocratic family treats a slave in subhuman ways.
High school history lesson on war	A story of a family's plight after a son is killed in battle, and the mother (or another or all family members) becomes despondent.

The teacher next conducts a discussion using the following sequence:

Teacher Questions	Student Responses
1. What happened in the episode? What did _____ do?	Enumerate facts from episode
2. How do you think (the person) felt when _____?	Infer feelings

The teacher repeats Question 2 for each key person in the episode.

3. Do you know of a situation where something like this happened to someone you know? Would you like to tell us about it?	Describe a similar situation
4. How do you think (the person or character) felt when _____?	Infer feelings

The teacher repeats Question 4 for each key person in the student-offered episode.

5. Based on our entire discussion, what can you say about how people feel when _____?	Generalize about feelings

The teacher follows up student responses throughout the discussion by asking, "Why do you think _____ felt that way?"

Illustration: Analyzing Values

The teacher presents to the class an intake episode that describes a person or some people in a situation that involves a value-laden choice or decision.[23] Situations such as those below could be read to the students, or the students could read them or see them on video.

Lesson Topic	Situation
Third-grade reading lesson about children who steal candy from a store	One of the children is asked whether he or she knows who stole the candy and must decide how to respond.
Eighth-grade health lesson on sexuality	A group of young teenagers is discussing supposed sexual encounters they and their friends have experienced. One of the group has to decide if he or she should admit to significantly less experience than the others report.
High school biology lesson on human physiology	A high school athlete is training for the coming football season and is afraid he is not strong and large enough to do well. He wants to use steroids. His girlfriend argues against his doing so.

Then the teacher conducts a discussion, using the following sequence:

Teacher Questions	Student Responses
1. What happened in the episode?	Enumerate facts from episode
2. Why do you think (the person) did (or decided) (the *action* or *decision*)?	Infer reasons for actions
3. If that was (the person's) reason for doing it, what do you think he (she) thinks is important?	Infer values behind reason
4. If you were in this situation, what would you do?	Predict own behavior
5. Do you know of a situation similar to this? Would you like to tell us about it? What did _____ do?	Describe a similar situation
6. Why do you think (the person) did (or decided) this (*action* or *decision*)?	Infer reasons for actions
7. If that was (the person's) reason for doing it, what do you think he or she thinks is important?	Infer values behind reason
8. Based on our entire discussion, what can you say about what people think is important?	Generalize about values

The teacher follows up student responses throughout the discussion by asking, "Why do you think that?"

Teaching and Learning History

This Educational Research section reports on an investigation into the teaching of a specific area of content—history. It describes a study by Matthew T. Downey and Linda S. Levstik in which two history educators analyzed what other researchers have been investigating about why and how history is taught in the schools.[24] That study asked several questions about the teaching and learning of history and reported how researchers have been answering those questions.

History was chosen as the focus of this section because the teaching of history has been debated publicly in recent years. However, the section is intended as an example of content-related research in all subject areas in general, not just history. As you read, consider what might be parallel issues and questions that concern the teaching of English, mathematics, science, foreign languages, and the other pre-K–12 subjects.

The questions Downey and Levstik asked, and their report on how the research they read was answering these questions, follow:

■ How much and how well is history being taught?

Data for the 1980s are not available; so we really do not know the answer to this question for the past decade. Through the 1970s, however, state course requirements and student enrollments held constant for American history and declined for world history. The world history courses that were eliminated were not replaced by increases in other social studies courses or by increases in enrollment in those courses.

Teachers of history rely heavily upon discussion, lecture, individual assignments, and weekly quizzes; little information exists as to how well they use these methods. One notable study reported wide variety in the quality of history instruction both across schools and in the same school.

■ How central is the textbook in history instruction?

Conventional wisdom says that history teachers rely excessively on texts, but actual studies are very limited, and two seem to question the assumption. One of these studies reports that there is little reading in history classes and that texts are used by students primarily as reference books to answer worksheet questions. The same study says, however, that many students actually avoided using texts as references by copying answers from other students and/or by completing their worksheets when the teacher reviews other students' answers. The second study reports that history teachers lecture and show films more than they rely on texts.

■ How much history do students know?

Recent tests of student knowledge in history, as well as studies in the 1940s, report what the test givers have called striking ignorance of history among students, but there is little agreement about what history and how much history students should know. Students who took the tests scored below the level that many people thought they should have scored, but the content of the tests and the expected level of satisfactory performance were based on subjective guesstimates made by the people who constructed the tests as much as on anything else.

■ In what ways do students understand the concept of time, and how do they develop the ability to think historically?

Although research is still limited on much of this, studies are underway, and there is evidence that students develop a variety of ways of understanding history, time, change, causation, and temporal relationships. However, the ties between age, cognitive development, historical thinking, and depth of historical understanding need much more exploration. For instance, possessing a sense of history, understanding historical descriptions, and comprehending complex historical explanations involve different levels of sophistication in thinking. One study of these areas of historical learning is particularly illustrative. According to Downey and Levstik, R. N. Hallam, studying students in the United Kingdom,

found that logical structures similar to those described by Piaget could be detected in historical thinking. His students responded to questions based on narrative historical passages in ways that seemed to him comparable to Piaget's stages of preoperational, concrete operational, and formal operational thinking. However, his history students reached the concrete and formal stages considerably later than Piaget's subjects had. Hallam's students reached the concrete operational stage at about age 13, rather than at age 7 or 8 for Piaget's students; formal operational thinking began at about age 16 in history, compared to age 12 in Piaget's research. He concluded that although students develop formal operational thinking in the study of history, it happens at a later [date than in the] study [of] mathematics and science.[25]

In contrast to approaches like Hallam's, other investigators question whether Piagetian ideas are appropriate for describing historical learning, because Piagetian thinking was derived from research on thinking about science and mathematics. Some say thinking about history is more open and includes historical perspective, both of which, they say, make cognitive development theories inadequate for explaining how children and young people think about history. At this time, these researchers are turning to a variety of alternative explanations.

■ What do studies such as these tell us about the present teaching of history?
   The studies show that much practice in teaching history is not based on research and that the ways in which history is taught

and learned needs to be studied more fully. To do this, research should include investigation of the relationships between child development and historical thinking as well as between historical content and the methods teachers use to teach it. It should also include close monitoring of what is happening in history classes and the documentation of effective practices.

In sum, although history has been taught for centuries, there is little evidence that proves what is good, appropriate, or poor practice. Much new information will be generated in the next few years, and knowledgeable teachers will use it to improve what they do and how well their students learn. New teachers will need to be informed.

Conclusion

If schools are to accomplish all the goals set for them, they must educate students in many ways—enable them to understand new information and ideas, help them develop better skills, stimulate in them increasingly sophisticated values, feelings, and sensitivities. To do this, teachers must select several types of content to insert into their lessons in ways that truly change their students. The task is made complex by the multiple purposes of schools and by the magnitude of the content that students should appropriately learn.

Teachers can make the tasks of selecting and teaching content manageable by (1) formulating educational objectives for their classes and (2) organizing the content they teach into an intellectual framework that makes sense to them. This chapter described content in the context of a particular conceptual structure—knowledge, skills (including thinking), and affective learning—in order to provide you with a simple way of understanding what content is and how it fits into the teaching-learning process.

The particular conceptual structure of content described in this chapter is not the only one and, in fact, is not even one of the most recently developed. It has been adopted by teachers for at least two decades. Some educators would call it a dated system, but it seems to be especially useful to beginning teacher-education students as they start to think of content as something more than the subject labels of the courses they studied in high school and college. We hope it will guide you as you face additional ideas about content in your future study.

Summary

The content taught in schools can be thought of in many ways. One way is to view it as having three dimensions—knowledge, skills, and affective learning. Each of these can be subdivided into facts, concepts, and generalizations; thinking and other skills; and values, feelings, sensitivities, and decision making. Content in all three areas is important for students to learn and appropriate for classroom instruction.

In thinking about content, it is useful to separate the idea of *information*—the "stuff" that students should know—from broader concepts of knowledge. When this is done, it is possible to view knowledge as facts, concepts, and generalizations drawn from numerous academic disciplines with various levels of abstraction. In this broader context, knowledge has structure, and that structure makes it understandable and perhaps easier to teach.

Skills are tasks or activities one is able to do. Learning them involves understanding and proficiency. Thinking, reading, and writing are especially important skills, but many others are also appropriate for school instruction. Values, feelings, sensitivities, and decision making can and should be taught in schools, along with knowledge and skills.

Study Questions

1. Think of your college academic major or subject-matter teaching field outside education and select five to ten important ideas from that subject that all students should learn before they finish high school. What criteria did you use to select those five to ten ideas? Would other students in this class agree with your choices?

2. Suppose that you are teaching all basic subjects at a fifth- or sixth-grade level and the last month of the school year is about to start. You realize that (a) you have much more than a month's worth of information to cover with your class, (b) more than half of the students in the class are well below grade level in reading and mathematics, and (c) the class as a whole seems to be particularly prejudiced toward students who are ethnically and racially different from themselves. Knowing that you will not be able to teach everything that you would like in the remaining month, to which goals or areas of content would you give highest priority? Why?

3. How would you respond if you were asked to comment on the following discussion between two high school teachers:
   Mr. Johnson: I realize that most of the students read and write very poorly, but my job is to teach history, not language arts.
   Mr. Smith: I disagree. All of us must teach reading and writing even if it cuts into our subject matter.

4. Should all students be required to take a knowledge and skills test at each grade level and in each high school subject before passing? If so, who should decide what each test covers? What should happen to the students who repeatedly fail?

Key Terms

Academic disciplines	Fact	Process of instruction
Affective learning	Feelings	Scientific inquiry
Artistic skills	Generalizations	Scientific method
Citizenship participation skills	Guided practice	Sensitivities
Concept	Idea	Skills
Conceptualizing	Knowledge	Social skills
Content	Levels of abstraction	Socializing institutions
Cultural expectations	Metacognition	Spiral instruction
Cultural literacy	Methods of inquiry	Structure of knowledge
Decision making	Motor skills	Thinking
Disciplines	Problem solving	Values
Educational objectives	Process of discovery	

For Further Reading

Adler, M. J. (1982). *The Paideia proposal.* New York: Macmillan.

Baron, J., & Sternberg, R. (Eds.). (1987). *Teaching thinking skills: Theory and practice.* New York: W. H. Freeman.

Beyer, B. K. (1988). Developing a scope and sequence for thinking skill instruction. *Educational Leadership, 45*(7), 26–30.

Beyer, B. K. (1987). *Practical strategies for the teaching of thinking.* Boston: Longman.

Bruner, J. S. (1960). *The process of education.* Cambridge: Harvard University Press.

Dewey, J. (1933). *How we think.* Lexington, MA: D. C. Heath.

Eisner, E. W. (1994). *The educational imagination: On the design and evaluation of school programs* (3rd ed.). New York: Macmillan.

Eisner, E. W. (1993). The education of vision. *Educational Horizons, 21*(2), 80–85.

Fraenkel, J. R. (1977). *How to teach about values: An analytical approach.* Englewood Cliffs, NJ: Prentice-Hall.

Harmin, M. (1990). *How to plan a program for moral education.* Alexandria, VA: Association for Supervision and Curriculum Development.

Kohlberg, L. (1975). The cognitive-developmental approach to moral education. *Phi Delta Kappan, 56*(10), 670–677.

Resnick, L. B. (1987). *Education and learning to think.* Washington, DC: Academic Press.

Schwab, J. J. (1962). The concept of structure of a discipline. *Educational Record, 43*(3), 197–205.

Taba, H. (1962). *Curriculum development: Theory and practice.* New York: Harcourt, Brace and World.

The Curriculum and Lessons

Designs for Learning

N ow that you have explored the various dimensions of content and how teachers use it to produce learning in students, this chapter turns to the ways in which content is combined with approaches to teaching, learning activities, and instructional materials to become school curricula, units, and lessons. The school curriculum is the school's plan of instruction, the design of what, when, and how students should be taught; which content should be covered; and what the students should have learned by the time they graduate or finish a specific grade level. It is put together by school leaders and committees of teachers who identify what students most need to know and to be able to do and how the school can provide for those needs. Units of instruction and lesson plans are both subdivisions and extensions of the curriculum. They cover segments of the content outlined in the curriculum, and they elaborate more specifically on how it will be taught.

This chapter describes a continuum of action that occurs in many curriculum development efforts, from the selection of content by curriculum developers to the preparation of a single lesson. Different types of curricula are explained, and partial examples of units are provided.

The chapter Snapshot consists of weekly class schedules for four very different students. These list the subject-matter components of the curriculum for each student and reflect the fact that the curriculum is not the same for everyone. The Reflecting on Practice section describes what happens when the teacher who planned a lesson described in the chapter actually teaches it to her first-grade students. The Educational Research section provides a college student's assessment of potential impacts of the information highway on school curricula.

SNAPSHOT

T he four weekly class schedules presented in this Snapshot are for a high school student in an academic program, a high school student in a general-vocational program, a second-grade student, and a middle school student.[1] As you read, consider:

- What differences in emphasis do you notice among the four programs?
- What educational priorities are reflected in the subjects studied by each student?
- How would you compare these programs with the schedules of students whom you know?

High School Student (Academic Program)
Name: William Holloway

Class: Grade 11

Period	*Monday*	*Tuesday*	*Wednesday*	*Thursday*	*Friday*
1	Algebra II	Algebra II	Algebra II	Algebra II	Algebra II
Homeroom					
2	English III	English III	English III	English III	English III
3	American History	American History	American History	American History	American History
4	French II	French II	French II	French II—Lab	French II
Lunch					
5	Chemistry	Chemistry	Art	Chemistry	Chemistry
6	Chemistry	Physical Education	Art	Physical Education	Art

High School Student (General-Vocational Program)
Name: Brad Swartz   Class: Grade 9

Period	Monday	Tuesday	Wednesday	Thursday	Friday
1	Math I	Math I	Math I	Math I	Math I
Homeroom					
2	English I	English I	English I	English I	English I
3	Data Processing	Music	Physical Education	Music	Data Processing
Lunch					
4	Auto Mechanics	Data Processing	Auto Mechanics	Data Processing	Auto Mechanics
5	Auto Mechanics	Data Processing	Auto Mechanics	Physical Education	Auto Mechanics
6	Social Studies	Social Studies	Social Studies	Social Studies	Social Studies

Second-Grade Student
Name: Kathy Wray   Class: Grade 2

Period		Monday	Tuesday	Wednesday	Thursday	Friday
8:00–8:30	Directions for the Day	→				
	Individual Reading					
8:30–9:00	Reading (Direct Instruction)	→				
9:00–9:30	Phonics Practice	→				
9:30–10:00	Spelling		Writing	Spelling	Writing	Spelling
10:00–10:20	Language Arts Practice	→				
10:20–10:30	Restroom	→				
10:30–11:00	Art		Music	Art	Library	Music
11:00–11:30	Math (Direct Instruction)	→				
11:30–12:00	Math Practice	→				
12:00–12:30	Lunch	→				
12:30–12:45	Restroom/Break	→				
12:45–1:00	Story Time	→				
1:00–1:30	Social Studies	→				
1:30–2:00	Physical Education	→				
2:00–2:30	Science		Science	Health	Science	Science
2:30–2:45	Clean up and prepare for dismissal	→				

Middle School Student
Name: Jill Driscoll   Class: Grade 6

Period	Monday	Tuesday	Wednesday	Thursday	Friday
1	Language Arts	Language Arts	Language Arts	Language Arts	Language Arts
2	World Cultures	World Cultures	World Cultures	World Cultures	World Cultures
3	Introduction to Computers	Music	Introduction to Computers	Music	Introduction to Computers
4	Mathematics	Mathematics	Mathematics	Mathematics	Mathematics
Lunch					
5	Earth Science	Earth Science	Exploratory	Earth Science	Earth Science
6	Earth Science	Art	Exploratory	Library	Art
7	Physical Education	Physical Education	Physical Education	Physical Education	Assembly

The Curriculum

If students are going to learn the knowledge, skills, and affective content that teachers, school leaders, and parents expect, their instruction must be organized rationally and sensibly. It must follow a design, and the design must take into account many factors discussed in this text—purposes of schools, processes of human development, philosophies of education, theories of learning, currently accepted approaches to instruction, and the nature of content. In short, school instruction must follow a plan, and such a plan is called the curriculum. The schedules in the Snapshot of this chapter reflect how four students' curricula are organized.

When educators design a curriculum, they decide what to teach, what to leave out, what to emphasize, what to skim over lightly. They also plan a sequence—what comes first, second, third, and so on—from year to year and from September to June. In addition, they develop ways of connecting the various elements of what is taught so that their students' instructional experiences are interrelated to some degree. Some of these connections are little more than the sequencing of lessons, but there are others—reading is related to language arts, and both are often connected with social studies; science lessons are based on an assumption that students can use certain arithmetic and mathematics skills; content from history and literature overlap and include values instruction. In schools with well-developed curricula, formal instructional content is also tied to the social life of the school community—clubs, sports, personal friendships, and informal student-teacher relationships.

Choices at three levels

In making curricular choices, educators usually start with content—what they think should be covered in various subjects at each grade level. Then they arrange classes, units, lessons, teaching strategies, learning activities, and instructional materials in ways that they believe will produce the greatest amount of learning most efficiently. Ideally, similar choices actually occur at three levels—curriculum planners design curricular frameworks for schools, committees of teachers or teachers working individually use the school curriculum to formulate units, and individual teachers use the units to plan class lessons. As a result, teachers actually end up with a plan of what to do with each of their classes each Monday morning, and for the most part, that plan makes sense and is appropriate for the students they teach.

This chapter emphasizes this method of designing curricula, but the teaching world is rarely ideal. Sometimes curricula are put together haphazardly, with little thought. Sometimes there is little sequencing, coordination, and articulation across grades and subjects. In some places teachers more or less do their own thing, shifting focus when they feel like it. Some schools have no written curriculum at all.

Different starting points

Though the curriculum development procedure just introduced is excellent, not all good curriculum plans, units, and lessons have to start with the selection of content. It is just as important to acknowledge that teachers frequently develop good lesson plans without having access to either units or curricula. Often teachers begin planning lessons by adopting particular texts and then organize their teaching around that decision. Some start by selecting teaching strategies they want to use—lectures, small groups, seat work, discussion—or learning activities they want their students to engage in—cooperative learning, drill and practice, class reports, note taking.

The pages that follow trace the process of curriculum development from the selection of content for schoolwide curriculum frameworks to the organization of a specific lesson plan for a class. The presentation is significantly and intentionally idealized for your ease of understanding as a student just beginning your study of curriculum.

Bases for Selecting Content

One of the factors that influences which content is taught is the pool of knowledge, skills, and values that are appropriate to be studied. In selecting knowledge to be taught, curriculum developers and teachers turn to the scholarly fields of study—the disciplines mentioned earlier. They search the disciplines for information and ideas that will be most useful, understandable, and interesting for their students. Similarly, they search for skills and value perspectives. However, because there is so much more information and there are so many more skills and value positions than can possibly be taught, and because all of them are not of equal worth, curriculum developers must make choices.

Available content

To make these selections, educators must look at criteria outside the disciplines for guidance; and when they do, these other criteria become a second influence on what is taught. One such influence involves the culture and society that the school serves and in which the students live. Educators analyze the society by asking such questions as the following: What are the traditions and long-term assumptions undergirding this society? What needs and problems does the society face? What does it expect and require of its citizens? Which values does it support?[2]

Culture and society

Answers to questions such as these provide teachers with ideas of two types: (1) answers about what society expects of them as teachers and (2) answers about which competencies and qualities their students will need in order to survive, participate, and prosper in the society. From such answers teachers discern what to teach and what students need to learn.

Much of Chapters 1, 7, 8, 9, and 10 addressed these points. Those chapters describe, respectively, the current context in which schools function, the purposes and goals for schools in recent decades, the historical assumptions, traditions, and political pressures that affect schools today, and philosophies of education.

The nature of learners and the learning process also influences which content is taught. On a general level, this factor includes ideas about the developmental stages of students, their interests, their strengths and weaknesses, their characteristics and needs, and how they learn. In a particular classroom, it also includes data about specific individuals in the class. Is this student average, college bound, a potential dropout, vocationally oriented, or special? Such questions direct teachers toward what to teach their students, as well as when and how to teach it.[3]

Learners and learning

Chapters 5 and 6 focus on these ideas in their descriptions of human development and theories of learning.

The Process of Selection

Ideally, the content to be taught to a group of students depends on the educational objectives set for them. The complex process of identifying those objectives occurs on at least three levels, each presented here. Although these levels appear to be discrete, in reality they are intertwined.[4]

Broad aims of education, which set general directions and emphases about what is taught, are typically set at national, state, and school district levels. They reflect broad cultural values and educational philosophies, and they provide an overall di-

Broad aims of education

rection for school programs to follow. They focus attention toward some subject matter and away from others, but only in very general terms. Usually, they are too abstract to be adequate guides for specific curricular decisions. Most are stated in words similar to the following:

to transmit cultural traditions	to provide for economic self-sufficiency
to develop basic literacy	to promote positive self-concepts
to cultivate civic responsibility	

School-level goals

Somewhat more specific, middle-range educational goals are usually set at the school-district and school-building levels. These follow from the broader aims but are more focused and more specific. They describe schoolwide goals and, sometimes, student behaviors that would demonstrate that they have been attained. Goals at this level include the following:

to develop critical thinking	to improve study habits
to encourage participation in political activity	to appreciate good literature
to enhance mathematical computational skills	

Objectives at this level set directions for curriculum planners and teachers. They serve as the guidelines around which school programs are organized. They provide the criteria for a second-level decision in the process of content selection.

Class-level objectives

Objectives at an even more specific level describe learning outcomes sought at the various grade levels, in particular subjects, and for particular units of instruction. They reflect decisions made about broader aims and goals, and they fit within their scope and limits. They are more specific, however, and are therefore useful in defining what students should learn. The following are objectives of this type. The students will be able:

to distinguish between long- and short-vowel sounds

to list the sequence of events in a story

to perform at or above the minimum standard on 50 percent of the physical fitness skill activities

to explain the process of photosynthesis

to solve quadratic equations

to write a clear, well-organized, two-page critique of a short story.

Good objectives at this level serve as the primary basis on which teachers decide which content to teach. They tell teachers which content to cover and which ideas, skills, and values to emphasize. They also suggest which learning experiences teachers might provide, the materials they might use, and how they might assess what the students have learned.

Making Content Choices

Relevance

In the end, the decision on what to teach is a matter of professional judgment by curriculum planners and classroom teachers. As a matter of judgment, it involves personal choices and individual priorities. As teachers make these choices, they ask themselves questions: What is important? What is meaningful? What is relevant to the needs of the school and my students? Such questions take time to answer and frequently generate heated disagreements within curriculum committees. They are the questions that caused dissension in the saber-tooth society of the Chapter 11 Snapshot. Behind them are many related and subsidiary questions: Relevant *to what?* Relevant *for whom?* Relevant *by what standard?* These are questions to keep in mind as you proceed with your studies.[5]

When time and resources are scarce, how should educators decide what content is "relevant" in the curriculum? Relevant for whom? By what standard?

Because choices of content are subjective, teachers who make them have to resort to their own values and beliefs as personal guides.[6] One such guide that they are likely to turn to is their own ideas about why schools exist—that is, the general roles, functions, and purposes of schools as they see them.

Teachers who have a traditional view of schools believe that the primary purpose of school is to transmit past cultural traditions to students, to inculcate in the students a loyalty to those traditions, and to perpetuate them. They tend to select content that has stood the test of time and are more likely to stress history, classical languages, a fundamental approach to reading, and basic computational skills in mathematics rather than contemporary issues, Asian cultures, write-to-read approaches to reading instruction, and computer applications. These teachers are not likely to change the curriculum frequently.[7]

On the other hand, teachers who have a present- or future-oriented view of schools believe that the most important task for schools is to enable students to cope with rapid social changes in modern society. They typically evaluate content in terms of its current and future utility for students and are likely to emphasize world studies, modern languages, computer mathematics, and environmental science. They are more noticeably open to changing the curriculum to keep up with the times.[8]

Teachers who hold a *reconstructionist* view of the role of schools see schools as more active institutions than do the traditional or the present- and future-oriented teachers. *Reconstructionists* believe that schools should go beyond helping students cope with change and should *push for social change* to make the society better. Teachers who accept this view choose content that questions the social status quo, advocates change, and encourages students to participate in that change; they tend to support issue-oriented school studies such as human relations, civil rights, women's studies, environmental courses, and fitness education.[9]

In a somewhat different vein, but just as important to the decision about the content to be taught, is the concept of how schools relate to other social institutions. For instance, teachers who do not see much interaction between the functions of

> **Teachers are curriculum decision makers**

> **Schools that advocate change**

> **Schools and other social institutions**

schools and those of families, churches, and other community institutions will have different ideas about what should be taught than will people who believe that contemporary schools must fill educational voids left by changing families and churches. Normally, the first group will want schools to focus primarily on transmitting knowledge and on training in academic skills; the second group will consider the development of personal character, personality, and individual values more important. Teachers in the second group are also more inclined toward a concern for student self-concept and personal security. They see school more as a broad socializing agency than as a narrow academic one.[10]

Curriculum Organization

Patterns of instruction

In addition to selecting content, curriculum planners arrange content and learning experiences by subject, grade level, course, unit, and lesson. When they are successful, they form patterns of instruction that cut across all dimensions of content and provide for continuous, sequential, integrated, and cumulative learning.

If the task is done well, it involves a number of steps, several of which were mentioned earlier. They include

1. defining school aims and goals
2. diagnosing students' needs
3. formulating educational objectives
4. translating objectives into patterns of learning
5. selecting and organizing content and learning experiences
6. choosing ways of evaluating learning outcomes.

Curriculum framework

The effort results in three kinds of documents that guide instruction. The first is a *curriculum framework*, which arranges content in particular patterns, assigns it to certain grade levels and subjects or classes, and puts it into identified sequences. The second is usually thought of as a series of *units of instruction* for each subject or class, at each grade level. The third is the *lesson plan* that teachers develop and follow for each class. All three are described in the discussion that follows.

Units of instruction
Lesson plans

From a student's perspective the curriculum looks like a list of sequential courses, units within courses, activities, and assignments. Different students take different courses, as the chapter Snapshot illustrates; but each student follows some curriculum that is based on a set of objectives and assumptions about what that student should learn.

Curriculum Frameworks

Typically, patterns of curriculum organization are described and compared, as if they emphasize particular points on a continuum, with *subject-centered* approaches on one side and *student-centered* ones on the other. (See Figure 12-1.) Such a way of describing curricula is, of course, simplistic, but it is also useful in showing the characteristics of each pattern. The descriptions that follow therefore follow the continuum model. Remember, however, that (1) the curricula of most schools are not exclusively of one design but a combination of patterns, (2) most programs fit somewhere toward the middle of the continuum, and (3) within any school there is variety from class to class and teacher to teacher.[11]

FIGURE 12-1   Selected curriculum patterns arranged from the most subject-centered to the most student-centered.

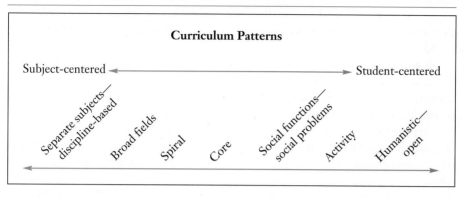

Subject-Centered Curricula

In recent years, subject-centered approaches to curriculum organization have been more prevalent than student-centered ones, especially in secondary schools. This discussion considers three such curriculum patterns. As a group, they reflect the following directions, although they do so in varying degrees.[12]

- They look on learning primarily as cognitive development and the acquisition of knowledge and information.
- They see the teacher's main job as the provision of instruction.
- They base the subject matter to be taught on preselected objectives that include concepts, generalizations, skills, and values to be learned.
- They expect teachers to plan instruction before teaching starts and to organize it around content rather than around conditions specific to the learning situation.
- They assume that certain subject matter should be taught to all students.
- They stress academic learning.

The oldest and most widely followed type of subject-centered approach to curriculum organization is the *separate-subjects*, or *discipline-based*, curriculum. This pattern has two primary goals, both derived from the content to be learned by the students:

Separate-subjects curriculum

1. the acquisition of information and ideas contained in the subjects being taught
2. the development of the mental discipline gained from studying those subjects

For instance, mathematics is taught so that students learn the basic content of mathematics and the ability to "think like a mathematician."

In the separate-subjects curriculum, content is divided into fairly discrete areas of study—composition, literature, history, geography, arithmetic, algebra, biology, chemistry, and so forth. Each class is separate from the rest and is taught in its own time slot. There is little overlap across classes or time blocks.

This pattern evolves from the idea that knowledge is logically separated into a number of well-defined disciplines, such as those of the research scholars, and that it can be learned best when taught in similar units. Advocates of the pattern believe that such an approach teaches students the solid content that they should know, and teaches it in such a way as to stimulate their abilities to think and solve problems. They suggest that the separate-subjects organization helps students order and clarify the complex and conflicting ideas that they confront in their rapidly changing world.

Expository methods of instruction are used most often with the separate-subjects curriculum: lecture, assigned reading, discussion, recitation, question-and-answer, and written exercise. The primary resources are teacher presentations, textbooks, films and videos, and other information-giving formats.

Among the educators who support a rigid view of the separate-subjects curriculum are those who advocate *basic education*. They suggest that all students should study a set of basic subjects and great books. They recommend a strong academic education, comparable to the liberal education of early Europe. Proponents of this view have included Arthur Bestor, William Bagley, James Koerner, Hyman Rickover, and William Bennett. Mortimer Adler's *Paideia Proposal* is a description of such a curriculum and a call for its implementation in American schools.[13]

Critics of the separate-subjects curriculum say it divides content into isolated components more than is appropriate for elementary and secondary school instruction, overemphasizes the learning of factual information at a time of rapid change, slights the teaching of critical thinking, and neglects differences among students and the problems they face. They note that the real life of students is not divided into subjects. Usually they prefer interdisciplinary curriculum patterns or curricula that focus more on the students than on the content to be learned.

Because of the back-to-basics and accountability movements, the separate-subjects curriculum has been very much in vogue in recent years, as have other subject-centered approaches. School reformers and parents alike have demanded that students learn the content—and "the content" is easier to identify when it is categorized by subject or discipline. Also, subject divisions usually conform to teacher interests and areas of expertise, the coverage of separate textbooks and tests, typical organization of high school departments, and the labels under which grades are awarded. In short, experts and lay persons alike see subjects as easily recognized units of knowledge that students should know.[14]

Broad-fields curriculum

The *broad-fields curriculum* (also called *integrated* or *fused*) is a second type of subject-centered approach to curriculum organization. It also stresses the acquisition of knowledge and the development of mental discipline, but it arranges content into broader, more general fields of study than does the separate-subjects pattern. For example, social studies or problems of democracy classes are taught instead of separate courses in history, government, and geography; language arts instead of reading, composition, literature, and spelling; and general science instead of biology, physics, and chemistry. This type of organization assumes that broader study will provide more useful or more functional knowledge for students, both immediately and in their adult lives. Because it permits broader and more general coverage of content, it allows for, but does not necessitate or require, the elimination of some factual detail.

This pattern was developed several decades ago during a movement when educators were trying to make the curriculum more consistent with the way students naturally see the world around them. It was an effort to avoid what many saw as the unnecessary compartmentalization of separate subjects and a way of integrating studies so they would be compatible with student interests. This type of organization has been practiced more in elementary than in secondary schools and, for a time, was rather common in junior high schools and middle schools. It is less popular today than in the past.

Critics of the broad-fields curriculum fit into two groups—those who prefer separate subjects and those who believe it is too much like the separate-subjects pattern. Those who prefer separate subjects charge that the more generalized curriculum is often too broad, too general, and lacking in depth. They also suggest that it neglects some of the mental-discipline aspects of separate-subjects patterns. Those who dislike the broad-fields curriculum because of its similarity to separate subjects charge that it is more tied to subjects and disciplines than to students, that in most situations the content is not really integrated, and that it often compresses several courses into the teaching time usually devoted to one or two, and without real integration.[15]

The *spiral,* or *structure of knowledge,* curriculum is a third type of subject-centered approach. Its content is organized around the knowledge to be taught, as are the separate-subjects and broad-fields patterns; but it is different from them in at least two ways. First, as described earlier, the spiral curriculum places more emphasis on the structure of knowledge—that is, on concepts and generalizations. Second, it is designed to fit sequentially with students' developmental thinking stages.

Content taught to students in the spiral curriculum is arranged around two things—the main ideas and the methods of inquiry used in the disciplines being studied. Students are expected to learn those big ideas and to develop those ways of thinking. They study the ideas simply at first and then in subsequent classes recycle to those ideas for increasingly deeper and more sophisticated learning.

The spiral pattern of curriculum organization was developed primarily in the 1950s and 1960s, evolved from the Piagetian idea of development, and is articulated best in the writings of Jerome Bruner and Hilda Taba.[16] Curriculum projects funded by the federal government in the 1960s in response to *Sputnik,* especially those in mathematics and science, used it extensively. Renewed interest in it has emerged since the recent school reform and back-to-basics pushes.[17]

The spiral curriculum evolved in response to the criticism that most subject-centered learning was static, not appropriate for students in a rapidly changing world. As a substitute, it is expected to teach more meaningful subject matter and to emphasize thinking skills more than other curriculum patterns. Ideally, it replaces memorization of facts and rote learning with higher-level student understanding of big ideas and student inquiry into those ideas. The pattern is based on the presumption that students who learn big ideas and the skill of inquiry will be able to use what they have learned to understand their world throughout their lifetime.

Advocates of the spiral curriculum argue that students taught in this way actually learn how to learn. They say that students thus better understand what they learn and are more able to use that understanding in future learning. They also note that knowledge learned in this way is not bound by subject divisions and is consistent with the cognitive development of students.

Some critics of this pattern charge that teaching ideas and methods of inquiry requires so much classroom time that many basic facts are not covered. Others say that it is still too subject-centered, is insufficiently tied to student interests, and is too theoretical for many students. Some also say that it requires teacher understanding of subjects and disciplines beyond the level that many teachers—especially elementary teachers, who teach a number of subjects—possess.

Spiral curriculum

FIGURE 12-2   Spiral curriculum. This figure is adapted from curriculum organization patterns developed by the Taba Curriculum Development Center, San Francisco, California. See Taba, H., Durkin, M. C., Fraenkel, J. R., & McNaughton, A. J. (1971). *A teacher's handbook to elementary social studies* (2nd ed.). Menlo Park: CA: Addison-Wesley, p. 29.

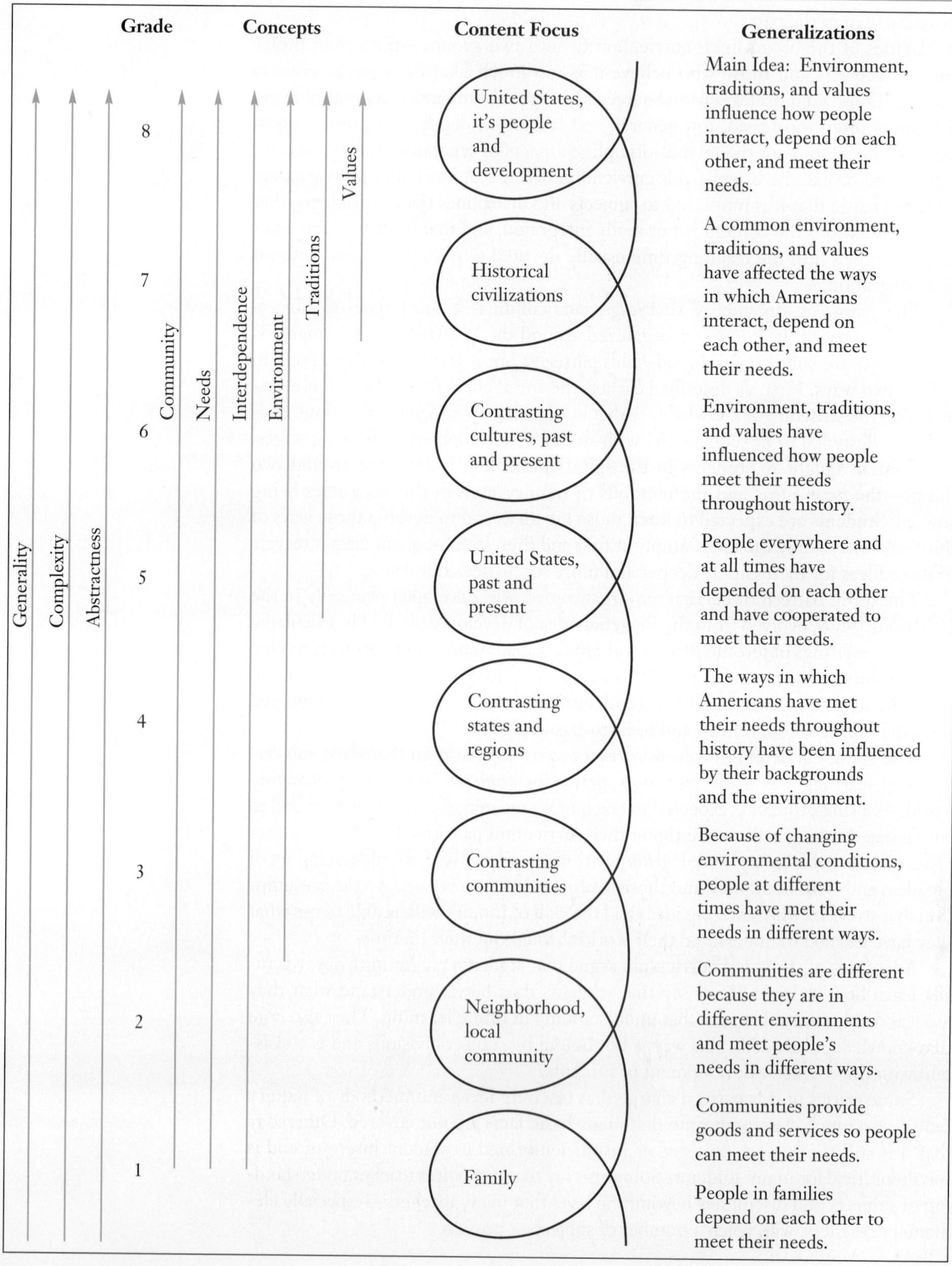

Grade	Concepts	Content Focus	Generalizations
8		United States, it's people and development	Main Idea: Environment, traditions, and values influence how people interact, depend on each other, and meet their needs.
7		Historical civilizations	A common environment, traditions, and values have affected the ways in which Americans interact, depend on each other, and meet their needs.
6		Contrasting cultures, past and present	Environment, traditions, and values have influenced how people meet their needs throughout history.
5		United States, past and present	People everywhere and at all times have depended on each other and have cooperated to meet their needs.
4		Contrasting states and regions	The ways in which Americans have met their needs throughout history have been influenced by their backgrounds and the environment.
3		Contrasting communities	Because of changing environmental conditions, people at different times have met their needs in different ways.
2		Neighborhood, local community	Communities are different because they are in different environments and meet people's needs in different ways.
1		Family	Communities provide goods and services so people can meet their needs.

People in families depend on each other to meet their needs. |

Left axis labels: Generality, Complexity, Abstractness

Concepts (vertical labels): Community, Needs, Interdependence, Environment, Traditions, Values

Figure 12-2 consists of a diagram that illustrates a structure-of-knowledge curriculum pattern for elementary school studies. The content focus for each grade level is listed in the spiral part of the diagram. The key concepts to be learned through the years are to the left of the spiral. The sequence of generalizations to be learned are to the right. The three arrows at the far left of the diagram indicate that the ideas studied become more general, more complex, and more abstract with each cycle.

Student-Centered Curricula

Whereas subject-centered curricula emphasize the information taught to students, *student-centered curricula* focus on student needs, interests, and activities. Generally, they are assumed to be less cognitively oriented and more concerned with affective aspects of student development. Proponents say they stimulate intrinsic motivation in students.

Student-centered curriculum organizations are less popular now than they were near the middle of the twentieth century, but examples can still be found throughout the country, more of them at elementary than secondary levels.

As a group, student-centered curricula usually reflect the following directions:[18]

- They look on learning primarily as experiences provided for students.
- They see the teacher's main job as stimulator and facilitator of student activity.
- They organize learning around the needs and interests of the students rather than the content.
- They assume the teacher will select and arrange content as learning proceeds.
- As often as possible, they individualize goals for students in order to meet their unique needs and qualities.
- They stress student individuality, creativity, and development in affective dimensions.

Early in the twentieth century, John Dewey set the foundation for most student-centered approaches to instruction, and his disciples and the progressive edu-

One of the goals shared by proponents of the various forms of student-centered curricula is to enhance students' intrinsic motivation for learning.

cation movement gave it impetus. Over the years, many variations developed, from those one step away from subject-centered patterns to those that are so focused on student interests and activities that they are accused of having little direction or substance.

This discussion considers four patterns of student-centered curricula. The first, the core curriculum, would be closest to the midpoint on a subject-centered–student-centered continuum. The last, the open curriculum, would be on the far end of the student-centered side.

Core curriculum

The *core curriculum* is a student-centered approach to curriculum organization that also contains a number of subject-centered characteristics. This pattern is similar to the broad-fields curriculum in that it combines subjects into broad fields of study. It is different in that its organizing bases are student needs, problems, and interests rather than content. Whereas broad-field curriculum developers begin by asking which large areas of content fit together well for students, core-curriculum developers ask which broad student needs, problems, and interests should be addressed. Broad-field curriculum leaders select content and fit it to students; core-curriculum people look at the student first, then select the content.

The core curriculum is more frequently found in middle schools than at other grade levels. Typically, it is organized around questions or themes that the students study across subject lines and over an extended time. The pattern usually involves cooperative planning between teacher and students and engages students in a variety of individual and group activities, such as research and writing projects. Questions that might serve as guides for core-curriculum units of study would include these: What persistent problems do people face today? How is the world being modified by technology? Themes that might serve the same purposes are People and Their Environment and Rapid Change in America.

The core curriculum was developed near the middle of the twentieth century and was most widespread during the 1950s and 1960s. Its designers hoped to accomplish all of the following: to address the needs and interests of students, to promote active learning, to relate learning significantly to the lives of students, and to integrate learning across subjects. Ideally, it possibly could do all this, but it has rarely existed in ideal form.

Most often, programs labeled as *core curriculum* are actually less ambitious than the ideal. Some are theme- or problem-oriented programs that combine studies across two or three subject areas, but without as much focus on students as core curriculum idealists would expect. Others are not really interdisciplinary but instead are simple time arrangements in school schedules that permit teachers to cross subject lines in their teaching when their desires and student interests suggest they do so. The subjects most often combined in core curricula are social studies and language arts, science and social studies, and mathematics and science.

The primary criticism of the core curriculum is that it does not work the way it is supposed to. This seems to happen primarily because it requires broad teacher competence in many subject fields, extensive cooperation among teachers, and considerable interdisciplinary planning. It also often requires school arrangements that are not easy to provide, such as flexible space and schedules, cross-age grouping, and a large supply of readily available supplemental materials. In addition, it does not match the separate-subjects orientation of most teaching materials and the way school administrators and college entrance committees expect grades to be assigned. In short, the core curriculum has not become a dominant pattern of curriculum organization because it seems to be too hard to implement.[19]

The *social functions*, or *social problems*, pattern of curriculum organization is similar to the core curriculum, but it places less significance on content that students must learn. Usually organized around themes focused on life situations that students face (or will face as adults), this pattern is assumed to provide more realistic and useful learning than other patterns. A social functions unit of instruction, for example, might address such themes as the following: productive work experiences, health and physical well-being, successful family life, use of leisure time, and understanding human nature.

Social functions curriculum

The social functions idea was pushed strongly as a result of the progressive education movement and was probably at its height in popularity in the 1940s. Its attraction has faded with the demand for academic excellence of the post-*Sputnik* era. It seems to have suffered from some of the same difficulties of implementation that apply to the core curriculum.

In addition, critics of the social functions curriculum point out that the pattern often lacks adequate structure, substance, and depth and that its content seems to fluctuate from class to class and from year to year. Because of this, teachers who attempt to pattern their instruction in this way sometimes have difficulty deciding what to teach and which topics to stress.[20]

As with the two student-centered approaches already described, the focus of an *activity-centered* curriculum is determined by the needs and interests of students. However, the content of this pattern is more flexible than that of the other two, and the information to be covered in a particular lesson is often not planned because the teacher cannot anticipate which student interests will surface. The pattern is based on the belief that student learning must be active, tied to student experience, and as lifelike as possible. Learning by doing and student problem solving are significant.

Activity-centered curriculum

The content for an activities-centered curriculum is arranged around what students do in the classroom, and those activities are frequently set by cooperative teacher-student planning. The ideas presented to students are chosen from many fields and are taught when the students' need for information arises during the course of completing classroom tasks. For example, teachers might plan instruction around a specific problem-solving task, such as confronting a local pollution problem; or around a research task, such as finding an explanation for a chemical reaction in a class science demonstration. In each situation, the information is woven into the tasks students perform.

Like the social functions pattern, the activity-centered curriculum was most popular before the midpoint of the twentieth century and was an outgrowth of the progressive education movement. The pattern has been used primarily in elementary schools and is still included as a significant aspect of many elementary programs. It has been followed only rarely at the secondary level and when followed, has almost always been combined with a more subject-oriented general curriculum scheme. For instance, when teachers plan problem-solving and research activities in science and/or social studies classes, they usually select the content in each subject before they decide on the activities.

Much of the rationale for the activities-centered curriculum is derived from the ideas and proposals of John Dewey, although many educators believe that some of what has been done in the name of activity-centered instruction is really an overextension of Dewey's recommendations. William Kilpatrick, a Dewey disciple, was probably the most outspoken advocate for activity-centered instruction.[21] He stressed the need for teachers to meet student interests and to adjust their teaching when student interests changed, even if they changed abruptly. This would mean that precise lesson planning is virtually impossible and usually undesirable.

Although many versions of the activity-centered curriculum have been followed over the years, the people most critical of it usually think of its most extreme applications. In doing so, they criticize activity-centered programs as being so flexible that they lack substantive content and direction. They say that students miss necessary content simply because it does not fit with their interests at the time. They believe that instruction must be more cognitively focused and teacher directed.

The activity-centered pattern has also suffered from the same difficulties of implementation mentioned for the core curriculum—the need for broad teacher expertise, flexible school space and schedules, multiple supplemental materials, and the expectation that students need to learn certain defined content. Often teachers avoid the pattern because they prefer a curriculum that has more structure and is easier to plan.[22]

Open education

The *humanistic curriculum* and *open education* are as much philosophies of instruction as they are patterns of curriculum organization. Although those who espouse each would argue that they are different enough to justify being described as two separate curricular patterns, their characteristics are similar enough for them to be presented together here. They occupy an extreme end of the subject-centered–student-centered continuum.

Humanistic and open education rose to prominence in the 1950s and 1960s as reactions to a heavy emphasis on cognitive learning in the schools. Both ideas sup-

Although the purest forms of "open education" are no longer in vogue, the movement's emphasis on self-directed learning and program flexibility continues to influence contemporary classrooms.

port instruction that encourages the development of student self-concepts, personal growth, feelings, and expression. Instruction that teaches students to be docile, to conform, and to follow strict school rules is not emphasized.

Ideally, teachers who follow the patterns facilitate, rather than direct, learning; they also set expectations so that all students can succeed. These teachers encourage their students to explore ideas freely, to question openly, and to feel good about their learning experiences. They foster student self-determination, independence, self-acceptance, and consciousness development. They create a nonthreatening classroom atmosphere of trust, mutual respect, cooperation, and friendliness. They accept cognitive development as an important role for schools but not at the expense of individual personal development in the affective domain.

Open classrooms are usually large, flexible spaces with movable furniture and walls. The teacher's station is often less prominent than the teacher's desk in more traditional classrooms. Students are typically free to explore at different interest centers in the area, individually and in small groups. Large numbers of books, videos, tapes and tape recorders, and other learning materials are available. There is less direct, whole-class instruction than in more cognitively oriented classrooms.

The rationale for humanistic and open education is based on work by psychologists Abraham Maslow and Carl Rogers, who see "self-actualization" and "the teaching of the total human being" as primary school goals.[23] Arthur Combs and Donald Snygg, who stressed the importance of motivation and positive student self-concepts in learning, advanced the ideas.[24]

In the late 1960s, humanistic and open education were pursued enthusiastically in the British infant schools, and those efforts became examples for advocates elsewhere. Many elementary schools in the United States shifted their programs in this direction, especially at the primary grades. New school buildings were often constructed with large areas called "pods" instead of traditional classrooms in order to provide flexible teaching space and to accommodate different size classes and cross-grade groupings.

By the mid-1970s, a reaction against open education had set in in the United States. Critics considered it an inefficient way of teaching, one that neglected important cognitive goals of schools; and in the back-to-basics trends of the late 1970s and early 1980s, those views became widespread. Educators, parents, and legislators became concerned about what students were missing. They wanted more direct teaching of knowledge, more teacher-planned instruction, and less left to chance.

Although few open education or heavily humanistic patterns of curriculum organization have survived into the 1980s, their existence in the 1970s moderated the earlier trends toward more rigid and overly cognitive approaches to teaching in most schools. Even though the pendulum has swung back and curricula in general are now more cognitively oriented than open education enthusiasts would like, schools frequently allow for more student self-direction, more program flexibility, and more concern for student affective development than had been the case before the advent of the open education movement.

Many of the open education programs that have continued to the present time are intended as alternative school options for particular types of students. Typically, their targets are high-risk students and students with special needs—students for whom positive self-concepts and continuing success are absolutely critical.[25]

In the Snapshot of this chapter, you were asked to analyze several student schedules in terms of the educational priorities that the schedules reflected. Refer again to those schedules and see whether you can place each of them on the subject-centered–student-centered continuum you just read about. As you do this, think about why you classify each in the way that you do.

Units of Instruction

Units of instruction are plans that many teachers use to organize what they do in their classes so that their students reach the objectives set for them. Teachers rely on units to arrange content, classroom activities, teaching strategies, and instructional resources into patterns of instruction. They follow them as outlines for their daily lesson plans so that they can translate school goals and the general curriculum into day-to-day classroom experiences for students.

Units of instruction vary in many ways—in form, length, amount of sophistication, degree of specificity, and so forth—but most have certain key components, including

- objectives to be achieved by the students
- content to be learned
- teaching strategies for the teacher to use
- learning activities for the students to experience
- resources to be used
- evaluation devices to assess student performance.

Although thorough study of units of instruction is not necessary at this point, a brief glimpse at the introductory parts of sample units should indicate the general thrust or focus of individual units and illustrate how they are used to implement the school curriculum and guide daily classroom instruction (Figure 12-3). The ex-

FIGURE 12-3   Examples of units of instruction for various subjects and grade levels. Note that only the introductory portion of each unit is shown.

Subject Area	Expressive Arts—Art (Grade K)			Mathematics (Grade 1)		
Content Focus	Texture			Addition		
Concepts	texture rough smooth	hard soft feel		addition number count	symbol equal	set group

Generalizations	Objects have a texture.
	Sometimes objects feel different
	   from the way they look.
				Addition is the joining of two sets of numbers
				   or objects.
				Addition using numbers requires the use of the
				   addition and equals symbols.		

Skills	Describing how objects feel
	Organizing objects into appropriate
	   categories (such as hard, soft, rough,
	   and smooth)
	Creating objects with different textures
				Putting items into sets
				Joining sets together
				Computing solutions to addition problems		

Affective Learning	Appreciation of beauty in different forms Creativity (in creating own art forms)			Cooperation (with peers in group situations) Honesty (in correcting own work)		

(continued)

amples that follow include only the parts of units that show the general focus and the content to be taught. They represent various subject areas and grade levels. (Complete units would include more detail on each of the items mentioned in these samples plus detailed descriptions of unit objectives, topics to be covered, activities, materials, and evaluation.)

Note that the skill and affective learnings listed in a number of the samples are not necessarily tied to the concepts and generalizations to be taught. They have just been plugged in. See, for example, "cooperation" and "honesty" in the second sample unit, which is on mathematics for grade 1. These two values are not tied substantively to the mathematics content of the lesson on addition, but the teacher can use the lesson as a means to teach the values *along with* the mathematics content. Plugging in objectives such as these enables the teacher to accomplish multiple skill and affective objectives while also teaching the intended cognitive content.

FIGURE 12-3 (*Continued*)

Subject Area	Reading/Language Arts (Grade 2)	Social Studies (Grade 4)
Content Focus	Long and short vowels	Physical characteristics of a community
Concepts	vowels word consonants word patterns sound long and short symbols	needs change neighborhood wants adaptation occupations goods growth transport services dependence responsibility
Generalizations	A word's pattern will usually determine whether the vowel sound is long or short. Short-vowel sounds and long-vowel sounds have different word patterns.	A community is made up of people who depend on one another. Communities help people meet needs by supplying goods and services. People in the community have a variety of responsibilities, roles, and occupations. Communities change over time and often grow in size and complexity. Each community is unique. I am important in my community.
Skills	Recognizing vowel patterns in words Distinguishing short-vowel words from long-vowel words Identifying groups of words that fit into the long- or short-vowel patterns Locating short- and long-vowel words in printed matter	Finding information on an assigned topic (research) Organizing information into a report to others Writing reports Presenting oral reports Asking appropriate questions of guest speakers
Affective Learning	Taking turns with other students (in reading groups) Respecting other students' ideas Perseverance (in pursuing a difficult learning task)	Acceptance of responsibility Cooperation with others on a group task Development of confidence in oneself (in preparing and presenting a report to others) Feeling of comfort in presenting ideas before peers

(*continued*)

FIGURE 12-3 (*Continued*)

Subject Area	Physical Education/ Health (Grade 6)		Science (Grade 8)	
Content Focus	Drug education—amphetamines and barbiturates		Heat and temperature	
Concepts	amphetamines stimulants barbiturates depressants hallucinogens emphysema cancer AIDS	over-the-counter drugs addiction drug dependency nicotine alcohol abuse peer pressure	heat temperature mass unit of heat	calorie nutrition melting point freezing
Generalizations	Drugs are chemical substances that speed up or slow down body activities. Drugs often make people feel better or happy for a limited time. They sometimes enable people to avoid reality. Drugs, if abused, are harmful to the body. Some drugs cause dependency, even if not physically addictive. Heavy users of various types of drugs are more susceptible to cancer, emphysema, AIDS, and other diseases than are nonusers.		Solids, liquids, and gases expand when heated. Water expands when it is heated and when it freezes. Air changes temperature faster than water. Gases rise when heated. When materials of different temperatures are mixed, the temperatures moderate.	
Skills	Conducting chemical experiments Gathering health data (research) Interpreting charts and graphs		Conducting laboratory experiments Measuring heat content of foods Converting Celsius and Fahrenheit temperatures Interpreting thermometers and other heat-measuring devices	
Affective Learning	Realization that drug abuse is serious Desire to avoid abuse of drugs, alcohol, and tobacco Belief that one should help those with drug problems Willingness to take public position against drug abuse Ability to withstand peer pressure concerning drugs		Cooperation (with classmates in conducting experiments) Realization of role of caloric intake on weight control Awareness of caloric content of different foods	

(*continued*)

FIGURE 12-3   (*Continued*)

Subject Area	History (Grade 10)	English (Grade 12)
Content Focus	Early commerce in feudal Europe	The play *Death of a Salesman* by Arthur Miller
Concepts	commerce manor manufacture trade principality cottage industry feudalism militarism feudal village craft the medieval feudal parish artisan church Middle Ages	symbolism love (of family members) idiom pride theme identity foreshadowing despair character hostility (toward loved ones) traits materialism tragic hero competition hope
Generalizations	Feudal manors were largely self-sufficient economic communities. Feudalism developed because of economic needs and needs for protection. Princes of medieval times provided protection and economic security in return for loyalty and work. Medieval craft associations were early European systems of vocational education. The feudal system combined political, military, economic, social, and religious systems or ways of living.	Although people in modern, materialistic society search for personal values and identity and strive to maintain dignity, these efforts are difficult. (as with Willy) Empty dreams of getting ahead through competition can cause a person to reject a more natural and simple life in which he or she could be himself or herself. (as with Biff) People who live in their dreams instead of reality often fail. People sometimes act with hostility toward people they love. Some business cultures prize competition and images of success to the exclusion of other values. At times people are judged by the amount of money they make and how well they are or appear to be liked by others.
Skills	Reading maps Drawing (of trade routes) Researching (of assigned topics in library) Writing reports	Recognizing and interpreting symbolism Inferring feelings reflected through characters of a play Identifying themes in a play Analyzing characters Comparing and contrasting playwright styles and techniques Discussing personal literary interpretations with class peers
Affective Learning	Sensitivity to the hard life of medieval manors and towns Appreciation of the difference between a class-based and a class-free society Respect for the skill of crafts persons despite the perceived status of the craft Respect for the opportunity provided by public, tax-supported education	Greater sensitivity to the ideals of integrity, loyalty, positive human character traits.

Something to Think About

One of the most difficult and complicating conditions that affects any curriculum plan and the teaching that is based on it is the fact that every student assigned to a class is not present every day. In fact, absenteeism seems to have risen in recent years and is so prevalent in some schools that high absentee rates are the norm. Yet curricula are designed as if all students are in school every day, and the teachers who follow the curriculum of any school are expected to educate all students. The new accountability demands hold them responsible for doing so.

Ben Stein, a journalist, sat in on classes at Birmingham High School in Van Nuys, California, during the 1985–86 school year and kept a diary of his observations.[26] Two of his diary entries are as follows:

November 25, 1985

It's raining, and the students in Miss Silver's class are frantic because of the rain. There are also only about 25 out of 40 here today. I ask Jamie, sitting in front of me, why there is so much absenteeism. "Well, it's raining," she says. "Yes, but do these kids have to walk to school?" "No, but they get up in the morning, and they look out the window, and it's raining, and they think it's a drag to go out in the rain, so they might as well stay in bed, have a cup of coffee, watch soap operas and then maybe get up to work at their jobs after school."

"But what about their parents? Don't their parents make them go to school?"

"No, because almost all of the parents are at work, and don't know what their kids are doing."

Class begins, and the students are. . . .

December 18, 1985

Miss Silver is in a bad mood. "It's class progress-report day," she says, stamping her foot. "I'm in a really terrible mood, so don't even talk to me today."

Outside, the sun is shining and the air is crisp and dry. The students are absent in droves. I ask Debbie, a diminutive girl with curly hair, where all the students are. "Well, it's a beautiful day, so they're probably at the beach," she says.

"But I thought they didn't come when it was raining." "I don't know," says John. "I think maybe kids don't like to be here when it's raining and also when it's sunny. Also maybe when it's cloudy, because when it's cloudy kids like to go to the tanning salon."

- Should curricula be designed to provide for absent students such as those described in the diary excerpts? If so, how can this be done?
- What should the teacher who uses the curriculum do to educate absent students?
- How accountable should teachers and schools be for seeing that students attend school? How should they deal with the problem of excessive absenteeism?
- Should teachers adjust their teaching to accommodate absent students regardless of their reason for being absent?

Lesson Plans

Lesson plans are the guides or outlines that teachers develop as maps for the lessons they expect to teach. Ideally, they are developed from the school's previously prepared curriculum framework and units of instruction, but they often come from many sources, as will be explained in Chapter 13. The plans organize content, teaching strategies, activities, and materials in a format that tells the teacher what to do step by step during a designated period of time on a particular school day.

The design and format of lesson plans varies greatly from school to school, teacher to teacher, and even from year to year for the same teacher. Therefore, multiple examples of specific lesson plans, such as you would see in methods classes, are not presented here. Instead, one lesson plan is outlined, so that you can get a feel for how lesson plans in general flow from curriculum outlines and units of instruction.

Variety of designs

The lesson plan in Figure 12-4 (page 468) was developed for a primary-level class by Lynn Myers.[27] The subsequent Reflecting on Practice section describes what happened when Ms. Myers taught the lesson to her students. As you study the plan, consider the following questions:

- What knowledge, skills, and values does Ms. Myers expect the students to learn from the lesson? Which elements of the lesson help achieve each of the objectives she listed on her plan?
- In what ways does she work toward several different objectives at the same time?
- Why does she devote so much energy toward skill and affective-learning goals when the content focus is animals?
- Where on the subject-centered–student-centered continuum would you place this lesson? Why?
- How might a teacher of secondary school students plan a lesson that would incorporate similar combinations of objectives across all dimensions of subject matter?

The Hidden Curriculum

Students learn more in school than the content specifically planned for them in the curriculum, and that learning outside the regular instructional program is often called the *hidden curriculum*. Although not purposely planned and often different from student to student, the hidden curriculum is, nonetheless, an important part of school learning and can affect students dramatically. It must be considered by school leaders and teachers as they decide how they want to influence the students for whom they are responsible.[28]

The hidden curriculum has a number of dimensions. One aspect includes the unexpected ideas, skills, and values that students pick up from their study even though their teachers had not expected them to do so. Some of these are good, and some are not. The good parts are those that are consistent with intended instruction. For example, students frequently learn new ideas in their reading that teachers thought they already knew; they gain insights from comments of other students;

Unintended content

FIGURE 12-4   Ms. Myers's lesson plan for a unit on animals (Grade 1).

Subject Area	Animals (Grade 1)
Content Focus	Differences among animals
Objectives	
Concepts	Types of animals Kinds of animal "skin" Shelter or "houses" for animals Where animals live (land, water, air, underground)
Generalizations	There are many kinds of animals, and they look different. Animals need food and shelter, but they eat different things and have different "houses." Animals live in different places on earth.
Types of Thinking	Recognizing differences Making comparisons Combining ideas into sentences
Learning Skills	Reading (stories) Writing (ideas from story) Listening (to group members read) Spelling

Social Skills	Group participation
	    Lead Share
	    Follow group leader Take turns

Affective Learning	Developing a concern for animals Developing a willingness to share (class materials) Cooperating (with other students in a group) Appreciating the need to stay on task and complete individual work
Lesson Sequence	1. Students sit together on mat for instruction. 2. Describe the lesson topic. 3. Tell the students they will work in groups and explain the group arrangement—6 groups of 4 each. 4. Announce to the whole class who the group leaders are. 5. Describe the contents of each book. Give one book to each group leader. 6. Tell students that each book contains a piece of paper for each child in the group who uses that book. 7. Explain that children in each group are to take turns reading parts of their book to each other as the other group members look at the words and pictures. 8. Tell each group to discuss the story at the end of the reading. 9. Tell them to return to their desks after the discussion and individually write paragraphs about what they have learned. 10. Explain that these are to be first drafts of writing and that they will be revised tomorrow. Remind them about what a first draft is. 11. Give group leaders time to pick a location in the classroom for their group to meet. 12. Tell the others to join their group leaders. 13. Monitor group and individual work. 14. Collect completed paragraphs. 15. Have students begin practicing spelling as they complete paragraphs.
Evaluation	Check for each objective through • Observing group and individual work • Questioning students individually • Reading individual responses
Resources	Animal books Writing paper (for each student)

T his Reflecting on Practice describes what happened when Lynn Myers taught the lesson she had planned. As you read, consider:

- How closely did the lesson follow the plan, and where did it deviate? How would you explain the deviations?
- As you compare what happened in the actual lesson with the plan, what assumptions do you think Ms. Myers made as she planned the lesson? For instance, what assumptions did she make about the previous knowledge of the students, about student maturity, and about the students' ability to follow directions?

When the class enters the room from recess, the children sit on the large mat at the front as Ms. Myers picks up her materials from her desk. She sits on the chair in the midst of the students and begins.

"Today we are going to work in groups. There will be six groups with four people in each. I have already picked the groups and a leader for each one. The leaders know who they are. We will learn about animals and will practice our reading and writing skills. Listen carefully to the directions so that you know what to do."

(Ms. Myers tells the class who the group leaders are.)

"Each group will have one of these books. (Ms. Myers holds up six small reading books.) They describe different things about animals—food animals eat, 'houses' animals live in, the kinds of 'skin' animals have, things animals do, special skills some animals have, and locations where animals live.

"After I finish these directions, each group leader will take a book and choose a place in the classroom for his or her group to study. Remember, leaders must see that everyone does his or her part and everyone else must follow the leader's suggestions.

"When your group is settled, the leader should start reading the book to the group, and the others should sit close enough to see the words and pictures. After a short while, the leader should give the book to someone else to read. Each person should take a turn so that everyone has an equal chance to read.

"When your group is finished reading the whole story, have a discussion about what you learned. Have the group discussion just as we usually do. Take turns, be courteous, and listen to your leader.

"At the end of the discussion, group leaders will give each person a piece of paper like this one. There are four pieces in each book. Then each person will go to his or her desk to start writing.

"When you get to your desk, put your name on the paper and write a paragraph that answers this question: 'What did I learn about animals from the book?' (Ms. Myers points to the question on the chalkboard.) If you forget the question, just look up here.

"Your paragraph will be a first draft, or a rough copy. Who remembers what a first draft is? (Through questions and explanations Ms. Myers reminds the class what a first draft is.) I will read your paragraphs tonight and give them back to you tomorrow. Tomorrow, we will fix them up. Then you can read them to your friends, and we will put them on the bulletin board.

"Remember when you are doing the first draft, you do not have to worry about the grown-up way to spell every word. If you are not sure how to spell a word, have a good guess and circle it. Tomorrow, we will take time to look up words and fix them.

"When you finish writing, give me your paragraph and begin your spelling practice. The page numbers are written on the chalkboard."

At this point, Ms. Myers tells the students which groups they are in, gives each leader a book, allows the leaders to pick the classroom spot where his or her group will meet, and tells the other students to join their leaders. She has assigned group membership so that each has about equal numbers of the following: high- and low-ability readers, outgoing and quiet personalities, and girls and boys. Because it is still before the midpoint in the school year, all the leaders are students with rather dominant personalities. She believes this helps the groups to stay on task. As the year progresses, she will designate less dominant children to be leaders and will help them develop leadership characteristics.

As the groups read the books, Ms. Myers and an aide move among them, suggesting how the children should sit so that they can see and hear, listening to what is being said, encouraging participation, managing behavior, answering questions, and monitoring group progress.

As the groups complete their discussions, Ms. Myers and the aide collect the books and help each student get started writing at his or her desk. As the writing proceeds, both adults monitor and guide the writing.

When individual students complete their paragraphs, they give them to Ms. Myers and begin their daily spelling practice.

they learn to think better in the process of doing an assignment; and they formulate values by learning about others' views and by confronting value choices.

Unexpected school learning can also be harmful. Students can learn (or think they have learned) ideas that can be erroneous, negative, and contrary to school goals. They can overgeneralize information about particular people and create stereotypes. Some students can see values intended to be presented as negative as attractive instead. Students sometimes use shortcuts, such as plagiarism and mass-published synopses, instead of developing their own skills and completing assignments; they sometimes use such methods and attain good grades.

School organization

A second aspect of the hidden curriculum comes from the ways in which the institutions are set up—*how* schools are organized, *how* they function day to day, and *how* teachers teach. Often these variables send unintended messages to students, and those messages may either support or conflict with what teachers and school administrators think they are teaching. When there is conflict between this part of the hidden curriculum and what the school expects to teach, such circumstances as these can occur. Students can be forced into conformity because the school organization demands it, even though the school program is intended to encourage creativity and originality. They can find attractive role models among students, adults, or media figures that school leaders had hoped would be unattractive. They can be encouraged to compete and cheat instead of to cooperate and do honest schoolwork. Sometimes this aspect of the hidden curriculum provides students with significant practice at outwitting, outguessing, deceiving, and confronting teachers and other authorities.

School cultures

A third aspect of the hidden curriculum is closely associated to school organization, but it has less to do with structure and rules and more to do with social atmosphere. It consists of the amorphous *school culture* and *social subtleties* that pervade a school—the traditions, rituals, peer associations, and friendships mentioned in Chapter 4. These aspects of school life, including relationships among students, among teachers and students, and among administrators and students, can stimulate personal achievement, individual responsibility, and self-confidence; or they can stifle them. They can foster a sense of belonging or instill a feeling of rejection. They can promote positive self-images or induce alienation.

Student-to-student interactions have particularly strong impact. Students who are part of the "in" group have different learning experiences from those who are not; as do those who are known as being highly intelligent, those who are considered desired dates, those who have cars, and those who excel in school activities. Peer associations frequently have direct influences on school learning as a whole. Students who have close friends among their school peers and who are socially comfortable in the school environment frequently achieve in ways that their more isolated and uncomfortable counterparts do not.

Just as planned and intended school learning extends beyond the classroom and into homework assignments, out-of-school projects, and everyday applications of learning in real life, the hidden curriculum extends beyond the school walls. Uncaring comments by teachers, rigid school rules, failed tests, and unoffered and unaccepted invitations to the school dance are remembered for a lifetime, as are friendly words of encouragement, exceptions to the rules, academic successes, and making the team. School plays, athletic competition, club leadership responsibilities, and

Were school theatrical productions part of the hidden curriculum in your own education? What are some of the learnings students take away from this kind of experience?

personal friendships are all part of school learning, as are peer rejections, disappointments, lost elections for campus offices, and the breakup of intense relationships. Often these experiences are more significant and longer lasting than academic learning and grades in courses.

Although these aspects of school learning are not part of the planned school curriculum, they are learning experiences; they must be taken into consideration by school personnel as they think about what they teach and what they want to accomplish. Although the hidden curriculum is not purposefully planned, it is part of what students learn at school, and, therefore, is content of a sort.

Conclusion

Curriculum frameworks, units, and lesson plans are the on-paper designs of what and how students are expected to learn in school. But there is always a difference between what those plans call for and what individual students actually learn. Sometimes the on-paper plans are simply not followed, possibly for sound reasons; even when they are, some are not as successful as the designer had hoped. Even good plans that work well with particular classes and students do not work with others.

On the other hand, effective teaching and learning rarely occur if school leaders and teachers do not design, organize, and follow good curriculum frameworks and lessons. A lack of curriculum conceptualization and planning leads to confusion, overlap, and oversight in the resulting curriculum.

Therefore, as you think about curriculum matters in the future, you should keep two important guiding principles in mind: Good teaching requires thorough planning, but thorough planning does not guarantee good teaching.

EDUCATIONAL RESEARCH

The Information Highway and Schools

This Educational Research section is different from the other Educational Research sections in this text in several ways: (1) It is a condensed and edited version of a paper that was written by a first-year college undergraduate student who used the first edition of this text in an introduction to teacher education course in 1994; (2) it reports on information that she read about in *Education Week* over a few weeks during the term she was enrolled in the class; and (3) it presents her conclusions—not those of experienced educational researchers or analysts. One of our reasons for presenting this student work here is to illustrate to you the type of "educational research" beginning teacher education students might do as they keep themselves informed about the professional happenings of the day. As we indicate a number of times in this book, today's teachers must be continuous learners, always reading and always updating their ideas. We believe that this professional researcher-learner approach to teaching should begin in your first course and never stop, short of your retirement from the profession.

The focus of this student's paper is on the *information highway* and its potential effect on schools. Her paper provides you with information about recent developments in technology, electronics, and communication that will greatly impact what is taught in schools in the near future as well as teaching methods. All beginning teachers need to understand these developments because of their certain effect on their professional lives.

The Electronic Community When we look to the classroom of the future, we see computers available for nearly every student in every school, technologically interactive lectures presented to thousands of students hundreds of miles away from the lecturer, students from all over the world communicating with each other, and computer programs tailored to meet students' individual needs and challenge their interests. In short, classrooms of the future will be connected to a growing information highway.

Although Peter West is partially accurate when he says in an article, "The Last Mile," "While everyone talks about the information highway, there is no common definition for what it means in any context, least of all education," there is enough of a general definition for us to talk about the concept.[29] The information highway is essentially a global electronic network, with linkages by means of fiber-optic or copper cabling through which people and their computers communicate. For example, Internet, one of a number of information highway networks, provides access to a pool of electronic data from throughout the world that a person can access via personal computers. Through its use, one can send electronic mail ("e-mail" for short), read numerous electronic bulletin boards, consult

several electronic encyclopedias, search through library collections and reference services, "tap into" on-line news services, share curriculum materials and instructional ideas, and much more.[30]

The most important questions about the information highway for teachers are, Where do schools fit into the system? How do they connect? Do the costs outweigh the benefits for students and teachers?

A recent study, "Computers in American Schools," found that only 35 percent of America's high schools reported using an external computer network, and only 16 percent reported using the network daily or weekly.[31] But, these statistics might be changing. For example, the Computer Curriculum Corporation (CCC) of California will install more than 7,500 computers and accompanying software in one Florida school district; furthermore, CCC has guaranteed that all students who use their system will exceed learning goals set for them by teachers, parents, or the students themselves. Another corporation, Jostens Learning, has a ten-year contract to provide elementary classrooms in West Virginia with $70 million worth of computer technology and so far has put 7,924 computers into classrooms. The same company has contracts with Atlanta and Chicago schools to provide about $25 million worth of equipment for classrooms.[32] One of the largest newspapers in North Carolina has offered electronic news and access to Internet over telephone lines free of charge.[33]

Earlier this year, two telecommunications powerhouses, Bell Atlantic Corporation and Tele-Communications Inc. (TCI), announced both a plan to merge and entrance into the educational market. Although

the merger has since been called off, the planned education program is still likely to happen in the near future under some corporate sponsorship. The specific Bell Atlantic-TCI program called for linking more than 25 percent of our nation's schools to the information highway. If the plan materializes, the linked schools will see cable-television programs, connect with data networks, and have access to Internet, all free of charge. Additional services will be offered with a charge.[34]

Another large telecommunications corporation, Pacific Bell, has also made plans to bring the information highway to schools. The company has promised to provide access to its network for all of the 6,500 public schools within its service area by 1996. A unique aspect of Pacific Bell's plan is that it does not involve fiber-optic cabling. The system will use something called "integrated service digital networks" (ISDN) and copper wiring. ISDN service will allow voice and video signals as well as computer data to be sent over telephone lines that are already in place.[35] Some critics of the plan say that this technology is not as advanced as fiber optics and does not have fiber-optic speed and capacity, but supporters note that right now less than 10 percent of classrooms have basic telephone service and, in that context, even the Pacific Bell system would be a monumental leap forward.[36]

An alliance of four distance-learning programming powers proposes to launch a satellite-based Interactive Distance Education Alliance Network (IDEANET). IDEANET will serve thirty-three states and the District of Columbia when it is in place, and it will provide an interactive television and computer network. As one representative of IDEANET states, "This network will serve as the schools' on-ramp to the 'information superhighway'."[37] If successful, the network will reach 2,000 schools nationwide.[38]

A program sponsored by Compaq Computer Corporation, America's third largest provider of computer technology but only a recent entry into the education market, is intended to provide the equipment students need to connect to the information highway. The program combines a computer leasing program with donated computers. For example, the company provided one school district in Tucson, Arizona, 300 free computers, 60 of which are laptops, which students can take from class to class and to their homes, from where they have access to their school's technology system via a modem.[39]

In a parallel effort, the American Federation of Teachers has formed a deal with Prodigy and America Online to allow its 835,000 teachers to sample services on the highway. Both Prodigy and America Online offer news, educational games, reference materials, encyclopedia, e-mail, and many other services. For the service, teachers are asked only to fill in periodic evaluations and after a year issue a "grade" to each company.[40]

Big business, however, is not the only party interested in the information highway; so is the federal government. The vice president of the United States, Al Gore, has taken a personal interest in the information highway. Congress has also been urged to get involved. The National Coordinating Committee on Technology in Education and Training recently released a statement titled, "The National Information Infrastructure: Requirements

for Education and Training," which encourages Congress to set a goal to connect each U.S. classroom to the information highway by the turn of the century. Suggestions as to how to fund such information highway connections for schools range from federal and state taxes to donations and fees paid by users.[41]

One voice in the "how-can-we-make-this-happen" arena comes from the Public Broadcasting Service (PBS), which is hoping to persuade Congress to require that all advanced telecommunications networks reserve a certain amount of capability, possibly up to 20 percent, for educational programming. Already, a bill introduced into the House of Representatives by Rep. Edward J. Markey of Massachusetts would require that the Federal Communications Commission reserve the appropriate information highway capacity for educational programming.[42] Even the famous filmmaker George Lucas has called on lawmakers to insure that every school has access to on-line services and Internet.[43]

So what is the bottom line? There are at least two opposing perspectives on this issue. On one side is the enthusiasm of the big telecommunication companies who are racing to break into the educational market. These companies are beginning to invest huge amounts of money into the future of the information highway in schools, as we have seen. On the other side, however, is the caution of people who are asking serious questions about costs for "hooking up" schools. Their concern focuses on what many call "the last mile." They ask about costs and other problems related to the wiring of school buildings, maintenance of equipment, payment for on-line services, and

training teachers to utilize the technology. They also ask how these costs and problems compare to the expected benefits for students.

A related set of questions includes the following: How does existing technology and equipment that schools already have fit into the information highway? (For example, Kentucky has already spent millions of dollars on satellite dishes and the technology related to them.) Will the information highway lead to the school, the classroom, or the individual student desk? How are teachers and students to navigate it?[44]

In my opinion, the information highway is an exciting prospect for schools, teachers, and students. I believe, however, that the issues regarding costs need to be dealt with now, before much more implementation occurs, in order to avoid problems down the line. Someone must address the costs of hooking schools to the information highway and set down a timeline that is possible to follow. That timeline must include budgeting, because only through budgeting will the full potential of the highway be realized by schools. As part of that process, the issues of equal access for all schools and students must be addressed.

A particular concern to me as a future educator is how am I to be trained in the use of this technology. I think teachers must be trained, or the technology will not be utilized to its fullest potential.

A second concern that I have has to do with the impact of technology on teaching and students. I would like to see teaching remain as "human" as possible. I would not like teachers to be replaced in the classroom by the computer; neither would I like computers to become the primary interacter for students.

One of the special aspects of teaching and learning is the learning that comes from interacting with other people. I would like to see that element of learning preserved into the technology age.

In conclusion, the information highway truly has the potential to greatly change teaching and learning. Many corporations are competing to bring this technology to the classroom, but it would be wise to listen to the voices of caution in order to avoid at least some of the potential problems. Let's move into the future through technology, but let's not forget the human quality that we all possess and that makes us different from the machines that we utilize.

Summary

Curriculum frameworks, units of instruction, and lesson plans are devices that educators use to organize their instruction. Developing curricula involves putting together goals, content, teaching strategies, activities, and materials. The process includes setting educational objectives at three levels—the school district level, the school level, and the class or subject level.

Curricula can have various emphases, and the different types of emphasis are usually thought of on a continuum that extends from those that are very content-centered and subject-specific to those that are very student-centered and integrated. Units of instruction are more focused and more detailed. Lesson plans are more specific and precise than units and, at least ideally, are developed from units.

Students learn more than the content planned for them in the prepared curriculum and intentionally taught in teachers' lessons. Much of that unplanned-for learning comes from the hidden curriculum of schools.

Study Questions

1. Make a list of all the subjects you studied during the last two or three years of high school. Then consider what value each course held for you. Think in terms of its value to you while you were still in high school, now that you are a college student, and potentially for your later life.
2. Review the five purposes for schools listed in Chapter 1. Then consider the same questions asked in Question 1 above, but this time in terms of those five purposes.
3. In which ways do different school curricula prepare students for different social

and economic levels of life? In which ways do they channel students in these directions more narrowly than they might?

4. Make a list of the five or six subjects typically studied anywhere between kindergarten and grade 12 that you believe are the most important for all students. Justify each of your choices.

Key Terms

Activity-centered curriculum

Basic education

Broad aims of education

Broad-fields curriculum

Class-level objectives

Core curriculum

Curriculum

Curriculum framework

Discipline-based curriculum

Expository methods of instruction

Hidden curriculum

Humanistic curriculum

Information highway

Lesson plans

Open education

Reconstructionism

Reconstructionists

Relevance

Self-actualization

Separate-subjects curriculum

Social-functions curriculum

Social-problems curriculum

Spiral curriculum

Structure of knowledge curriculum

Student-centered curriculum

Subject-centered curriculum

Units of instruction

For Further Reading

Apple, M. W. (1982). *Education and power.* Boston: Routledge and Kegan Paul.

Apple, M. W. (1983). Curriculum in the year 2000: Tensions and possibilities. *Phi Delta Kappan, 64*(5), 321–326.

Banks, J. R., et al. (1992). *Building learner-centered schools: Three perspectives.* New York: Teachers College, Columbia University, National Center for Restructuring Education.

Brophy, J. (1992). Probing the subtleties of subject-matter teaching. *Educational Leadership, 49*(7), 4–8.

Counts, G. S. (1932). *Dare the schools build a new social order?* New York: John Day.

Eisner, E. W. (1994). The educational imagination: On the design and evaluation of school programs (3rd ed.). New York: Macmillan.

Eisner, E. W. (1990). Creative curriculum development and practice. *Journal of Curriculum and Supervision, 6*(1), 62–73.

Jackson, P. W. (1968). *Life in classrooms.* New York: Holt, Rinehart and Winston.

Joyce, B., Weil, M., & Showers, B. (1992). *Models of teaching* (4th ed.). Boston: Allyn and Bacon.

Kilpatrick, W. H. (1918). The project method. *Teachers College Record, 19*(4), 319–335.

Taba, H. (1962). Curriculum development. *Theory and practice.* New York: Harcourt, Brace and World.

Tyler, R. W. (1949). *Basic principles of curriculum and instruction.* Chicago: University of Chicago Press.

The Act of Teaching
Planning, Implementing, and Evaluating

CONTRIBUTING AUTHORS
Carolyn M. Evertson
Marcy Singer Gabella
Ann M. Neely
Catherine H. Randolph

Carolyn M. Evertson, Marcy Singer Gabella, Ann M. Neely, and Catherine H. Randolph are the primary authors of this chapter. Charles and Lynn Myers provided the Educational Research section.

This chapter provides a brief sketch of the process of teaching. It explains the process as consisting of three intertwined parts—(1) the actual teaching of lessons, (2) the planning that precedes the teaching, and (3) the evaluation of students and the lessons taught. It labels that three-part process as *the act of teaching*.

As teachers think about their lessons, they take into consideration many elements and ideas (most of which are described in earlier chapters). They take into account their talents as teachers, goals and objectives of their instruction, the nature of students, theories of learning, the culture of the school and their classes, philosophies of education, content, and the school's curriculum framework. Using their own style, they fit all the parts together and, somehow, make it all work. When it does work, students learn what the teachers want them to learn.

The chapter is built around images of a teacher who leads a sixth-grade writing class. The chapter begins with an examination of the context for the act of teaching, and then it focuses in on planning and evaluation. The first section presents teaching as an interactive activity embedded in the cultural context of the classroom. The planning section analyzes the kind of thinking teachers do as they design classes. The evaluation section describes how teachers assess the effectiveness of lessons and use that information for continuous planning.

The chapter contains three interrelated Snapshots, all about one teacher as she teaches and thinks about her sixth-grade writing class. The first episode shows her teaching the class and the other two describe some of her planning and evaluation of her work. The three as a group illustrate how a teacher uses reflective practice to improve teaching. The Educational Research section surveys researchers' and educational thinkers' ideas about reflective practice. Because reflective practice is so much a focus of this chapter, there is no Reflecting on Practice section.

SNAPSHOT

The first Snapshot for this chapter describes a lesson in a sixth-grade writing class.[1] Students in the class meet with their teacher for writing for 45 minutes, four days a week. The episode that is presented shows the class "in motion." It is about midyear, and the students and teacher are relying on a predictable set of routines and expectations for how the class period will progress. Students begin independent work with only a few instructions; the teacher circulates and spends time with a few students, while others work alone or obtain help from nearby peers. As you read this Snapshot, consider the following questions:

- What kinds of activities are students engaged in?
- What kinds of skills must students already have learned in order to work in this way?
- What can you infer about the culture of this class and how it has operated in the past?
- What kinds of "teaching" activities is the teacher performing?

Ms. Harding's Writing Class, February

There is a bustle and chatter as students enter the classroom and find their seats. The electric pencil sharpener hums, and students bombard the teacher and one another with questions and laughter. The teacher signals the beginning of writing class, saying, "Thank you for entering so quickly and quietly so we can get started. We have lots to do today."

The class settles into its daily routine. The teacher runs down her checklist of who turned in an entry for a local essay contest. She then announces who has published writing by sharing it with the class: "Jonathan published a piece of writing entitled, 'Alan Hood.'" As she calls students' names, they come to the front of the room and collect a certificate that says *"You did it! You published a fantastic piece of writing!"* When all the certificates have been distributed, the class applauds the authors.

The teacher turns next to the stack of final drafts that have been turned in. "Bethany, will you read your story, 'My Bratty Sister'?" Bethany nods, comes to the front, and reads aloud. Most students listen; one in the front gets up to get a dictionary from a bookcase on the side wall; another reads a paperback. The teacher continues leading a session of sharing final drafts. As she selects one, she comments, "This is interesting. Brian's rough draft was twelve pages long. His final draft is a page and a half. Let's talk about that. What made you decide to do it that way, Brian?" The student talks about his strategy of leaving out the things he thought got in the way of the action.

The sharing continues. Sometimes an especially good piece earns spontaneous applause from the class. After the last work is read, the teacher comments, "I continue to be impressed with this class and the writing you're doing. All of that came in just yesterday!" There are "oohs" and "aahs" as the class responds with surprise.

"All right, I want you to use the rest of our time today

for your own writing. Remember the due date for all writing is just two weeks away. Let's see how everyone is doing. How many of you are just getting an idea?" Hands go up. "Okay. If you're planning a story, you may want to pick up a planning sheet from the bookshelf. You can write down your characters, setting, and so forth. How many are in the process of writing a draft? Okay. How many have a draft completed and are ready to share it with a friend and get some feedback?" She continues through the writing process, checking for people who are likely to need her help, and getting all the students focused on what they're doing. "Okay. You have about twenty minutes left. I'll set the timer for fifteen minutes, and then you may use the class library if you want to."

Students settle into their writing as the teacher moves to one of the writers who indicated he needed an idea. She sits down in a nearby empty seat and begins talking with him about a trip he took the previous summer. Students, seated around the room in groups of four, begin to write. There is a steady hum of quiet talk as students pause to chat, to ask for an idea, to read aloud what they have just written, or to take a break. There is movement of various kinds: a student turning in a finished draft, another getting a thesaurus, another taking a rough draft to a knowledgeable peer across the room, another seeking out the teacher, who has moved to a new desk to brainstorm with another student. The noise level ranges from silence to busy hum to dull roar and back again, as students share what they create. Occasionally the teacher quiets a particularly noisy group.

The timer goes off, and a few students move to the library to find books. The next group of students gathers outside the classroom door. Their muffled murmur calls them to the teacher's attention. "Okay," she says, rising, "Time to get going." "Noooo," mutters Ian, who is still looking for the perfect word starting with O to fit into his poem. "I'll take your journals on your way out the door," the teacher continues. "See you tomorrow."

The Teaching Process

Three overlapping components

The act of teaching involves at least three primary components: planning, teaching, and evaluating. It is tempting to think of teaching in a linear way, as if the components occur as three sequential steps—planning, implementing plans, and, finally, evaluating the effectiveness of the plans and their implementation. In fact, however, planning, implementing, and evaluating are ongoing and overlapping parts of the teaching process, as the Snapshots in this chapter illustrate. Although it is necessary to describe these activities separately in this chapter, it is important to recognize that this separation is artificial. The first Snapshot shows a complex learning setting where the teacher evaluates and modifies her plans as she teaches. As she checks with students regarding their progress with their writing, she is gathering information about where her energies should be spent during the class period; in this case, she selects students who appear to need her individual help. The responses to shared writing and the contributions students make to the discussion of Brian's revisions help her gauge their progress toward her goals for them as writers and readers and provide information about how the class should progress in the coming days and weeks. As a result of information gathered on the day this Snapshot took place, for example, Ms. Harding brought in drafts of her own writing and shared how she revises her work.

The intent of the first Snapshot is to give you a picture of *the act of teaching* in progress. It will serve as a framework for the rest of the chapter, within which we will explore how the act of teaching takes place and how teachers make plans and evaluate their teaching on an ongoing basis. First, let's consider the complex setting in which instruction takes place—the classroom.

The Classroom Environment

Classrooms are complicated places. In classrooms, groups of twenty to thirty-five individuals meet daily to interact, share information, and learn. Over time, each group takes on characteristics that make it different from all other groups that meet or have met in a particular room or building. In the following section, we discuss how these differences come about and how they are related to the act of teaching.

Classrooms as Cultures

You have already read in Chapter 4 about how schools can be thought of as organizational cultures. Now it will be helpful to extend this idea to examine classrooms as smaller but similar cultures. Chapter 4 pointed out how the larger school culture and existing student subcultures may affect what students and teachers do within a particular classroom. Additionally, however, it is important to recognize that, over time, each class and classroom setting becomes a unique culture of its own. Within those cultures, students and teachers have particular roles and expectations for each other; they interact in more or less predictable ways; they may even develop common ways of using certain terms, thus developing a language of their own.

Understood roles and expectations

As an example, reflect upon the classroom in the Snapshot. In some classrooms, one aspect of the teacher's role might be to provide help to any student in need. However, in this classroom, the task of providing help is shared and becomes part of the role of both students and teacher. Students know when and for what reasons they may leave their seats, and they know that they are expected to talk with one another as they write. The class shares a definition of what it means to be a "published" writer that is different from what the term *published* would mean to someone who was unfamiliar with how the group operates. Each of these elements, along with many others, serves to identify this group as a particular culture, "Ms. Harding's 11:00 writing class."

One more important element of classroom cultures is that, as teachers and students develop roles and expectations for how they interact, they are also developing working definitions of the abstract concepts "teaching" and "learning." For instance, some classroom observers are likely to define *teaching* and *learning* as things that happen only when the teacher is standing in front of the class. (In fact, this might have been your view before you studied Chapter 2.) However, these definitions appear not to apply to the class described in the Snapshot. In this episode, both the students and the teacher accept definitions of teaching and learning that include students teaching one another and learning on their own and in cooperation with their peers. More illustrations of different classroom environments and cultures are presented in the models of instruction in Chapter 14. For our purposes here, however, it is important to recognize that the ways teachers and students interact and the assumptions on which they base that interaction have effects on the instruction and learning that actually develop and operate in the day-to-day life of the classroom. As teachers plan, implement plans, and evaluate students and their teaching, the cultures of their classrooms shape their actions and are at the same time shaped *by* their actions and the actions of their students.

Particular definitions of "teaching" and "learning"

Classrooms as Communicative Environments

How does a classroom's culture develop? Remember that the Snapshot you read at the start of this chapter took place at midyear in this classroom. On the first day of school, neither teacher nor students knew exactly what to expect or how this year was going to develop. Over time, as the students and teacher received and interpreted messages from one another, they established patterns of communicating and behaving that were acceptable to both. Sometimes, the students or Ms. Harding may have called attention to "the way we do things around here"; more often, however, this negotiation was an unspoken part of the act of teaching. Verbally and nonverbally, teachers and students develop classroom culture through communication, and the patterns of communication established in a classroom serve as evidence of the kind of culture that has developed there. The next sections of this chapter describe the particular features that make classroom communication unique.

Talk in Classrooms

Much of the time in any classroom is taken up with talk; and, in most classrooms, most of that talk is directed from teachers to students. More than two decades ago, Ned Flanders studied verbal communication in classrooms and found that someone was talking about two-thirds of the time; when someone was talking, about two-thirds of the time the talker was the teacher.[2] Although we would like to think that typical classrooms of today involve more balanced talking patterns and more varied exchanges of ideas than those found by Flanders, most present-day classroom communication patterns are probably not much different.

Classroom talk: Who is talking?

In addition to the fact that teachers usually dominate classroom communication, classroom talk has a number of other characteristics that make it noticeably different from talk in other settings.[3] One of these differences was illustrated by Hugh Mehan[4] and is presented here. Notice the differences between these two short verbal exchanges:

SPEAKER 1: What time is it?	SPEAKER A: What time is it?
SPEAKER 2: 10:45.	SPEAKER B: 10:45.
SPEAKER 1: Very good!	SPEAKER A: Thank you!

It is easy to deduce that the exchange on the left is probably taking place between a teacher and a student and the exchange on the right is probably not. Speaker 1 apparently already knows what time it is and asks the question as a kind of test, which he or she then evaluates, providing feedback with the comment "Very good!" The gratitude expressed by Speaker A, on the other hand, implies that he or she had a genuine need for the information Speaker B supplied.

In many instances, as in this example, teacher talk follows patterns that are quickly recognized by all of us who have spent time in schools. Typically, as in the example above, teachers ask questions to which they already know the answers and they evaluate the answers that they receive. Teachers also may ask questions that are really directives. For instance, depending on the context, the question, "Kevin, do you need help?" can actually mean any of the following:

"Kevin, I am sincerely asking if you need help; do you?"
"Kevin, I know you need help; I am now ready to help you."
"Kevin, go back to your seat and be quiet!"

Each of these questions has a different meaning, and what is meant varies with the context in which it is raised, even though the teacher uses the exact same words. Interestingly, however, regardless of the meaning a teacher intends to convey with a question or statement, most students in the class are likely to know exactly what the teacher means. They know that because they are part of the classroom culture and understand the assumptions on which that culture is based. Similarly, teachers also use cultural understandings to interpret and respond to student questions.

The patterns described here are typical of much classroom talk; however, that does not mean that they are the only patterns established in classrooms. Teachers who work consciously to encourage student exploration of ideas through talk may allow patterns of talk that are much less teacher-centered to develop in their classrooms.

Talk and Learning

We have already discussed how definitions of teaching and learning are developed as teachers and students interact in classrooms. If teachers control classroom talk, as they do in the typical communication patterns just described, they also control how these definitions develop.[5] It is important for teachers to be aware of the amount and kinds of talk that occur in their classrooms in order to be sure that the messages communicated through these interactions are consistent with the messages the teachers intend to communicate. For example, if a teacher's goal is to encourage independent, creative thought in students, classroom talk that remains highly teacher-centered is unlikely to be helpful. Similarly, if a teacher asks, "How do you think the child in the story felt when the wind howled so loudly?" he or she should not reject a student response that does not match the possible answers the

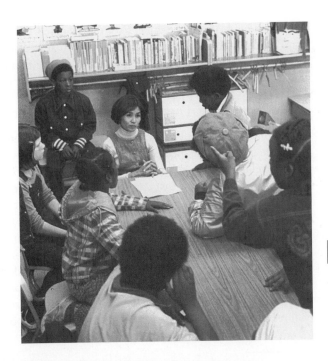

Teachers should constantly assess whether the patterns of talk in their classrooms are conveying the messages they want students to receive.

teacher had anticipated. If teachers accept only predetermined responses consistently, students come to realize that when the teacher asks, "What do you think?" he or she really means "What do I want you to say you think?"

Studies have reported, however, that teachers are frequently unaware of the extent to which their talk dominates classes and that they often do not know whether their talk accomplishes what they want it to do.[6] To be more aware of the impact of talk in their classrooms, teachers need to plan, monitor, and evaluate their teaching in ways that are conscious of the quality, quantity, and direction of classroom talk. They need to consider who is talking, when, and for what purposes and whether the patterns of communication that are developing are beneficial for all students. For example, in one particular study, boys received more teacher verbal contacts than girls in a number of classrooms, and many of these contacts varied in type as well as frequency.[7] The teacher's verbal comments to boys frequently contained a high proportion of critical statements and statements intended to control behavior: "Don't do that." "I told you not to push others." "Put that book away." Another study reported that although girls seemed to receive fewer verbal contacts, more of the contacts they received dealt with instructional content than with directions or behavior control.[8]

Another factor that teachers need to consider as they assess classroom communication is whether the interaction patterns of a particular classroom are an appropriate match for the home cultures of the students in that classroom. Numerous studies have illustrated how conflicts between communication patterns that students are used to at home and those at school result in students being misjudged by teachers and classmates or left out of classroom interaction altogether. For example, Susan Philips studied home and school communication patterns on the Warm Springs Indian Reservation.[9] She found that while communication at school was characterized by competition and individual student display of performance, the students' home learning patterns involved much more cooperation, with little pres-

Classroom cultures and home cultures

sure for individual performance. Programs such as the Kamehameha Early Education Project in Hawaii have worked actively to alter classroom communication patterns to match more closely the patterns that are familiar to the students and to create conditions under which students are more likely to be successful.[10]

Summary: The Classroom Environment

Although there are many ways of looking at what happens during classroom lessons, when one takes the perspective that classrooms are cultural settings, then classroom activity can be understood as a process of communication that affects what is learned and by whom. This view casts teachers as communicators and as *orchestrators* of the communication process. Teachers talk, listen, direct conversations, and so forth. Students are active participants in the communicative system. These roles and these characteristics of classrooms provide the context within which teachers' plans are enacted, communicated, and shaped through interaction.

Teachers as orchestrators

The classroom excerpt presented in the first Snapshot of this chapter is a result of a series of plans, decisions, and modifications that took place during the months that led to the day at midyear when the episode occurred. The next section of this chapter shows how those plans were developed and modified.

Planning Learning Experiences

The class you read about in the Snapshot at the beginning of this chapter took place about midway through the school year. You saw an episode from a single day in Ms. Harding's classroom, but it would be a mistake to assume that the planning for that day's class could be isolated into a single planning event. Actually, this class at midyear was in part a result of all the classes that came before it and the roles and expectations that had been established through those earlier classes. Because of these facts, it is more appropriate to think of a lesson such as that described in the Snapshot as if it were one of many frames taken from a movie instead of thinking of it as a single photograph. Planning for Ms. Harding's class, then, can be thought of as having begun at least as early as the previous year, as Ms. Harding thought about her goals and ideas for the coming year, a thinking process in which she drew upon all her knowledge and experience as a teacher. The second Snapshot for this chapter, which follows, illustrates how she began developing her ideas and plans months before the episode described in the earlier Snapshot occurred.

SNAPSHOT

As you read this Snapshot, consider the following questions:

- What goals does Ms. Harding have for her first unit for next year?
- Where does she get her ideas?
- Do any aspects of her planning process surprise you?

Ms. Harding—Lunchtime, Late in the School Year

It is late in May, and Ms. Harding sits chatting with another sixth-grade teacher over lunch. Lately, Ms. Harding has been reflecting on the past year, and she is beginning to formulate ideas and make plans for next year. She tells her friend, "I've written down a lot of thoughts lately, about writing. . . . I didn't like using poetry as my first unit. The kids just didn't get as excited about it as I wanted them to. So I'm trying to think of something else. I could do short stories, but that's pretty complicated for a first unit. I was thinking maybe newspaper articles. Everyone's read the newspaper. . . ."

"Yes," her friend responds. "I tried that once. With newspapers, kids can go a lot of different directions."

"That's true. I'm not sure I want that for the first unit. I want something more focused, so I can work through it with them step by step. It works better for me to give them more structure at first and more freedom later. Maybe we could do biography. That's an idea."

"How would you do it?"

"Well. . . . Good question. I'd have to bring in biographies to show them. That could be hard, to find some that aren't too long to share in class."

"One of the anthologies that we used as a text in my old district had a section of short biographies and autobiographies. I'll look at home and see if I can dig it up. You know, if you did biographies, I wonder if we could find a way to tie them into one of my social studies units. Of course, that might be easier later in the year, when things will be a little less hectic."

"That's a great idea. Okay, so we'll save the biographies. So I'm back where I started. Ummm . . . What about children's stories? That would be fun. It's perfect, because everyone can relate to them. Everyone will know what a children's book is. They'll be able to talk about their favorites—it'll get everyone involved. I'll

think some more about that, but I like that idea. Children's stories."

Summer

Over the summer, Ms. Harding continues to think about her children's story unit. She laughs to herself that suddenly she's obsessed—everywhere she goes she sees children's stories. She has found a couple of books with some ideas, and she dips into them occasionally, noting suggestions she can adapt to suit her. She starts a file of newspaper clippings with allusions to fairy tales and Mother Goose. Ideas pop into her head at the most unlikely times—at a baseball game, over dinner, stuck in traffic. She lets them "cook," figuring that the best ones will stay with her.

Late in the summer, Ms. Harding sits down to write a letter to parents describing what students will do in her class in the coming year, and the unit starts to come together in her head. She blocks out a unit plan, allocating topics to the six weeks that make up the first marking period:

Week 1: Introduction; share favorite stories

Week 2: Continue sharing stories; discuss characteristics of children's stories

Week 3: Begin writing children's stories

Week 4: Continue writing and revising for content

Week 5: Edit drafts for mechanics

Week 6: Share final drafts with the class

As the first day of school gets closer, she begins to make more specific lesson plans. She revises her letter to parents, which she will share with students on the first day of class.

In this Snapshot, several factors come into play as Ms. Harding begins to plan for her writing class. Notice that her thinking begins with reflection and evaluation. She is dissatisfied with the way she began the previous school year. In addition to this evaluation, Ms. Harding draws on her past experience with the subject and with other sixth graders. She thinks about the learning and social goals she has for a first unit, and she considers the connections that could be made between her curriculum and the experiences students will be having in their other classes. As with Ms. Harding, when most teachers begin to think about future lessons and plan their work, their thoughts are usually random. They also occur at various times, both in and out of school. Teachers do not limit planning time to the thirty minutes scheduled during the school day or to the time they set aside for work in the evenings. Lesson plans are often made in rush-hour traffic, at the grocery store, while jogging, or in the early morning. A student teacher once said, "It seems as if I'm always planning

Reflection as a starting point

for my class. I'll be at a party, having a conversation, and in the back of my head I'm thinking of how something will fit into a lesson."

The second Snapshot also illustrates how planning can take place on a number of levels. Ms. Harding has *macro-level planning* decisions to make about her overall goals for her students and about the broad topic areas that will make up her year or a unit. Her macro-level planning answers questions such as "What do I want my students to be able to do at the end of the year? What kinds of thinking do I want to encourage this year? What kind of atmosphere do I want for my classroom?" As the time she will actually begin teaching comes closer, her planning becomes more specific, and she makes more *micro-level planning* decisions about particular lessons. Questions needing micro-level answers include "What am I going to do in class next Tuesday? What materials do I need to have ready? What can students do at home to explore what we will do in class?"

During and after the thinking process described in the second Snapshot, a teacher would translate his or her thoughts and dreams about a unit or lesson into written lesson plans. Ms. Harding keeps a list of the topics she will discuss during a particular unit and jots down the activities she anticipates will occur on a given day. These lists form an outline of her thinking and a reminder of the decisions she has made about the lessons, and she updates them throughout the unit as she learns from her students about their knowledge and needs. Such a list for the lesson you read about in the first Snapshot in this chapter might have looked like this:

Wednesday: Drafting/Revising

- collect remaining contest entries
- share completed drafts (make certificates!); Brian's revisions— how/why?
- writing time; check in on progress (*due in two weeks*)
- journals due

Ms. Harding's written plans are not sophisticated or detailed, and they do not fit a precise format. However, as an experienced teacher, Ms. Harding is able to work from such notes and expand them as she teaches. Less experienced teachers or experienced teachers who are teaching in new areas frequently make much more specific written plans.

Just as the planning process does not start from scratch, it does not end when teaching the lesson begins. Even the best planning involves many teacher assumptions, anticipations about how "things will go," and guesses about what is likely to happen at each step in the lesson. As a result, teachers make adjustments and "replan on their feet" as the lesson develops.

Approaches to Planning

Each teacher has an individual style for planning, but planning styles as a whole tend to follow similar processes and have many common elements. Over the years, researchers who have studied how teachers plan have described planning in two ways: the *rational-choice approach* and the *lesson-image approach*.

The Rational-Choice Approach to Lesson Planning

The *rational-choice approach* to planning was originally articulated by Ralph Tyler (1949), and in the years since has been adapted by others, including Hilda Taba

Macro-level planning

Micro-level planning

(1962) and James Popham and Eva Baker (1970).[11] The approach identifies four tasks that teachers must accomplish through planning and suggests that these tasks are best handled in a sequence of four steps. The four steps are

1. specifying behavioral objectives
2. identifying students' entry behavior (knowledge, skills, and affective learning)
3. selecting and sequencing learning activities so that students move from entry behavior to the objectives
4. evaluating the outcomes of instruction in order to improve planning

These steps present a logical and organized way of planning for instruction, and the rational-choice approach has become the model taught most consistently in colleges of education and used most often in statewide teacher evaluation programs.

At this stage in your study, it is probably obvious that good lessons are not simply made up on a teacher's whim. They are well thought out and are derived from many factors, circumstances, and contexts that affect teachers' thinking—including their knowledge of student needs and backgrounds and their understanding of course content, as well as the influences of school leaders, the community, and the expectations other teachers have for their students. At the same time, however, it is also important to realize that, in practice, teachers rarely follow the planning tasks outlined in the rational-choice approach as sequentially and as neatly as the steps suggest. Instead, teachers typically begin their planning as Ms. Harding did, by jotting down ideas from their mental notes that describe the activities and materials they will use. In their thinking, they shift back and forth between goals and objectives on one hand, and activities, materials, and many other considerations that come to mind on the other. They do this in recurring cycles, considering how activities will meet goals and what goals will be met by particular activities and so forth.

The tasks represented by the four steps of the rational-choice approach are similar to the tasks of planning you have already seen in Ms. Harding's planning process. Although she does not pursue the tasks in step-by-step fashion, she does consider her desired goals and her knowledge of student abilities, and she develops units and activities that contribute to these goals while meeting student needs. Also, as is illustrated in a later section of this chapter, she evaluates her teaching and students' experiences in her classroom and uses these evaluations as a means of improving her curriculum and instruction.

Teachers' Lesson Images

Researchers who studied elementary teachers' planning processes in the late 1970s found that many of the teachers they studied first thought about the activities they would use, the content they would teach, specific student needs, and the materials or resources available.[12] They also used information gained from evaluating their previous lessons. The researchers also found that teachers' written plans usually took the form of brief outlines or lists of topics to be covered. They concluded that the teacher's planning was mainly a mental process, much of which was not committed to paper. The teachers in this study indicated that the act of planning itself served two functions. The first and most obvious one was that planning was a means of organizing instruction; and the second, less obvious, function was that it served as a psychological resource for the teachers, a source of confidence, security, and direction.

A related study found that there is a difference between the comprehensive

Planning is a mental process

planning activities that teachers conducted in their heads and their written plans.[13] In addition to the written plans, teachers develop "lesson images" as a result of their planning. These images contain the details that are seldom recorded in written plans but which teachers visualize and plan for specifically. Those "images" are, in fact, the teachers' plans.

Studies have also focused on the thinking and decision making that teachers engage in as they plan.[14] In essence, they report that the process is multifaceted and much more involved than most people presume. Among these studies, Robert Yinger examined teacher thinking while the teachers actually engaged in planning. He concluded that teachers see the planning process primarily as a task of solving problems. The problem is the need for their students to learn; the solution is a realistic sequence of activities that will promote that learning.

It appears that beginning teachers' planning tends to resemble more closely the rational-choice approach, but as teachers gain experience, they shift more to the use of lesson images and to varied and personal ways of planning.[15] This shift might occur, at least in part, because experienced teachers have more knowledge to draw upon and feel more secure in planning without detailed written plans. Whatever the process looks like, skilled teachers (experienced or novice) keep the overall goals they have for their students in mind as they develop specific activities.

Planning as a problem-solving task (margin note)

Goals and Objectives for Lessons

Whether formally, as in the rational-choice approach, or less formally, through lesson images, the beginnings of planning are in the goals and objectives teachers have for their classes. (Chapter 12 describes the nature of goals and objectives and how they are typically developed.) At the very beginning of the planning process, skilled teachers think through their goals at both the macro and micro levels discussed earlier, using them as a basis for selecting the topics and activities for a particular day. Teachers also know how to fit a day's set of activities, a particular activity, or a specific lesson format into the larger goals they have for a unit or a year. As they engage in this process, they select and manipulate all the instructional devices and classroom elements available to them—content, activities, materials, their own instructional skills, and so forth; at the same time, they avoid, moderate, or adapt to potential hindrances to reaching the goals—student misbehavior, time limits, different ability levels, and interruptions. The main task, as in all planning, is in making things fit together to encourage student learning. Teachers also know that it is important to communicate these goals to their students, because, without the sense of purpose that knowledge of the goals and objectives can provide, students will see classes as nothing more than a series of activities or disconnected exercises.

Goals set for students, whether they are set by teachers, school leaders, or the broader community, determine to a great extent what students learn, what teachers teach, and, therefore, what teachers *plan* to teach. They are, in effect, what teachers expect their teaching to accomplish if it is successful; these goals are what teachers want their students to learn. (The tie between goals for lessons and broader and longer-range goals and purposes for student learning is explained in Chapter 12.)

Lesson goals or objectives that are used by teachers to develop lessons can be divided according to the types of content described in Chapter 11—knowledge, thinking skills, skills other than thinking, and affective learning. For any given lesson or unit, teachers' goals and the activities they plan to achieve them may span several of these categories. For example, Ms. Harding's lesson included the follow-

Types of lesson objectives (margin note)

ing objectives for her students: (1) to learn information about writing (knowledge), (2) to begin to see their writing from the perspective of an outside reader (thinking skill), (3) to improve their abilities to read and write (skills other than thinking), and (4) to develop responsibility, independence, cooperation, and acceptance of the ideas of others (affective learning).

As teachers plan for and evaluate their teaching, goals other than those tied directly to subject-matter knowledge must also be weighed. The question teachers must consider is how the subject-matter content of a lesson interacts with the skill and affective objectives for the lesson. If you return to the first Snapshot of Ms. Harding's class, you can infer that among her affective goals is the desire that students will view each other as knowledgeable writers and seek each other out for help; therefore, she accepts quiet talk and movement around the room as appropriate behavior. Her objectives for knowledge, skill, and affect are all compatible.

A final point about teachers' goals for students is that, because they come in many forms, they must be assessed in many different ways. Some are easily measured: The students will spell eight of ten words correctly. Others are much less tangible; for example, a teacher may want students to develop an appreciation for a particular visual artistic image or work of literature purely for its aesthetic value. To develop this appreciation, the teacher may simply want the students to share the feeling of enjoying the work, to be encouraged to explore it and similar works further, and to develop a sense that meaning can be found in such forms of expression. This type of aim comes close to what Elliot Eisner has called *expressive outcomes*.[16] Eisner uses the term *outcome* rather than *objective* because, unlike an objective, the precise result desired is not determined in advance. It is the experience itself that is valued.

Goals and outcomes

Expressive outcomes

Whatever a teacher's intentions for an activity, it is important that student learning be assessed through a form of evaluation sensitive to those goals. For example, when the outcome is highly expressive, as in the example just given, an objective test limited to the students' knowledge of specific facts or characteristics of the piece would be inappropriate.

It is important to remember that teachers do not select goals for their teaching in a vacuum. As described in Chapter 12, school systems establish goals that teachers are to pursue and students are to reach. The impact of these predetermined goals varies from district to district, school to school, and teacher to teacher. Although teachers often have considerable autonomy, their teaching must be consistent with these goals. They must shape their own objectives and plans for students based on these expectations. The next section of this chapter discusses a variety of influences on teachers' goal setting, planning, and teaching.

Influences on Planning and Teaching

Teachers' plans begin with their beliefs about the kinds of activities that will lead to student learning. In his classic treatise *Experience and Education* (first published in 1938), John Dewey described learning as the widening and deepening of the individual's experience. The broadening of experience results from an ongoing cycle of interaction between an individual and that individual's environment. The cycle revolves through "the formation of ideas, acting upon ideas, observation of the conditions which result, and organization of facts for future use."[17] Through this cycle of interaction, prior experiences become tools for understanding present situations; solving problems in the present becomes a vehicle for understanding in the future.

Learning experience as cycles of interaction

Dewey thus defines educative experiences as those that expand the learners' opportunities for future growth.

Two ideas are especially important here. The first is the notion of *continuity*. With this term, Dewey captures the idea that learning is a contingent process. What students learn depends on their prior learning and experiences, and what they learn today affects future learning and experiences. Therefore, as teachers plan, they must think about activities in terms of what learning experiences have preceded them and what may follow.

The second important idea here is *interaction*. Dewey uses the term to convey the idea that students do not learn as individuals isolated in a vacuum, nor does learning take place solely within the learner's head. Instead, learning experiences involve an interaction between the learner and the *objective conditions* (the "givens") of the world outside the learner. These objective conditions exist in the world at large and in the classroom. Those in the world at large include such things as pressure for good grades, family and community aspirations for students' futures, and out-of-school and extracurricular demands on students' time. Inside classrooms, these objective conditions include the personal characteristics of students and teachers, the subject-matter content, and available materials, as well as the elements of classroom culture mentioned earlier in this chapter. The act of teaching is influenced by all these objective conditions, those from outside the classroom as well as those within it. Thus, teachers must take into account not only the subject matter and the learner, but also the physical and social contexts of the classroom and school and how learners and subject matter interact within that context.

We now look at these conditions as influences that affect how teachers plan and teach. As we begin this examination, it is important to remember that teaching, learning, and the classroom setting are all complex; and, as a result, the number of factors good teachers take into account (consciously and unconsciously) as they plan are numerous. Many of these factors are illustrated in Figure 13-1; they include teacher background and beliefs, student backgrounds and needs, external expectations, organizational demands, and subject-matter attributes. Each of these groups of influences and some of the influences within them are explained in more detail on the following pages.

Teacher Backgrounds and Beliefs

The amount of experience teachers have with teaching and with children is one factor that influences planning and teaching. To state the point simply, past experiences help enrich teachers' mental images of lessons. Because experienced teachers have more images of previous lessons on which to draw, they are able to plan more knowledgeably. Additionally, seasoned teachers are able to use their past experiences to teach with more flexibility and responsiveness to student needs.

Because beginning teachers lack experience, they must often compensate by planning to a greater extent than might be necessary for more experienced teachers, and they may be reluctant to modify those plans once they are teaching in the classroom. As they gain experience, however, their continued planning gradually comes to resemble replanning, rather than initial planning. Each experience influences the next.

A second influence on planning and teaching is the teacher's own teaching philosophy—the teacher's view of teaching and learning in general. Such philosophies usually begin developing during preservice teacher-preparation years and continue to be developed and refined as teachers gain experience with students and teaching.

FIGURE 13-1   Influences on teacher planning.

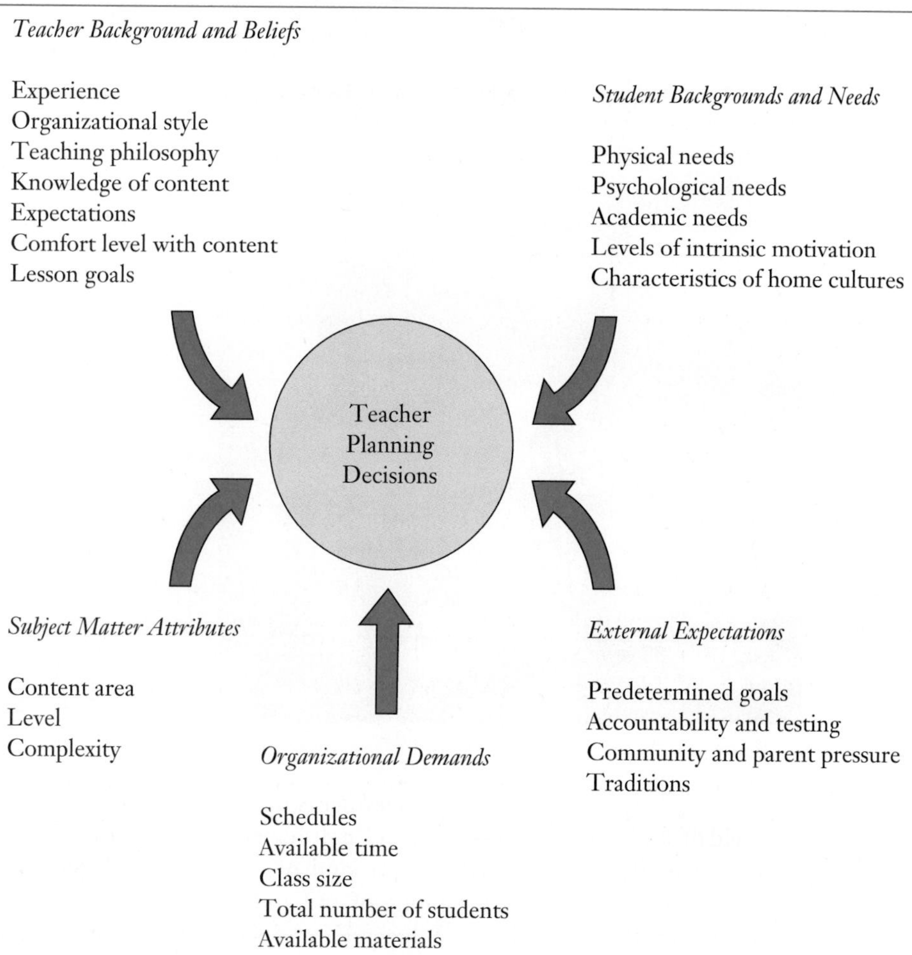

Teacher Background and Beliefs

Experience
Organizational style
Teaching philosophy
Knowledge of content
Expectations
Comfort level with content
Lesson goals

Student Backgrounds and Needs

Physical needs
Psychological needs
Academic needs
Levels of intrinsic motivation
Characteristics of home cultures

Teacher
Planning
Decisions

Subject Matter Attributes

Content area
Level
Complexity

Organizational Demands

Schedules
Available time
Class size
Total number of students
Available materials

External Expectations

Predetermined goals
Accountability and testing
Community and parent pressure
Traditions

Teaching philosophies are, as explained in Chapter 10, not limited to how the teacher views teaching and learning, but are part of that teacher's general makeup as a person.

Teachers' knowledge of content is a third influence on how and what they plan. Teachers obviously cannot plan to teach content they do not know; but even if they know the content to some extent, it is not unusual for their knowledge to be limited enough to affect both planning and teaching. In such an event, planning is necessarily restricted and usually less creative than it might be. In fact, teachers who feel their knowledge of content in some particular area is inadequate tend to avoid teaching it, teach it superficially, or teach it in only an expository style. Many resort to long lectures and limit student questions. One situation in which this phenomenon seems to be prevalent is in the teaching of science at the elementary level. Frequently, primary grade teachers admit that they avoid teaching science because they do not feel comfortable with their own level of understanding of the topics to be taught. On the other hand, teachers who know their content well usually plan more varied and flexible lessons, because they can readily manipulate and arrange information to fit their students' levels of understanding and their own specific instructional plans.

Lee Shulman and his colleagues have described knowledge of content in terms of three dimensions: subject-matter knowledge, pedagogical knowledge, and cur-

Knowledge of content

Teachers' lesson planning involves not just their content knowledge, but their experience, beliefs, and values.

ricular knowledge.[18] *Subject-matter knowledge* is the kind of knowledge any specialist in a field of study would have—what an English major would know about literature, for example. *Pedagogical knowledge* is a kind of content knowledge particular to teachers; it involves an understanding of and ability to predict how students will learn content. Pedagogical knowledge guides teachers' choices of examples, explanations, and student tasks. Finally, *curricular knowledge* refers to the teacher's knowledge of content as it is reflected in the variety of materials to which students have been and will be exposed. For example, curricular knowledge would include knowledge of how familiar students in a mathematics class are likely to be with two-digit addition based on the school district's curriculum.

Knowledge of content also affects the ways in which teachers determine the goals for their lessons. As they plan, they must address questions such as: What should the students know when they are finished? Where am I going with this lesson? How much is reasonable to expect from students in this area? When they are unsure about what is important about the content, it is hard for them to decide what their students should know.

Student Backgrounds and Needs

Student needs affect teachers' plans in significant ways. Because students are different, their needs are varied and change over time. Students come to school with various *physical needs* that cannot be ignored. Those who are hungry, tired, or sick are unlikely to benefit much from even the most exciting lesson. They are likely to need rest and withdraw psychologically. Students with physical handicaps or who are vision- or hearing-impaired also have particular physical needs, which may range from special seating requirements to the use of high-tech equipment.

Physical needs

Students also come to school with a wide variety of *psychological* and *emotional* needs that affect their classroom performance. Students who need greater self-esteem, increased peer affiliation, and security may be difficult to involve in lessons. Students who are easily bored require challenges and variety. Other students may be especially anxious and fearful of taking risks in the classroom. They may need reassurance and encouragement before they try a classroom task and risk embarrassment. Still other students dominate and have to be kept busy.

A great deal of educational research has focused on determining effective strategies for teaching students with varied academic abilities and different *academic needs*. Studies have demonstrated, for example, that effective methods for teaching high- and low-ability students often differ, that low-ability students often benefit academically from teaching strategies that provide for a slower pace and divide content into small steps with ample opportunities for practice, and that higher-achieving students may require a faster pace, more challenge, and opportunities for discussion and interaction about the task.[19]

Student *motivational levels* affect the time and energy required of teachers to capture students' attention and focus their energy on learning tasks. Slower students may lack motivation because of past failures whereas boredom may be the issue with faster students. In either case, lessons must challenge and provide variety. Recent research on motivation focuses on a theory that the effort a person is willing to invest in a task is determined by the degree to which the person (1) expects to be able to succeed and (2) values either participation in the task or access to the rewards that successful completion will bring. In other words, students do not invest effort in tasks at which they do not believe they will succeed or in tasks that they do not value.[20] Planning effective lessons therefore requires that teachers be aware of students' perception and valuation of the tasks they are asked to complete.

Psychological needs

Academic needs

Motivation

Something to Think About

Earlier chapters of this text contain several case studies describing particular students with special needs. Remembering those individuals, consider the questions below. The case studies and the pages on which they can be found are

William, sixth grade   page 153

Sherry, eleventh grade   pages 153–154

James   pages 187–188

Mark   pages 228–229

Jamie   page 229

Saundra   pages 229–230

- How would the presence of each of these students influence the mental images of lessons being planned by their teachers?
- In what ways will the teaching of lessons be more complicated because these students are in class?

Student cultural backgrounds

As we briefly discussed earlier in this chapter, students' *cultural backgrounds* may affect how they can be expected to react to both content and methods of presentation, and teachers must plan accordingly. For instance, some cultural norms consider challenging a teacher's statement and looking a teacher in the eye as disrespectful. Other cultures deemphasize competition, especially among peers. Students whose cultures have strong sanctions against competition may not be willing to participate in team competitions, number fact drills, and other activities that require them to stand apart from their peers.

Class personality

Teachers often remark that each class has its own personality—a synergistic combination of unique individuals—that can often be altered by the addition or subtraction of only one individual. Some classes abound with cooperation and enthusiasm; others do not. Some classes seem to catch on quickly; others need much more instruction, direction, and review. Such characteristics of class groups naturally influence the planning of lessons and the ways teachers imagine those lessons as they plan.

Student role-players

Finally, students in a class, like all persons in groups, play certain roles, and these roles affect classroom dynamics. Successful teachers plan with these students in mind and use them to accomplish their instructional goals. For example, nearly everyone remembers from their own school days the students who assumed the roles of court jester, brain, goody-goody, troublemaker, nonconformist, and victim.[21] As teachers plan, they know that the ways they interact with these different personalities affect how well their lessons progress.

External Expectations

As teachers plan and teach, they face constraints that are external to themselves and their individual classrooms. Often these constraints emanate from decisions made by school administrators, from public pressures, and from traditional practices and assumptions that have been in place for some time—"the way it is done here." In recent years, external influences have placed ever-increasing pressures on teachers and have affected what they plan and how they do so.

Predetermined goals

One form of external pressure on teacher planning involves the *goals and expectations established by school systems.* As was discussed in Chapter 12, school systems establish objectives that teachers are to pursue and students are to reach. Although teachers often have considerable autonomy, their teaching must be consistent with these goals; thus, they are not wholly free to teach anything they want. This influences planning and teaching.

Often school system goals and expectations have been in place for a long time and are traditional, though this is not always the case. In recent years, for example, many school systems have required that such subject matter as the contributions of minority groups to American culture, substance abuse, teenage pregnancy, death, and safe sex be taught—topics that only a few years earlier were unusual, if not directly excluded from the curriculum. When such topics become official additions to school programs, teachers must, of course, plan their teaching to include them.

Accountability

Increased pressure for teacher and school *accountability* is another external influence on planning. One effect of this pressure is that teachers' plans are expected to be more precise than in the past and to reflect specific intended learning outcomes. Although teachers have reported for years that they decide early in the planning process exactly what they want students to learn, many have rarely stated these goals in behavioral terms or have committed them to detailed written form. Now, however, teachers are frequently required to write formal behavioral objectives for lessons. Often the requirements specify that lesson objectives be exact statements of what students are to learn, how the learning will be evaluated, and the level of learning that will be accepted. In some cases, these objectives are then used as measures of the teachers' performance.

When school systems require this type of documentation, many teachers shift the emphasis of their teaching toward content that is easier to describe in terms of behavioral objectives and easier to assess on objective tests than content they might otherwise have used. For example, they may feel a pressure to teach and assess knowledge of information that can be memorized and recalled instead of values and skills that cannot be recorded in multiple-choice fashion.

Standardized achievement tests, given yearly in many school districts, and other forms of *systemwide testing*, are examples of the influence of teacher accountability on planning. Test scores are often used to determine the achievement gains for individual students and classes as a whole. Sometimes they are the critical factor in determining whether students pass to the next grade. They are also considered a clear reflection of teacher performance.

Testing

If test scores receive a great amount of attention, teachers often prepare their students to take the tests. This situation has raised concern among educators who believe many teachers feel forced to let standardized tests dictate too many of their planning and teaching decisions. They believe teachers, to be effective, must retain the authority to make planning decisions that reflect their teaching situation and personal professional judgments.

Community and parental pressure also have their impact on teacher planning, and the pressure pushes two ways. Sometimes teachers are expected to include certain topics, materials, or teaching techniques; at other times they are expected to exclude them or treat them with extreme caution. Topics that have been pushed for both inclusion and exclusion are sex education, drug education, child abuse, AIDS education, and numerous local issues that involve values and emotions in controversy. At times, certain texts and other student-used materials become controversial in local communities, raising the potential for censorship of books, materials, and teachers. At other times, parents question teachers' use of classroom strategies, such as values clarification and open discussion of value-laden issues.

Community and parent pressures

Traditions—the ways things have been done in schools and communities—also influence teacher planning. For example, teachers have to plan for at least some of the following events: sport rivalries (football and basketball take time when there are big games or tournaments), Columbus Day, Thanksgiving, end-of-semester exams, Christmas break, snow days, Martin Luther King Day, prom, spring break, spring fever, and senior cut day. Most also have to turn in grades by deadline dates and have to ensure that a sufficient number of grades has been recorded for each report-card grading period.

Traditions

Other external influences on planning include such conditions as student absenteeism and interruptions. Teachers must adjust to and even anticipate both. Students who miss work must be able to catch up as much as is possible, and teachers must replan lessons that are delayed or seriously disrupted. Sometimes these interferences are fairly minor and not difficult to accommodate, but persistent and large-scale absences occur in virtually all classes, and special assemblies, field trips, and pull-out programs are common in most schools.

Other external influences

Organizational Demands

All teachers function within organizational structures and procedures. Some of these are based at the school system level, some at the building level, and some at the classroom level. At the classroom level, teachers organize time, space, materials, the curriculum, and the use of students' time. They also manage student behavior. Similar structures, processes, and routines exist for entire schools and for whole school systems. Each imposes constraints on teacher planning and influences teachers' lessons.

Schedules

The schedules that school systems establish for schools, that schools establish for activities in the building, and that teachers establish for classes are one type of organizational influence that affects planning. The yearly calendar determines when students are in school, and daily schedules determine what happens within each day. Examples of such schedules for elementary and secondary students are shown in the Snapshot of Chapter 12.

When teachers plan and develop images of their lessons, they must fit their instruction within these schedules. They must provide for lunch, recess, resource classes, pull-out programs, music, physical education, pep rallies, unexpected changes in schedules, and so forth.

Available time

The *time available* for instruction also greatly influences the planning process. Secondary school teachers usually have firmly set amounts of class time for the entire year and must plan their lessons within those limits. Class periods are just so long, and there are just so many of them. Elementary school teachers have somewhat more latitude, but they also face time expectations, at least as guidelines. Within these limits teachers determine the amount of time to be devoted to specific lessons and topics. This determination rests on teacher predictions of the amount of time needed to complete lessons successfully. Teacher plans, therefore, reflect a matching of time available with the time needed to teach lessons effectively. Figures 13-2 and 13-3 show typical teacher schedules.

The planning process is not just a matter of fitting self-contained lessons into isolated hours, days, and weeks. Lessons must fit together, and learning must be incremental. As a result, teachers plan with different lengths of instructional time in mind—daily, weekly, and long-range—and how they conceive of these periods of time also influences the plans they develop. The goal of all planning is that students receive an intellectually meaningful education, in whatever time spans are available.

Class size and total numbers of students being taught

Another important influence on teacher planning is the combination of *class size* and the *total number of students* the teacher instructs. Understandably, teachers with large classes and large total numbers of students plan differently from those with fewer students. They think of the numbers of students they expect to teach and design lessons that they believe will serve those students best—as a group and as individual learners. Some activities work well with small numbers, and others do not; the same is true for large groups.

Some activities are more demanding of teachers than others, and teachers are more likely and more able to pursue the more demanding ones if student numbers are small rather than large. For example, teachers with a large number of students may find thorough evaluation of a large number of writing assignments impractical. (Note that the teacher whose schedule appears in Figure 13-3 teaches three sections of English composition and, presumably, has numerous pieces of student writing to read and respond to regularly.) Similarly, large numbers of students might require more copies of reading materials than are available.

FIGURE 13-2   An elementary teacher's weekly schedule.

TIME	MONDAY	TUESDAY	WEDNESDAY	THURSDAY	FRIDAY
Ms. Adams		TEACHER'S WEEKLY SCHEDULE			
8:00–8:20	Lunch count Attendance check Morning meetings				→
8:20–9:50	Reading groups Language arts	Handwriting	→	→	Reading test
	Spelling words Restrooms Snack break	Spelling drill	Spelling pretests	Spelling games	Weekly spelling test →
9:50–10:30	Math				→
10:30–11:00	P.E.				→
11:00–11:20	Finish morning work				→
11:20–12:00	Lunch				→
12:00–1:00	Library	Silent reading	Art	Journal writing	Music
	Silent reading	Journal writing	Oral reading		Oral reading
1:00–2:00	Science				→
2:00–2:45	Social studies			→	Friday activities

Even when teachers have average numbers of students, they often find that, to instruct all students effectively and to provide for individual needs, they must plan several simultaneous activities. They frequently plan to divide their larger classes into smaller groups in order to conduct multiple activities at the same time. This, of course, adds complexity to the planning process and to teaching.

Teachers' plans are also influenced greatly by the materials and resources that are accessible and available to them. For instance, in order to plan a literature-based reading and language arts program, a teacher must have a wide variety and large number of books that interest children. Similarly, a science teacher who wants students to conduct experiments must have the necessary laboratory equipment. When such resources are lacking, teachers may be prevented from planning lessons they would most like to implement. Alternatively, they may be especially creative and industrious about finding materials that will work. In either case, they must plan in advance, and the planning is more difficult than when resources abound.

Materials and resources

FIGURE 13-3   A secondary English teacher's weekly schedule.

Ms. Brown	TEACHER'S WEEKLY SCHEDULE				
TIME	MONDAY	TUESDAY	WEDNESDAY	THURSDAY	FRIDAY
8:00–8:20	Home Room	Home Room	Home Room	Home Room	Home Room
8:25–9:15	English Lit II	English Comp I (Sect. a)	English Lit II	English Comp I (Sect. a)	English Lit II
9:20–10:10	AP English	AP English	AP English	AP English	AP English
10:15–11:05	English Comp I (Sect. b)	English Comp I (Sect. c)	English Comp I (Sect. b)	English Comp I (Sect. c)	English Comp I (Sect. b)
11:10–12:00	Preparing Marking	Preparing Marking	Preparing Marking	Preparing Marking	Preparing Marking
12:00–12:40			LUNCH		
12:45–1:35	English Comp I (Sect. a)	English Lit II	English Comp I (Sect. a)	English Lit II	English Comp I (Sect. a)
1:40–2:30	English Comp I (Sect. c)	English Comp I (Sect. b)	English Comp I (Sect. c)	English Comp I (Sect. b)	English Comp I (Sect. c)
2:35–3:25	Debate	Debate	Debate	Debate	Debate

Subject Matter Attributes

Content area

As discussed in Chapters 11, 12, and earlier in this chapter, the content or subject matter taught also influences teacher plans and images of lessons. For example, English composition, mathematics, laboratory science, and history are different enough to necessitate different teaching approaches and classroom activities. Even within a particular subject area, planning varies with the level of instruction—

Level of instruction

advanced placement, general level, or remedial—and with the content emphasis for the day or the unit. Planning also varies depending on the complexity of the ideas, skills, and affective aspects of learning encompassed in the content to be taught. Teachers have to match their assessment of their students' abilities and prior learning with the levels of difficulty of the content they are considering teaching. If the level of difficulty is above or noticeably below their assessment of what their students can grasp, they need to modify their plans. Teachers know that what they teach determines to a great extent how they teach, and this affects how they design their lessons.

Conclusions about Planning

It should be obvious by this point that the act of teaching requires substantial planning, that planning is a complex process, and that many factors influence how and what teachers plan for their lessons. Approaching lesson planning in a rational way that starts with goals and objectives seems logical, and such a beginning is particularly recommended for new teachers because it puts in focus what students will have learned when the lesson is successful. This focus then becomes a guide for lesson development. But, because teaching is so multifaceted and because so many factors influence both teaching and planning, a strict rational-choice approach to planning is not realistic for most teachers. As a result, most experienced teachers plan around their images of classes and of successful students. The process they use is intricate and may appear confusing to an outsider. For success, teaching and planning demand skilled, perceptive, reflective, and intelligent classroom experts. Regardless of the planning approach an individual teacher uses, as teachers plan, they move constantly between their desired outcomes for students and strategies for accomplishing them.

Evaluation

The preceding discussions of teaching and planning have each referred indirectly to an element of the act of teaching that we now discuss more directly: evaluation. During the communicative process that makes up activity in classrooms, teachers constantly monitor the feedback they receive from students about their understanding of and reaction to the content and activities of the day. Then they assess that feedback by matching it against what they anticipated. They also monitor and assess their own feelings and reactions to how the lesson is developing. They ask themselves, Are activities occurring in the ways I anticipated? Is the timing right? Are the levels of student understanding and skill development what I thought they would be? What adjustments am I making as the lesson proceeds? Are some students ahead of others? Are some behind? How am I accommodating the differences?

Monitoring and assessing lessons

All of these reactions and reflections form the basis for teachers' evaluations of their teaching. They are typically informal and are an ongoing part of the practice of a skillful and reflective teacher. Teachers use this information both to evaluate lessons and to inform their planning for future classroom experiences. The following Snapshot illustrates how Ms. Harding evaluates the success of her writing program.

Ms. Willis's visit gives Ms. Harding a chance to reflect on her teaching by comparing her perceptions with those of someone else. Ms. Willis is able to help her think through one aspect of her teaching that has been bothering her—grading. At the same time, Ms. Willis keeps Ms. Harding from being too self-critical. Nonjudgmental talk with a peer is an invaluable source of information teachers have about their classrooms.

Following the discussion described in the third Snapshot, Ms. Harding recognized that some ways she had organized her class conflicted with the goals she had

As you read this Snapshot, consider the following questions:

- What factors does Ms. Harding consider in her assessment of student progress?

- What advantages can you see in doing peer observations with other teachers? What is Ms. Willis able to see that Ms. Harding might miss? How is the experience potentially beneficial for Ms. Willis as well as Ms. Harding?

- What risks are involved in such observations?

Midyear Revisited

Ms. Harding sits down for lunch with Ms. Willis, who teaches next door. "So," she asks, "what did you think?"

Earlier that day, during her planning period, Ms. Willis had come into Ms. Harding's writing class to borrow some materials. "I'm glad you invited me to stay," she says. "I always forget how much I learn in someone else's classroom."

"Okay, okay. But what did you think?"

"It was interesting. I was noticing how independently the students were working. Do you have any trouble getting them motivated?"

"Some of them. I'm kind of frustrated, actually. I hoped at this point in the year to be seeing writing of better quality. Some of them are doing really well, but I think they're the ones who were doing pretty well at the beginning of the year anyway. The others . . . well, they wait until the end of the marking period and just write something as fast as they can to turn in. No thinking, no revising—it's pitiful."

"So you just collect work at the end of the marking period? How do they know what they should be doing?"

"Well, I've always had trouble figuring out how to grade writing when I teach this way, so this year I told them, three pieces is an 'A,' two pieces a 'B,' and so forth. So some of them work really hard and get three

pieces done and stop, and some wait until the last minute, like I said, and crank out three short, sloppy things. I wanted to focus less on grading the product and emphasize the process instead, but it's not working that way."

"What are you doing to emphasize the process? I can see how the grades would get students focused on the product."

"Well, we talk about it a lot. I guess I'm seeing that that's not enough."

"Do you mean like at the beginning of class? I noticed that you asked the students three questions: who was writing a draft, who was sharing with a friend, and who was revising. Do they really know how to do all of that?"

"It's the same thing, some do, some don't. Maybe I need to spend more time on the parts of the writing process. That discussion we had with Brian about how he revised his work . . . we need to do more of that. It was great to have a specific example like that."

"It was great to see Brian talk about his writing that way—he seemed so confident. I have a hard time getting him to participate in my class. I guess I just thought he was shy, so I didn't push him."

"Yeah, I had the same reaction at first. Some of these kids, though, when they're talking about their own ideas, it's a whole different thing."

"They all seemed pretty engaged. Everybody was working on something, and they kept at it even when you were sitting down with Joel. And, you could tell they hated to leave. And the pieces they shared at the beginning of class weren't bad."

"Yeah, I feel pretty good about it overall. It just needs some fine-tuning. It seems like they're enjoying writing, and that's always my first goal. Now that we've gotten that far, I need to emphasize the quality of what they're doing more. Mostly I need another way to do grades, so it doesn't just turn into a matter of how many pages they can crank out."

Getting nonjudgmental feedback from peers can ease the loneliness of teachers' decision making and improve the quality of their self-evaluations.

for students. For example, she wanted the students to focus on the process of creating writing and to take time to revise their work; but the grading system she established actually worked against these goals. As a result of this realization, she began thinking and reading about other ways of evaluating student writing, and she made adjustments until she developed a system that was more consistent with her goals.

Ms. Harding's conversation with Ms. Willis highlighted some areas that concern her about her teaching. As you saw in the second Snapshot for this chapter, she used this information as she planned for the following year, building in more support for the stages in the writing process. Similar discussions throughout the year shaped her day-to-day teaching as well.

The purpose of reflection and self-evaluation is for teachers to improve their own teaching. The third Snapshot illustrates informal self-evaluation. Evaluation can also be more formal, usually at the end of a lesson or unit and often at points during a lesson that the teacher selects as likely times to gather valuable information. Formally and informally, it is critical that teachers evaluate the effectiveness of their lessons. Teachers must consider all aspects of their lessons, including elements such as classroom interactions, student work, and student feedback. Then they must ask themselves, Did the students learn what I intended for them to learn? What else did they learn? What did I learn?

Informal self-evaluation

Formal self-evaluation

Sources for Self-Evaluation

As teachers evaluate their lessons, either formally or informally, they use a variety of sources of information. Some of these sources include:

- evidence of student interest and engagement in the lesson
- quality of work produced by students
- type and quantity of student questions and responses during the lesson
- explicit feedback about the lesson solicited from students

■ observation of specific student actions as they engage in activities individually and in groups

■ student success on tests and other outcome measures designed to document their progress

As the wording of this list suggests, some of these sources are more helpful for evaluating individual lessons, while others are more appropriate for evaluation at the end of a unit. Also, some say more about individual student performance, while others more adequately assess the appropriateness of the teacher's planning and lesson implementation.

Because teachers develop goals and objectives as a major part of their planning and use them as guides throughout the teaching process, they are able to assess how well their lessons succeeded in enhancing student learning and the appropriateness of their goals. They can compare what happened with what they expected to happen, examine the benefits and drawbacks of the ways they handled unexpected events, and determine whether the learning outcomes they had envisioned were appropriate for their students. In the process, they can also reflect on the communication patterns that evolved in the lessons, and they can pinpoint weaknesses in their planning and preparation for class.

Conclusions about Evaluation

Several key points about lesson evaluation should be emphasized. First, for good teaching, lesson evaluation is necessary and must be taken seriously. It is a central component of teaching. Second, lesson evaluation involves informal, unwritten reflection about how things went as well as more formal analyses of lessons. Third, as we have stressed throughout this chapter, lesson evaluation is not only something that comes at the end of the process of teaching lessons, but is also the first step in planning for future lessons. Ongoing evaluation is the way teachers continually improve their work.

EDUCATIONAL RESEARCH

Reflective Practice

Throughout this text, teachers have been described as reflective, decision-making professionals, and the description of the act of teaching in this chapter underscores both char-

acteristics.[22] This Educational Research section describes some of the research and thinking behind the evolution of reflection and decision making to their present position of prominence in defining what teachers are and do.

A cynical educator of teachers once tried to distinguish between noticeably good experienced teachers and average-to-poor experienced teachers. He said good teachers are those who have taught

differently each year of their career, always learning and always getting better; and average-to-poor teachers are those who have repeated their first year of teaching throughout their careers. The distinction that the college professor was drawing is the essential difference between reflective, decision-making teachers and those who are not.

Reflective, decision-making teachers are always thinking, or reflecting, carefully about their teaching—past, present, and future—and deciding consciously and rationally how to teach from tomorrow forward based on the results of that reflection. Their teaching is built year after year on experience, new information, and careful thought rather than on unsubstantiated trial and error, hunch, and whim.

The idea of reflective practice is not limited to teaching, however. It fits with all professions that require thought and decision making.

Many researchers believe that John Dewey's ideas about inquiry form a basis for understanding reflective thinking. Dewey wrote about reflecting thinking as early as 1903 and elaborated upon his ideas extensively in *How We Think* and *Logic: The Theory of Inquiry*.[23] For him, reflective thinking is essentially a systematic way of understanding problems, selecting and implementing solutions, and assessing the results. It is solving problems in a rational manner. For teachers, the most general problem that needs solving is the need for students to learn. More specific subproblems involve questions such as, How should I teach next week's mathematics lessons? How much content should I cover? How can I do it with the wide range of abilities in my third-period class? When should I lecture? When should the students practice problems individually in class? What is an appropriate assignment for homework? In every case, the teacher has to decide what to do and how to do it.

More recently Donald Schon has described many of the problems that reflective practitioners face as being different from those of the theoretical researcher.[24] He shows that the problems cut across professions. They encompass the everyday decisions that practitioners make—the ones that do not fit the solutions that theoretical researchers have devised, the ones that are "muddied" by the situations of the real world of practice. For teachers, they are like the questions we just noted. Schon illustrates his point with the following example:

A teacher of arithmetic, listening to a child's question, becomes aware of a kind of confusion and, at the same time, a kind of intuitive understanding, for which she has no readily available response. Because the unique case falls outside the categories of existing theory and technique, the practitioner cannot treat it as an instrumental problem to be solved by applying one of the rules in her store of professional knowledge. The case is not "in the book." If she is to deal with it competently, she must do so by a kind of improvisation, inventing, and testing in the situation strategies of her own devising.[25]

Schon's ideas that teachers, such as the one in his illustration, need to improvise, invent, and test solutions when they face everyday classroom problems tie directly to the concept of reflective practice. It is through experience that teachers gain much of the knowledge that they need to make decisions such as these and through reflective practice that good teachers make good decisions.

So, how do we characterize these everyday decisions that teachers make? What are those decisions like, and how do they relate to reflective practice? Robert Fitzgibbons, a philosopher of education, has described three types of teacher decisions: (1) those concerned basically with *educational outcomes;* (2) those concerned with *what is taught;* and (3) those concerned with *how teaching should* take place.[26] In essence, teachers need to decide, for each of their lessons, what they should try to accomplish, what content to cover, how much to cover, how detailed to be, what teaching strategies to use, which student activities to organize, and so on. Not one of these questions has a set answer. All depend on the specific situation and the context in which they are being raised. Only the teacher facing the questions can answer them. It is that individual teacher who must figure out what to do. Studies of reflective practice are actually studies into how good teachers do this.

Joellen Killion and Guy Todnem say that reflective teachers build personal theories about teaching and learning as a main part of their reflection and that their reflection consists of three types, depending on when it occurs: (1) reflections *on* practice, (2) reflection *in* practice, and (3) reflection *for* practice.[27] *Reflection on practice* occurs after the teaching has taken place and the teacher is looking back, *assessing how things went. Reflection in practice* occurs as the teaching is happening and the teacher is *monitoring how things are going. Reflection for practice* occurs as a result of the first two types. It takes place as teachers use their ideas about past practices *to plan for new lessons.* For Killion and Todnem, reflecting *on* and *in* practice is necessary, but reflection *for* practice is the crucial element for good teaching. It uses past experience and thought to build increasingly better teaching. It is the component of teacher decision making that makes each year of teaching fit the image of a spiral—always getting better—rather than that of a circle—simply repeating last year.[28]

Some researchers have identified a hierarchy in the way teachers reflect upon their practice and tie the levels of reflection to the amount of experience teachers have. For example, Max Van Manen describes three levels based on what seems to be of prime concern to the teachers doing the reflection: (1) reflection concerned with the application in classrooms of knowledge and skills that the teacher has learned, (2) reflection about the assumptions that underly specific classroom practices and their consequences, and (3) reflection on the moral and ethical bases for teaching one way rather than another or teaching with one content focus instead of another.[29] Illustrations of each level follow. A new teacher at Van Manen's first reflection level might be thinking, I know this content and I practiced conducting group work like this in my practica. Can I do it tomorrow with a whole class of real students? A slightly more experienced teacher at Van Manen's second reflection level might think, Why do my college professors and all these other teachers think cooperative learning is so good? Does it really help students learn better? An experienced teacher at Van Manen's third level of reflection might think, Is cooperative learning really good for these students? Is it appropriate of me to insist that students from different ethnic backgrounds and with different intellectual abilities study together and get to know one another better?

Other researchers have examined teacher reflection in terms of *elements* or things teachers do in the process of reflecting. Georgea Sparks-Langer and Amy Colton, who have synthesized research on teachers' reflective thinking, see three elements of this type, which they have labeled: (1) the cognitive

element, (2) the critical element, and (3) the narrative element. The *cognitive element* of reflection consists of two intellectual teacher acts: First, gaining the knowledge that teachers need to think seriously about their teaching and, second, constructing the intellectual *schemata* of facts, concepts, generalizations, and experiences they use to make sense out of that information and to apply it to their classroom practice.[30] For example, before teachers can reflect productively about developing a plan for maintaining appropriate student classroom behavior, they need to know something about the nature of human behavior, peer interactions, rewards and punishment, and so on (knowledge); and they have to have formulated what they know on all these points into some generalizations about what that information means in terms of how they see themselves as managers of student behavior (schemata).

A point of major significance about the cognitive element of the reflection process that you will want to keep in mind as a teacher education student is that reflective expertise develops over time. You cannot learn all of what you need to know in college classes and simply do it in pre-K–12 classrooms.[31] Only practicing teachers have the experience needed to develop the intellectual schemata necessary to put theoretical knowledge to use in the specific situations teachers face. This characteristic of reflection, as much as any other, separates beginning and novice teachers. Even when you get to student teaching, your cooperating teachers will seem to know more about how to do things than you do. They will know more, and that is normal.

The *critical element* of reflection

can be explained by comparing it to cognitive reflection. Whereas cognitive reflection tends to stress questions about what works most effectively in creating the learning desired in students, critical reflection engages political, moral, ethical, and values questions. These questions go beyond, Will it work? They ask things such as, Is it right to do this? For example, embarrassing a student before his peers might get him to do his homework, but is it something the teacher should do?

The *narrative element* is the developing of the teacher's own interpretation of the situation. Some researchers refer to it as the *voice of teachers, themselves.* This element shows up in the accounting or recording processes that teachers use to sift through their classroom experiences, make sense out of them, and apply them to future lessons. They take many forms: written journals, logs, self-interviews, conferences, conversations with colleagues (possibly like those in the Snapshots for this chapter), and so on.

In summary, researchers have identified reflective thinking as an intellectual tool good teachers use to make the multitude of decisions that are a major task of their professional work. Teachers use it before, during, and after their lessons as an organized and rational way of deciding what to do in the future each time they face a class of students. As Dewey described it, it is part of the problem-solving inquiry process that addresses the critical teacher question, What are the best ways I can teach my students? Reflection is not a simple process, however. Different researchers have identified many types, characteristics, and elements. Further research will discover more.

Conclusion

Teaching is more than standing before students and telling them what they should know and what to do. It is a complex process that involves multiple interactions among many individuals in a classroom cultural setting, thorough planning, and constant reflection and evaluation. Good teachers take each of these steps seriously, although each step and the process as a whole may look different for different teachers.

The act of teaching is a culmination of everything a teacher has learned prior to the point of planning and implementing a specific lesson. It involves the teacher's knowledge, skills, and values concerning (1) purposes for schools, (2) effective teaching strategies, (3) child development, (4) theories of learning, (5) how schools and classrooms operate as organizational cultures, (6) philosophy, (7) subject-matter content, and (8) curriculum. It requires a teacher to put everything together to encourage desired learning in students.

Teaching lessons—
a culminating effort

Because of its complexity, teaching can be analyzed from a number of perspectives. The perspectives presented in this chapter describe the act of teaching as three intertwined processes. Teaching and learning are explained as communicative processes that take place in classrooms, which are seen as cultural settings. Planning is presented as a process that involves reflection upon previous experience, goal setting, and decision making, with the aim of developing learning experiences for students. Evaluation is described as a continuous process of monitoring, assessing, and adjusting. The cycle of lesson planning, teaching, and evaluation depicted in Figure 13-4 is one way of describing *the act of teaching* in graphic form.

FIGURE 13-4   Cycle of lesson planning, implementing, evaluating, and replanning.

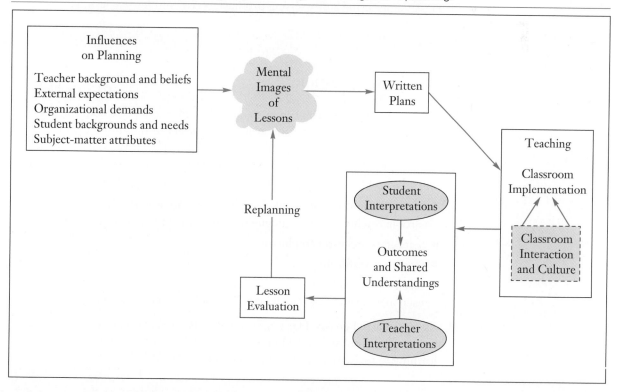

The central lesson to be learned from this chapter is that classrooms are highly complex, and the difficulty of the act of teaching lies in the fact that it is embedded in this complex setting. The best teachers may make the act of teaching look seamless, and a casual observer may conclude that it is easy. Even though most of us have sat in classrooms for thirteen or more years, too often we retain an outsider's perspective, which is much like that of a spectator at an athletic event or an artistic performance. We recognize the results of good teaching (a good game or a good show), but we may overlook how much knowledge, skill, and hard work were behind those results. When we see poor teaching, it is tempting to judge rather than to explain, with comments like, "He is a bad teacher." "She can't teach." We hope, now that you have finished thirteen chapters of this text, that you can not only recognize the different results of good and bad teaching, but can also begin to understand what contributes to each. To the extent you are able to understand this, you are no longer just a spectator.

Summary

Lesson planning involves much reflection and occurs on two levels: macro-level planning and micro-level planning. Two approaches to planning are the rational-choice approach and the lesson-image approach. There are at least five types of influences or sets of pressures that affect teacher planning and lessons: teacher background and beliefs, student background and needs, external expectations, organizational demands, and subject-matter attributes.

Evaluation of lessons includes monitoring and assessing both students and the lessons themselves, formally and informally, and using the information generated from that monitoring and assessing to adjust, revise, and reteach lessons.

Study Questions

1. Think about teachers you had in elementary and secondary school and select the one who you think probably planned his or her lessons most thoroughly; also select the one who you think probably planned the least. What evidence did you consider in making each selection? How was the teaching of the two individuals different in style, effect, motivating quality, and so on?

2. Below are several analogies that have been used to describe the function(s) of classroom teachers. In your judgment, how is each accurate or inaccurate?
   - teacher as orchestra conductor
   - teacher as traffic director
   - teacher as driving instructor with twenty-five or thirty beginning drivers, each in a separate car but all being instructed at the same time

3. Assume that, when Ms. Harding read students' drafts of their writing, she determined that more than half of them were making little or no progress in learning to revise their work. What should she do? Why?

4. Select a subject, a grade level, and a topic for a lesson you would want to teach to a class of elementary or secondary school students. What types of things would you need to know in order to develop useful mental images of that lesson?

Key Terms

Academic needs	Lesson-image approach	Rational-choice approach
Class personality	to lesson planning	to lesson planning
Continuity	Lesson objectives	Schemata
Cultural backgrounds	Macro-level planning	Student needs
Curricular knowledge	Micro-level planning	Subject matter attributes
Emotional needs	Motivation	Subject matter knowledge
Evaluation	Objective conditions	Student role players
Expressive outcomes	Organizational demands	System-wide testing
External expectations	Pedagogical knowledge	Teachers as orchestrators
Interaction	Physical needs	Teachers' lesson images
Lesson goals	Psychological needs	The act of teaching

For Further Reading

Brophy, J., & Good, T. (1974). *Teacher-student relationships: Causes and consequences*. New York: Holt, Rinehart and Winston.

Brophy, J., & Evertson, C. M. (1981). *Student characteristics and teaching*. New York: Longman.

Eisner, E. (1994). *The educational imagination: On the design and evaluation of school programs*. (3rd ed.). New York: Macmillan.

Evertson, C. M., & Weade, R. (1991). The social construction of classroom lessons. In H. Waxman & H. Walberg (Eds.), *Effective teaching: Current research* (pp. 135–159). Chicago: University of Chicago Press.

Mehan, H. (1979). *Learning lessons: Social organization in the classroom*. Cambridge, MA: Harvard University Press.

Neely, A. (1985). Teacher planning: Where has it been? Where is it now? Where is it going? *Action in Teacher Education*, 7(3), 25–29.

Neely, A. (1986). Integrating planning and problem solving in teacher education. *Journal of Teacher Education*, 37(3), 29–33.

Peterson, P. L., Marx, R. W., & Clark, C. M. (1978). Teacher planning, teacher behavior, and student achievement. *American Educational Research Journal*, 15(3), 417–432.

Sinclair, J. McH., & Brazil, D. (1982). *Teacher talk*. London: Oxford University Press.

Models of
Instruction

CONTRIBUTING AUTHORS
Alene H. Harris
Earline Kendall
Deborah W. Rowe
Jane Stallings
The Cognitive and Technology Group at Vanderbilt

This chapter was written by Alene H. Harris, Earline Kendall, Deborah W. Rowe, and the Cognitive and Technology Group at Vanderbilt. Jane Stallings was the primary author of the first edition of this chapter.

This chapter consists of descriptions of five models of instruction, each of which is a design or plan for teaching based on specific assumptions about purposes for schools, students, learning theory, educational philosophy, and curriculum theory; and each is intended to accomplish specific learning goals. You will notice that the models clearly reflect aspects of all the elements about teaching and learning that you have studied already in this text.

Many models could be described, but these five were selected because they reflect a variety of theoretical points of view, because they have had substantial impact on instructional practice, and because their effectiveness has been researched. The research that is described is rather technical and detailed, instead of in summary form. This is done intentionally, to provide you examples of specific educational research efforts and terminology. The models that are discussed are mastery learning, cooperative learning, the High/Scope cognitive-oriented curriculum, whole-language instruction, and technology-based anchored instruction.

The chapter organization differs from that of earlier chapters. Each model is described through a vignette of teacher-student interactions that is presented in the form of a Snapshot, and theoretical underpinnings and research results are provided for each model. Therefore, there are five chapter Snapshots and no Reflecting on Practice or Educational Research sections. As you read, compare and contrast elements of the models in order to consider which instructional strategies and student outcomes are most appealing to you.

SNAPSHOT

This first Snapshot, like the others in the chapter, describes a segment of a lesson that illustrates one of the instruction models.[1] As you read about this second-grade class, consider:

- What are the essential elements of the lesson?
- Which theories of learning that you read about in Chapter 6 support this type of lesson?
- Which students might this lesson affect positively?
- Which students might this lesson affect negatively?
- What do you think about this lesson?

Mastery Learning

Situation: A second-grade class is being taught the relationship between long vowel sounds and the silent *e*.

TEACHER: Today we will be studying the long vowel sounds. We will start with the long *a*. The long vowel sound says its name: a, e, i, o, u. [The teacher points to the word *name* written on the chalkboard.] The word *name* has a long *a*. Listen for the long *a* when we say the word *name*. Say it all together: Naaaaaaame.

STUDENTS: Naaaame.

TEACHER: Very good. I am going to show you a rule that will help you to know when to use the long vowel to pronounce words and when to use the short one. Words are pronounced with a long vowel sound when a silent *e* comes at the end of the word. What is this word? [Writes on chalkboard.]

ALL STUDENTS: At.

TEACHER: Very good. Now I will add a silent *e*. The new word is a-t-e. Remember the *a* now has a long vowel sound. It says its name. What is the new word?

FOUR STUDENTS: Ate.

TEACHER: Thank you Sarah, Bill, José, and Ann. Now, everyone say the word *ate*.

ALL STUDENTS: Ate.

TEACHER: Now let's look at these words and see what new words are formed when we add a silent *e*. In *hat* the *a* has a short vowel sound, but when we add an *e*, the word becomes *hate*, and the *a* has a long vowel sound. Say the new word.

SARAH, BILL, JOSÉ, AND ANN: Hate.

TEACHER: It seems you four understand the change the silent *e* makes in words. You can do the worksheet

matching the long vowel and short vowel words to the pictures.

As the four students begin working on their worksheets, the teacher talks to the rest of the class.

TEACHER: Let's look at some more words. *Mat* has a short vowel sound. What happens when we add an *e*? What happens to the sound, Cathy?

CATHY: It becomes *mate*.

TEACHER: Good. That's correct. Let's look at the next word. What happens to *mad* when we add an *e*, Jon?

The teacher proceeds with this line of discussion until all students understand the concept being taught. As students demonstrate that they have grasped the idea, the teacher directs them to their worksheets, as she did earlier with Sarah, Bill, José, and Ann. Then she continues with those remaining.

Later, the teacher collects all worksheets and checks each one to see whether everyone has learned what she intended. She plans additional instruction for those who did not.

Mastery Learning

The preceding instruction took place in a mastery learning classroom. The primary goal of that class, as well as the primary goal of the *mastery learning model* in general, is to make sure that *all* students achieve the lesson's objectives and to allow each of them enough time to do so. The teachers in mastery learning intend to teach all of the students all of the material. In most cases this means that the material must be structured so that students can work at different paces over different lengths of time.[2]

All students achieve

The teacher described in the first Snapshot allowed the four successful students to proceed with their independent work while she continued to help the others learn the relationship of long vowel sounds and the silent *e*. She continued to teach students about the relationship until all of them could read and pronounce the words in the day's lesson. She did this even though some children may have achieved the lesson objective in ninety minutes and others in only ten. All of them had to master the words and concept being taught in the lesson before they could proceed to the next lesson.

Mastery learning is, in essence, a process of instruction. In its initial form, teachers organize the instruction in a precise pattern, present information and skills

TABLE 14-1   Goals and Characteristics of Mastery Learning

Primary Goals	Characteristics
All students achieve objectives	Common objectives for all students
All students master material	Common material and tasks for all students
	Flexible amounts of time provided for different students to complete tasks
	Students work at different paces
	Structured lessons
	High rates of student success
	Close monitoring of students and frequent feedback

to the students according to the pattern, determine regularly how well each student is progressing, feed back information on that progress to the students, help students overcome difficulties through guidance and additional instruction or practice, and provide extra enrichment experiences for those who master the material quickly. Its goals and characteristics are summarized in Table 14-1.

Mastery learning is presented here as a model of instruction because it provides a relatively easy-to-understand illustration of how all the elements about teaching and learning that you have studied so far can be fitted together into a self-contained approach to teaching that cuts across grade levels and subject matter. It was selected as the first model of instruction for this chapter even though its popularity as a "packaged approach to instruction" has waned in recent years. Its influence on instruction of the 1990s is still prominent, however, because many mastery learning principles and characteristics are embodied in *outcome-based education*. In fact, many instructional theorists see mastery learning as a forerunner of outcome-based education.

When reviewed historically, mastery learning, competency-based education, and outcome-based education (OBE) are three terms used interchangeably by many educators for the past thirty years. The popularity of each of these terms can be associated with a decade: mastery learning, the 1970s; competency-based education, the 1980s; outcome-based education, the 1990s. According to one researcher, underlying principles of programs recognized under each of these titles can be traced back to the work of Benjamin Bloom, J. Thomas Hastings, and George F. Madaus in the early 1970s;[3] they put forth the following ideas:[4]

1. Educational processes should not restrict or limit students.
2. Both kind and quality of instruction should be appropriate to the needs of the student.
3. Time available for learning should vary according to the needs of the student.
4. The teacher should make clear the learning goals/objectives at the beginning of the instructional process.
5. Formative evaluation should be a major and integral part of the learning process.

6. When needed, reteaching/corrective measures should be used with a student.
7. When appropriate, a summative/final evaluation should be given.

Outcome-based education programs of recent times appear to rest on two fundamental principles: (1) instructional practice should be designed around clearly defined outcomes that all students must demonstrate and (2) schools must provide the opportunity for all students to reach those learning outcomes.[5] Guiding most outcome-based programs are at least five premises that address five separate components of instructional programs. Those are:

1. Philosophy: All students can learn; the teacher can/must organize learning to ensure success.
2. Curriculum: The curriculum must be organized around agreed-upon learning objectives.
3. Instruction: Time is a variable in student learning, not a constant—some students need more or less of it to learn.
4. Assessment: The instructional approach of teach-test-reteach-test provides formative feedback to students and also summative evaluation.
5. Organization: Teachers must work in and create an environment that allows flexibility in pacing and learning format.

Current proponents of outcome-based education maintain that it is a way to meet the needs of all students regardless of their home environment, ethnicity, economic status, or possible disabling condition. They also claim that teaching oriented toward outcomes creates a clearer curricular focus for instruction, enhances development of better and more appropriate instructional methods, and provides for more precise and more valid assessment of student achievement. Outcome-based education possibly has become the fastest-growing educational reform thrust of the 1990s. Many school systems and, indeed, entire state educational systems (Kentucky, Michigan, Minnesota, Washington, and Pennsylvania) have entered into long-term commitments to become outcome-based systems.[6] As of 1993, twenty-four states had developed or implemented some form of outcome-based programs and twelve others made outcomes a part of their accreditation or assessment processes.[7]

Educational Theory behind the Model

The underlying assumption of the mastery learning model was articulated in 1963 by John B. Carroll.[8] The assumption is that nearly all students can learn the basic school curriculum, although it takes some students longer than others. Stating it another way, the critical variable that determines what students learn is the *rate* at which they learn rather than their inherent *ability* to learn. Theorists of mastery learning describe three factors affecting learning rates: prerequisite knowledge, interest and motivation, and quality of instruction.

Rate of learning

Benjamin Bloom, the developer of the mastery learning model, believes that the differences in the amount of achievement that students show on final examinations are the results of nonmastery procedures used in schools. He says that what students already know, the time available to learn, and the quality of the instruction, not native ability, explain these differences. Some students are not given enough time or enough learning experiences to learn what is expected, so they master only part of the curriculum. Therefore, since students learn at different rates, they need to be provided different amounts of time to learn. Each needs to be given the amount of time he or she personally needs.[9]

Motivation for learning is an important element in this model. Advocates note that some students come to new units of study with low motivation because of previous failure and inadequate background information. These students fall further and further behind in achievement, and their attitudes become more negative. The solution to this problem, they say, is to provide prerequisite skills and time needed for all students to master the content of each lesson. As the students succeed at their work, they will become more positive about it.

There is some evidence that students in mastery programs, after gaining the prerequisite knowledge, progress increasingly faster in their lessons when compared with nonmastery students. Bloom suggests that under mastery learning the difference between good and poor learners in the time required to learn tends to be reduced to a vanishing point.[10] Critics of mastery learning question the degree to which slow learners speed up and suggest that fast learners slow down.

The Model in Practice

Mastery learning, as originally designed by Bloom and in the variations that have evolved from his original model, is a process of instruction that requires the learning of structured, hierarchical, sequential units of material. Despite these characteristics, it can be introduced into many classes without wholesale distortion of the content to be covered and without eliminating many of the other modes of instruction that the teacher employs. On the other hand, if mastery learning is to be pursued correctly, instructional objectives must be clear; the subject matter must be divided into short, individualized, incremental units; individualized evaluation must be provided; and individual student progress must be monitored. Teachers who incorporate the concept of mastery learning into their teaching can continue to teach the same information and ideas and can continue to lecture, form small discussion

Margin notes:
Motivation

Prerequisite skills

Slow learners catch up

Individual mastery

Techniques such as peer tutoring or small study groups can be adapted to serve the specific purposes of different teaching models, including mastery learning.

groups, and assign projects; but they must modify the ways they do these things in order to assure individual student mastery.

Frequently administered diagnostic assessments are critical to mastery learning. Teachers develop and administer brief tests to determine the students' mastery of the objectives. Students who score 15 percent or more incorrect go over the work again until they achieve mastery. To help children achieve mastery, teachers might plan individual work, such as special reading, worksheet assignments, or computer games; they might also plan peer tutoring, small-group study sessions, or academic group games. Students who master the material quickly are given *enrichments* that enable them to study the content more comprehensively.

Diagnostic assessments

Grading in mastery learning is not competitive. When students demonstrate mastery of the information, they receive an A. Until then, they receive an I, for incomplete.

The two principal formats for presenting mastery learning material are the original Bloom format, in which teachers teach the unit to the whole class, and a variation, in which students work through the units independently at their own speed. In either case, students are given tests at the end of each unit. If they do not achieve a score of 80 to 90 percent correct, they receive more instruction and are provided more time until they can achieve a mastery grade on a retest.

Two formats

The most widely followed version of the individualized format of mastery learning has been that designed by F. S. Keller.[11] It is called the Personalized System of Instruction. In contrast to the Bloom version, students in the Personalized System of Instruction use programmed materials, which they go through individually and at their own pace. Teachers monitor and assist students individually and are not concerned about keeping the class working together. There is little teacher-led interactive instruction. As the school year proceeds, the gap between what the faster and the slower students learn expands.

Both formats have some inherent problems. First, whole-group instruction requires that the teacher keep the group working on the same unit. If the teacher waits for all students to reach mastery of a unit before going on to the next unit and if some of the additional learning time comes from class time, fast learners are slowed and pay inevitable achievement costs. In the other case, when students work at their own pace, there is little time for teacher instruction for each student. For example, a fifty-minute period divided by twenty-five students allows an average of no more than two minutes per child. Obviously, some children receive more than two minutes, and others receive none at all. Also, some researchers report that children they studied using both formats of the model tended to consider that finishing worksheets first or quickly was a primary goal of their lessons. As a result, they tended to become competitive and rush through the materials.[12]

Possible problems

Assessing the Effectiveness of the Model

Programs based on mastery learning ideas have been embraced for more than two decades by hundreds of school systems in this nation and around the world. However, as with many educational innovations, the efforts often seem to have been undertaken without serious evaluation. A significant number of those who employed the program for the first time did not carry out studies to measure program effects; and where studies were conducted, they were often poorly designed. In the mid-1970s, J. H. Block and R. Burns summarized six studies of Bloom-style mastery learning efforts that were conducted in elementary schools.[13] They report that, in general, the studies are flawed. Among the six, two had nonequivalent control groups; five had post-test scores but no pretest scores; five used criterion tests to assess mastery; and only one used standardized achievement test scores.[14] Of the five studies that used criterion tests at the end of the units, only three reported significant positive results for mastery students compared to control groups.

Mixed results

In the one study that used standardized test scores, Anderson gathered comparative scores for eighteen classes. Of these, three mastery classes performed significantly better on the tests than did the control groups. Eight of the other mastery classes scored higher than control groups, but the differences were not great enough to be statistically significant. Three control groups scored statistically higher than the mastery groups, and four control groups scored higher than mastery classrooms, but without statistically significant differences. These findings from both criterion tests and standardized achievement tests may indicate a positive trend for mastery programs, but they certainly do not provide a ringing vote of confidence in the superiority of the performance of the mastery students.

Because the goal of mastery learning, at least Bloom's version, is to enable all students, especially the slow ones, to achieve and because flexible use of time is at the heart of its approach, understanding the ways in which fast and slow learners fare in comparison with each other is important in assessing the model's effectiveness. Research and analyses have contributed some insight to the following questions: Do the differences between fast and slow learners decrease, increase, or remain stable over time? Are faster learners held back, waiting for slower learners? If so, does this holding back increase, decrease, or remain stable over time?[15]

In one study, students in four elementary classrooms were examined during ten consecutive lessons. Over that period, the differences between the time required by fast and slow learners to learn the intended content remained stable. The time needed to bring slower students to mastery did not lessen. Faster students were consistently held back with alternative activities while they waited for slower children to catch up.[16]

A second study compared all students in one school who began first grade in September 1977 and who were in the mastery learning program for the next four years. Results indicated that differences in the rate of learning between fast and slow learners remained stable or increased over the four years. Many of the students who needed extra time during the early years were the same students who needed extra time toward the end of the study.[17]

Slow learners might not catch up

The results of the two studies conflict with mastery learning theorists' claims that mastery learning procedures minimize achievement differences and time differences simultaneously. M. Arlin states, "While it was possible to minimize *achievement* differences in both studies by insuring that most students achieved at similar levels, it was not possible to minimize the differences between students in the *time needed* to achieve this mastery."[18] These results suggest that educators may be disappointed if they implement mastery programs with the expectation that the time it takes for fast and slow students to learn will equalize.

A number of investigators have raised philosophical and practical questions about how mastery learning is implemented. Some insist that when teachers spend sizable amounts of their time helping lower-ability students master the content, the higher-ability students are slighted and are often expected to wait for the others. Although the Personalized System of Instruction version of mastery learning is less susceptible to this criticism, it is criticized because it limits interactive instruction and student-to-student social interaction.

Something to Think About

Two teachers in a faculty lounge are talking about the strengths and weaknesses of mastery learning. Both express themselves with conviction, the first saying:

> As far as I can tell, my good students are always being held back by the slow ones. The good ones are wasting time and become bored; and the slow ones are embarrassed because everyone knows they need extra time and more work to learn the same things the others master more quickly. They become frustrated. I think individualizing instruction is a better approach.

The second colleague responds:

> As far as I am concerned, mastery learning is a godsend for my slow students. If we didn't teach this way, they would be ignored. Being put on the spot is not as bad as being neglected totally.

If you were a teacher who chose to enter this conversation in the lounge, what position would you take? What would you say?

Other critics suggest that mastery learning is too narrow, too behavioristic, too structured, and too rigid. They say that it reduces student and teacher creativity and insight; that it focuses learning on only a few specific sets of information and skills; that it teaches students to study only materials that will be tested; that it punishes weak students by assigning them more work; and that it is too demanding of teacher time, energy, and competence in materials development.[19]

Too rigid?

There are additional criticisms: There is not enough general agreement among educators about specific instructional goals to formulate appropriate mastery materials. The assessment tests that are needed for evaluation of student mastery are not developed to the point that most teachers can use them competently. There are not enough efficient and appropriate *corrective* materials available for teachers to meet the needs of their students.[20]

The greatest vote of confidence for mastery learning comes from the school districts that have used the model over some time and indicate that their test scores have improved. This positive reaction might be explained by the fact that mastery learning includes the expectation that most students can learn what is being taught in the classroom. That is, there is a belief that everyone can succeed—the self-fulfilling prophecy phenomenon.

Everyone can succeed

It appears that this combination of criticisms and positive results concerning mastery learning has led to less use of the precisely developed version of the model at the same time that several of its more general characteristics have been incorporated into the more pervasive and less precise idea of outcome-based instruction. The need to teach students who achieve at widely varied rates and the complexities involved in developing precise mastery learning packages has led educators to apply the ideas of individualized instruction, frequently administered assessments, and success for all in ways more flexible than those of the rigid mastery learning format.

A second model for instruction is cooperative learning.[21] As you read the lesson description that follows in this Snapshot, consider the following questions:

- What are the essential elements of the lesson?
- Which theories of learning that you read about in Chapter 6 support this type of lesson?
- Which prior organization and classroom management skills that you read about in Chapter 3 must be in place for this format to be successful?
- Which students might this lesson affect positively?
- Which students might this lesson affect negatively?
- What do you think about this lesson?

Cooperative Learning

Situation: A sixth-grade teacher has organized a mathematics class of thirty students into cooperative work groups. The teacher has grades for previous work indicating which students have high, middle, and low mathematics scores and has formed five groups so that each group has equal numbers of students at each level. The students have been assigned seats so that low achievers are sitting between high or middle achievers.

TEACHER: For the next three weeks of our math lessons, we will be working part of each week in groups. I will still be explaining some things to you, but then you will have the opportunity to work together as a team to teach one another.

As a team member, you can earn points for your team in three ways—by completing your homework, by completing it correctly, and by showing improvement on weekly quizzes. Each of you can earn one point for each completed homework assignment. Since there are five people on each team and four days of homework per week, how many points could each team earn if everyone on the team completes all assignments?

STUDENTS: Twenty.

TEACHER: Right. Points for your team will also be awarded by the number of homework problems correct. Remember, going too fast and getting wrong answers on homework won't help you learn to do math, so check those answers. Agreed?

STUDENTS: (Nod)

TEACHER: Also, remember when you work together that helping means assisting or explaining—not doing the work for the other person. If one person on your team does other team members' work for them, then those people are not likely to learn the material and get right answers on the quizzes. The point of these lessons will be to improve your own math skills and to help one another *learn* to do mathematics.

Finally, you can each earn another set of points for your team on your weekly quiz. Does each of you remember your math average for last grading period?

STUDENTS: (Think and nod)

TEACHER: By competing with your own grade averages, you can earn up to 30 points for your team on each quiz and test. Here is how it will work. (The teacher draws the following chart on the board. Students study it carefully and nod.)

QUIZ SCORE	TEAM POINTS
more than 10 points below your average	0
from 1 to 10 points below your average	10
your average to 10 points above	20
more than 10 points above your average	30
all perfect papers	30

During the next few minutes, each group should select a name and assign each person a work role for this week: group facilitator, homework checker, record keeper, sergeant-at-arms, timekeeper. Homework checkers check the homework each morning, record keepers record the number of correct problems for their group on the graph on the bulletin board, sergeants-at-arms remind people to use quiet voices during work periods, facilitators make certain that everyone has turns to get to help or share ideas during group problem-solving time, and timekeepers remind us of the time to help us pace ourselves and get work finished on time. (The teacher displays an overhead projection with the title and job description of each work role.)

STUDENTS: (Talk quietly in groups as the teacher circles among the groups. Groups choose names including Math Monsters, The Comets, Fantastic Five, and Too Cool for School; they begin to assign work roles.)

Cooperative Learning

The preceding interaction occurred in a mathematics classroom in which the teacher followed the *cooperative learning model*. This model, as explained in Chapter 3, has two types of primary goals. The first is to improve student understanding and skills in the subject being taught. The second is for the students to develop cooperative group skills and to gain an appreciation for the different individuals and subcultures represented in classrooms. As the students work toward these goals, they are expected to raise the value they place on academic learning and develop more positive attitudes toward people of different racial and ethnic backgrounds.[22]

The model works toward its goals through arrangements that require student cooperation. In some approaches, students on a given class team cooperate with one another in academic games and tournaments in order to compete effectively with other teams. Teams whose members do not cooperate rarely win.

Several cooperative learning programs have been developed during the past fifteen to twenty years. The most notable ones include Student Team-Academic Divisions (STAD), Teams-Games-Tournaments (TGT), Team Assisted Individualization (TAI), Cooperative Integrated Reading and Composition (CIRC), Jigsaw II, Learning Together (LT), and Group Investigation (GI). Shlomo Sharan classifies the variety of learning models into two groups: peer tutoring and group investigation.[23] While the models vary in structure and have different types of tasks for the students to perform, the intent of each one is to increase student cooperation while also improving student academic achievement.

In some program formats, students work on a learning task as a group. This format is presumed to encourage truly cooperative learning and peer tutoring. In other formats, the task is divided, and group members work independently, seeking help as needed. In the end, both formats reward learning and reinforce cooperation, although the specific ways in which rewards are achieved may differ. The goals and characteristics of cooperative learning programs are summarized in Table 14-2.

Educational Theory behind the Model

Although the Snapshot scenario on cooperative learning describes the forming of teams that are about to compete in homework and on quizzes, the essential activity for the students on the teams is to help one another do well in mathematics. The model was developed around this characteristic of cooperation because cooperative learning enthusiasts believe that most classroom environments encourage competition rather than cooperation and that, aside from teams in athletics, music, and

Student cooperation

Group rewards

TABLE 14-2   Goals and Characteristics of Cooperative Learning

Primary Goals	Characteristics
Improved student understanding and skill development	Assignments and tasks that require student cooperation in groups
Development of skills of interpersonal cooperation	Group rewards, but individual grades
	Structured lessons and student tasks
Positive attitudes toward different individuals and cultures	Peer teaching

drama, schools and classrooms offer few opportunities for students to develop co-operative skills. They want to change this situation because students and adults, in order to be successful in the world of work, in communities, and in families, must be able to cooperate, as well as compete, with others.

Proponents of cooperative learning believe that important life skills such as speaking, listening, arriving at consensus, and problem solving can be taught through cooperative learning experiences. They also suggest that students who have opportunities to work with students different from themselves and to experience one another as teammates will reduce some of their stereotypical attitudes regarding racial groups, low achievers, mainstreamed disabled students, males, and females. In the process of working together, they are assumed by cooperative learning propo-nents to learn to appreciate one another's strengths and to develop friendships that transcend ethnic, racial, gender, and other group divisions. This, in turn, is expected to improve racial and other group relations in schools.

Proponents of cooperative learning presume that it encourages students to help and support peers in their group, rather than compete against all their classmates. As in team sports, in which individual excellence is encouraged because it benefits the whole team, team competition in the classroom results in greater student sup-port of others' achievements. Proponents also state that students learn better from cooperative learning.

Cooperative learning theorists also believe that when students learn from one another, both high- and low-ability children benefit. As they see it, the high-ability child achieves a higher level of understanding in the process of helping slower chil-dren, and the lower-ability child benefits from the other children's assistance.

Cooperative models are also believed to be more motivational than the indi-vidual competitive models characteristic of most classrooms because the competi-tive models are motivational only for those children who perceive they have a chance of winning. Studies show that many academically disadvantaged children expect to do poorly no matter how hard they try, and eventually they cease trying. They simply choose not to compete.[24] See Chapter 5 for further explanation of this point.

The group reward structure is expected to increase motivation for low-ability students. Evidence suggests that simply being a member of a successful group, re-gardless of the child's own performance, allows the child some of the advantages of success, satisfaction, and peer esteem.[25] Group competition presumably pits groups of equal ability against each each other, and consequently all groups and all students can experience winning on occasion.

Reduce stereotypes (margin note)

Achievement gains (margin note)

Motivation (margin note)

The Model in Practice

As with mastery learning, cooperative learning is a process of instruction that can be implemented at various grade levels and in different subject-matter areas. Teach-ers simply need to understand the concept and apply it to their teaching. In order to follow specific cooperative learning models properly, teachers need to organize their students, learning activities, and assessments according to that model; but they have significant flexibility within those bounds, and they do not have to follow a specific formula in order to do cooperative learning. As a result, many teachers are using some form of the cooperative learning model without special training or di-rect contact with the people who developed and tested it. Thus, the model has been disseminated easily.

The general idea of cooperative learning dates back for decades, but serious research-oriented program development and testing of specific cooperative learning models has occurred primarily since about 1970.

Prominent leaders in the field of cooperative learning have been Robert Slavin at Johns Hopkins University and David and Roger Johnson at the University of Minnesota. The methods developed by Slavin and Johnson and Johnson approach cooperative learning from different educational perspectives and with different educational goals. Slavin seeks to improve students' learning by orienting peer norms to support academic achievement; Johnson and Johnson, to improve students' social interactions and self-esteem.

The most thoroughly researched cooperative learning programs are those developed by Robert Slavin. These include Student Teams-Achievement Divisions (STAD), Teams-Games-Tournaments (TGT), Team Assisted Individualization (TAI), Cooperative Integrated Reading and Composition (CIRC), and Jigsaw II.

In *Student Teams-Achievement Divisions,* students are divided into four- or five-member teams so that each team contains high, average, and low achievers; boys and girls; and representatives of the racial, ethnic, and social groups in the class. At the start of each new set of lessons, the teacher presents new material to the class. The team members then study and practice the material in their groups, often working in pairs. They complete worksheets, quiz one another, discuss problems, and practice exercises. Their task is to enable everyone in their group to learn the material. At the end, the teacher administers assessments that the students must complete individually.

STAD

Using students' individual assessment scores, the teacher determines the number of points each student contributes to his or her team. Individuals provide the best scores for their team by showing *improvement* from previous performance or by achieving a perfect grade. Because improvement is an important element in an individual's score, academically weak students can contribute significantly to the team. They are not automatically the weak team members. The teacher sees to it that weekly team scores and notable individual performances are publicly recognized.

Students who participate in STAD need to cooperate, so that everyone learns and scores highly on the quizzes. Teams without members who improve their grades and produce perfect scores do not win.

Teams-Games-Tournaments is much like STAD in that it involves teacher introduction of content, worksheets, team study, individual assessment, team recognition, and equal opportunity for success. It is different in that quizzes are replaced by tournaments between members of different teams. The process is as follows: Team members prepare one another for the tournament by studying and practicing together. The teacher matches individuals from each team with academically comparable tournament competitors and changes the matchings with each new set of lessons to reflect students' current content mastery and assure that all students have the best chance of success; individuals compete weekly, and the weekly scores are compiled and reported as team scores. Teams stay together for about six weeks.

TGT

Team Assisted Individualization is individualized, rather than class-organized or class-paced, instruction. It was designed for use with programmed, sequential mathematics instruction. Teams are organized as with STAD and TGT, but each student works through individualized programmed units chosen to match his or her ability level.

TAI

Team members work in pairs or small groups as they complete their different exercises, but each must proceed through the materials in sequence and must complete periodic checkouts with at least an 80 percent score. When all checkouts are completed, each student takes a test over the content studied. Team scores consist of the sums of individual scores and the number of tests each team member completes in a particular amount of time. The critical factor for each student's contribution to the team is his or her weekly progress.

CIRC

Cooperative Integrated Reading and Composition was designed for the teaching of reading, writing, and language arts at the upper elementary grades.[26] CIRC consists of three principal elements: basal reader-related activities, direct teacher instruction in reading comprehension, and integrated language arts and writing. Students work in heterogeneous teams, and all activities follow a regular cycle of teacher presentation, team practice, independent practice, peer reassessment, additional practice, and testing.

Jigsaw II

Jigsaw II is a revision of an earlier version called Jigsaw, and both are cooperative learning techniques useful when lesson material is in a narrative form such as a chapter or story. In Jigsaw II, as with STAD and TGT, students study in teams of four or five members. Each student studies the whole assignment given by the teacher but is expected to be the team "expert" on one specific element of the task. For example, each student is responsible for a particular part of a short story or a section of a textbook chapter. The most significant difference between Jigsaw II and Jigsaw is that in Jigsaw each student reads only the material for which he or she is the expert; there is no common study of the entire assignment.

When the specific assignment has been studied, the "experts" from all teams who have been assigned the same tasks meet to discuss their work and assist each other. Then the "experts" return to their own team and teach the other members about their assigned portion. On completion of the intrateam instruction, students take individual quizzes, and the individual results are compiled into team scores based on improvement, as with STAD.

Learning Together

Johnson and Johnson's *Learning Together* is a widely used cooperative learning method. It emphasizes four elements:[27]

1. *face-to-face interaction* (students work in four- to five-member groups)
2. *positive interdependence* (students work together to achieve a group goal)
3. *individual accountability* (students must show individual content mastery) and
4. *interpersonal and small-group skills* (students must be taught effective ways to work together and to discuss how well their groups are working to achieve their goals)

Groups are heterogeneous, the focus is on team building and group self-assessment, and teachers often use team grades rather than team recognition.[28]

Group Investigation

One other significant cooperative learning model is *Group Investigation*, an approach dating back to John Dewey and recently refined and researched by Shlomo and Yael Sharan and Rachel Hertz-Lazarowitz at the University of Tel Aviv.[29] Group Investigation organizes students into groups that prepare group projects or complete class assignments, and it requires prior training in communication and social skills. Group Investigation is appropriate for students' investigating and/or solving a multifaceted topic and/or problem, such as the biology of a rain forest.[30]

Assessing the Effectiveness of the Model

Because cooperative learning attempts to accomplish a number of goals, assessment of its effectiveness must be based on multiple criteria. The effects reported here are in terms of academic achievement, intergroup relations, mainstreaming, and self-esteem. The data are drawn primarily from a summary of research studies compiled by Slavin in 1990 and are based on precise and controlled implementations of specific cooperative learning models.

Slavin reports that the effects of cooperative learning on academic achievement are clearly positive.[31] His review of sixty-eight studies of cooperative learning methods revealed that forty-nine studies (72 percent) showed significantly positive results in favor of cooperative learning and only eight (12 percent) favored the control groups. The review also found some cooperative learning methods to be much more effective than others. Specifically, those that emphasized group goals and individual accountability (STAD, TGT, and TAI) were consistently more effective for increasing student academic achievement than were other forms of cooperative learning. Studies of the Learning Together model found significant positive effects on student achievement only when the model incorporated group goals and individual accountability. From these studies, Slavin draws the conclusion that "cooperative learning methods can be an effective means of increasing student achievement, but only if they incorporate group goals and individual accountability."[32] Thus, it seems that individual student responsibilities—individual quizzes and test scores and *not* group grades—are as important to academic achievement as the team cooperation.

Academic achievement

The idea that cooperative learning might enhance intergroup relations is derived from two research findings of earlier and more general studies. First, studies of cooperation among people indicate that people who cooperate learn to like each other.[33] Second, research on school desegregation notes that students with different racial and ethnic backgrounds do not integrate socially just because they go to the same school.[34] If both findings are valid, cooperative learning that requires student

Intergroup relations

Although additional research is needed, studies suggest that cooperative learning improves interpersonal and intergroup relations.

cooperation across racial and ethnic groups in schools should result in students' liking each other better.

According to several studies, students who participate in cooperative learning do, in fact, increase their intergroup relations with other students.[35] In most of these studies, students were asked to list their best friends before and after they participated in cooperative learning. The two lists were then compared to determine the number of students from other racial and ethnic groups listed each time by the same student. An increase in the number of cross-group friendships was assumed to indicate improved intergroup relations.

Studies involving each of the cooperative learning methods described here have shown positive effects on intergroup relations, with the strongest and most consistent effects resulting from STAD, TGT, and TAI.

Mainstreaming

Several studies have also been conducted to determine the effect of cooperative learning on attitudes among students in classrooms containing mainstreamed students with disabling conditions. The limited data available indicate that the experience of cooperative learning led to reduced rejection of the mainstreamed children, while all children in the classes gained in self-esteem and achievement. Results of this kind were found when academically handicapped students participated in STAD classes and when emotionally handicapped students participated in TGT classes.[36]

Self-esteem

Students who have participated in cooperative learning also seem to develop improved self-esteem, although the evidence is not completely consistent.[37] Some studies indicate an increase in students' social self-esteem, some an increase in students' academic self-esteem, and others indicate no change. Eleven of fifteen studies investigating the effects of cooperative learning on students' self-esteem found positive effects on some aspect of self-esteem. It would seem that—more than the control group students—students in these classes liked their classmates and were better liked by their classmates.

In summary, the cooperative learning model of instruction seems to produce a variety of positive results much of the time. These results include improvement in academic achievement, social relationships, cooperative work skills, and self-esteem. The results appear in a wide range of studies in different schools, at different grade levels, and with different students. The data, however, are not universally positive and are limited for the most part to controlled experimental situations. Longitudinal studies are needed to examine the long-term positive effects of cooperative work groups upon students and teachers.

SNAPSHOT

A third model of instruction, the High/Scope cognitive-oriented curriculum, is illustrated in this Snapshot.[38] As you read the observation report of a kindergarten class, consider the following questions:

- What are the essential elements of the lesson?
- Which theories of learning in Chapter 6 support this type of lesson?
- Which philosophies of education in Chapter 9 are consistent with this type of lesson?

- Which students might this lesson affect positively?
- Which students might this lesson affect negatively?
- What do you think about this lesson?

The High/Scope Cognitive-Oriented Curriculum

8:00–8:10: Arrival

When the kindergarten children first arrive at school, the teacher or an aide gives them symbols (animal shapes made from construction paper), a different one for each child. Each child's symbol is taped to his or her cubby. The children go directly to a small-group planning area.

8:10–8:20: Planning Time

During the first fifteen minutes of Planning Time, the children plan what they are going to do in their work centers.

TEACHER: José, what did you do yesterday?

JOSÉ: Made this truck.

TEACHER: What do you plan to do today?

JOSÉ: Fix the wheels.

Each child in turn describes a plan for a project.

8:20–9:15: Project Time

Children carry out their projects independently, requesting assistance as necessary. The teacher or aide asks questions or guides the child toward solving problems.

9:15–9:30: Evaluation Time

Children reassemble in their small groups to evaluate their projects.

TEACHER: José, what did you do today?

JOSÉ: I fixed the wheels on my truck.

TEACHER: How did you do that?

JOSÉ: I put some washers on each wheel.

TEACHER: How does it work?

JOSÉ: It moves easier now.

TEACHER: What do you plan to do tomorrow?

JOSÉ: I am going to fix the steering wheel.

9:30–10:15: Instruction Time

The teacher has arranged big and little circles and squares cut from construction paper on the table. She holds up a large and small red circle. She holds the big one up high and asks, "Big or little?" The group answers, "Big!" This process is repeated, using different shapes and objects. The children then paste the shapes on pieces of paper—little circles and squares on one sheet and big ones on another. Either the teacher or an aide is always in the art area, eliciting oral responses from the children and encouraging conversation related to what they are doing.

In the small-motor area, children work with big and little cars and blocks. They make roads and garages with the blocks. The teacher constantly emphasizes the size relations of the objects—for example, big garages are for big cars—and encourages verbal responses from the children.

10:15–10:45: Cleanup Time

During a short meeting at the beginning of Cleanup Time, the children select areas they will clean up. The teacher and aide emphasize the size relations of the objects the children are putting away; for instance, two children are responsible for finding all the big blocks. Children go to the bathroom and get drinks as needed.

10:45–11:00: Juice and Group Time

Cookies and juice are distributed to the class. There are cookies of two sizes, and each child selects one big and one little cookie. There is a brief discussion about the juice cups being full and empty as the children pour their own juice and drink it.

11:00–11:20: Story Time

A story is read to the group. The teacher asks interpretive questions.

11:20–11:45: Circle Time

The children go outside today to play on the playground equipment. The teacher emphasizes spatial concepts as the children play. For instance, as the children use the slide, the teacher stresses *up/down* and *high/low*.

11:45: Dismissal

Children go to their cubbies for their coats and hats. As the children put on their clothing, the teacher and aide relate body parts to articles of clothing—for example, *hat/head*. While waiting for the bus, the children sing "The wheels on the bus go round and round," using hand motions.

The High/Scope Cognitive-Oriented Curriculum

The classroom interaction described in this Snapshot occurred during a lesson from a cognitive development model of instruction that was first developed in the early 1960s to serve children from low-income families. It was used initially in the Perry Preschool Program in Ypsilanti, Michigan.[39] The program was based on the sequential cognitive development theory of Jean Piaget.

Since those early days, the model has evolved significantly, and it is now usually known as the High/Scope program. The model rests on the assumption that appropriately designed cognitively oriented school experiences can stimulate student cognitive abilities. It acknowledges that enhancing cognitive skills is a difficult and long process and, therefore, ought to be started at the preschool level, especially for children from low-income homes whose out-of-school experiences may not be cognitively stimulating.

Children in the program start learning at the motor level, when they use their own bodies and physical experiences to explore elementary concepts. They touch, taste, smell, and manipulate things. Then they learn labels for the things and experiences they have been exploring. Eventually, they become familiar with symbols that they can use to represent the objects, events, and experiences. In short, their learning proceeds from the concrete to the abstract.

Interaction with environment

Learning experiences are organized so that children interact actively with their environment. These experiences help them to classify things, so that they learn about size, order, and temporal and spatial relationships. The experiences also help them sort items and put them in sequence through their use of touch, smell, taste, and visual appearance. The teacher asks the children questions about specific items they encounter, questions that prompt them to think about various attributes of each item—how it looks, smells, feels, tastes, and how it can be used. The teacher also asks them to compare items for similarities and differences.

Structured routines

Daily routines that help students manage their use of time and space and develop control over their behavior are significant program elements. These routines involve the students directly in planning, conducting, and evaluating their activities and behavior. The different segments of the class described in the Snapshot illustrate this characteristic of the program in a lesson developed in the early years of the Perry Preschool Program. At that point, the program's classroom routines were rather rigid and teacher dominated, but through years of revision they have become more flexible. Table 14-3 summarizes the goals and characteristics of this model.

Parental contact

The initial Perry Preschool Program also contained significant contact with and involvement of parents. Students attended the preschool for five half-days each week, and program staff members visited parents in their homes for one and one-half hours a week. Staff members encouraged parents to structure home activities along the lines of the in-school pattern and to involve the children in accomplishing home tasks.

Educational Theory behind the Model

The High/Scope cognitive-oriented curriculum model is based on the Piagetian ideas that explain a child's intelligence, logical thinking, and development in stages according to age and experience. Piaget's ideas, which have been described in Chap-

TABLE 14-3   Goals and Characteristics of the High/Scope Cognitive-Oriented Curriculum

Primary Goals	Characteristics
Stimulate cognitive abilities in young children according to Piagetian stages	Starts with concrete elements of students' physical environment and moves to the symbolic
Develop thinking skills	Includes skills of classifying, sorting, comparing
	Teacher questioning
	Daily routines
	Clearly designed curriculum, using all senses to learn

ters 5 and 6, are based on four cognitive developmental stages. Each is built on the previous one and requires the development of a new set of abilities. The order of stages holds true for all children, but the ages at which children progress through them depend on the child's physical and social environment.

Primary to Piaget's theory is the notion that children learn through involvement in and manipulation of the environment. This is the process by which they develop knowledge about self and objects, learn about relationships among objects, and come to categorize things and events in their own lives. Through the four stages they coordinate and integrate new knowledge with what they have learned in the past. Gradually, children develop the ability to think logically.

Piaget said that at each stage of development the child has a characteristic way of looking at and thinking about the world. Because the stages were described earlier, they are only mentioned here: stage 1: sensorimotor (birth to 2 years); stage 2: preoperational (2 to 7 years); stage 3: concrete operations (7 to 11 years); stage 4: formal operations (11 to 14 years).

Although Piaget accumulated a persuasive body of data to support his theory of the stages of child development, it was not his purpose to implement his theory in school instructional programs. Some educators, however, have tried to put his theory into practice. For example, Irving Sigel translated some of Piaget's ideas into teaching strategies designed to stimulate children's thinking.[40] These strategies involve prescribed sequences of teacher questions, teacher-led group discussions, precisely planned student verbal interactions, carefully selected teaching materials and classroom environments, and activities designed to enhance the students' use and interpretation of language. Each teaching strategy is intended to fit the current cognitive level of the students being taught and is consistent with the content they are studying.

Sigel teaching strategies

The High/Scope cognitive-oriented curriculum is an effort to formulate a precise curriculum, establish classroom patterns, and forge school-parent contacts that apply Piagetian principles and applications of Sigel's theory to the early education of high-risk children. It is intended to structure the cognitive environment of children in ways that enhance their cognitive development. It was undertaken as a type of compensatory program with the knowledge that the out-of-school environment of the typical Perry Preschool student would not be cognitively oriented. The approach is expected to teach cognitive skills to students who are not likely to learn them in their everyday lives.

The Model in Practice

Experiences that fit student developmental stages

Teachers who use the High/Scope cognitive-oriented curriculum provide learning experiences that fit the students' current stages of development and foster development beyond that point. To do this, they prepare an environment and select or create activities that provide the children with the necessary experiences to progress through each stage. So that the instruction is responsive to the children's ideas, teachers must understand how the children in their class think and how they perceive the world. They must have a repertoire of activities that fit the students' development and must know how and when to use them.

For example, at certain developmental points, they need to provide activities that help young school children learn how to classify objects and grasp the idea of a series. When the students understand classification and series, they are better able to understand number concepts, and their teachers can proceed from this point. As they proceed, students learn a sense of time, cause and effect, spatial relationships, and, eventually, more abstract mental relationships.

Teacher guidance

The model requires teachers to assist and guide children in their learning; they do not simply tell or direct them. Teachers can guide young children by using concrete objects to help them understand new concepts and by questioning to help them understand relationships among items. Later, when the children are at the symbolic stage, the teacher can present more abstract concepts.

Learning environment and material

To teach according to the model's design, it is essential that the classroom be arranged so that the stage-appropriate learning experiences take place. Several learning centers and a wide variety of materials are necessary to achieve this. The materials and equipment can be ordinary items, but they must fit the different students' developmental stages. For instance, a teacher might take children on a scavenger hunt across the schoolyard to gather materials. In the process, the children would fill their bags with items they find along the way: seeds, gum wrappers, sucker sticks, paper clips, a leaf, a button, safety pins, stones. Back in the classroom, individual children could arrange or classify their findings into categories according to color, shape, or whatever. Then they could play What's My Set? In this game the children take turns guessing which characteristics the others used to classify their objects.[41]

Every day, children plan, execute their plans, and evaluate their performances. They know what to expect of time in school—a planning session, a work period in which to carry out the plans, a cleanup time when materials are returned to permanent storage areas, an evaluation period in which small groups of children discuss their accomplishments with teachers and aides, and an activity time during which the total group engages in some vigorous play.

More flexible in recent years

Over the years, the cognitive-oriented curriculum has moved considerably away from a tight teacher-planned structure and from teacher verbal dominance toward increased teacher reaction to student verbal cues. One observer has described the shift as a move from students responding to teachers, to teachers responding to students. Compared to the early years of the Perry Preschool Program, the curriculum involves less teacher verbal bombardment of students, less teacher pushing to accelerate students' cognitive development, and more initiation of classroom interactions by students.

Assessing the Effectiveness of the Model

The High/Scope cognitive-oriented curriculum is one of the most thoroughly evaluated models of instruction. Evaluation, however, has focused tightly on the model as it has been tested by its original developers and has been used under experimentally controlled conditions. Data on how successfully it has been used by schools and teachers in less controlled conditions and with limited training are less abundant.

Observation studies made by Jane Stallings during the evaluation of the Follow Through Planned Variation Project and reported in 1974 indicated that children in the High/Scope cognitive-oriented curriculum model classrooms use concrete objects in their learning activities more often than children in other educational models.[42] When working by themselves, children use objects such as weights, measures, and games to carry out their work plans.

That study also compared the effects of education models. Compared to children in classes in which a programmed-instruction model is used, children in the High/Scope model more frequently initiated conversations with adults, asked questions, and made statements to adults regarding their work.

Because of the precise nature of the model, some educators have asked about the extent to which teachers who are not directly associated with the Perry Preschool Program can implement the cognitive-oriented model satisfactorily. One study indicated that teachers trained in this program implemented it effectively in five Follow Through locations: Greenwood, Mississippi; Fort Walton Beach, Florida; New York City; Greeley, Colorado; and Denver, Colorado.[43]

Teachers' ability to use the model

A longitudinal study followed 128 children who participated in the Perry Preschool program.[44] By the mid-1980s, the generalization made about the academic achievement effects of the program was that the students who participated in the program were usually ahead of their primary-grade schoolmates initially, but the positive gains faded as they reached the end of first grade or during second grade.[45]

As recently as 1993, High/Scope reported data from the continuing longitudinal study of 123 of the former Perry Preschool students.[46] At that time, the former Perry students were about 27 years of age. The data indicate that, when compared with a control group, the former Perry students had (1) significantly higher monthly earnings, (2) a higher percentage of home ownership, (3) higher levels of schooling, (4) a lower percentage receiving social services over the prior ten years, and (5) fewer arrests.[47]

Throughout the three decades of the High/Scope longitudinal study, effects of participation in the preschool program have been reflected in higher scores on IQ tests, higher school achievement when the participants were tested at age 14, higher general literacy when tested at age 19, fewer assignments to special education classes, and more reporting of homework when assessed at age 15.[48]

Conclusions drawn from the longitudinal study as of 1993 include the following:[49]

- Participation in the Perry Preschool Program created a "framework" for adult success and alleviated at least some effects of the students' childhood poverty.

- Interventions in the school lives of program participants after they left Perry Preschool—such as remedial instruction, special education, and "criminal justice measures"—did not seem to improve the life course of the participants.
- Effects of the program were different for males and females when compared to the control group. Females were more likely to remain in school through high school and graduate; males were less likely to become involved in criminal and other antisocial behavior and more likely to assume greater social responsibility.
- The Perry Preschool experiences seemed to enable the participants to interact positively with other people and to handle social tasks that led to success in school and in the community.
- The costs of the program were outweighed by the economic benefits received by the participants over the three decades of the study.

What characteristics of the model would explain these findings? Given the impressive nature of 4-year-old children, it may be that a curriculum that requires children every day to (1) examine what they did yesterday, (2) decide what they plan to do today, (3) execute their plan, (4) evaluate their product, and (5) plan for tomorrow might well affect the ways in which students plan and face consequences for the rest of their lives.

More specifically, High/Scope officials believe that the Preschool Project features that bring about the positive results that accrue to its participants are[50]

- its active learning approach that encourages the children to initiate their own developmentally appropriate learning activities
- its parent involvement and outreach efforts to parents such as weekly home visits and parent group meetings
- the fact that the program reaches children at ages 3 and 4, just prior to their beginning school
- the fact that the program lasts for two school years, five days a week, with at least two and one-half hours of classroom time each day
- its low student-staff ratio
- its systematic staff training and close staff supervision

SNAPSHOT

The fourth Snapshot for this chapter describes classroom teaching that implements an approach to instruction called "whole language."[51] We refer to whole-language instruction as an *approach* rather than a model because there are different ways of implementing the whole-language philosophy and there is no set pattern of teaching it, as there is with the other four types of instruction described in this chapter. As you read the lesson description, consider the following questions:

- What lesson characteristics set whole-language instruction apart from other ways of teaching reading that you know about?

- Which theories of learning in Chapter 6 support this type of lesson?
- Which philosophies of education in Chapter 10 are consistent with this type of teaching?
- Which students might this lesson affect positively?
- Which students might this lesson affect negatively?
- What do you think about this lesson?

Whole-Language Instruction

Ms. Galloway teaches second grade in an inner-city public school. A typical morning in her classroom begins with a five- to ten-minute "town meeting."

Here she and students gather informally on a rug at the front of the room to allow them to share important events and observations that have occurred overnight. They also discuss class business and make plans for the day. Following this opening, she begins a two and one-half hour reading and writing workshop period, which on most days starts with "whole-class focus" time. While students are still gathered on the rug, Ms. Galloway presents a ten- to fifteen-minute mini-lesson to the entire class. These lessons always begin with a reading or writing experience selected to highlight the literacy strategy targeted for emphasis. Some days, she reads from children's literature or a student-composed piece and focuses discussion on particular strategies used by the student author to express meanings or on particular features of print. On other days, she composes a piece on the overhead, thinking aloud as she writes. Children offer suggestions for both content and strategies.

As the mini-lesson ends, Ms. Galloway offers a series of invitations for children's activities during "workshop" time. During this two and one-half hour block of time, children work independently, in small peer groups, and with the teacher to draft, revise, and edit either books, articles for the class newspaper, or reports of research on their personal inquiries. Some days children meet in literature discussion groups to talk about books related to class themes that they are reading together. Children know they can use this time for a variety of types of reading and writing, and they develop their own activities in response to invitations and suggestions from the teacher. Ms. Galloway, on the other hand, divides her time among several kinds of activities: circulating around the room for brief conferences that let her "take stock" of and provide support for the children and their work. As she does this, she participates as a member of the writing or reading discussion groups, presents small group lessons on skills needed by children as they read and write, or holds formal one-on-one conferences with students concerning their reading and writing. Observation of students is an important part of all these activities, and she typically records notes on dated sheets listing each child's name. It is these observations that she uses to guide her selection of topics for whole-class and small-group mini-lessons.

As the "workshop" portion of the class comes to a close, children gather again on the rug for "wrap-up and sharing." Some students have signed up to sit in the Author's Chair to read their recently completed pieces to the class and to receive peer comments and questions. There will also be an informal discussion of children's accomplishments for the morning. Some will be presented by the children themselves, and some by Ms. Galloway.

Though the language arts period ends, reading and writing will continue all day. For example, every day after lunch, Ms. Galloway reads children's literature to the class. Though she may later draw mini-lessons from these readings, at this time of the day the focus is on enjoyment and interpretation. In the afternoon, students will use reading and writing as they work on various content-area projects. This afternoon period is similar in structure to the morning workshop except that Ms. Galloway now focuses her attention on highlighting math skills and strategies and on helping students use both literacy and observation skills to pursue projects related to important math and content themes. Sometimes these themes are the same as those of the morning reading and writing time, and at the other times they differ. In either case, students read information and storybooks and write about the results of their projects.

Whole Language

Ms. Galloway, the classroom teacher in the Snapshot, uses a whole-language approach for her second-grade reading and writing instruction. She engages her students in reading and writing in her class even though the students are beginning readers and writers. She starts by discussing various literary works and the meanings that the students are able to draw from those works. Then, she uses student interest in the ideas they are discussing to teach them at least three things: (1) the content they are reading about, (2) how to read, and (3) how to write. For many observers, the whole-language approach to teaching reading seems to move in a reverse order

Meaning and understanding come first

from more traditional methods. Students do not learn the mechanics of reading and practice reading skills first, with meaning and understanding deferred until the mechanics and skills are firmly in grasp. Instead, they read, discuss, and write about meaningful topics and *in the process* learn to read and write. In short, they learn to read by reading and learn to write by writing.

Whole-language teachers focus on the meaning that students find in what they read and write by having them read selected pieces of literature as their reading text. When they follow the reading by asking the students to discuss what they've read, the students actually supply their own meaning. Student-supplied meaning comes from the students' ideas, which are based not only on what the students think of the author's intention, but also on the experiences and interests that the students bring to their reading. Because the meaning is supplied by the students, it is at their ability level. In the process of reading, discussing, and writing about what the literature means to them, the students develop their ideas and skills. At first, the reading and writing are unconventional (they don't follow standard language rules), but the students know in their own ways what they are reading and writing about. With practice and teacher guidance, their reading and writing "gets better" or becomes more conventional.

At student levels of understanding

The whole-language approach was not originally developed by university researchers as a "model of instruction"; instead, it evolved from teacher use in classrooms. As a result, it does not have a precise set of classroom activities for teachers and students to follow—at least, not in a way similar to the three approaches to instruction already described in this chapter.[52] Instead, it is a combination of beliefs about learning, teaching, curriculum, and the nature of teacher-student relationships.[53] It also has more than one agreed-upon set of definitions and styles of implementation. Whole-language classrooms reflect the variations of teacher experiences and classroom settings. Because the approach is more philosophical and theory-based, rather than activity-based, it has been adapted by teachers for working with every age level from preschoolers to adult learners.

Not a precise model

The whole-language approach evolved in the United States in the mid-1970s as a grass roots movement among teachers who rejected behaviorist views of learning and sought to apply sociopsycholinguistic, cognitive, and sociocultural theories of learning to their reading and writing instruction.[54] The first of these perspectives, *sociopsycholinguistics*, considers how learners construct hypotheses about language as they interact with others. The second, *cognitive psychology*, concerns itself with the mental acts individual learners perform in an attempt to understand and produce language. The third perspective, *sociocultural theories*, focuses on the ways socially and culturally rooted actions influence both the ways children understand language and the meanings they form.

Grass roots movement

The whole-language approach has been widely used and adopted by state, provincial, and national educational agencies in a number of other English-speaking countries, including New Zealand, Australia, England, and Canada for at least three decades. Though the early emphasis of this approach was almost entirely on reading and writing instruction, whole-language educators currently apply their theoretical beliefs across curricular areas, often integrating literacy instruction into other subject areas through thematic units and student-directed inquiry projects. Table 14-4 summarizes the goals and characteristics of the whole-language approach.

TABLE 14-4   Goals and Characteristics of the Whole-Language Approach to Instruction

Primary Goals	Characteristics
Students learn to read by reading	Authentic, whole texts
Students learn to write by writing	Purposeful literacy activities
Students use reading and writing for personally meaningful purposes	Focus on meaning
	Immersion in literate environment
Students use reading and writing to learn about content areas	Integration of reading, writing, speaking, and listening
Students develop social collaboration among students and teachers	Integration of literacy instruction across curriculum areas
	Thematic instruction
	Use literacy for inquiry
	Learner-directed inquiry
	Learner-selected activities
	Social interaction
	Intense teacher observation of students

Educational Theory behind the Approach

Whole-language instruction has two major theoretical roots. First, it is based on a *transactional theory* of reading and writing.[55] That theory looks upon both reading and writing as "transactions" between the students doing the reading and writing and the ideas they are reading and writing about. According to this theory, as students read, they learn the meaning of the material they read by understanding that text in relation to their personal experiences, interests, and abilities. Thus, reading is more than the passing of information from author to reader. It also involves student construction of new meanings and interpretations as they interact with the reading. In short, students help bring meaning to their reading; they do not simply read to find out what the author intended. (The concept of *constructivism* as described in Chapter 6 helps explain this further.)

Reading as transactions

A second theoretical underpinning of this approach is the *sociopsycholinguistic perspective* on literacy learning mentioned earlier. Research in this area has highlighted similarities in the ways children learn oral and written language. Key ideas are that children learn about language by inventing and trying out hypotheses about its (1) *form* (the way words are put together to form sentences), (2) *function* (the purposes for which talk and writing are used), and (3) *meaning* (the ideas that speakers and writers express) in order to communicate and get things done in everyday activities. For example, in this kind of informal learning, *form follows function*. That is to say, long before children use adult forms of grammar or spelling, they are able to express their meanings and to get things done through childlike talk (Me goed!) and writing. For example, they might write the following: *WWG to the rit Mos i W*

A sociopsycholinguistic perspective

to go $L Sor to mean *When we go to the right mall, I want to go to "It's a Dollar" store.* The children's early attempts at talking and writing are characteristically unconventional, or childlike. However, over time, the students form more conventional hypotheses about language forms because of their desire to communicate more effectively. As this happens, the children learn language from "the whole" to "the parts." That is, in their attempts to communicate whole meanings, they form increasingly more fine-grained hypotheses about how the parts of language, such as letters, words, sentences, and so on, are put together to express those meanings. In other words, the children learn to read and write using reading and writing to communicate. While doing so, they are motivated and have the opportunity to observe language closely enough to construct more and more sophisticated hypotheses about language. Unconventional reading and writing—including errors—is a necessary part of literacy learning and needs to be valued as part of the constructive nature of literacy learning.

The learning environment

Research suggests that this kind of active language learning is encouraged by a learning environment in which children are surrounded by talk and print; where whole, natural language is used in familiar, purposeful situations; where they have many opportunities to observe more experienced language users (such as older students and adults) talking and writing; and where they have opportunities to participate as talkers and writers with peers and adults who know them well.[56] Thus, oral and written language learning are both viewed as having social and cognitive components. Language learning occurs *socially* as children interact with parents, siblings, peers, and others; and it occurs *cognitively* as individual children construct hypotheses about *what* can be said, *how* to say it in talk or writing, and *why* one might say it. The whole-language view concerning the cognitive components of literacy learning is further supported by the constructivist notions of cognitive psychologists such as Jean Piaget, while the social learning theories of Lev Vygotsky provide support for the role of social interaction in the construction of culturally based meanings and language strategies.[57]

The Approach in Practice

As mentioned earlier, whole language is defined not by a set of activities, but by a set of related beliefs about teaching, learning, curriculum, and social relationships within the classroom. There are, however, some commonly agreed-upon characteristics of whole-language instruction.

Authentic texts

In whole-language classrooms, teachers use authentic texts of a variety of sorts (for example, signs, notes, charts, children's literature) because of their belief that whole, meaningful texts support students' literacy learning. The primary focus of classroom literacy experiences remains on meaning, with literacy skills and strategies taught in context as students need them to construct these meanings. A key concern of teachers is that students find reading and writing to be personally useful, relevant, and meaningful. Whole-language teachers attempt to provide opportunities for students to use literacy in ways similar to those used by readers and writers outside of school. For example, a number of teachers structure writing experiences so that children engage in many of the same kinds of activities as publishing writers. This might occur as students engage in an "authoring cycle," which includes exploration of writing topics, drafting, conferencing with peers and teachers, self-editing, revising, editing by outside editors, and publishing.[58] This focus on literacy-in-use has led many whole-language teachers to integrate literacy experiences and instruc-

Student-constructed meaning

The whole-language approach calls for creating a supportive learning community filled with opportunities for reading, writing, discussion, and learning from peers as well as from the teacher.

tion across curricular areas through thematic units. When this is done, students are taught to use literacy to read about, learn about, and write about math, science, history, literature, and so on. Many whole-language teachers also invite students to use other communication systems, such as math, art, and drama, to develop and present personal inquiry projects. Such projects might include writing and producing plays or three-dimensional displays depicting the history and customs of other cultures.

Though whole-language teaching occurs in widely varying settings, teachers at all grade levels are concerned about immersing students in a literate environment, promoting social interaction, and developing a supportive learning community. Learners need many and repeated opportunities to observe demonstrations of literacy at work in a variety of situations. If they are to form more sophisticated hypotheses about literacy, they need to have opportunities to observe the ways peers and teachers apply literacy and to have continued access to the published writing of both peers and professional authors. To accomplish these goals, whole-language classrooms are filled with print and with opportunities for reading, writing, and researching. Teachers promote interaction among learners during reading and writing. Students work in pairs or small groups to discuss interpretations of their reading and to provide feedback to one another on their writing. Teachers also provide demonstrations by reading and writing with the students. Given the theory of literacy learning described above, it is important that these social interactions promote a climate of collaboration in which students are encouraged to learn from one another, to develop a shared understanding of the varying experiences and perspectives of class members, and to take the risk of discussing their initial guesses and responses to questions that arise. The classroom must also support students' efforts

Variety of settings

Interaction among learners

to put their ideas in writing even though their first drafts may not be entirely correct in spelling, grammar, and so on.

Various strategies

Because the kinds of literacy strategies needed by learners varies according to their current hypotheses about literacy and the demands of the particular reading or writing situation, the types of lessons teachers plan and the sequence in which teachers introduce reading and writing strategies and skills also varies from class to class and child to child. Frequently teachers use a piece of the children's writing or a published text they are reading as the context for presenting a mini-lesson on a literacy skill to individuals, small groups, or the whole class. For example, teachers may draw attention to the way an author grabs the reader's attention with the lead paragraph of a book or the way descriptive words are used to build a rich image of a setting or character. Teachers also provide individual instruction, feedback, and suggestions in one-on-one reading and writing conferences with students. Groupings of children for mini-lessons are flexible and change frequently. Teachers use anecdotal observations and student reading and writing portfolios as a means of tracking student progress and determining which students will benefit from a particular lesson.

Student ownership of learning

Overall, teachers arrange the environment, monitor the development of understanding and skills, provide relevant materials, demonstrate literacy-in-use, conduct diagnostic mini-lessons, and invite learners to participate in and plan literacy events. Students take ownership of their own learning because they need and want to use reading and writing to communicate.

Assessing the Effectiveness of the Approach

Because of variation in definitions of whole-language instruction and because the approach is implemented across a wide range of age levels and with a wide range of classroom practices, assessment of the effectiveness of the approach has been difficult. Two general types of research have been conducted with mixed results. The first type of study compares student reading performance in whole-language classrooms with performance in classrooms emphasizing direct instruction in decoding skills.[59] Most of this research has been conducted with beginning readers in the primary grades. There is currently considerable debate about the general conclusions that should be drawn from this body of research. For example, Steven A. Stahl and Patricia D. Miller (1989) conducted a statistical meta-analysis of 45 quantitative studies comparing the reading achievement of whole-language or Language Experience Approach classrooms to students enrolled in classrooms using basal reader approaches.[60] Of the comparisons between the whole language and basal reader approaches, 22 percent favored whole-language approaches, 12 percent favored basal reading programs, and 66 percent showed no significant differences between the approaches. These authors interpret their findings as suggesting that, overall, the two approaches produce approximately equal outcomes on reading instruction. Additional analyses led them to suggest that whole-language instruction was more effective than basal reader approaches in kindergarten, but for first grade the approaches were more equal. These authors also conclude that in the twelve relevant studies analyzed, basal reader approaches were more effective with populations of disadvantaged students and students of lower socioeconomic status. Stahl and Miller note several limitations of their work, including its focus on primary-grade children and the fact that effects on writing were not studied and that studies using ethnographic research methods were not included.

Approximately equal outcomes on decoding skills

Although other researchers have agreed with the conclusions drawn in the Stahl and Miller study,[61] a number of other writers have challenged the validity of some aspects of the Stahl and Miller interpretations.[62] This second group of researchers argues that the effectiveness of whole-language instruction cannot be fairly evaluated using only standardized measures of reading achievement because these tests tend to measure students' abilities to complete skill exercises such as marking long and short vowels or identifying the main idea of a paragraph, rather than their ability to use these skills in the course of purposeful reading. They also note that the wide variety of teaching practices labeled as whole language make a clear understanding of differential effects problematic.

A second approach to evaluating the effectiveness of whole-language instruction is descriptive ethnography. Studies of this type provide in-depth descriptions and theoretical explanations for children's literacy learning activities in whole-language classrooms. Frequently these studies use interviews and observations to tap students' reading and writing strategies and their views of themselves as readers. Two such studies found similar results in that primary-grade children in whole-language classrooms had a greater repertoire of reading strategies for dealing with problems in decoding words, felt better about themselves as readers, focused more on meaning and the purposeful nature of written language, and were more independent in both reading and writing.[63] On standardized reading test scores, one of these studies found no significant differences between the whole-language students and a matched group who had received basal reader instruction.[64]

Greater repertoire of reading strategies

As this brief review suggests, children are learning to read and write with the whole-language approach. However, the mixed results of existing experimental research that compares the whole-language approach to others (usually direct instruction in decoding skills) fails to provide clear evidence as to which approach produces better outcomes in reading. Results of ethnographic and descriptive studies suggest that primary-grade students in whole-language classes do, indeed, learn what teachers teach. That is, whole-language students' reading and writing strategies, beliefs about reading and writing, and approaches to solving problems reflect the emphases of whole-language classrooms. By far the most important outcome of this line of research is to show the limitations of current assessments of whole-language instruction. It appears that general questions about the effectiveness of whole-language approaches need to be rephrased as more specific questions about the effectiveness of the various approaches in helping children learn a variety of specific kinds of literacy attitudes, strategies, and functions. Additionally, future research must address a wider age range of students.

More research needed

SNAPSHOT

A fifth model of instruction is technology-based anchored instruction.[65] As you read the lesson description in this Snapshot, consider the following questions:

■ What are the essential elements of the lesson, including how the lesson is "anchored"?

■ Which theories of learning described in Chapter 6 support this type of lesson?

■ How does this type of lesson fit with the ideas about the *information highway* reported in the Educational Research section of Chapter 12?

■ Which students might this lesson affect positively?

- Which students might this lesson affect negatively?
- What do you think about this lesson?

Technology-Based Anchored Instruction

Situation: A sixth-grade math class is working on an episode from the videodisc-based mathematical problem-solving series, *The Adventures of Jasper Woodbury*. The episode, titled *The Big Splash*, challenges students to help the main character, Chris, develop a business plan that he can present to the principal of his school. All of the information students need to develop this plan is contained in the video.

Synopsis of *The Big Splash*: Chris's school is having a Fun Fair to raise money to buy a new camera for the school TV station. Chris wants to set up a dunking booth at the fair. Students would buy tickets for the opportunity to try to dunk their teachers in a pool of water. Chris needs to develop a business plan to get his dunking booth project approved by the school and to obtain a loan from the school principal. The plan must include an estimate of revenue and expenses for the dunking booth and must meet several constraints set by the principal with respect to the maximum amount of the loan and the requisite profit.

The video shows Chris collecting information that he will later use to develop his plan. Chris's goal—the goal that students viewing the video are going to help him achieve—is to develop the best plan for the dunking booth. Many different plans can be generated based on the information presented. For example, there are different options for deciding how to fill the dunking booth with water. Each option differs in terms of cost, risk, and the amount of time it takes.

The business plan challenge also involves some important statistical concepts. Chris conducts a survey to collect information on whether students at his school would be interested in dunking a teacher and how much they would pay to do so. Data from the survey can be used by students to extrapolate an estimate of revenue for the whole school.

Day 1

TEACHER: "You have seen *The Big Splash*, so you now know that your challenge is to help Chris develop a business plan for the dunking booth that he can present to his principal. We will spend the next two weeks working in small groups. Each group's task will be to come up with what they believe to be the best plan and to prepare a presentation on the plan that they will deliver to the rest of the class. You will begin by working on the expenses part of your plan."

"I do not expect that you will be able to remember all of the information that is shown in the video. You may need to refer back to it to find or verify information. This can be done very easily because the information is on videodisc. On a videodisc, every part of the video has a unique number. These are called frame numbers. We can search for and then play any part of the movie by simply entering its frame number on this remote control device. And it is very fast, too. It takes less than two seconds for the videodisc player to find a segment of video after you have entered its frame number."

"I have a list of the frame numbers for the major scenes in the episode. I will place the list next to the videodisc player so that you can refer to it when you are accessing information. You may use the videodisc player whenever you need to; but to avoid overcrowding at the player, only one member from each group may go the player at a time."

Later in the Lesson

WENDY: "Okay, so where do we start?"

KEISHA: "We need to start with how much money everything will cost."

AMANDA: "The dunking machine costs twenty-five dollars per day."

WENDY: "But the Fire Chief said that he'd give it to Chris for free, didn't he?"

AMANDA: "No, that was the water."

KEISHA: "Well, I'll go check the video, just to be sure."

(Keisha searches the movie to verify information.)

KEISHA: "It's twenty-five dollars a day."

WENDY: "Okay. Chris is only going to have to rent the machine for a day, so it'll cost him twenty-five dollars."

KEISHA: "So what else would he have to pay for?"

WENDY: "And the fee per load of water from the pool store is fifteen dollars."

AMANDA: "But if they got the water from the Fire Department it would be free."

WENDY: "Yeah, but if the firefighters were out on a call, they couldn't pump it in for Chris."

AMANDA: "The Fun Fair is on Friday at ten. Well, the firefighters said that they could be there at eight-thirty. So how long would it take to fill the pool?"

KEISHA: "The movie said that it pumps a thousand gallons per minute."

WENDY: "Let's try to figure out what it would cost to get the water from someone else, in case we couldn't get it from the fire people."

KEISHA: "Okay, the total amount of water that the pool can hold is twenty-five hundred gallons. Okay, the pool store truck can hold fifteen hundred gallons."

AMANDA: "They'd have to drive back and fill it up again."

WENDY: "We've got to figure out how many miles it takes to get from the pool store to the school 'cause there's a mileage charge for hauling water. And then it takes twenty minutes to drive from the pool store to the school and fifteen minutes to pump the water out. Are we going to have enough time to fill the pool before the fair starts?"

Technology-Based Anchored Instruction

The preceding interactions occurred in a mathematics classroom in which the teacher was using anchored instruction (AI), a technology-based course of study developed by the Cognition and Technology Group at Vanderbilt, an education research team at the Learning Technology Center, Peabody College, Vanderbilt University.[66] A primary goal of AI is to use technology to create meaningful and challenging *contexts* for learning. These contexts are intended to support a particular type of learning experience for the student and, consequently, are associated with a particular type of pedagogy. In this section, we describe features of these technology-based learning environments; in later sections we describe the pedagogy and its underlying theory.

Contexts for learning

Although the learning contexts, or *anchors*, are technology-based, the fact that they are technology-based is important only insofar as the technology can be used to create a particular type of learning environment. Effective anchors could be created without the use of technology. For example, a class could develop its own plan to raise money for a school, and that plan would involve a complex and relatively ill-defined problem from everyday life. The plan would constitute the anchor for the group's problem-solving task. However, the developers of AI suggest that interactive video is an easy-to-use and effective medium for these purposes. Many of the goals of AI would be difficult to accomplish if the anchors did not involve technology. Because developing anchors from scratch is time-consuming, teachers find technology-based anchors easier to use and less likely to present unanticipated problems. They also serve as examples for teachers who do develop their own anchors.

Anchors

The technological anchors have several key characteristics. First, in contrast to many educational videos, they are not lectures on tape. The anchors are short movies that *tell a story* and, at the end of each story, *pose a problem*. The information needed to solve the problem has been embedded in the story; however, as students watch the video for the first time, they are not aware of its significance. The information is merely "part of the story."

For example, *The Big Splash* tells the story of Chris trying to realize his goal of having a dunking booth at the fair. He is shown collecting information that will be used to develop a business plan. Students see him taking a survey and summarizing the data. This information is relevant to the problem, which the students will later solve, of estimating revenue for the dunking booth. However, at the time of their first viewing, the students do not know that this is the problem they will have to solve. Furthermore, the story never tells the students that the survey results can be used to estimate revenue from the whole school or how to use the survey results in this way. In essence, the anchors serve as contexts for problem solving rather than explanations of how to solve problems.

Complex problems

Another key characteristic of anchors is that they are *very complex*, and it is this characteristic that sets AI apart from other problem-based approaches to learning. In most mathematics classrooms, for example, story problems are a basic part of the curriculum.[67] But the problems are typically very simple. They usually involve one or, occasionally, two mathematical operations. Furthermore, story problems are well-formulated in the sense that their goals (that is, what is to be solved) are explicitly stated and—in most cases—only numbers relevant to their solutions are given. This means that the only challenge for students is to decide on a mathematical operation. Often, even this challenge is trivialized because students come to realize that the problems can be solved by applying the mathematical operation that is the focus of the chapter in which the problems appear.

In contrast to these typical mathematical story problems, solving the problems used in AI requires many steps, and the tasks students need to undertake are ill defined in the sense that only general problem-solving goals are stated. In *The Big Splash*, the stated goal is to develop a business plan. But, to accomplish this, the students must formulate subgoals for themselves, and frequently they discover how to do this only in the course of problem solving. For example, in the conversation between Wendy, Amanda, and Keisha described in the Snapshot, the subgoal of determining whether there is enough time on the day of the Fun Fair to execute a given plan for filling the pool is one that they formulate in the process of deciding what the expenses will be for filling the pool. These ill-defined problems are designed to be similar to problems in the real world. Like problems in the real world, it is not usually clear what data are relevant for solving these problems, and multiple solutions are often possible.

Real-world problems

Because the anchors are designed to be like real-world problems, the skills needed to solve them are often interdisciplinary. For example, in several of the episodes from *The Adventures of Jasper Woodbury*, students need relatively sophisticated map reading skills as well as geometry skills. The map skills are usually taught in social studies rather than mathematics classes. As a consequence of this design feature of the anchors, they have been used to integrate instruction across domains. The social studies and mathematics teacher may coordinate their lessons around an anchor or may even team teach an episode. Table 14-5 summarizes the goals and characteristics of technology-based anchored instruction.

Educational Theory behind the Model

Inert knowledge

Many years ago, Alfred Whitehead identified a major problem in schools, the problem of *inert knowledge*.[68] He explained that when a student learns something in one context, but fails to retrieve that knowledge later to solve problems, the knowledge is inert. In other words, it is knowledge that is available in students' heads for retrieval (that is, it has not been forgotten), but the students do not access it when relevant. Whitehead argued that schools were especially adept at creating inert knowledge in students but not at teaching students to apply that knowledge.

The developers of technology-based anchored instruction, the Cognition and Technology Group at Vanderbilt, suggest that one factor contributing to the problem of inert knowledge is that traditional school tasks often consist of drill and practice on isolated skills and procedures (for example, practicing multicolumn addition or multiplication).[69] Students are not provided with opportunities to practice applying these skills to real problems, and so they do not learn *when* or *how* to use them. Their knowledge is not "tagged" in memory, so to speak, with information about the conditions under which to apply it. For example, many students who possess the

TABLE 14-5   Goals and Characteristics of Technology-Based Anchored Instruction

Primary Goals	Characteristics
Improved conceptual understanding and transfer of information learned	Use of technology-based anchors that reflect real-world problems
	Emphasis on collaborative learning
Improved skill at defining and formulating problems	Emphasis on explanation, reasoning, and effective communication of ideas
Improved discussion skills	Emphasis on peer-to-peer communication
Development as an independent learner	Extended work on complex problems that have multiple solutions and require formulation
Positive attitudes toward challenging problems	Interdisciplinary anchors
	Change in teacher's role away from that of "dispenser of knowledge"
	Students assume greater intellectual autonomy

requisite mathematical skills still experience difficulty solving *The Big Splash*. It is likely that their difficulties may be attributable to their not having sufficient experience in using mathematics in the context of solving real problems.

Proponents of AI suggest that solving problems like *The Big Splash* helps students learn when and how to apply mathematics. They also argue that these experiences deepen students' *understanding* of the mathematical concepts themselves. An unfortunate consequence of isolated skills practice is that the skills often lack meaning for students. Students "learn" by memorizing a fact or procedure. Nevertheless, they may not "understand" the information.[70] In mathematics, students may have learned operations or procedures for manipulating number symbols, but have not developed an understanding of these procedures.[71] For example, when students first start working on problems like *The Big Splash*, they often remark to their teachers that they know what problem they want to solve, but they do not "know whether to add, subtract, multiply, or divide." Over time, students learn to represent the problems in ways that link them with mathematical procedures. For example, in *The Big Splash*, students need to determine how long it will take to fill a 2,500-gallon pool using a hose that pumps water at a rate of 1,000-gallons per minute. By encouraging students to reason about the situation in concrete terms, that is, how many gallons would be in the pool after one minute, after two minutes, and so forth, many students come to understand the mathematical operation in a more meaningful way.

The importance of understanding

Another aspect of AI that is intended to foster learning is that the anchors are specially designed in ways that help students take an *active role* in the learning process. If used in particular ways, video anchors will engage students in productive activities such as defining, formulating, and solving problems. By virtue of this characteristic, AI is consistent with a class of instructional theories known as *constructivist* theories.[72] These theories reject the idea that students learn by passively "soaking up" knowledge that is transmitted to them by teachers or others. Instead they assume that the more active or intent an individual is in trying to understand and explain new information in relation to what he or she already knows, the deeper the

Active learning

In constructivist approaches like technology-based anchored instruction, the teacher's role changes from that of an all-knowing dispenser of information to that of a coach who facilitates students' own construction of meaning. Which kind of teacher appeals to you more—a "sage on the stage" or a "guide on the side"?

learning. From this perspective, students learn more deeply if the teacher engages them in activities such as defining problems, clarifying misunderstandings, generating solutions, and so forth—instead of lecturing or "telling" students the answers.

Constructivist approaches such as AI involve a change in the traditional role of the teacher. The teacher's role moves away from that of "the expert who dispenses knowledge" and toward one in which the teacher acts as a "guide" or "coach." Students are expected to assume responsibility for constructing meaning and making sense of information.

The Model in Practice

The Adventures of Jasper Woodbury Problem Solving Series is being used in classrooms throughout the United States. The classrooms in which it is used are equipped with a videodisc player and a monitor. The videodisc is controlled using either a hand-held remote controller or specially designed computer software. Although *Jasper* involves the use of video materials and a particular pedagogical approach, teachers have a great deal of latitude in how they implement it in their own instruction. The following passage describes a typical instructional sequence:

> During the first session, the teacher shows the episode and teaches students how to use the remote control. The remaining class periods are devoted to problem solving. The task for students is to solve the challenge posed in the video and to develop a presentation on the results of their problem solving. Most teachers will ask students to report to the class on their problem-solving progress from time to time. This gives important information to both the teacher and other students. Because there are multiple solutions to each challenge, presentations give students new ideas to consider. They also give teachers information that they can use to guide the course of their instruction. For

example, the teacher may determine that enough students are having difficulty with a particular mathematical concept that a large group discussion is warranted.

Many teachers divide students into cooperative learning groups to work on the problem. Because of the complexity of the problems, the materials are effective for use in small groups. It is effective to have input from a number of students when they are brainstorming a plan for solving the problem. Furthermore, there is too much information in each video for any one individual to remember after a single viewing, so it is helpful to have input from several group members.

Depending on what the teacher perceives to be the skill level of the class, he or she might structure the small group work in different ways. If, for example, the class is relatively skilled, the teacher may impose very little structure. The teacher might simply ask students to solve the challenge posed at the end of the video. For other classes using *The Big Splash*, the teacher may ask groups to work first on expenses or may even focus the task more by asking groups to brainstorm ideas for ways to fill the pool with water. One approach that would not be consistent with AI would be for the teacher to tell students the various methods for filling the pool or to tell them the steps to follow in order to determine expenses (for example, find out the cost of renting the dunking machine, then find out the cost of renting the pool, and so forth). A goal of AI is to provide students with opportunities to define and formulate problems for themselves.

The role of the teacher

Two important aspects of AI relate to how teachers mediate group problem solving, and how they conduct the large group discussion that follows the group work.[73] Because a goal of AI is to have students assume responsibility for their learning, it is important that the teacher interact with students in ways that encourage them to explain their thinking and that promote interactions among peers. In other words, the shift in the teacher's role is away from that of the intellectual authority. Initially, this may be difficult for students, as well as teachers. In typical class situations, students are used to looking to the teacher to say whether something is correct or not, and they are not accustomed to having to explain their thinking to the satisfaction of their peers. Following is an excerpt from a teacher's interaction with a small group that illustrates how an AI teacher might facilitate the process:[74]

TEACHER:　*(Scans what students have written in their notebooks)*
"Darrius has something different written on his paper from the rest of you."

DARRIUS TO TEACHER: "I think that Chris will make two hundred and seventy dollars from the dunking booth."

TEACHER TO DARRIUS: "Darrius, don't tell me. Explain your thinking to the rest of your group. To work well as a group each one of you needs to understand what the others are thinking and work as a group to come to an agreement on the best way to solve the problem."

DARRIUS TO GROUP: "I think that Chris will make two hundred and seventy dollars from the dunking booth."

TEACHER TO KELLY: "Do you understand how Darrius got his estimate of revenue?"

KELLY: "No."

TEACHER: "Well, ask Darrius to explain how he got his answer."

(Darrius explains his thinking and the group looks to the teacher for confirmation)

TEACHER: "Joyce, do you think Darrius's reasoning is sound? If not, tell him why."

Whenever possible, AI teachers try to get students to evaluate whether an answer is reasonable by encouraging them to explain and discuss the answer with one another. Similar techniques are appropriate in leading large group discussions as well. The teacher's role is to elicit explanations from students, to point out when there is a disagreement, and to encourage students to try to reach some consensus. But what if the class or group reaches consensus, but the answer is wrong? In these situations, teachers indicate to students that they disagree and will suggest some new direction to explore in thinking about the problem. They will try to avoid being the source of the correct answer.

Some educators who have studied AI ask about its relationship to more basic instruction in mathematics skills. Proponents of AI believe that basic skills instruction is important and that students need to be able to execute basic mathematical procedures in a fluent manner.[75] They suggest, however, that basic skills instruction is more motivating and meaningful to students when it is conducted in the context of an anchor. For example, if the teacher's goal is to teach decimals to students, the teacher might select an anchor that involves use of decimals. The teacher might do some direct instruction on decimals in the context of solving the anchor. In this way, students may understand that the skill is a tool that can be used to solve a problem that they are invested in solving.

Similarly, if, in the course of working on an anchor, the teacher ascertains that several or all of the students need practice on a particular mathematical operation, the teacher will prescribe some drill and practice.

Assessing the Effectiveness of the Model

Anchored instruction is a relatively new approach to instruction, and most of the research on it has been conducted by its developers in mathematics at the middle school level. However, recently researchers have been exploring its applications in preservice teacher education programs and in teaching literacy skills to young children.[76]

One of the largest-scale studies on AI involved a field implementation of four episodes from *The Adventures of Jasper Woodbury*.[77] These anchors were used over the course of a school year by teachers in seventeen classes in seven states in the Southeast. In three-fourths of the classes, the *Jasper* instruction took the place of the students' regular mathematics instruction. In addition to these classes, the researchers recruited ten comparison classes that were matched on key student demographic variables, including socioeconomic status, location, gender, minority representation, and achievement (standardized mathematics scores). Comparison students did not receive instruction on *Jasper*. Both *Jasper* and the comparison students were administered a series of tests at the beginning and again at the end of the school year that were designed to assess the effects of the special instruction. One test examined students' skills at solving word problems. (This is the typical way in which students' problem-solving skills are taught and assessed in school.) In spite of the fact that *Jasper* students had not received additional practice on written word problems and, in actual fact, may have had less practice on these problems because of time spent on *Jasper*, they performed significantly better than the comparison students at the end of the year. Apparently *Jasper* students were able to transfer the skills they had acquired in the context of solving *Jasper* problems to written problems.

Students were also administered a series of tests designed to assess their abilities

Assessing word-problem skills

to define and formulate problems. They were given complex story problems in written form and were asked to identify goals that would need to be addressed to solve these problems. They were also shown mathematical formulations and were asked to identify the goal that each formula would satisfy. As noted earlier, these aspects of problem solving are unique to the *Jasper* anchors and are not part of traditional mathematical problem-solving instruction. As expected, *Jasper* students performed better than comparison students on the post-test.

The researchers also collected standardized mathematics achievement data from all seventeen sites because they were concerned that—having had less instruction in the basic curriculum—*Jasper* students might show a drop in achievement scores. These data were difficult to analyze because different states use different tests; however, the researchers examined the data on a class-by-class basis. For each class, they looked at achievement at the end of the school year before *Jasper* was implemented and compared it to achievement at the end of the school year during which *Jasper* was implemented. More of the *Jasper* classes showed an increase or no change in their scores.

Basic mathematics achievement

Finally, the researchers collected self-report measures of students' attitudes. *Jasper* students showed more desirable change relative to comparison students in five areas across the school year. *Jasper* students showed a reduction in math anxiety and increases in their beliefs about their ability to perform successfully in math. In addition, *Jasper* students were more interested in mathematics and more interested in solving complex problems than were comparison students. Finally, students were asked to rate how useful they thought mathematics was. *Jasper* students thought mathematics was more useful in solving problems that occurred outside of mathematics class than did comparison students.

Student attitudes

Although this study showed some positive changes in performance and attitudes, it is difficult, given the design of the study, to attribute the effects to the materials alone. The teachers who implemented AI were a select group of practitioners. The success of the program may depend on the skill of these teachers and, if these teachers had been the ones teaching the comparison students, their students might have performed at the level of the *Jasper* students. These issues need to be pursued in future research.

The results of field implementation of *Jasper* suggest that AI can have positive effects on student learning when it is compared with the traditional curriculum. But what about AI relative to other types of special instruction on mathematical problem solving? The Cognition and Technology Group at Vanderbilt has explored this question in two studies and has found similar patterns of results in both.[78] In these studies, the researchers compared two groups of sixth-grade students. One group received five hours of intensive instruction on how to solve word problems, including instruction on special strategies to use to solve these problems. A second group received five hours of AI from one of the episodes from *The Adventures of Jasper Woodbury*. The mathematical content taught to both groups was matched; both groups worked on rate, distance, and time problems. After the instruction, students received a written word-problem test, and a new *Jasper*-like anchor on video. In two separate studies, both groups performed equally well on word problems, but the *Jasper*-instructed students performed much better in complex problem-solving situations. The results suggest that there is value added for AI.

Research on AI is in its early stages, but the data collected thus far have been positive. Important questions that need to be addressed relate to the long-term and cumulative effects of the instruction. Also questions about the professional devel-

A variable to be studied—teacher skills

opment of teachers need to be explored. Thus far, AI has been studied with a small number of teachers who were specially trained in the use of the technology and pedagogy. The Cognition and Technology Group at Vanderbilt is currently investigating ways to facilitate professional development on a larger scale.

Other Models of Instruction

There are, of course, many models of instruction other than the five described in this chapter, and many of those models overlap. A valuable description of a number of other models is provided in *Models of Teaching* (4th ed.) by Bruce Joyce, Marsha Weil, and Beverly Showers (1992).[79] Those authors divide models into four "families," shown in Table 14-6.

TABLE 14-6   Models of Teaching—Four Families

Model	Primary Thrust
The social family	Models of this type fit learning to the students' nature as social creatures and expand their ability to relate appropriately to one another.
Partners in learning	To teach problem solving through cooperative learning and interaction
Role playing	To teach the study of values, social skills, and cooperative behavior
Jurisprudential inquiry	To teach clarification of values and conflict resolution
Adapting to individual differences	To teach cognitive and social tasks that fit the students' developmental stages
The information-processing family	Models of this type teach students to collect and organize information, to build and test hypotheses, and to form concepts.
Thinking inductively	To teach concept formation, development of generalizations and hypotheses, and inferences about causes
Attaining concepts	To teach concepts and how to form and use intellectual categories in thinking
Memorization	To teach mastery of information and the ability to generate mnemonics and facilitate mental associations
Learning from presentations	To teach students through structured courses and presentations
Inquiry training	To teach collecting and verifying information, developing concepts, and building and testing hypotheses
Synetics	To teach creative thinking particularly through participation in groups
The developing intellect	To teach according to stages of intellectual growth and to accelerate rates of development
The personal family	Models of this type focus on the development of students into thinking, feeling people.
Nondirective teaching	To teach self-understanding, personal-goal clarification, and acceptance of responsibility
Concepts of self	To teach self-growth and self-actualization
The behavioral systems family	Models of this type rely on students' tendency to modify their behavior in response to feedback.
Mastery learning, direct instruction, social learning theory	To teach through relatively small self-pacing, sequenced modules
Learning self-control	To teach appropriate behavior management and self-control
Learning through simulation	To teach through games and simulations that provide feedback about performance
Conditions of learning	To teach through an organized sequence of learning objectives and goals

Conclusion

The criteria used to select the five models of instruction presented here have been noted, along with the fact that the selection of these models does not imply that they are the best or that they are representative of models of instruction in general. They are simply five examples.

The objectives for the chapter are to (1) acquaint you with several models of instruction, (2) demonstrate for you the relationships between educational practice as reflected in these models and theories of child development, learning, philosophy, and views of content, (3) foster an understanding of the relationships between classroom practice and all the elements and factors teachers need to consider in their teaching, and (4) encourage you to reflect upon the concept of *the act of teaching* as it is illustrated in these models.

Summary

Models of instruction are designs or plans for teaching; they are based on particular assumptions and theories about students, learning, content, and teachers; and they are intended to accomplish specific learning goals. Although there are many models of teaching, only five were described in this chapter. Those described reflect a variety of theoretical perspectives, have had impact on classroom practice, and have a research base regarding their effectiveness.

Mastery learning is intended to assure that all students achieve lesson objectives and it allows each student enough time to do so. Students who do not learn as fast as others are retaught until they do.

Cooperative learning is intended to teach students to cooperate in order to learn academically and, thereby, to learn positive attitudes toward other students in class, including those with different racial and ethnic backgrounds. Students participate in learning teams, games, or tournaments that reward cooperation.

The High/Scope cognitive-oriented curriculum, developed initially at Ypsilanti, Michigan, concentrates on the sequential development of students' cognitive abilities, beginning in preschool. Student experiences follow Piagetian developmental steps and include active use of the classroom environment, teacher questioning, and precisely designed daily routines.

Whole-language instruction is an approach to teaching reading, writing, and other subjects that teaches children literacy with a focus on meaning and understanding before they have developed conventional reading and writing skills. Students learn to read by reading and learn to write by writing even though they do not do either through strict adherence to rules. It is a constructivist approach to teaching.

Technology-based anchored instruction uses technology to present students with problem-solving experiences or "anchors." The anchors are complex, ill-defined tasks, similar to real-world problems, which the students are supposed to solve. The process engages students in active learning and peer interaction. It teaches problem-solving skills.

The models of instruction presented in the chapter are intended as examples that show connections among theories of learning, philosophies of education, educational practice, and student growth. Understanding them should help teachers formulate their own philosophies and ideas about education in ways that guide what they do in classrooms and the ways in which their students learn.

Study Questions

1. Which characteristics of each model of instruction do you like? Which do you dislike?

2. Which underlying educational philosophies and theories of learning support each of the models? For which grade levels? For which subjects?

3. Which of the models of instruction do you prefer? How does your choice among models of instruction relate to the educational philosophy that you find most appealing?

4. How does your choice relate to the theory of learning that you find most attractive?

Key Terms

Anchored instruction
Authentic texts
Cognitive and
  Technology Group
  at Vanderbilt
Cognitive psychology
Cooperative Integrated
  Reading and
  Composition (CIRC)
Cooperative learning
Corrective materials
Diagnostic assessments
Enrichments
Formative evaluation
Group Investigation

Group rewards
High/Scope Cognitive
  Oriented Curriculum
Individual mastery
Inert knowledge
Jigsaw II
Learning Together
Mastery Learning
Models of instruction
Outcome-based
  education
Personalized System of
  Instruction
Self-esteem
Sociocultural theories

Sociopsycholinguistic
  perspective
Student-Teams
  Achievement Division
  (STAD)
Summative evaluation
Team Assisted
  Individualization
  (TAI)
Teams-Games-
  Tournaments (TGT)
Technology-Based
  Anchored Instruction
Transactional theory
Whole Language

For Further Reading

Mastery Learning

Anderson, L. W. (1988). Benjamin Bloom: His research and influence on education. *Teaching Education, 2*(1), 54–58.

Block, J. (1979). Mastery learning: The current state of the craft. *Educational Leadership, 37*(2), 114–117.

Bloom, B. (1981). *All our children learning.* New York: McGraw-Hill.

Bloom, B. S. (1982). *Human characteristics and school learning.* New York: McGraw-Hill.

Guskey, T. R. (1985). *Implementing mastery learning.* Belmont, CA: Wadsworth.

Cooperative Learning

Cohen, L. G. (1994). Restructuring the classroom: Conditions for productive small groups. *Review of Educational Research, 64*(1), 1–35.

Graves, N., & Graves, T. (1987). *Cooperative learning: A resource guide.* Santa Cruz, CA: International Association for the Study of Cooperative Education.

Johnson, D. W., Johnson, R. T., Holubec, E. J., & Roy, P. (1984). *Circles of learning.* Alexandria, VA: Association for Supervision and Curriculum Development.

Kagan, S. (1990). *Cooperative learning resources for teachers.* San Juan Capistrano, CA: Resources for Teachers.

Sharan, S. (1994). *Cooperative learning: Theory and research.* New York: Praeger.

Slavin, R. E. (1990). *Cooperative learning: Theory, research, and practice.* Englewood Cliffs, NJ: Prentice-Hall.

High/Scope Cognitive-Oriented Curriculum

Cohen, D. L. (1993, April 21). Perry Preschool graduates show dramatic new social gains at 27. *Education Week, 12*(30), 1, 16–17.

Ennis, R. (1985). Goals for critical thinking/reasoning curriculum. *Educational Leadership, 43*(2), 46.

Schweinhart, L., & Weikart, D. (1980). *Young children grow up: The effects of the Perry Preschool Program on youths through age 15.* Ypsilanti, MI: High/Scope Educational Research Foundation, Monograph No. 7.

Schweinhart, L. J., & Weikart, D. P. (1993). Changed lives, significant benefits: The High/Scope Perry Preschool Project to date. *High/Scope Resource*, Summer, 1, 10–14.

Sigel, I. E. (1969). The Piagetian system and the world of education. In E. Elkind & J. H. Flavell (Eds.), *Studies in cognitive development.* New York: Oxford University Press.

Whole-Language Instruction

Calkins, L. M. (1994). *The art of teaching writing* (2nd ed.). Portsmouth, NH: Heinemann.

Cambourne, B. (1988). *The whole story.* Auckland, New Zealand: Ashton Scholastic.

Goodman, K. (1986). *What's whole in whole language?* Portsmouth, NH: Heinemann.

Mills, H., & Clyde, J. A. (1990). *Portraits of whole language classrooms: Learning for all ages.* Portsmouth, NH: Heinemann.

Way to go. (1993). *Teacher Magazine, 4*(5), 25–29.

Weaver, C. (1994). *Reading process and practice. From socio-psycholinguistics to whole language* (2nd ed.). Portsmouth, NH: Heinemann.

Technology-Based Anchored Instruction

Bransford, J. D., & Vye, N. J. (1989). A perspective on cognitive research and its implications for instruction. In L. B. Resnick & L. Klopfer (Eds.), *Toward the thinking curriculum: Current cognitive research* (pp. 173–205). Alexandria, VA: ASCD.

Cognition and Technology Group at Vanderbilt. (1990). Anchored instruction and its relationship to situated cognition. *Educational Researcher, 19*(6), 2–10.

Cognition and Technology Group at Vanderbilt. (1992). The Jasper experiment: An exploration of issues in learning and instructional design. *Educational Technology Research and Development, 40*, 65–80.

Cognition and Technology Group at Vanderbilt. (1992). The Jasper series as an example of anchored instruction: Theory, program description, and assessment data. *Educational Psychologist, 27*, 291–315.

Sharp, D. L. M., Bransford, J. D., Vye, N. J., Goldman, S. R., Kinzer, C., & Soraci, S. (1992). Literacy in the age of integrated media. In M. Dreher & W. Slater (Eds.), *Elementary school literacy: Critical issues* (pp. 183–210). Norwood, MA: Christopher-Gordon.

5

Teachers

Unit 5, which consists of Chapters 15 and 16, looks at professional classroom teachers, at their lives and their work, today and in the years ahead. In addition to providing new information, it asks you to use the ideas you have gained from your study of the first fourteen chapters of this text and the course in which the text is being used to analyze and think about what teachers do and what their professional lives are like. It also asks you to consider how you feel about teaching as a career—the rewards and successes, the difficulties and burdens. Then it suggests that you seriously probe the question: Do I want to be a classroom teacher?

By studying the unit, you should gain information about several aspects of the professional lives of teachers at the present time and what those conditions are likely to be like for teachers through the next ten to twenty years. You should also begin the reflective, self-questioning process that raises and tentatively answers the questions you will want to keep before you as you decide if you want to be a classroom teacher and, if so, what kind and where?

Chapter 15 describes the day-to-day contexts in which classroom teachers function today. It provides brief glimpses at the nature of the job, some of the student needs that teachers address, and working conditions.

Chapter 16 projects into the next two decades or so and hints at what classroom teaching will involve for people about to begin a generation of teaching—people like you. Then, it provides information for those who will be looking for their first teaching jobs in the near future.

When you finish each chapter, you should have an understanding of the general concepts listed below and have begun to develop the skills noted.

CHAPTER 15
Professional Teachers: The Life and the Work

General Concepts

- Teachers are a diverse group who have similar professional goals and perform similar work.

- The job of teaching revolves around a number of contexts in which it takes place—the nature of classrooms and schools as workplaces, the characteristics of students, relationships between teachers and their students, interactions among teacher colleagues, teachers' associations with administrators and parents, and the roles and responsibilities teachers assume when they close the classroom door.

- Job conditions of teachers vary greatly, but most teachers seem to balance the good and the bad and enjoy their work.

Skill

- An ability to relate information about teaching today to your own values and plans as a prospective teacher

CHAPTER 16
Teaching the Next Generation: Is It for You?

General Concepts

- During the next generation, the most significant educational reforms will occur in classrooms, with teachers and students, rather than in legislatures and among policy boards. Financing will be critical.

- Teachers are the most critical variable in the education process.

- Teaching in the next generation will be influenced by many professional and societal conditions, including the continued professionalization of teachers, international events, changing technology, poverty, and the changing nature of the American family.

Skill

- An ability to reflect upon what it means to be a teacher and to continually update your perceptions of the kind of teacher you might become

Professional Teachers
The Life and the Work

Although many people believe they understand the lives and work of teachers because of their years in school as students, they often know less than they think. When we attended elementary and secondary schools, we were either very young or not particularly mature. We had only our perspective as students, and being the lesser part of the teacher-student partnership inevitably biased us in many ways. We had only a few teachers, who, for the most part, we saw only at school. Peers, parents, and gossip could prejudice us. In short, people who think they know about teaching because they have been students have only a limited understanding of teaching, and they have not experienced teaching personally and felt the emotions that go with the job.

Therefore, this chapter presents a view of teachers as practicing professionals. It analyzes in succession the work teachers do, the needs of students that teachers address, the conditions under which teachers perform, the rewards they accrue, and the standards they are expected to meet. The chapter concludes with a glimpse at teachers as part of a professional group.

The chapter Snapshot and Reflecting on Practice are teachers' reflections on their experiences. The Snapshot is a letter by a teacher who is well satisfied in her career. The Reflecting on Practice contains comments by beginning teachers about incidents in their own teaching. The Educational Research section reports on a survey of teachers' perceptions of their job.

SNAPSHOT

The Snapshot for this chapter is part of a letter written by Margaret Metzger about her professional life in teaching.[1] She wrote it to a former student who had just completed college and was considering a teaching career. As you read, consider:

- Would this letter sway you toward a career as a teacher? Why or why not?
- In what ways do you think Ms. Metzger's experiences and attitudes are representative of teachers in general?
- What do you think might be some negative aspects of Ms. Metzger's work that she does not mention?
- Think of your own contacts with teachers. Which aspects of their professional lives appeal to you? Which do not?

Dear Clare,

. . . By mid-August I start planning lessons and dreaming about classrooms. I also wonder whether I'll have the energy to start again with new classes. Yet after September gets under way, I wake up in the morning expecting to have fun at work. I know that teaching well is a worthwhile use of my life. I know that my work is significant.

I am almost 40 years old, and I'm happier in my job than anyone I know. That's saying a lot. My husband, who enjoys his work, has routine days when he comes home and says, "Nothing much happened today—just meetings." I never have routine days. When I am in the classroom, I usually am having a wonderful time.

I also hate this job. In March I want to quit because of the relentless dealing with 100 antsy adolescents day after day. I lose patience with adolescent issues. I think I'll screech if I have to listen to one more adolescent self-obsession. I'm physically exhausted every Friday. The filth in our school is an aesthetic insult. The unending petty politics drain me. Often I feel undermined on small issues by a school system that supports me well on [something as major as] academic freedom.

Like all jobs, teaching has inherent stresses. As you know from student teaching, you must know how to discipline a room full of adolescents; you need to have a sense of purpose about what you are teaching; you need to cope with the exhaustion; and as an English teacher you must get the paper grading under control. I am always saddened by the number of excellent teachers who leave teaching because they think these difficult problems are unsolvable.

A curious irony exists. I am never bored at work, yet my days are shockingly routine. I can tell you exactly what I have done every school day for the past 18 years at 10:15 in the morning (homeroom attendance), and I suspect I will do the same for the next 20 years. The structure of the school day has changed little since education moved out of the one-room schoolhouse. All teachers get tired of the monotonous routine of bookkeeping, makeup assignments, 22-minute lunches, and study-hall duties. . . .

. . . To most people, I am "just a teacher."

But this is the outside reality. The interior world of the teacher is quite different. Although you have come to some terms with the outward flatness of the career, I want to assure you that teachers change and grow. So little research has been done on stage development of teachers that the literature recognizes only three categories—intern, novice, and veteran. This is laughably oversimplified. There is life after student teaching; there is growth after the first year. You will some day solve many of the problems that seem insurmountable during your exhilarating student teaching and your debilitating first year.

Sometimes I am aware of my growth as a teacher, and I realize that finally, after all these years, I am confident in the classroom. On the very, very best days, when classes sing, I am able to operate on many levels during a single class: I integrate logistics, pedagogy, curriculum, group dynamics, individual needs, and my own philosophy. I feel generous and good-natured toward my students, and I am challenged by classroom issues. But on bad days, I feel like a total failure. . . .

I keep going because I'm intellectually stimulated. I enjoy literature, and I assign books I love and books I want to read. I expect class discussions and student papers to give me new insights into literature. . . .

To me, teaching poses questions worthy of a lifetime of thought. I want to think about what the greater writers are saying. I want to think about how people learn. I want to think about the values we are passing on to the next generation. Questions about teaching are like

puzzles to me; I can spend hours theorizing and then use my classroom as a laboratory. . . .

And then there are all the difficult, "normal" situations: students and parents who are "entitled," hostile, emotionally needy, or indifferent; students who live in chaotic homes, who are academically pressured, who have serious drug and alcohol problems. The list goes on and on. No school of education prepared me for the "Hill Street Blues" intensity and chaos of public schools. I received my combat training from other teachers, from myself, and mostly from the students. You will too. . . .

Ultimately, teaching is nurturing. The teacher enters a giving relationship with strangers, and then the teacher's needs must give way to students' needs. I want to work on my own writing; instead, I work on students' writing. My days are spent encouraging young people's growth. I watch my students move beyond me, thinking and writing better than I have ever done. I send them to colleges I could never afford. And I must strive to be proud, not jealous, of them. I must learn generosity of heart.

I am a more compassionate person because I have known teachers and students. I think differently about handicaps because I worked with Guy, who is quadriplegic from a rugby accident. Refugee problems have a human face because I've heard Nazmul tell stories about refugee camps in Bangladesh, and I've heard Merhdad tell about escaping from Iran, hidden in baggage on a camel. I have seen the school social worker give suicidal students his home phone number, telling them to call anytime. I have seen administrators bend all the rules to help individual students through personal crises. Every day I hear stories of courage and generosity. I admire other teachers.

Facing every new class is an act of courage and optimism. Years ago, the courage required was fairly primitive. I needed courage to discipline my classes, to get them into line, to motivate them to work. But now I need a deeper courage. I look at each new class and know that I must let each of these young people into my life in some significant way. The issue is one of heart. Can I open my heart to 200 or more adolescent strangers each year? Put bluntly, can I be that loving?

I hope to love my students so well that it doesn't even matter whether they like me. I want to love them in the way I love my own son—full of respect and awe for who they are, full of wanting for their growth, full of wonder at what it means to lead and to follow the next generation.

Clare, when you consider a life's work, consider not just what you will take to the task but what it will give you. Which job will give self-respect and challenge?

Which job will give you a world of ideas? Which job will be intellectually challenging? Which job will enlarge you and give you life in abundance? Which job will teach you lessons of the heart?

With deep respect,
Margaret Metzger

Professionals Who Educate

About the same time each weekday morning between September and June, more than 50 million American children, adolescents, and teenagers crawl out of bed, nibble breakfast, gather belongings, and stumble off to school. With varying degrees of anticipation or reluctance, they either walk to the neighborhood school, board school buses, or slide into cars. Within a short time all arrive at school. The pattern is usually routine and occurs with little fuss and confusion. It is what they expect to do.

The students

At the end of this daily procession, students enter classrooms where they pass the next six to seven hours of their lives under the control and responsibility of one or more teachers. The community expects it; the law requires it; and the students, whatever their personal feelings may be, normally conform to these expectations without serious question.

Once in classrooms, students engage in learning experiences that are designed and conducted by their teachers, experiences intended to transform them into more informed, better skilled, and increasingly sensitive human beings. For many, those experiences taken as a whole are the most significant and most challenging of their lives. And so they should be. Teachers are judged by the extent to which the experiences they provide students are successful in educating them.

Assumed competence

But because of the routine nature of schooling, few people actually consider what teachers do to educate their charges. Instead, they tend to think, without much evidence, that teachers know what they are doing, are well-intentioned, and are competent. They choose to believe that teachers' classroom activities are good, effective, and appropriate for each individual in the class. Typically, parents and others from outside the school get involved only when something appears to be wrong or when it is so unusually good that it deserves special notice.

In the course of their pre-K–12 schooling, most students spend about 15,000 hours under the direction of teachers, no matter what they might prefer to be doing, regardless of how much they are or are not learning, and perhaps without considering how skilled and informed those teachers happen to be. Except for sleeping and playing, that amount of time takes up more hours than any other discrete activity those students engage in. By comparison, most children, adolescents, and teenagers spend more time with teachers than they do with any other group of adults besides their parents; and for many the time spent with teachers is also longer than that spent with parents.[2]

Images of Teachers

Generally, teachers are like most educated Americans. They come in all sizes, shapes, colors, and personalities. They function with varying idiosyncrasies, degrees of physical and mental health, and levels of personal satisfaction. Not all are as satisfied as Margaret Metzger, but many are. Most are above average intellectually when compared with the population as a whole. They have diverse political, social, philosophical, and religious beliefs but seem to cluster toward the middle point on most continua. Sixty-five percent describe themselves as conservative, 36 percent say they are Democrats, 32 percent say they are Republicans, and almost one-third claim to be independent of political party affiliation. A few belong to minor parties.[3]

As noted in Chapter 1, 72 percent of pre-K–12 teachers are women. About 88 percent are white, almost 7 percent are black, 2.7 percent have Hispanic surnames, 1 percent are Native American, and 1 percent have Asian or Pacific Islander family origins. Their average age is 42. Over three-fourths are married and, of those not married, slightly more than one in ten has been married previously. About 80 percent of spouses of teachers are employed full-time outside the home.[4]

The average teacher in a pre-K–12 public school in recent years has been teaching for fifteen years or more and has spent about twelve of those years in the same school system. On average, elementary teachers teach twenty-four students in a class, and secondary teachers face about one hundred students in a typical five-period day. About two-thirds of all teachers belong to the National Education Association, 12 percent to the American Federation of Teachers, and about 20 percent do not belong to a union.[5]

In 1992–1993, the average school-year teaching salary for public school teachers was about $35,334.[6] A sizable number of teachers, especially male teachers, also hold second jobs in the summer, on weekends, or in the evening.

In spite of the fact that teachers are about as diverse as the American population in general, there are several patterns of behavior or roles that teachers as a group are perceived to follow. Sometimes these perceptions are accurate, but not always. Teachers are thought to be outgoing, widely read, well traveled, emotionally balanced, caring and sincere, and active in social and governmental affairs. They are assumed to be more "middle of the road" than the general population on most issues, more conservative in their ideas and actions, and more moral and ethical. They are expected to demonstrate models of behavior for children to follow. They are considered to be dedicated to an improved social order, but also preservers of past traditions and the status quo.[7]

In appearance, dress, lifestyle, and housing, teachers are thought to be middle class. To some extent, especially in traditional communities, they are assumed to be religious. They are considered to be less likely to do far-out or extreme things inside and outside the classroom. As a parent of elementary school children once said, "The teachers in this school might 'do' drugs and have very active sex lives but we do not want our children to think of them in those ways."

In the classroom and in their other school-related contact with students, teachers are supposed to transmit knowledge, develop skills, and instill values. Therefore, they are expected to be intelligent—at least more intelligent than most "average" people—knowledgeable of the subject matter they teach, and skilled in teaching methods. They should know content, teaching techniques, psychology, and the general things that intelligent people know. They also should know how to discipline

Diverse individuals

Middle of the road

Middle class

Knowledgeable

Something to Think About

Think for a few minutes about your own image of a teacher. For instance, write the title The American Teacher at the top of a blank sheet of paper. Then draw a human figure to fit the image you have in mind. (Put clothes on the figure that fit your image, and so forth.) After you have done that, consider these questions:

- Why did you draw the figure you did?
- Did you have a particular person or people in mind when you drew the figure? If so, why do you think that person or those people came to mind?
- In which ways is your image of Ms. Metzger, from the chapter Snapshot, similar to and different from the figure you drew? How do you account for this?

Compare your figure with those drawn by other students in this class.

students and motivate them to learn. They should be able to assess students and guide their learning toward appropriate obtainable goals.[8]

Substitute parents

Especially at the elementary school levels, teachers are often expected to be substitute parents. This involves a whole range of roles—service provider, authority figure, judge, nurturer, confidant, counselor, caring supporter, defender, arbitrator, and so forth. The roles vary in importance with different students and from time to time, and they have changed in recent years. Modeling behavior and setting expectations are now major responsibilities.

Beginning Teachers

Responsibilities

For beginning teachers, the professional expectations, roles, and responsibilities of teaching are sometimes overwhelming. In fact, the first year of teaching has often been described as an emotional roller coaster, but it is probably no more difficult or less rewarding than the first year of other professions that involve significant responsibility for the lives of others. It is intense, involves unexpected demands, includes troublesome worries about the welfare of students, and causes bothersome second thoughts about actions already taken—actions that sometimes affect students seriously and can hurt deeply.

Satisfied

But by the end of the first year in the profession, most new teachers are satisfied with what they have done and, in fact, are quite proud of themselves. They often admit they have learned more than they expected and sometimes realize they had known less than they thought. More importantly, they have learned how responsible and rewarding the job of teaching is and realize that no one can really understand all the facets of the life of a professional teacher without being one.

Reasons for Teaching

Why do people become teachers? The motives, of course, are many, and they range from very idealistic to very practical. However, when contemporary teachers are asked about their motives, they often mention a desire to work with young people, a liking for a particular subject, an interest in doing things they see teachers do, and a desire to perform a valuable public service. They also believe teaching provides status, job security, good retirement benefits, free time in summers, work schedules compatible with raising a family, a good "first career" while they prepare for a second, and a career that is easier to prepare for than other professions.[9]

Older teachers and those who have recently retired also mention two other reasons for teaching that no longer apply. Many men who entered teaching between the end of World War II and the early 1970s did so because teaching positions were readily available, and teaching was a step up the professional ladder from the work their fathers performed. Because they were military veterans, the government paid them to go to college, which was something they would not normally have expected to do. They were often the first in their family to attend college, and teaching was frequently the only profession they thought they knew. Teaching seemed less mysterious than the work of medical doctors, lawyers, and engineers.

During the same time, many women and minority group members entered teaching because it was one of the few professions open to them. They were not expected to be physicians, lawyers, and engineers and were often excluded from those fields.

The Profession of Teaching

The next several pages describe some of the aspects of the job of teaching by looking at what teachers do in several different contexts:

- in classrooms
- with students
- in the general school environment
- among professional peers
- as employees
- with parents
- behind the classroom door

However, as you read, remember that teaching involves more than the brief sketches presented here and that the various roles are intertwined.

Teachers in Classrooms

Classrooms are teachers' workplaces—where teachers practice their profession of instructing students and where they succeed or fail professionally. They are different from the workplaces of any other professional group. To begin with, classrooms are populated primarily by young people rather than adults and are designed with that in mind. They have a particular purpose, recognizable physical characteristics, and a *feeling* that sets them apart.

When compared with each other, classrooms have similar general characteristics but are different in detail. Most have walls, but those walls look different. All involve instruction, but it is never the same. All are controlled by a teacher, but no two teachers are exactly alike.[10]

Physical characteristics

Classrooms tend to have a typical size and shape. Except for open education pods, they are built like boxes along long hallways, behind doors that teachers close to separate their work from the intrusions of the outside world—doors with small windows that are often covered with paper. Classrooms contain desks, chalkboards, bright lights, books, a flag, audiovisual equipment, paper supplies, a trash can, a pencil sharpener, and a closet.

This sameness in the physical aspects of classrooms is illustrated in the writing of Philip W. Jackson:

> School bulletin boards may be changed but they are never discarded, the seats may be rearranged but thirty of them are there to stay, the teacher's desk may have a new plant on it but there it sits, as ubiquitous as the roll-down maps, the olive drab wastebasket, and the pencil sharpener on the window ledge. . . .
>
> Even the odors of the classroom are fairly standardized. . . . If a person stumbled into a classroom blindfolded, his nose alone, if he used it carefully, would tell him where he was.[11]

Crowded places

Classrooms are crowded places in which to work. They are not very large spaces for twenty, thirty, or more people, even if the people are often small in size; and they contain lots of furniture, equipment, and supplies. There is constant activity, and people frequently bump into each other.[12] Few other workplaces are so cramped, and few involve the same level of hustle and bustle. Teachers not only work in this congested environment, but they are also personally responsible for its smooth, productive operation.

Social contexts

Classrooms also have particular and consistent social contexts, as mentioned earlier. They are youth-dominated and learning-oriented, with an adult in charge. Under normal conditions, all activity is set to serve the learning needs of the students. Desks, teaching stations, learning centers, individual study alcoves, bulletin boards, electronic equipment, and so forth are all strategically located for that purpose. Verbal interactions are structured to accomplish it.[13]

Social conventions

As you have already begun to learn, classroom environments include a number of common social conventions. Some would say they are ritualistic. For example, the teacher sets the pattern of behavior, establishes standards, and gives directions. The students normally follow. The arrangements are so common that substitute teachers can take over without ever seeing the regular teacher, and nonteaching visitors can tell when something is wrong.[14] Most of the time someone is talking, and, more often than not, it is the teacher. Chalkboards are erased nightly, bulletin boards changed monthly, and desks straightened as often as needed. In tightly ordered rooms, loose paper is picked up from the floor at the end of each period. A corner of the board is used for assignments, reminders, and the posting of infractions. A hook near the door or the top drawer of the teacher's desk holds a hall pass.

Routine patterns

Classroom events follow regular routines and patterns. Schedules, periods, assignments, special activities, and pull-out programs are all arranged to fit with one another, and most are planned during the summer before school starts. Each year's instruction of students follows developmentally those before it. Subjects are sequenced through the school day. Art, music, and physical education are planned so that the one or two specialists in the building can see all students for about equal amounts of time each week. Nearly everything is scheduled around a few immovable events, particularly the bus schedule and lunch.

Even activities that teachers arrange within their own classrooms follow set patterns, and although teachers can make changes, they rarely do. Most think their job is more manageable if events occur predictably. Certain subjects are taught at the same time each day. For example, in elementary schools, reading is typically taught in the morning, when students are most alert. Lecture, recitation, seatwork, guided practice, individual study, enrichment, and assessment follow a consistent sequence.[15]

Both students and teachers perform their duties according to prescribed rules of behavior that everyone is expected to understand and obey. These are thought to be necessary because the students, regardless of their age, are not adults. They need direction to stay on task and to avoid classroom chaos. For example, students are to be in their seats when the bell rings, they are not to interrupt others, they are to look only at their own papers, they are not to run in the halls, they are not to smoke on school property. Teachers are expected to dress appropriately, speak correctly, treat everyone equitably, punish inappropriate behavior, assign homework, and have a positive attitude. Students and teachers who follow the rules are considered good.

Prescribed rules of behavior

For a variety of reasons, teachers need to do many things at once, a point already discussed in Chapter 3. This, in turn, means teachers must be skilled planners, organizers, and directors of all that occurs in their rooms.[16]

Many things at once

A major aspect of the many-things-at-once classroom is rapid-paced, teacher-led interactions. For example, all of the following might happen within seconds of the middle of a lesson: A teacher asks a question and glances toward John. John looks away because he does not want to be called on. Then he frowns in embarrassment as he peeks out of the corner of his eye toward his girlfriend. As he suspected, she is looking at him and knows he does not understand. Both blush. She looks away, hiding her feeling of sympathy for him. The teacher sees all this and calls on another student but makes a mental note to return to John shortly with an easier question so he can save face.

Rapid-paced interactions

The magnitude of the task of managing classroom activity can be illustrated with a comparison to the work of other professionals. Physicians usually treat one patient at a time, with the assistance of a nurse, a laboratory assistant, a receptionist, a pharmacist, and other support staff ready to respond at a moment's call; meanwhile, patients wait their turn, sometimes for hours, in rooms away from the physician. Specialists, even more buffered, await referrals. Engineers tackle individual phases of projects, frequently in a planned sequence, without a need to monitor the behavior and thoughts of a large number of other people in the same room; they can take a break when they feel like it without disrupting others. College professors teach more mature and patient students who are less demanding of attention, more likely to be motivated, and usually in class by choice.

Studies have found that teachers engage in as many as one thousand significant interpersonal interactions each day.[17] In the process of instruction, they communicate constantly with whole classes of individuals verbally and nonverbally, sometimes interacting differently with several students at the same time—listening to Janet respond, while motioning to Amy that her turn is next, watching Jill and Sarah whisper, nodding to Bill that he may sharpen his pencil, and nudging Jim's feet back under his desk.

Interruptions, disruptions, and delays are facts of classroom life. Students prompt some of these with unexpected questions, extraneous comments, inattention, misbehavior, and procrastination. Visitors, public-address announcements, special events, principals, and other teachers also intrude. But in spite of it all, bells ring as planned, and school ends on time.

Interruptions and delays

In order to be happy and productive, teachers must want to work in the unique environment of the classroom. They must be accepting of the crowded physical space, the routines and rules, the pace, and the multiple interactions. They must like coordinating the myriad of facets of classroom life so that all fit together and some-how foster learning.[18]

Teachers with Students

Cultivating relationships

The best standard by which teachers are judged is the extent to which they succeed in helping students learn. To succeed in this way, teachers cultivate positive rela-tionships with students. After all, teachers are in classrooms by choice, and when they agree to take a class, they accept the responsibility to teach every student re-gardless of individual abilities, motivations, state of cleanliness, personality quirks, and parental support. Students, on the other hand, have to be there. Their presence is not voluntary. Most cannot even choose their own teachers.

Relationships between teachers and students are complex professional associ-ations between superiors (teachers) and subordinates (students). They are domi-nated by the teacher's authority and enforced by custom and law. Students usually comply with teachers' wishes, rely on their help, and cultivate their support and favor. They do so publicly, before their peers, and with the threat of embarrassment and failure.[19]

Although these relationships are significant, often close, and sometimes intense, they are not as personal or as emotional as family relationships and friendships. They are also not as permanent. They are typically limited to certain hours in the day and for a school year.

Teacher authority

Because teachers possess authority over students, they usually control the rela-tionships and, therefore, must accept primary responsibility for them. They need to use their power carefully to establish, maintain, and cultivate positive associations. If they fail to do so, they often jeopardize student success, and teaching becomes less pleasant than it should be.

The authority that teachers have over students is characterized by Philip W. Jackson as follows:

> Seated at his desk the student is in the position to do something. It is the teacher's job to declare what that something shall be.
>   . . . When students do what the teacher tells them to do, they are, in ef-fect, abandoning one set of plans (their own) in favor of another (their teach-er's). At times, of course, these two sets of plans do not conflict and may even be quite similar. But at other times that which is given up in no way resembles the action called for by the teacher.[20]

Many personalities

Probably the most challenging aspect of the relationships between teachers and students is the fact that each class consists of many individual student personalities with which teachers must interact. Some students enjoy being in school, in particu-lar classes, and with specific teachers; others do not. Some are secure and find learn-ing easy, others are threatened and have difficulty. Some have personal styles that are compatible with the teacher's, some clash. Some are middle class, polite, clean, and neat; others are "at risk," rough, gruff, and dirty. Some are turned on, others are tuned out. In spite of it all, good teachers—such as Ms. Metzger who wrote the letter in the Snapshot of this chapter—interact warmly with all students.

Student dislike for school

Many of the students who dislike school seem to fall into two groups—those who find their school experience to be frightening and embarrassing and those who are bored by it.[21] Those in the first group often fail and frequently suffer publicly and painfully before their peers. Those in the second tend to endure in sleepy silence. In either case, much alienation seems to derive from what teachers do or have done to and with those students. When some teachers turn off students, other teachers are the only ones who can make the classrooms welcoming places again.

Although teacher-student relationships revolve primarily around instruction, what teachers do in other roles also has an important impact on their students. As noted earlier, besides being instructors in a strict sense, teachers are substitute parents, managers of behavior, confidants, advisors, arbitrators, role models, protectors, and evaluators. At critical times throughout every school year, what teachers do in these other roles has a greater effect on some students than their instruction. Virtually every adult remembers such instances from his or her own school days— a pat on the back, an enthusiastic congratulation, a forgiving glance, a patient ear, a confidential bit of advice, a discouraging frown, a moment of ridicule, a disappointing lack of interest, a public condemnation.

Many roles

Parents expect teachers to set standards of acceptable conduct and to punish those who transgress—to stop fighting, to prevent harassment, to prohibit the use of foul language, and to require proper dress and manners. They often want to be informed about their own children's inappropriate behavior and want other children's parents notified as well. When violations are serious, they want legal authorities notified, except, perhaps, when the culprit is their own child.[22]

Students frequently turn to teachers when they need guidance, advice, and affirmation. They do so partly because teachers are readily available, respected adults who usually can help or know someone who can and because they are not so emo-

Guidance and advice

Teachers are much more than academic experts. Students frequently turn to teachers for guidance, advice, and affirmation about issues ranging from the simple and common to the complex and profound.

tionally involved with the students as parents and relatives. Such requests vary with maturity and age, and they range from the simple and common to the complex and profound. For example:

Should I hit Betty back?
Should I smoke?
Is it okay to have sex with my boyfriend?
I'm an alcoholic. Will you help me?
My father is sexually abusing me. What should I do?
I'm pregnant. Will you help me get an abortion?
My parents threw me out of the house. Can you help me find a place to live?

Most teachers see questions such as these as part of the territory. When students need help, they try to provide it, even if their actions might be criticized and second-guessed. They believe that to ignore questions such as these is to neglect students whom they are pledged to serve.

Being protective

Teachers are frequently called on to step into situations in order to protect students who are unable to protect themselves. For example, they are asked to shield students from physical injury by stopping fights, from embarrassment before their peers by cutting off accusatory dialogues, from discrimination, and from other forms of mistreatment. They are expected to protect them against their own actions as well as those of other students, teachers, and the system. Sometimes they have to do so in spite of the rules and potential harmful consequences.

Evaluating

In a role that seems at times to contrast with several already described, teachers also evaluate their students. They set standards for student performance, encourage students to strive to meet them, test periodically, and fail those who do not measure up. In addition to academic achievement, they assess personal characteristics and qualities such as motivation, intellectual ability, behavior patterns, and potential. Like it or not, they separate students into good and bad on a number of criteria. For many teachers the role is a burden, but it too comes with the territory.[23]

As was illustrated in the Snapshot about Leonard Rucks in Chapter 1, recent education accountability movements emphasize the teacher's evaluative role and shift thinking on the subject away from that of the 1960s and 1970s, a time of flexible standards and softened expectations. The teachers of the 1990s are expected to enforce strict academic performance standards for students; if they shy away from the task of evaluation, they may be considered weak or contentious.

To be satisfied with a job in teaching, teachers must like interacting with students and building relationships with them. They must believe they can help them and be committed to trying. Of all the things that keep teachers in the profession, relationships with students are probably the most sustaining.[24]

Teachers in the General School Environment

Child- and youth-oriented environment

Because schools are child- or youth-oriented, their cultural environments differ from those of other workplaces, as was indicated earlier. Schedules, rules of conduct, dress regulations, standards of language usage, disciplinary procedures, degrees of formality, types of cafeteria food, and size of furniture are all decided upon because of the students. Rules are plentiful, restrictions tight, and administrative directives inhibiting. Compliance is expected.[25]

Although expectations are different for teachers than for students, teachers are caught up in the regulatory milieu. They are expected to model appropriate behav-

Paul Ong

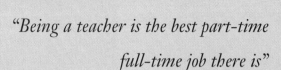

"Being a teacher is the best part-time full-time job there is"

*W*hen Paul Ong is asked about his career as a teacher, his modest self-descriptions mask his obvious dedication to teaching—and learning. He has taught all levels and ages of students, from elementary school through adult school, working for a time in administration along the way. In the 1970s he left teaching for a second career in business so that he could better support his own children as they went through college. In the 1980s he retired— only to find himself drawn back to the classroom, first as a substitute and then, at his principal's request, as a full-time teacher.

Ten years after his "retirement," Paul is still in the classroom, working in an inner-city junior high school where the vast majority of the students are Asian, black, and Hispanic. He has no plans to retire again any time soon. Being a teacher, he tells his retired friends, is the "best part-time full-time job there is."

*O*fficially, Paul currently teaches computer skills. But if you ask him about his teaching, what he talks about is practical wisdom—how to apply for a job, why education is the key to a better life, how to choose friends worth having, why time is anyone's most precious commodity. And no matter what the subject— whether computers, math, or science—he teaches vocabulary.

"Maybe it's because I remember being held back in the third grade for lack of proficiency in English—even though I was fluent in Chinese, Italian, and Spanish! To me, language is so important. When I taught math, people said,

'You're supposed to be teaching math, not English.' But I said, if they don't understand the language—if they don't know what 'corollary' means—then they can't succeed. Then it's my job, my duty, to teach them the language. It's the only way I will be able to get them to achieve."

"It's a great feeling

when a kid is able to do something

he didn't think he could do"

*P*aul talks about teaching with a quiet assurance that reflects not just long experience but, perhaps more important, a lifetime of reflecting on his work and pursuing more learning.

"Confidence is a huge part of teaching," he says. "That's why I've taken so many courses in my life. I have more graduate credits than undergraduate! When you have a conceptual understanding, you free yourself from having to follow a set path with a subject.

"We have so many students who are turned off because the person teaching is just regurgitating the textbook. I like to look at a textbook not as a bible, but as a reference. I try to give students exercises that are real, that are practical. They learn more that way. And, you know, it's a great feeling when a kid is able to do something he didn't think he could do."

April 12, 1994

3519 6100 Hayes ST
Oakland, Ca. 94606

Dear Mr. Ong

About the test I was doing. I thought it was hard because I didn't study. I thought I was going to get it all wrong but so I study it real hard and got it in my mind. When you gave me the paper, I look at it and said, "this look's easy." I began to do it. That test wasn't that hard at all. It was kind of fun doing it because I learn all the key's proper position. We should have more tests to test how well you do at Computer Class. Now I can type better at Computer Class because you taught us something that we never learn. Thank's alot.

Sincerely Your Friend,
AiChiem Saepharn

*"I find that the more I give,
the more I receive all around"*

*P*aul may describe teaching as a "part-time full-time" job, but his actions belie his words. He makes himself lunch in a closet next to his classroom so that the computer room can stay open for students. His "free time" is likely to go into repairing broken machines, teaching summer school, taking night classes, or shopping at a science museum for materials to use when he takes on teaching science next term.

"My wife says I'm always giving," he confesses. "But I find that the more I give, the more I receive all around. That's the great thing I get out of teaching: the more I can tell the students, the more they can tell me— the more I learn.

"People say a lot of bad things about schools. But even in our own families, we seldom talk about the positives of what's happening in our lives. And in schools there are so many positive things happening that they overshadow whatever the negatives are."

ior and to follow school norms. They do not smoke in the halls, wear their most beat-up casual shoes, call each other by nicknames in the presence of students, or use the time-honored expletives they might express at home.

To be happy, teachers need to like working in these student-oriented conditions. They must be willing to listen to incessant talk about sports heroes, rock music, and dates and appear interested. They must be open to—and expect—juvenile banter, student council debates, athletic competition, assemblies, dances, and pep rallies.

As with any work environment that includes a large number of people, schools have their share of disappointments, pains, and sadness; and when they occur, teachers, sometimes more than anyone else, feel the effects. Sometimes those sad occurrences happen directly to teachers; but more often than not, they happen to students, and the pain transfers to the teacher.

Realistic teachers must accept the fact that students sometimes fail, get hurt, and die. Some do not achieve as much as teachers hope or expect because they lack ability, motivation, or support from home. Some become hooked on drugs. Some are physically, emotionally, or sexually abused. Some are so alienated that they cannot be reached. And for students, even though they are young and deserving, life is often unfair.

Heartaches

Teachers among Professional Peers

Unlike most other professionals, teachers usually practice their profession in relative isolation—each in his or her own classroom out of the sight of colleagues. They rarely communicate with one another about professional matters of substance. Granted, they share ideas about teaching strategies and information on students, and they sometimes gossip. But they do not watch one another teach, critique one another's work, or purposely advise one another on how to teach better. Doctors, lawyers, businesspeople, and engineers all do this more regularly.

Isolation

One group of researchers into professional interactions among teachers describes teaching as a *flat* rather than a *hierarchical* profession.[26] They note that teachers typically think of one another as equally skilled and knowledgeable rather than dividing themselves into expert, average, and novice performers. They are uneasy when observed closely by peers and reluctant to act as if they know more or less than the others. Teachers who know more than their peers and display that knowledge openly tend to be disliked rather than respected, and those who admit they do not know enough are considered to be weak.

Flat profession

Although there has been significant change in recent years in many schools, most school systems generally have not arranged for skilled, experienced teachers to help those recently hired. All are expected to work competently and alone from the first day. Other teachers, even principals, are not expected to intervene and often do not. Those who frequently ask for help are looked down upon.

A significant thrust within educational reform movements of recent years is targeted toward making teaching more hierarchical. Most plans divide teachers into ranks based on regularly scheduled evaluations and label them accordingly. Those at higher ranks are considered more skilled and are assigned to help those lower on the scale. They also receive higher levels of pay.

Differentiation of professional roles

Although these schemes are becoming more common, most run counter to traditional professional norms among teachers. Their introduction has usually prompted teacher objection and has forced teachers to look differently at their professional relationships with colleagues. As a result, mentoring, cross-class observing, and peer counseling are all growing parts of teachers' professional lives.

In the eyes of most teachers, the traditional isolation from peers has both advantages and drawbacks. Although it frees teachers to do things their own way and avoid direct criticism, it also denies them support and makes the seeking of advice more conspicuous. It establishes a norm in which giving and receiving advice about classroom performance are not routine.

Socially active

This is not to say that teachers do not interact socially with one another or with other professionals. They probably do so as much as those in any other profession, and the extent to which they do probably depends more on individual personality than on anything else. Those who find each other compatible and like the same things tend to become friends and do things together in school and out.

Contrary to images of long ago, teachers tend to be outgoing and active socially. They dress fashionably, party, drink, and vacation at exciting locations. Despite what some small children think, teachers do relax, act silly, and get married—just like normal people.[27]

Teachers as Employees

Principals

Teachers work for many people—students, parents, school boards, communities—but, at least in traditional school settings, those with the most direct influence over them and their jobs are their building principals, whose impact is usually followed in importance by department chairs, curriculum supervisors, and central office administrators. Principals are the most immediate supervisor and the de facto school leaders.

Of course, principals and other superiors have different philosophies, personalities, styles of operation, idiosyncrasies, and habits; and each of these traits affects the job conditions of the teachers who work with them. Sometimes they cause problems for certain teachers; but good, experienced teachers usually size up their supervisors and act accordingly. They fit in most of the time, accommodate differences when they need to, and manipulate situations to their liking when they can. In a sense, they use the principal and other administrators to support their own professional goals. Usually, new teachers admire the skill, perception, and ease with which the old masters do this.

Fitting in and manipulating

Cultivating support

Like officials in all bureaucracies, principals and supervisors play many roles. In their work with teachers, good ones encourage, provide support, gather and disperse ideas and materials, facilitate normal operations, stimulate new efforts, manage crises, mediate disputes, and absorb blame. They also protect teachers from intrusions, criticisms, and abuse. As middle managers, they try to serve their superiors as well as their teachers and, when necessary, provide a buffer between the two. Because of multiple responsibilities and conflicting expectations, they are easy to disagree with and dislike. Smart teachers, however, see them as leaders whose support is invaluable, and they cultivate it.

Principals and supervisors rarely question teacher decisions unless someone complains—test scores are low, the classroom is noisy, someone hits someone, there is too much homework or not enough. In fact, recent proponents of accountability complain that school administrators tend to be so unintrusive that they know little about the quality of their teachers' performances.

Autonomy without neglect

This may be a problem, but good principals do not neglect their teachers. They check on beginning teachers closely and often advise them. They also look out for teachers with difficulties. If the teachers are doing well, they manage subtly. They see their main role with teachers as that of providing the conditions in which teachers can practice their skills to the maximum of their capabilities. A prophetic principal once said, "Good teachers teach well without direction from managers; good principals make it possible for them to do so."[28]

Teachers with Parents

Teachers interact with parents less often than most people think. In fact, when things run smoothly, there is likely to be little or no contact at all, especially for secondary teachers. When contact is made, the teacher usually initiates it, and it typically marks an exceptionally proud moment or a significant problem. Some teachers like the situation this way and see parents as complicating elements in the education of their children; others seek parental involvement even in normal times.

In any event, the job of teaching includes interacting with parents—informing them of progress and difficulties, consulting them on decisions, cooperating with them on matters of mutual responsibility, asking their help, and responding to their requests. Good teachers consider serving parents part of their job, and they conscientiously keep the channels of communication open. They understand parents' concern about their children's welfare. They want the parents' confidence.

Parental confidence

Of course, different parents devote varying amounts of attention to the education of their children. Of those involved the least, some are overwhelmed with other

As professionals, teachers need to be skillful at working with parents who display quite different levels of competence, interest, and understanding.

pressures—family matters, sickness, their own work; some are just normally busy; some do not understand school operations and are intimidated by teachers; some feel superior to teachers; and some just do not care. Those involved the most are normally helpful to teachers. They share information about their children, support teacher decisions at home, volunteer at school, and raise money. Some, however, are more bother than help. They want unfair amounts of attention for their children, think they always know what is best, publicly criticize teacher actions, and love a dispute. Even if their intentions are good, they are bothersome.

Cultivating relationships

For their students' sake and to accomplish their own professional goals, good teachers cultivate positive relationships with all kinds of parents. They inform them of their priorities, philosophies, and expectations and convince them that they are intelligent, caring, and skilled professionals who will be beneficial to their children. They win their support. Similarly, they try to understand parents because that understanding helps them teach the children.

Honest communication

Successful teachers usually interact well with parents. They possess good communication skills. They are honest and direct when things are not going well, as well as when they are. They praise parents with sincerity when they can, challenge their actions when those actions hurt their children, and report them for child abuse when necessary.

To do all this, teachers need to remember that parents do not pass tests to have children. They possess widely different levels of competence and perceptions about themselves, their children, the school, and the teacher. They range from highly intelligent to mentally retarded, from emotionally secure to nervous wrecks, from socially stable to drug addicts. Some have their children under control, others have no hope of that. Some understand their children's strengths and weaknesses, and others' perceptions of their children are absolutely invalid. Most love their children, but some do not. All, however, believe, or at least hope that teachers will make their children better and more successful human beings.[29]

Teachers behind the Classroom Door

When teachers close the classroom door, they are in charge. They set the agenda, direct the instruction, decide what to cover, and choose whom to praise and reprimand. Few other adults know what teachers do with their classes day to day and minute to minute. Even fewer would intrude on their authority. Most trust teachers to do the right thing and assume they are capable enough to do so. In a sense, the classroom is the teacher's palace. This amount of autonomy is not characteristic of most other types of employment, especially not of work that involves similar responsibility.

Something to Think About

Below are a number of comments that various teachers have heard over the years from parents. Each reflects a different perspective about the teacher-parent aspect of teaching.

I asked that Marsha be assigned to you because you're the best teacher in the school.

My husband left me last year, and I'm at a loss. I can't cope well, and Johnnie is devastated. His school work deteriorated in grade 8, and he's been in trouble with the law. Please help him this year. He needs it so badly, and I have no one else to turn to.

I'm sorry to say this, but Mike is a rotten kid. I can't do anything with him. Please don't call me about his school problems. I can't help.

I was never good at school, so I can see why my children have problems. But I am interested in how they do, and they better behave. Let me know how I can help. I always work at the school fair and bake cakes.

I used to be a teacher, and your teaching style is different from anything I was ever taught.

William did well last year for Ms. Miller. I don't know why he has so many problems since you became his teacher.

You seem to be an intelligent and capable teacher. The kids love you. Would you consider working for me in my business? I need a person like you. I'll pay you a heck of a lot more than you'll ever make as a teacher.

You must have been teaching a long time. When do you retire?

■ What do you think might have motivated each of these comments?
■ If you had been the teacher to whom each of the comments was made, what would you have said or done?

Most successful, experienced teachers like being their own boss and do not want interference, but autonomy has its burdens as well as its benefits, particularly for new teachers. If beginning teachers do not have the pressure of supervisors looking over their shoulder and do not have to justify their actions to them, they must also make most of their own decisions and live with the consequences. Although they have more professional freedom than people in other professions, they also have more personal responsibility.

Freedom with responsibility

Why teachers have so much autonomy is not clear, but they have had it for a long time—probably since the one-room schoolhouse. It is so ingrained that teachers today protect it as a matter of principle. They assume that they know what is best for their students and that outsiders can do no more than offer advice. They believe that outsider dictation about what and how they should teach, as well as close evaluation of their teaching according to external criteria, destroys classroom spontaneity and hurts children.[30]

This idea of classroom autonomy is reflected in the following statement of a cooperating teacher to his new student teacher:

When I close that door, it's the students and me. What we do determines how much they learn. There are policies, guidelines, and a curriculum; and I try to abide by them as much as is practical. But in reality, few other adults walk through that door while I am teaching. My students learn what they are supposed to learn and they like me. No one bothers me. I'm free to do what I think is best.

REFLECTING ON PRACTICE

The episodes in this section consist of firsthand comments by teachers about personal experiences during their first years on the job. They reflect some of the aspects of teaching described on the preceding pages. The first set of comments are those of students of the text authors. The latter are comments of the authors based on personal experiences. As you read, consider:

- Do the comments reflect teaching as you see it?
- In what ways do the comments highlight the noninstructional aspects of a teacher's work?
- Of the elements of teaching that are highlighted, which would you want changed? Why? How could those changes be accomplished?
- Which of the elements of teaching that are highlighted require adjustments in the ways you have thought about your teaching?

In the Classroom

Teaching seemed so easy when I observed classrooms as a college student. Then it seemed so complex when I had to do it in student teaching.

Questioning was especially difficult at first. I could not think of the right questions or phrase them so that the kids understood. Even when I did, I didn't listen to the answers. I must have agreed to lots of really stupid answers. Once I said "Correct!" when a student told me he didn't know the answer. You have to do ten things at once. Thirty sets of eyes looking at you. Thirty mouths ready to talk. All that energy needing direction. Sometimes I felt like an orchestra conductor, and all the musicians were ignoring me.

One day class was really going well. A discussion was flowing smoothly; everyone was into it. Then, within five minutes two kids left for a band trip, the secretary interrupted on the public-address system, Mary from next door asked to borrow a book, a parent showed up at the door, and the fire drill bell rang. We never did get back on track.

With Students

When I started, the other teachers said, "Be firm" and "Don't smile until Christmas," and I tried to follow their idea. I'm glad I did. It felt uncomfortable at first, but I was strict, not mean. I liked the kids and they could see that. They tried to test me but found that I was serious when I said our top priority was learning. We could have fun but only if we also learned.

I remember a boy asking me why I was not "soft" like other first-year teachers and a mother telling me that my reputation among her daughter's friends was "hard, serious, and friendly." I was proud of both comments. One day, I overheard one of my students talking to a new student about me. He said, "He's little, but don't mess with him. Do what he says. He means it. But he's okay. He's the best teacher I have. If you have a problem, he's the one to talk to." After hearing this, I would have taught the rest of the year without pay. My motto when it comes to students is be firm, friendly, fair; and care.

Among Professional Peers

When I first started, I felt so alone. Everyone was busy getting school started with his or her own classes. They were friendly but did not have time to reassure a scared new teacher, and I was also very busy. I saw other teachers only in the halls, at lunch, and in the parking lot. When I had control problems, I couldn't turn to anyone, and I didn't want anyone else to know.

Then Sarah sat down and talked with me. She sensed I was unhappy and befriended me. She became a source of support in every way. She knew what to say even when I didn't ask. Sarah got me through the first weeks and over the hump. She became my best friend. About the third week of school, Sarah took me to Friday afternoon happy hour with the faculty. We were the noisiest group in the tavern, probably sounded like kids at lunch. I quickly got to know most of the other teachers socially. They are a fun group, and they welcomed me openly. But you know, I know them well socially, and we all teach in the same school, but I have never seen most of them teach, nor they me.

The Needs of Students

The purpose of teaching is to serve the educational needs of students, and students have many needs. The next few pages describe some problematic aspects of students' lives that create needs that teachers must face. Because the purpose of this section is to draw attention to the elements of student lives that have significant impact upon what teachers do, the problems presented are those that severely affect students rather than more normal and commonplace conditions.

Although teachers never face the ideal class of academically hungry students who have no worries, weaknesses, or personal problems, most classes do consist of a preponderance of students who look like the stereotypical average school-age student. These students vary in intellectual ability but are friendly, possess middle-class values, attend school regularly, are comfortable with their lives and their learning, and like their teachers. They come from average homes, have enough to eat, dress appropriately, handle their personal problems adequately, and appear to be reasonably well adjusted.

Average students

But many students are not like this. They face conditions and crises that are great and sometimes long-lasting—conditions that present special challenges for their teachers. Some of those conditions are poverty; discrimination; physical, emotional, and intellectual disability; family trauma; abuse; neglect and alienation; drug and alcohol abuse; vandalism, delinquency, and violence.

Poverty

Although nearly all teachers in America are middle class, many of their students live in poverty. Some of these have only the very basics of life, if that. They live from day to day, often with insufficient food, inadequate clothing, and substandard housing. Some have never slept in a bed of their own or seen a pediatrician or family doctor. Some move among migrant labor camps and have no permanent place to call home. Some do not know of a single family member who holds a job or expects to get one. Insecurity and psychological strain are facts of life.

Because of conditions such as these, America began a national War on Poverty in 1964; it was intended to break the *cycle of poverty* that trapped so many children. Schools played a major part in the effort (as described in Chapter 7). But so far, the war has failed many families and children. Poverty is still present in the lives of children in most schools. In fact, according to recent statistics, 40 percent of the total U.S. population living in poverty are children under 18 years of age even though they make up only about 26 percent of the population; over 20 percent of all children under 18 live in poverty, the gap between the middle class and poor people in America is widening rapidly, and the lives of many children are getting worse.[31]

In order to develop a realistic personal grasp of the impact of poverty conditions in the United States on education and schools, pause for a few moments to analyze the statistics in Figure 15-1. These data are for the year 1992 and are indicative of

FIGURE 15-1   Statistics about poverty in the United States. *Source:* A variety of government sources as reported in *Newsweek,* 1993, October 18, p. 44.

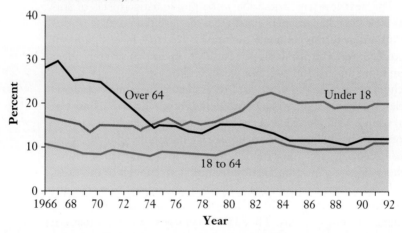

Poverty Rates by Age

Poverty threshold for one person in 1992 was $7,143.
Poverty threshold for a family of four in 1992 was $14,335

Poverty Groups

No. People	Percentage/Population
General	
36,880,000 = 14.5% of entire population	
27,372,000 = 13.9% of people in urban areas	
9,509,000 = 16.8% of people outside urban areas	
By Race	
18,308,000 = 9.6% of whites (non-Hispanic)	
10,613,000 = 33.3% of blacks	
6,655,000 = 29.3% of Hispanics	
912,000 = 12.5% of Asian/Pacific Islanders	
By Race (Families)	
7,960,000 = 11.7% of all families	
3,860,000 = 7.3% of white families (non-Hispanic)	
2,435,000 = 30.9% of black families	
1,395,000 = 26.2% of Hispanic families	
199,000 = 12.0% of Asian/Pacific Islander families	

No. People	Percentage/Population
By Race (Children)	
14,617,000 = 21.9% of all children under 18 years old	
8,955,000 = 16.9% of white children under 18	
4,938,000 = 46.6% of black children under18	
3,116,000 = 39.9% of Hispanic children under 18	
By Type of Household	
4,171,000 = 34.9% of all female-led households	
3,318,000 = 6.2% of all married-couple families	
1,835,000 = 49.8% of black female-led households	
486,000 = 13.0% of black married-couple families	
By Region	
14,763,000 = 16.9% of people in Southern states	
7,983,000 = 13.1% of people in Midwestern states	
7,907,000 = 14.4% of people in Western states	
6,227,000 = 12.3% of people in Northeastern states	

Something to Think About

The following case study of a poor child is not atypical.[32]

Gerry is 15 and in the eighth grade. He does not like school. He flunks most tests and is frustrated all the time. He plans to quit next year. Most of his friends already have.

No one in his family has finished high school. His mother stopped in the tenth grade, when she became pregnant. His father never returned after he was sent to reform school during ninth grade. His brother dropped out last year, supposedly to look for a job, and his sister, a sophomore, rarely attends and is flunking every course.

Gerry is never encouraged to study at home. No one else ever did, and there is no quiet place to do it even if he wanted to. His parents would not be able to help him if he got stuck, and he would not embarrass them by asking. No one else at home reads anything but occasional newspapers and magazines.

His parents have not visited the school since he was in fifth grade. They are uneasy about talking to teachers. He knows his teachers think his parents do not care about his education, but he is sure they do. They just do not know how to help. They are as frustrated as he is.

Gerry knows that some of his teachers want to help him but cannot. They talk about things he does not understand, go places he will never see, and own things he cannot get unless he steals them. They live in a different world. They do not understand.

■ What could teachers do to be successful with Gerry?
■ What would constitute success in this situation?

circumstances today. What do these numbers and percentages mean for how teachers teach students? What do they mean for continued public support for schools? What do they mean concerning the cultural, ethnic, and racial makeup of student populations and their teachers? How do they affect what schools are expected to accomplish?

Teachers must serve children from poor families as best they can, and that means devoting extra effort to them. They must help them compensate for the burdens of their disadvantaged position in society and enable them to learn anyway. They must reach them instructionally no matter how difficult they are to reach, provide them with the academic and other coping skills they need to succeed, give them hope, and ease the pain. The task is enormous and failure is frequent, but teachers find despair the worst enemy; they cannot afford it. For some students, teachers are the best hope of making it out of poverty, and many of those who do make it say that at least one teacher was critical to that success.[33]

Teachers—A way out

Discrimination

Many students suffer from discrimination of one form or another—because of race, ethnic or religious background, gender, or handicapping condition. For many, discrimination is direct, personal, current, and continuing. For others it is the result of past injustices inflicted upon them, their ancestors, or the group with which they identify. In either case, the experience is painful and produces economic, social, emotional, and sometimes physical scars. Frequently, it makes learning difficult and causes students to be behind in school in comparison with their more fortunate counterparts.

Confronting discrimination

To be successful with these students, teachers must confront the effects of discrimination, teach in ways that succeed in spite of the scars, and provide the knowledge and skills that enable students to achieve despite the burden. In addition, because serious prejudice is displayed in behaviors at school, teachers must watch for it and root it out. They must stand above the crowd and avoid being caught up in subtle bias and prejudicial assumptions that could cause them to discriminate themselves. They must not only fight the problem, but they must also be ever vigilant against becoming part of it.

Teachers need to do *more* for and with these children if they are going to achieve at the same level as their relatively unscarred classmates. Until now, however, broad-scale attempts at compensatory instruction for victims of discrimination have not been very successful. For example, studies show that greater percentages of black and other minority students still perform below the level of whites on academic criteria, and greater percentages fail to graduate from high school. Also, minority students are disproportionately assigned to special education classes and identified as problem students.[34]

Individual concentrated help

But there is hope. Concentrated work by individual teachers with individual students helps significantly, and such efforts occur in every school every day.

Physical, Emotional, and Intellectual Disability

Like students who suffer from poverty and discrimination, students with disabilities, even if they are not discriminated against, have conditions and needs that are out of the ordinary and require special teacher attention. Some have handicaps severe enough to require specially arranged instruction and consideration, while others have less serious conditions—such as diabetes, epilepsy, dyslexia, attention deficit disorder, mild retardation, chronic illness, and controlled emotional disorders—and require only limited adjustments.

Compensating for disabilities

Whatever the specific disabling condition or the severity of its effect on student learning, students who live with handicaps deserve to be educated to their fullest, and teachers are responsible for providing that service even if it is difficult or inconvenient. They must help students with disabling conditions learn in spite of their condition and aid them in dealing with the complications caused by it.

Family Stress

If sometime in the romantic past virtually all students came to school from stable, secure families with two knowledgeable, skilled, dedicated parents living in the same house and with one parent at home most of the day performing services for the rest of the family and waiting at the door when the children returned from school, that time no longer exists. Nowadays, students come from all sorts of homes. Some are strong and supportive, but many are under stress, on the verge of collapse, or already shattered. When there are problems at home, students are affected at school, and the circumstances must be of concern to teachers.

Because of dramatic changes in the nature of families, teachers cannot assume that parents are available to students during after-school hours. What implications does this fact have for teaching practice?

During the last few decades, the American family has undergone enormous change, and schools and teachers have not always kept up with the times. For example, single-parent homes are the norm for many schools; many poverty-level families have no adult male relatives in the home; increasingly parents are teenagers, and in 60 percent of American families with two parents, both parents now work outside the home, an increase of more than 20 percent in only twenty years.[35] Parents are at home less and busier and more fatigued when they are at home. Many are less able to concentrate on traditional, middle-class, one-parent-at-home parenting functions such as reading to the children, enforcing homework time, monitoring television, talking over milk and cookies, and participating in family outings.

Single and working parents

Therefore, more children and school-age youth are on their own more of the time. They arrive home on their own schedule, choose their own detours en route, have their own key, watch their own soap operas, and hang out away from home for much of their out-of-school time. Some younger children spend more time with babysitters than with either parent.

Latchkey children

Families live more isolated existences in more impersonal, urban environments than previously. They have less contact with extended family members, and they move more often. School children typically change neighborhoods and schools several times during their thirteen years of schooling.

Isolated, transient families

A rather extreme illustration of contemporary, urban family life for a class of elementary school children is portrayed in the case study reported below, which reports on a class taught in the mid-1980s by Lynn Myers:

> Of the 27 first graders, 21 lived with neither or only one of their own parents. Several lived with grandparents, rarely saw their mother, and did not know their father.
>
> Approximately one-third lived in a home that included an adult male who was not their father and was not married to their mother. They usually re-

ferred to him as "uncle" or "momma's boyfriend." His presence was considered to be temporary.

One child came from a home of five children who had the same mother but five different fathers. None of the fathers currently lived with the family, but a grandmother did.

During that year, nine children moved and transferred away from the school. Eight children transferred in. One child moved away and back again three times during the nine months, while her mother persistently tried to reconcile (unsuccessfully) with her alcoholic husband, who physically abused her and the child.

Contemporary teachers must constantly remember that at any given time one or more of their students are probably suffering under some form of significant family stress that affects how those students learn and function in school. They must tailor their teaching to help those students learn as best they can under the circumstances.

Child Abuse

The *battered child syndrome* is well known in American society today. In populated areas, cases are reported in the media constantly. Those reported, however, are only the worst cases and the ones known to authorities. Many more occur, and most of the victims go to school. With all of their physical and emotional scars, they sit before teachers who are pledged to teach them.

The abuse can be physical, sexual, and psychological. It is always emotional. It can occur as an isolated incident or be repeated frequently over long periods of time. It can show up as highly visible injuries and scars or be almost hidden. But in all its forms, it is traumatic.

A need to act

Most teachers knowingly confront child abuse sometime during their career, and some face it regularly. When they do, they are often the first people in positions of authority to notice it, and that fact places them in unique situations of responsibility. They must do something. If they do not act, they allow current abuses to continue, and they neglect a child who needs special treatment.

Often teachers want to shy away from child abuse situations. They are heart wrenching and messy. Intrusion could make the child more vulnerable. Accusations could open the teacher to threats, physical attack, and legal challenges. But as responsible adults, they cannot avoid action. They must step in, notify authorities, and stop the abuse.

Teachers' responsibilities, however, are not limited to the reporting of child abuse. They must teach the victims and, at the same time, help them succeed in spite of the circumstances. They must care for them emotionally as much as they can, help them cope, and protect them from further pain as much as possible.

Drug and Alcohol Abuse

Alcoholism and drug abuse are rampant in American society among adults and students. Majorities of high school students drink alcohol, at least occasionally, and apparently similar numbers use street drugs or abuse medicinal ones. At least one in twenty teenagers is already an alcoholic. Even elementary students are "hooked," sometimes from birth because of prenatal usage by their mothers. Drug and alcohol abuse is so prevalent in some homes and neighborhoods that it is the expected thing to do, even for children.[36]

Children of the drug-culture parents now appear in the primary grades of many schools. They have already suffered from prenatal usage and withdrawal. Some cannot concentrate or remember, are hyperactive, cannot hold their hands still, and in the worst cases are noticeably brain-damaged. Their conditions make normal learning impossible. Children of the drug culture

Many children and youth who do not abuse drugs and alcohol themselves still suffer from the consequences. When parents, siblings, and other relatives and friends are hooked, all close to them suffer. The impact is at least distracting, clearly emotional, and sometimes devastating.

Under the circumstances, teachers must face the reality that some of their students suffer because of alcohol and drug abuse, and they must act accordingly. They must be especially observant, understanding, and sympathetic toward students already suffering or at risk. They must intervene to try to stop harmful repercussions. They must teach about the harmful effects of alcohol and drug use. And they must adjust their teaching to compensate for alcohol- and drug-related handicaps that affect learning.

As with child abuse situations, teacher involvement in alcohol and drug abuse matters has its professional risks. The circumstances are personal, private, and messy. They almost always include family situations that are embarrassing to all and not normally a teacher's concern. Nevertheless, if they are harmful to their students, teachers who do not act are negligent. Another need to act

Vandalism, Delinquency, and Violence

Today's students are often victims of violent behavior. They may suffer directly, suffer under the threat of harm, or suffer from the repercussions of harm inflicted on those close to them. The harm might be physical or psychological. It might occur at school or in their out-of-school lives. They could be participants, perpetrators, or victims.

In the out-of-school world, thousands of people are attacked, intimidated, harassed, and otherwise harmed each day. Thousands more are frightened by what might happen. And that atmosphere of violence spills over into schools. Some students hurt, steal from, and extort money from others. Some badger, threaten, and assault teachers. Some vandalize school property and teachers' and other students' cars. A violent society

The causes of this behavior are diverse and often obscure. Modern society is large, complex, and impersonal; and schools are often the same. Society, in and out of school, is competitive and sometimes harsh. Whatever the causes, however, the conditions interfere with learning and disrupt teaching. They do not go away if ignored. Violence in schools

Therefore, teachers and school administrators must confront violence in schools and the effects of violence that intrude from outside. They must stop the abuse and remove the fear. They must make schools as safe and the lives of their students as secure as they can. They must protect potential victims, report perpetrators, and head off trouble before it starts.

Sometimes teachers have to step in physically to stop violence as it is occurring and get emergency help to do so, but more often teachers' roles are more subtle. They can counter a propensity toward violence by the way they manage students, by the behavior they model and expect in their classrooms, by how they reach out to potential troublemakers and victims, and by what they teach—especially in the value aspects of their instruction. These efforts do not always work, but they do help much of the time.

In addition to confronting trouble, teachers must also prevent it from pulling them away from their primary task. They must continue to teach effectively, whatever the conditions. Even in troubled schools, the students must continue to learn.

Addressing Student Needs

Helping with problems

This section began with the warning that it stresses problems in the lives of students, problems that are severe enough to intrude into classrooms and complicate what teachers do. It was presented in this way to emphasize that the job of teaching involves more than instructing students under ideal conditions. Teaching also involves meeting the broader needs of students. It does so for two reasons: (1) because those needs impinge upon what students learn and (2) because teachers are expected to address student needs beyond those that are narrowly academic.

Job Conditions

Teachers teach under all kinds of conditions, from ideal to intolerable, but most teaching situations are fairly close to the midpoint between those extremes. Individual teachers usually see both good and bad aspects in what they do, but for the most part, they take conditions into account, balance them out, and teach successfully.

Generally, teachers like their work. They usually find their goals achievable, the expectations of their superiors reasonable, limits on their freedom acceptable, responses from students stimulating, and feedback on their performance encouraging. They tend to fit comfortably into their classroom and school environment. They find their interactions with other people to their liking and the results of their efforts rewarding.

Although most teachers can easily find something legitimate to complain about, usually those situations are eventually corrected or gradually forgotten. In general, job conditions are on a par with those of most comparable professions and not much different from that which most beginning teachers expect from the start.

That is not to say that teaching is easy or that job conditions are always as they should be. Teaching is a hard, stressful, and sometimes burdensome profession, and anyone considering it as a career should face that fact realistically. Some specific negative work conditions are unavoidable, and others take time to correct. The next few paragraphs describe some of the positive and negative aspects of teaching.

The Positives

Teaching means helping children and young people learn and develop in good ways; and when noticeable changes occur, teachers feel an exhilarating sense of satisfaction—a feeling of accomplishment that motivates them to continue with determination. That satisfaction plus a belief among teachers that they are doing something worthwhile combine with extrinsic rewards—compensation, other monetary benefits, community respect—to constitute much of the positive side of the job of teaching.[37]

Feeling of satisfaction

The feeling of satisfaction is illustrated poignantly by Philip W. Jackson in *Life in Classrooms* (1968). One of his illustrations follows:

> When you see a child that has suddenly caught on and is enjoying reading or is going ahead to be an independent worker, you can't help but have satisfaction and know that you have done something for this particular child. You know that you aren't going to do wonders with every child. . . . But when you do see a child bloom, it's gratifying.[38]

The belief among teachers that they are doing good, useful, prized, and respected work rests on the assumption that teaching improves students' lives and the well-being of the entire community. These two quotes from anonymous teachers illustrate the idea:

> I think of teaching as missionary work. I have always wanted to serve others, and this is my way of doing it. I believe my work is important.

> By teaching, we help young people, and that helps everyone. We contribute to society and make people's lives more fulfilling.

Other positive aspects of the job that teachers frequently mention are

- The constant reinforcing feedback from students who are enjoying what the teacher is doing—"You can tell they like it by the smiles and attention."
- The openness and informality that teachers and students have with each other—"You do not have to perform like an employee performs for a boss. You can be yourself with students; they certainly are themselves."
- The autonomy—"When you close that door, you're the boss, at least until someone complains."
- The spontaneity of the classrooms—"Sometimes students say or do things that you would never expect and you change directions in response. It reminds you that you are working with active human minds. I find it exhilarating."
- A daily schedule and yearly calendar that are compatible with those of children—"Of course I have to work a lot after hours at home, but those hours are flexible, and I can be home most of the time that my children are there."

Although teacher salaries are not as high as they should be and do not attract many people to teaching from other professional careers, they are the primary external reward for teachers, and in the recent years of educational reform they have been getting better. (More on salaries appears in Chapter 16.)

Other extrinsic benefits that teachers normally receive are[39]

- job security (although enrollment declines in the 1970s and 1980s caused layoffs)
- annual salary increments
- secure and adequate retirement benefits
- adequate benefits, such as health insurance and leaves of absence
- opportunities for additional paid assignments such as coaching, club sponsorship, curriculum development, and summer teaching
- free time in the summer

The Negatives

Although the positive aspects of teaching tend to be general in nature, the negative aspects tend to be more specific conditions of work. Some of those conditions are, of course, simply a part of teaching—working in crowded classrooms, within bureaucracies, under strict time pressures, and surrounded by noise and confusion; but

Doing a good thing

Other positives

Salary

Other benefits

One of the challenges facing teachers is finding constructive ways to cope with such common sources of stress as inadequate funding and facilities.

other negative work conditions are specific irritants that sometimes can be modified or adjusted.[40] Points that teachers complain about most often include

rigid bureaucratic procedures
insensitive, impersonal, and impractical regulations
inadequate supplies and resources
too many students and classes that are too large
insufficient planning time
old and worn-out facilities

demanding and insensitive administrators
lack of student discipline
unprofessional colleagues
too much paperwork
criticism from parents and community groups
stress

Teachers also express concerns about

lack of adequate feedback and appreciation
inadequate pay
declining family interest in education
lack of support from parents
being held accountable for conditions they cannot control

censorship and challenges to academic freedom
vulnerability to legal liability action
denial of due process in employment matters
sex discrimination
loss of tenure rights
testing to prove their competence

increased student testing   limited opportunities for profes-
students' refusal to do homework   sional advancement
abuse from students

Negative conditions such as these are usually bothersome rather than defeating for most teachers, but they are matters of concern nonetheless, and they do impinge upon teacher performance. When they go on for long periods of time and occur in great numbers, frustrations build up, and teaching is not as enjoyable as it should be.

Bothersome rather than defeating

Teaching—On Balance

The extent to which individual teachers see their job in positive or negative terms depends on a number of things, including

1. the relative balance between positive and negative conditions that actually exist
2. the perspectives and attitudes of the teacher facing the conditions
3. the standard against which the conditions are being judged

In some circumstances, the rewards outweigh the trials and tribulations; in others the negative conditions are too numerous, intense, and frustrating to be balanced by the positive. Some teachers are so satisfied and proud of what they do that they take the negative conditions in stride and succeed happily despite them, while others are so troubled by bad conditions that the good never compensates for them. Sometimes teachers judge their job conditions against the way they should be, while others think of how much worse they could be. In any event, most teachers who remain in the classroom consider their work worthwhile and satisfying.

Teachers as a Professional Group

Like any group of professionals, teachers have much in common. They do the same kinds of work, have similar professional responsibilities and goals, experience comparable successes and frustrations, and confront common pressures. Some people say teachers even think alike, have similar lifestyles, and select their friends from among other teachers.

Possibly a very significant finding of recent research is the idea that teachers working together as a sincere *professional community* provides a very effective means for reforming schools, improving working conditions in schools, and enhancing student learning. Related to this is the belief that, when professional teacher groups possess the power to make important organizational, curricular, and personnel decisions (instead of top-level school administrators), there is hope for more successful schools.[41]

Collectively, teachers and other professional educators have professional power that they can, and do, use to affect the direction of American education. They help select political officials, direct public policy, shift educational priorities, and sway public decisions; insist that students be educated appropriately and treated fairly; and demand that they themselves be compensated adequately, treated justly, and consulted regularly. They also influence curriculum decisions, teacher evaluation standards, teaching procedures, and all sorts of matters that affect what and how they teach.

A group of professionals

In the past, many teachers were reluctant to use their collective power. They tended to see themselves as rather do-good public servants. During recent decades, however, they have become more outspoken on educational matters and have been more forceful as advocates for children and better schools. They have also become more visible proponents of their own welfare.

Organizations through which teachers and other educators wield influence include the following national groups:

Influential organizations

National Education Association (NEA)
American Federation of Teachers (AFT)
National Association of Secondary School Principals
National Association of Elementary School Principals
American Association of School Administrators
National Council for the Accreditation of Teacher Education
National School Boards Association
National Congress of Parents and Teachers
Council of Chief State School Officers
Association of Teacher Educators

Many of these groups have state and local affiliates or counterparts.

Unions

The two major national teachers' unions—the National Education Association and the American Federation of Teachers—along with their state and local affiliates, are the largest and most influential teacher bodies. Both exist to advocate for improved education and to represent the interests of teachers. In recent years, the two unions have conducted continuing discussions about some form of merger. Their main activities include:

- negotiating and collective bargaining for their members
- influencing legislative and regulatory policy
- supplying information to members
- protecting teachers against legal action and unfair outside pressures
- setting standards of professional practice
- providing personal support services (such as stress management consultation and financial advice)
- providing auxiliary membership services (such as insurance, investment programs, travel packages, and book clubs)

Both unions have significant political clout, especially as official bargaining agents and lobbyists. They actively support and oppose legislation and the election of candidates, and their actions are often very effective. For example, both have helped pass local and state education bond issues and tax levies over the years and have fought budget cuts for education. Both were particularly influential in the election of President Bill Clinton in 1992, and NEA was the primary force behind the establishment in 1979 of the U.S. Department of Education. Both unions have also been vocal in support of desegregated schools and programs that improve the welfare of students. They have opposed using public funds for private schools and for religious education.

Because of their power and large constituencies, the two organizations were represented on most major education reform commissions of the 1980s, and their influence continues. Most observers believe their concurrence with proposed reforms in the future is necessary if the reforms are to have a lasting impact. Currently, both unions are directly involved in efforts intended to change the ways in which teachers are evaluated, certified by states, and prepared by colleges.

The National Education Association is the oldest and largest teachers' union. NEA It was begun in 1857, and has approximately 2 million members—about two-thirds of all practicing teachers. It includes administrators and supervisors as well as teachers.

In addition to its bargaining and political activities, the NEA is active in teacher staff development and curricular matters. It also gathers data about schools, students, and teachers, which it disseminates to its members. Teachers use the data to improve their teaching; association affiliates use them to further their advocacy work. For example, the affiliates use comparative information on salaries, fringe benefits, negotiation arrangements, and job conditions to convince legislatures and school boards to be more supportive of their schools and teachers.

The NEA has been especially active in the move to place teachers in control of their own profession through the establishment of state professional standards boards that contain a teacher majority. In its view, these boards should control standards for teachers, police their own ranks, and monitor the conditions under which teachers work. They should operate similarly to the medical boards and bar associations established by physicians and attorneys.

The American Federation of Teachers was begun in 1916, is an affiliate of the AFT AFL-CIO labor organization, and currently has about 800,000 members, many of whom are employed in major American cities, including New York, Philadelphia, Boston, Washington, D.C., and Detroit. It does not admit administrators or supervisors.

The AFT focuses its energies more narrowly on teacher employment concerns than does the NEA and because of its AFL-CIO ties is more influential in national political matters that affect other school employees and union workers in other areas of employment.

Through its longtime national president, Albert Shanker, the AFT is a supporter of national standards and testing for teachers. Shanker has been outspoken in favor of making entry to the teaching profession more rigorous. The AFT also advocates a national professional standards board controlled by teachers.

Specialized Professional Organizations

In addition to unions, many teachers also join professional organizations that identify more closely with their specific teaching specialties or with a particular group of children and their specialized needs. Those who teach in special types of schools such as religious-affiliated and independent, private schools often join associations organized around these focuses. Teachers do this because these groups advocate for issues they believe in and because they are a way to communicate on such matters. Because the groups can speak on behalf of and with the support of their members, they, too, enhance the power of their teacher members. Organizations of these types include:

American Alliance for Health, Physical Education, Recreation, and Dance
American Association for Gifted Children
American Council of the Teaching of Foreign Languages
American Industrial Arts Association
American Vocational Association
Association for Childhood Education International
Council for Exceptional Children
International Reading Association

Modern Language Association
National Art Educational Association
National Association for the Education of Young Children
National Business Education Association
National Council for the Social Studies
National Council of Teachers of English
National Council of Teachers of Mathematics
National Science Teachers Association

Teachers and Group Membership

Teachers, like all professionals, benefit from professional group membership. Through it, they develop contacts, friendships, and a feeling that they are not alone in their job. They get to know people like themselves who do the same things, gain the same satisfactions, and experience similar frustrations. Those colleagues are available to them when needed to share excitements and provide support.

Pride of membership

In addition, professional group membership provides individual teachers with a general group identity—a sense of belonging that comes when one says, "I am a teacher" or "I am going to be a teacher." That sense of belonging makes a person part of a professional community, and being part of such a community carries with it a certain amount of professional respect, status, and pride. To outsiders, the person has special credentials.

Of course, if the profession is not well respected, the status attributed to it and its members is not high. Most observers would say that teaching is respected more than many professions, but not as much as some. Therefore, those who contemplate joining the group called teachers have at least two questions to consider:

■ Do I want to be called a teacher?
■ Will my work as a teacher add to the professional respectability of the group?

EDUCATIONAL RESEARCH

Assessing the Condition of Teaching

This Educational Research section presents selected findings from two recent efforts to survey teachers and assess the current condition of teaching. The reports include demographic data, teacher perceptions of school conditions, their opinions about the work they do, and their sense of satisfaction about being a teacher. Because this is the last Educational Research section in this text, the data are presented in raw form and you are asked to draw your own inferences from them. As you read the information presented, consider what the data may mean to you as a potential teacher. Do any of the data surprise or disappoint you?

The Research Division of the National Education Association conducts a survey of American public school teachers every five years, which it reports as *Status of the American Public School Teacher.* The most recent survey was completed in 1990–1991 and reported in 1992.[42] Selected data from that report are listed below.

■ Seventy-six percent of American public school teachers were married.
■ Seventy-three percent had children.
■ Fifty-three percent held at least a master's degree.
■ Thirty-five percent, including

most of the younger teachers, had to pass a competency test to enter or remain in teaching.

- The mean length of teaching experience was 15 years.
- First-year teachers made up only 3 percent of all public school teachers.
- The mean number of teachers teaching in an elementary school was 30, and the mean number in a secondary school was 63.
- Fifty percent of all public school teachers taught in elementary schools, just over 20 percent taught in middle schools or junior highs, and just under 30 percent taught in high schools.
- Twenty-five percent of all public high school teachers taught English, 14.5 percent taught mathematics.
- The mean class size for elementary teachers was 24.
- The mean number of students for secondary teachers was 93.
- The typical length of time teachers had for lunch was 31 minutes.
- The mean number of uncompensated hours teachers reported spending each week on school-related activities was almost 11 hours.
- Teachers reported spending 8.4 hours each week outside of the school day on instruction-related work, such as lesson preparation and paper grading.
- Fifty-nine percent of public school teachers said they would choose teaching again as their profession, 5.4 percent would not, and 17 percent probably would not; the others were not sure.
- Younger teachers were more likely to say they would teach again than older teachers.
- Sixty-five percent of public school teachers said they are or tend to be conservative; 35 percent said they are or tend to be liberal.
- Thirty-six percent were Demo-

crats; 32 percent were Republicans.

When American public school teachers of 1990–1991 were asked to identify the three main reasons why they originally became teachers, their responses broke down as follows:

Reason	% Teachers Who Listed This Reason
Desire to work with young people	65.9
Value or significance of education in society	37.2
Interest in subject-matter field	33.6
Influence of a teacher during a student's elementary or secondary school years	26.8
Never really considered anything else	23.8
Influence of family	22.7
Long summer vacation	20.7
Job security	16.7
Opportunity for a lifetime of self-growth	7.9

When the teachers were asked to indicate what helped or hindered them the most in providing the best services as teachers, the top six responses in each category were as follows:

Reason	% Teachers Who Listed This Reason
Helps	**%**
Interest in children and teaching	21.5
Training, education, and knowledge of subject matter	15.8
Cooperative and competent teacher colleagues	15.4
Help from administrators and specialists	15.0
School environment and freedom to teach	10.9
Good materials, resources, and facilities	5.8
Hindrances	
Incompetent and uncooperative administrators	16.2
Heavy work load and extra responsibilities	14.8
Lack of materials, resources, and facilities	12.4
Lack of funds and decent salaries	11.9
Negative attitudes of the public and parents	9.3
Class size	8.7

In 1990, The National Center for Education Information surveyed public and private school teachers *who were hired since 1985* about their opinions on a number of professional issues. The Center reported its data in *Profile of Teachers in the U.S.—1990*. Samples of those data are reported below.[43]

- Eighty-three percent of teachers hired since 1985 said that schools should adjust to the needs, interests, and learning styles of individual students, rather than expect students to adjust to the norms of the school.
- Only 13 percent thought students were the best judges of what they need to learn and when they are ready to learn it.
- Seventy-seven percent said academic achievement standards should be flexible enough for each student to feel successful.
- Seventy-four percent agreed that students are apt to feel pride in themselves only if they see in the curriculum examples of success, achievement, and contributions by members of their racial, linguistic, and religious group.
- Only 13 percent thought that students are best taught by teachers of their own race or ethnic group.
- Eighty percent believed that students can reach the highest levels of achievement regardless of socioeconomic background.

When the teachers hired since 1985 were asked to indicate if they agreed or not with a number of recent school reform proposals, the percentage who agreed was as follows:

Reform Proposal	% Agreed
Give teachers greater authority in the running of schools	90
Allow greater flexibility at the school building level in determining what and how students are taught	84
Establish national goals for education in this country	83
Demand that a student perform at grade level before he or she is passed on to the next grade	74
Let each individual school decide how the school will operate	65
Involve parents more directly in the running of schools	60
Recruit adults who have experience in careers other than education into teaching	56
Allow parents to send their children to the school of their choice	53
Recruit adults who have experience as managers or administrators in careers other than education into positions as superintendents and principals	28

Reform Proposal	% Agreed
Extend the school year	26
Extend the school day	16

The teachers hired since 1985 responded as follows when asked to choose up to three responses to this question: If you had to choose, which of these are most important to you?

	%
Chance to work with young people—see them develop	71%
A chance to use your mind and abilities	65
A good salary	45
Appreciation for a job well done	41
Job security	25
Medical and other benefits	18
A clean, quiet, comfortable place to work	16

When teachers hired since 1985 were asked how satisfied they were with different aspects of their job, the percent of those who responded as being satisfied are as follows:

	%
Relationship with other teachers	93%
Overall job satisfaction	83
Relationship with parents of students	83

Reform Proposal	% Agreed
Relationship with principal	80
Present curriculum	74
General working conditions	69
Present textbooks	67
Salary	45
Status of teachers in this community	42

The positive responses of teachers hired since 1985 when asked if they were satisfied with various aspects of their lives are reported below. For comparison purposes, responses on the same points by the general public in a 1988 Gallup Poll are also listed.

	Teachers Hired Since 1985 (%)	General Public (%)
Your health today	88	88
Your family life	84	94
The way things are going in your personal life	81	85
Your present housing	78	87
The job/work you do	77	76
Your free time—the time when you are not working at your job	70	87
Your standard of living	67	85
Your household income	51	69

Sources: National Education Association, 1992. *Status of the American Public School Teachers 1990–91.* Washington, D.C.: NEA. Reprinted by permission. National Center for Education Information data reprinted by permission of C. Emily Feistritzer, NCEI.

Conclusion

When people try to assess teaching as a career, they often compare teachers with other professionals. In doing so, they consider the work the different groups do, job conditions, compensation, degree of satisfaction, status, and so forth. Then they try to decide whether teaching is better or worse than the other jobs by determining the extent to which teaching measures up against the others. The process helps people decide whether they want to be teachers, but it is admittedly artificial for several reasons:

1. Professions differ in enough significant ways to make some comparisons artificial.
2. Professions change so rapidly and radically that comparisons quickly become dated.
3. Comparisons of this type do not place enough emphasis on the personal values and priorities of the individuals who are facing the career choice.

Probably a more useful way of determining whether teaching is a career for you is to ask yourself questions that compare teaching as you know it with what you want for yourself—your personal career goals and priorities. The four questions that follow might start that process for you.

- What do teachers do in their jobs?
- What are their professional lives like generally?
- Do you want to do that?
- Do you want to live like that?

This chapter is intended to help you raise questions such as these and to provide you with sufficient information to develop some responses to them. If it has been successful, you now have a basis on which to formulate further questions and answers as your study continues. In the years ahead, you will be able to balance the pluses and minuses of teaching within your own value system. Being a successful and satisfied teacher requires constant reflection at a professional level. Questions such as these are part of that process.

The Snapshot that opened this chapter presented Margaret Metzger's thoughtful assessment of why she is and remains a teacher. You might want to return to that letter again to stimulate your own thinking at this point. You might also want to consider the following incident:

> Professor Mark Shannon had just finished observing Tim Johnson, one of his social studies student teachers at John Overton Comprehensive High School in Nashville, Tennessee. As he approached his car in the parking lot, he noticed a note under the windshield wiper. It said,
>
> Dear Professor,
>
> Just a note to let you know what a great teacher Mr. Johnson is. We all respect him and learn a great deal from him.
>
> Yours truly,
The Students of John Overton High School
>
> Tim Johnson was hired as a regular teacher in that school the next year.

Summary

Although teachers are a diverse group of human beings, they are similar in having common professional goals and performing comparable work. Most are middle class, have served in classrooms for several years, seem to be relatively middle of the road on most issues, and are thought to be knowledgeable about what they do.

Beginning teachers soon realize that teaching is a complex job. Most seem to adjust quickly, however, and express satisfaction with the way they handle their first year in the classroom.

The job of teaching revolves around a number of contexts within which it takes place, including the nature of classrooms and schools as workplaces; the characteristics of the students being taught; the relationships developed between teachers and their students; the interactions that occur between teachers and their peers, their principal, and parents; and the roles and responsibilities assumed by teachers when they close the classroom door. The job is also greatly affected by the needs of the particular students each teacher faces. Students who experience particularly harsh living conditions—such as poverty, discrimination, abuse, and alienation—have special needs and present special challenges for their teachers.

Job conditions for teachers vary greatly, but most teachers seem to balance out the good and the bad. Typically, teachers list a feeling of doing worthwhile and respected work as the most positive aspect of teaching and mention day-to-day frustrations and specific deterrents to doing their work as the most persistent negatives.

Teachers join professional groups to share common concerns, marshal professional power, and influence educational and political decisions at local, state, and national levels. The National Education Association and the American Federation of Teachers are the two national teacher unions.

Study Questions

1. Make a list of ten to fifteen circumstances or conditions that teachers often face in a given day or week on the job, being sure to include about equal numbers of positive and negative items. Then rank the items from the most positive aspect to the most negative. Which items would cancel out items at the other end of the ranking?

2. Which types of teacher work conditions would be most likely to drive you out of teaching? Which aspects of the job would be likely to keep you in the classroom despite the negatives? Justify your thinking on each response.

3. Which types of issues and situations should have highest priority for attention by teacher unions? Why do you think so?

4. How involved should teachers get in out-of-school problems of students?

5. How involved should teacher unions and associations get in social issues?

Key Terms

Battered Child syndrome	Professional community	Teacher
Cycle of poverty	Routine patterns	autonomy
"Flat profession"	Social conventions	Teacher isolation
Hierarchial profession	Specialized professional	
Latch-key children	organizations	
Pride of membership	Stress	

For Further Reading

Arends, R. I. (1994). *Learning to teach*. New York: McGraw-Hill.

Brophy, J. E. (1982). How teachers influence what is taught and learned in classrooms. *Elementary School Journal, 83*, 1–13.

Csikszentmihalyi, M., & McCormack, J. (1986). The influence of teachers. *Phi Delta Kappan, 67*(6), 415–419.

Darling-Hammond, L. (1990). Teacher and teaching: Signs of a changing profession. In R. W. Houston, M. Haberman, & J. Sikula (Eds.), *Handbook of research on teacher education* (pp. 267–290). New York: Macmillan.

Ekstrom, R. B., Goertz, M. E., Pollack, J. M., & Rock, D. A. (1986). Who drops out of high school and why? Findings from a national study. *Teachers College Record, 87*(3), 356–373.

Elam, S. M., Rose, L. C., & Gallup, A. M. (1993). The 25th annual Phi Delta Kappa/Gallup Poll of the public's attitudes toward the public schools. *Phi Delta Kappan, 75*(2), 137–152. (Similar polls appear in *Phi Delta Kappan* each year in either the September or October issue.)

Frymier, J. (1992). Children who hurt, children who fail. *Phi Delta Kappan, 74*(3), 257–259.

Haselkorn, D., & Calkins, A. (1993). *Careers in teaching handbook*. Belmont, MA: Recruiting New Teachers.

Jackson, P. (1968). *Life in classrooms*. New York: Holt, Rinehart and Winston.

Lortie, D. C. (1975). *School teacher: A sociological study*. Chicago: University of Chicago Press.

McLaughlin, M. W. (1992). How district communities do and do not foster teacher pride. *Educational Leadership, 50*(1), 33–35.

National Education Association. (1992). *Status of the American public school teacher: 1990–91*. Washington, DC: National Education Association.

Teaching the Next Generation

Is It for You?

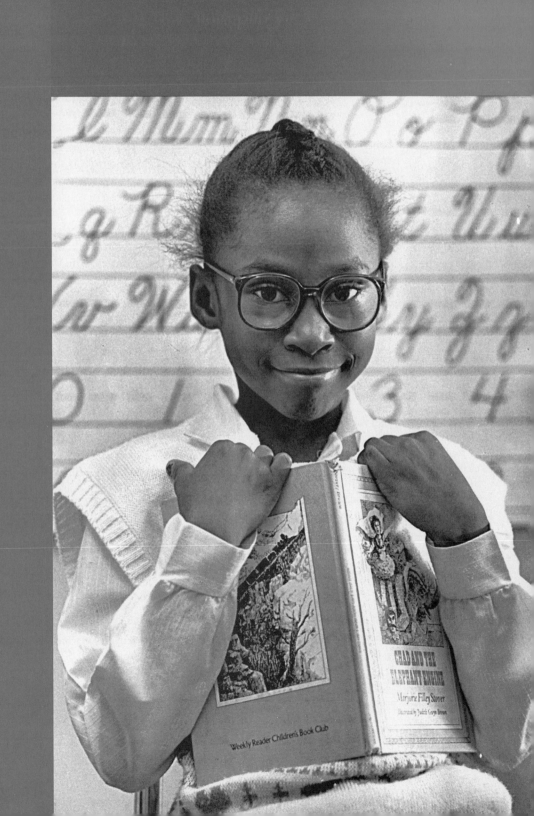

C hapter 15 surveyed key aspects of the professional work of contemporary teachers. It was intended to provide a brief glimpse at what teachers do and the situations they face day after day as practicing professionals. This chapter builds on that material. It extends current conditions and trends that affect schools and teaching into the next generation in order to provide a look at teaching during the late 1990s and beyond. It ends by asking you to consider this question: If that is what teaching will be about in the years ahead, do you want to be a teacher?

The chapter begins with a look at the ways in which educational reform agendas described earlier in this text are likely to be played out during the next decade or so, and it comes to focus on the central importance of the teacher. Next, it surveys key employment matters for beginning teachers—supply and demand, ideas about where to teach, and salary and compensation. It then describes several professional and societal conditions that are expected to have great impact on teaching through the turn of the century. Finally, it asks you to consider whether pre-K–12 classroom teaching is the career for you.

The Snapshot and Reflecting on Practice sections are different from those of previous chapters. The Snapshot asks you to take an instant picture of yourself, now, and to make an assessment of what you see. The Reflecting on Practice asks you to place that picture into the landscape in which the next generation of teachers can expect to work. Together, the two exercises should help describe what a teaching career would be like for you.

SNAPSHOT

I nstead of providing you with a Snapshot picture of teachers, students, schools, or events that affect teaching, as in other chapters, the Snapshot for this chapter asks you to take a picture of yourself—to look at yourself as a person preparing to make a career decision. It suggests points you should consider and also recommends that you add to the list.

To take a picture of yourself as a potential teacher, proceed as follows:

1. Look at yourself honestly in terms of the points listed below, as well as those that you add to the list.
2. Write a description of what you see.
3. Analyze that description as it relates to teaching.
4. Keep the description for use again at the end of the chapter.

Be careful. Do not construct a picture of a teacher who might be you. Record an honest picture, and *then* ask: Is this a picture of a teacher?

Points to consider:

- your personal strengths
- your weaknesses
- things you enjoy
- things you dislike
- attachments and associations that are important to you
- ways in which you relate to others
- things you aspire to do and achieve
- things you value
- where you expect to live
- the lifestyle you expect to follow
- the type of professional career you envision for yourself
- activities in which you anticipate engaging in your work
- activities you anticipate outside your professional work
- other points that occur to you as being relevant

Trends into the Twenty-First Century

The basic premises of the education reform movements of the 1980s and early 1990s were (1) that students were not learning as much as they should in school and (2) that schools and teaching had to be changed to correct the situation. Therefore, numerous efforts, described earlier in this text, were initiated to bring about change. The first stages of those initiatives are now in place, and early data about their impact are being collected, but clear results are not yet available. They will accumulate gradually during the years ahead.

The stages of the reform efforts that have been completed so far are probably the easiest to accomplish. They aroused interest, mobilized energy, put on pressure, provided tentative directions, and raised some resources for change; but they did so on a very general level and only in limited ways. Laws were written and regulations changed. Educators were told to do things differently; and, in some cases, more funding was provided.

Next, two major steps must occur. First, teachers and individual schools must   Results
harness and focus the energies of school reform so they have positive effects in their classrooms and with their students. They must turn the ideas, pressures for action, and plans into results. They must improve student learning. Second, elected officials and taxpayers must provide the resources and public support to enable teachers and educational leaders to accomplish what they say they want. They cannot demand more of teachers without helping them. They cannot simply stand aloof and criticize. They must accept their share of responsibility for the present unsatisfactory condition of many American public schools and their necessary role in making improvements.

The situation can be illustrated by a military analogy. The alarm has been sounded. The apparent enemies have been identified. The nation has been mobilized. The general battle plan has been developed. Some of the supplies have been secured, and supply routes have been designed. A new type of soldier (teacher) has been envisioned. Now reform must proceed in the trenches (classrooms) but with public psychological and financial support. Teachers, school administrators, and the public that hires and supports them will determine, as they all work together, whether the war will be won—whether students will learn as much as society expects.

Pursuing Reform and National Goals: The Next Steps

Because much of the work of schools and teachers in the late 1990s and the early twenty-first century will involve continued implementation of the education reform agendas first articulated in the 1980s and enacted into national legislation in 1994 as Goals 2000, teaching in the next generation needs to be understood in the context of that reform. That context can be understood if the education reform movement of the 1980s and early 1990s is looked upon as consisting of five interrelated agendas, as described in Chapter 1:[1]

1. back-to-basics and accountability
2. greater professionalization of teaching
3. more effective schools and teaching

4. more equitable education (not just equal amounts of education)
5. changing the content or subject matter taught

With the exception of the need for political leaders and citizens to provide the funds necessary to carry out education improvements, much of the responsibility for the specific thrusts of reform in education has now shifted from legislatures and policymakers to schools and teachers. School leaders and teachers are now deciding what students need to learn and how they should be taught so that they learn it. Once teachers do this, they undertake the teaching and, if all goes well, produce the learning desired. As this happens, students are assessed to see whether the process produces the results expected. Data from assessments will indicate how successful the schools and teachers have been. Those results, in turn, will indicate appropriate future directions.[2]

Changing professional environment

As teachers do all of this, they continue to teach students much as teachers have done for years. But all is not the same. The professional environment is changing. In fact, it is already significantly different in many ways from that which teachers faced in the early 1980s:[3]

- There are now nationally proclaimed Goals 2000 for all schools, teachers, and students to try to reach.
- Student achievement data are collected and compared school by school, statewide, and nationally.
- State and national professional standards boards are beginning to oversee teaching.
- Poor, minority, and nonachieving students are the focus of great attention, but effective ways of reaching them have still not been identified.
- Questions about content are being debated.

The collection and comparison of student achievement data are based on the assumption that schools and their teachers are accountable for what students do and do not learn. Those data and the tests that produce them are used as yardsticks against which teachers, schools, school systems, and states will be judged. They will increasingly influence what is taught and enable everyone to see how the local students, schools, and states do in comparison with others.

Educators at all levels use the results either as justification for what they are doing or as guides for how to improve. Doing better on next year's test becomes an implicit goal, and the criteria for deciding how to improve becomes the anticipated content of that test. Those whose results are not good promise that their students' scores will get better, and teachers teach more directly for the tests.

Toward a nation's report card

If current trends continue, either newly developed subject-matter tests, the National Assessment of Educational Progress, or similar instruments will, in effect, serve as a national blueprint for education. Unlike the way these instruments were used in the past, data from the assessments in the form of student scores in certain core subjects will be reported comparatively as a nation's report card. As a result, school curricula can be expected gradually to conform to the areas of knowledge assessed on the tests, and those who want their area of interest included in the curriculum will push to have it covered on the tests. Some semblance of a de facto national curriculum will emerge.[4]

National criteria for "good teachers"

The development of national assessments for teachers means that what is thought to constitute good teaching will become more definite and more explicit. Those developing the instruments have already been deciding what teachers need to know and be able to do. They are using those decisions to set assessment criteria. Teachers who are assessed have to do well in terms of those standards.[5]

Because the assessment data are being compared in a traditionally competitive society, individual teachers, the colleges that prepared them, and the school systems that hire them want to appear to be better than those with whom they are compared. Because they want to improve their test results, they set their priorities in terms of test content. This, in turn, will pressure teachers to show their competence in certain prescribed ways.

The push for state and national boards to set standards for licensing teachers and to control entry into the profession of teaching is affecting many aspects of education—who becomes teachers, the qualifications they possess, the college programs that prepare them. Advocates for such boards say they should be controlled by teachers; set higher and more relevant standards than in the past; end emergency licensing; and be willing to suspend, revoke, withdraw, and deny licenses and program approval.[6]

National standards for teachers

Moves in this direction shift more of the control and responsibility over teachers from public and community officials to teachers themselves. They put teachers in charge of broader educational policies, and doing this changes the nature of the profession. They put teachers in the position of deciding who can be certified to teach, who can be hired by school systems, and what should be done when no qualified teacher can be found for a position. Local and state school boards of education have been making these decisions until now.

The continued concern about teaching poor and minority-group students and the special challenges involved in doing so will dominate teaching throughout the next generation. Schools and teachers will keep struggling at the task of teaching these students more effectively, but noticeably successful approaches will probably continue to be elusive. Americans will continue to believe that education can overcome poverty, and they will retain the hope that teachers will find a way to make it happen. Whether they are willing to provide the needed increased funding, however, is not at all clear.

Focus on poor students

Although more will be said about this later in the chapter, it is important to note that schools generally still continue to be less than successful in educating hard-to-teach students. Studies consistently report that poor and minority students are achieving less and dropping out of school in greater proportions than students as a whole. Schools are still not succeeding anywhere close to the level that they should with the following student groups: blacks, Hispanics, those from families of lower socioeconomic status, those from single-parent families, those from large families, those living in large cities, those in the South, and those with weak self-concepts. Other studies report that people such as these who do not achieve in school are not likely to do so in the adult world.[7]

Questions about the content that should be taught will change the school curriculum during the late 1990s, although some of the directions of that change are not clear and may not be clear for some time. Teachers will be expected to teach certain prescribed common core subjects and to do so with more adherence to set norms and demonstrated success than in years past. Tests will be available for high schools to assess student knowledge in "the basic subjects"—at least reading, writing, mathematics, history, geography, civics, and science—and communities, if not legislatures, will demand that passing the tests be required for graduation. Teachers will be expected to provide the basics, to make students culturally literate, to teach

Changing content

Something to Think About

Some critics of education reform say that two conflicting reform pressures on teachers—to be more accountable to others and to be more profession-ally responsible for their own classes—are incompatible, unfair, and impos-sible for teachers to meet. These critics say that teachers cannot be scruti-nized more closely against standards set by politicians, school boards, and commissions and at the same time be held accountable personally for the lack of success of their students. They also say that if teachers are not trusted to set the direction and standards for the education of their students, they should not be responsible for the results.

■ Do you see a significant contradiction as these critics do?
■ If so, what do you think should be done to avoid it?

students to think, and to inculcate the correct values. Student test results will be checked to see if teachers successfully achieve this. It will be interesting to watch what happens when significant numbers of students fail the tests, especially in school systems that provide less school capital—the financial support for teacher salaries, supplies, and other resources—than do school systems nearby.

In a sense, this means that schools and teachers will gradually become more accountable for *what* students learn as well as for how much and how effectively they learn. Teachers will be less able to slide over a topic on the basis of their own professional judgment or because students are not interested in it. Students will need to know the prescribed information and to develop the prescribed skills and values. Those items will be covered on the test. There is an irony here. Teachers will have more decision-making authority in many ways, but they will also have to teach more of what others want and do it with a degree of conformity.

Different kinds of professionals

As teachers continue teaching through the changed education environment and assume the additional responsibilities that reform has thrust upon them, they, in fact, will gradually become different kinds of professionals than were teachers of the past. They will be caught up in a nationwide process of rethinking what schools should accomplish and how schools and teachers should operate. This means that teachers of the next generation will take on more responsibility in a more complex educational world. Instead of teaching just as they were taught, they will have to be better professionals than the teachers who taught them in each of the follow-ing ways:[8]

1. as *executive-like managers* who select priorities of instruction and oversee the running of their schools
2. as *decision makers* who decide what and how to teach, in what depth, to which students, at which times, and for which tests
3. as *subject-matter scholars* who understand the content they teach well enough to manipulate it so that it can be learned by their students
4. as *abstract thinkers* who can pull together ideas from child development, learning theory, philosophy, sociology, anthropology, and the various sub-

ject areas taught in the school and who can bring these to bear on what they do in the classroom

5. as *infinitely skilled practitioners* who can make all this work.

Much of each of these aspects of teaching is not new, but the level of complexity involved in each is. The pleasant, dedicated, caring teachers of past times who continue to function as artisans will not be adequate in the future. Successful teachers of the twenty-first century will have to be more intelligent, better informed, more insightful, and more highly skilled than most of their professional predecessors if the dreams of education reform and Goals 2000 are to be attained.

Schools will also have to be different, not only in what occurs in them but also in their governance and organization. Much as the Carnegie Task Force on Teaching as a Profession suggested, schools will need to be places where skilled teachers *decide* and *do* what is necessary to produce appropriate student learning rather than places where they follow the dictates of tight curriculum frameworks and rigid, status quo-seeking managers.[9] These changes will be especially threatening to many—to communities and parents who want to run the schools so tightly that they prescribe what is taught and how to teach it, to principals who want controlled and orderly schools, and to teachers who want administrators to make decisions for them.

Different kinds of schools

If the reform agendas are to come to fruition, dramatically different kinds of teachers will staff classrooms. Their day-to-day work will be startlingly more sophisticated. The demands on them to show success will be more persistent. Their roles and responsibilities will be more complex. Their levels of competence will have to be much higher. Many of the people who used to pursue successful careers in teaching will no longer be capable of doing so.

The Importance of Teachers

Virtually everyone who has studied contemporary education in America agrees that teachers are the critical variable in the education process. They also agree that the extent to which student learning will improve in the years ahead depends directly on the abilities of the teachers available to teach those students. In light of this consensus, it would be useful at this point to reflect again about the characteristics of effective teaching itemized in Chapter 3 and the ideas about school cultures described in Chapter 4. It is also useful to remember that, until recently, average citizens and many professional educators alike have often said they could identify good teaching when they saw or experienced it but could not define it or list its critical characteristics. Many even said teachers were born, not made, and were artists whose abilities were too abstract to be isolated and labeled. Many paid little attention to the school culture in which teachers teach.

Identifying critical characteristics

Ideas such as these are no longer acceptable. Regardless of how artistic teaching might be or whether teachers are born or not, experts believe that characteristics of good teachers and good teaching can be identified with greater assurance, and many are in the process of doing so. The data being generated are making the elements of teaching and school operation more understandable.

At this point, however, there is a lot more to be learned. Both the criteria and expertise for identifying good teaching are still inadequate. David Berliner, a lead-

Finding the experts

ing researcher into the characteristics of expert teachers, suggests that most teacher-of-the-year competitions are so superficial and unscientific that they are insulting. He notes that judges of Olympic competitors usually have twenty to thirty years of prior experience; judges of teachers have comparatively little. Cattle show judges must train more intensively or have more experiences as unofficial judges than many of those who evaluate teachers.[10]

Competencies of Future Teachers

Areas of competence

Nevertheless, we know enough to identify areas in which teachers of the next century have to be more competent than their predecessors. These areas of necessary competence for future teachers are discussed in the following sections.

Knowledge

Teachers have to know more information and understand it better. Although they still need to be well versed in the tricks of the trade, more importantly they need theoretical knowledge—ideas from pedagogy, history, psychology, sociology, philosophy, subject-matter disciplines, and so forth—that will help them answer questions as yet unraised. They need knowledge that is deep and sophisticated enough to be applied in all kinds of classrooms, all of them bombarded by the multitude of changing circumstances and pressures already described. For example, they need to have enough background knowledge and depth of understanding to grasp the concepts associated with the idea of "multiculturalism" and to determine what that idea means for their own personal teaching. They need to be able to evaluate other popular new concepts regularly as they surface throughout their teaching careers.

Intelligence, Insight, and Reflection

Teachers have to be able to think reflectively, flexibly, abstractly, and conceptually. They must simultaneously process all sorts of information. They must constantly assess their own teaching and the learning that teaching did or did not produce and then use that assessment information to revise what they do next. At the same time, they must take in new and competing ideas, use them to reconfigure what they believe, and apply them to what they do with students.

For example, when teaching strategies do not work as well as expected for fourth-period English, the teacher needs to figure out why and decide how to adjust. When educational theorists suggest that teachers should rely less on stimulus-response techniques to motivate students and should base their teaching more on student intrinsic motivations, teachers need to be able to understand the point, assess its validity for their own teaching, and modify their classroom strategies accordingly. It is simply no longer adequate to teach by doing things the way Mr. Washington or Ms. Jones always did them, the way a college professor suggested, or the way they are outlined in the teacher's guide.

Organizing Ability

Because more activity than ever before seems to be occurring both in and around classrooms these days, teachers have to be especially competent organizers, planners, and managers. They need to arrange such things as ideas, classroom events, subject-matter content, developmental skills, student strengths and weaknesses, and their own teaching strategies in ways that bring meaning to what they do. They need to have a clear idea of what they intend to accomplish so that they can balance everything. They need to formulate and pursue routines and procedures that enhance, rather than stifle, teaching and learning.

Technical Skills

As always, teachers have to be skilled in the technical aspects of their jobs—to formulate objectives, motivate students, diagnose difficulties, correct or reinforce behavior, vary activities, utilize complicated equipment, evaluate materials, sequence lessons, pace instruction, monitor student progress, provide feedback, ask questions, manage time, keep students on task, assess performance, and so forth. They have to do all this and make it lead to demonstrable student learning.

Caring

Teachers will even have to be more caring than their predecessors—not because teachers of the past did not care about their students, but because more and more students of most teachers will be harder to teach, less like the teacher who teaches them, and probably more alienated. Many of them will have comparatively less student capital, as described in Chapter 5, and their teachers will have to care enough to make sure they succeed anyway. Many of the students, frankly, will be harder to like and care about. Teachers who do not care deeply about them will not succeed with them and will not be happy trying.

Confidence

Teachers have to be secure and confident professionals who are convinced that they know what they are doing, that it is the right thing to do, and that they can do it.

Over time, today's teachers need to develop a high degree of confidence in their ability to adapt to complex and changing circumstances.

Teaching nowadays is too complex for the cookbook teacher who might have survived in the past, too demanding for the unsure and the marginally qualified. Even the experts strain at times to keep up.

Ability to Handle Complexity

Interwoven among all of the above is the fact that teachers face a more complex set of tasks and more complex circumstances than their predecessors. Students, social conditions, expectations for schools, teachers themselves, and the very act of teaching all seem to be more complicated than what we remember of the good old days. The teacher of the one-room schoolhouse (such as Priscilla Hope, described in Chapter 6) simply could not cope with the current multitude of teacher roles and the magnitude of present conditions; but teachers today and tomorrow must be able to succeed in that environment (Figure 16-1).

Of course, the need to be competent in many ways is really not new to teachers. Good teachers have possessed the abilities noted above and have performed ably under similar circumstances for years. Now, however, the needs seem to be more pressing, and the level of competence required seems to be more difficult to achieve.

A critical question that underscores all of these points about the importance of

FIGURE 16-1   As college teacher-education faculty think about how best to prepare teachers, they often develop conceptualizations of what their graduates should look like—what characteristics or competencies they should possess. This drawing represents one institution's conceptualization of the graduates it recommends for teacher licensure.

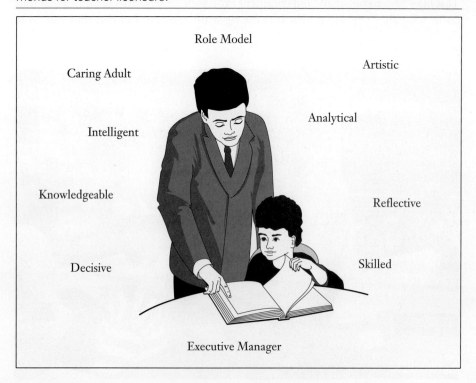

teachers is this: *Can America attract to teaching enough people who possess the capabilities it wants in its teachers?* One skeptic described the situation this way:

> Since about 1983, Americans have said they want teachers comparable in ability to leading business and industry executives. But they are willing to pay them no more than they pay assembly line workers; moreover the working conditions of schools are more like the plant floor than the board room.[11]

Others are more positive, and those who are say that current educational changes, reform-generated improvements, and nationally verbalized goals for all support their position.

Teacher Supply and Demand

During the 1950s and early 1960s, Americans had babies in record numbers, and the baby boom swelled pre-K–12 school enrollments greatly through the 1960s and early 1970s. Then the boom turned to bust. The boomers completed school, their parents were beyond childbearing age, and they were not yet old enough to have school-age children of their own in great numbers.

These demographic trends had a direct effect on the need for teachers. At first, the need outstripped the number of teachers available, and school systems were forced to hire almost anyone with a college degree who was willing to teach. When news of the demand spread, more college students pursued teaching. Gradually, the supply caught up to and eventually passed the demand. *(margin: Effects of the 1960s and 1970s)*

When the bust hit schools about 1973, the supply of qualified teachers suddenly outdistanced the demand in most teaching fields and regions of the country. Fewer students attended pre-K–12 grades, but large numbers of boomers were still being graduated from college, and many of them still wanted to teach. Again, the news spread, and this time fewer college students chose careers in teaching.[12]

The impact of the shifts in the numbers of teachers hired in the 1960s and 1970s was not limited to those years, however. Because many teachers were employed before 1973 and few between 1973 and the mid-1980s, the average age of teachers crept up each year. As a result, a disproportionate number of teachers either retired in the 1980s or will retire in the 1990s. An illustration of the phenomenon was reflected in 1984 in a high school in upstate New York, where no teacher in the building had been teaching for fewer than seventeen years—that is, since 1967. *(margin: Older teachers)*

More recently, the supply-demand situation has changed again. Since the mid-1980s, student enrollments have been increasing as children of the baby boomers enter elementary school and move through the grades and as the birthrates among certain population groups remains high, especially among Hispanic Americans. The need for teachers is expanding again.

During the last years of the 1980s and early 1990s, the general demand for teachers across the nation and in all fields increased by about 4 percent a year, although different grade levels, subject areas, and regions of the country experienced higher demands than others, and some still had oversupplies. The higher demand is expected to remain for some time. *(margin: Increased demand)*

This increased demand has already led to an increased supply of teachers, and most predictions suggest that the demand and supply are likely to be in relative *(margin: Increased supply and quality)* balance for the next decade or so. It also appears that the supply of *skilled* and *competent* teachers will continue at a high enough level to avoid deterioration in the quality of new teachers. The overall quality of teachers should actually increase as better-educated and more skilled new teachers replace those who retire.

More detailed information about teacher supply and demand is reflected in data reported below. These data include information on school enrollment, the supply of teachers, teacher quality, and influences that affect supply-and-demand equations.

Enrollment

School enrollment in the United States has gradually increased since 1984 and will continue to do so for a number of years. Reasons for this are

■ The bulge in school enrollments caused by baby-boomer children will continue for a number of years as those children pass through the system.[13]
■ There has been a large number of women of childbearing age in recent years, and, even though some of them are having fewer children per family than earlier generations, their total numbers are higher.[14]
■ Birthrates among Hispanic and black Americans are expected to remain high, and many women in those groups are in their childbearing years.[15]

Teacher numbers

The number of new college graduates who *completed teacher-education programs* with a bachelor's degree rose during the 1950s, 1960s, and early 1970s to almost 200,000 in the peak years of 1972–73 (Figure 16-2). Then it fell to less than 90,000 in 1985–86. Since the mid-1980s, the number of teacher-education graduates has gradually increased again.[16]

The number of people *employed as new teachers* averaged about 138,000 per year between 1972 and 1985 and rose to an average of about *190,000* between 1986 and 1988. Since then the numbers have remained at or above that level.

High percentages of current teachers are expected to retire or leave teaching

FIGURE 16-2   Bachelor's degrees earned in education, 1950–1991.

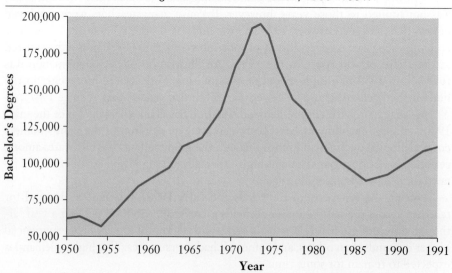

SOURCE: T. D. Snyder & C. M. Hoffman (1993). *Digest of educational statistics.* Washington, DC: U.S. Office of Education, p. 288.

for other reasons in the next decade or so. As a result, the late 1990s and early twenty-first century should witness a high turnover rate and a greater number of new teaching jobs than in the recent past.[17]

Of course, general teacher supply-and-demand statistics and trends do not present an adequate picture of real supply-demand situations. Teachers are not interchangeable parts, and the need for teachers is not equal across fields and in all regions. As of the mid-1990s, this country needed more elementary teachers than secondary. Mathematics and special education teachers have been in great demand. Inner-city classrooms lacked sufficient numbers of qualified practitioners, while suburban schools had more qualified applicants than they needed. Enrollments in the South, Southwest, and California increased while they stabilized or declined elsewhere.

Teacher capabilities and quality are also critical in assessing supply-and-demand conditions. School systems will probably always be able to find someone to stand before nearly every class of children, but that is not the issue. The issue is whether schools can attract enough people who are good enough to do what teachers must do and what children deserve. If children are expected to learn more, they deserve especially qualified teachers.

Teacher quality

Recent data about the people who are becoming teachers are encouraging, but much progress still needs to be made. For example, in 1993, the average SAT score for college freshmen *who said they intended to teach* was 47 points below the national average. In comparison with earlier times, the gap had closed from 59 points in 1973 and 80 points below the average in 1982.[18] Although the gap has closed slightly, the average of intended teachers in the mid-1980s was still below all other college majors except four—agriculture, ethnic studies, home economics, and trade and vocational fields.[19] It is particularly important to note, however, that these scores are for college students who say they *intend* to be teachers, not students who successfully complete teacher-education programs, gain licenses to teach, and acquire teaching jobs. Recent teacher competency tests and other more stringent screening requirements are eliminating more of the academically weak students who would like to be teachers than in the past.

A similar uneven pattern is reflected in the credentials of some groups of practicing teachers. For example, in some states, one-third or more of high school science and mathematics teachers do not possess minimum state qualifications for their positions. Several states that set minimum-level basic skills standards for teachers in the middle of the 1980s have since lowered them to allow less-qualified practicing teachers and teacher applicants to be placed in classrooms. For example, in 1985, Louisiana reduced its National Teachers Exam cutoff scores because of teacher shortages in math and science; and Georgia and Alabama reduced test score standards when sued by practicing teachers who challenged the tests in court.[20] In many areas, pay for substitute teachers is so low that many substitutes have neither college degrees from four-year institutions nor adequate training in teaching or the subjects they are hired to teach.

Influencing the Equations

Three developments that are expected to influence teacher supply-and-demand conditions substantially over the next decade are (1) increased school system efforts to recruit high-quality teachers, including those from nontraditional sources; (2) general efforts to further professionalize teaching; and (3) the extent to which school systems spend funds necessary for hiring more teachers to match their rising enrollments.

A number of school districts and several states have developed plans to attract to teaching people from other careers—people with liberal arts degrees and little teacher training and older people who prepared to teach in the past but either never did so or have not done so for some time. Some of the plans are primarily recruiting efforts and flexible training arrangements that make teacher preparation possible for these people but retain the same expectations and quality checks as more traditional programs. Some substitute alternative criteria for the more traditional checks, and some drop most entry standards. The extent to which these plans attract high-quality teachers who remain in the classroom will not be known for several years, but if they do succeed, they will greatly affect supply-demand situations.

Reform efforts at further professionalizing teaching—such as the Clinton administration's Goals 2000: Educate America legislation, recent changes in state licensing standards, the new standards used by the National Council for the Accreditation of Teacher Education to approve teacher-education programs at colleges, as well as the recommendations of the Carnegie Forum on Education and the Economy, the Holmes Group, the National Governors' Association, and the Education Commission of the States—propose the setting of higher standards for selecting teachers and assume that this will result in a higher public regard for teachers that would, in turn, make teaching more attractive. (See Chapter 1 of this text.) These efforts generally call for intellectually sophisticated, inquiring teachers who challenge students with ideas and thought-provoking questions, who run their own schools, and who are the executive decision makers described earlier.[21] They envision a more select group of teachers with more status and power and better compensation.[22] If and when these things happen, the teacher supply-demand picture

Recruiting more members of minority groups to teaching is one of the most important tasks facing schools in the years ahead.

will be quite different from what it is today because the nature of the teaching force itself will have changed.

Of course, the number of teachers hired is tied directly to the amount of money school systems are willing or able to provide. If student numbers increase but funding does not, class size rises, not the number of classes and teachers. This phenomenon has been occurring in recent years in financially strapped school districts and where voter bond issues have been rejected.

Probably the most acute teacher supply-and-demand challenge ahead for schools is the need to attract more minority-group members to teaching. Today, a significantly lower percentage of minority-group members teach than attend school, and the situation is worsening. The problem was described in 1987 by Patricia Albjerg Graham, of the graduate school of education at Harvard University:

Minority teachers

> Simply stated, the problem is that, as minority enrollments in the public schools are rising, the number of minority teachers, especially black teachers, is shrinking. This is the case because proportionately fewer blacks are going to college than a decade ago and, of those who do go to college, fewer are choosing to become teachers and, of those seeking to become teachers, too few are passing the new teacher tests, especially in the southern states, where about half of the nation's black teachers are prepared. Throughout the seventies and into the eighties, blacks constituted about 8 percent of public school teachers, roughly half the proportion of black children in the schools. Today, however, blacks make up less than 7 percent of the teaching force, and that percentage is expected to decline even further by the end of the decade [1989], when black enrollments may well be substantially higher than the current level of about 16 percent.[23]

While minority teachers are in great demand, two factors work against more minority-group members' entering teaching. Those who perform well in college are in such demand for jobs in other fields that school systems cannot compete for them. Those who do not do well in college also perform poorly in terms of the new academic standards for entering teaching. Of course, the latter group would not make good role models in the classroom where majority and minority students need to interact with intelligent, articulate, and academically successful minority teachers.[24]

Something to Think About

In recent years school systems seem to have struggled to hire minority teachers, but there have simply not been enough qualified minority-group members to fill the positions available.

- What strategies should be used to attract more minority-group members to teaching positions?
- What are the advantages and disadvantages of each?

A Look Ahead

Although it is hard to predict precisely what teacher supply-and-demand conditions will be like in a decade or so, the following estimates seem to be reasonable:

- School systems will continue to strain to attract good teachers and compete with each other to do so. The more affluent districts will get the better teachers.
- Good teachers will be in demand in most parts of the country, at most grade levels, and in most fields.
- As long as qualitative standards remain in place, teacher numbers will not expand to satisfy the demand to the extent that they did in the 1960s.
- Minority teachers will be in particularly short supply.
- Teacher turnover will be high but much of it will be attributed to teachers changing schools rather than leaving teaching.
- Some school systems will not pay what is necessary for an adequate number of qualified teachers for their students.
- Marginally qualified and unqualified teachers will be hired by school systems that cannot get better ones.
- The less-qualified teachers will be teaching poorer students whose parents lack political clout.

Sellers' market

In summary, the next decade or two will be a sellers' market for highly qualified prospective teachers, although there will be regional variations. But the people most in demand will also be sought by other professions. Some will never teach; others will be attracted away after teaching only a short time. School systems will compete for the best, but many of them will have to settle for less.

Where to Teach

To the extent that qualified new teachers enter a sellers' market in the next generation, they will make decisions about where to teach; and all teaching positions are not equal. Conditions vary greatly, and jobs that appeal to some will not appeal to others. A number of varying circumstances that teacher applicants will want to consider as they look for jobs are noted in this section.

However, two parts of the question of where to teach are not addressed directly. First, the general characteristics and circumstances of teaching have already been treated in earlier chapters of this text. Second, the attractions or detractions of a specific job are too individually variable to be described usefully here. Therefore, comments included here are directed toward three points: teaching in different regions of the country, in different types of communities, and in different types of schools.

Regions of the Country

Personal preference

Probably the prime considerations about which part of the country prospective teachers find most attractive have more to do with personal background and preferences than regional ways of life or teaching conditions. Factors such as where a person grew up, location of relatives, jobs of spouses, climate, proximity to cultural

Is having to conduct tutoring sessions in a hallway because of overcrowding an intolerable situation—or just another everyday challenge? Grappling with questions like these can help you decide where you are most willing and eager to teach.

events, and so forth should not be undervalued. Prospective teachers will regret choosing jobs that require them to live where they will not be happy.

Regional enrollment trends

On the other hand, teaching and schools in different regions of the country are, in fact, different and positions in international schools, foreign countries, U.S. armed forces schools, Vista and Peace Corps locations are particularly so. Within the fifty United States, school enrollments will increase most in the South, the Southwest, and California. They will increase most in urban schools with high percentages of minority and poor children. Enrollments will be more steady in the Northeast and the upper Midwest and will decline in rural areas. These trends and the financial resources of the schools involved will affect the number and types of teaching positions available. They will also affect teaching conditions.

School improvements

The states of the Southeast, where schools have been weakest historically, made serious commitments during the 1980s to doing better and have shown some gains. In most of these states, tax increases have provided more money for schools, and many quality-improving reforms have begun. Yet, because of where these states started in comparison with other states, even these special efforts have not been enough to bring conditions to a par with more advanced states. Even where there have been gains, reform energy has been running out and necessary funds have often not been provided in adequate amounts.

Urban conditions

In all regions, many urban schools will have monumental problems. They will experience the biggest barriers to success, the greatest limits on resources, and the students with the greatest need. Their teaching jobs will be the easiest to find and the most difficult to perform. For talented, committed teachers with the right predilections, those jobs will be the most satisfying, as well as the most demanding.

Variations

Generally, experts predict that schools as a whole nationally will get better for the next decade or two, although many see urban schools as an exception to the trend. Some areas and states will advance faster than others, at least for a time. Those that develop fastest at one point will eventually slow and be passed by others.

In any event, there will probably be more variation in teacher employment and conditions in schools within regions than across them.

College graduates considering teaching positions in different regions of the country should first consider where they would like to live, but more specific considerations are probably best left to the time when applicants are in the midst of their job search. Decisions made too early can exclude good options and may be based on conditions that are likely to change. Like most contemporary American professionals, those who begin teaching in the late 1990s and early twenty-first century will be less tied to one position than their predecessors. They will have opportunities to change jobs during their career. If conditions in one locale turn out to be less than optimal, they will be able to look around and move on.

Types of Communities

Because communities vary greatly and because schools are an extension of the communities in which they are located, prospective teachers should think carefully about the locale in which they anticipate teaching and living. Rural, suburban, and urban areas have different types of social environments, lifestyles, and atmospheres in which to work. They vary, for example, in basic, important matters such as cost of living, how close one lives to school, how one travels to and from work, and how long it takes to do so. A short walk, a long drive through heavy traffic, or a subway ride are three significantly different ways of starting the day. Teachers who like living and working in one environment may not enjoy doing so in the others.

A thorough discussion of the benefits and burdens of living and teaching in various community settings is not necessary here, but it is important to acknowledge that teaching involves daily interaction with students, administrators, peers, and parents who are influenced by the culture in which they live; as a result, teachers cannot separate their work in the schools of a community from the community itself. Those who try to do so seem to complicate their jobs unnecessarily. It seems only logical that those who take jobs in communities where they fit in comfortably have a greater chance of enjoying their work.

As with decisions about regions of the country, whether a person teaches in an urban, suburban, or rural community is primarily a matter of personal preference. However, if prospective teachers are motivated to teach because of a desire to do good, they should seriously consider urban positions, simply because urban students need good teachers most desperately. Besides, younger teachers usually find city life more exciting and have fewer family responsibilities of the sort that make city work and life impractical for others. Both authors of this book have spent most of their pre-K–12 teaching careers in urban schools and recommend teaching there.

Types of Schools

Within communities, schools vary as much as they are alike, and those variations affect the experience of teaching in each. Some of the basic differences are:

- age and grade level of students
- comprehensiveness of curriculum
- proportional numbers of students with different social and economic backgrounds
- number of at-risk and special-needs students
- educational philosophy

- tightness of administrative regulation
- style of school leadership
- level of expectations for student performance
- degree to which academics are stressed

Of course, private, religious-affiliated, and public schools differ greatly and in many ways. Also, many school systems have special-focused alternative schools that may appeal to teachers with particular interests.

Because Chapter 4 has discussed differences among schools, no further description is provided here. However, prospective teachers need to remember that the general nature and day-to-day activities of any teaching position depend greatly on the environment in which that teaching takes place—the school atmosphere, the students, teaching peers, administrators, secretaries, custodians, and the less tangible accompanying circumstances. All these affect the job. They make it exciting, pleasant, tolerable, burdensome, or horrible.

Different teachers evaluate schools by different criteria. Some like working where others would fear to tread. And, of course, things change over time. People who are considering a teaching career need to assess teaching positions in terms of their own preferences and predilections, both on the basis of what they see in the school and what they expect it to be like some years ahead.

Public or private

A matter of choice

Salaries and Compensation

Although teacher salaries are not as high as many people believe they should be and do not attract significant numbers of individuals away from other professions, they are the primary external reward for teaching. For years, teacher salaries have been below the average salaries of most other professions that require four years of college preparation, but they have been getting better in recent years. As a result, they are less of a deterrent to teaching than they once were.

Generalizing about teacher salaries is difficult because (1) they change each year, (2) they vary from state to state and district to district, (3) they are adjusted for years of service, extent of professional study, career ladder category, and type of assignment, and (4) they can be supplemented by performing extra duties. Comparison with other occupations is also complex because (1) those other salaries change and vary, (2) most teachers are paid for nine or ten months' work a year without paid vacations, and (3) teachers rarely receive on-the-job training within the school day and at school expense, a typical benefit in other fields.

Nevertheless, general data about teacher salaries are presented in the discussion that follows. Those data show recent average salaries for beginning teachers and for all teachers in each state. They also reflect trends in recent years and as projected for several years to come.

As noted earlier, the average teacher salary for *all* public school teachers in the United States for the school year 1992–93 was about $35,334 (Figure 16-3). That amount compares with $4,995 in 1959–60; $8,635 in 1969–70; $15,970 in 1979–80; and $25,313 in 1985–86. So in the thirty-three years between 1959–60 and 1992–93 average teacher salaries rose more than seven times. They doubled in the years between 1980 and 1993.[25]

These figures are distorted, however, by at least two factors—inflation (although Figure 16-3 adjusts for inflation) and the fact that the average age of teachers

Average salary

FIGURE 16-3 Average annual salaries for teachers (in constant 1990–91 dollars) since 1978 and projected through 2003.

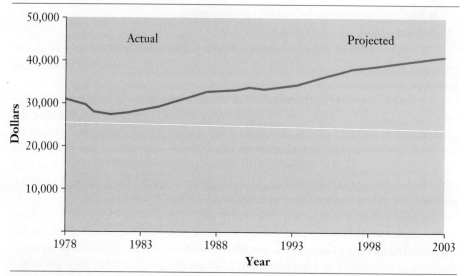

SOURCE: D. E. Gerald & W. J. Hussar. (1992). *Projections of educational statistics to 2003.* Washington, DC: National Center for Education Statistics, pp. 79, 83; National Education Association. (1992). *Estimates of state school statistics.* Washington, DC: National Education Association.

has been increasing in recent years. As a result, the average teacher salary in the late 1990s is for a teacher with more years of experience than the average salary a number of years earlier, and dollar-for-dollar it does not buy as much. Several studies report that recent salary increases have had the effect only of restoring teacher buying power to a level comparable to what it was in the early 1970s.[26] In any event, real gains are now being made again, at least in some areas.

The average salary of all *beginning* teachers in the United States in 1992–1993 was $23,054 (Figure 16-4). That figure compares to $8,063 in 1974–1975, $11,676 in 1980–1981, and $16,692 in 1985–1986. The percentage increases as of 1992 were just short of 300 percent since 1974, almost 200 percent since 1980, and nearly 40 percent since 1985.[27]

First-year, twelve-month salaries of bachelor's degree recipients in various professions in 1992–1993 were[28]

Engineering	$34,700	Economics/finance	$28,700
Computer specialist	$31,600	Liberal arts	$27,700
Chemistry	$30,900	Business administration	$27,700
Math/statistics	$29,800	Sales/marketing	$27,100
Accounting	$29,100	Teaching	$23,054

If teaching salaries are considered to represent only nine months' work, as some people insist, the twelve-month equivalent of the $23,054 in 1992–1993 was $30,739, an amount more than the average yearly salary for accounting, business administration, economics/finance, liberal arts, math/statistics, and sales/marketing.

Salary schedules

Averages, of course, obscure variations in salaries within the teaching force, and those variations are quite extensive. Table 16-1 shows salaries by state. Table 16-2 is an example of a typical teacher salary schedule for 1992–93. It reports on salaries

FIGURE 16-4 Average beginning salaries of teachers (in constant 1990–91 dollars) between 1976 and 1992.

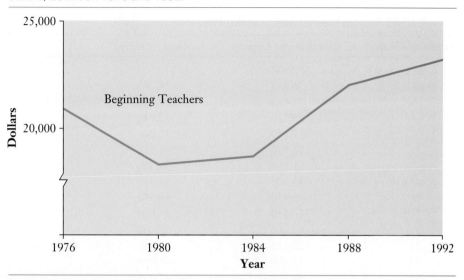

SOURCE: N. Alsalam, G. E. Fischer, L. T. Ogle, G. T. Rogers, & T. M. Smith. (1993). *The condition of education 1993.* Washington, DC: National Center for Education Statistics.

TABLE 16-1 Average Salaries of Public School Teachers, 1992–93, and Percent Change Since 1982–83 (in constant dollars)

State	Salary	% Change	State	Salary	% Change
Connecticut	$48,343	60.5%	Arizona	32,403	5.6
Alaska	45,728	−7.4	Virginia	32,356	20.1
New York	44,999	23.9	Florida	31,172	17.4
Michigan	43,604	16.7	Kentucky	31,115	16.5
New Jersey	42,680	36.4	West Virginia	30,301	20.4
Pennsylvania	41,215	33.9	Maine	30,250	28.1
California	40,221	17.2	Iowa	30,130	7.7
Maryland	38,753	16.4	Wyoming	30,080	−12.6
D.C.	38,702	0.0	Texas	29,935	5.4
Illinois	38,632	19.1	Missouri	29,382	15.4
Massachusetts	38,223	20.4	South Carolina	29,270	21.9
Rhode Island	37,510	11.4	North Carolina	29,108	13.9
Wisconsin	36,477	16.8	Tennessee	28,960	14.7
Hawaii	36,470	1.2	Nebraska	28,768	13.7
Delaware	36,217	20.9	Georgia	28,757	13.7
Oregon	35,880	13.6	Montana	27,617	−3.5
Washington	35,780	4.8	Arkansas	27,598	26.4
Minnesota	35,093	5.6	Alabama	27,490	7.4
Indiana	35,068	19.8	Idaho	27,011	5.7
United States (as a whole)	35,000	16.4	Utah	26,997	−6.4
			Oklahoma	26,529	−0.1
Vermont	34,824	47.3	New Mexico	26,464	−10.6
Nevada	34,119	6.4	Louisiana	26,074	−2.6
Ohio	34,100	17.3	North Dakota	25,211	−7.6
New Hampshire	33,931	41.1	Mississippi	24,367	17.1
Colorado	33,541	7.5	South Dakota	24,289	7.2
Kansas	32,863	24.1			

SOURCE: National Education Association. (1994, May). *NEA Today, 12*(9), 8.

TABLE 16-2 Typical Teacher Salary Scale, 1992–93

Experience Step	Baccalaureate Degree	Master's Degree*
0–1	$25,940	$27,700
2	26,850	28,790
3	27,780	29,850
4	28,710	30,940
5	29,650	32,090
6	30,580	33,230
7	31,510	34,340
8	32,450	35,430
9	33,410	36,550
10	34,340	37,660
11	35,280	38,800
12	36,240	39,940
13	37,190	41,090
14	38,150	42,230
15	39,140	43,370
** 20	40,640	44,870

High school employees shall receive an additional 10% instructional supplement if regularly scheduled to teach six periods.

*Add $1,000 for Specialist in Education Degree from an accredited university.
 Add $2,000 for Specialist in Education Degree if in the area of assignment.
 Add $1,900 for Doctoral Degree from an accredited university.
 Add $2,800 for Doctoral Degree if in the area of assignment.

**To be eligible employees must have a minimum of twenty (20) years of teaching or administrative service in Collier County Public Schools.

A maximum of five (5) years of experience may be transferred to Collier County.

Salaries are computed on the basis of 196 working days. All instructional positions which are more or fewer than 196 days will be computed at the daily rate of 1/196 of the instructional salary.

SOURCE: Literature distributed by the Personnel Department, Collier County (Florida) Public Schools.

for each year of service based on traditional increments—years of teaching experience and amount of college education.

New bases for increments

However, recent reforms have introduced other bases for awarding differential salaries—career ladder ranks, incentive pay plans, and merit awards. Most of these are intended (1) to reward teachers who are believed to be performing noticeably better than their peers, (2) to compensate more for teaching in areas of greatest need, and (3) to attract more and better qualified people to teaching.

Two of the most interesting developments concerning teacher salaries in recent years are state efforts to extend teacher employment through the summer with additional pay and to raise teacher pay to match salaries of occupations that require similar amounts of academic preparation. Some of the recent plans for extended teacher contracts provide up to 25 percent more pay annually for the extra work.

In summary, teacher salaries have been increasing faster in recent years than in the past. There are sincere efforts in some states to increase them further, to make them comparable to those of other fields, and to tie them to performance criteria. The key questions for the years ahead are whether the commitments in these directions will remain strong enough to bring about permanent improvement and whether enough money will be provided to finance the efforts. In any event, it seems logical to predict that teachers of the late 1990s and the new century will be paid comparatively better than those of the 1980s and earlier. On the other hand, most teacher salaries will still be lower than many people believe they should be.

Future Conditions

Now that you are nearing the end of this text, this section of this last chapter describes five very general societal conditions that many experts think will be among the significant situations and circumstances that schools and teachers of the next generation will have to address. The conditions described represent trends that have already begun, and all have been mentioned to some degree earlier in this book. They are presented here not as new information, but as ideas to stimulate your thinking about the challenges of teaching in the twenty-first century—the time when you will be in the classroom if you continue into teaching. The first is tied directly to teaching itself; the others are more truly societal in scope. After the five conditions are described, we, the authors, state our personal views of how schools and teachers will face the challenges noted.

The Continued Professionalization of Teaching

Optimists believe that teaching will continue to evolve to a higher level of professionalism in the years ahead. They expect to see teachers of recognized quality and status who inspire public confidence and respect. Their scenario includes high standards of accountability for students, teachers, and schools, as well as the means to attain those expectations. Many of them see Goals 2000 legislation, particularly the *opportunity to learn* standard, as a driving force for improvement. As one prognosticator expressed it, "Teachers will be doing significant, high-quality work; they will be respected; and they will be compensated at a level that more closely approximates what they deserve."

This expectation involves implemented reforms in teacher education, induction, and certification—bachelor's degrees in liberal arts, fifth-year training in professional education, year-long supervised internships, tests in professional knowledge and teaching subject matter, sophisticated ongoing teacher evaluation, and higher standards at each checkpoint. It also includes greater selectivity and a restricted supply of teachers, even though more people will seek credentials. Many who wish to enter teaching will be rejected because of lack of qualifications. All of this should lead to higher pay, better working conditions, and greater attractions to teaching for better qualified people.

In this view, teachers will be intelligent, reflective, abstract thinkers who have high expectations for their students and themselves; they will set high standards for their colleagues and drive out the weak; and they will decide how and what to teach, control their own curricula, and manage their own schools. Their job will be more complex and more demanding than only a few years ago, but they will be prepared to handle it.

Less optimistic observers believe that some of these predictions will occur, but they anticipate fewer successes. They say that teachers cannot become more professional if they are consistently held to tighter accountability standards imposed by lay-person-dominated school boards and other political bodies. They also question if taxpayers are willing to provide the money needed to reach these goals. However,

Implemented reforms

Selectivity and restricted supply

Teachers in control

even the doubters think the profession of teaching is moving toward a higher, more complex, more demanding plane; and they consider much of the evolution irreversible, at least for the next generation.

America and International Events

Much of the current driving force for change in education has surfaced in part because of the traditional American belief that the United States is the best and most powerful nation on earth. But, in the 1970s, many Americans began to have doubts about that position of prominence. When this happened, they looked to schools to see what went wrong and to determine what to do to make things better. In short, Americans saw schools both as a major cause of the problem and as a potential part of the solution.

At the start of the 1990s, Americans still believed that the United States was "on top" on most matters of national importance. For example, no political system was as stable as that of the United States.

So, as of 1990, the fixing that Americans thought to be necessary to make America stronger was considered doable. Many of the problems that had developed resulted from neglect, not from inherent flaws in basic ideas or conditions. A little more attention to neglected areas, including the major one of schools, was expected to stabilize the country again.

During the 1990s and beyond, the idea of an invincible American nation has been and will continue to be severely challenged internationally. Competition of all types—of ideas, of economic systems, of military might—will not always end in apparent American wins. For example, it is probably safe to assume the following:

- The United States will continue as a debtor nation, with poor balances of trade and under the financial control of foreign investors.
- Segments of its major industries will be unable to compete internationally.
- Middle Eastern oil will not always be a reliable or convenient resource.
- Consumers will continue to reject some American products because they are not as good as those of international competitors.
- Americans will lose Olympic and other international athletic competitions, perhaps more often.
- Minority-group members and those already poor will become comparatively poorer.
- American military troops will not be able to stop violence in every nation of the world.
- More nations will question America's righteousness and reject its leadership.

As Americans realize that these things are happening, their sense of national pride will be shaken, and they will experience forms of national self-doubt. That, in turn, will disturb their faith in their institutions, including schools. What all this will mean for schools is, of course, a matter for conjecture; but as it happens, schools will face a different national environment and psychological atmosphere from that of most of the twentieth century.

Changing Technology and Media

Much has been written about changing technology and its expected impact on American lives in the years ahead. Technological changes are making life more complex, communication instantaneous, skilled jobs more difficult, and teaching more complicated.

(margin notes)

Schools—Problem and solution

Nation on top

Fixing

Not really invincible

Shaken faith

People used to get credit at the store because the manager knew and trusted them, but few managers know their customers any more. There are too many customers, and managers change jobs too often. The decision as to who gets credit is based on computer data and company regulations, not personal, face-to-face judgments. The personal touch is lost. Computers record information on everyone, and God help us when the computer is wrong or the data are lost!

Radio, television, and information highways report world events in living rooms within minutes, maybe seconds, of their happening—events that require an education to understand. The telephone relays family problems across distances for others to share the anxiety, when in the past the difficulty would have passed before they could know about it and begin to worry. Americans view athletic competition on television from the other side of the world and watch participants they do not know competing in events they may not understand; yet often they develop instant favorites, especially if their uniform is emblazoned with a symbol of their own country.

People are sometimes bombarded with more information than they can understand or would even care to know. The weather report takes ten minutes when all the listener may want to know is whether it will rain or not. Financial news may absolutely baffle many of us, but somehow it affects personal bank accounts. Two politicians can argue endlessly over a moral issue, and both may appear to be right. Teachers may teach children content beyond the comprehension of parents, but it sounds important.

Currently paychecks can be deposited directly into the bank, loan payments automatically withdrawn, purchases electronically charged, overdrafts approved, and interest deducted without the people involved ever seeing the money. Some people find themselves hopelessly in debt without realizing what happened. They know they are in trouble when the bank balance on their television screen says so, or when they get nasty letters that some computer wrote them.

Commuters get up at six in the morning to sit in traffic jams in order to get to the office by eight. They arrive at home late and grouchy because the traffic reporter in the radio helicopter told everyone else to use their route home because of an accident on the freeway. When they arrive, dinner is burned because the children put it in the oven at the 5:15 commercial break as directed. Some people have it even worse. They get stuck in underground commuter trains because the grid system computer says there are too many trains on the same track because a door got stuck on car 33 on the Red Line.

Work, as we have often said, is becoming more complicated, as reflected in this 1987 news article:

> Ypsilanti, Mich.—Lavester Frye works at an assembly table eight hours a day building automobile horns, setting a metal plate on a metal dish with one hand, adding a tiny ring with the other.
>
> In the 22 years he has worked at the Ford Motor Co., it never really has mattered that he didn't finish high school. He always has had jobs like this one, jobs that depend more on his hands than his mind.
>
> But Frye has been told that his job will become more complicated. To improve productivity, the company is phasing in an intricate statistical system of quality control.
>
> The news made Frye feel nervous and unprepared, and when he looked at the charts he would be expected to keep under the new system, he was even more troubled by what he saw: decimal points. "A long time ago at school, I had decimals, but it faded out of my mind," he said.

Lost personal touch

Instant communication

Baffling information

Electronic transactions

Lots of people

Complexity at work

On this factory floor, amidst the assembly lines, the huge hulking furnaces and the din of metal on metal, the ability to put a decimal point in the proper place suddenly has become a ticket to a job.

Like thousands of other workers across the country, Frye is experiencing firsthand the transformation of the American workplace in pursuit of competitive advantage. He also sees—and feels, painfully—that, in this race to keep up with other countries, a critical and often missing factor is education.[29]

Biological engineering

Biological scientists are making breakthroughs almost daily. They can make infertile couples fertile, artificially inseminate women, find out when fetuses are defective, correct some defects before or after conception, recommend abortion when risks are high, and in essence engineer the conception, prenatal development, and birth of babies. Some say these discoveries are wonderful, others say they are immoral. Either way, they create choices for prospective parents that did not exist a few years ago.

TV—The "third parent"

Television is often called a third parent in contemporary American society—the children's friend, source of values, attractive picture of the world, and fantasy. It tells children that life consists of excitement, violence, personal confrontation, and Rambo-like physical conflicts—but that in the end (after thirty to sixty minutes) problems are usually solved and goodness prevails. It also shows a world of physical attraction and sexuality, in which few are lonely or neglected and in which life is routinely easy and families supportive. Television has become so powerfully intrusive in the lives of many children and youth that in their minds it has replaced the real world.[30]

Poverty

Much has already been said in this text about poverty in America and its implications for schools and teachers; the main points made earlier that project into the future are repeated here:

■ Many schoolchildren are very poor.
■ Their numbers are increasing.
■ The gap between poor and middle-class children is widening.
■ Schools are and will be expected to educate these children out of poverty.
■ So far, schools have not been able to do this.

As of 1992, about 22 percent of American children, including 46.6 percent of black American children and 39.9 percent of Hispanic children, lived in poverty.[31] The figures have not improved since. (Also see the statistics in Figure 15-1.)

Lack of education

The relationship between poverty and lack of education surfaces all of the time. For example, in 1987 California social-services officials responsible for establishing a new work-training program for unemployed welfare recipients found that 60 percent of the applicants could not read, write, or do the arithmetic necessary for the lowest-level jobs available. Many who had completed high school read below the sixth-grade level. Although jobs were available, these people could not handle them, and the state had not provided the millions of dollars necessary for remedial education.[32]

In a 1986 speech Donna E. Shalala, who later became Secretary of Health and Human Services in the Clinton administration, described the situation this way:

Walk down any city street or into any public school, visit a shelter for the homeless or the maternity or pediatric ward of any public hospital, and you'll see that poor children are in desperate trouble. They are living on welfare, going without proper medical care, and dropping out of school. They are going hungry—in rural communities as well as on the streets of big cities. And they are experimenting with drugs.

The facts are tragic . . .

In education, the statistics are staggering. The school dropout rate is 25 percent overall and more than 50 percent for blacks and Hispanics. Of the small number of children who go on to college, many need remedial help to succeed there.

School dropouts

There is no question that children are now by far the most impoverished group in the United States. As Senator Daniel Moynihan has said, "We may be the first society in history of which it can be said that the children are worse off than their parents." Clearly, an article of faith that was at the very foundation of our nation is in grave danger.

We Americans have always believed that each succeeding generation would outreach the one before. . . .

Twenty, thirty, forty years hence we will need our children to work, to be the teachers and the doctors—even the lawyers—for future generations of children, to say nothing of paying the Social Security taxes that will make our retirement possible.

Our destiny as individuals, as families, as a nation is tied to the destiny of children, all of them—black, Hispanic, Asian, and American Indian, as well as white. As educators, we must convince America that all children, rich and poor, deserve an equal opportunity to grow and learn. That is the challenge as we approach the next century.[33]

Future adults

Something to Think About

A number of educational thinkers question the extent to which schools can and should be expected to enable poor children to overcome the conditions in which they live. They usually say that poverty involves too much that needs to be overcome for the schools to succeed at the task and that other agencies and elements of society must be involved in the effort more than some people think. Some say poverty is endemic to American economic and social conditions and that it will not be overcome without radical changes in the American way of life.

- Do you think schools can and should be expected to play the dominant role in helping poor children overcome the conditions in which they live? If so, how should they do this?
- What should other agencies and other elements of society do for poor children?
- What should not be expected of schools in this regard?

Changing Families

Because the changing conditions in American families were described earlier, only a few statistics are noted here as reminders.

- Three out of every five children in elementary school during the 1990s will live with only one parent before reaching age 18.
- Two-thirds of married women with children of school age are in the work force.
- One-half of all children between ages 5 and 14 change residences at least once in five years.
- The largest age group of poor Americans is children, who are six times more likely to be living below the poverty line than people over 65 years of age.
- About 20 percent of all births are to teenagers, most of whom are poor, undereducated, and unmarried.
- Each day in America 40 teenagers give birth to their third child.

In essence, many families of the twenty-first century will be unable to fulfill the supportive and educative functions of real or idealized families of older times. Other institutions may try to fill the void and compensate for the neglect. Schools and teachers will continue to be expected to shoulder much of the burden.

Teaching in the Years Ahead—As We See It

The conditions just listed for the late 1990s and the next century will pose formidable challenges for schools and teachers. They will require competence and commitment in big doses. But teaching will still provide the satisfactions and rewards that past teachers have enjoyed and will probably supply them more generously. Of course, teaching will be difficult, but teachers will be up to the task.

Educating future generations

Nothing will change the fact that children of future generations deserve to be educated at least as well as children of the past. They deserve it in their own right; but besides that, our future well-being depends on them as effective, educated participants in society. One statistic alone illustrates the point. In 1945, twenty-seven workers supported the American Social Security system for each retired person who drew from its reserves. In 1995, that ratio became three workers for every retiree. One of those three workers is nonwhite, and most have grown up in poor, unstable family circumstances. Most are undereducated. America simply cannot afford a large undereducated population.

Of course, it is unrealistic to rely on schools to cure all societal ills. On the other hand, it is only logical to expect schools and teachers to do their part. That is why schools were established. That is why we have teachers.

Do You Want to Be a Teacher?

Obviously, you have considered the question of whether you want to be a teacher often—before you ever took this course or began reading this text, during your time in the course, and again now. And, you will continue to raise it many times again in the future, especially if you continue toward a teaching career. If you become a teacher, you will then often ask, "Should I continue teaching?"

The Reflecting on Practice that follows is intended to focus your thinking toward the future and to help you search methodically for an answer. Before you begin that exercise, however, you might want to reflect on what you have learned so far

*Is teaching the next genera-
ton for you? There is no
simple way to answer that
question—or to foresee the
unique challenges, frustrations, and rewards await-
ing you if you answer
"yes."*

about teaching and schools and compare your presently held ideas with those you
had when you first considered teaching as a career.

- Do you see teaching differently from the way you saw it before? If so,
  in what ways?
- Do these differences mean that a career in teaching for you would be different from the way you envisioned earlier?
- Would these differences make teaching more or less appealing to you?

REFLECTING ON PRACTICE

Now that you are about to finish this text, it is time to project ahead, to think
about teaching in the next generation. This Reflecting on Practice section
asks you to develop your own description of teaching in the future by doing
several things in succession:

1. Imagine a teacher, a school, and a class of students ten years after the year
   you expect to take your first teaching job. Pick the grade level, type of
   school, and type of community that you would most likely teach in, but do
   not be selective in any other way.

   Make the scene realistic based on what you have learned in this course
   and your other studies. The teacher is not necessarily you. He or she is
   simply a realistic representation of a teacher for that time, school, class,
   and community.
2. Write down what you see.
3. Compare what you have written with the Snapshot description that you
   wrote about yourself at the beginning of this chapter.
4. Ask yourself whether that person from the Snapshot fits into this scene.

Summary

The impact of education reform will continue in teaching and schools for the next generation, but the most significant activity will occur in classrooms and with teachers and students rather than in state legislatures and among policy boards. The continuing reform will include agendas such as (1) back-to-basics and accountability, (2) greater professionalization of teaching, (3) more effective teaching and schools, (4) more equitable education, and (5) changes in content. Making schools better will cost more money.

Virtually everyone who understands teaching sees teachers as the most critical variable in the education process. Because of the increasing complexity of teaching, teachers in the future will have to be more competent in more diverse ways. Finding enough capable teachers for all classes will be difficult. Attracting qualified minority teachers will be particularly hard.

Deciding where to teach is a personal decision for most teacher candidates and depends on personal preferences and values. Some of the main considerations for most people are region of the country, type of community, and type of school.

Teacher salaries have always been low in comparison to those in other professions, but they have increased in the last few years. Some states have pledged to make teaching more attractive by improving compensation and working conditions.

Teaching in the next generations will be influenced by many professional and societal conditions, including the continued professionalization of teaching, international competition, changing technology, poverty, and the changing nature of the American family.

Study Questions

1. If a high school student who is thinking about becoming a teacher asked you what you think are the positive and negative aspects of teaching, what would you say?

2. In what ways will teaching in the year 2010 be significantly different from today? In what ways will it be the same?

3. Which aspects of today's teachers' jobs do you think most need to be preserved without change in the years ahead?

4. What is the most important reason that you are considering (or might consider) a career in teaching? What is the greatest deterrent to your doing so?

Key Terms

Goals 2000	Abstract thinkers	Subject-matter scholars
National Assessment of Educational Progress	Skilled practitioners	Reflective thinking
Executive-like managers	Theoretical knowledge	Conceptual thinking
Decision makers		Technical skills of teaching

For Further Reading

Because this is the last chapter in this text and because the thrust of the chapter has been on teaching in the next generation, this section is different from those of earlier chapters. We suggest that you keep up with conditions and circumstances that will affect teaching and schools in the years ahead and help with your questions about teaching. To do this, we recommend you purchase a handbook that has been referred to earlier and read regularly four types of periodicals.

- Haselkorn, D., & Calkins, A. (1993). *Careers in teaching handbook.* Belmont, MA: Recruiting New Teachers
- a general periodical about teaching and schools, such as *Education Week*
- a general professional journal on issues that affect teaching and schools, such as *Phi Delta Kappan* and *Educational Leadership*
- a professional journal in your educational area of interest, such as a publication of one of the specialty organizations listed in Chapter 15
- a general weekly newsmagazine, such as *Newsweek*

The Teacher-Student Interaction Observation System

The Teacher-Student Interaction Observation System is intended for use by students who have completed Chapter 2. It supplies an additional analytical way of looking at classroom instruction and reinforces ideas and skills covered in the chapter. It is organized just like the Student On-Task/Off-Task Observation System in Chapter 2 and can be pursued independently from class instruction. The Reflecting on Practice section of the material provides an opportunity for practicing the use of the system; and after you have completed it, you should be able to use the system when observing in real classrooms.

The Teacher-Student Interaction Observation System supplies data on the oral interaction, or verbal exchange, between the teacher and individual students. It lists the times a teacher talks to each student and the form of that communication—statement, question, praise, reprimand, and so forth. The form on which the observer records the data is called the Teacher-Student Interaction Seating Chart. As with the off-task instrument, it is an observer-designed seating chart appropriate to the arrangement of the class being observed. If the class is organized with traditional rows of seats and the teacher plans to talk with the whole group at once, the chart might look like Figure A-1.

Explanation

The purpose of the Teacher-Student Interaction System is to record each time the teacher speaks to individual students. The data are collected continuously throughout a class period. The instrument is intended to be used primarily in classes in which there is a pattern of teacher-student verbal interaction, such as direct instruction, recitation, drill, and teacher-led discussion, rather than when students are studying individually, reading silently, watching a film, or taking a test. When teacher comments are directed to the class as a whole, the observer notes the symbols in the teacher box.

Directions

1. Prepare for the observation by developing a boxlike seating chart similar to that in Figure A-1. The boxes need to be large enough for several entries to be made in each. (Little or no space is needed between boxes.)
2. Enter the teacher's name, school, date, and the beginning time of the observation on the form.
3. As soon as the teacher begins the lesson, record each teacher question or statement. Note particularly those that are directed to a specific student. Record continuously until the end of the lesson or until you have observed

FIGURE A-1   Teacher-Student Interaction Seating Chart.

TEACHER-STUDENT INTERACTION SEATING CHART

Teacher: _____ School: _____

Date: _____ Time: _____
                                          (beginning)   to   (end)

(front of classroom)

Teacher

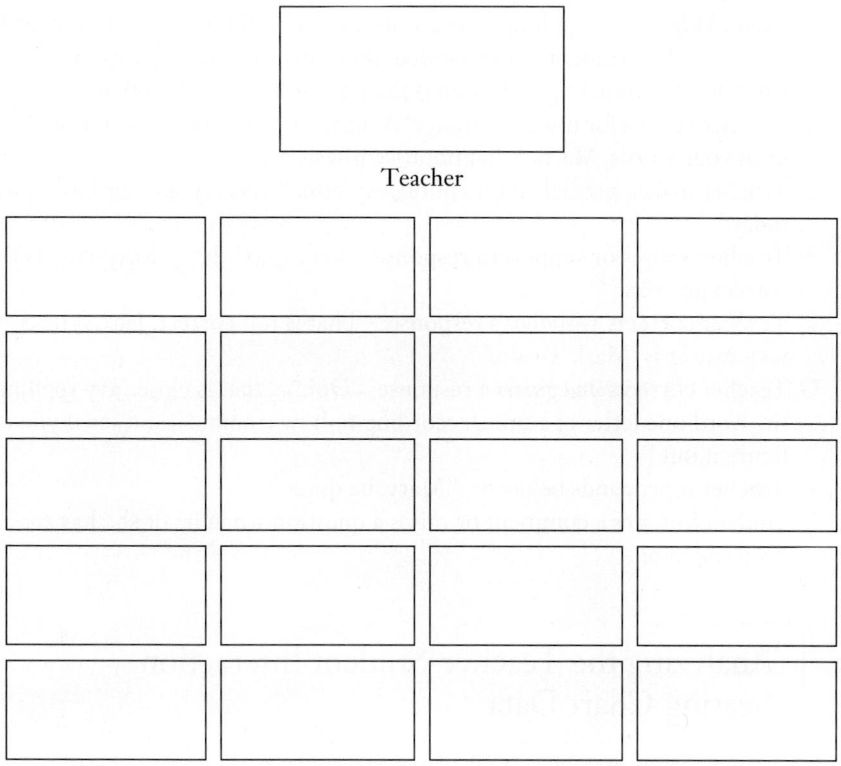

Codes

?	= Asks a direct question	+	= Praises or supports a response
⊙	= Asks an open-ended question	C	= Corrects a response
⅔	= Checks for understanding	G	= Corrects and guides a response
✓	= Makes a general or social	—	= Reprimands behavior
	comment or response	*	= Student initiated comment

SOURCE: Jane Stallings.

for the length of time you had planned. Record each continuous set of teacher-student interactions in a single line in that student's box, and start a new line if the teacher returns to that student later.

4. Record the time when you stop.
5. Note that when the teacher directs a student to respond rather than asking

him or her a question, the comment is still recorded as a question because its purpose is to prompt a student answer. (See "Allen, take Number 1," in the first teacher comment in the Reflecting on Practice that follows.)

An example of a completed observer seating chart appears in Figure A-2.

Data Recorded and Codes

? Teacher asks a student a direct question or directs the student to respond: "Sam, What is the spelling of the word *voyage*?" "Frankie, spell number 4."

⑦ Teacher asks a student a open-ended, thought-provoking question: "Karen, what do you think might happen if the girl in the story does that?"

√̃ Teacher checks for understanding: "Maria, you said, 'photosynthesis.' Tell us in your words, Maria, what photosynthesis means."

√ Teacher makes a social comment or response: "Tracy, your hair looks nice today."

+ Teacher praises or supports a response: "Very good, José; 'forty-two' is the correct answer."

C Teacher corrects a student's response: "That is not correct, Jack. The correct answer is 'Mark Twain.'"

G Teacher corrects *and guides* a response: "Donna, that is close. Try spelling the word one letter at a time, according to how it sounds, and see if you can figure it out."

− Teacher reprimands behavior: "Mary, be quiet."

* Student initiates a comment or raises a question when he or she has *not* been called on.

Analyzing the Teacher-Student Interaction Seating Chart Data

In Figure A-2, you will notice that the number and types of comments that the teacher made to each student are recorded. The sequence of interaction with each student is also discernible.

It is also clear that several elements of teacher-student interaction are not recorded. For example, the chart does not report the overall sequence of the teacher's comments. The teacher might have talked alternately with two students a number of times in succession or might have interspersed those two comments with interactions with other students. The chart does not indicate how long each teacher comment was; nor does it note how long the intervals between comments were. The chart does not report when students were off task, and it contains no information about nonverbal teacher-student interaction.

With the data that are reported, however, the observer can determine the following:

1. how many students the teacher spoke to
2. how many times the teacher addressed particular students
3. the types of teacher communication with each student

FIGURE A-2   Partially completed Teacher-Student Interaction Seating Chart.

TEACHER-STUDENT INTERACTION SEATING CHART

Teacher: Mr. Smith   School: Fall-Hamilton

Date: March   Time: 2:15   to   2:50
                                    (beginning)   (end)

(front of classroom)

✓ ✓ ✓ ✓

Teacher

Tracy	Maria	Betty	Joe
✓	?＋	⑦＋ ⅔＋	✓
?G＋	?＋	?⅔G＋	?＋

Jose	Susan	Robert	Dora
⑦⅔＋	⑦⅔＋	*	⑦⅔G?＋
?＋	?＋?G＋	?C	
	*	✓	

Ursula	Daniel	Ellen	Bill
—	⑦G＋	?⅔⑦＋	?GC?＋
	?C	?＋	

Sharon	Jack	Lee	Mary
—	?＋	?C?＋	
—		＝	

Thomas	Sarah	Andrew	Calvin

Codes

?	= Asks a direct question		＋	= Praises or supports a response
⑦	= Asks an open-ended question		C	= Corrects a response
⅔	= Checks for understanding		G	= Corrects and guides a response
✓	= Makes a general or social comment or response		—	= Reprimands behavior
			*	= Student initiated comment

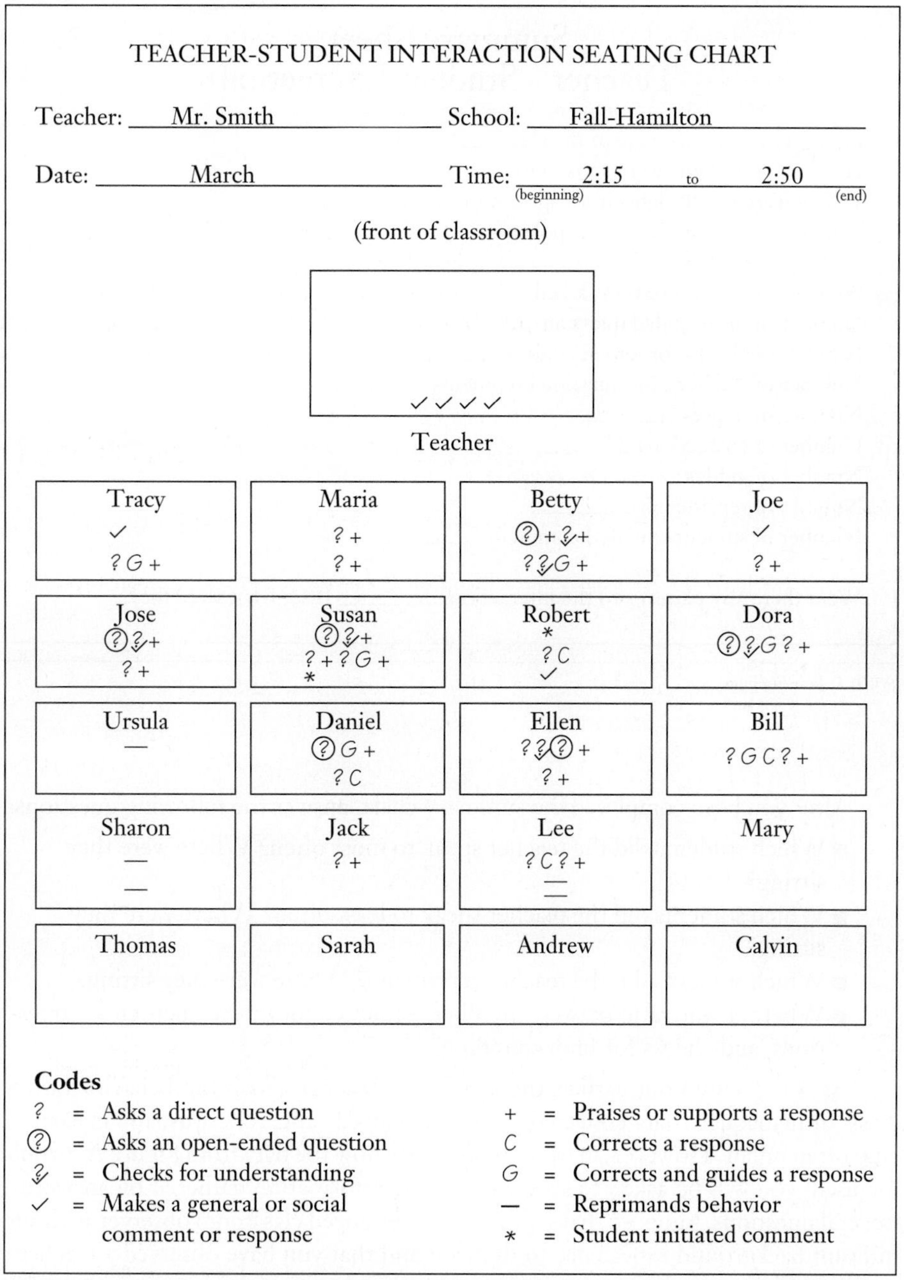

SOURCE: Jane Stallings.

4. the frequency of each type of communication
5. whether the place where students sat reflects a pattern in the interaction

The data in Figure A-2 can be summarized by completing a summary chart like the one shown in Figure A-3. To do this for the information recorded on the seating chart in Figure A-2, complete the summary sheet in Figure A-3.

FIGURE A-3   Teacher-Student Interaction Summary Chart.

Summary Sheet
Teacher - Student Interaction

How many students were in the class? _____
How many students were spoken to ? _____
Where were the students most spoken to sitting? _____
Where were the students not spoken to sitting? _____

Number of direct questions asked _____
Number of open-ended questions asked _____
Number of checks for understanding _____
Number of teacher non-question comments _____
Number of praises _____
Number of corrections _____
Number of guides _____
Number of reprimands _____
Number of student-initiated comments _____

Were there any patterns to the interaction? _____ If so, what were they?

SOURCE: Jane Stallings.

After you have completed the summary chart, answer the following questions:

■ Which students did the teacher speak to most often? Where were they sitting?
■ Which students did the teacher speak to least often? Where were they sitting?
■ Which students did the teacher reprimand? Where were they sitting?
■ What was the ratio between numbers of direct questions, open-ended questions, and checks for understanding?

As was pointed out earlier, the analysis of teacher classroom behavior on the basis of inadequate data collected by inexperienced observers is usually inaccurate and often unfair. However, in order to illustrate how the data from Figure A-3 could be used, you will be asked to speculate on the information gathered by answering several questions. Suppose that you are an experienced classroom observer with significant background experience to draw on and that you have observed a teacher a number of times and have consistently recorded data such as those on the seating chart in Figure A-2 and on the summary sheet in Figure A-3.

■ What significant findings would you infer from these data?
■ What explanation would you offer for the findings and patterns you see?
■ What recommendations would you make to the teacher?

REFLECTING ON PRACTICE

N ow that you have learned about the Teacher-Student Interaction Observation System, analyze the teacher-student interaction recorded on the transcript printed here. The transcript reports all teacher-student oral interactions for ten minutes of a teacher-led, whole-class discussion involving the same English teacher and students described in the second exercise in Chapter 2. The time is now two days later.

1. Make a Teacher-Student Interaction Seating Chart as in Figure A-1. The students are seated as they were for the observation of the same class in Chapter 2. You will need to refer to this section to make an accurate seating chart.
2. Fill in the boxes of the seating chart based on the transcript.
3. Make and complete a summary chart as in Figure A-3.
4. Respond to the questions.

Interaction Transcript

TEACHER: Let's begin the grammar assignment I just handed you. As I call on you, please read the adverb phrase you find in each sentence.
Allen, take Number 1.

ALLEN: Beside the base.

TEACHER: Good. How do you know that phrase is an adverb and not an adjective?

ALLEN: It tells where the player stood.

TEACHER: So it would modify which word?

ALLEN: Stood.

TEACHER: Yes.
Hope, take Number 2.

HOPE: With a spin.

TEACHER: How do you know *with a spin* functions adverbially?

HOPE: Because it tells how he threw the ball.

TEACHER: And it would modify what word?

HOPE: Threw.

TEACHER: Right.
Charlie, do the next one.

CHARLIE: For the winning point.

TEACHER: Good. And how would you prove that phrase is an adverb?

CHARLIE: It is an adverb because it tells—uh—how?

TEACHER: Think again.
Efram, please put all four of your chair legs on the floor.

CHARLIE: Well, I think it modifies *batted*, and I guess it tells why.

TEACHER: Yes.
Felicia, Number 4.

FELICIA: In the red hat.

TEACHER: Oops. I'll agree that's a prepositional phrase, but is it adverbial? Look again.

FELICIA: With his left hand.

TEACHER: Good. And how do you know that is an adverbial phrase?

FELICIA: [Stares at paper but makes no response.]

TEACHER: Louise, can you explain it?

LOUISE: It has to be adverbial because it tells how he threw the ball.

TEACHER: Exactly.
Now look at *in the red hat*. Who can explain that phrase?
Allen?

ALLEN: It's an adjective phrase pointing out which boy.

TEACHER: You're so right.
Class, continue working on this sheet for the next few minutes. Raise your hand if you need help.

[Students work as Ms. Lloyd walks from desk to desk, looks over shoulders, and comments to students.]

TEACHER: Patty, let's make a deal. The classroom is really not the place for personal grooming. If you won't comb your hair in class, I won't brush my teeth here. Okay? [Patty giggles and puts her comb away, and the teacher moves on.]
Good work, Quillen.
Rosa, your penmanship is improving, and I'm pleased with your efforts.
Sam, look again at Number 8.
Tara, please put your shoes back on.

NAN: I need help with Number 8.

TEACHER: Where are the subject and the verb? [Nan points to them.] Yes, good. Now *think*. Does any phrase tell how, when, where, or why?

NAN: This one here? [Points again.]

TEACHER: Yes, you've got it.

HOPE: I need help telling adjective and adverb phrases apart.

TEACHER: Hope, you must look at what the phrases *do* in the sentences; that determines what they are. What can an adverb do?

HOPE: An adverb can tell *how, when, where, why,* and *to what extent.*

TEACHER: You're right. And if a prepositional phrase does any of those, then it is an adverbial phrase. Okay? [Hope nods.]
Efram, the number of chair legs touching the floor should always be four.
[Efram shrugs and sits up straight.]

TEACHER: All right. Is everyone finished through Number 8? [All students nod.] Good. Put this sheet in your folder and finish it for homework tonight. [All students comply.] Now let's change gears and focus on last night's literature assignment.
What words or phrases come to mind when you hear the name *Rip Van Winkle?*
Gary?

GARY: I guess *a long sleep* and also *henpecked.*

TEACHER: Why do you say *henpecked?*

GARY: Because Dame Van Winkle was always fussing at him.

DIANA: The word *lazy* comes to my mind, and I think his wife had good reason to nag!

TEACHER: How so?

DIANA: Well, if I had a husband who never worked or helped around the house but went around playing with kids and fixing broken fences for other women, you can bet I'd say something!

TEACHER: You definitely have a point there.
Let's go back to the idea of a long sleep. Just suppose you went to sleep tonight and woke up twenty years from now. What are some things you think really might be different?

EFRAM: You can bet the cars would sure be different.

TEACHER: How, so, Efram?

EFRAM: Well, probably they'd use some fuel besides gasoline.

TEACHER: Can you think of any general effect that might have on life?

EFRAM: Hmmm. Well, maybe it wouldn't pollute the air so much, and people could breathe better in the cities.

TEACHER: That's an interesting idea.

SAM: In twenty years there would be a whole lot more people.

TEACHER: Can you think of any ways that might affect life in general?

SAM: You'd probably have to stand in lines longer at Disney World.

TEACHER: Could well be.
Patty, this is not the place to file your nails. [Patty returns the file to her purse.]

MARY: I think movies and television would be different, probably all 3-D and maybe with smells, too.

TEACHER: Interesting.

QUILLEN: Everything would be computerized and then some.

TEACHER: How might that make life different from what we know now?

QUILLEN: Well, it might save a lot of time on things. Maybe there would even be a computerized homework machine. Or maybe a computerized teacher.
Ms. Lloyd, do you think you could be replaced by a computer?

TEACHER: Not this year.

Addresses of State Offices of Teacher Licensure and Certification

As you pursue your teacher-education studies, you might want to keep yourself up-to-date on the requirements for teacher licensure and certification in the state or states where you will most likely teach. The addresses and phone numbers of the state offices that can supply you with that information are listed below:

STATE OFFICES OF TEACHER LICENSURE & CERTIFICATION

ALABAMA
Certification—Division of Professional Services
Department of Education
Gordon Persons Building
50 North Ripley Street
Montgomery, AL 36130-3901
205-242-9977

ALASKA
Teacher Education and Certification
Department of Education
Alaska State Office Building
Pouch F
Juneau, AK 99811-1894
907-465-2831

ARIZONA
Teacher Certification Unit
Department of Education
1535 West Jefferson Street
P.O. Box 25609
Phoenix, AZ 85007
602-542-4368

ARKANSAS
Office of Teacher Education and Licensure
Department of Education
#4 Capitol Mall, Room 106B/107B
Little Rock, AR 72201
501-682-4342

CALIFORNIA
Commission on Teacher Credentialing
1812 9th Street
Sacramento, CA 95814
916-445-7254

COLORADO
Teacher Certification
Department of Education
201 East Colfax Avenue
Denver, CO 80203-1799
303-866-6628

CONNECTICUT
Bureau of Certification and Accreditation
Department of Education
P.O. Box 2219
Hartford, CT 06145
203-566-4561

DELAWARE
Office of Certification
Department of Public Instruction
Townsend Building
P.O. Box 1402
Dover, DE 19903
302-739-4688

DISTRICT OF COLUMBIA
Division of Teacher Services
District of Columbia Public Schools
415 12th Street, N.W.
Room 1013
Washington, D.C. 20004-1994
202-724-4250

FLORIDA
Division of Human Resource Development
Teacher Certification Offices
Department of Education, FEC, Rm. 201
325 West Gaines Street
Tallahassee, FL 32399-0400
904-488-5724

GEORGIA
Professional Standards Commission
Department of Education
1454 Twin Towers East
Atlanta, GA 30334
404-656-2604

HAWAII
Office of Personnel Services
Department of Education
P.O. Box 2360
Honolulu, HI 96804
808-586-3420

IDAHO
Teacher Education and Certification
Department of Education
Len B. Jordan Office Building
650 West State Street
Boise, ID 83720
208-334-3475

ILLINOIS
Certification and Placement
State Board of Education
100 North First Street
Springfield, IL 62777-0001
217-782-2805

INDIANA
Professional Standards Board
Department of Education
State House, Room 229
Indianapolis, IN 46204-2790
317-232-9010

IOWA
Board of Education Examiners
State of Iowa
Grimes State Office Building
Des Moines, IA 50319-0146
515-281-3245

KANSAS
Certification, Teacher Education & Accreditation
Department of Education
120 SE Tenth Avenue
Topeka, KS 66612
913-296-2288

KENTUCKY
Teacher Education and Certification
Department of Education
500 Mero Street, Rm. 1820
Frankfort, KY 40601
502-564-4606

LOUISIANA
Teacher Certification
Department of Education
P.O. Box 94064
626 North 4th Street
Baton Rouge, LA 70804-9064
504-342-3490

MAINE
Department of Education
Certification and Placement
State House Station 23
Augusta, ME 04333
207-289-5800

MARYLAND
Division of Certification and Accreditation
Department of Education
200 West Baltimore Street
Baltimore, MD 21201
410-333-2142

MASSACHUSETTS
Bureau of Teacher Certification
Department of Education
350 Main Street
Malden, MA 02148
617-338-3300

MICHIGAN
Teacher/Administrator Preparation and Certification
Department of Education
P.O. Box 30008
608 West Allegan Street
Lansing, MI 48909
517-373-3310

MINNESOTA
Personnel and Licensing
Department of Education
616 Capitol Square Building
550 Cedar Street
St. Paul, MN 55101
612-296-2046

MISSISSIPPI
Office of Teacher Certification
Department of Education
P.O. Box 771
Jackson, MS 39205
601-359-3483

MISSOURI
Teacher Education
Missouri Teacher Certification Office
Department of Elementary and Secondary Education
P.O. Box 480
Jefferson City, MO 65102-0480
314-751-3486

MONTANA
Certification Services
Office of Public Instruction
State Capitol
Helena, MT 59620
406-444-3150

NEBRASKA
Teacher Certification/Education
301 Centennial Mall, South
Box 94987
Lincoln, NE 68509
402-471-2496

NEVADA
Teacher Licensure
Department of Education
1850 East Sahara, Suite 200
State Mail Room
Las Vegas, NV 89158
702-486-6457

NEW HAMPSHIRE
Bureau of Teacher Education and Professional Standards
Department of Education
State Office Park South
101 Pleasant Street
Concord, NH 03301-3860
603-271-2407

NEW JERSEY
Teacher Certification and Academic Credentials
Department of Education
3535 Quakerbridge Road, CN 503
Trenton, NJ 08625-0503
609-292-2070

NEW MEXICO
Educator Preparation and Licensure
Department of Education
Education Building
Santa Fe, NM 87501-2786
505-827-6587

NEW YORK
Office of Teacher Certification
Department of Education
Cultural Education Center, Room 5A 11
Albany, NY 12230
518-474-3901

NORTH CAROLINA
Division of Certification
Department of Public Instruction
114 West Edenton Street
Raleigh, NC 27603-1712
919-733-4125; 919-733-0377

NORTH DAKOTA
Teacher Certification Division
Department of Public Instruction
600 East Blvd. Avenue
Bismarck, ND 58505-0440
701-224-2264

OHIO
Teacher Certification
Department of Education
65 South Front Street, Room 1012
Columbus, OH 43266-0308
614-466-3593

OKLAHOMA
Department of Education
2500 North Lincoln Blvd., Room 211
Oliver Hodge Education Building
Oklahoma City, OK 73105-4599
405-521-3337

OREGON
Teacher Standards and Practices Commission
580 State Street, Room 203
Salem, OR 97310
503-378-3586

PENNSYLVANIA
Bureau of Teacher Preparation and Certification
Department of Education
333 Market Street, 3rd Floor
Harrisburg, PA 17126-0333
717-787-2967

PUERTO RICO
Teacher Certification Division
Department of Education
Box 190759
Hato Rey, PR 00919
809-758-4949

RHODE ISLAND
School and Teacher Accreditation,
Certification and Placement
22 Hayes Street
Roger Williams Building, 2nd Floor
Providence, RI 02908
401-277-2675

SOUTH CAROLINA
Teacher Education and Certification
Department of Education
1015 Rutledge
1429 Senate Street
Columbia, SC 29201
803-734-8466

SOUTH DAKOTA
Office of Certification
Division of Education and Cultural Affairs
Kneip Office Building
700 Governor's Drive
Pierre, SD 57501
605-773-3553

TENNESSEE
Office of Teacher Licensing
Department of Education
6th Floor, North Wing
Cordell Hull Building
Nashville, TN 37243-0377
615-741-1644

TEXAS
Division of Personnel Records
William B. Travis Office Building
1701 North Congress Avenue
Austin, TX 78701
512-463-8976

UTAH
Certification and Personnel Development
State Office of Education
250 East 500 South
Salt Lake City, UT 84111
801-538-7740

VERMONT
Licensing Division
Department of Education
Montpelier, VT 05620
802-828-2445

VIRGINIA
Office of Professional Licensure
Department of Education
P.O. Box 2120
Richmond, VA 23216-2120
804-225-2022

WASHINGTON
Director of Professional Preparation
Office of the Superintendent of Public Instruction
Old Capitol Building
Box 47200
Olympia, WA 98504-7200
206-753-6775

WEST VIRGINIA
Office of Professional Preparation
Department of Education
Capitol Complex, Room B-337, Bldg. 6
Charleston, WV 25305
304-558-2703; 1-800-982-2378

WISCONSIN
Bureau of Teacher Education, Licensing and Placement
Department of Public Instruction
125 South Webster Street
P.O. Box 7841
Madison, WI 53707-7841
608-266-1027

WYOMING
Certification and Licensing Unit
Department of Education
2300 Capitol Avenue
Hathaway Building
Cheyenne, WY 82002-0050
307-777-6261

ST. CROIX DISTRICT
Department of Education
Educational Personnel Services
2133 Hospital St.
Christianstead
St. Croix, Virgin Islands 00820
809-773-5844

ST. THOMAS/ST. JOHN DISTRICT
Educational Personnel Services
Department of Education
44-46 Kongens Grade
St. Thomas, Virgin Islands 00802
809-744-0100

U.S. DEPARTMENT OF DEFENSE OVERSEAS DEPENDENT SECTION
Teacher Recruitment
2461 Eisenhower Avenue
Alexandria, VA 22331-1100
703-325-0690

SOURCE: This list is drawn from Haselkorn, D., & Calkins, A. (1993). *Careers in teaching handbook.* Belmont, MA: Recruiting New Teachers, pp. 65–69.

Glossary

Abstract thinker. A role expected of teachers of the future that involves thinking on theoretical levels and then drawing on knowledge from many disciplines to decide what to do in the classroom.

Academic disciplines. Categories of knowledge that have their own identified conceptual focuses and methods of inquiry.

Academic engaged rate. The ratio between the amount of time students are actually engaged in academic learning tasks and the total time they are in class.

Academic freedom. The freedom of teachers and students to hold and express ideas without arbitrary interference by others with power.

Academic learning time. The time in class during which students are actively engaged in academic tasks and are succeeding at a high rate.

Academic needs. Student needs associated with what they know and do not know and with their academic abilities.

Academic purposes of schools. Purposes of schools associated with intellectual development and learning information and ideas; the purposes are usually reflected in academic subjects.

Accelerated Schools Project. A network of schools that attempts to improve how schools work with difficult-to-teach students by replacing remedial instruction with accelerated instruction; a second-wave proposal for school reform developed by Henry M. Levin.

Accommodation. The mental process of changing one's patterns of thinking to incorporate newly learned information and ideas.

Accountability. Being held responsible for one's actions and the results of those actions; a concept applied to students, teachers, and schools by educational reformers.

Accreditation of teacher education. A process whereby regional, state, and national organizations, or states themselves, evaluate teacher education institutions and programs and publicly announce if each meets established standards.

Acculturation. A process by which an individual acquires the characteristics and beliefs of a culture; usually considered to be a purpose of schools.

Active learning. Learning activities in which students participate in an active way as contrasted with activities in which they listen or watch passively.

Active teaching. Teaching during which the teacher is actively interacting with students who are engaged in learning tasks.

Activity-centered curriculum. A type of child-centered, integrated curriculum plan arranged around student classroom activities.

Act of teaching. A specialized use of the term in this text to mean the three-part process of planning, teaching, and evaluating lessons.

Adaptation. The mental process of changing one's ideas and/or behavior as a result of interacting with one's environment.

Adaptive behavior. Learned behavior derived from accommodating to one's environment.

Advanced organizers. An active teaching technique by which teachers start the lesson by letting students know how the lesson will progress and what to expect.

Aesthetics. The branch of the study of values that deals with the question, What is beauty?

Aesthetic value judgments. Judgments about beauty.

"A free appropriate public education." A quote from the Supreme Court *Pennsylvania Association of Retarded*

Children v. *Commonwealth of Pennsylvania* decision and repeated in Public Law 94-142 that ensures students with disabilities an appropriate education.

Affective learning. The learning of values, feelings, and sensitivities, as opposed to *cognitive learning*.

Age-grouped societies. Subgroups within broader society divided primarily by age.

Age of Reason. A time in the development of Western education that roughly parallels the eighteenth century, characterized by a strong interest in science and empirical investigation; also called the *Enlightenment*.

"All deliberate speed." An order of the United States Supreme Court that schools be desegregated in a prompt and timely manner.

Allocated time. The time provided in class for students to be engaged in learning tasks.

Alternative certification. Ways of receiving state certificates to teach without completing traditional teacher education programs.

Alternative schools. Schools that are set up to meet student needs that are not being met by regular schools; often intended for students who are hard to teach for some reason.

Analytical observation. The purposeful viewing of a situation with particular attention to its component parts and essential features.

Analyzing. An aspect of thinking that involves examining something in detail by separating it into its component parts to find out its nature.

Analyzing values. A specific set of teaching strategies that are used to teach students to think about their own and others' values.

Anchored instruction. A problem-solving task for a group of students that forms a meaningful and challenging context for their learning, usually associated with the Technology-Based Anchored Instruction model of instruction.

Applying knowledge. An aspect of thinking that involves putting knowledge to use, as in problem solving.

Apprentice. A beginner or learner; a person who is learning a trade by helping a worker skilled in that trade.

Apprenticeship. The condition or period of being an apprentice.

Apprentice teacher. A new teacher who is still learning classroom skills characteristic of a more experienced or master teacher.

Approval of others stage of moral development. The third stage of moral development identified by Lawrence Kohlberg; the stage at which moral behavior is guided by a desire to look like a good person in the eyes of others.

Aristotelian philosophy. A way of thinking or form of logic developed by the Greek philosopher Aristotle that uses deduction and is characterized by syllogism.

Artistic skills. Abilities that people use to create something or to perform, such as painting, dancing, and singing.

Assertive discipline. A specific counseling-based approach to behavior control that includes guides for teachers to follow as they formulate their personal discipline plan.

Assimilation. (1) The mental process of integrating newly formed ideas with one's current patterns of thinking; (2) the integration of cultural traits as different cultural groups intermix.

Association theory. A theory about behavior and memory that says learning occurs because the mind makes associations, or mental con-

nections, between certain items and events.

At-risk. A condition under which a person, family, nation, or other entity is particularly vulnerable.

Attention deficit hyperactivity disorder. A complex learning disorder characterized by a cluster of several symptoms including difficulty staying on task and controlling one's behavior, not listening, and engaging in risky behavior.

Attribution. The bases or reasons students use to explain their successes or failures, such as, "I failed the test because the teacher is too hard."

Authenticity. The quality of being one's own person; genuine, reliable.

Authentic people. Those who believe in their own freedom to think and act, utilize their own ideas, and accept their own responsibility.

Authentic texts. Student readings that consist of real literature and other forms of real writing, such as signs and notices, rather than writings put together specifically for reading lessons.

Authority. Legitimate power over others.

"Average students." Students whose characteristics are not significantly different from those of most other students.

Axiology. A branch of philosophy that focuses on the study of the nature of values.

Back-to-basics. A movement in education, especially since the 1970s, that emphasizes the teaching of core academic subjects such as English, mathematics, history, and science.

Baseline behavior. The behavior measured or assessed before learning takes place or before an experiment starts.

Basic education. A view of education that emphasizes the study of basic academic subjects such as English,

history, mathematics, science; stresses literacy and the study of great literary works.

Basics. Subjects that many consider essential, usually including reading, writing, English, mathematics, science, and social studies.

Battered child syndrome. A set of characteristics often seen in children who are abused or otherwise consistently mistreated.

Behavioral expectations. The student classroom behaviors expected by teachers.

Behavioral objectives. The anticipated results or products of instruction, usually stated in terms of the behaviors that teachers expect students to be able to exhibit as a result of instruction; also called *educational objectives* and *instructional objectives*.

Behavioral research. Investigations that focus on analyzing how and why people and groups act as they do.

Behavioral stages of development. Developmental stages of student behavior at which certain generalized patterns of classroom behavior can be expected (as identified by Jere Brophy and Carolyn Evertson).

Behavior disorder. A condition in which a student exhibits problem behavior.

Behaviorism. The belief that all behavior is caused and, therefore, predictable and susceptible to modification.

Behavior modification. The use of conditioning to change behavior.

Behavior theory. A theory that says that behavior is learned and extrinsically influenced.

Belief. The acceptance of an idea or proposition as true or acceptance that a situation or an object actually exists.

Bilingual education. Education programs for non-native-English-speaking students that attempt to teach in the students' native language as well as in English.

Block grants. Funds provided by the federal government during the 1980s under the Reagan administration that replaced categorical aid and had fewer strings attached.

Blue-backed speller. A spelling book written by Noah Webster and first published in 1783 that was used nationwide for many years.

Bourgeoisie. The social class between the very wealthy and the working class; according to Marxist doctrine, the class antithetical to the working class (the proletariat).

Brisk pace (as a classroom characteristic). An instructional tempo that maintains momentum and student motivation and helps students stay on task.

Broad aims of education. Statements about general directions and emphases about what content should be taught in schools; usually set at national, state, and district levels.

Broad-fields curriculum. A type of subject-centered curriculum arranged around broad, integrated subject areas such as social studies and language arts.

Cardinal Principles of Secondary Education **(1918).** The report of the Commission on the Reorganization of Secondary Education of the National Education Association (NEA) that recommended that schools emphasize teaching about seven broad areas of life.

Career ladder. A system of job classification that contains successively higher levels of responsibility and salary through which employees, such as teachers, can advance by means of evaluation, training, and/or experience.

Carnegie Task Force on Teaching as a Profession. One of the groups that proposed remedies to improve

schools in one of the early second-wave reform reports; it focused its concerns on improving teaching and teacher education; it is the primary force behind the National Board of Professional Teaching Standards.

Carriers. Individuals in a tribe or an organization who tell the folk stories and legends and pass on the traditions.

Categorical aid. Funds provided to local public schools by the state and federal governments for specific purposes; contrast with *general aid*.

Causal attribution. A psychological theory that says that people explain their behavior by crediting their successes and failures to various causes.

Centering. A characteristic of the thinking of young children before the Piagetian concrete operational stage, whereby children focus on only one aspect of a problem, usually the most obvious one.

Cerebral palsy. A physically disabling condition that is usually caused by oxygen deprivation at birth.

Ceremonials. Rites, rituals, or ceremonies.

Chapter I. An abbreviated reference to Chapter I of the Education Consolidation and Improvement Act of 1981; provides federal aid to programs for low-income families.

Checking for understanding. A technique of instruction in which the teacher monitors student responses and practice to determine if and how well they understand, rather than just recall, the ideas presented; often done through questioning and written assignments.

Child benefit theory. The idea that some public funding of instruction in private schools is constitutional if its primary effect is to benefit the student rather than to support the school.

Citizenship education. A purpose of schooling that gives students the knowledge, skills, and values to be effective political, economic, and social participants in society.

Citizenship participation skills. Abilities that people use to play active roles in their society, such as leading others, staying informed, and making decisions.

Clarifying (as used in Chapter 10). The step in the process of philosophizing that addresses the question, What do you mean?

Classical humanism. A type of rational study characteristic of the Renaissance that emphasizes classical literature and culture.

Classical realists. Traditional realists who believe that some moral values can be arrived at by rigorous thought and who, on a continuum, are closer to idealists in their thinking than to materialistic realists.

Classifying. Organizing things into categories and assigning labels to each category.

Class-level objectives. Objectives established for instruction at particular grade levels, often set for each subject taught.

Class personality. The combination of individual student personality characteristics that give a class its own personality or character.

Classroom climate. The physical, psychological, social, and interpersonal atmosphere of a classroom.

Classroom culture. The values, belief systems, and norms present in a classroom.

Classroom ecology. The physical aspects of a classroom environment.

Classroom effectiveness. The degree to which classroom conditions enhance teaching and learning.

Classroom milieu. The interpersonal atmosphere, or the "feeling" aspect, of a classroom environment.

Classroom routines. Conscious patterns of classroom procedure that are followed consistently by the teacher and students throughout a school year.

Classroom structures. The procedures, routines, and rules of a classroom as established by the teacher's management plan.

Classroom verbal interaction. Interaction in a classroom through the use of words.

Coalition of Essential Schools. A network of schools that attempts to make schools more effective by focusing attention on nine common principles about how schools should operate and what they should accomplish; a second-wave proposal for school reform developed by Theodore Sizer.

Cognition. The process of knowing, learning, and/or thinking.

Cognitive. Of or pertaining to the processes of knowing, thinking, or learning.

Cognitive and Technology Group at Vanderbilt. A team of educational researchers at the Learning Technology Center, Peabody College, Vanderbilt University.

Cognitive behavior modification systems. Approaches to behavior change, based on behavior theory and cognition, that emphasize the students' role in understanding and controlling their own behavior change.

Cognitive-development theory. A learning theory that says learning is an active process of information acquisition that includes perceiving, encoding, and retrieving from memory; the theory also holds that learning increases in sophistication as people increase their interactions with their environment. Also called *information-processing theory*.

Cognitive domain. The area of educational objectives and learning that focuses on information, ideas, and thinking.

Cognitive growth. The increasing of one's intellectual ability to transform and manipulate information.

Cognitive learning. The learning of information, ideas, and thinking skills, as opposed to *affective learning*.

Cognitive psychology. A psychological theory that sees learning as a process of information acquisition that includes perceiving, encoding, and retrieving from memory.

Cognitive research. Investigations into how people know and learn, often with a particular focus on thinking.

Coherence. Sticking together; having all parts connected in a proper way; clear.

Commission on the Reorganization of Secondary Education of NEA (1918). The commission that recommended that high schools teach content that addresses student needs, interests, and abilities as well as the needs of society; reported its recommendations in *Cardinal Principles of Secondary Education*.

Committee of Ten on Secondary Schools of the NEA (1893). The committee that recommended that high schools "train the mind" and prepare students for college; recommended that the curriculum consist of nine academic subjects.

Common education. Education provided by schools intended for all children and youth of the society.

Common schools. (1) Schools of American colonial times established by towns to provide rudimentary education to the town's children; (2) tax-supported schools of the nineteenth century established through state authorization.

Communication apprehension. Anxiousness of fearfulness about participating in oral communication.

Compensatory education. Educational efforts intended to make up for social, economic, and educational deficiencies in students' out-of-school lives.

Comprehending. An aspect of thinking that involves intellectually grasping the meaning of something.

Comprehensive education. A broad education that includes academic, general, and vocational studies; intended to serve all types of students.

Comprehensive high schools. General secondary schools offering programs in both vocational and general academic subjects, but in which the majority of the students are not enrolled in programs of vocational education.

Compulsory schooling. Requiring by law that children and youth attend school.

Computer ethics. Guidelines for the fair and honest use of computer technology and software.

Computing. An aspect of thinking that involves calculating numbers or items.

Concept. A category or representation into which or under which specifics are grouped.

Conceptualizing. A thinking process that involves categorizing things or putting things into groups; also referred to as developing concepts.

Conceptual thinking. Thinking about broad ideas and categories, as distinct from lower levels of thinking that focus on specific facts.

Conditioned reflex. A response or reaction to a stimulus based on repeated association of the reaction to the stimulus, often to the point that the reaction is virtually automatic; for example, Pavlov's dog salivating when hearing a bell ring.

Conditioning. The idea from association theory that some thing or some event causes a particular automatic behavior in people and animals.

Consent of the governed. The principle that governments derive their power from the people and can be removed by the people.

Constitutional authority. Legitimate power held by a government because it is authorized by a constitution.

Constructivism. The idea that learning is a process by which students construct meaning through their own interpretation of things and events based on their personal interactions with the environment.

Contemporary philosophies. Philosophies that have developed in recent times, including reconstructionism, futurism, behaviorism, essentialism, and perennialism.

Content. The knowledge, skills, and affective learning students are taught in school.

Continuity. An idea about learning articulated by John Dewey that sees learning as continuous; what students learn in a lesson depends on prior learning and experiences and affects future learning.

Continuous progress. A characteristic of instruction that enables large numbers of students to progress continuously with high rates of success and a minimum of confusion.

Contract. A binding legal agreement between people; used by John Locke to explain the relationship between people and their government.

Conversational dance. Communication and social interactions between infants and caregivers that prompt the beginnings of social understanding; also referred to as *turn taking*.

Cooperative Integrated Reading and Composition (CIRC). A type of cooperative learning of integrated language arts and writing that combines teacher presentations, individual study, and peer group work.

Cooperative learning. A model of instruction that organizes students into teams of varying abilities and economic and cultural backgrounds in order to encourage academic achievement and interpersonal understanding.

Coping behavior. Actions whereby individuals deal with difficulties, stress, and conflict without relinquishing their goals.

Copyright laws. Laws that guide the use of creative materials by others in order to give the creators proper credit and compensation for their work and creativity.

Core curriculum. A curriculum plan that is slightly more subject-centered than student-centered but combines both subject-centered and student-centered characteristics; one that is arranged around broad, integrated fields yet is attentive to student needs, interests, and experiences.

Corporal punishment. Punishment that involves inflicting pain through physical contact.

Corrective materials. Materials assigned to students in Mastery Learning who need additional work to master the task they are studying.

Correlation. A connection or mutual relationship between or among two or more elements.

Correlational studies. Studies that show that one phenomenon is associated with another, although the one might not necessarily cause the other.

Counseling and therapy-based behavior modification systems. Approaches to behavior change based on principles drawn from counseling psychology and psychotherapy.

Court schools. Schools sponsored by Renaissance-era princes for the children of prominent friends of the prince.

Creation science. The biblical explanation of the origin of the human race.

Criterion tests. Assessments that compare scores or performances against an identified standard.

Critical theory. A contemporary philosophy that argues against authoritarianism, social control, and oppression by the privileged.

Cultural backgrounds. The group associations and experiences that shape people's patterns of behavior, values, beliefs, traditions, and norms.

Cultural capital. Resources that students possess or can draw on because of their identification with a cultural group and its traditions, heritage, and sources of support.

Cultural expectations. What a culture values and the behaviors that are expected of its members.

Cultural literacy. The possession of a common set of knowledge about one's culture that advocates such as E. D. Hirsch suggest should be known by all who expect to function competently in contemporary society.

Cultural organizations. Organizations in which people share common values and beliefs, patterns of thinking and behaving, history, and traditions.

Cultural pluralism. The recognition of the diverse cultural, language, and ethnic groups and heritages in American society.

Cultural-sociological dimensions of individual-environment interaction. Types of interaction between individuals and their environment that concern cultural and sociological elements such as religion, laws, traditions, and community.

Culture. The patterns of behavior, values, beliefs, traditions, and norms that characterize a group.

Culture of the school. The shared values, beliefs, traditions, sense of purpose, feeling of belonging, and history of a school organization.

Curricular knowledge. Knowledge of content as it is reflected in curriculum materials.

Curriculum. A plan of instruction for a school system, school, or area of subject matter; the design of what, when, and how students should be taught; a plan of what content should be taught at which grade levels.

Curriculum framework. A document that outlines the plan of instruction for a school system, school, or area of subject matter.

Cycle of poverty. The phenomenon that children who grow up in poverty conditions tend to accept poverty as a permanent way of life and continue to live under similar circumstances as adults.

Dames' schools. A low-level primary school in the colonial and other early periods, usually conducted by an untrained woman in her own home.

Decentering. The ability to see something from more than one perspective, particularly from perspectives other than one's personal point of view.

Decision maker. A role expected of teachers of the future that involves deciding what and how and in what depth to teach, how to assess students, and many more issues about the education of students.

Decision making. The intellectual process of making decisions and choices.

Decision-making skill. The ability to decide, make judgments, or reach conclusions through rational processes and with firmness of mind.

Decoding. Translating a coded message into an uncoded one or into one tht is more readily interpretable.

Deductive reasoning. Reasoning from a general principle to a specific, from a principle to an unknown, or from a premise to a logical conclusion.

De facto segregation. The forced separation of people due to conditions and practices other than those enacted by law.

De jure segregation. The forced separation of people by legislation and other legal means.

Denominational schools. Schools sponsored by churches, prevalent during American colonial times and the early nineteenth century.

Desegregation. The process of correcting past practices of racial or any other form of illegal segregation.

Developing mental operations. A pattern of thinking associated with the Piagetian concrete operational stage in which representations such as maps and symbols can be manipulated; includes adding, subtracting, ordering, and classifying.

Diagnostic assessments. Evaluations intended to assess student prior knowledge and abilities so that appropriate instruction can be provided.

Dialectical theory. A concept of development that focuses on the interaction between individuals and their environment.

Differential instruction. Teaching that accommodates differences among individual learners.

Direct instruction. A teaching pattern that emphasizes the teacher's telling the students what to do and the students following these directions; often conducted in lessons that have several rather small parts that fall in a set sequence.

Discipline-based curriculum. A type of subject-centered curriculum arranged around specific content disciplines such as English, history, or mathematics; also called *separate-subjects curriculum.*

Disciplines. Categories of knowledge associated with academic study.

Diversity. A quality or state characterized by different elements or variety.

Dominated communities. Local political communities that are controlled by a single strong leader or a few powerful people.

Down's syndrome. A genetically caused form of mental retardation.

Drill and practice questioning. An active teaching technique that consists of fast-paced questions that have right and wrong answers; usually used to review and reinforce factual information and basic skills.

Druggies. A nickname for youth who use illicit drugs.

Due process of law. Legal procedures designed to ensure that people are treated fairly in terms of the law.

Dyslexia. A learning disability associated with reading that involves an inability to decode or interpret symbolic forms such as printed words.

Eclectic. Selecting from various sources.

Economic capital. Resources that students possess or can draw on because of their (or their family's) economic well-being.

Educable mentally retarded. One of the names for the category of people with mild mental retardation.

Educational capital. Resources that students possess or can draw on because of acquired knowledge and skills.

Educational equity. The goal that schools provide an equally high-quality education for every student.

Educationally handicapped. Those whose lack of education or inadequate education hampers their functioning in society.

Educational malpractice. Improper conduct by education professionals that injures students or hinders their learning.

Educational objectives. The anticipated results or products of instruction, usually stated in terms of the behaviors that teachers expect students to be able to exhibit as a result of instruction; also called *behavioral objectives* and *instructional objectives.*

Educational outcome. The result or product of instruction, usually stated in terms of what students learn.

Educational Policies Commission, NEA and American Association of School Administrators (1938). The commission that recommended that schools focus on teaching the whole child and suggested four broad topics to be covered; issued the report *The Purposes of Education in American Democracy.*

Educational Policies Commission, NEA and American Association of School Administrators (1944). The commission that recommended schools emphasize "life adjustment" education by meeting the "ten imperative needs of youth"; issued the report *Education for All American Youth.*

Education for All American Youth **(1944).** The report of the Educational Policies Commission that recommended that schools emphasize "life adjustment" education by meeting the "ten imperative needs of youth."

Education for All Handicapped Children Act (1975). See Public Law 94-142.

Education for Work Act (1994). Federal legislation proposed by the Clinton administration; intended to help schools develop programs that lead directly to jobs.

Effective schools. Schools that successfully and efficiently produce academic achievement in their students.

Egocentrism. Self-centeredness.

Emotional development. The increasing of one's emotional sophistication and stability, including how to feel and control one's emotions.

Emotionality. Possessing and/or exhibiting emotion.

Emotionally disturbed. An emotional state or condition outside of the normal range.

Emotional needs. Student needs such as self-esteem, peer affiliation, and personal security; also thought of as *psychological needs.*

Empathy. Sharing the perspectives, feelings, and emotions of another person; putting oneself "in another's shoes."

Encouragement (as used in Chapter 3). A teaching technique that urges more student effort and improvement, as distinct from praise, which also includes teacher approval.

Engaged time. The time during which students are actually involved in purposeful classroom activity.

Enlightenment. A time in the development of Western education that roughly parallels the eighteenth century, characterized by a strong interest in science and empirical investigation; also called the *Age of Reason.*

Enrichments. Supplemental instructional experiences provided for students to enable them to study more comprehensively or in greater depth.

Epistemology. A branch of philosophy that focuses on the study of the nature of knowledge.

Equality of input. The idea of equity in education that stresses equal amounts and quality of school services for all students, as distinct from *equality of results.*

Equality of results. The idea of equity in education that stresses the providing of different amounts and quality of school services in order to enable students with different abilities and backgrounds to learn as much as all students in general, as distinct from *equality of imput.*

Equal protection of the law. A right guaranteed in the Fourteenth Amendment to the U.S. Constitution that protects individuals from biased or discriminatory treatment.

Equity. Fairness, justice, impartiality; as applied to schooling, the idea that all students should receive an equal education.

Essentialism. The belief that truth and knowledge consist of an identifiable and indispensable common core of information and ideas.

Establishment of religion. Governmental establishment or support of a particular religion or religious practice; an act that is unconstitutional in the United States under the First Amendment.

Ethical principles stage of moral development. The highest stage of moral development identified by Lawrence Kohlberg; the stage at which moral behavior is guided by one's conscience and belief of what is right and just.

Ethical value judgments. Judgments about right and wrong, good and bad.

Ethics. The branch of the study of values that deals with the questions, What is good, and what is right and wrong?

Ethnocentrism. An attitude that one's own ethnic group, nation, or culture is superior to all others.

Ethnographic research. Investigations that study people, groups, or cultures primarily through observation and the analysis of descriptive data.

Ethnography. The study of people, groups, or cultures primarily through observation and analysis of descriptive data.

Ethos. The fundamental characteristics, spirit, or "feel" of a culture or group that relay its beliefs, customs, and practices.

Ethos of achievement. An underlying sentiment or attitude of a school or classroom that promotes accomplishment.

Evaluating. An aspect of thinking that involves determining worth, value, or quality of something.

Evaluation (as one of the parts of the act of teaching). The processes of monitoring and assessing teaching to determine if objectives are being met.

Evangelicalism. The belief that truth and knowledge rest on the Christian gospels and their teachings.

Excellence in education. The goal that schools provide the best possible education for each individual student.

Executive-like manager. A role expected of teachers of the future that involves selecting priorities for instruction and overseeing the running of schools.

Exemplary practice. Doing something so well that it serves as an example for others to follow.

Existentialism. The belief that what is true and real is tied to personal existence rather than abstract principles, and that individuals are totally free to act and are responsible for their actions.

Expectations. That which students anticipate in terms of success or failure when they face challenges such as taking tests.

Experimentalism. The belief that experience and scientific experimentation are adequate sources of knowledge.

Exploring feelings. A specific set of teaching strategies that are used to teach students to think about their own and others' feelings.

Expository methods of instruction. Instruction in which the teacher presents facts or ideas such as through lecturing, showing videos, or assigning reading.

Expressive outcomes. Outcomes that are less tangible than content-based objectives, such as "develop an appreciation" for something; the kind of outcomes that depend more on what students experience in a lesson than the specific knowledge or skill they acquire.

External expectations. Things that teachers are expected to accomplish with their students beyond the goals the teachers themselves set; expectations of school administrators and the community at large.

External motivation. The stimulation of student learning that comes from the offering of rewards or threats of penalties from outside the students themselves.

Fact. A specific element of information.

Fair use guidelines. Relatively unofficial but generally agreed upon guidelines for the use of copyrighted materials.

Feelings. Internal emotional and moral sensations that people experience as they respond to others, to events, and to circumstances.

Financial authority. Legitimate power held by a government because it has control over finances.

First-line service provider. A concept from Deming's total quality management thinking that stresses the importance of the people in an organization who provide the face-to-face service to those whom the organization serves; for schools, it is the teachers.

Fixed-interval schedule of reward. A reward schedule in which the re-

ward occurs after determined and consistent periods of time or number of responses.

"Flat profession." A characterization of the teaching profession as being nonhierarchical; that is, not having novice, experienced, and expert levels as do many other professions; a view that virtually all teachers are comparably skilled and knowledgeable.

Folklore. Legends, sayings, and stories about the past of a cultural group.

Folkways. Ways of thinking, feeling, and behaving in a culture that are considered "the right way" by most members of the group.

Follow Through program. A federal program intended to help high-risk children maintain academic achievement gains through grades K–3, intended primarily to extend support provided for younger children by Head Start.

Formative evaluation. Assessment during the time learning is taking place; used to determine what is being learned and how lessons should be modified to enhance learning.

Foundation program formula. A formula whereby states provide matching funds to local public schools to ensure an amount of revenue considered to be the minimum necessary for the adequate education of students.

Four-basic-question approach to classroom observation. A specific way of observing in classrooms that is guided by four questions: What is the teacher doing? What are the students doing? Why is the teacher doing that? Why are the students doing that?

Fractionated communities. Local political communities that are controlled by two or a few competing power groups.

Fragmented type of state policymaking. State-level policymaking processes characterized by clashes among statewide education interest groups.

Franklin's academy. A high school established in colonial Pennsylvania at the urging of Benjamin Franklin that prepared students for employment rather than for college.

"Free appropriate public education." A stipulation incorporated into Public Law 94-142 and other legislation that requires schools to educate handicapped children and youth on the same basis as they do nonhandicapped children.

Freedom of expression. The freedom of individuals to express personal views without the arbitrary interference of others.

Friends Public Schools. Schools established and sponsored by Quakers in colonial Pennsylvania.

Fundamentalists. Bible-believing Christians; typically those who believe in a literal interpretation of the Bible.

Fused curriculum. Similar to a broad-fields curriculum but with the subject matter divisions even less noticeable; also called an *integrated curriculum.*

Futurism. The belief that individuals need to prepare intellectually and emotionally to live in an unknown future world.

Gender-based play. Children's play that is often associated with one gender and subcultures that develop around genders, such as rough and competitive games for boys and cooperative play for girls.

Gender-role expectations. The belief or assumption that men and women possess or follow expected values, abilities, and roles based on gender.

Gender schema. A set of beliefs, concepts, and attributes that one acquires due to his or her gender.

General aid. Funding provided to local public schools by the state and federal governments without clear directives that it should be spent for specific purposes; contrast with *categorical aid.*

Generalizations. Valid statements of relationships among concepts; general conclusions.

Generalizing. An aspect of thinking that involves formulating broad principles from specific instances.

G.I. Bill of Rights. Federal legislation that provided funding for World War II and Korean conflict veterans to attend college.

Gifted students. Students with exceptional abilities of some kind.

Goals 2000. Federal legislation of the early 1990s that specifies eight goals that public schools of the United States should reach by the year 2000.

Groovers. A nickname for youth who seem to "go with the flow" or whose behavior seems to fit smoothly with what is normally expected of them.

Group investigation. A type of cooperative learning in which students prepare group projects and complete whole-class assignments.

Group rewards. Grade points and other incentives given to all members of a cooperative learning group because of the group's accomplishments.

Guided practice. Student use of new ideas and skills as they practice recent learning under the direct supervision of the teacher.

Guild. A medieval union of craftspeople.

Handicapped. Possessing an impairment that limits one's activities.

Hands-on experiences. Student learning experiences in which students handle objects or do experiments rather than listen to the teacher, view a presentation, or read.

Head bangers. A nickname for youth who are into heavy metal rock music.

Head Start. A federally funded program for preschool children from socioeconomic backgrounds that lack academic experiences; intended to help them prepare academically for their start of school.

Hearing impaired students. Students whose hearing is below the normal range.

Heroes and heroines. Prominent members of a tribe or an organization that embody the essential character of the group.

Hidden curriculum. What students learn from the school environment other than the content intentionally planned for them.

Hierarchical profession. A profession that has many stages and status levels, usually based on skill and experience, such as probationary, novice, experienced, and expert.

High/Scope Cognitive-Oriented Curriculum. A structured cognitive, developmental model of instruction for preschool students that was developed initially as The Perry Preschool Program in Ypsilanti, Michigan.

History (as a characteristic of classroom environments). The characteristic of classroom environments identified by Walter Doyle that develops because students and the teacher meet as the same group day after day and share common experiences, routines, and norms.

Holistic education. A Neo-Thomist concept of education with the general aim of developing the person as a person in a way that balances intellectual development and religious faith.

Hornbook. A type of primer used in American colonial schools, consisting of a sheet of parchment mounted on a wooden board and covered with a thin transparent horn, often containing the alphabet and other information to be learned.

Humanistic curriculum. A curriculum that emphasizes the development of student self-concepts, personal growth, and expression.

Hypothesize. To make a thoughtful prediction about something based on prior knowledge and relevant generalizations.

Hypothetical thinking. Thinking that considers possibilities rather than only what is tied to established facts.

Idea. A thought, mental conception, or image; something a person thinks, knows, or imagines.

Idealism. The belief that what is true or real is a matter of perceptions that are based on ideas of the mind rather than on physical objects.

Idealists. Those who believe that what is true or real is a matter of perceptions that are based on ideas of the mind rather than on physical objects.

Ideals. Ideas that embody perfection.

Idea of progress. A belief that the world can be made better through the use of reason and scientific investigation, characteristic of Enlightenment thinking.

Identity-seeking behavior. Behavior associated with a developing sense of potency, independence, and experimentation; usually seen in adolescents.

"I" messages. Statements that begin with the word "I" that are a technique used to facilitate communication in the *Teacher Effectiveness Training* approach to handling student misbehavior.

Immediacy (as a characteristic of classroom environments). A characteristic of classroom environments identified by Walter Doyle that calls attention to the fact that things happen very quickly.

Incentives. The offering of rewards to students by the teacher to encourage learning or good student behavior.

Inclusion. The idea that all students, regardless of their capabilities or disabilities, should be included in classes with their age-level peers instead of being taught in special education classes; an extension of the mainstreaming concept.

Independent practice. Student application and practice of what has been learned without close teacher supervision.

Individual education plan. A written plan of instruction designed to meet the needs of an individual student and to accommodate his or her specific abilities; used most often for special students.

"Individual excellence." The idea that what is considered to be excellent for an individual is determined by comparing that individual's achievement only against his or her own potential.

Individual mastery. The point at which an individual student has learned (mastered) the learning task that he or she is studying.

Individual psychological dimensions of individual-environment interaction. Types of interaction between individuals and their environment that concern individual traits or tendencies such as sociability, shyness, personal values, sensitivity, and artistic talent.

Individual reward structures. Systems of rewarding students that have no effect on the probability of others being rewarded.

Individual rights and standards stage of moral development. The fifth stage of moral development identified by Lawrence Kohlberg; the stage at which moral behavior is guided by a desire to follow rules but also use one's own judgment when appropriate.

Inductive process. The process of forming general principles from specific instances.

Inductive reasoning. Thinking that involves bringing specifics together to formulate or prove a general principle.

Inert communities. Local political communities that have no visible power structure.

Inert knowledge. Knowledge that students learn but fail to retrieve for use when it would be appropriate to do so, such as when it could help them solve a problem.

Inference. The aspect of thinking that involves making mental connections among ideas and drawing conclusions based on reasoning rather than observable fact.

Inferring. An aspect of thinking that involves drawing mental connections among phenomena, such as cause and effect.

Influences on planning. Factors that affect teachers' thinking about the lessons they plan and how they plan them.

Informal players. Individuals in a tribe or an organization who preserve tradition and transmit the group's history and reminiscence; at times, informal players counterbalance the power of the chief.

Information highway. Telecommunication network of interconnected computer systems that transmit data worldwide.

Information-processing theory. A learning theory that says learning is an active process of information acquisition that includes sensory input, encoding, and retrieving from memory; also called *cognitive-development theory*.

Inner-biological dimensions of individual-environment interaction. Types of interaction between individuals and their environment that concern physiological maturational changes and health changes.

Input. Supplying information and ideas for students to learn, such as through lecture or assigned reading.

Input-output research. Investigations that compare data at the beginning of a process with data at the end of the process; for example, how well students can perform addition at the start of the school year and at the end of the year.

Insight. A sudden and unexplained realization or clear understanding of something.

Instructional objectives. The anticipated results or products of instruction, usually stated in terms of the behaviors that teachers expect students to be able to exhibit as a result of instruction; also called *behavioral objectives* and *educational objectives.*

Instructional time. Classroom time in which instruction is actually occurring.

Instrumentalism. The belief that the mind and ideas are instruments to be used by individuals to plan actions and to adjust to their environment.

Integrated curriculum. Similar to a broad-fields curriculum but with the subject matter divisions even less noticeable; also called a *fused curriculum.*

Intellectual accomplishments (as used in Chapter 5). Intellectual abilities that children are able to perform for the first time at certain developmental stages after not being able to do so at less mature levels.

Intellectual capital. Resources that students possess or can draw on because of their intelligence.

Intellectually gifted. Either an intellectual ability reflected in scores of over 145 on the Stanford-Binet or WISC-R intelligence tests, or intellectual ability well above the norm.

Interaction (as a characteristic of learning). An idea articulated by John Dewey that notes that learning is not limited to what happens in a student's head; it involves student interaction with elements of the environment in the classroom and in the outside world.

Interactive instructional practices. Approaches to teaching in which teachers and students actively interact with each other.

Intermittent ratio schedule of reward. A reward schedule in which the reward occurs randomly.

Interpreting (as used in Chapter 10). The step in the process of philosophizing that addresses the question, How should these data be understood?

Interventions. Techniques that teachers use to stop or correct student misbehavior.

Intrapersonal regulation. The idea that learning involves a developmental aspect in which students and children internalize regulating interactions by their teachers, parents, and caregivers and control their own behavior in a pattern similar to that taught by the teacher.

Intrinsic motivation. The stimulation of student learning that comes from personal needs or internal drives, such as enjoyment of learning and a sense of satisfaction or the belief that the learning is valuable.

Isolation (as used in Chapter 3). An intervention strategy used to stop student misbehavior by separating the misbehaving student from all others for a period of time.

Jigsaw II. A type of cooperative learning in which different team members become experts in different parts of the task, which then need to be fitted together for all to learn and the team to succeed.

Jim Crow. A term used to describe policies and practices of racial segregation and discrimination.

Jocks. A nickname for youth who play or are deeply involved in sports.

Judicial authority. Legitimate power held by a government because it is authorized by decisions of the courts.

Judicial review. The principle that the U.S. Supreme Court has the authority to interpret the federal constitution and judge if other court decisions and actions by government are constitutional.

Justifying (as used in Chapter 10). The step in the process of philosophizing that addresses the question, How do you know?

Knowledge. Facts, information, and ideas that people acquire through learning.

Knowledgeable classroom observation. Classroom observation that is guided by previous knowledge and/or experience.

Knowledge base of education. The core ideas and information about teaching and schools that professional educators need to know to understand their field.

Kohlberg's stages of moral development. Stages and levels in moral reasoning, as identified by Lawrence Kohlberg.

Land grant college. A college maintained to carry out the purposes of the first Morrill Act of 1862 and the supplementary legislation that granted public lands to states for the establishment of colleges to provide practical education such as agricultural and mechanical arts.

Latch-key children. Children who arrive home from school to a house without an adult present and who, therefore, carry their own house key.

Latin grammar school. An early type of school that was attended after primary school, emhasizing the study of Latin, literature, history, mathematics, music, and dialectics.

Law of effect. A principle within association theory that says intellectual associations are strengthened through success and rewards but not weakened through negative consequences.

Law of scattered effect. A principle within association theory that says behaviors that are similar to behaviors followed by a reward also tend to be learned.

Lead teachers. Teachers within teaching teams who hold leadership roles among their colleagues.

Leap of faith. A way of discovering meaning or God that relies on a belief that transcends reason and that is not provable intellectually.

Learn by doing. An emphasis in educational theory, popularized by John Dewey, that stresses student activity as part of learning.

Learned helplessness. A condition in which individuals come to believe that they cannot succeed, usually a result of persistent failure.

Learning communities. Communities, such as schools, in which all participants are constantly learning how to do their work and fulfill their roles better, where all participants learn from each other.

Learning disability. A condition that makes learning more difficult than would normally be expected.

Learning outcomes. The learning that students are expected to achieve by the time they reach certain grade levels or are ready to graduate from school.

Learning styles. The individual ways that students learn, including the ways they process information, whether they like competition or cooperation, and the environmental conditions—amount of light and background noise—under which they learn best.

Learning theory. A set of assumptions or generalizations about the nature of learning that are supported by philosophical and scientific principles and that suggest the direction of further investigation about how learning takes place.

Learning time. Classroom time in which students are actually learning.

Learning together. A type of cooperative learning that emphasizes interpersonal dependence and the learning of interpersonal, small-group skills.

"Least restrictive environment." A belief and legal stipulation that disabled students be educated in classes and other instructional settings as close to those provided for nondisabled students as possible; a quote from the Supreme Court *Pennsylvania Association of Retarded Children* v. *Commonwealth of Pennsylvania* decision and repeated in Public Law 94-142 that ensures that students with disabilities receive an appropriate education.

Legislative authority. Legitimate power held by a government because it is authorized by legislation passed by a legislature (for example, Congress).

Lemon test. Three guidelines in the *Lemon* v. *Kurtzman* court decision that are used by courts to decide whether specific funding of private education in religious schools is constitutional.

Lesson goals. Goals established by teachers that identify what they want the lesson to accomplish and that guide their teaching of the lesson; also called *lesson objectives*.

Lesson-image approach to lesson planning. Planning lessons by formulating images of what the lesson will eventually look like and then fitting all the parts together coherently.

Lesson objectives. Objectives established by teachers that identify what they want the lesson to accomplish and that guide their teaching of the lesson; also called *lesson goals*.

Lesson plans. Teachers' plans about how they will provide instruction for specific classes on particular days, usually involving step-by-step directions for a period or particular length of time.

Levels of abstraction. The successive layering of facts, concepts, and generalizations from specific facts to broad generalizations.

Liberal arts. Subjects or branches of learning that served as the foci of education during the Middle Ages—grammar, logic, rhetoric, arithmetic, geometry, music, and astronomy.

Life adjustment education. A focus of schooling prominent in the 1940s and 1950s that stressed the whole child and his or her adjustment to adult life in general rather than a more narrow focus on academics.

Local disparate type of state policymaking. State-level policymaking processes characterized by noticeable political relationships between local leaders and state politicians.

Longitudinal study. A study that follows the subjects for an extended period of time.

Loyalty oath. Pledges under oath, required of public employees in the 1950s and earlier, that stated that the individual did not advocate actions against the United States and did not belong to groups that did so.

Macro-level planning. Teacher planning that focuses on overall goals for students and the broad topics to be covered over a unit or longer period of teaching time.

Magnet schools. Schools with special foci intended to draw students from throughout a school district to learn a special field of study; a school arrangement used to attract racially integrated student populations to schools that would otherwise be overwhelmingly of a single race.

Mainstreaming. The process of integrating students with disabilities into programs and classes with nondisabled peers.

Maintenance bilingual program. Instruction provided in a non-native-English-speaking student's native language with the purpose of helping the student retain the native language as he or she also learns English.

Manipulation of privileges. An intervention strategy used to stop student misbehavior by withdrawing privileges that students like, or by threatening to do so.

Marxism. The belief that reality is material and that social classes have struggled over time to control the means of production.

Master teacher. An experienced teacher whose classroom performance is considered to be an example for others to follow.

Mastery Learning. A model of instruction that enables all students to learn the material intended through the completion of designed learning tasks, flexible allotments of time, and frequent assessment and reteaching.

Materialistic realists. Realists who believe either that moral values are to be determined based on their consequences on society or that moral values are rooted in natural moral laws.

Materialists. Those who are more concerned with material things than with spiritual, intellectual, or cultural values.

McGuffey Readers. School reading books written by William McGuffey and first published in 1836 that were used nationwide for many years.

Melting pot. The idea that people who immigrate to the United States should abandon their cultural distinctions and become more like other Americans.

Mental images. A mental picture of what a situation that has not yet been confronted would be like, such as how a lesson that is being planned will actually occur.

Mental linkages. The intellectual connecting of new ideas to previously learned knowledge and past experience.

Mentally retarded. Either an intellectual ability reflected in scores under 70 on the Stanford-Binet or WISC-R intelligence tests, or intellectual ability well below the norm.

Metacognition. Thinking about how one thinks.

Metaphysical beliefs. Beliefs about the nature of reality.

Metaphysics. A branch of philosophy that focuses on the study of the nature of reality.

Methods of inquiry. The types of investigation that academic disciplinarians use to explore their fields, conduct research, and discover new knowledge.

Micro-level planning. Teacher planning of specific components of lessons.

Middle childhood. Childhood roughly between ages 6 and 10.

Middle schools. Schools designed for teaching adolescents, usually for grades 5 or 6 through 7 or 8, typically organized around interdisciplinary teams of teachers with flexible schedules so that teachers can maintain close contact with individual students.

Mnemonic. Intellectual associations such as familiar words, letter patterns, sayings, and jingles that learners use to memorize or remember information.

Modeling. Demonstrating or acting as one wants others to act; providing examples of ideas, processes, or skills that students are to learn.

Models of instruction. Particular approaches to teaching that are based on specific learning theories and intended to accomplish selected learning goals.

Monolithic type of state policymaking. State-level policymaking processes characterized by a coalition of statewide political groups who make educational decisions.

Montessori method. A method of teaching initially developed by Maria Montessori for use with young mentally handicapped children; individualized instruction that uses multisensory materials and exercises and encourages student interaction with the environment, peers, and teachers.

Moral development. The idea that as people grow and learn they pass through stages associated with what they believe is right, good, and just.

Moral education. Education about right and wrong behavior.

Moral growth. The increasing of one's moral reasoning ability.

Morrill Act of 1862. Federal legislation that provided funds to states to establish land grant colleges.

Motivation. The stimulation and sustaining of action.

Motor skills. Abilities that use body movement, such as eye-hand coordination, drawing, jumping, and running.

Multicultural education. Instruction that recognizes cultural differences and the contributions of different ethnic, cultural, language, and social groups and heritages in American society.

Multiculturalism. The belief that schools should reflect and teach in ways that address the diverse racial, ethnic, religious, language, and social traditions and heritages of America.

Multidimensionality. A characteristic of classroom environments identified by Walter Doyle that calls attention to the fact that a large number of tasks and events occur in classrooms.

Mystique. A cluster of beliefs, attitudes, and feelings associated with a person, culture, group, organization, or activity.

Myth. Stories, often exaggerated or fictitious, about historical events and people that reinforce cultural traditions and customs.

National Assessment of Educational Progress. National government-sponsored tests of student academic achievement, which in recent years have been used to compare student performance across schools, school districts, and states.

National Board of Professional Teaching Standards. A national board established as part of the educational reform efforts of the 1980s and 1990s that sets standards and procedures for certifying especially competent experienced teachers.

National Council for the Accreditation of Teacher Education. The national organization that oversees and accredits colleges, schools, and departments of eduction that educate teachers and other professionals who work in schools.

National Defense Education Act (1958). Federal legislation that funneled money to schools for teacher education, curriculum development, and equipment, especially in mathematics, science, and foreign languages; a response to *Sputnik*.

Natural laws. Assumed principles that govern the ways the universe, including humans, operates.

Natural state of humans. An idea developed during the Enlightenment, associated primarily with Jean-Jacques Rousseau, that humans are born in a natural state that is good and that their interaction with society corrupts them.

Neo-Thomists. A philosophy derived from Thomism developed by St. Thomas Aquinas that brings together ideas of truth and religious faith through inductive and deductive reasoning.

New England Primer. A reading book used in schools in colonial New England.

Non-native-English speakers. Individuals who did not learn English as their primary language as children.

Nonverbal communication. Communication without the use of words.

Normal schools. Schools for the training of teachers.

Normative development. Development consistent with normal expectations.

Normative futurists. Futurists who suggest the person of the future should possess a prescribed set of characteristics.

Norms. A standard of behavior or achievement; a pattern or model that others are compared to.

Object lesson. A method of teaching that develops lessons around concrete objects with which the students have direct contact.

Objective conditions. The "givens" of the world outside the learner that affect his or her learning, such as pressure for grades, personal characteristics of other students in a class, and the nature of the content being studied.

Observation sweep. The scanning of the full classroom one time by a classroom observer for the purpose of recording individual student activity.

Observation system. A specific approach or set of techniques used to view a situation for the purpose of collecting valid data about that situation.

Off-task behavior. Student behavior that is not productive and not what the teacher expects.

Off-task rate. The ratio between the number of times students are off task compared to the number of times they could have been off task.

"Old Deluder Satan" Act. An early colonial education law (1647) that required colonial towns of at least fifty households to provide education for youth.

On-task behavior. Student behavior that is consistent with what the teacher expects.

Open curriculum. A curriculum that emphasizes student self-development and is especially flexible so that teachers can fit the content to student needs and interests.

Open education. A curriculum that emphasizes the development of student self-concepts, personal growth, and expression; similar to humanistic curriculum.

Operant behavior. A principle within behavior theory that says behavior is learned because of the consequences of actions rather than because of the stimuli that elicit them.

Opportunity-to-learn standards. The expectation that schools, school leaders, and government officials provide the resources necessary for students to have an equal opportunity to learn.

Optimal error rate. The ratio between correct and incorrect student responses that leads to the greatest student achievement.

Ordered classrooms. Classrooms that are more focused on learning and content and less flexible than others; usually a characteristic that distinguishes secondary school classrooms from elementary classrooms.

Ordering. Arranging things methodically, often placing them in a sequence.

Ordinance of 1785. Federal act that set aside land in the Northwest Territory to be sold to finance schools.

Organization. A group or association of people drawn together for the purpose of accomplishing some end or work.

Organizational culture. Pattern of behavior, values, beliefs, traditions, and norms that characterize specific organizations.

Organizational demands (as influences on teaching). Characteristics of school operations that influence teacher planning and teaching, such as schedules, length of periods, lunch time, and interruptions.

Organizational saga. The shared mythology of an organization.

Organizational style. The way different people arrange their thinking about tasks they face as well as the various elements of the task in order to complete the task or solve a problem.

Outcome-based education. A view of education that rests on the principles that instruction should be designed around outcomes that all students should be able to demonstrate as a result of the instruction and that all schools must provide the opportunities for all students to reach these outcomes.

Outer-physical dimensions of individual-environment interaction. Types of interaction between individuals and their environment that concern phenomena outside of the individuals, such as climate, terrain, and other elements of and changes in the physical environment.

Overlapping. The ability of a teacher to be engaged in more than one teaching task at a time.

Over learning. Learning that results from a teaching technique in which the teacher conducts drill or repetitive practice for a longer time than is necessary for initial learning of ideas or skills being taught; the technique is used to prompt quick recall or to enable students to recall the ideas or to reuse the skills a long time after the learning has taken place.

Pairing. In association theory, the aspect of teaching in which the teacher exposes the learner to two things at about the same time so that the learner learns to associate them with each other; an example is Pavlov's experiment where a dog associates food with the ringing of a bell.

Participation mystiques. Ceremonies, activities, and rituals that members

of cultures participate in to demonstrate and enhance their feeling of belonging to the group.

Pedagogical knowledge. The type of content knowledge particular to teachers; the knowledge of content that guides teachers' determination of how to teach the content and how students will learn it.

Peer perceptions. The ways in which someone is viewed by people of equal status or position; for example, the way students are seen by other students.

Peer tutoring. Students helping other students learn by providing resource help and guidance; a type of cooperative instruction.

Perception. The process of becoming aware of something, usually through the senses.

Perceptual growth. The increasing of one's ability to detect elements in his or her environment.

Perennialism. The belief that truth and knowledge are universal, permanent, and not subject to change or cultural evolution.

Personal capital. Resources that students possess or can draw on due to personal self-assurance.

Personal development. Growth and learning associated with becoming a good, mature, social human being who feels good about one's self and possesses the knowledge and skill to succeed in life.

Personal fable. A feeling or belief that an individual's emotional experiences are both unique to the person experiencing them and important to everyone else; usually associated with adolescence.

Personal idealism. The belief that reality and value are centered in a personality, an absolute mind, a supreme being, God.

Personal idealists. Idealistic philosophers who see ultimate reality as a person, an absolute mind, a supreme being, God.

Personalized System of Instruction. An individualized form of Mastery Learning, developed by F. S. Keller.

Philosophizing. The intellectual process of thinking something through in order to form a conclusion or make a decision.

Physical needs. Student needs such as hunger, fatigue, and sickness.

Piagetian theory. A learning theory that combines cognitive and developmental theory, attributes learning to interaction between individuals and their environment, and acknowledges that learning occurs over time and in stages; developed primarily by Jean Piaget.

Planning as problem solving. An approach to lesson planning that begins with the idea that there is a problem to be solved. The "problem" is that the students need to learn certain information, ideas, skills, and so forth.

Planning routine. The particular approach that a person, such as a teacher, uses in developing plans.

Pluralistic communities. Local political communities that are characterized by multiple competing power groups.

Power of the purse. The power that accrues to a governmental entity because it has power over finances.

Pragmatism. The belief that what is true and real is known through human experience and inquiring thought.

Praise. The teaching technique of saying something positive or complimentary about a student's action, response, or achievement.

Preferential value judgments. Those value judgments based on one's preferences or likes and dislikes rather than those based on inherent right and wrong, truth, justice, or beauty.

Prejudice. A judgment (either positive or negative) made without knowing the facts or in spite of the facts; intolerance or irrational dislike for others; unreasonable bias.

Prerequisite skills and knowledge. Skills and knowledge that students must possess in order to profit from the instruction about to be provided.

Preventive approach. A philosophy of and approach to teaching that attempts to educate every child so that no one ever falls behind the achievement of the peer group or grade level; in this approach, remedial instruction is not necessary.

Pride of membership. A sense of dignity that people feel due to belonging to a particular group.

Problem solving. A process of thinking in which one who confronts unexplained information or a problem situation is able to formulate an appropriate explanation or solution.

Process of discovery. The intellectual process of figuring things out.

Process of instruction. The combination of procedures teachers use to create learning in students.

Process of investigation. The manner in which investigators raise questions about their areas of study and the way they conduct their research.

Process-product research. Investigations that compare instructional processes or activities (processes) with results or outcomes (products).

Professional community. A group of people who associate and identify with one another because they belong to an accepted group that involves advanced training and a recognized level of knowledge and skills.

Professionalization of teaching. A movement toward making teachers more expert, holding them more responsible for the results of their teaching, and giving them more

control over their professional decisions.

Professional standards board. A body of professionals, such as teachers, that sets standards of acceptable practice and assesses how well individual members of the profession meet these standards.

Programmed instruction. Instruction organized around methods and materials that provide immediate reinforcement to the learner and then proceed in small increments as the learner responds correctly to questions and activities.

Progressive education. An education philosophy and thrust prominent during the 1930s and 1940s that emphasized education of the whole child, organizing instruction around student needs and interests, and popularized the idea "learning by doing."

Proletariat. The social class made up of working people; according to Marxist doctrine, the class exploited by the bourgeoisie (the middle class).

Prompts. Subtle teacher suggestions that guide and encourage student responses or remind students of previously learned ideas and information.

Property right. The right of possession or ownership.

Protestant Reformation. The European religious movement in the sixteenth century that was aimed at reforming the Roman Catholic Church but resulted in forming Protestant churches.

Psychological needs. Student needs such as self-esteem, peer affiliation, and personal security; also called *emotional needs*.

Public Law 94-142. The Education for All Handicapped Children Act, 1975; the federal act that applied the concept of equity in education to students with disabilities and prescribed that disabled children

and youth be provided a free appropriate public education in the least restricted environment.

Publicness. A characteristic of classroom environments identified by Walter Doyle that calls attention to the fact that events occur in the open and are witnessed by all present.

Public schools. (1) Community-operated, tax-supported schools of the nineteenth and twentieth centuries; (2) common schools of American colonial times, which were public in purpose but not tax-supported.

"Pull-out" programs. Special school programs that require the students who participate in them to leave their regular class for extra instruction.

Punishment-obedience stage of moral development. The first stage of moral development identified by Lawrence Kohlberg; the stage at which moral behavior is guided by fear of punishment as a consequence of what one does.

***Purposes of Education in American Democracy* (1938).** The report of the Educational Policies Commission of NEA that recommended teaching "the whole child."

Purposive behavior. The learning theory that animals engage in behavior based on insight and to accomplish a purpose (for example, rats want to get to food at the end of a maze), instead of simple trial and error.

Pygmalion effect. An idea that student performance is often influenced both positively and negatively by the expectations that they and their teachers have for them; high expectations lead to high performance and low expectations lead to poor performance; an idea suggested by a study entitled *Pygmalion in the Classroom*.

Rate of success. The proportion of times students get the right answer or solve problems correctly in their school work.

Rational-choice approach to lesson planning. Planning lessons thoughtfully, beginning with the establishment of behavioral objectives and moving sequentially from that point.

Readiness. A time in a student's development when he or she has the prerequisite knowledge and abilities to learn what is intended.

Realism. The belief that what is true and real rests on entities and objects that have substance apart from the mind's consciousness of them.

Realists. Those who believe that what is true and real rests on entities and objects that have substance apart from the mind's consciousness of them.

Reality. A concept of being that engages the question, "What is real?" The answer one supplies for the question depends on one's personal philosophy or metaphysical position.

Reality therapy. A counseling-based approach to handling student misbehavior, based on the thinking of William Glasser.

Reason. To think logically and draw conclusions; the ability to think logically and draw conclusions.

Reasonableness test. A basis used by courts to decide issues concerning expression and privacy, which, in essence, states that authorities must have a good reason to restrict students' freedoms or invade their privacy.

Reciprocity-needs stage of moral development. The second stage of moral development identified by Lawrence Kohlberg; the stage at which moral behavior is guided by the idea, "If I do the right thing, others will do the right thing to me."

Reconstructionism. The belief that society can be improved and that

individuals and institutions have a responsibility to encourage the process.

Reconstructionists. Educational thinkers and curriculum developers who believe that society can be improved and that individuals and institutions have a responsibility to encourage the process.

Redundancy. A technique of instruction that includes repetition in the teaching of main points and key concepts to be learned.

Reflective skill. The ability to think in an organized way about what one has done and to use that information to guide future actions.

Reflective thinking. Thinking in a systematic way that involves looking back at past experiences for information to formulate a conclusion, make a decision, solve a problem, or guide future actions.

Regulatory authority. Legitimate power held by a government because it is authorized by government rules and regulations.

Reinforcement theory. A theory that says that the consequences of actions encourage or discourage behavior and that learning occurs because certain behaviors are rewarded or punished.

Released time for religious education. The public school practice of releasing students from instruction during part of a school day so they can be taught religion off public school property by someone who is not a paid public school teacher.

Relevance. Pertinence; having to do with that which is important or meaningful.

Religious existentialists. Existentialists who also believe in God.

Religious realists. Realists whose thinking combines reason and revelation in forming moral values; often also thought of as Thomist philosophers because of the influ-

ence of St. Thomas Aquinas on their thinking.

Remedial education. Education targeted toward students who did not learn something when it was taught earlier; designed to help such students make up what they missed.

Remediation. Instruction tailored to students who have fallen behind the level of achievement that would normally be expected of them; intended to help them catch up.

Renaissance. The great rebirth of art, literature, and learning in Europe in the fourteenth, fifteenth, and sixteenth centuries; any rebirth or revival like this.

Representation. A configuration, drawing, painting, photograph, model, or image intended to resemble something or someone.

Researcher perceptions of classrooms. What is seen in classroom activity when viewed by skilled observers who have research experience.

Retarded. Delayed in development; slower than or below normal rates or levels of development.

Rewards. Positive teacher actions that encourage and reinforce good student behavior.

Reward structure. The context or set of assumptions that a teacher arranges with classes that guide how and when students are rewarded for good behavior or achievement.

"Rising tide of mediocrity." An expression used in the 1983 report *A Nation at Risk*; intended to convey the criticism that schools and students are striving only to be mediocre rather than excellent.

Rites. Ceremonies, observances, or rituals performed according to cultural rules, customs, or traditions.

Rituals and ceremonies. Events at which members of a tribe or organization have an opportunity to experience shared values and to be bonded together in a common quest.

Routine patterns. Ways of operating that are consistently the same over time.

Rules (law and order) stage of moral development. The fourth stage of moral development identified by Lawrence Kohlberg; the stage at which moral behavior is guided by a respect for authority and duty.

Schedule of rewards. In operant behavior theory, the timing pattern of when rewards occur to reinforce behavior.

Schema or schemata. Organized mental structures that enable an individual to interpret new information in terms of existing knowledge.

Scholasticism. An approach to study during the Middle Ages that combined reliance on religious faith and reason in the search for truth and meaning.

Scholastics. Christian teachers of the Middle Ages who subscribed to scholasticism.

School capital. Resources schools need to educate their students adequately and to be held accountable for doing so.

School culture. The patterns of behavior, values, beliefs, traditions, and norms that characterize a school.

School district decentralization. The practice of dividing large school districts into a number of smaller organizational units.

School effectiveness. The extent to which a school efficiently produces expected student learning.

School ethos. The cultural environment of a school, including its habits, beliefs, dispositions, and other distinguishing characteristics.

School financing equalization. The idea that all school districts of a state should have access to comparable amounts of revenues.

School-level goals. Statements of purpose or guidelines around which school instructional programs are organized.

School Power. A collaborative school, parent, and community plan for school reform developed by James P. Comer; a second-wave proposal for school reform.

Scientific inquiry. Thinking that precedes thought steps such as those described as the scientific method.

Scientific method. An approach to research and investigation and a pattern of thinking that involves the steps of identifying a problem, gathering relevant data, formulating a hypothesis, and testing the hypothesis.

Self-actualization. Fully developing one's abilities and ambitions.

Self-concept. An individual's image of himself or herself and his or her identity, abilities, and worth.

Self-esteem. Belief in oneself; self-respect; how people see themselves.

Self-fulfilling prophecy. The idea that teacher expectations actually cause students to perform above or below the level of achievement at which they would normally be expected to perform.

Self-regulaton. An internal personal intellectual directive that tells a person what to do and not to do; an intellectual accomplishment that develops during the Piagetian concrete operational stage.

Sensitivities. The capacities to respond to others and to situations in a perceptive, humane, and empathetic way.

Sensory handicap. An impairment of one of the senses; for example, hearing or sight.

"Separate but equal." A doctrine that holds that equality of treatment is accorded when people of different races are provided substantially equal facilities, even though the facilities are separate.

Separate-subjects curriculum. A type of subject-centered curriculum arranged around specific content disciplines such as English, history, or mathematics; also called *discipline-based curriculum.*

Separation of church and state. The U.S. constitutional principle that prohibits government from establishing or prohibiting religious practice.

Separation of powers. The principle that each of the three branches of the federal government—legislative, executive, and judicial—have separate and distinct areas of responsibility.

Seriation. An arrangement of items in a sequence; the act of arranging items in a sequence.

Setting the stage for teaching. Planning and organizing all elements of instruction ahead of time to ensure that teaching will occur as intended.

Seven liberal arts. A curriculum initially developed during the Middle Ages that consisted of the trivium (grammar, rhetoric, logic) and the quadrivium (arithmetic, geometry, music, astronomy).

Severe or profound programs. Special education instructional programs for students with great degrees of mental retardation.

Shared values and beliefs. Ideas and principles for which a tribe or an organization stands.

"Should do" statements. Policy statements that prescribe what teachers and schools should do.

Simultaneity. A characteristic of classroom environments identified by Walter Doyle that calls attention to the fact that many things happen at the same time.

Site-based management. Running schools by placing as much authority as possible in the hands of the local-building-level professionals and parents.

Skill. The ability to do something with proficiency.

Skilled practioner. A role expected of teachers of the future that involves the ability to use the teaching techniques in classrooms that produce student learning.

Sociability. The ability of people to communicate and interact positively with others.

Social behavior. A person's actions as a member of a group or a society; often behavior approved by the dominant cultural group.

Social capital. Resources that students possess or can draw on because of their social environment—family, friends, neighborhood, community.

Social cognition. The learning of rules and patterns of interpersonal relationships.

Social conventions. Common practices or assumed ways of behaving that develop within cultures and organizations; established standards and patterns for how things are usually done.

Social development. The increasing of one's social knowledge and skills, including how to interact with others.

Social environment. The aspect of one's surroundings made up of other people and one's interactions with them.

Social-functions curriculum. A type of child-centered, integrated curriculum plan arranged around social activities or life situations that students face or will face as adults.

Socialization. The gradual initiation of children and youth into the values, beliefs, and assumptions of a culture.

Socializing institutions. Institutions established by societies for the purpose of transmitting cultural values to younger generations and instilling in them a commitment to those values.

Social-problems curriculum. A type of child-centered, integrated curriculum plan arranged around social problems students face or will face as adults.

Social skills. Abilities that people use to interact with others, such as interacting pleasantly, leading, cooperating, and helping.

Social system of classrooms. The formal and informal rules that guide interpersonal actions and relationships in classrooms.

Sociocultural theories. Ideas that student understanding and the meanings they form have social and cultural roots.

Sociolinguistic research. Investigations that focus on the interactions of language and social structures.

Sociopsycholinguistic perspective. The constructivist idea about learning that students construct meaning about what they study through their interaction with others, including their classmates and teachers.

Socratic method. A method of teaching developed by Socrates that uses questioning of students in dialogue style.

Soft imperatives. Subtle but firm teaching techniques used to stop or correct student misbehavior.

Sophists. Teachers of ancient Greece who traveled from place to place.

Specialized professional organizations. Groups that teachers belong to because they identify with specific subject matter specialities or particular groups of children.

Spectator perceptions of classrooms. What is seen in classroom activity when viewed by individuals with little or no background knowledge about or experience with classroom instruction.

Spina bifida. An opening along a person's spine that allows neural tissue to bulge, causing serious motor problems.

Spiral curriculum. A curriculum arranged around a hierarchy of concepts that are taught several times through the years, each time with added sophistication and depth; also called *structure of knowledge curriculum.*

Spiral instruction. Teaching concepts and skills in a repeating fashion so that with successive returns to the concepts and skills, they are taught with increasing sophistication and depth.

Spirit. Life, will, consciousness, thought as essences of being rather than that which is material.

Spiritual reality. A view of nature that sees ultimate reality as nonmaterial and consisting of ideas and matters of the mind.

Sputnik. The first man-made satellite to orbit the earth, launched by the former Soviet Union in 1957.

Stereotyping. Viewing a group as if all individuals are the same; a view that allows for no individuality.

Stories and legends. Miscellaneous reflections that are passed from generaton to generation in a tribe or an organization and that carry the group's traditions and values.

Stress. Emotional and physical pressure.

Structural routines. Tightly drawn patterns of action that occur regularly without modification.

Structure of knowledge. The manner in which knowledge is organized into disciplines and levels of abstraction.

Structure of knowledge curriculum. A curriculum arranged around a hierarchy of concepts that are taught several times through the years, each time with added sophistication and depth; also called *spiral curriculum.*

Structuring of lessons. The planning and organizing of lessons into predetermined sequences.

Student accountability. The idea that students are responsible for their own behavior, actions, successes, and failures.

Student alerting techniques. Teacher techniques of classroom presentation and questioning that keep students involved in learning tasks.

Student capital. Resources that students possess or can draw on to help their learning.

Student-centered curriculum. A curriculum arranged around the needs, interests, and experiences of students.

Student engaged time. The classroom time in which students are actually involved in learning.

Student needs. The various kinds of personal needs students have that affect their learning, including physical needs, psychological (emotional) needs, and academic needs.

Student on-task observation system. A particular approach to classroom observation that focuses on when individual students are or are not doing what the teacher expects.

Student performance contracts. A cognitive behavior modification technique used by teachers to handle student misbehavior and keep them on task.

Student role players. Students in classes that play certain roles, such as the class leader, class clown, and class peacemaker.

Student-Teams Achievement Division (STAD). A type of cooperative learning that has teams of students study together and prepare cooperatively for individual tests and that includes group as well as individual grades.

Subculture. A small group within a larger group that has its own values, beliefs, and patterns of behavior.

Subject-centered curriculum. A curriculum arranged around organized fields of knowledge such as English, language arts, history, mathematics, science, or social studies.

Subjectivity period. A developmental period of infants until about 8 months, during which infants respond to external stimuli but fail to separate objects in the external environment from their own actions.

Subject matter attributes. Characteristics of different types of subject matter that affect how they are taught.

Subject matter knowledge. Knowledge that makes up a subject or academic discipline; the knowledge that an expert in the field of study would know.

Subject-matter scholar. A role expected of teachers of the future that involves understanding content well enough to be able to manipulate it so that it can be learned by students.

"Success for All" program. A plan to improve how schools educate hard-to-teach students by making a commitment to and following strategies that reach all students; a second-wave plan for school reform developed by Robert E. Slavin.

Summative evaluation. Assessment at the end of a lesson, unit of study, or grading period to assign a grade or designate if the teaching has succeeded or not.

Syllogism. A form of deductive reasoning in which two statements are made from which a logical conclusion can be drawn.

Symbolic activity (as used in Chapter 4). Actions that people and groups engage in to give meaning to their life and work; (as used in Chapter 5) intellectually manipulating symbols such as language, signs, and images.

Symbols. An object, idea, or event that represents something—often something abstract.

Synchrony of interactions. An idea from dialectical theory that states that the coordination of the interactions in all four dimensions of

interaction between individuals and their environment determines an individual's behavior at any given time.

Syndical type of state policymaking. State-level policymaking processes characterized by cooperation among state officials, interest groups, and citizens concerning educational matters.

Synthesizing. An aspect of thinking that involves drawing specifics or separate parts into a whole.

Systematic study. Knowledgeable study conducted in an organized, preplanned, step-by-step manner.

Systematizing (as used in Chapter 10). The step in the process of philosophizing that addresses the question, How do these findings form a coherent pattern?

System-wide testing. Tests of students system-wide that are used to assess accountability and to compare student and class performances.

Taboos. Culturally prohibited or disapproved behaviors.

Tabula rasa. The idea expressed by John Locke that the human mind is a blank slate at birth and that all knowledge is learned through the senses.

Teacher as born artist. The simplistic idea that good teachers are born with a special set of talents rather than that they learn how to teach well.

Teacher as craftsperson. The outdated idea that teachers learn to teach by observing master teachers and then practicing the same teaching techniques until they do them just as well as the master.

Teacher as orchestrator. The idea that teachers lead many communication interactions in classrooms as they teach, much like orchestra conductors lead an orchestra.

Teacher as ringmaster. The idea that teachers are similar to circus ringmasters because they have so many things to do to manage classrooms and produce learning.

Teacher autonomy. A characteristic of teaching in which teachers function independently and without close control from others.

Teacher Effectiveness Training. A specific therapy-based approach to behavior control that focuses on analyzing interpersonal conflict situations.

Teacher expectations. Results that teachers expect of lessons in terms of student learning and behavior.

Teacher isolation. The fact that the teaching activities of teachers are rather unknown to and not seen by other teaching professionals, even colleagues in the same building.

Teacher objectives. Learning goals that teachers set for their lessons and use to guide their teaching.

Teachers' lesson images. Teachers' mental pictures of what the lessons they are planning will look like as they put all the elements of the lesson together in an appropriate sequence.

Teachers' private behavior. The actions of teachers that are not associated with their professional work.

Teaching as communication. The idea that teaching is primarily a process of communication between the teacher and students.

Teaching certificate. A document that attests to the fact that a person has met specified teacher requirements.

Teaching effectiveness. The degree to which teacher behavior produces student learning.

Teaching functions. Types of teacher behaviors that researchers have discovered as they have analyzed classroom practice.

Teaching license. Official authorization granted by a state that allows a person to teach.

Teaching routines. Classroom patterns planned and established by the teacher and followed by stu-

dents so that classes can be effective.

Team Assisted Individualization (TAI). A type of cooperative learning in mathematics in which students assist each other but each student completes an individualized sequentially programmed unit.

Teams-Games-Tournaments (TGT). A type of cooperative learning in which teams of students learn by preparing for academic competition with other teams.

Technical skills of teaching. Specific skills teachers use to teach students effectively, such as behavior management techniques, ways of asking questions, and techniques of reinforcing correct responses.

Technology-Based Anchored Instruction. A model of instruction that uses technology to create problem-solving learning experiences around which to construct student lessons.

"Ten imperative needs of youth" (1944). The ten areas recommended for emphasis in the school curriculum for "life adjustment" education by the Educational Policies Commission of 1944.

Tenure. The status of holding a position on a permanent basis as long as one fulfills the requirements of the position.

Theory. An assumption or generalization supported by philosophies and/or scientific principles that support hypotheses, explain phenomena, and suggest appropriate action or the direction of further investigation.

Theory of values. Ideas about the nature of values that guide other philosophical beliefs.

Therapy-based behavior control systems. Approaches to behavior control based on ideas from counseling and psychotherapy.

Thinking. The intellectual process of remembering, figuring something

out, reflecting, determining, resolving, or reasoning; using the mind to form conclusions, draw inferences, make decisions, and formulate explanations.

Time as a teaching technique. The combination of teaching techniques that use time in particular ways to promote learning, such as wait time.

Time on task. The time during a class period when an individual student is engaged in the tasks the teacher expects.

Tort laws. Laws that govern civil suits concerning wrongful acts, injury, and damage but not involving breach of contract.

Total quality management. The idea or belief that what a business or school does is based on the primary goal of serving its customers or clients; all aspects of the effort are assessed in terms of how well they contribute to that goal.

Trade-off. Prioritizing goals and exchanging those of lesser value for those of greater value.

Tradition. A belief, custom, practice, or convention that is passed from generation to generation.

Traditional realists. Realists who believe in the reality of abstract ideas.

Trainable mentally retarded. One of the names for the category of people who are moderately (as distinct from "mildly") mentally retarded.

"Training the mind." An approach to teaching based on a belief that students learn to think better through practicing difficult thought problems.

Transactional theory. The constructivist idea about learning that sees reading and writing as interactions between the students doing the reading and writing and the ideas they are reading and writing about.

Transitional bilingual programs. Instruction provided in a non-native-

English-speaking student's native language for a temporary time while the student is also taught English, with the expectation that English will replace the native language.

Transitional class. Classes that consist of students who have finished a year at one elementary grade level but are not yet ready for the next grade; usually with low teacher-student ratios to enhance student academic performance.

Tree huggers. A nickname for youth who are particularly concerned about the environment.

Trial-and-error learning. Learning in which the learner tries various responses somewhat randomly until one response or a combination of responses results in success, satisfaction, or a reward of some type.

Tribal mystique. The idea that tribes and other groups possess distinctive shared values and beliefs, heroes and heroines, rituals and ceremonies, stories and legends, and informal players.

Turn taking (as used in Chapter 5). Communication and social interactions between infants and caregivers that prompt the beginnings of social understanding; also referred to as *conversational dance*.

Ultimate reality. The greatest or most fundamental form of being real.

Units of instruction. A plan of instruction that many teachers develop for a class so that the students reach the objectives set for them, usually involving lesson sequences that coordinate content, activities, teaching strategies, and resources.

Universal values. Never-changing ideas about worth, esteem, or standards.

Unpredictability (as a characteristic of classroom environments). A characteristic of classroom environments identified by Walter Doyle that calls attention to the fact that many classroom events happen unexpectedly.

Use of time. A term used to denote the ways in which teachers make use of classroom time.

Value. The idea that something possesses worth; the attachment of worth or esteem to something; a standard that people endorse, maintain, and try to live up to.

Verbal communication. Transmitting information through language.

Vernacular. The native language of a country or region; the everyday language of ordinary people.

Visually impaired students. Students whose vision is below the normal range.

Vocational preparation. A purpose of schools associated with teaching students job skills.

Wait time. The time after teachers ask a question and before they call on a student to respond, during which the students do not know who will be responsible for answering.

War on poverty. A large-scale federal program of the Lyndon B. Johnson administration that focused on helping people living in poverty conditions in America.

White flight. The migration of white people away from an area, usually from areas with an increasing minority population.

Whole child. The view of students as total human beings who require education in social and personal development as well as academics, as distinct from education focused on academics alone.

Whole-language approach. An approach to teaching reading and writing that emphasizes student understanding of their reading and writing, authentic texts, and purposeful literary activities. Especially in the early grades it stresses the use of personally meaningful authentic literature and writing.

Withitness. The ability of a teacher to know what is happening in the classroom at all times as well as to anticipate what is about to occur.

Zone of action. The physical area in a classroom that is likely to involve the most teacher-student interaction.

Zone of proximal development. The area of growth from the point at which a child stands developmentally at a particular time to the state of development he or she could be expected to reach with guidance.

Notes

Chapter 1

1. The two episodes described in this Snapshot are composites based on classes of several teachers known by the authors.

2. The Subscription Office of *Education Week* is P.O. Box 2094, Marion, OH 43306-2084.

3. Jefferson, T. (1816, January 6). Letter to Colonel Yancey. Cited in H. A. Washington (Ed.). (1854). *The writings of Thomas Jefferson* (Vol. 6, p. 517). Washington, DC: Taylor and Maury.

4. Snyder, T. D. (1993). *Digest of education statistics, 1992*. Washington, DC: National Center for Education Statistics, p. 11.

5. Gerald, D. E., & Hussar, W. J. (1992). *Projections of educational statistics to 2003*. Washington, DC: National Center for Education Statistics, pp. 6–7; Kominski, R., & Adams, A. (1993). School enrollment—social and economic characteristics of students: October 1991. *Current Population Reports*, Ser. P-20 (p. 12). Washington, DC: U.S. Department of Commerce.

6. U.S. Bureau of the Census. (1992). *Poverty in the United States: 1991*. Washington, DC: U.S. Department of Commerce, pp. 4–5.

7. U.S. Bureau of the Census. (1991). Households, families, marital status, and living arrangements: March 1991. *Current Population Reports*, Ser. P-20. Washington, DC: U.S. Department of Commerce.

8. Hodgkinson, H. L. (1992). *Demographic look at tomorrow*. Washington, DC: Institute for Educational Leadership, p. 4.

9. *Newsweek*. (1993, August 30), pp. 18–29; *Kids Count Data Book*. (1992). Washington, DC: Center for the Study of Social Policy; Hodgkinson, H. (1993). American education: The good, the bad, and the task. *Phi Delta Kappan*, 74(8), 619–623; Hodgkinson, H. (1991). Reform versus reality. *Phi Delta Kappan*, 73(1), 8–16.

10. Csikszentmihalyi, M., & McCormack, J. (1986). The influence of teachers. *Phi Delta Kappan*, 67(6), 415–419.

11. National Education Association. (1992). *Status of the American public school teacher: 1990–1991*. Washington, DC: National Education Association, pp. 18, 78.

12. Elam, S. M., Rose, L. C., & Gallup, A. M. (1993). The 25th annual Phi Delta Kappa/Gallup Poll of the public's attitudes toward the public schools. *Phi Delta Kappan*, 75(2), 137–152. Poll reports appear annually in the September or October issue of *Phi Delta Kappan*.

13. National Commission on Excellence in Education. (1983). *A nation at risk: The imperative for educational reform*. Washington, DC: U.S. Department of Education; The College Board. (1983). *Academic preparation for college: What students need to know and be able to do*. New York: The College Board; Boyer, E. (1983). *High school: A report on secondary education in America*. New York: Harper and Row; Goodlad, J. L. (1983). *A place called school: Prospects for the future*. New York: McGraw-Hill; Sizer, T. (1984). *Horace's compromise: The dilemma of the American high school*. Boston: Houghton Mifflin; Bennett, W. J. (1986). *First lessons: A report on elementary education in America*. Washington, DC: U.S. Department of Education; Darling-Hammond, L. (1984). *Beyond the commission reports: The coming crisis in teaching*. Santa Monica, CA: RAND Corporation.

14. Mirga, T. (1987, May 13). Indiana lawmakers approve reform bill. *Education Week*, 6(33), 11–12.

15. Carnegie Task Force on Teaching as a Profession. (1986). *A nation prepared: Teachers for the 21st century*. New York: Carnegie Forum on Education and the Economy; Holmes Group. (1986). *Tomorrow's teachers: A report of the Holmes Group*. East Lansing, MI: Holmes Group; National Commission for Excellence in Teacher Education. (1985). *A call for change in teacher education*. Washington, DC: American Association for Colleges for Teacher Education; California Commission on the Teaching Profession. (1985). *Who will teach our children?* Sacramento, CA: California Commission on the Teaching Profession; Commission for Educational Quality of the Southern Regional Education Board. (1985). *Improving teacher education: An agenda for higher education and the schools*. Atlanta, GA: Southern Regional Education Board; National Governors' Association. (1986). *Time for results: The governors' 1991 report on education*. Washington, DC: National Governors' Association; National Academy of Education. (1987). *The nation's report card: Improving the assessment of student achievement*. Cambridge, MA: National Academy of Education; Goodlad, J. I. (1992). On taking school reform seriously. *Phi Delta Kappan*, 73(3), 232–238; Goodlad, J. I. (1990). Why our schools don't get much better—And how they might. *Teacher Education Quarterly*, 17(4), 5–21; Gollnick, D. M., & Kunkel, R. C. (1986). The reform of national accreditation. *Phi Delta Kappan*, 68(4), 310–314; Warner, A. R. (1993). Reforming national accreditation in Teacher Education. *Journal of Educational Reform*, 2(2), 149–153; Wise, A. E., & Leibbrand, J. (1993). Accreditation and the cre-

ation of a profession of teaching. *Phi Delta Kappan, 75*(2), 133–136, 154–157; Stedman, J. B., and others. (1993). *Goals 2000: Educate America act overview and analysis.* Washington, DC: Library of Congress; *Improving America's schools act of 1993: The reauthorization of the elementary and secondary education act and amendments to other acts.* (1993). Washington, DC: U.S. Department of Education.

16. The National Educational Goals. (1994, May). *NEA Today*, p. 3; Earley, P. M. (1994, April 11). *AACTE Briefs, 15*(7), 1, 7; text of statement on education goals adopted by governors (1990, March 7). *Education Week, 9*(24), 16.

17. Edmonds, R. (1983). A final report on the research project: Search for effective schools. East Lansing, MI: Michigan State University; Edmonds, R. (1984). School effects for the urban poor. *Educational Leadership, 37*(1), 15–24.

18. Fullan, M. (1992). Getting reform right: What works and what doesn't. *Phi Delta Kappan, 73*(10), 744–752; Fullan, M. (1992). Visions that bind. *Educational Leadership, 44*(5), 19–22; Fullan, M. (1985). Change processes and strategies at the local level. *Elementary School Journal, 85*(3), 391–421; Fullan, M. (1992). *The meaning of educational change.* New York: Teachers College Press.

19. Sizer, T. (1992). *Horace's school: Redesigning the American school.* Boston: Houghton Mifflin; Sizer, T. R. (1992). The substance of schooling. *American School Board Journal, 179*(1), 27–29; Sizer, T. R. (1991). No pain, no gain. *Educational Leadership, 48*(8), 32–34; Sizer, T. R. (1988). A visit to an "essential" school. *School Administrator, 38*(1), 28–34; Comer, J. P. (1993). *School power: Implications of an intervention project.*

New York: The Free Press; Comer, J. P. (1988). Educating poor minority children. *Scientific American, 259*(5), 42–48; Comer, J. P. (1992). Organizing schools around child development. *Social Policy, 23*(3), 28–30; Haynes, N. M., & Comer, J. P. (1993). The Yale School Development Program: Process outcomes, and policy implications. *Urban Education, 28*(2), 166–199; Levin, H. M., & Hopfenberg, W. W. (1991). Don't remediate: Accelerate. *Principal, 70*(3), 11–13; Brandt, R. (1992). On building learning communities: A conversation with Hank Levin. *Educational Leadership, 5*(1), 19–23; Legters, N., & Slavin, R. E. (1992). *Elementary students at risk: A status report.* Baltimore: Center for Research on Effective Schooling for Disadvantaged Students; Slavin, R. E. (1991). Success for all: Ending reading failure from the beginning (research directions). *Language Arts, 68*(5), 404–409; Slavin, R. E. (1990). Success for all: First year outcomes of a comprehensive plan for reforming urban education. *American Educational Research Journal, 27*(2) 255–278; Slavin, R. E., & Madden, N. A. (1989). What works for students at risk: A research synthesis. *Educational Leadership, 46*(5), 4–13; Slavin, R. E., Karweit, N. L., & Madden, N. A. (1989). *Effective programs for students at risk.* Boston: Allyn and Bacon.

20. Sizer, T. (1992). *Horace's school: Redesigning the American school.* Boston: Houghton Mifflin, pp. 207–209.

21. This plan was outlined in Levin, H. M., & Hopfenberg, W. W. (1991). Don't remediate: Accelerate. *Principal, 70*(3), 11–13.

22. Levin, H. M., & Hopfenberg, W. W. (1991). Don't remediate: Accelerate. *Principal, 70*(3), 11–13.

23. Comer, J. P. (1993). *School power: Implications of an intervention project.* New York: The Free Press, pp. 31, 38, 39, 41.

24. Comer, J. P. (1993). *School power: Implications of an intervention project.* New York: The Free Press.

25. Slavin, R. E., & Madden, N. A. (1989). What works for students at risk: A research synthesis. *Educational Leadership, 46*(5), 4–13; Slavin, R. E., Karweit, N. L., & Madden, N. A. (1989). *Effective programs for students at risk.* Boston: Allyn and Bacon.

26. Darling-Hammond, L. (1988). The futures of teaching. *Educational Leadership, 46*(3), 4–10; Meek, A. (1988). On teaching as a profession: A conversation with Linda Darling-Hammond. *Educational Leadership, 46*(3), 11–17.

27. Rutter, M., Maughan, B., Mortimore, D., Ouston, J., & Smith, A. (1979). *Fifteen thousand hours: Secondary schools and their effects on children.* Cambridge, MA: Harvard University Press.

28. Ornstein, A. C. (1985). Research on teaching: Issues and trends. *Journal of Teacher Education, 36*(6), 27–31.

29. Coleman, J., Campbell, E., Hobson, C., McPartland, J., Mood, A., Weinfield, F., & York, R. (1966). *Equality of educational opportunity.* Washington, DC: U.S. Dept. of Health, Education, and Welfare; Jencks, C. S., Smith, M., Ackland, H., Bane, M. F., Cohen, D., Gintis, H., Heyns, B., & Michelson, S. (1972). *Inequality: A reassessment of the effect of family and schooling in America.* New York: Basic Books.

Chapter 2

1. Lynn Myers, the teacher of this second-grade class, is one of the authors of this text. The class episode reported here is drawn from her teaching at Fall-Hamilton

Elementary School, Nashville, Tennessee.

2. Shirley Bassler, the teacher of this algebra class, is a teacher at Father Ryan High School, Nashville, Tennessee. This class episode was recorded during one of her classes by Alene Harris, a trained classroom observer and a contributing author of this text.

3. Goodlad, J. I. (1984). *A place called school: Prospects for the future.* New York: McGraw-Hill, pp. 93–94.

4. Carew, J., & Lightfoot, S. L. (1979). *Beyond bias: Perspectives on classrooms.* Cambridge: Harvard University Press, p. 53.

5. Morine-Dershimer, G. (1985). *Talking, listening, and learning in elementary classrooms.* New York: Longman, pp. 78–79.

6. Stallings, J. A. (1977). *Learning to look.* Belmont, CA: Wadsworth. Also see Stallings, J. A., & Freiberg, H. J. (1991). Observation for the improvement of teaching. In Waxman, H. C., & Walberg, H. J., *Effective teaching: Current research.* Berkeley, CA: McCutchan.

7. Goodlad, J. I., Klein, M. F., & associates. (1974). *Looking behind the classroom door* (2nd ed.). Worthington, OH: Charles A. Jones, p. 78.

8. One of the first observation systems used widely for the analysis of teacher-student interactions was the Flanders Interaction Analysis System. See Flanders, N. (1970). *Analyzing teacher behavior.* Reading, MA: Addison-Wesley. For a comprehensive discussion of classroom observation and analysis, see Evertson, C. E., & Green, J. L. (1986). Observation as inquiry and method. In M. C. Wittrock (Ed.), *Handbook of research on teaching: Third edition* (pp. 162–213). New York: Macmillan.

9. For additional information on this and other observation systems developed by Stallings, see Stallings, J. A., & Freiberg, H. J. (1991). Observation for the improvement of teaching. In Waxman, H. C., & Walberg, H. J., *Effective teaching: Current research.* Berkeley, CA: McCutchan. For information on a parallel observation system, see Evertson, C. M., & Burry, J. A. (1988, April). *Capturing classroom context: The observation system as lens for assessment.* Paper presented at the annual meeting of the American Educational Research Association, New Orleans.

10. Coleman, J., Campbell, E., Hobson, C., McPartland, J., Mood, A., Weinfield, F., & York, R. (1966). *Equality of educational opportunity.* Washington, DC: U.S. Dept. of Health, Education, and Welfare.

11. See, for example, Brophy, J. (1979). Teacher behavior and its effects. *Journal of Educational Psychology, 71,* 733–750; Brophy, J. E. (1983). Classroom organization and management. *Elementary School Journal, 83*(4), 265–286; Emmer, E., Evertson, C., & Anderson, L. (1980). Effective classroom management at the beginning of the school year. *Elementary School Journal, 80*(5), 219–231; Evertson, C., & Emmer, E. T. (1988). Effective management at the beginning of the school year in junior high classes. *Journal of Educational Psychology, 74*(4), 485–498.

12. Berliner, D. C., & Casanova, U. (1993). *Putting research to work in your classroom.* Jefferson City, MO: Scholastic; Hopkins, D. (1993). *A teacher's guide to classroom research* (2nd ed.). Philadelphia: Open University Press; Gage, N. L., & Berliner, D. C. (1989). Nurturing the critical, practical, and artistic thinking of teachers. *Phi Delta Kappan, 71*(3), 212–214.

Chapter 3

1. The classes described in this Snapshot were observed by Jane Stallings.

2. Csikszentmihalyi, M., & McCormack, J. (1986). The influence of teachers. *Phi Delta Kappan, 67*(6), 415–419.

3. Doyle, W. (1977). Paradigms for research on teacher effectiveness. *Review of Research in Education, 5,* 163–199; Doyle, W. (1980). *Classroom management.* West Lafayette, IN: Kappa Delta Pi; Doyle, W. (1986). Classroom organization and management. In M. C. Wittrock (Ed.), *Handbook of research on teaching: Third edition* (pp. 392–431). New York: Macmillan.

4. Brophy, J. E., & Good, T. L. (1986). Teacher behavior and student achievement. In M. C. Wittrock (Ed.), *Handbook of research on teaching: Third edition* (pp. 328–375). New York: Macmillan; Good, T. L. (1983). New direction in research on teacher and student expectations. *Midwestern Educational Researcher, 6*(1), 7–10, 17, 33; Brophy, J. E. (1988). Research on teacher effects: Uses and abuses. *Elementary School Journal, 89*(1), 3–21.

5. Stallings, J. (1975). Implications and child effects of teaching practices in Follow Through classrooms. *Monographs of the Society for Research in Child Development, 40*(7–8), 50–93.

6. Fisher, C., Filby, N., Marliave, R., Cahen, L., Dishaw, M., Moore, J., & Berliner, D. (1978). *Teaching behaviors, academic learning time, and student achievement: Final Report of Phase III-B, Beginning teacher evaluation study.* San Francisco: Far West Laboratory. Also see Berliner, D., & Casanova, U. (1989). Effective schools: Teachers make the difference. *Instructor, 99*(3), 14–15.

7. Brophy, J. E., & Good, T. L.

(1986). Teacher behavior and student achievement. In M. C. Wittrock (Ed.), *Handbook of research on teaching: Third edition* (pp. 328–375). New York: Macmillan.

8. Berliner, D. C. (1979). Tempus educare. In P. Peterson & W. Walberg (Eds.), *Research on teaching: Concepts, findings, and implications.* Berkeley, CA: McCutchan; Fisher, C., Berliner, D., Filby, N., Marliare, R., Cahen, L., & Dishaw, M. (1980). Teaching behaviors, academic learning time, and student achievement: An overview. In C. Denham & A. Lieberman (Eds.), *Time to learn.* Washington, DC: National Institute of Education.

9. Denham, C., & Lieberman, A. (Eds.). (1980). *Time to learn.* Washington, DC: National Institute of Education.

10. Brophy, J., & Evertson, C. (1976). *Learning from teaching: A developmental perspective.* Boston: Allyn and Bacon: Brophy, J. (1979). Teacher behavior and its effects. *Journal of Educational Psychology, 71,* 733–750; Rosenshine, B. (1983). Teaching functions in instructional programs. *Elementary School Journal, 83*(4), 335–351.

11. Brophy, J. E., & Good, T. L. (1986). Teacher behavior and student achievement. In M. C. Wittrock (Ed.), *Handbook of research on teaching: Third edition* (pp. 328–375). New York: Macmillan.

12. Stallings, J., Needels, M., & Stayrook, N. (1978). *The teaching of basic reading skills in secondary schools, Phase II and Phase III.* Menlo Park, CA: SRI International.

13. Berliner, D. C. (1983). Developing concepts of classroom environments: Some light on the T in classroom studies of ATI. *Educational Psychologist, 18*(1), 1–13; Gage, N. L. (1984). What do we know about teacher effectiveness? *Phi Delta Kappan, 66*(2), 87–93;

Gage, N. L., & Berliner, D. C. (1991). *Educational Psychology* (5th ed.). Boston: Houghton Mifflin.

14. See Hansford, B. (1988). *Teachers and classroom communication.* Sydney, Australia: Harcourt Brace Jovanovich, pp. 166–187.

15. See Anderson, D. J. (1982). The search for school climate: A review of the research. *Review of Educational Research, 25,* 368–420.

16. Doyle, W. (1979). Making managerial decisions in classrooms. In D. L. Duke (Ed.), *Classroom management* (78th yearbook of the National Society for the Study of Education, Part 2). Chicago: University of Chicago Press; Doyle, W. (1984). How order is achieved in classrooms: An interim report. *Journal of Curriculum Studies, 16*(3), 259–277. Doyle, W. (1986). Classroom organization and management. In M. C. Wittrock (Ed.), *Handbook of research on teaching: Third edition* (pp. 392–431). New York: Macmillan.

17. Evertson, C. M., Emmer, E. T., Clements, B. S., & Worsham, M. E. (1994). *Classroom management for elementary teachers.* Boston: Allyn and Bacon; Emmer, E. T., Evertson, C. E., Clements, B. S., & Worsham, M. E. (1994). *Classroom management for secondary teachers.* Boston: Allyn and Bacon; Harris, A. H. (1991). Proactive classroom management: Several ounces of prevention. *Contemporary Education, 62,* 156–160.

18. Kounin, J. S. (1970). *Discipline and group management in classrooms.* New York: Holt, Rinehart and Winston; Emmer, E., Evertson, C., & Anderson, L. (1980). Effective classroom management at the beginning of the school year. *Elementary School Journal 80*(5), 219–231; Evertson, C., & Emmer, E. T. (1982). Effective management for the beginning

of the school year in junior high school classes. *Journal of Educational Psychology, 74*(4), 485–498.

19. Brophy, J. E., & Good, T. L. (1986). Teacher behavior and student achievement. In M. C. Wittrock (Ed.), *Handbook of research on teaching: Third edition* (pp. 328–375). New York: Macmillan; Doyle, W. (1986). Classroom organization and management. In M. C. Wittrock (Ed.), *Handbook of research on teaching: Third edition* (pp. 392–431). New York: Macmillan.

20. Emmer, E., Evertson, C., & Anderson, L. (1980). Effective classroom management at the beginning of the school year. *Elementary School Journal 80*(5), 219–231; Evertson, C., & Emmer, E. T. (1982). Effective management at the beginning of the school year in junior high school classes. *Journal of Educational Psychology, 74*(4), 485–498.

21. Kounin, J. S. (1970). *Discipline and group management in classrooms.* New York: Holt, Rinehart and Winston.

22. Kounin, J. S. (1970). *Discipline and group management in classrooms.* New York: Holt, Rinehart and Winston; Brophy, J. E. (1983). Classroom organization and management. *Elementary School Journal, 83*(4), 265–286.

23. Kounin, J. S. (1970). *Discipline and group management in classrooms.* New York: Holt, Rinehart and Winston; Brophy, J. E. (1983). Classroom organization and management. *Elementary School Journal, 83*(4), 265–286.

24. Brophy, J. E. (1983). Classroom organization and management. *Elementary School Journal, 83*(4), 265–286.

25. Kounin, J. S. (1970). *Discipline and group management in classrooms.* New York: Holt, Rinehart and Winston; Brophy, J. E. (1983). Classroom organization

and management. *Elementary School Journal, 83*(4), 265–286.

26. Brophy, J. E. (1983). Classroom organization and management. *Elementary School Journal, 83*(4), 265–286.

27. Brophy, J. E. (1983). Classroom organization and management. *Elementary School Journal, 83*(4), 265–286.

28. Emmer, E., Evertson, C., & Anderson, L. (1980). Effective classroom management at the beginning of the school year. *Elementary School Journal 80*(5), 219–231; Brophy, J. E. (1983). Classroom organization and management. *Elementary School Journal, 83*(4), 265–286; Good, T. L., & Brophy, J. E. (1986). *Educational psychology* (3rd ed.). New York: Longman; Evertson, C., & Emmer, E. T. (1982). Effective management for the beginning of the school year in junior high school classes. *Journal of Educational Psychology, 74*(4), 485–498; Smith, L. M., & Geoffrey, W. (1968). *The complexities of an urban classroom.* New York: Holt, Rinehart and Winston.

29. Brophy, J. E. (1983). Classroom organization and management. *Elementary School Journal, 83*(4), 265–286.

30. Doyle, W. (1986). Classroom organization and management. In M. C. Wittrock (Ed.), *Handbook of research on teaching: Third edition* (pp. 392–431). New York: Macmillan; Kounin, J. S. (1970). *Discipline and group management in classrooms.* New York: Holt, Rinehart and Winston; Emmer, E., Evertson, C., & Anderson, L. (1980). Effective classroom management at the beginning of the school year. *Elementary School Journal 80*(5), 219–231; Evertson, C., & Emmer, E. T. (1982). Effective management at the beginning of the school year in junior high school classes. *Journal*

of *Educational Psychology, 74*(4), 485–498.

31. Erickson, F., & Mohatt, G. (1982). Cultural organization of participation structures in two classes of Indian students. In G. Spindler (Ed.), *Doing the ethnography of schooling.* New York: Holt, Rinehart and Winston; Borman, K. M., Lippincott, N. S., Matey, C. M., & Obermiller, P. (1978, March). Characteristics of family and classroom control in an urban Appalachian neighborhood. Paper presented at the annual meeting of the American Educational Research Association, Toronto; Berliner, D., & Casanova, U. (1989). Changing minds to change behavior. *Instructor, 98*(6), 20–21; Doyle, W. (1986). Classroom organization and management. In M. C. Wittrock (Ed.), *Handbook of research on teaching: Third edition* (pp. 392–431). New York: Macmillan.

32. Brophy, J. E. (1983). Classroom organization and management. *Elementary School Journal, 83*(4), 265–286.

33. Gordon, T. (1993). *Teacher effectiveness training.* New York: Time Books–Random House.

34. Gordon, T. (1993). *Teacher effectiveness training.* New York: Time Books–Random House; Brophy, J. E. (1983). Classroom organization and management. *Elementary School Journal, 83*(4), 265–286.

35. Glasser, W. (1965). *Reality therapy: A new approach to psychology.* New York: Harper and Row; Glasser, W. (1975). *Schools without failure.* New York: Harper and Row; Glasser, W. (1990). *The quality school: Managing students without coercion.* New York: Harper and Row.

36. Glasser, W. (1975). *Schools without failure.* New York: Harper and Row.

37. Canter, L., & Canter, M. (1976).

Assertive discipline: A take-charge approach for today's educator. Seal Beach, CA: Canter and Associates; Canter, L. (1988). Assertive discipline and the search for the perfect classroom. *Young Children, 43*(2), 24.

38. Canter, L. (1989). More than names on the board and marbles in a jar. *Phi Delta Kappan, 71*(1), 57–61; Charles, D. M. (1991). *Building classroom discipline: Four models to practice* (4th ed.). New York: Longman.

39. Emmer, E. T., & Aussiker, A. (1990). School and classroom discipline programs: How well do they work? In O. C. Moles (Ed.), *Student discipline strategies* (pp. 129–165). Albany, NY: State University of New York Press.

40. Evertson, C. M., & Harris, A. H. (1992). What we know about managing classrooms. *Educational Leadership, 49*(7), 74–78.

41. Brophy, J., & Evertson, C. (1976). *Learning from teaching: A developmental perspective.* Boston: Allyn and Bacon.

42. Brophy, J. E. (1983). Classroom organization and management. *Elementary School Journal, 83*(4), 265–286.

43. Becker, W. C. (1977). Teaching reading and language to the disadvantaged—What we have learned from field research. *Harvard Educational Review, 47*(4), 518–543.

44. Peterson, P. L., Wilkinson, L. C., & Hallinan, M. (Eds.). (1984). *The social contexts of instruction: Group organization and group process.* Orlando, FL: Academic Press; Slavin, R. E. (1993). Ability grouping in the middle grades: Achievement efforts and alternatives. *Elementary School Journal, 93*(5), 535–552.

45. Green, J. L., & Smith, P. (1983). Teaching and learning: A linguistic perspective. *Elementary School Journal, 83*(4), 353–391; Good, T. (1979). Teacher effectiveness

in the elementary school: What we know about it now. *Journal of Teacher Education, 30*(2), 52–64.

46. Weinstein, D. E. (1982). Training students to use elaboration learning strategies. *Contemporary Educational Psychology, 7*(4), 301–311.

47. Brophy, J. E., & Good, T. L. (1986). Teacher behavior and student achievement. In M. C. Wittrock (Ed.), *Handbook of research on teaching: Third edition* (pp. 328–375). New York: Harper and Row; Good, T., & Brophy, J. (1984). *Looking in classrooms* (3rd ed.). New York: Harper and Row; Doyle, W. (1986). Classroom organization and management. In M. C. Wittrock (Ed.), *Handbook of research on teaching: Third edition* (pp. 392–431). New York: Macmillan.

48. Slavin, R. E. (1992). Putting research to work: Cooperative learning. *Instructor, 102*(2), 46–47; Slavin, R. E. (1990). *Cooperative learning: Theory, research, and practice.* Englewood Cliffs, NJ: Prentice-Hall; Slavin, R. E. (1990). Research on cooperative learning: Consensus and controversy. *Educational Leadership, 47*(4), 52–54; Slavin, R. E. (1988). Cooperative learning and student achievement. *Educational Leadership, 46*(2), 31–33; Slavin, R. E. (1980). Cooperative learning. *Review of Educational Research, 50*(2), 315–342; Slavin, R. E. (1980). Effects of student teams and peer tutoring on academic achievement and time on task. *Journal of Experimental Education, 48*, 252–257; Slavin, R. E. (1981). Student team learning. *Elementary School Journal, 82*(1), 5–17.

49. Brophy, J. E. (1983). Classroom organization and management. *Elementary School Journal, 83*(4), 265–286; Soar, R. S., & Soar, R. M. (1983, February). Context

effects in the teaching-learning process. In D. C. Smith (Ed.), *Essential knowledge for beginning educators.* Washington, DC: American Association of Colleges for Teacher Education; Good, T. (1979). Teacher effectiveness in the elementary school: What we know about it now. *Journal of Teacher Education, 30*(2), 52–64; Good, T., Grouws, D., & Ebmeier, M. (1983). *Active mathematics teaching.* New York: Longman; Rosenshine, B. (1983). Teaching functions in instructional programs. *Elementary School Journal, 83*(4), 335–351.

50. Brophy, J. E., & Good, T. L. (1986). Teacher behavior and student achievement. In M. C. Wittrock (Ed.), *Handbook of research on teaching: Third edition* (pp. 328–375). New York: Macmillan.

51. Brophy, J. E., & Good, T. L. (1986). Teacher behavior and student achievement. In M. C. Wittrock (Ed.), *Handbook of research on teaching: Third edition* (pp. 328–375). New York: Macmillan.

52. Brophy, J. E., & Good, T. L. (1986). Teacher behavior and student achievement. In M. C. Wittrock (Ed.), *Handbook of research on teaching: Third edition* (pp. 328–375). New York: Macmillan; Doyle, W. (1984). How order is achieved in classrooms: An interim report. *Journal of Curriculum Studies, 16*(3), 259–277; Emmer, E., Evertson, C., & Anderson, L. (1980). Effective classroom management at the beginning of the school year. *Elementary School Journal 80*(5), 219–231; Evertson, C., & Emmer, E. T. (1982). Effective management for the beginning of the school year in junior high school classes. *Journal of Educational Psychology, 74*(4), 485–498; Rosenshine, B., & Stevens, R. (1986). Teaching functions. In M. C. Wittrock (Ed.), *Handbook of re-*

search on teaching: Third edition* (pp. 376–391). New York: Macmillan.

53. Anderson, L., Evertson, D., & Brophy, J. (1979). An experimental study of effective teaching in first-grade reading groups. *Elementary School Journal, 79*(4), 193–223; Rosenshine, B. (1983). Teaching functions in instructional programs. *Elementary School Journal, 83*(4), 335–351; Hawley, W., & Rosenholtz, S. J. (1984). Good schools: What research says about improving student achievement. *Peabody Journal of Education, 61*(4), 1–178; Bennett, D. (1982). Should teachers be expected to learn and use direct instruction? *Association for Supervision and Curriculum Development Update, 24*, 5.

54. See Bransford, J. D. (1979). *Human cognition.* Belmont, CA: Wadsworth.

55. See Rosenshine, B. (1983). Teaching functions in instructional programs. *Elementary School Journal, 83*(4), 335–351.

56. Brophy, J. E., & Good, T. L. (1986). Teacher behavior and student achievement. In M. C. Wittrock (Ed.), *Handbook of research on teaching: Third edition* (pp. 328–375). New York: Macmillan.

57. Rosenthal, R., & Jacobson, L. (1968). *Pygmalion in the classroom: Teacher expectations and pupils' intellectual development.* New York: Holt, Rinehart and Winston. For an update that is technical, see Rosenthal, R. (1991). Teacher expectancy effects: A brief update 25 years after the pygmalion experiment. *Journal of Research in Education, 1*(1), 3–12.

58. Brophy, J., & Good, T. (1974). *Teacher-student relationships: Causes and consequences.* New York: Holt, Rinehart and Winston. Also see Cooper, H. M., & Good, T. L. (1982). *Pygmalion grows up.* New York: Longman;

and Hamilton, S. F. (1983). The social side of schooling: Ecological studies of classrooms and schools. *Elementary School Journal, 83*(4), 313–334.

59. Brophy, J., & Good, T. (1974). *Teacher-student relationships: Causes and consequences.* New York: Holt, Rinehart and Winston.

60. Morine-Dershimer, G., & Tenenberg, M. (1981). *Participant perspectives on classroom discourse.* Final report to National Institute of Education, Executive Summary, April (Ed. 210 107).

61. Morine-Dershimer, G. (1982). Pupil perceptions of teacher praise. *Elementary School Journal, 82*(5), 421–434.

62. Brophy, J. (1981). Teacher praise: A fundamental analysis. *Review of Educational Research, 51*(1), 5–32; Morine-Dershimer, G. (1982). Pupil perceptions of teacher praise. *Elementary School Journal, 82*(5), 421–434; Brophy, J. E., & Good, T. L. (1986). Teacher behavior and student achievement. In M. C. Wittrock (Ed.), *Handbook of research on teaching: Third edition* (pp. 328–375). New York: Macmillan.

63. Cobb, J. A. (1972). Relationship of discrete classroom behaviors to fourth-grade academic achievement. *Journal of Educational Psychology, 63*(1), 74–80; Cobb, J. A., & Hops, H. (1972). *Survival skills in the educational setting: Their implications for research and implementation. Report No. 13.* Eugene, OR: Oregon University Department of Education.

64. Chance, P. (1992). The rewards of learning. *Phi Delta Kappan, 74*(3), 200–207.

65. Slavin, R. E. (1978). Student teams and comparisons among equals: Effects on academic performance. *Journal of Educational Psychology, 70*(4), 532–538; Slavin, R. E. (1980). Cooperative learning. *Review of Educational Research, 50*(2); 315–342; Slavin, R. E., (1980). Effects of student teams and peer tutoring on academic achievement and time on task. *Journal of Experimental Education, 48,* 252–257; Slavin, R. E. (1981). Student team learning. *Elementary School Journal, 82*(1), 5–17; Johnson, D., Johnson, R., & Scott, L. (1978). The effect of cooperative and individual instruction on students attitudes and achievement. *Journal of Social Psychology, 104,* 207–216.

66. Emmer, E. T. (1988). Praise and the instructional process. *Journal of Classroom Instruction, 23*(2), 32–39; Nelsen, J., Lott, L., & Glenn, H. S. (1993). *Positive discipline in the classroom.* Rocklin, CA: Prima; Brophy, J. (1981). Teacher praise: A fundamental analysis. *Review of Educational Research, 51*(1), 5–32; Brophy, J., & Evertson, C. (1976). *Learning from teaching: A developmental perspective.* Boston: Allyn and Bacon; Soar, R. S., & Soar, R. M. (1983, February). Context effects in the teaching-learning process. In D. C. Smith (Ed.), *Essential knowledge for beginning educators.* Washington, DC: American Association of Colleges for Teacher Education.

67. Nelsen, J., Lott, L., & Glenn, H. S. (1993). *Positive discipline in the classroom.* Rocklin, CA: Prima.

68. Hitz, R., & Driscoll, A. (1989). *Praise in the classroom.* ERIC EDO-PS-89-1; ERIC ED 313-08.

69. Berliner, D. C. (1985). Laboratory settings and the study of teacher education. *Journal of Teacher Education, 36*(6), 2–8. Berliner refers to the work of McKay, D. A., & Marland, P. W. (1978, February). *Thought processes of teachers.* Paper presented at the annual meeting of the American Educational Research Association, Toronto; and Jackson, P. (1968). *Life in classrooms.* New York: Holt, Rinehart and Winston.

70. Gage, N. (1978). *The scientific basis of the art of teaching.* New York: Teachers College Press; Gage, N. L. (1984). What do we know about teacher effectiveness? *Phil Delta Kappan, 67*(6), 415–419.

Chapter 4

1. Deal, T., & Kennedy, A. (1982). *Corporate cultures.* Reading, MA: Addison-Wesley; Peters, T., & Waterman, R. (1982). *In search of excellence.* New York: Harper and Row.

2. Waller, W. (1932). *The sociology of teaching.* New York: Wiley, p. 103.

3. Clark, B. (1983). The organizational saga in higher education. In J. Baldridge & T. Deal (Eds.), *The dynamics of organizational change in education* (pp. 373–382). Berkeley, CA: McCutchan.

4. Sarason, S. (1971). *The culture of the school and the problems of change.* Boston: Allyn and Bacon.

5. Deal, T. (1982). Alternative schools: Struggle for identity. *Changing Schools, 10*(2), 8–9; Swidler, A. (1979). *Organization without authority.* Cambridge: Harvard University Press.

6. Deal, T. (1982). Alternative schools: Struggle for identity. *Changing Schools, 10*(2), 8–9.

7. Swidler, A. (1979). *Organization without authority.* Cambridge: Harvard University Press, p. viii.

8. Fullan, M. (1985). Change processes and strategies at the local level. *Elementary School Journal, 85*(3), 391–421. Also see Fullan's more recent ideas in Fullan, M. G., & Stiegelbauer, S. (1991). *The new meaning of educational change* (2nd ed.). New York: Teachers College Press.

9. Deal, T., Gunnar, H., & Wiske,

S. (1977). *Linking knowledge to schools: The process of change in six sites.* Andover, MA: The Network.

10. McDill, E., & Rigsby, L. (1973). *Structure and process in secondary schools.* Baltimore: Johns Hopkins University Press.

11. For more information, see *Elementary School Journal, 85*(3).

12. Shanker, A. (1970, February). Charles W. Hunt Lecture. Annual meeting of the American Association of Colleges for Teacher Education, Chicago.

13. See Waller, W. (1932). *The sociology of teaching.* New York: Wiley, especially p. 108.

14. Bolman, L. G., & Deal, T. E. (1993). *Becoming a teacher leader: From isolation to collaboration.* Thousand Oaks, CA: Corwin Press; Cohen, E., Deal, T., Meyer, J., & Scott, W. (1979). Technology and teaming in the elementary school. *Sociology of Education, 53,* 20–33; Deal, T., Meyer, J., & Scott, W. (1983). Organizational influences on educational innovation. In J. Baldridge & T. Deal (Eds.), *The dynamics of organizational change in education.* Berkeley, CA: McCutchan; Meyer, J., & Rowan, B. (1977). Institutional organizations—Formal structure as myth and ceremony. *American Journal of Sociology, 83,* 440–463.

15. Gordon, W. (1957). *The social system of the high school.* New York: The Free Press.

16. McDill, E., & Rigsby, L. (1973). *Structure and process in secondary schools.* Baltimore: Johns Hopkins University Press.

17. Wolcott, H. F. (1973). *The man in the principal's office: An ethnography.* New York: Holt, Rinehart and Winston.

18. Stein, B. (1986, November). High school diary. *Los Angeles Magazine,* 174–175.

19. Brookover, W. B., & Lezotte, L. W. (1979). *Changes in school characteristics coincident with changes in student achievement.* Occasional paper no. 17. East Lansing: Michigan State University, College of Urban Development; Edmonds, R. (1983). *A final report on the research project: Search for effective schools.* East Lansing: Michigan State University and Washington, DC: National Institute of Education.

20. See, for example, Lezotte, L. W. (1992). Learn from effective schools. *Social Policy, 22*(3), 34–36; Lezotte, L. W. (1989). Base school improvement on what we know about effective schools. *American School Board Journal, 176*(8), 18–20.

21. Fullan, M. (1985). Change process and strategies at the local level. *Elementary School Journal, 85*(3), 391–421; Fullan, M., & Stiegelbauer, S. (1991). *The new meaning of educational change* (2nd ed.). New York: Teachers College Press; Fullan, M. G., & Miles, M. B. (1992). Getting reform right: What works and what doesn't. *Phi Delta Kappan, 73*(10), 744–752.

22. Deming, W. E. (1982). *Quality, productivity, and competitive position.* Cambridge, MA: Massachusetts Institute of Technology, Center for Advanced Engineering Study; Senge, P. M. (1990). *The fifth discipline: The art and practice of the learning organization.* New York: Doubleday. For studies of how these theories and ideas, as well as culture as a general idea, apply to education, see Lezotte, L. W. (1992). *Creating the total quality effective school.* Ann Arbor, MI: Effective School Products; Murphy, J., & Hallinger, P. (1993). *Restructuring schooling: Learning from ongoing efforts.* Thousand Oaks, CA: Corwin Press; Deal, T. E. (1990). Reframing reform. *Educational Leadership, 47*(8), 6–7, 9, 11–12; Kaufman, R., & Zahn, D. (1993). *Quality management plus: The continuous improvement of education.* Thousand Oaks, CA: Corwin Press; Rowan, B., Raudenbush, W., & Kang, S. (1990). Organizational design in high schools: A multilevel analysis. *American Journal of Education, 99*(2), 238–266; McLaughlin, M. W., & Talbert, J. E. (1993). Contexts that matter for teaching and learning: Strategic opportunities for meeting the nation's educational goals. Palo Alto, CA: Center for Research on the Context of Secondary School Teaching.

23. Stein, B. (1986, November). High school diary. *Los Angeles Magazine,* 177–178.

24. Lightfoot, S. (1983). *The good high school: Portraits of character and culture.* New York: Basic Books.

25. See, for example, Wolcott, H. F. (1985). On ethnographic intent. *Educational Administration Quarterly, 21*(3), 187–203.

26. Fisher, Marc. (1987, May 22). The forgotten land surrounded by drugs. *The Washington Post,* 96.

Chapter 5

1. The two case studies presented in this Snapshot are based on information about students known to the authors of this text.

2. Flavell, J. H. (1992). Cognitive development: Past, present, and future. *Developmental psychology, 28*(6), 998–1005; Flavell, J. H. (1985). *Cognitive development* (2nd ed.). Englewood Cliffs, NJ: Prentice-Hall; Kagan, J. (1986). *The nature of the child.* New York: Basic Books. (See chapter on connectedness.)

3. See de Villiers, P. A., & de Villiers, J. G. (1979). *Early language.* Cambridge: Harvard University Press; Olson, D. P. (1980). *The social foundations of language and thought.* New York: W. W. Norton.

4. Riegel, K. F. (1976). The dialectics of human development. *American Psychologist, 31*(10), 689–700; Sameroff, A. J. (1975). Transactional models in early social relations. In K. F. Riegel (Ed.), *The development of dialectical operations.* Basel: S. Karger; Sameroff, A. J. (1993). Stability of intelligence from preschool to adolescence: The influence of social and family risk factors. *Child Development, 64*(1), 80–97.

5. Gibson, E. J. (1969). *Principles of perceptual learning and development.* New York: Appleton-Century-Crofts.

6. Gibson, E. J. (1969). *Principles of perceptual learning and development.* New York: Appleton-Century-Crofts.

7. Gibson, E. J. (1969). *Principles of perceptual learning and development.* New York: Appleton-Century-Crofts.

8. See Wadsworth, B. J. (1989). *Piaget's theory of cognitive development* (4th ed.). White Plains, NY: Longman.

9. McCall, R. B. (1979). The development of intellectual functioning in infancy and the prediction of later IQ. In J. Osofsky (Ed.), *Handbook of infant development.* New York: Wiley.

10. McCall, R. B. (1979). The development of intellectual functioning in infancy and the prediction of later IQ. In J. Osofsky (Ed.), *Handbook of infant development.* New York: Wiley.

11. Vygotsky, L. S. (1978). *Mind in society: The development of higher psychological processes.* Translation and summary version. (M. Cole, V. John-Steiner, S. Scribner, & E. Souberman, Eds.). Cambridge: Harvard University Press.

12. Zivin, G. (1986). Processes of expressive behavior development. *Merrill-Palmer Quarterly, 36*(2), 103–140; Zivin, G. (1979). *The development of self-regulation through private speech.* New York: Wiley; Berk, L. E. (1985, July). Why young children talk to themselves. *Young Children,* pp. 46–52; Trotter, R. J. (1987, May). You've come a long way, baby. *Psychology Today,* pp. 34–45.

13. Piaget, J. (1965). *The moral judgment of the child.* New York: The Free Press.

14. Kohlberg, L. (1970). The child as moral philosopher. In P. Cramer (Ed.), *Readings in developmental psychology today* (pp. 109–115). Del Mar, CA: CRM Books; Kohlberg, L. (1981). *Essays on moral development. Vol. 1: The philosophy of moral development.* New York: Harper and Row; Kohlberg, L. (1984). *Essays on moral development. Vol. 2: The psychology of moral development.* San Francisco: Harper and Row; Power, F. C., Higgins, A., & Kohlberg, L. (1989). *Lawrence Kohlberg's approach to moral education.* New York: Columbia University Press.

15. Gilligan, C. (1993). *In a different voice.* Cambridge: Harvard University Press. Also see Gilligan, C., & Attanucci, J. (1988). Two moral orientations: Gender differences and similarities. *Merrill-Palmer Quarterly, 34*(3), 223–237.

16. Campos, J. J., Barrett, C. K., Lamb, M. E., Goldsmith, H. H., & Sternberg, C. C. (1983). Socioemotional development. In P. H. Mussen (Ed.), *Handbook of child psychology* (4th ed.). *Vol. 2. Infancy and developmental psychology.* New York: Wiley; Campos, J. J., et al. (1989). Emergent themes in the study of emotional development and emotion regulation. *Developmental Psychology, 25*(3), 394–402.

17. Mangelsdorf, M., Kestenbaum, R., Lang, S., & Andreas, D. (1990). Infant-proneness-to-distress temperament, maternal personality, and mother-infant attachment: Associations and goodness of fit. *Child Development, 61,* 820–831.

18. Dunn, J. (1983). Sibling relationships in early childhood. *Child Development, 54,* 787–811; Brown, J. R., & Dunn, J. (1992). Talk with your mother or your sibling? Developmental changes in early family conversations about feelings. *Child Development, 63*(2), 336–349; Dunn, J. J., et al. (1991). Young children's understanding of other people's feelings and beliefs: Individual differences and their antecedents. *Child Development, 62*(6), 1352–1366; Munn, P., & Dunn, J. (1989). Temperament and the developing relationship between siblings. *International Journal of Behavioral Development, 12*(4), 433–451.

19. Vygotsky, L. S. (1978). *Mind in society: The development of higher psychological processes.* (M. Cole, V. John-Steiner, S. Scribner, & E. Souberman, Eds.). Cambridge: Harvard University Press.

20. Dunn, J. (1983). Sibling relationships in early childhood. *Child Development, 54,* 787–811; Zajonc, R. B., & Hall, E. (1986, February). Mining new gold from old research. *Psychology Today,* pp. 46–51.

21. Huston, A. C. (1983). Sex-typing. In P. H. Mussen (Ed.), *Handbook of child psychology* (4th ed.). *Vol. 4. Socialization, personality, and social development* (pp. 387–468). New York: Wiley.

22. Dweck, C. S., & Bush, E. S. (1976). Sex differences in learned helplessness: I. Differentiation debilitation with peer and adult evaluators. *Developmental Psychology, 12,* 147–156; Dweck, C. S., Davidson, W., Nelson, S., & Enna, B. (1978). Sex differences in learned helplessness: II. The contingence of evaluative feedback in the classroom. III. An experimental analysis. *Developmental Psychology, 14,* 268–276.

23. Elkind, D. (1970, April 5). Erik Erikson's eight ages of man. *New York Times Magazine*, 25–27+.

24. Elkind, D. (1981). *Children and adolescents* (3rd ed.). New York: Oxford University Press (see especially chapter on egocentrism in children and adolescents); Harter, S. (1983). Developmental perspectives on the self-esteem. In P. H. Mussen (Ed.), *Handbook of child psychology* (4th ed.). *Vol. 4. Socialization, personality, and social development.* New York: Wiley.

25. Elkind, D. (1981). *Children and adolescents* (3rd ed.). New York: Oxford University Press.

26. For more information, see Coleman, J. S., Hoffer, T., & Kilgore, S. (1982). *Achievement in high school: Public and private schools compared.* New York: Basic Books; Coleman, J. S. (1981). Quality and equality in American education: Public and Catholic schools. *Phi Delta Kappan, 63*(3), 159–164; Coleman, J. S. (1988, February). *Social capital in the development of human capital: The ambiguous position of private schools.* Paper presented at the annual conference of The National Association of Independent Schools, New York; Coleman, J. S. (1991). *Parental involvement in education. Policy perspective series.* Washington, DC: Office of Educational Research and Improvement; Coleman, J. S. (1990). *Equality and achievement in education.* Boulder, CO: Westview Press; Haynes, N. M., & Comer, J. P. (1993). The Yale school development program: Process, outcomes, and policy implications. *Urban Education, 28*(2), 166–169; Comer, J. P. (1993). The potential effects of community organizations on the future of our youth. *Teachers College Record, 94*(3), 658–661.

27. Archer, J. (1992). Childhood gender roles: Social context and organization. In H. McGurk (Ed.), *Childhood social development: Contemporary perspectives* (pp. 31–61). Hillsdale, NJ: Lawrence Erlbaum.

28. Whiting, B. B., & Edwards, C. P. (1988). *Children of different worlds: The formation of social behavior.* Cambridge, MA: Howard University Press.

29. David, D. S., & Brannon, R. (1976). The male sex role: Our culture's blueprint for manhood, and what it has done for us lately. In D. S. David & R. Brannon (Eds.), *The forty-nine percent majority: The male sex-role.* Reading, MA: Addison-Wesley.

30. Hilton, T. L., & Berglund, G. W. (1974). Sex differences in mathematics achievement—a longitudinal study. *Journal of Educational Research, 67,* 231–237.

31. Terman, L. (1925–1959). *Genetic studies in genius* (Vols. I–V). Stanford: Stanford University Press.

32. Van Tassel-Baska, J. (1989). Profiles of precocity: A three-year study of talented adolescents. In J. Van Tassel-Baska and P. Olszewski-Kubilius (Eds.), *Patterns of influence on gifted learners* (pp. 29–39). New York: Teachers College Press; Van Tassel-Baska, J. (1992). *Planning effective curriculum for gifted learners.* Denver: Love; Whitmore, J. R. (1988). Gifted children at risk for learning difficulties. *Teaching Exceptional Children, 20*(4), 10–14; Gross, M. (1993). *Exceptionally gifted children.* New York: Routledge.

33. Horowitz, F. D., & O'Brien, M. (1985). *The gifted and talented: Developmental perspectives.* Washington, DC: American Psychological Association.

34. American Association on Mental Retardation. (1992). *Mental retardation: Definition, classification, and systems of supports* (9th ed.). Washington, DC: Author.

35. See MacMillan, D. (1977). *Mental retardation in school and society.* Boston: Little, Brown.

36. For a more detailed definition, see Bryan, T. H., & Bryan, J. H. (1986). *Understanding learning abilities* (3rd ed.). Palo Alto: Mayfield.

37. Sawyer, D. J. (1992). Dyslexia: Introduction to the special series. *Journal of Learning Disabilities, 25*(1), 38–39; Richardson, S. O. (1992). Historical perspectives on dyslexia. *Journal of Learning Disabilities, 25*(1), 40–47; Kamhi, A. G. (1992). Response to historical perspective. *Journal of Learning Disabilities, 25*(1), 48–52.

38. Bashir, A. S., & Scavuzzo, A. (1992). Children with language disorders: Natural history and academic success. *Journal of Learning Disabilities, 25*(1), 53–65.

39. Bashir, A. S., & Scavuzzo, A. (1992). Children with language disorders: Natural history and academic success. *Journal of Learning Disabilities, 25*(1), 53–65; Sawyer, D. J. (1992). Dyslexia: Introduction to the special series. *Journal of Learning Disabilities, 25*(1), 38–39.

40. Abramowitz, A. J., & O'Leary, S. G. (1991). Behavioral interventions for the classroom: Implications for students with ADHD. *School Psychology Review, 20*(2), 220–234; Barklely, R. A. (1981). *Hyperactive children: A handbook for diagnosis and treatment.* New York: Guilford Press; McCall, R. B. (1989). A.D.D. alert. *Learning, 17*(5), 66–69; *ADHD teachers handbook.* (1992). Nashville: Metropolitan Public Schools.

41. See Fotheringham, J. B., Hambley, W. D., & Haddad-Curran, H. W. (1983). *Prevention of intellectual handicaps.* Ontario: Association for the Mentally Retarded.

42. Gilfand, D. M., Jenson, W. R., & Drew, C. J. (1982). *Understanding child behavior disorders.* New York: Holt, Rinehart and Winston.

43. This episode is based on conver-

sations between the Chris referred to in the story and Charles Myers, one of the authors of this text.

44. Sutherland, A. T. (1984). *Disabled we stand*. Bloomington: Indiana University Press.

45. Dunn, L. M. (1968). Special education for the mentally retarded: Is much of it justifiable? *Exceptional Children, 35*(1), 5.

46. Dunn, L. M. (1968). Special education for the mentally retarded: Is much of it justifiable? *Exceptional Children, 35*(1), 6.

47. Dunn, L. M. (1968). Special education for the mentally retarded: Is much of it justifiable? *Exceptional Children, 35*(1), 6.

48. Dunn, L. M. (1968). Special education for the mentally retarded: Is much of it justifiable? *Exceptional Children, 35*(1), 11.

Chapter 6

1. Quoted in Marrow, A. J. (1969). *The practical theorist: The life and work of Kurt Lewin*. New York: Basic Books.

2. See Babkin, B. P. (1949). *Pavlov: A biography*. Chicago: University of Chicago Press.

3. Watson, J. B. (1970). *Behaviorism*. New York: W. W. Norton; Watson, J. B., & Rayner, R. (1920). Conditional emotional reactions. *Journal of Experimental Psychology, 3*, 1–14; also see Horowitz, F. D. (1992). John B. Watson's legacy: Learning and environment. *Developmental Psychology, 28*(3), 360–367.

4. Watson, J. B. (1970). *Behaviorism*. New York: W. W. Norton, p. 104.

5. Guthrie, E. R. (1952). *The psychology of learning*. New York: Harper and Row.

6. See Biehler, R. F., & Snowman, J. (1989). *Psychology applied to teaching* (6th ed.). Boston: Houghton Mifflin.

7. Rachlin, H. (1970). *Introduction to modern behaviorism*. San Francisco: W. H. Freeman.

8. Thorndike, E. L. (1931). *Human learning*. New York: Century.

9. Thorndike, E. L. (1911). *Animal intelligence*. New York: Hafner, p. 131.

10. Skinner, B. F. (1974). *About behaviorism*. New York: Knopf; Skinner, B. F. (1977). Herrnstein and the evolution of behaviorism. *American Psychologist, 32*(12), 1006–1012; see also Sparzo, F. J. (1992). B. F. Skinner's contributions to education: A retrospective appreciation. *Contemporary Education, 63*(3), 225–233.

11. Skinner, B. F. (1969). *Contingencies of reinforcement: A theoretical analysis*. New York: Appleton-Century-Crofts.

12. Keller, F. S. (1968). Good-bye teacher. . . . *Journal of Applied Behavior Analysis, 1*(1), 79–89.

13. Mood, A. M. (1970). Do teachers make a difference? In *Do teachers make a difference? A report on recent research in pupil achievement*. Washington, DC: Bureau of Educational Personnel Development, Office of Education, U.S. Department of Health, Education, and Welfare.

14. Premack, D. (1965). Reinforcement theory. In D. Levine (Ed.), *Nebraska Symposium on Motivation, 13*. Lincoln: University of Nebraska Press, pp. 150–151.

15. See Gage, N. L., & Berliner, D. C. (1991). *Educational psychology* (5th ed.). Boston: Houghton Mifflin, pp. 294–297.

16. Winett, R. A., & Winkler, R. C. (1972). Current behavior modification in the classroom: Be still, be quiet, be docile. *Journal of Applied Behavior Analysis, 5*(4), 499–504.

17. O'Leary, K., & O'Leary, S. (Eds.). (1977). *Classroom management: The successful use of behavior modification*. New York: Pergamon Press.

18. Tolman, E. C. (1951). *Collected papers in psychology*. Berkeley: University of California Press.

19. Gagné, R. M. (1974). *Essentials of learning for instruction*. New York: Holt, Rinehart and Winston. Also see Gagné, R. M. (1988). Some reflection on thinking skills. *International Science, 17*(4), 387–390.

20. Ericsson, K. A., & Simon, H. A. (1980). Verbal reports as data. *Psychological Review, 87*(3), 215–251.

21. Gagné, E. D. (1985). *The cognitive psychology of school learning*. Boston: Little, Brown.

22. Bereiter, C. (1980). Development in writing. In L. W. Gregg & E. R. Steinberg (Eds.), *Cognitive processes in writing* (pp. 73–93). Hillsdale, NJ: Lawrence Erlbaum; Birnbaum, J. C. (1982). The reading and composing behavior of selected fourth- and seventh-grade students. *Research in the Teaching of English, 16*(3), 241–260.

23. Gagné, E. D. (1985). *The cognitive psychology of school learning*. Boston: Little, Brown.

24. Piaget, J. (1952). *The language and thought of the child*. London: Routledge and Kegan Paul; Piaget, J. (1967). *Six psychological studies*. New York: Random House; also see Beilin, H. (1992). Piaget's enduring contribution to developmental psychology. *Developmental Psychology 28*(2), 191–204.

25. Piaget, J., & Inhelder, B. (1969). *The psychology of the child*. New York: Basic Books.

26. For a compatible approach, see Bruner, J. S. (1990). *Acts of meaning*. Cambridge: Harvard University Press; Bruner, J. S. (1966). *Toward a theory of instruction*. Cambridge: Harvard University Press.

27. Siegler, R. S. (1976). Three aspects of cognitive development. *Cognitive Psychology, 8*, 481–520; Siegler, R. S. (1981). Developmental sequences within and between concepts. *Monographs of the*

Society for Research in Child Development, 46(2), Serial No. 189.

28. Siegler, R. S. (1976). Three aspects of cognitive development. *Cognitive Psychology, 8*, 481–520.

29. Vygotsky, L. S. (1978). *Mind in society: The development of higher psychological processes.* Translation and summary version. M. Cole, V. John-Steiner, S. Scribner, & E. Souberman (Eds.). Cambridge: Harvard University Press.

30. Wheatley, G. H. (1991). Constructivist perspectives on science and mathematics learning. *Science Education, 75*(1), 9–21; von Glasersfeld, E. (1990). *Constructivism as a scientific method.* London: Pergamon Press.

31. Barron, L. C., & Goldman, E. S. (1994). Integrating technology with teacher preparation. In B. Means (Ed.), *Technology and education reform.* San Francisco: Jossey-Bass, p. 81.

32. Clements, D. H., & Battista, M. T. (1990). Constructivist learning and teaching. *Arithmetic Teacher, 38*(1), 34–35.

33. Clements, D. H., & Battista, M. T. (1990). Constructivist learning and teaching. *Arithmetic Teacher, 38*(1), 34–35; Resnick, L. B. (1987). *Education and learning to think.* Washington, DC: National Academy Press; von Glasersfeld, E. (1987). Learning as a constructive activity. In C. Janvier (Ed.), *Problems of representation in the teaching and learning of mathematics.* Hillsdale, NJ: Lawrence Erlbaum; Yackel, E., Cobb, P., Wood, T., & Merkel, G. (1990). Experience, problem solving and discourse as central aspects of constructivism. *Arithmetic Teacher, 38*(4), 34–35; Barron, L. C., & Goldman, E. S. (1994). Integrating technology with teacher preparation. In B. Means (Ed.), *Technology and education reform.* San Francisco: Jossey-Bass; Steffe, L. P., & Cobb, P. (1988). *Construction of arithmetical meanings and strategies.* New York: Springer-Verlag; Cobb, P. (1988). The tension between theories of learning and instruction in mathematics education. *Educational Psychologist, 23*(3), 87–103.

34. Cobb, P. (1988). The tension between theories of learning and instruction in mathematics education. *Educational Psychologist, 23*(3), 87–103; Steffe, L. P., & Cobb, P. (1988). *Construction of arithmetical meanings and strategies.* New York: Springer-Verlag; Cobb, P., Yackel, E., & Wood, T. (1992). A constructivist alternative to the representational view of mind in mathematics education. *Journal of Research in Mathematics Education, 23*(1), 2–33.

35. Cobb, P., Yackel, E., & Wood, T. (1992). A constructivist alternative to the representational view of mind in mathematics education. *Journal of Research in Mathematics Education, 23*(1), 2–33; Leinhardt, G. (1992). What research on learning tells about teaching. *Education Leadership, 49*(7), 20–25; Cognitive and Technology Group at Vanderbilt. (1990). Anchored instruction and its relationship to situated cognition. *Educational Researcher, 19*(6), 2–10; Cognitive and Technology Group at Vanderbilt. (1993). The Jasper experiment: Using video to furnish real-world problem-solving contexts. *Arithmetic Teacher, 40*(8), 474–478; Barron, L. C., & Goldman, E. S. (1994). Integrating technology with teacher preparation. In B. Means (Ed.), *Technology and education reform.* San Francisco: Jossey-Bass; National Council of Teachers of Mathematics. (1989). *Curriculum and evaluation standards for school mathematics.* Reston, VA: National Council of Teachers of Mathematics; Wood, T., & Yackel, E. (1990). The development of collaborative dialogue within small group interaction. In L. P. Steffe, & T. Wood (Eds.), *Transforming children's mathematics education: An international perspective.* Hillsdale, NJ: Lawrence Erlbaum; Yackel, E., Cobb, P., Wood, T., Wheatley, G., & Merkel, G. (1990). The importance of social interactions in children's construction of mathematical knowledge. In T. Cooney (Ed.), *1990 Yearbook of the National Council of Teachers of Mathematics.* Reston, VA: National Council of Teachers of Mathematics.

36. National Council of Teachers of Mathematics. (1989). *Curriculum and evaluation standards for school mathematics.* Reston, VA: Author; National Council of Teachers of Mathematics. (1991). *Professional standards for teaching mathematics.* Reston, VA: Author.

Chapter 7

1. The three case studies presented in this Snapshot are based on information about students known personally to the authors of this text.

2. National Education Association. (1893). *Report of the committee on secondary school studies.* Washington, DC: Government Printing Office.

3. Commission on the Reorganization of Secondary Education. (1918). *Cardinal principles of secondary education.* Washington, DC: Government Printing Office.

4. Educational Policies Commission. (1938). *The purposes of education in American democracy.* Washington, DC: National Education Association and American Association of School Administrators.

5. Educational Policies Commission. (1944). *Education of all American youth.* Washington, DC: National Education Association and American Association of School Administrators.

6. Educational Policies Commission. (1944). *Education of all

American youth. Washington, DC: National Education Association and American Association of School Administrators.

7. Conant, J. B. (1959). *The American high school today*. New York: McGraw-Hill.

8. Gardner, J. W. (1961). *Excellence: Can we be equal and excellent too?* New York: Harper and Brothers, pp. 128–131.

9. For an in-depth discussion of excellence, see Fantini, M. D. (1989). Changing conceptions of equality: Moving from equality of opportunity to equality of results. *Equity and Excellence*, 24(2), 21–33; Fantini, M. D. (1986). *Regaining excellence in education*. Columbus, OH: Charles E. Merrill.

10. For thorough discussions of racial desegregation, see Hawley, W. D. (Ed.). (1981). *Effective school desegregation: Equity, quality, and feasibility*. Beverly Hills, CA: Sage; Rossell, C. H., & Hawley, W. D. (Eds.). (1983). *The consequences of school desegregation*. Philadelphia: Temple University Press.

11. Rossell, C. H., & Hawley, W. D. (Eds.). (1983). *The consequences of school desegregation*. Philadelphia: Temple University Press.

12. For more information about different forms of desegregation, see Rossell, C. H. (1990). How effective are voluntary plans with magnet schools? *Education Evaluation and Policy Analysis*, 10(4), 325–342; Rossell, C. H. (1988). The carrot or the stick for school desegregation policy? *Urban Affairs Quarterly*, 25(3), 474–499.

13. For more information about compensatory education and compensatory programs, see Lehr, J. B., & Harris, H. W. (1988). *At-risk, low achieving students in the classroom*. Washington, DC: National Education Association; Schwartz, W., & Hawley, C. (Eds.). (1991). *Overcoming risk: An annotated bibliography of publi-*

cations developed by ERIC clearinghouses. Charleston, WV: ERIC Clearinghouse on Rural Education and Small Schools; Frymier, J. (1992). Children who hurt, children who fail. *Phi Delta Kappan*, 74(3), 257–259; Barnett, S. (1993, May 19). Does Head Start fade out? *Education Week*, 12(34), 40.

14. Excerpted from interviews conducted by Anne Turnbaugh Lockwood and reported in *Newsletter: National Center on Effective Secondary Schools*, School of Education, University of Wisconsin—Madison, Fall 1986. Used by permission of Anne Turnbaugh Lockwood. The school and city are not identified because the project is part of a national research effort.

15. For more information on bilingual education, see Rossell, C. H. (1990). The research on bilingual education. *Equity and Choice*, 6(2), 29–36; Rossell, C. H., & Baker, K. (1988). Selecting and exiting students in bilingual education programs. *Journal of Law and Education*, 17(4), 589–623.

16. For more information on multicultural education, see Heath, S. B., & McLaughlin, M. W. (Eds.). (1993). *Identity and inter-city youth: Beyond ethnicity and gender*. New York: Teachers College Press; Estrada, K., & McLaren, P. (1993). A dialogue on multiculturalism and democratic culture. *Educational Researcher*, 22(3), 27–33; Banks, J. A. & McGee Banks, C. A. (1995). Handbook of research on multicultural education. New York: Macmillan; Banks, J. A. (1994). *An introduction to multicultural education* (3rd ed.). Boston: Allyn and Bacon; Banks, J. A. (1994). *Multiethnic education: Theory and practice*. Boston: Allyn and Bacon; Sleeter, C. E., & Grant, C. A. (1994). *Making choices for multicultural education: Five approaches to race, class, and gender*. New York: Macmillan;

Gollnick, D. M., & Chinn, P. C. (1993). *Multicultural education in a pluralistic society* (4th ed.). New York: Macmillan; National Council for the Social Studies. (1992). Curriculum guidelines for multicultural education. *Social Education*, 56(5), 274–294.

Chapter 8

1. This description of education in Athens was developed by the authors of this book from a variety of historical accounts of the period.

2. From Records of the Governor and Company of the Massachusetts Bay in New England, Vol. II, 6–7. Boston, 1853. Reproduced in Cubberley, E. P. (1920). *Readings in the history of education*. Boston: Houghton Mifflin.

3. From Records of the Governor and Company of the Massachusetts Bay in New England, Vol. II, 203. Boston, 1853. Reproduced in Cubberley, E. P. (1920). *Readings in the history of education*. Boston: Houghton Mifflin.

4. Reproduced in Brumbaugh, M. G. (1969). *Life and works of Christopher Dock*. New York: Arno Press, pp. 105–111.

5. For additional information on the Friends Public Schools, see Myers, C. B. (1968). *Public secondary schools in Pennsylvania during the American Revolutionary era 1760–1800*. Ph.D. dissertation, George Peabody College for Teachers.

6. Myers, C. B. (1968). *Public secondary schools in Pennsylvania during the American Revolutionary era 1760–1800*. Ph.D. dissertation, George Peabody College for Teachers.

7. Jefferson, T. (1816, January 6). Letter to Colonel Yancey. Cited in H. A. Washington (Ed.). (1854). *The writings of Thomas*

Jefferson (Vol. VI, p. 517). Washington, DC: Taylor and Maury.

8. National Education Association. (1893). *Report of the committee on secondary school studies.* Washington, DC: Government Printing Office.

9. Commission on the Reorganization of Secondary Education. (1918). *Cardinal principles of secondary education.* Washington, DC: Government Printing Office.

10. Cuban, L. (1982). Persistent instruction: The high school curriculum, 1900–1980. *Phi Delta Kappan, 64*(2), 113–118.

Chapter 9

1. Charles Myers, the college supervisor of student teaching in this episode, is one of the authors of this text.

2. Tom Johnson was a teacher education student at our university before he accepted the teaching position described in this episode.

3. This episode is based on the following news reports: Bradley, A. (1993). Not making the grade. *Education Week, 13*(2), 1, 19–21; Bradley, A. (1994). Board votes to reinstate ousted algebra teacher. *Education Week, 13*(26), 11.

4. Public schools operate under the direct legal authority of official governmental bodies; private schools are, of course, less directly controlled by governments, but they must conform to governmental rules and laws intended to protect American citizens and the public at large.

5. For more detailed information on state politics and education, see Spring, J. (1993). *Conflicts of interests: The politics of American education* (2nd ed.). New York: Longman, pp. 119–144; and Spring, J. (1991). *American education: An introduction to social and political as-*

pects (5th ed.). New York: Longman, pp. 176–189.

6. Spring, J. (1993). *Conflicts of interests: The politics of American education* (2nd ed.). New York: Longman, pp. 119–120.

7. Iannaccone, L. (1967). *Politics in education.* New York: Center for Applied Research in Education; also see Spring, J. (1993). *Conflicts of interests: The politics of American education* (2nd ed.). New York: Longman, pp. 121–122.

8. McGivney, J. H. (1984). State educational governance patterns. *Educational Administration Quarterly, 20*(2), 43–63; also see Spring, J. (1993). *Conflicts of interests: The politics of American education* (2nd ed.). New York: Longman, pp. 119–121.

9. For more detailed information on local politics and education, see Spring, J. (1993). *Conflicts of interests: The politics of American education* (2nd ed.). New York: Longman, pp. 145–175; and Spring, J. (1991). *American education: An introduction to social and political aspects* (5th ed.). New York: Longman, pp. 155–175.

10. McCarty, D., & Ramsey, C. (1971). *The school managers: Power and conflict in American public education.* Westport, CT: Greenwood; also see Spring, J. (1993). *Conflicts of interests: The politics of American education* (2nd ed.). New York: Longman, pp. 146–160.

11. Boyd, W. (1976). The public, the professionals, and educational policy making: Who governs? *Teachers College Record, 77*(4), 547–549; Zeigler, L. H., & Jennings, M. K. (1974). *Governing American schools: Political interaction in local school districts.* North Scituate, MA: Duxbury Press.

12. See Spring, J. (1993). *Conflicts of interests: The politics of American education* (2nd ed.). New York: Longman, pp. 165–170; Johnson, S. M. (1984). *Teachers' unions in the schools.* Philadelphia: Tem-

ple University Press; McDonnell, L., & Pascal, A. (1979). *Organized teachers in American schools.* Santa Monica, CA: RAND Corporation.

13. Also see Spring, J. (1993). *Conflicts of interests: The politics of American education* (2nd ed.). New York: Longman, pp. 95–118.

14. See Spring, J. (1991). *American education: An introduction to social and political aspects* (5th ed.). New York: Longman, pp. 109–122.

15. Zirkel, P. A., & Richardson, S. N. (1988). *A digest of Supreme Court decisions affecting education* (2nd ed.). Bloomington, IN: Phi Delta Kappa, pp. 89–90; Data Research. (1993). *U.S. Supreme Court education cases* (3rd ed.). Rosemount, MN: Data Research, Inc., pp. 4–5.

16. Zirkel, P. A., & Richardson, S. N. (1988). *A digest of Supreme Court decisions affecting education* (2nd ed.). Bloomington, IN: Phi Delta Kappa, p. 93; Data Research. (1993). *U.S. Supreme Court education cases* (3rd ed.). Rosemount, MN: Data Research, Inc., pp. 12–13.

17. Zirkel, P. A., & Richardson, S. N. (1988). *A digest of Supreme Court decisions affecting education* (2nd ed.). Bloomington, IN: Phi Delta Kappa, pp. 98–99; Data Research. (1993). *U.S. Supreme Court education cases* (3rd ed.). Rosemount, MN: Data Research, Inc., pp. 19–20.

18. Zirkel, P. A., & Richardson, S. N. (1988). *A digest of Supreme Court decisions affecting education* (2nd ed.). Bloomington, IN: Phi Delta Kappa, pp. 103, 109–110; Data Research. (1993). *U.S. Supreme Court education cases* (3rd ed.). Rosemount, MN: Data Research, Inc., pp. 32–35; Ornstein, A. C., & Levine, D. U. (1993). *Foundations of education* (5th ed.). Boston: Houghton Mifflin, p. 405; Johnson, J. A., Dupuis, V. L., Musial, D., & Hall, G. E. (1994). *Introduction to*

the foundations of American education (9th ed.). Boston: Allyn and Bacon, pp. 255–256.

19. Zirkel, P. A., & Richardson, S. N. (1988). *A digest of Supreme Court decisions affecting education* (2nd ed.). Bloomington, IN: Phi Delta Kappa, p. 103; Data Research. (1993). *U.S. Supreme Court education cases* (3rd ed.). Rosemount, MN: Data Research, Inc., pp. 34–35.

20. Zirkel, P. A., & Richardson, S. N. (1988). *A digest of Supreme Court decisions affecting education* (2nd ed.). Bloomington, IN: Phi Delta Kappa, p. 128; Data Research. (1993). *U.S. Supreme Court education cases* (3rd ed.). Rosemount, MN: Data Research, Inc., pp. 31–32; Johnson, J. A., Dupuis, V. L., Musial, D., & Hall, G. E. (1994). *Introduction to the foundations of American education* (9th ed.). Boston: Allyn and Bacon, pp. 256–257.

21. Data Research. (1994). *1994 deskbook encyclopedia of American school law*. Rosemount, MN: Data Research, Inc., pp. 378–379; Johnson, J. A., Dupuis, V. L., Musial, D., & Hall, G. E. (1994), *Introduction to the foundations of American education* (9th ed.). Boston: Allyn and Bacon, pp. 256–257.

22. See Chapter 7 of this text.

23. McCarthy, M. M. (1991). Severely disabled children: Who pays? *Phi Delta Kappan, 72*(1), 68–69; Data Research. (1993). *U.S. Supreme Court education cases* (3rd ed.). Rosemount, MN: Data Research, Inc., pp. 212–213.

24. McCarthy, M. M. (1991). Severely disabled children: Who pays? *Phi Delta Kappan, 72*(1), pp. 66–71.

25. Spring, J. (1993). *Conflicts of interests: The politics of American education* (2nd ed.). New York: Longman, pp. 207–209; Spring, J. (1991). *American education: An introduction to social and political aspects* (5th ed.). New York:

Longman, pp. 256–257; Data Research. (1993). *U.S. Supreme Court education cases* (3rd ed.). Rosemount, MN: Data Research, Inc., pp. 98–99.

26. Childs, R. A. (1990). *Legal issues in testing*. Washington, DC: American Institutes for Research; Spring, J. (1991). *American education: An introduction to social and political aspects* (5th ed.). New York: Longman, pp. 257–258.

27. Spring, J. (1991). *American education: An introduction to social and political aspects* (5th ed.). New York: Longman, pp. 233–234; Zirkel, P. A., & Richardson, S. N. (1988). *A digest of Supreme Court decisions affecting education* (2nd ed.). Bloomington, IN: Phi Delta Kappa, p. 17; Data Research. (1993). *U.S. Supreme Court education cases* (3rd ed.). Rosemount, MN: Data Research, Inc., pp. 42–44, 83–84.

28. Spring, J. (1991). *American education: An introduction to social and political aspects* (5th ed.). New York: Longman, p. 235; Zirkel, P. A., & Richardson, S. N. (1988). *A digest of Supreme Court decisions affecting education* (2nd ed.). Bloomington, IN: Phi Delta Kappa, p. 17; Data Research. (1993). *U.S. Supreme Court education cases* (3rd ed.). Rosemount, MN: Data Research, Inc., pp. 42–44, 83–84.

29. Ornstein, A. C., & Levine, D. U. (1993). *Foundations of education* (5th ed.). Boston: Houghton Mifflin, p. 305; Data Research. (1993). *U.S. Supreme Court education cases* (3rd ed.). Rosemount, MN: Data Research, Inc., pp. 44–45.

30. Spring, J. (1991). *American education: An introduction to social and political aspects* (5th ed.). New York: Longman, pp. 233–235.

31. Spring, J. (1991). *American education: An introduction to social and political aspects* (5th ed.). New York: Longman, pp. 235–236;

Keim, A. N. (Ed.). (1972). *Compulsory education and the Amish*. Boston: Beacon; Data Research. (1993). *U.S. Supreme Court education cases* (3rd ed.). Rosemount, MN: Data Research, Inc., p. 84.

32. Spring, J. (1991). *American education: An introduction to social and political aspects* (5th ed.). New York: Longman, p. 237; Data Research. (1993). *U.S. Supreme Court education cases* (3rd ed.). Rosemount, MN: Data Research, Inc., pp. 105–106; Zirkel, P. A., & Richardson, S. N. (1988). *A digest of Supreme Court decisions affecting education* (2nd ed.). Bloomington, IN: Phi Delta Kappa, p. 40.

33. Zirkel, P. A., & Richardson, S. N. (1988). *A digest of Supreme Court decisions affecting education* (2nd ed.). Bloomington, IN: Phi Delta Kappa, pp. 17–19; Data Research. (1993). *U.S. Supreme Court education cases* (3rd ed.). Rosemount, MN: Data Research, Inc., pp. 46–48.

34. Zirkel, P. A., & Richardson, S. N. (1988). *A digest of Supreme Court decisions affecting education* (2nd ed.). Bloomington, IN: Phi Delta Kappa, p. 19; Data Research. (1993). *U.S. Supreme Court education cases* (3rd ed.). Rosemount, MN: Data Research, Inc., p. 48.

35. Data Research. (1993). *U.S. Supreme Court education cases* (3rd ed.). Rosemount, MN: Data Research, Inc., pp. 45–46; Spring, J. (1991). *American education: An introduction to social and political aspects* (5th ed.). New York: Longman, p. 240.

36. Johnson, J. A., Dupuis, V. L., Musial, D., & Hall, G. E. (1994). *Introduction to the foundations of American education* (9th ed.). Boston: Allyn and Bacon, p. 245; Zirkel, P. A., & Richardson, S. N. (1988). *A digest of Supreme Court decisions affecting education* (2nd ed.). Bloomington, IN: Phi

Delta Kappa, pp. 22–24; Data Research. (1993). *U.S. Supreme Court education cases* (3rd ed.). Rosemount, MN: Data Research, Inc., pp. 52–53.

37. Spring, J. (1991). *American education: An introduction to social and political aspects* (5th ed.). New York: Longman, pp. 240–241; Zirkel, P. A., & Richardson, S. N. (1988). *A digest of Supreme Court decisions affecting education* (2nd ed.). Bloomington, IN: Phi Delta Kappa, p. 18; Data Research. (1993). *U.S. Supreme Court education cases* (3rd ed.). Rosemount, MN: Data Research, Inc., pp. 46–47.

38. Connors, E. T. (1988). *Religion and the schools: Significant court decisions in the 1980s.* Bloomington, IN: Phi Delta Kappa.

39. Huefner, S. (1991). The establishment clause as antiremedy. *Phi Delta Kappan, 73*(1), 72–77.

40. Spring, J. (1991). *American education: An introduction to social and political aspects* (5th ed.). New York: Longman, pp. 240–241; Zirkel, P. A., & Richardson, S. N. (1988). *A digest of Supreme Court decisions affecting education* (2nd ed.). Bloomington, IN: Phi Delta Kappa, p. 33.

41. Walsh, M. (1992). Court curbs schools from providing Chapter 1 aid on church grounds. *Education Week, 11*(16), 8.

42. Zirkel, P. A., & Richardson, S. N. (1988). *A digest of Supreme Court decisions affecting education* (2nd ed.). Bloomington, IN: Phi Delta Kappa, p. 36; Walsh, M. (1991). Court upholds rule on Chapter 1 aid to religious schools. *Education Week, 10*(37), 5.

43. Walsh, M. (1994). Church-state controversy rattles Hasidic enclave. *Education Week, 13*(26), I, 10–11; Walsh, M. (1994, May–June). Testing the boundaries. *Teacher Magazine,* pp. 6–7.

44. Spring, J. (1991). *American education: An introduction to social and political aspects* (5th ed.). New York: Longman, pp. 237–238; Zirkel, P. A., & Richardson, S. N. (1988). *A digest of Supreme Court decisions affecting education* (2nd ed.). Bloomington, IN: Phi Delta Kappa, p. 20; Data Research. (1993). *U.S. Supreme Court education cases* (3rd ed.). Rosemount, MN: Data Research, Inc., pp. 91–92.

45. Spring, J. (1991). *American education: An introduction to social and political aspects* (5th ed.). New York: Longman, pp. 238–239; Zirkel, P. A., & Richardson, S. N. (1988). *A digest of Supreme Court decisions affecting education* (2nd ed.). Bloomington, IN: Phi Delta Kappa, p. 20; Data Research. (1993). *U.S. Supreme Court education cases* (3rd ed.). Rosemount, MN: Data Research, Inc., pp. 92–93.

46. Data Research. (1993). *U.S. Supreme Court education cases* (3rd ed.). Rosemount, MN: Data Research, Inc., p. 95; Zirkel, P. A., & Richardson, S. N. (1988). *A digest of Supreme Court decisions affecting education* (2nd ed.). Bloomington, IN: Phi Delta Kappa, p. 34.

47. Rossow, L. F., & Hininger, J. A. (1991). *Students and the law.* Bloomington, IN: Phi Delta Kappa, pp. 25–27; Data Research. (1993). *U.S. Supreme Court education cases* (3rd ed.). Rosemount, MN: Data Research, Inc., pp. 116–117; Walsh, M. (1990). Efforts of decision on extracurriculars raise thorny issues. *Education Week, 9*(39), pp. 1, 12.

48. Data Research. (1993). *U.S. Supreme Court education cases* (3rd ed.). Rosemount, MN: Data Research, Inc., pp. 97–98; Ornstein, A. C., & Levine, D. U. (1993). *Foundations of education* (5th ed.). Boston: Houghton Mifflin, p. 301.

49. Data Research. (1993). *U.S.*

Supreme Court education cases (3rd ed.). Rosemount, MN: Data Research, Inc., pp. 97–98; Ornstein, A. C., & Levine, D. U. (1993). *Foundations of education* (5th ed.). Boston: Houghton Mifflin, p. 301.

50. Data Research. (1993). *U.S. Supreme Court education cases* (3rd ed.). Rosemount, MN: Data Research, Inc., pp. 93–94; Zirkel, P. A., & Richardson, S. N. (1988). *A digest of Supreme Court decisions affecting education* (2nd ed.). Bloomington, IN: Phi Delta Kappa, p. 32.

51. Ornstein, A. C., & Levine, D. U. (1993). *Foundations of education* (5th ed.). Boston: Houghton Mifflin, p. 301; McGough, M. (1990). Menorah wars. *The New Republic, 202*(6), 12–43.

52. Verhovek, S. H. (1990, August 30). School ordered to remove crucifixion mural. *New York Times,* p. B12.

53. Spring, J. (1991). *American education: An introduction to social and political aspects* (5th ed.). New York: Longman, pp. 240–244.

54. Spring, J. (1993). *Conflicts of interests: The politics of American education* (2nd ed.). New York: Longman, pp. 199–202.

55. Zirkel, P. A., & Richardson, S. N. (1988). *A digest of Supreme Court decisions affecting education* (2nd ed.). Bloomington, IN: Phi Delta Kappa, p. 36; Data Research. (1993). *U.S. Supreme Court education cases* (3rd ed.). Rosemount, MN: Data Research, Inc., pp. 95–96.

56. Zirkel, P. A., & Richardson, S. N. (1988). *A digest of Supreme Court decisions affecting education* (2nd ed.). Bloomington, IN: Phi Delta Kappa, p. 47; Data Research. (1993). *U.S. Supreme Court education cases* (3rd ed.). Rosemount, MN: Data Research, Inc., pp. 87–88.

57. Rossow, L. F., & Hininger, J. A. (1991). *Students and the law.*

Bloomington, IN: Phi Delta Kappa, pp. 8–9; Data Research. (1993). *U.S. Supreme Court education cases* (3rd ed.). Rosemount, MN: Data Research, Inc., p. 107; Zirkel, P. A., & Richardson, S. N. (1988). *A digest of Supreme Court decisions affecting education* (2nd ed.). Bloomington, IN: Phi Delta Kappa, p. 41.

58. Data Research. (1993). *U.S. Supreme Court education cases* (3rd ed.). Rosemount, MN: Data Research, Inc., p. 107; Zirkel, P. A., & Richardson, S. N. (1988). *A digest of Supreme Court decisions affecting education* (2nd ed.). Bloomington, IN: Phi Delta Kappa, p. 41.

59. Rossow, L. F., & Hininger, J. A. (1991). *Students and the law.* Bloomington, IN: Phi Delta Kappa, p. 9; Data Research. (1993). *U.S. Supreme Court education cases* (3rd ed.). Rosemount, MN: Data Research, Inc., pp. 112–113; Spring, J. (1991). *American education: An introduction to social and political aspects* (5th ed.). New York: Longman, pp. 250–251; Zirkel, P. A., & Richardson, S. N. (1988). *A digest of Supreme Court decisions affecting education* (2nd ed.). Bloomington, IN: Phi Delta Kappa, p. 50.

60. Fischer, L., Schimmel, D., & Kelly, C. (1991). *Teachers and the law* (3rd ed.). New York: Longman, pp. 121–123.

61. Rossow, L. F., & Hininger, J. A. (1991). *Students and the law.* Bloomington, IN: Phi Delta Kappa, pp. 11–13; Zirkel, P. A., & Richardson, S. N. (1988). *A digest of Supreme Court decisions affecting education* (2nd ed.). Bloomington, IN: Phi Delta Kappa, p. 51; Data Research. (1993). *U.S. Supreme Court education cases* (3rd ed.). Rosemount, MN: Data Research, Inc., pp. 114–115; Spring, J. (1991). *American education: An introduction to social and political aspects* (5th ed.).

62. Spring, J. (1991). *American education: An introduction to social and political aspects* (5th ed.). New York: Longman, pp. 251–252; Zirkel, P. A., & Richardson, S. N. (1988). *A digest of Supreme Court decisions affecting education* (2nd ed.). Bloomington, IN: Phi Delta Kappa, p. 47; Data Research. (1993). *U.S. Supreme Court education cases* (3rd ed.). Rosemount, MN: Data Research, Inc., pp. 111–113.

63. Rossow, L. F., & Hininger, J. A. (1991). *Students and the law.* Bloomington, IN: Phi Delta Kappa, pp. 15–20; Zirkel, P. A., & Richardson, S. N. (1988). *A digest of Supreme Court decisions affecting education* (2nd ed.). Bloomington, IN: Phi Delta Kappa, pp. 49–50; Data Research. (1993). *U.S. Supreme Court education cases* (3rd ed.). Rosemount, MN: Data Research, Inc., pp. 125–126.

64. See Ornstein, A. C., & Levine, D. U. (1993). *Foundations of education* (5th ed.). Boston: Houghton Mifflin, pp. 292–293.

65. Rossow, L. F., & Hininger, J. A. (1991). *Students and the law.* Bloomington, IN: Phi Delta Kappa, pp. 21–24.

66. Rossow, L. F., & Hininger, J. A. (1991). *Students and the law.* Bloomington, IN: Phi Delta Kappa, pp. 22–24; Data Research. (1994). *1994 deskbook encyclopedia of American school law.* Rosemount, MN: Data Research, Inc., pp. 168, 480–481.

67. Rossow, L. F., & Hininger, J. A. (1991). *Students and the law.* Bloomington, IN: Phi Delta Kappa, pp. 34–35; Zirkel, P. A., & Richardson, S. N. (1988). *A digest of Supreme Court decisions affecting education* (2nd ed.). Bloomington, IN: Phi Delta Kappa, p. 43; Data Research. (1993). *U.S. Supreme Court education cases*

New York: Longman, pp. 251–252.

(3rd ed.). Rosemount, MN: Data Research, Inc., pp. 119–120.

68. Data Research. (1993). *U.S. Supreme Court education cases* (3rd ed.). Rosemount, MN: Data Research, Inc., pp. 120–121; Zirkel, P. A., & Richardson, S. N. (1988). *A digest of Supreme Court decisions affecting education* (2nd ed.). Bloomington, IN: Phi Delta Kappa, p. 140.

69. Data Research. (1993). *U.S. Supreme Court education cases* (3rd ed.). Rosemount, MN: Data Research, Inc., pp. 127–128.

70. Data Research. (1993). *U.S. Supreme Court education cases* (3rd ed.). Rosemount, MN: Data Research, Inc., pp. 121–122; Zirkel, P. A., & Richardson, S. N. (1988). *A digest of Supreme Court decisions affecting education* (2nd ed.). Bloomington, IN: Phi Delta Kappa, p. 45; Ornstein, A. C., & Levine, D. U. (1993). *Foundations of education* (5th ed.). Boston: Houghton Mifflin, pp. 294–295.

71. Spring, J. (1991). *American education: An introduction to social and political aspects* (5th ed.). New York: Longman, p. 246.

72. Newman, J. W. (1994). *America's teachers: An introduction to education* (2nd ed.). New York: Longman, pp. 119–120.

73. Fischer, L., Schimmel, D., & Kelly, C. (1991). *Teachers and the law* (3rd ed.). New York: Longman, pp. 3–15; Newman, J. W. (1994). *America's teachers: An introduction to education* (2nd ed.). New York: Longman, pp. 120–124.

74. Zirkel, P. A., & Richardson, S. N. (1988). *A digest of Supreme Court decisions affecting education* (2nd ed.). Bloomington, IN: Phi Delta Kappa, p. 55; Data Research. (1993). *U.S. Supreme Court education cases* (3rd ed.). Rosemount, MN: Data Research, Inc., pp. 145–146.

75. Spring, J. (1991). *American educa-*

tion: An introduction to social and political aspects (5th ed.). New York: Longman, pp. 246–247; Zirkel, P. A., & Richardson, S. N. (1988). *A digest of Supreme Court decisions affecting education* (2nd ed.). Bloomington, IN: Phi Delta Kappa, p. 64; Data Research. (1993). *U.S. Supreme Court education cases* (3rd ed.). Rosemount, MN: Data Research, Inc., pp. 146–147.

76. Zirkel, P. A., & Richardson, S. N. (1988). *A digest of Supreme Court decisions affecting education* (2nd ed.). Bloomington, IN: Phi Delta Kappa, pp. 72–76; Data Research. (1993). *U.S. Supreme Court education cases* (3rd ed.). Rosemount, MN: Data Research, Inc., pp. 150–151, 154–155, 167–168.

77. Zirkel, P. A., & Richardson, S. N. (1988). *A digest of Supreme Court decisions affecting education* (2nd ed.). Bloomington, IN: Phi Delta Kappa, p. 78; Newman, J. W. (1994). *America's teachers: An introduction to education* (2nd ed.). New York: Longman, pp. 132–133; Fischer, L., Schimmel, D., & Kelly, C. (1991). *Teachers and the law* (3rd ed.). New York: Longman, p. 127.

78. Zirkel, P. A., & Richardson, S. N. (1988). *A digest of Supreme Court decisions affecting education* (2nd ed.). Bloomington, IN: Phi Delta Kappa, pp. 70–71, 76–77; Data Research. (1993). *U.S. Supreme Court education cases* (3rd ed.). Rosemount, MN: Data Research, Inc., pp. 155–156, 164–165.

79. Zirkel, P. A., & Richardson, S. N. (1988). *A digest of Supreme Court decisions affecting education* (2nd ed.). Bloomington, IN: Phi Delta Kappa, p. 77; Data Research. (1993). *U.S. Supreme Court education cases* (3rd ed.). Rosemount, MN: Data Research, Inc., pp. 156–157.

80. Data Research. (1994). *1994 deskbook encyclopedia of American school law*. Rosemount, MN: Data Research, Inc., pp. 294–295, 360–361; Data Research. (1993). *U.S. Supreme Court education cases* (3rd ed.). Rosemount, MN: Data Research, Inc., pp. 149–150, 152–153, 158–159; Zirkel, P. A., & Richardson, S. N. (1988). *A digest of Supreme Court decisions affecting education* (2nd ed.). Bloomington, IN: Phi Delta Kappa, p. 105.

81. Newman, J. W. (1994). *America's teachers: An introduction to education* (2nd ed.). New York: Longman, p. 123; Data Research. (1993). *U.S. Supreme Court education cases* (3rd ed.). Rosemount, MN: Data Research, Inc., pp. 159–160; Zirkel, P. A., & Richardson, S. N. (1988). *A digest of Supreme Court decisions affecting education* (2nd ed.). Bloomington, IN: Phi Delta Kappa, p. 81; Fischer, L., Schimmel, D., & Kelly, C. (1991). *Teachers and the law* (3rd ed.). New York: Longman, pp. 24–26, 212.

82. Zirkel, P. A., & Richardson, S. N. (1988). *A digest of Supreme Court decisions affecting education* (2nd ed.). Bloomington, IN: Phi Delta Kappa, pp. 67–68; Data Research. (1993). *U.S. Supreme Court education cases* (3rd ed.). Rosemount, MN: Data Research, Inc., pp. 147–149.

83. Zirkel, P. A., & Richardson, S. N. (1988). *A digest of Supreme Court decisions affecting education* (2nd ed.). Bloomington, IN: Phi Delta Kappa, pp. 65–66; Data Research. (1993). *U.S. Supreme Court education cases* (3rd ed.). Rosemount, MN: Data Research, Inc., pp. 143–144.

84. Spring, J. (1991). *American education: An introduction to social and political aspects* (5th ed.). New York: Longman, pp. 240–244; Fischer, L., Schimmel, D., & Kelly, C. (1991). *Teachers and the law* (3rd ed.). New York: Longman, p. 350.

85. Fischer, L., Schimmel, D., & Kelly, C. (1991). *Teachers and the law* (3rd ed.). New York: Longman, p. 137; Ornstein, A. C., & Levine, D. U. (1993). *Foundations of education* (5th ed.). Boston: Houghton Mifflin, p. 279.

86. Newman, J. W. (1994). *America's teachers: An introduction to education* (2nd ed.). New York: Longman, p. 130.

87. Ornstein, A. C., & Levine, D. U. (1993). *Foundations of education* (5th ed.). Boston: Houghton Mifflin, pp. 279–280.

88. Spring, J. (1991). *American education: An introduction to social and political aspects* (5th ed.). New York: Longman, pp. 251–252; Zirkel, P. A., & Richardson, S. N. (1988). *A digest of Supreme Court decisions affecting education* (2nd ed.). Bloomington, IN: Phi Delta Kappa, p. 47; Data Research. (1993). *U.S. Supreme Court education cases* (3rd ed.). Rosemount, MN: Data Research, Inc., pp. 111–113.

89. Fischer, L., Schimmel, D., & Kelly, C. (1991). *Teachers and the law* (3rd ed.). New York: Longman, pp. 138–140.

90. Spring, J. (1991). *American education: An introduction to social and political aspects* (5th ed.). New York: Longman, p. 249; Zirkel, P. A., & Richardson, S. N. (1988). *A digest of Supreme Court decisions affecting education* (2nd ed.). Bloomington, IN: Phi Delta Kappa, pp. 56–57; Data Research. (1993). *U.S. Supreme Court education cases* (3rd ed.). Rosemount, MN: Data Research, Inc., pp. 132–133.

91. Zirkel, P. A., & Richardson, S. N. (1988). *A digest of Supreme Court decisions affecting education* (2nd ed.). Bloomington, IN: Phi Delta Kappa, p. 59; Data Research. (1993). *U.S. Supreme Court education cases* (3rd ed.). Rosemount, MN: Data Research, Inc., pp. 136–137.

92. Zirkel, P. A., & Richardson, S. N.

(1988). *A digest of Supreme Court decisions affecting education* (2nd ed.). Bloomington, IN: Phi Delta Kappa, p. 60; Data Research. (1993). *U.S. Supreme Court education cases* (3rd ed.). Rosemount, MN: Data Research, Inc., pp. 138–139.

93. Spring, J. (1991). *American education: An introduction to social and political aspects* (5th ed.). New York: Longman, pp. 249–250; Zirkel, P. A., & Richardson, S. N. (1988). *A digest of Supreme Court decisions affecting education* (2nd ed.). Bloomington, IN: Phi Delta Kappa, p. 63; Data Research. (1993). *U.S. Supreme Court education cases* (3rd ed.). Rosemount, MN: Data Research, Inc., pp. 141–142.

94. Zirkel, P. A., & Richardson, S. N. (1988). *A digest of Supreme Court decisions affecting education* (2nd ed.). Bloomington, IN: Phi Delta Kappa, p. 66; Data Research. (1993). *U.S. Supreme Court education cases* (3rd ed.). Rosemount, MN: Data Research, Inc., pp. 144–145.

95. Spring, J. (1991). *American education: An introduction to social and political aspects* (5th ed.). New York: Longman, p. 250.

96. Fischer, L., Schimmel, D., & Kelly, C. (1991). *Teachers and the law* (3rd ed.). New York: Longman, pp. 235–237.

97. Ornstein, A. C., & Levine, D. U. (1993). *Foundations of education* (5th ed.). Boston: Houghton Mifflin, pp. 245–247; Johnson, J. A., Dupuis, V. L., Musial, D., & Hall, G. E. (1994). *Introduction to the foundations of American education* (9th ed.). Boston: Allyn and Bacon, pp. 219–220.

98. Zirkel, P. A., & Richardson, S. N. (1988). *A digest of Supreme Court decisions affecting education* (2nd ed.). Bloomington, IN: Phi Delta Kappa, pp. 10–11; Data Research. (1993). *U.S. Supreme Court education cases* (3rd ed.).

Rosemount, MN: Data Research, Inc., p. 197.

99. Ornstein, A. C., & Levine, D. U. (1993). *Foundations of education* (5th ed.). Boston: Houghton Mifflin, pp. 246–247; Johnson, J. A., Dupuis, V. L., Musial, D., & Hall, G. E. (1994). *Introduction to the foundations of American education* (9th ed.). Boston: Allyn and Bacon, p. 220.

100. Ornstein, A. C., & Levine, D. U. (1993). *Foundations of education* (5th ed.). Boston: Houghton Mifflin, pp. 246–248; Johnson, J. A., Dupuis, V. L., Musial, D., & Hall, G. E. (1994). *Introduction to the foundations of American education* (9th ed.). Boston: Allyn and Bacon, pp. 220–221.

101. Ornstein, A. C., & Levine, D. U. (1993). *Foundations of education* (5th ed.). Boston: Houghton Mifflin, p. 248.

102. National Conference of State Legislatures. (1991). *Recent changes in state, local, and state-local tax levels.* Denver: National Conference of State Legislatures. For additional information about state financing of schools, see Ornstein, A. C., & Levine, D. U. (1993). *Foundations of education* (5th ed.). Boston: Houghton Mifflin, pp. 238–250; Ornstein, A. C. (1988). State financing of public schools: Policies and prospects, *Urban Education, 23*(2), pp. 188–207.

103. National Conference of State Legislatures. (1991). *Recent changes in state, local, and state-local tax levels.* Denver: National Conference of State Legislatures.

104. Ornstein, A. C., & Levine, D. U. (1993). *Foundations of education* (5th ed.). Boston: Houghton Mifflin, p. 236.

105. Snyder, T. D., & Hoffman, C. M. (1993). *Digest of educational statistics 1993.* Washington, D.C.: National Center for Education Statistics, p. 151.

106. For additional information about state financing of schools, see Ornstein, A. C., & Levine, D. U. (1993). *Foundations of education* (5th ed.). Boston: Houghton Mifflin, pp. 250–254.

107. Ornstein, A. C., & Levine, D. U. (1993). *Foundations of education* (5th ed.). Boston: Houghton Mifflin, pp. 254–256.

108. Bradley, A. (1993). Consortium drafts model standards for new teachers. *Education Week, 12*(20), 1, 14; Edelfelt, R., & Raths, J. (1992). National teacher certification: A quality guarantee? *Education Week, 11*(35), 26; Viadero, D. (1990). 4 midwest states create regional teaching credential. *Education Week, 9*(37), 5; Diegmueller, K. (1990). S.R.E.B. proposes reciprocal teacher certification. *Education Week, 10*(1), 10; also see Haselkorn, D., & Calkins, A. (1993). *Careers in teaching handbook.* Belmont, MA: Recruiting New Teachers.

109. Wise, A. E. (1994). Professionalization and standards: A unified system of quality assurance. *Education Week, 13*(36), 48; Wise, A. E., & Leibbrand, J. (1993). Accreditation and the creation of a profession of teaching. *Phi Delta Kappan, 75*(2), 133–136, 154–157; Diegmueller, K. (1993). NCATE analysis of education schools to help forge partnerships with states. *Education Week, 12*(26), 27; Bradley, A. (1993). Consortium drafts model standards for new teachers. *Education Week, 12*(20), 1, 14.

110. Fischer, L., Schimmel, D., & Kelly, C. (1991). *Teachers and the law* (3rd ed.). New York: Longman, pp. 224–230; Rossow, L. F., & Hininger, J. A. (1991). *Students and the law.* Bloomington, IN: Phi Delta Kappa, pp. 16–20, 22–24.

111. For more information on tenure laws and tenure rights, see

Fischer, L., Schimmel, D., & Kelly, C. (1991). *Teachers and the law* (3rd ed.). New York: Longman, pp. 21–35; Spring, J. (1991). *American education: An introduction to social and political aspects* (5th ed.). New York: Longman, pp. 245–250.

112. See Zirkel, P. A., & Gluckman, I. B. (1991). Educational malpractice. *Principal, 71*(1), pp. 61–62; Zirkel, P. A., & Gluckman, I. B. (1991). A legal brief: Educational Malpractice. *NASSP Bulletin 75*(537), pp. 110–114. Ornstein, A. C., & Levine, D. U. (1993). *Foundations of education* (5th ed.). Boston: Houghton Mifflin, pp. 284–285; Johnson, J. A., Dupuis, V. L., Musial, D., & Hall, G. E. (1994). *Introduction to the foundations of American education* (9th ed.). Boston: Allyn and Bacon, p. 283.

113. For more information on teacher responsibilities in dealing with child abuse, see Fischer, L., Schimmel, D., & Kelly, C. (1991). *Teachers and the law* (3rd ed.). New York: Longman, pp. 76–86.

114. Fischer, L., Schimmel, D., & Kelly, C. (1991). *Teachers and the law* (3rd ed.). New York: Longman, pp. 103–118, especially p. 110.

115. See for example, Spring, J. (1991). *American education: An introduction to social and political aspects* (5th ed.). New York: Longman, pp. 64–83; Berube, M. (1988). *Teacher politics: The influence of unions.* Westport, CT: Greenwood Press; Spring, J. (1993). *Conflicts of interests: The politics of American education* (2nd ed.). New York: Longman, pp. 129–131, 165–170; Newman, J. W. (1994). *America's teachers: An introduction to education.* New York: Longman, pp. 89–117.

116. See, for example, the standards of the National Council of Teachers of Mathematics, which are published as two documents, *Curriculum and evaluation standards for school mathematics* (1989) and *Professional standards for teaching mathematics* (1991). Reston, VA: National Council of Teachers of Mathematics.

117. Wise, A. E. (1994). Professionalization and standards: A unified system of quality assurance. *Education Week, 13*(36), 48, 37; Wise, A. E., & Leibbrand, J. (1993). Accreditation and the creation of a profession of teaching. *Phi Delta Kappan, 75*(2), 133–136, 154–157; National Board of Professional Teaching Standards. (1990). *Toward high and rigorous standards for the teaching profession.* Washington, D.C.: National Board of Professional Teaching Standards; Porter, J. W. (1990). A call for national certification of teachers. *NASSP Bulletin, 74*(528), pp. 64–70.

118. For additional information about multicultural and multiethnic education in general as well as about specific efforts by special interests groups to influence the curriculum, see Banks, J. A. (1994). *An introduction to multicultural education* (3rd ed.). Boston: Allyn and Bacon; Banks, J. A. (1994). *Multiethnic education: Theory and practice.* Boston: Allyn and Bacon; Bullard, S. (1992). Sorting through the multicultural rhetoric. *Educational Leadership, 49*(5), pp. 8–11; Scherer, M. (1992). School snapshot: Focus on African-American culture. *Educational Leadership, 49*(5), pp. 17, 19; Gollnick, W. A. (1990). The reappearance of the vanishing American. *The College Board Review, 155*(6), pp. 30–36; Spring, J. (1993). *Conflicts of interests: The politics of American education* (2nd ed.). New York: Longman, pp. 35–43, 96–101.

119. For more information about school tax policy and public reaction, see Augenblick, J. (1991). *School finance: A primer.* Denver: Education Commission of the States; U.S. Advisory Commission on Intergovernmental Relations. (1991). *Changing public attitudes on government and taxes.* Washington, D.C.: Government Printing Office; Odden, A. R. (Ed.). (1992). *Rethinking school finance: An agenda for the 1990s.* San Francisco: Jossey-Bass; Swanson, A. D., & King, R. A. (1991). *School finance: Its economics and politics.* New York: Longman.

120. For discussions of these activities, see McNeil, J. (1988). An overview: Curriculum politics: Local, state and federal. *NAASP Bulletin, 72*(509), pp. 60–69; Apple, M. W. (1991). Conservative agendas and progressive possibilities: Understanding the wider politics of curriculum and teaching. *Education and Urban Society, 23*(3), pp. 279–291; Ornstein, A. C. (1992). The censored curriculum: The problem with textbooks today. *NASSP Bulletin, 76*(547), pp. 1–9; Apple, M. W. (1990). Is there a curriculum voice to reclaim? *Phi Delta Kappan, 71*(7), pp. 526–530.

121. Hanushek, E. A. (1981). Throwing money at schools. *Journal of Policy Analysis and Management, 1,* 19–41; Hanushek, E. A. (1986). The economics of schooling. *Journal of Economic Literature, 24,* 1141–1177; Hanushek, E. A. (1989). The impact of differential expenditures on school performance. *Educational Researcher, 18*(4), 45–65; Hanushek, E. A. (1991). When school finance

122. Hedges, L. V., Laine, R. D., & Greenwald, R. (1994). Does money matter? A meta-analysis of studies of the effect of differential school inputs on student outcomes. *Educational Researcher, 23*(3), 5–14; Harp, L. (1994). Analysis links achievement and spending. *Education Week, 13*(26), 1, 12.

123. Hanushek, E. A. (1981). Throwing money at schools. *Journal of Policy Analysis and Management, 1*, 19–41; Hanushek, E. A. (1986). The economics of schooling. *Journal of Economic Literature, 24*, 1141–1177; Hanushek, E. A. (1989). The impact of differential expenditures on school performance. *Educational Researcher, 18*(4), 45–65; Hanushek, E. A. (1991). When school finance "reform" may not be a good policy. *Harvard Journal on Legislation, 28*, 423–456.

124. Hanushek, E. A. (1989). The impact of differential expenditures on school performance. *Educational Researcher, 18*(4), 47.

125. Hedges, L. V., Laine, R. D., & Greenwald, R. (1994). Does money matter? A meta-analysis of studies of the effect of differential school inputs on student outcomes. *Educational Researcher, 23*(3), 13.

Chapter 10

1. All three descriptions of teachers in this Snapshot are hypothetical, but the actions, characteristics, and philosophical positions presented are drawn from teachers whom the authors of this text have known.

2. See Simpson, D. J., & Jackson, M. J. B. (1984). *The teacher as philosopher: A primer in philosophy of education.* Toronto: Methuen; Soltis, J. F. (1978). *An introduction to the analysis of educational concepts* (2nd ed.). Reading, MA: Addison-Wesley.

3. For more information on the activity of clarifying, see Barrow, R., & Woods, R. (1988). *An introduction to philosophy of education* (3rd ed.). London: Routledge; Chambers, J. H. (1989). *The achievement of education: An examination of key concepts in educational practice.* Lanham, MD: University Press of America.

4. For more information on the activity of justification, see Fitzgibbons, R. E. (1981). *Making educational decisions: An introduction to philosophy of education.* New York: Harcourt Brace Jovanovich; Simpson, D. J., & Jackson, M. J. B. (1984). *The teacher as philosopher: A primer in philosophy of education.* Toronto: Methuen.

5. Sockett, H. (1993). *The moral base of teacher professionalism.* New York: Teachers College Press.

6. For more discussion of interpretation and systemization, see Power, E. J. (1982). *Philosophy of education: Studies in philosophies, schooling and educational policies.* Englewood Cliffs, NJ: Prentice-Hall; Simpson, D. J., & Jackson, M. J. B. (1984). *The teacher as philosopher: A primer in philosophy of education.* Toronto: Methuen.

7. For more detailed analyses of these philosophies of education, see Griese, A. A. (1981). *Your philosophy of education: What is it?* Santa Monica, CA: Goodyear; O'Neill, W. F. (1990). *Educational ideologies: Contemporary expressions of educational philosophy.* Dubuque, IA: Kendall/Hunt.

8. Butler, J. D. (1968). *Four philosophies and their practice in education and religion* (3rd ed.). New York: Harper and Row; Brightman, E. S., & Beck, R. N. (1963). *An introduction to philosophy* (3rd ed.). New York: Holt, Rinehart and Winston; Knight, G. R. (1990). *Issues and alternatives in educational philosophy.* Berrien Springs, MI: Andrews University Press.

9. Martin, W. O. (1969). *Realism in education.* New York: Harper and Row; Broudy, H. S. (1961). *Building a philosophy of education.* Englewood Cliffs, NJ: Prentice-Hall; Maritain, J. (1938). *True humanism.* New York: Charles Scribner's Sons.

10. See O'Neill, W. F. (1990). *Educational ideologies: Contemporary expressions of educational philosophy.* Dubuque, IA: Kendall/Hunt; Dewey, J. (1933). *How we think.* Boston: D. C. Heath; James, W. (1946). *Talk to teachers.* New York: Holt, Rinehart and Winston.

11. For more information on progressivism, see Knight, G. R. (1990). *Issues and alternatives in educational philosophy.* Berrien Springs, MI: Andrews University Press; Kilpatrick, W. H. (1951). *Philosophy of education.* New York: Macmillan; Graham, P. A. (1967). *Progressive education: From Arcady to academe.* New York: Teachers College Press.

12. See Knight, G. R. (1990). *Issues and alternatives in educational philosophy.* Berrien Springs, MI: Andrews University Press; Holt, J. (1967). *How children learn.* New York: Pitman; Neill, A. S. (1960). *Summerhill: A radical approach to child rearing.* New York: Hart; Rogers, C. (1983). *Freedom to learn* (rev. ed.). Columbus, OH: Charles E. Merrill.

13. See Power, E. J. (1982). *Philosophy of education: Studies in philosophies, schooling and educational policies.* Englewood Cliffs, NJ: Prentice-Hall; Vandenberg, D. (1971). *Being and education: An essay in existential phenomenology.* Englewood Cliffs, NJ: Prentice-Hall; Greene, M. (1973). *Teacher*

as stranger. Belmont, CA: Wadsworth.

14. Knight, G. R. (1990). *Issues and alternatives in educational philosophy* (2nd ed.). Berrien Springs, MI: Andrews University Press; Brameld, T. (1965). *Toward a reconstructed philosophy of education.* New York: Dryden Press; Counts, G. S. (1946). *Education and the promise of America.* New York: Macmillan; Stanley, W. O. (1952). *Education and social integration.* New York: Teachers College Press.

15. Stanley, W. (1992). *Curriculum for utopia: Social reconstruction and critical pedagogy in postmodern era.* Albany: State University of New York Press.

16. See Knight, G. R. (1990). *Issues and alternatives in educational philosophy.* Berrien Springs, MI: Andrews University Press; Shane, H. (1973). *The educational significance of the future.* Bloomington, IN: Phi Delta Kappa; Toffler, A. (1980). *The third wave.* New York: William Morrow.

17. See Bigge, M. L. (1982). *Educational philosophies for teachers.* Columbus, OH: Charles E. Merrill; Skinner, B. F. (1968). *The technology of teaching.* Englewood Cliffs, NJ: Prentice-Hall; Watson, J. B. (1924). *Behaviorism.* New York: W. W. Norton.

18. See Knight, G. R. (1990). *Issues and alternatives in educational philosophy.* Berrien Springs, MI: Andrews University Press; Adler, J. A. (1982). *The paideia proposal: An educational manifesto.* New York: Macmillan; Hutchins, R. M. (1968). *The learning society.* New York: Praeger.

19. See Power, E. J. (1982). *Philosophy of education: Studies in philosophies, schooling and educational policies.* Englewood Cliffs, NJ: Prentice-Hall; Bestor, A. E. (1955). *The restoration of learning.* New York: Knopf; Rickover, H. G. (1962). *Swiss schools and ours: Why theirs are better.* Boston: Atlantic Monthly Press.

20. See Peterson, M. L. (1986). *Philosophy of education: Issues and options.* Downers Grove, IL: InterVarsity Press; Gaebelein, F. F. (1968). *The pattern of God's truth.* Chicago: Moody Press; Lewis, C. S. (1969). *The best of C. S. Lewis.* Washington, DC: Christianity Today.

21. Ozmon, H. A., & Craver, S. M. (1990). *Philosophical foundations of education* (4th ed.). Columbus, OH: Charles E. Merrill; Bowles, S., & Gintis, H. (1976). *Schooling in capitalist America: Educational reform and the contradictions of economic life.* New York: Basic Books; Apple, M. W. (1990). *Ideology and curriculum* (2nd ed.). New York: Routledge.

22. See Apple, M. (1993). *Official knowledge: Democratic education in a conservative age.* New York: Routledge, Chapman and Hall; Freire, P. (1973). *Pedagogy of the oppressed* (M. B. Ramos, trans.). New York: Seabury Press; Giroux, H. A. (1988). *Teachers as intellectuals: Toward a critical pedagogy of learning.* Granby, MA: Bergin and Garvey; Habermas, J. (1974). *Theory and practice.* London: Heinemann; Kincheloe, J. (1993). *Toward critical politics of teacher thinking: Mapping the postmodern.* Westport, CT: Bergin and Garvey; McLaren, P. (1993). *Schooling as a ritual performance: Towards a political economy of educational symbols and gestures* (2nd ed.). London: Routledge and Kegan Paul.

Chapter 11

1. Peddiwell, J. A. [Benjamin, H.]. (1939). *The saber-tooth curriculum.* New York: McGraw-Hill.

2. For more discussion of selecting content, see Taba, H. (1962). *Curriculum development: Theory and practice.* New York: Harcourt Brace and World, pp. 1–87, 194–228; Bruner, J. S. (1960). *The process of education.* Cambridge, MA: Harvard University Press; Tyler, R. W. (1949). *Basic principles of curriculum and instruction.* Chicago: University of Chicago Press; Klausmeier, H. J., & Harris, C. W. (1966). *Analysis of concept learning.* New York: Academic Press. The Taba, Bruner, and Tyler works were written some time ago, but they are classics in their influence on instruction. Also see Joyce, B., Weil, M., & Showers, B. (1992). *Models of teaching* (4th ed.). Boston: Allyn and Bacon; Ryan, K. (1988). Teacher education and moral education. *Journal of Teacher Education, 39*(5), 18–23. Martin, B. L., & Briggs, L. J. (1986). *The affective and cognitive domains: Integration for instruction and research.* Englewood Cliffs, NJ: Educational Technology Publications; Gagné, R. M., & Briggs, L. J. (1979). *Principles of instructional design* (2nd ed.). New York: Holt, Rinehart and Winston.

3. For more information on the structure of knowledge, see Taba, H. (1962). *Curriculum development: Theory and practice.* New York: Harcourt Brace and World, pp. 172–192, 211–215; Schwab, J. J. (1962). The concept of structure in a discipline. *Educational Record, 43*(3), 197–205. Also see two chapters by Schwab in G. W. Ford & L. Pugno (Eds.). (1964). *The structure of knowledge and the curriculum.* Chicago: Rand McNally; Bruner, J. S. (1960). *The process of education.* Cambridge, MA: Harvard University Press.

4. See Bruner, J. S. (1960). *The process of education.* Cambridge, MA: Harvard University Press; Taba, H. (1962). *Curriculum development: Theory and practice.* New York: Harcourt Brace and World, pp. 76–83, 211–218, 290–301; Weil, M., & Joyce, B. R. (1978).

Information processsing models of teaching. Englewood Cliffs, NJ: Prentice-Hall.

5. Hirsch, E. D. (1987). *Cultural literacy: What every American needs to know.* Boston: Houghton Mifflin; Hirsch, E. D. (1988). Cultural literacy: Let's get specific. *NEA Today, 6*(6), 15–21. For a general overview of Hirsch's ideas, see *Education Week, 6*(27), 1987, April 1. For a related perspective, also see Bloom, A. D. (1987). *The closing of the American mind.* New York: Simon and Schuster.

6. For more discussion of thinking, see Taba, H. (1962). *Curriculum development: Theory and practice.* New York: Harcourt Brace and World, pp. 211–218; Dewey, J. (1933). *How we think.* Boston: D. C. Heath; Baron, J. (1990). Thinking about consequences. *Journal of Moral Education, 19*(2), 77–87; Beyer, B. K. (1990). What philosophy offers to the teaching of thinking. *Educational Leadership, 47*(5), 55–60; Beyer, B. K. & Backes, J. D. (1990). Integrating thinking skills into the curriculum. *Principal, 69*(3), 18–21; Beyer, B. K. (1988). Developing a scope and sequence for thinking skill instruction. *Educational Leadership, 45*(7), 26–30; Beyer, B. K. (1985). Critical thinking: What is it? *Social Education, 49*(4), 271–276; Eisner, E. W. (1991). What really counts in schools. *Educational Leadership, 48*(5), 10–11, 14–17; Scriven, M. (1976). *Reasoning.* New York: McGraw-Hill; Norris, S. P. (1985). Synthesis of research on critical thinking. *Educational Leadership, 42*(8), 40–45.

7. For additional ideas about teaching thinking skills, see Weil, M., & Joyce, B. R. (1978). *Information processing models of teaching.* Englewood Cliffs, NJ: Prentice-Hall; Alvino, J. (1990). Building better thinkers: A blueprint for instruction. *Learning, 18*(6), 40–41; *Critical thinking, special collection number 3.* (1991). Bloomington, IN. ERIC Clearinghouse on Reading and Communication, ED334556; Marzano, R. J. (1991). *Cultivating thinking in English and the language arts.* Urbana, IL: National Council of Teachers of English; Parker, W. C. (1988). Thinking and learning concepts. *Social Studies, 79*(2), 70–73; Baron, J., & Brown, R. V. (1991). *Teaching decision making to adolescents.* Hillsdale, NJ: Lawrence Erlbaum; Parker, W. C. (1987). Teaching thinking: The persuasive approach. *Journal of Teacher Education, 36*(3), 50–58; Chance, P. (1986). *Thinking in the classroom: A survey of programs.* New York: Teachers College Press; Wassermann, S. (1992). *Asking the right questions: The essence of teaching.* Bloomington, IN: Phi Delta Kappa Educational Foundation; Hartman, H., & Sternberg, R. J. (1993). Abroad BACEIS for improving thinking. *Instructional Science, 21*(5), 401–425; Sternberg, R. J., & Lubart, T. I. (1991). Creating creative minds. *Phi Delta Kappan, 72*(8), 608–614: Raths, L. E., Wasserman, S., Jonas, A., & Rothstein, A. M. (1986). *Teaching for thinking* (2nd ed.). New York: Teachers College Press; Baron, J., & Sternberg, R. (Eds.). (1987). *Teaching thinking skills: Theory and practice.* New York: W. H. Freeman; Costa, A. L. (Ed.). (1985). *Developing minds: A resource book for teaching thinking.* Alexandria, VA: Association for Supervision and Curriculum Development; Sternberg, R. J. (1984). How can we teach intelligence? *Educational Leadership, 42*(1), 38–48; Nickerson, R. S. (1984). Kinds of thinking taught in current programs. *Educational Leadership, 42*(1), 26–36; Copple, C., Sigel, I. E., & Saunders, R.

(1984). *Educating the young thinker: Classroom strategies for cognitive growth.* Hillsdale, NJ: Lawrence Erlbaum; Sigel, I. E. (1984). A constructionist perspective for teaching thinking. *Educational Leadership, 42*(3), 18–21; Joyce, B. (1985). Models for teaching thinking. *Educational Leadership, 42*(8), 4–7.

8. Dewey, J. (1933). *How we think.* Boston: D. C. Heath.

9. Suchman, J. R. (1962). *The elementary school training program in scientific inquiry.* (Report 216 of Project VIII.) Report to the U.S. Office to Education. Urbana, IL: University of Illinois Publications Office. Also see Suchman, J. R. (1966). *Inquiry development program: Developing inquiry.* Chicago: Science Research Associates.

10. Taba, H., Durkin, M. C., Fraenkel, J. R., & McNaughton, A. J. (1971). *A teacher's handbook to elementary social studies* (2nd ed.). Menlo Park, CA: Addison-Wesley. Also see Fraenkel, J. R. (1992). Hilda Taba's contribution to social studies education. *Social Education, 56*(3), 172–178.

11. For more information, see Rafoth, M. A., et al. (1993). *Strategies for learning and remembering; Study skills across the curriculum. Analysis and action series.* Washington, DC: National Education Association; Bonds, C. W., et al. (1992). Developing independence in learning. *Clearing House, 66*(1), 56–59; Harrison, C. J. (1991). Metacognition and motivation. *Reading Improvement, 28*(1), 35–39; Costa, A. L. (1984). Mediating the metacognitive. *Educational Leadership, 42*(3), 57–62.

12. Brown, A. L. (1982). Learning how to learn from reading. In J. Langer & M. T. Smith-Burke (Eds.), *Reader meets author/bridging the gap.* Newark, DE: IRA. Also see Wham, M. A. (1987). Metacognition and classroom in-

struction. *Reading Horizons, 27*(2), 95–102.

13. Baker, L., & Brown, A. L. (1984). Metacognitive skills and reading. In P. D. Pearson (Ed.), *Handbook of reading research*. New York: Longman; McLain, K. V. (1991). Metacognition in reading comprehension: What it is and strategies for instruction. *Reading Improvement, 28*(3), 169–172; Patricia, E. (1991). SQ3R + What I know sheet = One strong strategy. *Journal of Reading, 35*(1), 50–52; Spires, H. (1990). Metacognition and reading: Implications for instruction. *Reading, 24*(3), 151–156; Blakey, E. & Spence, S. (1990). Developing metacognition. *ERIC Digest*, Syracuse, NY: ERIC Clearing House on Information Resources.

14. For more information on teaching skills, see Taba, H. (1962). *Curriculum development: Theory and practice*. New York: Harcourt Brace and World, pp. 225–228; Singer, R. M. (1980). *Motor learning and human performance* (3rd ed.). New York: Macmillan.

15. Fraenkel, J. R. (1977). *How to teach about values: An analytical approach*. Englewood Cliffs, NJ: Prentice-Hall; Harmin, M. (1990). *How to plan a program for moral education*. Alexandria, VA: Association for Supervision and Curriculum Development; Harmin, M. (1988). Value clarity, high morality: Let's go for both. *Educational Leadership, 45*(8), 23–30; Wynne, E. A., & Ryan, K. (1993). Curriculum as a moral educator. *American Educator, 17*(1), 20–24, 44–46, 48; Kirschenbaum, H. (1992). A comprehensive model for values education and moral education. *Phi Delta Kappan, 73*(10), 771–776; Taba, H. (1962). *Curriculum development: Theory and practice*. New York: Harcourt Brace and World, pp. 68–70, 220–223;

Raths, L. E., Harmin, M., & Simon, S. B. (1966). *Values and teaching*. Columbus, OH: Charles E. Merrill; Kohlberg, L. (1975). The cognitive-developmental approach to moral education. *Phi Delta Kappan, 56*(10), 670–677; Kohlberg, L., Levine, C., & Hewer, A. (1984). The current formulation of the theory. In L. Kohlberg (Ed.), *Essays on moral development* (Vol. 2, pp. 320–386). San Francisco: Harper and Row.

16. Fraenkel, J. R. (1977). *How to teach about values: An analytical approach*. Englewood Cliffs, NJ: Prentice-Hall; Taba, H. (1962). *Curriculum development: Theory and practice*. New York: Harcourt Brace and World, pp. 68–70, 223–225; Raths, L. E., Harmin, M., & Simon, S. B. (1966). *Values and teaching*. Columbus, OH: Charles E. Merrill.

17. Fraenkel, J. R. (1977). *How to teach about values: An analytical approach*. Englewood Cliffs, NJ: Prentice-Hall; Taba, H. (1962). *Curriculum development: Theory and practice*. New York: Harcourt Brace and World, pp. 68–70, 223–225; Raths, L. E., Harmin, M., & Simon, S. B. (1966). *Values and teaching*. Columbus, OH: Charles E. Merrill.

18. Baron, J., & Brown, R. V. (Eds.). (1991). *Teaching decision-making to adolescents*. Hillsdale, NJ: Lawrence Erlbaum; Elias, M. J., & Tobias, S. E. (1990). *Problem solving/decision making for social and academic success*. Washington, DC: National Education Association; Elias, M. J., & Clabby, J. F. (1992). *Building social problem-solving skills: Guidelines for a school-based program*. San Francisco: Jossey-Bass.

19. Taba, H. (1962). *Curriculum development: Theory and practice*. New York: Harcourt Brace and World, pp. 68–70, 220–223.

20. For more information on teaching values, feelings, sensitivities,

and decision making, see Fraenkel, J. R. (1977). *How to teach about values: An analytical approach*. Englewood Cliffs, NJ: Prentice-Hall; Galbraith, R. E., & Jones, T. M. (1976). *Moral reasoning*. Anoka, MN: Grenhaven; Simon, S. B., Howe, L. W., & Kirschenbaum, H. (1972). *Values clarification*. New York: Hart; Brady, L. (1974). *Do we dare? A dilemma approach to moral development*. Sydney, Australia: Dymock's; Brady, L. (n.d., approx. 1975). *Values taught and caught: Personal development for secondary schools*. Sydney, Australia: Dymock's.

21. Taba, H., Durkin, M. C., Fraenkel, J. R., & McNaughton, A. J. (1971). *A teacher's handbook to elementary social studies* (2nd ed.). Menlo Park, CA: Addison-Wesley.

22. This illustration is based on a lesson design developed by the Taba Curriculum Development Center. See Taba, H., Durkin, M. C., Fraenkel, J. R., & McNaughton, A. J. (1971). *A teacher's handbook to elementary social studies* (2nd ed.). Menlo Park, CA: Addison-Wesley, p. 78.

23. This illustration is based on a lesson design developed by the Taba Curriculum Development Center. See Taba, H., Durkin, M. C., Fraenkel, J. R., & McNaughton, A. J. (1971). *A teacher's handbook to elementary social studies* (2nd ed.). Menlo Park, CA: Addison-Wesley, pp. 81–82.

24. Downey, M. T., & Levstik, L. S. (1988). Teaching and learning history: The research base. *Social Education, 52*(5), 336–342.

25. Hallam, R. N. (1966). *An investigation into some aspects of the historical thinking of children and adolescents*. Unpublished M. Ed. thesis, University of Leeds; discussed in Downey, M. T., & Levstik, L. S. (1988). Teaching and learning history: The research base. *Social Education, 52*(5), 336–

342. Also see Hallam, R. N. (1967). Logical thinking in history. *Educational Review, 19*(June), 183–202.

Chapter 12

1. The schedules presented here are composites of typical schedules reviewed by the authors of this text.

2. Taba, H. (1962). *Curriculum development: Theory and practice.* New York: Harcourt, Brace and World, pp. 31–75, 179–194.

3. See Taba, H. (1962). *Curriculum development: Theory and practice.* New York: Harcourt, Brace and World, pp. 76–120, 132–171; also see Chapters 5 and 7 of this text.

4. For more thorough discussions of the process of selecting content in terms of educational objectives, see Taba, H. (1962). *Curriculum development: Theory and practice.* New York: Harcourt, Brace and World, pp. 194–230; Ornstein, A. C. (1992). The textbook curriculum. *Educational Horizons, 70*(4), 167–169; Mehaffy, G. L. (1992). Social studies in the age of reform: Symbolic and substantive change. *International Journal of Social Education, 7*(2), 76–82; Joyce, B., Weil, M., & Showers, B. (1992). *Models of teaching* (4th ed.). Boston: Allyn and Bacon; Ornstein, A. C., & Levine, D. U. (1993). *Foundations of education* (5th ed.). Boston: Houghton Mifflin, pp. 487–496; Kibler, R. J., Baker, L. L., & Miles, D. T. (1981). *Behavioral objectives and instruction* (2nd ed.). Boston: Allyn and Bacon; Gronlund, N. E. (1978). *Stating objectives for classroom instruction.* New York: Macmillan. Also see Bloom, B. S., & Krathwohl, D. R. (1956). *Taxonomy of educational objectives: Cognitive domain.* New York: David McKay; Krathwohl, D. R. (1956). *Taxonomy of educational objectives:*

Affective domain. New York: David McKay; Maslow, A. H. (1988). On the shoulders of giants. *Educational Forum, 52*(3), 203–208.

5. For more discussion of the question of relevance, see Taba, H. (1962). *Curriculum development: Theory and practice.* New York: Harcourt, Brace and World, pp. 76–79; Ryan, K., & Cooper, J. M. (1995). *Those who can, teach* (7th ed.). Boston: Houghton Mifflin, pp. 350–352.

6. Of course, they can always turn to higher authority—the curriculum guide, the textbook, a more experienced teacher—but if they do, it is still their own choice to follow this course. When they yield to authority, they choose, in effect, to allow others to make the choice, or at least to influence it significantly.

7. For example, see Taba, H. (1962). *Curriculum development: Theory and practice.* New York: Harcourt, Brace and World, pp. 18–22; Ryan, K., & Cooper, J. M. (1995). *Those who can, teach* (7th ed.). Boston: Houghton Mifflin, pp. 127–130, 134–136; Johnson, J. A., Dupuis, V. L., Musial, D., & Hall, G. E. (1994). *Introduction to the foundations of American education* (9th ed.). Boston: Allyn and Bacon, pp. 412–415. Also see sections on perennialism and essentialism in Chapter 10 of this text.

8. For example, see Taba, H. (1962). *Curriculum development: Theory and practice.* New York: Harcourt, Brace and World, pp. 40–46, 53–75; Ryan, K., & Cooper, J. M. (1995). *Those who can, teach* (7th ed.). Boston: Houghton Mifflin, pp. 130–134, 290–292; Johnson, J. A., Dupuis, V. L., Musial, D., & Hall, G. E. (1994). *Introduction to the foundations of American education* (9th ed.). Boston: Allyn and Bacon, pp. 419–424. Also see sections on pragmatism and futurism in Chapter 10 of this text.

9. For example, see Taba, H. (1962). *Curriculum development: Theory and practice.* New York: Harcourt, Brace and World, pp. 22–28, 65–73; Roth, R. A. (1992). Dichotomous paradigms for teacher education: The rise and fall of the empire. *Action in Teacher Education, 14*(1), 1–9; Stanley, W. B. (1985). Social reconstruction for today's social education. *Social Education, 49*(5), 384–389; Counts, G. S. (1932). *Dare the schools build a new social order?* New York: John Day; Apple, M. W. (1982). *Education and power.* Boston: Routledge and Kegan Paul; Apple, M. W., & Weis, L. (1983). *Ideology and practice in schooling.* Philadelphia: Temple University Press. For a critical pedagogy perspective, see McLaren, P. (1989). *Life in schools: An introduction to critical pedagogy in the foundations of education.* New York: Longman. Also see sections on reconstructionism and Marxism in Chapter 10 of this text.

10. For more discussion on this point, see Ornstein, A. C., & Levine, D. U. (1993). *Foundations of education* (5th ed.). Boston: Houghton Mifflin, pp. 318–336.

11. For discussions of the field of curriculum, see Klein, M. F. (1992). A perspective on the gap between curriculum theory and practice. *Theory into Practice, 31*(3), 191–197; Klein, M. (1992, December). *Integrating the curriculum: Re-examination of a new truism.* Paper presented at the annual meeting of the Reading Forum, Sanibel Island, FL; Brophy, J. (1992). Probing the subtleties of subject-matter teaching. *Educational Leadership, 49*(7), 4–8; Brophy, J. (1992). The de-facto national curriculum in U.S. elementary social studies: Critique of a representative sample. *Journal of Curriculum Studies, 24*(5), 401–447; Eisner,

E. W. (1990). Creative curriculum development and practice. *Journal of Curriculum and Supervision, 6*(1), 62–73; Banks, J. A., et al. (1992). *Building learner-centered schools: Three perspectives.* New York: Teachers College, National Center for Restructuring Education; Ornstein, A. C. (1987). The field of curriculum: What approach? What definition? *High School Journal, 70,* 208–216; McNeil, J. D. (1985). *Curriculum: A comprehensive introduction* (3rd ed.). Boston: Little, Brown; Miller, J. P., & Seller, W. (1986). *Curriculum perspectives and practice.* New York: Longman. Also see Schwab, J. J. (1969). The practical: Language for the curriculum. *School Review, 78*(1), 1–23; and Cuban, L. (1982). Persistent instruction: The high school classroom, 1900–1980. *Phi Delta Kappan, 64*(2), 113–118.

12. See Brophy, J. (1992). Probing the subtleties of subject-matter teaching. *Educational Leadership, 49*(7), 4–8; Klein, M. F. (1992). A perspective on the gap between curriculum theory and practice. *Theory into Practice, 31*(3), 191–197; Ornstein, A. C., & Levine, D. U. (1993). *Foundations of education* (5th ed.). Boston: Houghton Mifflin, pp. 521–531, 539–544; Taba, H. (1962). *Curriculum development: Theory and practice.* New York: Harcourt, Brace and World, pp. 382–393; Johnson, J. A., Dupuis, V. L., Musial, D., & Hall, G. E. (1994). *Introduction to the foundations of American education* (9th ed.). Boston: Allyn and Bacon, pp. 456–459, 461–462.

13. Adler, M. J. (1982). *The Paideia proposal.* New York: Macmillan.

14. For more information on separate-subjects curricula, see Brophy, J. (1992). Probing the subtleties of subject-matter teaching. *Educational Leadership, 49*(7); Klein, M. F. (1992). A per-

spective on the gap between curriculum theory and practice. *Theory into Practice, 31*(3), 191–197; Taba, H. (1962). *Curriculum development: Theory and practice.* New York: Harcourt, Brace and World, pp. 382–393; Ornstein, A. C., & Levine, D. U. (1993). *Foundations of education* (5th ed.). Boston: Houghton Mifflin, pp. 522–530; Johnson, J. A., Dupuis, V. L., Musial, D., & Hall, G. E. (1994). *Introduction to the foundations of American education* (9th ed.). Boston: Allyn and Bacon, pp. 456–458.

15. For more information on broad-field curricula, see Klein, M. (1992, December). *Integrating the curriculum: Re-examination of a new truism.* Paper presented at the annual meeting of the Reading Forum, Sanibel Island, FL; Taba, H. (1962). *Curriculum development: Theory and practice.* New York: Harcourt, Brace and World, pp. 392–395; Johnson, J. A., Dupuis, V. L., Musial, D., & Hall, G. E. (1994). *Introduction to the foundations of American education* (9th ed.). Boston: Allyn and Bacon, pp. 458–459.

16. Bruner, J. S. (1960). *The process of education.* Cambridge, MA: Harvard University Press; Taba, H. (1962). *Curriculum development: Theory and practice.* New York: Harcourt, Brace and World.

17. See Taba, H., Durkin, M. C., Fraenkel, J. R., & McNaughton, A. J. (1971). *A teacher's handbook to elementary social studies* (2nd ed.). Menlo Park, CA: Addison-Wesley, especially p. 29.

18. See Banks, J. R., et al. (1992). *Building learner-centered schools: Three perspectives.* New York: Teachers College, Columbia University, National Center for Restructuring Education; Eisner, E. W. (1990). Creative curriculum development and practice. *Journal of Curriculum and Supervision, 6*(1), 62–73; Klein, M. F.

(1992). A perspective on the gap between curriculum theory and practice. *Theory into Practice, 31*(3), 191–197; Ornstein, A. C., & Levine, D. H. (1993). *Foundations of education* (5th ed.). Boston: Houghton Mifflin, pp. 531–539; Johnson, J. A., Dupuis, V. L., Musial, D., & Hall, G. E. (1994). *Introduction to the foundations of American education* (9th ed.). Boston: Allyn and Bacon, pp. 459–462.

19. For more information on the core curriculum, see Taba, H. (1962). *Curriculum development: Theory and practice.* New York: Harcourt, Brace and World, pp. 407–412; Orstein, A.C. & Levine, D. U. (1993). *Foundations of education* (5th ed.) Boston: Houghton Mifflin, pp. 539–540; Johnson, J. A. Dupuis, V. L., Musial, D., & Hall, G. E. (1994). *Introduction to the foundations of American education* (9th ed.). Boston: Allyn and Bacon, pp. 458–460.

20. For more information on social functions and social problems curricula, see Taba, H. (1962). *Curriculum development: Theory and practice.* New York: Harcourt, Brace and World, pp. 396–400; Kilpatrick, W. H. (Ed.). (1933). *The educational frontier.* New York: Appleton-Century.

21. Kilpatrick, W. H. (1918). The project method. *Teachers College Record, 19*(4), 319–335; Kilpatrick, W. H. (1951). *Philosophy of education.* New York: Macmillan.

22. For more information on activity-centered curricula, see Taba, H. (1962). *Curriculum development: Theory and practice.* New York: Harcourt, Brace and World, pp. 400–407; Ornstein, A. C., & Levine, D. H. (1993). *Foundations of education* (5th ed.). Boston: Houghton Mifflin, pp. 434–436.

23. Maslow, A. H. (1962). *Toward a psychology of being.* New York: Van Nostrand Reinhold; Maslow, A. H. (1970). *Motivation and personality* (2nd ed.). New York:

Harper and Row; Rogers, C. R. (1961). *On becoming a person.* Boston: Houghton Mifflin; Rogers, C. R. (1983). *Freedom to learn for the 80's.* Columbus, OH: Charles E. Merrill.

24. Combs, A., & Snygg, D. (1959). *Individual behavior* (2nd ed.). New York: Harper and Row. Also see Combs, A. (Ed.). (1962). *Perceiving, behaving, becoming: 1962 ASCD yearbook.* Washington, DC: Association for Supervision and Curriculum Development.

25. For more information about humanistic and open education, see Ornstein, A. C., & Levine, D. H. (1993). *Foundations of education* (5th ed.). Boston: Houghton Mifflin, pp. 536–537; Apple, M. W. (1983). Curriculum in the year 2000: Tensions and possibilities. *Phi Delta Kappan, 64*(5), 321–326; Silberman, C. A. (1971). *Crisis in the classroom.* New York: Random House; Berman, L. M., & Roderick, J. A. (Eds.). (1977). *Feelings, values, and the art of growing: 1977 ASCD yearbook.* Washington, DC: Association for Supervision and Curriculum Development; Eisner, E. W. (1983). The art and craft of teaching. *Educational Leadership, 40*(4), 4–13; Eisner, E. W. (1994). *The educational imagination* (3rd ed.). New York: Macmillan.

26. Stein, B. (1986, November). High school diary. *Los Angeles Magazine,* pp. 168–175.

27. Ms. Myers's plan and teaching are drawn from several plans and lessons she taught at Fall-Hamilton Elementary School, Nashville, Tennessee. The basic concept of the lesson was developed and taught initially by Margaret Duncan, Armidale City Public School, Armidale, New South Wales, Australia. (A number of educators who reviewed early drafts of this chapter felt that this lesson plan was too advanced for first grade. It is a "whole-language-type" lesson that has been successful for Ms. Myers's and Ms. Duncan's first grades in the United States and in Australia.)

28. For more information on the hidden curriculum, see Ornstein, A. C., & Levine, D. H. (1993). *Foundations of education* (5th ed.). Boston: Houghton Mifflin, p. 333; Jackson, P. W. (1968). *Life in classrooms.* New York: Holt, Rinehart and Winston; Lightfoot, S. L. (1983). *The good high school.* New York: Basic Books; Cusick, P. A. (1983). *The egalitarian ideal and the American high school.* New York: Longman; Eisner, E. W. (1994). *The educational imagination* (3rd ed.). New York: Macmillan.

29. West, P. (1994). The last mile. *Education Week, 13*(23), 33.

30. West, P. (1994). The last mile. *Education Week, 13*(23), 31–34.

31. West, P. (1994). The last mile. *Education Week, 13*(23), 31–34.

32. West, P. (1994). 7,500-computer deal announced for Florida district. *Education Week, 13*(18), 6.

33. West, P. (1994). On-line service for N.C. students launched. *Education Week, 13*(26), 8.

34. West, P. (1994). The last mile. *Education Week, 13*(23), 31–34; West, P. (1994). Plan to offer data links to schools still on, firms say. *Education Week, 13*(24), 7.

35. West, P. (1994). California firm to furnish schools with data links. *Education Week, 13*(22), 6.

36. West, P. (1994). California firm to furnish schools with data links. *Education Week, 13*(22), 6.

37. West, P. (1994). Distance-learning network launched. *Education Week, 13*(21), 10.

38. West, P. (1994). Distance-learning network launched. *Education Week, 13*(21), 10.

39. West, P. (1994). Compaq computer firm develops K-12 sales strategy. *Education Week, 13*(21), 8.

40. Portner, J. (1994). A.F.T. puts 2 on-line services to technological test. *Education Week, 13*(23), 10.

41. West, P. (1994). Policy on school access to data networks urged. *Education Week, 13*(28), 5; West, P. (1994). Technology advisor seeks to help put theory into practice. *Education Week, 13*(23), 20.

42. West, P. (1994). PBS drafts measure seeking space for education on electronic networks. *Education Week, 13*(25), 20.

43. Technology. (1994). *Education Week, 13*(28), 5.

44. West, P. (1994). The last mile. *Education Week, 13*(23), 33.

Chapter 13

1. The class segment described in this Snapshot and the parallel episodes described in the two remaining Snapshots in this chapter were developed by Catherine Randolph and Marcy Singer Gabella based on classroom observations.

2. Flanders, N. (1970). *Analyzing teacher behavior.* Reading, MA: Addison-Wesley.

3. Cazden, C. (1986). Classroom discourse. In M. C. Wittrock (Ed.), *Handbook of research on teaching: Third edition* (pp. 432–463). New York: Macmillan; Edwards, A. D., & Furlong, V. J. (1978). *The language of teaching: Meaning in classroom interaction.* London: Heinemann; Mehan, H. (1979). *Learning lessons: Social organization in the classroom.* Cambridge, MA: Harvard University Press.

4. Mehan, H. (1979). "What time is it, Denise?": Asking known information questions in classroom discourse. *Theory into Practice, 18*(4), 285–294.

5. Green, J., & Smith, D. (1983). Teaching and learning: A linguistic perspective. *The Elementary School Journal, 83*(4), 352–391.

6. Hansford, B. C. (1988). *Teachers*

and classroom communication. Sydney, Australia: Harcourt Brace Jovanovich.

7. Brophy, J., & Good, T. (1974). *Teacher-student relationships: Causes and consequences.* New York: Holt, Rinehart and Winston.

8. Brophy, J., & Evertson, C. (1981). *Student characteristics and teaching.* New York: Longman.

9. Philips, S. U. (1983). *The invisible culture: Communication in classroom and community in the Warm Springs Indian reservation.* New York: Longman.

10. Au, K. H. (1980). Participation structures in a reading lesson with Hawaiian children: Analysis of a culturally appropriate instructional event. *Anthropology & Education Quarterly, 11,* 91–115.

11. Tyler, R. (1949). *Basic principles of curriculum and instruction.* Chicago: University of Chicago Press; Taba, H. (1962). *Curriculum development, theory and practice.* New York: Harcourt, Brace and World; Popham, J. W., & Baker, E. L. (1970). *Systematic instruction.* Englewood Cliffs, NJ: Prentice-Hall.

12. Clark, C. M., & Yinger, R. J. (1979). Research on teacher planning: A progress report. *Journal of Curriculum Studies, 11*(2), 175–177.

13. Morine, G., & Vallance, E. (1975). *A study of teacher and pupil perceptions of classroom interactions (BTES Special Report B).* San Francisco: Far West Laboratory for Education Research and Development.

14. Morine, G. (1976). *A study of teacher planning* (Technical Report 76-3-1, Beginning Teacher Evaluation Study). San Francisco: Far West Laboratory for Education Research and Development; Peterson, P. L., Marx, R. W., & Clark, C. M. (1978). Teacher planning, teacher behavior, and student achievement. *American*

Educational Research Journal, 15(3), 417–432; Yinger, R. J. (1977). *A study of teacher planning: Description and theory development using ethnographic and information-processing methods.* Unpublished doctoral dissertation, Michigan State University; Yinger, R. J. (1979). Routines in teacher planning. *Theory into Practice, 19*(2), 163–169; Yinger, R. J., & Clark, C. M. (1981, July). *Reflective journal writing: Theory and practice.* East Lansing: Institute for Research on Teaching, Michigan State University (ERIC: ED 208 411).

15. Neely, A. (1985). Teacher planning: Where has it been? Where is it now? Where is it going? *Action in Teacher Education, 7*(3), 25–29; Neely, A. (1986). Integrating planning and problem solving in teacher education. *Journal of Teacher Education, 37*(3), 29–33.

16. Eisner, E. (1994). *The educational imagination: On the design and evaluation of school programs.* (3rd ed.). New York: Macmillan.

17. Dewey, J. (1938). *Experience and education.* New York: Macmillan.

18. Shulman, L., Sykes, G., & Phillips, D. (1983, November). *Knowledge growth in a profession: The development of knowledge in teaching.* Proposal submitted to the Spencer Foundation, Stanford University School of Education, Stanford, CA.

19. Brophy, J. E., & Evertson, C. M. (1976). *Learning from teaching: A development perspective.* Boston: Allyn and Bacon; Brophy, J. E., & Good, T. L. (1986). Teacher behavior and student achievement. In M. C. Wittrock (Ed.), *Handbook of research on teaching: Third edition* (pp. 328–375). New York: Macmillan.

20. Ames, R., & Ames, C. (Eds.). *Research on motivation in education:* Vol. 1. *Student motivation.* Orlando, FL: Academic Press; Ames

& Ames, (Eds.). (1985). *Research on motivation in education:* Vol. 2. *The classroom milieu.* Orlando, FL: Academic Press.

21. Smith, L., & Geoffrey, W. (1968). *Complexities of an urban classroom: An analysis toward a general theory of teaching.* New York: Holt, Rinehart and Winston; Damico, S. B., & Purkey, W. W. (1978). Class clowns: A study of middle school students. *American Educational Research Journal, 15*(3), 391–398; Davis, J. (1972). Teachers, kids and conflict: Ethnography of a junior high school. In J. P. Spradley & D. W. McCurdy, *The cultural experience: Ethnography in complex society* (pp. 103–119). Chicago: Science Research Associates.

22. Three of the most informative explanations of reflective practice and ones we relied on more than any other sources for this section are Brubacher, J. W., Case, C. W., & Reagan, T. G. (1994). *Becoming a reflective educator: How to build a culture of inquiry in the schools.* Thousand Oaks, CA: Corwin Press; Pasch, M., Sparks-Langer, G. M., Gardner, Starko, A., & Moody, (1991). *Teaching as decision making: Instructional practices for the successful teacher.* New York: Longman; and Sparks-Langer, G. M., & Colton, A. B. (1991). Synthesis of research on teachers' reflective thinking. *Educational Leadership, 48*(6), 37–44.

23. Dewey, J. (1910). *How we think.* Boston: D. C. Heath; Dewey, J. (1933). *How we think: A restatement of the relations of reflective thinking to the educative process.* (2nd ed.). Lexington, MA: D. C. Heath; Dewey, J. (1938). *Logic: The theory of inquiry.* New York: Henry Holt; Brubacher, J. W., Case, C. W., & Reagan, T. G. (1994). *Becoming a reflective educator: How to build a culture of inquiry in the schools.* Thousand

Oaks, CA: Corwin Press, pp. 18–19, 38.

24. Schon, D. A. (1983). *The reflective practitioner: How professionals think in action*. New York: Basic Books; Schon, D. (1987). *Educating the reflective practitioner*. San Francisco: Jossey-Bass.

25. Schon, D. (1987). *Educating the reflective practitioner*. San Francisco: Jossey-Bass, p. 5.

26. Fitzgibbons, R. (1981). *Making educational decisions: An introduction to philosophy of education*. New York: Harcourt Brace Jovanovich, pp. 13–14; Brubacher, J. W., Case, C. W., & Reagan, T. G. (1994). *Becoming a reflective educator: How to build a culture of inquiry in the schools*. Thousand Oaks, CA: Corwin Press, pp. 17–18.

27. Killion, J. P., & Todnem, G. R. (1991). A process for personal theory building. *Educational Leadership*, *48*(6), 14–16; Brubacher, J. W., Case, C. W., & Reagan, T. G. (1994). *Becoming a reflective educator: How to build a culture of inquiry in the schools*. Thousand Oaks, CA: Corwin Press, pp. 19–20.

28. Killion, J. P., & Todnem, G. R. (1991). A process for personal theory building. *Educational Leadership*, *48*(6), 14–16; Brubacher, J. W., Case, C. W., & Reagan, T. G. (1994). *Becoming a reflective educator: How to build a culture of inquiry in the schools*. Thousand Oaks, CA: Corwin Press, pp. 19–20.

29. Van Manen, M. J. (1977). Linking ways of knowing with ways of being practical. *Curriculum Inquiry*, *6*, 205–208. Also see Zeichner, K. M., & Liston, D. P. (1987). Teaching student teachers to reflect. *Harvard Educational Review*, *57*(10), 23–48.

30. Sparks-Langer, G. M., & Colton, A. B. (1991). Synthesis of research on teachers' reflective thinking. *Educational Leadership*, *48*(6), 37–44; Berliner, D. (1986). In pursuit of the expert pedagogue. *Educational Researcher*, *15*(7), 5–13.

31. One of the best delineations of the types of knowledge that teachers need is that by Shulman, L. S. (1987). Knowledge and teaching: Foundations of the new reform. *Harvard Educational Review*, *57*(1), 1–22.

Chapter 14

1. The class segment described in this Snapshot is drawn from classroom observations by Jane Stallings.

2. Gagné, R. M. (1988). Mastery learning and instructional design. *Performance Improvement Quarterly*, *1*(1), 7–18; Stallings, J. A., & Stipek, D. (1986). Research on early childhood and elementary school teaching programs. In M. C. Wittrock (Ed.), *Handbook of research on teaching: Third edition* (pp. 727–753). New York: Macmillan.

3. Ford, M. (1990). *The development of a guide on outcome-based learning for McCook Community College*. Unpublished paper (ERIC ED 326 259).

4. Bloom, B. J., Hastings, T., & Madaus, G. F. (1971). *Handbook on formative and summative evaluation of student learning*. McGraw-Hill. Also see Anderson, L. W. (1988). Benjamin Bloom: His research and influence on education. *Teaching Education*, *2*(1), 54–58.

5. Spady, W. G., Filby, N., & Burns, R. (1986). *Outcome-based education: A summary of essential features and major implications*. San Francisco: Far West Laboratory; Burns, R. (1987). *Models of instructional organization: A casebook on mastery learning and outcome-based education*. San Francisco: Far West Laboratory.

6. Capper, C. A., & Jamison, M. T. (1992, April). *Outcome-based education reexamined. From structural functionalism to poststructuralism*. Paper presented at the annual meeting of the American Educational Research Association, San Francisco.

7. Zlatos, B. (1993, September). Outcome-based outrage. *The Executive Educator*, *15*, 12–16.

8. Carroll, J. B. (1963). A model for school learning. *Teachers College Record*, *64*(8), 723–733.

9. Bloom, B. S. (1968). Learning for mastery. *Education Comment (UCLA-CSIED)*, *1*(2), 1–12.

10. Bloom, B. S. (1982). *Human characteristics and school learning*. New York: McGraw-Hill.

11. Keller, F. S. (1968). Good-bye teacher. . . . *Journal of Applied Behavior Analysis*, *1*(1), 79–89.

12. Buckholdt, D., & Wodarski, J. (1974, August). *The effect of different reinforcement systems on cooperative behaviors exhibited by children in classroom contexts*. Paper presented at the annual meeting of the American Psychological Association, New Orleans; Levine, J. (1983). Social comparison and education. In J. Levine and M. Wang (Eds.), *Teacher and student perceptions: Implications for learning* (pp. 29–55). Hillsdale, NJ: Lawrence Erlbaum.

13. Block, J. H., & Burns, R. (1976). Mastery learning. In L. S. Shulman (Ed.), *Review of research in education*, Vol. 4 (pp. 3–49). Itasca, IL: F. E. Peacock.

14. Anderson, L. (1976, April). *The effects of a mastery learning program on selected cognitive, affective and interpersonal variables in grades 1 through 6*. Paper presented at the annual meeting of the American Educational Research Association, San Francisco; Anderson, L. (1976). An empirical investigation of the individual differences in time to learn. *Journal of Educational Psychology*, *68*(2), 226–233.

15. Arlin, M. (1984). Time, equality,

and mastery learning. *Review of Educational Research, 54*(1), 65–86; Arlin, M. (1984). Time variability in mastery learning. *American Educational Research Journal, 21*(1), 103–120; Slavin, R. E. (1990). Mastery learning re-considered. *Review of Educational Research, 60*(2), 300–302; Kulik, C. L., Kulik, J. A., & Bengert-Drowns, R. L. (1990). Effectiveness of mastery learning programs: A meta-analysis. *Review of Educational Research, 60*(2), 265–299; Kulik, J. A., et al. (1990). Is there better evidence on mastery learning? A response to Slavin. *Review of Educational Research, 60*(2), 303–307.

16. Arlin, M. (1984). Times, equality, and mastery learning. *Review of Educational Research, 54*(1), 65–86; Arlin, M. (1984). Time variability in mastery learning. *American Educational Research Journal, 21*(1), 103–120.

17. Arlin, M. (1984). Time variability in mastery learning. *American Educational Research Journal, 21*(1), 103–120.

18. Arlin, M. (1984). Time variability in mastery learning. *American Educational Research Journal, 21*(1), 103–120.

19. Groff, P. (1974). Some criticisms of mastery learning. *Today's Education, 63*(4), 88–91.

20. Horton, L. (1979). Mastery learning: Sound in theory, but. . . . *Educational Leadership, 37*(2), 154–156.

21. The class segment described in this Snapshot was written by Alene Harris and Jane Stallings, based on classroom observations by Jane Stallings.

22. Slavin, R. E. (1991). Synthesis of research on cooperative learning. *Educational Leadership, 48*(5), 71–82; Slavin, R. E. (1990). *Cooperative learning: Theory, research, and practice.* Englewood Cliffs, NJ: Prentice-Hall; Slavin, R. E. (1982). *Cooperative learning: Stu-*

dent teams. Washington, DC: National Education Association; Johnson, D. W., & Johnson, R. T. (1990). *Cooperation and competition: Theory and practice.* Edina, MN: Interaction Book Company; Johnson, D. W., & Johnson, R. T. (1975). *Circles of learning.* Englewood Cliffs, NJ: Prentice-Hall; Sharan, S. (1990). *Cooperative learning: Theory and research.* New York: Praeger; Davidson, N., & O'Leary, P. (1990). How cooperative learning can enhance mastery learning. *Educational Leadership, 47*(5), 30–34.

23. Sharan, S. (1980). Cooperative learning in small groups. Recent methods and effects on achievement, attitudes, and ethnic relations. *Review of Educational Research, 50*(2), 341–371.

24. Covington, M., & Beery, R. (1976). *Self-worth and whole learning.* New York: Holt, Rinehart and Winston. Also see Joyce, B. R. (1991). Common misconceptions about cooperative learning and gifted students. Response to Allan. *Educational Leadership, 48*(6), 72–74.

25. Ames, C. (1981). Competitive versus cooperative reward structures: The influence of individual and group performance factors on achievement attributions and affect. *American Educational Research Journal, 18*(3), 273–288.

26. Slavin, R. E. (1990). *Cooperative learning: Theory, research, and practice.* Englewood Cliffs, NJ: Prentice-Hall.

27. Johnson, D. W., Johnson, R. T., Holubec, E. J., & Roy, P. (1984). *Circles of learning.* Alexandria, VA: Association of Supervision and Curriculum Development.

28. Slavin, R. E. (1990). *Cooperative learning: Theory, research, and practice.* Englewood Cliffs, NJ: Prentice-Hall.

29. Slavin, R. E. (1990). *Cooperative learning: Theory, research, and*

practice. Englewood Cliffs, NJ: Prentice-Hall.

30. For references to Learning Together and Group Investigations, see Slavin, R. E. (1982). *Cooperative learning: Student teams.* Washington, DC: National Education Association, pp. 7–8, and Slavin, R. E. (1990). *Cooperative learning: Theory, research, and practice.* Englewood Cliffs, NJ: Prentice-Hall, pp. 94–100, 111.

31. Slavin, R. E. (1990). *Cooperative learning: Theory, research, and practice.* Englewood Cliffs, NJ: Prentice-Hall.

32. Slavin, R. E. (1990). *Cooperative learning: Theory, research, and practice.* Englewood Cliffs, NJ: Prentice-Hall, pp. 31–32.

33. See Slavin, R. E. (1982). *Cooperative learning: Student teams.* Washington, DC: National Education Association.

34. See Gerard, H. B., & Miller, N. (1975). *School desegregation: A long-range study.* New York: Plenum Press.

35. See Slavin, R. E. (1990). *Cooperative learning: Theory, research, and practice.* Englewood Cliffs, NJ: Prentice-Hall.

36. Ballard, M., Carman, L., Gottlieb, J., & Kaufman, M. (1977). Improving the social status of mainstreamed retarded children. *Journal of Educational Psychology, 69*(5), 605–611; Blaney, N. T., Stephen, S., Rosenfield, D., Aronson, E., & Sikes, J. (1977). Interdependence in the classroom: A field study. *Journal of Educational Psychology, 69*(2), 121–128; Madden, N. A., & Slavin, R. E. (1983). Effects of cooperative learning on the social acceptance of mainstreamed academically handicapped students. *Journal of Special Education, 17*(2), 171–182; Slavin, R. E. (1977). Classroom reward structure: An analytical and practical review. *Journal of Educational Research, 47*, 633–650; Joyce, B. R. (1991).

Misconceptions about cooperative learning and gifted students: Response to Allan. *Educational Leadership, 48*(6), 72–74.

37. Slavin, R. E. (1990). *Cooperative learning: Theory, research, and practice.* Englewood Cliffs, NJ: Prentice-Hall.

38. The class segment described in this Snapshot is a composite drawn from classroom observations by Jane Stallings and descriptions of sample classes that appear in Weikart, D. P., Rogers, L., Adcock, C., & McClelland, D. (1970). *The cognitively oriented curriculum: A framework for preschool teachers.* Ypsilanti, MI: High/Scope Educational Research Foundation (ERIC, ED 044 535).

39. For additional information on this model, see Stallings, J. A., & Stipek, D. (1986). Research on early childhood and elementary school teaching programs. In M. C. Wittrock (Ed.), *Handbook of research on teaching: Third edition* (pp. 729–732). New York: Macmillan; Lalli, R. (1977). *An introduction to the cognitively oriented curriculum for elementary grades.* Ypsilanti, MI: High/Scope Educational Research Foundation; McClelland, D., Smith, S. A., Kluge, J., Hudson, A., & Taylor, C. (1970). *The cognitive curriculum.* Ypsilanti, MI: High/Scope Educational Research Foundation (ERIC, ED 049 832).

40. Sigel, I. E. (1969). The Piagetian system and the world of education. In D. Elkind & J. Flavell (Eds.), *Studies in cognitive development.* New York: Oxford University Press.

41. Stallings, J. A. (1977). *Learning to look.* Belmont, CA: Wadsworth, pp. 123–166.

42. Stallings, J. A., & Kaskowitz, D. H. (1974). *Follow Through classroom observation evaluation, 1972–1973.* Menlo Park, CA: Stanford Research Institute.

43. Stallings, J. A., & Kaskowitz, D. H. (1974). *Follow Through classroom observation evaluation, 1972–1973.* Menlo Park, CA: Stanford Research Institute.

44. Schweinhart, L., & Weikart, D. (1980). *Young children grow up: The effects of the Perry Preschool program on youths through age 15.* Ypsilanti, MI: High/Scope Educational Research Foundation, Monograph No. 7.

45. See Stallings, J. A., & Stipek, D. (1986). Research on early childhood and elementary school teaching programs. In M. C. Wittrock (Ed.), *Handbook of research on teaching: Third edition* (pp. 729–732). New York: Macmillan.

46. Schweinhart, L. J., & Weikart, D. P. (1993). Changed lives, significant benefits: The High/Scope Perry Preschool Project to date. *High/Scope Resource,* Summer, 1, 10–14.

47. Schweinhart, L. J., & Weikart, D. P. (1993). Changed lives, significant benefits: The High/Scope Perry Preschool Project to date. *High/Scope Resource,* Summer, 1, 10–14; Cohen, D. L. (1993, April 21). Perry Preschool graduates show dramatic new social gains at 27. *Education Week, 12*(30), 1, 16–17.

48. Schweinhart, L. J., & Weikart, D. P. (1993). Changed lives, significant benefits: The High/Scope Perry Preschool Project to date. *High/Scope Resource,* Summer, 11.

49. Schweinhart, L. J., & Weikart, D. P. (1993). Changed lives, significant benefits: The High/Scope Perry Preschool Project to date. *High/Scope Resource,* Summer, 11.

50. Schweinhart, L. J., & Weikart, D. P. (1993). Changed lives, significant benefits: The High/Scope Perry Preschool Project to date. *High/Scope Resource,* Summer, 12–13.

51. The class segment described in this Snapshot is drawn from classroom observation by Deborah Rowe.

52. Altwerger, B., Edelsky, C., & Flores, B. (1987). Whole language: What's new? *The Reading Teacher, 41,* 144–154; Goodman, K. (1986). *What's whole in whole language?* Portsmouth, NH: Heinemann; Goodman, K. (1992). I didn't found whole language. *The Reading Teacher, 46,* 188–199; Watson, D. (1989). Defining and describing whole language. *Elementary School Journal, 90,* 129–141; Way to go. (1993). *Teacher Magazine, 4*(5), 25–29.

53. Goodman, K. (1992). Why whole language is today's agenda in education. *Language Arts, 69,* 354–363; Smith, M. C., & Wham, M. A. (1993). The dialects of the whole language versus traditional instruction. *Reading Psychology, 14*(3), 205–227.

54. Goodman, K. (1992). I didn't found whole language. *The Reading Teacher, 46,* 188–199.

55. Rosenblatt, L. (1978). *The reader, the text, the poem.* Carbondale: Southern Illinois University Press; Goodman, K. (1984). Unity in reading. In O. Niles & A. Purves (Eds.), *Becoming readers in a complex society.* 83rd yearbook of the National Society for the Study of Education (pp. 79–114). Chicago: University of Chicago Press; Harste, J., Woodward, V., & Burke, C. (1984). *Language stories and literacy lessons.* Portsmouth, NH: Heinemann.

56. Halliday, M. (1975). *Learning how to mean: Explorations in the development of language.* London: Edward Arnold; Halliday, M. (1978). Meaning and the construction of reality in early childhood. In H. L. Pick, Jr., & E. Saltzman (Eds.), *Modes of perceiving and processing information* (pp. 67–96). Hillsdale, NJ:

Lawrence Erlbaum; Holdaway, D. (1979). *The foundations of literacy.* Sydney: Ashton Scholastic; Teale, W. (1986). The beginnings of reading and writing: Written language development during the preschool and kindergarten years. In M. R. Sampson (Ed.), *The pursuit of literacy: Early reading and writing* (pp. 1–29). Dubuque, IA: Kendall/Hunt.

57. Piaget, J., & Inhelder, V. (1969). *The psychology of the child.* New York: Basic Books; Vygotsky, L. (1978). *Mind in society.* Cambridge, MA: Harvard University Press.

58. Harste, J., Short, K., & Burke, C. (1988). *Creating classrooms for authors.* Portsmouth, NH: Heinemann.

59. See, for example, Stahl, S., & Miller, P. (1989). Whole language and language experience approaches for beginning reading: A quantitative research synthesis. *Review of Educational Research, 59,* 87–116; Hiebert, E. H., & Fisher, C. W. (1990). Whole language: Three themes for the future. *Educational Leadership, 47*(6), 62–64.

60. Stahl, S., & Miller, P. (1989). Whole language and language experience approaches for beginning reading: A quantitative research synthesis. *Review of Educational Research, 59,* 87–116.

61. McKenna, M., Robinson, R., & Miller, J. (1993). Whole language and research: The case for caution. In D. Leu & C. Kinzer (Eds.), *Examining central issues in literacy research, theory, and practice.* Forty-second yearbook of the National Reading Conference (pp. 141–152). Chicago: National Reading Conference.

62. Schickedanz, J. (1990). The jury is still out on the effects of whole language and language experience approaches for beginning reading: A critique of Stahl and Miller's study. *Review of Educa-*

tional Research, 60, 127–132; McGee, L., & Lomax, R. (1990). On combining apples and oranges: A response to Stahl and Miller. *Review of Educational Research, 60,* 133–140.

63. Freppon, P. (1988). *An investigation of children's concepts of the purpose and nature of reading in different instructional settings.* Unpublished doctoral dissertation, University of Cincinnati; Stice, C., & Bertrand, N. (1988, December). *The texts and textures of literacy learning in whole language versus traditional/skills classrooms.* Paper presented at the annual meeting of the National Reading Conference, Tucson.

64. Stice, D., & Bertrand, N. (1988, December). *The texts and textures of literacy learning in whole language versus traditional/skills classrooms.* Paper presented at the annual meeting of the National Reading Conference, Tucson.

65. The video episode described in this Snapshot is part of *The Adventures of Jasper Woodbury Problem Solving Series* developed by members of the Cognition and Technology Group at Vanderbilt University and available through Optical Data Corporation, Warren, NJ. The class segment described in this Snapshot is drawn from classroom observations by Nancy Vye.

66. Cognition and Technology Group at Vanderbilt. (1992). The Jasper experiment: An exploration of issues in learning and instructional design. *Educational Technology Research and Development, 40,* 65–80; Cognition and Technology Group at Vanderbilt. (1990). Anchored instruction and its relationship to situated cognition. *Educational Researcher, 19*(6), 2–10.

67. Silver, E. A. (Ed.). (1985). *Teaching and learning mathematical problem solving.* Hillsdale, NJ: Lawrence Erlbaum.

68. Whitehead, A. N. (1929). *The aims of education.* New York: Macmillan.

69. Bransford, J. D., & Vye, N. J. (1989). A perspective on cognitive research and its implications for instruction. *Toward the thinking curriculum: Current cognitive research* (pp. 173–205). Alexandria, VA: Association for Supervision and Curriculum Development.

70. Resnick, L. B., & Klopfer, L. E. (Eds.). (1989). *Toward the thinking curriculum: Current cognitive research.* Alexandria, VA: Association for Supervision and Curriculum Development.

71. Schoenfeld, A. H. (1985). *Mathematical problem solving.* New York: Academic Press.

72. Resnick, L. B. (1987). *Education and learning to think.* Washington, DC: National Academy Press; Brown, J. S., Collins, A., & Duguid, P. (1989). Situated cognition and the culture of learning. *Educational Researcher, 18,* 32–41; Cognition and Technology Group at Vanderbilt. (1990). Anchored instruction and its relationship to situated cognition. *Educational Researcher, 19*(6), 2–10; Gragg, C. I. (1940, October). Because wisdom can't be told. *Harvard Alumni Bulletin,* 78–84.

73. The pedagogy is consistent with other constructivist-oriented approaches. For other examples, see Resnick, L. B., Bill, V., Lesgold, S., & Leer, M. (1991). Thinking in arithmetic class. In B. Means, C. Chelemer, & M. S. Knapp (Eds.), *Teaching advanced skills to at-risk students: Views from research and practice.* San Francisco: Jossey-Bass; Lampert, M. (1986). Knowing, doing and teaching mathematics. *Cognition and Instruction, 3*(4), 305–342; Peterson, P. L. (1992). Revising their thinking: Keisha Coleman and her third grade mathematics class. In H. Marshall (Ed.), *Re-*

defining student learning: Roots of educational change (pp. 151–176). Norwood, NJ: Ablex.

74. The class segment described here is drawn from classroom observations by Nancy Vye.

75. Bransford, J. D., Sherword, R. S., Hasselbring, T. S., Kinzer, C. K., & Williams, S. M. (1990). Anchored instruction: Why we need it and how technology can help. In D. Nix & R. Spiro (Eds.), *Cognition, education, and multi-media: Exploring ideas in high technology* (pp. 115–141). Hillsdale, NJ: Lawrence Erlbaum; Bransford, J. D., & Vye, N. J. (1989). A perspective on cognitive research and its implications for instruction. *Toward the thinking curriculum: Current cognitive research* (pp. 173–205). Alexandria, VA: Association for Supervision and Curriculum Development.

76. Goldman, E. S., & Barron, L. C. (1990). Using hypermedia to improve the preparation of elementary teachers. *Journal of Teacher Education, 41*(3), 21–31; Goldman, E. S., Barron, L. C., & Witherspoon, M. L. (1991). Hypermedia cases in teacher education: A context for understanding research on teaching and learning of mathematics. *Action in Teacher Education, 13*(1), 28–36; Risko, V. J., Yount, D., & Towell, J. (1991). Video-based CASE analysis to enhance teacher preparation. In T. V. Rasinski, N. D. Radak, & J. Logan (Eds.), *Reading is knowledge* (pp. 87–96). Kent, OH: College Reading Association; Risko, V. J. (1992). Video-based instruction enhances analysis of classroom situations. *Association of Teacher Education Newsletter, 25*(5), 3; Risko, V. J., & Kinzer, C. K., Bigenho, F., Meltzer, L., & Carson, J. (1992). An argument for video-based case methodology for the redesign of reading methods courses. Paper pre-

sented at the meeting of the National Reading Association, San Antonio, TX. Sharp, D. L. M., Bransford, J. D., Vye, N. J., Goldman, S. R., Kinzer, C., & Soraci, S. (1992). Literacy in the age of integrated media. In M. Dreher & W. Slater (Eds.), *Elementary school literacy: Critical issues* (pp. 183–210). Norwood, MA: Christopher-Gordon; Bransford, J. D., Vye, N. J., Kinzer, C., & Risko, V. (1990). Teaching thinking and content knowledge: Toward an integrated approach. In B. Jones & L. Idol (Eds.), *Dimensions of thinking and cognitive instruction* (pp. 381–414). Hillsdale, NJ: Lawrence Erlbaum.

77. Pellegrino, J. W., Hickey, D., Heath, A., Rewey, K., Vye, N. J., & Cognition and Technology Group at Vanderbilt. (1991). Assessing the outcomes of an innovative instructional program: The 1990–1991 implementation of the "Adventures of Jasper Woodbury" (Tech. Rep. No. 91-1). Nashville, TN: Vanderbilt University, Learning Technology Center; Cognition and Technology Group at Vanderbilt. (1992). The Jasper series as an example of anchored instruction: Theory, program description, and assessment data. *Educational Psychologist, 27,* 291–315.

78. Cognition and Technology Group at Vanderbilt. (1994). From visual word problems to learning communities: Changing conceptions of cognitive research. In K. McGilly (Ed.), *Classroom lesson: Integrating cognitive theory and classroom practice* (pp. 157–200). Cambridge, MA: MIT Press/Bradford Books; Van Haneghan, Barron, L., Young, M., Williams, S., Vye, N. J., & Bransford, J. D. (1992). The Jasper series: An experiment with new ways to enhance mathematical thinking. In D. Halpern

(Ed.), *Enhancing thinking skills in the sciences and mathematics* (pp. 15–38). Hillsdale, NJ: Lawrence Erlbaum.

79. Joyce, B., Weil, M., & Showers, B. (1992). *Models of teaching* (4th ed.). Boston: Allyn and Bacon.

Chapter 15

1. Excerpted from Metzger, M. (1986). Reflections on a career in teaching. *Education Week, 6*(23), 28, 36.

2. Jackson, P. (1968). *Life in classrooms.* New York: Holt, Rinehart and Winston, pp. 5–6; Csikszentmihalyi, M., & McCormack, J. (1986). The influence of teachers. *Phi Delta Kappan, 67*(6), 415–419.

3. National Education Association. (1992). *Status of the American public school teacher: 1990–91.* Washington, DC: National Education Association; National Education Association. (1986). *Status of the American public school teacher: 1985–86.* Washington, DC: National Education Association; National Education Association. (1983). *Teacher opinion poll: Demographic highlights. Research memo.* Washington, DC: National Education Association; Educational Research Service. (1987). *Educator opinion poll.* Arlington, VA: Educational Research Service; Kottkamp, R. B., Provenzo, E. F., & Cohn, M. M. (1986). Stability and change in a profession: Two decades of teacher attitudes: 1964–1984. *Phi Delta Kappan, 67*(8), 559–567.

4. *Teaching's Next Generation.* (1993). Belmont, MA: Joint Project of the DeWitt Wallace–Reader's Digest Fund and Recruiting New Teachers; Darling-Hammond, L. (1990). Teachers and teaching: Signs of a changing profession. In R. W. Houston, M. Haberman, & J. Sikula (Eds.),

Handbook of research on teacher education (pp. 267–290). New York: Macmillan; Haberman, M. (1989). More minority teachers. *Phi Delta Kappan, 70*(10), 771–776; National Education Association. (1992). *Status of the American public school teacher: 1990–91.* Washington, DC: National Education Association; National Education Association. (1986). *Status of the American public school teacher: 1985–86.* Washington, DC: National Education Association; National Education Association. (1983). *Teacher opinion poll: Demographic highlights. Research memo.* Washington, DC: National Education Association.

5. National Education Association. (1992). *Status of the American public school teacher: 1990–91.* Washington, DC: National Education Association; National Education Association. (1983). *Teacher opinion poll: Demographic highlights. Research memo.* Washington, DC: National Education Association; Educational Research Service. (1987). *Educator opinion poll.* Arlington, VA: Educational Research Service.

6. NEA Research. (1993). *Estimates of school statistics 1992–93.* Washington, DC: National Education Association.

7. National Education Association. (1992). *Status of the American public school teacher: 1990–91.* Washington, DC: National Education Association; National Education Association. (1986). *Status of the American public school teacher: 1985–86.* Washington, DC: National Education Association.

8. See, for example, Elam, S. M., Rose, L. C., & Gallup, A. M. (1993). The 25th annual Phi Delta Kappa/Gallup Poll of the public's attitude toward the public schools. *Phi Delta Kappan, 75*(2), 137–152. (Poll reports appear annually in the September or October issue of *Phi Delta Kappan*); Clark, D. L. (1987). High school seniors react to their teachers and their schools. *Phi Delta Kappan, 68*(7), 503–509.

9. Ornstein, A. C., & Levine, D. U. (1993). *Foundations of education* (5th ed.). Boston: Houghton Mifflin, pp. 4–8.

10. Jackson, P. (1968). *Life in classrooms.* New York: Holt, Rinehart and Winston; Doyle, W. (1986). Classroom organizations and management. In M. C. Wittrock (Ed.), *Handbook of research on teaching: Third edition* (pp. 392–431). New York: Macmillan; Doyle, W. (1981). Research on classroom context. *Journal of Teacher Education, 32*(6), 3–6; Hamilton, S. F. (1983). The social side of schooling: Ecological studies of classrooms and schools. *Elementary School Journal, 83*(4), 313–334; Brophy, J. E. (1983). Classroom organization and management. *Elementary School Journal, 83*(4), 265–285. Many characteristics of classrooms are also mentioned in slightly different form in Chapters 3 and 13 of this text.

11. Jackson, P. (1968). *Life in classrooms.* New York: Holt, Rinehart and Winston, pp. 6–7.

12. Doyle, W. (1986). Classroom organizations and management. In M. C. Wittrock (Ed.), *Handbook of research on teaching: Third edition* (pp. 392–431). New York: Macmillan; Jackson, P. (1968). *Life in classrooms.* New York: Holt, Rinehart and Winston; Berliner, D. C. (1983). Developing concepts of classroom environments: Some light on the T in classroom studies of ATI. *Educational Psychologist, 18,* 1–13; Brophy, J. E. (1982). How teachers influence what is taught and learned in classrooms. *Elementary School Journal, 83,* 1–13.

13. Doyle, W. (1986). Classroom organizations and management. In M. C. Wittrock (Ed.), *Handbook of research on teaching: Third edition* (esp. pp. 403–409). New York: Macmillan; Berliner, D. C. (1983). Developing concepts of classroom environments: Some light on the T in classroom studies of ATI. *Educational Psychologist, 18,* 1–13; Doyle, W. (1981). Research on classroom context. *Journal of Teacher Education, 32*(6), 3–6.

14. Jackson, P. (1968). *Life in classrooms.* New York: Holt, Rinehart and Winston.

15. See, for example, Doyle, W. (1986). Classroom organizations and management. In M. C. Wittrock (Ed.), *Handbook of research on teaching: Third edition* (esp. pp. 395–403). New York: Macmillan.

16. See Brophy, J. E. (1983). Classroom organization and management. *Elementary School Journal, 83*(4), 265–285; Chapter 3 of this text; Smith, L. M., & Geoffrey, W. (1968). *The complexities of an urban classroom: An analysis toward a general theory of teaching.* New York: Holt, Rinehart and Winston.

17. Jackson, P. (1968). *Life in classrooms.* New York: Holt, Rinehart and Winston, p. 11.

18. For a review of research findings about classrooms and the teaching skills needed to handle them well, see Berliner, D. C. (1986). In pursuit of the expert pedagogue. *Educational Researcher, 15*(17), 5–13; Jackson, P. (1968). *Life in classrooms.* New York: Holt, Rinehart and Winston, p. 11.

19. Jackson, P. (1968). *Life in classrooms.* New York: Holt, Rinehart and Winston.

20. Jackson, P. (1968). *Life in classrooms.* New York: Holt, Rinehart and Winston, p. 30.

21. Jackson, P. (1968). *Life in classrooms.* New York: Holt, Rinehart and Winston, pp. 41–61.

22. See, for example, Zirkel, P. M., &

Reichner, H. F. (1987). Is *in loco parentis* dead? *Phi Delta Kappan, 68*(6), 466–469.

23. See Doyle, W. (1983). Academic work. *Review of Educational Research, 53*(2), 159–199.

24. See Hawley, R. A. (1983). Mr. Chips revisited. *Learning, 12*(5), 70–71.

25. See Chapter 4 of this text; Jackson, P. (1968). *Life in classrooms.* New York: Holt, Rinehart and Winston; Doyle, W. (1986). Classroom organizations and management. In M. C. Wittrock (Ed.), *Handbook of research on teaching: Third edition* (pp. 392–431). New York: Macmillan; Hamilton, S. F. (1983). The social side of schooling: Ecological studies of classrooms and schools. *Elementary School Journal, 83*(4), 313–334; Berliner, D. C. (1983). Developing concepts of classroom environments: Some light on the T in classroom studies of ATI. *Educational Psychologist, 18*, 1–13.

26. Glidewell, J. C., Tucker, S., Todt, M., & Cox, S. (1983). Professional support systems: The teaching profession. In A. Nadler, J. D. Fischer, & B. M. DePaulo (Eds.), *New directions in helping: Allied research in help-seeking and -receiving* (Vol. 3, pp. 198–212). New York: Academic Press. Instead of the term *flat*, these researchers use *norm of equality*.

27. See McLaughlin, M. W. (1992). How district communities do and do not foster teacher pride. *Educational Leadership, 50*(1), 33–35; Lieberman, A., & McLaughlin, M. W. (1992). Networks for educational change: Powerful and problematic. *Phi Delta Kappan, 73*(9), 673–677; McLaughlin, M. W., & Talbert, J. (1990). Constructing a personalized school environment. *Phi Delta Kappan, 72*(3), 230–235.

28. See McLaughlin, M. W. (1992).

How district communities do and do not foster teacher pride. *Educational Leadership, 50*(1), 33–35; Lieberman, A., & McLaughlin, M. W. (1992). Networks for educational change: Powerful and problematic. *Phi Delta Kappan, 73*(9), 673–677; McLaughlin, M. W., & Talbert, J. (1990). Constructing a personalized school environment. *Phi Delta Kappan, 72*(3), 230–235.

29. McLaughlin, M. W., & Shields, P. M. (1987). Involving low-income parents in the schools: A role for policy. *Phi Delta Kappan, 69*(2), 156–160.

30. Jackson, P. (1968). *Life in classrooms.* New York: Holt, Rinehart and Winston, pp. 129–133.

31. For more information about family conditions, poverty, and other demographics about children, see Struggling to save the black family. (1993, August 30). *Newsweek,* 18–28; America's poor showing. (1993, October 18). *Newsweek,* 44; U.S. Bureau of the Census. (1992). *Poverty in the United States, 1991.* Washington, DC: U.S. Government Printing Office; U.S. Bureau of the Census. (1992). *Household and family characteristics: March 1991.* Washington, DC: U.S. Government Printing Office; Hodgkinson, H. L. (1992). *Demographic look at tomorrow.* Washington, DC: Institute for Educational Leadership; Hodgkinson, H. L. (1991). Reform versus reality. *Phi Delta Kappan, 73*(1), 8–16; Hofferth, S. L. (1987). Implications of family trends for children: A research perspective. *Educational Leadership, 44*(5); 78–84; Cardenas, J., & First, J. M. (1985). Children at risk. *Educational Leadership, 43*(1), 4–8; Ekstrom, R. B., Goertz, M. E., Pollack, J. M., & Rock, D. A. (1986). Who drops out of high school and why? Findings from a national study. *Teachers College Record,*

87(3), 356–373; Here they come, ready or not. (1986, May 14). *Education Week, 5*(34), 13–37; LeCompte, M. D. (1987, May 13). The cultural context of dropping out. *Education Week, 6*(33), 21, 28.

32. This case study is a composite based on information about several students known to the authors of this text.

33. For example, see Haberman, M. (1992). The ideology of Star Teachers of children in poverty. *Educational Horizons, 70*(3), 125–129; Haberman, M. (1991). The pedagogy of poverty versus good teaching. *Phi Delta Kappan, 73*(4), 290–294; Levine, D. U., & Ornstein, A. C. (1993). Reforms that can work. *American School Board Journal, 180*(6), 31–34; Knapp, M. S., & Shields, P. M. (1990). Reconceiving academic instruction for the children of poverty. *Phi Delta Kappan, 71*(10), 753–758; Frymier, J., et al. (1992). *Growing up is risky business, and schools are not to blame. Final report. Phi Delta Kappa study of students at risk.* Volume 1. Bloomington, IN: Phi Delta Kappa; Frymier, J., et al. (1992). *Assessing and predicting risk among students in school. Final report, Phi Delta Kappa study of students at risk.* Volume 2. Bloomington, IN: Phi Delta Kappa.

34. Ekstrom, R. B., Goertz, M. E., Pollack, J. M., & Rock, D. A. (1986). Who drops out of high school and why? Findings from a national study. *Teachers College Record, 87*(3), 356–373; Edmonds, R. (1981). Making public schools effective. *Social Policy, 12*(2), 56–60; Graham, P. A. (1987). Black teachers: A drastically scarce resource. *Phi Delta Kappan, 68*(8), 598–605. Also see Dunn, L. M. (1968). Special education for the mentally retarded: Is much of it justifiable? *Exceptional Children, 35*(1), 5.

35. See Struggling to save the black family. (1993, August 30). *Newsweek*, 18–28; U.S. Bureau of the Census. (1992). *Poverty in the United States, 1991*. Washington, DC: U.S. Government Printing Office; Hodgkinson, H. L. (1992). *Demographic look at tomorrow*. Washington, DC: Institute for Educational Leadership; Alsalam, N. A., Fischer, G. E., Ogle, L. T., Rogers, G. T., & Smith, T. M. (1993). *The condition of education 1993*. Washington, DC: National Center for Education Statistics; Polakow, V. (1993). *Lives on the edge: Single mothers and their children in the Other America*. Chicago: University of Chicago Press; Hofferth, S. L. (1987). Implications of family trends for children: A research perspective. *Educational Leadership, 44*(5), 78–84; Cardenas, J., & First, J. M. (1985). Children at risk. *Educational Leadership, 43*(1), 4–8; Stern, J. P., & Williams, M. F. (Eds.). (1986). *The condition of education: A statistical report, 1986 edition*. Washington, DC: National Center for Education Statistics.

36. For more data and perspectives on drug and alcohol abuse among children, see, for example, Hawley, R. A. (1990). The bumpy road to drug-free schools. *Phi Delta Kappan, 72*(4), 310–314; Hawley, R. A. (1987). School children and drugs: The fancy that has not passed. *Phi Delta Kappan, 68*(9), K1–K8; Shannon, J. (1986). In the classroom stoned. *Phi Delta Kappan, 68*(1), 60–62; Cody, B. (1984). Alcohol and other drug abuse among adolescents. *Statistical Bulletin of Metropolitan Insurance Companies*, January–March, 4–13.

37. National Education Association. (1992). *Status of the American public school teacher: 1990–91*. Washington, DC: National Education Association.

38. Jackson, P. (1968). *Life in classrooms*. New York: Holt, Rinehart and Winston, p. 138.

39. See, for example, Jackson, P. (1968). *Life in classrooms*. New York: Holt, Rinehart and Winston, pp. 115–155. Provenzo, E. F., et al. (1989). Metaphors and meaning in the language of teachers. *Teachers College Record, 90*(4), 551–573; Educational Research Service. (1987). *Educator opinion poll*. Arlington, VA: Educational Research Service; National Education Association. (1992). *Status of the American public school teacher: 1990–91*. Washington, DC: National Education Association; National Education Association. (1983). *Nationwide teacher opinion poll, 1983*. Washington, DC: National Education Association; Kottcamp, R. B., Provenzo, E. F., & Cohn, M. M. (1986). Stability and change in a profession: Two decades of teacher attitudes: 1964–1984. *Phi Delta Kappan, 67*(559–567).

40. See, for example, Haberman, M., & Rickards, W. H. (1990). Urban teachers who quit: Why they leave and what they do. *Urban Education, 25*(3), 297–303; Frymier, J. (1987). Bureaucracy and the neutering of teachers. *Phi Delta Kappan, 69*(1), 9–14; McLaughlin, M. W., Pfeifer, R. S., Swanson-Owens, D., & Yee, S. (1986). Why teachers won't teach. *Phi Delta Kappan, 67*(6), 420–426; National Education Association. (1992). *Status of the American public school teacher: 1990–91*. Washington, DC: National Education Association; National Education Association. (1983). *Nationwide teacher opinion poll, 1983*. Washington, DC: National Education Association.

41. McLaughlin, M. W., & Talbert, J. E. (1993). *Contexts that matter for teaching and learning: Strategic opportunities for meeting the nation's educational goals*. Palo Alto,

CA: Center for Research on the Context of Secondary School Teaching; Ornstein, A. C. (1988). The changing status of the teaching profession. *Urban Education, 23*(3), 261–279.

42. National Education Association, Research Division. (1992). *Status of the American public school teacher 1990–91*. Washington, DC: National Education Association.

43. Feistritzer, C. E., Quelle, F., & Chester, D. T. (1990). *Profile of teachers in the U.S.—1990*. Washington, DC: National Center for Education Information.

Chapter 16

1. Finn, C. E. (1987). The two agendas of education reform. *Independent School, 46*(2), 5–13; Finn, C. E. (1992). Up from mediocrity. What next in school reform? *Policy Review*, no. 61, 80–83; Pipho, C. (1986). States move reform closer to reality. *Phi Delta Kappan, 68*(4), K1–K8; Wise, A. E. (1990). Six steps to teacher professionalism. *Educational Leadership, 47*(7), 57–60.

2. Some say these changes will assure more competent teachers and that this in turn will produce greater respect. Others, however, say such scrutiny and rigid standards have the opposite effect—they deprofessionalize teaching.

3. See, for example, Hirsch, E. D. (1993). The core knowledge curriculum—What's behind the success? *Educational Leadership, 50*(8), 23–25, 27–30; Hirsch, E. D. (1990). Reflections on cultural literacy and arts education. *Journal of Aesthetic Education, 24*(1), 1–6; Hirsch, E. D. (1987). *Cultural literacy: What every American needs to know*. Boston: Houghton Mifflin; Hirsch, E. D. (1988). Cultural literacy: Let's be specific. *NEA Today, 6*(6), 15–21; Estes, T. H., et al. (1988). Cultural literacy: What every educa-

tor needs to know. *Educational Leadership, 46*(1), 14–17; Benninga, J. S. (1988). The emerging synthesis in moral education. *Phi Delta Kappan, 69*(6), 415–418; Ryan, K. (1986). The new moral education. *Phi Delta Kappan, 68*(4), 228–233.

4. For more information on the use of national assessment data, see Alsalam, N., Fischer, G. E., Ogle, L. T., Rogers, G. T., & Smith, T. M. (1993). *The condition of education 1993.* Washington, DC: National Center for Education Statistics; Phillips, G. W., & Finn, C. E. (1990). State-by-state comparisons can benefit education. *Educational Leadership, 47*(7), 43–55; *The Nation's Report Card.* (1987). Washington, DC: U.S. Department of Education; McLarty, J. (1986). On making NAEP a national "blueprint" for education policy. *Education Week, 6*(9), 22; Olson, L. (1987). Bennett panel urges major expansion of NAEP. *Education Week, 6*(26), 1, 8–9; Comments of the Assessment Policy Committee on the Nation's Report Card. (1987). *Education Week, 6*(39), 22–23; Rothman, R. (1987). NAEP's policy board endorses redesign plan, with reservations. *Education Week, 6*(38), 6; Chiefs urge changes in NAEP by 1990. (1987). *Education Week, 6*(27), 7.

5. See, for example, Alsalam, N., Fischer, G. E. Ogle, L. T., Rogers, G. T., & Smith, T. M. (1993). *The condition of education 1993.* Washington, DC: National Center for Education Statistics. Shulman, L. S., & Sparks, D. (1992). Merging content knowledge and pedagogy. An interview with Lee Shulman. *Journal of Staff Development, 13*(1), 14–16; Shulman, L. S. (1987). Assessment of teaching: An initiative for the profession. *Phi Delta Kappan, 69*(1), 38–44.

6. See Wise, A. E., & Leibbrand, J.

(1993). Accreditation and the creation of a profession of teaching. *Phi Delta Kappan, 75*(2), 133–157; Wise, A. E. (1990). Policies for reforming teacher education. *Phi Delta Kappan, 72*(3), 200–202; Rodman, B. (1987). N.E.A. pursues its plan to establish state boards controlled by teachers. *Education Week, 6*(31), 1, 20; Olson, L., & Rodman, B. (1986). Teachers' unions vie for professional status, back national board. *Education Week, 6*(1), 12–13; Olson, L., & Rodman, B. (1987). Thorny issues face planners of board to certify teachers. *Education Week, 6*(21), 1, 28–29; Wise, A. E. (1986). Three scenarios for the future of teaching. *Phi Delta Kappan, 67*(9), 649–652.

7. For further discussion on several of these points, see Wise, A. E., & Gendler, T. (1989). Rich schools, poor schools: The persistence of unequal education. *College Board Review, 151*, 12–17, 36–37; Graham, P. A. (1987). Black teachers: A drastically scarce resource. *Phi Delta Kappan, 68*(8), 598–605; Shalala, D. E. (1986). It just makes sense to help poor children. *Chronicle of Higher Education, 33*(9), 96. Also see Snyder, T. D., & Hoffman, C. M. (1993). *Digest of education statistics.* Washington, DC: U.S. Office of Education; Snyder, T. D. (1992). *Digest of educational statistics 1992.* Washington, DC: U.S. Department of Education; Here they come, ready or not. (1986). *Education Week, 5*(34), 12–37; Ekstrom, R. B., Goertz, M. E., Pollack, J. M., & Rock, D. A. (1986). Who drops out of high school and why? Findings from a national study. *Teachers College Record, 87*(3), 356–373.

8. For more discussion on these points, see Brubaker, D. L., & Simon, L. H. (1993). *Teacher as decision maker: Real-life cases to hone your people skills.* Newbury

Park, CA: Corwin Press; Brubacher, J. W., Case, C. W., & Reagan, T. G. (1994). *Becoming a reflective educator: How to build a culture of inquiry in the schools.* Thousand Oaks, CA: Corwin Press; Zehm, S. J., & Kottler, J. A. (1993). *On being a teacher: The human dimension.* Newbury Park, CA: Corwin Press; Participants in teacher education. (1990). Section D of Houston, W. R., Haberman, M., & Sikula, J. (Eds.), *Handbook of research on teacher education.* New York: Macmillan, pp. 267–370; Berliner, D. C. (1986). In pursuit of the expert pedagogue. *Educational Researcher, 15*(7), 5–13; Berliner, D. C. (1985). Laboratory settings and the study of teacher education. *Journal of Teacher Education, 36*(6), 2–8; Wise, A. E. (1986). Three scenarios for the future of teaching. *Phi Delta Kappan, 67*(9), 649–652.

9. Carnegie Task Force on Teaching as a Profession. (1986). *A nation prepared: Teachers for the twenty-first century.* New York: Carnegie Forum on Education and the Economy.

10. Berliner, D. C. (1986). In pursuit of the expert pedagogue. *Educational Researcher, 15*(7), 8–9.

11. Myers, C. B. (1986, November). *Social studies teacher education in an era of "Haves" and "Have Nots."* Paper presented at the annual meeting of the National Council for the Social Studies, New York.

12. For more information on teacher supply and demand, see Darling-Hammond, L. (1990). Teachers and teaching: Signs of a changing profession. In Houston, W. R., Haberman, M., & Sikula, J. (Eds.), *Handbook of research on teacher education.* New York: Macmillan; Snyder, T. D. (1992). *Digest of educational statistics 1992.* Washington, DC: U.S. Department of Education; Olson, L., & Rodman, B. (1987). Is there a

teacher shortage? It's anyone's guess. *Education Week, 6*(30), 1, 14–16; Carnegie Foundation for the Advancement of Education. (1986). Future teachers: Will there be enough good ones? *Change, 18*(5), 27–30; Feistritzer, C. E. (1987). There's no shortage of good teachers. *Wall Street Journal,* p. 34.

13. See Figure 1-1 in this text; Gerald, D. E., & Hussar, W. J. (1992). *School enrollment expected to pass historic all-time high. Issue brief.* Washington, DC: National Center for Education Statistics; Gerald, D. E., & Hussar, W. J. (1992). *Projections of education statistics to 2003.* Washington, DC: National Center for Education Statistics; Bickers, P. M. (1987). *Indicators of future school enrollments.* Arlington, VA: Educational Research Service; Snyder, T. D. (1992). *Digest of educational statistics 1992.* Washington, DC: U.S. Department of Education.

14. See Figure 1-1 of this text; Here they come, ready or not. (1986). *Education Week, 5*(34), 12–37; Rist, M. C. (1986). The baby boomlet has begun, but it's more (and less) than you bargained for. *School Boards Association Journal, 173*(4), 35–40; Montague, W. (1987). Districts scramble to cope with building needs. *Education Week, 6*(36), 1, 19–20.

15. Bickers, P. M. (1987). *Indicators of future school enrollments.* Arlington, VA: Educational Research Service, p. 33.

16. See Darling-Hammond, L. (1990). Teachers and teaching: Signs of a changing profession. In Houston, W. R., Haberman, M., & Sikula, J. (Eds.), *Handbook of research on teacher education.* New York: Macmillan; Carnegie Foundation for the Advancement of Teaching. (1988). The rise and fall of education as a major. *Change, 20*(4), 27–32; Berger, J.

(1988). Allure of teaching reviving: Education school rolls surge. *New York Times,* p. A1; Kane, P. R. (1987). Young teachers: Who comes? Who stays? Who leaves? *Independent School, 46*(3), 43–46; Rothman, R. (1987). More college freshmen note interest in teaching as career. *Education Week, 6*(16), 12, 18; Snyder, T. D. (1992). *Digest of educational statistics 1992.* Washington, DC: U.S. Department of Education.

17. Gerald, D. E., & Hussar, W. J. (1992). *School enrollment expected to pass historic all-time high. Issue brief.* Washington, DC: National Center for Education Statistics; Olson, L., & Rodman, B. (1987). Thorny issues face planners of board to certify teachers. *Education Week, 6*(21), 1, 28–29.

18. Snyder, T. D. (1992). *Digest of educational statistics 1992.* Washington, DC: U.S. Department of Education, p. 127; Carnegie Task Force on Teaching as a Profession. (1986). *A nation prepared: Teachers for the twenty-first century.* New York: Carnegie Forum on Education and the Economy, p. 27.

19. Carnegie Task Force on Teaching as a Profession. (1986). *A nation prepared: Teachers for the twenty-first century.* New York: Carnegie Forum on Education and the Economy, p. 27.

20. Wise, A. E. (1991). We need more than redesign. *Educational Leadership, 49*(3), 7; Berry, B. (1988). Labor market choices and teacher reform: Policy options for the public schools of the twenty-first century. *Teaching and Teacher Education, 4*(1), 71–81; Darling-Hammond, L., & Berry, B. (1988). *The evolution of teacher policy.* RAND, p. 23; Rodman, B. (1988). Georgia, N.E.A. settle suit on teacher testing. *Education Week, 7*(24), 1, 17.

21. See Berliner, D. C. (1986). In

pursuit of the expert pedagogue. *Educational Researcher, 15*(7), 5–13.

22. Darling-Hammond, L. (1987). The educational reform dilemma. *Basic Education, 31*(6), 2–5; Wise, A. E. (1986). Three scenarios for the future of teaching. *Phi Delta Kappan, 67*(9), 649–652.

23. Graham, P. A. (1987). Black teachers: A drastically scarce resource. *Phi Delta Kappan, 68*(8), 598–605.

24. Rodman, B. (1988). The fiercest competition. *Education Week, 7*(19), 1, 13; Graham, P. A. (1987). Black teachers: A drastically scarce resource. *Phi Delta Kappan, 68*(8), 598–605.

25. See *Education Week.* (1989). *9*(1), 2; Carnegie Foundation for the Advancement of Education. (1988). *The condition of teaching: A state-by-state analysis, 1988.* Princeton, NJ: Carnegie; Snyder, T. D. (1992). *Digest of educational statistics 1992.* Washington, DC: U.S. Department of Education; Sedlak, M., & Schlossman, S. (1986). *Who will teach?* RAND, p. 6; National Education Association. (1986). *Status of the American public school teacher: 1985–86.* Washington, DC: National Education Association; The forgotten message: Excellence costs. (1988, April). *NEA Today,* pp. 4–5; National Education Association. (1992). *Estimates of state school statistics.* Washington, DC: National Education Association; for more up-to-date statistics also see recent issues of *Education Daily.*

26. See, for example, Darling-Hammond, L., & Berry, B. (1988). *The evolution of teacher policy.* RAND, pp. 38–49.

27. See Gerald, D. E., & Hussar, W. J. (1992). *Projections of education statistics to 2003.* Washington, DC: National Center for Education Statistics; The forgotten

message: Excellence costs. (1988, April). *NEA Today*, p. 5; *NEA Today*. (1989, April), p. 8.

28. *NEA Today*. (1993, March), p. 32.

29. *Washington Post*. (1987, April 14), p. A1.

30. See, for example, Stein, B. (1986). This is not your life: Television as the third parent. *Public Opinion*, *9*, 41–42.

31. U.S. Bureau of the Census, cited in *Newsweek*. (1993, October 18), p. 44.

32. Montague, W. (1987). "Workfare" applicants said to lack skills. *Education Week*, *6*(33), 5.

33. Shalala, D. E. (1986). It just makes sense to help poor children. *Chronicle of Higher Education*, *33*(9), 96.

Name Index

Subject Index

Photograph Credits

Page 5, Nita Winter; **8,** Virginia Blaisdell/Stock, Boston Inc.; **15,** Nita Winter; **18,** Elizabeth Crews; **35,** Frank Siteman/The Picture Cube; **47** (left), Nita Winter; **47** (right), Elizabeth Crews/The Image Works; **53,** Elizabeth Crews; **55,** Larry Wilson; **58** (left), Elizabeth Crews; **58** (right), MacDonald Photography/The Picture Cube; **64,** Elizabeth Crews; **70,** Elizabeth Crews; **83,** Tony Velez/The Image Works; **85,** Robert Finken/The Picture Cube; **88,** Stan Rowin/The Picture Cube; **96,** Elizabeth Crews/The Image Works; **101,** Elizabeth Crews/The Image Works; **106,** Richard Orton/The Picture Cube; **117,** Michaels/The Image Works; **119,** Larry Wilson; **123,** Sarah Putnam/The Picture Cube; **124,** Dan Chidester /The Image Works; **128,** Robert Finken/The Picture Cube; **136,** N. R. Rowan/Stock, Boston Inc.; **151,** Elizabeth Crews; **153,** Larry Wilson; **163,** Steve Takatsuno/The Picture Cube; **169,** Elizabeth Crews; **177,** Rick Mansfield/The Image Works; **182,** Meri Houtchens-Kitchens/The Picture Cube; **195,** Jean-Claude LeJeune/Stock, Boston Inc.; **197,** Brown Bros.; **203** (left), Richard Wood/The Picture Cube; **203** (right), Christopher Johnson/Stock, Boston Inc.; **205,** Spencer Grant/Stock, Boston Inc.; **210,** Elizabeth Crews; **212,** Archives of the History of American Psychology; **227,** Bob Kalman/The Image Works; **229,** Billy Barnes/Stock, Boston Inc.; **235,** John Coletti/The Picture Cube; **238,** Spencer Grant III/Stock, Boston Inc.; **242,** Elizabeth Crews; **249,** Elizabeth Crews; **263,** Meri Houtchens-Kitchens/The Picture Cube; **265,** The Bettmann Archives; **268,** Culver Pictures; **269,** The Bettmann Archives; **271,** Culver Pictures; **277,** The Bettmann Archives; **288,** North Wind Archives; **290,** Bob Daemmrich/Stock, Boston Inc.; **297,** Michael Siluk/The Image Works; **301,** Elizabeth Crews/The Image Works; **309,** Nita Winter; **327,** Frank Siteman/Stock, Boston Inc.; **342,** George Gardner/Stock, Boston Inc.; **354,** Ellis Herwig/The Picture Cube; **369,** Steve Takatsuno/The Picture Cube; **371,** Jeffrey Hamilton/Stock, Boston Inc.; **377,** Christopher Brown/Stock, Boston Inc.; **393,** Glassman/The Image Works; **411,** Michael Schwarz/The Image Works; **413,** Elizabeth Crews; **418,** Owen Franken/Stock, Boston Inc.; **422,** Richard Pasley/Stock, Boston Inc.; **425,** Elizabeth Crews/Stock, Boston Inc.; **437,** Elizabeth Crews; **445,** Elizabeth Crews/The Image Works; **447,** John Griffin/The Image Works; **451,** L. Kolvoord/The Image Works; **457,** Richard Orton/The Picture Cube; **460,** Elizabeth Crews; **471,** Elizabeth Crews; **479,** Jerry Howard/Stock, Boston Inc.; **481,** Jean-Claude LeJeune/Stock, Boston Inc.; **485,** Elizabeth Crews; **494,** Elizabeth Crews/The Image Works; **503,** Elizabeth Crews; **511,** Jean-Claude LeJeune/Stock, Boston Inc.; **513,** Larry Wilson; **516,** Elizabeth Crews; **525,** Spencer Grant/The Picture Cube; **537,** Elizabeth Crews; **544,** Elizabeth Crews/Stock, Boston Inc.; **555,** Bob Daemmrich/Stock, Boston Inc.; **557,** Robert Finken/The Picture Cube; **565,** Elizabeth Crews; **569,** Elizabeth Crews/The Image Works; **577,** Michael Weisbrot/Stock, Boston Inc.; **582,** Bob Daemmrich /The Image Works; **593,** Susie Fitzhugh/Stock, Boston Inc.; **601,** Spencer Grant/Stock, Boston Inc.; **606,** Nita Winter; **609,** Michael Weisbrot/The Image Works; **621,** Nita Winter/The Image Works; **Profile** of Paul Ong, Nita Winter; **Profile** of Sarah Smith, Bonnie Kamin.